Solaris 10 System Administration

Bill Calkins

Solaris 10 System Administration Exam Prep (CX-310-200 & CX-310-202)

International Standard Book Number: 0-7897-3461-3

Library of Congress Catalog Card Number: 2005934729

Printed in the United States of America

First Printing: December 2005

08 07 06 05 4 3 2 1

Trademarks

All terms mentioned in this book that are known to be trademarks or service marks have been appropriately capitalized. Que Certification cannot attest to the accuracy of this information. Use of a term in this book should not be regarded as affecting the validity of any trademark or service mark.

Warning and Disclaimer

Every effort has been made to make this book as complete and as accurate as possible, but no warranty or fitness is implied. The information provided is on an "as is" basis. The author and the publisher shall have neither liability nor responsibility to any person or entity with respect to any loss or damages arising from the information contained in this book or from the use of the CD or programs accompanying it.

Bulk Sales

Que Certification offers excellent discounts on this book when ordered in quantity for bulk purchases or special sales. For more information, please contact

U.S. Corporate and Government Sales
1-800-382-3419
corpsales@pearsontechgroup.com

For sales outside the United States, please contact

International Sales
international@pearsoned.com

PUBLISHER
Paul Boger

EXECUTIVE EDITOR
Jeff Riley

ACQUISITIONS EDITOR
Carol Ackerman

DEVELOPMENT EDITOR
Steve Rowe

MANAGING EDITOR
Charlotte Clapp

PROJECT EDITOR
Tonya Simpson

PRODUCTION EDITOR
Benjamin Berg

INDEXER
Aaron Black

PROOFREADER
Jenny Matlik

TECHNICAL EDITORS
Edgar Danielyan
Scott Howard

PUBLISHING COORDINATOR
Vanessa Evans

MULTIMEDIA DEVELOPER
Dan Scherf

BOOK DESIGNER
Gary Adair

PAGE LAYOUT
Nonie Ratcliff

Contents at a Glance

Table of Contents

Part I: Exam Preparation

Part II: Final Review

Part III: Appendixes

About the Author

Bill Calkins is a Sun Certified System Administrator for the Solaris operating environment. He is owner and president of Pyramid Consulting Inc., a computer training and consulting firm located near Grand Rapids, Michigan, specializing in the implementation and administration of Open Systems. He has more than 20 years of experience in Unix system administration, consulting, and training at more than 150 different companies. Bill has authored several Unix textbooks, which are currently best sellers and are used by universities and training organizations worldwide:

- *Solaris 2.6 Administrator Certification Training Guide Part I* (New Riders Publishing, ISBN: 157870085X)
- *Solaris 2.6 Administrator Certification Training Guide Part II* (New Riders Publishing, ISBN: 1578700868)
- *Solaris 7 Administrator Certification Training Guide: Parts I and II* (New Riders Publishing, ISBN: 1578702496)
- *Solaris 8 Training Guide (CX-310-011 and CX-310-012): System Administrator* (New Riders Publishing, ISBN: 1578702593)
- *Inside Solaris 9* (New Riders Publishing, ISBN: 0735711011)
- *Solaris 9 Training Guide (CX-310-014 and CX-310-015): System Administrator* (New Riders Publishing, ISBN: 0789729229)

In addition, Bill has worked with Sun Press and Prentice Hall as a technical editor and a major contributor to many of their Solaris titles.

Bill's professional interests include consulting, writing, teaching, and developing Web-based training materials.

Bill consults with Sun Microsystems Professional Services and assists in the development of Solaris training and testing materials for the education division at Sun Microsystems. Bill consults with the certification group at Sun Microsystems and assists with the development of Solaris certification materials and exams.

Bill works as an instructor in both corporate and university settings, and has helped thousands of administrators get their certification. His experience covers all varieties of Unix, including Solaris, HP-UX, AIX, IRIX, Linux, and SCO. When he's not working in the field, he writes Unix books and conducts training and educational seminars on various system administration topics. He draws on his many years of experience in system administration and training to provide a unique approach to Unix training.

Contributing Author

John Philcox is owner and director of Mobile Ventures Limited, a computer consultancy based in Cheltenham, Gloucestershire, in the United Kingdom, specializing in Unix systems and networks. He has more than 20 years experience in IT, 15 of those with the Sun operating system and Solaris environments. He is a certified Solaris system administrator as well as a professional member of the Institution of Analysts and Programmers and the Institute of Management of Information Systems. Philcox is also a member of Usenix and SAGE. He has worked in a number of large multivendor networks in both the public and private sectors of business.

John was the author of *Solaris System Management*, published by New Riders, and the technical editor on *Solaris 2.6 Administrator Certification Guide Part II*, *Solaris 7 and 8 Administrator Certification Guides*, *Solaris 8 Security*, and *Inside Solaris 9*, all with New Riders.

Acknowledgments

I'd like to thank John Philcox of Mobile Ventures Limited, who once again has helped me get this book together. As always, John, you've done a great job. You've been a great asset and have become a good friend to have along on all of my books and projects. I want to thank all the editors who have contributed to this book; I value your input greatly. With each book, our tech editors get more refined, and their work is a huge contribution to the quality of this book. It's been a great team effort, and the book would not be as complete without your help. A special thanks goes out to Scott Howard and Edgar Danielyan.

A big thanks to Sun Microsystems for letting me participate in the Solaris 10 beta program and the input that they have provided for this book. A special thanks to Yvonne Prefontaine at Sun for her contributions and the information that she provided in the intro of this book.

Thank you, the reader, for buying my books and providing comments to improve the content with each new release. This book would not be what it is if it were not for your valuable input over the years. May the material in this book help you better your skills, enhance your career, and achieve your goal to become certified. Best of luck!

A lot of people behind the scenes make a book like this happen. After several books, I still don't have a clue how it all works, but it's a great team effort. A big thanks to everyone who edits the text, sets the type, prints the pages, and ships the book. My efforts would be lost in a closet somewhere if it weren't for your hard work.

We Want to Hear from You!

As the reader of this book, *you* are our most important critic and commentator. We value your opinion and want to know what we're doing right, what we could do better, what areas you'd like to see us publish in, and any other words of wisdom you're willing to pass our way.

As an executive editor for Que Certification, I welcome your comments. You can email or write me directly to let me know what you did or didn't like about this book—as well as what we can do to make our books better.

Please note that I cannot help you with technical problems related to the topic of this book. We do have a User Services group, however, where I will forward specific technical questions related to the book.

When you write, please be sure to include this book's title and author as well as your name, email address, and phone number. I will carefully review your comments and share them with the author and editors who worked on the book.

Email: feedback@quepublishing.com

Mail: Jeff Riley
Executive Editor
Que Certification
800 East 96th Street
Indianapolis, IN 46240 USA

For more information about this book or another Que Certification title, visit our website at www.examcram.com. Type the ISBN (excluding hyphens) or the title of a book in the Search field to find the page you're looking for.

Introduction

Bill Calkins has been training Solaris System Administrators for more than 15 years. This book contains the training material that he uses in his basic and advanced Solaris administration courses that, over the years, have helped thousands of Solaris administrators become certified. This is our first edition of the *Solaris 10 System Administrator Exam Prep*. It began with the Training Guide for Solaris 2.6, 7, 8, 9, and is now the Exam Prep for Solaris 10. Instructors from universities and training organizations around the world have used the book as courseware in their Solaris Administration courses. In addition, administrators from around the world have used this book as a self-study when instruction from a Sun training center is either not available or not within their budget. Many of you have written with your success stories, suggestions, and comments. Your suggestions are what keep making this guide more valuable.

This book provides training materials for anyone interested in becoming a Sun Certified System Administrator for Solaris 10. When used as a study guide, this book will save you a great deal of time and effort searching for information you will need to know when taking the exam. This book covers the exam objectives in enough detail for the inexperienced administrator to learn the objectives and apply the knowledge to real-life scenarios. Experienced readers will find the material in this book to be complete and concise, making it a valuable study guide. This book is not a cheat sheet or cram session for the exam; it is a training manual. In other words, it does not merely give answers to the questions you will be asked on the exam. We have made certain that this book addresses the exam objectives in detail, from start to finish. If you are unsure about the objectives on the exam, this book will teach you what you need to know. After reading each chapter, assess your knowledge on the material covered using the review questions at the end of the chapter. When you have completed reading a section, use the practice exam at the end of the book and the ExamGear test engine on the CD-ROM to assess your knowledge of the objectives covered on each exam. This CD-ROM contains sample questions similar to what you are likely to see on the real exams. More sample questions are available at `www.UnixEd.com`, so make sure you visit this site to find additional training and study materials.

How This Book Helps You

This book teaches you how to administer the Solaris 10 operating system. It offers you a self-guided training course of all the areas covered on the certification exams by installing, configuring, and administering the Solaris 10 operating environment. You will learn all of the specific skills to administer a system and specifically to become a Sun Certified System Administrator for Solaris 10.

Throughout the book, we provide helpful tips and real-world examples that we have encountered as system administrators. In addition, we provide useful, real-world exercises to help you practice the material you have learned. The setup of this book is discussed in the following sections.

- **Organization**—This book is organized according to individual exam objectives. Every objective you need to know for installing, configuring, and administering a Solaris 10 system is in this book. We have attempted to present the objectives in an order that is as close as possible to that listed by Sun. However, we have not hesitated to reorganize them as needed to make the material as easy as possible for you to learn. We have also attempted to make the information accessible in the following ways:
    - This introduction includes the full list of exam topics and objectives.
    - Read the "Study and Exam Prep Tips" section early on to help you develop study strategies. This section provides you with valuable exam-day tips and information on exam/question formats such as adaptive tests and case study–based questions.
    - Each chapter begins with a list of the objectives to be covered, exactly as they are defined by Sun. Throughout each section, material that is directly related to the exam objectives is identified.
    - Each chapter also begins with an outline that provides you with an overview of the material and the page numbers where particular topics can be found.
- **Instructional Features**—This book is designed to provide you with multiple ways to learn and reinforce the exam material. The following are some of the helpful methods:
    - **Objective Explanations**—As mentioned previously, each chapter begins with a list of the objectives covered in the chapter. In addition, immediately following each objective is an explanation in a context that defines it more meaningfully.
    - **Study Strategies**—The beginning of each chapter also includes strategies for studying and retaining the material in the chapter, particularly as it is addressed on the exam.
    - **Exam Alerts**—Throughout each chapter you'll find exam tips that will help you prepare for exam day. These tips are written by those who have already taken the Solaris 10 certification exams.
    - **Key Terms**—A list of key terms appears near the end of each chapter.
    - **Notes**—These appear in the margin and contain various types of useful information such as tips on technology or administrative practices, historical background on terms and technologies, or side commentary on industry issues.

- **Cautions**—When using sophisticated information technology, mistakes or even catastrophes are always possible because of improper application of the technology. Warnings appear in the margins to alert you to such potential problems.
- **Step-by-Steps**—These are hands-on lab excercises that walk you through a particular task or function relevant to the exam objectives.
- **Exercises**—Found at the end of the chapters in the "Apply Your Knowledge" section, exercises are performance-based opportunities for you to learn and assess your knowledge.
- **Suggested Readings and Resources**—At the end of each chapter we've prepared a list of additional resources that you can use if you are interested in going beyond the objectives and learning more about topics that are presented in the chapter.

- **Extensive Practice Test Options**—The book provides numerous opportunities for you to assess your knowledge and practice for the exam. The practice options include the following:
    - **Exam Questions**—These questions appear in the "Apply Your Knowledge" section at the end of each chapter. They allow you to quickly assess your comprehension of what you just read in the chapter. Answers to the questions are provided later in a separate section titled "Answers to Exam Questions."
    - **Practice Exam**—A practice exam is included in the "Final Review" section for each exam (as discussed later).
    - **ExamGear**—The ExamGear software included on the CD-ROM provides further practice questions.

NOTE

ExamGear Software For a complete description of the ExamGear test engine, please see Appendix A, "What's on the CD-ROM."

- **Final Review**—This part of the book provides you with three valuable tools for preparing for the exam, as follows:
    - **Fast Facts**—This condensed version of the information contained in the book will prove extremely useful for last-minute review.
    - **Practice Exam**—A full practice exam is included with questions written in styles similar to those used on the actual exam. Use the practice exam to assess your readiness for the real exam.

- **Appendixes**—The book contains valuable appendixes as well, including a glossary and a description of what is on the CD-ROM (Appendix A).

These and all the other book features mentioned previously will enable you to thoroughly prepare for the exam.

Conventions Used in This Book

- **Commands**—In the steps and examples, the commands you type are displayed in a special `monospaced` font.
- **Arguments and Options**—In command syntax, command options and arguments are enclosed in < >. (The italicized words within the < > symbols stand for what you will actually type. You don't type the < >.)

  ```
  lp -d<printer name> <filename> <return>
  ```

- **Using the Mouse**—When using menus and windows, you will select items with the mouse. Here is the default mapping for a three-button mouse:

  Left button—Select

  Middle button—Transfer/Adjust

  Right button—Menu

  The Select button is used to select objects and activate controls. The middle mouse button is configured for either Transfer or Adjust. By default, it is set up for Transfer, which means this button is used to drag or drop list or text items. You use the left mouse button to highlight text, and then you use the middle button to move the text to another window or to reissue a command. The middle button can also be used to move windows around on the screen. The right mouse button, the Menu button, is used to display and choose options from pop-up menus.

- **Menu Options**—The names of menus and the options that appear on them are separated by a comma. For example, "Select File, Open" means to pull down the File menu and choose the Open option.
- **Code Continuation Character**—When a line of code is too long to fit on one line of a page, it is broken and continued to the next line. The continuation is preceded by a backslash.

Audience

This book is designed for anyone who has a basic understanding of Unix and wants to learn more about Solaris system administration. Whether you plan to become certified or not, this book is the starting point to becoming a Solaris System Administrator. It's the same training material that Bill uses in his Solaris System Administration classes. This book covers the basic as well as the advanced system administration topics you need to know before you begin administering the Solaris operating system. Our goal was to present the material in an easy-to-follow format, with text that is easy to read and understand. The only prerequisite is that you have used Unix, you have attended a fundamentals Unix class for users, or you have studied equivalent material so that you understand basic Unix commands and syntax. Before you begin administering Solaris, it's important that you have actually used Unix.

This book is also intended for experienced system administrators who want to become certified, update their current Solaris certification, or simply learn about the Solaris 10 operating environment. To pass the certification exams, you need to have a solid understanding of the fundamentals of administering Solaris. This book will help you review the fundamentals required to pass the certification exams.

The Sun Certified System Administrator Exams

To become a Sun Certified System Administrator, you need to pass two exams: CX-310-200 (Part I) and CX-310-202 (Part II). Part I is a prerequisite for Part II. You will not receive a certificate until you have passed both examinations. Also, if you are already certified in Solaris 2.6, 7, 8, or 9, you can use this book to take the upgrade exam, CX-310-203, to become certified on Solaris 10.

Beware of fakes. We have seen some Web sites promoting their own certification programs, so be sure to evaluate them carefully. Certification programs promoted by these sites are not the same as the Sun certification program, and you will not receive a certificate from Sun until you pass Sun's exams from a certified Sun testing center. Go to my Web site (`www.UnixEd.com`) for links to the real exams and information on Sun's certification program if you are in doubt. In addition, feel free to visit our online Solaris certification discussion forum at `www.UnixEd.com` where you can ask me questions directly.

Exam CX-310-200

Exam CX-310-200 objectives are covered in the following sections.

Manage File Systems

List the different types of file systems and file types in the Solaris operating environment. Understand how to add disk devices to a system and the device files associated with each disk. Understand how to use the format utility. Understand how to create, mount, and repair file systems. Understand all of the configuration files associated with managing file systems.

Install Software

Describe the methods used and the sequence of steps required to perform the Solaris 10 operating environment software installation on SPARC, x64, and x86-based systems. Identify the function of the package administration commands. Understand how to install, verify, and remove operating system patches.

Perform System Boot Procedures

Understand the entire boot process with knowledge of the various configuration files and startup scripts on SPARC, x64, and x86-based systems. Understand how to use and execute boot PROM commands. Understand the role of the Solaris Management Facility (SMF) in the boot process and become familiar with the SMF related commands. Understand the function of the files or directories accessed during the boot process. Understand the commands used to change the run level of a system to a specified state.

Perform User and Security Administration

Understand all aspects of administering users and groups. Understand how to set and verify file and directory permissions.

Manage Network Printers and System Processes

Describe the purpose, features, and functionality of the print management tools available in the Solaris operating environment. Understand the LP print service directory structure, and the Solaris operating environment printing process. Understand the commands that display information for all active processes on the system. Understand the effect of sending a specified signal to a process. Understand the various methods used to terminate an active process.

Perform System Backups and Restores

Understand the functional capabilities of the various backup, archive, and restore utilities in Solaris 10. Identify the commands and steps required to back up and restore a file system. Given a specific scenario, be prepared to develop a strategy for scheduled backups, and back up an unmounted file system using the appropriate commands.

Exam CX-310-202

Exam CX-310-202 objectives are covered in the following sections.

Describe Network Basics

Define the function of each layer within the seven-layer OSI model and TCP/IP model. List the features and functions of the Ethernet. Describe the characteristics of RARP and ARP. Identify the commands that display information about the local network interface. Describe the relationship between the RPC service and the `rpcbind` process and how to list registered RPC services. Identify the steps necessary to start and stop network services via the command line.

Manage Virtual File Systems and Core Dumps

Understand the benefits of using the automount utility and each of the types of automount maps. Understand how to configure, start, and stop the automounter. Understand the Solaris pseudo file systems. Understand swap and all of the steps required to create and add swap to the system. Understand how to manage the crash and core dump configuration.

Manage Storage Volumes

Explain the purpose, features, and functionalities of RAID, and identify the guidelines to follow when using RAID 0, RAID 1, and RAID 5, including hardware considerations. Define key SVM concepts, including volumes, soft partitions, hot spares, and state databases. Create the state database, build a mirror, and unmirror the root file system using SVM.

Control Access and Configure System Messaging

Understand the commands used to create, modify, and delete access control lists (ACLs) on files. Understand how to use and configure the Role-Based Access Control (RBAC) facility in Solaris 10. Understand `syslog` and how to configure it. Understand the syntax of the `syslog` configuration file and its effect on `syslog` behavior.

Set Up Naming Services

Understand the purpose of each type of name service available in Solaris 10 and be able to compare and contrast their functionality. Understand how to configure the name service switch file for each type of name service. Understand the processes and components of the NIS master server, NIS slave server, and NIS client. Know the steps required to configure an NIS master, slave, and client. Understand the steps required to add, update, and propagate an

NIS map. Understand how to configure the DNS and LDAP client. Configure, stop, and start the Name Service Cache Daemon (nscd) and retrieve naming service information using the getent command.

Solaris Zones

Learn consolidation issues and features of Solaris zones, and understand the different zone concepts including zone types, daemons, networking, and command scope. In a given scenario, create a Solaris zone, identify zone components and `zonecfg` resource parameters, allocate file system space, use the `zonecfg` command, describe the interactive configuration of a zone, and view the zone configuration file. Also, for a given scenario, understand how to use the `zoneadm` command to view, install, boot, halt, reboot, and delete a zone.

Perform Advanced Installation Procedures

Understand the purpose of the JumpStart server. You need to know all of the commands used to set up and modify a JumpStart session between a server and its clients. In a nutshell, you need to know everything about configuring a Solaris JumpStart session. Explain how to use the Flash installation feature, and describe requirements and limitations of this feature. Explain how to create, manipulate, and use a Flash archive during the installation process.

Exam CX-310-203 (Solaris 10 Upgrade Exam)

If you're already certified on Solaris 2.6, 7, 8, or 9, you'll only need to take the CX-310-203 upgrade exam to update your certification. Here are the objectives for that exam:

- Install Software
- Manage File Systems
- Perform System Boot and Shutdown Procedures for SPARC-, x64-, and x86-based systems
- Perform User and Security Administration
- Control Access and Configure System Messaging
- Perform Advanced Installation Procedures for SPARC- and x86-based systems

A complete description of each objective is described earlier in this section.

Summary

It's not uncommon for Sun to change the exam objectives or to shift them around after the exams have been published. It's highly recommended that before you start this book, you visit my Web site at `www.UnixEd.com` to get the most up-to-date list of exam objectives, the errata for this book, up-to-date sample exam questions, and any other last-minute notes about these exams. We will provide all of the information you need to pass the exam—all you need to do is devote the time. Learning the objectives is the first step; the next step is to practice. You need to have access to a system running Solaris 10 so that you can practice what you have learned. Unless you have a supernatural memory, it's going to be difficult to pass the exams without practice.

In the back of this book is the ExamGear software test CD that will prepare you for the questions you might see on the exam. The CD-ROM–based test engine has been designed by educational experts to help you learn as you test. It is a preview of the types of questions to expect on the exams and will test your knowledge on all the exam objectives. If you are weak in any area, the sample questions will help you identify that area so that you can go back to the appropriate chapter and study the topic. Each question on the CD-ROM has a flashcard to help you in case you get stuck. This flashcard contains brief, concise, textbook excerpts that explain why each answer is correct so you can learn as you test.

In addition, for an additional cost, you can purchase additional questions for the ExamGear test engine from our Web site. You'll obtain hundreds of questions that will take you deep into each exam objective providing a comprehensive skills assessment and evaluate your readiness and your retention of the materials.

Advice on Taking the Exam

More extensive tips are found in the "Study and Exam Prep Tips" and throughout the book, but keep in mind the following advice as you study for the exam:

- **Read all the material**—This book includes information not reflected in the exam objectives to better prepare you for the exam and for real-world experiences. Read all of the material to benefit from this.
- **Do the step-by-step lab exercises and complete the exercises in each chapter**—This will help you gain experience and prepare you for the scenario-type questions that you will encounter.
- **Use the questions to assess your knowledge**—Each chapter contains review questions and exam questions. Use these to asses your knowledge and determine where you need to review material.

- **Review the exam objectives**—Develop your own questions and examples for each topic listed. If you can develop and answer several questions for each topic, you should not find it difficult to pass the exam.
- **Relax and sleep before taking the exam**—Time for taking the examination is limited. However, if you have prepared and you know Solaris network administration, you will find plenty of time to answer all of the questions. Be sure to rest well for the stress that time limitations put on you as you take the exam.
- **Review all the material in the fast facts the night before or the morning you take the exam.**
- **If you don't know the answer to a question, just skip it and don't waste much time**—You'll need to complete the exam in the time allotted. Don't be lazy during the examination, and answer all the questions as quickly as possible. Any unfinished questions will be marked incorrect.
- **Visit my Web site, `www.UnixEd.com`. It contains the following:**
  - Late-breaking changes that Sun might make to the exam or the objectives. You can expect Sun to change the exams frequently. Make sure you check my Web site before taking the exam.
  - A FAQs page with frequently asked questions and errata regarding this book or the exams.
  - Links to other informative Web sites.
  - Additional practice questions and sample exams for the ExamGear test engine. The ExamGear test engine has hundreds of questions that you can use to further assess your retention of the material presented in the book. The exams feature electronic flash cards that take the place of those sticky notes that you've used as bookmarks throughout the book. Don't attempt the real exam until you can pass every section of the practice exams with a 95% or better score.
  - An online forum where you can discuss certification-related issues with me and other system administrators, including some that have already taken the exam.
  - Additional study materials, training programs, and online seminars related to Solaris certification.
  - You can also email me directly from this Web site with questions or comments about this book. I always personally try to answer each one.

When you feel confident, take the real exams and become certified. Don't forget to drop me an email and let me know how you did on the exam (`guru@UnixEd.com`).

Study and Exam Prep Tips

These study and exam prep tips provide you with some general guidelines to help prepare for the Sun Certified Security Administrator exam. The information is organized into two sections. The first section addresses your pre-exam preparation activities and covers general study tips. The second section offers some tips and hints for the actual test-taking situation. Before tackling those areas, however, think a little bit about how you learn.

Learning as a Process

To better understand the nature of preparation for the exams, it is important to understand learning as a process. You probably are aware of how you best learn new material. You might find that outlining works best for you, or you might need to "see" things as a visual learner. Whatever your learning style, test preparation takes place over time. Obviously, you cannot start studying for this exam the night before you take it. It is important to understand that learning is a developmental process; as part of that process, you need to focus on what you know and what you have yet to learn.

Learning takes place when we match new information to old. You have some previous experience with computers, and now you are preparing for this certification exam. Using this book, software, and supplementary material will not just add incrementally to what you know; as you study, you will actually change the organization of your knowledge as you integrate this new information into your existing knowledge base. This will lead you to a more comprehensive understanding of the tasks and concepts outlined in the objectives and of computing in general. Again, this happens as a repetitive process rather than a singular event. Keep this model of learning in mind as you prepare for the exam, and you will make better decisions concerning what to study and how much more studying you need to do.

Study Tips

There are many ways to approach studying, just as there are many different types of material to study. The following tips, however, should work well for the type of material covered on the certification exam.

Study Strategies

Although individuals vary in the ways they learn, some basic principles apply to everyone. You should adopt some study strategies that take advantage of these principles. One of these principles is that learning can be broken into various depths. Recognition (of terms, for example) exemplifies a more surface level of learning in which you rely on a prompt of some sort to elicit recall. Comprehension or understanding (of the concepts behind the terms, for example) represents a deeper level of learning. The ability to analyze a concept and apply your understanding of it in a new way represents an even deeper level of learning.

Your learning strategy should enable you to know the material at a level or two deeper than mere recognition. This will help you do well on the exam. You will know the material so thoroughly that you can easily handle the recognition-level types of questions used in multiple-choice testing. You also will be able to apply your knowledge to solve new problems.

Macro and Micro Study Strategies

One strategy that can lead to this deeper learning includes preparing an outline that covers all the objectives for the exam. You should delve a bit further into the material and include a level or two of detail beyond the stated objectives for the exam. Then expand the outline by coming up with a statement of definition or a summary for each point in the outline.

An outline provides two approaches to studying. First, you can study the outline by focusing on the organization of the material. Work your way through the points and subpoints of your outline with the goal of learning how they relate to one another. Be certain, for example, that you understand how each of the objective areas is similar to and different from the others. Next, you can work through the outline, focusing on learning the details. Memorize and understand terms and their definitions, facts, rules and strategies, advantages and disadvantages, and so on. In this pass through the outline, attempt to learn detail rather than the big picture (the organizational information that you worked on in the first pass through the outline).

Research has shown that attempting to assimilate both types of information at the same time seems to interfere with the overall learning process. To better perform on the exam, separate your studying into these two approaches.

Active Study Strategies

Develop and exercise an active study strategy. Write down and define objectives, terms, facts, and definitions. In human information-processing terms, writing forces you to engage in more active encoding of the information. Just reading over it exemplifies more passive processing.

Next, determine whether you can apply the information you have learned by attempting to create examples and scenarios on your own. Think about how or where you could apply the concepts you are learning. Again, write down this information to process the facts and concepts in a more active fashion.

Common Sense Strategies

Finally, you also should follow common sense practices when studying. Study when you are alert, reduce or eliminate distractions, take breaks when you become fatigued, and so on.

Pre-Testing Yourself

Pre-testing enables you to assess how well you are learning. One of the most important aspects of learning is what has been called metalearning. Metalearning has to do with realizing when you know something well or when you need to study some more. In other words, you recognize how well or how poorly you have learned the material you are studying.

For most people, this can be difficult to assess objectively on their own. Practice tests are useful in that they reveal more objectively what you have learned and what you have not learned. You should use this information to guide review and further study. Developmental learning takes place as you cycle through studying, assessing how well you have learned, reviewing, and assessing again until you think you are ready to take the exam.

You might have noticed the practice exam included in this book. Use it as part of the learning process. The ExamGear software on the CD-ROM also provides a variety of ways to test yourself before you take the actual exam. By using the practice exam, you can take an entire timed, practice test quite similar in nature to that of the actual Solaris exam. Set a goal for your pretesting. A reasonable goal would be to score consistently in the 95% range in all categories.

For a more detailed description of the exam simulation software, see Appendix A, "What's on the CD-ROM."

Exam Prep Tips

The Solaris certification exam reflects the knowledge domains established by Sun Microsystems for the Solaris OS administrators. The exam is based on a fixed set of exam questions. The individual questions are presented in random order during a test session. If you take the same exam more than once, you will see the same number of questions, but you won't necessarily see the same questions.

Solaris exams are similar in terms of content coverage, number of questions, and allotted time, but the questions differ. You might notice, however, that some of the same questions appear on, or rather are shared among, different final forms. When questions are shared among multiple final forms of an exam, the percentage of sharing is generally small.

Solaris exams also have a fixed time limit in which you must complete the exam.

Finally, the score you achieve on a fixed-form exam is based on the number of questions you answer correctly. The exam's passing score is the same for all final forms of a given fixed-form exam.

Table 1 shows the format for the exam.

TABLE 1 Time, Number of Questions, and Passing Score for the Exam

Exam	Time Limit in Minutes	Number of Questions	Passing %
Sun Certified System Administrator for the Solaris 10 Operating System: Part 1	90	59	61
Sun Certified System Administrator for the Solaris 9 Operating System: Part 2	90	61	62

Question types on both exams are multiple choice and drag & drop. As of this writing, there are no true/false or free response type questions.

Remember that you do not want to dwell on any one question for too long. Your 90 minutes of exam time can be consumed very quickly and any unfinished questions will be marked as incorrect

Correctly answered questions receive one point each. Many of the multi-choice questions are scenarios that have multiple correct answers. The question will inform you of the number of answers to select; however, if you get one answer wrong, the entire question is marked wrong and you do not receive a point.

When you finish the exam, you will receive the results with a report outlining your score for each section of the exam. You will not know which questions were correct or incorrect.

If you fail, you'll need to purchase another voucher and retake the exam after a two-week waiting period. Every exam will contain different questions.

If you feel that you were unfairly scored, you can request a review by sending an email to `who2contact@sun.com`.

Putting It All Together

Given all these different pieces of information, the task now is to assemble a set of tips that will help you successfully tackle the Solaris certification exam.

More Pre-Exam Prep Tips

Generic exam-preparation advice is always useful. Tips include the following:

- The certification exams are directed toward experienced Solaris system administrators—typically 6 to 12 months of experience. Although the Sun training courses will help you prepare, some of the material found on the exam is not taught in the Sun training courses; however, everything on the exam is found in this book. To pass the exam, you need to retain everything that I've presented in this book. To help you assess your skills, I've created the ExamGear test engine which you will use to assess your retention of the materials. In addition, you can purchase hundreds of additional ExamGear test questions from `http://www.UnixEd.com` to assess your knowledge of the material. I don't recommend taking the Sun certification exams until you consistently pass these practice exams with a 95% or higher in ALL categories.

- Become familiar with general terminology, commands, and equipment. Hands-on experience is one of the keys to success; it will be difficult, but not impossible, to pass the exam without that experience. Review the chapter-specific study tips at the beginning of each chapter for instructions on how to best prepare for the exam.
- Avoid using "brain dumps" available from various websites and newsgroups. Your exam may not match that particular user's exam and you'll obtain a false sense of readiness. In addition, brain dumps do not prepare you for the scenario type questions that you will receive on the exam, and may be illegal. You need to know the objectives and there is no shortcut for learning the material. Sun goes through a 13-step process to develop these exams and to prevent cheating—you cannot pass these exams without understanding the material. Besides, what good is the certification if you don't know the material? You'll never get through the job interview screening.
- Review the current exam-preparation guide on the Sun Web site. Visit my website, `www.unixed.com`, for late-breaking changes and up-to-date study tips from other administrators who have taken the exam. Use the forum to talk to others that have already taken the exam.
- Memorize foundational technical detail, but remember that you need to be able to think your way through questions as well.
- Take any of the available practice tests that assess your knowledge against the stated exam objectives—not the practice exams that cheat and promise to show you actual exam questions and answers. Sun knows that these exams and brain dumps are available and they change the questions too often for these types of practice exams to be useful. Too many users have written me to say that they thought they were prepared because they could pass the exam simulators, only to find the questions and answers were revised on the actual exam. I recommend the practice exams included in this book and the exams available using the ExamGear software on the CD-ROM. These are true skill assessment exams with flash cards to help you learn and retain while taking the exams. The test engine on this CD is designed to complement the material in this book and help you prepare for the real exam by helping you learn and assess your retention of the materials. If you know the material, you'll be able to handle any scenario-based question thrown at you. For more sample test questions, you can visit my website, `www.unixed.com`. I keep the questions up-to-date and relevant to the

objectives. In addition, through our Solaris Certification online forum, you can share your experiences with other Solaris administrators who are preparing for the exam, just like you, and learn from those who have gone through the process. In addition, this website will provide up-to-date links to the official Sun certification websites.

During the Exam Session

The following generic exam-taking advice that you have heard for years applies when taking this exam:

- Take a deep breath and try to relax when you first sit down for your exam session. It is important to control the pressure you might (naturally) feel when taking exams.
- You will be provided scratch paper. Take a moment to write down any factual information and technical detail that you committed to short-term memory.
- Many questions are scenarios that require careful reading of all information and instruction screens. These displays have been put together to give you information relevant to the exam you are taking.
- Read the exam questions carefully. Reread each question to identify all relevant details. You may find that all answers are correct, but you may be asked to choose the best answer for that particular scenario.
- Tackle the questions in the order they are presented. Skipping around will not build your confidence; the clock is always counting down.
- Do not rush, but also do not linger on difficult questions. The questions vary in degree of difficulty. Don't let yourself be flustered by a particularly difficult or verbose question.
- Note the time allotted and the number of questions appearing on the exam you are taking. Make a rough calculation of how many minutes you can spend on each question and use this to pace yourself through the exam.
- Take advantage of the fact that you can return to and review skipped or previously answered questions. Record the questions you cannot answer confidently, noting the relative difficulty of each question, on the scratch paper provided. After you have made it to the end of the exam, return to the more difficult questions.
- If session time remains after you have completed all questions (and if you aren't too fatigued!), review your answers. Pay particular attention to questions that seem to have a lot of detail or that involve graphics.

- As for changing your answers, the general rule of thumb here is *don't*! If you read the question carefully and completely the first time and felt like you knew the right answer, you probably did. Do not second-guess yourself. If, as you check your answers, one clearly stands out as incorrectly marked, then change it. If you are at all unsure, however, go with your first instinct.

If you have done your studying and follow the preceding suggestions, you should do well. Good luck!

PART I

Exam Preparation

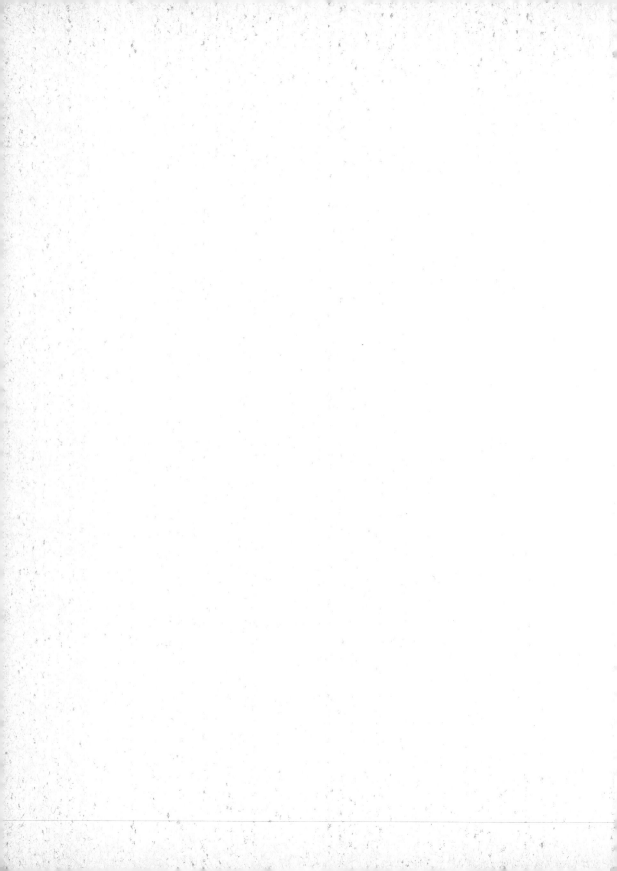

CHAPTER ONE

Managing File Systems

Objectives

The following objectives for Exam CX-310-200 are covered in this chapter:

Explain disk architecture including the UFS file system capabilities and naming conventions for devices for SPARC, x64, and x86-based systems.

- Device drivers control every device connected to your system, and some devices use multiple device drivers. This chapter explains device drivers so that you can recognize and verify all devices connected to your system. In addition, the Solaris operating system accesses devices, such as disks and tape drives, through device and path names. The system administrator must be familiar with the various path names that point to each piece of hardware connected to the system.

Explain when and how to list devices, reconfigure devices, perform disk partitioning, and relabel a disk in a Solaris operating environment using the appropriate files, commands, options, menus, and/or tables.

- The system administrator is responsible for adding and configuring new hardware on the system. This chapter describes how new devices are configured into the Solaris operating environment. You'll need to describe disk architecture and understand naming conventions for disk devices as used in the Solaris operating environment.
- You'll need to know how to set up the disks and disk partitions when installing the Solaris operating environment. However, to properly set up a disk, you first need to understand the concepts behind disk storage and partitioning. You then need to determine how you want data stored on your system's disks.

Explain the Solaris 10 OS file system, including disk-based, distributed, devfs, and memory file systems related to SMF, and create a new UFS file system using options for <1Tbyte and >1Tbyte file systems.

- You'll need to understand all of the file systems that are available in the Solaris operating environment. In addition, you'll need to know when to use each type of file system.

Explain when and how to create a new UFS using the `newfs` command, check the file system using `fsck`, resolve file system inconsistencies, and monitor file system usage using associated commands.

- You'll need to be familiar with all of the commands used to create, check, and repair file systems. The system administrator needs to know how to use these tools and understand the effect that the various command options will have on performance and functionality.

Describe the purpose, features, and functions of root subdirectories, file components, file types, and hard links in the Solaris directory hierarchy.

Explain how to create and remove hard links in a Solaris directory.

- You'll need to know how to create, remove, and identify a hard link and understand why they are used in the Solaris operating environment. You'll need to be able to identify and describe all of the file types available in the Solaris operating environment. You'll need to understand the purpose of each subdirectory located in the root file system and the type of information that is stored in these subdirectories.

Explain the purpose and function of the vfstab file in mounting UFS file systems, and the function of the mnttab file system in tracking current mounts.

- You'll need to maintain the table of file system defaults as you configure file systems to mount automatically at bootup. You'll also need to understand the function of the mounted file system table (mnttab) and the entries made in this file.

Explain how to perform mounts and unmounts, and either access or restrict access to mounted diskettes and CD-ROMs.

- Each file system type supports options that control how the file system will function and perform. You'll need to understand all of these custom file system parameters. The system administrator needs to be familiar with mounting and unmounting file systems and all of the options associated with the process.

Outline

Study Strategies

The following study strategies will help you prepare for the exam:

- This chapter introduces many new terms that you must know well enough to match to a description if they were to appear on the exam. Know the terms I've provided in the "Key Terms" section at the end of this chapter.
- Understand what a device driver is and the various device driver names. They are rather difficult to remember, but keep going over them until you can describe them from memory. Many questions on the exam refer to the various types of device names.
- Practice all the commands and step by steps until you can describe and perform them from memory. The best way to memorize them is to practice them repeatedly on a Solaris system.
- As with every chapter of this book, you'll need a Solaris 10 system on which to practice. Practice every step-by-step example that is presented until you can perform the steps from memory. Also, as you practice creating file systems, you'll need some unused disk space with which to practice. I recommend an empty, secondary disk drive for this purpose.
- Familiarize yourself with the various types of file systems described in this chapter, but specifically, pay close attention to the UFS type and UFS parameters. Most questions on the exam revolve around the UFS. In addition, make sure you understand the Solaris Volume Manager. You don't need to know how to use it—just understand what it does and why you would use it.
- Make sure that you practice disk slicing. Understand how to create and delete disk slices and pay close attention to the limitations inherent with standard disk slices. Practice partitioning a disk using the `format` utility and SMC GUI tools until you have the process memorized.
- Finally, understand how to mount and unmount a file system as well as how to configure the /etc/vfstab file. Make sure that you understand all of the commands described in this chapter that are used to manage and display information about file systems, such as `df`, `fsck`, and `prtvtoc`.

Introduction

Before we can describe file systems, it's important that you understand how Solaris views the disk drives and various other hardware components on your system. In particular, you need to understand how these devices are configured and named before you can create a file system on them or install the Solaris operating environment.

Device management in the Solaris 10 environment includes adding and removing peripheral devices from a system, such as tape drives, disk drives, printers, and modems. Device management also involves adding a third-party device driver to support a device if the device driver is not available in Sun's distribution of the Solaris operating environment. System administrators need to know how to specify device names if using commands to manage disks, file systems, and other devices.

This chapter describes disk device management in detail. It also describes disk device naming conventions as well as adding, configuring, and displaying information about disk devices attached to your system.

Device Drivers

Objective:

Describe the basic architecture of a local disk and the naming conventions for disk devices as used in the Solaris operating environment.

Explain when and how to list and reconfigure devices.

A computer typically uses a wide range of peripheral and mass-storage devices such as a small computer system interface (SCSI) disk drive, a keyboard, a mouse, and some kind of magnetic backup medium. Other commonly used devices include CD-ROM drives, printers, and various Universal Serial Bus (USB) devices. Solaris communicates with peripheral devices through device files or drivers. A *device driver* is a low-level program that allows the kernel to communicate with a specific piece of hardware. The driver serves as the operating system's "interpreter" for that piece of hardware. Before Solaris can communicate with a device, the device must have a device driver.

When a system is started for the first time, the kernel creates a device hierarchy to represent all the devices connected to the system. This is the autoconfiguration process, which is described later in this chapter. If a driver is not loaded for a particular peripheral, that device is not functional. In Solaris, each disk device is described in three ways, using three distinct naming conventions:

- **Physical device name**—Represents the full device pathname in the device information hierarchy.

- **Instance name**—Represents the kernel's abbreviation name for every possible device on the system.
- **Logical device name**—Used by system administrators with most file system commands to refer to devices.

System administrators need to understand these device names when using commands to manage disks and file systems. We discuss these device names throughout this chapter.

EXAM ALERT

Memorize these device names. You'll encounter them in several questions and it's important that you understand when and where each name is used. Make sure you can identify a particular device driver name when it is presented as a filename.

Physical Device Name

Before the operating system is loaded, the system locates a particular device through the device tree, also called the full device pathname. Full device pathnames are described in Chapter 3, "Perform System Boot and Shutdown Procedures." After the kernel is loaded, however, a device is located by its physical device pathname. Physical device names represent the full device pathname for a device. Note that the two names have the same structure. For example, the full device pathname for a SCSI disk at target 0 on a Sun Ultra 450 system is as follows:

```
/pci@1f,4000/scsi@3/disk@0,0
```

Now let's look at the corresponding physical device name from the operating system level. Use the `dmesg` command, described later in this section, to obtain information about devices connected to your system. By typing `dmesg` at the command prompt, you'll receive the following information about SCSI disks 3 and 4:

```
Jul 25 14:06:47 smokey genunix: [ID 936769 kern.notice] sd19 is\
 /pci@1f,0/pci@1/scsi@1,1/sd@3,0
Jul 25 14:06:48 smokey scsi: [ID 193665 kern.notice] sd20 at\
 glm1: target 4 lun 0
Jul 25 14:06:48 smokey genunix: [ID 936769 kern.notice] sd20 is\
 /pci@1f,0/pci@1/scsi@1,1/sd@4,0
```

This same information is also available in the `/var/adm/messages` file.

The physical device pathnames for disks 3 and 4 are as follows:

```
Jul 25 14:06:47 smokey scsi: [ID 193665 kern.notice] sd19 at glm1: target 3 lun 0
Jul 25 14:06:47 smokey genunix: [ID 936769 kern.notice] sd19 is\
/pci@1f,0/pci@1/scsi@1,1/sd@3,0
```

```
Jul 25 14:06:48 smokey scsi: [ID 193665 kern.notice] sd20 at glm1: target 4 lun 0
Jul 25 14:06:48 smokey genunix: [ID 936769 kern.notice] sd20 is\
/pci@1f,0/pci@1/scsi@1,1/sd@4,0
```

As you can see, the physical device name and the full device name are the same. The difference is that the full device pathname is simply a path to a particular device. The physical device is the actual driver used by Solaris to access that device from the operating system.

Physical device files are found in the `/devices` directory. The content of the `/devices` directory is controlled by the devfs file system. The entries in the `/devices` directory dynamically represent the current state of accessible devices in the kernel and require no administration. New device entries are added when the devices are detected and added to the kernel. The physical device files for SCSI disks 3 and 4 would be

```
/devices/pci@1f,0/pci@1/scsi@1,1/sd@3,0:<#>
/devices/pci@1f,0/pci@1/scsi@1,1/sd@4,0:<#>
```

for the block device and

```
/devices/pci@1f,0/pci@1/scsi@1,1/sd@3,0:<#>,raw
/devices/pci@1f,0/pci@1/scsi@1,1/sd@4,0:<#>,raw
```

for the character (raw) device, where <#> is a letter representing the disk slice. Block and character devices are described later in this chapter in the section titled "Block and Raw Devices."

The system commands used to provide information about physical devices are described in Table 1.1.

TABLE 1.1 Device Information Commands

Command	Description
`prtconf`	Displays system configuration information, including the total amount of memory and the device configuration, as described by the system's hierarchy. This useful tool verifies whether a device has been seen by the system.
`sysdef`	Displays device configuration information, including system hardware, pseudo devices, loadable modules, and selected kernel parameters.
`dmesg`	Displays system diagnostic messages as well as a list of devices attached to the system since the most recent restart.
`format`	The `format` command displays both physical and logical device names for all available disks.

NOTE

prtconf Output The output produced by the `prtconf` command can vary depending on the version of the system's PROM.

Type the `prtconf` command:

```
prtconf
```

The following output is displayed:

```
System Configuration:  Sun Microsystems  sun4u
Memory size: 128 Megabytes
System Peripherals (Software Nodes):

SUNW,Ultra-5_10
    scsi_vhci, instance #0
    packages (driver not attached)
        terminal-emulator (driver not attached)
        deblocker (driver not attached)
        obp-tftp (driver not attached)
        disk-label (driver not attached)
        SUNW,builtin-drivers (driver not attached)
        sun-keyboard (driver not attached)
        ufs-file-system (driver not attached)
    chosen (driver not attached)
    openprom (driver not attached)
        client-services (driver not attached)
    options, instance #0
    aliases (driver not attached)
    memory (driver not attached)
    virtual-memory (driver not attached)
    pci, instance #0
        pci, instance #0
            ebus, instance #0
                auxio (driver not attached)
                power, instance #0
                SUNW,pll (driver not attached)
                se, instance #0
                su, instance #0
                su, instance #1
                ecpp (driver not attached)
                fdthree, instance #0
                eeprom (driver not attached)
                flashprom (driver not attached)
                SUNW,CS4231, instance #0
            network, instance #0
            SUNW,m64B, instance #0
            ide, instance #0
                disk (driver not attached)
                cdrom (driver not attached)
                sd, instance #3
                dad, instance #1
        pci, instance #1
```

```
            scsi, instance #0 (driver not attached)
                disk (driver not attached)
                tape (driver not attached)
            scsi, instance #1
                disk (driver not attached)
                tape (driver not attached)
                sd, instance #0 (driver not attached)
```

*Output has been truncated.

Use the -v option to display detailed information about devices such as information about the attached SCSI disks:

```
dev_path=/pci@1f,0/pci@1/scsi@1,1/sd@2,0:a
            spectype=blk type=minor
            dev_link=/dev/dsk/c2t2d0s0
            dev_link=/dev/sd18a
dev_path=/pci@1f,0/pci@1/scsi@1,1/sd@2,0:a,raw
             spectype=chr type=minor
             dev_link=/dev/rdsk/c2t2d0s0
             dev_link=/dev/rsd18a
```

Next is an example of the output displayed by the `sysdef` command. Type the `sysdef` command:

```
sysdef
```

The following output is displayed:

```
* Hostid
*
  80a26382
*
* sun4u Configuration
*
*
* Devices
*
scsi_vhci, instance #0
packages (driver not attached)
        terminal-emulator (driver not attached)
        deblocker (driver not attached)
        obp-tftp (driver not attached)
        disk-label (driver not attached)
        SUNW,builtin-drivers (driver not attached)
        sun-keyboard (driver not attached)
        ufs-file-system (driver not attached)
chosen (driver not attached)
openprom (driver not attached)
```

```
        client-services (driver not attached)
options, instance #0
aliases (driver not attached)
memory (driver not attached)
virtual-memory (driver not attached)
pci, instance #0
        pci, instance #0
                ebus, instance #0
                        auxio (driver not attached)
                        power, instance #0
                        SUNW,pll (driver not attached)
                        se, instance #0
                        su, instance #0
                        su, instance #1
                        ecpp (driver not attached)
                        fdthree, instance #0
                        eeprom (driver not attached)
                        flashprom (driver not attached)
                        SUNW,CS4231, instance #0 (driver not attached)
                network, instance #0
                SUNW,m64B, instance #0 (driver not attached)
                ide, instance #0
                        disk (driver not attached)
                        cdrom (driver not attached)
                        sd, instance #1
                        dad, instance #1
```

*Output has been truncated.

```
* System Configuration
*
  swap files
swapfile             dev  swaplo blocks   free
/dev/dsk/c0t0d0s3   136,11     16 1052624 1052624
*
* Tunable Parameters
*
 2498560        maximum memory allowed in buffer cache (bufhwm)
    1914        maximum number of processes (v.v_proc)
      99        maximum global priority in sys class (MAXCLSYSPRI)
    1909        maximum processes per user id (v.v_maxup)
      30        auto update time limit in seconds (NAUTOUP)
      25        page stealing low water mark (GPGSLO)
       1        fsflush run rate (FSFLUSHR)
      25        minimum resident memory for avoiding deadlock (MINARMEM)
      25        minimum swapable memory for avoiding deadlock (MINASMEM)
*
* Utsname Tunables
*
```

```
    5.10  release (REL)
  ultra5  node name (NODE)
   SunOS  system name (SYS)
 Generic  version (VER)
*
* Process Resource Limit Tunables (Current:Maximum)
*
0x0000000000000100:0x0000000000010000   file descriptors
*
* Streams Tunables
*
     9  maximum number of pushes allowed (NSTRPUSH)
 65536  maximum stream message size (STRMSGSZ)
  1024  max size of ctl part of message (STRCTLSZ)
*
* IPC Messages module is not loaded
*
*
* IPC Semaphores module is not loaded
*
*
* IPC Shared Memory module is not loaded
*
*
* Time Sharing Scheduler Tunables
*
60      maximum time sharing user priority (TSMAXUPRI)
SYS     system class name (SYS_NAME)
```

*Output has been truncated.

Finally, here's an example of the device information for an Ultra system displayed using the dmesg command:

```
dmesg
```

The following output is displayed:

```
Aug  5 11:19:16 smokey reboot: [ID 662345 auth.crit] rebooted by root
Aug  5 11:19:22 smokey genunix: [ID 672855 kern.notice] syncing file systems...
Aug  5 11:19:22 smokey genunix: [ID 904073 kern.notice]  done
Aug  5 11:20:40 smokey genunix: [ID 540533 kern.notice]
SunOS Release 5.10 Version Generic 64-bit
Aug  5 11:20:40 smokey genunix: [ID 943906 kern.notice] Copyright 1983-2005\
 Sun Microsystems, Inc.  All rights reserved.
Aug  5 11:20:40 smokey Use is subject to license terms.
Aug  5 11:20:40 smokey genunix:[ID 678236 kern.info] Ethernet address= 8:0:20:c0:3f:29
Aug  5 11:20:40 smokey unix: [ID 673563 kern.info] NOTICE: Kernel Cage is ENABLED
Aug  5 11:20:40 smokey unix: [ID 389951 kern.info] mem = 131072K (0x8000000)
Aug  5 11:20:40 smokey unix: [ID 930857 kern.info] avail mem = 121143296
```

```
Aug  5 11:20:40 smokey rootnex: [ID 466748 kern.info] root nexus = \
 Sun Ultra 5/10 UPA/PCI (UltraSPARC-IIi 333MHz)
Aug  5 11:20:40 smokey rootnex: [ID 349649 kern.info] pseudo0 at root
Aug  5 11:20:40 smokey genunix: [ID 936769 kern.info] pseudo0 is /pseudo
Aug  5 11:20:40 smokey rootnex: [ID 349649 kern.info] scsi_vhci0 at root
Aug  5 11:20:40 smokey genunix: [ID 936769 kern.info] scsi_vhci0 is /scsi_vhci
Aug  5 11:20:40 smokey rootnex: [ID 349649 kern.info] pcipsy0 at root: UPA 0x1f 0x0
Aug  5 11:20:40 smokey genunix: [ID 936769 kern.info] pcipsy0 is /pci@1f,0
Aug  5 11:20:40 smokey pcipsy: [ID 370704 kern.info] PCI-device: pci@1,1, simba0
Aug  5 11:20:40 smokey genunix: [ID 936769 kern.info] simba0 is /pci@1f,0/pci@1,1
Aug  5 11:20:40 smokey simba: [ID 370704 kern.info] PCI-device: ide@3, uata0
Aug  5 11:20:40 smokey genunix: [ID 936769 kern.info] uata0 is /pci@1f,0/pci@1,1/ide@3
Aug  5 11:20:41 smokey uata: [ID 114370 kern.info] dad1 at uata0
Aug  5 11:20:41 smokey uata: [ID 347839 kern.info]  target 0 lun 0
Aug  5 11:20:41 smokey genunix: [ID 936769 kern.info] dad1 is\
 /pci@1f,0/pci@1,1/ide@3/dad@0,0
Aug  5 11:20:41 smokey dada: [ID 365881 kern.info]\
      <IBM-DJNA-370910 cyl 17660 alt 2 hd 16 sec 63>
Aug  5 11:20:41 smokey swapgeneric: [ID 308332 kern.info] root on\
  /pci@1f,0/pci@1,1/ide@3/disk@0,0:a fstype ufs
```

*Output has been truncated.

Use the output of the `prtconf` command to identify which disk, tape, and CD-ROM devices are connected to the system. As shown in the preceding `prtconf` and `sysdef` example, some devices display the `driver not attached` message next to the device instance. This message does not always mean that a driver is unavailable for this device. It means that no driver is currently attached to the device instance because there is no device at this node or the device is not in use. The operating system automatically loads drivers when the device is accessed, and it unloads them when it is not in use.

The system determines what devices are attached to it at startup. This is why it is important to have all peripherals powered on at startup, even if they are not currently being used. During startup, the kernel configures itself dynamically, loading needed modules into memory. Device drivers are loaded when devices, such as disk and tape devices, are accessed for the first time. This process is called autoconfiguration because all kernel modules are loaded automatically if needed. As described in Chapter 3, the system administrator can customize the way in which kernel modules are loaded by modifying the `/etc/system` file.

Device Autoconfiguration

Autoconfiguration offers many advantages over the manual configuration method used in earlier versions of Unix, in which device drivers were manually added to the kernel, the kernel was recompiled, and the system had to be restarted. Now, with autoconfiguration, the administrator simply connects the new device to the system and performs a reconfiguration startup. To perform a reconfiguration startup, follow the steps in Step by Step 1.1.

STEP BY STEP

1.1 Performing a Reconfiguration Startup

1. Create the `/reconfigure` file with the following command:

   ```
   touch /reconfigure
   ```

   The `/reconfigure` file causes the Solaris software to check for the presence of any newly installed devices the next time you turn on or start up your system.

2. Shut down the system using the shutdown procedure described in Chapter 3.

   If you need to connect the device, turn off power to the system and all peripherals after Solaris has been properly shut down.

   After the new device is connected, restore power to the peripherals first and then to the system. Verify that the peripheral device has been added by attempting to access it.

NOTE

Automatic Removal of /reconfigure The file named `/reconfigure` automatically gets removed during the bootup process.

An optional method of performing a reconfiguration startup is to type `boot -r` at the OpenBoot prompt.

NOTE

Specify a Reconfiguration Reboot As root, you can also issue the `reboot -- -r` command from the Unix shell. The `-- -r` passes the `-r` to the `boot` command.

During a reconfiguration restart, a device hierarchy is created in the `/devices` file system to represent the devices connected to the system. The kernel uses this to associate drivers with their appropriate devices.

Autoconfiguration offers the following benefits:

- Main memory is used more efficiently because modules are loaded as needed.
- There is no need to reconfigure the kernel if new devices are added to the system. When you add devices such as disks or tape drives other than USB and hot-pluggable devices, the system needs to be shut down before you connect the hardware so that no damage is done to the electrical components.

- Drivers can be loaded and tested without having to rebuild the kernel and restart the system.

> **NOTE**
>
> **devfsadm** Another option used to automatically configure devices on systems that must remain running 24×7, and one that does not require a reboot, is the `devfsadm` command.

Occasionally, you might install a new device for which Solaris does not have a supporting device driver. Always check with the manufacturer to make sure any device you plan to add to your system has a supported device driver. If a driver is not included with the standard Solaris release, the manufacturer should provide the software needed for the device to be properly installed, maintained, and administered.

Third-party device drivers are installed as software packages using the `pkgadd` command. At a minimum, this software includes a device driver and its associated configuration (.conf) file. The .conf file resides in the `/kernel/drv` directory. Table 1.2 describes the contents of the module subdirectories located in the `/kernel` directory.

TABLE 1.2 Kernel Module Subdirectories

Directory	Description
`drv/sparcv9`	Contains loadable device drivers and pseudo device drivers
`exec/sparcv9`	Contains modules used to run different types of executable files or shell scripts
`fs/sparcv9`	Contains file system modules such as ufs, nfs, procfs, and so on
`misc/sparcv9`	Contains miscellaneous system-related modules such as `swapgeneric` and `usb`
`sched/sparcv9`	Contains operating system schedulers
`strmod/sparcv9`	Contains System V STREAMS loadable modules (generalized connection between users and device drivers)
`sys/sparcv9`	Contains loadable system calls such as system semaphore and system accounting operations

USB Devices

Universal Serial Bus (USB) devices were developed to provide a method to attach peripheral devices such as keyboards, printers, cameras, and disk drives using a common connector and interface. Furthermore, USB devices are *hot-pluggable*, which means they can be connected or disconnected while the system is running. The operating system automatically detects when a USB device has been connected and automatically configures the operating environment to make it available.

The Solaris 10 operating environment supports USB devices on Sun Blade, Netra, Sunfire, and x86/x64-based system. In addition, a USB interface can be added to Sun systems that may not already have one.

When hot-plugging a USB device, the device is immediately displayed in the device hierarchy. For example, a full device pathname for a USB Zip drive connected to an Ultra system would appear as follows:

```
/pci@1f,4000/usb@5/storage@1
```

A printer would look like this:

```
/pci@1f,4000/usb@5/hub@3/printer@1
```

Be careful when removing USB devices, however. If the device is being used when it is disconnected, you will get I/O errors and possible data errors. When this happens, you'll need to plug the device back in, stop the application that is using the device, and then unplug the device.

As stated in the "Volume Management" section later in this chapter, removable media such as floppy diskettes and CD-ROMs can be inserted and automatically mounted. When attaching a hot-pluggable device, it's best to restart `vold` after attaching the USB device as follows:

```
pkill -HUP vold
```

Once `vold` identifies that the device has been connected, you'll see device names set up as follows:

```
zip1 -> /vol/dev/rdsk/c2t0d0/fat32        (USB Zip device)
zip0 -> /vol/dev/rdsk/c1t0d0/zip100       (USB Zip device)
jaz0 -> /vol/dev/rdsk/c3t0d0/jaz1gb       (USB Jaz device)
```

When disconnecting a USB device such as a Zip drive, unmount the device, stop `vold`, disconnect the device, and then restart `vold` as follows:

1. Stop any application that is using the device.
2. Unmount the USB device using the `volrmmount` command as follows:

   ```
   volrmmount -e zip0
   ```

   or the `eject` command as follows:

   ```
   eject zip0
   ```

   `zip0` is a nickname for the Zip device. The following nicknames are recognized:

   ```
   fd          /dev/rdiskette
   fd0         /dev/rdiskette
   ```

```
fd1             /dev/rdiskette1
diskette        /dev/rdiskette
diskette0       /dev/rdiskette0
diskette1       /dev/rdiskette1
rdiskette       /dev/rdiskette
rdiskette0      /dev/rdiskette0
rdiskette1      /dev/rdiskette1
floppy          /dev/rdiskette
floppy0         /dev/rdiskette0
floppy1         /dev/rdiskette1
cdrom0          /vol/dev/rdsk/cXtYdZ/label
zip0            /vol/dev/rdsk/cXtYdZ/label
jaz0            /vol/dev/rdsk/cXtYdZ/label
rmdisk0         /vol/dev/rdsk/cXtYdZ/label
```

The `-e` option simulates the ejection of the media. For a more up-to-date listing of nicknames that might have been added since this writing, consult the `volrmmount` man page.

3. As root, stop `vold`:

```
/etc/init.d/volmgt stop
```

4. Disconnect the USB device.
5. Start `vold`:

```
/etc/init.d/volmgt start
```

For more information on `vold` and USB devices, see the section titled “Volume Management” later in this chapter.

Instance Names

The instance name represents the kernel’s abbreviated name for every possible device on the system. For example, on an Ultra system, `dad0` represents the instance name of the IDE disk drive, `sd0` represents a SCSI disk, and `hme0` is the instance name for the network interface. Instance names are mapped to a physical device name in the `/etc/path_to_inst` file. The following shows the contents of a `path_to_inst` file:

```
more /etc/path_to_inst
```

```
#
#       Caution! This file contains critical kernel state
#
"/pseudo" 0 "pseudo"
"/scsi_vhci" 0 "scsi_vhci"
"/options" 0 "options"
"/pci@1f,0" 0 "pcipsy"
"/pci@1f,0/pci@1,1" 0 "simba"
"/pci@1f,0/pci@1,1/ide@3" 0 "uata"
"/pci@1f,0/pci@1,1/ide@3/sd@2,0" 3 "sd"
"/pci@1f,0/pci@1,1/ide@3/dad@0,0" 1 "dad"
"/pci@1f,0/pci@1,1/ebus@1" 0 "ebus"
"/pci@1f,0/pci@1,1/ebus@1/power@14,724000" 0 "power"
"/pci@1f,0/pci@1,1/ebus@1/se@14,400000" 0 "se"
"/pci@1f,0/pci@1,1/ebus@1/su@14,3083f8" 0 "su"
"/pci@1f,0/pci@1,1/ebus@1/su@14,3062f8" 1 "su"
"/pci@1f,0/pci@1,1/ebus@1/ecpp@14,3043bc" 0 "ecpp"
"/pci@1f,0/pci@1,1/ebus@1/fdthree@14,3023f0" 0 "fd"
"/pci@1f,0/pci@1,1/ebus@1/SUNW,CS4231@14,200000" 0 "audiocs"
"/pci@1f,0/pci@1,1/network@1,1" 0 "hme"
"/pci@1f,0/pci@1,1/SUNW,m64B@2" 0 "m64"
"/pci@1f,0/pci@1" 1 "simba"
"/pci@1f,0/pci@1/scsi@1" 0 "glm"
"/pci@1f,0/pci@1/scsi@1,1" 1 "glm"
"/pci@1f,0/pci@1/scsi@1,1/sd@1,0" 17 "sd"
"/pci@1f,0/pci@1/scsi@1,1/sd@2,0" 18 "sd"
"/pci@1f,0/pci@1/scsi@1,1/sd@3,0" 19 "sd"
"/pci@1f,0/pci@1/scsi@1,1/sd@4,0" 20 "sd"
#
```

Although instance names can be displayed using the commands `dmesg`, `sysdef`, and `prtconf`, the only command that shows the mapping of the instance name to the physical device name is the `dmesg` command. For example, you can determine the mapping of an instance name to a physical device name by looking at the `dmesg` output, as shown in the following example from an Ultra system:

```
sd19 is /pci@1f,0/pci@1/scsi@1,1/sd@3,0
dad1 is /pci@1f,0/pci@1,1/ide@3/dad@0,0
```

In the first example, `sd19` is the instance name and `/pci@1f,0/pci@1/scsi@1,1/sd@3,0` is the physical device name. In the second example, `dad0` is the instance name and `/pci@1f,0/pci@1,1/ide@3/dad@0,0` is the physical device name. After the instance name has been assigned to a device, it remains mapped to that device. To keep instance numbers consistent across restarts, the system records them in the `/etc/path_to_inst` file. This file is only read at startup, and it is updated by the `devfsadmd` daemon described later in this section.

Devices already existing on a system are not rearranged when new devices are added, even if new devices are added to `pci` slots that are numerically lower than those occupied by existing devices. In other words, the `/etc/path_to_inst` file is appended to, not rewritten, when new devices are added.

CAUTION

Do Not Remove! Do not remove the `path_to_inst` file; the system cannot start up without it. The system relies on information found in this file to find the root, usr, and swap devices. Make changes to this file only after careful consideration.

It is generally not necessary for the system administrator to change the `path_to_inst` file because the system maintains it. The system administrator can, however, change the assignment of instance numbers by editing this file and doing a reconfiguration startup. However, any changes made in this file are lost if the `devfsadm` command is run before the system is restarted.

NOTE

Resolving Problems with `/etc/path_to_inst` If you can't start up from the startup disk because of a problem with the `/etc/path_to_inst` file, you should start up from the CD-ROM (`boot cdrom -s`) and remove the `/etc/path_to_inst` file from the startup disk. To do this, start up from the CD-ROM using `boot cdrom -s` at the OpenBoot prompt. Use the `rm` command to remove the file named `/a/etc/path_to_inst`. The `path_to_inst` file will automatically be created the next time the system boots.

You can add new devices to a system without requiring a reboot. It's all handled by the `devfsadmd` daemon that transparently builds the necessary configuration entries for those devices capable of notifying the kernel when the device is added (such as USB, FC-AL, disks, and so on). Before Solaris 7, you needed to run several `devfs` administration tools such as `drvconfig`, `disks`, `tapes`, `ports`, and `devlinks` to add in the new device and create the `/dev` and `/devices` entries necessary for the Solaris operating environment to access the new device. These tools are still available but only for compatibility purposes; `drvconfig` and the other link generators are symbolic links to the `devfsadm` utility. Furthermore, these older commands are not aware of hot-pluggable devices, nor are they flexible enough for devices with multiple instances. The `devfsadm` command should now be used in place of all these commands; however, `devfsadmd`, the `devfsadm` daemon, automatically detects device configuration changes, so there should be no need to run this command interactively unless the device is unable to notify the kernel that it has been added to the system.

An example of when to use the `devfsadm` command would be if the system had been started but the power to the CD-ROM or tape drive was not turned on. During startup, the system did not detect the device; therefore, its drivers were not installed. This can be verified by issuing the `sysdef` command and examining the output for sd6, the SCSI target ID normally used for the external CD-ROM:

```
sd, instance #6 (driver not attached)
```

To gain access to the CD-ROM, you could halt the system, turn on power to the CD-ROM, and start the system backup, or you could simply turn on power to the CD-ROM and issue the following command at the command prompt:

```
devfsadm
```

When used without any options, `devfsadm` will attempt to load every driver in the system and attach each driver to its respective device instances. You can restrict `devfsadm` to only look at specific devices using the `-c` option as follows:

```
devfsadm -c disk -c tape
```

This restricts the `devfsadm` command to devices of class *disk* and *tape*. As shown, the `-c` option can be used more than once to specify more than one device class.

Now, if you issue the `sysdef` command, you'll see the following output for the CD-ROM:

```
sd, instance #6
```

You can also use the `devfsadm` command to configure only the devices for a specific driver such as "st" by using the `-i` option as follows:

```
devfsadm -i st
```

The `devfsadm` command will only configure the devices for the driver named "st."

Major and Minor Device Numbers

Each device has a major and minor device number assigned to it. These numbers identify the proper device location and device driver to the kernel. This number is used by the operating system to key into the proper device driver whenever a physical device file corresponding to one of the devices it manages is opened. The major device number maps to a device driver such as sd, st, or hme. The minor device number indicates the specific member within that class of devices. All devices managed by a given device driver contain a unique minor number. Some drivers of pseudo devices (software entities set up to look like devices) create new minor devices on demand. Together, the major and minor numbers uniquely define a device and its device driver.

Physical device files have a unique output when listed with the `ls -l` command, as shown in the following example:

```
cd /devices/pci@1f,0/pci@1,1/ide@3

ls -l
```

The system responds with this:

```
total 4
drwxr-xr-x   2 root     sys          512 Mar 24 13:25 dad@0,0
brw-r-----   1 root     sys      136,  8 Aug  5 11:31 dad@0,0:a
crw-r-----   1 root     sys      136,  8 Aug  5 11:57 dad@0,0:a,raw
brw-r-----   1 root     sys      136,  9 Aug  5 11:32 dad@0,0:b
crw-r-----   1 root     sys      136,  9 Aug  5 11:57 dad@0,0:b,raw
brw-r-----   1 root     sys      136, 10 Aug  5 11:57 dad@0,0:c
crw-r-----   1 root     sys      136, 10 Aug  5 11:57 dad@0,0:c,raw
brw-r-----   1 root     sys      136, 11 Aug  5 11:55 dad@0,0:d
crw-r-----   1 root     sys      136, 11 Aug  5 11:57 dad@0,0:d,raw
brw-r-----   1 root     sys      136, 12 Aug  5 11:32 dad@0,0:e
crw-r-----   1 root     sys      136, 12 Aug  5 11:57 dad@0,0:e,raw
brw-r-----   1 root     sys      136, 13 Aug  5 11:32 dad@0,0:f
crw-r-----   1 root     sys      136, 13 Aug  5 11:57 dad@0,0:f,raw
brw-r-----   1 root     sys      136, 14 Aug  5 11:32 dad@0,0:g
crw-r-----   1 root     sys      136, 14 Aug  5 11:57 dad@0,0:g,raw
brw-r-----   1 root     sys      136, 15 Aug  5 11:32 dad@0,0:h
crw-r-----   1 root     sys      136, 15 Aug  5 11:57 dad@0,0:h,raw
```

This long listing includes columns showing major and minor numbers for each device. The `dad` driver manages all the devices listed in the previous example, which have a major number of 136. Minor numbers are listed after the comma.

During the process of building the /devices directory, major numbers are assigned based on the kernel module attached to the device. Each device is assigned a major device number by using the name-to-number mappings held in the `/etc/name_to_major` file. This file is maintained by the system and is undocumented. The following is a sample of the `/etc/name_to_major` file:

```
more /etc/name_to_major
cn 0
rootnex 1
pseudo 2
ip 3
logindmux 4
icmp 5
fas 6
hme 7
p9000 8
p9100 9
sp 10
clone 11
sad 12
```

```
mm 13
iwscn 14
wc 15
conskbd 16
consms 17
ipdcm 18
dump 19
se 20
log 21
sy 22
ptm 23
pts 24
ptc 25
ptsl 26
bwtwo 27
audio 28
zs 29
cgthree 30
cgtwo 31
sd 32
st 33
...
...
envctrl 131
cvc 132
cvcredir 133
eide 134
hd 135
tadbat 136
ts102 137
simba 138
uata 139
dad 140
atapicd 141
```

To create the minor device entries, the `devfsadmd` daemon uses the information placed in the `dev_info` node by the device driver. Permissions and ownership information are kept in the `/etc/minor_perm` file.

Logical Device Name

The final stage of the autoconfiguration process involves the creation of the logical device name to reflect the new set of devices on the system. To see a list of logical device names for the disks connected to a SPARC system, execute a long listing on the `/dev/dsk` directory, as follows:

```
ls -l /dev/dsk

total 96
lrwxrwxrwx   1 root     root          46 Mar 23 15:05 c0t0d0s0 -> \
../../devices/pci@1f,0/pci@1,1/ide@3/dad@0,0:a
lrwxrwxrwx   1 root     root          46 Mar 23 15:05 c0t0d0s1 -> \
../../devices/pci@1f,0/pci@1,1/ide@3/dad@0,0:b
lrwxrwxrwx   1 root     root          46 Mar 23 15:05 c0t0d0s2 -> \
../../devices/pci@1f,0/pci@1,1/ide@3/dad@0,0:c
lrwxrwxrwx   1 root     root          46 Mar 23 15:05 c0t0d0s3 -> \
../../devices/pci@1f,0/pci@1,1/ide@3/dad@0,0:d
lrwxrwxrwx   1 root     root          46 Mar 23 15:05 c0t0d0s4 -> \
../../devices/pci@1f,0/pci@1,1/ide@3/dad@0,0:e
lrwxrwxrwx   1 root     root          46 Mar 23 15:05 c0t0d0s5 -> \
../../devices/pci@1f,0/pci@1,1/ide@3/dad@0,0:f
lrwxrwxrwx   1 root     root          46 Mar 23 15:05 c0t0d0s6 -> \
../../devices/pci@1f,0/pci@1,1/ide@3/dad@0,0:g
lrwxrwxrwx   1 root     root          46 Mar 23 15:05 c0t0d0s7 -> \
../../devices/pci@1f,0/pci@1,1/ide@3/dad@0,0:h
```

*Output has been truncated.

On the second line of output from the `ls -l` command, notice that the logical device name `c0t0d0s0` is linked to the physical device name, as shown in the following:

```
../../devices/pci@1f,0/pci@1,1/ide@3/dad@0,0:a
```

On Sun SPARC systems, you'll see an eight string logical device name for each disk slice that contains the controller number, the target number, the disk number, and the slice number (c#t#d#s#).

Controller number (c#) Identifies the host bus adapter (HBA), which controls communications between the system and disk unit. The controller number is assigned in sequential order, such as c0, c1, c2, and so on.

Target number (t#) Target numbers, such as t0, t1, t2, and t3, correspond to a unique hardware address that is assigned to each disk, tape, or CD-ROM. Some external disk drives have an address switch located on the rear panel. Some internal disks have address pins that are jumpered to assign that disk's target number.

Disk number (d#) The disk number is also known as the logical unit number (LUN). This number reflects the number of disks at the target location. The disk number is always set to 0 on embedded SCSI controllers.

Slice number (s#) A slice number ranging from 0 to 7.

X86-based Solaris systems have a different disk naming convention, but before describing the logical device name for a disk on an x86-based system, it's worth pointing out a fundamental difference between disk slicing on a SPARC system and disk slicing on an x86-based system. Disk partitioning on the Solaris for the x86 platform has one more level than that of Solaris for SPARC. On Solaris for SPARC, slices and partitions are one and the same; on Solaris for x86, slices are "subpartitions" of a PC partition. This was done to allow Solaris to coexist with other PC operating systems, such as for dual boot configurations.

This difference in slicing brings some differences in the naming of disk devices on a Solaris x86-based PC. Slices are created in the first Solaris partition on a drive and, for SCSI disks, are named the same as on the Solaris for SPARC (c#t#d0s#). However, because slices are within a PC partition, the PC partitions have their own device names. The entire drive is named c#t#d0p0, and the PC partitions (maximum of 4) are c#t#d0p1 through c#t#d0p4. To support the x86 environment, the `format` utility also has an added command called `fdisk` to deal with the PC partitions.

Solaris x86-based systems have 16 slices versus 8 for SPARC. On the x86 PC, slice 8 is used to hold boot code and slice 9 is used for alternate sectors on some types of disks. Higher slices are available for use, but not supported by format at this time.

The major differences between the logical device names used on SPARC-based systems versus x86-based systems are as follows:

- c is the controller number.
- t is the SCSI target number.
- s is the slice number.
- p represents the `fdisk` partition (not slice partition).
- d is the LUN number or IDE Drive Number.

If an IDE drive is used, *d* is used to determine MASTER or SLAVE and the *t* is not used for IDE drives. For example, two controllers are installed on an x86 PC:

- c0 is an IDE controller.
- c1 is a SCSI controller.

On an x86-based Solaris system, the following devices are listed in the `/dev/dsk` directory:

```
c0d0p0    c0d0s7    c1t0d0s4    c1t1d0s15    c1t2d0s12    c1t5d0s1     c1t6d0p3
c0d0p1    c0d0s8    c1t0d0s5    c1t1d0s2     c1t2d0s13    c1t5d0s10    c1t6d0p4
c0d0p2    c0d0s9    c1t0d0s6    c1t1d0s3     c1t2d0s14    c1t5d0s11    c1t6d0s0
c0d0p3    c1t0d0p0  c1t0d0s7    c1t1d0s4     c1t2d0s15    c1t5d0s12    c1t6d0s1
c0d0p4    c1t0d0p1  c1t0d0s8    c1t1d0s5     c1t2d0s2     c1t5d0s13    c1t6d0s10
```

```
c0d0s0     c1t0d0p2    c1t0d0s9    c1t1d0s6    c1t2d0s3    c1t5d0s14   c1t6d0s11
c0d0s1     c1t0d0p3    c1t1d0p0    c1t1d0s7    c1t2d0s4    c1t5d0s15   c1t6d0s12
c0d0s10    c1t0d0p4    c1t1d0p1    c1t1d0s8    c1t2d0s5    c1t5d0s2    c1t6d0s13
c0d0s11    c1t0d0s0    c1t1d0p2    c1t1d0s9    c1t2d0s6    c1t5d0s3    c1t6d0s14
c0d0s12    1t0d0s1     c1t1d0p3    c1t2d0p0    c1t2d0s7    c1t5d0s4    c1t6d0s15
c0d0s13    c1t0d0s10   c1t1d0p4    c1t2d0p1    c1t2d0s8    c1t5d0s5    c1t6d0s2
c0d0s14    c1t0d0s11   c1t1d0s0    c1t2d0p2    c1t2d0s9    c1t5d0s6    c1t6d0s3
c0d0s15    c1t0d0s12   c1t1d0s1    c1t2d0p3    c1t5d0p0    c1t5d0s7    c1t6d0s4
c0d0s2     c1t0d0s13   c1t1d0s10   c1t2d0p4    c1t5d0p1    c1t5d0s8    c1t6d0s5
c0d0s3     c1t0d0s14   c1t1d0s11   c1t2d0s0    c1t5d0p2    c1t5d0s9    c1t6d0s
c0d0s4     c1t0d0s15   c1t1d0s12   c1t2d0s1    c1t5d0p3    c1t6d0p0    c1t6d0s7
c0d0s      c1t0d0s2    c1t1d0s13   c1t2d0s10   c1t5d0p4    c1t6d0p1    c1t6d0s8
c0d06      c1t0d0s3    c1t1d0s14   c1t2d0s11   c1t5d0s0    c1t6d0p2    c1t6d0s9
```

It's easy to see which devices are IDE disks because they do not have a "t" in the logical device name, while the SCSI disks with "c1" have a target number listed. This system has one IDE drive and five SCSI drives listed, targets 0, 1, 2, 5, and 6 (t6 is typically the CD-ROM).

NOTE

In this text and in the examples, unless otherwise noted, I will be using SPARC-based logical device names.

On both SPARC-based and x86-based systems, the logical device name is the name that the system administrator uses to refer to a particular device when running various Solaris file system commands. For example, if running the `mount` command, use the logical device name `/dev/dsk/c0t0d0s7` to mount the file system `/home`:

```
mount /dev/dsk/c0t0d0s7 /home
```

Logical device files in the `/dev` directory are symbolically linked to physical device files in the `/devices` directory. Logical device names are used to access disk devices if you do any of the following:

- Add a new disk to the system.
- Move a disk from one system to another.
- Access (or mount) a file system residing on a local disk.
- Back up a local file system.
- Repair a file system.

Logical devices are organized in subdirectories under the `/dev` directory by their device types, as shown in Table 1.3.

TABLE 1.3 Device Directories

Directory	Description of Contents
/dev/dsk	Block interface to disk devices
/dev/rdsk	Raw or character interface to disk devices
/dev/rmt	Tape devices
/dev/term	Serial line devices
/dev/cua	Dial-out modems
/dev/pts	Pseudo terminals
/dev/fbs	Frame buffers
/dev/sad	STREAMS administrative driver
/dev/md	Metadevices managed by Solaris Volume Manager (SVM)
/dev/vx	Devices managed by Veritas Volume Manager

Block and Raw Devices

Disk drives have an entry under both the `/dev/dsk` and `/dev/rdsk` directories. The `/dsk` directory refers to the block or buffered device file, and the `/rdsk` directory refers to the character or raw device file. The "r" in `rdsk` stands for "raw." You may even hear these devices referred to as "cooked" and "uncooked" devices. If you are not familiar with these devices, refer to Chapter 2, "Installing the Solaris 10 Operating Environment," where block and character devices are described.

The `/dev/dsk` directory contains the disk entries for the block device nodes in `/devices`, as shown in the following command output:

```
# ls -l /dev/dsk
total 96
lrwxrwxrwx   1 root     root          46 Mar 23 15:05 c0t0d0s0 -> \
../../devices/pci@1f,0/pci@1,1/ide@3/dad@0,0:a
lrwxrwxrwx   1 root     root          46 Mar 23 15:05 c0t0d0s1 -> \
../../devices/pci@1f,0/pci@1,1/ide@3/dad@0,0:b
lrwxrwxrwx   1 root     root          46 Mar 23 15:05 c0t0d0s2 -> \
../../devices/pci@1f,0/pci@1,1/ide@3/dad@0,0:c
lrwxrwxrwx   1 root     root          46 Mar 23 15:05 c0t0d0s3 -> \
../../devices/pci@1f,0/pci@1,1/ide@3/dad@0,0:d
lrwxrwxrwx   1 root     root          46 Mar 23 15:05 c0t0d0s4 -> \
../../devices/pci@1f,0/pci@1,1/ide@3/dad@0,0:e
...
...
```

The `/dev/rdsk` directory contains the disk entries for the character device nodes in `/devices`, as shown in the following command:

```
# ls -l /dev/rdsk
total 96
lrwxrwxrwx    1 root      root          50 Mar 23 15:05 c0t0d0s0 -> \
../../devices/pci@1f,0/pci@1,1/ide@3/dad@0,0:a,raw
lrwxrwxrwx    1 root      root          50 Mar 23 15:05 c0t0d0s1 -> \
../../devices/pci@1f,0/pci@1,1/ide@3/dad@0,0:b,raw
lrwxrwxrwx    1 root      root          50 Mar 23 15:05 c0t0d0s2 -> \
../../devices/pci@1f,0/pci@1,1/ide@3/dad@0,0:c,raw
lrwxrwxrwx    1 root      root          50 Mar 23 15:05 c0t0d0s3 -> \
../../devices/pci@1f,0/pci@1,1/ide@3/dad@0,0:d,raw
lrwxrwxrwx    1 root      root          50 Mar 23 15:05 c0t0d0s4 -> \
../../devices/pci@1f,0/pci@1,1/ide@3/dad@0,0:e,raw
```

*Output has been truncated.

You should now have an understanding of how Solaris identifies disk drives connected to the system. The remainder of this chapter describes how to create file systems on these devices. It will also describe how to manage file systems and monitor disk space usage, some of the fundamental concepts you'll need for the first exam.

EXAM ALERT

Make sure you understand when to use a raw device and when to use a buffered device. You'll encounter several questions on the exam where you will need to select either the raw or buffered device for a particular command.

A File System Defined

A *file system* is a collection of files and directories stored on disk in a standard Unix file system (UFS) format. All disk-based computer systems have a file system. In Unix, file systems have two basic components: files and directories. A file is the actual information as it is stored on the disk, and a directory is a list of the filenames. In addition to keeping track of filenames, the file system must keep track of files' access dates, permissions, and ownership. Managing file systems is one of the system administrator's most important tasks. Administration of the file system involves the following:

- Ensuring that users have access to data. This means that systems are up and operational, file permissions are set up properly, and data is accessible.
- Protecting file systems against file corruption and hardware failures. This is accomplished by checking the file system regularly and maintaining proper system backups.
- Securing file systems against unauthorized access. Only authorized users should have access to files.

- Providing users with adequate space for their files.
- Keeping the file system clean. In other words, data in the file system must be relevant and not wasteful of disk space. Procedures are needed to make sure that users follow proper naming conventions and that data is stored in an organized manner.

You'll see the term *file system* used in several ways. Usually, *file system* describes a particular type of file system (disk-based, network based, or virtual). It might also describe the entire file tree from the root directory downward. In another context, the term *file system* might be used to describe the structure of a disk slice, described later in this chapter.

The Solaris system software uses the virtual file system (VFS) architecture, which provides a standard interface for different file system types. The VFS architecture lets the kernel handle basic operations, such as reading, writing, and listing files, without requiring the user or program to know about the underlying file system type. Furthermore, Solaris provides file system administrative commands that enable you to maintain file systems.

Defining a Disk's Geometry

Before creating a file system on a disk, you need to understand the basic geometry of a disk drive. Disks come in many shapes and sizes. The number of heads, tracks, and sectors and the disk capacity vary from one model to another. Basic disk terminology is described in Table 1.4.

TABLE 1.4 Disk Terminology

Disk Term	Description
Track	A concentric ring on a disk that passes under a single stationary disk head as the disk rotates.
Cylinder	The set of tracks with the same nominal distance from the axis about which the disk rotates.
Sector	Section of each disk platter. A sector holds 512 bytes.
Block	A data storage area on a disk. A disk block is 512 bytes.
Disk controller	A chip and its associated circuitry that control the disk drive.
Disk label	The first sector of a disk (block 0) that contains disk geometry and partition information. Also referred to as the Volume Table Of Contents (VTOC). To label a disk means to write slice information onto the disk. You usually label a disk after you change its slices using the `format` command.
Device driver	A kernel module that controls a hardware or virtual device.

A hard disk consists of several separate disk platters mounted on a common spindle. Data stored on each platter surface is written and read by disk heads. The circular path that a disk head traces over a spinning disk platter is called a *track*.

Each track is made up of a number of sectors laid end to end. A *sector* consists of a header, a trailer, and 512 bytes of data. The header and trailer contain error-checking information to help ensure the accuracy of the data. Taken together, the set of tracks traced across all the individual disk platter surfaces for a single position of the heads is called a *cylinder*.

Disk Controllers

Associated with every disk is a *controller*, an intelligent device responsible for organizing data on the disk. Some disk controllers are located on a separate circuit board, such as SCSI. Other controller types are integrated with the disk drive, such as Integrated Device Electronics (IDE) and Enhanced IDE (EIDE).

Defect List

Disks might contain areas where data cannot be written and retrieved reliably. These areas are called *defects*. The controller uses the error-checking information in each disk block's trailer to determine whether a defect is present in that block. When a block is found to be defective, the controller can be instructed to add it to a defect list and avoid using that block in the future. The last two cylinders of a disk are set aside for diagnostic use and for storing the disk defect list.

Disk Labels

A special area of every disk is set aside for storing information about the disk's controller, geometry, and slices. This information is called the disk's label or *volume table of contents (VTOC)*.

To label a disk means to write slice information onto the disk. You usually label a disk after defining its slices. If you fail to label a disk after creating slices, the slices will be unavailable because the operating system has no way of knowing about them.

Solaris supports two types of disk labels, the VTOC disk label and the EFI disk label. Solaris 10 (and later versions of Solaris 9) provides support for disks that are larger than 1 terabyte on systems that run a 64-bit Solaris kernel. The acronym EFI stands for Extensible Firmware Interface and this new label format is REQUIRED for all devices over 1TB in size, and cannot be converted back to VTOC.

The EFI label provides support for physical disks and virtual disk volumes. Solaris 10 also includes updated disk utilities for managing disks greater than 1 terabyte. The UFS file system is compatible with the EFI disk label, and you can create a UFS file system greater than 1 terabyte.

The traditional VTOC label is still available for disks less than 1 terabyte in size. If you are only using disks smaller than 1 terabyte on your systems, managing disks will be the same as in previous Solaris releases. In addition, you can use the `format -e` command to label a disk less than 1TB with an EFI label.

The advantages of the EFI disk label over the VTOC disk label are as follows:

- Provides support for disks greater than 1 terabyte in size.
- Provides usable slices 0–6, where slice 2 is just another slice.
- Partitions (or slices) cannot overlap with the primary or backup label, nor with any other partitions. The size of the EFI label is usually 34 sectors, so partitions start at sector 34. This feature means that no partition can start at sector zero (0).
- No cylinder, head, or sector information is stored in the EFI label. Sizes are reported in blocks.
- Information that was stored in the alternate cylinders area, the last two cylinders of the disk, is now stored in slice 8.
- If you use the `format` utility to change partition sizes, the unassigned partition tag is assigned to partitions with sizes equal to zero. By default, the format utility assigns the usr partition tag to any partition with a size greater than zero. You can use the partition change menu to reassign partition tags after the partitions are changed.
- Solaris ZFS (zettabyte file system) uses EFI labels by default. As of this writing, ZFS file systems are not implemented but are expected in a future Solaris 10 update.

The following lists restrictions of the EFI disk label:

- The SCSI driver, ssd or sd, currently supports only up to 2 terabytes. If you need greater disk capacity than 2 terabytes, use a disk and storage management product such as Solaris Volume Manager to create a larger device.
- Layered software products intended for systems with EFI-labeled disks might be incapable of accessing a disk without an EFI disk label.
- You cannot use the `fdisk` command on a disk with an EFI label that is greater than 1 terabyte in size.
- A disk with an EFI label is not recognized on systems running previous Solaris releases.
- The EFI disk label is not supported on IDE disks.
- You cannot boot from a disk with an EFI disk label.
- You cannot use the Solaris Management Console's Disk Manager tool to manage disks with EFI labels. Use the format utility to partition disks with EFI labels. Then, you can use the Solaris Management Console's Enhanced Storage Tool to manage volumes and disk sets with EFI-labeled disks.

- The EFI specification prohibits overlapping slices. The entire disk is represented by c#t#d#.
- The EFI disk label provides information about disk or partition sizes in sectors and blocks, but not in cylinders and heads.
- The following `format` options are either not supported or are not applicable on disks with EFI labels:
  - The `save` option is not supported because disks with EFI labels do not need an entry in the `format.dat` file.
  - The `backup` option is not applicable because the disk driver finds the primary label and writes it back to the disk.

Partition Tables

An important part of the disk label is the *partition table*, which identifies a disk's slices, the slice boundaries (in cylinders), and the total size of the slices. A disk's partition table can be displayed by using the `format` utility described in the "Disk Slices" section later in this chapter.

Solaris File System Types

Objective:

Describe the purpose, features, and functions of disk-based, networked, and pseudo file systems in a Solaris operating environment, and explain the differences among these file system types.

Solaris file systems can be put into three categories: disk-based, network-based, and virtual.

Disk-Based File Systems

Disk-based file systems reside on the system's local disk. As of this writing, the following are four types of disk-based file systems found in Solaris 10:

- **UFS (Unix File System)**—The Unix file system, which is based on the BSD FFS Fast file system (the traditional Unix file system). The UFS is the default disk-based file system used in Solaris.
- **HSFS (High Sierra File System)**—The High Sierra and ISO 9660 file system, which supports the Rock Ridge extensions. The HSFS file system is used on CD-ROMs and is a read-only file system.

- **PCFS (PC File System)**—The PC file system, which allows read/write access to data and programs on DOS-formatted disks written for DOS-based personal computers.
- **UDF (Universal Disk Format)**—The Universal Disk Format file system. UDF is the new industry-standard format for storing information on optical media technology called DVD (digital versatile disc).
- Not in Solaris 10 as of this writing, but worth noting is the zettabyte file system (ZFS), scheduled for a future Solaris 10 update, incorporating advanced data security and protection features, eliminating the need for `fsck` or other recovery mechanisms. By redefining file systems as virtualized storage, Solaris ZFS will enable virtually unlimited scalability.

Network-Based File Systems

Network-based file systems are file systems accessed over the network. Typically, they reside on one system and are accessed by other systems across the network.

The network file system (NFS) or remote file systems are file systems made available from remote systems. NFS is the only available network-based file system bundled with the Solaris operating environment. NFS is discussed in detail in Chapter 9, "Virtual File Systems, Swap Space, and Core Dumps."

Virtual File Systems

Virtual file systems, previously called pseudo file systems, are virtual or memory-based file systems that create duplicate paths to other disk-based file systems or provide access to special kernel information and facilities. Most virtual file systems do not use file system disk space, although a few exceptions exist. Cache file systems, for example, use a disk-based file system to contain the cache.

Some virtual file systems, such as the temporary file system, might use the swap space on a physical disk. The following is a list of some of the more common types of virtual file systems:

- **SWAPFS (Swap File System)**—A file system used by the kernel for swapping. Swap space is used as a virtual memory storage area when the system does not have enough physical memory to handle current processes.
- **PROCFS (Process File System)**—The Process File System resides in memory. It contains a list of active processes, by process number, in the `/proc` directory. Commands such as `ps` use information in the `/proc` directory. Debuggers and other development tools can also access the processes' address space by using file system calls.

- **LOFS (Loopback File System)**—The Loopback File System lets you create a new virtual file system, which can provide access to existing files using alternate pathnames. Once the virtual file system is created, other file systems can be mounted within it, without affecting the original file system.
- **CacheFS (Cache File System)**—The Cache File System lets you use disk drives on local workstations to store frequently used data from a remote file system or CD-ROM. The data stored on the local disk is the cache.
- **TMPFS (Temporary File System)**—The Temporary File System uses local memory for file system reads and writes. Because TMPFS uses physical memory and not the disk, access to files in a TMPFS is typically much faster than to files in a UFS. Files in the temporary file system are not permanent; they are deleted when the file system is unmounted and when the system is shut down or rebooted. TMPFS is the default file system type for the `/tmp` directory in the SunOS system software. You can copy or move files into or out of the `/tmp` directory just as you would in a UFS `/tmp`. When memory is insufficient to hold everything in the temporary file system, the TMPFS uses swap space as a temporary backing store, as long as adequate swap space is present.
- **MNTFS**—The MNTFS type maintains information about currently mounted file systems. MNTFS is described later in this chapter.
- **CTFS (Contract File System)**—The CTFS is associated with the `/system/contract` directory and is the interface for creating, controlling, and observing contracts. The service management facility (SMF) uses process contracts (a type of contract) to track the processes which compose a service.
- **DEVFS (Device file System)**—The DEVFS is used to manage the namespace of all devices on the system. This file system is used for the `/devices` directory. The devfs file system is new in Solaris 10 and increases system boot performance because only device entries that are needed to boot the system are attached. New device entries are added as the devices are accessed.
- **FDFS (File Descriptor File System)**—The FDFS provides explicit names for opening files by using file descriptors.
- **OBJFS (Object File System)**—The OBJFS (object) file system describes the state of all modules currently loaded by the kernel. This file system is used by debuggers to access information about kernel symbols without having to access the kernel directly.

Disk Slices

Objective:

Perform disk partitioning and relabel a disk in a Solaris operating environment using the appropriate files, commands, options, menus, and/or tables.

Disks are divided into regions called *disk slices* or *disk partitions*. A slice is composed of a single range of contiguous blocks. It is a physical subset of the disk (except for slice 2, which represents the entire disk). A Unix file system or the swap area is built within these disk slices. The boundaries of a disk slice are defined when a disk is partitioned using the Solaris `format` utility or the Solaris Management Console Disks Tool, and the slice information for a particular disk can be viewed by using the `prtvtoc` command. Each disk slice appears to the operating system (and to the system administrator) as though it were a separate disk drive.

Disk slicing differs between the SPARC and the x86 platforms. On the SPARC platform, the entire disk is devoted to the Solaris OS; the disk can be divided into 8 slices, numbered 0–7. On the x86 platform, the disk is divided into `fdisk` partitions using the `fdisk` command. The Solaris `fdisk` partition is divided into 10 slices, numbered 0–9.

NOTE

Slices Versus Partitions Solaris device names use the term *slice* (and the letter *s* in the device name) to refer to the slice number. Slices were called *partitions* in SunOS 4.*x*. This book attempts to use the term *slice* whenever possible; however, certain interfaces, such as the `format` and `prtvtoc` commands, refer to slices as partitions.

A *physical disk* consists of a stack of circular platters, as shown in Figure 1.1. Data is stored on these platters in a cylindrical pattern. Cylinders can be grouped and isolated from one another. A group of cylinders is referred to as a slice. A slice is defined with start and end points, defined from the center of the stack of platters, which is called the *spindle*.

Disk slices are defined by an offset and a size in cylinders. The offset is the distance from cylinder 0. To define a slice, the administrator provides a starting cylinder and an ending cylinder. A disk can have up to eight slices, named 0 to 7, but it is uncommon to use partition 2 as a file system. (See Chapter 2 for a discussion of disk-storage systems and sizing partitions.)

NOTE

Using Slice 2 As a Partition Sometimes a relational database uses an entire disk and requires one single raw partition. It's convenient in this circumstance to use slice 2, as it represents the entire disk, but is not recommended because you would be using cylinder 0. You should start your database partition on cylinder 1 so that you don't risk overwriting the disk's VTOC. UFS file systems are smart enough not to touch the VTOC, but some databases have proven to be not so friendly.

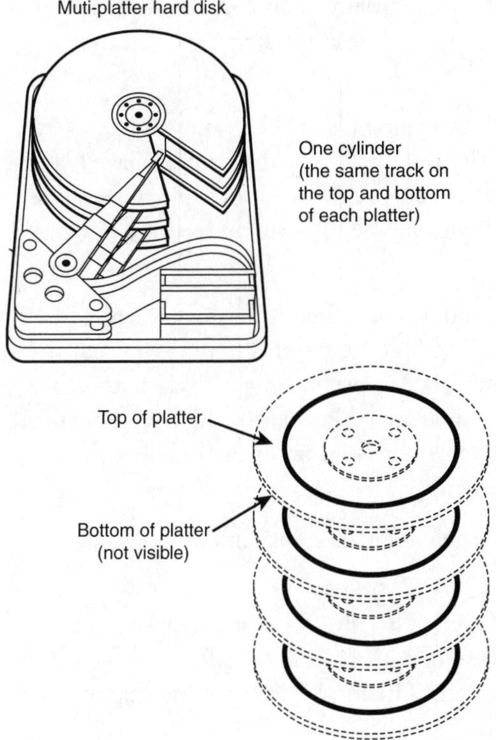

FIGURE 1.1 Disk platters and cylinders.

When setting up slices, remember these rules:

- Each disk slice holds only one file system.
- No file system can span multiple slices.
- After a file system is created, its size cannot be increased or decreased without repartitioning and destroying the partition directly before or after it.
- Slices cannot span multiple disks; however, multiple swap slices on separate disks are allowed.

When we discuss logical volumes later in this chapter, you'll learn how to get around some of these limitations in file systems.

Also follow these guidelines when planning the layout of file systems:

- Distribute the workload as evenly as possible among different I/O systems and disk drives. Distribute `/home` and swap directories evenly across disks. A single disk has limitations on how quickly data can be transferred. By spreading this load across more than one disk, you can improve performance exponentially. This concept is described in Chapter 10, "Managing Storage Volumes," where I describe striping using the Solaris Volume Manager.

- Keep projects or groups within their own file system. This enables you to keep better track of data for backups, recovery, and security reasons. Some disks might have better performance than others. For multiple projects, you could create multiple file systems and distribute the I/O workload by putting high-volume projects on separate physical disks.
- Use the faster drives for file systems that need quick access and the slower drives for data that might not need to be retrieved as quickly. Some systems have drives that were installed as original hardware along with newer, better performing, drives that were added on some time later. Maybe you have a database dedicated to a high-volume project. This would be a perfect candidate to put on the newer, faster disk while a less accessed project could go on the slower disk drive.
- It is not important for most sites to be concerned about keeping similar types of user files in the same file system.
- Occasionally, you might have some users who consistently create small or large files. You might consider creating a separate file system with more inodes for users who consistently create small files. (See the section titled "The inode" later in this chapter for more information on inodes.)

We discuss disk slices again in Chapter 2, where we describe setting up disk storage and planning the layout of your disk slices.

Displaying Disk Configuration Information

As described earlier, disk configuration information is stored in the disk label. If you know the disk and slice number, you can display information for a disk by using the print volume table of contents (`prtvtoc`) command. You can specify the volume by specifying any slice defined on the disk (for example, `/dev/rdsk/c0t3d0s2` or `/dev/rdsk/c0t3d0s*`). Regardless of which slice you specify, all slices defined on the disk will be displayed. If you know the target number of the disk but do not know how it is divided into slices, you can show information for the entire disk by specifying either slice 2 or s*. Step by Step 1.2 shows how you can examine information stored on a disk's label by using the `prtvtoc` command.

STEP BY STEP

1.2 Examining a Disk's Label Using the `prtvtoc` Command

1. Become superuser.
2. Type **`prtvtoc /dev/rdsk/`*`cntndnsn`*** and press Enter.

   Information for the disk and slice you specify is displayed. In the following steps, information is displayed for all of disk 3:

1. Become superuser.
2. Type **`prtvtoc /dev/rdsk/c0t3d0s2`** and press Enter.

   The system responds with this:

```
* /dev/rdsk/c0t3d0s2 (volume "") partition map
*
* Dimensions:
*     512 bytes/sector
*      36 sectors/track
*       9 tracks/cylinder
*     324 sectors/cylinder
*    1272 cylinders
*    1254 accessible cylinders
*
* Flags:
*   1: unmountable
*  10: read-only
*
*                         First   Sector  Last
* Partition Tag Flags  Sector  Count   Sector  Mount Directory
  2         5   01     0       406296  406295
  6         4   00     0       242352  242351
  7         0   00     242352  163944  406295  /files7
```

The `prtvtoc` command shows the number of cylinders and heads, as well as how the disk's slices are arranged.

The following is an example of running the `prtvtoc` command on a SCSI disk with an EFI label:

```
prtvtoc /dev/rdsk/c2t1d0s1
* /dev/rdsk/c2t1d0s1 partition map
*
* Dimensions:
*     512 bytes/sector
* 8385121 sectors
* 8385054 accessible sectors
*
```

```
* Flags:
*   1: unmountable
*  10: read-only
*
*                          First      Sector     Last
* Partition   Tag  Flags    Sector     Count      Sector  Mount Directory
       0       2    01          34     41006      41039
       1       2    00       41040   8327663    8368702   /mnt
       8      11    00     8368703     16384    8385086
```

Using the `format` Utility to Create Slices

Before you can create a file system on a disk, the disk must be formatted, and you must divide it into slices by using the Solaris `format` utility. Formatting involves two separate processes:

- Writing format information to the disk
- Completing a surface analysis, which compiles an up-to-date list of disk defects

When a disk is formatted, header and trailer information is superimposed on the disk. When the `format` utility runs a surface analysis, the controller scans the disk for defects. It should be noted that defects and formatting information reduce the total disk space available for data. This is why a new disk usually holds only 90–95% of its capacity after formatting. This percentage varies according to disk geometry and decreases as the disk ages and develops more defects.

The need to perform a surface analysis on a disk drive has dropped as more manufacturers ship their disk drives formatted and partitioned. You should not need to perform a surface analysis within the `format` utility when adding a disk drive to an existing system unless you think disk defects are causing problems. The primary reason that you would use `format` is if you want to view or change the partitioning scheme on a disk.

CAUTION

Always Back Up Your Data Formatting and creating slices is a destructive process, so make sure user data is backed up before you start.

The `format` utility searches your system for all attached disk drives and reports the following information about the disk drives it finds:

- Target location
- Disk geometry

- Whether the disk is formatted
- Whether the disk has mounted partitions

In addition, the `format` utility is used in disk repair operations to do the following:

- Retrieve disk labels
- Repair defective sectors
- Format and analyze disks
- Partition disks
- Label disks (write the disk name and configuration information to the disk for future retrieval)

The Solaris installation program partitions and labels disk drives as part of installing the Solaris release. However, you might need to use the `format` utility when doing the following:

- Displaying slice information
- Dividing a disk into slices
- Formatting a disk drive when you think disk defects are causing problems
- Repairing a disk drive

The main reason a system administrator uses the `format` utility is to divide a disk into disk slices.

EXAM ALERT

`format` Utility Pay close attention to each menu item in the format utility and understand what task each performs. Expect to see several questions pertaining to the format utility menus on Exam CX-310-200. Along with adding slices, make sure you know how to remove or resize slices. You may see a scenario where a production system is running out of swap and you need to go into the format utility and add another swap slice.

The process of creating slices is outlined in Step by Step 1.3.

NOTE

If you are using Solaris on an x86 or x64-based PC system, refer to the next Step by Step to create an FDISK partition before creating the slices.

STEP BY STEP

1.3 Formatting a Disk

1. Become superuser.

2. Type **`format`**.

   The system responds with this:

```
Searching for disks...done

AVAILABLE DISK SELECTIONS:
       0. c0t0d0 <IBM-DJNA-370910 cyl 17660 alt 2 hd 16 sec 63>
          /pci@1f,0/pci@1,1/ide@3/dad@0,0
       1. c2t1d0 <SUN4.2G cyl 3880 alt 2 hd 16 sec 135>
          /pci@1f,0/pci@1/scsi@1,1/sd@1,0
       2. c2t2d0 <SUN4.2G cyl 3880 alt 2 hd 16 sec 135>
          /pci@1f,0/pci@1/scsi@1,1/sd@2,0
       3. c2t3d0 <SUN4.2G cyl 3880 alt 2 hd 16 sec 135>
          /pci@1f,0/pci@1/scsi@1,1/sd@3,0
       4. c2t4d0 <SUN4.2G cyl 3880 alt 2 hd 16 sec 135>
          /pci@1f,0/pci@1/scsi@1,1/sd@4,0
```

3. Specify the disk (enter its number).

   The system responds with the format main menu:

```
FORMAT MENU:
    disk - select a disk
    type - select (define) a disk type
    partition - select (define) a partition table
    current - describe the current disk
    format - format and analyze the disk
    repair - repair a defective sector
    label - write label to the disk
    analyze - surface analysis
    defect - defect list management
    backup - search for backup labels
    verify - read and display labels
    save - save new disk/partition definitions
    inquiry - show vendor, product and revision
    volname - set 8-character volume name
    !<cmd> - execute <cmd>, then return
    quit
```

Table 1.5 describes the format main menu items.

TABLE 1.5 Format Main Menu Item Descriptions

Menu Item	Description
`disk`	Lists all the system's drives. Also lets you choose the disk you want to use in subsequent operations. This disk is referred to as the current disk.
`type`	Identifies the manufacturer and model of the current disk. Also displays a list of known drive types. Choose the Auto configure option for all SCSI-2 disk drives.
`partition`	Creates and modifies slices.
`current`	Describes the current disk (that is, device name, device type, number of cylinders, alternate cylinders, heads, sectors, and physical device name).
`format`	Formats the current disk by using one of these sources of information in this order: Information that is found in the `format.dat` file Information from the automatic configuration process Information that you type at the prompt if no format.dat entry exists This command does not apply to IDE disks. IDE disks are preformatted by the manufacturer.
`fdisk`	x86 platform only: Runs the fdisk program to create a Solaris fdisk partition.
`repair`	Used to repair a specific block on the current disk.
`label`	Writes a new label to the current disk. This is not the same as labeling the disk with `volname`.
`analyze`	Runs read, write, and compare tests.
`defect`	Retrieves and displays defect lists. This feature does not apply to IDE disks. IDE disks manage defects automatically.
`backup`	Searches for backup labels if the VTOC becomes corrupted or gets deleted.
`verify`	Displays information about the current disk such as device name, device type, number of cylinders, alternate cylinders, heads, sectors, and partition table.
`save`	Saves new disk and partition information.
`inquiry`	SCSI disks only—Displays the vendor, product name, and revision level of the current drive.
`volname`	Labels the disk with a new eight-character volume name that you specify. This is not the same as writing the partition table to disk using `label`.
`quit`	Exits the format menu. Ctrl+D will also exit the format utility from the main menu or from any submenu.

4. Type **`partition`** at the format prompt. The partition menu is displayed.

NOTE

Using Shortcuts in the `format` Utility It is unnecessary to type the entire command. After you type the first two characters of a command, the `format` utility recognizes the entire command.

```
format> partition
PARTITION MENU:
    0 - change '0' partition
    1 - change '1' partition
    2 - change '2' partition
    3 - change '3' partition
    4 - change '4' partition
    5 - change '5' partition
    6 - change '6' partition
    7 - change '7' partition
    select - select a predefined table
    modify - modify a predefined partition table
    name - name the current table
    print - display the current table
    label - write partition map and label to the disk
    !<cmd> - execute <cmd>, then return
    quit
```

5. Type **`print`** to display the current partition map.

   The system responds with this:

```
partition> print
Current partition table (original):
Total disk cylinders available: 3984 + 2 (reserved cylinders)
Part      Tag    Flag     Cylinders        Size            Blocks
0        root     wm       0 -  175      90.49MB    (176/0/0)    185328
1        swap     wu     176 - 1051     450.40MB    (876/0/0)    922428
2      backup     wu       0 - 3983       2.00GB    (3984/0/0) 4195152
3 unassigned      wm       0               0        (0/0/0)           0
4         usr     wm    1052 - 1635     300.27MB    (584/0/0)    614952
5         usr     wm    1636 - 3982       1.18GB    (2347/0/0) 2471391
6 unassigned      wm       0               0        (0/0/0)           0
7 unassigned      wm       0               0        (0/0/0)           0
```

The columns displayed with the partition table are

- **Part**—The slice number (0–7).
- **Tag**—This is an optional value that indicates how the slice is being used. The value can be any of the following names that best fits the function of the file system you are creating:

  unassigned, boot, root, swap, usr, backup, stand, var, home, alternates, reserved

  You may also see tags labeled `public` or `private`, which represent Sun StorEdge Volume Manager tags:

- **Flag**—Values in this column can be
  - **wm**—The disk slice is writable and mountable.
  - **wu**—The disk slice is writable and unmountable (such as a swap slice).
  - **rm**—The disk slice is read-only and mountable.
  - **ru**—The disk slice is read-only and unmountable.
- **Cylinders**—The starting and ending cylinder number for the disk slice.
- **Size**—The slice size specified as
  - mb—megabytes
  - gb—gigabytes
  - b—blocks
  - c—cylinders
- **Blocks**—The total number of cylinders and the total number of sectors per slice.

NOTE

Wasted Disk Space Wasted disk space occurs during partitioning when one or more cylinders have not been allocated to a disk slice. This may happen intentionally or accidentally. If there are unallocated slices available, then wasted space can possibly be assigned to a slice later on.

You can use the `name` and `save` commands in the partition menu to name and save a newly created partition table to a file that can be referenced by name later, when you want to use this same partition scheme on another disk. When issuing the `name` command, you'll provide a unique name for this partition scheme and then issue the `save` command to save the information to the `./format.dat` file. Normally this file is located in the `/etc` directory, so provide the full pathname for `/etc/format.dat` to update the master file.

6. After you partition the disk, you must label it by typing **`label`** at the partition prompt:

```
partition> label
```

You are asked for confirmation on labeling the disk as follows:

```
Ready to label disk, continue?
```

Enter **Y** to continue.

NOTE

Label Your Drive To label a disk means to write slice information onto the disk. If you don't label the drive when exiting the `format` utility, your partition changes will not be retained. Get into the habit of labeling at the partition submenu, but you can also label at the `format` utility main menu as well—you get two chances to remember before exiting the utility.

7. After labeling the disk, type **quit** to exit the partition menu:

```
partition> quit
```

8. Type **quit** again to exit the `format` utility:

```
format> quit
```

It's important to point out a few undesirable things that can happen when defining disk partitions with the `format` utility if you're not careful. First, be careful not to waste disk space. Wasted disk space can occur when you decrease the size of one slice and do not adjust the starting cylinder number of the adjoining disk slice.

Second, don't overlap disk slices. Overlapping occurs when one or more cylinders are allocated to more than one disk slice. For example, increasing the size of one slice without decreasing the size of the adjoining slice will create overlapping partitions. The `format` utility will not warn you of wasted disk space or overlapping partitions.

As described earlier in this chapter, Solaris on x86-based PCs treats disk drives slightly differently than on the SPARC-based systems. On an x86 system, once a disk drive has been physically installed and verified as working, you'll use the `format` command to slice the disk, but first an fdisk partition must be created on the new drive. Use the `format` command as follows:

STEP BY STEP

1.4 Using the `format` Command

1. As root, type `format` to get into the `format` utility.

```
format
```

The following menu appears:

```
AVAILABLE DISK SELECTIONS:
        0. c1t0d0 <FUJITSU-M1606S-512-6234 cyl 3455 alt 2 hd 6 sec 102>
           /pci@0,0/pci9004,8178@3/cmdk@0,0
        1. c1t1d0 <IBM-DFHSS1W!e-4141 cyl 4071 alt 2 hd 4 sec 135>
           /pci@0,0/pci9004,8178@3/cmdk@1,0
        2. c1t2d0 <DEFAULT cyl 2928 alt 2 hd 6 sec 120>
           /pci@0,0/pci9004,8178@3/cmdk@2,0
Specify disk (enter its number):
```

2. Enter the number corresponding to the new drive and the following menu will be displayed:

```
FORMAT MENU:
        disk       - select a disk
        type       - select (define) a disk type
        partition  - select (define) a partition table
```

```
          current     - describe the current disk
          format      - format and analyze the disk
          fdisk       - run the fdisk program
          repair      - repair a defective sector
          label       - write label to the disk
          analyze     - surface analysis
          defect      - defect list management
          backup      - search for backup labels
          verify      - read and display labels
          save        - save new disk/partition definitions
          inquiry     - show vendor, product and revision
          volname     - set 8-character volume name5
          quit
format>
```

3. Select the `fdisk` option and the following menu appears:

```
The recommended default partitioning for your disk is:
  a 100% "SOLARIS System" partition.

To select this, please type "y".  To partition your disk
differently, type "n" and the "fdisk" program will let you
select other partitions.
```

4. If you wish to use the entire drive for Solaris enter **y**. This will return to the format menu. If **n** is chosen, the fdisk menu will be displayed.

```
             Total disk size is 4073 cylinders
             Cylinder size is 540 (512 byte) blocks
                                           Cylinders
   Partition   Status    Type      Start   End   Length    %
   =========   ======    ========  =====   ===   ======   ===

THERE ARE NO PARTITIONS CURRENTLY DEFINED
SELECT ONE OF THE FOLLOWING:
     1.   Create a partition
     2.   Change Active (Boot from) partition
     3.   Delete a partition
     4.   Exit (Update disk configuration and exit)
     5.   Cancel (Exit without updating disk configuration)
Enter Selection:
```

5. Choose 1 to create a Solaris FDISK partition. This is not the same as a Solaris slice.

6. After creating the partition, choose 4 to exit and save. The format menu will return.

7. Choose `partition` and follow the Step by Step 1.3 procedure described earlier for formatting a disk, beginning at step number 4.

One more item of note: On standard UFS file systems, don't change the size of disk slices that are currently in use. When a disk with existing slices is repartitioned and relabeled, any existing data will be lost. Before repartitioning a disk, first copy all the data to tape or to another disk.

The Free Hog Slice

When using the `format` utility to change the size of disk slices, a temporary slice is automatically designated that expands and shrinks to accommodate the slice resizing operations. This temporary slice is referred to as the *free hog*, and it represents the unused disk space on a disk drive. If a slice is decreased, the free hog expands. The free hog is then used to allocate space to slices that have been increased. It does not, however, prevent the overlapping of disk slices as described in the previous section.

The free hog slice exists only when you run the `format` utility. It is not saved as a permanent slice.

Using the `format` Utility to Modify Partitions

If you need to change the size of slices on a particular disk, you can either re-create the disk slices as outlined in the previous section or use the `modify` option of the `format` utility.

CAUTION

Copy Your Data to Avoid Loss You will lose all data when changing partition sizes. Make sure that you copy your data either to another disk or to tape before continuing.

The `modify` option allows the root to create slices by specifying the size of each slice without having to keep track of starting cylinder boundaries. It also keeps track of any excess disk space in the temporary free hog slice. To modify a disk slice, follow the process outlined in Step by Step 1.5.

STEP BY STEP

1.5 Modifying a Disk Slice

1. Make a backup of your data. This process destroys the data on this disk slice.
2. As root, enter the partition menu of the `format` utility, as described in Step by Step 1.3.
3. After printing the existing partition scheme, type **`modify`** and press Enter.

NOTE

Mounted Partitions If you try to modify mounted partitions, you receive an error that states "Cannot modify disk partitions while it has mounted partitions."

When typing `modify`, you'll see the following output on a disk that does not have mounted partitions:

```
Select partitioning base:
        0. Current partition table (original)
        1. All Free Hog
Choose base (enter number) [0]?
```

4. Press Enter to select the default selection. The following is displayed:

```
Part      Tag    Flag   Cylinders      Size         Blocks
0         usr    wm     0 -   194      100.26MB     (195/0/0)    205335
1 unassigned     wu     195 - 1167     500.28MB     (973/0/0)   1024569
2      backup    wm     0 - 3983       2.00GB       (3984/0/0)  4195152
3 unassigned     wm     0               0           (0/0/0)           0
4 unassigned     wm     0               0           (0/0/0)           0
5 unassigned     wm     0               0           (0/0/0)           0
6 unassigned     wm     0               0           (0/0/0)           0
7 unassigned     wm     0               0           (0/0/0)           0

Do you wish to continue creating a new partition
table based on above table[yes]?
```

5. Press Enter to select the default selection. The following message is displayed:

```
Free Hog partition[6]?
```

6. Press Enter to select the default selection. If all the disk space is in use, the following message is displayed:

```
Warning: No space available from Free Hog partition.
Continue[no]?
```

7. Type **yes**. You'll be prompted to type the new size for each partition:

```
Enter size of partition '0' [205335b,195c,100.26mb,0.10gb]: 90m
Enter size of partition '1' [1024569b,973c,500.28mb 0.49gb]:450m
Enter size of partition '3' [0b, 0c, 0.00mb, 0.00gb]: <cr>
Enter size of partition '4' [0b, 0c, 0.00mb, 0.00gb]: <cr>
Enter size of partition '5' [0b, 0c, 0.00mb, 0.00gb]: <cr>
Enter size of partition '7' [0b, 0c, 0.00mb, 0.00gb]: <cr>
```

NOTE

Temporary Free Hog Slice 6 is not displayed because that is the temporary free hog.

When you are finished resizing the last partition, the following is displayed, showing you the revised partition map:

```
Part      Tag    Flag     Cylinders        Size          Blocks
0          usr    wm       0 -  175      90.49MB     (176/0/0)   185328
1 unassigned    wu     176 - 1051     450.40MB     (876/0/0)   922428
2       backup    wm       0 - 3983       2.00GB     (3984/0/0) 4195152
3 unassigned    wm       0                0          (0/0/0)          0
4 unassigned    wm       0                0          (0/0/0)          0
5 unassigned    wm       0                0          (0/0/0)          0
6 unassigned    wm    1052 - 3983       1.47GB    (2932/0/0)   3087396
7 unassigned    wm       0                0          (0/0/0)          0
Okay to make this the current partition table[yes]?
```

NOTE

The Free Hog Slice 6, the free hog, represents the unused disk space. You might want to allocate this space to another partition so that it does not go unused, or you can save it and allocate it another time to an unused partition.

8. Press Enter to confirm your modified partition map. You'll see the following message displayed:

   ```
   Enter table name (remember quotes):
   ```

9. Name the modified partition table and press Enter:

   ```
   Enter table name (remember quotes): c0t3d0.2gb
   ```

10. After you enter the name, the following message is displayed:

    ```
    Ready to label disk, continue?
    ```

11. Type **yes** and press Enter to continue.
12. Type **quit** (or **q**) and press Enter to exit the partition menu. The main menu is displayed.
13. Type **quit** and press Enter to exit the `format` utility.

Using the Solaris Management Console Disks Tool

You can also partition a disk and view a disk's partition information by using the graphical interface provided by the Solaris Management Console (SMC) Disks Tool. To view partition information, follow the procedure outlined in Step by Step 1.6.

STEP BY STEP

1.6 Viewing a Disk's Partition Information Using Disks Tool

1. As root, start up the SMC by typing

    ```
    smc &
    ```

2. In the left navigation window, select the This Computer icon, then click on the Storage icon as shown in Figure 1.2.

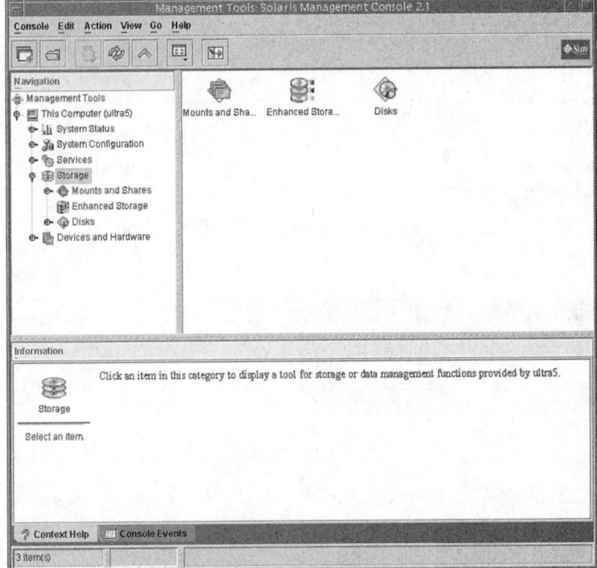

FIGURE 1.2 The SMC Storage icon.

3. From the SMC Main window, select the Disks icon as shown in Figure 1.3.

    The disk drives connected to your system will be displayed in the main window as shown in Figure 1.4.

4. Select the disk that you wish to view and the partition information for that disk will be displayed as shown in Figure 1.5.

    You can use the SMC Disks Tool to perform the following tasks:

    - Display information about a specific disk.
    - Create Solaris disk partitions.
    - List partitions.
    - Copy the layout of one disk to another disk of the same type.
    - Change the disk's label.

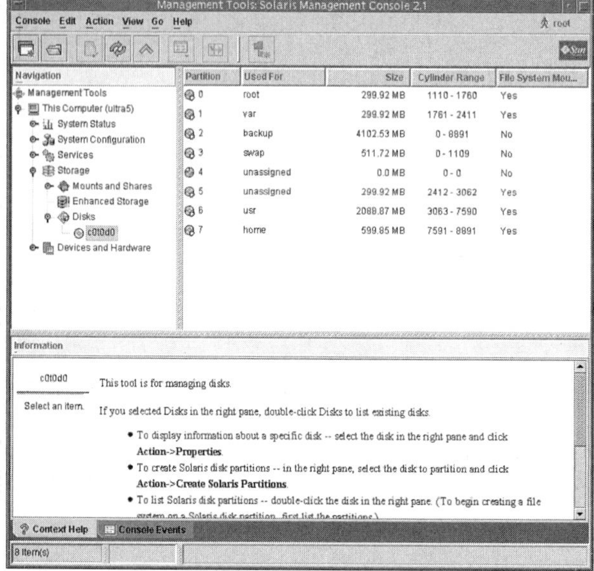

FIGURE 1.3 The SMC Disks icon.

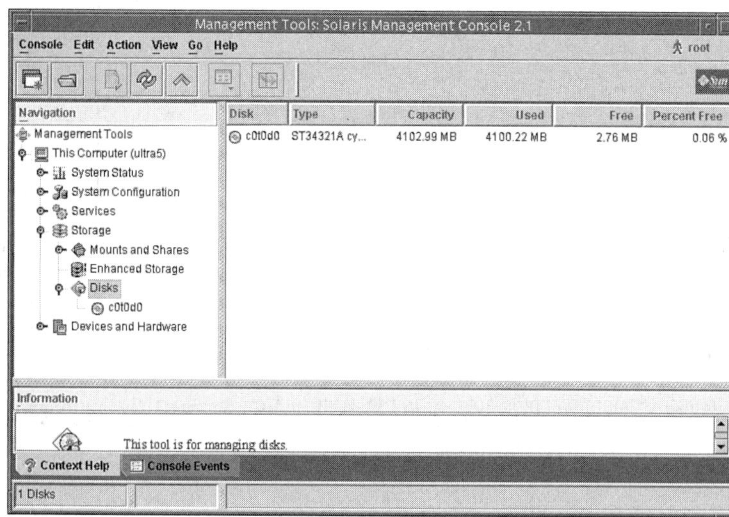

FIGURE 1.4 The SMC Disks tool.

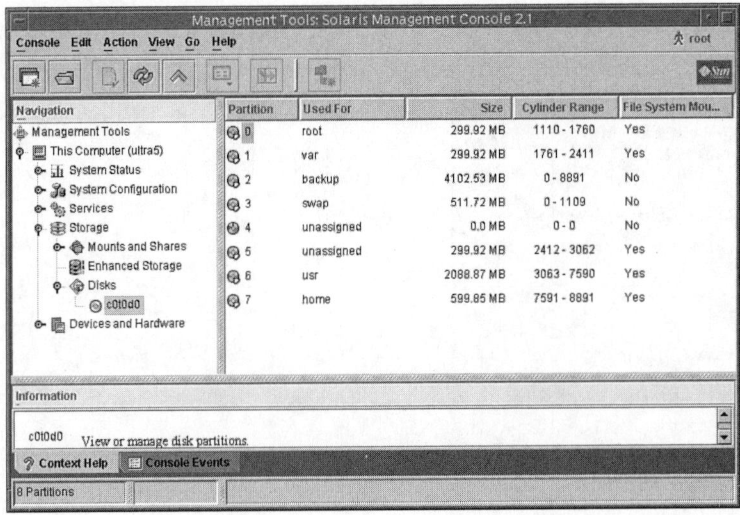

FIGURE 1.5 Selecting a disk.

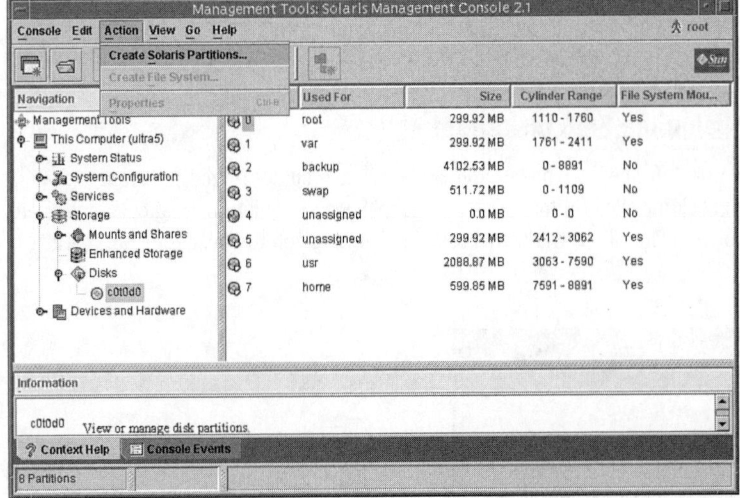

FIGURE 1.6 Partition a disk using Disks Tool.

To partition a disk using the SMC Disks Tool, follow the steps outlined in Step by Step 1.6. After selecting the disk that you want to partition, select the Create Solaris Partitions option from the pull-down Action menu as shown in Figure 1.6.

A Warning message will appear as shown in Figure 1.7.

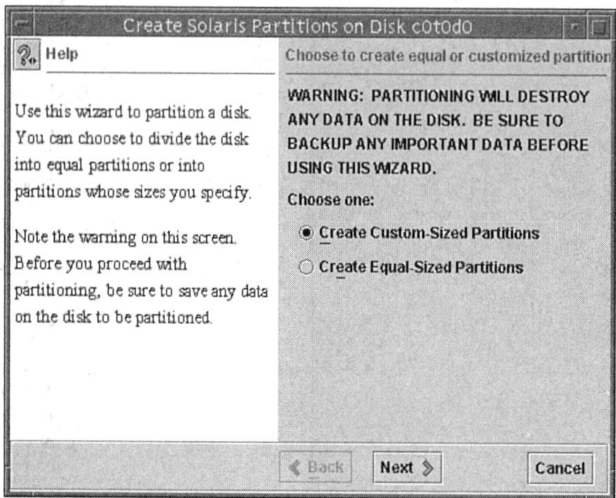

FIGURE 1.7 SMC warning message.

Click on the Next button and follow the prompts in each window to partition your disk. To partition a disk using the Disks Tool, follow the procedure outlined in Step by Step 1.7.

STEP BY STEP

1.7 Partitioning the Disk Using the SMC Disks Tool

1. In the window shown in Figure 1.7, specify whether you want to create custom-sized partitions or equal-sized partitions, then click the Next button. For this example, we are going to create custom-sized partitions. The window shown in Figure 1.8 will be displayed prompting you to specify the number of partitions to create.

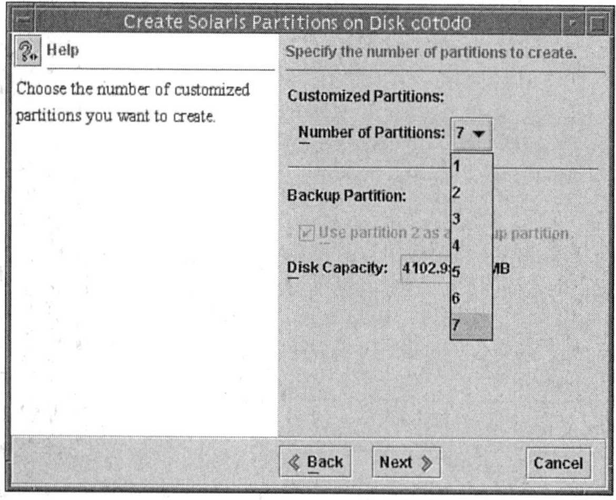

FIGURE 1.8 Specify number of partitions.

2. For this example, I selected 7 partitions and clicked on the Next button to continue. The next window prompts you to specify the size and use of the partition, as shown in Figure 1.9.

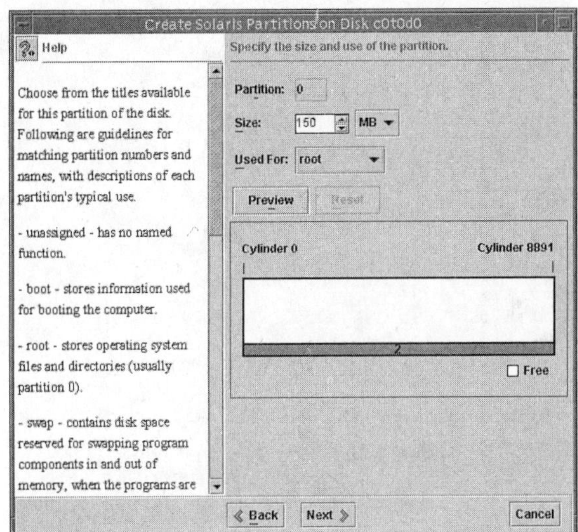

FIGURE 1.9 Specify the size and use of the partitions.

3. Next to the Size field, I selected `MB` and entered `150` into the Size field. Options for specifying size are MB (megabytes) or % (percentage of total disk).

   For the Used For field, I selected `root` because this is going to be the root partition. Options are `unassigned`, `boot`, `root`, `swap`, `usr`, `stand`, `var`, or `home`. Select the option that matches the function of the file system that you are creating. These options are described in the "Using the `format` Utility to Create Slices" section of this chapter.

   When you've made all of your selections, you can click on the Preview button to see a graphical layout of the disk. Click on the Next button when you are finished making all of your selections and you'll be asked to specify the size and use of the next partition. Continue sizing each partition. For this example, I left the remaining slices at 0 MB.

4. When you are finished sizing all of your partitions, you'll see a window summarizing all of your selections. Click Next and you'll see a warning window displayed as shown in Figure 1.10.

5. If you are satisfied with the partitions, click Finish. The new partitioning information is written and the `newfs` utility builds the partitions and creates each new file system.

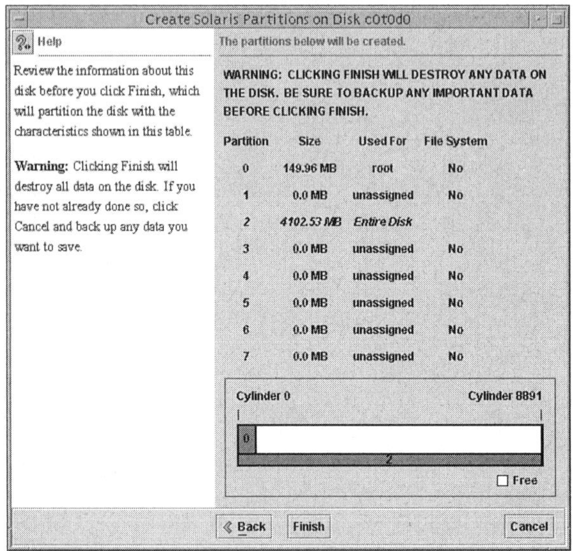

FIGURE 1.10 SMC warning window.

Recovering Disk Partition Information

It's always a good idea to save a disk's VTOC to a file using the `prtvtoc` command described earlier. This information can then be used later to restore the disk label if your current VTOC becomes corrupted or accidentally changed, or if you need to replace the disk drive.

NOTE

The disk label (VTOC) is stored in block 0 of each disk. The UFS file systems are smart enough not to touch the disk label, but be careful of any third party applications that create raw data slices. Ensure that these applications do not start at block 0; otherwise the disk label will be overwritten and the data on the disk will become inaccessible. I've seen some administrators start their raw slice at cylinder 2 or 3 just to ensure the disk label does not accidentally get overwritten.

By saving the output from the `prtvtoc` command into a file on another disk, you can reference it when running the `fmthard` command. The `fmthard` command updates the VTOC on hard disks. To recover a VTOC using `fmthard`, follow Step by Step 1.8.

STEP BY STEP

1.8 Recovering a VTOC

1. Run the `format` utility on the disk and label it with the default partition table.
2. Use the `fmthard` command to write the backup VTOC information back to the disk drive. The following example uses the `fmthard` command to recover a corrupt label on a disk named

/dev/rdsk/c0t3d0s2. The backup VTOC information is in a file named c0t3d0 in the /vtoc directory:

```
fmthard -s /vtoc/c0t3d0 /dev/rdsk/c0t3d0s2
```

Another use for the fmthard command is partitioning several disks with the same partitioning scheme. Get the VTOC information from the disk you want to copy (c0t0d0), and write the information to the new disk (c1t0d0) as follows:

```
prtvtoc /dev/rdsk/c0t0d0S0 ¦ fmthard -s - /dev/rdsk/c1t0d0s2
```

Logical Volumes

On a large server with many disk drives, standard methods of disk slicing are inadequate and inefficient. File systems cannot span multiple disks, and the size of the file system is limited to the size of the disk. Another problem with standard file systems is that they cannot be increased in size without destroying data on the file system.

Sun has addressed these issues with two software packages: the Solaris Volume Manager (SVM), called Solstice DiskSuite in previous Solaris releases, and the Veritas Volume Manager (VxVM). Both packages allow file systems to span multiple disks and provide for improved I/O and reliability compared to the standard Solaris file system. We refer to these types of file systems as *logical volumes (LVMs)*.

SVM is now part of Solaris 10. The Veritas Volume Manager is purchased separately and is not part of the standard Solaris operating system distribution. SVM is a lower cost solution and typically, SVM is used on Sun's multipacks and for mirroring the OS drives, whereas the Veritas Volume Manager package is used on the larger SPARC storage arrays. LVMs, the SVM, and the Veritas Volume Manager are described in Chapter 10.

Parts of a UFS

TIP

File Systems Although this section doesn't apply to any specific exam objective, the information is provided to help you better understand file systems in general.

UFS is the default disk-based file system used by the Solaris operating environment. It provides the following features:

- **State flags**—These show the state of the file system as clean, stable, active, or unknown. These flags eliminate unnecessary file system checks. If the file system is clean or stable, fsck (file system check) is not run when the system boots.

- **Extended fundamental types (EFT)**—These include a 32-bit user ID (UID), a group ID (GID), and device numbers.
- **Large file systems**—A UFS can be as large as 1 terabyte (TB) and can have regular files up to 2 gigabytes (GB). By default, the Solaris system software does not provide striping, which is required to make a logical slice large enough for a 1TB file system. However, the Solaris Volume Manager described in Chapter 10, provides this capability.
- **By default, a UFS can have regular files larger than 2GB**—You must explicitly use the `nolargefiles` mount option to enforce a 2GB maximum file size limit.
- **Logging**—UFS logging is the process of writing file system updates to a log before applying the updates to a UFS file system.
- **Multiterabyte file systems**—A multiterabyte file system enables creation of a UFS file system with up to approximately 16 terabytes of usable space, minus approximately one percent overhead. The system must be booted under a 64-bit kernel to support a multiterabyte file system. Systems booted under a 32-bit kernel are limited to a 1 TB file system.

During the installation of the Solaris software, several UFS file systems are created on the system disk. These are Sun's default file systems. Their contents are described in Table 1.6.

TABLE 1.6 Solaris Default File Systems

Slice	File System	Description
0	root	Root (/) is the top of the hierarchical file tree. It holds files and directories that make up the operating system. The root directory contains the directories and files critical for system operation, such as the kernel, the device drivers, and the programs used to boot the system. It also contains the mount point directories, in which local and remote file systems can be attached to the file tree. The root (/) file system is always in slice 0.
1	swap	Provides virtual memory or swap space. Swap space is used when you're running programs too large to fit in the computer's memory. The Solaris operating environment then "swaps" programs from memory to the disk and back, as needed. Although it is not technically required, it is common for the swap slice to be located in slice 1 unless /var is set up as a file system. If /var is set up, the interactive installation places /var on slice 1, and it places swap on slice 3. The /var file system is for files and directories likely to change or grow over the life of the local system. These include system logs, `vi` and `ex` backup files, printer and email spool files, backups of OS patches, and UUCP files. On a server, it's a good idea to have these files in a separate file system so that they cannot fill up the root slice.

TABLE 1.6 *Continued*

Slice	File System	Description
2	Entire Disk	Refers to the entire disk and is defined automatically by Sun's `format` utility and the Solaris installation programs. The size of this slice should not be changed.
3	/var	This slice is unassigned by default. In Solaris 10, if you let the Sun installation program auto layout the slices, it will place the /var directory under slice 0 with the root file system. However, if during the installation, /var is selected to have its own slice, the installation program will place /var onto slice 1 and will move swap to slice 3.
4		By default, slice 4 is unassigned and available for use.
5	/opt	This slice is unassigned by default. In Solaris 10, the /opt directory is put under slice 0 by default with the root file system. However, if during the installation, /opt is selected to have its own slice, the installation program will place /opt onto slice 5. /opt holds additional Sun software packages and optional third-party software that have been added to a system. If a slice is not allocated for this file system during installation, the /opt directory is put in slice 0, the root (/) file system.
6	/usr	This slice is unassigned by default. In Solaris 10, the /usr directory is put under slice 0 by default with the root file system. However, if during the installation, /usr is selected to have its own slice, the installation program will place /usr onto slice 6. /usr contains operating system commands—also known as executables—designed to be run by users. /usr also holds documentation, system programs (init and syslogd, for example), library routines, and system files and directories that can be shared with other users. Files that can be used on all types of systems (such as man pages) are in /usr/share. If /usr is placed on slice 0, slice 6 becomes an unallocated slice.
7	/export/home	Holds files created by users. On a standard system, /home is a mount point that points to /export/home and is managed by AutoFS. See Chapter 9 for more information.

Slice Numbers and Their Location on Disk

Although root may be located on slice 0, it doesn't necessarily mean that it is located first on the disk. For example, note the following partition scheme:

```
Part      Tag    Flag     Cylinders         Size            Blocks
  0      root     wm     258 -   759    1000.08MB    (502/0/0)      2048160
  1       var     wm     760 -  2265       2.93GB    (1506/0/0)     6144480
  2    backup     wm       0 - 39417      76.69GB    (39418/0/0)  160825440
  3      swap     wu       0 -   257     513.98MB    (258/0/0)      1052640
  4 unassigned    wm       0                 0       (0/0/0)              0
```

(continues)

(continued)

```
5 unassigned    wm    2266 -  2767    1000.08MB    (502/0/0)     2048160
6        usr    wm    2768 -  6783       7.81GB    (4016/0/0)   16385280
7       home    wm    6784 -  9293       4.88GB    (2510/0/0)   10240800
```

Notice how slice 3 starts at cylinder 0 and ends at cylinder 257. This puts slice 3 first on the disk. `root` is located on slice 0, which starts after slice 3 at cylinder 258. When using the interactive installation program to install the operating system, the swap partition is placed at the start of the disk beginning at cylinder 0 and the root partition is placed after the swap partition. A marginal performance increase is achieved by putting swap at the starting cylinder because of the faster rotation speeds on the outside perimeter of the disk. The interactive installation program is described in Chapter 2, "Installing the Solaris 10 Operating Environment."

You need to create (or re-create) a UFS only when you do the following:

- Add or replace disks.
- Change the slices of an existing disk.
- Do a full restore on a file system.
- Change the parameters of a file system, such as block size or free space.

The Root (/) File System

Objective:

Describe the purpose, features, and functions of root subdirectories, file components, file types, and hard links in the Solaris directory hierarchy.

Solaris comes with many file systems already created. These file systems were described earlier in this chapter. One of the most important file systems is the root file system. This file system is important because it is the first file system that is mounted when the system begins to boot. It is the file system that contains the kernel and all of the bootup scripts and programs. Without this file system, the system will not boot.

Furthermore, the root file system is at the top of the hierarchy of all file systems and contains all of the directory mount points for the other file systems. Taking a closer look at the contents of the root file system, we see that it contains many important directories, which are described in Table 1.7.

TABLE 1.7 Root Directories

Directory	Description of Contents
/	Root of the overall file system name space.
/bin	This is a symbolic link to the /usr/bin directory. See the section later in this chapter titled "Soft (Symbolic) Links."
/dev	Primary location for logical device names. Logical device names are described earlier in this chapter. Subdirectories within this directory are /dev/cfg—Symbolic links to physical ap_ids /dev/cua—Dial out devices for UUCP /dev/dsk—Block (buffered) disk devices /dev/fbs—Frame buffer device files /dev/fd—File descriptors /dev/md—Solaris Volume Manager metadisk devices /dev/pts—Pseudo terminal devices /dev/rdsk—Raw (character) disk devices /dev/rmt—Raw magnetic tape devices /dev/sad—Entry points for the STREAMS Administrative driver /dev/sound—Audio device and audio device control files /dev/swap—Default swap device /dev/term—Serial devices
/devices	This file system contains physical device names, which were described earlier in this chapter.
/etc	Platform-dependent administrative and configuration files and databases that are not shared among systems. Most configuration files in this directory define the machine's identity. A few subdirectories within the /etc directory that you need to be aware of are /etc/acct—Accounting system configuration information. /etc/cron.d—Configuration information for cron(1M). /etc/default—Default information for various programs. /etc/dfs—Configuration information for shared file systems. /etc/dhcp—Dynamic Host Configuration Protocol (DHCP) configuration files. /etc/inet—Configuration files for Internet services. /etc/init.d—Contains legacy RC scripts for transitioning between run levels. This directory has been significantly reduced from previous versions of Solaris with the introduction of SMF, which is described in Chapter 3, "Perform System Boot and Shutdown Procedures." /etc/lib—Shared libraries needed during booting. /etc/lp—Configuration information for the printer subsystem. /etc/mail—Mail subsystem configuration. /etc/nfs—NFS server logging configuration file. /etc/opt—Configuration information for optional packages. /etc/openwin—OpenWindows configuration files. /etc/rc<#>.d—Contains legacy RC scripts for transitioning between run levels. These are mainly hard links to the /etc/init.d directory and are described in Chapter 3. /etc/saf—Service Access Facility files.

(continues)

TABLE 1.7 *Continued*

Directory	Description of Contents
	`/etc/security`—Basic Security Module (BSM) configuration files. `/etc/skel`—Default profile scripts for new user accounts. This directory is discussed in Chapter 4, "User and Security Administration." `/etc/uucp`—UUCP configuration information.
`/export`	This directory contains commonly shared file systems such as user home directories.
`/home`	This is the system default directory (mount point) for user home directories. When you are running AutoFS (see Chapter 9, "Virtual File Systems, Swap Space, and Core Dumps"), you cannot create new entries in this directory.
`/kernel`	This directory contains platform-independent loadable kernel modules required as part of the boot process. `/kernel` includes the generic part of the core kernel that is platform independent, named `/kernel/genunix`.
`/lib`	Shared executable files and Service Management Facility (SMF) executables.
`/mnt`	Default temporary mount point for file systems. Use this empty directory to temporarily mount any file system.
`/opt`	This is a default directory for add-on and third party application packages.
`/platform`	This directory contains platform-specific objects that need to reside on the root file system. It contains a series of directories, one per supported platform.
`/sbin`	The single-user `bin` directory contains essential commands used in the booting process. These commands are available when `/usr/bin` is not mounted. It contains many system administration commands and utilities.
`/usr`	The mount point for the `/usr` file system. The name "usr" is an acronym for Unix System Resources. Important subdirectories in `/usr` are `/usr/bin`—Most standard system commands are located here. `/usr/ccs`—C-compilation programs and libraries. `/usr/demo`—Demonstration programs. `/usr/dt`—CDE programs and files. `/usr/include`—Header files for C programs and other executables. `/usr/java`—Java programs and libraries. `/usr/lib`—Program libraries and databases. `/usr/openwin`—OpenWindows programs and files. `/usr/opt`—Configuration information for optional packages. `/usr/pub`—Files for online manual pages and character processing. `/usr/sadm`—System administration files and directories. `/usr/spool`—A symbolic link to `/var/spool`. `/usr/share`—A location for sharable files. Bundled Solaris software gets loaded here.

(continues)

TABLE 1.7 *Continued*

Directory	Description of Contents
	/usr/snadm—Files related to system and network administration. /usr/tmp—Symbolic link to /var/tmp. /usr/ucb—Berkeley compatibility package binaries.
/var	Directory for varying files such as logs, status files, mail, print files, and so on.

In addition, Solaris 10 introduces additional in-memory system directories and subdirectories that are described in Table 1.8. These in-memory directories are maintained by the kernel and system services. With the exception of `/tmp`, do not attempt to manually create, alter, or remove files from these directories.

TABLE 1.8 In-Memory System Directories

Directory	Description
/dev/fd	A directory containing special files relating to current file descriptors in use by the system.
/devices	The primary directory for physical device names.
/etc/mnttab	A memory-based file, in its own file system, which contains details of currently mounted file systems.
/etc/svc/volatile	A directory that contains log files and reference files relating to the current state of system services.
/proc	This directory stores current process-related information. Every process has its own subdirectory in /proc.
/system/contract	A file system used for creating, controlling, and observing contracts, which are relationships between processes and system resources. These process contracts are used by the Service Management Facility (SMF) to track the processes that compose a service. See Chapter 3 for a description of the SMF.
/system/object	This directory, used primarily for DTrace activity, describes the state of all modules currently loaded by the kernel.
/tmp	A memory-resident directory for temporary files. Be careful storing files in /tmp; this directory is cleared during the boot sequence.
/var/run	This directory contains lock files, special files, and reference files for a variety of system processes and services.

As you browse the directories in the root file system, you'll notice many file types. The file type can usually be identified by looking at the first character of the first column of information displayed when issuing the `ls -l` command.

A typical listing may look like this when listing the contents of the /etc directory:

```
ls -l /etc
total 583
lrwxrwxrwx   1 root     root           14 Aug  9 19:18 TIMEZONE -> ./default/init
drwxr-xr-x   6 root     other         512 Aug  9 20:51 X11
drwxr-xr-x   2 adm      adm           512 Aug 10 09:24 acct
lrwxrwxrwx   1 root     root           14 Aug  9 19:31 aliases -> ./mail/aliases
drwxr-xr-x   7 root     bin           512 Aug 10 09:34 apache
drwxr-xr-x   2 root     bin           512 Aug 10 09:26 apache2
drwxr-xr-x   2 root     other         512 Aug  9 20:29 apoc
-rw-r--r--   1 root     bin           226 Sep 13 14:17 auto_home
-rw-r--r--   1 root     bin           248 Aug  9 19:29 auto_master
lrwxrwxrwx   1 root     root           16 Aug  9 19:18 autopush -> ../sbin/autopush
drwxr-xr-x   2 root     other         512 Aug  9 20:19 bonobo-activation
drwxr-xr-x   2 root     sys           512 Aug  9 19:18 certs
lrwxrwxrwx   1 root     root           18 Aug  9 19:18 cfgadm -> ../usr/sbin/cfgadm
lrwxrwxrwx   1 root     root           18 Aug  9 20:18 chroot -> ../usr/sbin/chroot
    <output has been truncated>
```

The information displayed in the long listing is in the form of columns and is as follows (reading from left to right):

- **Column 1**—Ten characters that describe the mode of the file. The first character displays the file type where

d	The entry is a directory.
D	The entry is a door.
l	The entry is a symbolic link.
b	The entry is a block special file.
c	The entry is a character special file.
p	The entry is a FIFO (or "named pipe") special file.
s	The entry is an AF_UNIX address family socket.
-	The entry is an ordinary file.

The next nine characters in column one describe the file's permission mode, which is described in detail in Chapter 4.

- **Column 2**—Displays the number of links to the file
- **Column 3**—Displays the file's owner
- **Column 4**—Displays the file's group
- **Column 5**—Displays the file size in bytes

- **Column 6**—Date/Time of the file's last modification
- **Column 7**—File name

The -> after a file name denotes a symbolic link, as follows:

```
lrwxrwxrwx   1 root   root    14 Feb 26  2005 TIMEZONE -> ./default/init
drwxr-xr-x   2 adm    adm    512 Feb 27  2005 acct
lrwxrwxrwx   1 root   root    14 Feb 26  2005 aliases -> ./mail/aliases
lrwxrwxrwx   1 root   root    16 Feb 26  2005 autopush -> ../sbin/autopush
lrwxrwxrwx   1 root   root    18 Feb 26  2005 cfgadm -> ../usr/sbin/cfgadm
lrwxrwxrwx   1 root   root    18 Feb 26  2005 chroot -> ../usr/sbin/chroot
lrwxrwxrwx   1 root   root    16 Feb 26  2005 clri -> ../usr/sbin/clri
```

A link is a pointer to another file or directory. Links provide a mechanism for multiple file names to reference the same data on disk. In Solaris, there are two types of links:

- Soft (symbolic) links
- Hard links

Both of these are discussed in the following sections.

Soft (Symbolic) Links

Sometimes symbolic links are used for shortcuts; other times we use them to link to a filename from each user's home directory to a centralized location or file. For example, perhaps we want to have a common directory named `documents` where every user stores their documents. This directory exists as `/export/data/documents`. In each user's directory, we create a link named documents that points to `/export/data/documents`. As a user, whenever I store something in the directory named `$HOME/documents`, the file actually gets directed to `/export/data/documents`. We can identify links when we perform a long listing on a directory as follows:

> **NOTE**
>
> Notice the use of the `-i` option used with the **ls** command and the results displayed. This option is used to display the inode number (in the left column of the output) that has been assigned to each file and directory. I'll describe why this inode number is relevant to links later in this section when I describe hard links.

```
ls -li $HOME
```

The system displays the following:

```
75264 drwxr--r--   2 bcalkins staff  512 Jun  6 20:36 dir1
78848 drwxrwxr-x   2 bcalkins staff  512 Jun  6 20:38 dir2
```

```
82432 drw-r--r--    2 bcalkins staff  512 Jun  6 20:39 dir3
3593 lrwxrwxrwx     1 bcalkins staff  22 Jun 17 17:09 documents\
 -> /export/data/documents
```

Output has been truncated.

Notice the file that has an *l* as the first character of column 2. This is a soft or *symbolic* link. The sixth field shows a file size of 22 bytes and the last field shows which file or directory this link is pointing to. Each file has a unique inode number identified in column 1; the importance of this column is discussed later in this chapter.

When storing a file in $HOME/documents, the system is redirecting it to be stored in `/export/data/documents`. Now when changing to the `/export/data/documents` directory and issuing the `ls -li` command:

```
cd /export/data/documents
ls -li
```

The system displays the following:

```
125461     drwxr-xr-x    2 root     other    512 Jun 17 17:09 documents
```

Notice that the file that has a *d* as the first character of column 2. This is the directory that the `$HOME/documents` link points to. The first column shows the inode number, and the sixth column shows the file size as 512 bytes.

Symbolic links can point to files anywhere on the network. The file or directory could exist in another file system, on another disk, or on another system on the network.

The syntax for creating a symbolic link is as follows:

```
ln -s source-file link-name
```

For example, you might have a file named `file1` that has the following contents:

```
This is the contents of file1
```

To create a symbolic link named `link1`, which will be linked to the existing file named `file1`, you issue the following command:

```
ln -s file1 link1
```

Now when you list the contents of the directory you see two files:

```
3588 -rw-r--r--   1 bcalkins staff          30 Jun 17 17:51 file1
3594 lrwxrwxrwx   1 bcalkins staff           5 Jun 17 18:09 link1 -> file1
```

See the link named `link1` pointing to `file1`? If you display the contents of `link1`, it shows the following:

```
This is the contents of file1
```

If you remove `file1`, the source file, `link1` will still exist, but it points to a file that does not exist. Type the following:

```
cat link1
```

The `cat` command can't print out the contents of the file, so you get this message:

```
cat: Cannot open link1
```

When you re-create `file1`, `link1` will contain data again.

Hard Links

Objective:

Explain how to create and remove hard links in a Solaris directory.

A hard link is more difficult to determine, because they are not so obvious when viewed with the `ls -li` command. For example, when you go to the `/etc/rc2.d` directory and type

```
ls -li
```

the system displays the following:

```
total 102
<output has been truncated>
      2123 -rwxr--r--    5 root     sys           1718 Jan 21   2005 S47pppd
      2102 -rwxr--r--    2 root     sys            327 Jan 21   2005 S70uucp
      1368 -rwxr-xr-x    2 root     other         1558 Jan  9   2005 S72autoinstall
       241 -rwxr--r--    2 root     sys           1262 Jan 21   2005 S73cachefs.daemon
      1315 -rwxr--r--    2 root     sys           1028 Jan 21   2005 S81dodatadm.udaplt
       237 -rwxr--r--    2 root     sys            256 Jan 21   2005 S89PRESERVE
      2103 lrwxrwxrwx    1 root     root            31 Aug 10 09:49 S89bdconfig ->\
 ../init.d/buttons_n_dials-setup
      1898 -rwxr--r--    5 root     sys           3506 Jan 10   2005 S90wbem
      2100 -rwxr--r--    5 root     sys           1250 Jan 10   2005 S90webconsole
<output has been truncated>
```

The first character in the second column of information displays the file type as a regular file (-). The third column, link count, shows a number greater than 1. It displays the number of links used by this inode number. These are hard links, but they are not identified as links and the display does not show which file they are linked to.

Think of a hard link as a file that has many names. In other words, they all share the same inode number. As described in the section titled "The inode" later in this chapter, a file system identifies a file not by its name, but by its inode number. Looking at the file named `S90wbem` in the previous listing, we see an inode number of 1898. List all file names in this file system that share this inode number as follows:

```
find / -mount -inum 1898 -ls
```

The system displays the following list of files:

```
1898   4 -rwxr--r--    5 root    sys      3506 Jan 10  2005 /etc/init.d/init.wbem
1898   4 -rwxr--r--    5 root    sys      3506 Jan 10  2005 /etc/rc0.d/K36wbem
1898   4 -rwxr--r--    5 root    sys      3506 Jan 10  2005 /etc/rc1.d/K36wbem
1898   4 -rwxr--r--    5 root    sys      3506 Jan 10  2005 /etc/rc2.d/S90wbem
1898   4 -rwxr--r--    5 root    sys      3506 Jan 10  2005 /etc/rcS.d/K36wbem
```

All six of these files have the same inode number; therefore, they are the same file. You can delete any one of the filenames, and the data will still exist.

In this example, the file is named `file1` in `$HOME`:

```
3588 -rw-r--r--    3 bcalkins staff         30 Jun 17 17:51 file1
```

The contents of this file are displayed with the `cat` command:

```
This is the contents of file1
```

The syntax for creating a hard link is as follows:

```
ln source-file link-name
```

To create a hard link named `link1`, which will be linked to the existing file named `file1`, issue the following command:

```
ln file1 link1
```

Now when I list the contents of the directory, I see two files:

```
3588 -rw-r--r--    2 bcalkins staff         30 Jun 17 17:51 file1
3588 -rw-r--r--    2 bcalkins staff         30 Jun 17 17:51 link1
```

Both files share the same inode number, the number of links is two, and the file size is 30 bytes. If I display the contents of `link1`, it shows the following:

```
This is the content of file1
```

If I remove `file1`, the source file, `link1` still exists and still contains the data. The data will not be deleted until I destroy the last file that shares this inode number.

A hard link cannot span file systems; it can only point to another file located within its file system. The reason is that hard links all share an inode number. Each file system has its own set of inode numbers; therefore, a file with inode number 3588 in the `/export/home` file system may not even exist in the `/var` file system.

An advantage of a symbolic link over a hard link is that you can create a symbolic link to a file that does not yet exist. You cannot create a hard link unless the source file already exists. Here's what happens when you create a symbolic link to a file that does not exist:

```
ln -s  nonexistentfile link5
```

When you list the file:

```
ls -l link5
```

The system responds with

```
lrwxrwxrwx  1 bcalkins staff  14 Jun 17 18:24 link5 -> nonexistentfile
```

Now, here's what happens when you create a hard link to a file that does not exist:

```
ln noexistentfile link6
```

The system responds with

```
ln: cannot access noexistentfile
```

Removing a Link

Remove a link using the `rm` command as follows:

```
rm <linkname>
```

For example, to remove the link named `link1`, type

```
rm link1
```

NOTE

Removing Files and Links When you remove a file, it's always a good idea to remove the symbolic links that pointed to that file, unless you plan to use them again if the file gets re-created.

Another advantage of symbolic links over hard links is that a symbolic link can link directories or files, whereas a hard link can link only files.

Components of the UFS

When you create a UFS, the disk slice is divided into cylinder groups. The slice is then divided into blocks to control and organize the structure of the files within the cylinder group. Each block performs a specific function in the file system. A UFS has the following four types of blocks:

- **Boot block**—Stores information used when booting the system
- **Superblock**—Stores much of the information about the file system
- **Cylinder Group**—File systems are divided into cylinder groups to improve disk access.
- **Inode**—Stores all information about a file except its name
- **Storage or data block**—Stores data for each file

The Boot Block

The boot block stores the code used in booting the system. Without a boot block, the system does not boot. Each file system has 15 sectors of space (sectors 1–15) allocated at the beginning for a boot block; however, if a file system is not to be used for booting, the boot block is left blank. The boot block appears only in the first cylinder group (cylinder group 0) and is the first 8KB in a slice.

The Superblock

The superblock resides in the 16 sectors (sectors 16–31) following the boot block and stores much of the information about the file system. Following are a few of the more important items contained in a superblock:

- Size and status of the file system
- Label (file system name and volume name)
- Size of the file system's logical block
- Date and time of the last update
- Cylinder group size
- Number of data blocks in a cylinder group
- Summary data block
- File system state (clean, stable, or active)
- Pathname of the last mount point

Without a superblock, the file system becomes unreadable. Because it contains critical data, the superblock is replicated in each cylinder group and multiple superblocks are made when the file system is created.

A copy of the superblock for each file system is kept up-to-date in memory. If the system gets halted before a disk copy of the superblock gets updated, the most recent changes are lost and the file system becomes inconsistent. The `sync` command saves every superblock in memory to the disk. The file system check program `fsck` can fix problems that occur when the `sync` command hasn't been used before a shutdown.

A summary information block is kept with the superblock. It is not replicated but is grouped with the first superblock, usually in cylinder group 0. The summary block records changes that take place as the file system is used, listing the number of inodes, directories, fragments, and storage blocks within the file system.

Cylinder Groups

Each file system is divided into cylinder groups with a minimum default size of 16 cylinders per group. Cylinder groups improve disk access. The file system constantly optimizes disk performance by attempting to place a file's data into a single cylinder group, which reduces the distance a head has to travel to access the file's data.

The inode

An inode contains all the information about a file except its name, which is kept in a directory. A filename is associated with an inode, and the inode provides access to data blocks. An inode is 128 bytes. The inode information is kept in the cylinder information block and contains the following:

- The type of the file (regular, directory, block special, character special, link, and so on)
- The mode of the file (the set of read/write/execute permissions)
- The number of hard links to the file
- The user ID of the file's owner
- The group ID to which the file belongs
- The number of bytes in the file
- An array of 15 disk-block addresses
- The date and time the file was last accessed
- The date and time the file was last modified
- The date and time the file was created

inodes are numbered and each file system maintains its own list of inodes. inodes are created for each file system when the file system is created. The maximum number of files per UFS is determined by the number of inodes allocated for a file system. The number of inodes depends on the amount of disk space that is allocated for each inode and the total size of the file system. Table 1.9 displays the default number of inodes created by the `newfs` command based on the size of the file system.

TABLE 1.9 Default Number of inodes

Disk Size	Density
Less than 1GB	2048
Less than 2GB	4096
Less than 3GB	6144
3GB to 1 Tbyte	8192
Greater than 1 Tbyte or file systems created with the `-T` option	1048576

You can change the default allocation by using the `-i` option of the `newfs` command. Also, the number of inodes will increase if a file system is expanded with the `growfs` command. The `newfs` command is described later in this chapter and `growfs` is described in Chapter 10, "Managing Storage Volumes."

The Storage Block

Storage blocks, also called data blocks, occupy the rest of the space allocated to the file system. The size of these storage blocks is determined at the time a file system is created. Storage blocks are allocated, by default, in two sizes: an 8KB logical block size and a 1KB fragmentation size.

For a regular file, the storage blocks contain the contents of the file. For a directory, the storage blocks contain entries that give the inode number and the filename of the files in the directory.

Free Blocks

Blocks not currently being used as inodes, indirect address blocks, or storage blocks are marked as free in the cylinder group map. This map also keeps track of fragments to prevent fragmentation from degrading disk performance.

Creating a UFS

Objective:

Explain when and how to create a new UFS using the `newfs` command, check the file system using `fsck`, resolve file system inconsistencies, and monitor file system usage using associated commands.

Use the `newfs` command to create UFS file systems. `newfs` is a convenient front end to the `mkfs` command, the program that creates the new file system on a disk slice.

On Solaris 10 systems, information used to set some of the parameter defaults, such as number of tracks per cylinder and number of sectors per track, is read from the disk label. `newfs` determines the file system parameters to use, based on the options you specify and information provided in the disk label. Parameters are then passed to the `mkfs` (make file system) command, which builds the file system. Although you can use the `mkfs` command directly, it's more difficult to use and you must supply many of the parameters manually. (The use of the `newfs` command is discussed more in the next section.)

You must format the disk and divide it into slices before you can create a file system on it. `newfs` makes existing data on the disk slice inaccessible and creates the skeleton of a directory structure, including a directory named `lost+found`. After you run `newfs`, the slice is ready to be mounted as a file system.

CAUTION

Cleaning Sensitive Data from a Disk Removing a file system using the `newfs` or `rm` commands, or simply formatting the disk, is not sufficient to completely remove data bits from the disk. In order to wipe a hard disk clean of sensitive information, so that the data is beyond the recovery limits of any data recovery software or utility, use the `analyze` option within the `format` utility's main menu. When the `analyze` menu appears, select the `purge` option. Purging data from the disk complies with Department of Defense (DoD) wipe disk standards for completely removing data bits from a disk. This procedure destroys all the file systems on the disk.

To create a UFS on a formatted disk that has already been divided into slices, you need to know the raw device filename of the slice that will contain the file system (see Step by Step 1.9). If you are re-creating or modifying an existing UFS, back up and unmount the file system before performing these steps.

STEP BY STEP

1.9 Creating a UFS

1. Become superuser.
2. Type `newfs /dev/rdsk/<device-name>` and press Enter. You are asked if you want to proceed. The `newfs` command requires the use of the raw device name, not the buffered device name. If the buffered device name is used, it will be converted to a raw device name. For more information on raw (character) and buffered (block) devices, refer to the "Block and Raw Devices" section that appeared earlier in this chapter.

CAUTION

Prevent Yourself from Erasing the Wrong Slice Be sure you have specified the correct device name for the slice before performing the next step. The `newfs` command is destructive and you will erase the contents of the slice when the new file system is created. Be careful not to erase the wrong slice.

3. Type **y** to confirm.

The following example creates a file system on `/dev/rdsk/c2t1d0s1`:

1. Become superuser by typing `su`, and enter the root password.
2. Type `newfs /dev/rdsk/c2t1d0s1`.

   The system responds with this:

```
# newfs /dev/rdsk/c2t1d0s1
newfs: construct a new file system /dev/rdsk/c2t1d0s1: (y/n)? y
/dev/rdsk/c2t1d0s1:     8337600 sectors in 3860 cylinders of 16 tracks, 135
sectors
        4071.1MB in 84 cyl groups (46 c/g, 48.52MB/g, 6080 i/g)
super-block backups (for fsck -F ufs -o b=#) at:
 32, 99536, 199040, 298544, 398048, 497552, 597056, 696560, 796064, 895568,
 7354112, 7453616, 7553120, 7652624, 7752128, 7851632, 7948832, 8048336,
 8147840, 8247344,
```

The `newfs` command uses conservative and safe default values to create the file system. We describe how to modify these values later in this chapter. Here are the default parameters used by the `newfs` command:

- The file system block size is 8192.
- The file system fragment size (the smallest allocable unit of disk space) is 1024 bytes.
- The percentage of free space is now calculated as follows: (64MB/partition size) × 100, rounded down to the nearest integer and limited to between 1% and 10%, inclusive.
- The number of inodes allocated to a file system (see Table 1.9, titled "Default Number of inodes").

Understanding Custom File System Parameters

Before you choose to alter the default file system parameters assigned by the `newfs` command, you need to understand them. This section describes each of these parameters:

- Logical block size
- Fragment size
- Minimum free space
- Rotational delay (gap)
- Optimization type
- Number of inodes and bytes per inode

Logical Block Size

The *logical block size* is the size of the blocks that the Unix kernel uses to read or write files. The logical block size is usually different from the physical block size (usually 512 bytes), which is the size of the smallest block that the disk controller can read or write.

You can specify the logical block size of the file system. After the file system is created, you cannot change this parameter without rebuilding the file system. You can have file systems with different logical block sizes on the same disk.

By default, the logical block size is 8192 bytes (8KB) for UFS file systems. The UFS supports block sizes of 4096 or 8192 bytes (4KB or 8KB, with 8KB being the recommended logical block size).

To choose the best logical block size for your system, consider both the performance desired and the available space. For most UFS systems, an 8KB file system provides the best performance, offering a good balance between disk performance and use of space in primary memory and on disk.

> **NOTE**
>
> **sun4u Only** The sun4u architecture does not support the 4KB block size.

As a general rule, a larger logical block size increases efficiency for file systems in which most of the files are large. Use a smaller logical block size for file systems in which most of the files are small. You can use the `quot -c` file system command on a file system to display a complete report on the distribution of files by block size.

Fragment Size

As files are created or expanded, they are allocated disk space in either full logical blocks or portions of logical blocks called fragments. When disk space is needed to hold data for a file, full blocks are allocated first, and then one or more fragments of a block are allocated for the remainder. For small files, allocation begins with fragments.

The capability to allocate fragments of blocks to files rather than whole blocks saves space by reducing the fragmentation of disk space that results from unused holes in blocks.

You define the fragment size when you create a UFS. The default fragment size is 1KB. Each block can be divided into one, two, four, or eight fragments, resulting in fragment sizes from 512 bytes (for 4KB file systems) to 8192 bytes (for 8KB file systems only). The lower boundary is actually tied to the disk sector size, typically 512 bytes.

NOTE

Fragment Size for Large Files The upper boundary might equal the full block size, in which case the fragment is not a fragment at all. This configuration might be optimal for file systems with large files when you are more concerned with speed than with space.

When choosing a fragment size, look at the trade-off between time and space: A small fragment size saves space but requires more time to allocate. As a general rule, a larger fragment size increases efficiency for file systems in which most of the files are large. Use a smaller fragment size for file systems in which most of the files are small.

Minimum Free Space

The minimum free space is the percentage of the total disk space held in reserve when you create the file system. Before Solaris 7, the default reserve was always 10%. Since Solaris 7, the minimum free space is automatically determined. This new method of calculating free space results in less wasted disk space on large file systems.

Free space is important because file access becomes less efficient as a file system gets full. As long as the amount of free space is adequate, UFS file systems operate efficiently. When a file system becomes full, using up the available user space, only `root` can access the reserved free space.

Commands such as `df` report the percentage of space available to users, excluding the percentage allocated as the minimum free space. When the command reports that more than 100% of the disk space in the file system is in use, some of the reserve has been used by `root`.

If you impose quotas on users, the amount of space available to the users does not include the free space reserve. You can change the value of the minimum free space for an existing file system by using the `tunefs` command.

Optimization Type

The optimization type is either space or time. When you select space optimization, disk blocks are allocated to minimize fragmentation and optimize disk use.

When you select time optimization, disk blocks are allocated as quickly as possible, with less emphasis on their placement. With enough free space, the disk blocks can be allocated effectively with minimal fragmentation. Time is the default.

You can change the value of the optimization type parameter for an existing file system by using the `tunefs` command.

Number of inodes and Bytes per inode

The number of inodes determines the number of files you can have in the file system because each file has one inode. The number of bytes per inode determines the total number of inodes created when the file system is made: the total size of the file system divided by the number of bytes per inode.

A file system with many symbolic links will have a lower average file size and the file system will require more inodes than a file system with a few very large files. If your file system will have many small files, you can use the `-i` option with `newfs` to specify the number of bytes per inode, which will determine the number of inodes in the file system. For a file system with very large files, give this parameter a lower value.

NOTE

Number of inodes Having too many inodes is much better than running out of them. If you have too few inodes, you could reach the maximum number of files on a disk slice that is practically empty.

The `mkfs` Command

EXAM ALERT

Expect to see several questions on creating, fixing, and managing file systems. All questions related to creating file systems will use newfs. It's important to understand the file system options described in this mkfs section, but don't be too concerned about understanding the mkfs method of creating file systems. Most system administrators use newfs and that is what you will be tested on.

Although it's highly recommended that the newfs command be used to create file systems, it's also important to see what is happening "behind the scenes" with the mkfs utility. The syntax for mkfs is as follows:

```
/usr/sbin/mkfs <options> <character device name>
```

The mkfs options are described in Table 1.10.

TABLE 1.10 The mkfs Command

Option	Description
-F	Used to specify the file system type. If this option is omitted, the /etc/vfstab and /etc/default/fs files are checked to determine a file system type.
-m	Shows the command line that was used to create the specified file system. No changes are made to the file system.
-V	Verbose. Shows the command line, but does not execute anything.
-o <specific options>	A list of options specific to the type of file system. The list must have the following format: -o followed by a space, followed by a series of keyword [=value] pairs, separated by commas, with no intervening spaces. apc=<*n*>—Reserved space for bad block replacement on SCSI devices. The default is 0. N—Prints the file system parameters without actually creating the file system. nsect=<*n*>—The number of sectors per track on the disk. The default is 32. ntrack=<*n*>—The number of tracks per cylinder on the disk. The default is 16. bsize=<*n*>—Logical block size, either 4096 (4KB) or 8192 (8KB). The default is 8192. The sun4u architecture does not support the 4096 block size. fragsize=<*bytes*>—The smallest amount of disk space, in bytes, to allocate to a file. The value must be a power of 2 with a minimum value of 512 and a maximum of the logical block size. Thus, if the logical block size is 4096, legal values are 512, 1024, 2048, and 4096. If the logical block size is 8192, 8192 is also a legal value. The default is 1024. cgsize=<*cyls*>—The number of cylinders per cylinder group. The default is 16.

(continues)

TABLE 1.10 *Continued*

Option	Description
	`free=`*<n>*—The minimum percentage of free space to maintain in the file system. This space is off-limits to normal users. After the file system is filled to this threshold, only the superuser can continue writing to the file system. This parameter can be subsequently changed using the `tunefs` command. The default is 10%; however, on large file systems, the `minfree` value is determined automatically.
	`rps=`*<rps>*—The rotational speed of the disk, specified in revolutions per second. The default is `60`.
	`nbpi=`*<value>*—The `value` specified is the number of bytes per inode, which specifies the density of inodes in the file system. The number is divided into the total size of the file system to determine the fixed number of inodes to create. It should reflect the expected average size of files in the file system. If fewer inodes are desired, a larger number should be used. To create more inodes, a smaller number should be given. The default is `2048`.
	`opt=`*<value>*—Space or time optimization preference. The value can be `s` or `t`. Specify `s` to optimize for disk space. Specify `t` to optimize for speed (time). The default is `t`. Generally, you should optimize for time unless the file system is more than 90% full.
	`gap=`*<milliseconds>*—Rotational delay. This option is obsolete in Solaris 10. The value is always set to 0.
	`nrpos=`*<n>*—The number of different rotational positions into which to divide a cylinder group. The default is `8`.
	`maxcontig=`*<blocks>*—The maximum number of blocks belonging to one file that are allocated contiguously before inserting a rotational delay. For a 4KB file system, the default is `14`; for an 8KB file system, the default is `7`. This parameter can subsequently be changed using the `tunefs` command.

`mkfs` constructs a file system on the character (or raw) device found in the `/dev/rdsk` directory. Again, it is highly recommended that you do not run the `mkfs` command directly, but instead use the friendlier `newfs` command, which automatically determines all the necessary parameters required by `mkfs` to construct the file system. In the following example, the `-v` option to the `newfs` command outputs all the parameters passed to the `mkfs` utility. Type the following:

```
newfs -v /dev/rdsk/c2t4d0s1
```

The system outputs the following information and creates a new file system on /dev/rdsk/c2t4d0s1:

```
newfs: construct a new file system /dev/rdsk/c2t4d0s1: (y/n)? y
```

The following output appears on the screen:

```
mkfs -F ufs /dev/rdsk/c2t4d0s1 8359200 135 16 8192 1024 96 1 120 8192 t 0 -1 8 128 n
/dev/rdsk/c2t4d0s1:      8359200 sectors in 3870 cylinders of 16 tracks, 135 sectors
        4081.6MB in 85 cyl groups (46 c/g, 48.52MB/g, 6080 i/g)
super-block backups (for fsck -F ufs -o b=#) at:
 32, 99536, 199040, 298544, 398048, 497552, 597056, 696560, 796064, 895568,
 7453616, 7553120, 7652624, 7752128, 7851632, 7948832, 8048336, 8147840,
 8247344, 8346848,
```

You'll see in the output that all the mkfs parameters used to create the file system are displayed. The second line of output describes the disk. The third line describes the UFS file system being created. The remaining lines of output list the beginning sector locations of the backup superblocks.

The newfs command also creates a lost+found directory for the UFS file system. This directory is used by the fsck command and described later in this chapter.

The fstyp Command

A good command to use to view file system parameters is the fstyp command. Use the -v option to obtain a full listing of a file system's parameters:

```
fstyp -v /dev/rdsk/c0t0d0s6
```

The system responds with this:

```
ufs
magic    11954   format   dynamic time     Fri Jul 19 18:51:52 2002
sblkno   16      cblkno   24      iblkno   32      dblkno   480
sbsize   3072    cgsize   2048    cgoffset 32      cgmask   0xfffffff0
ncg      28      size     205065  blocks   192056
bsize    8192    shift    13      mask     0xffffe000
fsize    1024    shift    10      mask     0xfffffc00
frag     8       shift    3       fsbtodb  1
minfree 10%      maxbpg   2048    optim    time
maxcontig 16     rotdelay 0ms     rps      90
csaddr   480     cssize   1024    shift    9       mask     0xfffffe00
ntrak    15      nsect    63      spc      945     ncyl     434
cpg      16      bpg      945     fpg      7560    ipg      3584
nindir   2048    inopb    64      nspf     2
nbfree   23678   ndir     50      nifree   100200  nffree   161
cgrotor 2        fmod     0       ronly    0       logbno   0
```

```
fs_reclaim is not set
file system state is valid, fsclean is 2
blocks available in each rotational position
cylinder number 0:
   position 0:      0   4   8  12  16  20  24  28
   position 1:     32  36  40  44  48  52  56
   position 2:      1   5   9  13  17  21  25  29
   position 3:     33  37  41  45  49  53  57
   position 4:      2   6  10  14  18  22  26  30
   position 5:     34  38  42  46  50  54  58
   position 6:      3   7  11  15  19  23  27  31
   position 7:     35  39  43  47  51  55  59
cylinder number 1:
   position 0:     63  67  71  75  79  83  87  91
   position 1:     60  95  99 103 107 111 115
   position 2:     64  68  72  76  80  84  88  92
   position 3:     61  96 100 104 108 112 116
```

*Output has been truncated.

NOTE

Copy the mkfs Options It's always a good idea to print the `mkfs` options used on a file system along with information provided by the `prtvtoc` command. Put the printout in your system log so that if you ever need to rebuild a file system because of a hard drive failure, you can re-create it exactly as it was before.

File System Operations

This section describes the Solaris utilities used for creating, checking, repairing, and mounting file systems. Use these utilities to make file systems available to the user and to ensure their reliability.

Synchronizing a File System

The UFS file system relies on an internal set of tables to keep track of inodes as well as used and available blocks. When a user performs an operation that requires data to be written to the disk, the data to be written is first copied into a buffer in the kernel. Normally, the disk update is not handled until long after the write operation has returned. At any given time, the file system, as it resides on the disk, might lag behind the state of the file system represented by the buffers located in physical memory (RAM). The internal tables finally get updated when the buffer is required for another use or when the kernel automatically runs the `fsflush` daemon (at 30-second intervals).

If the system is halted without writing out the memory-resident information, the file system on the disk will be in an inconsistent state. If the internal tables are not properly synchronized with data on the disk, inconsistencies result, data may be lost, and file systems will need repairing. File systems can be damaged or become inconsistent because of abrupt termination of the operating system in these ways:

- Experiencing power failure
- Accidentally unplugging the system
- Turning off the system without the proper shutdown procedure
- Performing a Stop+A (L1+A)
- Encountering a software error in the kernel
- Encountering a hardware failure that halts the system unexpectedly

To prevent unclean halts, the current state of the file system must be written to disk (that is, synchronized) before you halt the CPU or take a disk offline.

Repairing File Systems

EXAM ALERT

Understand all aspects of repairing a file system. Know everything from unmounting a faulty file system, checking a file system, creating a new file system, and restoring data to that file system.

During normal operation, files are created, modified, and removed. Each time a file is modified, the operating system performs a series of file system updates. When a system is booted, a file system consistency check is automatically performed. Most of the time, this file system check repairs any problems it encounters. File systems are checked with the `fsck` (file system check) command.

CAUTION

Never run the **fsck** command on a mounted file system. This could leave the file system in an unstable state and could result in the loss of data. Because the `/` (root), `/usr`, and `/var` file systems cannot be unmounted, these file systems should only have `fsck` run on them while in single-user mode.

Reboot the system immediately after running the `fsck` on these mounted file systems.

The Solaris `fsck` command uses a state flag, which is stored in the superblock, to record the condition of the file system. Following are the possible state values:

- `FSCLEAN`—If the file system was unmounted properly, the state flag is set to `FSCLEAN`. Any file system with an `FSCLEAN` state flag is not checked when the system is booted.
- `FSSTABLE`—On a mounted file system, this state indicates that the file system has not changed since the last `sync` or `fsflush`. File systems marked as `FSSTABLE` can skip `fsck` before mounting.
- `FSACTIVE`—The state flag gets set to `FSACTIVE` when a file system is mounted and modified. The `FSACTIVE` flag goes into effect before any modifications are written to disk, however. The exception is when a file system is mounted with UFS logging and the flag is set to `FSLOG`, as described later. When a file system is unmounted properly, the state flag is then set to `FSCLEAN`. A file system with the `FSACTIVE` flag must be checked by `fsck` because it might be inconsistent. The system does not mount a file system for read/write unless its state is `FSCLEAN`, `FSLOG`, or `FSSTABLE`.
- `FSBAD`—If the root file system is mounted when its state is not `FSCLEAN` or `FSSTABLE`, the state flag is set to `FSBAD`. A root file system flagged as `FSBAD` as part of the boot process is mounted as read-only. You can run `fsck` on the raw root device and then remount the root file system as read/write.
- `FSLOG`—If the file system was mounted with UFS logging, the state flag is set to `FSLOG`. Any file system with an `FSLOG` state flag is not checked when the system is booted. See the section titled "Mounting a File System with UFS Logging Enabled," where I describe mounting a file system from the command line later in this chapter.

`fsck` is a multipass file system check program that performs successive passes over each file system, checking blocks and sizes, pathnames, connectivity, reference counts, and the map of free blocks (possibly rebuilding it). `fsck` also performs cleanup. The phases (passes) performed by the UFS version of `fsck` are described in Table 1.11.

TABLE 1.11 `fsck` Phases

`fsck` Phase	Task Performed
Phase 1	Checks blocks and sizes
Phase 2	Checks pathnames
Phase 3	Checks connectivity
Phase 4	Checks reference counts
Phase 5	Checks cylinder groups

Normally, `fsck` is run noninteractively at bootup to preen the file systems after an abrupt system halt in which the latest file system changes were not written to disk. Preening automatically fixes any basic file system inconsistencies but does not try to repair more serious errors. While preening a file system, `fsck` fixes the inconsistencies it expects from such an abrupt halt. For more serious conditions, the command reports the error and terminates. It then tells the operator to run `fsck` manually.

Determining Whether a File System Needs Checking

File systems must be checked periodically for inconsistencies to avoid unexpected loss of data. As stated earlier, checking the state of a file system is automatically done at bootup; however, it is not necessary to reboot a system to check whether the file systems are stable as described in Step by Step 1.10.

STEP BY STEP

1.10 Determining the Current State of the File System

1. Become a superuser.
2. Type **`fsck -m /dev/rdsk/`*`cntndnsn`*** and press Enter. The state flag in the superblock of the file system you specify is checked to see whether the file system is clean or requires checking. If you omit the device argument, all the UFS file systems listed in `/etc/vfstab` with an `fsck` pass value of greater than `0` are checked.

In the following example, the first file system needs checking, but the second file system does not:

```
fsck -m /dev/rdsk/c0t0d0s6

** /dev/rdsk/c0t0d0s6
ufs fsck: sanity check: /dev/rdsk/c0t0d0s6 needs checking
fsck -m /dev/rdsk/c0t0d0s7
** /dev/rdsk/c0t0d0s7
ufs fsck: sanity check: /dev/rdsk/c0t0d0s7 okay
```

Running `fsck` Manually

You might need to manually check file systems when they cannot be mounted or when you've determined that the state of a file system is unclean. Good indications that a file system might need to be checked are error messages displayed in the console window or system crashes that occur for no apparent reason.

When you run `fsck` manually, it reports each inconsistency found and fixes innocuous errors. For more serious errors, the command reports the inconsistency and prompts you to choose a response. Sometimes corrective actions performed by `fsck` result in some loss of data. The amount and severity of data loss can be determined from the `fsck` diagnostic output. The procedure outlined in Step by Step 1.11 describes how to check a file system by running the `fsck` command manually.

STEP BY STEP

1.11 Manually Checking File Systems

1. Log in as root and unmount the file system.
2. After the file system is unmounted, type **`fsck /dev/rdsk/`*`<device>`*** and press Enter.

   If you do not specify a device, all file systems in the `/etc/vfstab` file with entries greater than `0` in the `fsck pass` field are checked, including root (/). As stated earlier, you must be in single-user mode to run fsck on root. You can also specify the mount point directory as an argument to `fsck`, and as long as the mount point has an entry in the `/etc/vfstab` file, `fsck` will be able to resolve the path to the raw device. The `fsck` command requires the raw device filename.
3. Any inconsistency messages are displayed. The only way to successfully change the file system and correct the problem is to answer `yes` to these messages.

> **NOTE**
>
> **Supply an Automatic Yes Response to fsck** The `fsck` command has a `-y` option that automatically answers `yes` to every question. But be careful: If `fsck` asks to delete a file, it will answer `yes` and you will have no control over it. If it doesn't delete the file, however, the file system remains unclean and cannot be mounted.

4. If you corrected any errors, type **`fsck /dev/rdsk/`*`<device>`*** and press Enter. `fsck` might not be capable of fixing all errors in one execution. If you see the message `FILE SYSTEM STATE NOT SET TO OKAY`, run the command again and continue to run `fsck` until it runs clean with no errors.
5. Rename and move any files put in `lost+found`. Individual files put in the `lost+found` directory by `fsck` are renamed with their inode numbers, so figuring out what they were named originally can be difficult. If possible, rename the files and move them where they belong. You might be able to use the `grep` command to match phrases with individual files and use the `file` command to identify file types, ownership, and so on. When entire directories are dumped into `lost+found`, it is easier to figure out where they belong and move them back.

> **NOTE**
>
> **Locating the Alternate Superblock** Occasionally the file system's superblock can become corrupted and `fsck` will ask you for the location of an alternate superblock. This information can be obtained by typing
>
> ```
> newfs -Nv <raw device name>
> ```

The labelit Command

After you create the file system with newfs, you can use the labelit utility to write or display labels on unmounted disk file systems. The syntax for labelit is as follows:

```
labelit <-F <fstype>> <-V> <special> < fsname volume >
```

Labeling a file system is optional. It's required only if you're using a program such as volcopy, which will be covered soon. The labelit command is described in Table 1.12.

TABLE 1.12 The labelit Command

Parameter	Description
<special>	This name should be the physical disk slice (for example, /dev/dsk/c0t0d0s6).
<fsname>	This represents the mount point (for example, root [/], /home, and so on) of the file system.
<volume>	This can be used to represent the physical volume name.
-F *<fstype>*	This specifies the file system type on which to operate. The file system type should either be specified here or be determinable from the /etc/vfstab entry. If no matching entry is found, the default file system type specified in /etc/default/fs is used.
-V	This prints the command line but does not perform an action.

NOTE

View Current Labels If fsname and volume are not specified, labelit prints the current values of these labels. Both fsname and volume are limited to six or fewer characters.

The following is an example of how to label a disk partition using the labelit command. Type the following:

```
labelit -F ufs /dev/rdsk/c0t0d0s6 disk1 vol1
```

The system responds with this:

```
fsname:  disk1
volume:  vol1
```

The volcopy Command

The administrator (root) can use the volcopy command to make a copy of a labeled file system. This command works with UFS file systems, but the file system must be labeled with the `labelit` utility before the `volcopy` command is issued. To determine whether a file system is a UFS, issue this command:

```
fstyp  /dev/rdsk/c0t0d0s6
```

The system responds with this:

```
ufs
```

The `volcopy` command can be used to copy a file system from one disk to another.

The syntax for `volcopy` is as follows:

```
volcopy <options> <fsname> <srcdevice> <volname1> <destdevice> <volname2>
```

`volcopy` is described in Table 1.13.

TABLE 1.13 The volcopy Command

Option	Description
`-F` ***<fstype>***	This specifies the file system type on which to operate. This should either be specified here or be determinable from the `/etc/vfstab` entry. If no matching entry is found, the default file system type specified in `/etc/default/fs` is used.
`-V`	This prints the command line but does not perform an action.
`-a`	This requires the operator to respond `yes` or `no`. If the `-a` option is not specified, `volcopy` pauses 10 seconds before the copy is made.
`-o` ***<options>***	This is a list of options specific to the type of file system. The list must have the following format: `-o` followed by a space, followed by a series of `keyword [=value]` pairs, separated by commas, with no intervening spaces.
<fsname>	This represents the mount point (for example, `/`, `/u1`, and so on) of the file system being copied.
<srcdevice> / ***<destdevice>***	This is the disk partition specified using the raw device (for example, `/dev/rdsk/clt0d0s7`, `/dev/rdsk/clt0d1s7`, and so on).
<srcdevice> / ***<volname1>***	This is the device and physical volume from which the copy of the file system is being extracted.
<destdevice> / ***<volname2>***	This is the target device and physical volume.

NOTE

fsname and volname Limits fsname and volname are limited to six or fewer characters and are recorded in the superblock. volname can be a dash (-) to use the existing volume name.

The following example copies the contents of /home1 (/dev/rdsk/c0t0d0s6) to /home2 (/dev/rdsk/c0t1d0s6):

```
volcopy -F ufs home1 /dev/rdsk/c0t0d0s6 home2 /dev/rdsk/c0t1d0s6 vol2
```

Other commands can also be used to copy file systems—ufsdump, cpio, tar, and dd, to name a few. These commands are discussed in Chapter 7, "Performing System Backups and Restorations."

Tuning File Systems

A situation might arise in which you want to change some of the parameters that were set when you originally created the file system. Perhaps you want to change the minfree value to free some additional disk space on a large disk drive. Using the tunefs command, you can modify the following file system parameters:

- maxcontig
- rotdelay
- maxbpg
- minfree
- optimization

See Table 1.14 for a description of these options.

CAUTION

tunefs can destroy a file system in seconds. Always back up the entire file system before using tunefs.

The syntax for tunefs is as follows:

```
tunefs [ -a <maxcontig> ] [ -d <rotdelay> ] [ -e <maxbpg> ]
[ -m <minfree> ] [ -o [ <value> ] <special>/<file system>
```

The tunefs command is described in Table 1.14.

TABLE 1.14 The `tunefs` Command

Option	Description
-a <***maxcontig***>	Specifies the maximum number of contiguous blocks that are laid out before forcing a rotational delay (see the -d option). The default value is 1 because most device drivers require an interrupt per disk transfer. For device drivers that can chain several buffers into a single transfer, set this to the maximum chain length.
-d <***rotdelay***>	This option is obsolete in Solaris 10. The value is always set to 0.
-e <***maxbpg***>	Sets the maximum number of blocks that any single file can allocate from a cylinder group before it is forced to begin allocating blocks from another cylinder group. Typically, this value is set to approximately one quarter of the total blocks in a cylinder group. The intent is to prevent any single file from using up all the blocks in a single cylinder group. The effect of this limit is to cause big files to do long seeks more frequently than if they were allowed to allocate all the blocks in a cylinder group before seeking elsewhere. For file systems with exclusively large files, this parameter should be set higher.
-m <***minfree***>	Specifies the percentage of space held back from normal users (the minimum free space threshold). The default value is 10%; however, on large file systems, the `minfree` value is determined automatically.
-o <***value***>	Changes the optimization strategy for the file system. The value is either `space` or `time`. Use `space` to conserve space; use `time` to organize file layout and minimize access time. Generally, optimize a file system for time unless it is more than 90% full.
<***special***>/<***file system***>	Enters either the special device name (such as `/dev/rdsk/c0t0d0s6`) or the file system name (such as `/home`).

The file system does not need to be unmounted before using `tunefs`.

To change the minimum free space (`minfree`) on a file system from 10% to 5%, type the following:

```
tunefs -m5 /dev/rdsk/c0t0d0s6
minimum percentage of free space changes from 10% to 5%
```

The manual page of `tunefs` recommends that `minfree` be set at 10%; if you set the value under that, you lose performance. This means that 10% of the disk is unusable. This might not have been too bad in the days when disks were a couple hundred megabytes in size, but on a 9GB disk, you're losing 900MB of disk space. The mention of loss of performance in the manual page is misleading. With such large disk drives, you can afford to have `minfree` as low as 1%. This has been found to be a practical and affordable limit. In addition, performance does not become an issue because locating free blocks even within a 90MB area is efficient.

A rule of thumb is to use the default 10% `minfree` value for file systems up to 1GB and then adjust the `minfree` value so that your `minfree` area is no larger than 100MB. As for performance, applications do not complain about the lower `minfree` value. The one exception is the root (/) file system, in which the system administrator can use his judgment to allow more free space just to be conservative, in case root (/) ever becomes 100% full.

NOTE

Viewing the minfree Value On large file systems, the `minfree` is automatically determined so that disk space is not wasted. Use the `mkfs -m` command described next if you want to see the actual `minfree` value that `newfs` used.

Later, if you want to see what parameters were used when creating a file system, issue the `mkfs` command:

```
mkfs -m /dev/rdsk/c2t1d0s1
```

The system responds with this:

```
mkfs -F ufs -o nsect=135,ntrack=16,bsize=8192,fragsize=1024,cgsize=46,free=1,\
rps=120,nbpi=8179,opt=t,apc=0,gap=0,nrpos=8,maxcontig=128,mtb=n\
 /dev/rdsk/c2t1d0s1 8337600
```

Mounting File Systems

Objective:

Explain how to perform mounts and unmounts.

File systems can be mounted from the command line by using the `mount` command. The commands in Table 1.15 are used from the command line to mount and unmount file systems.

TABLE 1.15 File System Commands

Command	Description
`mount`	Mounts specified file systems and remote resources
`mountall`	Mounts all file systems specified in a file system table (vfstab)
`umount`	Unmounts specified file systems and remote resources
`umountall`	Unmounts all file systems specified in a file system table

NOTE

/sbin/mountall is actually a shell script that first checks the state of each file system specified in the /etc/vfstab file before issuing the `mount -a` command. If the file system flag indicates that the file system is not mountable, `mountall` will prompt for the root password on the console and try to fix the file system with `fsck` before running the `mount -a` command.

After you create a file system, you need to make it available. You make file systems available by mounting them. Using the `mount` command, you attach a file system to the system directory tree at the specified mount point, and it becomes available to the system. The root file system is mounted at boot time and cannot be unmounted. Any other file system can be mounted or unmounted from the root file system with few exceptions.

The syntax for `mount` is as follows:

```
mount -F <fstype> <options> [ -o <specific_options> ] <-O > device_to_mount mountpoint
```

Table 1.16 describes options to the `mount` command.

TABLE 1.16 The mount Command Options

Option	Description
`-F <fstype>`	Used to specify the file system type `<fstype>` on which to operate. If **fstype** is not specified, it must be determined from the `/etc/vfstab` file or by consulting `/etc/default/fs` or `/etc/dfs/fstypes`.
`-g`	Globally mount the file system. On a clustered system, this globally mounts the file system on all nodes of the cluster.
`-m`	Mounts the file system without making an entry in `/etc/mnttab`.
`-r`	Mounts the file system as read-only.
`-O`	Overlay mount. Allows the file system to be mounted over an existing mount point, making the underlying file system inaccessible. If a mount is attempted on a preexisting mount point without setting this flag, the mount fails, producing the error `device busy`.
`-p`	Prints the list of mounted file systems in the `/etc/vfstab` format. This must be the only option specified.
`-v`	Prints the list of mounted file systems in `verbose` format. This must be the only option specified.
`-V`	Echoes the complete command line but does not execute the command. `umount` generates a command line by using the options and arguments provided by the user and adding to them information derived from `/etc/mnttab`. This option should be used to verify and validate the command line.

(continues)

TABLE 1.16 *Continued*

Option	Description
`-o`	Specifies `fstype`-specific options. These are generic options that can be specified with the `-o` option. If you specify multiple options, separate them with commas (no spaces)—for example, `-o ro,nosuid`. Additionally, file system specific options are described later in this chapter and in their respective man pages (such as `man mount_ufs` and `man mount_nfs`). `devices` | `nodevices`—Allow or disallow the opening of device-special files. The default is devices. `exec` | `noexec`—Allow or disallow executing programs in the file system. `rw`|`ro`—Specifies read/write or read-only. The default is read/write. `nbmand` | `nonbmand`—Allow or disallow non-blocking mandatory locking semantics on this file system. Non-blocking mandatory locking is disallowed by default. `nosuid`—Disallows setuid execution and prevents devices on the file system from being opened. The default is to enable setuid execution and to allow devices to be opened. `remount`—With `rw`, remounts a file system with read/write access. `m`—Mounts the file system without making an entry in `/etc/mnttab`. `largefiles`—Specifies that a file system might contain one or more files larger than 2GB. It is not required that a file system mounted with this option contain files larger than 2GB, but this option allows such files within the file system. `largefiles` is the default. `nolargefiles`—Provides total compatibility with previous file system behavior, enforcing the 2GB maximum file size limit.

NOTE

Determining a File System's Type Because the `mount` commands need the file system type to function properly, the file system type must be explicitly specified with the `-F` option or determined by searching the following files:

`/etc/vfstab`—Search the FS type field for the file system type.

`/etc/default/fs`—Search for a local file system type.

`/etc/dfs/fstypes`—Search for a remote file system type.

If the file system type is not found in any of these locations, the system will report an error.

EXAM ALERT

Be very familiar with the mount options for a UFS file system along with the defaults used when an option is not specified. The exam has several questions related to creating and repairing file systems. You need to know all aspects of mounting and unmounting a file system on a production (active) system.

The following examples illustrate the options described in Table 1.16.

A file system has been created on disk `c0t0d0` on slice `s0`. The directory to be mounted on this disk slice is `/home2`. To mount the file system, first create the directory called `/home2` and then type the following:

```
mount /dev/dsk/c0t0d0s0 /home2
```

If the file system has been mounted, you return to a command prompt. No other message is displayed.

When the UFS file system is mounted with no options, a default set of file system specific options are used—they are explained in Table 1.17. Options specific to the UFS file system are also described in the `mount_ufs` man pages.

TABLE 1.17 Mount Default Options for a UFS File System

Option	Description
`read/write`	Indicates that file system can be read and written to.
`setuid`	Permits the execution of setuid programs in the file system.
`devices`	Allow the opening of device-special files.
`intr`	Allows keyboard interrupts to kill a process that is waiting for an operation on a locked file system.
`logging`	Indicates that logging is enabled for the UFS file system. This is the default for the Solaris 10 OS.
`largefiles`	Allows for the creation of files larger than 2 Gbytes. A file system mounted with this option can contain files larger than 2 Gbytes.
`xattr`	Supports extended attributes not found in standard Unix file systems.
`onerror=panic`	Specifies the action that the UFS file system should take to recover from an internal inconsistency on a file system. An action can be specified as: panic—Causes a forced system shutdown. This is the default. lock—Applies a file system lock to the file system. umount—Forcibly unmounts the file system.

In the next example, the `-v` option is used with the `mount` command to display a list of all mounted file systems:

```
mount -v
```

The system responds with this:

```
# mount -v
/dev/dsk/c0t0d0s0 on / type ufs \
read/write/setuid/devices/intr/largefiles/logging/xattr/onerror=panic/dev=2200008 \
on Fri Aug  5 11:32:05 2005
/devices on /devices type devfs read/write/setuid/devices/dev=4380000 \
 on Fri Aug  5 11:31:47 2005 ctfs on /system/contract type ctfs \
```

```
read/write/setuid/devices/dev=43c0001 on Fri Aug  5 11:31:47 2005
proc on /proc type proc read/write/setuid/devices/dev=4400000 on\
 Fri Aug  5 11:31:47 2005
mnttab on /etc/mnttab type mntfs read/write/setuid/devices/dev=4440001 \
on Fri Aug  5 11:31:47 2005

swap on /etc/svc/volatile type tmpfs read/write/setuid/devices/xattr/dev=4480001 \
on Fri Aug  5 11:31:47 2005

objfs on /system/object type objfs read/write/setuid/devices/dev=44c0001 on \
Fri Aug  5 11:31:47 2005

/dev/dsk/c0t0d0s6 on /usr type ufs \
read/write/setuid/devices/intr/largefiles/logging/xattr/onerror=panic/dev=220000e \
on Fri Aug  5 11:32:06 2005
fd on /dev/fd type fd read/write/setuid/devices/dev=4640001 \
on Fri Aug  5 11:32:06 2005
/dev/dsk/c0t0d0s1 on /var type ufs \
read/write/setuid/devices/intr/largefiles/logging/xattr/onerror=panic/dev=2200009 \
on Fri Aug  5 11:32:09 2005
swap on /tmp type tmpfs read/write/setuid/devices/xattr/dev=4480002 \
on Fri Aug  5 11:32:09 2005
swap on /var/run type tmpfs read/write/setuid/devices/xattr/dev=4480003 \
on Fri Aug  5 11:32:09 2005
/dev/dsk/c0t0d0s4 on /data type ufs \
read/write/setuid/devices/intr/largefiles/logging/xattr/onerror=panic/dev=220000c \
on Fri Aug  5 11:32:16 2005
/dev/dsk/c0t0d0s5 on /opt type ufs \
read/write/setuid/devices/intr/largefiles/logging/xattr/onerror=panic/dev=220000d \
on Fri Aug  5 11:32:16 2005
/dev/dsk/c0t0d0s7 on /export/home type ufs \
read/write/setuid/devices/intr/largefiles/logging/xattr/onerror=panic/dev=220000f \
on Fri Aug  5 11:32:16 2005
```

The following example mounts a file system as read-only:

```
mount -o ro /dev/dsk/c0t0d0s0 /home2
```

The next example uses the `mount` command to mount a directory to a file system as read/writeable, disallow setuid execution, and allow the creation of large files:

```
mount -o rw,nosuid,largefiles /dev/dsk/c0t0d0s0 /home2
```

Type `mount` with no options to verify that the file system has been mounted and to review the mount options that were used:

```
mount
```

The system responds with information about all mounted file systems, including `/home2`:

```
/home2 on /dev/dsk/c0t0d0s0 read/write/nosuid/largefiles on\
 Tue Jul 16 06:56:33 2005
```

NOTE

Using SMC to View Current Mounts You can also use the SMC Mounts Tool to view information about mounted file systems. The information provided is similar to the information displayed when you issue the `mount` command with no options. To access the Mounts Tool, follow the Step by Step procedure for using the SMC Usage Tool described in the section titled "Displaying a File System's Disk Space Usage."

Mounting a File System with Large Files

On a Solaris system, a large file is a regular file whose size is greater than or equal to 2GB. A small file is a regular file whose size is less than 2GB. Some utilities can handle large files, and others cannot. A utility is called *large file–aware* if it can process large files in the same manner that it does small files. A large file–aware utility can handle large files as input and can generate large files as output. The `newfs`, `mkfs`, `mount`, `umount`, `tunefs`, `labelit`, and `quota` utilities are all large file–aware for UFS file systems.

NOTE

Due to file system overhead, the largest file size that can be created on a multiterabyte file system is approximately 1 Tbyte. The data capacity of a 1 Tbyte file system is approximately 1 Tbyte minus 0.5% overhead and the recommended 1% free space.

On the other hand, a utility is called *large file–safe* if it causes no data loss or corruption when it encounters a large file. A utility that is large file–safe cannot properly process a large file, so it returns an appropriate error. Some examples of utilities that are not large file–aware but are large file–safe include the `vi` editor and the `mailx` and `lp` commands. A full list of commands that are large file–aware and large file–safe can be found in the online manual pages.

The `largefiles` mount option lets users mount a file system containing files larger than 2GB. The `largefiles` mount option is the default state for the Solaris 10 environment. The `largefiles` option means that a file system mounted with this option might contain one or more files larger than 2GB.

You must explicitly use the `nolargefiles` mount option to disable this behavior. The `nolargefiles` option provides total compatibility with previous file system behavior, enforcing the 2GB maximum file size limit.

NOTE

Mounting Largefile File Systems After you mount a file system with the default `largefiles` option and large files have been created, you cannot remount the file system with the `nolargefiles` option until you remove any large files and run `fsck` to reset the state to `nolargefiles`.

Mounting a File System with UFS Logging Enabled

The UFS logging feature eliminates file system inconsistency, which can significantly reduce the time of system reboots. UFS logging is the default in Solaris 10 and does not need to be specified when mounting a file system. Use the `nologging` option in the `/etc/vfstab` file or as an option to the `mount` command to disable UFS logging on a file system.

UFS logging is the process of storing file system operations to a log before the transactions are applied to the file system. Because the file system can never become inconsistent, `fsck` can usually be bypassed, which reduces the time to reboot a system if it crashes or after an unclean halt.

The UFS log is allocated from free blocks on the file system. It is sized at approximately 1MB per 1GB of file system, up to a maximum of 64MB. The default is logging for all UFS file systems.

NOTE

fsck on Logged File Systems Is it ever necessary to run `fsck` on a file system that has UFS logging enabled? The answer is yes. It is usually unnecessary to run `fsck` on a file system that has UFS logging enabled. The one exception to this is when the log is bad. An example of this is when a media failure causes the log to become unusable. In this case, logging puts the file system in an error state, and you cannot mount it and use it until `fsck` is run. The safest option is to always run `fsck`. It will quit immediately if logging is there and the file system is not in an error state.

Unmounting a File System

Unmounting a file system removes it from the file system mount point and deletes the entry from `/etc/mnttab`. Some file system administration tasks, such as `labelit` and `fsck`, cannot be performed on mounted file systems. You should unmount a file system if any of the following three conditions exist:

- The file system is no longer needed or has been replaced by a file system that contains software that is more current.
- When you check and repair it by using the `fsck` command.
- When you are about to do a complete backup of it.

To unmount a file system, use the `umount` command:

```
umount <mount-point>
```

`<mount-point>` is the name of the file system you want to unmount. This can be either the directory name in which the file system is mounted or the device name path of the file system. For example, to unmount the `/home2` file system, type the following:

```
umount /home2
```

Alternatively, you can specify the device name path for the file system:

```
umount /dev/dsk/c0t0d0s0
```

NOTE

Shutting Down the System File systems are automatically unmounted as part of the system shutdown procedure.

The `fuser` Command

Before you can unmount a file system, you must be logged in as the administrator (root) and the file system must not be busy. A file system is considered busy if a user is in a directory in the file system or if a program has a file open in that file system. You can make a file system available for unmounting by changing to a directory in a different file system or by logging out of the system. If something is causing the file system to be busy, you can use the `fuser` command, described in Table 1.18, to list all the processes that are accessing the file system and to stop them if necessary.

NOTE

Informing Users Always notify users before unmounting a file system.

The syntax for `fuser` is as follows:

```
/usr/sbin/fuser [options] <file>|<file system>
```

Replace `<file>` with the filename you are checking, or replace `<file system>` with the name of the file system you are checking.

TABLE 1.18 The `fuser` Command Options

Option	Description
`-c`	Reports on files that are mount points for file systems and on any files within that mounted file system.
`-f`	Prints a report for the named file but not for files within a mounted file system.
`-k`	Sends the `SIGKILL` signal to each process.
`-u`	Displays the user login name in parentheses following the process ID.

The following example uses the fuser command to find out why /home2 is busy:

```
fuser -cu /home2
```

The system displays each process and user login name that is using this file system:

```
/home2:     8448c(root)    8396c(root)
```

The following command stops all processes that are using the /home2 file system by sending a SIGKILL to each one. Don't use it without first warning the users:

```
fuser -c -k /home2
```

Using the fuser command as described is the preferred method for determining who is using a file system before unmounting it. Added in Solaris 8 was another, less desirable method for unmounting a file system, using the umount command with the -f option, as follows:

```
umount -f /home2
```

The -f option forcibly unmounts a file system. Using this option can cause data loss for open files and programs that access files after the file system has been unmounted; it returns an error (EIO). The -f option should be used only as a last resort.

You can also use the fuser command to check on any device such as the system console. By typing:

```
fuser /dev/console
```

The system displays the processes associated with that device as follows:

```
/dev/console:     459o    221o
```

/etc/mnttab

When a file system is mounted, an entry is maintained in the mounted file system table called /etc/mnttab. The file /etc/mnttab is really a file system that provides read-only access to the table of mounted file systems for the current host. The mount command adds entries to this table, and umount removes entries from this table. The kernel maintains the list in order of mount time. For example, the first mounted file system is first in the list, and the most recently mounted file system is last. When mounted on a mount point, the file system appears as a regular file containing the current mnttab information. Each entry in this table is a line of fields separated by spaces in this form:

```
<special> <mount_point> <fstype>  <options>  <time>
```

Table 1.19 describes each field.

TABLE 1.19 /etc/mnttab Fields

Field	Description
<*special*>	The resource to be mounted (that is, /dev/dsk/c0t0d0s0)
<*mount_point*>	The pathname of the directory on which the file system is mounted
<*fstype*>	The file system type
<*options*>	The list of mount options used to mount the file system
<*time*>	The time at which the file system was mounted

Following is a sample /etc/mnttab file:

```
# more /etc/mnttab
/dev/dsk/c0t0d0s0       /       ufs     \
rw,intr,largefiles,logging,xattr,onerror=panic,dev=2200008      1127941982
/devices        /devices        devfs   dev=4380000     1127941959
ctfs    /system/contract        ctfs    dev=43c0001     1127941959
proc    /proc   proc    dev=4400000     1127941959
mnttab  /etc/mnttab     mntfs   dev=4440001     1127941959
swap    /etc/svc/volatile       tmpfs   xattr,dev=4480001       1127941959
objfs   /system/object  objfs   dev=44c0001     1127941959
/dev/dsk/c0t0d0s6       /usr    ufs     \
rw,intr,largefiles,logging,xattr,onerror=panic,dev=220000e      1127941982
fd      /dev/fd fd      rw,dev=4640001  1127941982
/dev/dsk/c0t0d0s1       /var    ufs     \
rw,intr,largefiles,logging,xattr,onerror=panic,dev=2200009      1127941983
swap    /tmp    tmpfs   xattr,dev=4480002       1127941983
swap    /var/run        tmpfs   xattr,dev=4480003       1127941983
/dev/dsk/c0t0d0s5       /opt    ufs     \
rw,intr,largefiles,logging,xattr,onerror=panic,dev=220000d      1127941991
/dev/dsk/c0t0d0s7       /export/home    ufs     \
rw,intr,largefiles,logging,xattr,onerror=panic,dev=220000f      1127941991
-hosts  /net    autofs  nosuid,indirect,ignore,nobrowse,dev=4700001     1127942006
auto_home       /home   autofs  indirect,ignore,nobrowse,dev=4700002    1127942006
smokey:vold(pid487)     /vol    nfs     ignore,noquota,dev=46c0001      1127942024
/vol/dev/dsk/c0t2d0/s10_software_companion      /cdrom/s10_software_companion   hsfs\
ro,nosuid,noglobal,maplcase,rr,traildot,dev=16c0001     1127942029
/dev/dsk/c2t1d0s1       /mnt    ufs     rw,intr,largefiles,logging,xattr,\
onerror=panic,dev=800089        1128021589
```

Before Solaris 8, the /etc/mnttab file was a text file. The downside of being a text file was that it could get out of sync with the actual state of mounted file systems, or it could be manually edited. Now this file is a mntfs file system that provides read-only information directly from the kernel about mounted file systems for the local hosts.

You can display the contents of the mount table by using the `cat` or `more` commands, but you cannot edit them.

You can also view a mounted file system by typing `/sbin/mount` from the command line as shown earlier in this section.

Creating an Entry in the /etc/vfstab File to Mount File Systems

Objective:

Explain the purpose and function of the vfstab file in mounting UFS file systems, and the function of the mnttab file system in tracking current mounts.

The `/etc/vfstab` (virtual file system table) file contains a list of file systems, with the exception of the `/etc/mnttab` and `/var/run`, to be automatically mounted when the system is booted to the multiuser state. The system administrator places entries in the file, specifying what file systems are to be mounted at bootup. The following is an example of the `/etc/vfstab` file:

```
# cat /etc/vfstab
#device         device           mount            FS       fsck     mount    mount
#to mount       to fsck          point            type     pass     at boot  options
#
fd        -       /dev/fd  fd       -       no       -
/proc     -       /proc    proc     -       no       -
/dev/dsk/c0t0d0s3       -        -       swap     -        no       -
/dev/dsk/c0t0d0s0       /dev/rdsk/c0t0d0s0       /        ufs      1        no       -
/dev/dsk/c0t0d0s6       /dev/rdsk/c0t0d0s6       /usr     ufs      1        no       -
/dev/dsk/c0t0d0s1       /dev/rdsk/c0t0d0s1       /var     ufs      1        no       -
/dev/dsk/c0t0d0s7       /dev/rdsk/c0t0d0s7       /export/home     ufs      2        yes      -
/dev/dsk/c0t0d0s5       /dev/rdsk/c0t0d0s5       /opt     ufs      2        yes      -
/devices          -      /devices         devfs    -        no       -
ctfs      -       /system/contract        ctfs     -        no       -
objfs     -       /system/object  objfs   -        no       -
swap      -       /tmp     tmpfs    -       yes      -
```

EXAM ALERT

You'll need to make entries in the vfstab file on the exam. Understand the syntax and know how to create a new line in this file for both a UFS file system and swap.

Each column of information follows this format:

- **device to mount**—The buffered device that corresponds to the file system being mounted.

- **device to `fsck`**—The raw (character) special device that corresponds to the file system being mounted. This determines the raw interface used by `fsck`. Use a dash (-) when there is no applicable device, such as for swap, `/proc`, `tmp`, or a network-based file system.
- **mount point**—The default mount point directory.
- **FS type**—The type of file system.
- **`fsck` pass**—The pass number used by `fsck` to decide whether to check a file. When the field contains a `0` or a non-numeric value, the file system is not checked. When the field contains a value of `1`, the `fsck` utility gets started for that entry and runs to completion. When the field contains a value greater than `1`, that device is added to the list of devices to have the `fsck` utility run. The `fsck` utility can run on up to eight devices in parallel. This field is ignored by the `mountall` command.
- **mount at boot**—Specifies whether the file system should be automatically mounted when the system is booted. These file systems get mounted when SMF starts up the `svc:/system/file` system service instances.

NOTE

vfstab Entries for root (/), /usr, and /var For root (`/`), `/usr`, and `/var` file systems (if they are separate file systems), the `mount at boot field` option is no. The kernel mounts these file systems as part of the boot sequence before the `mountall` command is run. The `mount` command explicitly mounts the file systems root (`/`), `/usr`, and `/var` when SMF starts up the `svc:/system/file` system service instances.

- **`mount` options**—A list of comma-separated options (with no spaces) used when mounting the file system. Use a dash (-) to use default `mount` options.

Type the `mount` command with the `-p` option to display a list of mounted file systems in `/etc/vfstab` format:

```
mount -p
```

The system responds with this:

```
/dev/dsk/c0t0d0s0 - / ufs - no rw,intr,largefiles,logging,xattr,onerror=panic
/devices - /devices devfs - no
ctfs - /system/contract ctfs - no
proc - /proc proc - no
mnttab - /etc/mnttab mntfs - no
swap - /etc/svc/volatile tmpfs - no xattr
objfs - /system/object objfs - no
```

```
/dev/dsk/c0t0d0s6 - /usr ufs - no rw,intr,largefiles,logging,xattr,onerror=panic
fd - /dev/fd fd - no rw
/dev/dsk/c0t0d0s1 - /var ufs - no rw,intr,largefiles,logging,xattr,onerror=panic
swap - /tmp tmpfs - no xattr
swap - /var/run tmpfs - no xattr
/dev/dsk/c0t0d0s4 - /data ufs - no rw,intr,largefiles,logging,xattr,onerror=panic
/dev/dsk/c0t0d0s5 - /opt ufs - no rw,intr,largefiles,logging,xattr,onerror=panic
/dev/dsk/c0t0d0s7 - /export/home ufs - no rw,intr,largefiles,logging,xattr,\
onerror=panic
```

The `-p` option is useful for obtaining the correct settings if you're making an entry in the `/etc/vfstab` file.

Volume Management

Objective:

Explain how to perform access or restrict access to mounted diskettes and CD-ROMs.

Volume management (not to be confused with Solaris Volume Manager [SVM] described in Chapter 10) with the `vold` daemon is the mechanism that manages removable media, such as the CD-ROM and floppy disk drives.

Mounting and unmounting a file system requires root privileges. How do you let users insert, mount, and unmount CD-ROMs and USB flash disks without being the administrator (root)? After a file system has been mounted and you remove the medium, what happens to the mount? Usually when you disconnect a disk drive while it is mounted, the system begins displaying error messages. The same thing happens if you remove a flash disk or CD-ROM while it is mounted.

Volume manager, with its `vold` daemon, provides assistance to overcome these problems. The `vold` daemon simplifies the use of disks and CDs by automatically mounting them. Volume manager provides three major benefits:

- By automatically mounting removable disks and CDs, volume management simplifies their use.
- Volume manager enables the user to access removable disks and CDs without having to be logged in as root.
- Volume manager lets the administrator (root) give other systems on the network automatic access to any removable disks and CDs that the users insert into your system.

To begin, let's look at the two devices that the system administrator needs to manage: the floppy disk drive and the CD-ROM. Volume manager provides access to both devices through the /vol/dev directory. In addition, Volume Manager creates links to the removable disk, CD-ROM, and USB devices through various directories, as shown in Table 1.20.

TABLE 1.20 Volume Manager Directories and Links

Link	Description
/vol/dev/diskette0	The directory providing block device access for the medium in floppy drive 0
/vol/dev/rdiskette0	The directory providing character device access for the medium in floppy drive 0
/vol/dev/aliases/floppy0	The symbolic link to the character device for the medium in floppy drive 0
/dev/rdiskette	The directory providing character device access for the medium in the primary floppy drive, usually drive 0
/vol/dev/aliases/cdrom0	Symbolic link to the directory providing character device access for the medium in the primary CD-ROM or DVD-ROM drive
/vol/dev/aliases/zip0	Symbolic link to the directory providing character device access for the medium in the primary Zip drive
/vol/dev/aliases/jaz0	Symbolic link to the directory providing character device access for the medium in the primary Jaz drive
/vol/dev/aliases/PCMCIA	Symbolic link to the directory providing character device access for the medium in the primary PCMCIA drive
/vol/dev/aliases/rmdisk0	Symbolic link to the directory providing character device access for the primary generic removable media that is not a Zip, Jaz, CD-ROM, floppy, DVD-ROM, or PCMCIA memory card
/vol/dev/dsk/	Symbolic link to the directory providing access to the CD-ROM buffered, or block, device
/vol/dev/rdsk/	Symbolic link to the directory providing access to the CD-ROM character, or raw, device
/cdrom/cdrom0	The symbolic link to the buffered device for the medium in CD-ROM or DVD-ROM drive 0
/floppy/floppy0	The symbolic link to the buffered device for the medium in floppy drive 0
/rmdisk/zip0	The symbolic link to the first mounted Zip medium in the local Zip drive
/rmdisk/jaz0	The symbolic link to the first mounted Jaz medium in the local Jaz drive
/pcmem/pcmem0	The symbolic link to the first mounted PCMCIA drive

The vold daemon automatically creates the mount point and mounts file systems when removable media containing recognizable file systems are inserted into the devices. For example, when a CD is inserted, vold automatically creates a mount point in the /cdrom directory and mounts the CD-ROM file system onto this mount point. It then creates a symbolic link to /vol/dev/aliases/cdrom0 and /cdrom/cdrom0 as described in the previous table.

NOTE

Most CDs and DVDs are formatted to the ISO 9660 standard, which is portable. So, most CDs and DVDs can be mounted by volume management. However, CDs or DVDs with UFS file systems are not portable between architectures. So, they must be used on the architecture for which they were designed. For example, a CD or DVD with a UFS file system for a SPARC platform cannot be recognized by an x86 platform. Likewise, an x86 UFS CD cannot be mounted by volume management on a SPARC platform. The same limitation generally applies to diskettes. However, some architectures share the same bit structure, so occasionally a UFS format specific to one architecture will be recognized by another architecture. Still, the UFS file system structure was not designed to guarantee this compatibility.

With a removable disk, however, the file system is not automatically mounted until you issue the volcheck command. The volcheck command instructs vold to look at each device and determine whether new media has been inserted into the drive. On some removable disks such as floppy disks, vold cannot continually poll the disk drive like it does on a CD because of the hardware limitation in these removable drives. Continuously polling a removable disk for media causes a mechanical action in the disk drive and causes the drive to wear out prematurely.

All USB devices are hot-pluggable, which means that the device is added and removed without shutting down the OS or the power. USB storage devices will be mounted by vold without any user interaction. When you hot-plug a USB device, the device is immediately seen in the system's device hierarchy, as displayed in the prtconf command output. When you remove a USB device, the device is removed from the system's device hierarchy, unless the device is in use.

If the USB device is in use when it is removed, the device node remains, but the driver controlling this device stops all activity on the device. Any new I/O activity issued to this device is returned with an error. In this situation, the system prompts you to plug in the original device. If the device is no longer available, stop the applications. After a few seconds, the port becomes available again.

The rmformat command is used to format, label, partition, and perform various functions on removable media such as USB storage devices. For example, to use the rmformat command to format a Zip drive, type the following:

```
rmformat -F quick /vol/dev/aliases/zip0
```

The system displays the following information:

```
Formatting will erase all the data on disk.
Do you want to continue? (y/n) y
.....................................................................
```

The -F option is used with one of the following options:

- `quick` Starts a format without certification or format with limited certification of certain tracks on the media.
- `long` Starts a complete format. For some devices this might include the certification of the whole media by the drive itself.
- `force` Provided to start a long format without user confirmation before the format is started. For drives that have a password protection mechanism, it clears the password while formatting. This feature is useful when a password is no longer available. On those media which do not have such password protection, force starts a long format.

After formatting the device, you can use the newfs command to create a file system on the device as follows:

```
/usr/sbin/newfs -v /vol/dev/aliases/zip0
```

You can also use the rmformat -l command to list the removable media devices on the system. Using this command provides detailed information about the device, such as the name used by vold and both the logical and physical device names as follows:

```
rmformat -l
```

The system displays the following information:

```
Looking for devices...
     1. Volmgt Node: /vol/dev/aliases/rmdisk1
        Logical Node: /dev/rdsk/c5t0d0s2
        Physical Node: /pci@1e,600000/usb@b/hub@2/storage@4/disk@0,0
        Connected Device: TEAC     FD-05PUB         1026
        Device Type: Floppy drive
```

The vold daemon is the workhorse behind Volume Manager. It is automatically started by the /etc/init.d/volmgt script. vold reads the /etc/vold.conf configuration file at startup. The vold.conf file contains the Volume Manager configuration information. This information includes the database to use, labels that are supported, devices to use, actions to take if certain media events occur, and the list of file systems that are unsafe to eject without unmounting. The vold.conf file looks like this:

```
# ident "@(#)vold.conf  1.26    00/07/17 SMI"
#
# Volume Daemon Configuration file
#

# Database to use (must be first)
db db_mem.so
```

```
# Labels supported
label cdrom label_cdrom.so cdrom
label dos label_dos.so floppy rmdisk
label sun label_sun.so floppy rmdisk

# Devices to use
use cdrom drive /dev/rdsk/c*s2 dev_cdrom.so cdrom%d
use floppy drive /dev/rdiskette[0-9] dev_floppy.so floppy%d
use rmdisk drive /dev/rdsk/c*s2 dev_rmdisk.so rmdisk%d

# Actions
eject dev/diskette[0-9]/* user=root /usr/sbin/rmmount
eject dev/dsk/* user=root /usr/sbin/rmmount
insert dev/diskette[0-9]/* user=root /usr/sbin/rmmount
insert dev/dsk/* user=root /usr/sbin/rmmount
notify rdsk/* group=tty user=root /usr/lib/vold/volmissing -p
remount dev/diskette[0-9]/* user=root /usr/sbin/rmmount
remount dev/dsk/* user=root /usr/sbin/rmmount

# List of file system types unsafe to eject
unsafe ufs hsfs pcfs udfs
```

Each section in the `vold.conf` file is labeled with its function. Of these sections, you can safely modify the devices to use, which are described in Table 1.21, and actions, which are described in Table 1.22.

The "Devices to Use" section of the file describes the devices for `vold` to manage. `vold` has the following syntax:

```
use <device> <type> <special> <shared_object> <symname> < options >
```

TABLE 1.21 `vold.conf` Devices to Use

Parameter Field	Description
`<device>`	The type of removable media device to be used. Valid values are `cdrom`, `floppy`, `pcmem`, and `rmdisk`.
`<type>`	The device's specific capabilities. The valid value is `drive`.
`<special>`	The device or devices to be used. The path usually begins with /dev.
`<shared_object>`	The name of the program that manages this device. `vold` expects to find this program in /usr/lib/vold.
`<symname>`	The symbolic name that refers to this device. The `symname` is placed in the device directory.
`<options>`	The user, group, and mode permissions for the medium inserted (optional).

The `<special>` and `<symname>` parameters are related. If `<special>` contains any shell wildcard characters (that is, has one or more asterisks or question marks in it), `<symname>` must have a %d at its end. In this case, the devices that are found to match the regular expression are sorted and then numbered. The first device has a 0 filled in for the %d, the second device found has a 1, and so on.

If the special specification does not have shell wildcard characters, the symname parameter must explicitly specify a number at its end.

The "Actions" section of the file specifies which program should be called if a particular event (action) occurs. The syntax for the Actions field is as follows:

```
insert <regex> < options > <program> <program_args>
eject <regex> < options > <program> <program_args>
notify <regex> < options> <program> <program_args>
```

The different actions are listed in Table 1.22.

TABLE 1.22 vold.conf Actions

Parameter	Description
insert|eject|notify	The media action prompting the event.
<regex>	This Bourne shell regular expression is matched against each entry in the /vol file system that is being affected by this event.
<options>	Which user or group name this event is to run (optional).
<program>	The full pathname of an executable program to be run if regex is matched.
<program_args>	Arguments to the program.

In the default vold.conf file, you see the following entries under the "Devices to Use" and "Actions" sections:

```
# Devices to use
use cdrom drive /dev/rdsk/c*s2 dev_cdrom.so cdrom%d
use floppy drive /dev/rdiskette[0-9] dev_floppy.so floppy%d
use rmdisk drive /dev/rdsk/c*s2 dev_rmdisk.so rmdisk%d
# Actions

eject dev/diskette[0-9]/* user=root /usr/sbin/rmmount
eject dev/dsk/* user=root /usr/sbin/rmmount
insert dev/diskette[0-9]/* user=root /usr/sbin/rmmount
insert dev/dsk/* user=root /usr/sbin/rmmount
notify rdsk/* group=tty user=root /usr/lib/vold/volmissing -p
remount dev/diskette[0-9]/* user=root /usr/sbin/rmmount
remount dev/dsk/* user=root /usr/sbin/rmmount
```

When a CD is inserted into the CD-ROM named /dev/dsk/c0t6d0, the following happens:

1. vold detects that the CD has been inserted and runs the /usr/sbin/rmmount command. rmmount is the utility that automatically mounts a file system on a CD-ROM

and floppy. It determines the type of file system, if any, that is on the medium. If a file system is present, `rmmount` creates a mount point in the `/cdrom` directory and mounts the CD-ROM file system onto this mount point. It then creates a symbolic link to `/vol/dev/aliases/cdrom0` and `/cdrom/cdrom0` as described in the previous table.

If the medium is read-only (either a CD-ROM or a floppy with the write-protect tab set), the file system is mounted as read-only. If a file system is not identified, `rmmount` does not mount a file system.

2. After the mount is complete, the action associated with the media type is executed. The action allows other programs to be notified that a new medium is available. For example, the default action for mounting a CD-ROM or a floppy is to start the File Manager.

   These actions are described in the configuration file `/etc/rmmount.conf`. Following is an example of the default `/etc/rmmount.conf` file:

```
# ident "@(#)rmmount.conf        1.12     00/08/29 SMI"
#
# Removable Media Mounter configuration file.
#

# File system identification
ident hsfs ident_hsfs.so cdrom
ident ufs ident_ufs.so cdrom floppy rmdisk
ident pcfs ident_pcfs.so floppy rmdisk
ident udfs ident_udfs.so cdrom floppy rmdisk

# Actions
action cdrom action_filemgr.so
action floppy action_filemgr.so
action rmdisk action_filemgr.so

# Mount
mount * hsfs udfs ufs -o nosuid
```

3. If the user issues the `eject` command, `vold` sees the media event and executes the action associated with that event. In this case, it runs `/usr/sbin/rmmount`. `rmmount` unmounts mounted file systems and executes actions associated with the media type called out in the `/etc/rmmount.conf` file. If a file system is “busy” (that is, it contains the current working directory of a live process), the `eject` action fails.

The system administrator can modify `vold.conf` to specify which program should be called if media events happen, such as eject or insert. If the `vold.conf` configuration file is modified, `vold` must be told to reread the `/etc/vold.conf` file. Signal `vold` to re-read the configuration file by sending a `-HUP` signal to the process as follows:

```
pkill -HUP vold
```

Several other commands help you administer Volume Manager on your system. They are described in Table 1.23.

TABLE 1.23 Volume Manager Commands

Command	Description
`rmmount`	Removable media mounter. Used by `vold` to automatically mount a `/cdrom`, `/floppy`, Jaz, or Zip drive if one of these media types is installed.
`volcancel`	Cancels a user's request to access a particular CD-ROM or floppy file system. This command, issued by the system administrator, is useful if the removable medium containing the file system is not currently in the drive.
`volcheck`	Checks the drive for installed media. By default, it checks the drive pointed to by `/dev/diskette`.
`volmissing`	Specified in `vold.conf`, and notifies the user if an attempt is made to access a removable media type that is no longer in the drive.
`vold`	The Volume Manager daemon, controlled by `/etc/vold.conf`.
`volrmmount`	Simulates an insertion so that `rmmount` will mount the media, or simulates an ejection so that `rmmount` will unmount the media.

To some, volume management might seem like more trouble than it's worth. To disable volume management, remove (or rename) the file `/etc/rc3.d/S81volmgt`. Then issue the command `/etc/init.d/volmgt stop`. If you want to have volume management on the CD but not the floppy disk, comment out the entries in the "Devices to Use" and "Actions" sections of the `vold.conf` file with a #, as follows:

```
# Devices to use
use cdrom drive /dev/rdsk/c*s2 dev_cdrom.so cdrom%d
#use floppy drive /dev/rdiskette[0-9] dev_floppy.so floppy%d
use rmdisk drive /dev/rdsk/c*s2 dev_rmdisk.so rmdisk%d

# Actions
#eject dev/diskette[0-9]/* user=root /usr/sbin/rmmount
eject dev/dsk/* user=root /usr/sbin/rmmount
#insert dev/diskette[0-9]/* user=root /usr/sbin/rmmount
insert dev/dsk/* user=root /usr/sbin/rmmount
notify rdsk/* group=tty user=root /usr/lib/vold/volmissing -p
remount dev/diskette[0-9]/* user=root /usr/sbin/rmmount
remount dev/dsk/* user=root /usr/sbin/rmmount
```

With the changes made to `/etc/vold.conf`, when the `vold` daemon starts up, it manages only the CD-ROM and not the floppy disk.

Using Volume Management

`vold` is picky. Knowing this is the key to keeping `vold` from crashing or not working for some reason. With other computers, such as Windows PCs, you can eject CD-ROMs with no problems. With Solaris, `vold` isn't that robust, so the system administrator needs to follow a few ground rules when using volume management:

- Always use `vold` commands for everything to do with CD-ROMs and floppy disks. Use the commands listed in Table 1.23 to accomplish your task.
- Never press the button to eject a CD when a CD is already in the machine. This could cause `vold` to stop working. Use the `eject cdrom` command instead.
- If you can't stop or start `vold` using the `/etc/init.d/volmgt` script, you need to restart the system to get `vold` working properly.

I have found that the most reliable way to use floppy disks is via the Removable Media Manager GUI in the Common Desktop Environment (CDE) or Java Desktop Environment (JDE). Problems seem to be minimized when using floppy disks if I go through the media manager GUI versus the command line. Step by Step 1.12 describes how to access the Removable Media Manager GUI.

STEP BY STEP

1.12 Accessing the Removable Media Manager GUI

1. Open the File Manager GUI from the CDE front panel located at the bottom of the screen, as shown in Figure 1.11.

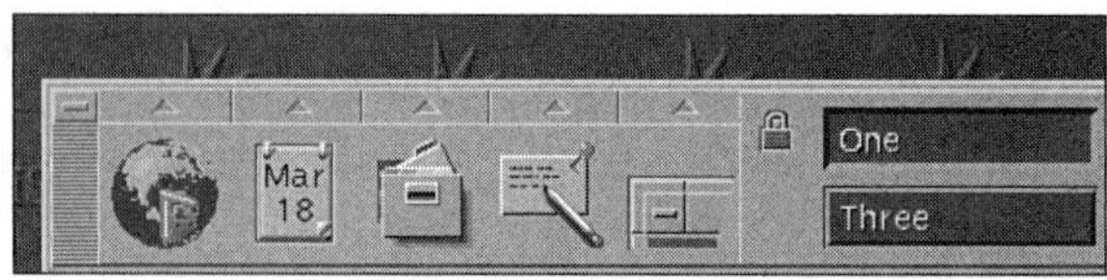

FIGURE 1.11 Front panel.

   The File Manager appears.

2. Click the File menu located in the menu bar, as shown in Figure 1.12.

   A pull-down menu will appear.

3. Select Removable Media Manager from the pull-down menu. The Removable Media Manager appears, as shown in Figure 1.13.

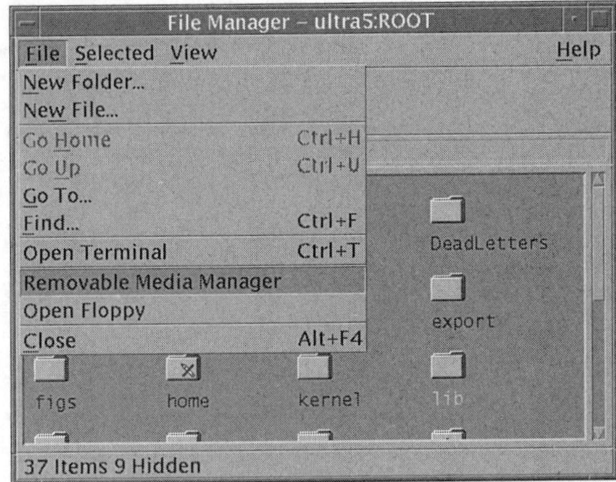

FIGURE 1.12 File Manager.

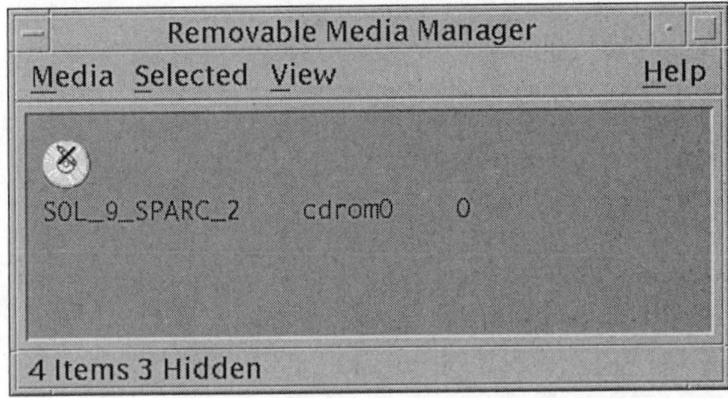

FIGURE 1.13 Removable Media Manager.

Troubleshooting Volume Manager

You might have problems with mounting a floppy or a CD-ROM. First, check to see if Volume Manager knows about the device. The best way to do this is to look in `/vol/dev/rdiskette0` and see if something is there. If not, the `volcheck` command has not been run or a hardware problem exists. If references to `/vol` lock up the system, it means that the daemon has died, and you need to restart the `vold` daemon as described earlier.

If `vold` is working properly, insert a formatted floppy disk and type `volcheck` followed by an `ls -l` as follows:

```
volcheck
ls -l /vol/dev/rdiskette0
```

The system responds with this:

```
total 0
crw-rw-rw-   1 nobody   nobody    91,  7 Oct 13 14:56 unlabeled
```

NOTE

Unlabeled Volumes The volume is unlabeled; therefore, the file in `/vol/dev/rdiskette0` is called unlabeled.

Check to make sure that a link exists in `/floppy` to the character device in `/vol/dev/rdiskette0`. Type the following:

```
ls -l /floppy
```

The system responds with this:

```
total 18
lrwxrwxrwx   1 root     nobody        11 Oct 13 14:56 floppy0 ->\
 ./noname
```

NOTE

Diskettes that are not named (that is, they have no "label") are assigned the default name of noname.

If a name is in `/vol/dev/rdiskette0`, as previously described, and nothing is mounted in `/floppy/<name_of_media>`, it's likely that data on the medium is an unrecognized file system. For example, perhaps it's a tar archive, a cpio backup, or a Macintosh file system. Don't use Volume Manager to get to these file types. Instead, access them through the block or character devices found in `/vol/dev/rdiskette0` or `/vol/dev/diskette0`, with user tools to interpret the data on them, such as `tar`, `dd`, or `cpio`.

If you're still having problems with Volume Manager, one way to gather debugging information is to run the `rmmount` command with the debug (`-D`) flag. To do this, edit `/etc/vold.conf` and change the lines that have `/usr/sbin/rmmount` to include the `-D` flag. For example:

```
insert /vol*/dev/diskette[0-9]/* user=root /usr/sbin/rmmount -D
```

This causes various debugging messages to appear on the console.

To see debugging messages from the Volume Manager daemon, run the daemon, `/usr/sbin/vold`, with the `-v -L10` flags. It logs data to `/var/adm/vold.log`. This file might contain information that could be useful in troubleshooting.

You might also want to mount a CD-ROM on a different mount point using volume management. By default, `vold` mounts the CD-ROM on the mount point `/cdrom/cdrom0`, but you can mount the CD-ROM on a different mount point by following the instructions in Step by Step 1.13.

STEP BY STEP

1.13 Mounting a CD-ROM on a Different Mount Point

1. If Volume Manager is running, bring up the File Manager and eject the CD-ROM by issuing the following command:

   ```
   eject cdrom
   ```

2. Stop the volume-management daemon by typing the following:

   ```
   /etc/init.d/volmgt stop
   ```

3. Create the directory called `/test`:

   ```
   mkdir /test
   ```

4. Insert the CD-ROM into the CD drive and issue this command:

   ```
   /usr/sbin/vold -d /test &
   ```

Now, instead of using the `/vol` directory, `vold` will use `/test` as the starting directory.

Displaying a File System's Disk Space Usage

Several options are available in Solaris for displaying disk usage. This chapter describes four commands:

- `df`—Displays information about currently mounted file systems and mount point, disk space allocation, usage, and availability.
- **SMC Usage Tool**—A GUI tool to display information about currently mounted file systems and mount point, disk space allocation, usage, and availability.
- `du`—Displays the disk usage of each file in each subdirectory. This command is described in the "Displaying Directory Size Information" section of this chapter.
- `quot`—Displays disk space used by each user. This command is described in the "Controlling User Disk Space Usage" section later in this chapter.

Use the `df` command and its options to see the capacity of each file system mounted on a system, the amount of space available, and the percentage of space already in use.

NOTE

Full File Systems File systems at or above 90% of capacity should be cleared of unnecessary files. You can do this by moving them to a disk, or you can remove them after obtaining the user's permission.

The following is an example of how to use the `df` command to display disk space information. The command syntax is as follows:

```
df -F fstype -g -k -t <directory>
```

Table 1.24 explains the `df` command and its options.

TABLE 1.24 The `df` Command

Command	Description
`df`	With no options, lists all mounted file systems and their device names. It also lists the total number of 512-byte blocks used and the number of files.
`<directory>`	Is the directory whose file system you want to check. The device name, blocks used, and number of files are displayed.
`-F` *`<fstype>`*	Displays the unmounted file systems, their device names, the number of 512-byte blocks used, and the number of files on file systems of type `fstype`.
`-h`	Scales disk space values to a more “human” readable format.
`-k`	Lists file systems, kilobytes used, free kilobytes, percent capacity used, and mount points.
`-t`	Displays total blocks as well as blocks used for all mounted file systems.

The following example illustrates how to display disk space information with the `df` command. Type the following:

```
df -k
```

The system responds with this:

```
File system             kbytes    used   avail capacity  Mounted on
/dev/dsk/c0t0d0s0       384847  233835  112528    68%    /
/devices                     0       0       0     0%    /devices
ctfs                         0       0       0     0%    /system/contract
proc                         0       0       0     0%    /proc
mnttab                       0       0       0     0%    /etc/mnttab
swap                    535968    1008  534960     1%    /etc/svc/volatile
objfs                        0       0       0     0%    /system/object
/dev/dsk/c0t0d0s6      5117182 2916567 2149444    58%    /usr
fd                           0       0       0     0%    /dev/fd
/dev/dsk/c0t0d0s1       577286   56583  462975    11%    /var
swap                    534960       0  534960     0%    /tmp
swap                    535000      40  534960     1%    /var/run
/dev/dsk/c0t0d0s4       480815  105097  327637    25%    /data
/dev/dsk/c0t0d0s5      1091142    1806 1034779     1%    /opt
/dev/dsk/c0t0d0s7       480815    2073  430661     1%    /export/home
```

In this example, we used the `-h` option to output the information in a more readable format so that you can see the difference:

```
df -h
```

The system responds with this:

```
File system              size   used  avail capacity  Mounted on
/dev/dsk/c0t0d0s0        376M   228M   110M    68%    /
/devices                   0K     0K     0K     0%    /devices
ctfs                       0K     0K     0K     0%    /system/contract
proc                       0K     0K     0K     0%    /proc
mnttab                     0K     0K     0K     0%    /etc/mnttab
swap                     523M  1008K   522M     1%    /etc/svc/volatile
objfs                      0K     0K     0K     0%    /system/object
/dev/dsk/c0t0d0s6        4.9G   2.8G   2.0G    58%    /usr
fd                         0K     0K     0K     0%    /dev/fd
/dev/dsk/c0t0d0s1        564M    55M   452M    11%    /var
swap                     522M     0K   522M     0%    /tmp
swap                     522M    40K   522M     1%    /var/run
/dev/dsk/c0t0d0s4        470M   103M   320M    25%    /data
/dev/dsk/c0t0d0s5        1.0G   1.8M  1011M     1%    /opt
/dev/dsk/c0t0d0s7        470M   2.0M   421M     1%    /export/home
```

Notice that the `-h` option scales the values to a more readable format.

In both examples, you'll see disk usage information displayed for each currently mounted file system.

You can also use the Solaris Management Console (SMC) Usage tool, which provides a graphical display of the available disk space for all mounted file systems. To use the Usage tool, follow the procedure outlined in Step by Step 1.14.

STEP BY STEP

1.14 Using the SMC Usage Tool

1. Launch the SMC by typing

   ```
   smc&
   ```

2. In the left navigation window, select the This Computer icon from the left navigation pane, then select the Storage icon, and then click on the Mounts and Shares icon as shown in Figure 1.14.

   A window will open, prompting you to enter the root password. The Mounts and Shares tools will be displayed as shown in Figure 1.15.

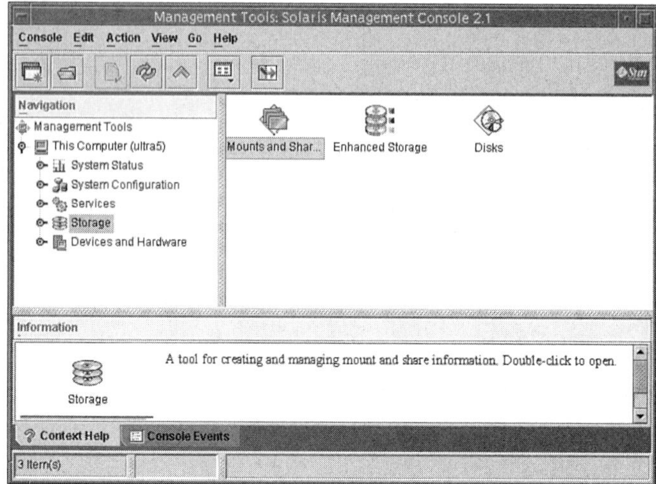

FIGURE 1.14 Selecting the Storage icon.

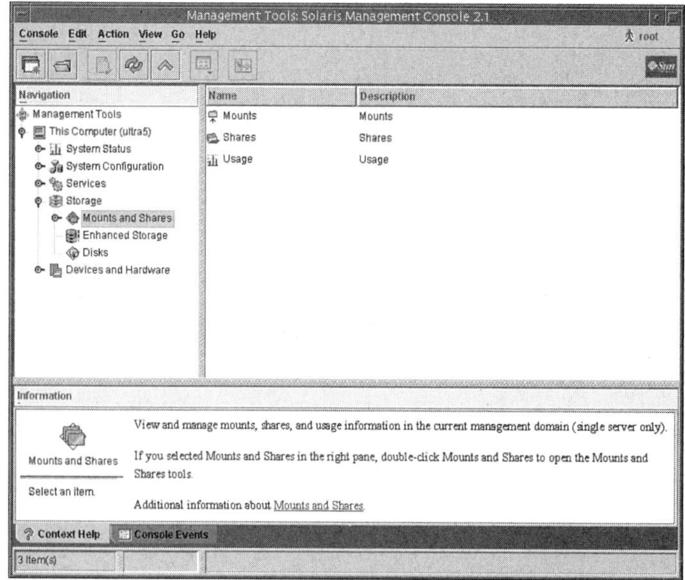

FIGURE 1.15 Mounts and Shares tools.

3. Select the Usage icon and the window shown in Figure 1.16 will be displayed.

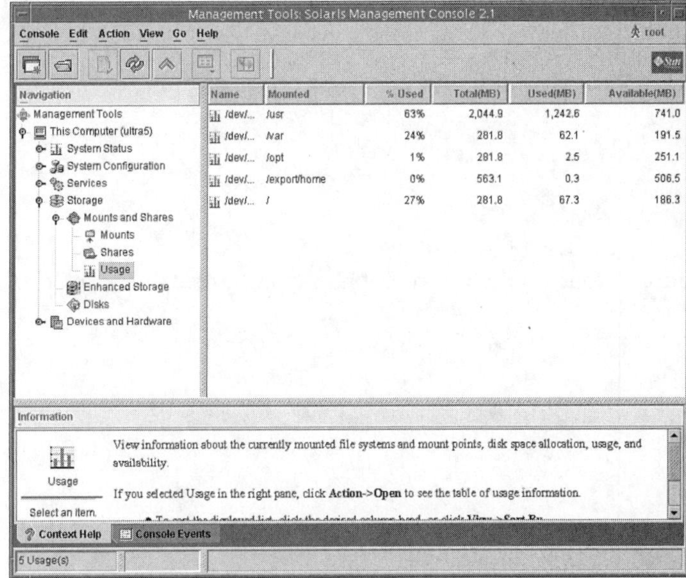

FIGURE 1.16 SMC Usage tool.

Displaying Directory Size Information

By using the `df` command, you display file system disk usage. You can use the `du` command to display the disk usage of a directory and all its subdirectories in 512-byte blocks. When used with the `-h` option, values are scaled to a more readable format.

The `du` command shows you the disk usage of each file in each subdirectory of a file system. To get a listing of the size of each subdirectory in a file system, type `cd` to the pathname associated with that file system and run the following pipeline:

```
du -s *| sort -r -n
```

This pipeline, which uses the reverse and numeric options of the `sort` command, pinpoints large directories. Use `ls -l` to examine the size (in bytes) and modification times of files within each directory. Old files or text files greater than 100KB often warrant storage offline.

The following example illustrates how to display the amount of disk space being consumed by the `/var/adm` directory using the `du` command. The largest files are displayed first, and the `-k` option displays the file size in 1024 bytes. Type the following:

```
du -k /var/adm|sort -r -n
```

The system responds with this:

```
2230     /var/adm
1785     /var/adm/sa
4        /var/adm/acct
```

```
1       /var/adm/streams
1       /var/adm/sm.bin
1       /var/adm/passwd
1       /var/adm/log
1       /var/adm/exacct
1       /var/adm/acct/sum
1       /var/adm/acct/nite
1       /var/adm/acct/fiscal
```

In this example we use the `-h` option to output the information in a more readable format so that you can see the difference:

```
du -h /var/adm¦sort -r -n
```

The system responds with this:

```
   4K   /var/adm/acct
 2.3M   /var/adm
 1.8M   /var/adm/sa
   1K   /var/adm/streams
   1K   /var/adm/sm.bin
   1K   /var/adm/passwd
   1K   /var/adm/log
   1K   /var/adm/exacct
   1K   /var/adm/acct/sum
   1K   /var/adm/acct/nite
   1K   /var/adm/acct/fiscal
```

NOTE

The sort Command Notice that the files are not listed by file size. This is because the `-n` option to the `sort` command sorts data numerically, not by file size. The number 4 is a larger number, numerically, than the number 2. The `-n` option does not take into account that 4KB is smaller in size than 2.3MB.

Information on File Systems

The `df` command gives you capacity information on each mounted file system. The output of `df` and `fsck` is often misunderstood. This section goes into more detail about these two commands and describes their output so that you can better understand the information displayed. I begin with the `fsck` command. Remember, run `fsck` only on unmounted file systems, as shown in the following example. Type the following:

```
umount /mnt
fsck /dev/rdsk/c2t1d0s1
```

The system responds with this:

```
** /dev/rdsk/c2t1d0s1
** Last Mounted on /mnt
** Phase 1 - Check Blocks and Sizes
** Phase 2 - Check Pathnames
** Phase 3 - Check Connectivity
** Phase 4 - Check Reference Counts
** Phase 5 - Check Cyl groups
2 files, 9 used, 4099509 free (13 frags, 512437 blocks, 0.0% fragmentation)
```

`fsck` first reports some things related to usage, as shown in Table 1.25.

TABLE 1.25 `fsck` Output

Field	Description
`files`	Number of files in the file system
`used`	Number of data blocks used
`free`	Number of data blocks free (fragments and whole blocks)

NOTE

Fragment Size A fragment is one data block in size, and a block consists of a number of data blocks, typically eight.

Then `fsck` reports more details of the free space, as shown in Table 1.26.

TABLE 1.26 `fsck` Output

Field	Description
`frags`	The number of free fragments (from fragmented blocks)
`blocks`	The number of free blocks (whole unfragmented blocks)
`% fragmentation`	Free fragments as a percentage of the whole disk size

Fragmentation does not refer to fragmentation in the sense of a file's disk blocks being inefficiently scattered across the whole file system, as you see in a Microsoft Windows file system.

In Solaris, a high percentage of fragmentation implies that much of the free space is tied up in fragments. In the previous example, fragmentation was 0%. High fragmentation affects creation of new files—especially those larger than a few data blocks. Typically, high fragmentation is caused by creating large numbers of small files.

Now let's review the output from the `df` command:

```
mount /dev/dsk/c2t1d0s1 /mnt
df -k /mnt
```

The system responds with this:

```
File system            kbytes    used   avail capacity  Mounted on
/dev/dsk/c2t1d0s1     4103598    4089 3894330     1%    /mnt
```

The `4103598` value in the output represents the total file system size in kilobytes. It includes the 5% `minfree` that you specified earlier with the `tunefs` command. The output is summarized in Table 1.27.

TABLE 1.27 Output from `df`

Field	Description
`4089KB used`	The amount of space used in the file system.
`3894330KB available`	Space available in the file system. This value is equal to the file system size minus the `minfree%` minus the space used (`4103598` – `5%` – `4089`). Because logging is enabled on this file system, a small amount of space is used for logging. The log size is 1MB per 1GB of space up to a max of 64MB.
`1% capacity`	Space used as a percentage, calculated as follows: kilobytes used/(kilobytes available – `minfree%`).

Controlling User Disk Space Usage

Quotas let system administrators control the size of UFS file systems by limiting the amount of disk space that individual users can acquire. Quotas are especially useful on file systems where user home directories reside. After the quotas are in place, they can be changed to adjust the amount of disk space or number of inodes that users can consume. Additionally, quotas can be added or removed as system needs change. Also, quota status can be monitored. Quota commands enable administrators to display information about quotas on a file system or search for users who have exceeded their quotas.

After you have set up and turned on disk and inode quotas, you can check for users who exceed their quotas. You can also check quota information for entire file systems by using the commands listed in Table 1.28.

TABLE 1.28 Commands to Check Quotas

Command	Description
`quota`	Displays the quotas and disk usage within a file system for individual users on which quotas have been activated
`repquota`	Displays the quotas and disk usage for all users on one or more file systems

You won't see quotas in use much today because the cost of disk space continues to fall. In most cases, the system administrator simply watches disk space to identify users who might be using more than their fair share. As you saw in this section, you can easily do this by using the `du` command. On a large system with many users, however, disk quotas can be an effective way to control disk space usage.

Another option for managing user space is the use of soft partitions described in Chapter 10. With soft partitions, each user's home directory can be created within its own disk partition and would be limited to the space allocated to that partition.

The `quot` Command

Use the `quot` command to display how much disk space, in kilobytes, is being used by users. You do not need to implement disk quotas to use this command. The `quot` command can only be run by root. The syntax for the `quot` command is

```
quot -options <file system>
```

The `quot` command has two options:

`-a`	Reports on all mounted file systems
`-f`	Includes the number of files

To display disk space being used by all users on all mounted file systems, type the following:

```
quot -af
```

The system responds with the following output:

```
/dev/rdsk/c0t0d0s0 (/):
68743     4370   root
  162       18   lp
   31       14   uucp
    1        1   adm
/dev/rdsk/c0t0d0s6 (/usr):
1270388 50748    root
 1254       19   lp
  766       15   uucp
   10        3   bin
    1        1   adm
/dev/rdsk/c0t0d0s1 (/var):
63327     5232   root
  208        9   adm
   22       27   lp
   16       17   uucp
    4        4   daemon
    4        8   nobody
```

```
    2        2    smmsp
    1        3    bill
    1        1    bin
/dev/rdsk/c0t0d0s5 (/opt):
 2608      253    root
    2        2    lp
/dev/rdsk/c0t0d0s7 (/export/home):
  212      131    root
   68       56    wcalkins
   58       39    bill
    5        5    sradmin
    4        4    jer
    4        4    jradmin
    2        2    tom
```

The columns of information displayed represent kilobytes used, number of files, and owner, respectively.

To display a count of the number of files and space owned by each user for a specific file system, enter

```
quot -f /dev/dsk/c0t0d0s7
```

The system responds with the following:

```
/dev/rdsk/c0t0d0s7:
  212      131    root
   68       56    wcalkins
   58       39    bill
    5        5    sradmin
    4        4    jer
    4        4    jradmin
    2        2    tom
```

Summary

This concludes the discussion of file systems. This chapter discussed the various device drivers and device names used in Solaris 10. I described the Solaris commands and utilities used to obtain information about these devices and drivers. In addition to the devices that come standard with Solaris, this chapter also described Solaris Volume Manager and the added functionality it provides.

Device drivers are discussed in several chapters of this book because they are used in many aspects of the system administrator's job. Devices are referenced when we install and boot the operating system (see Chapter 2, "Installing the Solaris 10 Operating Environment," and Chapter 3, "System Startup and Shutdown"), when creating and mounting file systems, when setting up printers (see Chapter 6, "Managing the LP Print Service"), and in general troubleshooting of system problems. It is very important that you have a good understanding of how device drivers are configured and named in the Solaris operating system.

This chapter also introduced you to the many options available for constructing file systems using the `mkfs` and `newfs` commands. Other Solaris utilities for managing, labeling, copying, and tuning file systems were also presented.

The process of creating a file system on a disk partition was described. Many file system creation parameters that affect performance were presented. This chapter also detailed all the parts of a file system so that, as you create file systems, you are familiar with terminology you'll encounter.

The `mount` and `umount` commands were described. In this chapter, I explained how to display mount options currently in use on a particular file system. In addition, the chapter showed you how to determine what process or user is using a file system before you unmount it.

In addition to showing how to manually mount file systems, this chapter described the Volume Manager for automatically mounting file systems on CD-ROM and disk. All the Volume Manager commands and associated configuration files were presented and explained.

Finally, the system administrator must monitor all file systems regularly. Commands and utilities used to monitor and manage file systems were described in detail.

Now that we've discussed devices, device and driver names, disk slices, and file systems, the next chapter will introduce the Solaris installation process.

Key Terms

- Block device
- Block size
- Character device
- Cylinder
- Device autoconfiguration
- Device driver

- Device hierarchy
- Device tree
- Disk label
- Disk partition
- Disk quota
- Disk slice
- Disk-based file system
- FDISK
- File system
- File system `minfree` space
- File system type
- Fragment
- Free block
- Free hog slice
- Hard link
- Hot-pluggable
- inode
- Instance name
- Large files
- Large file–aware
- Large file–safe
- Logical device name
- Logical volume
- Major device number
- Minor device number
- Mounted file system table (`mnttab`)
- Network-based file system
- Partition table
- Physical device name
- Reconfiguration startup
- Sector
- Storage block
- Superblock
- Swap
- Symbolic link
- UFS logging
- Virtual file system
- Volume manager
- Volume name

Exercises

1.1 Device Autoconfiguration

This exercise demonstrates three different methods that can be used to perform a reconfiguration boot so that the kernel recognizes new devices attached to the system.

Estimated time: 15 minutes

1. From the OpenBoot prompt, type the following:

   ```
   boot -r
   ```

   The system performs a reconfiguration boot and a login prompt appears.

2. Log in as root and create an empty file named `/reconfigure` as follows:

```
touch /reconfigure
```

Now reboot the system as follows:

```
/usr/sbin/shutdown -y -g0 -i6
```

The system performs a reconfiguration boot, and a login prompt appears.

3. Log in as root and issue the following command:

```
reboot -- -r
```

The system performs a reconfiguration boot, and a login prompt appears.

1.2 Displaying Information About Devices

In this exercise, you'll use a few of the Solaris commands to display information about devices connected to your system.

Estimated time: 5 minutes

1. Use the `dmesg` command to determine the mapping of an instance name to a physical device name. Type the following:

```
dmesg
```

In the output, identify the instance name assigned to each disk drive and peripheral attached to your system. On a system with IDE disks, you'll see entries similar to the following:

```
sd0 is /pci@1f,0/pci@1,1/ide@3/sd@2,0
```

On a system with SCSI disks, you'll see something like this:

```
sd17 is /pci@1f,0/pci@1/scsi@1,1/sd@1,0
```

2. Use the `prtconf` command to see which drivers are attached to the instance names identified in the previous step.

For example, you should see an entry something like this:

```
sd, instance #0
```

1.3 Adding a New Device

In this exercise, you'll use the `devfsadm` command to add in a new device without rebooting the system.

Estimated time: 15 minutes

1. Connect a tape drive, disk drive, or CD-ROM to the system and perform a reconfiguration reboot.

2. Log in and issue the dmesg command to verify that the device has been installed. You should see an entry something like this if you're adding an SCSI disk drive:

```
sd17 is /pci@1f,0/pci@1/scsi@1,1/sd@1,0
```

   Check to see that a driver is attached by issuing the prtconf command.

3. Halt the system, turn off the new device, and boot the system back up using the boot command. Do not do a reconfiguration reboot.

4. Issue the prtconf command. It should display (driver not attached) next to the instance device name for that device.

5. Issue the devfsadm command.

6. Issue the prtconf command again. The message (driver not attached) next to the instance device name should be gone and the device is now available for use.

1.4 Displaying Disk Configuration Information

In this exercise, you determine the disk geometry and slice information of your disk drive.

Estimated time: 20 minutes

1. Log in as root.

2. Display and record your current disk configuration information using the prtvtoc command, as shown here:

```
prtvtoc <raw disk device name>
```

   How are the disk slices arranged? What disk geometry does it display?

3. Now, follow these steps to look at your disk information using the format utility:

   ❍ **A.** Type format. The Main menu appears, displaying your disk drives. You're going to select the disk numbered 0, so note all of the information on that line.

   ❍ **B.** Type 0. This will select the first disk listed. The Format menu will appear.

   ❍ **C.** Type partition. The Partition menu will appear.

   ❍ **D.** Type print. All of your disk partition information will be displayed.

   ❍ **E.** Press Ctrl+D. You'll exit the format utility.

1.5 Creating a File System

The following exercise requires that you have a spare disk drive connected to your system or a spare, unused slice on a disk. You will practice creating a disk slice and creating a file system.

Estimated time: 30 minutes

1. Practice creating a slice on your spare disk drive using the steps outlined in the earlier section titled "Using the `format` Utility to Create Slices."
2. Create a file system on the new or unused slice using the `newfs` command as follows:

   ```
   newfs <raw device name>
   ```

3. Create a directory in the root partition named `/test`, as shown here:

   ```
   mkdir /test
   ```

4. Mount the new file system to support large files using the following command:

   ```
   mount -o largefiles <block device name> /test
   ```

5. Unmount the file system, as shown here:

   ```
   umount /test
   ```

6. View the contents of the `/etc/vfstab` file on your system by typing `cat /etc/vfstab`.
7. Add the following line to the `/etc/vfstab` file for the file system you've just created so that it gets mounted automatically at boot time:

   ```
   <raw device> <block device name> /test  ufs  2   yes  -
   ```

8. Reboot the system:

   ```
   /usr/sbin/shutdown -y -g0 -i6
   ```

9. Verify that the file system was mounted automatically:

   ```
   mount4p1
   ```

1.6 Tuning a File System

In this exercise, you'll modify some of the file system parameters that were specified when the file system was originally created with the **newfs** command.

Estimated time: 15 minutes

1. Log in as root.
2. List all of the parameters currently in use on the file system by typing the following:

   ```
   newfs -v <raw device name>
   ```

3. Open another window. Leave the information displayed in step 2 in the window for referencing later. In the new window, type the `tunefs` command to change the `minfree` value to 5% on the file system as follows:

   ```
   tunefs -m5 <raw device name>
   ```

4. View the new file system parameters, but this time you'll use the `mkfs` command as follows:

```
mkfs -m <raw device name>
```

   Compare the parameters displayed with the parameters that were displayed earlier in the other window.

5. Try the `fstyp` command for viewing the file system parameters as follows:

```
fstyp -v <raw device name>
```

1.7 Using Volume Manager

In this exercise, you'll utilize Volume Manager to automatically mount a CD-ROM.

Estimated time: 10 minutes

1. Insert a CD-ROM into the CD-ROM player.
2. Type the `mount` command with no options to verify that the device was mounted. What is the mount point that was used?
3. Eject the CD-ROM as follows:

```
eject cdrom
```

4. Type the following command to look for the Volume Manager process named `vold`:

```
pgrep -l vold
```

5. Turn off the Volume Manager by typing the following:

```
/etc/init.d/volmgt stop
```

6. Type the following command to look for the Volume Manager process named `vold`:

```
pgrep -l vold
```

7. Insert the CD into the CD-ROM player. Did it mount the CD?
8. Restart the Volume Manager daemon by typing the following:

```
/etc/init.d/volmgt start
```

9. Type the `mount` command with no options to list all mounted file systems. Is the CD mounted now?

Exam Questions

1. Which of the following represents the kernel's abbreviated name for every possible device on the system?

   ❍ **A.** Instance name

   ❍ **B.** Logical device

   ❍ **C.** Physical device name

   ❍ **D.** Pseudo device name

2. Physical device files are found in which of the following?

   ❍ **A.** `/kernel/drv`

   ❍ **B.** `/dev`

   ❍ **C.** `/platform`

   ❍ **D.** `/devices`

3. Which of the following displays device configuration information, including system hardware, pseudo devices, loadable modules, and selected kernel parameters?

   ❍ **A.** `messages`

   ❍ **B.** `prtconf`

   ❍ **C.** `dmesg`

   ❍ **D.** `sysdef`

4. When you see the **driver not attached** message, it means which of the following?

   ❍ **A.** The device for this driver is not attached.

   ❍ **B.** A driver is unavailable for this device.

   ❍ **C.** No driver is currently attached to the device instance because there is no device at this node or the device is not in use.

   ❍ **D.** The kernel needs to be reconfigured to attach the device.

5. The conf files reside in what file system?

   ❍ **A.** `/kernel/drv`

   ❍ **B.** `/dev`

   ❍ **C.** `/devices`

   ❍ **D.** `/platform`

6. Which of the following are mapped to a physical device name in the /etc/path_to_inst file?

❍ **A.** Logical devices

❍ **B.** Instance names

❍ **C.** Physical devices

❍ **D.** Pseudo devices

7. You can determine the mapping of an instance name to a physical device name by doing what? Choose all that apply.

❍ **A.** Looking at output from the `dmesg` command

❍ **B.** Viewing the `/var/adm/messages` file

❍ **C.** Looking at output from the `sysdef` command

❍ **D.** Looking at output from the `prtconf` command

8. The system relies on information found in which of the following files to find the root, usr, or swap device?

❍ **A.** `/etc/vfstab`

❍ **B.** `/etc/path_to_inst`

❍ **C.** `kernel`

❍ **D.** `/kernel/drv/`

❍ **E.** `/etc/driver`

9. Which of the following commands creates logical links to device nodes in the **/dev** and **/devices** directories?

❍ **A.** `boot -r`

❍ **B.** `drvconfig`

❍ **C.** `devfsadm`

❍ **D.** `devlinks`

10. Which of the following commands is used to inform the system about newly installed device drivers?

❍ **A.** `devlinks`

❍ **B.** `drvconfig`

❍ **C.** `add_drv`

❍ **D.** `devfsadm`

11. Which of the following is the daemon responsible for handling both reconfiguration boot processing and updating `/dev` and `/devices` in response to dynamic reconfiguration event notifications from the kernel?

❍ **A.** `devfsadmd`

❍ **B.** `inetd`

❍ **C.** `devfsdadm`

❍ **D.** `svc.startd`

12. Your external CD-ROM was not turned on when the system was last booted with a reconfiguration reboot. To gain access to the CD-ROM, you could halt the system, turn on power to the CD-ROM, and start the system back up, or you could issue which of the following commands at the command prompt?

❍ **A.** `drvconfig cdrom`

❍ **B.** `add_drv cdrom`

❍ **C.** `devfsadm`

❍ **D.** `drvconfig -d`

13. Which of the following indicates the general device driver for devices such as disk, tape, or serial line?

❍ **A.** Minor device number

❍ **B.** Major device number

❍ **C.** Device tree

❍ **D.** Pseudo device

14. The minor device number:

❍ **A.** Indicates the general device driver for devices such as disk, tape, or serial line.

❍ **B.** Indicates the specific member within a driver.

❍ **C.** Uniquely defines a device and its device driver.

❍ **D.** Identifies the proper device location and device driver to the kernel.

15. Logical device files in the `/dev` directory are symbolically linked to which of the following in the `/devices` directory?

   ❍ **A.** Instance names

   ❍ **B.** Pseudo device files

   ❍ **C.** Full device path names

   ❍ **D.** Physical device files

16. Which of the following is a link from the `/dev` directory to the physical device name located in the `/devices` directory?

   ❍ **A.** Full device path name

   ❍ **B.** Pseudo device name

   ❍ **C.** Logical device name

   ❍ **D.** Instance name

17. `/dev/dsk/c0t0d0s7` is what type of device?

   ❍ **A.** Logical device name

   ❍ **B.** Pseudo device name

   ❍ **C.** Full device path name

   ❍ **D.** Instance name

18. Which of the following commands creates entries in the `/dev` directory for disk drives attached to the system?

   ❍ **A.** `devfsadm`

   ❍ **B.** `add_drv`

   ❍ **C.** `drvconfig`

   ❍ **D.** `boot -r`

19. Which directory contains the disk entries symbolically linked to the block device nodes in `/devices`?

   ❍ **A.** `/kernel/drv`

   ❍ **B.** `/dev/rdsk`

   ❍ **C.** `/vol/dev/aliases`

   ❍ **D.** `/dev/dsk`

20. Which of the following best describes a physical device name?

❍ **A.** It represents the full device pathname of a device.

❍ **B.** It is equivalent to the SCSI target ID of a device.

❍ **C.** It represents the actual name of a device, such as a disk, tape, and so on.

❍ **D.** It represents the kernel's abbreviated name for a device on the system.

21. In the standard device file naming convention "cXtYdZ," what does the "tY" portion of the filename identify?

❍ **A.** The controller card to which this device is attached

❍ **B.** The SCSI target address of the device

❍ **C.** The LUN of the device

❍ **D.** The function number as contained on the "Core I/O" board

22. Which of the following is a character device name?

❍ **A.** `/dev/dsk/c0t3d0s0`

❍ **B.** `/dev/rdsk/c0t3d0s0`

❍ **C.** `/dev/cua`

❍ **D.** `/devices/sbus@1,f8000000/esp@0,40000/sd@3,0:a`

23. What best describes an instance name?

❍ **A.** The kernel's abbreviated name for every possible device on the system

❍ **B.** A symbolic link to a physical device file

❍ **C.** The full device pathname of a device

❍ **D.** The SCSI address of a disk drive

24. Logical devices are organized in subdirectories under which directory?

❍ **A.** `/dev`

❍ **B.** `/devices`

❍ **C.** `/kernel`

❍ **D.** `/`

25. What best describes a logical device name?

❍ **A.** It is a symbolic link to a physical device file.

❍ **B.** It represents the kernel's abbreviated name for every possible device on the system.

❍ **C.** It represents the full device pathname of a device.

❍ **D.** It defines the SCSI address of a disk device.

26. What statement is *not* true about disk slices on standard Solaris?

❍ **A.** Each slice can hold only one file system.

❍ **B.** A file system cannot span multiple disk slices.

❍ **C.** A file system cannot be increased or decreased.

❍ **D.** Slices can span multiple disks.

27. Where is disk configuration information stored?

❍ **A.** On the disk label

❍ **B.** In several locations on the disk

❍ **C.** In the superblock

❍ **D.** In the partition table

28. Which of the following stores the procedures used to boot the system?

❍ **A.** Boot block

❍ **B.** Superblock

❍ **C.** inode

❍ **D.** Disk label

29. Which of the following commands will display partition information about a disk?

❍ **A.** `prtvtoc`

❍ **B.** `sysdef`

❍ **C.** `df -k`

❍ **D.** `sysinfo`

30. Which of the following is *not* a virtual file system?

- ❍ **A.** `/export/home`
- ❍ **B.** `Tmpfs`
- ❍ **C.** `Cachefs`
- ❍ **D.** `Procfs`

31. Which of the following tasks cannot be performed with the `format` utility?

- ❍ **A.** Repairing defective sectors
- ❍ **B.** Partitioning
- ❍ **C.** Retrieving corrupted disk labels
- ❍ **D.** Displaying disk usage

32. Which of the following does the superblock *not* contain?

- ❍ **A.** Size and status of the file system
- ❍ **B.** Cylinder group size
- ❍ **C.** Pathname of the last mount point
- ❍ **D.** Boot information

33. What information does the inode contain? Choose all that apply.

- ❍ **A.** The type of the file
- ❍ **B.** File directory information
- ❍ **C.** The number of bytes in the file
- ❍ **D.** Logical volume information

34. What is *not* true about logical block sizes?

- ❍ **A.** The logical block size is the size of the blocks the Unix kernel uses to read or write files.
- ❍ **B.** By default, the logical block size is 8192 bytes.
- ❍ **C.** A larger logical block size increases efficiency for file systems in which most of the files are large.
- ❍ **D.** A small logical block size increases efficiency for file systems in which most of the files are large.

35. What determines the number of inodes to be created in a new file system?

❍ **A.** The number of inodes depends on the amount of disk space that is allocated for each inode and the total size of the file system.

❍ **B.** 2048 inodes are created per 1GB of file system space.

❍ **C.** The number is dynamic and the kernel assigns inodes as required by the number of files in a file system.

❍ **D.** By default, one inode is allocated for each 2KB of data space.

36. In Solaris, which of the following is referred to as the smallest allocable unit of disk space?

❍ **A.** Fragment

❍ **B.** Data block

❍ **C.** Logical block

❍ **D.** Byte

37. What is another name for swap space and the total physical memory combined?

❍ **A.** Virtual memory

❍ **B.** Random Access Memory

❍ **C.** Partition C or Slice 2

❍ **D.** Static memory

38. When should a file system be checked with `fsck`? Choose all that apply.

❍ **A.** If the file system was unmounted improperly

❍ **B.** After a power outage

❍ **C.** Whenever a file system cannot be mounted

❍ **D.** When data has been accidentally deleted

39. What does `fsck` do when it preens a file system?

❍ **A.** Forces checking of the file system

❍ **B.** Checks and fixes the file system noninteractively

❍ **C.** Checks writeable file systems only

❍ **D.** Only checks to determine if a file system needs checking

40. Which of the following files contains a list of file systems to be automatically mounted at bootup?

- ❍ **A.** `/etc/fstab`
- ❍ **B.** `/etc/dfs/dfstab`
- ❍ **C.** `/etc/vfstab`
- ❍ **D.** `/etc/rc2.d/S74autofs`

41. The `mountall` command

- ❍ **A.** Mounts the CD-ROM and floppy automatically
- ❍ **B.** Mounts all file systems specified in the file system table
- ❍ **C.** Shares all files systems so that they can be mounted
- ❍ **D.** Mounts the tape in the tape drive

42. What command(s) is/are used to display disk space information?

- ❍ **A.** `du`
- ❍ **B.** `df`
- ❍ **C.** `quota`
- ❍ **D.** `repquota`
- ❍ **E.** All of the above

43. Which of the following mount options is used to mount file systems that have files larger than 2GB?

- ❍ **A.** `largefiles`
- ❍ **B.** `nolargefiles`
- ❍ **C.** `lf`
- ❍ **D.** `nlf`

44. What should you do to disable UFS logging on a file system?

- ❍ **A.** Use the `-o` logging option with the `mount` command.
- ❍ **B.** Use the `-l` option with the `mount` command.
- ❍ **C.** You don't need to do anything; `nologging` is the default when mounting a file system.
- ❍ **D.** Use the logging feature in the `newfs` command when creating the file system.

45. Which of the following represents the correct format for an entry in the `/etc/vfstab` file?

❍ **A.** device to mount, device to fsck, mount point, FS type, fsck pass, mount at boot, mount options

❍ **B.** device to fsck, device to mount, mount point, FS type, fsck pass, mount at boot, mount point

❍ **C.** mount point, device to mount, device to fsck, mount point, FS type, fsck pass, mount at boot

❍ **D.** mount point, device to fsck, device to mount, mount point, FS type, fsck pass, mount at boot

46. Which of the following commands shows you the disk usage of each file in each subdirectory of a file system?

❍ **A.** `du`

❍ **B.** `df`

❍ **C.** `ls`

❍ **D.** `printenv`

47. Which of the following commands displays disk space occupied by mounted file systems?

❍ **A.** `df`

❍ **B.** `du`

❍ **C.** `ls`

❍ **D.** `printenv`

48. Which of the following causes high fragmentation?

❍ **A.** Creating large numbers of small files

❍ **B.** Creating large numbers of large files

❍ **C.** Not enough disk space

❍ **D.** A file's disk blocks being inefficiently scattered across the whole file system

49. Output from `df -k` does *not* contain which of the following fields?

❍ **A.** Total size in kilobytes

❍ **B.** Fragmentation

❍ **C.** Capacity

❍ **D.** Kilobytes available

50. Which of the following is the recommended way to create a file system?

- ❍ **A.** `mkfs`
- ❍ **B.** `format`
- ❍ **C.** `tunefs`
- ❍ **D.** `newfs`

51. Which of the following commands do you use to write or display labels on unmounted disk file systems?

- ❍ **A.** `format`
- ❍ **B.** `prtvtoc`
- ❍ **C.** `newfs`
- ❍ **D.** `labelit`

52. Which of the following commands do you issue to determine whether a file system is a UFS?

- ❍ **A.** `fstyp`
- ❍ **B.** `prtvtoc`
- ❍ **C.** `format`
- ❍ **D.** `newfs -v`

53. Which of the following commands is used to change the `minfree` value of a file system?

- ❍ **A.** `mkfs`
- ❍ **B.** `tunefs`
- ❍ **C.** `newfs`
- ❍ **D.** `format`

54. Which of the following commands do you use to view a full listing of file system parameters?

- ❍ **A.** `fstyp`
- ❍ **B.** `mkfs`
- ❍ **C.** `newfs`
- ❍ **D.** `prtvtoc`

55. A large file is a regular file whose size is greater than or equal to which of the following?

❍ **A.** 1TB

❍ **B.** 1GB

❍ **C.** 5GB

❍ **D.** 2GB

56. Which of the following commands is *not* large file–aware?

❍ **A.** `labelit`

❍ **B.** `vi`

❍ **C.** `mkfs`

❍ **D.** `mount`

57. Which of the following types of utility is able to handle large files as input and to generate large files as output?

❍ **A.** Large file–compatible

❍ **B.** Large file–safe

❍ **C.** Large file–aware

❍ **D.** Large file–capable

58. Which of the following options to the `mount` command provides total compatibility with previous file system behavior, enforcing the 2GB maximum file size limit?

❍ **A.** `-o compat`

❍ **B.** `largefiles`

❍ **C.** `-nolargefiles`

❍ **D.** `-o nolargefiles`

59. Which of the following options do you type the `mount` command with to display a list of mounted file systems in `/etc/vfstab` format?

❍ **A.** `-p`

❍ **B.** `-v`

❍ **C.** `-f`

❍ **D.** `-a`

60. Which of the following examples uses the `mount` command to map a directory to a file system as read/writeable, disallow `setuid` execution, and enable the creation of large files:

- ❍ **A.** `mount -o rw,nosuid,large /dev/dsk/c0t0d0s0 /home2`
- ❍ **B.** `mount -o rw,nosuid,largefiles /dev/dsk/c0t0d0s0 /home2`
- ❍ **C.** `mount -o rw,nosuid,largefiles /dev/rdsk/c0t0d0s0 /home2`
- ❍ **D.** `mount -o rw,suid,largefiles /dev/dsk/c0t0d0s0 /home2`

61. When a file system is mounted, where are entries maintained?

- ❍ **A.** `/etc/mnttab`
- ❍ **B.** `/etc/vfstab`
- ❍ **C.** `/etc/fstab`
- ❍ **D.** `/mnt`

62. Which of the following tasks can be performed on a mounted file system?

- ❍ **A.** `labelit`
- ❍ **B.** `fsck`
- ❍ **C.** `tunefs`
- ❍ **D.** `newfs`

63. If something is causing the file system to be busy, which of the following commands can you use to list all the processes accessing the file system?

- ❍ **A.** `fuser`
- ❍ **B.** `mount`
- ❍ **C.** `ps`
- ❍ **D.** `finger`

64. Which of the following commands stops all processes that are using the `/home2` file system?

- ❍ **A.** `fuser -c -k /home2`
- ❍ **B.** `fuser -k /home2`
- ❍ **C.** `kill -9 /home2`
- ❍ **D.** `umount /home2`

65. Which of the following is the mechanism that manages removable media, such as the CD-ROM and floppy disk drives?

- ❍ **A.** `autofs`
- ❍ **B.** NFS
- ❍ **C.** `vold`
- ❍ **D.** `init`

66. **`vold`** does all of the following except for what?

- ❍ **A.** Gives other systems on the network automatic access to any disks and CDs the users insert into your system
- ❍ **B.** Automatically mounts disks and CDs
- ❍ **C.** Enables the user to access disks and CDs without having to be logged in as root
- ❍ **D.** Automatically mounts a file system located on another system when that file system is accessed

67. Which of the following is the directory that provides character device access for the media in the primary floppy drive?

- ❍ **A.** `/vol/dev/diskette0`
- ❍ **B.** `/dev/rdiskette`
- ❍ **C.** `/vol/dev/aliases/floppy0`
- ❍ **D.** `/floppy/floppy0`

68. Which of the following contains the volume management configuration information used by `vold`?

- ❍ **A.** `/etc/init.d/volmgt`
- ❍ **B.** `/etc/vfstab`
- ❍ **C.** `/etc/vold.conf`
- ❍ **D.** `/etc/inittab`

69. Which of the following files can the system administrator modify to specify the program that should be called if media events happen, such as eject or insert?

- ❍ **A.** `/etc/vold.conf`
- ❍ **B.** `/etc/rmmount.conf`
- ❍ **C.** `/etc/inittab`
- ❍ **D.** `/etc/mnttab`

70. Which of the following actions notifies the user if an attempt is made to access a CD or disk that is no longer in the drive?

❍ **A.** `vold`

❍ **B.** `volcheck`

❍ **C.** `volmissing`

❍ **D.** `rmmount`

71. Which of the following commands is used to format a floppy disk and add a volume label?

❍ **A.** `format -d`

❍ **B.** `labelit`

❍ **C.** `format`

❍ **D.** `fdformat`

72. Which of the following should you issue to stop the volume management daemon?

❍ **A.** `vold stop`

❍ **B.** `/etc/init.d/volmgt stop`

❍ **C.** `ps -ef¦grep vold, then kill the process ID for vold`

❍ **D.** `volcancel`

73. Which of the following commands displays capacity information on each mounted file system?

❍ **A.** `du`

❍ **B.** `format`

❍ **C.** `prtvtoc`

❍ **D.** `df`

74. Which of the following commands is used to instruct the system to mount the floppy automatically?

❍ **A.** `volcheck`

❍ **B.** `vold`

❍ **C.** `mount`

❍ **D.** `automount`

75. You can type `mount /opt` on the command line and not get an error message if which of the following conditions exits?

❍ **A.** `/opt` is listed in the `/etc/rmtab`.

❍ **B.** `/opt` is listed in the `/etc/mnttab`.

❍ **C.** `/opt` is listed in the `/etc/vfstab`.

❍ **D.** `/opt` is listed in the `/etc/dfs/dfstab`.

76. Volume Manager provides access to the CD-ROM and floppy devices through which of the following directories?

❍ **A.** `/vol/dev`

❍ **B.** `/dev/vol`

❍ **C.** `/dev`

❍ **D.** `/vold`

77. Which of the following is *not* true about volume management?

❍ **A.** Volume Manager is started via the `/etc/init.d/volmgt` script.

❍ **B.** Volume Manager automatically mounts CDs and floppy disks.

❍ **C.** Volume Manager reads the `/etc/vold.conf` configuration file at startup.

❍ **D.** Volume Manager automatically checks and performs an `fsck` on file systems at bootup.

78. Which directory contains configuration files used to define a machine's identity?

❍ **A.** `/dev`

❍ **B.** `/usr`

❍ **C.** `/etc`

❍ **D.** `/opt`

❍ **E.** `/var`

79. Which type of link cannot span file systems?

❍ **A.** Symbolic link

❍ **B.** Hard link

❍ **C.** Hardware link

❍ **D.** Software link

80. Which type of link can point to a file that does not exist?

❍ **A.** Symbolic link

❍ **B.** Hard link

❍ **C.** Hardware link

❍ **D.** Software link

81. You can remove a link using which of the following commands?

❍ **A.** `unlink`

❍ **B.** `rm`

❍ **C.** `rmdir`

❍ **D.** `rm -l`

❍ **E.** `rmlink`

83. Which task cannot be performed by the SMC Disks Tool?

❍ **A.** View partition information.

❍ **B.** Format a disk.

❍ **C.** Partition a disk.

❍ **D.** Copy one disk's partition scheme to another disk.

Answers to Review Questions

1. A. The instance name represents the kernel's abbreviation name for every possible device on the system. For more information, see the "Device Drivers" section.

2. D. Physical device files are found in the `/devices` directory. For more information, see the "Physical Device Name" section.

3. D. The `sysdef` command displays device configuration information, including system hardware, pseudo devices, loadable modules, and selected kernel parameters. For more information, see the "Physical Device Name" section.

4. C. When you see the `driver not attached` message, it means no driver is currently attached to the device instance because there is no device at this node or the device is not in use. For more information, see the "Physical Device Name" section.

5. A. The .conf files reside in the `/kernel/drv` directories. For more information, see the "Device Autoconfiguration" section.

6. **B.** Instance names are mapped to a physical device name in the /etc/path_to_inst file. For more information, see the "Instance Names" section.

7. **A, B.** You can determine the mapping of an instance name to a physical device name by looking at the `dmesg` output and by viewing the `/var/adm/messages` file. For more information, see the "Instance Names" section.

8. **A, B.** The system relies on information found in both the `/etc/vfstab` file and the `/etc/path_to_inst` file to find the root, usr, and swap device. For more information, see the "Instance Names" section.

9. **C.** The `devfsadm` command a creates logical links to device nodes in /dev and `/devices` and loads the device policy. For more information, see the "Instance Names" section.

10. **D.** The `devfsadm` command is used to inform the system about newly installed device drivers. For more information, see the "Instance Names" section.

11. **A.** The `devfsadmd` daemon is the daemon responsible for handling both reconfiguration boot processing and updating `/dev` and /devices in response to dynamic reconfiguration event notifications from the kernel. For more information, see the "Instance Names" section.

12. **C.** An example of when to use the `devfsadm` command would be if the system has been started, but the power to the CD-ROM or tape drive was not turned on. During startup, the system did not detect the device; therefore, its drivers were not installed. The `devfsadm` command will perform these tasks. For more information, see the "Instance Names" section.

13. **B.** The major device number indicates the general device driver for devices such as disk, tape, or serial line. For more information, see the "Major and Minor Device Numbers" section.

14. **B.** The minor device number indicates the specific member within a driver. For more information, see the "Major and Minor Device Numbers" section.

15. **D.** The logical device name is a link from the `/dev` directory to the physical device name located in the `/devices` directory. For more information, see the "Logical Device Name" section.

16. **C.** The logical device name is a link from the `/dev` directory to the physical device name located in the `/devices` directory. For more information, see the "Logical Device Name" section.

17. **A.** The logical device name is a link from the `/dev` directory to the physical device name located in the `/devices` directory. The following is an example of a logical device name: `/dev/dsk/c0t0d0s7`. For more information, see the "Logical Device Name" section.

18. **A.** The `devfsadm` command can be used to create entries in the `/dev` directory for disk drives attached to the system. For more information, see the "Instance Names" section.

19. **D.** The `/dev/dsk` directory contains the disk entries for the block device nodes in `/devices`. For more information, see the "Block and Raw Devices" section.

20. **A.** A physical device name represents the full device pathname of the device. Physical device files are found in the `/devices` directory and have the following naming convention:

```
/devices/sbus@1,f8000000/esp@0,40000/sd@3,0:a
```

For more information, see the "Physical Device Name" section.

21. **B.** The fields of the logical device name cXtYdZ are as follows:

    - `cX`—Refers to the SCSI controller number
    - `tY`—Refers to the SCSI bus target number
    - `dZ`—Refers to the disk number (always 0, except on storage arrays)

    For more information, see the "Logical Device Name" section.

22. **B.** In the character device name `/dev/rdsk/c0t3d0s0`, the `/rdsk` directory refers to the character or raw device file. The *r* in *rdsk* stands for *raw*. For more information, see the "Block and Raw Devices" section.

23. **A.** The instance name represents the kernel's abbreviated name for every possible device on the system. For example, `sd0` and `sd1` represent the instance names of two SCSI disk devices. For more information, see the "Instance Names" section.

24. **A.** Logical device names are used with most Solaris file system commands to refer to devices. Logical device files in the `/dev` directory are symbolically linked to physical device files in the `/devices` directory. For more information, see the "Logical Device Name" section.

25. **A.** Logical device files in the `/dev` directory are symbolically linked to physical device files in the `/devices` directory. For more information, see the "Logical Device Name" section.

26. **D.** On a standard Solaris file system, a file system cannot span multiple disks or slices. It's only possible when using virtual file systems (that is, Solaris Volume Manager). For more information, see the "Disk Slices" section.

27. **A.** Disk configuration information is stored on the disk label. For more information, see the "Displaying Disk Configuration Information" section.

28. **A.** The boot block stores the procedures used in booting the system. Without a boot block, the system does not boot. For more information, see the "Components of the UFS" section.

29. **A.** The slice information for a particular disk can be viewed by using the `prtvtoc` command. For more information, see the "Disk Slices" section.

30. **A.** The following are virtual file systems: `swapfs`, `procfs`, `lofs`, `cachefs`, `tmpfs`, and `mntfs`. For more information, see the "Virtual File Systems" section.

31. **D.** The `format` utility is used to retrieve corrupted disk labels, repair defective sectors, format and analyze disks, partition disks, and label disks. For more information, see the "Using the `format` Utility to Create Slices" section.

32. D. Here are a few of the more important things contained in a superblock:

- Size and status of the file system
- Label (file system name and volume name)
- Size of the file system's logical block
- Date and time of the last update
- Cylinder group size
- Number of data blocks in a cylinder group
- Summary data block
- File system state (clean, stable, or active)
- Pathname of the last mount point

For more information, see the "The Superblock" section.

33. A, C. An inode contains all of the information about a file except its name, which is kept in a directory. The inode information is kept in the cylinder information block and contains the following:

- The type of the file (regular, directory, block special, character special, link, and so on)
- The mode of the file (the set of read/write/execute permissions)
- The number of hard links to the file
- The user id of the file's owner
- The group id to which the file belongs
- The number of bytes in the file
- An array of 15 disk-block addresses
- The date and time the file was last accessed
- The date and time the file was last modified
- The date and time the file was created

For more information, see the "The inode" section.

34. D. As a general rule, a larger logical block size increases efficiency for file systems in which most of the files are large. Use a smaller logical block size for file systems in which most of the files are small. For more information, see the "Logical Block Size" section.

35. A. The number of inodes depends on the amount of disk space that is allocated for each inode and the total size of the file system. For more information, see the "inode" section.

36. A. The file system fragment size is the smallest allocable unit of disk space, which by default is 1024 bytes. For more information, see the "Information on File Systems" section.

37. **A.** Swap space plus the total amount of physical memory is also referred to as virtual memory. For more information, see the "Virtual File Systems" section.

38. **A, B, C.** `fsck` should be run after a power outage, when a file system is unmounted improperly, or whenever a file system cannot be mounted. For more information, see the "Repairing File Systems" section.

39. **B.** Normally, `fsck` is run noninteractively at bootup to preen the file systems after an abrupt system halt. Preening automatically fixes any basic file system inconsistencies and does not try to repair more serious errors. While preening a file system, `fsck` fixes the inconsistencies it expects from such an abrupt halt. For more serious conditions, the command reports the error and terminates. For more information, see the "Repairing File Systems" section.

40. **C.** The `/etc/vfstab` file contains a list of file systems to be automatically mounted when the system is booted to the multiuser state. For more information, see the "Creating an Entry in the `/etc/vfstab` File to Mount File Systems" section.

41. **B.** The `mountall` command mounts all file systems specified in the file system table (vfstab). For more information, see the "Mounting File Systems" section.

42. **E.** The following commands can be used to display disk space usage: `du`, `df`, `quota`, `repquota`. For more information, see the "Displaying a File System's Disk Space Usage" section.

43. **A.** The `largefiles` mount option lets users mount a file system containing files larger than 2GB. For more information, see the "Mounting File Systems" section.

44. **A.** Use the `-o nologging` option of the `mount` command to disable UFS logging on a file system. Logging is the default. For more information, see the "Mounting File Systems" section.

45. **A.** The correct format for the `/etc/vfstab` file is as follows:

    device to mount, device to fsck, mount point, FS type, fsck pass, mount at boot, mount options.

    For more information, see the "Creating an Entry in the `/etc/vfstab` File to Mount File Systems" section.

46. **A.** Use the `du` (directory usage) command to report the number of free disk blocks and files. For more information, see the "Displaying a File System's Disk Space Usage" section.

47. **A.** The `df` command with no options lists all mounted file systems and their device names. It also lists the total number of 512-byte blocks used and the number of files. For more information, see the "Displaying a File System's Disk Space Usage" section.

48. **A.** Typically, creating large numbers of small files causes high fragmentation. The solution is to either create a larger file system or to decrease the block size (finer granularity). For more information, see the "Displaying a File System's Disk Space Usage" section.

49. **B.** The `df -k` command does not display the percentage of fragmentation. For more information, see the "Displaying a File System's Disk Space Usage" section.

50. **D.** `newfs` is the friendly front end to the `mkfs` command. The `newfs` command automatically determines all the necessary parameters to pass to `mkfs` to construct new file systems. `newfs` was added in Solaris to make the creation of new file systems easier. It's highly recommended that the `newfs` command be used to create file systems. For more information, see the "Creating a UFS" section.

51. **D.** After you create the file system with `newfs`, you can use the `labelit` utility to write or display labels on unmounted disk file systems. For more information, see the "Creating a UFS" section.

52. **A.** Use the `fstyp` command to determine a file system type. For example, use it to check whether a file system is a UFS. For more information, see the "The `fstyp` Command" section.

53. **B.** Use the `tunefs` command to change the `minfree` value of a file system. For more information, see the "Tuning File Systems" section.

54. **A.** Use the `fstyp` command to view file system parameters. Use the `-v` option to obtain a full listing of a file system's parameters. For more information, see the "The `fstyp` Command" section.

55. **D.** A large file is a regular file whose size is greater than or equal to 2GB. For more information, see the "Mounting a File System with Large Files" section.

56. **B.** A utility is called large file–aware if it can process large files in the same manner that it does small files. A large file—aware utility can handle large files as input and can generate large files as output. The `vi` command is not large file–aware. For more information, see the "Mounting a File System with Large Files" section.

57. **C.** As stated in the previous question and answer, a utility is called large file–aware if it can process large files in the same manner that it does small files. A large file–aware utility can handle large files as input and can generate large files as output. For more information, see the "Mounting a File System with Large Files" section.

58. **D.** The `-o nolargefiles` option of the `mount` command provides total compatibility with previous file system behavior, enforcing the 2GB maximum file size limit. For more information, see the "Mounting a File System with Large Files" section.

59. **A.** Type the `mount` command with the `-p` option to display a list of mounted file systems in `/etc/vfstab` format. For more information, see the "Creating an Entry in the `/etc/vfstab` File to Mount File Systems" section.

60. **B.** The following command uses the `mount` command to map a directory to a file system as read/writeable, disallow `setuid` execution, and enable the creation of large files (more than 2GB in size):

    ```
    mount -o rw,nosuid,largefiles /dev/dsk/c0t0d0s0\
    /home2
    ```

    For more information, see the "Mounting a File System with Large Files" section.

61. **A.** When a file system is mounted, an entry is maintained in the mounted file system table called `/etc/mnttab`. This file is actually a read-only file system and contains information about devices that are currently mounted. For more information, see the "Mounting File Systems" section.

62. **C, D.** Do not use the following commands on a mounted file system: `fsck`, and `labelit`. `newfs` cannot be run on a mounted file system—it generates an error. For more information, see the "Unmounting a File System" section.

63. **A.** If something is causing the file system to be busy, you can use the `fuser` command to list all of the processes accessing the file system and to stop them if necessary. For more information, see the "The `fuser` Command" section.

64. **A.** The following command stops all processes that are using the `/home2` file system by sending a `SIGKILL` to each one: `fuser -c -k /home2`. For more information, see the "The `fuser` Command" section.

65. **C.** The `vold` daemon is the mechanism that manages removable media, such as the CD-ROM and floppy disk drives. For more information, see the "Volume Management" section.

66. **D.** `vold` does not automatically mount a file system located on another system when that file system is accessed. The facility responsible for that task is AutoFS. For more information, see the "Volume Management" section.

67. **B.** `/dev/rdiskette` and `/vol/dev/rdiskette0` are the directories providing character device access for the medium in the primary floppy drive, usually drive 0. For more information, see the "Volume Management" section.

68. **C.** `vold` reads the `/etc/vold.conf` configuration file at startup. The `vold.conf` file contains the Volume Manager configuration information used by `vold`. For more information, see the "Volume Management" section.

69. **A.** The "Actions" section of the `vold.conf` file specifies which program should be called if a particular event (action) occurs such as eject or insert. For more information, see the "Volume Management" section.

70. **C.** The `volmissing` action in the `vold.conf` file notifies the user if an attempt is made to access a CD or diskette that is no longer in the drive. For more information, see the "Volume Management" section.

71. **D.** Use the `fdformat` command to format a floppy disk, and then add a volume label. For more information, see the "Troubleshooting Volume Manager" section.

72. **B.** Run the following run control script to stop the volume management daemon: `/etc/init.d/volmgt stop`. For more information, see the "Troubleshooting Volume Manager" section.

73. **D.** The `df` command gives you capacity information on each mounted file system. For more information, see the "Displaying a File System's Disk Space Usage" section.

74. A. The `volcheck` command instructs `vold` to look at each device and determine if new media has been inserted into the drive. The system administrator issues this command to check the drive for installed media. By default, it checks the drive to which `/dev/diskette` points. For more information, see the "Volume Management" section.

75. C. You can type `mount /opt` on the command line and not get an error message if `/opt` is listed in the `/etc/vfstab` file. For more information, see the "Creating an Entry in the `/etc/vfstab` File to Mount File Systems" section.

76. A. Volume Manager provides access to the floppy disk and CD-ROM devices through the `/vol/dev` directory. For more information, see the "Volume Management" section.

77. D. Volume management does not automatically `fsck` file systems at bootup. It does, however, automatically mount CD-ROM and file systems when removable media containing recognizable file systems are inserted into the devices. For more information, see the "Volume Management" section.

78. C. The `/etc` directory contains configuration files that define a system's identity. For more information, see the "The Root (/) File System" section.

79. B. A hard link cannot span file systems, but a symbolic link can. For more information, see the "Hard Links" section.

80. A. An advantage of a symbolic link over a hard link is that you can create a symbolic link to a file that does not yet exist. For more information, see the "Soft (Symbolic) Links" section.

81. B. Remove a link using the `rm` command. For more information, see the "Soft (Symbolic) Links" section.

82. B. The SMC Disks Tool cannot be used to format a disk. For more information, see the "Using the Solaris Management Console Disks Tool" section.

Suggested Readings and Resources

- Calkins, Bill. *Inside Solaris 9*. New Riders Publishing, 2002.
- *Solaris 10 System Administration Guide: Devices and File Systems*, 2005, Sun Microsystems, Part number 817-5093-11. This manual is available online at `docs.sun.com`.

CHAPTER TWO

Installing the Solaris 10 Operating Environment

Objectives

The following test objectives for exam CX-310-200 are covered in this chapter:

This chapter describes how to install and manage the Solaris 10 operating system software. This chapter will prepare you for the following exam objectives:

Explain how to install the Solaris operating system from CD/DVD, including installation and upgrade options, hardware requirements, Solaris operating system software components (software packages, clusters, and groups) on SPARC, x64, and x86-based systems.

- There are many different methods that can be used to install the Solaris 10 operating environment (OE). Which method you use depends on whether you are upgrading the operating system from a previous release, installing the operating system from scratch, or installing several systems that are configured exactly the same way. You also need to know if your system meets the minimum hardware requirements for the Solaris 10 OE.

  In addition to installing Solaris on Sun SPARC systems, you must also understand how to install the OS on x86- and x64-based systems.

Perform Solaris 10 OS package administration using command-line interface commands and manage software patches for the Solaris OS, including preparing for patch administration and installing and removing patches using the `patchadd` and `patchrm` commands.

- When installing the operating system, you'll need to understand how Sun packages their software into packages and groups. You'll need to understand how to install, list, verify, and remove individual software packages using the command line interface commands described in this chapter.

  In addition, you'll need to understand how software updates are distributed via software patches. You'll need to understand how to obtain, install, list, and remove these patches using the various command line interface utilities.

Outline

Study Strategies

The following strategies will help you prepare for the exam:

- Understand each of the seven methods used to install the operating system. Primarily, you need to know the difference between each method as well as where and when to use each one.
- Know all of the hardware requirements for installing the Solaris 10 operating environment on SPARC and x86/x64-based systems.
- Become familiar with all of the tools used to manage software on a Solaris system. Understand which tool is best for a particular circumstance.
- Understand how to patch the operating system. Pay special attention to how to obtain patches, the various methods used to install and remove them, and how to verify patches on your system.
- Practice all of the commands presented in this chapter until you can perform them and describe them from memory. In addition, practice installing the Solaris 10 OE and adding/removing software packages no less than three times or until you can perform all of the tasks from memory.
- Finally, understand all of the terminology and concepts described in this chapter as well as the terms outlined at the end of the chapter. Each term and concept is likely to appear on the exam.

Introduction

The Solaris installation process consists of three phases: system configuration, system installation, and post-installation tasks such as setting up printers, users, and networking. This chapter describes the various system configurations and the installation of the Solaris operating system on a standalone system.

Once the software is installed, the system administrator is responsible for managing all software installed on a system. Installing and removing software is a routine task that is performed frequently. This chapter explains how to add and remove additional applications after the operating system has already been installed.

Installing the Solaris 10 Software

When installing the operating system onto a machine, you'll be performing one of two types of installations: initial or upgrade.

You'll perform an initial installation either on a system that does not have an existing Solaris operating system already installed on it or when you want to completely wipe out the existing operating system and reinstall it.

An upgrade is performed on a system that is already running Solaris 7, Solaris 8, Solaris 9, or a previous release of Solaris 10. An upgrade will save as many modifications as possible from the previous version of Solaris that is currently running on your system.

CAUTION

Upgrading to a New Software Group You cannot upgrade your system to a software group that is not currently installed on the system. For example, you cannot upgrade to the Developer Solaris Software group if you previously installed the End User Solaris Software group. You can, however, add software that is not currently part of the installed software group to a system.

Another option when upgrading your system is to take advantage of the Solaris live upgrade, which enables an upgrade to be installed while the operating system is running and can significantly reduce the downtime associated with an upgrade. The process involves creating a duplicate boot environment on an unused disk slice and upgrading the duplicate boot environment. When you're ready to switch and make the upgraded boot environment active, you simply activate it and reboot. The old boot environment remains available as a fallback to the original boot environment and allows you to quickly reactivate and reboot the old environment. This is useful if you need to back out of the upgrade and go back to the previous operating system release.

Regardless of whether you are going to perform an initial installation or an upgrade, you need to first determine whether your hardware meets the minimum requirements to support the Solaris 10 environment.

Requirements and Preparation for Installing the Solaris 10 Software

The first step in the installation is to determine whether your system type is supported under Solaris 10. Second, you need to decide which system configuration you want to install and whether you have enough disk space to support that configuration.

In preparation for installing Solaris 10 on a system, use Table 2.1 to check whether your system type is supported. Also, make sure you have enough disk space for Solaris and all of the packages you plan to install. (The section "Software Terminology" later in this chapter will help you estimate the amount of disk space required to hold the Solaris operating system.)

If your system is running a previous version of Solaris, you can determine your system type using the `uname -m` command. The system will respond with the platform group and the platform name for your system. Compare the system response to the Platform Group column in Table 2.1. For example, to check for Sun platforms that support the Solaris 10 environment, use the command `uname -m`. On a Sun Ultra5, the system returns `sun4u` as the platform name and on an x86/x64 system, the command will return `i86pc` as the platform name.

NOTE

`OpenBoot` Commands To determine the system type on a system that is not currently running some version of Solaris, you'll need to use the `OpenBoot` commands described in the next chapter.

TABLE 2.1 Sun Platforms That Support the Solaris 10 Environment

System	Platform Name	Platform Group
Workstation Systems	Sun Blade 100	SUNW,Sun-Blade-100
	Sun Blade 150	SUNW,Sun-Blade-100
	Sun Blade 1000	SUNW,Sun-Blade-1000
	Sun Blade 1500	SUNW,Sun-Blade-1000
	Sun Blade 2000	SUNW,Sun-Blade-1000
	Sun Blade 2500	SUNW,Sun-Blade-1000
	Ultra 2	SUNW,Ultra-2
	Ultra 5	SUNW,Ultra-5_10
	Ultra 10	SUNW,Ultra-5_10

(continues)

Table 2.1 *Continued*

System	Platform Name	Platform Group
	Ultra 30	SUNW,Ultra-30
	Ultra 60	SUNW,Ultra-60
	Ultra 80	SUNW,Ultra-80
	Ultra 450	SUNW,Ultra-4
Entry/Workgroup Servers	Sun Fire V100	SUNW,UltraAX-i2
	Sun Fire V120	SUNW,UltraAX-i2
	Sun Fire V210	SUNW,Sun-Fire-V210
	Sun Fire V240	SUNW,Sun-Fire-V240
	Sun Fire V250	SUNW,Sun-Fire-V250
	Sun Fire 280R	SUNW,Sun-Fire-280R
	Sun Fire V440	SUNW,Sun-Fire-V440
	Sun Fire V480	SUNW,Sun-Fire-480
	Sun Fire V490	SUNW,Sun-Fire-490
	Sun Fire V880	SUNW,Sun-Fire-880
	Sun Fire V890	SUNW,Sun-Fire-890
	Sun Fire B100s	SUNW,Serverblade1
	Sun Fire B10n	SUNW,Serverblade1
	Sun Enterprise 2	SUNW,Ultra-2
	Sun Enterprise Ultra 5S	SUNW,Ultra-5_10
	Sun Enterprise Ultra 10S	SUNW,Ultra-5_10
	Sun Enterprise 250	SUNW,Ultra-250
	Sun Enterprise 450	SUNW,Ultra-4
	Sun Enterprise 220R	SUNW,Ultra-60
	Sun Enterprise 420R	SUNW,Ultra-80
Mid-Range and Mid-Frame Servers	Sun Fire V1280	SUNW,Netra-T12
	Sun Fire 3800	SUNW,Sun-Fire
	Sun Fire 4800	SUNW,Sun-Fire
	Sun Fire 4810	SUNW,Sun-Fire
	Sun Fire 6800	SUNW,Sun-Fire
	Sun Fire E2900	SUNW,Sun-Fire
	Sun Fire E4900	SUNW,Sun-Fire
	Sun Fire E6900	SUNW,Sun-Fire
	Sun Enterprise 3000	SUNW,Ultra-Enterprise
	Sun Enterprise 4000	SUNW,Ultra-Enterprise
	Sun Enterprise 5000	SUNW,Ultra-Enterprise
	Sun Enterprise 6000	SUNW,Ultra-Enterprise
	Sun Enterprise 3500	SUNW,Ultra-Enterprise
	Sun Enterprise 4500	SUNW,Ultra-Enterprise
	Sun Enterprise 5500	SUNW,Ultra-Enterprise
	Sun Enterprise 6500	SUNW,Ultra-Enterprise

TABLE 2.1 *Continued*

System	Platform Name	Platform Group
High-End Servers	Sun Fire E20K	SUNW,Sun-Fire-Enterprise-20K
	Sun Fire E25K	SUNW,Sun-Fire-Enterprise-25K
	Sun Fire 12K	SUNW,Sun-Fire-12000
	Sun Fire 15K	SUNW,Sun-Fire-15000
	Sun Enterprise 10000	SUNW,Ultra-Enterprise
Netra Servers	Netra 20	SUNW,Netra-T4
	Netra 120	SUNW,UltraAX-i2
	Netra 240	SUNW,Netra-240
	Netra 440	SUNW,Netra-440
	Netra 1280	SUNW,Netra-T12
	Netra T1 AC200/DC200	SUNW,UltraAX-i2
	Netra X1	SUNW,UltraAX-i2
	Netra ct 400	SUNW,UltraSPARC-IIi-Netract
	Netra ct 800	SUNW,UltraSPARC-IIi-Netract
	Netra CT 820	SUNW,Netra-CP2300
	Netra CP2300	SUNW,Netra-CP2300
	Netra t1 100	SUNW,UltraSPARC-IIi-cEngine
	Netra t1 105	SUNW,UltraSPARC-IIi-cEngine
	Netra t 1120	SUNW,Ultra-60
	Netra t 1125	SUNW,Ultra-60
	Netra t 1400	SUNW,Ultra-80
	Netra t 1405	SUNW,Ultra-80

Table 2.1 outlines a general list of Sun systems that support Solaris 10. For a complete, up-to-date listing of all hardware that is compatible with the Solaris 10 OE, including all x86/x64-based systems, go to `http://www.sun.com/bigadmin/hcl/`. This site features a searchable database to quickly locate equipment in three categories: Sun Certified, Test Suite Certified, and Reported to Work. X86- and x64-based systems are available from many vendors, and the components can vary from system to system. Use this site to track down the specific components that are installed in your system to determine if it is compatible with Solaris 10. Overall, your x86/x64-based system needs to have a 120MHz or faster processor with hardware floating-point support required, a minimum of 128MB of RAM, and 12GB of disk space.

Check slice 2 by using the `format` command to determine whether your disk drive is large enough to hold Solaris. See Chapter 1, "Managing File Systems," for the correct use of this command. As described in Chapter 1, slice 2 represents the entire disk.

Minimum System Requirements

The computer must meet the following requirements before you can install Solaris 10 using the interactive installation method:

- The system must have a minimum of 128MB of RAM (256MB is recommended). Sufficient memory requirements are determined by several factors, including the number of active users and applications you plan to run.

EXAM ALERT

Minimum Memory Requirements Although Sun states that 128MB of RAM is the minimum required, it is possible to install Solaris 10 on a system that has 64MB of RAM. With less than 128MB, the system will run sluggishly. It's important that you use Sun's RAM recommendations when you encounter this question on the exam. Also, pay close attention to the question and understand the difference between "minimum" and "recommended."

- The media is distributed on CD-ROM and DVD only, so a CD-ROM or DVD-ROM drive is required either locally or on the network. You can use all of the Solaris installation methods to install the system from a networked CD-ROM or DVD-ROM.
- A minimum of 2GB of disk space is required. See the next section for disk space requirements for the specific Solaris software you plan to install. Also, remember to add disk space to support your environment's swap space requirements.
- When upgrading the operating system, you must have an empty 512MB slice on the disk. The swap slice is preferred, but you can use any slice that will not be used in the upgrade such as root (`/`), `/usr`, `/var`, and `/opt`.
- The system must be a SPARC-based or supported x86/x64-based system.

Software Terminology

The operating system is bundled in packages on the distribution media. Packages are arranged into software groups. The following sections describe the Solaris bundling scheme.

Software Packages

A *software package* is a collection of files and directories in a defined format. It describes a software application, such as manual pages and line printer support. The Solaris 10 entire distribution contains approximately 900 software packages that require 6.5 gigabytes of disk space.

A Solaris software package is the standard way to deliver bundled and unbundled software. Packages are administered by using the package administration commands, and they are generally identified by a SUNWxxx naming convention when supplied by Sun Microsystems. SUNW is Sun Microsystems's ticker symbol on the stock exchange, hence the SUNW prefix.

Software Groups

Software packages are grouped into *software groups*, which are logical collections of software packages. Sometimes these groups are referred to as clusters. For example, the online manual pages software group contains one package. Some software groups contain multiple packages, such as the CDS software cluster, which contains the CDE man pages, CDE desktop applications, CDE daemons, and so on.

For SPARC systems, software groups are grouped into six configuration groups to make the software installation process easier. During the installation process, you will be asked to install one of the six configuration groups. These six configuration groups are reduced networking support, core system support, end-user support, developer system support, entire distribution, and entire distribution plus OEM system support. The following list describes each software group:

- **Reduced networking support**—Sun recommends 736MB to support the software, swap, and disk overhead required to support this software group. This group contains the minimum software that is required to boot and run a Solaris system with limited network service support. The Reduced Networking software group provides a multi-user text-based console and system administration utilities. This software group also enables the system to recognize network interfaces, but does not activate network services. A system installed with the Reduced Networking software group could, for example, be used as a thin-client host in a network.
- **Core system support**— Sun recommends 777MB to support the software, swap, and disk overhead required to support this software group. This software group contains the minimum software required to boot and run Solaris on a system. It includes some networking software and the drivers required to run the OpenWindows (OW) environment, but it does not include the OpenWindows software.
- **End-user system support**—Sun recommends 3.6 GB to support the software, swap, and disk overhead required to support this software group. This group contains the core system support software plus end-user software, which includes OW compatibility and the Common Desktop Environment (CDE) software.
- **Developer system support**—Sun recommends 4.6GB to support the software, swap, and disk overhead required to support this cluster. This software group contains the end-user software plus libraries, include files, man pages, and programming tools for developing software. Compilers and debuggers are purchased separately and are not included. However, you can use the open source GCC compiler supplied on the Solaris Companion CD.
- **Entire distribution**—Sun recommends 4.7GB to support the software, swap, and disk overhead required to support this software group. This software group contains the entire Solaris 10 release, which includes additional software needed for servers.

- **Entire distribution plus OEM system support**—Sun recommends 4.8GB to support the software, swap, and disk overhead required to support this software group. This software group contains the entire Solaris 10 release software plus extended hardware support for non-Sun SPARC systems.

NOTE

Recommended Space Requirements Swap space and necessary file system overhead is included in the disk space recommendations for each software group. A minimum of 512MB is required for swap space, but more space might be needed.

In addition, as new releases of Solaris 10 are made available, the size of these software groups might change.

Solaris Media

The Solaris 10 operating system software is distributed on a DVD or CD-ROM set numbered 1 through 4 and is referred to as "the installation media kit." The single DVD contains the contents of the entire CD set and is bootable. CD 1 of the CD set is the only bootable CD. From this CD, you can access both the Solaris installation graphical user interface (GUI) and the console-based installation. This CD also enables you to install selected software products from both the GUI and the console-based installation. The remaining CDs of the CD set contain the following:

- Solaris packages
- Extra value software which includes supported and unsupported software
- Installers
- Localized interface software and documentation

For those of you who have used previous versions of Solaris, the Supplemental CD and Installation CD are longer supplied.

System Configuration to Be Installed

Before installing the operating system, you need to determine the system configuration to be installed. The configurations are defined by the way they access the root (`/`) and `/usr` file systems and the swap area. The system configurations are as follows:

- Server
- Standalone

Each of these system configurations are discussed in the following sections.

Servers

A *server* is a system that provides services or file systems, such as home directories or mailboxes, to other systems on the network. An operating system server is a server that provides the Solaris software to other systems on the network.

There are file servers, startup servers, database servers, license servers, print servers, mail servers, web servers, installation servers, NFS servers, and even servers for particular applications. Each type of server has a different set of requirements based on the function it will serve. For example, a database server will be disk and memory intensive, but it probably will not have many logged-in users. Therefore, when this system is configured, special thought needs to be put into setting up the file systems and fine tuning kernel parameters that relate to disk I/O and memory usage to optimize system performance.

A server system typically has the following file systems installed locally:

- The root (`/`) and `/usr` file systems plus swap space
- The `/var` file system which supports the print spooler, mail repository, and software spooler.
- The `/export`, `/export/swap`, and `/export/home` file systems, which support client systems and provide home directories for users
- The `/opt` directory or file system for storing application software

Servers can also contain the following software to support other systems:

- Solaris CD-ROM image and boot software for networked systems to perform remote installations
- A JumpStart directory for networked systems to perform custom JumpStart installations

The server must meet a few minimum requirements before Solaris 10 can be installed:

- The Solaris 10 release supports all `sun4u` platforms.
- To run a graphical user interface (GUI) installation, the system must have a minimum of 256MB of RAM. As a server, however, it is typical to have 512MB of RAM or more.
- The disk needs to be large enough to hold the Solaris operating system, swap space, and additional software. Plan on a minimum of 9GB of disk space, but realistically the server should have 18GB to 36GB or more depending on the resources that this server will be providing.

Clients

A *client* is a system that uses remote services from a server. Some clients have limited disk storage capacity or perhaps none at all, so they must rely on remote file systems from a server to function.

Other clients might use remote services (such as installation software) from a server, but they don't rely on a server to function. A standalone system, which has its own hard disk containing the root (`/`), `/usr`, and `/export/home` file systems and swap space, is a good example of this type of client.

Standalone Systems

On a standalone system, the operating system is loaded on a local disk, and the system is set to run independently of other systems. The operating system might be networked to other standalone systems. A networked standalone system can share information with other systems on the network, but it can function autonomously because it has its own hard disk with enough space to contain the root (`/`), `/usr`, and `/export/home` file systems and swap space. The standalone system has local access to operating system software, executables, virtual memory space, and user-created files. Sometimes the standalone system will access the server for data or access a CD-ROM or tape drive from a server if one is not available locally.

Disk Storage

Before you begin to install a system, you need to think about how you want data stored on your system's disks. With one disk, the decision is easy. When multiple disks are installed, you must decide which disks to use for the operating system, the swap area, and the user data.

As described in Chapter 1, "Managing File Systems," Solaris breaks disks into pieces called *partitions*, or *slices*. A Solaris disk can be divided into a maximum of seven slices.

Why would you want to divide the disk into multiple slices? Some administrators don't; they use the entire disk with one slice. By using one slice, all of the space on the disk is available for anyone to use. When the system administrator creates a slice, the space in that slice is available only to the file system that is mounted on it. If another file system on the same disk runs out of space, it cannot borrow space from the other slice without repartitioning the disk. However, having multiple slices can provide some advantages. The following list describes some of the reasons why you might want to consider partitioning disks into multiple slices:

- Slices allow finer control over tasks such as creating backups. Unix commands such as `ufsdump` work on entire file systems. For backups, you might want to separate data and swap space from the application software so that backups are completed faster with a `ufsdump`. For example, you might want to back up only data on a daily basis. On the other hand, you'll need to take the system down to single-user mode to back up / and /usr, so separating the data will make your backup complete much more quickly and will result in less downtime.

- If one file system becomes corrupted, the others remain intact. If you need to perform a recovery operation, you can restore a smaller file system more quickly. Also, when data is separated from system software, you can modify file systems without shutting down the system or reloading operating system software.
- Slices allow you to control the amount of disk storage allocated to an activity or type of use. For example, /var can grow rapidly because it stores mail, log files, and patch backups. To keep /var from filling up the root (/) file system, we typically create a slice specifically for the /var file system.
- If file systems are mounted remotely from other systems, you can share only the data that needs to be accessed, not the entire system disk.

The installation process gives you the option of creating slices. Start with the default partition scheme supplied with the installation program, which is to set up a file system for root (/) and swap. This scheme sets up the required slices and provides you with the sizes required, based on the software group you select to install. The following is a typical partitioning scheme for a system with a single disk drive:

- **root (/) and /usr**—Solaris creates the root (/) slice by default. It is also recommended that you create a slice for /usr. The auto_layout function of the installation program determines how much space you need in root (/) and /usr. Most of the files in these two slices are static. Information in these file systems will not increase in size unless you add software packages later. If you plan to add third-party software after the installation of Solaris, make sure you increase the root (/) and /usr slices to accommodate the additional files you plan to load. If the root (/) file system fills up, the system will not operate properly.
- **Swap**—This area on the disk doesn't have files in it. In Unix, you're allowed to have more programs than will fit into memory. The pieces that aren't currently needed in memory are transferred into swap to free up physical memory for other active processes. Swapping into a dedicated slice is a good idea for two reasons: Swap slices are isolated so that they aren't put on tape with the daily backups, and a swap slice can be laid out on a disk in an area to optimize performance.
- **/export/home**—On a single-disk system, everything not in root (/), /usr, or swap should go into a separate slice. /export/home is where you would put user-created files.

- `/var` **(optional)**—Solaris uses this area for system log files, print spoolers, and email. The name `/var` is short for variable; this file system contains system files that are not static but are variable in size. One day the print spooler directory might be empty; another day it might contain several 1MB files. This separate file system is created to keep the root (`/`) and `/usr` file systems from filling up with these files. If the `/var` file system does not exist, make sure you make root (`/`) larger.
- `/opt` **(optional)**—By default, the Solaris installation program loads optional software packages here. Also, third-party applications are usually loaded into `/opt`. If this file system does not exist, the installation program puts the optional software in the root file system. If the `/opt` file system does not exist, make sure you make root (`/`) larger.

File systems provide a way to segregate data, but when a file system runs out of space, you can't "borrow" from a file system that has some unused space. Therefore, the best plan is to create a minimal number of file systems with adequate space for expansion. This concept is discussed in Chapter 1, "Managing File Systems," and the ability to make file systems larger is described in Chapter 10, "Managing Storage Volumes."

Basic Considerations for Planning Partition (Slice) Sizes

Planning disk and partition space depends on many factors: the number of users, the application requirements, and the number and size of files and databases. The following are some basic considerations for determining your disk space requirements:

- Allocate additional disk space for each language selected (for example, Chinese, Japanese, and Korean).
- If you need printing or mail support, create a slice for a separate `/var` file system and allocate additional disk space. You need to estimate the number and size of email messages and print files to size this slice properly. In addition to this space, if you intend to use the crash dump feature `savecore`, allocate additional space in `/var` equal to twice the amount of physical memory.
- Allocate additional disk space on a server that will provide home file systems for users. Again, the number of users and the size of their files will dictate the size of this file system. By default, home directories are usually located in the `/export` file system.
- Allocate additional disk space on an operating system server for JumpStart clients if this server will be used as a JumpStart installation server.

- Make sure you allocate enough swap space. The minimum size for the swap slice is 512MB. Factors that dictate the amount of swap space are the concurrent number of users and the application requirements. Consult with your application vendor for swap-space requirements. Vendors usually give you a formula to determine the amount of swap space you need for each application. In addition, the swap slice will be used for core dumps and should contain enough space to hold a complete core dump—that is, exceed the size of the installed RAM. See Chapter 9 for more information on configuring core dumps.

NOTE

Sizing the Swap Area In the past, system administrators sized their swap based on the amount of RAM installed in their system. A simple rule of "set your minimum swap space at two times the amount of physical memory" was used. With newer systems now containing several gigabytes of RAM, this rule is no longer relevant. See Chapter 9, "Virtual File Systems, Swap, and Core Dumps" for more information on swap.

- Determine the software packages you will be installing and calculate the total amount of disk space required. When planning disk space, remember that the Solaris Interactive Installation program lets you add or remove individual software packages from the software group that you select.
- Create a minimum number of file systems. By default, the Solaris Interactive Installation program creates file systems for only root (`/`) and swap, although `/export` is also created when space is allocated for operating system services. Creating a minimum number of file systems helps with future upgrades and file system expansion because separate file systems are limited by their slice boundaries. Be generous with the size of your file systems, especially root (`/`) and `/usr`. Even when using logical volumes, these file systems cannot be increased without completely reloading the operating system.
- For each file system you create, allocate an additional 30% more disk space than you need to allow for future Solaris upgrades. This is because each new Solaris release needs approximately 10% more disk space than the previous release. By allocating an additional 30% more space for each file system, you'll allow for several Solaris upgrades before you need to repartition your system disk.
- Calculate additional disk space for copackaged or third-party software.
- If you will be using Solaris Volume Manager (SVM), you'll need to allocate an empty slice for the `metadb` replicas. See Chapter 10, "Managing Storage Volumes," for more information on SVM.

Slice Arrangements on Multiple Disks

Although a single large disk can hold all slices and their corresponding file systems, two or more disks are often used to hold a system's slices and file systems.

NOTE

Conventional File Systems Using conventional Solaris file systems, you cannot split a slice between two or more disks. Solaris Volume Manager is described in Chapter 9 and allows us to overcome this limitation. For this chapter, however, I'm going to describe the use of conventional file systems.

For example, a single disk might hold the root (`/`) file system, a swap area, and the `/usr` file system, and a second disk might be used for the `/export/home` file system and other file systems containing user data. In a multiple-disk arrangement, the disk containing the root (`/`) and `/usr` file systems and swap space is referred to as the *system disk* or *boot disk*. Disks other than the system disk are called *secondary disks* or *nonsystem disks*.

Locating a system's file systems on multiple disks allows you to modify file systems and slices on the secondary disks without shutting down the system or reloading the operating system software. Also, using multiple disks allows you to distribute the workload as evenly as possible among different I/O systems and disk drives, such as distributing the `/home` and swap slices evenly across disks.

Having more than one disk increases input/output (I/O) volume. By distributing the I/O load across multiple disks, you can avoid I/O bottlenecks.

NOTE

Improving System Performance with Multiple Swap Slices A good way to improve system performance is to create more than one swap slice and assign each one to a separate disk drive. When the system needs to access swap, the disk I/O is spread evenly across the multiple disk drives.

Methods of Installing the Solaris 10 Software

You can use one of seven methods to install the Solaris software:

- Solaris Interactive installation using the graphical user interface (GUI)
- Solaris Interactive installation using the command line interface (CLI)
- Solaris JumpStart

- Solaris Custom JumpStart
- Solaris Flash Archives
- Solaris WAN Boot Installation
- Solaris Upgrade Method

Each of these is discussed in the following sections.

Solaris Interactive Installation

The Solaris Interactive Installation program, `suninstall`, guides you step by step through installing the Solaris software. You'll be allowed to do a complete installation/reinstallation, perform an upgrade, or install a Solaris Flash archive. I like to refer to this installation as the conventional interactive installation. If you've installed previous versions of Solaris, this is the original interactive installation. With this installation, you need to know more about Solaris and other software products before installing them. The Interactive program does not allow you to install all of the software (Solaris software and copackaged software) at once; it installs only the SunOS software. After you install the Solaris software, you must install the other copackaged software by using the copackaged installation programs.

If your system does not have a directly attached CD-ROM or DVD-ROM drive, you can specify a drive that is attached to another system. The only requirement is that both systems must be attached to the same subnet.

JumpStart

JumpStart provides the capability to install Solaris on a new system by inserting the CD-ROM into the CD-ROM drive and turning on power to the system. No interaction is required. The software components installed are specified by a default profile that is selected based on the model and disk size of the system.

All new SPARC-based systems have the JumpStart software (a preinstalled boot image) preinstalled on the boot disk. You can install the JumpStart software on existing systems by using the `re-preinstall` command.

Custom JumpStart

The Custom JumpStart method, formerly called autoinstall, allows you to automatically—and identically—install many systems with the same configuration without having to configure each of them individually. Custom JumpStart requires upfront setup of configuration files before the systems can be installed, but it's the most cost effective way to automatically install

Solaris software for a large installation. Custom JumpStart provides the best solution for performing hands-off installation across the network.

NOTE

JumpStart Configuration on New Systems On a new system, the installation software is specified by a default profile based on the system's model and the size of its disks; you don't have a choice of the software to be installed. Make sure this JumpStart configuration is suited to your environment. The system loads the end-user distribution group and sets up minimal swap space. Slices and their sizes are set up by using default parameters that might not be suitable for the applications you plan to install.

When might you want to use JumpStart? For example, suppose you need to install the Solaris software on 50 systems. Of these 50 systems to be installed, 25 are in engineering as standalone systems with the entire distribution software group, and 25 are in the IT group with the developer distribution software group. JumpStart enables you to set up a configuration file for each department and install the operating system on all the systems. This process facilitates the installation by automating it, ensuring consistency between systems and saving you time and effort.

EXAM ALERT

JumpStart Exam Objective Custom JumpStart is an objective on the CX-310-202 exam and is described in detail in Chapter 13, "Solaris Zones." However, there are a couple of basic questions about Custom JumpStart on the CX-310-200 exam which you need to know, such as

- Why would you use JumpStart over another type of installation such as Web Start Flash or interactive?
- Which installation method is designed to allow hands off installation across the network?

Solaris Flash Archives

The Solaris Flash Archive installation enables you to use a single reference installation (Flash Archive) of the Solaris OE on a system, which is called the *master system*. After installing the operating system onto the master system, you can add or delete software and modify system configuration information as necessary. You then create a flash archive from this master system and can use this archive to replicate that installation on a number of systems, which are called clone machines. Then, you can replicate that installation on a number of systems, which are called clone systems.

You can also replicate (clone) systems with a Solaris Flash initial installation that overwrites all files on the system or with a Solaris Flash update that only includes the differences between two system images. A differential update changes only the files that are specified and is restricted to systems that contain software consistent with the old master image.

You may also be wondering what makes Web Start Flash different from custom JumpStart.

When you use any of the Solaris installation methods and you do not select to install a Solaris Flash archive, the installation method installs each Solaris package individually. The package-based installation method is time consuming because the installation method must extract each individual package from the installation media and then update the package map for each package. A Flash archive installs Solaris onto your system much faster because it is simply copying an image onto your drive and does not install the operating system package by package.

If you have many different Solaris configurations that you want to install on your systems, you need a Solaris Flash archive for each configuration. Solaris Flash archives are large files and require a significant amount of disk space. Also, after you create a Solaris Flash archive, you cannot change the archive. If you have many different installation configurations or if you want the flexibility to change your installation configuration, you might consider using the custom JumpStart installation method.

Custom JumpStart employs a command-line installation method that enables you to automatically install or upgrade several systems, based on profiles that you create. Custom Jumpstart can be configured to install Solaris from a Solaris Flash archive. The JumpStart configuration files define specific software installation requirements. You can also incorporate shell scripts to include preinstallation and postinstallation tasks. This is not a capability within the Solaris Flash archive.

If you have multiple systems to install, the custom JumpStart installation method might be the most efficient way for you to install your systems. However, if you plan to install only a few systems, the custom JumpStart installation method is less efficient. This is because the creation of a custom JumpStart environment and its associated configuration files is very time consuming.

WAN Boot

The WAN boot installation method enables you to boot and install software over a wide area network (WAN) by using HTTP. Utilizing the WAN boot method of installation, you can install the Solaris OS on SPARC-based systems over a wide area network. WAN boot can be used with security features to protect data confidentiality and installation image integrity.

The WAN boot installation method enables you to transmit an encrypted Solaris Flash archive over a WAN to a remote SPARC-based client. The WAN boot programs then install the client system by performing a custom JumpStart installation.

WAN boot is an advanced installation method and is covered in Chapter 13.

Solaris Live Upgrade

Solaris Live Upgrade allows you to create a copy of the current operating environment and upgrade the copy while the system is running in the original environment. Solaris Live Upgrade utilizes Solaris Volume Manager (SVM) to create a mirror of the OS (SVM is covered in chapter 10). Once complete, you'll reboot to the upgraded version of the OS. If problems are encountered with the upgrade, you can boot back to the previous version, significantly reducing any downtime. For example, let's say that you are upgrading the OS using the Upgrade option in the interactive installation. If the power failed halfway through the upgrade and the system was powered off, your operating system would be incomplete and you would be unable to boot. Using Live Upgrade, because you're upgrading a copy of the OS, you simply boot to the original version of the OS and start over.

To perform a live upgrade, the SUNWlur and SUNWluu software packages must be installed. The packages are installed with the entire distribution software group in Solaris 10; however, the system you are upgrading is probably running an older version of the OS, therefore, you'll need to install the Solaris 10 Live Upgrade packages on your current OS. The release of the Solaris Live Upgrade packages must match the release of the OS you are upgrading to. For example, if your current OS is the Solaris 8 release and you want to upgrade to the Solaris 10 release, you need to install the Solaris Live Upgrade packages from the Solaris 10 release. Solaris versions 7, 8, 9, or 10 can be upgraded to the most recent version of Solaris 10 using Live Upgrade.

EXAM ALERT

Performing a live upgrade is beyond the scope of this chapter and is not covered in detail on the exam. For the exam, you'll need to describe a Solaris Live Upgrade and understand how it differs from the other installation methods, including a Solaris Interactive upgrade.

Upgrading the Operating System

An operating system upgrade merges the new version of the Solaris operating environment with the existing files on the system's disk. An upgrade saves as many modifications that you have made to the previous version of the Solaris operating environment as possible.

NOTE

Backups Make sure that you back up your entire system and check the backup before performing an upgrade.

You can upgrade any system that is running the Solaris 7, 8, or 9 software. You can also update the Solaris 10 Update release if your system is running an older version of the Solaris 10 software. In this chapter, I will be describing how to perform an initial installation and will not be performing an upgrade. You'll see, however, in the later section "Using the Interactive Installation Process (`suninstall`)," that after the system identification portion of the installation process is complete, `suninstall` will ask you if you want to perform an upgrade.

You cannot upgrade your system to a software group that is not installed on the system. For example, if you previously installed the end-user Solaris software group on your system, you cannot use the upgrade option to upgrade to the developer Solaris Software group. However, during the upgrade, you can add software to the system that is not part of the currently installed software group.

If you are already running the Solaris 10 operating environment and have installed individual patches, be aware of the following when upgrading to a Solaris 10 Update release:

- Any patches that were supplied as part of the Solaris 10 Update release are reapplied to your system. You cannot back out these patches.
- Any patches that were previously installed on your system and are not included in the Solaris 10 Update release are removed.

The Solaris Installation PrecheckList

Before you begin installing the operating system, it's important to make sure you have everything you'll need. Adequate planning and preparation will save you time and trouble later. If the system is currently running a version of Solaris, make a full backup of all file systems before reloading the operating system. Even if the file systems are on separate disks than the operating system, make sure you have backups in place. As the saying goes, "better safe than sorry." I recommend completing the installation worksheet in Table 2.2 so that all of the information you'll need is handy during the installation.

TABLE 2.2 Installation Worksheet

Item or Option	Issue	Status
Network	Is the system connected to a network?	Yes/No
Hostname	The name for the system. Hostnames should be short, easy to spell, and lowercase, and they should have no more than 64 characters. If the system is on a network, the hostname should be unique.	
DHCP	Will the system use the Dynamic Host Configuration Protocol (DHCP) to configure its network interface?	Yes/No

(continues)

TABLE 2.2 *Continued*

Item or Option	Issue	Status
IP address	If not using DHCP, supply the static IP address for the system. This information must come from your site IP coordinator. `192.9.200.1` is one example of an IP address. IP addresses must be unique for every system on your network. For a large site or a site that has a presence on the Internet, you should apply for a unique IP address from the NIC to ensure that no other network node shares your address.	
Subnet	If not using DHCP, is the system part of a subnet? If using a subnet, make sure you also get the subnet mask used at your site. On an existing system, this information can be obtained from the `/etc/netmasks` file.	Yes/No
IPv6	You'll be asked if support for IPv6, the next generation Internet protocol, should be installed.	Yes/No
Kerberos	Do you want to configure Kerberos security on this system? Kerberos provides selectable, strong, user- or server-level authentication based on symmetric key cryptography. Ask your in-house security personnel if Kerberos security is required. If yes, gather the following: Default realm: Administration server: First KDC: Additional KDCs:	Yes/No
Name service	NIS, NIS+, DNS, LDAP, or NONE. You'll need to specify which name service your system will be using (or NONE if you're not using one). On a running system, you can check which name service is being used by examining the `/etc/nsswitch.conf` file.	
Domain name	If the system uses a name service, supply the name of the domain in which the system resides. On a running system, this information can be obtained using the `/usr/bin/domainname` command.	
Default router	Do you want to specify a default IP router (gateway) or let the Solaris Web Start installation program find one? If you want to specify a default route, provide the following information. Router IP address:	
Time zone	You'll need to specify the geographic region and time zone in which this system will be operated. Geographic region: Offset from GMT: Time zone file:	
Power management	Do you want to use power management? (Only available on SPARC systems that support power management)	Yes/No

TABLE 2.2 *Continued*

Item or Option	Issue	Status
Proxy server configuration	Do you have a direct connection to the Internet, or do you need to use a proxy server to gain access to the Internet? If you use a proxy server, provide the following: Host: Port:	
Locales	For which geographic regions do you want to install support?	
Software group	Which Solaris Software group do you want to install? (Reduced Networking Support, Entire Plus OEM, Entire, Developer, End User, or Core)	
Custom package selection	Do you want to add or remove software packages from the Solaris software group that you install?	
Select disks	On which disk(s) do you want to install the Solaris software? (for example, `c0t0d0`)	
Preserve data	Do you want to preserve data on any of the disk partitions? (Only available when using `suninstall`)	Yes/No
Autolayout file systems	Do you want the installation program to automatically lay out file systems on your disks? If yes, which file systems should be used for autolayout? If no, you'll need to provide file system configuration information and you should have the layout of your disk slices prepared in advance.	Yes/No
Mount remote file systems	Does this system need to access software on another file system? If yes, provide the following information about the remote file system: Server: IP address: Remote file system: Local mount point: (Only available when using `suninstall`)	Yes/No
Root password	During the installation, you will be asked to assign a password to the root user account.	
Language	Determine the language to be used to install the Solaris 10 operating environment.	

You can use the `sysidcfg` file to preconfigure this information for a system. You must create a unique `sysidcfg` file for every system that requires different configuration information. You can use the same `sysidcfg` file to preconfigure parameters that are common between systems such as time zone, domain name, and so on. You'll need a system specific `sysidcfg` file to specify parameters that are unique to each system, such as IP address, hostname, and root password. The `sysidcfg` file is covered in detail in Chapter 13.

Next, verify that you have enough disk space for Solaris 10 and all the co-packaged and third-party software you plan to add. (Refer to the section "Software Groups" earlier in this chapter.) Normally, a server would have several gigabytes (GB) of disk space available for the operating system, so you'll be installing the full distribution software group. Also, you need to check with your software vendor regarding space requirements for any third-party software packages as well as swap space requirements.

Using the Interactive Installation Process (`suninstall`)

After gathering the information for the installation worksheet, you are ready to begin the installation process. The following steps outline the process for installing Solaris 10 on a Sun SPARC system using the `suninstall` interactive installation method. With the conventional interactive installation, Solaris is installed by using the Solaris install tool, `suninstall`, a friendly and easy-to-use interface that will carry out a dialog for installing the operating system. The dialog will ask you several questions about the installation. This section provides an overview of the installation process using the conventional interactive installation program, `suninstall`.

`suninstall` brings up various menus and asks for your input. For this example, I'll be using a character-based terminal. Those of you using a bitmapped display will see the same dialog, but it will be graphical. You'll be able to use your mouse to click on your selections. The `suninstall` interface allows you to go back to previous screens if you make a mistake, and it doesn't actually do anything to your system until the installation program reaches the end and tells you it is about to start the loading process. During the installation, help is always available via the Help button.

CAUTION

Reinstalling the OS Destroys Data The following procedure reinstalls your operating system. That means it destroys all data on the target file systems.

If you're upgrading or installing Solaris on a running system, use the steps in Step by Step 2.1 to shut down and then perform the installation.

STEP BY STEP

2.1 Shutting Down and Installing on a Running System

1. Become root.
2. Issue the `shutdown` command. This command, described in chapter 3, brings the system to a single-user state by halting the window system and leaving you with a single root prompt on the console. It takes about a minute.

3. Issue the `halt` command. This command puts you into the PROM. You'll know you're in the PROM when you receive either an `ok` or a > prompt.
4. Put the Solaris 10 CD-ROM 1 into the CD-ROM player and boot from the CD-ROM. If your system has a DVD-ROM, place the Solaris 10 DVD into the drive and boot from the DVD. For this example, I'll be installing from CD-ROM media.
5. At the `ok` prompt, type **`boot cdrom`**.

   This command will start the default GUI installation on a bit-mapped console if your system has at least 384MB of RAM installed. If your system has less than 384MB of ram, enter **`boot cdrom - nowin`** for the CLI (command line interface) version of the installation program. If the console does not support graphics, you'll automatically be put into the CLI version of the installation.

For x86 and x64 systems only

If you are installing Solaris onto an x86- or x64-based system, you will not have the `ok` prompt, so you'll need to follow these steps:

a. Place the CD (or DVD) into the CD-ROM drive and boot to the CD. Your system's BIOS must be configured to boot from the CD-ROM.

b. You'll be presented with a hardware configuration screen where you'll have the option of modifying device settings or continuing. You must press the ESC key within five seconds to interrupt the installation and modify device settings; otherwise the installation will continue.

c. Select an install type. For the example, select Solaris Interactive.

d. On the Solaris Installation Program screen, press F2_Continue. If the installation program detects the type of keyboard, display, and mouse on your system, the Select a Language screen is displayed. If the installation program does not detect the type of keyboard, display, and mouse on your system, the `kdmconfig` - Introduction screen is displayed.

The `kdmconfig` utility detects the drivers that are necessary to configure the keyboard, display, and mouse on your system. The `kdmconfig` utility displays the results of this search in the `kdmconfig` - View and Edit Window System Configuration screen.

If the `kdmconfig` utility cannot detect the video driver for your system, the `kdmconfig` utility selects the 640x480 VGA driver. The Solaris installation GUI cannot be displayed with the 640x480 VGA driver. As a result, the Solaris installation text installer is displayed. To use the Solaris installation GUI, use the `kdmconfig` utility to select the correct video driver for your system.

a. When you are finished, select No changes needed - Test/Save and Exit and press F2_Continue. The `kdmconfig` Window System Configuration Test screen appears. Press F2_Continue.

b. The screen refreshes and the `kdmconfig` Window System Configuration Test palette and pattern screen appears.

Move the pointer and examine the colors that are shown on the palette to ensure that they are displayed accurately.

(continues)

(continued)

If the colors are not displayed accurately, click No. If possible, press any key on the keyboard, or wait until `kdmconfig` exits the `kdmconfig` Window System Configuration Test screen automatically.

If the colors are displayed accurately, your graphic controller card is configured correctly. Click `Yes` and after a few seconds, the Select a Language screen is displayed as shown, and the installation will begin.

NOTE

You can enter the installation program and complete all of the selections, but no changes will be made to the disk until you click the Begin Installation button at the end of the installation process.

The system starts from the CD-ROM, the installation program is loaded into memory, and it begins configuring devices. Ignore any messages such as cables not connected or network interfaces that fail to respond. After a few minutes, you'll enter the system identification section of the installation. The installation program will open a dialog, asking you various questions about your locale and language as follows:

```
Select a Language
   0. English
   1. French
   2. German
   3. Italian
   4. Japanese
   5. Korean
   6. Simplified Chinese
   7. Spanish
   8. Swedish
   9. Traditional Chinese

Please make a choice (0 - 9), or press h or ? for help:
```

6. Select a language by entering the corresponding number and press Enter. In the example, I selected 0 for English. The system responded with the following menu querying your terminal type:

```
What type of terminal are you using?
 1) ANSI Standard CRT
 2) DEC VT52
 3) DEC VT100
 4) Heathkit 19
 5) Lear Siegler ADM31
 6) PC Console
 7) Sun Command Tool
 8) Sun Workstation
 9) Televideo 910
```

```
 10) Televideo 925
 11) Wyse Model 50
 12) X Terminal Emulator (xterms)
 13) Other
Type the number of your choice and press Return:
```

This menu only comes up when you're using a character-based screen. You will not see this menu if you're using a bitmapped display.

7. For this example, I selected item 3 and pressed the Return key. The following menu displays next:

```
--The Solaris Installation Program--

The Solaris installation program is divided into a series of \
short sections where you'll be prompted to provide information \
for the installation. At the end of each section, you'll be able\
 to change the selections you've made before continuing.

  About navigation...
        - The mouse cannot be used
        - If your keyboard does not have function keys, or they do not
          respond, press ESC; the legend at the bottom of the screen
          will change to show the ESC keys to use for navigation.
```

Again, this menu of options will only be displayed when using a character-based screen. On a bitmapped display, you will not see this menu.

8. I pressed the F2 key to continue. The following menu displays next:

```
----Identify This System ----

On the next screens, you must identify this system as networked or \
non-networked, and set the default time zone and date/time.

If this system is networked, the software will try to find the \
information it needs to identify your system; you will be prompted \
to supply any information it cannot find.

  > To begin identifying this system, press F2.
```

9. Press the F2 key to continue. The following menu will be displayed:

```
---Network Connectivity----

Specify Yes if the system is connected to the network by one of \
the Solaris or vendor network/communication Ethernet cards that \
are supported on the Solaris CD. See your hardware documentation \
for the current list of supported cards.
Specify No if the system is connected to a network/communication card that is not \
supported on the Solaris CD, and follow the instructions listed under Help.
```

```
Networked
      [X] Yes
      [ ] No

F2_Continue    F6_Help
```

If the system is connected to a Sun-supported network/communication card, select `Yes`. If the system is connected to a network card that is not supported on the Solaris CD-ROM, select `No` and complete the installation of Solaris software as follows:

a. Install the unbundled network/communication card.

b. As root, run the `/usr/sbin/sys-unconfig` program to return the system to its "as-manufactured" state. This command is entered with no options and simply unconfigures your system's hostname, network information, service domain name, time zone, IP address, subnet mask, and root password. When `sys-unconfig` is finished, it performs a system shutdown.

c. Attach the network adapter to the system.

d. At the `ok` prompt, type **`boot -r`**.

e. Provide network information as prompted on the screen, and the network will now be aware of the system.

f. After making your selection, press the F2 key to continue. The following menu will be displayed:

```
Primary Network Interface

On this screen you must specify which of the following network \
adapters is the system's primary network interface.  \
Usually the correct choice is the lowest number.  \
However, do not guess; ask your system administrator \
if you're not sure.

> To make a selection, use the arrow keys to highlight the \
option and press Return to mark it [X].

Primary network interface

[X] hme0
[ ] qfe0
[ ] qfe1
[ ] qfe2
[ ] qfe3
F2_Continue    F6_Help
```

Specify the primary network interface for your system. This information is requested if the software detects multiple Ethernet cards or network adapter cards on your system. This screen will be displayed if you're installing a gateway from a CD-ROM; on this system, I have the primary network adapter and four additional network adapters installed.

In most cases, the correct choice is to select the lowest-numbered interface. However, if you don't know, ask your system or network administrator.

CAUTION

Specify the Correct Network Interface If you specify the incorrect primary network interface, your system might not be able to find a name service.

In this example, I selected `hme0` as the interface and pressed F2 to continue and the following menu was displayed:

```
---DHCP ----

On this screen you must specify whether or not this system \
should use DHCP for network interface configuration.  \
Choose Yes if DHCP is to be used, or No if the interfaces \
are to be configured manually.

NOTE: DHCP support will not be enabled, if selected, until \
after the system reboots.

Use DHCP
[ ] Yes
[X] No

F2_Continue    F6_Help
```

10. For more information on DHCP, see Chapter 12, "Naming Services." For this example, I selected `No` and pressed F2 to continue. The following menu displays next:

```
---Host Name ----

Enter the host name which identifies this system on the network. \
The name must be unique within your domain; creating a duplicate \
host name will cause problems on the network after you install Solaris. \

A host name must be at least two characters; it can contain \
letters, digits, and minus signs (-).

Host name:___ultra5___________

F2_Continue    F6_Help
```

11. Enter a unique hostname. In this example, I entered `ultra5` for the hostname and pressed F2 to continue. The following menu displays next:

```
---IP Address----
```

```
Enter the Internet Protocol (IP) address for this network interface. \
It must be unique and follow your site's address conventions, or a \
system/network failure could result.

IP addresses contain four sets of numbers separated by periods \
(for example 129.200.9.1).

IP address: 192.168.0.125

F2_Continue    F6_Help
```

12. This menu displays if you did not select DHCP earlier in the process. Internet addresses are usually assigned by network or system administrators according to local and Internetwork policies. Because creating duplicate IP addresses can cause network problems, do not guess or make up a number; check with your system or network administrator for help. See Chapter 8, "The Solaris Network Environment," for more information on IP addresses. For this example, I set the IP address to `192.168.1.198` and pressed F2 to continue. The following menu displays next:

```
---Subnets ---

On this screen you must specify whether this system is \
part of a subnet.  If you specify incorrectly, the system \
will have problems communicating on the network after you reboot.

> To make a selection, use the arrow keys to highlight \
the option and press Return to mark it [X].

System part of a subnet
[ ] Yes
[X] No

F2_Continue    F6_Help
```

13. Specify whether your system is on a network that has subnets. If the network to which your system is connected is divided into subnets (usually using routers or gateways), answer Yes. If you do not know if your network has subnets, do not guess; check with your system administrator for help. For this example, my system was not part of a subnet, so I selected `No` and pressed F2 to continue. The following menu displays next:

```
---IPv6---

Specify whether or not you want to enable IPv6, the next generation Internet \
  Protocol, on this network interface.  Enabling IPv6 will have no effect if \
  this machine is not on a network that provides IPv6 service.  IPv4 service \
  will not be affected if IPv6 is enabled.

    To make a selection, use the arrow keys to highlight \
    the option and press Return to mark it [X].
```

```
Enable IPv6
 [ ] Yes
 [X] No

F2_Continue    F6_Help
```

14. Specify whether this system will use IPv6, the next generation Internet protocol described in Chapter 8. This system will not use IPv6, so I selected No and pressed F2 to continue. The following menu displays next:

```
---Default Route---

To specify the default route, you can let the software try to detect one
upon reboot, you can specify the IP address of the router, or you can choose
None.  Choose None if you do not have a router on your subnet.

    To make a selection, use the arrow keys to highlight \
    your choice and press Return to mark it [X].

Default Route for hme0
[X] Detect one upon reboot
[ ] Specify one
[ ] None

F2_Continue    F6_Help
```

15. Specify whether a default route is needed and, if so, specify an IP address to the router (gateway) in the network. The router is used to forward all network traffic that is not addressed to the local subnet. See Chapter 8, for more information. If you know the address of your default router, select Specify One. If not, you can select Find One, and the system will try to locate the default router. In this example, I selected Find One and pressed F2. The following summary menu displays next:

```
---Confirm Information for hme0 ---
> Confirm the following information.  If it is correct, press F2;
    to change any information, press F4.


                  Networked: Yes
                   Use DHCP: No
                  Host name: ultra5
                 IP address: 192.168.1.198
    System part of a subnet: No
                Enable IPv6: No
              Default Route: Detect one upon reboot
```

16. Confirm the settings by pressing F2 and the next menu is displayed:

```
Configure Security Policy:
```

```
Specify Yes if the system will use the Kerberos security \
mechanism. Specify No if this system will use standard UNIX \
security.

Configure Kerberos Security
 [ ] Yes
 [X] No

F2_Continue    F6_Help
```

This specifies the type of security policy being implemented on this system. If no special security policy is desired, select No and normal Unix security will be implemented.

> **NOTE**
>
> **Kerberos Security** Using Kerberos requires coordination with your network administrator. You will need to know certain information, such as the fully qualified domain name of one or more KDCs. If you do not have this information or don't know what this is, you can add it later to the /etc/krb5/krb5.conf file.

17. On this system, I will be using normal Unix security, so I selected No and pressed F2. The following confirmation menu displays next:

```
Confirm Information

> Confirm the following information.  If it is correct, \
press F2; to change any information, press F4.

Configure Kerberos Security: No

F2_Continue    F4_Change    F6_Help
```

18. If everything looks okay, press F2 to continue. The following menu displays next:

```
Name Service

On this screen you must provide name service information. \
Select the name service that will be used by this system, \
or None if your system will either not use a name service \
at all, or if it will use a name service not listed here.

> To make a selection, use the arrow keys to highlight \
the option and press Return to mark it [X].

Name service

[ ] NIS+
[ ] NIS
```

```
[ ] DNS
[ ] LDAP
[X] None

F2_Continue    F6_Help
```

Specify the name service you will be using. Refer to Chapter 12, for more information.

19. This system will not be using a name service, only local `/etc` files, so I selected `None` and pressed F2 to continue. The following confirmation menu displays next:

```
Confirm Information

> Confirm the following information.  If it is correct, \
press F2; to change any information, press F4.

Name service: None

F2_Continue    F4_Change    F6_Help
```

20. If everything looks okay, press F2 to continue. The following menu displays next:

```
Subnets

On this screen you must specify whether this system is \
part of a subnet.  If you specify incorrectly, the system \
will have problems communicating on the network after you reboot.

> To make a selection, use the arrow keys to highlight \
the option and press Return to mark it [X].

System part of a subnet
[ ] Yes
[X] No

F2_Continue    F6_Help
```

21. This question was asked earlier, and it's asked again. If your system is part of a subnet, answer `Yes`. For this example, the system is not part of a subnet, so I answered `No` and pressed F2 to continue. The following menu displays next:

```
Time Zone

On this screen you must specify your default time zone.  \
You can specify a time zone in three ways:  select one of \
the geographic regions from the list, select other - offset \
from GMT, or other - specify time zone file.

> To make a selection, use the arrow keys to highlight \
the option and press Return to mark it [X].
```

```
Continents and Oceans
  -  [ ] Africa
     [X] Americas
     [ ] Antarctica
     [ ] Arctic Ocean
     [ ] Asia
     [ ] Atlantic Ocean
     [ ] Australia
     [ ] Europe
     [ ] Indian Ocean

F2_Continue    F6_Help
```

22. The next two menus will ask you to provide information about your default time zone. First select your region and press F2 to continue. A subsequent menu will appear, asking for specifics about that particular region, as follows:

```
Time Zone

> To make a selection, use the arrow keys to highlight \
the option and press Return to mark it [X].

Countries and Regions
  -   [X] United States
      [ ] Anguilla
      [ ] Antigua & Barbuda
      [ ] Argentina
      [ ] Aruba
      [ ] Bahamas
      [ ] Barbados
      [ ] Belize
      [ ] Bolivia
      [ ] Brazil
      [ ] Canada
      [ ] Cayman Islands
      [ ] Chile
F2_Continue    F5_Cancel    F6_Help
```

23. Continue to make your selection on subsequent menus to specify your time zone and press F2 to continue. The following menu will appear, asking you to verify the date and time:

```
Date and Time

  > Accept the default date and time or enter new values.

Date and time: 2005-08-08 15:42

    Year   (4 digits) : 2005
    Month  (1-12)     : 08
```

```
    Day    (1-31)      : 08
    Hour   (0-23)      : 15
    Minute (0-59)      : 42

F2_Continue    F6_Help
```

24. Modify the time as required and press F2 to continue. The following confirmation screen will display:

```
Confirm Information

  > Confirm the following information.  If it is correct, \
press F2; to change any information, press F4.

System part of a subnet: No
       Time zone: United States / Michigan
                  (US/Michigan)
   Date and time: 2005-08-08 15:42:00

F2_Continue    F4_Change    F6_Help
```

25. If everything is correct, press F2 to continue and the following menu will open asking you to set the root password:

```
--Root Password ------------

  Please enter the root password for this system.

  The root password may contain alphanumeric and special characters.  For
  security, the password will not be displayed on the screen as you type it.

  > If you do not want a root password, leave both entries blank.


    Root password: ****
    Root password: ****
```

26. Set the root password by entering it twice and press F2 to continue.

27. The system identification portion of the installation is complete. Following the system identification portion of the installation, you'll see the following dialog displayed:

```
---Solaris Interactive Installation ---------------

  On the following screens, you can accept the defaults or you can customize
  how Solaris software will be installed by:

        - Selecting the type of Solaris software to install
        - Selecting disks to hold software you've selected
        - Selecting unbundled products to be installed with Solaris
        - Specifying how file systems are laid out on the disks
```

```
    After completing these tasks, a summary of your selections (called a
    profile) will be displayed.

    There are two ways to install your Solaris software:

     - "Standard" installs your system from a standard Solaris Distribution.
       Selecting "Standard" allows you to choose between initial install
       and upgrade, if your system is upgradable.
  "Flash" installs your system from one or more Flash Archives.
  F2_Standard    F4_Flash     F5_Exit    F6_Help
```

CAUTION

The Initial Option Destroys Data All data on the operating system slices will be lost. These slices include / (root), /usr, /opt, and /var.

28. The upgrade option is available if you are currently running Solaris 7, 8, or 9 and you want to upgrade to Solaris 10. As described earlier in this chapter, the upgrade option preserves all customizations you made in the previous version of Solaris. For this example, I pressed F4 to select the Initial option, which is a complete reinstallation of the software, and the following menu was displayed:

```
--- Eject a CD/DVD Automatically?-----------------------------

    During the installation of Solaris software, you may be using one or more
    CDs/DVDs. You can choose to have the system eject each CD/DVD automatically
    after it is installed or you can choose to manually eject each CD/DVD.


              [X] Automatically eject CD/DVD
              [ ] Manually eject CD/DVD


       F2_Continue    F3_Go Back    F5_Exit
```

29. I selected the option to have the CD automatically ejected when complete. After pressing F2 to continue, you'll be asked about rebooting after the installation completes as shown in the following menu:

```
--- Reboot After Installation? ---------------------------------

    After Solaris software is installed, the system must be rebooted. You can
    choose to have the system automatically reboot, or you can choose to
    manually reboot the system if you want to run scripts or do other
    customizations before the reboot.  You can manually reboot a system by using
    the reboot(1M) command.
```

```
        [X] Auto Reboot
        [ ] Manual Reboot


    F2_Continue    F3_Go Back    F5_Exit
```

30. I selected Auto Reboot and pressed F2 to continue. You'll get a message that the system is initializing and loading the install media. The system will hesitate for approximately 60 seconds as the media is being loaded from the CD followed by a license agreement as shown below:

```
--License ---------------------------------

Sun Microsystems, Inc. ("Sun")
SOFTWARE LICENSE AGREEMENT

READ THE TERMS OF THIS AGREEMENT ("AGREEMENT") CAREFULLY BEFORE
OPENING SOFTWARE MEDIA PACKAGE. BY OPENING SOFTWARE MEDIA
PACKAGE, YOU AGREE TO THE TERMS OF THIS AGREEMENT. IF YOU ARE
ACCESSING SOFTWARE ELECTRONICALLY, INDICATE YOUR ACCEPTANCE OF
THESE TERMS BY SELECTING THE "ACCEPT"(OR EQUIVALENT) BUTTON AT
THE END OF THIS AGREEMENT. IF YOU DO NOT AGREE TO ALL OF THE
TERMS, PROMPTLY RETURN THE UNUSED SOFTWARE TO YOUR PLACE OF
PURCHASE FOR A REFUND OR, IF SOFTWARE IS ACCESSED ELECTRONICALLY,
SELECT THE "DECLINE" (OR EQUIVALENT) BUTTON AT THE END OF THIS
AGREEMENT. IF YOU HAVE SEPARATELY AGREED TO LICENSE TERMS
 ("MASTER TERMS") FOR YOUR LICENSE TO THIS SOFTWARE, THEN SECTIONS
1-6 OF THIS AGREEMENT ("SUPPLEMENTAL LICENSE TERMS") SHALL
SUPPLEMENT AND SUPERSEDE THE MASTER TERMS IN RELATION TO THIS
SOFTWARE.

1. Definitions.

     F2_Accept License    F5_Exit
```

31. Read the Licensing terms and if you agree, press F2 to accept the agreement. The next menu that is displayed will ask you to select the geographic regions for which support will be installed as follows:

```
-- Select Geographic Regions ------------------------

  Select the geographic regions for which support should be installed.

  > [ ] Asia
  > [ ] Northern Africa
  > [ ] Middle East
  > [ ] South America
  > [ ] Central America
  > [ ] Australasia
  > [ ] Southern Europe
  > [ ] Northern Europe
```

```
> [ ] Eastern Europe
> [ ] Central Europe
> [ ] North America
> [ ] Western Europe
```

32. A selection is optional. Select a region or leave it unselected and press F2. I did not select a region, I pressed F2 and the following menu was displayed:

```
--- Select System Locale -------------------------

  Select the initial locale to be used after the system has been installed.

    [X]     POSIX C ( C )


     F2_Continue    F3_Go Back    F5_Exit    F6_Help
```

33. Leaving the default selection of POSIX C as my locale, I pressed F2 to continue and the following screen is displayed:

```
--Solaris Interactive Installation ------

On the following screens, you can accept the defaults or you can customize
  how Solaris software will be installed by:

        - Selecting the type of Solaris software to install
        - Selecting disks to hold software you've selected
        - Selecting unbundled products to be installed with Solaris
        - Specifying how file systems are laid out on the disks

  After completing these tasks, a summary of your selections (called a
  profile) will be displayed.

  There are two ways to install your Solaris software:

   - "Standard" installs your system from a standard Solaris Distribution.
     Selecting "Standard" allows you to choose between initial install
     and upgrade, if your system is upgradable.
   - "Flash" installs your system from one or more Flash Archives.

     F2_Standard    F3_Go Back    F4_Flash    F5_Exit    F6_Help
```

34. Press F2 to continue and the following software installation menu appears asking you to select additional products to install. These are Extra products and applications that can be installed from the Installation CD or DVD after the OS installation is complete.

```
---Select Products ----------------------------------

  Select the products you would like to install.
```

```
> [ ] Solaris 10 Extra Value Software.................    0.00 MB
> [ ] Solaris 10 Documentation........................    0.00 MB
> [ ] Java Enterprise System..........................    0.00 MB
> [ ] Solaris Software Companion CD...................    0.00 MB


 Move left, right, up, down using the arrow keys

 F2_Continue    F3_Go Back    F4_Product Info    F5_Exit    F6_Help
```

35. For the example, I did not select any additional software products to install. Select F2 to continue and the next window asks if there are any applications from other sources to install as follows:

```
---Additional Products -----------------------------------

  To scan for additional products, select the location you wish to scan.
  Products found at the selected location that are in a Web Start Ready
  install form will be added to the Products list.

  Web Start Ready product scan location:

      [X]  None
      [ ]  CD/DVD
      [ ]  Network File System



    F2_Continue    F3_Go Back    F5_Exit
```

36. For the example, I have no other application to install so I selected none and pressed F2 to continue. The next window asks me to select the software group that I would like installed:

```
--- Select Software ----------------------------------

  Select the Solaris software to install on the system.

  NOTE: After selecting a software group, you can add or remove software by
  customizing it. However, this requires understanding of software
  dependencies and how Solaris software is packaged.

      [ ]  Entire Distribution plus OEM support ....... 4779.00 MB
      [X]  Entire Distribution ........................ 4737.00 MB
      [ ]  Developer System Support ................... 4602.00 MB
      [ ]  End User System Support .................... 3555.00 MB
      [ ]  Core System Support ........................  777.00 MB
      [ ]  Reduced Networking Core System Support .....  736.00 MB


    F2_Continue    F3_Go Back    F4_Customize    F5_Exit    F6_Help
```

> **NOTE**
>
> **Default Software Group** The Entire Distribution software group is selected by default. After you select the software group you want to install, if you press F4, you will see an interactive menu that allows you to select and deselect software packages within a particular software group.

37. Unless you don't have enough disk space, I recommend selecting the Entire Distribution so that the entire Solaris OE gets installed. After making your selection, press F2 to continue, and Select Disks menu will appear as follows:

```
---Select Disks ---------------------------

  On this screen you must select the disks for installing Solaris software.
  Start by looking at the Suggested Minimum field; this value is the
  approximate space needed to install the software you've selected. Keep
  selecting disks until the Total Selected value exceeds the Suggested Minimum
  value.
  NOTE: ** denotes current boot disk

  Disk Device                                          Available Space
  ==============================================================
  [ ]    c0t0d0                                               78528 MB

                                          Total Selected:       0 MB
                                       Suggested Minimum:    3591 MB

     F2_Continue     F3_Go Back     F4_Edit     F5_Exit     F6_Help
```

38. Select the disk on which to install the operating system. This disk becomes your boot disk. Press the F2 key after making your selection and the Preserve Data menu will appear as follows:

```
--- Preserve Data? ---------------------------

  Do you want to preserve existing data? At least one of the disks you've
  selected for installing Solaris software has file systems or unnamed slices
  that you may want to save.


     F2_Continue     F3_Go Back     F4_Preserve     F5_Exit     F6_Help
```

39. If you wish to preserve data on any of your partitions, press F4. I backed up my data before starting the installation, so I had no data to preserve. I was completely reinstalling the OS and building new disk slices, so I pressed F2 to continue and all file systems were erased. This provides the most flexibility for laying out a new partition scheme on this disk. After pressing F2, the following menu is displayed:

```
---Automatically Layout File Systems? ------------------------------
```

```
Do you want to use auto-layout to automatically layout file systems?
Manually laying out file systems requires advanced system administration
skills.



    F2_Auto Layout    F3_Go Back    F4_Manual Layout    F5_Exit    F6_Help
```

40. Press F2. The system automatically lays out the file systems. Sizes are determined by the software packages you selected. If you plan to add additional software, you can modify the file system sizes in later steps. You'll next see the following dialog:

```
Automatically Layout File Systems

On this screen you must select all the file systems you want \
auto-layout to create, or accept the default file systems shown.

NOTE: For small disks, it may be necessary for auto-layout to \
break up some of the file systems you request into smaller file \
systems to fit the available disk space. So, after auto-layout \
completes, you may find file systems in the layout that you did \
not select from the list below.

                File Systems for Auto-layout
                ========================================
                [X]  /
                [ ]  /opt
                [ ]  /usr
                [ ]  /usr/openwin
                [ ]  /var
                [X]  swap

F2_Continue    F5_Cancel    F6_Help
```

41. Make your selection(s) and press F2.

NOTE

`/usr`, `/var`, and `/opt` I recommend adding `/usr`, `/var`, and `/opt` as separate file systems. `/usr` provides a separate file system for most of the Solaris binary files. `/var` allows space for system log files, spooled software packages, and many other things that can take up a large amount of disk space. It's not recommended that you make `/var` part of the root file system. `/usr` and `/opt` will provide space for additional software packages that you will add later. Again, it's not recommended that `/opt` and `/usr` be part of the root file system.

For this example, I selected these additional file systems. You'll see the following dialog:

```
--- File System and Disk Layout ------------------------------------
```

```
The summary below is your current file system and disk layout, based on the
information you've supplied.

NOTE: If you choose to customize, you should understand file systems, their
intended purpose on the disk, and how changing them may affect the operation
of the system.

    File sys/Mnt point Disk/Slice                                        Size
    ========================================================================
    /                  c0t0d0s0                                    193      MB
    /var               c0t0d0s1                                    111      MB
    overlap            c0t0d0s2                                    78528    MB
    swap               c0t0d0s3                                    513      MB
    /opt               c0t0d0s5                                    27       MB
    /usr               c0t0d0s6                                    4056     MB
    /export/home       c0t0d0s7                                    73625    MB


   F2_Continue     F3_Go Back     F4_Customize     F5_Exit     F6_Help
```

42. At this point, you can further customize the slice sizes by pressing F4. You'll then be given a menu to select new sizes for each slice. I'm going to change a few slice sizes, so I'm going to press F4. The following menu displays:

```
--- Customize Disk: c0t0d0 ------------------------------------
  Boot Device: c0t0d0s0

  Entry: /                        Recommended:  148 MB     Minimum:  126 MB
================================================================================
  Slice   Mount Point                 Size (MB)
     0    /                                193
     1    /var                             111
     2    overlap                         78528
     3    swap                             513
     4                                       0
     5    /opt                              27
     6    /usr                            4056
     7    /export/home                   73625
================================================================================
                          Capacity:      78528 MB
                         Allocated:      78525 MB
                    Rounding Error:          3 MB
                              Free:          0 MB


   F2_OK     F4_Options     F5_Cancel     F6_Help
```

43. I begin by decreasing the size of `/export/home` to 5,000MB. Then I'll increase / to 1,000MB. I'll allocate 3,000MB to `/var`, 8,000MB to `/usr`, and 1,000MB to `/opt`. I'm then going to add another slice called `/data` and make it 60,012MB. When you're satisfied with the way the slices are sized, press F2 to continue. The following dialog will display:

```
--- File System and Disk Layout ------------------

  The summary below is your current file system and disk layout, based on the
  information you've supplied.

  NOTE: If you choose to customize, you should understand file systems, their
  intended purpose on the disk, and how changing them may affect the operation
  of the system.

      File sys/Mnt point Disk/Slice                                   Size
      ========================================================================
      /                  c0t0d0s0                                1000    MB
      /var               c0t0d0s1                                3000    MB
      overlap            c0t0d0s2                                78528   MB
      swap               c0t0d0s3                                513     MB
      /data              c0t0d0s4                                60012   MB
      /opt               c0t0d0s5                                1000    MB
      /usr               c0t0d0s6                                8000    MB
      /export/home       c0t0d0s7                                5000    MB


    F2_Continue    F3_Go Back    F4_Customize    F5_Exit    F6_Help
```

44. Double-check your selections and press F2 when you're ready to go to the next step. This is a good time to verify all of your selections. Make sure swap is adequate for the type of server you are installing. It seems you can never have too much swap space or space on the `/var`, `/opt`, and `/usr` file systems. In other words, err on the side of being too large, not too small.

NOTE

Allow Space for Upgrades Sun recommends adding 30% to each file system that you create to enable you to upgrade to future Solaris versions. In the past, each new Solaris release has required approximately 10% more disk space than the previous release. By allowing 30% extra space, you can upgrade several times before you need to increase slice sizes.

Many servers today come with 72GB disk drives. I use the entire drive for the operating system. Most of my servers also run a third-party performance-monitoring package that can create huge log files in `/var`. Operating system patches can also use up a lot of space in `/var`. You'll find that you're constantly adding patches to a server because of the vast array of applications and hardware components you're supporting. I usually go crazy a little and allocate a few gigabytes to each of the file systems.

Also, it's difficult to estimate your swap requirements on a server. These servers can run for months without a reboot and might be supporting several database applications or users. Again, allocate ample swap—no less than twice the amount of RAM. System performance will not be degraded if you allocate too much swap space. Too much swap space will simply waste disk space. Disk space is cheap, however, compared to the cost of running out of swap and crashing an application during peak production times. When you're satisfied with your selections, press F2 and the following dialog will display:

```
Mount Remote File Systems?

Do you want to mount software from a remote file server? \
This may be necessary if you had to remove software because \
of disk space problems.

F2_Continue  F3_Go Back  F4_Remote Mounts  F5_Exit  F6_Help
```

45. Press F2 to continue, unless you want to set up remote mounts.

NOTE

Setting Up Mount Points I usually wait until after the initial software installation to set up these mounts. Many times, the system is not connected to a production network at this point, so the mount points are unavailable. It's also a personal preference to save this task for the post-installation phase, when I set up users, printers, and so on. I have a checklist of all the things I need to do after software installation, and setting up mount points is one of them.

Next you'll see the following dialog:

```
--- Profile ---------------------------------

  The information shown below is your profile for installing Solaris software.
  It reflects the choices you've made on previous screens.

  ============================================================================

                Installation Option: Initial
                        Boot Device: c0t0d0
                    Client Services: None
                      System Locale: C ( C )

                           Software: Solaris 10, Entire Distribution

          File System and Disk Layout: /                   c0t0d0s0 1000 MB
                                       /var                c0t0d0s1 3000 MB
                                       swap                c0t0d0s3  513 MB
                                       /opt                c0t0d0s5 1000 MB
                                       /usr                c0t0d0s6 8000 MB
                                       /export/home        c0t0d0s7 5000 MB

     F2_Begin Installation     F4_Change     F5_Exit     F6_Help
```

46. Verify the information and press F2 if you agree.

CAUTION

By pressing F2 to begin the installation, all file systems, except any that were preserved, will be destroyed. If you press F5 to cancel, the installation will be aborted, all changes will be lost, and the disk will be unchanged.

NOTE

Slice Sizing Slice sizes and disk space requirements were discussed earlier in this chapter. Review the sections titled "Software Groups" and "Disk Storage" if you are unsure of the slices and sizes that have been set up by the installation program.

You'll see the following dialog as the software is being installed:

```
Preparing system for Solaris install

Configuring disk (c0t0d0)
        - Creating Solaris disk label (VTOC)

Creating and checking UFS file systems
        - Creating / (c0t0d0s0)
        - Creating /var (c0t0d0s1)
        - Creating /data (c0t0d0s4)
        - Creating /opt (c0t0d0s5)
        - Creating /usr (c0t0d0s6)
        - Creating /export/home (c0t0d0s7)
Beginning Solaris software installation

Solaris Initial Install
       MBytes Installed:     1.00
       MBytes Remaining:   3010.14
```

A meter will appear at the bottom of the screen, showing the progress of the installation. When it reaches 100%, the system will reboot. After it boots up, you'll see the following screen:

```
This system is configured with NFS version 4, which uses a domain
        name that is automatically derived from the system's name services.
        The derived domain name is sufficient for most configurations. In a
        few cases, mounts that cross different domains might cause files to
        be owned by "nobody" due to the lack of a common domain name.

        Do you need to override the system's default NFS version 4 domain
        name (yes/no) ? [no] :
```

Respond with `No` to continue. The system will reboot and prompt you for the next media choice.

47. Select the CD option, insert the Solaris 2 CD-ROM and click OK to continue. As the installation continues, you'll continue to be prompted to load and unload the remaining CDs. After the system completes loading all CDs, the system will reboot and the login screen will be displayed.

NOTE

Depending on the Energy Star version for your particular system, you may be prompted to enable the automatic power saving feature of your system. If your system uses Energy Star version 3 or later, you are not prompted for this information.

This completes the installation of the Solaris operating system.

You'll find various log files associated with the installation in the `/var/sadm` directory. For example, the `/var/sadm/install_data/install_log` contains all messages generated by the installation program.

Configuring Power Management

You can manually configure the power management configuration for your system by using the `pmconfig` command. A user has permission to change the Power Management configuration of his or her system using `pmconfig` only if the user is allowed to do so according to PMCHANGEPERM keyword of `/etc/default/power` file.

`pmconfig` first resets the Power Management state back to its default and then reads the new Power Management configuration from /etc/power.conf and issues the commands to activiate the new configuration. The `pmconfig` utility is run at system boot. This utility can also be run from the command line after manual changes have been made to the `/etc/power.conf` file. For editing changes made to the `/etc/power.conf` file to take effect, users must run `pmconfig`.

The following is what the /etc/power.conf file looks like on a system that has power management configured:

```
more /etc/power.conf
# Copyright (c) 1996 - 2001 by Sun Microsystems, Inc.
# All rights reserved.
#
#pragma ident    "@(#)power.conf 1.16    01/03/19 SMI"
#
# Power Management Configuration File
#
# This entry keeps removable media from being powered down unless the
# console framebuffer and monitor are powered down
# (See removable-media(9P))
```

```
device-dependency-property removable-media /dev/fb


autopm                  default
# Auto-Shutdown         Idle(min)       Start/Finish(hh:mm)      Behavior
autoshutdown            60              17:00 7:00               shutdown
autopm                  default
statefile               /export/home/.CPR
```

In this example, power management is configured to autoshutdown the system when it has been idle for 60 minutes anytime between the time of 5:00 p.m. and 7:00 a.m. To disable autoshutdown, change the following lines in the /etc/power.conf file:

```
# Auto-Shutdown Idle(min)   Start/Finish(hh:mm)  Behavior
autoshutdown     60             17:00 7:00       noshutdown
```

Note that shutdown has been changed to noshutdown in the /etc/power.conf file.

The dtpower GUI also allows the configuration of /etc/power.conf file. For ease-of-use, it is recommended that you use dtpower GUI to configure the parameters in the /etc/power.conf file.

Tools for Managing Software

After installing the Solaris operating environment, you'll find it necessary to install additional software packages, or perhaps remove software from the system. In addition, you'll most likely need to install operating system patches on an on-going basis. Solaris provides the tools for adding and removing software from a system. These are described in Table 2.3.

Sun and its third-party vendors deliver software products in a form called a software package. As I described earlier, a package is a collection of files and directories in a defined format that conforms to the Application Binary Interface (ABI), a supplement to the System V Interface Definition. The Solaris operating environment provides a set of utilities that interpret the ABI format and provides the means to install or remove a package or to verify its installation.

TABLE 2.3 Tools for Managing Software

Command	Description
Managing Software from the Command Line	
pkgadd	Adds software packages to the system.
pkgrm	Removes software packages from the system.
pkgchk	Checks the accuracy of a software package installation.
pkginfo	Displays software package information.

(continues)

TABLE 2.3 *Continued*

Command	Description
`pkgask`	Stores answers in a response file so that they can be supplied automatically during an installation.
`pkgparam`	Displays package parameter values.
`pkgtrans`	Translates an installable package from one format to another.
Managing Software from the Graphical User Interface	
Solaris Product Registry	Manages all of your Solaris software.
Web Start Installer	Installs or removes a software package with a GUI or text-based installer wizard.

Use the `pkgadd` or `pkgrm` commands directly from the command line to load or remove software packages. The `pkgadd` and `pkgrm` commands can be incorporated into scripts to automate the software-installation process. Many third-party vendors use `pkgadd` in scripts as a means of installing their software.

The Solaris Product Registry, also a front-end GUI for the software package commands described in Table 2.5, is a system for maintaining records of the software products installed on a Solaris system. The Product Registry includes a GUI tool to make managing your Solaris software easier. The Product Registry enables you to install, list, or uninstall Solaris software packages or clusters.

Also included on many CD-ROMs that ship with Solaris is the installer utility, which invokes a Web Start install wizard sequence that leads the user through a sequence of installation windows. This installer utility is found in the top-level directory on many CD-ROMs that ship with Solaris. When the installer is on a CD-ROM being accessed from a desktop file manager, double-click the installer to start the installation sequence. If the user is not currently the system's root user, the system will request the root user password.

Adding and Removing Software Packages

When you add a software package, the `pkgadd` command decompresses and copies files from the installation media, such as the CD-ROM, to a local system's disk. When you use packages, files are delivered in package format and are unusable as they are delivered. The `pkgadd` command interprets the software package's control files and then decompresses the product files and installs them on the system's local disk.

You should know the following before installing additional application software:

- Sun packages always begin with the prefix SUNW, as in SUNWvolr, SUNWadmap, and SUNWtcsh. Third-party packages usually begin with a prefix that corresponds to the company's stock symbol.

- You can use the pkginfo command or the Solaris Product Registry to view software already installed on a system.
- Clients might have software that resides partially on a server and partially on the client. If this is the case, adding software for the client requires adding packages to both the server and the client.
- You need to know where the software will be installed, and you need to make sure you have a file system with enough disk space to store the application software. If you know the name of the software package, you can use the pkgparam command to determine where the package will be loaded. For example, to find out information about the SUNWman package, type the following:

  ```
  pkgparam -d /cdrom/sol_10_305_sparc_4/Solaris_10/Product SUNWman SUNW_PKGTYPE
  ```

  SUNW_PKGTYPE is a special parameter that reports where a Solaris software package will be installed. If the package does not have the SUNW_PKGTYPE parameter set, the pkgparam command returns an empty string. For Sun packages, this usually means that the package will be installed in /opt.

  The system responds with the location where the application will be stored:

  ```
  usr
  ```

NOTE

Obtaining pkgid Information It's not always clear what the pkgid is for a particular software package or application until it is actually installed. Sometimes the release documentation that comes with the package will tell you the name of the pkgid. Other times you might need to call the vendor to get the pkgid information.

CAUTION

Use pkgrm To Remove Software When you remove a package, the pkgrm command deletes all the files associated with that package unless those files are also shared with other packages. If the files are shared with other packages, a system message will warn you of that fact, and you will be asked if you want to remove them anyway. Be sure you do not delete application software without using pkgrm. For example, some system administrators delete an application simply by removing the directory containing the application software. With this method, files belonging to the application that might reside in other directories are missed. With pkgrm, you'll be assured of removing all files associated with the application and not damaging installation of other packages.

Although the pkgadd and pkgrm commands do not log their output to a standard location, they do keep track of the product installed or removed. The pkgadd and pkgrm commands store information in a software product database about a package that has been installed or removed. By updating this database, the pkgadd and pkgrm commands keep a record of all software products installed on the system.

Using a Spool Directory

For convenience, you can copy frequently installed packages to a spool directory. If you copy packages to the default spool directory, /var/spool/pkg, you do not need to specify the source location of the package when using the pkgadd command. The pkgadd command, by default, will look in the /var/spool/pkg directory for any packages specified on the command line.

NOTE

Spooling Packages Versus Installing Them Copying packages to a spool directory is not the same as installing the packages on a system.

You can add a software package to a spool directory by following the steps described in Step by Step 2.2.

STEP BY STEP

2.2 Adding a Package to the Spool Directory

1. Log in as root.
2. Make sure the spool directory exists.
3. Add a software package to a spool directory using the pkgadd command, as follows:

```
pkgadd -d <device-name> -s <spool directory> <pkgid>
```

in which

- -d *<device-name>* specifies the absolute path to the software package. *<device-name>* can be the path to a device, a directory, or a spool directory.
- -s *<spool directory>* specifies the name of the spool directory where the software package will be spooled. You must specify a *<spool directory>*, a directory where the software will be put.
- *<pkgid>* is optional. It is the name of one or more packages, separated by spaces, to be added to the spool directory. If omitted, pkgadd copies all available packages.

4. Use the pkginfo command to verify that the package has been copied to the spool directory, as follows:

```
pkginfo -d <spool directory> ¦ grep <pkgid>
```

The pkginfo command will return a line of information about the package if it has been copied to the spool directory properly. If it returns an empty command line, the package has not been successfully copied to the spool directory.

The following is an example of how to copy a software package to the /var/spool/pkg directory:

```
pkgadd -d /cdrom/sol_10_305_sparc_4/Solaris_10/Product -s /var/spool/pkg SUNNWman
```

The system responds with

```
Transferring <SUNWman> package instance
```

Now type the following to list the packages in the /var/spool/pkg directory:

```
pkginfo -d /var/spool/pkg <cr>
```

The system responds with

```
system      SUNWman On-Line Manual Pages
```

Installing Software from the Command Line

Use the pkgadd command to install additional software packages from the command line. In the previous section, we used pkgadd to add software to a spool directory. To install this software on the system, type

```
pkgadd <cr>
```

Any software that has been spooled to the /var/spool/pkg directory will be listed. In this example, I spooled a package named SFWgawk. After typing the pkgadd command, the system responds with

```
The following packages are available:
  1  SFWgawk      gawk - pattern scanning and processing language \
                (sparc) 3.0.6,REV=2002.03.27.20.41
Select package(s) you wish to process (or 'all' to process \

all packages). (default: all) [?,??,q]:
```

After pressing the Return key, you may see a message like the following:

```
Using </opt> as the package base directory.
## Processing package information.
```

```
## Processing system information.
## Verifying package dependencies.
WARNING:
    The <SFWgcmn> package "Common GNU package" is a
    prerequisite package and should be installed.
Do you want to continue with the installation of <SFWgawk> [y,n,?]
```

Enter y to install the prerequisite package. When finished, you'll see a message as follows:

```
Installation of <SFWgawk> was successful.
The following packages are available:
  1  SFWgawk     gawk - pattern scanning and processing language \
                (sparc) 3.0.6,REV=2002.03.27.20.41
Select package(s) you wish to process (or 'all' to process \
all packages). (default: all) [?,??,q]:
```

Enter q to finish and you'll return to the shell prompt.

Removing Software Using pkgrm

You can remove software packages from the command line using the pkgrm command. For example, to remove the software package named SUNWman, type

```
pkgrm SUNWman <cr>
```

The system responds with

```
The following package is currently installed:
   SUNWman  On-Line Manual Pages
            (sparc) 43.0,REV=75.0

Do you want to remove this package? [y,n,?,q]
```

Enter y and press the Enter key. You'll see a list of files being removed followed by a message similar to this one:

```
## Updating system information.
Removal of <SUNWman> was successful.
```

Solaris Product Registry

The Solaris Product Registry enables you to do the following:

- View a list of installed and registered software and some software attributes.
- Find and launch an installer.

- Install additional software products.
- Uninstall software.

The main difference between the Product Registry and the other tools is that the Product Registry is designed to be compatible with more of the newer installation wizards and Web Start 3.0.

To start up the Solaris Product Registry, type the following:

```
/usr/bin/prodreg
```

The Product Registry window shown in Figure 2.1 appears.

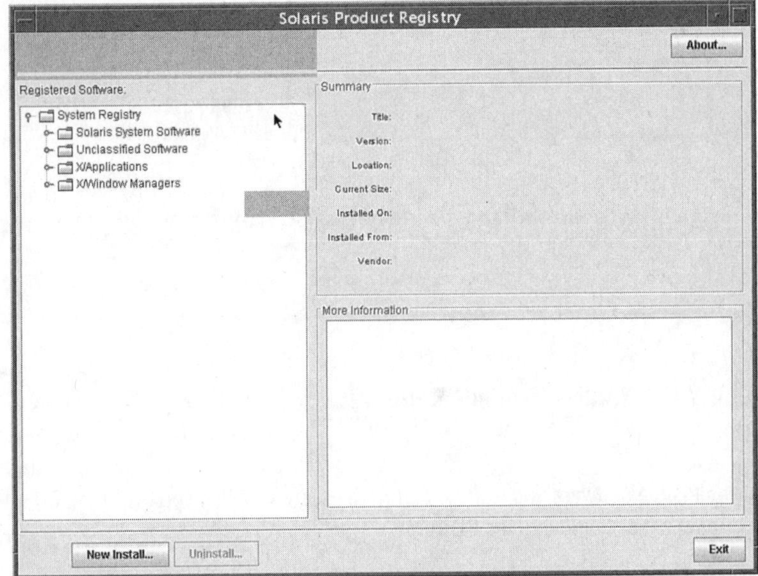

FIGURE 2.1 The Product Registry window.

To view the contents of the system registry, double-click the magnifying glass next to Solaris System Software. The registry will be expanded and the contents listed. Click any folder listed to get more information on that package. I clicked on Entire Distribution and then Apache Web Server, and the information shown in Figure 2.2 was displayed.

Along with listing information about all installed software products on your system, use the Solaris Product Registry to check the integrity of software products installed on the system. Follow the steps outlined for listing installed software. After you see the package you want to check, click its name in the window titled Software Installed in Solaris Registry. If all or part of the product is missing, the message `Missing files in one or more components` displays after the Installed From attribute.

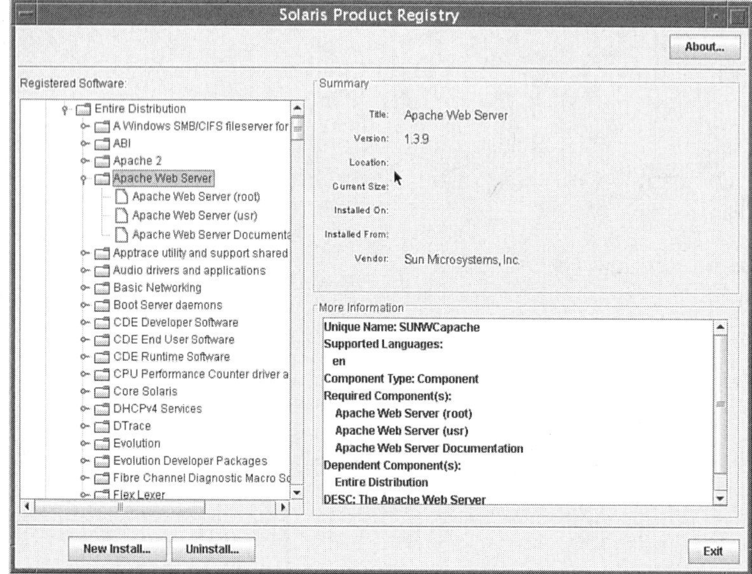

FIGURE 2.2 Apache Web Server information.

You can install a software package with the Solaris Product Registry by following the steps described in Step by Step 2.3.

STEP BY STEP

2.3 Installing Software Using the Solaris Product Registry

1. Log in as root.
2. Insert the CD-ROM that contains the software you want to add to the system. When you insert the CD-ROM, the Volume Manager automatically mounts the CD-ROM.
3. Start the Solaris Product Registry as outlined earlier in this section.
4. Click the New Install button at the bottom of the Solaris Product Registry window. The Product Registry displays the Select Installer dialog box, which initially points to the `/cdrom` directory.
5. When you find the installer you want, click its name in the Files box and then click OK.
6. The installer you selected launches Web Start installer. Follow the directions displayed by the installer you selected to install the software. For more information on the Web Start installer, see the next section.

You can also use the Product Registry to remove software by following these steps:

You can remove a software package with the Solaris Product Registry by following the steps described in Step by Step 2.4.

STEP BY STEP

2.4 Uninstalling Software Using the Solaris Product Registry

To uninstall software, go into the Solaris Product Registry window and follow these steps:

1. Click the System Registry folder in the window titled Software Installed in Solaris Registry and click the software package you want to remove. Read the software attributes to make sure this is the software you want to uninstall.
2. Click the Uninstall button at the bottom of the Solaris Product Registry window. The software product you selected is uninstalled.

Web Start Installer

The Web Start installer enables you to add software to a system on which you have installed the Solaris operating environment. The Solaris Web Start program installs only those components in the software groups that you skipped when you initially installed the Solaris operating environment. You cannot change to another software group after installing or upgrading.

To add software to your system using the Web Start installer, see Step by Step 2.5.

STEP BY STEP

2.5 Adding Software Using Web Start

1. Log in to the system as root.
2. Load the CD-ROM into the CD-ROM drive.

   This procedure assumes that the system is running volume management (`vold`). See Chapter 1, "Managing File Systems," for more details.
3. Change directories to find the Solaris Web Start installer. It is a file named "installer" that's usually located in the top-level directory of the CD-ROM.
4. Execute the installer by typing **`./installer`** or by double-clicking the Installer icon in the File Manager or Solaris Product Registry window (as described in the preceding section). You can run the installer in a GUI interface or from the command line. To run the installer from the command line, execute the installer as follows:

   ```
   ./installer -nodisplay
   ```

In the following example, I've installed the Solaris CD-ROM labeled "Solaris 10 Companion CD" into the CD-ROM drive. vold automatically mounts the CD-ROM

1. After inserting the CD into the CD-ROM drive, type the following to begin the installation:

```
/cdrom/cdrom0/installer -nodisplay
```

The following dialog begins:

```
Select the type of installation you want for each product.

      No Install  Default Install  Custom Install  Product
      ----------  ---------------  --------------  -------
 0.   [ ]         [X]              [ ]             Application/Accessibility
 1.   [ ]         [X]              [ ]             Application/Editors
 2.   [ ]         [X]              [ ]             Application/Networking
 3.   [ ]         [X]              [ ]             Application/Publishing
 4.   [ ]         [X]              [ ]             Application/Utilities
 5.   [ ]         [X]              [ ]             Desktop/Environment
 6.   [ ]         [X]              [ ]             Development/Languages
 7.   [ ]         [X]              [ ]             Development/Libraries
 8.   [ ]         [X]              [ ]             Development/Tools
 9.   [ ]         [X]              [ ]             System/Daemons
 10.  [ ]         [X]              [ ]             X/Applications
 11.  [ ]         [X]              [ ]             X/Window Managers
 12.                                               Done
   Enter the number next to the product you wish to change.  Select "Done" when
   finished [12]:
```

2. Deselect items 1–9 and press Enter to continue. The following messages are displayed on the screen:

```
Checking disk space.

The following items will be installed:

Product: X/Applications
Location: /opt
Size: 101.15 MB
----------------------
stardic - Star Dictionary online translation tool, v1.3.1    3.14 MB
xterm - Terminal emulator for X Windows, v196    395.32 KB
sane -  Scanner Applications, v1.0.12    8.82 MB
rxvt - ouR eXtended Virtual Terminal, v2.7.10    177.44 KB
xcpustate - display CPU states and statistics, v2.5    40.05 KB
xmcd - Motif CD Audio Player, v3.2.1    5.66 MB
gimp - GNU Image Manipulation Program, v1.2.1    41.16 MB
vnc - Virtual Network Computing, v3.3.7    1.57 MB
xmms - X MultiMedia System, v1.2.10    6.04 MB
asclock - the AfterStep clock, v1.0    34.19 MB
```

```
Product: X/Window Managers
Location: /opt
Size: 14.34 MB
--------------------------
afterstep - X11 window manager, v1.8.8    37.55 MB
WindowMaker - X11 Window Manager, v0.80.2    7.91 MB
fvwm - X11 virtual window manager, v2.4.3    3.08 MB


Ready to Install

1. Install Now
2. Start Over
3. Exit Installation

   What would you like to do [1]?
```

3. Press Enter to Install Now and a license agreement is displayed. Press y to accept the agreement and continue the install. The system will show you the progress of the installation and, when complete, will display the following message:

```
Installing X/Window Managers
¦-1%--------------25%-----------------50%-----------------75%--------------100%¦


Installation details:

    Product              Result     More Info
 1. X/Applications       Installed  Available
 2. X/Window Managers    Installed  Available

 3. Done
```

4. Press Enter to complete the installation.

Listing and Verifying Installed Packages

At any time, you can use the Software Product Registry or issue the `pkginfo` command from the command line to obtain a complete listing of the software installed on a system. The Product Registry GUI will display information about installed software, as described in the previous section and as shown in Figure 2.3.

Figure 2.3 illustrates the `pkginfo` command used from the command line, piped to `more` to show the display of information one page at a time.

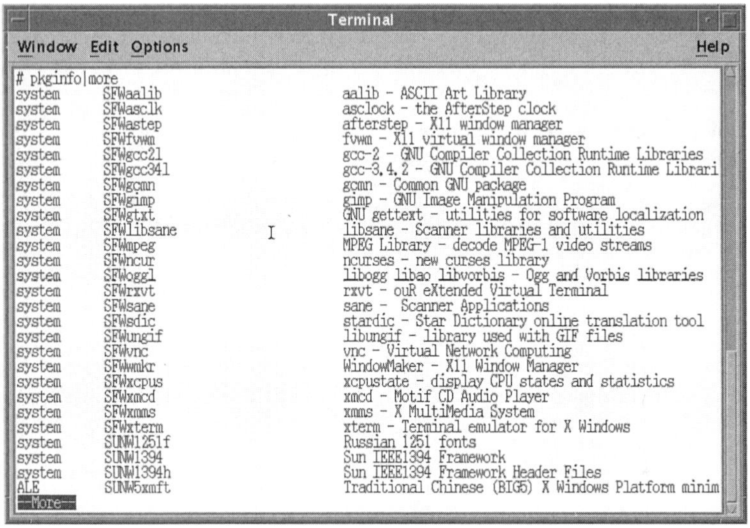

```
# pkginfo|more
system     SFWaalib        aalib - ASCII Art Library
system     SFWasclk        asclock - the AfterStep clock
system     SFWastep        afterstep - X11 window manager
system     SFWfvwm         fvwm - X11 virtual window manager
system     SFWgcc21        gcc-2 - GNU Compiler Collection Runtime Libraries
system     SFWgcc341       gcc-3.4.2 - GNU Compiler Collection Runtime Librari
system     SFWgcmn         gcmn - Common GNU package
system     SFWgimp         gimp - GNU Image Manipulation Program
system     SFWgtxt         GNU gettext - utilities for software localization
system     SFWlibsane      libsane - Scanner libraries and utilities
system     SFWmpeg         MPEG Library - decode MPEG-1 video streams
system     SFWncur         ncurses - new curses library
system     SFWoggl         libogg libao libvorbis - Ogg and Vorbis libraries
system     SFWrxvt         rxvt - ouR eXtended Virtual Terminal
system     SFWsane         sane -  Scanner Applications
system     SFWsdic         stardic - Star Dictionary online translation tool
system     SFWungif        libungif - library used with GIF files
system     SFWvnc          vnc - Virtual Network Computing
system     SFWwmkr         WindowMaker - X11 Window Manager
system     SFWxcpus        xcpustate - display CPU states and statistics
system     SFWxmcd         xmcd - Motif CD Audio Player
system     SFWxmms         xmms - X MultiMedia System
system     SFWxterm        xterm - Terminal emulator for X Windows
system     SUNW1251f       Russian 1251 fonts
system     SUNW1394        Sun IEEE1394 Framework
system     SUNW1394h       Sun IEEE1394 Framework Header Files
ALE        SUNW5xmft       Traditional Chinese (BIG5) X Windows Platform minim
--More--
```

FIGURE 2.3 The `pkginfo` output.

Table 2.4 lists some of the files and directories used with package administration.

TABLE 2.4 Software Package Files and Directories

File or Directory Name	Description
`/var/sadm/install/contents`	This file contains a complete record of all the software packages installed on the local system disk. It references every file and directory belonging to every software package and shows information about each software component, such as its default permission level and the package to which it belongs.
/opt/*<pkgname>*	The preferred location for the installation of unbundled packages.
/etc/opt/*<pkgname>*	The preferred location for log files of unbundled packages.

The `/var/sadm` directory is extremely important, especially when changes are made to the software installed on your system in any form. This directory is used to record the changes made to the system when installing or removing software and patches. Many Solaris change management utilities rely upon the information inside `/var/sadm` for an accurate picture of what actually resides on the system.

`/var/sadm/install/contents` is a file that can be used to determine which package an individual file belongs to. You can also use it to determine which files are associated with a certain software group. For example, to find out what things are associated with the `format` command:

```
grep /etc/format /var/sadm/install/contents
```

The system displays the following information:

```
/etc/format=../usr/sbin/format s none SUNWcsr
/etc/format.dat v none 0644 root sys 6986 55261 1106350052 SUNWcsr
```

`/var/sadm/pkg/<package name>` is the directory where all the information about your software packages is stored. It is critical to keep this directory intact and up to date by using the standard package installation commands described in this section.

Quite often, system administrators may be tempted to remove the files from `/var/sadm` when their `/var` file system begins to fill up.

CAUTION

Do Not Remove Files from `/var/sadm` DO NOT remove files from `/var/sadm`. The removal of files from this directory may not impact the system for quite some time, but as soon as a patch or package needs to be applied or removed from the system, you will run into a variety of problems.

Software Patches

Another system administration task is managing system software patches. A *patch* is a fix to a reported software problem. Sun will ship several software patches to customers so that problems can be resolved before the next release of software. The existing software is derived from a specified package format that conforms to the ABI.

Patches are identified by unique alphanumeric strings. The patch base code comes first, and then a hyphen, and then a number that represents the patch revision number. For example, patch 110453-01 is a Solaris patch to correct a known problem.

You might want to know more about patches that have previously been installed. Table 2.5 shows commands that provide useful information about patches already installed on a system.

TABLE 2.5 Helpful Commands for Patch Administration

Command	Function
`showrev -p`	Shows all patches applied to a system.
`pkgparam <pkgid> PATCHLIST`	Shows all patches applied to the package identified by `<pkgid>`.
`pkgparam <pkgid> PATCH INFO <patch-number>`	Shows the installation date and name of the host from which the patch was applied. `<pkgid>` is the name of the package (for example, SUNWadmap), and `<patch-number>` is the specific patch number.
`patchadd -R <client_root_path> -p`	Shows all patches applied to a client, from the server's console.

(continues)

TABLE 2.5 *Continued*

Command	Function
`patchadd -p`	Shows all patches applied to a system.
`patchrm <patchname>`	Removes a specified patch. *<patchname>* is the name of the patch to be removed.
`smpatch`	A new tool in Solaris 10 for managing patches.
`Patch Tool`	A Solaris Management Console Tool for managing patches.

The tools in Table 2.5 are tools you might already be accustomed to if you've managed patches using earlier versions of the Solaris operating environment. In Solaris 10, Patch Manager helps you manage patches by displaying information about installed patches. It also assists you in adding patches to one or more systems concurrently, removes patches, analyzes a system's patch requirements, and downloads patches from the SunSolve Online service.

I'll first describe how to manage patches using the conventional tools described in Table 2.5, and then I'll describe Patch Manager.

Installing a Patch

Sun customers can access security patches and other recommended patches via the World Wide Web or anonymous FTP. You can download patches from the SunSolve website, which (as of this writing) is at `http://sunsolve.sun.com`. Sun customers who have purchased a service contract can access an extended set of patches and a complete database of patch information. (This information is also available via the World Wide Web or FTP, and it is regularly distributed on CD-ROM.)

You can obtain individual patches or groups of patches called a *patch cluster*. Detailed information about how to install and remove a patch is provided in the README file included with each patch, which contains specific information about the patch.

Patches come in three different formats. Solaris 10 patches come in ZIP format, such as `104945-02.zip`. For Solaris 10 patches, use the `unzip` command to extract the patch files, as follows:

```
/usr/bin/unzip 104945-02.zip
```

Other times, a patch may come in as a jar file indicated by a .jar suffix in the name, for example `120292-01.jar`. To extract the jar file, type

```
jar xvf 120292-01.jar
```

For Solaris 2.6 and earlier operating environments, patches might come in compressed TAR format, such as `104945-02.tar.Z`. Use the `zcat` command to decompress this type of patch file and the `tar` command to create the patch directories, as follows:

```
/usr/bin/zcat 104945-02.tar.Z | tar xvf -
```

Other Solaris patches might come as GZIP compressed TAR files, such as `102945-02.tar.gz`. To extract a GZIP compressed TAR file, use the `gzcat` command to decompress and create the patch directories, as follows:

```
/usr/bin/gzcat 104945-02.tar.gz | tar xvf -
```

The `patchadd` command is used to install directory-format patches to a Solaris 10 system. It must be run as root. The syntax is as follows:

```
patchadd [ -d ] [ -u ] [ -B backout_dir ]
```

The `patchadd` command is described in Table 2.6.

TABLE 2.6 `patchadd` Command Options

Command Option	Description
`-d`	Does not create a backup of the files to be patched. The patch cannot be removed when this option has been used to install the patch. By default, `patchadd` saves a copy of all files being updated so that the patch can be removed if necessary. Do not use the `-d` option unless you're positive the patch has been tested.
`-p`	Displays a list of the patches currently applied.
`-u`	Installs the patch unconditionally, with file validation turned off. The patch is installed even if some of the files to be patched have been modified since their original installation.
`-B` *<backout_dir>*	Saves backout data to a directory other than the package database. Specify *<backout_dir>* as an absolute pathname.
`-M` *<patch_dir>* *<patch_id>*	Specifies the patches to be installed. Specify patches to the `-M` option by directory location and by patch number.
<patch_dir>	is the absolute pathname of the directory that contains the spooled patches. The *<patch_id>* is the patch number of a particular patch.
`-M` *<patch_dir>* *<patch_file list>*	Specifies the patches to be installed. Specify patches to the `-M` option by directory location and the name of a file containing a patch list. To use the directory location and a file containing a patch list, specify *<patch_dir>* as the absolute pathname of the directory containing the file with a list of patches to be installed. Specify *<patch_list>* as the name of the file containing the patches to be installed. See the example in the "Installing a Patch" sectionof this chapter.

(continues)

TABLE 2.6 *Continued*

Command Option	Description
`-R <client_root_path>`	Locates all patch files generated by `patchadd` under the directory `<client_root_path>`. `<client_root_path>` is the directory that contains the bootable root of a client from the server's perspective. Specify `<client_root_path>` as the absolute pathname to the beginning of the directory tree under which all patch files generated by `patchadd` are to be located. See the example in the "Installing a Patch" section of this chapter.

NOTE

`patchadd` Options Additional options to the `patchadd` command can be found online in the Solaris system manual pages.

Installing a Patch

The following examples describe how to add patches to your system. A word of caution is in order before you install patches, however. It has been my personal experience—Murphy's Law, you might say—that things can go wrong. Because you're modifying the operating system with a patch, I highly recommend that you back up your file systems before loading patches. Although it can be a time-consuming and seemingly unnecessary task, I once encountered a power failure during a patch installation that completely corrupted my system. Another time, the patch installation script was defective, and the patch did not load properly. Without a backup, I would have had to reinstall the entire operating system.

The following example installs a patch to a standalone machine:

```
patchadd /var/spool/patch/104945-02
```

The following example installs multiple patches. The `patchlist` file specifies a file containing a list of patches to install:

```
patchadd -M /var/spool/patch patchlist
```

Many times, a patch or patch cluster contains a script named `install_patch` or `install_cluster`. Simply executing this script will install the patch or patch cluster.

The following example displays the patches installed on a client system named client1:

```
patchadd -R /export/root/client1 -p
```

When you're installing a patch, the `patchadd` command copies files from the patch directory to the local system's disk. More specifically, `patchadd` does the following:

- It determines the Solaris version number of the managing host and the target host.
- It updates the patch package's pkginfo file with information about patches made obsolete by the patch being installed, other patches required by this patch, and about patches incompatible with this patch.
- It moves outdated files and directories to the /var directory.
- It logs the patch installation to the /var/sadm/patch/(*patch-id*) directory.
- It updates the /var/sadm/pkg/<*pkg-name*>/pkginfo file.

The patchadd command will not install a patch under the following conditions:

- If the package is not fully installed on the host.
- If the patch architecture differs from the system architecture.
- If the patch version does not match the installed package version.
- If an installed patch already exists with the same base code and a higher version number.
- If the patch is incompatible with another, already-installed patch. (Each installed patch keeps this information in its pkginfo file.)
- If the patch being installed requires another patch that is not installed.

When a patch is installed, files that are replaced are moved into the /var/sadm/pkg/<*pkgname*>/save directory. Files in this directory are used if you ever need to back out of a patch. These files are used to restore the system to the prepatch installation state. Backing out a patch returns files and directories stored in the /var directory to their original locations and removes the versions installed by the patch. If you remove files in this directory, you will not be able to backout a patch.

showrev -p gets its information from /var/sadm/pkg/<*pkgname*>/save as well, specifically from the pkginfo file in each pkg directory. This directory contains old information about the package as it existed prior to a patch install and contains backups of critical files for the package.

The file that you see in this directory will be different depending on the package, but the save information for the patch IDs that have been installed should always exist and will look something like this:

```
ls -l /var/sadm/pkg/SUNWcsu/save <cr>
total 8
drwxr-xr-x   2 root     other        512 Oct 10 15:25 112233-02
drwxr-xr-x   2 root     other        512 Oct 10 15:20 112963-01
drwxr-xr-x   2 root     other        512 Oct 10 15:27 112964-02
drwxr-xr-x   2 root     other        512 Oct 10 15:08 112998-02
```

Looking into each directory, we see a file named `undo.Z` as follows:

```
ls 112233-02 <cr>
undo.Z
```

If a file doesn't exist here, the patch was installed with the `-d` option. You did not save the backout information and the patch cannot be backed out. This file will not always be in .Z format. Sometimes it will be just a regular uncompressed file.

A patch cluster contains a selected set of patches, conveniently wrapped for one-step installation. Typically, they will be named "10_recommended". Clusters consist of operating system patches (including security fixes) deemed to be of universal interest. To install a patch cluster, follow these steps:

1. Uncompress or unzip the patch cluster and extract the tar file.
2. Change to the directory that contains the patch cluster, read the README file for any specific instructions, and run the `install_cluster` script.

Removing a Patch

Sometimes a patch does not work as planned and needs to be removed from the system. The utility used to remove, or "back out of," a patch is the `patchrm` command, described in Table 2.7. Its syntax is as follows:

```
patchrm [ -f ] [ -B backout_dir ]
```

TABLE 2.7 `patchrm` Command Options

Command Options	Description
`-f`	Forces the patch removal regardless of whether the patch was superseded by another patch.
`-B` *<backout_dir>*	Removes a patch whose backout data has been saved to a directory other than the package database. This option is needed only if the original backout directory, supplied to the `patchadd` command at installation time, has been moved. Specify *<backout_dir>* as an absolute pathname.

The following example removes a patch from a standalone system:

```
patchrm 104945-02
```

The `patchrm` command removes a Solaris 10 patch package and restores previously saved files—restoring the file system to its state before a patch was applied—unless any of the following four conditions exist:

- The patch was installed with `patchadd -d`. (The `-d` option instructs `patchadd` not to save copies of files being updated or replaced.)
- The patch has been made obsolete by a later patch.
- The patch is required by another patch already installed on the system.
- The `patchrm` command calls `pkgadd` to restore packages saved from the initial patch installation.

Historical information about all installed patches that are able to be uninstalled using `patchrm` is stored in the `/var/sadm/patch` directory.

Patch Manager (smpatch)

Patch Manager is provided in Solaris 10 to assist you in managing patches on your system. Specifically, Patch Manager uses the `/usr/sbin/smpatch` utility to do the following:

- Analyze your system to determine if patches need to be installed.
- Download patches.
- Install patches.
- Remove patches.

The syntax for the `smpatch` utility is as follows:

```
smpatch subcommand  <subcommand_option>
```

The `smpatch` requires you to enter a *subcommand*, which are outlined in Table 2.8

TABLE 2.8 smpatch Subcommands

Subcommand	Description
`add`	Applies one or more patches to one or more systems. You must specify at least one patch to apply. By default, patches are applied to the local system. This subcommand attempts to apply only the patches you specify. If you specify a patch that depends on another that has not been applied, the `add` command fails to apply the patch you specified.
`analyze`	Analyzes a system to generate a list of the appropriate patches. After analyzing the system, use the `update` subcommand or the `download` and `add` subcommands to download and apply the patches to your systems. The smpatch analyze command depends on network services that are not available while the system is in single-user mode.

(continues)

Table 2.8 *Continued*

Subcommand	Description
`download`	Downloads patches from the Sun patch server to a system. You can optionally specify which patches to download. You can also specify the name of a system and download the appropriate patches to that system.
`get`	Lists one or more of the `smpatch` configuration parameter values.
`order`	Sorts a list of patches into an order that can be used to apply patches.
`remove`	Removes a single patch from a single system.
`set`	Sets the values of one or more configuration parameters.
`unset`	Resets one or more configuration parameters to the default values.
`update`	Updates a single local or remote system by applying appropriate patches. This subcommand analyzes the system and then downloads the appropriate patches from the Sun patch server to your system. After the availability of the patches has been confirmed, the patches are applied based on the patch policy.

Each subcommand has specific options, which are described in Table 2.9.

TABLE 2.9 `smpatch` Subcommands and Options

Option	Description
Subcommand Options Supported by the *add* Command	
`-i` *`patch_id1`* `-i` *`patch_id2`*	Specifies the patch or patches that you want to install. You can list one or several patches to install, or you can specify the `-x` option to specify a file that contains the list of patches.
`-x mlist=`*`patchlist_file`*	Use this option instead of the `-i` option when you have many patches to install. With this option, you specify a file (*`patchlist_file`*) that contains the list of patches you want to install.
Subcommand Options for the *add* Subcommand	
`-d` *<patchdir>*	Specifies the directory where the patches are located. If you do not specify this option, the default patch spool directory (`/var/sadm/spool`) is assumed. The patch directory has the following syntax: *`system_name`*`:`*`/directory_path`*, where *`system_name`* is the name server containing the files and *`/directory_path`* is a fully qualified, shared directory. You can specify just the *`/directory_path`* if the directory is an NFS-mounted network directory or is located on the machine on which you want to install the patches.
`-h`	Displays information on how to use the command.
`-n` *`system_name1`* `-n` *`system_name2`*	Specifies the host or list of *`system_name2`* `...` systems on which you want to install the patches. You can specify the `-x mlist=`*`system_name_file`* operand instead of specifying this option.

TABLE 2.9 *Continued*

Option	Description
-x mlist=*systemlist_file*	Specifies a file that contains the list of systems (machines) to which you want to install patches. You can specify the -n *system_name1* option instead of specifying this operand.
Options for the analyze Subcommand	
-h	Displays the command's usage statement.
-n *system_name*	Specifies the system you want to analyze.
The *download* Subcommand Requires One of the Following Subcommand Options	
-I *patch_id1* -i *patch_id2*	Specifies the patch or patches *patch_id2* ... that you want to download. You can specify the -x idlist= *patch_id_file* operand instead of this option, or you can omit this argument in favor of the -n *download_system* option.
-x idlist=*patchlist_file*	Specifies the file containing the list of patches you want to download. You can specify this operand instead of specifying the -i *patch_id1* option.
Optional Subcommand Arguments for the download Subcommand	
-n *download_system*	Specifies the machine on which you want to download the recommended patches.
-d *downloaddir*	Specifies the directory where the patches are downloaded. This directory must have write permission and be accessible to the *download_system*. If you do not specify this option, the default patch spool directory (/var/sadm/spool) located on the download system is assumed.
The remove Subcommand Requires the Following Options	
-i *patch_id*	Specifies the patch you want to remove.
-n systemname	Specifies the system on which you want to remove the recommended patches. (Optional)

To use the analyze subcommand, the system needs to be connected to the Internet so that it can access the SunSolve site for patch information. To analyze a system, login as root and type the following command:

```
smpatch analyze
```

The system responds with a list of patches:

```
120199-01 SunOS 5.10: sysidtool Patch
119145-02 SunOS 5.10: usr/snadm/lib Patch
119252-02 SunOS 5.10: System Administration Applications Patch
```

```
119315-02 SunOS 5.10: Solaris Management Applications Patch
119313-02 SunOS 5.10: WBEM Patch
119250-02 SunOS 5.10: usr/sbin/install.d/pfinstall Patch
119534-02 SunOS 5.10: Flash Archive Patch
119254-02 SunOS 5.10: Install and Patch Utilities Patch
119783-01 SunOS 5.10 : bind patch
119065-01 SunOS 5.10: fc-cache patch
119812-01 X11 6.6.2: Freetype patch

. . . <output has been truncated > . . .
```

The following example analyzes the system named `zeus` and downloads the assessed patches from the SunSolve Online database to the default patch spool directory:

```
/usr/sadm/bin/smpatch download
```

The system responds with the following:

```
120199-01 has been validated.
119145-02 has been validated.
119252-02 has been validated.
119315-02 has been validated.
119313-02 has been validated.
119250-02 has been validated.
119534-02 has been validated.
[Output has been truncated.]
```

The patches get downloaded to the `/var/sadm/spool` directory as jar files. Extract the files using `jar xvf` as described earlier in this chapter.

After extracting the jar file, install a patch from the download directory, by typing

```
smpatch add -i 120469-01
```

The system responds with:

```
add patch 120469-01
Patch 120469-01 has been successfully installed.
Validating patches...
Loading patches installed on the system...
Done!
Loading patches requested to install.
Done!
Checking patches that you specified for installation.
Done!
Approved patches will be installed in this order:
120469-01
```

I've generated a list of the patches I downloaded and want to install onto this system. To install the patches in this list, I type the following:

```
smpatch add -x idlist=/var/sadm/spool/patchlist
```

The system responds with

```
add patch 120469-01
Validating patches...
Loading patches installed on the system...
Done!
Loading patches requested to install.
Done!
The following requested patches are already installed on the system
Requested to install patch 120469-01 is already installed on the system.
No patches to check dependency.
add patch 120292-01
Package SUNWmysqlS from patch 120292-01 is not installed on the system.
The original package SUNWmysqlS that 120292-01 is attempting to install to does \
not exist on this system.
wordlist too large
Patch 120292-01 failed to be copied to the pspool directory.
Validating patches...
Loading patches installed on the system...
Done!
Loading patches requested to install.
Done!
Checking patches that you specified for installation.
Done!
Approved patches will be installed in this order:
120292-01
add patch 120251-01
Patch 120251-01 has been successfully installed.
Validating patches...
Loading patches installed on the system...
Done!
Loading patches requested to install.
Done!
Checking patches that you specified for installation.
Done!
Approved patches will be installed in this order:
120251-01
add patch 120198-02
Patch 120198-02 has been successfully installed.
Validating patches...
Loading patches installed on the system...
Done!
Loading patches requested to install.
Done!
```

```
Checking patches that you specified for installation.
Done!
Approved patches will be installed in this order:
120198-02
```

Patch Tool

Patch Tool, a GUI-based tool for installing patches, is available in the Solaris Management Console (SMC), and mimics the `smpatch` command.

Access this Patch Tool by typing the following:

```
smc <cr>
```

The Solaris Management Tool is displayed as shown in Figure 2.4.

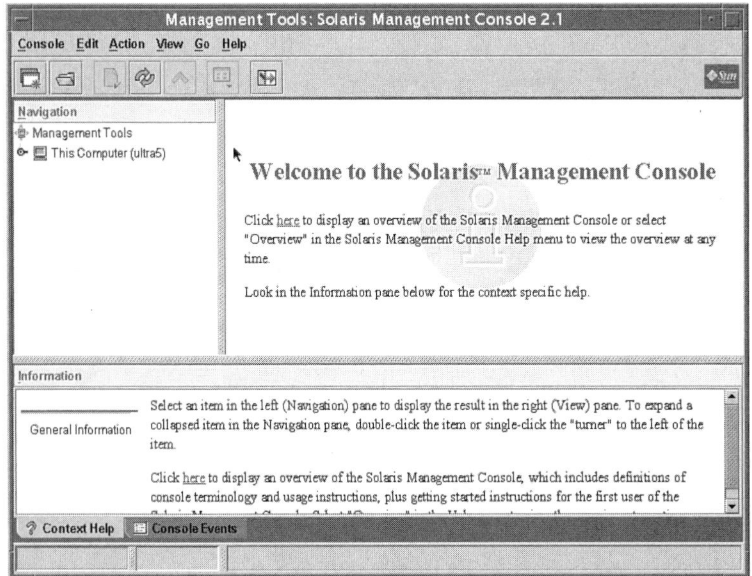

FIGURE 2.4 Solaris Management Tool.

In the left pane, click on the This Computer icon. The icon will expand as shown in Figure 2.5, displaying icons for various SMC tools.

Click on the System Configuration icon. The System Configuration icon will expand and icons for the System Configuration tools will be displayed as shown in Figure 2.6.

Click on the Patches icon, shown in Figure 2.6, enter the root password when prompted, and the main window on the Management Console will display information about any patches installed on the system. If the window is blank, no patches are installed.

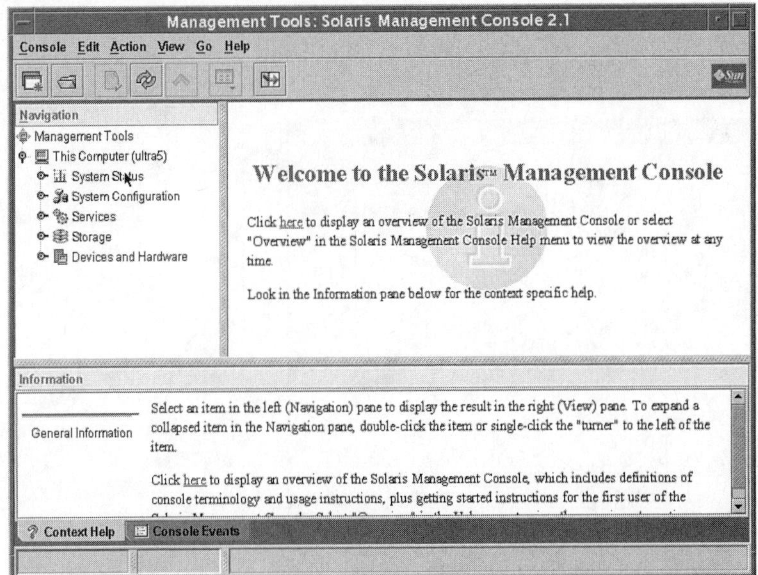

FIGURE 2.5 System Configuration tools.

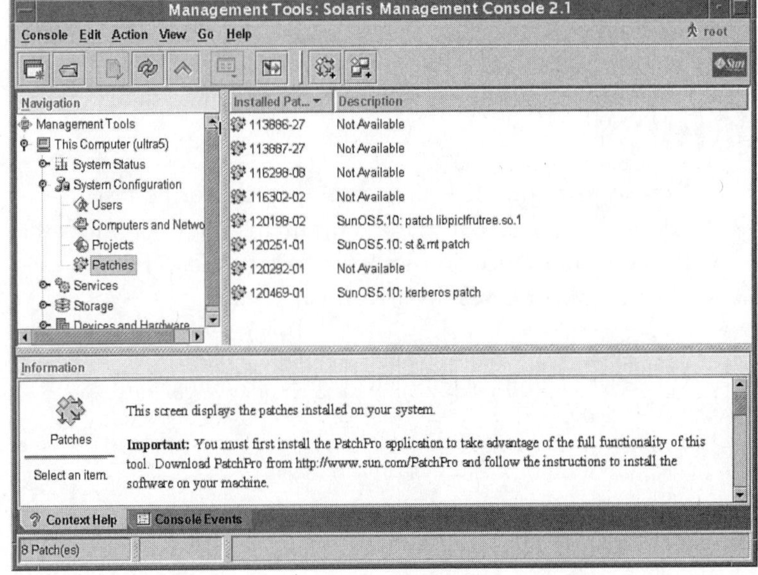

FIGURE 2.6 System Configuration icons.

When you click on Action from the top toolbar, you have the option to add patches, analyze your system for patches, and download patches using the GUI as shown in Figure 2.7.

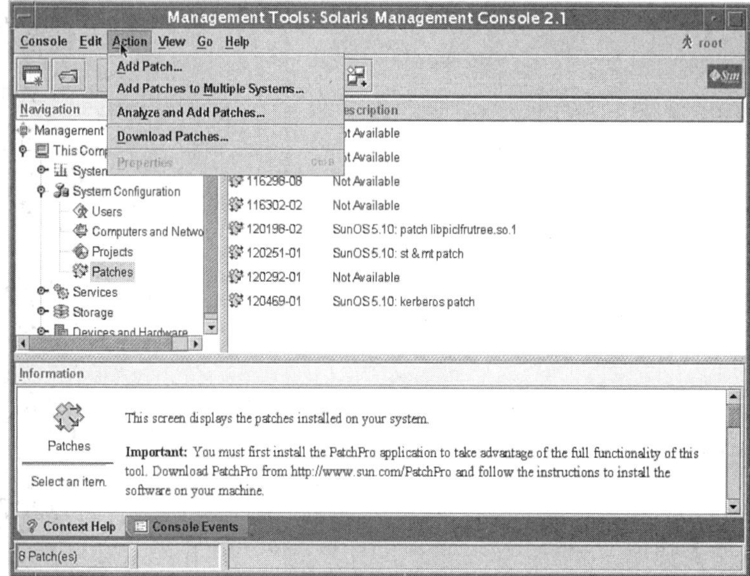

FIGURE 2.7 Patch actions.

General Guidelines

Some software packages do not conform to the ABI; therefore, they cannot be installed by using the Solaris Product Registry or the `pkgadd` command. For installation of products that do not conform to the ABI, follow the vendor's specific installation instructions. Here are a few additional guidelines to follow when installing new software on a system:

- Always be cautious with third-party or public-domain software. Make sure the software has been tested and is free of trojans and malicious code before installing it on a production system.
- Make sure the software package is supported under Solaris 10.
- Always read the vendor's release notes for special loading instructions. They might contain kernel parameters that need to be modified or suggest software patches that need to be applied.
- Do not install patches unless directed by Sun or one of your software providers. Some patches have not been tested thoroughly, especially when used in conjunction with other software patches. Adverse system performance could result.

NOTE

Recommended Patch Sets For each release of software, Sun usually has a prebundled set of patches called "Recommended and Security Patches." These patches have been thoroughly tested, and Sun recommends adding these patches to every system after the initial software installation is complete.

Adding and removing software packages is one of the simpler tasks you will encounter in system administration. As with all computer software, you should first load new software packages or patches on a nonproduction system for test purposes. Only after the software has been thoroughly tested should you install it on a production system.

Summary

This chapter described how to prepare for and install the Solaris operating environment on a machine. You learned how to install the Solaris 10 operating environment onto a standalone system using the interactive installation program `suninstall`. The interactive installation program provides a dialog that allows the system administrator to select software packages and create file systems on the new server.

This chapter also described Software Package Administration, beginning with the methods Sun uses to package their bundled and unbundled operating system software. Then you learned about the tools and methods used to install, verify, and remove these software packages on a Solaris system.

The chapter also explained that occasionally, software deficiencies are discovered and need to be repaired. You learned how to obtain, install, and, if necessary, uninstall software patches.

Now that you understand how to install the Solaris operating environment, the next chapter will describe system startup and shutdown procedures.

Key Terms

- Platform group
- Platform name
- Installation media
- Disk slice
- Disk partition
- Software package
- Software group
- Configuration group
- Swap space
- Server
- Client
- JumpStart
- Standalone system
- Power management
- Hostname
- Initial installation
- IP address
- IPv6
- Solaris Interactive installation
- Upgrade (as it pertains to the Solaris Interactive method of installation)
- Solaris Live upgrade
- Web Start Installer
- WAN Boot
- Solaris Flash Archive
- Solaris product registry
- Software package
- Software patch
- Patch Manager

- Software spool directory
- Bundled software package
- Unbundled software package
- Compressed tar file
- Compressed jar file
- Patchlist file

Exercises

2.1 Preparing to Install the Solaris 10 Operating Environment

In this exercise, you will perform the steps necessary to prepare for a Solaris 10 operating system install on a networked standalone system.

Estimated time: 15 minutes

1. Identify your system type using the following command:

   ```
   uname -m
   ```

   Is it a supported platform type listed in Table 2.1, and do you have the Solaris 10 Installation media kit for that platform?

2. Identify the peripherals connected to your system and determine the device name for the CD-ROM and the disk drive that will be used as the boot device. Use the `prtconf`, `sysdef`, and `dmesg` commands to identify these devices.

   Make sure your system meets the minimum system requirements for Solaris 10. If it does not meet the minimum requirements, you will not be able to install Solaris 10. Check the amount of RAM as follows:

   ```
   prtconf|grep Memory
   ```

   Does the system have a CD-ROM?

   Check the amount of disk space using the `format` command and listing the size of slice 2, making sure that you select the correct device name for your boot disk.

NOTE

The `format` Command Chapter 4 describes the use of the `format` command.

3. Determine the software cluster that you want to install and determine the amount of disk space it will require. Compare this value with the total size of your disk, which was determined in the previous step. For example, if the size of disk slice 2 is 1.3GB, and I want to install the Entire Distribution cluster, I do not have enough disk space to complete the installation.

4. Plan your storage requirements as described in the "Disk Storage" section of this chapter. Determine the file systems and slice sizes that you will want the installation program to create.

5. Obtain the following information that will be required by the Solaris 10 installation program:
   - What is the hostname of the system? Use the `hostname` command to determine the hostname on an existing system or ask your network administrator to assign a hostname.
   - Does it have a static IP address or DHCP? Use the `ifconfig` command to determine the IP address on an existing system or ask your IP coordinator to assign an IP address. For more information on using the `ifconfig` command to determine a system's IP address, see Chapter 8, "The Solaris Network Environment."
   - Does Ipv6, the next generation Internet protocol, need to be enabled?

NOTE

Enabling the IPv6 Services Enabling IPv6 will have no effect if this machine is not on a network that provides IPv6 service. IPv4 service will not be affected if IPv6 is enabled.

   - Is a name service used, such as NIS, NIS+, DNS, or LDAP? See Chapter 12, "Naming Services," for more information on name services.
   - Should Kerberos security be configured? Ask your in-house security personnel if this is required.
   - What is the geographic region of your time zone (Eastern, Central, Alaska)?
   - During the installation, you will be asked to assign a password to the root user account.
   - Determine the language to be used to install the Solaris 10 operating environment.

2.2 Installing Solaris 10 Using the Interactive Installation Program

For this exercise, you'll use the interactive installation program to install the Solaris 10 operating environment onto your system.

Estimated time: 1–2 hours depending on the speed of your system and CD-ROM

Warning: This exercise will destroy all data on your hard drive.

1. Insert the Solaris 10 CD #1 into the CD-ROM drive.
2. If the system is currently running, either log in as root and shut the system down or abort the operating system by pressing Stop+A.
3. Boot the operating system from the CD as follows:

```
boot cdrom <return>
```

4. The interactive installation program will begin. Refer to the section titled "Using the Interactive Installation Process (`suninstall`)" in this chapter, and follow the steps outlined in that section for installing the operating system.

2.3 Software Package Administration

This exercise takes you through the task of installing, verifying, and removing software on a Solaris system using the command line.

Estimated time: 20 minutes

1. List the software packages that are currently installed on your system by typing the following:

   ```
   pkginfo
   ```

2. Display a long-format listing of information for the SUNWman package installed on your system:

   ```
   pkginfo -l SUNWman
   ```

   What is listed for the status, install date, number of files, and number of blocks used by this package?

3. Remove the SUNWman package from your system with the following:

   ```
   pkgrm SUNWman
   ```

   Verify that the software package has been removed by repeating step 1.

   Now, we'll reinstall the software package. Log in as root and insert Solaris 10 CD #4 into the CD-ROM drive. Use `pkgadd` to spool the SUNWman package into the default spool area as follows:

   ```
   pkgadd -d /cdrom/sol_10_305_sparc_4/Solaris_10/Product\
   -s /var/spool/pkg SUNWman
   ```

4. Use the following commands to verify the presence of SUNWman in the default spool area:

   ```
   pkginfo -d /var/spool/pkg
   ```

5. Observe the messages displayed and verify that the package is installed in `/var/spool/pkg`.

6. Reinstall the SUNWman package from the spool area as follows:

   ```
   pkgadd
   ```

7. Select the SUNWman package when you are prompted and the package will be reinstalled.

8. To remove the SUNWman package from the spool area, type the following:

   ```
   pkgrm -s /var/spool/pkg
   ```

   Select the SUNWman package and it will be removed from the spool directory.

9. You can now use the `pkgchk` command to check the completeness, pathname, file contents, and file attributes of the SUNWman package:

   ```
   pkgchk SUNWman
   ```

Exam Questions

1. What is the minimum amount of RAM required to install Solaris 10?

   ❍ **A.** 256MB

   ❍ **B.** 64MB

   ❍ **C.** 96MB

   ❍ **D.** 128MB

2. What is the best command used to find out the name of your hardware's platform group and name?

   ❍ **A.** `uname -a`

   ❍ **B.** `sysdef`

   ❍ **C.** `arch`

   ❍ **D.** `uname -m`

3. What is a software group?

   ❍ **A.** A group of files and directories that describe a software application

   ❍ **B.** A logical collection of software packages

   ❍ **C.** Any software that can be installed on Solaris

   ❍ **D.** A collection of files that make up a software application

4. What is a software package?

   ❍ **A.** A group of files and directories that describe a software application

   ❍ **B.** A logical collection of software packages

   ❍ **C.** A collection of files that make up a software application

   ❍ **D.** A collection of files and directories

5. Which is *not* one of the six software groups in Solaris 10?

   ❍ **A.** Entire system support

   ❍ **B.** Reduced networking support

   ❍ **C.** Developer system support

   ❍ **D.** Entire distribution plus OEM system support

6. What are the default file systems created by the Solaris installation program?

❍ **A.** /, `/opt`, `/usr`, `/var`, and swap

❍ **B.** /, `/usr`, `/var`, and swap

❍ **C.** /, `/usr`, and swap

❍ **D.** / and swap

7. Which of the following is *not* a valid method of installing Solaris 10?

❍ **A.** Installing over a wide-area network using HTTP

❍ **B.** Interactive

❍ **C.** Installing from a remote CD-ROM on a system on the same subnet

❍ **D.** Web Start

8. Which of the following statements is *not* true of a software package?

❍ **A.** A software package is a group of files and directories that describe a software application, such as manual pages and line printer support.

❍ **B.** A software package is a standard way to deliver bundled and unbundled software.

❍ **C.** Software packages are grouped into software clusters.

❍ **D.** Software packages are administered using the `installf` command.

9. On a Sun system, what is the first step in installing a new operating system?

❍ **A.** Informing the users

❍ **B.** Repartitioning the hard drive

❍ **C.** Finding the source distribution media

❍ **D.** Performing a full backup

10. Which is *not* a valid software configuration group to choose during installation of the Solaris 10 operating environment?

❍ **A.** Core

❍ **B.** Client

❍ **C.** End-User

❍ **D.** Developer

11. For which of the following is custom JumpStart used?

❍ **A.** To install the Solaris software on 50 identical systems

❍ **B.** To start a system that refuses to boot

❍ **C.** To set up AutoClient systems on a server

❍ **D.** To interactively guide you, step by step, in installing the Solaris software

12. Which of the following is a system that provides services to other systems in its networked environment?

❍ **A.** Server

❍ **B.** Client

❍ **C.** File server

❍ **D.** AutoClient server

13. Which of the following is a system that uses remote services from a server, has limited disk space, and requires a server to function?

❍ **A.** AutoClient server

❍ **B.** File server

❍ **C.** Client

❍ **D.** Standalone

14. Which type of installation preserves data and system configuration information?

❍ **A.** Initial

❍ **B.** Upgrade

❍ **C.** Preserve

❍ **D.** Interactive

15. What are the three phases of the installation process?

❍ **A.** System configuration, installation, and post installation

❍ **B.** Power on, boot from CD, execute the installation program

❍ **C.** Boot from CD, start installation program, post installation

❍ **D.** Boot from CD, system configuration, software installation

16. During installation, what is the default software group that is selected to be installed?

❍ **A.** End-user distribution

❍ **B.** Core distribution

❍ **C.** Developer distribution

❍ **D.** Entire distribution

17. What is the kernel architecture of an ultra 5?

❍ **A.** sun4m

❍ **B.** sun4c

❍ **C.** sun4u

❍ **D.** sun4

18. Which information is *not* required to install a server system?

❍ **A.** The server's Ethernet address

❍ **B.** The server's hostname

❍ **C.** The server's IP address

❍ **D.** The server's geographic region

19. Which of the following commands is used to show software package information?

❍ **A.** `pkgadd`

❍ **B.** `pkgchk`

❍ **C.** `pkgparam`

❍ **D.** `pkginfo`

20. Which of the following commands verifies the accuracy of a software package installation?

❍ **A.** `pkgadd`

❍ **B.** `pkgchk`

❍ **C.** `pkgask`

❍ **D.** `pkginfo`

21. Which of the following methods are used to remove software packages from a system?

❍ **A.** `pkgrm`

❍ **B.** `rm -r`

❍ **C.** AdminTool

❍ **D.** All of the above

22. What do software packages names usually start with?

❍ **A.** An abbreviation of the software package

❍ **B.** The company's stock symbol

❍ **C.** SUNW

❍ **D.** Anything the vendor chooses

23. Which of the following commands prepares a compressed tar patch file (with a ".Z" extension) for installation and saves approximately 25% on temporary disk space usage?

❍ **A.** `installpatch -u 104945-02.tar.Z`

❍ **B.** `installpatch -f 104945-02.tar.Z`

❍ **C.** `/usr/bin/zcat 104945-02.tar.Z ¦ tar xvf -`

❍ **D.** `unzip 104945-02.tar.Z ¦ tar xvf -`

24. Which of the following commands show(s) all patches applied to a system? Choose all that apply.

❍ **A.** `patchadd -p`

❍ **B.** `pkginfo`

❍ **C.** `showrev -p`

❍ **D.** `smpatch`

25. Which of the following commands is used to remove a patch from a system?

❍ **A.** `uninstall`

❍ **B.** `pkgrm -s`

❍ **C.** `patchrm`

❍ **D.** `rm -r /var/sasdm/pkg/<pkgname>/save`

26. Sun distributes software patches in which of the following forms? Choose all that apply.

❍ **A.** Sun FTP site

❍ **B.** Email

❍ **C.** CD-ROM

❍ **D.** Magnetic tape

27. The Solaris Product Registry enables you to do which of the following? Choose all that apply.

❍ **A.** View a list of installed software.

❍ **B.** Uninstall software.

❍ **C.** Launch the installer.

❍ **D.** Directly edit software packages with the registry editor.

28. When installing a patch using the `patchadd` command, which of the following options does not create a backup of the files to be patched?

❍ **A.** `-f`

❍ **B.** `-p`

❍ **C.** `-B`

❍ **D.** `-d`

29. Select all of the conditions that will prevent a patch from being installed.

❍ **A.** The patch being installed requires another patch that is not installed.

❍ **B.** The patch is incompatible with another, already installed patch.

❍ **C.** The patch was removed.

❍ **D.** The patch version is not the most up-to-date version.

❍ **E.** All of the above.

30. Which method of installation creates a copy of the OS, upgrades the copy, and allows you to fall back to the original version of the OS if you encounter problems?

❍ **A.** Custom JumpStart

❍ **B.** Upgrade

❍ **C.** Live upgrade

❍ **D.** Solaris Flash Archive

Answers to Exam Questions

1. **C.** The system on which you will be installing Solaris 10 must have a minimum of 128MB of RAM; however, 256MB of RAM is recommended. For more information, see the "Minimum System Requirements" section.

2. **D.** To determine your system type, use the `uname -m` command. The system will respond with the platform group and the platform name for your system. For more information, see the "Requirements and Preparation for Installing the Solaris 10 Software" section.

3. **B.** Software packages are grouped into software clusters, which are logical collections of software packages. For more information, see the "Software Terminology" section.

4. **A.** A software package is a collection of files and directories in a defined format. It is a group of files and directories that describe a software application. For more information, see the "Software Terminology" section.

5. **A.** The six software groups are reduced networking support, core system support, end-user support, developer system support, entire distribution, and entire distribution plus OEM system support. For more information, see the "Software Groups" section.

6. **D.** The default partition scheme setup with the interactive installation program is root (/) and swap. For more information, see the "Disk Storage" section.

7. **D.** Web Start is not a method of installing the OS. Web Start installers are used to install software packages, and Solaris Flash Archives are used when cloning systems. For more information on the methods of installation, refer to the section titled "Methods of Installing the Solaris 10 Software."

8. **D.** The `installf` command is used to add a file to the software installation database, not to administer software packages. For more information, see the "Software Terminology" section.

9. **D.** The first step in installing the operating system, or a patch, is to run a full backup to tape because the installation process destroys all data on the disk. For more information, see the "The Solaris Installation Prechecklist" section.

10. **B.** The six configuration groups are reduced networking support, core system support, end-user support, developer system support, entire distribution, and entire distribution plus OEM system support. For more information, see the "Software Groups" section.

11. **A.** Custom JumpStart allows you to automatically and identically install many systems with the same configuration without having to configure each of them individually. For more information, see the "Custom Jumpstart" section.

12. **A.** A server is a system that provides services or file systems, such as home directories or mail files, to other systems on the network. For more information, see the "Servers" section.

13. **C.** A client is a system that uses remote services from a server. Some clients have limited disk storage capacity, or perhaps none at all; these clients must rely on remote file systems from a server to function. For more information, see the "Servers" section.

14. **B.** The Upgrade option updates the Solaris software to the new release, preserving data, and saving as many modifications to the previous version of Solaris software as possible. For more information, see the "Upgrading the Operating System" section.

15. **A.** The three phases of the installation process are system configuration, installation, and post installation. For more information, see the "Introduction" section.

16. **D.** During the interactive installation, the entire distribution software group is selected by default. For more information, see the "Using the Interactive Installation Process (`suninstall`)" section.

17. **C.** sun4u is the kernel architecture for all Sun UltraSPARC systems. For more information, see the "Requirements and Preparation for Installing the Solaris 10 Software" section.

18. **A.** The server's Ethernet address is not required to install a server system. During the installation, you will be prompted to enter the IP address, the hostname, and the geographic region. For more information, see the "The Solaris Installation Prechecklist" section.

19. **D.** The `pkginfo` command displays software package information. For more information, see the "Tools for Managing Software" section.

20. **B.** The `pkgchk` command checks the accuracy of a software package installation. For more information, see the "Tools for Managing Software" section.

21. **A.** The `pkgrm` command removes software packages from the system. For more information, see the "Tools for Managing Software" section.

22. **B.** Software package names usually start with the company's stock symbol. For more information, see the "Adding and Removing Software Packages" section.

23. **C.** Patches might come in compressed tar format, for example 104945-02.tar.Z. Use the `zcat` command to decompress this type of patch file. For more information, see the "Installing a Patch" section.

24. **A, C.** Use the `patchadd -p` command or the `showrev -p` command to show all patches that have been applied to a system. For more information, see the "Installing a Patch" section.

25. **C.** Use the `patchrm` command to remove a patch from a system. For more information, see the "Installing a Patch" section.

26. **A, B, C.** Software patches are delivered to the customer in the following ways: from Sun's FTP site, via email, or on CD-ROM. For more information, see the "Installing a Patch" section.

27. **A, B, C.** The Solaris Product Registry enables you to view all installed software, uninstall software, or launch the installer to install additional software. For more information, see the "Tools for Managing Software" section.

28. **D.** The `-d` option for the `patchadd` command does not create a backup of the files to be patched. For more information, see the "Installing a Patch" section.

29. **A, B.** The following conditions can prevent a patch from being installed:

    - The patch being installed requires another patch that is not installed.
    - The patch is incompatible with another, already installed patch.

    For more information, see the "Installing a Patch" section.

30. **C.** Live upgrade allows you to create a copy of the current operating environment and upgrade the copy while the system is running in the original environment.

    For more information, see the "Solaris Live Upgrade" section.

Suggested Readings and Resources

1. Websites

    - `docs.sun.com`—Solaris 10 Installation Guide by Sun Microsystems
    - `docs.sun.com`—Solaris 10 System Administration Guide: Basic Administration by Sun Microsystems

CHAPTER THREE

Perform System Boot and Shutdown Procedures

Objectives

The following objectives for the Solaris System Administrator Exam are covered in this chapter:

Explain boot PROM fundamentals, including OpenBoot Architecture Standard, boot PROM, NVRAM, POST, Abort Sequence, and displaying POST to serial port on SPARC systems.

Explain the BIOS settings for booting, abort sequence, and displaying POST.

Execute basic boot PROM commands for a SPARC system.

Perform system boot and shutdown procedures, including identifying the system's boot device, creating and removing custom device aliases, viewing and changing NVRAM parameters, and interrupting an unresponsive system.

Explain the Service Management Facility and the phases of the boot process.

Use Service Management Facility or legacy commands and scripts to control both the boot and shutdown procedures.

- ▶ You need to understand the primary functions of the OpenBoot environment, which includes the programmable read-only memory (PROM). You need to have a complete understanding of how to use many of the OpenBoot commands and how to set and modify all the configuration parameters that control system bootup and hardware behavior.
- ▶ You must understand the entire boot process, from the proper power-on sequence to the steps you perform to bring the system into multiuser mode.
- ▶ You must be able to identify the devices connected to a system and recognize the various special files for each device.
- ▶ Occasionally, conventional shutdown methods might not work on an unresponsive system or on a system that has crashed. This chapter introduces when and how to use these alternative shutdown methods to bring the system down safely.
- ▶ You must understand how the Service Management Facility (SMF) controls which processes and services are started at various stages of the boot process. You need to understand how to use SMF or legacy commands and scripts to control both the boot and shutdown procedures.

Outline

Study Strategies

The following study strategies will help you prepare for the exam:

- When studying this chapter, you should practice on a Sun system each step-by-step process that is outlined. In addition to practicing the processes, you should practice the various options described for booting the system.
- You should display the hardware configuration of your Sun system by using the various OpenBoot commands presented in this chapter. You need to familiarize yourself with all the devices associated with your system. You should be able to identify each hardware component by its device pathname.
- You should practice creating both temporary and permanent device aliases. In addition, you should practice setting the various OpenBoot system parameters that are described in this chapter.
- You should practice booting the system by using the various methods described. You need to understand how to boot into single-user and multiuser modes and how to specify an alternate kernel or system file during the boot process.
- During the boot process, you should watch the system messages and familiarize yourself with every stage of the boot process. You should watch the system messages that are displayed at bootup. You need to understand each message displayed during the boot process from system power-on to bringing the system into multiuser mode.
- You need to thoroughly understand the Service Management Facility (SMF), service states, and milestones. You'll need to understand how the `scv.startd` daemon uses information from the service configuration repository to determine required milestones and how it processes the manifests located in the `/var/svc/manifest` directory. In addition you must understand legacy run control scripts, run levels, and how they affect the system services.
- You should practice shutting down the system. You should make sure you understand the advantages and disadvantages of each method presented.

Introduction

System startup requires an understanding of the hardware and the operating system functions that are required to bring the system to a running state. This chapter discusses the operations that the system must perform from the time you power on the system until you receive a system logon prompt. In addition, it covers the steps required to properly shut down a system. After reading this chapter, you'll understand how to boot the system from the OpenBoot programmable read-only memory (PROM) and what operations must take place to start up the kernel and Unix system processes.

Booting a System

Objective:

Explain the phases of the boot process.

Bootstrapping is the process a computer follows to load and execute the bootable operating system. The term comes from the phrase "pulling yourself up by your bootstraps." The instructions for the bootstrap procedure are stored in the boot PROM.

The boot process goes through the following phases:

1. **Boot PROM phase**—After you turn on power to the system, the PROM displays system identification information and runs self-test diagnostics to verify the system's hardware and memory. It then loads the primary boot program, called `bootblk` from its location on the boot device into memory.

2. **Boot programs phase**—The `bootblk` program finds and executes the secondary boot program (called `ufsboot`) from the Unix file system (UFS) and loads it into memory. After the `ufsboot` program is loaded, the `ufsboot` program loads the two-part kernel.

3. **Kernel initialization phase**—The kernel initializes itself and begins loading modules, using `ufsboot` to read the files. When the kernel has loaded enough modules to mount the root file system, it unmaps the `ufsboot` program and continues, using its own resources.

4. **`init` phase**—The kernel creates a user process and starts the `/sbin/init` process. The `/sbin/init` process reads the `/etc/inittab` file for instructions on starting other processes, one of which is the `svc.startd` daemon (`/lib/svc/bin/svc.startd`).

5. **`svc.startd` phase**—The `svc.startd` daemon starts the system services and boots the system to the appropriate milestone. Specifically, `svc.startd` starts the following system services:

- Checks and mounts file systems
- Configures the network and devices
- Initiates various startup processes and performs system maintenance tasks
- In addition, `svc.startd` executes the legacy run control (rc) scripts for compatibility.

TIP

Boot Phases For the exam, you need to make sure you thoroughly understand each boot phase and the order in which each phase is run. The first two phases are described in this section, with the description of OpenBoot. The kernel, `init`, and `svc.startd` phases are described later in the chapter, in the sections "The Kernel" and "System Run States."

Powering On the System

Before you power on the system, you need to make sure everything is plugged in properly. Check the small computer system interface (SCSI) cables that connect any external devices to the system (such as disk drives and tape drives) to make sure they are properly connected. Check your network connection. Also make sure that the keyboard and monitor are connected properly. Loose cables can cause your system to fail during the startup process.

CAUTION

Connecting Cables with the Power Turned Off Always connect your cables before turning on the hardware; otherwise, you could damage your system.

The correct sequence for powering on your equipment is to first turn on any peripherals (that is, external disk drives or tape drives) and then turn on power to the system.

The Boot PROM and Program Phases

The bootstrap process begins after power-up, when the startup routines located in the hardware's PROM chip are executed. Sun calls this the *OpenBoot firmware*, and it is executed immediately after you turn on the system.

The primary task of the OpenBoot firmware is to test the hardware and to boot the operating system either from a mass storage device or from the network. OpenBoot contains a program called the *monitor* that controls the operation of the system before the kernel is available and before the operating system has been booted. When a system is turned on, the monitor runs a power-on self-test (POST) that checks such things as the hardware and memory on the system.

If no errors are found, the automatic boot process begins. OpenBoot contains a set of instructions that locate and start up the system's boot program and eventually start up the Unix operating system.

NOTE

Automatic System Recovery Sun server class systems can recognize failed components and disable the board that contains the failed component. If the server is configured with multiple central processing unit (CPU)/memory and input/output (I/O) boards, the system can boot in a degraded yet stable condition, even with failed components. See your server's *System Reference Manual* for details on automatic system recovery.

The boot program is stored in a predictable area (sectors 1–15) on the system hard drive, CD-ROM, or other bootable device and is referred to as the *bootblock* (`bootblk`). The bootblock is responsible for loading the secondary boot program (`ufsboot`) into memory, which is located in the UFS file system on the boot device. The path to `ufsboot` is recorded in the bootblock, which is installed by the Solaris `installboot` utility.

`ufsboot` locates and loads the two-part kernel. The *kernel* (which is covered in detail later in this chapter) is the part of the operating system that remains running at all times until the system is shut down. It is the core and the most important part of the operating system. The kernel consists of a two-piece static core called `genunix` and `unix`. `genunix` is the platform-independent generic kernel file, and `unix` is the platform-specific kernel file. When the system boots, `ufsboot` combines these two files into memory to form the running kernel.

The OpenBoot Environment

Objective:

Execute basic boot PROM commands for a SPARC system.

- Explain boot PROM fundamentals, including OpenBoot Architecture Standard, boot PROM, NVRAM, POST, Abort Sequence, and displaying POST to serial port on SPARC systems.

The hardware-level user interface that you see before the operating system starts is called the OpenBoot PROM (OBP). OpenBoot is based on an interactive command interpreter that gives you access to an extensive set of functions for hardware and software development, fault isolation, and debugging. The OBP firmware is stored in the system's PROM chip.

Sun UltraSPARC systems use a programmable boot PROM that allows new boot program data to be loaded into the PROM by "flashing" the PROM with software. This type of PROM is called a flash PROM (FPROM).

The NVRAM chip stores user-definable system parameters, also referred to as NVRAM variables or EEPROM parameters. The parameters allow administrators to control variables such as the default boot device and boot command. The NVRAM also contains writeable areas for user-controlled diagnostics, macros, and device aliases. NVRAM is where the system identification information is stored, such as the host ID, Ethernet address, and time-of-day (TOD) clock. On older systems, a single lithium battery backup provides backup for the NVRAM and clock. Newer systems contain a non-removable Serial Electronically Erasable Programmable Read-Only Memory (SEEPROM) chip that does not require a battery. Other newer systems may contain a removable system configuration card to hold the system configuration information. Many software packages use the host ID for licensing purposes; therefore, it is important that the NVRAM chip can be removed and placed into any replacement system board. Because NVRAM contains unique identification information for the machine, Sun sometimes refers to it as the identification programmable read-only memory (ID PROM).

OpenBoot is currently at version 5 but is available only on high-end Sun servers (SunFire and higher). Depending on the age of your system, you could have PROM version 3, 4, or 5 installed. The original boot PROM firmware, version 1, was first introduced on the Sun SPARCstation 1. The first version of the OpenBoot PROM was version 2, and it first appeared on the SPARCstation 2 system. OpenBoot versions 3 and 4 are the versions that are currently available on the Ultra series systems and Enterprise servers. Versions 3, 4 and 5 of the OpenBoot architecture provide a significant increase in functionality over the boot PROMs in earlier Sun systems. One notable feature of the OpenBoot firmware is a programmable user interface based on the interactive programming language Forth. In Forth, sequences of user commands can be combined to form complete programs. This capability provides a powerful tool for debugging hardware and software. Another benefit of versions 3, 4, and 5 is the Flash update feature. You can update the version 3, 4, and 5 firmware without replacing the PROM chip, but you will not be tested on updating the firmware on the exam.

To determine the version of the OpenBoot PROM, type

```
/usr/bin/prtdiag -v
```

or

```
prtconf -v
```

NOTE

No OpenBoot Environment on the Intel Platform The Intel environment has no OpenBoot PROM or NVRAM. On Intel systems, before the kernel is started, the system is controlled by the basic input/output system (BIOS), the firmware interface on a PC. Therefore, many features provided by OpenBoot are not available on Intel systems.

Entry-Level to High-End Systems

Every Sun workstation and server except the midrange, midframe, and high-end servers has only one system board and holds only one boot PROM and NVRAM chip.

Sun's midrange, midframe, and high-end servers, such as the Enterprise and Sun Fire, can be configured with multiple CPU/memory and I/O boards.

The following are some things you should be aware of on multiple-CPU systems:

- A multiple-CPU system has a clock board to oversee the backplane communications.
- The `host ID` and Ethernet address are on the clock board and are automatically downloaded to the NVRAM on all CPU boards when the POST is complete.
- PROM contents on each CPU are compared and verified via checksums.
- The CPU that is located in the lowermost card cage slot is the master CPU board.
- Each CPU runs its own individual POST.
- If these systems are configured with redundant CPU/memory and I/O boards, they can run in a degraded yet stable mode, even when some components have failed. Such systems are usually described as fault-tolerant or fault-resilient.

Accessing the OpenBoot Environment

You can get to the OpenBoot environment by using any of the following methods:

- Halting the operating system.
- Pressing the Stop and A keys simultaneously (Stop+A). On terminals that are connected to the serial port and do not have a Stop key, you press the Break key. This will stop the operating system and transfer control to the OpenBoot monitor. In some cases, this may lead to data loss or corruption, and therefore should be used with caution.
- When the system is initially powered on. If your system is not configured to start up automatically, it stops at the user interface (the monitor prompt). If automatic startup is configured, you can make the system stop at the user interface by pressing Stop+A after the display console banner is displayed but before the system begins starting the operating system.
- When the system hardware detects an error from which it cannot recover. (This is known as a *watchdog reset*.)

System Control Switch

On those servers with a power button and system control switch located on the system's front panel, the ability to turn the system on or off is controlled by the key position on the system control switch.

The four-position system control switch (key) located on the system's front panel controls the power-on modes of the system and prevents unauthorized users from powering off the system or reprogramming system firmware. Table 3.1 describes the function of each system control switch setting:

TABLE 3.1 Function of Each System Control Switch Setting

Position	Description
Normal	This key position allows the system Power button to power the system on or off. If the operating system is running, pressing and releasing the Power button initiates a graceful software system shutdown. Pressing and holding the Power button in for five seconds causes an immediate hardware power off. which could cause disk corruption and loss of data—this should be used only as last resort.
Locked	This key position disables the system Power button to prevent unauthorized users from powering the system on or off. It also disables the keyboard L1-A (Stop-A) command, terminal Break key command, and ~# tip window command, preventing users from suspending system operation to access the system ok prompt. The Locked setting, used for normal day-to-day operations, also prevents unauthorized programming of the system boot PROM.
Diagnostics	This key position forces the power-on self-test (POST) and OpenBoot Diagnostics software to run during system startup and system resets. The Power button functions the same as when the system control switch is in the Normal position.
Forced Off	This key position forces the system to power off immediately and to enter 5-volt standby mode. It also disables the system Power button. Use this setting when AC power is interrupted and you do not want the system to restart automatically when power is restored. With the system control switch in any other position, if the system were running prior to losing power, it restarts automatically once power is restored. The Forced Off setting also prevents a Remote System Control (RSC) session from restarting the system. However, the RSC card continues to operate using the system's 5-volt standby power.

NOTE

Alternative Methods for Stopping a System An alternative sequence that can be used to stop the system is Enter+~+Ctrl+B, which is equivalent to Stop+A. There must be an interval of more than 0.5 seconds between characters, and the entire string must be entered in less than 5 seconds. You can use this method only with serial devices acting as consoles and not for systems with keyboards of their own. To enable this alternative sequence, you must first modify the `/etc/default/kbd` file by removing the # from the entry:

```
#KEYBOARD_ABORT=alternate
```

To disable the abort key sequence, make the following entry to the `/etc/default/kbd` file:

```
KEYBOARD_ABORT=disable
```

Remember to uncomment the line by removing the "#".

Then you save the changes and, as root, type

```
kbd -i
```

to put the changes into effect.

On a server with a physical keyswitch, the alternative BREAK does not work when the key is set to the Secure position.

If your console is connected to the serial port via a modem, you can send a break (Stop+A or L1+A) through the `tip` window by typing ~# (tilde and then the pound sign).

CAUTION

Using Stop+A Sparingly Forcing a system into the OpenBoot PROM by using Stop+A or Break abruptly breaks execution of the operating system. You should use these methods only as a last resort to restart the system. When you access the `ok` prompt from a running system, you are suspending the operating environment software and placing the system under firmware control. Any processes that were running under the operating environment software are also suspended, and the state of such software may not be recoverable.

The diagnostics and commands that you run from the `ok` prompt have the potential to affect the state of the system. Don't assume that you will be able to resume execution of the operating environment software from the point at which it was suspended. Although the `go` command will resume execution in most circumstances, as a rule, each time you drop the system down to the `ok` prompt, you should expect to have to reboot it to get back to the normal operating state.

OpenBoot Firmware Tasks

The IEEE Standard 1275 defines the OpenBoot architecture and the primary tasks of the OpenBoot firmware are as follows:

- Test and initialize the system hardware.
- Determine the hardware configuration.

- Start the operating system from either a mass storage device or a network.
- Provide interactive debugging facilities for configuring, testing, and debugging.
- Allow modification and management of system startup configuration, such as NVRAM parameters.
- Servers such as the Sun Fire provide environmental monitoring and control capabilities at both the operating system level and the OpenBoot firmware level to monitor the state of the system power supplies, fans, and temperature sensors. If it detects any voltage, current, fan speed, or temperature irregularities, the monitor generates a warning message to the system console and ultimately it will initiate an automatic system shutdown sequence.

Specifically, the following tasks are necessary to initialize the operating system kernel:

1. OpenBoot displays system identification information and then runs self-test diagnostics to verify the system's hardware and memory. These checks are known as a POST—power-on self test.
2. OpenBoot will then probe system bus devices, interpret their drivers, build a device tree, and then install the console. After initializing the system, OpenBoot displays a banner on the console.
3. OpenBoot will check parameters stored in NVRAM to determine how to boot the operating system.
4. OpenBoot loads the primary startup program, `bootblk`, from the default startup device.
5. The `bootblk` program finds and executes the secondary startup program, `ufsboot`, and loads it into memory. The `ufsboot` program loads the operating system kernel.

The OpenBoot Architecture

Objective:

Explain boot PROM fundamentals, including OpenBoot Architecture Standard

TIP

The OpenBoot Device Tree In this section, pay close attention to the OpenBoot device tree. You're likely to see this topic on the exam.

The OpenBoot architecture provides an increase in functionality and portability compared to the proprietary systems of some other hardware vendors. Although this architecture was first implemented by Sun Microsystems as OpenBoot on SPARC (Scaleable Processor Architecture) systems, its design is processor independent. The following are some notable features of OpenBoot firmware:

- **Plug-in device drivers**—A device driver can be loaded from a plug-in device such as an SBus card. The plug-in device driver can be used to boot the operating system from that device or to display text on the device before the operating system has activated its own software device drivers. This feature lets the input and output devices evolve without changing the system PROM.
- **The FCode interpreter**—Plug-in drivers are written in a machine-independent interpreted language called FCode. Each OpenBoot system PROM contains an FCode interpreter. This enables the same device and driver to be used on machines with different CPU instruction sets.
- **The device tree**—Devices called *nodes* are attached to a host computer through a hierarchy of interconnected buses on the device tree. A node representing the host computer's main physical address bus forms the tree's root node. Both the user and the operating system can determine the system's hardware configuration by viewing the device tree.

  Nodes with children usually represent buses and their associated controllers, if any. Each such node defines a physical address space that distinguishes the devices connected to the node from one another. Each child of that node is assigned a physical address in the parent's address space. The physical address generally represents a physical characteristic that is unique to the device (such as the bus address or the slot number where the device is installed). The use of physical addresses to identify devices prevents device addresses from changing when other devices are installed or removed.
- **The programmable user interface**—The OpenBoot user interface is based on the programming language Forth, which provides an interactive programming environment. It can be quickly expanded and adapted to special needs and different hardware systems. Forth is used not only by Sun but also utilized in the OpenFirmware boot ROMs provided by IBM, Apple, and Hewlett-Packard.

NOTE

Forth If you're interested in more information on Forth, refer to American National Standards Institute (ANSI) Standard X3.215-1994 (see `www.ansi.org`).

The OpenBoot Interface

Objective:

Execute basic boot PROM commands for a SPARC system.

The OpenBoot firmware provides a command-line interface for the user at the system console called the *Forth Monitor*.

The Forth Monitor is an interactive command interpreter that gives you access to an extensive set of functions for hardware and software diagnosis. Sometimes you'll also see the Forth Monitor referred to as *new command mode*. These functions are available to anyone who has access to the system console.

The Forth Monitor prompt is `ok`. When you enter the Forth Monitor mode, the following line displays:

```
Type help for more information
ok
```

Getting Help in OpenBoot

At any time, you can obtain help on the various Forth commands supported in OpenBoot by using the `help` command. The `help` commands from the `ok` prompt are listed in Table 3.2.

TABLE 3.2 OpenBoot `help` Commands

Command	Description
`help`	Displays instructions for using the help system and lists the available help categories.
`help` *<category>*	Shows help for all commands in the category. You use only the first word of the category description.
`help` *<command>*	Shows help for an individual command.

Because of the large number of commands, help is available only for commands that are used frequently.

The following example shows the `help` command with no arguments:

```
ok help
```

The system responds with the following:

```
Enter 'help command-name' or 'help category-name' for more help
(Use ONLY the first word of a category description)
Examples:  help system  -or-  help nvramrc
```

```
Categories:
boot (Load and execute a program)
nvramrc (Store user defined commands)
system configuration variables (NVRAM variables)
command line editing
editor (nvramrc editor)
resume execution
devaliases (Device Aliases)
diag (Diagnostic commands)
ioredirect (I/O redirection commands)
misc (Miscellaneous commands)
ok
```

If you want to see the help messages for all commands in the category `diag`, for example, you type the following:

```
ok help diag
```

The system responds with this:

```
test <device>  Run the selftest method for specified device
test-all       Execute test for all devices with selftest method
watch-net      Monitor network connection
probe-scsi     Show attached SCSI devices
ok

ok help misc
```

The system responds with this:

```
reset-all     Reset system (similar to a power-cycle)
power-off     Power off system
sync          Reenter operating system to sync the disks
eject-floppy  Eject floppy from drive
ok

ok help boot
```

The system responds with this:

```
boot [<device-specifier>:<device-arguments>] [boot-arguments]
Examples:
boot              Default boot (values specified in NVRAM variables)
boot disk1:h      Boot from disk1 partition h
boot myunix -as   Boot from default device. Pass boot program "myunix -as"

Booting from network
boot <network-device>:[dhcp,][server-ip],[boot-filename],[client-ip],
[router-ip],[boot-retries],[tftp-retries],[subnet-mask] [boot-arguments]
ok
```

PROM Device Tree (Full Device Pathnames)

Objective:

Display devices connected to the bus.

- Identify the system's boot device.

NOTE

The Device Tree Versus Device Pathname The terms *device tree* and *device pathname* are often interchanged, and you'll see both used. They both mean the same thing.

OpenBoot deals directly with the hardware devices in the system. Each device has a unique name that represents both the type of device and the location of that device in the device tree. The OpenBoot firmware builds a device tree for all devices from information gathered at the POST. Sun uses the device tree to organize devices that are attached to the system. The device tree is loaded into memory, to be used by the kernel during boot to identify all configured devices. The paths built in the device tree by OpenBoot vary, depending on the type of system and its device configuration. The following example shows a full device pathname for an internal disk on a peripheral component interconnect (PCI) bus system such as an Ultra 5:

```
/pci@1f,0/pci@1,1/ide@3/disk@0,0
```

Typically, the OBP uses `disk` and `cdrom` for the boot disk and CD-ROM drive.

The following example shows the disk device on an Ultra system with a PCI-SCSI bus and a SCSI target address of 3:

```
/pci@1f,0/pci@1/scsi@1,1/sd@3,0
```

A *device tree* is a series of node names separated by slashes (`/`). The top of the device tree is the root device node. Following the root device node, and separated by a leading slash `/`, is a list of bus devices and controllers. Each device pathname has this form:

```
driver-name@unit-address:device-arguments
```

The components of the device pathname are described in Table 3.3.

TABLE 3.3 Device Pathname Parameters

Parameter	Description
driver-name	This is the root device node, which is a human-readable string that consists of 1 to 31 letters, digits, and the following punctuation characters: , (comma) . (period) _ (underscore) + (plus sign) - (minus sign) Uppercase and lowercase characters are distinct from one another. In some cases, the driver name includes the name of the device's manufacturer and the device's model name, separated by a comma. Typically, the manufacturer's uppercase, publicly listed stock symbol is used as the manufacturer's name (for example, `SUNW,hme0`). For built-in devices, the manufacturer's name is usually omitted (for example, `scsi` or `pci`). @ must precede the address parameter; it serves as a separator between the driver name and unit address.
unit-address	A text string that represents the physical address of the device in its parent's address space. The exact meaning of a particular address depends on the bus to which the device is attached. In this example, `/sbus@3,0/SUNW,fas@3,0/sd@0,0` `sbus@3,0` represents the I/O board in slot 1, located on the back of the system, and `SUNW,fas@3,0` is the onboard fast/wide SCSI controller of the same board. The following are common device driver names: **fas**—Fast/wide SCSI controller. **hme**—Fast (10/100Mbps) Ethernet. **isp**—Differential SCSI controllers and the SunSwift card. **ge**—Sun Gigabit Ethernet. **eri**—FastEthernet. **ce**—Gigaswift Ethernet. **qfe**—Quad FastEthernet. **dmfe**—Davicom FastEthernet. **glm**—UltraSCSI controllers. **scsi**—SCSI devices. **sf**—SCSI-compliant nexus driver that supports the Fibre Channel Protocol for SCSI on Private Fibre Channel Arbitrated Loops (FC-ALs). **soc**—Serial optical controller (SOC) device driver.

TABLE 3.3 *Continued*

Parameter	Description
	`socal`—The Fibre Channel host bus adapter, which is an SBus card that implements two full-duplex Fibre Channel interfaces. Each Fibre Channel interface can connect to an FC-AL. **`iprb`**—An Intel network interface found on x86/x64 based systems. The network interface driver will change depending on which one of many possible third party network interfaces you have installed on your x86/x64 platform. Others are `dnet` (Sohoware), `elxl` (3COM), `spwr` (SMC), and `nei` (Linksys). `sd@0,0` is the SCSI disk (`sd`) set to target `id 0`. (In this case, it is an internal disk because only internal disks should be controlled by the onboard SCSI controller of the I/O board in slot 1.)
`device-arguments`	A text string whose format depends on the particular device. *`device-arguments`* can be used to pass additional information to the device's software. In this example: `/pci@1f,0/pci@1,1/ide@3/atapicd@2,0:f` the argument for the disk device is `f`. The software driver for this device interprets its argument as a disk partition, so the device pathname refers to partition `f` on a CD-ROM.

You use the OpenBoot command `show-devs` to obtain information about the device tree and to display device pathnames. This command displays all the devices known to the system directly beneath a given device in the device hierarchy. `show-devs` used by itself shows the entire device tree. The syntax is as follows:

```
ok show-devs
```

The system outputs the entire device tree, as follows:

```
/SUNW,UltraSPARC-IIi@0,0
/pci@1f,0
/virtual-memory
/memory@0,10000000
/aliases
/options
/openprom
/chosen
/packages
/pci@1f,0/pci@1
/pci@1f,0/pci@1,1
/pci@1f,0/pci@1/scsi@1,1
/pci@1f,0/pci@1/scsi@1
/pci@1f,0/pci@1/scsi@1,1/tape
/pci@1f,0/pci@1/scsi@1,1/disk
```

```
/pci@1f,0/pci@1/scsi@1/tape
/pci@1f,0/pci@1/scsi@1/disk
/pci@1f,0/pci@1,1/ide@3
/pci@1f,0/pci@1,1/SUNW,m64B@2
/pci@1f,0/pci@1,1/network@1,1
/pci@1f,0/pci@1,1/ebus@1
/pci@1f,0/pci@1,1/ide@3/cdrom
/pci@1f,0/pci@1,1/ide@3/disk
/pci@1f,0/pci@1,1/ebus@1/SUNW,CS4231@14,200000
/pci@1f,0/pci@1,1/ebus@1/flashprom@10,0
/pci@1f,0/pci@1,1/ebus@1/eeprom@14,0
/pci@1f,0/pci@1,1/ebus@1/fdthree@14,3023f0
/pci@1f,0/pci@1,1/ebus@1/ecpp@14,3043bc
/pci@1f,0/pci@1,1/ebus@1/su@14,3062f8
/pci@1f,0/pci@1,1/ebus@1/su@14,3083f8
/pci@1f,0/pci@1,1/ebus@1/se@14,400000
/pci@1f,0/pci@1,1/ebus@1/SUNW,pll@14,504000
/pci@1f,0/pci@1,1/ebus@1/power@14,724000
/pci@1f,0/pci@1,1/ebus@1/auxio@14,726000
/openprom/client-services
/packages/ufs-file-system
/packages/sun-keyboard
/packages/SUNW,builtin-drivers
/packages/disk-label
/packages/obp-tftp
/packages/deblocker
/packages/terminal-emulator
ok
```

Commands that are used to examine the device tree are listed in Table 3.4.

TABLE 3.4 Commands for Browsing the Device Tree

Command	Description
`.properties`	Displays the names and values of the current node's properties.
`dev` *<device-path>*	Chooses the specified device node and makes it the current node.
`dev` *<node-name>*	Searches for a node with the specified name in the subtree below the current node and chooses the first such node found.
`dev ..`	Chooses the device node that is the parent of the current node.
`dev /`	Chooses the root machine node.
`cd /`	Same as `dev /`
`device-end`	Leaves the device tree.
<device-path> `find-device`	Chooses the specified device node, similar to `dev`.
`ls`	Displays the names of the current node's children.
`pwd`	Displays the device pathname that names the current node.

TABLE 3.4 *Continued*

Command	Description
`see <wordname>`	Decompiles the specified word.
`show-devs <device-path>`	Displays all the devices known to the system directly beneath a given device in the device hierarchy. `show-devs` used by itself shows the entire device tree.
`show-disks`	Displays only the disk devices currently connected to the system.
`show-nets`	Displays only the network interface devices currently connected to the system.
`words`	Displays the names of the current node's methods.
`<device-path>" select-dev`	Selects the specified device and makes it the active node.

You can examine the device path from a Unix shell prompt by typing the following:

```
prtconf -p
```

The system displays the following information:

```
System Configuration:  Sun Microsystems  sun4u
Memory size: 128 Megabytes
System Peripherals (PROM Nodes):

Node 'SUNW,Ultra-5_10'
    Node 'packages'
        Node 'terminal-emulator'
        Node 'deblocker'
        Node 'obp-tftp'
        Node 'disk-label'
        Node 'SUNW,builtin-drivers'
        Node 'sun-keyboard'
        Node 'ufs-file-system'
    Node 'chosen'
    Node 'openprom'
        Node 'client-services'
    Node 'options'
    Node 'aliases'
    Node 'memory'
    Node 'virtual-memory'
    Node 'pci'
        Node 'pci'
            Node 'ebus'
                Node 'auxio'
                Node 'power'
                Node 'SUNW,pll'
                Node 'se'
                Node 'su'
```

```
                Node 'su'
                Node 'ecpp'
                Node 'fdthree'
                Node 'eeprom'
                Node 'flashprom'
                Node 'SUNW,CS4231'
            Node 'network'
            Node 'SUNW,m64B'
            Node 'ide'
                Node 'disk'
                Node 'cdrom'
        Node 'pci'
            Node 'scsi'
                Node 'disk'
                Node 'tape'
            Node 'scsi'
                Node 'disk'
                Node 'tape'
   Node 'SUNW,UltraSPARC-IIi'
```

OpenBoot Device Aliases

Objective:

Create and remove custom device aliases.

Device pathnames can be long and complex. Device aliases, like Unix file system aliases, allow you to substitute a short name for a long name. An alias represents an entire device pathname, not a component of it. For example, the alias `disk0` might represent the following device pathname:

```
/pci@1f,0/pci@1,1/ide@3/disk@0,0
```

OpenBoot provides the predefined device aliases listed in Table 3.5 for commonly used devices, so you rarely need to type a full device pathname. Be aware, however, that device aliases and pathnames can vary on each platform. The device aliases shown in Table 3.5 are from a Sun Ultra 5 system.

TABLE 3.5 Predefined Device Aliases

Alias	Device Pathname
disk	/pci@1f,0/pci@1,1/ide@3/disk@0,0
disk0	/pci@1f,0/pci@1,1/ide@3/disk@0,0
disk1	/pci@1f,0/pci@1,1/ide@3/disk@1,0
disk2	/pci@1f,0/pci@1,1/ide@3/disk@2,0

TABLE 3.5 *Continued*

Alias	Device Pathname
disk3	/pci@1f,0/pci@1,1/ide@3/disk@3,0
cdrom	/pci@1f,0/pci@1,1/ide@3/cdrom@2,0:f
net	/pci@1f,0/pci@1,1/network@1,1

If you add disk drives or change the target of the startup drive, you might need to modify these device aliases. Table 3.6 describes the `devalias` commands, which are used to examine, create, and change OpenBoot aliases.

TABLE 3.6 The `devalias` Commands

Command	Description
`devalias`	Displays all current device aliases
`devalias_`*`<alias>`*	Displays the device pathname that corresponds to *`alias`*
`devalias_<alias>` *`<device-path>`*	Defines an alias that represents *`device-path`*

NOTE

Don't Use Existing `devalias` Names If an alias with the same name already exists, you'll see two aliases defined: a `devalias` with the old value and a `devalias` with the new value. It gets confusing as to which `devalias` is the current `devalias`. Therefore, it is recommended that you do not reuse the name of an existing `devalias`, but choose a new name.

The following example creates a device alias named `bootdisk`, which represents an Integrated Drive Electronics (IDE) disk with a target ID of 3 on an Ultra 5 system:

```
devalias bootdisk /pci@1f,0/pci@1,1/ide@3/disk@3,0
```

To confirm the alias, you type `devalias`, as follows:

```
ok devalias
```

The system responds by printing all the aliases, like this:

```
bootdisk                 /pci@1f,0/pci@1,1/ide@3/disk@3,0
screen                   /pci@1f,0/pci@1,1/SUNW,m64B@2
net                      /pci@1f,0/pci@1,1/network@1,1
cdrom                    /pci@1f,0/pci@1,1/ide@3/cdrom@2,0:f
disk                     /pci@1f,0/pci@1,1/ide@3/disk@0,0
disk3                    /pci@1f,0/pci@1,1/ide@3/disk@3,0
disk2                    /pci@1f,0/pci@1,1/ide@3/disk@2,0
disk1                    /pci@1f,0/pci@1,1/ide@3/disk@1,0
disk0                    /pci@1f,0/pci@1,1/ide@3/disk@0,0
```

```
ide                    /pci@1f,0/pci@1,1/ide@3
floppy                 /pci@1f,0/pci@1,1/ebus@1/fdthree
ttyb                   /pci@1f,0/pci@1,1/ebus@1/se:b
ttya                   /pci@1f,0/pci@1,1/ebus@1/se:a
keyboard!              /pci@1f,0/pci@1,1/ebus@1/su@14,3083f8:forcemode
keyboard               /pci@1f,0/pci@1,1/ebus@1/su@14,3083f8
mouse                  /pci@1f,0/pci@1,1/ebus@1/su@14,3062f8
name                   aliases
```

You can also view device aliases from a shell prompt by using the `prtconf -vp` command.

User-defined aliases are lost after a system reset or power cycle unless you create a permanent alias. If you want to create permanent aliases, you can either manually store the `devalias` command in a portion of NVRAM called NVRAMRC or you can use the `nvalias` and `nvunalias` commands. The following section describes how to configure permanent settings in the NVRAM on a Sun system.

OpenBoot NVRAM

Objective:

List, change, and restore default NVRAM parameters.

- View and change NVRAM parameters from the shell.

System configuration variables are stored in system NVRAM. These OpenBoot variables determine the startup machine configuration and related communication characteristics. If you modify the values of the configuration variables, any changes you make remain in effect even after a power cycle. Configuration variables should be adjusted cautiously, however, because incorrect settings can prevent a system from booting.

Table 3.7 describes OpenBoot's NVRAM configuration variables, their default values, and their functions.

TABLE 3.7 NVRAM Variables

Variable	Default	Description
`auto-boot?`	`true`	The system starts up automatically after power-on or reset if `auto-boot?` is `true`. If it is set to false, the system stops at the OpenBoot prompt (`ok`) after power-on or reset.
`boot-command`	`boot`	The command that is executed if `auto-boot?` is `true`.
`boot-device`	`disk` or `net`	The device from which to start up.
`boot-file`	Empty string	Arguments passed to the started program.

TABLE 3.7 *Continued*

Variable	Default	Description
`diag-device`	`net`	The diagnostic startup source device.
`diag-file`	Empty string	Arguments passed to the startup program in diagnostic mode.
`diag-switch?`	`false`	Whether to run in diagnostic mode.
`fcode-debug?`	`false`	Whether name fields are included for plug-in device FCodes.
`input-device`	`keyboard`	A console input device (usually `keyboard`, `ttya`, or `ttyb`).
`nvramrc`	Empty	The contents of NVRAMRC.
`oem-banner`	Empty string	A custom original equipment manufacturer (OEM) banner (enabled with `oem-banner? true`).
`oem-banner?`	`false`	If `true`, use custom OEM banner.
`oem-logo`	No default	A byte array custom OEM logo (enabled with `oem-logo? true`). Displayed in hexadecimal.
`oem-logo?`	`false`	If `true`, use custom OEM logo; otherwise, use the Sun logo.
`output-device`	`screen`	A console output device (usually `screen`, `ttya`, or `ttyb`).
`sbus-probe-list`	`0123`	Which SBus slots to probe and in what order.
`screen-#columns`	`80`	The number of onscreen columns (characters/line).
`screen-#rows`	`34`	The number of onscreen rows (lines).
`security-#badlogins`	No default	The number of incorrect security password attempts.
`security-mode`	none	The firmware security level (options: none, `command`, or `full`).
`security-password`	No default	The firmware security password (which is never displayed).
`use-nvramrc?`	`false`	If `true`, execute commands in NVRAMRC during system startup.

NOTE

OpenBoot Versions Because older SPARC systems use older versions of OpenBoot, they might use different defaults or different configuration variables from those shown in Table 3.7. This text describes OpenBoot version 4.

You can view and change the NVRAM configuration variables by using the commands listed in Table 3.8.

TABLE 3.8 Commands for Viewing and Modifying Configuration Variables

Command	Description
`password`	Sets the security password.
`printenv`	Displays the current value and the default value for each variable. To show the current value of a named variable, you type the following:
	`printenv <parameter-name>`
`setenv <variable> <value>`	Sets `<variable>` to the given decimal or text `<value>`. Changes are permanent, but they often take effect only after a reset.
`set-default <variable>`	Resets the value of a specified `<variable>` to the factory default.
`set-defaults`	Resets ALL OpenBoot variable values to the factory defaults.

The following examples illustrate the use of the commands described in Table 3.8. All commands are entered at the `ok` OpenBoot prompt.

You use the `printenv` command, with no argument, to display the current value and the default value for each variable:

```
ok printenv
```

The system responds with this:

```
Variable Name         Value                          Default Value
tpe-link-test?        true                           true
scsi-initiator-id     7                              7
keyboard-click?       false                          false
keymap
ttyb-rts-dtr-off      false                          false
ttyb-ignore-cd        true                           true
ttya-rts-dtr-off      false                          false
ttya-ignore-cd        true                           true
ttyb-mode             9600,8,n,1,-                   9600,8,n,1,-
ttya-mode             9600,8,n,1,-                   9600,8,n,1,-
pcia-probe-list       1,2,3,4                        1,2,3,4
pcib-probe-list       1,2,3                          1,2,3
mfg-mode              off                            off
diag-level            max                            max
#power-cycles         89
system-board-serial#
system-board-date
fcode-debug?          false                          false
output-device         screen                         screen
input-device          keyboard                       keyboard
load-base             16384                          16384
```

```
boot-command            boot                  boot
auto-boot?              false                 true
watchdog-reboot?        false                 false
diag-file
diag-device             net                   net
boot-file
boot-device             disk:a disk net       disk net
local-mac-address?      false                 false
ansi-terminal?          true                  true
screen-#columns         80                    80
screen-#rows            34                    34
silent-mode?            false                 false
use-nvramrc?            false                 false
nvramrc
security-mode           none
security-password
security-#badlogins     0
oem-logo
oem-logo?               false                 false
oem-banner
oem-banner?             false                 false
hardware-revision
last-hardware-update
diag-switch?            false                 false
```

NOTE

The printenv Command Depending on the version of OpenBoot that you have on your system, the printenv command might show slightly different results. This example uses a system running OpenBoot version 3.31.

To set the auto-boot? variable to false, you type the following:

```
ok setenv auto-boot? false
```

The system responds with this:

```
auto-boot? =    false
```

You can verify the setting by typing the following:

```
ok printenv auto-boot?
```

The system responds with this:

```
auto-boot? =      false
```

To reset the variable to its default setting, you type the following:

```
ok set-default auto-boot?
```

The system does not respond with a message—only another OpenBoot prompt. You can verify the setting by typing the following:

```
ok printenv auto-boot?
```

The system responds with this:

```
auto-boot? =      true
```

To reset all variables to their default settings, you type the following:

```
ok set-defaults
```

The system responds with this:

```
Setting NVRAM parameters to default values.
```

It's possible to set variables from the Unix command line by issuing the `eeprom` command. You must be logged in as root to issue this command, and although anyone can view a parameter, only root can change the value of a parameter. For example, to set the `auto-boot?` variable to `true`, you type the following at the Unix prompt (note the use of quotes to escape the ? from expansion by the shell):

```
eeprom 'auto-boot?=true'
```

Any non-root user can view the OpenBoot configuration variables from a Unix prompt by typing the following:

```
/usr/sbin/eeprom
```

For example, to change the OpenBoot parameter `security-password` from the command line, you must be logged in as root and issue the following command:

```
example# eeprom security-password=
Changing PROM password:
New password:
Retype new password:
```

CAUTION

Setting the OpenBoot Security Mode Setting the security mode and password can be dangerous: If you forget the password, the system is unable to boot. It is nearly impossible to break in without sending the CPU to Sun to have the PROM reset. OpenBoot security is discussed more in the section "OpenBoot Security," later in this chapter.

The security mode password you assign must be between zero and eight characters. Any characters after the eighth are ignored. You do not have to reset the system after you set a password; the security feature takes effect as soon as you type the command.

With no parameters, the `eeprom` command displays all the OpenBoot configuration settings, similar to the OpenBoot `printenv` command.

Use the `prtconf` command with the `-vp` options to view OpenBoot parameters from the shell prompt as follows:

```
prtconf -vp
```

The system responds with a great deal of output, but you'll see the following OpenBoot information embedded in the output:

```
. . . . <output truncated>
ansi-terminal?:  'true'
        screen-#columns:  '80'
        screen-#rows:  '34'
        silent-mode?:  'false'
        use-nvramrc?:  'false'
        nvramrc:
        security-mode:  'none'
        security-password:
        security-#badlogins:  '0'
        oem-logo:
        oem-logo?:  'false'
        oem-banner:
        oem-banner?:  'false'
        hardware-revision:
        last-hardware-update:
        diag-switch?:  'false'
        name:  'options'

    Node 0xf002ce38
        screen:  '/pci@1f,0/pci@1,1/SUNW,m64B@2'
        net:  '/pci@1f,0/pci@1,1/network@1,1'
        cdrom:  '/pci@1f,0/pci@1,1/ide@3/cdrom@2,0:f'
        disk:  '/pci@1f,0/pci@1,1/ide@3/disk@0,0'
        disk3:  '/pci@1f,0/pci@1,1/ide@3/disk@3,0'
        disk2:  '/pci@1f,0/pci@1,1/ide@3/disk@2,0'
        disk1:  '/pci@1f,0/pci@1,1/ide@3/disk@1,0'
        disk0:  '/pci@1f,0/pci@1,1/ide@3/disk@0,0'
        ide:  '/pci@1f,0/pci@1,1/ide@3'
. . . <output truncated>
```

NOTE

Resetting NVRAM Variables On non-USB style keyboards, not USB keyboards, if you change an NVRAM setting on a SPARC system and the system no longer starts up, you can reset the NVRAM variables to their default settings by holding down Stop+N while the machine is powering up. When you issue the Stop+N key sequence, you hold down Stop+N immediately after turning on the power to the SPARC system; you then keep these keys pressed for a few seconds or until you see the banner (if the display is available).

These are both good techniques for forcing a system's NVRAM variables to a known condition.

You can use the NVRAM commands listed in Table 3.9 to modify device aliases so that they remain permanent, even after a restart.

TABLE 3.9 NVRAM Commands

Command	Description
`nvalias` *<alias> <device-path>*	Stores the command `devalias` *<alias> <device-path>* in NVRAMRC. (The alias persists until the `nvunalias` or `set-defaults` command is executed.) This command turns on `use-nvramrc?`.
`nvunalias` *<alias>*	Deletes the corresponding alias from NVRAMRC.

For example, to permanently create a device alias named `bootdisk` that represents a SCSI disk with a target ID of 3 on an Ultra 5 system, you type the following:

```
nvalias bootdisk /pci@1f,0/pci@1,1/ide@3/disk@3,0
```

Because disk device pathnames can be long and complex, the `show-disks` command is provided to assist you in creating device aliases. Type the `show-disks` command and a list of disk devices is shown as follows:

```
ok show-disks
a) /pci@1f,0/pci@1,1/ide@3/cdrom
b) /pci@1f,0/pci@1,1/ide@3/disk
c) /pci@1f,0/pci@1,1/ebus@1/fdthree@14,3023f0
q) NO SELECTION
Enter Selection, q to quit:
```

Type `b` to select an IDE disk and the system responds with the following message:

```
/pci@1f,0/pci@1,1/ide@3/disk has been selected.
Type ^Y ( Control-Y ) to insert it in the command line.
e.g. ok nvalias mydev ^Y for creating devalias mydev for
/pci@1f,0/pci@1,1/ide@3/disk
```

Now create a device alias named `mydisk` followed by `ctrl+y` as follows:

```
nvalias mydisk ^Y
```

The system pastes the selected device path as follows:

```
ok nvalias mydisk /pci@1f,0/pci@1,1/ide@3/disk
```

Now all you need to do is add the target number and logical unit number (for example, `sd@0,0` or `disk@0,0`) to the end of the device name as follows:

```
ok nvalias mydisk /pci@1f,0/pci@1,1/ide@3/disk@0,0
```

NOTE

Specifying the Disk Slice If the boot slice of the disk device that you wish to boot to is not slice 0, you will need to add the disk slice letter to the end of the device name as follows:

```
ok nvalias mydisk /pci@1f,0/pci@1,1/ide@3/disk@0,0:b
```

In the example, I used the letter "b," which corresponds to disk slice 1. This is one area where you'll find disk slices identified by an alpha character and not a number. The letter "a" corresponds to slice 0, "b" is slice 1, etc. If no letter is specified, "a" for slice 0 is assumed. For example, `/pci@1f,0/pci@1,1/ide@3/disk@0,0` is the same as specifying `/pci@1f,0/pci@1,1/ide@3/disk@0,0:a`.

To remove an alias, type `nvunalias <aliasname>`. For example, to remove the `devalias` named *`mydisk`*, type

```
ok nvunalias mydisk
```

The alias named `mydisk` will no longer be listed after the next OpenBoot `reset`.

The `nvedit` Line Editor

Optionally, you can use `nvedit` to create your device aliases. On systems with a PROM version of 1.x or 2.x, the `nvalias` command might not be available and you must use `nvedit` to create custom device aliases. `nvedit` is an OpenBoot line editor that edits the NVRAMRC directly, has a set of editing commands, and operates in a temporary buffer. The following is a sample `nvedit` session:

```
ok setenv use-nvramrc? true
```

TIP

Learning `nvedit` This section is included for information purposes, to show an additional method for modifying the NVRAM. The `nvedit` line editor will not be covered on the certification exam.

The system responds with the following:

```
use-nvramrc? =      true
ok nvedit

  0: devalias bootdisk /pci@1f,0/pci@1,1/ide@3/disk@0,0
1: <Control-C>
ok nvstore
ok reset-all
   Resetting ......
ok boot bootdisk
```

The preceding example uses `nvedit` to create a permanent device alias named `bootdisk`. The example uses Ctrl+C to exit the editor. It also uses the `nvstore` command to make the change permanent in the NVRAMRC. Then, it issues the `reset-all` command to reset the system and then boots the system from `bootdisk` by using the `boot bootdisk` command.

Table 3.10 lists some of the basic commands you can use while in the `nvedit` line editor.

TABLE 3.10 `nvedit` Commands

Command	Meaning
Ctrl+A	Moves backward to beginning of the line.
Ctrl+B	Moves backward one character.
Esc+B	Moves backward one word.
Ctrl+C	Exits the script editor, returning to the OpenBoot command interpreter. The temporary buffer is preserved but is not written back to the script. You use `nvstore` afterward to write it back.
Ctrl+D	Erases the next character.
Esc+D	Erases from the cursor to the end of the word, storing the erased characters in a save buffer.
Ctrl+E	Moves forward to the end of the line.
Ctrl+F	Moves forward one character.
Esc+F	Moves forward one word.
Ctrl+H	Erases the previous character.
Esc+H	Erases from the beginning of the word to just before the cursor, storing erased characters in a save buffer.
Ctrl+K	Erases from the cursor position to the end of the line, storing the erased characters in a save buffer. If at the end of a line, it joins the next line to the current line (that is, deletes the new line).
Ctrl+L	Displays the entire contents of the editing buffer.
Ctrl+N	Moves to the next line of the script-editing buffer.

TABLE 3.10 *Continued*

Command	Meaning
Ctrl+O	Inserts a new line at the cursor position and stays on the current line.
Ctrl+P	Moves to the previous line of the script-editing buffer.
Ctrl+Q	Quotes the next character (that is, allows you to insert control characters).
Ctrl+R	Retypes the line.
Ctrl+U	Erases the entire line, storing the erased characters in a save buffer.
Ctrl+W	Erases from the beginning of the word to just before the cursor, storing erased characters in a save buffer.
Ctrl+Y	Inserts the contents of the save buffer before the cursor.
Return (Enter)	Inserts a new line at the cursor position and advances to the next line.
Delete	Erases the previous character.
Backspace	Erases the previous character.

OpenBoot Security

Anyone who has access to a computer keyboard can access OpenBoot and modify parameters unless you set up the security variables. These variables are listed in Table 3.11.

TABLE 3.11 OpenBoot Security Variables

Variable	Description
`security-mode`	Restricts the set of operations that users are allowed to perform at the OpenBoot prompt.
`security-password`	Specifies the firmware security password. (It is never displayed.) You should not set this variable directly; you set it by using `password`.
`security-#badlogins`	Specifies the number of incorrect security password attempts.

CAUTION

Setting the OpenBoot Security Mode It is important to remember your security password and to set it before setting the security mode. If you later forget this password, you cannot use your system; you must call your vendor's customer support service to make your machine bootable again.

If you are able to get to a Unix prompt as root, you can use the `eeprom` command to either change the security-mode parameter to none or reset the security password.

To set the security password, you type the password at the `ok` prompt, as shown in the following:

```
New password (only first 8 chars are used): <enter password>
Retype new password: <enter password>
```

Earlier in this chapter you learned how to change the OpenBoot parameter `security-password` from the command line.

After you assign a password, you can set the security variables that best fit your environment.

You use `security-mode` to restrict the use of OpenBoot commands. When you assign one of the three values shown in Table 3.12, access to commands is protected by a password. The syntax for setting `security-mode` is as follows:

```
setenv security-mode <value>
```

TABLE 3.12 OpenBoot Security Values

Value	Description
`full`	Specifies that all OpenBoot commands except `go` require a password. This security mode is the most restrictive.
`command`	Specifies that all OpenBoot commands except `boot` and `go` require a password.
`none`	Specifies that no password is required. This is the default.

The following example sets the OpenBoot environment so that all commands except `boot` and `go` require a password:

```
setenv security-mode command
```

With `security-mode` set to `command`, a password is not required if you enter the `boot` command by itself or if you enter the `go` command. Any other command requires a password, including the `boot` command with an argument.

The following are examples of when a password might be required when `security-mode` is set to `command`:

Example	Description
`ok boot`	No password is required.
`ok go`	No password is required.
`ok reset-all`	You are prompted to enter a password.

Note that with `Password`, the password is not echoed as it is typed.

If you enter an incorrect security password, there is a delay of about 10 seconds before the next startup prompt appears. The number of times that an incorrect security password can be typed is stored in the `security-#badlogins` variable, but you should not change this variable.

OpenBoot Diagnostics

You can run various hardware diagnostics in OpenBoot to troubleshoot hardware and network problems. The diagnostic commands are listed in Table 3.13.

TABLE 3.13 OpenBoot Diagnostic Commands

Command	Description
`.env`	On servers, this command is used to obtain status information about the system's power supplies, fans, and temperature sensors.
`probe-scsi`	Identifies devices attached to the internal SCSI bus.
`probe-scsi-all`	Identifies devices attached to any SCSI bus.
`probe-ide`	Identifies IDE devices attached to the PCI bus.
`probe-fcal-all`	Identifies devices on all fibre channel loops.
`reset-all`	Resets the entire system, similar to a power cycle.
`test` *<device-specifier>*	Executes the specified device's self-test method. For example, `test floppy` tests the floppy drive (if installed), and `test net` tests the network connection.
`test-all` *<device-specifier>*	Tests all devices that have built-in self-test methods below the specified device tree node. If *<device-specifier>* is absent, all devices beginning from the root node are tested.
`watch-clock`	Tests the clock function.
`watch-net`	Monitors the network connection.

The following examples use some of the diagnostic features of OpenBoot.

To identify peripheral devices currently connected to the system, such as disks, tape drives, or CD-ROMs, you use OpenBoot `probe` commands. To identify the various probe commands and their syntax, you use the OpenBoot `sifting` command, as follows:

```
sifting probe
```

The system responds with this:

```
(f006c444) probe-all
(f006bf14) probe-pci-slot
(f006baa4) probe-scsi-all
(f0060de8) probe-pci
. . . <output has been truncated>
```

The OpenBoot `sifting` command, also called a `sifting` dump, searches OpenBoot commands to find every command name that contains the specified string.

This first example uses the OpenBoot `probe` command, `probe-scsi`, to identify all the SCSI devices attached to a particular SCSI bus:

```
ok probe-scsi
```

This command is useful for identifying SCSI target IDs that are already in use or to make sure that all devices are connected and identified by the system. The system responds with this:

```
Target 1
  Unit 0   Disk     IBM      DDRS34560SUN4.2GS98E
Target 3
  Unit 0   Disk     IBM      DDRS34560SUN4.2GS98E
```

NOTE

OpenBoot probe Commands The most common OpenBoot `probe` commands are `probe-scsi` and `probe-scsi-all`, which are used to obtain a free open SCSI target ID number before adding a tape unit, a CD-ROM drive, a disk drive, or any other SCSI peripheral. Only devices that are powered on will be located, so you need to make sure everything is turned on. You can use this command after installing a SCSI device to ensure that it has been connected properly and that the system can see it. You can also use this command if you suspect a faulty cable or connection. If you have more than one SCSI bus, you use the `probe-scsi-all` command, but only after a `reset-all` has been issued; otherwise the system is likely to lock up.

This example uses the `probe-ide` command to identify all IDE devices connected to the PCI bus:

```
ok probe-ide
  Device 0  ( Primary Master )
         ATA Model: ST34321A
  Device 1  ( Primary Slave )
        Not Present
  Device 2  ( Secondary Master )
        Removable ATAPI Model: CRD-8322B
  Device 3  ( Secondary Slave )
        Not Present
```

This example tests many of the system components, such as video, the network interface, and the floppy disk:

```
ok test all
```

To test the disk drive to determine whether it is functioning properly, you put a formatted, high-density disk into the drive and type the following:

```
ok test floppy
```

The system responds with this:

```
Testing floppy disk system. A formatted disk should be in the drive.
Test succeeded.
```

You type **`eject-floppy`** to remove the disk.

Table 3.14 describes other OpenBoot commands you can use to gather information about the system.

TABLE 3.14 System Information Commands

Command	Description
`banner`	Displays the power-on banner
`show-sbus`	Displays a list of installed and probed SBus devices
`.enet-addr`	Displays the current Ethernet address
`.idprom`	Displays ID PROM contents, formatted
`.traps`	Displays a list of SPARC trap types
`.version`	Displays the version and date of the startup PROM
`.speed`	Displays CPU and bus speeds
`show-devs`	Displays all installed and probed devices

The following example uses the `banner` command to display the CPU type, the installed RAM, the Ethernet address, the host ID, and the version and date of the startup PROM:

```
ok banner
```

The system responds with this:

```
Sun Ultra 5/10 UPA/PCI (UltraSPARC-IIi 270MHz), No Keyboard
OpenBoot 3.31, 128 MB (60 ns) memory installed, Serial #10642306.
Ethernet address 8:0:20:a2:63:82, Host ID: 80a26382.
```

This example uses the `.version` command to display the OpenBoot version and the date of the startup PROM:

```
ok .version
```

The system responds with this:

```
Release 3.31 Version 0 created 2001/07/25 20:36
OBP 3.31.0 2001/07/25 20:36
POST 3.1.0 2000/06/27 13:56
```

NOTE

Checking the OpenBoot Version from a Shell Prompt You can display the OpenBoot version from a shell prompt by typing this:

```
/usr/sbin/prtdiag -v
```

The system displays the following system diagnostic information and the OpenBoot version is displayed at the end of the output:

```
System Configuration:  Sun Microsystems  sun4u Sun Ultra 5/10 UPA/PCI
(UltraSPARC-IIi 270MHz)
System clock frequency: 90 MHz
Memory size: 128 Megabytes
======================== CPUs ========================
                    Run   Ecache   CPU    CPU
Brd  CPU   Module   MHz     MB    Impl.   Mask
---  ---  -------  -----  ------  ------  ----
 0    0     0       270    0.2    12       1.3
======================== IO Cards ========================
     Bus#  Freq
Brd  Type  MHz   Slot  Name                              Model
---  ----  ----  ----  --------------------------------  ---------------------
 0   PCI-1  33     1   ebus
 0   PCI-1  33     1   network-SUNW,hme
 0   PCI-1  33     2   SUNW,m64B                         ATY,GT-C
 0   PCI-1  33     3   ide-pci1095,646.1095.646.3
 0   PCI-2  33     1   pci-pci1011,25.4
No failures found in System
===========================
======================== HW Revisions ========================
ASIC Revisions:
---------------
Cheerio: ebus Rev 1
System PROM revisions:
----------------------
  OBP 3.31.0 2001/07/25 20:36   POST 3.1.0 2000/06/27 13:56
```

This example shows how to use the `.enet-addr` command to display the Ethernet address:

```
ok .enet-addr
```

The system responds with this:

```
8:0:20:1a:c7:e3
```

To display the CPU information, type the following:

```
.speed
```

The system responds with this:

```
CPU  Speed : 270.00MHz
UPA  Speed : 090.00MHz
PCI  Bus A : 33MHz
PCI  Bus B : 33MHz
```

Input and Output Control

The console is used as the primary means of communication between OpenBoot and the user. The console consists of an input device that is used for receiving information supplied by the user and an output device that is used for sending information to the user. Typically, the console is either the combination of a text/graphics display device and a keyboard, or an ASCII terminal connected to a serial port.

The configuration variables that are related to the control of the console are listed in Table 3.15.

TABLE 3.15 Console Configuration Variables

Variable	Description
`input-device`	Specifies the console input device (usually `keyboard`, `ttya`, or `ttyb`).
`output-device`	Specifies the console output device (usually `screen`, `ttya`, or `ttyb`).
`screen-#columns`	Specifies the number of onscreen columns. The default is 80 characters per line.
`screen-#rows`	Specifies the number of onscreen rows. The default is 34 lines.

You can use the variables in Table 3.15 to assign the console's power-on defaults. These values do not take effect until after the next power cycle or system reset.

If you select `keyboard` for `input-device` and the device is not plugged in, input is accepted from the `ttya` port as a fallback device. If the system is powered on and the keyboard is not detected, the system looks to `ttya`—the serial port—for the system console and uses that port for all input and output.

You can define the communication parameters on the serial port by setting the configuration variables for that port. These variables are shown in Table 3.16.

TABLE 3.16 Port Configuration Variables

Variable	Default Value
`ttyb-rts-dtr-off`	`false`
`ttyb-ignore-cd`	`true`
`ttya-rts-dtr-off`	`false`

(continues)

TABLE 3.16 *Continued*

Variable	Default Value
ttya-ignore-cd	true
ttyb-mode	9600,8,n,1,-
ttya-mode	9600,8,n,1,-

The value for each field of the ttya-mode variable is formatted as follows:

<baud-rate>,*<data-bits>*,*<parity>*,*<stop-bits>*,*<handshake>*

The values for these fields are shown in Table 3.17.

TABLE 3.17 Fields for the ttya-mode Variable

Field	Values
<baud-rate>	110, 300, 1200, 4800, 9600, 19200
<data-bits>	5, 6, 7, 8
<parity>	n (none), e (even), o (odd), m (mark), s (space)
<stop-bits>	1, 1.5, 2
<handshake>	- (none), h (hardware: rts/cts), s (software: xon/xoff)

OpenBoot PROM Versions

Before you can run Solaris 10, your version of OpenBoot must meet the minimum firmware level for your system.

Sun Ultra systems must have PROM version 3.25.*xx* or later to use the Dynamic Host Configuration Protocol (DHCP) network boot, and must be aware of milestones that are used by the Service Management Facility in Solaris 10 and described later in this chapter. For examples in this book, I'm using OpenBoot version 3.31.

On Sun Ultra systems, you can install an updated version of the PROM's firmware to keep your PROM (and your version of OpenBoot) up-to-date. Updating your PROM is not covered on the exam, but if you would like more information on performing this procedure, visit http://sunsolve.sun.com and search the Sunsolve knowledgebase using the keywords **flash prom**.

Booting a System

Objective:

Boot the system; access detailed information.

- Explain how to perform a system boot.

Up to this point, this chapter describes the OpenBoot diagnostic utilities, variables, and parameters. At the OpenBoot PROM, the operating system is not yet running. In fact, the OpenBoot PROM will work fine if the operating system is not even loaded. The primary function of the OpenBoot firmware is to start up the system. Starting up is the process of loading and executing a standalone program (for example, the operating system or the diagnostic monitor). In this discussion, the standalone program that is being started is the two-part operating system kernel. After the kernel is loaded, the kernel starts the Unix system, mounts the necessary file systems, and runs `/sbin/init` to bring the system to the `initdefault` state that is specified in `/etc/inittab`. This process is described in the "System Run States" section, later in this chapter.

Starting up can be initiated either automatically or with a command entered at the user interface. On most SPARC-based systems, the bootstrap process consists of the following basic phases:

1. The system hardware is powered on.
2. The system firmware (the PROM) executes a POST. (The form and scope of POSTs depend on the version of the firmware in the system.)
3. After the tests have been completed successfully, the firmware attempts to autoboot if the appropriate OpenBoot configuration variable (`auto-boot?`) has been set.

The OpenBoot startup process is shown here:

```
Sun Ultra 5/10 UPA/PCI (UltraSPARC-IIi 333MHz), No Keyboard
OpenBoot 3.31, 128 MB (50 ns) memory installed, Serial #12599081.
Ethernet address 8:0:20:c0:3f:29, Host ID: 80c03f29.

Initializing Memory
Rebooting with command: boot
Boot device: disk  File and args:
SunOS Release 5.10 Version Generic 64-bit
Copyright 1983-2005 Sun Microsystems, Inc.  All rights reserved.
Use is subject to license terms.
Hostname: smokey
checking ufs filesystems
```

```
/dev/rdsk/c0t0d0s5: is logging.
/dev/rdsk/c0t0d0s7: is logging.
/dev/rdsk/c0t0d0s4: is logging.
smokey console login:
```

The startup process is controlled by a number of configuration variables, as described in Table 3.19.

TABLE 3.19 Boot Configuration Variables

Variable	Description
`auto-boot?`	Controls whether the system automatically starts up after a system reset or when the power is turned on. The default for this variable is `true`. When the system is powered on, the system automatically starts up to the default run level.
`boot-command`	Specifies the command to be executed when `auto-boot?` is `true`. The default value of `boot-command` is `boot`, with no command-line arguments.
`diag-switch?`	Causes the system to run in diagnostic mode if the value is `true`. This variable is `false` by default.
`boot-device`	Contains the name of the default startup device used when OpenBoot is not in diagnostic mode.
`boot-file`	Contains the default startup arguments used when OpenBoot is not in diagnostic mode. The default is no arguments. (See Table 3.20 for details on when this variable is used.)
`diag-device`	Contains the name of the default diagnostic mode startup device. The default is `net`. (See Table 3.20 for details on when this variable is used.)
`diag-file`	Contains the default diagnostic mode startup arguments. The default is no arguments. (See Table 3.20 for details on when this variable is used.)

Typically, `auto-boot?` is set to `true`, `boot-command` is set to `boot`, and OpenBoot is not in diagnostic mode. Consequently, the system automatically loads and executes the program and arguments described by `boot-file` from the device described by `boot-device` when the system is first turned on or following a system reset.

The boot Command

The `boot` command has the following syntax:

```
boot <device specifier> [arguments]
```

All arguments and options are optional.

The `boot` command and its options are described in Table 3.20.

TABLE 3.20 `boot` **Command Arguments and Options**

Argument	Description
<device specifier>	The full device name or `devalias` of the boot device. Typically this boot device is *<full device name>*—For example, `/sbus/esp@0,800000/sd@3,0:a` indicates a SCSI disk (`sd`) at target 3, `lun0` on the SCSI bus, with the `esp` host adapter plugged in to slot 0. `cdrom`—Boot from CD in the CDROM drive. `disk`—Boot from the hard drive. `net`—Boot from the network
[*arguments*]	The name of the program to be booted (for example, stand/diag) and any program arguments. You can also specify the name of the standalone program to be started up (for example, `kernel/sparcv9/unix`). The default on a Sun SPARC system is to start up `kernel/sparcv9/unix` from the root partition.

The following options control the behavior of the `boot` command:

Option	Description
`-a`	The startup program interprets this flag to mean "Ask me," so it prompts for the name of the standalone program to load.
`-m verbose`	Allows customization of the boot console output.
`-m milestone` *<level>*	Allows the operator to enter which milestone to enter upon bootup.
`-r`	Triggers device reconfiguration during startup.
`-s`	Boots to the single-user milestone.
`-v`	Boots in verbose mode. When this option is set, all system messages are displayed.
flags	The boot program passes all startup flags to *[argument]*. The startup flags are not interpreted by boot. (See the section "The Kernel," later in this chapter, for information on the options that are available with the default standalone program, `kernel/sparcv9/unix`.)

A noninteractive boot (`boot`) automatically boots the system by using default values for the boot path. You can initiate a noninteractive boot by typing the following command from the OpenBoot prompt:

```
ok boot
```

The system boots without requiring any additional interaction.

An interactive boot (`boot -a`) stops and asks for input during the boot process. The system provides a dialog box in which it displays the default boot values and gives you the option of changing them. You might want to boot interactively to make a temporary change to the system file or kernel. Booting interactively enables you to test your changes and recover easily if you have problems. To do this, follow the process in Step by Step 3.1.

TIP

The Interactive Boot Process For the exam, you should make sure you understand what each step of an interactive boot process is asking for. For example, you should know the name of the default kernel, know what the default modules are and where they are located, understand what the `/etc/system` file is used for, and what is meant by the default root file system. Each of these are described in the section "The Kernel," later in this chapter.

STEP BY STEP

3.1 The Interactive Boot Process

1. At the `ok` prompt, type `boot -a` and press Enter. The boot program prompts you interactively.
2. Press Enter to use the default kernel as prompted, or type the name of the kernel to use for booting and then press Enter.
3. Press Enter to use the default modules directory path as prompted, or type the path for the modules directory and then press Enter.
4. Press Enter to use the default `/etc/system` file as prompted, or type the name of the system file and then press Enter.

NOTE

A Missing `/etc/system` File If the `/etc/system` file is missing at bootup, you see this message:

```
Warning cannot open system file!
```

The system still boots, however, using all "default" kernel parameters. Because by default the lines in the `/etc/system` file are all commented by the asterisk (`*`) character, `/etc/system` is actually an "empty" file. The kernel doesn't use anything from this file until you edit this file and enter an uncommented line. You can specify `/dev/null` (an empty file) for the system filename, and the system still boots. In fact, if the `/etc/system` file gets corrupted and the system won't boot from the `/etc/system` file, you can specify a file named `/dev/null` to get the system to boot.

5. Press Enter to use the default root file system type as prompted (that is, `ufs` for local disk booting or `nfs` for diskless clients).
6. Press Enter to use the default physical name of the root device as prompted or type the device name.

The following output shows an example of an interactive boot session:

```
ok boot -a
Resetting ...


Sun Ultra 5/10 UPA/PCI (UltraSPARC-IIi 270MHz), No Keyboard
OpenBoot 3.31, 128 MB (60 ns) memory installed, Serial #10642306.
Ethernet address 8:0:20:a2:63:82, Host ID: 80a26382.

Rebooting with command: boot -a
Boot device: /pci@1f,0/pci@1,1/ide@3/disk@0,0  File and args: -a
Enter filename [kernel/sparcv9/unix]:
Enter default directory for modules [/platform/SUNW,Ultra-5_10/kernel /platform/
sun4u/kernel /kernel /usr/kernel]:
Name of system file [etc/system]:
SunOS Release 5.10 Version Generic 64-bit
Copyright 1983-2005 Sun Microsystems, Inc.  All rights reserved.
Use is subject to license terms.
root filesystem type [ufs]:
Enter physical name of root device
[/pci@1f,0/pci@1,1/ide@3/disk@0,0:a]:
Hostname: ultra5
/dev/rdsk/c0t0d0s5: is logging.
/dev/rdsk/c0t0d0s7: is logging.
/dev/rdsk/c0t0d0s4: is logging.
ultra5 console login:
```

To view more detailed information during the boot process, you use the `boot -v` or `boot -m verbose` options to the `boot` command:

```
ok boot -m verbose
```

The system outputs more detailed boot messages as follows:

```
Boot device: /pci@1f,0/pci@1,1/ide@3/disk@0,0:a  File and args: -m verbose
SunOS Release 5.10 Version Generic 64-bit
Copyright 1983-2005 Sun Microsystems, Inc.  All rights reserved.
Use is subject to license terms.
[ network/loopback:default starting (loopback network interface) ]
[ system/filesystem/root:default starting (root file system mount) ]
[ network/pfil:default starting (packet filter) ]
Sep 20 11:15:54/74: system start time was Tue Sep 20 11:15:39 2005
[ milestone/name-services:default starting (name services milestone) ]
[ network/physical:default starting (physical network interfaces) ]
[ system/filesystem/usr:default starting (read/write root file systems mounts) ]
[ system/device/local:default starting (Standard Solaris device configuration.) ]
[ system/filesystem/minimal:default starting (minimal file system mounts) ]
[ milestone/devices:default starting (device configuration milestone) ]
[ system/identity:domain starting (system identity (domainname)) ]
```

```
[ system/manifest-import:default starting (service manifest import) ]
[ milestone/network:default starting (Network milestone) ]
[ system/cryptosvc:default starting (cryptographic services) ]
[ system/identity:node starting (system identity (nodename)) ]
[ network/initial:default starting (initial network services) ]
[ system/sysevent:default starting (system event notification) ]
Hostname: ultra5
[ system/device/fc-fabric:default starting (Solaris FC fabric device configuration.) ]
[ system/coreadm:default starting (system-wide core file configuration) ]
[ system/keymap:default starting (keyboard defaults) ]
[ system/name-service-cache:default starting (name service cache) ]
[ system/rmtmpfiles:default starting (remove temporary files) ]
[ milestone/single-user:default starting (single-user milestone) ]
[ system/picl:default starting (platform information and control) ]
[ network/service:default starting (layered network services) ]
[ system/power:default starting (power management) ]
[ application/print/cleanup:default starting (print cleanup) ]
[ system/filesystem/local:default starting (local file system mounts) ]
checking ufs filesystems
/dev/rdsk/c0t0d0s5: is logging.
/dev/rdsk/c0t0d0s7: is logging.
[ system/cron:default starting (clock daemon (cron)) ]
[ application/font/fc-cache:default starting (FontConfig Cache Builder) ]
[ system/sysidtool:net starting (sysidtool) ]
[ network/rpc/bind:default starting (RPC bindings) ]
[ system/sysidtool:system starting (sysidtool) ]
[ network/nfs/status:default starting (NFS status monitor) ]
[ network/nfs/mapid:default starting (NFS ID mapper) ]
[ milestone/sysconfig:default starting (Basic system configuration milestone) ]
[ network/inetd:default starting (inetd) ]
[ network/nfs/nlockmgr:default starting (NFS lock manager) ]
[ system/sac:default starting (SAF service access controller) ]
[ system/utmp:default starting (utmpx monitoring) ]
[ system/console-login:default starting (Console login) ]

ultra5 console login: Sep 20 11:16:38/214: network/nfs/client:default starting
Sep 20 11:16:40/216: system/filesystem/autofs:default starting
Sep 20 11:16:43/220: network/ssh:default starting
Sep 20 11:16:43/221: system/dumpadm:default starting
Sep 20 11:16:44/223: system/system-log:default starting
Sep 20 11:16:45/227: system/fmd:default starting
Sep 20 11:16:45/229: network/smtp:sendmail starting
Sep 20 11:16:46/231: milestone/multi-user:default starting
Sep 20 11:17:00/235: system/zones:default starting

ultra5 console login: ultra5 console login:
```

If you are not at the system console to watch the boot information, you can use the Unix `dmesg` command to redisplay information that was displayed during the boot process, or you can view the information in the /var/adm/messages file. The dmesg command displays the contents of a fixed-size buffer. Therefore, if the system has been up for a long time, the initial boot messages may have been overwritten with other kernel log entries.

To view messages displayed during the boot process, you can use one of the following methods:

- At a Unix prompt, type **/usr/sbin/dmesg** and press Enter.

NOTE

Viewing dmesg Output Several pages of information are displayed when you use this method, so I recommend that you pipe the dmesg command to more, as shown here: /usr/sbin/dmesg¦more.

- At a Unix prompt, type **more /var/adm/messages** and press Enter.

New in Solaris 10 is the concept of services, described in the Service Management Facility (SMF) section of this chapter. With SMF, there are additional tools for viewing system startup messages. Refer to the section on SMF for additional information.

When you specify an explicit device alias, such as disk3, with the boot command, the machine starts up from the specified startup device, using no startup arguments. Here's an example:

```
boot disk3
```

In this case, the system boots from the disk drive defined by the device alias named disk3. It then loads kernel/sparcv9/unix as the default standalone startup program.

Various options affect the behavior of the boot command. You use the following syntax to specify any of the options listed in Table 3.20 with the boot command:

```
boot [options]
```

When you specify options with the boot command, the machine starts up from the default startup device. Here's an example:

```
boot -a
```

The -a option instructs the boot command to ask for the name of the standalone program to load. If you specify kernel/sparcv9/unix, which is the default, you are prompted to enter the directory that contains the kernel modules. (See the section "The Kernel," later in this chapter, for details on kernel modules.)

You can mix options and arguments with the boot command by using the following syntax:

```
boot [argument]<program filename> - <flags>
```

When you specify the `boot` command with an explicit startup device and option, the machine starts up from the specified device using the specified option. Here's an example:

```
boot disk3 -a
```

This gives the same prompts as the previous example, except that you are specifying the boot device and not using the default boot device. The system starts up the bootblock from the disk drive defined by the device alias named `disk3`.

During the startup process, OpenBoot performs the following tasks:

1. The firmware resets the machine if a client program has been executed since the last reset. The client program is normally an operating system or an operating system's loader program, but `boot` can also be used to load and execute other kinds of programs, such as diagnostics programs. For example, if you have just issued the `test net` command, when you next type `boot`, the system resets before starting up.
2. The boot program is loaded into memory, using a protocol that depends on the type of selected device. You can start up from disk, CD-ROM, or the network.
3. The loaded boot program is executed. The behavior of the boot program can be controlled by the `argument` string, if one is passed to the `boot` command on the command line.

The program that is loaded and executed by the startup process is a secondary boot program, the purpose of which is to load the standalone program. The second-level program is either `ufsboot`, when you're starting up from a disk, or `inetboot`, when you're starting up from the network.

If you're starting up from disk, the bootstrap process consists of two conceptually distinct phases: primary startup and secondary startup. The PROM assumes that the program for the primary startup (`bootblk`) is in the primary bootblock, which resides in sectors 1 through 15 of the startup device. The bootblock is created by using the `installboot` command. The software installation process typically installs the bootblock for you, so you don't need to issue this command unless you're recovering a corrupted bootblock.

To install a bootblock on disk `c0t3d0s0`, for example, you type the following:

```
installboot /usr/platform/'uname -i'/lib/fs/ufs/bootblk \
 /dev/rdsk/c0t3d0s0
```

You cannot see the bootblock, as it resides outside the file system area. It resides in a protected area of the disk and will not be overwritten by a file system. The program in the bootblock area loads the secondary startup program, `ufsboot`.

When you're executing the `boot` command, if you specify a filename, that filename is the name of the standalone startup program to be loaded. If the pathname is relative (that is, it does not begin with a slash), `ufsboot` looks for the standalone program in a platform-dependent search path which is `/platform/'uname-m'` and `/platform/'uname -i'`.

NOTE

Determining Your System's Platform Name You can use the `uname -i` command to determine your system's platform name. For example, on a Sun Ultra 5, the path is `/platform/SUNW,Ultra-5_10`. You use the command `uname -m` to find the hardware classname of a system; for an Ultra 5, the hardware classname is `sun4u`. `ufsboot` will search in both the `/platform/'uname-m'` and `/platform/'uname -i'` directories for the kernel files.

On the other hand, if the path to the filename is absolute, `boot` uses the specified path. The startup program then loads the standalone program and transfers control to it.

The following example shows how to specify the standalone startup program from the OpenBoot `ok` prompt:

```
ok boot disk5 kernel/sparcv9/unix -s
```

In this example, the PROM looks for the primary boot program (`bootblk`) on `disk5` (`/pci@1f,0/pci@1,1/ide@3/disk@5,0`). The primary startup program then loads `/platform/'uname -m'/ufsboot`. `ufsboot` loads the appropriate two-part kernel. The core of the kernel is two pieces of static code called `genunix` and `unix`, where `genunix` is the platform-independent generic kernel file and `unix` is the platform-specific kernel file. When `ufsboot` loads these two files into memory, they are combined to form the running kernel. On systems running the 64-bit mode OS, the two-part kernel is located in the directory:

```
/platform/'uname -m'/kernel/sparcv9
```

Typical secondary startup programs, such as `kernel/sparcv9/unix`, accept arguments of the form `<filename> -<flags>`, where *`filename`* is the path to the standalone startup program and `-<flags>` is a list of options to be passed to the standalone program. The example starts up the operating system kernel, which is described in the next section. The `-s` flag instructs the kernel to start up in single-user mode.

The Kernel

After the `boot` command initiates the kernel, the kernel begins several phases of the startup process. The first task is for OpenBoot to load the two-part kernel. The secondary startup program, `ufsboot`, which is described in the preceding section, loads the operating system kernel. The core of the kernel is two pieces of static code called `genunix` and `unix`. `genunix` is the platform-independent generic kernel file, and `unix` is the platform-specific kernel file. The platform-specific kernel used by `ufsboot` for systems running in 64-bit mode is named `/platform/'uname -m'/kernel/sparcv9/unix`. Solaris 10 only runs on 64-bit systems; however, early versions of Solaris gave you the option of running in 32-bit or 64-bit mode. On previous versions of Solaris, the 32-bit platform-specific kernel was named `/platform/'uname -m'/kernel/unix`. Now, in Solaris 10, `/platform/'uname -m'/kernel/unix` is merely a link to the 64-bit kernel located in the `sparcv9` directory. When `ufsboot` loads `genunix` and `unix` into memory, they are combined to form the running kernel.

The kernel initializes itself and begins loading modules, using `ufsboot` to read the files. After the kernel has loaded enough modules to mount the root file system, it unmaps the `ufsboot` program and continues, using its own resources. The kernel creates a user process and starts the `/sbin/init` daemon, which starts other processes by reading the `/etc/inittab` file. (The `/sbin/init` process is described in the "System Run States" section, later in this chapter.)

The kernel is dynamically configured in Solaris 10. The kernel consists of a small static core and many dynamically loadable kernel modules. Many kernel modules are loaded automatically at boot time, but for efficiency, others—such as device drivers—are loaded from the disk as needed by the kernel.

A kernel module is a software component that is used to perform a specific task on the system. An example of a loadable kernel module is a device driver that is loaded when the device is accessed. Drivers, file systems, `STREAMS` modules, and other modules are loaded automatically as they are needed, either at startup or at runtime. This is referred to as *autoconfiguration*, and the kernel is referred to as a *dynamic kernel*. After these modules are no longer in use, they can be unloaded. Modules are kept in memory until that memory is needed. This makes more efficient use of memory and allows for simpler modification and tuning.

The `modinfo` command provides information about the modules that are currently loaded on a system. The modules that make up the kernel typically reside in the directories `/kernel` and `/usr/kernel`. Platform-dependent modules reside in the `/platform/'uname -m'/kernel` and `/platform/'uname -i'/kernel` directories.

When the kernel is loading, it reads the `/etc/system` file where system configuration information is stored. This file modifies the kernel's parameters and treatment of loadable modules. It specifically controls the following:

- The search path for default modules to be loaded at boot time as well as the search path for modules not to be loaded at boot time
- The modules to be forcibly loaded at boot time rather than at first access
- The root type and device
- The new values to override the default kernel parameter values

The following is an example of the default /etc/system file:

```
login: login: root
Password:
Last login: Tue Jul 26 22:23:37 on console
Sun Microsystems Inc.   SunOS 5.10      Generic January 2005
# cd /sbi
/sbi: does not exist
# cd /sbin
# ls init
init
# ls -l init
-r-xr-xr-x   1 root     sys        48984 Jan 22  2005 init
# cd /etc
# ls init
init
# ls -l init
lrwxrwxrwx   1 root     root          12 Feb 25 14:26 init -> ../sbin/init
# more /etc/system
*ident  "@(#)system     1.18    97/06/27 SMI" /* SVR4 1.5 */
*
* SYSTEM SPECIFICATION FILE
*

* moddir:
*
*       Set the search path for modules.  This has a format similar to the
*       csh path variable. If the module isn't found in the first directory
*       it tries the second and so on. The default is /kernel /usr/kernel
*
*       Example:
*               moddir: /kernel /usr/kernel /other/modules



* root device and root filesystem configuration:
*
*       The following may be used to override the defaults provided by
*       the boot program:
*
*       rootfs:         Set the filesystem type of the root.
*
*       rootdev:        Set the root device.  This should be a fully
*                       expanded physical pathname.  The default is the
*                       physical pathname of the device where the boot
*                       program resides.  The physical pathname is
*                       highly platform and configuration dependent.
*
```

```
*       Example:
*               rootfs:ufs
*               rootdev:/sbus@1,f8000000/esp@0,800000/sd@3,0:a
*
*       (Swap device configuration should be specified in /etc/vfstab.)



* exclude:
*
*       Modules appearing in the moddir path which are NOT to be loaded,
*       even if referenced. Note that `exclude' accepts either a module name,
*       or a filename which includes the directory.
*
*       Examples:
*               exclude: win
*               exclude: sys/shmsys



* forceload:
*
*       Cause these modules to be loaded at boot time, (just before mounting
*       the root filesystem) rather than at first reference. Note that
*       forceload expects a filename which includes the directory. Also
*       note that loading a module does not necessarily imply that it will
*       be installed.
*
*       Example:
*               forceload: drv/foo



* set:
*
*       Set an integer variable in the kernel or a module to a new value.
*       This facility should be used with caution.  See system(4).
*
*       Examples:
*
*       To set variables in 'unix':
*
*               set nautopush=32
*               set maxusers=40
*
*       To set a variable named 'debug' in the module named 'test_module'
*
*               set test_module:debug = 0x13
```

CAUTION

Modifying the /etc/system File A system administrator will modify the /etc/system file to modify the kernel's behavior. By default, the contents of the /etc/system file are completely commented out and the kernel is using all default values. A default kernel is adequate for average system use and you should not modify the /etc/system file unless you are certain of the results. A good practice is to always make a backup copy of any system file you modify, in case the original needs to be restored. Incorrect entries could prevent your system from booting. If a boot process fails because of an unusable /etc/system file, you should boot the system by using the interactive option boot -a. When you are asked to enter the name of the system file, you should enter the name of the backup system filename or /dev/null, to use default parameters.

The /etc/system file contains commands that have this form:

```
set <parameter>=<value>
```

For example, the setting for the kernel parameter nfs:nfs4_nra is set in the /etc/system file with the following line:

```
set nfs:nfs_nra=4
```

This parameter controls the number of read-ahead operations that are queued by the NFS version 4 client.

Commands that affect loadable modules have this form:

```
set <module>:<variable>=<value>
```

NOTE

Editing the /etc/system File A command must be 80 or fewer characters in length, and a comment line must begin with an asterisk (*) or hash mark (#) and end with a hard return.

For the most part, the Solaris OE is self-adjusting to system load and demands minimal tuning. In some cases, however, tuning is necessary.

If you need to change a tunable parameter in the /etc/system file, you can use the sysdef command or the mdb command to verify the change. sysdef lists all hardware devices, system devices, loadable modules, and the values of selected kernel-tunable parameters. The following is the output that is produced from the sysdef command:

```
* Hostid
*
  80a26382
*
* sun4u Configuration
```

```
*
*
* Devices
*
scsi_vhci, instance #0
packages (driver not attached)
        terminal-emulator (driver not attached)
        deblocker (driver not attached)
        obp-tftp (driver not attached)
        disk-label (driver not attached)
        SUNW,builtin-drivers (driver not attached)
        sun-keyboard (driver not attached)
        ufs-file-system (driver not attached)
chosen (driver not attached)
openprom (driver not attached)
        client-services (driver not attached)
options, instance #0
aliases (driver not attached)
memory (driver not attached)
virtual-memory (driver not attached)
pci, instance #0
        pci, instance #0
                ebus, instance #0
                        auxio (driver not attached)
                        power, instance #0
                        SUNW,pll (driver not attached)
                        se, instance #0
                        su, instance #0
                        su, instance #1
                        ecpp (driver not attached)
                        fdthree, instance #0
                        eeprom (driver not attached)
                        flashprom (driver not attached)
                        SUNW,CS4231, instance #0 (driver not attached)
                network, instance #0
                SUNW,m64B, instance #0
                ide, instance #0
                        disk (driver not attached)
                        cdrom (driver not attached)
                        sd, instance #1
                        dad, instance #1
        pci, instance #1

Output has been truncated . . . . . . .

* System Configuration
*
  swap files
```

```
swapfile             dev  swaplo blocks   free
/dev/dsk/c0t0d0s3   136,11     16 1052624 1052624
*
* Tunable Parameters
*
 2498560          maximum memory allowed in buffer cache (bufhwm)
    1914          maximum number of processes (v.v_proc)
      99          maximum global priority in sys class (MAXCLSYSPRI)
    1909          maximum processes per user id (v.v_maxup)
      30          auto update time limit in seconds (NAUTOUP)
      25          page stealing low water mark (GPGSLO)
       1          fsflush run rate (FSFLUSHR)
      25          minimum resident memory for avoiding deadlock (MINARMEM)
      25          minimum swapable memory for avoiding deadlock (MINASMEM)
*
* Utsname Tunables
*
    5.10  release (REL)
  ultra5  node name (NODE)
   SunOS  system name (SYS)
 Generic  version (VER)
*
* Process Resource Limit Tunables (Current:Maximum)
*
0x0000000000000100:0x0000000000010000   file descriptors
*
* Streams Tunables
*
     9  maximum number of pushes allowed (NSTRPUSH)
 65536  maximum stream message size (STRMSGSZ)
  1024  max size of ctl part of message (STRCTLSZ)
*
* IPC Messages module is not loaded
* IPC Semaphores module is not loaded
* IPC Shared Memory module is not loaded
* Time Sharing Scheduler Tunables
*
60      maximum time sharing user priority (TSMAXUPRI)
SYS     system class name (SYS_NAME)
```

The mdb command is used to view or modify a running kernel and must be used with extreme care. The use of mdb is beyond the scope of this book; however, more information can be obtained from The Solaris Modular Debugger Guide available at http://docs.sun.com.

NOTE

Kernel Tunable Parameters in Solaris 10 You'll find in Solaris 10 that many tunable parameters that were previously set in `/etc/system` have been removed. For example, IPC facilities were previously controlled by kernel tunables, where you had to modify the `/etc/system` file and reboot the system to change the default values for these facilities. Because the IPC facilities are now controlled by resource controls, their configuration can be modified while the system is running. Many applications that previously required system tuning to function might now run without tuning because of increased defaults and the automatic allocation of resources.

Configuring the kernel and tunable parameters is a complex topic to describe in a few sections of a chapter. This introduction to the concept provides enough information for the average system administrator and describes the topics you'll need to know for the exam. If you are interested in learning more about the kernel and tunable parameters, refer to the additional sources of information described at the end of this chapter.

The `init` Phase

Objective:

The `init` phase has undergone major changes in Solaris 10. Even if you are experienced on previous versions of Solaris OE, this section introduces the `svc.startd` daemon and the Service Management Facility (SMF), which are new in Solaris 10 and will be tested heavily on the exam.

After control of the system is passed to the kernel, the system begins the last stage of the boot process—the `init` stage. In this phase of the boot process, the `init` daemon (`/sbin/init`) reads the `/etc/default/init` file to set any environment variables for the shell that `init` invokes. By default, the CMASK and variables are set. These values get passed to any processes that `init` starts. Then, `init` reads the `/etc/inittab` file and executes any process entries that have `sysinit` in the action field so that any special initializations can take place before users log in.

After reading the `/etc/inittab` file, `init` starts the `svc.startd` daemon, which is responsible for starting and stopping other system services such as mounting file systems and configuring network devices. In addition, `svc.startd` will execute legacy run control (rc) scripts, which are described later in this section.

The `/sbin/init` command sets up the system based on the directions in `/etc/inittab`. Each entry in the `/etc/inittab` file has the following fields:

```
id:runlevel:action:process
```

Table 3.23 provides a description of each field.

TABLE 3.23 Fields in the inittab File

Field	Description
id	A unique identifier
rstate	The run level(s)
action	How the process is to be run
process	The name of the command to execute

Valid action keywords are listed in Table 3.24:

TABLE 3.24 inittab action Field Values

Field	Description
sysinit	Executes the process before init tries to access the console via the console prompt. init waits for the completion of the process before it continues to read the inittab file.
powerfail	Indicates that the system has received a powerfail signal.

The following example shows a default /etc/inittab file:

```
ap::sysinit:/sbin/autopush -f /etc/iu.ap
sp::sysinit:/sbin/soconfig -f /etc/sock2path
smf::sysinit:/lib/svc/bin/svc.startd    >/dev/msglog 2<>/dev/msglog </dev/console
p3:s1234:powerfail:/usr/sbin/shutdown -y -i5 -g0 >/dev/msglog 2<>/dev/msglog
```

The init process performs the following tasks based on the entries found in the default /etc/inittab file:

Line 1: Initializes the STREAMS modules used for communication services.

Line 2. Configures the socket transport providers for network connections.

Line 3. Initializes the svc.startd daemon for SMF.

Line 4. Describes the action to take when the init daemon receives a power fail shutdown signal.

The Solaris Management Facility (SMF) Service

Objective:

Explain the Service Management Facility and the phases of the boot process.

- Use Service Management Facility or legacy commands and scripts to control both the boot and shutdown procedures.

In Solaris 10, the `svc.startd` daemon replaces the `init` process as the master process starter and restarter. Where in previous versions of Solaris, `init` would start all processes and bring the system to the appropriate "run level" or "init state." Now SMF, or more specifically, the `svc.startd` daemon, assumes the role of starting system services.

NOTE

SMF Services A service can be described as an entity that provides a resource or list of capabilities to applications and other services. This entity can be running locally or remote, but at this phase of the boot process, the service is running locally. A service does not have to be a process; it can be the software state of a device or a mounted file system. Also, a system can have more than one instance of a service, such as with multiple network interfaces, multiple mounted file systems, or a set of other services.

The advantages of using SMF to manage system services over the traditional Unix startup scripts that, in the past, were run by the `init` process are

- SMF automatically restarts failed services in the correct order, whether they failed as the result of administrator error, software bug, or were affected by an uncorrectable hardware error. The restart order is defined by dependency statements within the SMF facility.
- The system administrator can view and manage services as well as view the relationships between services and processes.
- Allows the system administrator to back up, restore, and undo changes to services by taking automatic snapshots of service configurations.
- Allows the system administrator to interrogate services and determine why a service may not be running.
- Allows services to be enabled and disabled either temporarily or permanently.
- Allows the system administrator to delegate tasks to non-root users, giving these users the ability to modify, enable, disable, or restart system services.
- Large systems boot and shutdown faster because services are started and stopped in parallel according to dependencies setup in the SMF.
- Allows customization of output sent to the boot console to be either be as quiet as possible, which is the default, or to be verbose by using `boot -m verbose` from the OpenBoot prompt.
- Provides compatibility with legacy RC scripts.

Those of you who have experience on previous versions of Solaris will notice a few differences immediately:

- The boot process creates fewer messages. All of the information that was provided by the boot messages in previous versions of Solaris is located in the `/var/svc/log` directory. You still have the option of booting the system with the `boot -v` option, which provides more verbose boot messages.
- Because SMF is able to start services in parallel, the boot time is substantially quicker than in previous versions of Solaris.
- Since services are automatically restarted if possible, it may seem that a process refuses to die. The `svcadm` command should be used to disable any SMF service that should not be running.
- Many of the scripts in `/etc/init.d` and `/etc/rc*.d` have been removed, as well as entries in the `/etc/inittab` file so that the services can be administered using SMF. You'll still find a few RC scripts that still remain in the `/etc/init.d` directory such as `sendmail`, `nfs.server`, and `dhcp`, but most of these legacy RC scripts simply execute the `svcadm` command to start the services through the SMF. Scripts and `inittab` entries that may still exist from legacy applications or are locally developed will continue to run. The legacy services are started after the SMF services so that service dependencies do not become a problem.

The *service instance* is the fundamental unit of administration in the SMF framework, and each SMF service has the potential to have multiple versions of it configured. A service instance is either enabled or disabled with the `svcadm` command described later in this chapter. An instance is a specific configuration of a service, and multiple instances of the same service can run in the same Solaris instance. For example, a web server is a service. A specific web server daemon that is configured to listen on port 80 is an instance. Another instance of the web server service could have different configuration requirements listening on port 8080. The service has system-wide configuration requirements, but each instance can override specific requirements, as needed.

Services are represented in the SMF framework as *service instance objects*, which are children of service objects. These instance objects can inherit or override the configuration settings of the parent service object. Multiple instances of a single service are managed as child objects of the service object.

Services are not just the representation for standard long-running system services such as `httpd` or `nfsd`. Services also represent varied system entities that include third-party applications such as Oracle software. In addition, a service can include less traditional entities such as the following:

- A physical network device
- A configured IP address
- Kernel configuration information

The services started by `svc.startd` are referred to as *milestones*. The milestone concept replaces the traditional run levels that were used in previous versions of Solaris. A milestone is a special type of service that represents a group of services. A milestone is made up of several SMF services. For example, the services that instituted run levels S, 2, and 3 in previous version of Solaris are now represented by milestone services named:

`milestone/single-user` (equivalent to run level S)

`milestone/multi-user` (equivalent to run level 2)

`milestone/multi-user-server`(equivalent to run level 3)

Other milestones that are available in the Solaris 10 OE are

`milestone/name-services`

`milestone/devices`

`milestone/network`

`milestone/sysconfig`

An SMF manifest is an XML (Extensible Markup Language) file that contains a complete set of properties that are associated with a service or a service instance. The properties are stored in files and subdirectories located in `/var/svc/manifest`. Manifests should not be edited directly to modify the properties of a service. The service configuration repository is the authoritative source of the service configuration information, and the service configuration repository can only be manipulated or queried using SMF interfaces, which are command-line utilities described later in this section.

Each service instance is named with a Fault Management Resource Identifier or FMRI. The FMRI includes the service name and the instance name. For example, the FMRI for the `ftp` service is `svc:`*`/network/ftp`*`:default`, where *`network/ftp`* identifies the service and `default` identifies the service instance.

You may see various forms of the FMRI that all refer to the same service instance, as follows:

```
svc://localhost/network/inetd:default
svc:/network/inetd:default
network/inetd:default
```

An FMRI for a legacy service will have the following format:

```
lrc:/etc/rc3_d/S90samba
```

where the `lrc` (legacy run control) prefix indicates that the service is not managed by SMF. The pathname `/etc/rc3_d` refers to the directory where the legacy script is located, and `S90samba` is the name of the run control script. See the section titled "Using the Run Control Scripts to Stop or Start Services" later in this chapter for information on run control scripts.

The service names will include a general functional category which include the following:

- Application
- Device
- Milestone
- Network
- Platform
- Site
- System

Service Dependencies

In earlier versions of Solaris, processes were started at bootup by their respective shell scripts, which ran in a pre-determined sequence. Sometimes, one of these shell scripts failed for various reasons. Perhaps it was an error in the script or one of the daemons did not start for various reasons. When a script failed, the other scripts were started regardless, and sometimes these scripts failed because a previous process failed to start. Tracking the problem down was difficult for the system administrator.

To remedy the problem with sequencing scripts, Sun uses the SMF to manage the starting and stopping of services. The SMF understands the dependencies that some services have on other services. With SMF, if a service managed by the SMF fails or is terminated, all dependent processes will be taken offline until the required process is restarted. The interdependency is started by means of a service contract, which is maintained by the kernel and is where the process interdependency, the restarter process, and the startup methods are all described.

Most service instances have dependencies on other services or files. Those dependencies control when the service is started and automatically stopped. When the dependencies of an enabled service are not satisfied, the service is kept in the offline state. When the service instance dependencies are satisfied, the service is started or restarted by the `svc.startd` daemon. If the start is successful, the service is transitioned to the online state. There are four types of service instance dependencies listed below.

- `require_all` The dependency is satisfied when all cited services are running (online or degraded), or when all indicated files are present.
- `require_any`—The dependency is satisfied when one of the cited services is running (online or degraded), or when at least one of the indicated files is present.
- `optional_all`—The dependency is satisfied when all of the cited services are running (online or degraded), disabled, in the maintenance state, or when cited services are not present. For files, this type is the same as `require_all`.

- `exclude_all`—The dependency is satisfied when all of the cited services are disabled, in the maintenance state, or when cited services or files are not present.

Each service or service instance must define a set of methods that start, stop, and optionally refresh the service. These methods can be listed and modified for each service using the `svccfg` command described later in this chapter.

A service instance is satisfied and started when its criteria, for the type of dependency, are met. Dependencies are satisfied when cited services move to the online state. Once running (online or degraded), if a service instance with a `require_all`, `require_any`, or `optional_all` dependency is stopped or refreshed, the SMF considers why the service was stopped and uses the `restart_on` attribute of the dependency to decide whether to stop the service. `restart_on` attributes are defined in Table 3.25x

TABLE 3.25 `restart_on` Values

Event	None	Error	Restart	Refresh
stop due to error	no	yes	yes	yes
non-error stop	no	no	yes	yes
refresh	no	no	no	yes

A service is considered to have stopped due to an error if the service has encountered a hardware error or a software error such as a core dump. For `exclude_all` dependencies, the service is stopped if the cited service is started and the `restart_on` attribute is not `none`.

You can use the `svcs` command, described later in this chapter, to view service instance dependencies and to troubleshoot failures. You'll also see how to use the `svccfg` command to modify service dependencies.

SMF Command-line Administration Utilities

The SMF provides a set of command-line utilities used to administer and configure the SMF. Table 3.26 describes these utilities.

TABLE 3.26 SMF Command-line Utilities

Command	Description
`inetadm`	Used to configure and view services controlled by the `inetd` daemon. Described in more detail in Chapter 8, "The Solaris Network Environment."
`svcadm`	Used to perform common service management tasks such as enabling, disabling, or restarting service instances.
`svccfg`	Used to display and manipulate the contents of the service configuration repository.

TABLE 3.26 SMF Command-line Utilities

Command	Description
svcprop	Used to retrieve property values from the service configuration repository with output that is appropriate for use in shell scripts.
svcs	Used to obtain a detailed view of the service state of all service instances in the configuration repository.

To report the status of all enabled service instances and get a list of the various services that are running, use the svcs command with no options as follows:

```
svcs ¦ more
```

The svcs command obtains information about all service instances from the service configuration repository and displays the state, start time, and FMRI of each service instance as follows:

```
STATE          STIME    FMRI
legacy_run     14:10:49 lrc:/etc/rc2_d/S10lu
legacy_run     14:10:49 lrc:/etc/rc2_d/S20sysetup
legacy_run     14:10:50 lrc:/etc/rc2_d/S40llc2
legacy_run     14:10:50 lrc:/etc/rc2_d/S42ncakmod
legacy_run     14:10:50 lrc:/etc/rc2_d/S47pppd
legacy_run     14:10:50 lrc:/etc/rc2_d/S70uucp
Output has been truncated . . . .
online         14:09:37 svc:/system/svc/restarter:default
online         14:09:48 svc:/network/pfil:default
online         14:09:48 svc:/network/loopback:default
online         14:09:48 svc:/milestone/name-services:default
online         14:09:50 svc:/system/filesystem/root:default
online         14:09:54 svc:/system/filesystem/usr:default
online         14:09:56 svc:/system/device/local:default
online         14:09:57 svc:/milestone/devices:default
online         14:09:57 svc:/network/physical:default
online         14:09:58 svc:/milestone/network:default
```

NOTE

Listing Legacy Services You'll notice that the list includes legacy scripts that were used to start up processes. Legacy services can be viewed, but cannot be administered with SMF.

The state of each service is one of the following:

- **degraded**—The service instance is enabled, but is running at a limited capacity.
- **disabled**—The service instance is not enabled and is not running.

- **legacy_run**—The legacy service is not managed by SMF, but the service can be observed. This state is only used by legacy services that are started with RC scripts.
- **maintenance**—The service instance has encountered an error that must be resolved by the administrator.
- **offline**—The service instance is enabled, but the service is not yet running or available to run.
- **online**—The service instance is enabled and has successfully started.
- **uninitialized**—This state is the initial state for all services before their configuration has been read.

Running the svcs command without options will display the status of all enabled services. Use the -a option to list all services, including disabled services as follows:

```
svcs -a
```

The result is a listing of all services as follows:

```
. .. . <output has been truncated>
disabled       15:48:41 svc:/network/shell:kshell
disabled       15:48:41 svc:/network/talk:default
disabled       15:48:42 svc:/network/rpc/ocfserv:default
disabled       15:48:42 svc:/network/uucp:default
disabled       15:48:42 svc:/network/security/krb5_prop:default
disabled       15:48:42 svc:/network/apocd/udp:default
online         15:47:44 svc:/system/svc/restarter:default
online         15:47:47 svc:/network/pfil:default
online         15:47:48 svc:/network/loopback:default
online         15:47:50 svc:/system/filesystem/root:default
. .. . <output has been truncated>
```

To display information on selected services, you can supply the FMRI as an argument to the svcs command as follows:

```
svcs -l network
```

With the -l option, the system displays detailed information about the network service instance. The network FMRI specified in the previous example is a general functional category and is also called the network milestone. The information displayed by the previous command is as follows:

```
fmri         svc:/milestone/network:default
name         Network milestone
enabled      true
state        online
next_state   none
```

```
state_time    Wed Jul 27 14:09:58 2005
alt_logfile   /etc/svc/volatile/milestone-network:default.log
restarter     svc:/system/svc/restarter:default
dependency    require_all/none svc:/network/loopback (online)
dependency    require_all/none svc:/network/physical (online)
```

Use the `-d` option to view which services are started at the `network:default` milestone, as follows:

```
svcs -d milestone/network:default
```

The system displays

```
STATE          STIME    FMRI
online         Jul_27   svc:/network/loopback:default
online         Jul_27   svc:/network/physical:default
```

Another milestone is the `multi-user` milestone, which is displayed as follows:

```
svcs -d milestone/multi-user
```

The system displays all of the services started at the `multi-user` milestone:

```
STATE          STIME    FMRI
online         Jul_27   svc:/milestone/name-services:default
online         Jul_27   svc:/milestone/single-user:default
online         Jul_27   svc:/system/filesystem/local:default
online         Jul_27   svc:/network/rpc/bind:default
online         Jul_27   svc:/milestone/sysconfig:default
online         Jul_27   svc:/network/inetd:default
online         Jul_27   svc:/system/utmp:default
online         Jul_27   svc:/network/nfs/client:default
online         Jul_27   svc:/system/system-log:default
online         Jul_27   svc:/network/smtp:sendmail
```

Many of these services have their own dependencies, services that must be started before they get started. We refer to these as sub-dependencies. For example, one of the services listed is the `svc:/network/inetd:default` service. A listing of the sub-dependencies for this service can be obtained by typing

```
svcs -d network/inetd
```

The system displays the following dependencies:

```
STATE          STIME    FMRI
disabled       15:47:57 svc:/network/inetd-upgrade:default
online         15:47:48 svc:/network/loopback:default
online         15:48:01 svc:/milestone/network:default
online         15:48:30 svc:/milestone/name-services:default
```

```
online          15:48:33 svc:/system/filesystem/local:default
online          15:48:34 svc:/network/rpc/bind:default
online          15:48:36 svc:/milestone/sysconfig:default
```

The `-d` option, in the previous example, lists the services or service instances upon which the `multi-user` service instance is dependent. These are the services that must be running before the `multi-user` milestone is reached. The `-D` option shows which other services depend on the `milestone/multi-user` service as follows:

```
svcs -D milestone/multi-user
```

The system displays the following output indicating that the `dhcp-server` and `multi-user-server` services are dependent on the `multi-user` service:

```
STATE          STIME    FMRI
online         Jul_27   svc:/network/dhcp-server:default
online         Jul_27   svc:/milestone/multi-user-server:default
```

To view processes associated with a service instance, use the `-p` option as follows:

```
svcs -p svc:/network/inetd:default
```

The system displays processes associated with the `svc:/network/inetd:default` service. In this case, information about the `inetd` process is shown as follows:

```
STATE          STIME    FMRI
online         Jul_27   svc:/network/inetd:default
               Jul_27        231 inetd
```

Viewing processes using `svcs -p` instead of the traditional `ps` command makes it easier to track all of the processes associated with a particular service.

If a service fails for some reason and cannot be restarted, you can list the service using the `-x` option as follows:

```
svcs -x
```

The system will display:

```
svc:/application/print/server:default (LP print server)
 State: disabled since Thu Sep 22 18:55:14 2005
Reason: Disabled by an administrator.
   See: http://sun.com/msg/SMF-8000-05
   See: lpsched(1M)
Impact: 2 dependent services are not running.  (Use -v for list.)
```

The example shows that the LP print service has not started and provides an explanation that the service has not been enabled.

Starting and Stopping Services Using SMF

To disable services in previous versions of Solaris, the system administrator had to search out and rename the relevant RC script(s) or comment out statements in a configuration file such as modifying the `inetd.conf` file when disabling `ftp`.

SMF makes it much easier to locate services and their dependencies. To start a particular service using SMF, the service instance must be enabled using the `svcadm enable` command. By enabling a service, the status change is recorded in the service configuration repository. The enabled state will persist across reboots as long as the service dependencies are met. The following example demonstrates how to use the `svcadm` command to enable the ftp server:

```
svcadm  enable network/ftp:default
```

To disable the `ftp` service, use the `disable` option as follows:

```
svcadm  disable network/ftp:default
```

To verify the status of the service, type

```
svcs network/ftp
```

The system displays the following:

```
STATE          STIME    FMRI
online         16:07:08 svc:/network/ftp:default
```

The `svcadm` command allows the following subcommands:

- **`Enable`**—Enables the service instances.
- **`Disable`**—Disables the service instances.
- **`Restart`**—Requests that the service instances be restarted.
- **`Refresh`**—For each service instance specified, `refresh` requests that the assigned restarter update the service's running configuration snapshot with the values from the current configuration. Some of these values take effect immediately (for example, dependency changes). Other values do not take effect until the next service restart.
- **`Clear`**—For each service instance specified, if the instance is in the maintenance state, signal to the assigned restarter that the service has been repaired. If the instance is in the degraded state, request that the assigned restarter take the service to the online state.

The `svcadm` command can also be used to change milestones. In the following step by step, I'll use the `svcadm` command to determine my current system state (milestone) and then change the system default milestone to single-user.

STEP BY STEP

3.2 Changing Milestones

1. First, check to see what the default milestone is set to for your system by using the `svcprop` command. This command will retrieve the SMF service configuration properties for my system

```
# svcprop restarter¦grep milestone
```

The system responds with the following, indicating that my system is set to boot to the multi-user milestone by default:

```
options/milestone astring svc:/milestone/multi-user:default
```

2. I'll check to see which milestone the system is currently running at:

```
svcs ¦ grep milestone
```

The system responds with

```
disabled       16:16:36 svc:/milestone/multi-user-server:default
online         16:16:36 svc:/milestone/name-services:default
online         16:16:43 svc:/milestone/devices:default
online         16:16:45 svc:/milestone/network:default
online         16:16:57 svc:/milestone/single-user:default
online         16:17:03 svc:/milestone/sysconfig:default
online         16:17:16 svc:/milestone/multi-user:default
```

From the output, I see that `multi-user-server` is not running, but `multi-user` is running.

3. To start the transition to the single-user milestone, type

```
svcadm milestone single-user
```

The system responds with the following, prompting for the root password and finally entering single-user mode:

```
Root password for system maintenance (control-d to bypass): <enter root password>
single-user privilege assigned to /dev/console.
Entering System Maintenance Mode

Sep 22 17:22:09 su: 'su root' succeeded for root on /dev/console
Sun Microsystems Inc.   SunOS 5.10      Generic January 2005
#
```

4. Verify the current milestone with the following command:

```
svcs -a ¦ grep milestone
```

The system responds with:

```
disabled       16:16:36 svc:/milestone/multi-user-server:default
disabled       17:21:37 svc:/milestone/multi-user:default
```

```
disabled        17:21:37 svc:/milestone/sysconfig:default
disabled        17:21:39 svc:/milestone/name-services:default
online          16:16:43 svc:/milestone/devices:default
online          16:16:45 svc:/milestone/network:default
online          16:16:57 svc:/milestone/single-user:default
```

The output indicates that the multi-user and multi-user-server milestones are disabled, and the single-user milestone is the only milestone that is currently online.

5. Finally, I'll bring the system backup to the multi-user-server milestone:

```
svcadm milestone milestone/multi-user-server:default
```

Issuing the svcs command again shows that the multi-user-server milestone is back online:

```
svcs -a ¦grep milestone
online          16:16:43 svc:/milestone/devices:default
online          16:16:45 svc:/milestone/network:default
online          16:16:57 svc:/milestone/single-user:default
online          17:37:06 svc:/milestone/name-services:default
online          17:37:12 svc:/milestone/sysconfig:default
online          17:37:23 svc:/milestone/multi-user:default
online          17:37:31 svc:/milestone/multi-user-server:default
```

At bootup, svc.startd retrieves the information in the service configuration repository and starts services when their dependencies are met. The daemon is also responsible for restarting services that have failed and for shutting down services whose dependencies are no longer satisfied.

In the following example, users cannot telnet into the server, so I check on the telnet service using the svcs -x command as follows:

```
svcs -x telnet
```

The results show that the service is not running:

```
svc:/network/telnet:default (Telnet server)
 State: disabled since Fri Sep 23 10:06:46 2005
Reason: Temporarily disabled by an administrator.
   See: http://sun.com/msg/SMF-8000-1S
   See: in.telnetd(1M)
   See: telnetd(1M)
Impact: This service is not running.
```

I'll enable the service using the svcadm command as follows:

```
svcadm enable svc:/network/telnet:default
```

After enabling the service, check the status using the `svcs` command as follows:

```
# svcs -x telnet
```

The system responds with:

```
svc:/network/telnet:default (Telnet server)
 State: online since Fri Sep 23 10:20:47 2005
   See: in.telnetd(1M)
   See: telnetd(1M)
Impact: None.
```

Also, if a service that has been running but stops, try restarting the service using the `svcadm restart` command as follows:

```
svcadm restart svc:/network/telnet:default
```

Starting Services During Boot

Under SMF, the boot process is much quieter than previous versions of Solaris. This was done to reduce the amount of uninformative "chatter" that might obscure any real problems that might occur during boot.

Some new boot options have been added to control the verbosity of boot. One that you may find particularly useful is `-m verbose`, which prints a line of information when each service attempts to start up. This is similar to previous versions of Solaris where the boot messages were more verbose.

You can also boot the system using one of the milestones as follows:

```
boot -m milestone=single-user
```

The system will boot into single-user mode where only the basic services are started as shown when the `svcs` command is used to display services.

```
STATE          STIME    FMRI
disabled       17:10:27 svc:/system/filesystem/local:default
disabled       17:10:27 svc:/system/identity:domain
disabled       17:10:27 svc:/system/sysidtool:net
disabled       17:10:28 svc:/system/cryptosvc:default
disabled       17:10:28 svc:/network/initial:default
disabled       17:10:28 svc:/network/rpc/bind:default
disabled       17:10:28 svc:/system/sysidtool:system
disabled       17:10:28 svc:/milestone/sysconfig:default
Output has been truncated . . . . .
```

This method of booting is slightly different than using the `boot -s` command. When the system is explicitly booted to a milestone, exiting the console administrative shell will not transition the system to multi-user mode, as `boot -s` does. To move to multi-user mode after `boot -m milestone=single-user`, use the following command:

```
svcadm milestone milestone/multi-user-server:default
```

The milestones that can be specified at boot time are

- none
- single-user
- multi-user
- multi-user-server
- all

If you boot a system using one of the milestones and you do not include the `-s` option, the system will stay in the milestone state that you booted the system in. The system will not go into multi-user state automatically when you press Ctrl+D. You can however, get into the multi-user state by using the following command and all services will be restored:

```
svcadm milestone all
```

To boot the system without any milestones, type

```
boot -m milestone=none
```

The `boot` command instructs the `svc.startd` daemon to temporarily disable all services except for the master restarter named `svc:/system/svc/restarter:default` and start `sulogin` on the console. The "none" milestone can be very useful in troubleshooting systems that have failures early in the boot process.

To bring the system back down to single-user mode from multi-user mode, type

```
svcadm milestone milestone/single-user
```

The `-d` option can be used with the previous example to cause `svcadm` to make the given milestone the default boot milestone, which persists across reboots. This would be the equivalent of setting the default run level in the `/etc/inittab` file on previous versions of Solaris.

Other options that can be used with `svcadm` include

- `-r`—Enables each service instance and recursively enables its dependencies.
- `-s`—Enables each service instance and then waits for each service instance to enter the `online` or `degraded` state. `svcadm` will return early if it determines that the service cannot reach these states without administrator intervention.
- `-t`—Temporarily enables or disables each service instance. Temporary `enable` or `disable` only lasts until reboot.

SMF Message Logging

In addition to the system logging methods described earlier in this chapter, each service has a log file in the `/var/svc/log` directory (or the `/etc/svc/volatile` directory, for services started before the single-user milestone) indicating when and how the system was started, whether it started successfully, and any messages it may have printed during its initialization. If a severe problem occurs during boot, you will be able to log in on the console in maintenance mode, and you can use the `svcs` command to help diagnose the problem, even on problems which would have caused boot to hang. Finally, the new `boot -m` boot option allows the system administrator to configure the boot process to be more verbose, printing a simple message when each service starts.

Creating New Service Scripts

Objective:

Use Service Management Facility or legacy commands and scripts to control both the boot and shutdown procedures.

As you customize your system, you'll create custom scripts to start and stop processes or services on your system. The correct procedure for incorporating these scripts into the SMF is as follows:

- Determine the process for starting and stopping your service.
- Establish a name for the service and the category this service falls into.
- Determine whether your service runs multiple instances.
- Identify any dependency relationships between this service and any other services. Practically every service has a dependency so that the service does not startup too soon in the boot process.
- If a script is required to start and stop the process, create the script and place it in a local directory such as `/lib/svc/method`.
- Create a service manifest file for your service in the `/var/svc/manifest/site` directory. This XML file describes the service and any dependency relationships. Service manifests are incorporated into the repository either by using the `svccfg` command or at boot time. See the `service_bundle(4)` manual page for a description of the contents of the SMF manifests.
- Incorporate the script into the SMF using the `svccfg` utility.

The following step by step describes the process of setting up and enabling an existing service instance.

STEP BY STEP

3.3 Enable the NFS Server Service

In the following example, I'll configure SMF to share the NFS resources on an NFS server.

1. Log in as root or use a role that includes the Service Management rights profile.
2. The NFS server services are not running as displayed by the following `svcs` command:

   ```
   svcs -a¦ grep -i nfs
   ```

   The system displays the following information about the NFS services:

   ```
   disabled        15:47:56 svc:/network/nfs/cbd:default
   disabled        15:47:59 svc:/network/nfs/server:default
   online          15:48:36 svc:/network/nfs/mapid:default
   online          15:48:36 svc:/network/nfs/status:default
   online          15:48:37 svc:/network/nfs/nlockmgr:default
   online          15:48:44 svc:/network/nfs/client:default
   online          15:54:26 svc:/network/nfs/rquota:default
   ```

   Notice that `svc:/network/nfs/server:default` is disabled.

3. Set up the required NFS configuration file on the server. To share a file system named `/data`, I need to configure the `/etc/dfs/dfstab` file as described in Chapter 9. I add the following line to the NFS server configuration file:

   ```
   share -F nfs -o rw /data
   ```

4. Enable the NFS service as follows:

   ```
   svcadm enable svc:/network/nfs/server
   ```

5. Verify that the NFS server service is running by typing:

   ```
   svcs -a ¦ grep -i nfs
   ```

   The system displays the following information:

   ```
   disabled        15:47:56 svc:/network/nfs/cbd:default
   online          15:48:44 svc:/network/nfs/client:default
   online          11:22:26 svc:/network/nfs/status:default
   online          11:22:26 svc:/network/nfs/nlockmgr:default
   online          11:22:27 svc:/network/nfs/mapid:default
   online          11:22:28 svc:/network/nfs/server:default
   online          11:22:28 svc:/network/nfs/rquota:default
   ```

This next step by step describes how to create a new service and incorporate it into the SMF. Taking the time to convert your existing RC scripts to SMF allows them to take advantage of automated restart capabilities that could be caused by hardware failure, unexpected service failure, or administrative error. Participation in the service management facility also brings enhanced visibility with `svcs` (as well as future-planned GUI tools) and ease of management with `svcadm` and other Solaris management tools. The task requires the creation of a short XML file and making a few simple modifications to the service RC script. The following step by step will take you through the process.

STEP BY STEP

3.4 Converting an RC Script to SMF

Before I start, I'll take an existing legacy RC script and place it under SMF control as a service. This script is named `/etc/init.d/legacy` and has the following entries:

```
#!/sbin/sh
case "$1" in
'start')
        /usr/local/legacyprog
        ;;

'stop')
        /usr/bin/pkill -x -u 0 legacyprog
        ;;

*)
        echo "Usage: $0 { start | stop }"
        exit 1
        ;;

esac
exit 0
```

I'll move this script to `/lib/svc/method/legacyservice`.

The most complex part of this procedure is writing the SMF manifest in XML. Currently, these manifests need to be created with an editor, but in the future, expect a GUI-based tool to aid in the creation of the manifest file. The `service_bundle(4)` man page describes this XML-based file, but you need to be familiar with the XML programming language, and that is beyond the scope of this book. Here's a copy of my manifest for the service we are going to implement; I named it `/var/svc/manifest/site/legacyservice`, and I'll describe the contents of the file in this section.

```
<?xml version="1.0"?>
<!DOCTYPE service_bundle SYSTEM
"/usr/share/lib/xml/dtd/service_bundle.dtd.1">
```

```
<!--
ident "@(#)newservice.xml 1.2 04/09/13 SMI"
-->
<service_bundle type='manifest' name='OPTnew:legacyservice'>

<service
        name='site/legacyservice'
        type='service'
        version='1'>

<single_instance/>

<dependency
        name='usr'
        type='service'
        grouping='require_all'
        restart_on='none'>
        <service_fmri value='svc:/system/filesystem/local' />
</dependency>

<dependent
        name='newservice'
        grouping='require_all'
        restart_on='none'>
        <service_fmri value='svc:/milestone/multi-user' />
</dependent>

<exec_method
        type='method'
        name='start'
        exec='/lib/svc/method/legacyservice start'
        timeout_seconds='30' />

<exec_method
        type='method'
        name='stop'
        exec='/lib/svc/method/legacyservice stop'
        timeout_seconds='30' />

<property_group name='startd' type='framework'>
<propval name='duration' type='astring' value='transient'
/>
</property_group>

<instance name='default' enabled='true' />

<stability value='Unstable' />
```

```
<template>
        <common_name>
                <loctext xml:lang='C'>
                New service
                </loctext>
        </common_name>
</template>
</service>
</service_bundle>
```

Now let's take a closer look at the XML-based manifest file and the steps I took to create it.

1. My file starts out with a standard header. After the header, I specify the name of the service, the type of service, the package providing the service, and the service name as follows:

   ```
   <?xml version="1.0"?>
   <!DOCTYPE service_bundle SYSTEM
   "/usr/share/lib/xml/dtd/service_bundle.dtd.1">
   <!--
   ident "@(#)newservice.xml 1.2 04/09/13 SMI"
   -->

   <service_bundle type='manifest' name='OPTnew:legacyservice'>
   ```

2. I specify the service category, type, name, and version. These categories aren't used by the system, but help the administrator in identifying the general use of the service. These categories types are

   application—Higher level applications, such as apache

   milestone—Collections of other services, such as name-services

   platform—Platform-specific services, such as Dynamic Reconfiguration daemons

   system—Solaris system services, such as coreadm

   device—Device-specific services

   network—Network/Internet services, such as protocols

   site—Site specific descriptions

   The service name describes what is being provided, and includes both any category identifier and the actual service name, separated by '/'. Service names should identify the service being provided. In this example, the entry I'll make to my manifest file is as follows:

   ```
   <service
           name='site/legacyservice'
           type='service'
           version='1'>
   ```

3. Identify whether your service will have multiple instances. The instance name describes any specific features about the instance. Most services deliver a "default" instance. Some (such as Oracle) may want

to create instances based on administrative configuration choices. This service will have a single instance, so I'll make the following entry in the manifest:

```
<single_instance />
```

4. Define any dependencies for this service. I added the following entry to the manifest:

```
<dependency
        name='usr'
        type='service'
        grouping='require_all'
        restart_on='none'>
        <service_fmri value='svc:/system/filesystem/local' />
</dependency>
```

The first entry states that the *legacyservice* requires the *filesystem/local* service.

5. We now need to identify dependents. If I want to make sure that my service is associated with the multi-user milestone and that the multi-user milestone requires this service, I add the following entry to the manifest:

```
<dependent
         name='testservice'
         grouping=require_all'
         restart_on='none'>
            <service_fmri value='svc:/milestone/multi-user' />
      <dependent>
```

By having the ability to identify dependents, I'm able to deliver a service that is a dependency of another service (milestone/multi-user) which I don't deliver. I can specify this in my *legacyservice* manifest without modifying the *milestone/multi-user* manifest, which I don't own. It's an easy way to have a service run before a Solaris default service.

If all the dependent services have not been converted to SMF, you'll need to convert those too, as there is no way to specify a dependent on a legacy script.

To avoid conflicts, it is recommended that you preface the dependent name with the name of your service. For example, if you're delivering a service (`legacyservice`) that must start before `syslog`, use the following entry:

```
<dependent
   name='legacyservice_syslog'
```

6. Specify how the service will be started and stopped. SMF interacts with your service primarily by its methods. The stop and start methods must be provided for services managed by `svc.startd`, and can either directly invoke a service binary or a script which handles care of more complex setup. The refresh method is optional for `svc.startd` managed services. I'll use the following start and stop methods:

```
<exec_method
        type='method'
```

```
        name='start'
        exec='/lib/svc/method/legacyservice start'
        timeout_seconds='30' />

<exec_method
        type='method'
        name='stop'
        exec='/lib/svc/method/legacyservice stop'
        timeout_seconds='30' />
```

Timeouts must be provided for all methods. The timeout should be defined to be the maximum amount of time in seconds that your method might take to run on a slow system or under heavy load. A method which exceeds its timeout will be killed. If the method could potentially take an unbounded amount of time, such as a large file system `fsck`, an infinite timeout may be specified as '0'.

7. Identify the service model—will it be started by `inetd` or `svc.startd`? My service will be started by `svc.startd`. `svc.startd` provides three models of service, which are

   Transient services—These are often configuration services, which require no long-running processes to provide service. Common transient services take care of boot-time cleanup or load configuration properties into the kernel. Transient services are also sometimes used to overcome difficulties in conforming to the method requirements for contract or wait services. This is not recommended and should be considered a stopgap measure.

   Wait services—These services run for the lifetime of the child process, and are restarted when that process exits.

   Contract services—These are the standard system daemons. They require processes which run forever once started to provide service. Death of all processes in a contract service is considered a service error, which will cause the service to restart.

   The default service model is *contract*, but may be modified. For this example, I'm going to start the service with `svc.startd`. As a transient service, it will be started once and not restarted by adding the following lines to the manifest:

```
<property_group name='startd' type='framework'>
<propval name='duration' type='astring' value='transient'
/>
</property_group>
```

8. The next step is to create the instance name for the service by making the following entry:

```
<instance name='default' enabled='true' />
```

9. Finally, create template information to describe the service providing concise detail about the service. I'll assign a common name in the C locale. The common name should

   Be short (40 characters or less)

   Avoid capital letters aside from trademarks like Solaris

Avoid punctuation

Avoid the word service (but do distinguish between client and server)

I make the following entry in the manifest to describe my service as "New service":

```
<template>
        <common_name>
                <loctext xml:lang='C'>
                New service
                </loctext>
        </common_name>
</template>
```

10. Once the manifest is complete, is a good idea to verify the syntax using the `xmllint` program as follows:

```
xmllint --valid /var/svc/manifest/site/legacyservice
```

The `xmllint` program will parse the XML file and identify any errors in the code before you try to import it into SMF. The `scvcfg` program also can validate your file as follows, but the output is not as verbose as the `xmllint` command:

```
svccfg validate /var/svc/manifest/site/legacyservice
```

11. Once you've validated the syntax of your XML file, the new service needs to be imported in SMF by issuing the `svccfg` command as follows:

```
svccfg import /var/svc/manifest/site/legacyservice
```

12. The service should now be visible using the `svcs` command as follows:

```
# svcs legacyservice
STATE          STIME    FMRI
-              svc:/site/legacyservice:default
```

13. You can also see which services the `legacyservice` depends on by using the `svcs -d` command as follows:

```
svcs -d legacyservice
STATE          STIME    FMRI
online         Sep_20   svc:/system/filesystem/local:default
```

14. As a final step, enable the service using the `svcadm` command as follows:

```
svcadm -v enable legacyservice
svc:/site/legacyservice:default enabled.
```

15. At any time, I can view the properties of a service using the `svccfg` command as follows:

```
svccfg -v -s legacyservice
```

The system responds with the following prompt:

```
svc:/site/legacyservice>
```

Use the `listprop` subcommand at the `svccfg` prompt to list the service properties:

```
svc:/site/legacyservice> listprop
usr                          dependency
usr/entities                 fmri      svc:/system/filesystem/local
usr/grouping                 astring   require_all
usr/restart_on               astring   none
usr/type                     astring   service
general                      framework
general/entity_stability     astring   Unstable
general/single_instance      boolean   true
dependents                   framework
dependents/newservice        astring   svc:/milestone/multi-user
startd                       framework
startd/duration              astring   transient
start                        method
start/exec                   astring   "/lib/svc/method/legacyservice start"
start/timeout_seconds        count     30
start/type                   astring   method
stop                         method
stop/exec                    astring   "/lib/svc/method/legacyservice stop"
stop/timeout_seconds         count     30
stop/type                    astring   method
tm_common_name               template
tm_common_name/C             ustring   "New service"
svc:/site/legacyservice>
```

Legacy Services

Objective:

Use Service Management Facility or legacy commands and scripts to control both the boot and shutdown procedures.

Solaris 10 still supports legacy RC scripts referred to as legacy services, but you will notice that the `/etc/inittab` file used by the `init` daemon has been significantly reduced. In addition, RC scripts that were located in the `/etc/init.d` directory and linked to the `/etc/rc#.d` directory have also been reduced substantially. For many of the scripts that remain, simply run the `svcadm` command to start the appropriate service.

SMF-managed services no longer use RC scripts or `/etc/inittab` entries for startup and shutdown, so the scripts corresponding to those services have been removed. In future releases of Solaris, more services will be managed by SMF, and these directories will become less and less populated. RC scripts and /etc/inittab entries that manage third-party–provided or locally developed services will continue to be run at boot. These services may not run at exactly the same point in boot as they had before the advent of SMF, but they are guaranteed to not run any earlier—any services which they had implicitly depended on will still be available.

For those readers who are experienced on Solaris versions prior to Solaris 10, you are accustomed to starting and stopping services via rc scripts. For instance, to stop and start the sshd daemon, you would type:

```
/etc/init.d/sshd stop
/etc/init.d/sshd start
```

In SMF, the correct procedure to start sshd is to type

```
svcadm enable -t network/ssh:default
```

To temporarily stop sshd, you would type

```
svcadm disable -t network/ssh:default
```

Or simply type

```
svcadm restart network/ssh:default
```

to stop and restart the sshd daemon.

Prior to Solaris 10, to send a HUP signal to the ssh daemon, we would have typed

```
kill -HUP `cat /var/run/sshd.pid`
```

In Solaris 10, the correct procedure is to type

```
svcadm refresh network/ssh:default
```

Using the Run Control Scripts to Stop or Start Services

Although it is recommended that you use SMF to start and stop services as described in the previous section, "Creating New Service Scripts," functionality still exists to allow the use of run control scripts to start and stop system services at various run levels. Run control scripts were used in previous versions of Solaris to start and stop system services before SMF was introduced.

A run level is a system state (run state), represented by a number or letter that identifies the services and resources that are currently available to users. The who -r command can still be used to identify a systems run state as follows:

```
who -r
```

The system responds with the following indicating that `run-level 3` is the current run state:

```
.        run-level 3  Aug  4 09:38     3      1  1
```

Since the introduction of SMF in Solaris 10, we now refer to these run states as milestones, and Table 3.26 describes how the legacy run states coincide with the Solaris 10 milestones.

TABLE 3.26 The System Run States

Run State (milestone)	Description
`0`	Stops system services and daemons. Terminates all running processes. Unmounts all file systems.
`S, s (single-user)`	Single-user (system administrator) state. Only root is allowed to log in at the console, and any logged-in users are logged out when you enter this run level. Only critical file systems are mounted and accessible. All services except the most basic operating system services are shut down in an orderly manner.
`1`	Single-user (system administrator) state. If the system is booted into this run level, all local file systems are mounted. All services except the most basic operating system services are shut down.
`2 (multi-user)`	Normal multiuser operation, without network file systems (NFSs) shared: directories; locks interfaces and starts processes; starts the `con` daemon; cleans up the `uucp tmp` files; starts the `lp` system; and starts the `sendmail` daemon and `syslog`.
`3 (multi-user-server)`	Normal multi-use operation of a file server, with NFSs shared. Completes all the tasks in run state 2 and starts the NFS daemons.
`4`	Alternative multi-user state (currently not used).
`5`	Power-down state. Shuts down the system so that it is safe to turn off power to the system. If possible, automatically turns off system power on systems that support this feature.
`6`	Reboot state.

To support legacy applications that still use them, run control scripts have been carried over from Solaris 9. With run control scripts, each `init` state (milestone) has a corresponding series of run control scripts—which are referred to as `rc` scripts and are located in the `/sbin` directory—to control each `run` state. These `rc` scripts are as follows:

- `rc0`
- `rc1`
- `rc2`
- `rc3`

- rc5
- rc6
- rcS

NOTE

Run Control Scripts Solaris startup scripts can be identified by their `rc` prefix or suffix, which means *run control.*

You can still use the `init` command to transition to between the various run states. The `init` daemon will simply pass the required run state to the `svc.startd` daemon for execution.

The SMF will execute the `/sbin/rc<n>` scripts, which in turn execute a series of other scripts that are located in the `/etc` directory. For each `rc` script in the `/sbin` directory, a corresponding directory named `/etc/rc<n>.d` contains scripts to perform various actions for that run state. For example, `/etc/rc3.d` contains files that are used to start and stop processes for run state 3.

The `/etc/rc<n>.d` scripts are always run in ASCII sort order shown by the `ls` command and have names of this form:

```
[K,S][#][filename]
```

A file that begins with `K` is referred to as a *stop script* and is run to terminate (kill) a system process. A file that begins with `S` is referred to as a *start script* and is run to start a system process. Each of these start and stop scripts is called by the appropriate `/sbin/rc#` script. For example, the `/sbin/rc0` script runs the scripts located in the `/etc/rc0.d` directory. The `/sbin/rc#` script will pass the argument `start` or `stop` to each script, based on their prefix and whether the name ends in `.sh`. There are no arguments passed to scripts that end in `.sh`.

All run control scripts are also located in the `/etc/init.d` directory, and all scripts must be `/sbin/sh` scripts. These files are hard linked to corresponding run control scripts in the `/etc/rc<n>.d` directories.

These run control scripts can also be run individually to start and stop services. For example, you can turn off NFS server functionality by typing **`/etc/init.d/nfs.server stop`** and pressing Enter. After you have changed the system configuration, you can restart the NFS services by typing `/etc/init.d/nfs.server start` and pressing Enter. If you notice, however, many of these RC scripts simply have `svcadm` commands embedded in them to perform the task of stopping and starting the service.

In addition to the `svcs -p` command, you can still use the `pgrep` command to verify whether a service has been stopped or started:

```
pgrep -f <service>
```

The `pgrep` utility examines the active processes on the system and reports the process IDs of the processes. See Chapter 5, "Managing System Processes," for details on this command.

Adding Scripts to the Run Control Directories

If you add a script to the run control directories, you put the script in the `/etc/init.d` directory and create a hard link to the appropriate `rc<n>.d` directory. You need to assign appropriate numbers and names to the new scripts so that they will be run in the proper ASCII sequence, as described in the previous section.

To add a new run control script to a system, follow the process in Step by Step 3.5.

STEP BY STEP

3.5 Adding a Run Control Script

1. Become the superuser.
2. Add the script to the `/etc/init.d` directory:

   ```
   # cp <filename> /etc/init.d
   # cd /etc/init.d
   # chmod 744 <filename>
   # chown root:sys <filename>
   ```

3. Create links to the appropriate `rc<n>.d` directory:

   ```
   # ln  <filename> /etc/rc2.d/S<nnfilename>
   # ln  <filename> /etc/rc<n>.d/K<nnfilename>
   ```

4. Use the `ls` command to verify that the script has links in the specified directories:

   ```
   # ls -li /etc/init.d/<filename> /etc/rc?.d/[SK]*<filename>
   ```

The following example creates an `rc` script named `program` that starts up at run level `2` and stops at run level `0`. Note the use of hard links versus soft links:

```
# cp program /etc/init.d
# cd /etc/init.d
# chmod 744 program
# chown root:sys program
# ln  /etc/init.d/program  /etc/rc2.d/S99program
 # ln  /etc/init.d/program  /etc/rc0.d/K01program
```

You can verify the links by typing this:

```
# ls -li /etc/init.d/program /etc/rc?.d/[SK]*program
```

The system displays the following:

```
389928 -rwxr--r--   3 root     sys              69 Oct 26 23:31 /etc/init.d/program
389928 -rwxr--r--   3 root     sys              69 Oct 26 23:31 /etc/rc0.d/K01program
389928 -rwxr--r--   3 root     sys              69 Oct 26 23:31 /etc/rc2.d/S99program
```

NOTE

Disabling a Run Control Script If you do not want a particular script to run when the system is entering a corresponding `init` state, you can change the uppercase prefix (`S` or `K`) to some other character; I prefer to prefix the filename with an underscore. Only files beginning with uppercase prefixes of `S` or `K` are run. For example, you could change `S99mount` to `_S99mount` to disable the script.

System Shutdown

Objective:

Complete a system shutdown.

- Interrupt a hung system.
- Given a scenario involving a hung system, troubleshoot problems and deduce resolutions.

Solaris has been designed to run continuously—7 days a week, 24 hours a day. Occasionally, however, you need to shut down the system to carry out administrative tasks. Very seldom, an application might cause the system to go awry, and the operating system must be stopped to kill off runaway processes, and then be restarted.

You can shut down the system in a number of ways, using various Unix commands. With Solaris, taking down the operating system in an orderly fashion is important. When the system boots, several processes are started; they must be shut down before you power off the system. In addition, information that has been cached in memory and has not yet been written to disk will be lost if it is not flushed from memory and saved to disk. The process of shutting down Solaris involves shutting down processes, flushing data from memory to the disk, and unmounting file systems.

CAUTION

Improper Shutdown Can Corrupt Data Shutting down a system improperly can result in loss of data and the risk of corrupting the file systems.

NOTE

Protecting Against Power Loss To avoid having your system shut down improperly during a power failure, you should use an uninterruptible power supply (UPS) that is capable of shutting down the system cleanly before the power is shut off. Be sure to follow the UPS manufacturer's recommendations for maintenance to eliminate the risk of the UPS becoming the cause of an improper shutdown.

Commands to Shut Down the System

When you're preparing to shut down a system, you need to determine which of the following commands is appropriate for the system and the task at hand:

`/usr/sbin/shutdown`

`/sbin/init`

`/usr/sbin/halt`

`/usr/sbin/reboot`

`/usr/sbin/poweroff`

Stop+A or L1+A

CAUTION

Aborting the Operating System Using the Stop+A key sequence (or L1+A) abruptly breaks execution of the operating system and should be used only as a last resort to restart the system.

The first three commands—`/usr/sbin/shutdown`, `/sbin/init`, and `/usr/sbin/halt`—initiate shutdown procedures, kill all running processes, write data to disk, and shut down the system software to the appropriate run level. The `/usr/sbin/reboot` command does all these tasks as well, and it then boots the system back to the state defined as `initdefault` in `/etc/inittab`. The `/usr/sbin/poweroff` command is equivalent to `init` state `5`.

The `/usr/sbin/shutdown` Command

You use the `shutdown` command to shut down a system that has multiple users. The `shutdown` command sends a warning message to all users who are logged in, waits for 60 seconds (by default), and then shuts down the system to single-user state. The command option `-g` lets you choose a different default wait time. The `-i` option lets you define the `init` state to which the system will be shut down. The default is `S`.

The `shutdown` command performs a clean system shutdown, which means that all system processes and services are terminated normally, and file systems are synchronized. You need superuser privileges to use the `shutdown` command.

When the `shutdown` command is initiated, all logged-in users and all systems mounting resources receive a warning about the impending shutdown, and then they get a final message. For this reason, the `shutdown` command is recommended over the `init` command on a server with multiple users.

> **NOTE**
>
> **Sending a Shutdown Message** When using either `shutdown` or `init`, you might want to give users advance notice by sending an email message about any scheduled system shutdown.

The proper sequence of shutting down the system is described in Step by Step 3.6.

STEP BY STEP

3.6 Shutting Down a System

1. As superuser, type the following to find out if users are logged in to the system:

```
# who
```

2. A list of all logged-in users is displayed. You might want to send an email message or broadcast a message to let users know that the system is being shut down.
3. Shut down the system by using the `shutdown` command:

```
# shutdown -i<init-state> -g<grace-period> -y
```

Table 3.27 describes the options available for the `shutdown` command.

TABLE 3.27 Options for the `shutdown` Command

Option	Description
`-i<init-state>`	Brings the system to an `init` state that is different from the default, `S`. The choices are `0`, `S`, `1`, `2`, `5`, and `6`.
`-g<grace-period>`	Indicates a time (in seconds) before the system is shut down. The default is 60 seconds.
`-y`	Continues to shut down the system without intervention; otherwise, you are prompted to continue the shutdown process after 60 seconds. If you use the `shutdown -y` command, you are not prompted to continue; otherwise, you get the message `Do you want to continue? (y or n)`.

The /sbin/init Command

You use the init command to shut down a single-user system or to change its run level. The syntax is as follows:

```
init <run-level>
```

<run-level> is any run level described in Table 3.21. In addition, <run-level> can be a, b, or c, which tells the system to process only /etc/inittab entries that have the a, b, or c run level set. These are pseudo-states, which can be defined to run certain commands but which do not cause the current run level to change. <run-level> can also be the keyword Q or q, which tells the system to reexamine the /etc/inittab file.

You can use init to place the system in power-down state (init state 5) or in single-user state (init state 1). For example, to bring the system down to run level 1 from the current run level, you type the following:

```
init 1
```

The system responds with this:

```
svc.startd: Changing to state 1.
svc.startd: Killing user processes: done.
svc.startd: The system is ready for administration.
Requesting System Maintenance Mode
(See /lib/svc/share/README for more information.)

Root password for system maintenance (control-d to bypass):<enter root password>
single-user privilege assigned to /dev/console.
Entering System Maintenance Mode

Aug  4 09:18:13 su: 'su root' succeeded for root on /dev/console
Sun Microsystems Inc.    SunOS 5.10       Generic January 2005
```

NOTE

The telinit Command The /etc/telinit command is the same as the init command. It is simply a link to the /usr/sbin/init command.

The /usr/sbin/halt Command

You use the halt command when the system must be stopped immediately and it is acceptable not to warn current users. The halt command shuts down the system without delay and does not warn other users on the system of the shutdown.

The `/usr/sbin/reboot` Command

You use the `reboot` command to shut down a single-user system and bring it into multi-user state. `reboot` does not warn other users on the system of the shutdown.

The Solaris `reboot`, `poweroff`, and `halt` commands stop the processor and synchronize the disks, but they perform unconditional shutdown of system processes. These commands are not recommended because they do not shut down any services and unmount any remaining file systems. They will, however, attempt to kill active processes with a SIGTERM, but the services will not be shut down cleanly. Stopping the services without doing a clean shutdown should only be done in an emergency or if most of the services are already stopped.

The speed of such a reboot is useful in certain circumstances, such as when you're rebooting from the single-user run state. Also, the capability to pass arguments to OpenBoot via the `reboot` command is useful. For example, this command reboots the system into run level `s` and reconfigures the device tables:

```
reboot -- -rs
```

The `/usr/sbin/poweroff` Command

The `poweroff` command is equivalent to the `init 5` command. As with the `reboot` and `halt` commands, the `poweroff` command synchronizes the disks and immediately shuts down the system, without properly shutting down services and unmounting all file systems. Users are not notified of the shutdown. If the hardware supports it, the `poweroff` command also turns off power.

NOTE

The `init` and `shutdown` Commands Using `init` and using `shutdown` are the most reliable ways to shut down a system because these commands shutdown services in a clean orderly fashion and shut down the system with minimal data loss. The `halt`, `poweroff`, and `reboot` commands do not shutdown services properly and are not the preferred method of shutting down the system.

Stopping the System for Recovery Purposes

Occasionally, a system might not respond to the `init` commands described earlier in this chapter. A system that doesn't respond to anything, including `reboot` or `halt`, is called a "crashed" or "hung" system. If you try to use the commands discussed in the preceding sections but get no response, on non-USB style keyboards, you can press Stop+A or L1+A to get back to the boot PROM. (The specific Stop key sequence depends on your keyboard type.) On terminals connected to the serial port, you can press the Break key, as described in the section "Accessing the OpenBoot Environment," earlier in this chapter.

Some OpenBoot systems provide the capability of commanding OpenBoot by means of pressing a combination of keys on the system's keyboard, referred to as a *keyboard chord* or *key combination*. These keyboard chords are described in Table 3.28. When issuing any of these commands, you press the keys immediately after turning on the power to your system, and you hold down the keys for a few seconds until the keyboard light-emitting diodes (LEDs) flash. It should be noted, however, that these keyboard chords only work on non-USB keyboards and not USB style keyboards.

TABLE 3.28 Keyboard Chords

Command	Description
Stop	Bypasses the POST. This command does not depend on the security mode. (Note that some systems bypass the POST as a default; in such cases, you use Stop+D to start the POST.)
Stop+A	Interrupts any program currently running and puts the system at the OpenBoot prompt, ready to accept OpenBoot PROM commands.
Stop+D	Enters diagnostic mode (sets the `diag-switch?` variable to `true`).
Stop+F	Enters Forth on the `ttya` port instead of probing. Uses `fexit` to continue with the initialization sequence. This chord is useful if hardware is broken.
Stop+N	Resets the contents of NVRAM to the default values.

NOTE

Disabling Keyboard Chords The commands in Table 3.26 are disabled if PROM security is on. Also, if your system has full security enabled, you cannot apply any of these commands unless you have the password to get to the `ok` prompt.

To change the default abort sequence on the keyboard, you need to edit the `/etc/default/kbd` file. In that file, you can enable and disable keyboard abort sequences, and change the keyboard abort sequence. After modifying this file, you issue the `kbd -i` command to update the keyboard defaults.

The process of breaking out of a hung system is described in Step by Step 3.7.

TIP

Interrupting a Hung System Step by Step 3.5 describes an objective that is sure to be on the exam. Make sure that you understand each step and the order in which the steps are executed.

STEP BY STEP

3.7 Breaking Out of a Hung System

1. Use the abort key sequence for your system (Stop+A or L1+A).

   The monitor displays the ok PROM prompt.

2. Type the sync command to manually synchronize the file systems:

   ```
   ok sync
   ```

   The sync procedure synchronizes the file systems and is necessary to prevent corruption. During the sync process, the system will panic, synchronize the file systems, perform a crash dump by dumping the contents of kernel memory to disk, and finally perform a system reset to start the boot process.

3. After you receive the login: message, log in and type the following to verify that the system is booted to the specified run level:

   ```
   # who -r
   ```

4. The system responds with the following:

   ```
   run-level 3  Jun 9 09:19  3   0  S
   ```

Turning Off the Power to the Hardware

Only after shutting down the file systems should you turn off the power to the hardware. You turn off power to all devices after the system is shut down. If necessary, you should also unplug the power cables. When power can be restored, you use the process described in Step by Step 3.8 to turn on the system and devices.

STEP BY STEP

3.8 Turning Off the Power

1. Plug in the power cables.
2. Turn on all peripheral devices, such as disk drives, tape drives, and printers.
3. Turn on the CPU and monitor.

Summary

This chapter provides a description of the OpenBoot environment, the PROM, NVRAM, and the kernel. It describes how to access OpenBoot and the various commands that are available to test and provide information about the hardware.

This chapter describes the OpenBoot architecture, and it explains how OpenBoot controls many of the hardware devices. By using the programmable user interface available in OpenBoot, you can set several parameters that control system hardware and peripherals.

The device tree and OpenBoot device names are explained in this chapter. Throughout this book, the text refers to various device names used in Solaris. It's important that you understand each one of them. Along with device names, this chapter explains how to set temporary and permanent device aliases.

The system startup phases are described in this chapter, and you have learned how Solaris processes and services are started, from bootup, to loading and initializing the two-part kernel, to continuing to the multi-user milestone. You can further control these services through the Service Management Facility.

This chapter describes how important it is to shut down the system properly because the integrity of the data can be compromised if the proper shutdown steps are not performed. All the various commands used to shut down a system in an orderly manner are outlined.

Chapter 4, "User and Security Administration," describes how to protect your system and data from unauthorized access.

Key Terms

- Autoconfiguration
- Boot
- Bootblock
- Bootstrapping
- Service Contract
- Dependency
- Sub-dependencies
- Device alias
- Device tree
- Dynamic kernel
- Full device name
- `init` state
- Interactive boot
- Kernel
- Loadable module
- Multiuser mode
- NVRAM
- OBP
- OpenBoot
- POST

- PROM
- Reconfiguration boot
- Run control script
- Run level
- Service Management Facility (SMF)
- Service
- Service Instance Object
- Single-user mode
- `ufsboot`

Exercises

CAUTION

Don't Do This on a Production System! Because some of the steps involved in the following exercises could render a system unbootable if they're not performed properly, you should not perform these exercises on a production system.

3.1 Using OpenBoot Commands

In this exercise, you will halt the system and use the OpenBoot commands to set parameters and gather basic information about your system.

Estimated time: 30 minutes

1. Issue the OpenBoot command to display the banner, as follows:

```
banner
```

2. Set parameters to their default values, as follows:

```
reset-all
```

3. Set the `auto-boot?` parameter to `false` to prevent the system from booting automatically after a reset. From the OpenBoot `ok` prompt, type the following:

```
setenv auto-boot? false
```

Verify that the parameter has been set by typing the following:

```
printenv auto-boot?
```

4. Display the list of OpenBoot help topics, as follows:

```
help
```

5. Use the `banner` command to get the following information from your system:

   ROM revision

   Amount of installed memory

   System type

   System serial number

   Ethernet address

   Host ID

6. Display the following list of OBP parameters by using the `printenv` command:

   ```
   output-device
   input-device
   auto-boot?
   boot-device
   ```

7. Use the following commands to display the list of disk devices attached to your system:

   ```
   probe-scsi
   probe-scsi-all
   probe-ide
   ```

   Explain the main differences between these commands.

CAUTION

Preventing a System Hang If any of these commands returns a message warning that your system will hang if you proceed, enter `n` to avoid running the command. Run `reset-all` before running `probe-` again and then respond `y` to this message.

8. List the target number and the device type of each SCSI device attached to your system by using the OpenBoot commands in step 7.

9. From the OpenBoot prompt, identify your default boot device as follows:

   ```
   printenv boot-device
   ```

10. Use the `show-disks` OpenBoot command to get a listing of the disk drives on your system, as follows:

    ```
    show-disks
    ```

11. Create a permanent device alias named `bootdisk` that points to the IDE master disk, as follows:

    ```
    nvalias bootdisk  /pci@1f,0/pci@1,1/ide@3/disk@0,0
    ```

    You'll need to select a SCSI disk if your system does not have IDE disks attached to it.

12. Reset the system and verify that the device alias is set properly by typing the following:

    ```
    reset-all
    ```

    After the system resets, type the following:

    ```
    devalias bootdisk
    ```

13. Now, set the system up so that it boots into single-user mode without any user intervention:

    ```
    setenv boot-command 'boot -s'
    ```

14. I suggest changing the `auto-boot?` parameter back to `true` and resetting the system to validate that your `boot-command` parameter is set properly as follows:

    ```
    setenv auto-boot? true
    reset-all
    ```

15. Boot the system, log on as root, and use the `eeprom` command to list all NVRAM parameters.
16. Use the `eeprom` command to list only the setting of the `boot-device` parameter, as follows:

    ```
    eeprom boot-device
    ```

17. Reset `boot-device` to its default parameter from the OpenBoot prompt, as follows:

    ```
    set-default boot-device
    ```

18. From the OpenBoot prompt, remove the alias `bootdisk`, as follows:

    ```
    nvunalias bootdisk
    ```

19. Reset the system and verify that `bootdisk` is no longer set, as follows:

    ```
    reset-all
    printenv
    ```

20. Set all the OpenBoot parameters back to their default values, as follows:

    ```
    set-defaults
    ```

3.2 Booting the System

This exercise takes you through the steps of powering on and booting the system.

Estimated time: 5 minutes

1. Turn on power to all the peripheral devices, if any exist.
2. If the OpenBoot parameter `auto-boot` is set to `false`, you should see the `ok` prompt shortly after you power on the system. If the system is set to `auto-boot`, you should see a message similar to the following displayed onscreen:

    ```
    SunOS Release 5.10 Version Generic 64-bit
    Copyright 1983-2005 Sun Microsystems, Inc.  All rights reserved.
    Use is subject to license terms.
    ```

You should see the system begin the boot process. Interrupt the boot process by pressing Stop+A. The `ok` prompt appears.

3. At the `ok` prompt, type `boot` to boot the system.

3.3 Booting an Alternate Kernel

In this exercise, you'll practice booting from a backup copy of the `/etc/system` file. You should use this process if your `/etc/system` file ever becomes corrupt or unbootable.

Estimated time: 15 minutes

1. Log in as root.
2. Create a backup copy of the `/etc/system` file by typing this:

```
cp /etc/system /etc/system.orig
```

3. Now remove the `/etc/system` file by typing this:

```
rm /etc/system
```

4. Halt the system by typing this:

```
/usr/sbin/shutdown -y -g0 -i0
```

5. At the `ok` prompt, boot the system by using the interactive option to supply the backup name of the `/etc/system` file. You do that by typing this:

```
boot -a
```

6. You are prompted to enter a filename for the kernel and a default directory for modules. Press Return to answer each of these questions. When you are prompted with this message to use the default `/etc/system` file

```
Name of system file [etc/system]:
```

   enter the following:

```
/etc/system.orig
```

7. Later you'll be asked to enter the root file system type and the physical name of the root device. At that point, press Return to answer both questions.
8. When the system is ready, log in as root and put the original `/etc/system` file back in place:

```
cp /etc/system.orig /etc/system
```

Review Questions

1. The hardware-level user interface that you see before the operating system has been started is called what?

   ❍ **A.** OpenBoot

   ❍ **B.** EEPROM

   ❍ **C.** Firmware

   ❍ **D.** Boot PROM

2. Which of the following is where the system identification information, such as the hostid, is stored?

   ❍ **A.** Firmware

   ❍ **B.** OpenBoot

   ❍ **C.** NVRAM

   ❍ **D.** Kernel

3. What tasks are performed by OpenBoot? (Select the two best answers.)

   ❍ **A.** Executing POST

   ❍ **B.** Loading `bootblk`

   ❍ **C.** Executing `ufsboot`

   ❍ **D.** Loading the operating system kernel

4. Which of the following is *not* a task of the OpenBoot firmware?

   ❍ **A.** Testing and initializing the system hardware

   ❍ **B.** Loading the kernel

   ❍ **C.** Starting up the operating system from either a mass storage device or from a network

   ❍ **D.** Allowing modification and management of system startup configuration, such as NVRAM parameters

5. Which of the following is attached to a host computer through a hierarchy of interconnected buses on the device tree?

   ❍ **A.** SBus cards

   ❍ **B.** SCSI peripherals

   ❍ **C.** Plug-in device drivers

   ❍ **D.** Nodes

6. What is `/pci@1f,0/pci@1,1/ide@3/disk@0,0`?

   ❍ **A.** Full device pathname

   ❍ **B.** Physical device

   ❍ **C.** Logical device

   ❍ **D.** Instance

7. Which of the following is used to obtain information about devices and to display device pathnames in OpenBoot?

   ❍ **A.** `show-devs`

   ❍ **B.** `dmesg`

   ❍ **C.** `pwd`

   ❍ **D.** `sysdef`

8. Which of the following commands creates a temporary device alias named `bootdisk`?

   ❍ **A.** `setenv bootdisk /pci@1f,0/pci@1,1/ide@3/disk@0,0`

   ❍ **B.** `set bootdisk /pci@1f,0/pci@1,1/ide@3/disk@0,0`

   ❍ **C.** `nvalias bootdisk /pci@1f,0/pci@1,1/ide@3/disk@0,0`

   ❍ **D.** `devalias bootdisk /pci@1f,0/pci@1,1/ide@3/disk@0,0`

9. If you want to create permanent aliases in NVRAM (that show up after a reboot), which of the following commands should you use?

   ❍ **A.** `devalias`

   ❍ **B.** `nvalias`

   ❍ **C.** `setenv`

   ❍ **D.** `eeprom`

10. Which NVRAM variable specifies the device from which to start up?

   ❍ **A.** `boot-device`

   ❍ **B.** `boot-file`

   ❍ **C.** `output-device`

   ❍ **D.** `input-device`

11. If a system will not start due to a bad NVRAM variable, which of the following, performed before you see the OpenBoot prompt, resets the NVRAM variables to their default settings?

- ❍ **A.** `set-default` *`<variable>`*
- ❍ **B.** Stop+N
- ❍ **C.** `set-defaults`
- ❍ **D.** Ctrl+N

12. Which of the following can restrict the set of operations that users are allowed to perform at the OpenBoot prompt?

- ❍ **A.** `security-password`
- ❍ **B.** `security-mode`
- ❍ **C.** `set-secure`
- ❍ **D.** `set-security`

13. Which of the following is used in OpenBoot to test all devices that have built-in self-test methods below the specified device tree node?

- ❍ **A.** `diag`
- ❍ **B.** `probe-scsi`
- ❍ **C.** `test-all`
- ❍ **D.** `test`

14. Which option do you use with the OpenBoot `boot` command so that you are prompted for the name of the standalone program to load?

- ❍ **A.** `-v`
- ❍ **B.** `-f`
- ❍ **C.** `-s`
- ❍ **D.** `-a`

15. What resides in blocks 1–15 of the startup device?

- ❍ **A.** `bootblk`
- ❍ **B.** `superblock`
- ❍ **C.** `kernel`
- ❍ **D.** `ufsboot`

16. Which of the following loads the operating system kernel?

- ❍ **A.** `ufsboot`
- ❍ **B.** `openBoot`
- ❍ **C.** `bootblk`
- ❍ **D.** `init`

17. Which of the following commands lists all hardware devices, system devices, loadable modules, and the values of selected kernel tunable parameters?

- ❍ **A.** `more /var/adm/messages`
- ❍ **B.** `adb`
- ❍ **C.** `dmesg`
- ❍ **D.** `sysdef`

18. What key combination would you enter to interrupt a system that is not responding?

- ❍ **A.** Ctrl+B
- ❍ **B.** Ctrl+C
- ❍ **C.** Stop+A
- ❍ **D.** Ctrl+Alt+Delete
- ❍ **E.** Ctrl+Break

19. What is the function of the auto-boot parameter that is set in the OpenBoot PROM?

- ❍ **A.** Boots automatically after power-on or reset
- ❍ **B.** Sets the default boot device
- ❍ **C.** Reboots after a watchdog reset
- ❍ **D.** Automatically performs a system reboot when a system core file has been generated

20. Which of the following commands is used to set the `auto-boot` parameter?

- ❍ **A.** `setenv auto-boot?=false`
- ❍ **B.** `set auto-boot=false`
- ❍ **C.** `eeprom auto-boot?=false`
- ❍ **D.** `nvset`

21. To display all OpenBoot parameter settings, such as `boot-device` and `ttya-mode`, what should you type?

❍ **A.** `nvalias`

❍ **B.** `devalias`

❍ **C.** `printenv`

❍ **D.** `show all`

22. To check the target IDs on all the SCSI devices connected to all the SCSI controllers, what should you type?

❍ **A.** `test-all`

❍ **B.** `probe-scsi`

❍ **C.** `probe-scsi-all`

❍ **D.** `test-scsi`

23. The kernel reads which of the following files when loading? (This is where system configuration information is stored.)

❍ **A.** `/etc/system`

❍ **B.** `kernel/sparcv9/unix`

❍ **C.** `/etc/inittab`

❍ **D.** `/kernel/unix`

24. Select the sequence of events that best describes the boot process.

❍ **A.** Boot PROM phase, boot program phase, kernel initialization phase, `init` phase, and `svc.startd` phase

❍ **B.** Boot program phase, boot PROM phase, kernel initialization phase, `svc.startd` phase, and `init` phase

❍ **C.** Boot program phase, boot PROM phase, `init` phase, kernel initialization phase, `svc.startd` phase

❍ **D.** Boot PROM phase, boot program phase, `svc.startd` phase, kernel initialization phase

25. What consists of a small static core and many dynamically loadable modules?

- ❍ **A.** The kernel
- ❍ **B.** `ufsboot`
- ❍ **C.** The shell
- ❍ **D.** The bootblock

26. After reading the `/etc/inittab` file, which daemon does the init process startup?

- ❍ **A.** `sched`
- ❍ **B.** `/sbin/rc1`
- ❍ **C.** `ufsboot`
- ❍ **D.** `svc.startd`

27. How can system messages displayed at bootup be viewed later?

- ❍ **A.** By issuing the `dmesg` command
- ❍ **B.** By viewing the `/var/adm/messages` file
- ❍ **C.** By issuing the `sysdef` command
- ❍ **D.** By viewing logs in the `/var/svc/log directory`

28. To boot a system into a single-user state, which commands are entered at the `ok` prompt?

- ❍ **A.** `boot`
- ❍ **B.** `boot -s`
- ❍ **C.** `boot -a`
- ❍ **D.** `boot -m milestone=single-user`

29. Which command, typed at the `ok` prompt, stops and asks for boot information during the boot process?

- ❍ **A.** `boot -i`
- ❍ **B.** `boot -a`
- ❍ **C.** `boot -v`
- ❍ **D.** `boot -s`

30. Which of the following programs is responsible for executing `ufsboot`?

- ❍ A. `bootblk`
- ❍ B. `kernel`
- ❍ C. `init`
- ❍ D. `boot`

31. What command do you use to change run levels?

- ❍ A. `run`
- ❍ B. `init`
- ❍ C. `kill`
- ❍ D. `su`

32. This XML-based file contains a complete set of properties that are associated with a SMF service or a service instance. Where are these files stored?

- ❍ A. `/var/svc/method`
- ❍ B. `/lib/svc/method`
- ❍ C. `/var/svc/manifest`
- ❍ D. `/var/svc/profile`

33. Which command is used to transition your system into the single-user milestone from the multi-user milestone?

- ❍ A. `svcadm milestone single-user`
- ❍ B. `svcadm milestone/single-user`
- ❍ C. `init -s`
- ❍ D. `init single-user`

34. Which of the following is NOT the valid FMRI name of a service instance?

- ❍ A. `svc://localhost/network/inetd:default`
- ❍ B. `lrc:/etc/rc3_d/S90samba`
- ❍ C. `network/inetd:default`
- ❍ D. `svc:/inetd:default`

35. Which command is used to obtain a detailed view of the service state of all service instances in the configuration repository?

- ❍ **A.** `inetadm -a`
- ❍ **B.** `svcs -a`
- ❍ **C.** `svcadm -a`
- ❍ **D.** `svcprop -l`

36. Which of the following service states indicates that the service is configured to run, but is not yet running or available to run?

- ❍ **A.** offline
- ❍ **B.** maintenance
- ❍ **C.** disabled
- ❍ **D.** degraded

37. Which SMF command displays the services that must be running before the multi-user milestone is reached?

- ❍ **A.** `svcs -d milestone/multi-user`
- ❍ **B.** `svcs -D milestone/multi-user`
- ❍ **C.** `svcs -p milestone/multi-user`
- ❍ **D.** `svcs -l milestone/multi-user`

Answers to Review Questions

1. **A.** The hardware-level user interface that you see before the operating system starts is called the OpenBoot PROM (OBP). For more information, see the section "The OpenBoot Environment."
2. **C.** Non-Volatile RAM (NVRAM) is where the system identification information—such as the host ID, Ethernet address, and TOD clock—is stored. For more information, see the section "The OpenBoot Environment."
3. **A, B.** The two primary tasks of the OpenBoot firmware are to run the POST and to load the bootblock. For more information, see the section "The OpenBoot Environment."
4. **B.** OpenBoot runs POSTs to initialize the system hardware. It also loads the primary startup program, `bootblk`, from the default startup device. The `bootblk` program finds and executes the secondary startup program, `ufsboot`, and loads it into memory. From that point, the `ufsboot` program loads the operating system kernel. For more information, see the section "The OpenBoot Environment."

5. **D.** Devices called *nodes* are attached to a host computer through a hierarchy of interconnected buses on the device tree. A node that represents the host computer's main physical address bus forms the tree's root node. For more information, see the section "The OpenBoot Architecture."

6. **A.** A full device pathname is a series of node names separated by slashes (/). The root of the tree is the machine node, which is not named explicitly but is indicated by a leading slash. Each device pathname has this form:

   ```
   driver-name@unit-address:device-arguments
   ```

   For more information, see the section "PROM Device Tree (Full Device Pathnames)."

7. **A.** The OpenBoot command `show-devs` is used to obtain information about devices and to display device pathnames. For more information, see the section "PROM Device Tree (Full Device Pathnames)."

8. **D.** You use the `devalias` command as follows to create a temporary device alias named `bootdisk`:

   ```
   devalias bootdisk  /pci@1f,0/pci@1,1/ide@3/disk@0,0
   ```

   For more information, see the section "OpenBoot Device Aliases."

9. **B. or D.** You use the `nvalias` command from the OpenBoot PROM or the `eeprom` command from the Unix prompt to create a permanent alias in NVRAM that remains in effect even after a reboot. For more information, see the section "OpenBoot Device Aliases."

10. **A.** The NVRAM variable named `boot-device` contains the name of the default startup device. For more information, see the section "Booting a System."

11. **B.** To reset the NVRAM variables to their default settings, you hold down the Stop+N keys simultaneously while the machine is powering up. For more information, see the section "OpenBoot NVRAM."

12. **B.** The OpenBoot command `security-mode` restricts the set of operations that users are allowed to perform at the OpenBoot prompt. For more information, see the section "OpenBoot Security."

13. **C.** The OpenBoot command `test-all` tests all devices that have built-in self-test methods below the specified device tree node. For more information, see the section "OpenBoot Diagnostics."

14. **D.** You issue the OpenBoot `boot` command with the `-a` option to be prompted for the name of the standalone program to load. For more information, see the section "The `boot` Command."

15. **A.** The bootblock resides in blocks 1–15 of the startup device. For more information, see the section "The `boot` Command."

16. **A.** The secondary startup program, `ufsboot`, loads the two-part operating system kernel. For more information, see the section "Booting a System."

17. **D.** You use the `sysdef` command to list all hardware devices, system devices, and loadable modules, as well as the values of selected kernel tunable parameters. For more information, see the section "The Kernel."

18. **C.** You interrupt a system that is not responding by pressing Stop+A. For more information, see the section "Stopping the System for Recovery Purposes."

19. **A.** `auto-boot?` controls whether the system automatically starts up after a system reset or when the power is turned on. The default for this variable is `true`. When the system is powered on, the system automatically starts up to the default run level. For more information, see the section "OpenBoot NVRAM."

20. **C.** `eeprom auto-boot?=false` is used to set the `auto-boot?` parameter from the Unix shell. Option A is wrong because the "=" sign should not be used with the `setenv` command. Option B is wrong because there is not a `set` command at the OpenBoot prompt, and using `set` from the Unix shell will not set an OpenBoot parameter. Option D is wrong because there is not an `nvset` command. For more information, see the section "OpenBoot NVRAM."

21. **C.** At the OpenBoot prompt, you use the `printenv` command to display all OpenBoot parameter settings. For more information, see the section "OpenBoot NVRAM."

22. **C.** You use the `probe-scsi-all` command to check the target IDs on all the SCSI devices that are connected to all the SCSI controllers. For more information, see the section "OpenBoot Diagnostics."

23. **A.** When the kernel is loading, it reads the `/etc/system` file, where system configuration information is stored. This file modifies the kernel's parameters and treatment of loadable modules. For more information, see the section "The Kernel."

24. **A.** The boot process goes through the following five phases: boot PROM phase, boot programs phase, kernel initialization phase, `init` phase, and `svc.startd` phase. For more information, see the section "Booting a System."

25. **A.** The kernel consists of a two-piece static core that is made up of `genunix` and `unix`. `genunix` is the platform-independent generic kernel file, and `unix` is the platform-specific kernel file. When the system boots, `ufsboot` combines these two files and many dynamically loadable modules into memory to form the running kernel. For more information, see the section "The Kernel."

26. **D.** The `init` process reads the `/etc/inittab` file and executes any process entries that have `sysinit` in the action field, so that any special initializations can take place before users log in. After reading the `/etc/inittab` file, `init` starts the `svc.startd` daemon, which is responsible for starting and stopping other system services such as mounting file systems and configuring network devices. In addition, `svc.startd` will execute legacy run control (rc) scripts. For more information, see the section "The `init` Phase."

27. **B.** The boot process creates fewer messages. All of the information that was provided by the boot messages in previous versions of Solaris is now located in the `/var/svc/log` directory. For more information, see the section "The Solaris Management Facility (SMF) Service."

28. **B, D.** You issue the `boot -s` command or the `boot -m milestone=single-user` at the OpenBoot `ok` prompt to boot the system into single-user mode. For more information, see the section "Booting a System." You can also boot to a specific milestone using the `boot -m` command.

29. **B.** The `boot -a` command performs an interactive boot. With this option, you are prompted to enter the name of the kernel, the default modules directory, the name of the system file, the root file system type, and the device name for the root device. For more information, see the section "Booting a System."

30. **A.** The `bootblk` program finds and executes the secondary boot program, called `ufsboot`, from the UFS and loads it into memory. For more information, see the section "Booting a System."

31. **B.** You use the `init` command to change run levels. For more information, see the section "System Run States."

32. **C.** An SMF manifest is an XML (Extensible Markup Language) file that contains a complete set of properties that are associated with a service or a service instance. The properties are stored in files and subdirectories located in `/var/svc/manifest`. For more information, see the section "The Solaris Management Facility (SMF) Service."

33. **A.** Use the `svcadm milestone single-user` command to switch into the single-user milestone. For more information, see the section "Starting Services During Boot."

34. **D.** A valid FMRI instance names take the form of:

    ```
    svc://localhost/network/inetd:default
    svc:/network/inetd:default
    network/inetd:default
    ```

    `svc:/inetd:default` does not contain the service category name.

    `lrc:/etc/rc3_d/S90samba` is an FMRI for a legacy run control script not managed by SMF.

    For more information, see the section "The Solaris Management Facility (SMF) Service."

35. **B.** Running the `svcs` command without options will display the status of all enabled services. Use the `-a` option to list all services, including disabled services. For more information, see the section "SMF Command-line Administration Utilities."

36. **A.** The offline status indicates that a service instance is enabled (configured to run), but the service is not yet running or available to run. A disabled service is configured not to start. For more information, see the section "SMF Command-line Administration Utilities."

37. **A.** The `-d` option for the `svcs` command lists the services or service instances upon which the multi-user service instance is dependent on. For more information, see the section "SMF Command-line Administration Utilities."

Suggested Readings and Resources

For more information on the OpenBoot environment and the boot process, refer to *Inside Solaris 9* by Bill Calkins, 2002, New Riders.

For more information on the Service Management Facility (SMF), refer to the "Managing Services" section of the *Solaris 10 System Administration Guide: Basic Administration*, 2005, Sun Microsystems, Part Number Part No: 817-1985-11. This manual is available online at `docs.sun.com`.

For more information on the Solaris kernel and tuning the Solaris kernel parameters, refer to the following publications:

- *The Solaris Tunable Parameters Reference Manual*, 2005, Sun Microsystems, Part number 817-0404-10. This manual is available online at `docs.sun.com`.
- *Sun Performance and Tuning: Java and the Internet*, by Adrian Cockroft, 1998, Prentice Hall.
- *Solaris Internals: Core Kernel Architecture*, by Jim Mauro and Richard McDougall, 2000, Prentice Hall.
- *Resource Management*, by Richard McDougall, Adrian Cockcroft, Evert Hoogendoorn, Enrique Vargas, Tom Bialaski, and Everet Hoogendoorn, 1999, Prentice Hall.

CHAPTER FOUR

User and Security Administration

Objectives

The following objectives for Exam CX-310-200 are covered in this chapter:

Explain and perform Solaris 10 OS user administration, and manage user accounts and initialization files.

- You need to know how to use the commands and utilities to set up user accounts, and you need to understand which files are configured and how the information is formatted in those files.

  When you set up user accounts, you can customize each user's session by using initialization files that are run each time the user logs in. This chapter describes how to administer each initialization file.

Monitor system access by using appropriate commands.

- You also need to control access to the operating system via user logins. Only users who have active logins should have access to the system. You need to control the level of access that each user will have. In addition to controlling system access, you need to monitor the system for unauthorized use.

Perform system security administration tasks by switching users on a system, and by becoming root and monitoring `su` attempts.

- Users sometimes obtain logins and passwords from other users. You need to monitor the system for any user that may be switching to a user account that they have not been authorized to use—this includes monitoring unauthorized use of the root account.

Control system security through restricting FTP access and using `/etc/hosts.equiv` and `$HOME/.rhosts` files and SSH fundamentals.

- You need to understand the vulnerabilities that are presented to your system by network services such as FTP, Telnet, and other forms of remote access. You need to restrict access to these facilities and ensure that unauthorized users do not gain access to your system over the network via an unsecured network service.

Restrict access to data in files through the use of group membership, ownership, and special file permissions.

- As a system administrator, you need to be able to assign access to directories and files by using the standard Solaris permissions scheme. Understanding this permission scheme and applying it to user and group IDs is necessary for controlling access to critical system data.

Outline

Study Strategies

The following study strategies will help you prepare for the exam:

- As you read this chapter, you should practice the step-by-step examples on a Solaris 10 system. You should practice the steps until you are able to perform them from memory.
- You should make sure you understand each of the attributes associated with a user account, such as the user ID (UID), primary group, default shell, and so on.
- You should practice using the command-line tools for adding, modifying, and removing user accounts, and you should pay attention to details. These commands will appear on the Sun exam, so you need to make sure you understand them thoroughly. You should continue practicing these commands until you can perform them from memory. You should modify the account attributes, such as the default shell, group, and UID value. You should modify variables in the initialization files for each user to see the results.
- You should pay special attention to the section "Controlling File Access." You need to understand everything discussed in that section because the exam tests heavily on those topics. You should know the commands described and understand permission values that are set on a file or directory.
- You should memorize all the configuration files described in this chapter. You won't need to understand how they are structured—just understand what they are used for and how they can be used to monitor and control security on a system.
- Various commands and files are described in the section "Auditing Users." You need to understand the commands and log files that are described in that section. Also, as you read through the "Controlling Network Security" section, you should pay special attention to the concept of trusted hosts and restrictions on superuser access and understand how to restrict these services
- You should study the terms at the end of the chapter. These terms might appear in questions on the exam, so you need to understand what they mean.

Introduction

Managing user accounts can be simple or complex, depending on the size of the network. Today, many Solaris servers are simply database servers or Web servers, and users do not log directly in to these systems. In addition, Solaris workstations may only require login accounts for one or two users. On the other hand, in a university setting, a server may hold hundreds of user login accounts. Managing these accounts is very complex because the accounts change every semester. The system administrator is not only responsible for managing user accounts but also for ensuring that system security is not compromised.

This chapter describes how to manage user accounts while maintaining a reasonable level of security on a system.

Administering User Accounts

Objective:

Explain and perform Solaris 10 OS user administration, and manage user accounts and initialization files.

Access to a system is allowed only through user login accounts that are set up by the system administrator. A user account includes information that a user needs to log in and use a system—a user login name, a password, the user's home directory, and login initialization files. Each of these items is described later in this chapter.

The following methods and tools are available in Solaris for adding new user accounts to a system:

- **User and Group Manager**—A graphical user interface (GUI) that is available in the Solaris Management Console.
- **The `/usr/sadm/bin/smuser` command**—A command that can be executed from the command line.
- **The `useradd` command**—A command that can be executed from the command line.

As with many Unix commands, the command-line method of adding user accounts can be difficult for inexperienced administrators. For this reason, Sun has added user account administration to the Solaris Management Console (SMC).

Managing User and Group Accounts with the SMC

The SMC is a GUI that is designed to ease several routine system administration tasks. When you use the SMC, you are presented with a menu-like interface that is much easier to use than the ASCII interface supplied at the command prompt. This chapter describes how to use the SMC and the command line to administer user accounts on a system.

Adding User Accounts with the SMC

To perform administrative tasks such as adding user accounts, SMC will prompt you for the root password or an authorized RBAC account before allowing permission to add, create, and modify user accounts. Chapter 11, "Controlling Access and Configuring System Messaging," provides more information on RBAC.

> **NOTE**
>
> **Editing User Accounts Files** When you're adding or modifying user accounts, the SMC edits the files `/etc/passwd`, `/etc/shadow`, and `/etc/group`. These files are described later in this chapter. As root, you could edit these files directly, but that is not recommended. Errors in any of these files could cause adverse effects on the system.

The first step in setting up a new user account is to have the user provide the information you need in order to administer the account. You also need to set up proper permissions so that the user can share information with other members of his or her department. You need to know the user's full name, department, and any groups with which the user will be working. It's a good idea for the system administrator to sit down with the user and compile an information sheet (like the one shown in Table 4.1) so that you have all the information you need when you set up the account.

TABLE 4.1 User Information Data Sheet

Item
User name:
UID:
Primary group:
Secondary groups:
Comment:
Default shell:
Password status and aging:
Home directory server name:
Home directory path name:
Mail server:

(continues)

TABLE 4.1 *Continued*

Item
Department name:
Department administrator:
Manager:
Employee name:
Employee title:
Employee status:
Employee number:
Start date:
Desktop system name:

To use the SMC to add a new user login account, you should follow the procedure described in Step by Step 4.1.

EXAM ALERT

Using the SMC to Add a New User For the exam, you will not be asked to use the SMC to add a new user account, but you do need to know what tool within the SMC is used to add a user account. You also need to know what information the SMC asks for.

STEP BY STEP

4.1 Adding a New Login Account

1. Start the SMC by typing **smc** at the command prompt. The SMC Welcome window appears, as shown in Figure 4.1.
2. In the left pane of the Welcome window, click the This Computer icon. The icon expands, displaying five additional icons, as shown in Figure 4.2.
3. Click the System Configuration icon, and the system configuration icons appear in the main pane of the window, as shown in Figure 4.3. One of these icons is Users.

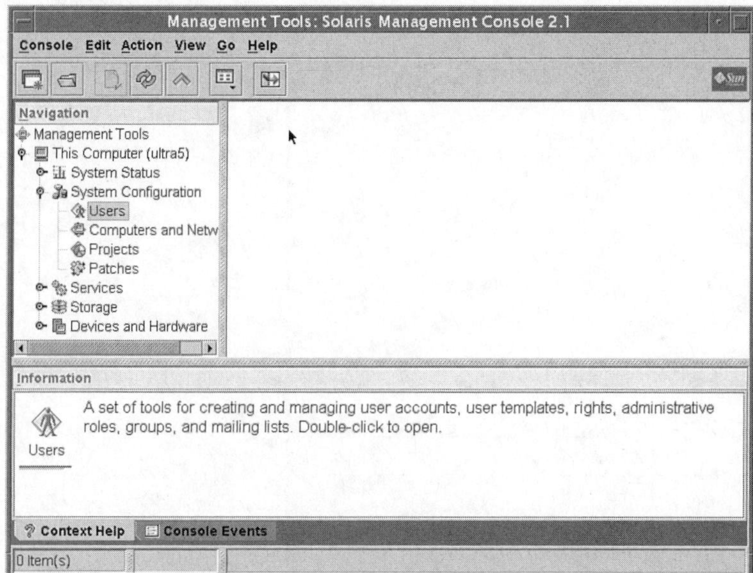

FIGURE 4.1 The SMC Welcome window.

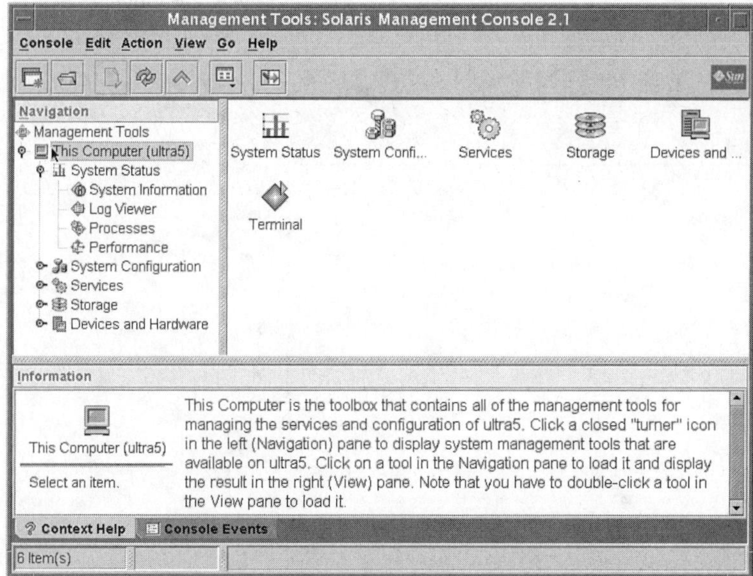

FIGURE 4.2 SMC tools.

4. Click the Users icon. You are prompted to enter a username and password. You can either enter the root password or enter your roll name and password if you have an RBAC account. After you enter the correct name and password, the User Accounts tool is loaded and displayed in the main pane of the window, as shown in Figure 4.4.

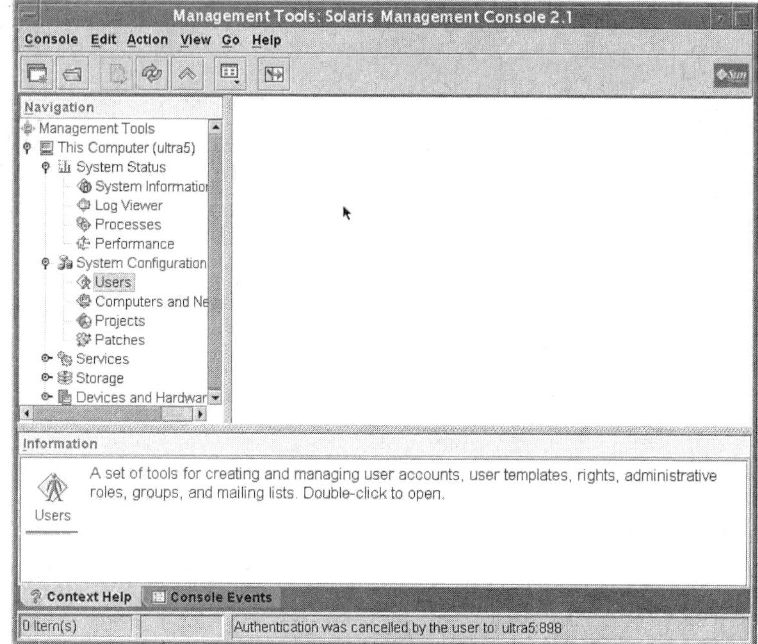

FIGURE 4.3 System configuration tools.

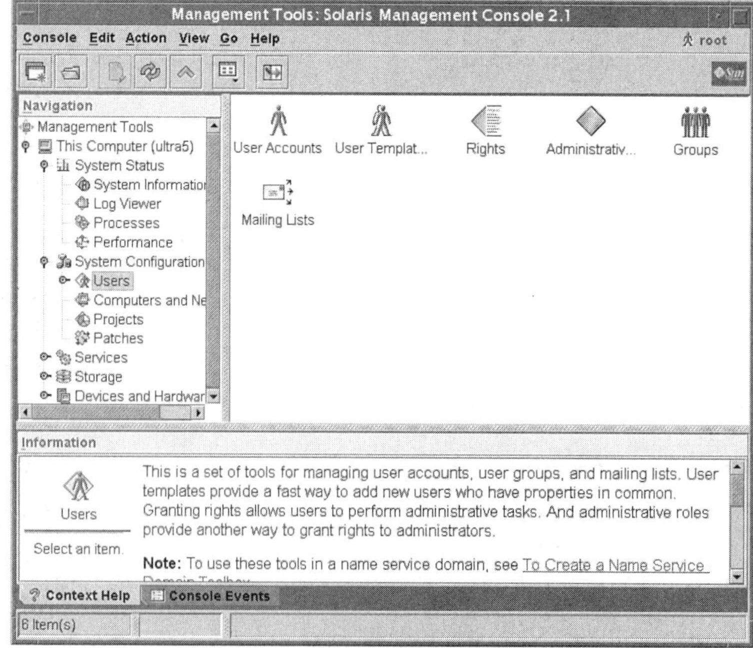

FIGURE 4.4 The Users Accounts tool.

5. Click the User Accounts icon. Current user accounts are displayed, then choose the Action menu and Add User, as shown in Figure 4.5.

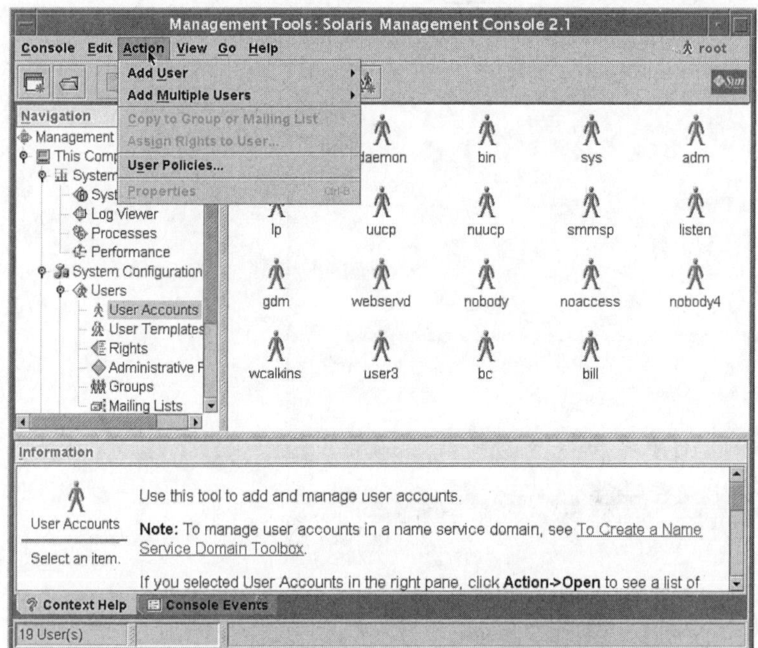

FIGURE 4.5 Displaying current user accounts.

6. From the top toolbar, select Action, Add User. Slide the mouse to the right, and you see two options for adding users, as shown in Figure 4.6. Select the With Wizard option.

   The Add User Wizard appears, as shown in Figure 4.7.

7. In the first wizard window that appears, all the fields are blank. Table 4.2 describes the information needed in this screen. If you aren't sure how to complete a field, read the Help screen in the left pane after you click on that field. After you enter the information in the first wizard window, click the Next button.

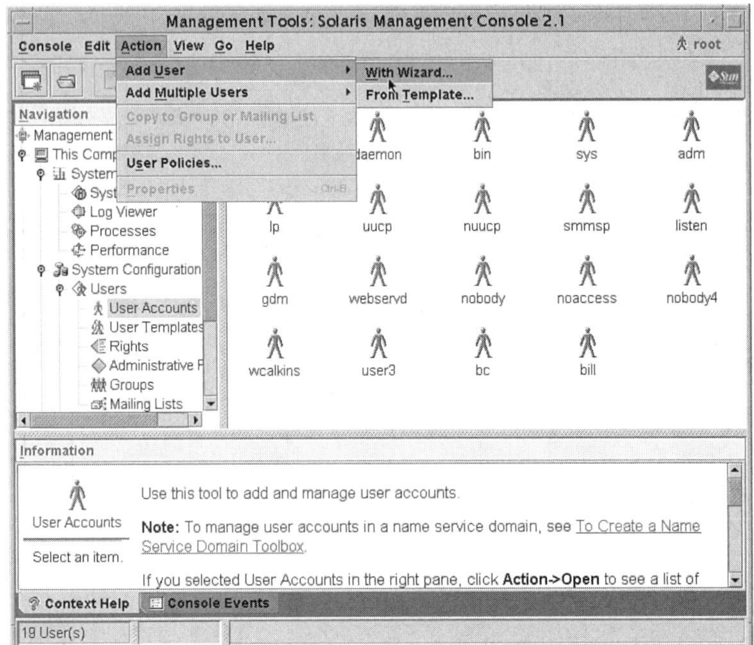

Figure 4.6 Adding a new user.

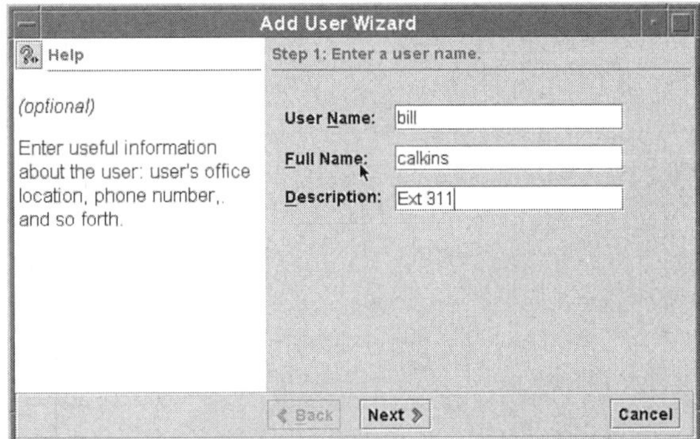

Figure 4.7 The Add User Wizard.

TABLE 4.2 Add User Fields

Field	Description
User Name	A unique login name that is entered at the Solaris login prompt. You should choose a name that is unique to the organization. The name can contain two to eight uppercase characters (A–Z), lowercase characters (a–z), or digits (0–9), but no underscores or spaces. The first character must be a letter, and at least one character must be a lowercase letter. The system allows you to use more than eight characters for the login name, but only the first eight characters are recognized.

TABLE 4.2 *Continued*

Field	Description
User ID	The unique UID. The SMC automatically assigns the next available UID; however, in a networked environment, you need to make sure this number is not duplicated by another user on another system. All UIDs must be consistent across the network. A UID is typically a number between 100 and 60,002, but it can be as high as 2,147,483,647. Note that Solaris releases prior to Solaris 9 use 32-bit data types to contain the UIDs, but UIDs in those versions are constrained to a maximum useful value of 60,000. Starting with the Solaris 2.5.1 release and compatible versions, the limit on UID values has been raised to the maximum value of a signed integer, or `2,147,483,647`. UIDs over `60,000` do not have full functionality and are incompatible with many Solaris features, so you should avoid using UIDs over `60,000`.
Primary Group	The primary group name for the group to which the user will belong. This is the group that the operating system will assign to files created by the user. `Group 10` (staff) is a predefined group that is sufficient for most users.
Full Name and Description	Optional comment fields. You can enter in these fields any comments, such as the full username, employee number, or phone number.
Password	The password status. You can select the following options: **User Account is Locked**—This is the default. If you choose this option, the user account is created and the account locked. **User Must Use This Password at First Login**—The account will have a password that you set in advance.
Home Directory	A field that points to an existing directory or specifies a new directory to create. This will be the location of the user's home directory and where the user's personal files will be stored. You should not include the username in this field. The username will automatically be added to the end of the path when the directory is created. Refer to the section "The Home Directory," later in this chapter.

8. Another window appears, asking you to enter a user ID (UID). Enter a UID and click Next.
9. In the third window of the wizard, you can either select to have the account locked or specify the password that the user will use the first time he or she logs in, as shown in Figure 4.8. Then click the Next button at the bottom of the window.

NOTE

Changing a Password from the Command Line A user can type the Unix command `passwd` at any time from the command prompt to change his or her password.

10. After you enter the user password information, a fourth window opens, asking you to select the primary group for that user. Select a group from the pull-down menu, as shown in Figure 4.9, and click the Next button.

FIGURE 4.8 The Enter the User's Password window.

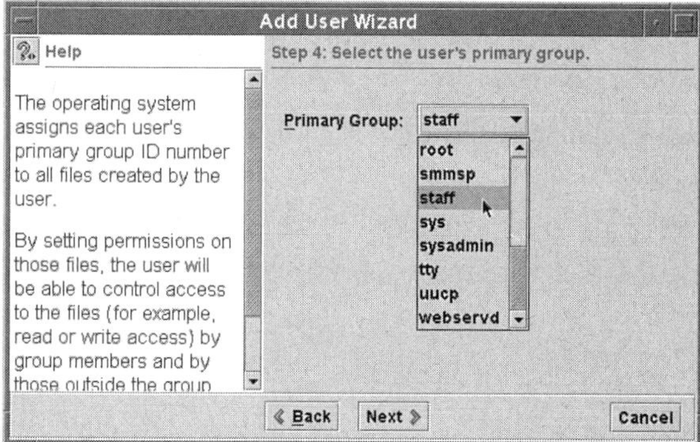

FIGURE 4.9 Selecting the user's primary group.

11. The fifth wizard window asks you to set the user's home directory, as shown in Figure 4.10. Fill in the information for the user's home directory and click the Next button.

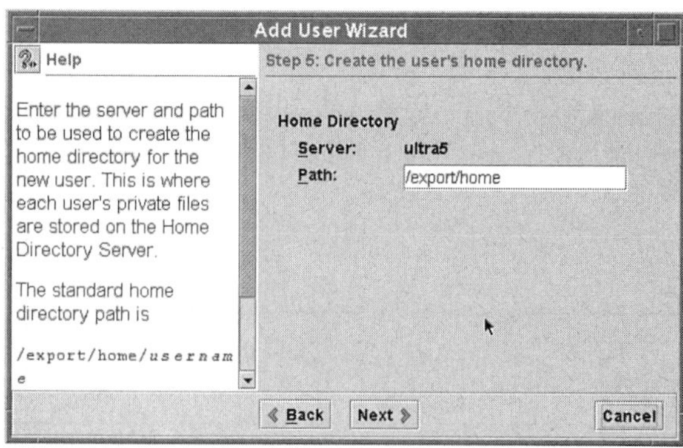

FIGURE 4.10 Selecting the user's home directory.

12. The sixth window displays the user's mail server and mailbox information, as shown in Figure 4.11. Click the Next button to continue.

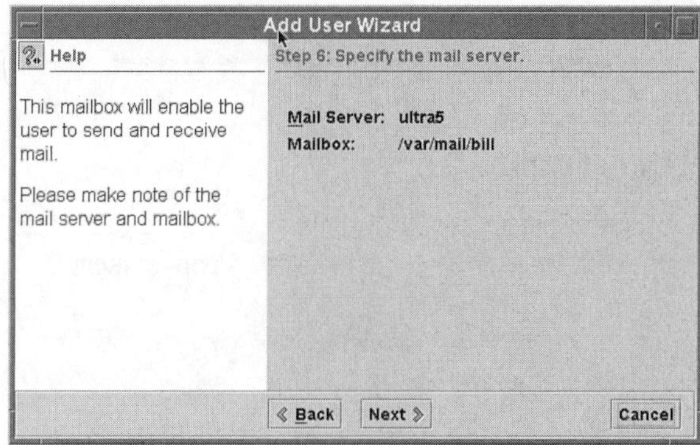

FIGURE 4.11 The user's mailbox and mail server information.

13. The next window displays a summary of the new user information, as shown in Figure 4.12. If the information is correct, click the Finish button, and you are returned to the main SMC window. Otherwise, click Back to go back and re-enter the information.

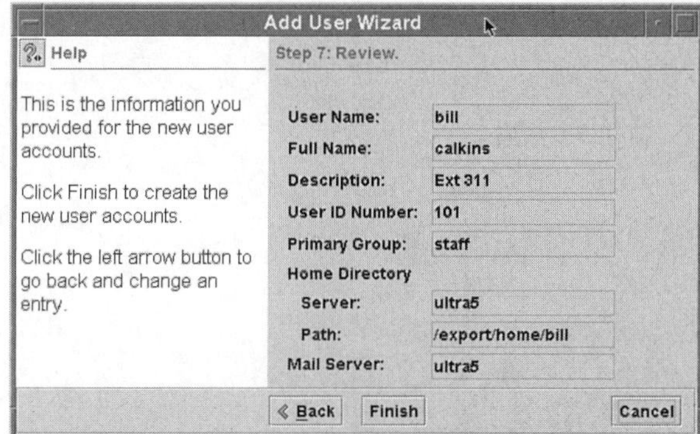

FIGURE 4.12 New user summary information.

When you use the Add User Wizard to create an account, the following defaults are assigned to the account:

- The default shell is the Bourne shell (`/bin/sh`).
- No secondary groups are set up.

To modify these settings, refer to the section "Modifying User Accounts with the SMC," later in this chapter.

Refer to the man pages for a description of this command.

Deleting User Accounts with the SMC

When a user account is no longer needed on a system, you need to delete it. Step by Step 4.2 describes how to perform this task.

STEP BY STEP

4.2 Using the SMC to Delete Existing User Accounts

1. Follow the steps in Step by Step 4.1 for adding a new login account through the SMC. When you get to the User Accounts tool (refer to Figure 4.5), right-click the user you want to delete. A pop-up menu appears, as shown in Figure 4.13.

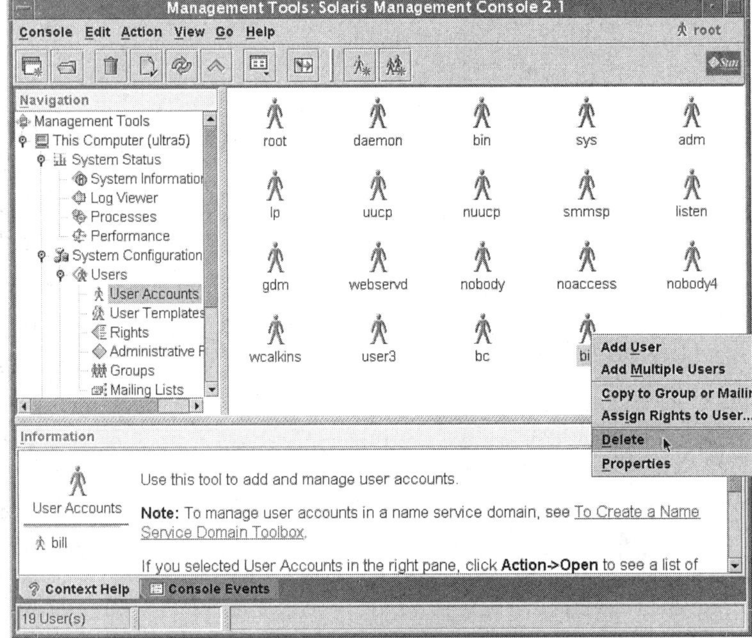

FIGURE 4.13 Deleting a user account.

2. Select Delete from the pop-up menu. A confirmation window appears, as shown in Figure 4.14.

   Select whether you want to delete the user's home directory and/or mailbox. Then click the Delete button at the bottom of the window to delete the account.

FIGURE 4.14 The Delete User confirmation window.

CAUTION

When selecting to remove the home directory, make sure that you are certain of the directory that will be removed. If you need data from this directory, do not remove it. Sometimes a user's home directory might point to an important directory such as "/" root. In this case, removing the home directory would remove important system files.

Modifying User Accounts with the SMC

If a login needs to be modified—to change a password or disable an account, for example—you can use the SMC to modify the user account settings, as described in Step by Step 4.3.

STEP BY STEP

4.3 Modifying User Accounts with the SMC

1. Follow the steps described in Step by Step 4.1 for adding a new login account through the SMC. When you get to the User Accounts tool (refer to Figure 4.5), double-click the user you want to modify. The window shown in Figure 4.15 appears.
2. Modify any of the following items in the User Properties window:
   - Change the username.
   - Change the full name.
   - Change the description of the account.
   - Change the login shell. By default the user is assigned to the Bourne shell (`/bin/sh`).
   - Change the account availability. This option allows you to specify a date on which the account is locked.
   - Lock an account to prevent logins using this user name.
   - Assign additional groups.

- Make the user a member of a project. Projects are described later in this chapter.
- Change the home directory.
- Share the home directory with other users or groups.
- Assign roles and grant rights to the account (see Chapter 11).
- Change the password or set password options, such as how often passwords should be changed, or expire passwords after a specified period of inactivity.

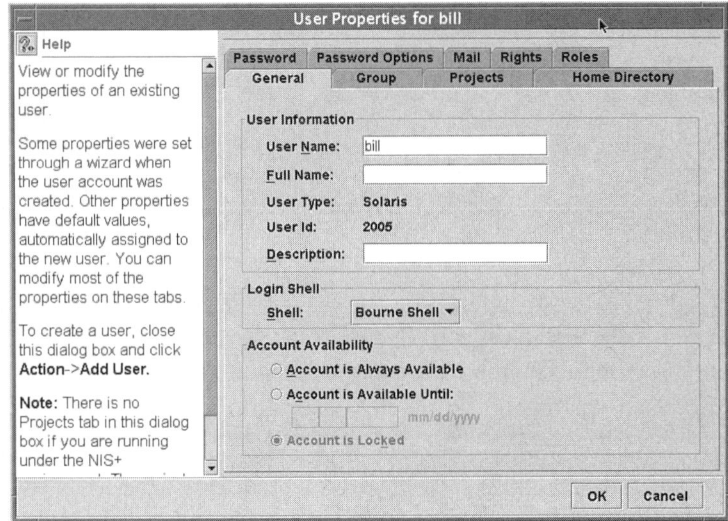

FIGURE 4.15 The User Properties window.

Adding Groups with the SMC

As a system administrator, you might need to add a group that does not already exist on the system. Perhaps a new group of users called `engrg` (from the Engineering Department) needs to be added. Step by Step 4.4 shows how to add this group to the system by using the SMC.

STEP BY STEP

4.4 Adding Groups with the SMC

1. Follow the steps described in Step by Step 4.1 for adding a new login account through the SMC. When you get to the Users tool (refer to Figure 4.4), double-click the Groups icon. The list of groups appears in the Groups tool, as shown in Figure 4.16.
2. From the top toolbar, select Action, Add Group, as shown in Figure 4.17.

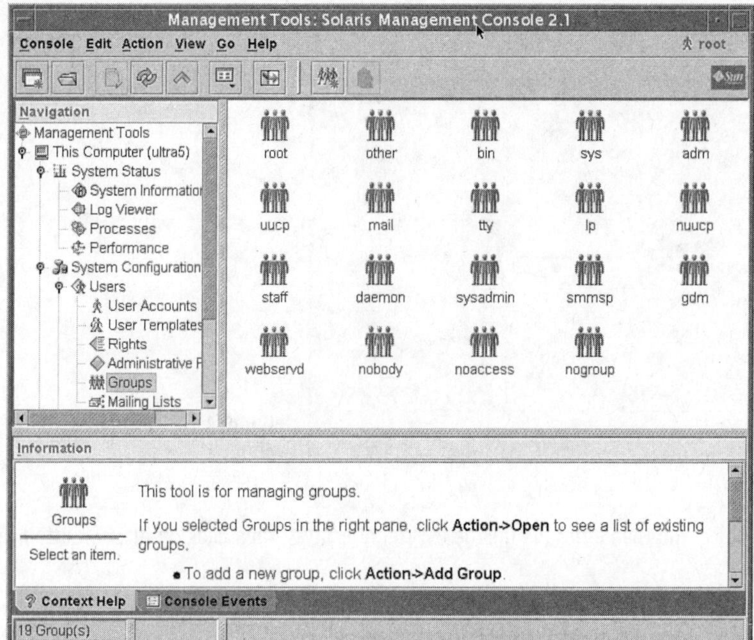

FIGURE 4.16 The Groups tool.

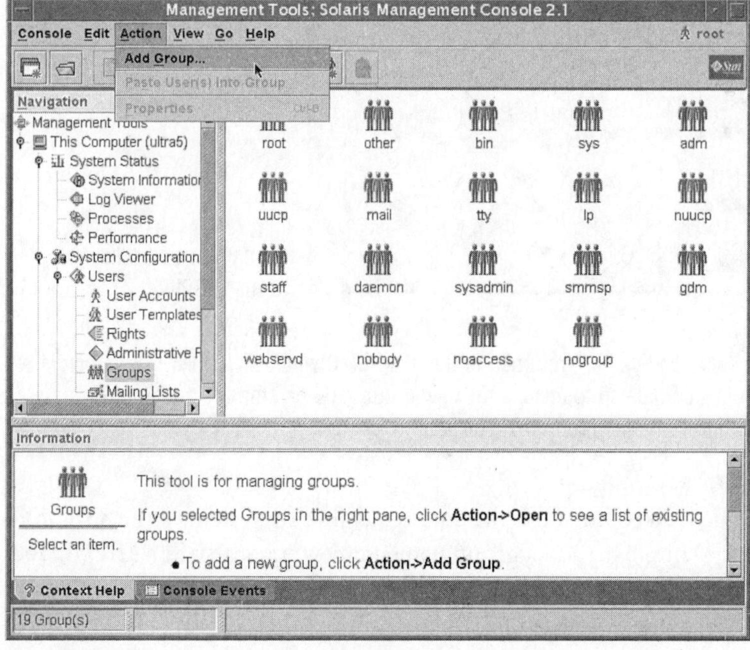

FIGURE 4.17 Adding a group.

The Add Group window appears, as shown in Figure 4.18.

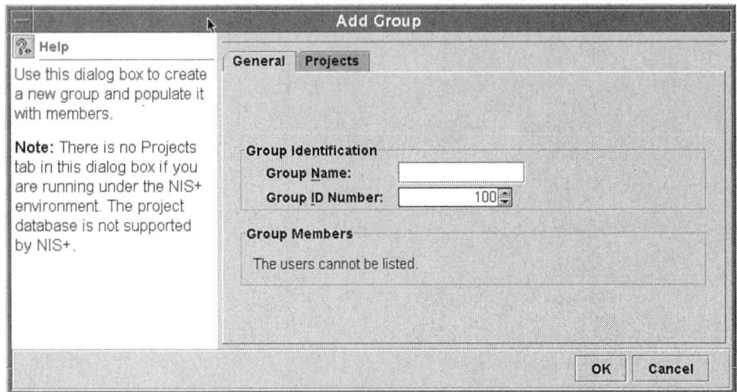

FIGURE 4.18 The Add Group window.

3. Enter the group name `engrg` and then enter the unique GID number **`200`**, then click on the OK button, as shown in Figure 4.19.

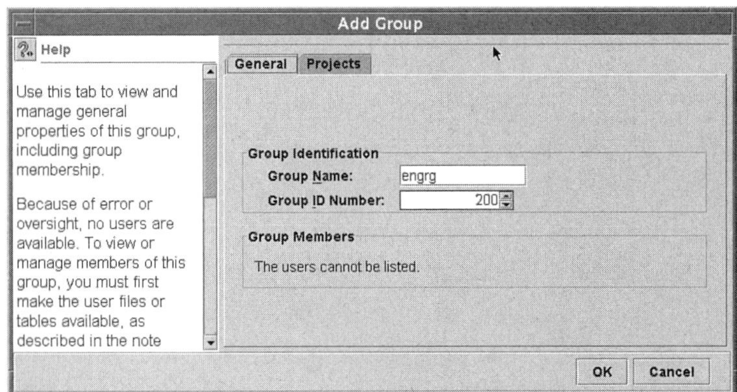

FIGURE 4.19 Adding the `engrg` group.

4. Click OK when you're finished, and you are returned to the main SMC window. The list of groups displayed in the Groups window is updated to include the new group. You can modify the group by double-clicking the icon that represents the group that you want to change.

The `/usr/sadm/bin/smgroup add` command is the command-line equivalent of the SMC tool for adding a new group. For example, to add a group named `development` with a GID of **`300`**, you enter this:

```
/usr/sadm/bin/smgroup add — -g 300 -n development
```

The system responds with this:

```
Authenticating as user: root
Type /? for help, pressing <enter> accepts the default denoted by [ ]
Please enter a string value for: password :: <Enter the Root Password>
Loading Tool: com.sun.admin.usermgr.cli.group.UserMgrGroupCli from ultra5
```

Refer to the man pages for a complete description of the `smgroup` command.

Managing User and Group Accounts from the Command Line

You can manage user accounts from the command line as well as through the SMC. Although using the command line is more complex than using the SMC GUI interface, the command line allows more options and provides a little more flexibility.

Solaris supplies the user administration commands described in Table 4.3 for setting up and managing user accounts.

TABLE 4.3 Account Administration Commands

Command	Description
`useradd`	Adds a new user account
`userdel`	Deletes a user account
`usermod`	Modifies a user account
`groupadd`	Adds a new group
`groupmod`	Modifies a group (for example, changes the GID or name)
`groupdel`	Deletes a group

NOTE

SMC Versus Conventional Administration Commands The SMC has its own command-line equivalents, such as `smuser` and `smgroup`. The difference between the SMC commands and the commands outlined in Table 4.3 is that the SMC can also update the name service. The commands in Table 4.3 only update the local files.

Adding User Accounts from the Command Line

You can add new user accounts on the local system by using the `useradd` command. This command adds an entry for the new user into the `/etc/passwd` and `/etc/shadow` files, which are described later in this chapter, in the section "Where User Account Information Is Stored."

Just like the SMC, the `-m` option to the `useradd` command copies all the user initialization files found in the `/etc/skel` directory into the new user's home directory. User initialization files are covered in the section "Setting Up Shell Initialization Files," later in this chapter.

The syntax for the `useradd` command is as follows:

```
useradd [-c comment] [-d dir] [-e expire]  [-f inactive]  [-g group] \
 [  -G group  [  , group...]] [ -m [-k skel_dir]] [-u uid  [-o]] \
 [-s shell]  [-A  authorization   [,authorization...]]
 [-P profile  [,profile...]] \
[-R role  [,role...]] [-p projname] [-K key=value] <loginname>
```

Table 4.4 describes these options.

TABLE 4.4 useradd Command Options

Option	Description
`-A` *<authorization>*	One or more comma-separated authorizations.
`-b` *<base-dir>*	The default base directory for the system if `-d` is not specified.
`-u` *<uid>*	Sets the unique UID for the user.
`-o`	Allows a UID to be duplicated. The default is not to let you choose a UID that is already in use.
`-g` *<gid>*	Specifies a predefined GID or name for the user that will be the user's primary group.
`-G` *<gid>*	Defines the new user's secondary group memberships. You can enter multiple groups, but they must be separated by commas. A user can belong to up to 15 additional groups. The number of groups can be increased to 32 by changing the kernel parameter `ngroups_max`.
`-m`	Creates a new home directory if one does not already exist.
`-s` *<shell>*	Defines the full pathname for the shell program to be used as the user's login shell. The default is `/bin/sh` if a shell is not specified.
`-c` *<comment>*	Specifies the user's full name, location, and phone number, in a comment.
`-d` *<dir>*	Specifies the home directory of the new user. It defaults to `<base-dir>/<account-name>`, where `<base-dir>` is the base directory for new login home directories and `<account-name>` is the new login name.
`-D` *<dir>*	Display the default values for `group`, `basedir`, `skel-dir`, and so on.
	When used with the `-g`, `-b`, `-f`, `-e`, `-A`, `-P`, `-p`, `-R`, or `-K` options, the `-D` option sets the default values for the specified fields.
`-e` *<expiration>*	Sets an expiration date on the user account. Specifies the date on which the user can no longer log in and access the account. After the specified date, the account is locked. Use the following format to specify the date: *mm/dd/yy*.

TABLE 4.4 *Continued*

Option	Description
`-f <inactive>`	Sets the number of inactive days allowed on a user account. If the account is not logged in to during the specified number of days, the account is locked.
`-k <skeldir>`	Specifies an alternate location for the user initialization template files. Files from this directory are copied into the user's home directory when the `-m` option is specified. The default location is `/etc/skel`.
`-p <project-name>`	Specifies the name of the project that the user is associated with.
`-P <profile>`	Specifies an execution profile for the account. See Chapter 11 for information on execution profiles.
`-R <role>`	Specifies a role for the account. See Chapter 11 for information on roles.
`<login-name>`	Specifies the user login name to be assigned to this account.

Many additional options are available, although most of them are not used as often as the ones in Table 4.4. Additional options to the `useradd` command apply specifically to RBAC accounts and are described in Chapter 11. You can also refer to the man pages to find a listing of all the options to the `useradd` command.

The following example creates a new login account for Bill Calkins:

```
useradd -u 3000 -g other -d /export/home/bcalkins -m -s /bin/sh \
 -c "Bill Calkins, ext. 2345" bcalkins
```

The login name is `bcalkins`, the UID is `3000`, and the group is `other`. In this example, you instruct the system to create a home directory named `/export/home/bcalkins`. The default shell is `/bin/sh`, and the initialization files are to be copied from the `/etc/skel` directory.

NOTE

Assigning a UID If the `-u` option is not used to specify a UID, the UID defaults to the next available number above the highest number currently assigned. For example, if UIDs `100`, `110`, and `200` are already assigned to login names, the next UID that is automatically assigned is `201`.

The `/usr/sadm/bin/smuser add` command is the command-line equivalent of the SMC tool for adding a new user. The advantage of using `smuser` over the `useradd` command is that `smuser` interacts with naming services, can use autohome functionality, and is well suited for remote management.

The `smuser` command has several subcommands and options. The syntax to add a user using `smuser` is

```
smuser add  [ auth args ] - [subcommand args]
```

A few of the more common arguments that can be used with the add subcommand are described in Table 4.5.

TABLE 4.5 add Subcommand Arguments

Argument	Description
-c <*comment*>	A short description of the login, typically the user's name and phone extension. This string can be up to 256 characters.
-d <*directory*>	Specifies the home directory of the new user. This string is limited to 1,024 characters.
-g <*group*>	Specifies the user's primary group membership.
-G <*group*>	Specifies the user's secondary group membership.
-n <*login*>	Specifies the user's login name.
-s <*shell*>	Specifies the user's login shell.
-u <*uid*>	Specifies the user ID of the user you want to add. If you do not specify this option, the system assigns the next available unique UID greater than 100.
-x autohome=Y¦N	Sets the home directory to automount if set to Y.

The following example adds a new user named "bcalkins" and a comment field of "Bill Calkins ext. 100":

```
# /usr/sadm/bin/smuser add — -n bcalkins -c "Bill Calkins Ext 100"
Authenticating as user: root

Type /? for help, pressing <enter> accepts the default denoted by [ ]
Please enter a string value for: password :: <ENTER ROOT PASSWORD>
Loading Tool: com.sun.admin.usermgr.cli.user.UserMgrCli from smokey
Login to smokey as user root was successful.
Download of com.sun.admin.usermgr.cli.user.UserMgrCli from smokey
was successful.
```

After you press Enter, the system asks for the root password to authenticate Bill Calkins before adding the new login account. The next step would be to set a password for the account using the passwd command as follows:

```
# passwd bcalkins
passwd: Changing password for bcalkins
New Password: <ENTER PASSWORD>
Re-enter new Password: <RE_ENTER PASSWD>
passwd: password successfully changed for bcalkins
```

Options that can be used with the passwd command are described in Table 4.6.

TABLE 4.6 passwd Options

Option	Description
-s *<name>*	Shows password attributes for a particular user. When used with the -a option, attributes for all user accounts are displayed.
-d <name>	Deletes password for name and unlocks the account. The login name is not prompted for a password.
-e *<name>*	Changes the login shell, in the /etc/passwd file, for a user.
-f <name>	Forces the user to change passwords at the next login by expiring the password.
-h *<name>*	Changes the home directory, in the /etc/passwd file, for a user.
-l *<name>*	Lock a user's account. Use the -d or -u option to unlock the account.
-N *<name>*	Makes the password entry for *<name>* a value that cannot be used for login but does not lock the account.
-u <name>	Unlocks a locked account.

To force a user to change his or her password at the next login, type

```
# passwd -f bcalkins
passwd: password information changed for bcalkins
#
```

To change a user's home directory, type

```
# passwd -h bcalkins
```

The system responds with

```
Default values are printed inside of '[]'.
To accept the default, type <return>.
To have a blank entry, type the word 'none'.
```

Enter the new home directory when prompted:

```
Home Directory [/home/wcalkins]: /home/bcalkins
passwd: password information changed for bcalkins
```

Modifying User Accounts from the Command Line

You use the usermod command to modify existing user accounts from the command line. You can use usermod to modify most of the options that were used when the account was originally created.

The following is the syntax for the usermod command:

```
usermod [ -u uid [-o]] [-g group] [ -G group [ ,  group...]]
[  -d dir  [-m]]  [-s shell]  [-c comment]  [-l new_name] [-f inactive]
[-e expire]  [-A  authorization2   [,  authorization]]  [-P  profile
[,  profile]] [-R role  [, role]] [-K key=value] <loginname>
```

The options used with the usermod command are the same as those described for the useradd command, except for those listed in Table 4.7.

TABLE 4.7 usermod Command Options

Option	Description
-l <new-login-name>	Changes a user's login name on a specified account
-m	Moves the user's home directory to the new location specified with the -d option

Additional options to the usermod command apply specifically to RBAC accounts and are described in Chapter 11.

The following example changes the login name for user bcalkins to wcalkins:

```
usermod -d /export/home/wcalkins -m -s /bin/ksh -l wcalkins bcalkins
```

This example also changes the home directory to /export/home/wcalkins and default shell to /bin/ksh.

NOTE

Modifying the Home Directory When you're changing the home directory, unless the -d and -m options are used, existing files still must be manually moved from the old home directory to the new home directory. In all cases, symbolic links, application-specific configuration files, and various other references to the old home directory must be manually updated.

To set a user's account expiration date, you enter this:

```
usermod -e 10/15/2006 wcalkins
```

The account is now set to expire October 15, 2006. Notice the entry made to the /etc/shadow file:

```
wcalkins:1luzXWgmH3LeA:13005::::::
```

The syntax of the /etc/shadow file is described later in this chapter, in the section "Where User Account Information Is Stored."

The /usr/sadm/bin/smuser modify command is the command-line equivalent of the SMC tool for modifying an existing user account.

Deleting User Accounts from the Command Line

You use the `userdel` command to delete a user's login account from the system. You can specify options to save or remove the user's home directory. The syntax for the `userdel` command is as follows:

```
userdel [-r] <login-name>
```

`-r` removes the user's home directory from the local file system. If this option is not specified, only the login is removed; the home directory remains intact.

CAUTION

Make sure you know where the user's home directory is located before removing it. Some users have `/` as their home directory, and removing their home directory would remove important system files.

The following example removes the login account for `bcalkins` but does not remove the home directory:

```
userdel bcalkins
```

The `/usr/sadm/bin/smuser delete` command is the command-line equivalent of the SMC tool for deleting an existing user account.

Adding Group Accounts from the Command Line

You use the `groupadd` command to add new group accounts on the local system. This command adds an entry to the `/etc/group` file. The syntax for the `groupadd` command is as follows:

```
groupadd [-g <gid>] -o <group-name>
```

Table 4.8 describes the `groupadd` command options.

TABLE 4.8 `groupadd` Command Options

Option	Description
`-g <gid>`	Assigns the GID *<gid>* for the new group.
`-o`	Allows the GID to be duplicated. In other words, more than one group with *group-name* can share the same GID.

The following example adds to the system a new group named `acct` with a GID of `1000`:

```
groupadd -g 1000 acct
```

NOTE

Assigning a GID If the -g option is not used to specify a GID, the GID defaults to the next available number above the highest number currently assigned. For example, if group IDs 100, 110, and 200 are already assigned to group names, the next GID that is automatically assigned is 201.

The /usr/sadm/bin/smgroup add command is the command-line equivalent of the SMC tool for creating a new group.

Modifying Group Accounts from the Command Line

You use the groupmod command to modify the definitions of a specified group. The syntax for the groupmod command is as follows:

```
groupmod [-g <gid>] -o [-n <name>] <group-name>
```

Table 4.9 describes the groupmod command options.

TABLE 4.9 groupmod Command Options

Option	Description
-g <gid>	Assigns the new GID <gid> for the group.
-o	Allows the GID to be duplicated. In other words, more than one group with *group-name* can share the same GID.
-n <name>	Specifies a new name for the group.

The following example changes the engrg group GID from 200 to 2000:

```
groupmod -g 2000 engrg
```

Any files that had the group ownership of “engrg” are now without a group name. A long listing would show a group ownership of 200 on these files, the previous GID for the engrg group. The group 200 no longer exists on the system, so only the GID is displayed in a long listing.

The /usr/sadm/bin/smgroup modify command is the command-line equivalent of the SMC tool for modifying an existing group.

Deleting Group Accounts from the Command Line

You use the groupdel command to delete a group account from the local system. The syntax for the groupdel command is as follows:

```
groupdel <group-name>
```

The following example deletes the group named `acct` from the local system:

```
groupdel acct
```

The `/usr/sadm/bin/smgroup delete` command is the command-line equivalent of the SMC tool for deleting an existing group.

Setting Up Shell Initialization Files

Objective:

When you set up user accounts, you can customize each user's session by using initialization files that are referenced each time the user logs in. This chapter describes how to administer each initialization file.

As a system administrator, when you're setting up a user's home directory, you need to set up the shell initialization files for the user's login shell (also called *user initialization files*). A *shell initialization file* is a shell script that runs automatically each time the user logs in. The initialization file sets up the work environment and customizes the shell environment for the user. The primary job of the shell initialization file is to define the user's shell environment, such as the search path, environment variables, and windowing environment. Each Unix shell has its own shell initialization file (or files), located in the user's home directory, as described in the following sections.

C Shell Initialization Files

C shell initialization files run in a particular sequence after the user logs in to the system. For the C shell, initialization files are run in the following sequence:

1. Commands in `/etc/.login` are executed.
2. Commands from the `$HOME/.cshrc` file (located in the user's home directory) are executed. In addition, each time the user starts a new shell or opens a new window in the CDE, commands from `$HOME/.cshrc` are run.
3. The shell executes commands from the `$HOME/.login` file (located in the user's home directory). Typically, the `$HOME/.login` file contains commands to specify the terminal type and environment.
4. When startup processing is complete, the C shell begins reading commands from the default input device, the terminal.

Although it is not part of the initialization of the shell, when the C shell terminates, it performs commands from the `$HOME/.logout` file (if that file exists in the home directory).

Bourne Shell Initialization Files

Bourne shell initialization files run in a particular sequence after the user logs in to the system. For the Bourne shell, initialization files are run in the following sequence:

1. Commands in `/etc/profile` are executed.
2. Commands from the `$HOME/.profile` file (located in the user's home directory) are executed. Typically, the `$HOME/.profile` file contains commands to specify the terminal type and environment.
3. When startup processing is complete, the Bourne shell begins reading commands from the default input device, the terminal.

Korn Shell Initialization Files

Korn shell initialization files run in a particular sequence after the user logs in to the system. For the Korn shell, initialization files are run in the following sequence:

1. Commands in `/etc/profile` are executed.
2. Commands from the `$HOME/.profile` file (located in the user's home directory) are executed. Typically, the `$HOME/.profile` file contains commands to specify the terminal type and environment.
3. If the `$HOME/.kshrc` file is present, commands located in this file are executed. In addition, this initialization file gets read (and the commands get executed) every time a new Korn shell is started after login.
4. When startup processing is complete, the Korn shell begins reading commands from the default input device, the terminal.

Additional Shells Included with Solaris 10

Solaris 10 also includes, as part of the operating environment, the `bash`, `zsh`, and `tcsh` shells. These shells, especially `bash` and `tcsh`, are gaining popularity with system administrators and contain extra options and functions. You can find further details about these shells and their additional functionality by consulting the man pages for them.

NOTE

The Effect of CDE on Shell Initialization Files Initialization files are executed in the order specified for each of the shells, except when you're logging in to the CDE, where the `$HOME/.dtprofile` file is also run. If the `DTSOURCEPROFILE` variable is not set to `TRUE` in the `.dtprofile` file, the `$HOME/.profile` file will not be run.

When you're using CDE, it may be necessary to add the following lines in the `$HOME/.profile` to get the `.kshrc` file to work properly in the Korn shell:

```
set -ha
ENV=$HOME/.kshrc
```

Without this entry, aliases and environment variables might not get passed to subshells (that is, additional shells spawned by the Korn shell). Therefore, when you open a new window in the CDE, alias and environment variables are set in the initial shell but are not set in subsequent shells, even though they are listed in the `$HOME/.kshrc` file. The preceding entries fix this problem.

Default Initialization Files

When a user logs in to the system, the user's login shell is invoked. The shell program looks for its initialization files in the correct order for the shell. The shell program then executes the commands contained in each file and, when it is finished, displays the shell prompt on the user's screen.

Default user initialization files (such as `.cshrc`, `.profile`, and `.login`) are created automatically in the user's home directory when a new user account is added. You can predefine the contents of these files, or you can choose to use the system default files. The Solaris 10 system software provides default user initialization files for each shell in the `/etc/skel` directory on each system. These files are listed in Table 4.10.

TABLE 4.10 Default Initialization Files

Filename	Description
`local.cshrc`	The default `.cshrc` file for the C shell
`local.login`	The default `.login` file for the C shell
`local.profile`	The default `.profile` file for the Bourne and Korn shells

You can use these initialization files as a starting point and modify them to create a standard set of files that provides a work environment that is common to all users. You can also modify them to provide a working environment for different types of users.

Customizing User Initialization Files

When a user logs in to a system, the shell initialization files determine the work environment. The shell startup scripts can be modified to set environment variables and directory paths that are needed by a specific user. These startup scripts are located in the user's home directory.

When you are setting up user initialization files, it might be important to allow the users to customize their own initialization files. You can do this by having centrally located and globally distributed user initialization files called *site initialization files*. With these files, you can continually introduce new functionality to all the user work environments by editing one initialization file.

The *local initialization file*, located in the user's home directory, allows user-specific configuration. A local initialization file lets users further customize their own work environment.

Site initialization files are located in the `/etc` directory and can be edited only by root. They are designed to distribute sitewide changes to all user work environments. Individual user initialization files are located in each user's home directory and can be customized by the owner of the directory. When a user logs in, the site initialization file is run first, and then the initialization file located in the user's home directory is run.

NOTE

Sitewide Shell Initialization Files You should not use system initialization files located in the `/etc` directory (`/etc/profile`, `/etc/.login`) to manage an individual user's work environment. Files in that folder are site initialization files, which are considered to be global files and are meant to be generic and used to set work environments for all users. The system runs these startup files first and then runs each user's startup files, located in the home directories.

The most commonly customized aspects of shell startup scripts are environment variables. Table 4.11 describes the most common environment and shell variables, including some that you might want to customize in user initialization files.

TABLE 4.11 Shell and Environment Variables

Variable	Description
LOGNAME	Defines the user's login name. This variable is set by the login program and wouldn't normally be modified.
HOME	Defines the path to the user's home directory. The `cd` command uses this variable when an argument is not specified. This variable is set by the login program and wouldn't normally be modified.
SHELL	Defines the path to the default shell. This variable normally isn't modified manually by the user.

TABLE 4.11 *Continued*

Variable	Description
LPDEST	Sets the user's default printer.
PWD	Is set to the current working directory. This variable changes automatically each time the user changes directories. This variable isn't modified manually by the user.
PS1	Defines the shell prompts for the Bourne and Korn shells.
PATH (or path in the C shell)	Lists, in order, the directories that the shell searches to find the program to run when the user enters a command. If the directory is not in the search path, users must enter the complete pathname of a command. The default PATH variable is automatically defined in .profile (Bourne or Korn shell) or .cshrc (C shell) as part of the login process. The order of the search path is important. When identical commands exist in different locations, the first command found with that name is used. For example, suppose PATH is defined (in Bourne and Korn shell syntax) as PATH=/bin:/usr/bin:/usr/sbin:$HOME/bin and a file named sample resides in both /usr/bin and $HOME/bin. If the user enters the command sample without specifying its full pathname, the version found in /usr/bin is used.
prompt	Defines the shell prompt for the C shell.
TERM (or term in the C shell)	Defines the terminal. This variable should be reset in /etc/profile or /etc/.login. When the user invokes a program that uses advanced terminal properties such as an editor, the system looks for a file with the same name as the definition of this environment variable. The system searches the directory /usr/share/lib/terminfo to determine the terminal characteristics.
MAIL	Sets the path to the user's mailbox.
MANPATH	Sets the search path for system man pages.
umask	Sets the default user mask. Although umask is a command and not a variable, it is used to set the file-mode creation mask of the current shell execution environment, as described in the section "The Default User Mask," later in this chapter.

TIP

Modifying the Shell Prompt Some users find it helpful to make their login name, the hostname, and the current directory part of the prompt. Here's how you set it up in the Korn shell:

```
PS1="$(whoami)@$(hostname) [\$PWD] #"
```

The resulting prompt looks like this:

```
root@ultra5 [/usr/bin] #
```

Step by Step 4.5 shows how to modify the shell environment by changing some of the variables in the shell startup file. It suggests some changes and shows the shell-specific syntax to use.

STEP BY STEP

4.5 Verifying and Changing a User's Environment

1. Log in as the user. This enables you to see the user's environment as the user would see it. You can use `su - <username>` to achieve this.
2. Set the user's default path to include the home directory as well as directories or mount points for the user's windowing environment and applications. To change the path setting, add or modify the line for PATH.

   For the Bourne or Korn shell, this is the syntax:

   ```
   PATH=/<dirname1>:/<dirname2>:/<dirname3>:.; export PATH
   ```

   For example, you could enter the following line in the user's `$HOME/.profile` file:

   ```
   PATH=$PATH:/usr/bin:/$HOME/bin:/net/glrr/files1/bin:.;export PATH
   ```

   For the C shell, notice that in the syntax, the colons are replaced with spaces:

   ```
   set path =(/<dirname1> /<dirname2> /<dirname3> .)
   ```

   For example, you could enter the following line in the user's `$HOME/.cshrc` file:

   ```
   set path=($path /usr/bin $HOME/bin /net/glrr/files1/bin .)
   ```

> **NOTE**
>
> **Modifying the PATH Variable** Prefixing `$PATH` (Korn shell) or `$path` (C shell) appends changes to the user's path settings that are already set by the site initialization file. When you set the PATH variable with this procedure, initial path settings are not overwritten and are not lost. Also note the dot (`.`) at the end of the list to denote the current working directory. The dot should always be at the end of the path for users and should not be used in the path for root, as discussed in the section "Setting the Correct Path," later in this chapter.

3. Make sure the environment variables are set to the correct directories for the user's windowing environments and third-party applications. To do so, enter `env`, and you see the following:

   ```
   $env
   HOME=/export/home
   HZ=100
   LOGNAME=bill
   MAIL=/var/mail/bill
   PATH=/usr/bin:
   SHELL=/bin/sh
   TERM=xterm
   TZ=US/Michigan
   ```

4. Add or change the settings of environment variables.

   For the Bourne or Korn shell, the syntax is as follows:

   ```
   VARIABLE=<value>;export VARIABLE
   ```

   The following example sets the user's default mail directory:

   ```
   MAIL=/var/mail/bcalkins;export MAIL
   ```

   For the C shell, the syntax is as follows:

   ```
   setenv VARIABLE <value>
   ```

   The following example sets the history to record the last 100 commands in C shell:

   ```
   set history = 100
   ```

The Home Directory

The *home directory* is the portion of a file system that is allocated to a user for storing private files. The amount of space you allocate for home directories depends on the kinds of files the user creates and the type of work performed. An entire file system is usually allocated specifically for home directories, and the users all share this space. As the system administrator, you need to monitor user home directories so that one user does not use more than his or her fair share of space. You can use disk quotas to control the amount of disk space a user can occupy. (Disk quotas are discussed in Chapter 1, "Managing File Systems.") Or you can use soft partitions, which are described in Chapter 10.

A home directory can be located either on the user's local system or on a remote file server. Although any directory name can be used for a home directory, it is customary that home directories are named using this convention: `/export/home/<username>`. When you put the home directory in `/export/home`, it is available across the network in case the user logs in from several different stations. For a large site, you should store home directories on a server.

Regardless of where their home directories are located, users usually access them through a mount point named `/home/<username>`. When AutoFS is used to mount home directories, you are not permitted to create any directories under the `/home` mount point on any system. The system recognizes the special status of `/home` when AutoFS is active. For more information about AutoFS and automounting home directories, see Chapter 9, "Virtual File Systems, Swap Space, and Core Dumps."

To access a home directory anywhere on the network, a user should always refer to it as `$HOME`, not as `/export/home/<username>`. The latter is machine specific, and its use should be discouraged. In addition, any symbolic links created in a user's home directory should use relative paths (for example, `../../../x/y/x`) so that the links will be valid no matter where the home directory is mounted. The location of user home directories might change. By not using machine-specific names, you maintain consistency and reduce system administration.

Projects

The concept of *projects* was introduced in Solaris 8. Projects are included in Solaris 10, and they allow much-improved tracking of resources and usage. The project concept is extremely useful when multiple projects use the same system and are charged for their usage of the system. With projects, it is now simple to identify and subsequently charge each project based on the resources used. In addition, a system administrator supporting multiple projects can perform duties associated with those projects so that his or her time is also booked to the project requesting the service. The system administrator would do this by using the `newtask` command. (See the `newtask` man page for further details about this command.)

You establish projects by using the configuration file `/etc/project`. The following example shows the standard `/etc/project` file:

```
system:0::::
user.root:1::::
noproject:2::::
default:3::::
group.staff:10::::
```

As you can see from this example, all members of the `staff` group (`GID 10`) belong to the project `group.staff`.

You can edit this file to create new projects and assign users and groups of users to the projects. Accounting software can produce reports on usage based on the projects specified in the `/etc/project` file.

For further information on projects, see the man page entry for projects as well as the entry for the `projects` command, which lists the projects a user or group belongs to.

Name Services

If you are managing user accounts for a large site, you might want to consider using a *name service* such as Network Information Service (NIS), Network Information Service Plus (NIS+), or Lightweight Directory Access Protocol (LDAP). A name service lets you store user account information in a centralized manner instead of storing it in every system's `/etc` file. When you use a name service for user accounts, users can move from system to system, using the same user account without having sitewide user account information duplicated in every system's `/etc` file. Using a name service also promotes centralized and consistent user account information. NIS, NIS+, and LDAP are discussed in Chapter 12, "Naming Services."

System Security

Objective:

Restrict access to data in files through the use of group membership, ownership, and special file permissions.

In addition to setting up user accounts, keeping the system's information secure is one of a system administrator's primary tasks. System security involves protecting data against loss due to a disaster or system failure. In addition, the system administrator must protect systems from the threat of unauthorized access and protect data on the system from unauthorized users. Bad disasters often come from authorized personnel—even system administrators—destroying data unintentionally. Therefore, the system administrator is presented with two levels of security: protecting data from accidental loss and securing the system against intrusion or unauthorized access.

The first scenario—protecting data from accidental loss—is easy to achieve with a full system backup scheme that you run regularly. Regular backups provide protection in the event of a disaster. If a user accidentally destroys data, if the hardware malfunctions, or if a computer program simply corrupts data, you can restore files from the backup media. (Backup and recovery techniques are covered in Chapter 7, "Performing System Backups and Restorations.")

The second form of security—securing the system against intrusion or unauthorized access—is more complex. This book cannot cover every security hole or threat, but it does discuss Unix security fundamentals. Protection against intruders involves the following:

- **Controlling physical security**—You need to limit physical access to the computer equipment.
- **Controlling system access**—You need to limit user access via passwords and permissions.
- **Controlling file access**—You need to limit access to data by assigning file access permissions.
- **Auditing users**—You need to monitor user activities to detect a threat before damage occurs.
- **Controlling network security**—You need to protect against access through phone lines, serial lines, or the network.
- **Securing superuser access**—You need to reserve superuser access for system administrator use only.

The following sections describe these facets of security.

Controlling Physical Security

Physical security is simple: You need to lock the door. You should limit who has physical access to the computer equipment to prevent theft or vandalism. In addition, you should limit access to the system console. Anyone who has access to the console ultimately has access to the data. If the computer contains sensitive data, you need to keep it locked in a controlled environment with filtered power and adequate protection against fire, lightning, flood, and other disasters. You should restrict access to protect against tampering with the system and its backups. Anyone with access to the backup media could steal it and access the data. Furthermore, if a system is logged in and left unattended, anyone who can use that system can gain access to the operating system and the network. You need to make sure your users log out or lock their screens before walking away. In summary, you need to be aware of your users' computer surroundings, and you need to physically protect them from unauthorized access.

Controlling System Access

Controlling access to systems involves using passwords and appropriate file permissions. To control access, all logins must have passwords, and those passwords must be changed frequently. *Password aging* is a system parameter that you set to require users to change their passwords after a certain number of days. Password aging lets you force users to change their passwords periodically or prevent users from changing their passwords before a specified interval. You can set an expiration date for a user account to prevent an intruder from gaining undetected access to the system through an old and inactive account. For a high level of security, you should require users to change their passwords periodically (for example, every six weeks or every three months for lower levels of security). You should change system administration passwords (such as root and any other user who has administrative privileges through an RBAC account) monthly or whenever a person who knows the root password leaves the company or is reassigned. Each user should have his or her own account, and no user should disclose his or her password to anyone else.

Several files that control default system access are stored in the `/etc/default` directory. Table 4.12 describes a few of the files in the `/etc/default` directory.

TABLE 4.12 Files in the `/etc/default` Directory

Filename	Description
`/etc/default/passwd`	Controls the default policy on password aging.
`/etc/default/login`	Controls system login policies, including the policy on root access. The default is to limit root access to the console.
`/etc/default/su`	Specifies where attempts to use `su` to become root are logged and where those log files are located. This file also specifies whether attempts to use `su` to become root are displayed on a named device (such as a system console).

You can set default values in the /etc/default/passwd file to control user passwords. Table 4.13 lists the options that can be controlled through the /etc/default/passwd file.

TABLE 4.13 Flags in /etc/default/passwd

Flag	Description
MAXWEEKS	Specifies the maximum time period for which a password is valid. The MAXWEEKS value can be overridden by entries in the /etc/shadow file.
MINWEEKS	Specifies the minimum time period before the password can be changed. The MINWEEKS value can be overridden by entries in the /etc/shadow file.
PASSLENGTH	Specifies a minimum password length for all regular users. The value can be 6, 7, or 8.
WARNWEEKS	Specifies a time period after which the system warns of the password's expiration date. This entry does not exist in the file by default, but it can be added. The WARNWEEKS value can be overridden by entries in the /etc/shadow file.

Additional controls have been added to Solaris 10 that can be set in the /etc/default/passwd file and are as follows:

- NAMECHECK=NO — Sets the password controls to verify that the user is not using the login name as a component of the password.
- HISTORY=0 — HISTORY can have a value from 0–26. Setting a value higher than 0 forces the passwd program to log up to 26 changes to the user's password. The value entered specifies the number of changes to log preventing a user from reusing the same password for up to 26 changes. When the HISTORY value is set to zero (0), the password log for all users will be removed the next time a user changes his password. No password history will be checked if the flag is not present or has zero value.
- DICTIONLIST= — Causes the passwd program to perform dictionary word lookups.
- DICTIONDBDIR=/var/passwd — The location of the dictionary where the generated dictionary databases reside. This directory must be created manually.

Complexity of the password can be controlled using the following parameters:

- MINDIFF=3 — The old and new passwords must differ by at least the MINDIFF value.
- MINALPHA=2 — Password must contain at least this number of alpha characters.
- MINUPPER=0 — Password must contain at least this number of uppercase characters.

`MINLOWER=0`	Password must contain at least this number of lowercase characters.
`MAXREPEATS=0`	The password must not contain more consecutively repeating characters than specified by the `MAXREPEATS` value.
`MINSPECIAL=0`	Password must contain at least this number of special characters.
`MINDIGIT=0`	Password must contain at least this number of digits.
`MINNONALPHA=1`	Describes the same character classes as `MINDIGIT` and `MINSPECIAL` combined; therefore you cannot specify both `MINNONALPHA` and `MINSPECIAL` (or `MINDIGIT`). You must choose which of the two options to use.
`WHITESPACE=YES`	Determines whether whitespace characters are allowed.

NOTE

Privileged users, such as root, are not forced to comply with password aging and password construction requirements. A privileged user can create a null password by entering a carriage return in response to the prompt for a new password. Therefore privileged users should be extra vigilant not to use bad (that is, easy to guess) passwords.

As a system administrator, your job is to ensure that all users have secure passwords. A system cracker can break weak passwords and put an entire system at risk. You should enforce the following guidelines on passwords:

- Passwords should contain a combination of six to eight letters, numbers, or special characters. Don't use fewer than six characters.
- Use a password with nonalphabetic characters, such as numerals or punctuation.
- Mix upper- and lowercase characters.
- The password must not contain any sequences of four or more letters (regardless of how you capitalize them) that can be found in a dictionary. Also, reversing the order of the letters doesn't do any good because a standard way of cracking a password is to try all the words in a dictionary, in all possible upper-/lowercase combinations, both forward and backward. Prefixing and/or appending a numeral or punctuation character to a dictionary word doesn't help either; on a modern computer, it doesn't take too long to try all those possible combinations, and programs exist (and are easy to get) to do exactly that.
- Use a password that is easy to remember, so you don't have to write it down. Never write down a password or email or give your password to anyone! You should be able to type it quickly, without having to look at the keyboard. This makes it harder for someone to steal your password by watching over your shoulder.

- Nonsense words made up of the first letter of every syllable in a phrase, such as `swotrb` for "Somewhere Over the Rainbow," work well for a password. Choose two short words and concatenate them together with a punctuation character between them (for example, `dog;rain`, `book+mug`, `kid?goat`).

NOTE

Dictionaries and Password Cracking Be aware that in addition to the standard American or English dictionaries, there are also crackers' dictionaries. These are collections of common computer terms and phrases, names, slang and jargon, easily typed key sequences (such as `asdfg` and `123456`), and commonly used phrases that one might be tempted to use for a password. These crackers' dictionaries are frequently updated and shared; programs to crack passwords are distributed with copies of these dictionaries.

The following are poor choices for passwords:

- Proper nouns, names, login names, and other passwords that a person might guess just by knowing something about the user.
- The user's name—forward, backward, or jumbled.
- Names of the user's family members or pets.
- Information that is easily obtained about you, such as the following:

  Car license plate numbers

  Telephone numbers

  Social Security numbers

  Employee numbers
- Names related to a hobby or an interest.
- Seasonal themes, such as Santa in December.
- Any word in the dictionary (English or foreign language).
- Simple keyboard patterns (such as `asdfgh`).
- Passwords the user has used previously.
- A password with fewer than six characters.
- A password of all digits, or all the same letter. This significantly decreases the search time for a cracker.

Where User Account Information Is Stored

When no network name service is used, user account and group information is stored in files located in the /etc directory. Even when you're using a name service, these local files still exist in the /etc directory, but most of the account information is stored in the name server's database. Refer to Chapter 12 for more information.

Most user account information is stored in the /etc/passwd file; however, password encryption and password aging details are stored in the /etc/shadow file. Only root can view the /etc/shadow file. Group information is stored in the /etc/group file. Users are put together into groups based on their file access needs; for example, the acctng group might be users in the Accounting Department.

Each line in the /etc/passwd file contains several fields separated by colons (:), and each line is formatted as follows:

```
<username>:<password>:<uid>:<gid>:<comment>:<home-directory>:<login-shell>
```

Table 4.14 defines the fields in the /etc/passwd file.

TABLE 4.14 Fields in the /etc/passwd File

Field	Description
<username>	Contains the user or login name. A username should be unique and should consist of one to eight letters (A–Z, a–z) and numerals (0–9), but no underscores or spaces. The first character must be a letter, and at least one character must be a lowercase letter.
<password>	Contains an x, which is a placeholder for the encrypted password that is stored in the /etc/shadow file and that is used by the pwconv command, which is described later in this section.
<uid>	Contains a UID number that identifies the user to the system. UID numbers for regular users should range from 100 to 60,000, but they can be as high as 2,147,483,647. All UID numbers should be unique. UIDs lower than 100 are reserved. To minimize security risks, you should avoid reusing UIDs from deleted accounts.
<gid>	Contains a GID number that identifies the user's primary group. Each GID number must be a whole number between 0 and 60,000 (60,001 and 60,002 are assigned to nobody and noaccess, respectively). GIDs can go as high as 2,147,483,647, but GIDs higher than 60,002 might not be supported across other Unix platforms. GID numbers lower than 100 are reserved for system default group accounts.
<comment>	Usually contains the user's full name.
<home-directory>	Contains the user's home directory pathname.
<login-shell>	Contains the user's default login shell.

Each line in the /etc/shadow file contains several fields, separated by colons (:). The lines in the /etc/shadow file have the following syntax:

```
<username>:<password>:<lastchg>:<min>:<max>:<warn>:<inactive>:<expire>
```

Table 4.15 defines the fields in the /etc/shadow file.

TABLE 4.15 Fields in the /etc/shadow File

Field	Description
<username>	Specifies the user or login name.
<password>	Might ontain one of the following entries: a 13-character encrypted user password; the string *LK*, which indicates an inaccessible (locked) account; or the string NP, which indicates no valid password on the account and you cannot login directly to this account.
<lastchg>	Indicates the number of days between January 1, 1970, and the last password modification date.
<min>	Specifies the minimum number of days required between password changes.
<max>	Specifies the maximum number of days the password is valid before the user is prompted to specify a new password.
<inactive>	Specifies the number of days that a user account can be inactive before it is locked.
<expire>	Specifies the absolute date when the user account expires. Past this date, the user cannot log in to the system.

You should refrain from editing the /etc/passwd file directly, and you should never edit the /etc/shadow file directly. Any incorrect entry can prevent you from logging in to the system. These files are updated automatically, using one of the Solaris account administration commands or the SMC, as described earlier in this chapter.

If you must edit the /etc/passwd file manually, you should use the pwck command to check the file. The pwck command scans the password file and notes any inconsistencies. The checks include validation of the number of fields, login name, UID, GID, and whether the login directory and the program to use as shell exist.

Some experienced system administrators edit the /etc/passwd file directly for various reasons, but only after creating a backup copy of the original /etc/passwd file. (Chapter 12 describes this procedure.) For example, you might want to restore an /etc/passwd file from backup—perhaps because the original was corrupted or was incorrectly modified.

Use the /usr/ucb/vipw command to edit the /etc/passwd file. /usr/ucb/vipw edits the password file while setting the appropriate locks, and does any necessary processing after the password file is unlocked. If the password file is already being edited, you will be told to try again later. /usr/ucb/vipw also performs a number of consistency checks on the password entry for root and will not allow a password file with a "mangled" root entry to be installed. It also checks the /etc/shells file to verify that a valid login shell for root has been defined.

After modifying the /etc/passwd file, you run the pwconv command. This command updates the /etc/shadow file with information from the /etc/passwd file.

The pwconv command relies on the special value of x in the password field of the /etc/passwd file. The x indicates that the password for the user already exists in the /etc/shadow file. If the /etc/shadow file does not exist, pwconv re-creates everything in it from information found in the /etc/passwd file. If the /etc/shadow file does exist, the following is performed:

- Entries that are in the /etc/passwd file and not in the /etc/shadow file are added to the shadow file.
- Entries that are in the /etc/shadow file and not in the /etc/passwd file are removed from the shadow file.

Each line in the /etc/group file contains several fields, separated by colons (:). The lines in the /etc/group file have the following syntax:

```
<group-name>:<group-password>:<gid>:<user-list>
```

Table 4.16 defines the fields in the /etc/group file.

TABLE 4.16 Fields in the /etc/group File

Field	Description
<group-name>	Contains the name assigned to the group. For example, members of the Accounting Department group might be called acct. A group name can have a maximum of nine characters.
<group-password>	Usually contains an asterisk or is empty. See the information on the newgrp command in the section "Effective UIDs and GIDs," later in this chapter.
<gid>	Contains the group's GID number, which must be unique on the local system and should be unique across the entire organization. Each GID number must be a whole number between 0 and 60,002, but it can be as high as 2,147,483,647. However, GIDs above 60,002 might not be supported on some Unix platforms. Numbers lower than 100 are reserved for system default group accounts, so don't use them. User-defined groups can range from 100 to 60,000 (60,001 and 60,002 are reserved and assigned to nobody and noaccess, respectively).
<user-list>	Contains a list of groups and a comma-separated list of usernames that represent the user's secondary group memberships. Each user can belong to a maximum of 16 secondary groups.

NOTE

UID Values Earlier Solaris software releases use 32-bit data types to contain the GIDs, but GIDs are constrained to a maximum useful value of `60,000`. Starting with Solaris 2.5.1 and compatible versions, the limit on GID values has been raised to the maximum value of a signed integer, or `2,147,483,647`. GIDs greater than `60,000` do not have full functionality and are incompatible with many Solaris features, so you should avoid using them.

By default, all Solaris 10 systems have default groups already defined in the `/etc/group` file. Those entries are outlined in Table 4.17:

TABLE 4.17 Default Group File Entries

Entry	Description
`root::0:`	Super user group
`other::1:root`	Optional group
`bin::2:root,daemon`	Administrative group associated with running system binaries
`sys::3:root,bin,adm`	Administrative group associated with system logging or temporary directories
`adm::4:root,daemon`	Administrative group associated with system logging
`uucp::5:root`	Group associated with `uucp` functions
`mail::6:root`	Electronic mail group
`tty::7:root,adm`	Group associated with `tty` devices
`lp::8:root,adm`	Line printer group
`nuucp::9:root`	Group associated with `uucp` functions
`staff::10:`	General administrative group
`daemon::12:root`	Group associated with routine system tasks
`sysadmin::14:`	Administrative group associated with legacy Admintool and Solstice AdminSuite tools
`smmsp::25:`	Daemon for Sendmail message submission program
`gdm::50:`	Group reserved for the GNOME Display Manager daemon
`webservd::80:`	Group reserved for WebServer access
`nobody::60001:`	Group assigned for anonymous NFS access
`noaccess::60002:`	Group assigned to a user or a process that needs access to a system through some application but without actually logging in
`nogroup::65534:`	Group assigned to a user who is not a member of a known group

Other than the staff group, you should not use these groups for users. Also, some system processes and applications might rely on these groups, so you should not change the GIDs or remove these groups from the /etc/group file unless you are absolutely sure of the effect on the system.

If you edit the /etc/group file manually, you should use the grpck command to verify all entries in the group file. This verification includes a check of the number of fields, the group name, and the GID, as well as a check to ensure that all login names appear in the password file.

A user can display the list of groups that they belong to by typing the groups command as follows:

```
#groups
```

Their primary and secondary groups are listed as follows:

```
root other bin sys adm uucp mail tty lp nuucp daemon
```

A user can change their primary group using the newgrp command as follows:

```
# newgrp other
```

The root user has changed his or her primary group from root to other as displayed by the id command:

```
# id
uid=0(root) gid=1(other)
```

Restricted Shells

System administrators can use restricted versions of the Korn shell (rksh) and the Bourne shell (rsh) to limit the operations allowed for a particular user account. Restricted shells are especially useful for ensuring that time-sharing users and users' guests on a system have restricted permissions during login sessions. When an account is set up with a restricted shell, users cannot do the following:

- Change directories to a directory above their home directory
- Set the $PATH variable
- Specify path or command names that begin with /
- Redirect output

You can also provide users with shell procedures that have access to the full power of the standard shell but that impose a limited menu of commands.

NOTE

Don't Confuse `rsh` You should not confuse the restricted shell `/usr/lib/rsh` with the remote shell `/usr/bin/rsh`. When you specify a restricted shell, you should not include the following directories in the user's path—`/bin`, `/sbin`, or `/usr/bin`. Doing so allows the user to start another shell (a nonrestricted shell).

Controlling File Access

Objective:

Restrict access to data in files through the use of group membership, ownership, and special file permissions.

After you have established login restrictions, you need to control access to the data on the system. Some users only need to look at files; others need the ability to change or delete files. You might have data that you do not want anyone else to see. You control data access by assigning permission levels to a file or directory.

Three levels of access permission are assigned to a Unix file to control access by the owner, the group, and all others. You display permissions by using the `ls -la` command. The following example shows the use of the `ls -la` command to display permissions on files in the `/users` directory:

```
ls -la    /users
```

The system responds with this:

```
drwxr-xr-x   2   bill   staff   512   Sep 23 07:02        .
drwxr-xr-x   3   root   other   512   Sep 23 07:02        ..
-rw-r--r--   1   bill   staff   124   Sep 23 07:02        .cshrc
-rw-r--r--   1   bill   staff   575   Sep 23 07:02        .login
```

The first column of information displays the type of file and its access permissions for the user, group, and others. The `r`, `w`, `x`, and `-` symbols are described in Table 4.18. The third column displays the owner of the file—usually the user who created the file. The owner of a file (and the superuser) can decide who has the right to read it, to write to it, and—if it is a command—to execute it. The fourth column displays the group to which this file belongs—normally the owner's primary group.

TABLE 4.18 File Access Permissions

Symbol	Permission	Means That Designated Users...
r	Read	Can open and read the contents of a file.
w	Write	Can write to the file (that is, modify its contents), add to it, or delete it.
x	Execute	Can execute the file (if it is a program or shell script).
-	Denied	Cannot read, write to, or execute the file.

When you list the permissions on a directory, all columns of information are the same as for a file, with one exception. The `r`, `w`, `x`, and `-` found in the first column are treated slightly different for a directory than for a file, as described in Table 4.19.

TABLE 4.19 Directory Access Permissions

Symbol	Permission	Means That Designated Users...
r	Read	Can list files in the directory.
w	Write	Can add files or links to or remove files or links from the directory.
x	Execute	Can open or execute files in the directory and can make the directory and the directories beneath it current.
-	Denied	Cannot read, write, or execute.

You use the commands listed in Table 4.20 to modify file access permissions and ownership, but you need to remember that only the owner of the file or root can assign or modify these values.

TABLE 4.20 File Access Commands

Command	Description
chmod	Changes access permissions on a file. You can use either symbolic mode (letters and symbols) or absolute mode (octal numbers) to change permissions on a file.
chown	Changes the ownership and optionally the group ownership of a file.
chgrp	Changes the group ownership of a file.

Use the `chmod` command to change the permissions on a file to `rwxrwxrwx` as follows:

```
chmod rwxrwxrwx <filename>
```

Use the `chown` command to change the ownership on a file to `bcalkins` as follows:

```
chown bcalkins <filename>
```

Use the `chgrp` command to change group ownership of a file to `engrg` as follows:

```
chgrp engrg <filename>
```

The `chown` command can be used to change both the user and group ownership of a file as follows:

```
chown bcalkins:engrg <filename>
```

Sometimes you don't have access to a file or directory if you use your current login and you want to switch from one login ID to another. As long as you know the login name and password, you can quickly switch to that login by using the `su` command, which is described in the following section.

Effective UIDs and GIDs

The `su` (switch user) command enables a user to become another user without logging off the system. To use the `su` command, you must supply the password for the user you are attempting to log in as. The root user can run `su` to any account without being prompted for passwords.

System administrators often use the `su` command. For example, as a safety precaution, rather than using the root account as a regular login, you might use a regular, nonroot login whenever you are not performing administration functions. When root access is required, you can quickly become the superuser by using the `su` command. When you are finished performing the task, you can exit the superuser account and continue working using your normal, nonroot account.

If the user enters the correct password, `su` creates a new shell process, as specified in the `shell` field of the `/etc/passwd` file for that particular user. In the following example, `user1` runs the `su` command to become `user2`:

```
su user2
```

An option to the `su` command is `-`. This option specifies a complete login. The specified user's `.profile` file is run, and the environment is changed to what would be expected if the user actually logged in as the specified user.

Without the `-` option, the environment is passed along from the original login, with the exception of `$PATH`, which is controlled by `PATH` and `SUPATH` in the `/etc/default/su` file (which is described later in this chapter). When the administrator uses `su` to access the root account from an untrusted user's account, the `-` option should always be used. If it is not used, the administrator is logged in as root, using a `PATH` variable defined for a nonroot user. This could result in the administrator inadvertently running commands specified in the user's shell initialization files.

A user can also switch his or her primary group by using the `newgrp` command. The `newgrp` command logs a user in to a new group by changing a user's real and effective GIDs. The user remains logged in, and the current directory is unchanged. The execution of `su` and `newgrp` always replaces the current shell with a new shell. The execution of `newgrp` always replaces the current shell with a new shell, even if the command terminates with an error (unknown group).

Any variable that is not exported is reset to null or its default value. Exported variables retain their values.

With no operands and options, `newgrp` changes the user's real and effective GIDs back to the primary group specified in the user's password file entry.

A password is demanded if the group has a password (in the second field of the `/etc/group` file), the user is not listed in `/etc/group` as being a member of that group, and the group is not the user's primary group. The only way to create a password for a group is to use the `passwd` command and then cut and paste the password from `/etc/shadow` to `/etc/group`. Group passwords are antiquated and not often used.

The Default User Mask

When a user creates a file or directory, the *user mask* controls the default file permissions assigned to the file or directory. The `umask` command should set the user mask in the `/etc/default/login` file or a user initialization file, such as `/etc/profile` or `.cshrc`. You can display the current value of the user mask by typing **`umask`** and pressing Enter.

The user mask is set with a three-digit octal value, such as `022`. The first digit of this value sets permissions for the user, the second sets permissions for the group, and the third sets permissions for others. To set the user mask to `022`, you type the following:

```
umask 022
```

By default, the system sets the permissions on a file to `666`, granting read and write permission to the user, group, and others. The system sets the default permissions on a directory or executable file to `777`, or `rwxrwxrwx`. The value assigned by `umask` is subtracted from the default. To determine what `umask` value you want to set, you subtract the value of the permissions you want from `666` (for a file) or `777` (for a directory). The remainder is the value to use with the `umask` command. For example, suppose you want to change the default mode for files to `644` (`rw-r--r--`). The difference between `666` and `644` is `022`, so you would use this value as an argument to the `umask` command.

Setting the `umask` value has the effect of granting or denying permissions in the same way that `chmod` grants them. For example, the command `chmod 644` denies write permission to the group, while others, such as `umask 022`, deny write permission to the group and others.

Sticky Bits

The *sticky bit* is a permission bit that protects the files within a directory. If the directory has the sticky bit set, a file can be deleted only by the owner of the file, the owner of the directory, or root. This prevents a user from deleting other users' files from public directories. A `t` or `T` in the access permissions column of a directory listing indicates that the sticky bit has been set, as shown here:

```
drwxrwxrwt   5 root     sys          458 Oct 17 23:04 /tmp
```

You use the chmod command to set the sticky bit. The symbols for setting the sticky bit by using the chmod command in symbolic mode are listed in Table 4.21.

TABLE 4.21 Sticky Bit Modes

Symbol	Description
t	Sticky bit is on; execution bit for others is on.

Access Control Lists (ACLs)

Objective:

Restrict access to data in files through the use of group membership, ownership, and special file permissions.

ACLs (pronounced *ackls*) can provide greater control over file permissions when the traditional Unix file protection in the Solaris operating system is not enough. The traditional Unix file protection provides read, write, and execute permissions for the three user classes: owner, group, and other. An ACL provides better file security by allowing you to define file permissions for the owner, owner's group, others, and specific users and groups, and allows you to set default permissions for each of these categories.

For example, assume you have a file you want everyone in a group to be able to read. To give everyone access, you would give "group" read permissions on that file. Now, assume you want only one person in the group to be able to write to that file. Standard Unix doesn't let you set that up; however, you can set up an ACL to give only one person in the group write permissions on the file. Think of ACL entries as an extension to regular Unix permissions.

ACL entries are the way to define an ACL on a file, and they are set through the ACL commands. ACL entries consist of the following fields, separated by colons:

```
entry_type:uid¦gid:perms
```

ACL entries are defined in Table 4.22.

TABLE 4.22 ACL Entries

ACL Field	Description
entry_type	The type of ACL entry on which to set file permissions. For example, entry_type can be user (the owner of a file) or mask (the ACL mask).
uid	The username or identification number.
gid	The group name or identification number.
perms	The permissions set on entry_type. Permissions are indicated by the symbolic characters rwx or an octal number, as used with the chmod command.

Setting ACL Entries

Set ACL entries on a file or directory by using the setfacl command:

```
$ setfacl -s user::perms,group::perms,other:perms,mask:perms,\
acl_entry_list filename ...
```

TIP

Setting Versus Modifying an ACL The -s option sets a new ACL, but also replaces an entire existing ACL with the new ACL entries. You should read any exam questions on this topic very carefully, as it can be easily confused with the -m option to modify an existing ACL.

The ACL entries that can be specified with the setfacl command are described in Table 4.23.

TABLE 4.23 ACL Entries for Files and Directories

ACL Entry	Description
u[ser]::<perms>	File owner permissions.
g[roup]::<perms>	File group permissions.
o[ther]:<perms>	Permissions for users other than the file owner or members of the file group.
m[ask]:<perms>	The ACL mask. The mask entry indicates the maximum permissions allowed for users (other than the owner) and for groups. The mask is a quick way to change permissions on all the users and groups. For example, the mask:r-- mask entry indicates that users and groups cannot have more than read permissions, even though they might have write/execute permissions. The mask permission will override any specific user or group permissions.
u[ser]:<uid>:<perms>	Permissions for a specific user. For <uid>, you can specify either a username or a numeric UID.
g[roup]:<uid>:<perms>	Permissions for a specific group. For <gid>, you can specify either a group name or a numeric GID.
d[efault]:u[ser]::<perms>	Default file owner permissions.
d[efault]:g[roup]::<perms>	Default file group owner permissions.
d[efault]:o[ther]:<perms>	Default permissions for users other than the file owner or members of the file group.
d[efault]:m[ask]:<perms>	Default ACL mask.
d[efault]:u[ser]:<uid>:<perms>	Default permissions for a specific user. For <uid>, you can specify either a username or a numeric UID.
d[efault]:g[roup]:<gid>:<perms>`	Default permissions for a specific group. For <gid>, you can specify either a group name or a numeric GID.

EXAM ALERT

ACL Entries Make sure you understand the ACL entries and how they work. It is quite common to get a question on the exam that gives you the ACL for a number of users/groups, such as Bill, Emily, and the "Accounts" group, and then asks which permissions does "Bill" have? Additionally, make sure you take into account the ACL mask.

The following example sets the user permissions to read/write, sets the group permissions to read-only, and other permissions to none on the `txt1.doc` file. In addition, the user bill is given read/write permissions on the file, and the ACL mask permissions are set to read/write, which means that no user or group can have execute permissions.

```
$ setfacl -s user::rw-,group::r--,other:---,mask:rw-,user:bill:rw-\txt1.doc
```

In addition to the ACL entries for files, you can set default ACL entries on a directory that apply to files created within the directory. For example, I'll use the `setfacl` command to add execute privileges on the `/export/home/bholzgen` directory for user `bcalkins`. This privilege on a directory allows the user `bcalkins` to change to that directory and do a long listing with the `ls -l` command to display the files in the directory. Before I set the ACL on this directory, let's look at the default permission that currently exists on this directory:

```
drwxr-xr-x   2 bholzgen   staff    512 Jul 30 12:41 bholzgen
```

Now, issue the command to set the default ACL privileges:

```
setfacl -s user::rwx,g::r--,o:---,d:user::rwx,d:group::r--,d:o:---\
,d:m:r-x,d:user:bcalkins:r-x /export/home/bholzgen
```

NOTE

Default ACL Entries When you set default ACL entries for specific users and groups on a directory for the first time, you must also set default ACL entries for the file owner, file group, others, and the ACL mask.

Use the `getfacl` command with the `-d` switch to display the default ACL entries for the `/export/home/bholzgen` directory as follows:

```
getfacl -d /export/home/bholzgen
```

The system responds with the following:

```
# file: /export/home/bholzgen
# owner: bholzgen
# group: staff
```

```
default:user::rwx
default:user:bcalkins:rwx       #effective:rwx
default:group::r--              #effective:r--
default:mask:rwx
default:other:---
```

Now, the only people allowed to change into the `/export/home/bholzgen` directory are `bholzgen` and `bcalkins`. No other members, except root, will be able to access this directory—not even members of the same group.

Checking the New File Permissions

Check the new file permissions with the `ls -l` command. The plus sign (+) to the right of the mode field indicates that the file has an ACL:

```
$ ls -l
 total 210
 -rw-r-----+    1 mike  sysadmin   32100  Sep 11 13:11 txt1.doc
 -rw-r--r--     1 mike  sysadmin   1410   Sep 11 13:11 txt2.doc
 -rw-r--r--     1 mike  sysadmin   1700   Sep 11 13:11 labnotes
```

Verifying ACL Entries

To verify which ACL entries were set on the file, use the `getfacl` command:

```
$ getfacl txt1.doc
```

The system responds with this:

```
# file: txt1.doc
# owner: mike
# group: sysadmin
user::rw-
user:bill:rw-       #effective:rw-
group::r--          #effective:r--
mask:rw-
other:---
```

Copying a File's ACL to Another File

Copy a file's ACL to another file by redirecting the `getfacl` output as follows:

```
getfacl <filename1> ¦ setfacl  -f  -  <filename2>
```

The following example copies the ACL from `file1` to `file2`:

```
getfacl file1 ¦ setfacl -f - file2
```

Issuing the getfacl command, you can verify that the change has been made:

```
getfacl file*

# file: file1
# owner: root
# group: other
user::rw-
user:bcalkins:rw-          #effective:rw-
group::r--                 #effective:r--
mask:rw-
other:---

# file: file2
# owner: root
# group: other
user::rw-
user:bcalkins:rw-                 #effective:rw-
group::r--                 #effective:r--
mask:rw-
other:---
```

Modifying ACL Entries on a File

Modify ACL entries on a file by using the setfacl command:

```
setfacl -m <acl_entry_list> <filename1> [filename2 ...]
```

The arguments for the setfacl command are described in Table 4.24.

TABLE 4.24 setfacl Arguments

Argument	Description
-m	Modifies the existing ACL entry.
<acl_entry_list>	Specifies the list of one or more ACL entries to modify on the file or directory. You can also modify default ACL entries on a directory. (See Table 11.2 for the list of ACL entries.)
<filename>	Specifies the file or directory.

Deleting ACL Entries from a File

To delete an ACL entry from a file, use the setfacl -d *<acl_entry_list>* command. The following example illustrates how to remove an ACL entry for user bcalkins on file1 and file2:

```
setfacl -d u:bcalkins file1 file2
```

Use the getfacl command, described earlier, to verify that the entries have been deleted.

Setting the Correct Path

Setting your path variable (`$PATH`) correctly is important; if you do not set it correctly, you might accidentally run a program introduced by someone else that harms the data or your system. That kind of program, which creates a security hazard, is called a *Trojan horse*. For example, a substitute `su` program could be placed in a public directory where you, as system administrator, might run it. Such a script would look just like the regular `su` command. The script would remove itself after execution, and you would have trouble knowing that you actually ran a Trojan horse.

The path variable is automatically set at login time through the `/etc/default/login` file and the shell initialization files `.login`, `.profile`, and/or `.cshrc`. Setting up the user search path so that the current directory (`.`) comes last prevents you and your users from running a Trojan horse. The path variable for superuser should not include the current directory (`.`).

NOTE

Checking Root's Path Solaris provides a utility called the *Automated Security Enhancement Tool (ASET)* that examines the startup files to ensure that the path variable is set up correctly and does not contain a dot (`.`) entry for the current directory. ASET is discussed later in this chapter.

The `setuid` and `setgid` Programs

When *set-user identification* (`setuid`) permission is set on an executable file, a process that runs the file is granted access based on the file's owner (usually root) rather than on the user who created the process. This enables a user to access files and directories that are normally available only to the owner. For example, the `setuid` permission on the `passwd` command makes it possible for a user to modify the `/etc/passwd` file to change passwords. When a user executes the `passwd` command, that user assumes the privileges of the root ID, which is UID `0`. The `setuid` permission can be identified by using the `ls -l` command. The `s` in the permissions field of the following example indicates the use of `setuid`, and the second `s` indicates the use of `setgid`:

```
ls -l /usr/bin/passwd
  -r-sr-sr-x   1 root     sys    10332 May  3 08:23 /usr/bin/passwd
```

Many executable programs must be run by root (that is, by the superuser) in order to work properly. These executables run with the UID set to `0` (`setuid=0`). Anyone running these programs runs them with the root ID, which creates a potential security problem if the programs are not written with security in mind.

On the other hand, the use of `setuid` on an executable program presents a security risk. A determined user can usually find a way to maintain the permissions granted to him or her by the `setuid` process, even after the process has finished executing. For example, a particular command might grant root privileges through setuid. If a user could break out of this command, he or she could still have the root privileges granted by setuid on that file. An intruder who accesses a system will look for any files that have the setuid bit enabled.

Except for the executables shipped with Solaris that have setuid set to root, you should disallow the use of setuid programs—or at least restrict and keep them to a minimum. A good alternative to using setuid on programs is to use an RBAC account, as described in Chapter 11.

NOTE

Locating setuid Programs To find files that have setuid permissions, you should become superuser. Then you can use the find command to find files that have setuid permissions set, as in this example:

```
# find / -user root -perm -4000 ---ls >/tmp/<filename>
```

The *set-group identification* (setgid) permission is similar to setuid, except that with setgid the process's effective GID is changed to the group owner of the file, and a user is granted access based on permissions granted to that group. By using the ls -l command, you can see that the file /usr/bin/mail has setgid permissions:

```
-r-x--s--x   1 bin   mail   61076 Nov  8 2001  /usr/bin/mail
```

The following example illustrates how to set the UID on an executable file named myprog1:

```
chmod 4711  myprog1
```

You can verify the change by entering this:

```
ls -l myprog1
```

The system responds with this:

```
-rws--x--x   1   root   other   25   Mar   6   11:52   myprog1
```

The following example illustrates how to set the GID on an executable file named myprog1:

```
chmod 2751 myprog1
```

You can verify the change by entering this:

```
ls -l myprog1
```

The system responds with this:

```
-rwxr-s--x   1   root   other   25   Mar   6   11:58   myprog1
```

A user can set the UID or GID permission for any file he or she owns.

Auditing Users

The following sections describe a few of the commands used to view information about users who have logged in to the system.

Monitoring Users and System Usage

As a system administrator, you need to monitor system resources and watch for unusual activity. Having a method to monitor the system is useful, especially when you suspect a breach in security. For example, you might want to monitor the login status of a particular user. In that case, you could use the `logins` command to monitor a particular user's activities, as described in Step by Step 4.6.

STEP BY STEP

4.6 Monitoring a User's Activity

1. Become superuser.
2. Display a user's login status by using the `logins` command:

   ```
   # logins -x -l <username>
   ```

   For example, to monitor login status for the user `calkins`, enter the following:

   ```
   # logins -x -l calkins
   ```

   The system displays the following information:

   ```
   calkins      200     staff          10   Bill S. Calkins
                        /export/home/calkins
                        /bin/sh
                        PS 030195 10 7 -1
   ```

   The following is the information displayed in the output of the `logins` command:

Field	Description
`calkins`	The login name
`200`	The UID
`staff`	The primary group
`10`	The GID
`Bill S. Calkins`	The comment field of the `/etc/passwd` file
`/export/home/calkins`	The user's home directory
`/bin/sh`	The user's default login shell

`PS 030195 10 7 -1`	The password aging information: the last date the password was changed, the number of days required between changes, the number of days allowed before a change is required, and the warning period

You should monitor user logins to ensure that their users' passwords are secure. A potential security problem is for users to use blank passwords (that is, users using carriage returns for passwords) or no password at all. When an account does not have a password, the password prompt will not be presented at login. Simply enter the user name, and you are in. You can periodically check user logins by using the method described in Step by Step 4.7.

STEP BY STEP

4.7 Checking for Users with No Passwords

1. Become superuser.
2. Display users who have no passwords by using the `logins` command:

   ```
   # logins -p
   ```

   The system responds with a list of users who do not have passwords.

Another good idea is to watch anyone who has tried to access the system but failed. You can save failed login attempts by creating the `/var/adm/loginlog` file with read and write permission for root only. After you create the `loginlog` file, all failed login activity is automatically written to this file after five failed attempts. This file does not exist by default; you, as the system administrator, must create it. To enable logging to this file as root, you can create the file as follows:

```
touch /var/adm/loginlog
```

Then set the permission on the file to `600`:

```
chmod 600 /var/adm/loginlog
```

The `loginlog` file contains one entry for each failed attempt. Each entry contains the user's login name, the `tty` device, and the time of the failed attempt. If a person makes fewer than five unsuccessful attempts, none of the attempts is logged.

The following is an example of an entry in which someone tried to log in as root but failed:

```
# more /var/adm/loginlog
root:/dev/pts/5:Wed Apr 11 11:36:40 2002
root:/dev/pts/5:Wed Apr 11 11:36:47 2002
root:/dev/pts/5:Wed Apr 11 11:36:54 2002
root:/dev/pts/5:Wed Apr 11 11:37:02 2002
```

The `loginlog` file might grow quickly. To use the information in this file and to prevent the file from getting too large, you must check it and clear its contents occasionally. If this file shows a lot of activity, someone might be attempting to break in to the computer system.

Checking Who Is Logged In

You use the Solaris `who` command to find out who is logged in to a system. To obtain the information it gives you, the `who` command examines the `/var/adm/utmpx` and `/var/adm/wtmpx` files. The `utmpx` file contains user access and accounting information for the `who` command (as well as for the `write` and `login` commands). The `wtmpx` file contains the history of user access and accounting information for the `utmpx` file.

Without arguments, the `who` command lists the login account name, terminal device, login date and time, and where the user logged in. Here is an example:

```
# who
root        pts/3        May 11 14:47     (10.64.178.2)
root        pts/1        May 10 15:42     (sparc1.PDESIGNINC.COM)
root        pts/2        May 10 15:53     (sparc1.PDESIGNINC.COM)
root        pts/4        May 11 14:48     (pluto)
```

Table 4.25 lists some of the most common options used with the `who` command.

TABLE 4.25 Common Options Used with the who Command

Options	Description
`-a`	Processes `/var/adm/utmpx` or the named file with `-b`, `-d`, `-l`, `-p`, `-r`, `-t`, `-T`, and `-u` options turned on.
`-b`	Indicates the time and date of the last reboot, as shown in the following example: `who -b`
`-m`	Outputs only information about the current terminal. Here's an example: `who -m`
`-n <x>`	Takes a numeric argument, `<x>`, which specifies the number of users to display per line. `<x>` must be at least 1. The `-n` option can be used only with the `-q` option.

`-q`	Displays only the names and the number of users currently logged on. When this option, which stands for *quick who*, is used, all other options are ignored. The following is an example of the `-q` and `-n` options being used together: `who -q -n2`
	The system responds with this:
	`root      bcalkins`
	`sburge      czimmerman`
	`# users=4`

`-r`	Indicates the current run level of the `init` process. Here's an example of the output returned by `who -r`: `.      run-level 3   Oct 18 09:02      3      0  S`
`-s`	Lists only the name, line, and time fields. This is the default when no options are specified.

The `rusers` command is similar to the `who` command, but it can be used to list users logged in on a remote host. To use `rusers`, the `rpc.rusers` daemon must be running. Check whether the `rpc.rusers` daemon is running by typing

```
svcs rusers
```

For more information on the `svcs` command, refer to Chapter 3.

To list users logged into other systems on your network, use the `rusers` command as follows:

```
# rusers -l
Sending broadcast for rusersd protocol version 3...
root          smokey:pts/1                Aug 12 10:07      29 (192.168.1.87)
root          ultra5:pts/1                Aug 12 17:33      (billsgateway.wca)
Sending broadcast for rusersd protocol version 2...
#
```

The `whoami` Command

The command `whoami` displays the effective current username. It is a lot like the `who` command used with the `am` and `i` options. These two options to the `who` command limit the output to describing the invoking user, which is equivalent to the `-m` option. `am` and `i` must be separate arguments.

`whoami` is a carryover from Berkeley Software Distribution (BSD) Unix. This old BSD command is found under the `/usr/ucb` directory with other BSD commands. `/usr/ucb/whoami` displays the login name that corresponds to the current effective UID. If you have used `su` to temporarily change to another user, `/usr/ucb/whoami` reports the login name associated with that user ID. For example, suppose you are logged in as `root` and issue the following `su` command to become `wcalkins`:

```
su - wcalkins
```

Now issue the `who am i` command:

```
who am i
```

The system reports that you are logged in as `root`. The `who am i` command looks up the entry for your current tty in the `utmpx` file:

```
root   pts/7        Oct 18 19:08
```

Next, you can issue the `/usr/ucb/whoami` command:

```
/usr/ucb/whoami
```

The system reports your current effective UID as follows:

```
wcalkins
```

The whodo Command

The whodo command produces formatted and dated output from information in the /var/adm/utmpx, /tmp/ps_data, and /proc/pid files. It displays each user logged in and the active processes owned by that user. The output of the whodo command shows the date, time, and machine name. For each user who is logged in, the system displays the device name, UID, and login time, followed by a list of active processes associated with the UID. The process list includes the device name, process ID, CPU minutes and seconds used, and process name. You issue the whodo command as follows:

```
whodo
```

The system responds with this:

```
Thu May 11 15:16:56 EDT 2001
holl300s

pts/3          root      14:47
    pts/3            505     0:00 sh
    pts/3            536     0:00 whodo

pts/1          root      15:42
    pts/1            366     0:00 sh
    pts/1            514     0:00 rlogin
    pts/1            516     0:00 rlogin

pts/2          root      15:53
    pts/2            378     0:00 sh

pts/4          root      14:48
    pts/4            518     0:00 sh
```

You use the -l option with the whodo command to get a long listing:

```
whodo -l
```

The system responds with this:

```
  1:11pm  up 4 day(s), 18 hr(s), 20 min(s)  3 user(s)
User    tty       login@   idle   JCPU  PCPU  what
root    console   Mon 9am  22:00              /usr/dt/bin/sdt_shell -c    u
root    pts/4     Mon 9am  22:00   4          -ksh
```

The fields displayed are the user's login name; the name of the tty the user is on; the time of day the user logged in; the idle time (which is the time since the user last typed anything in *hours*:*minutes*); the CPU time used by all processes and their children on that terminal (in *minutes*:*seconds*); the CPU time used by the currently active processes (in *minutes*:*seconds*); and the name and arguments of the current process.

The `last` Command

The Solaris `last` command looks in the `/var/adm/wtmpx` file for information about users who have logged in to the system. The `last` command displays the sessions of the specified users and terminals in reverse chronological order, displaying the most recent login first. For each user, `last` displays the time when the session began, the duration of the session, and the terminal where the session took place. The `last` command also indicates whether the session is still active or was terminated by a reboot.

For example, the command `last root console` lists all of root's sessions, as well as all sessions on the console terminal:

```
# last root console ¦more
```

The system responds with this:

```
root    pts/1    10.64.178.2          Tue May 30 11:24   still logged in
root    pts/1    10.64.178.2          Fri May 26 14:26 - 15:47  (01:20)
root    pts/1    10.64.178.2          Fri May 26 11:07 - 13:37  (02:29)
root    pts/1    10.64.178.2          Fri May 26 10:12 - 10:23  (00:11)
root    pts/1    10.64.178.2          Fri May 26 09:40 - 09:42  (00:02)
root    console :0                    Wed May 24 16:36 - 16:38  (00:01)
root    console :0                    Wed May 24 16:20 - 16:36  (00:15)
root    pts/3    10.64.178.2          Wed May 24 13:52 - 14:22 (1+00:30)
root    pts/1    ultra5.PDESIGNINC    Mon May 22 15:14 - 15:15  (00:00)
root    pts/2    sparc21.PDESIGNINC   Wed May 10 15:53 - 15:47  (23:53)
```

Controlling Network Security

Objective:

Control system security through restricting FTP access and using `/etc/hosts.equiv` and `$HOME/.rhosts` files, and SSH fundamentals.

The most difficult system administration issue to address is network security. When you connect your computer to the rest of the world via a network such as the Internet, someone can find an opening and breach your security. The following sections describe a few fundamental recommendations for tightening up a system in a networked environment.

Securing Network Services

Solaris is a powerful operating system that executes many useful services such as FTP and HTTP services. However, some of the services aren't needed and can pose potential security risks, especially for a system that is connected to the Internet. The first place to start tightening up a system is by disabling unneeded network services.

In past releases of Solaris, these services were managed by `inetd`, which obtained its instructions from the `/etc/inetd.conf` file. In Solaris 10, you'll notice that this file is substantially smaller because inetd is now started by the SMF, which is described in Chapter 3. The `inetd` daemon is configured using the `inetadm` command, which is described in Chapter 8.

By default, `inetd` is configured for 40 or more services, but you probably need only some of them. You can list all of the network services and view their state with the `inetadm` command as follows:

```
# inetadm
ENABLED   STATE          FMRI
enabled   online         svc:/network/rpc/gss:default
enabled   online         svc:/network/rpc/mdcomm:default
enabled   online         svc:/network/rpc/meta:default
enabled   online         svc:/network/rpc/metamed:default
enabled   online         svc:/network/rpc/metamh:default
disabled  disabled       svc:/network/rpc/rex:default
enabled   online         svc:/network/rpc/rstat:default
enabled   online         svc:/network/rpc/rusers:default
disabled  disabled       svc:/network/rpc/spray:default
disabled  disabled       svc:/network/rpc/wall:default
 <output is truncated> . . .
```

You can deactivate unnecessary services by disabling them. For example, to disallow Telnet connections to the system, you would disable it as follows:

```
inetadm -d telnet
```

To disable FTP, type

```
inetadm -d ftp
```

You can verify that the FTP service has been disabled by typing

```
inetadm|grep ftp
```

The system responds with

```
disabled  disabled       svc:/network/ftp:default
```

You also can type

```
svcs ftp
```

The system responds with

```
STATE          STIME    FMRI
disabled        9:02:23 svc:/network/ftp:default
```

You can disable `nfs`, `spray`, `rexec`, `finger`, and many other Internet services in a similar manner.

It is critical that you turn off all unneeded network services because many of the services that are run by `inetd`, such as `rexd`, pose serious security vulnerabilities. `rexd` is a daemon that is responsible for remote program execution. On a system that is connected to the rest of the world via the Internet, this could create a potential entry point for a hacker. You should absolutely disable TFTP unless it's required, as with a JumpStart server. TFTP is managed by the SMF, under the service identifier `svc:/network/tftp/udp6:default`. Administrative actions on this service, such as enabling, disabling, or requesting restart, can be performed using `svcadm`. Responsibility for initiating and restarting this service is delegated to `inetd`. Use `inetadm` to make configuration changes and to view configuration information for this service. The service status can be queried using the `svcs` command.

You might also want to disable `finger` so that external users can't figure out the usernames of your internal users—which would make breaking in much easier. Whether you keep the other services much depends on the needs of your site. Disable `finger` as follows:

```
inetadm -d finger
```

Other services that you may want to consider disabling are

- `svc:/network/nfs/client:default`
- `svc:/network/nfs/server:default`
- `svc:/system/filesystem/autofs:default`
- `svc:/network/smtp:sendmail`
- `svc:/network/rpc/rusers:default`
- `lrc:/etc/rc2_d/S99dtlogin`
- `lrc:/etc/rc3_d/S76snmpdx`

The `lrc` services are disabled through their respective run control scripts.

The /etc/default/login File

One way to protect your system from unauthorized access—regardless of whether it's on the Internet or not —is via the `/etc/default/login` file. You need to make sure the following line is not commented:

```
CONSOLE=/dev/console
```

With this entry, root is allowed to log in only from the secure system console and not via the network by using `telnet` or `rlogin`. However, this entry does not disallow a user from using the `su` command to switch to root after logging in as a regular user if he or she knows the root password.

Modems

Modems are always a potential point of entry for intruders. Anyone who discovers the phone number to which a modem is attached can attempt to log in. Low-cost computers can be turned into automatic calling devices that search for modem lines and then try endlessly to guess passwords and break in. If you must use a modem, you should use it for outgoing calls only. An outgoing modem will not answer the phone. If you allow calling in, you should implement a callback system. A callback system guarantees that only authorized phone numbers can connect to the system. Another option is to have two modems that establish a security key between them. This way, only modems with the security key can connect with the system modem and gain access to the computer.

Trusted Hosts

Along with protecting passwords, you need to protect your system from a root user coming in from across the network. For example, say `systemA` is a trusted host from which a user can log in without being required to enter a password. A user who has root access on `systemA` could access the root login on `systemB` simply by logging in across the network, if `systemA` is set up as a trusted host on `systemB`. When `systemB` attempts to authenticate root from `systemA`, it relies on information in its local files—specifically, `/etc/hosts.equiv` and `/.rhosts`. Because of the many risks posed by `rlogin` and other `r` commands, you should not use them. Instead, you should use the Secure Shell (SSH) commands, which are described in the section "The Secure Shell (`ssh`)," later in this chapter.

The `/etc/hosts.equiv` File

The `/etc/hosts.equiv` file contains a list of trusted hosts for a remote system, one per line. An `/etc/hosts.equiv` file has the following structure:

```
system1
system2 user_a
```

If a user attempts to log in remotely by using `rlogin` from one of the hosts listed in this file, and if the remote system can access the user's password entry, the remote system enables the user to log in without a password.

When an entry for a host is made in `/etc/hosts.equiv` (for example, the sample entry for `system1` shown earlier), the host is trusted and so is any user at that machine. If the username is also mentioned, as in the second entry shown in the previous example, the host is trusted only if the specified user is attempting access. A single line of `+` in the `/etc/hosts.equiv` file indicates that any host is trusted.

NOTE

Don't Trust Everyone Using a + in the `hosts.equiv` or `.rhosts` file is very bad practice and could pose a serious security problem because it specifies that *all* systems are trusted. You should get into the habit of listing the trusted systems and not using the + sign. Better yet, you should use a more secure alternative to `rlogin`, such as the Secure Shell (`ssh`).

TIP

Security and the `/etc/hosts.equiv` File The `/etc/hosts.equiv` file presents a security risk. If you maintain an `/etc/hosts.equiv` file on your system, this file should include only trusted hosts in your network. The file should not include any host that belongs to a different network or any machines that are in public areas. Also, you should never put a system name into the `/etc/hosts.equiv` file without a username or several names after it.

The `.rhosts` File

The `.rhosts` file is the user equivalent of the `/etc/hosts.equiv` file. It contains a list of hosts and users. If a host/user combination is listed in this file, the specified user is granted permission to log in remotely from the specified host without having to supply a password. Note that an `.rhosts` file must reside at the top level of a user's home directory because `.rhosts` files located in subdirectories are not consulted. Users can create `.rhosts` files in their home directories; this is another way to allow trusted access between their own accounts on different systems without using the `/etc/hosts.equiv` file.

The `.rhosts` file presents a major security problem. Although the `/etc/hosts.equiv` file is under the system administrator's control and can be managed effectively, any user can create an `.rhosts` file that grants access to whomever the user chooses—without the system administrator's knowledge.

NOTE

Disabling `.rhosts` and `hosts.equiv` Files To disable `.rhosts` and `/etc/hosts.equiv` access altogether while still allowing the `rlogin` protocol, you comment the lines that reference `pam_rhosts_auth.so.1` from `/etc/pam.conf`. This forces `rlogin` to use a password during authentication and effectively disables `in.rshd` and `in.rexecd`.

The only secure way to manage `.rhosts` files is to completely disallow them.

Restricting FTP

File Transfer Protocol (FTP) is a common tool for transferring files across a network. Although most sites leave FTP enabled, you need to limit who can use it. Solaris contains various configuration files in the `/etc/ftpd` directory to control access to the FTP server. One of these files is a file named /etc/ftpd/ftpusers, which is used to restrict access via FTP. The /etc/ftpd/ftpusers file contains a list of login names that are prohibited from running an FTP login on the system. The following is an example of a default /etc/ftpd/ftpusers file:

```
# more /etc/ftpd/ftpusers

# ident "@(#)ftpusers   1.5     04/02/20 SMI"
#
# List of users denied access to the FTP server, see ftpusers(4).
#
root
daemon
bin
sys
adm
lp
uucp
nuucp
smmsp
listen
gdm
webservd
nobody
noaccess
nobody4
```

Names in the /etc/ftpd/ftpusers file must match login names in the /etc/passwd file.

NOTE

Root Access to FTP The default in Solaris 10 is to not allow FTP logins by root. It is dangerous to allow root access via FTP because that would allow anyone who knows the root password to have access to the entire system.

The FTP server in.ftpd reads the /etc/ftpd/ftpusers file each time an FTP session is invoked. If the login name of the user trying to gain access matches a name in the /etc/ftpd/ftpusers file, access is denied.

The /etc/ftpd/ftphosts file is used to allow or deny access to accounts from specified hosts. The following example allows the user ftpadmin to connect via FTP from the explicitly listed addresses 208.164.186.1, 208.164.186.2, and 208.164.186.4; and deny the specified ftpadmin user to connect from the site 208.164.186.5:

```
# Example host access file
#
# Everything after a '#' is treated as comment,
```

```
# empty lines are ignored
allow ftpadmin 208.164.186.1 208.164.186.2 208.164.186.4
deny ftpadmin 208.164.186.5
```

The file `/etc/shells` contains a list of the shells on a system. Whereas the `/etc/ftpd/ftpusers` file contains a list of users not allowed to use FTP, the `/etc/shells` file enables FTP connections only to those users running shells that are defined in this file. If this file exists and an entry for a shell does not exist in this file, any user running the undefined shell is not allowed FTP connections to this system.

The `/etc/shells` file does not exist by default. If the file does not exist, the system default shells are used. The following are the system default shells:

`/bin/bash`	`/bin/tcsh`	`/usr/bin/ksh`
`/bin/csh`	`/bin/zsh`	`/usr/bin/pfcsh`
`/bin/jsh`	`/sbin/jsh`	`/usr/bin/pfksh`
`/bin/ksh`	`/sbin/sh`	`/usr/bin/pfsh`
`/bin/pfcsh`	`/usr/bin/bash`	`/usr/bin/sh`
`/bin/pfksh`	`/usr/bin/csh`	`/usr/bin/tcsh`
`/bin/pfsh`	`/usr/bin/jsh`	`/usr/bin/zsh`
`/bin/sh`		

You can create the `/etc/shells` file by using the `vi` editor and listing each shell that you want to be recognized by the system. The following is an example `/etc/shells` file:

```
# more /etc/shells
        /sbin/sh
        /bin/sh
        /bin/ksh
```

NOTE

`/etc/shells` May Deny Access If you don't list all the default shells in the `/etc/shells` file, as done in the previous example, users using those shells are not allowed access.

Securing Superuser Access

The Unix superuser (root) is immune from restrictions placed on other users of the system. Any Unix account with a UID of `0` is the superuser. All Unix systems have a default superuser login named root. The user of this account can access any file and run any command. This login is valuable because any user who might have gotten himself or herself into trouble by removing access permissions, forgetting his or her password, or simply needing a file from an area to which he or she doesn't have access can be helped by root.

However, root access can be dangerous. Root can delete anything, including the operating system. The root login is both dangerous and necessary. System administrators must not give the root password to anyone and should use it themselves only when required. If it becomes necessary to grant superuser privileges to non-root users, you should utilize `roles`, as described in Chapter 11.

Restricting Root Access

Root access needs to be safeguarded against unauthorized use. You should assume that any intruder is looking for root access. You can protect the superuser account on a system by restricting access to a specific device through the `/etc/default/login` file. For example, if superuser access is restricted to the console, the superuser can log in only at the console, which should be in a locked room. Anybody who remotely logs in to the system to perform an administrative function must first log in with his or her login and then use the `su` command to become superuser.

Step by Step 4.8 describes the procedure for restricting root from logging in to the system console from a remote system.

STEP BY STEP

4.8 Restricting Root Access

1. Become superuser.
2. Edit the `/etc/default/login` file and uncomment the following line:

   ```
   CONSOLE=/dev/console
   ```

In Step by Step 4.8, you set the variable `CONSOLE` to `/dev/console`. If the variable `CONSOLE` were set as follows with no value defined, root could not log in from anywhere, not even from the console:

```
CONSOLE=
```

With the `CONSOLE` value set to nothing, the only way to get into the system as root is to first log in as a regular user and then become root by issuing the `su` command. If the system console is not in a controlled environment, the option of not being able to log in to the console as root might be useful.

Monitoring Superuser Access

Solaris can be set up to log all attempts to become superuser. The logs that contain this information are useful when you're trying to track down unauthorized activity. Whenever someone issues the `su` command to switch from being a user to being root, this activity is logged in the file `/var/adm/sulog`. The `sulog` file lists all uses of the `su` command—not only those used to switch from being a user to being superuser. The entries in the `sulog` file show the date and time the command was entered, whether the command was successful, the port from which the command was issued, and the name of the user and the switched identity.

To monitor who is using the `su` command, the `sulog` logging utility must be turned on in the `/etc/default/su` file. By default, `su` logging is enabled. Step by Step 4.9 describes how to turn on logging of the `su` command if it has been disabled.

STEP BY STEP

4.9 Monitoring Superuser Access

1. Become superuser.
2. Edit the `/etc/default/su` file and uncomment the following line:

   ```
   SULOG=/var/adm/sulog
   ```

Through the `/etc/default/su` file, you can also set up the system to display a message on the console each time an attempt is made to use the `su` command to gain superuser access from a remote system. This is a good way to immediately detect when someone is trying to gain superuser access to the system on which you are working. Step by Step 4.10 describes how to display root access attempts to the console.

STEP BY STEP

4.10 Monitoring Superuser Access Attempts

1. Become superuser.
2. Edit the `/etc/default/su` file and uncomment the following line:

   ```
   CONSOLE=/dev/console
   ```

3. Use the `su` command to become root. Verify that a message is printed on the system console.

The Secure Shell (ssh)

The Secure Shell (ssh) enables users to securely access a remote system over an insecure network. You use the Secure Shell to do the following:

- Log in to a remote system (by using ssh).
- Copy files over the network between hosts (by using scp or sftp).

Before the Secure Shell was available, remote connections were—and still can be—handled via rlogin, rsh, and rcp. These commands create insecure connections and are prone to security risks.

With the Secure Shell, you establish secure communication between two hosts on an insecure network. The two hosts are referred to as the *client* (the host that requests the connection) and the *server* (the host being connected to). The Secure Shell daemon, sshd, starts up on each host at system boot, when the svc:/network/ssh:default service has been enabled by the SMF. The sshd daemon listens for connections, and it handles the encrypted authentication exchange between the hosts. When authentication is complete, the user can execute commands and copy files remotely.

The ssh on the client side is controlled by the /etc/ssh/ssh_config file and by ssh command line options. The ssh_config file controls which types of authentication are permitted for accessing the server. Optionally, a user can also provide ssh settings in his or her own $HOME/.ssh/config file.

The sshd on the server side is controlled by the /etc/ssh/sshd_config file, which is controlled by the system administrator.

Normally, each user wanting to use SSH with authentication runs the ssh-keygen command once to create the authentication key in $HOME/.ssh/identity, $HOME/.ssh/id_dsa, or $HOME/.ssh/id_rsa. The client maintains the private key, and the server is provided with the public key that is needed to complete authentication. Public-key authentication is a stronger type of authentication than typical password authentication because the private key never travels over the network. To create a public/private key for public key authentication, follow Step by Step 4.11.

STEP BY STEP

4.11 Setting Up Public Key Authentication for Solaris Secure Shell

In the following step by step, you'll set up Public Key Authentication so that bcalkins can log in to a remote host using ssh. For this step by step, you'll need two systems. One will be the client, and the other will be the remote host.

1. Make sure both systems have a user account named `bcalkins`, a password assigned to the account, and an established home directory named `/export/home/bcalkins`.
2. Make sure each account has a `.ssh` directory in the `/export/home/bcalkins` home directory. If not, you can create the `.ssh` directory by running the `ssh-keygen` command described in step 7.
3. As root, enable host-based authentication on the client by adding the following line to the `/etc/ssh/ssh_config` file:

```
HostbasedAuthentication yes
```

4. On the remote host, enable host based authentication by adding the following line to the `/etc/ssh/sshd_config` file:

```
HostbasedAuthentication yes
```

5. Start up `sshd` on the remote host if it is not currently running by typing

```
svcadm svc:/network/ssh:default
```

   If the `ssh` service is already running, restart it.

6. On the remote host, ensure that the `sshd` daemon can access the list of trusted hosts by setting `IgnoreRhosts` to no in the `/etc/ssh/sshd_config` file as follows

```
IgnoreRhosts no
```

7. On the client, log in as `bcalkins` and create the client's public key. To generate the public key on the client, issue the following command:

```
ssh-keygen -t rsa
```

   Use the `-t` option to specify the type of algorithm; `rsa`, `dsa`, or `rsa1`. The system responds with

```
Generating public/private rsa key pair.
Enter file in which to save the key (//.ssh/id_rsa):
```

   When you press Enter, the system responds with

```
Created directory '/export/home/bcalkins/.ssh'.
Enter passphrase(empty for no passphrase):
```

   The `passphrase` is used for encrypting the private key. A good `passphrase` is 10–30 characters long, mixes alphabetic and numeric characters, and avoids simple English prose and English names. A carriage return entry means that no `passphrase` is used; this type of blank `passphrase` is strongly discouraged for user accounts. The `passphrase` is not displayed when you type it in, as shown here:

```
Enter same passphrase again:
```

   Enter the `passphrase` again to confirm it. The system responds with

```
Your identification has been saved in /export/home/bcalkins/.ssh/id_rsa.
Your public key has been saved in /export/home/bcalkins/.ssh/id_rsa.pub.
```

```
The key fingerprint is:
c9:8e:d8:f9:69:6e:01:e7:c4:82:05:8a:8e:d3:03:56 root@ultra5
```

8. The key fingerprint is displayed as a colon-separated series of two-digit hexadecimal values. You should check to make sure the path to the key is correct. In this example, the path is `/export/home/bcalkins/.ssh/id_rsa.pub`. At this point, you have created a public/private key pair. Now, copy the public key and append the key to the `$HOME/.ssh/authorized_keys` file in your home directory on the remote host.

9. When the public key has been created on the client and copied to the remote host, you can start using the Secure Shell to log in to the remote system by typing this line, where *<hostname>* is the name of the remote host that you want to connect to:

   ```
   ssh <hostname>
   ```

   The first time you run `ssh`:

   ```
   ssh 192.168.0.252
   ```

   you're prompted with questions regarding the authenticity of the remote host as follows:

   ```
   The authenticity of host '192.168.0.252' can't be established.
    RSA key fingerprint in md5 is: \
   78:28:11:cb:41:81:a2:73:50:5a:d4:49:bb:12:85:03
    Are you sure you want to continue connecting(yes/no)? yes
   ```

   This is a normal message for initial connections to the remote host. If you enter `yes`, the system responds with

   ```
   Warning: \
   Permanently added '192.168.0.252' (RSA) to the list of known hosts.
   Enter passphrase for key '/export/home/bcalkins/.ssh/id_rsa':
   ```

   After you enter your `passphrase`, the system will log you into the remote host.

   ```
   Last login: Wed Oct 19 20:43:57 2005 from ultra5
   Sun Microsystems Inc.   SunOS 5.10      Generic January 2005
   ```

To copy files by using the Secure Shell, you start the secure copy program by typing the `scp` command, using the following syntax:

```
scp <sourcefile> <username>@<hostname>:</destinationdir>
```

Table 4.26 describes the arguments to the `scp` command.

TABLE 4.26 scp Command Arguments

Argument	Description
<sourcefile>	The name of the local file that you want to copy
<username>	The username on the remote host to which you want to connect
<hostname>	The name of the remote system to which the file will be copied
<destinationdir>	The name of the directory on the remote host to which you will copy the file

You should type the secure `passphrase` when prompted. The system responds by displaying the following:

- The filename
- The percentage of the file transferred as it is being copied
- The quantity of data transferred as it is being transferred
- The estimated time of arrival when the entire file will be copied to the remote directory

This example copies the file named `file1` to the home directory of `bcalkins` on the remote host:

```
scp file1 bcalkins@192.168.0.252:~
```

The system responds with this:

```
Password:
```

If you enter the user login password, you are then logged in to the remote host:

```
file1   100%   |*************************************|  12540   0:00
```

For more information on using the Secure Shell, refer to the `ssh` and `sshd` man pages.

ASET

The Solaris 10 system software includes ASET (Automated Security Enhancement Tool), which helps you monitor and control system security by automatically performing tasks that you would otherwise do manually. ASET performs the following seven tasks, each of which makes specific checks and adjustments to system files and permissions to ensure system security:

- Verifies appropriate system file permissions
- Verifies system file contents

- Checks the consistency and integrity of /etc/passwd and /etc/group file entries
- Checks the contents of system configuration files
- Checks environment files (.profile, .login, and .cshrc)
- Verifies appropriate electrically erasable programmable read-only memory (EEPROM) settings
- Ensures that the system can be safely used as a network relay

The ASET security package provides automated administration tools that let you control and monitor a system's security. You specify a low, medium, or high security level at which ASET runs. At each higher level, ASET's file-control functions increase to reduce file access and tighten system security.

ASET tasks are disk intensive and can interfere with regular activities. To minimize their impact on system performance, you should schedule ASET to run when the system activity level is lowest—for example, once every 24 or 48 hours, at midnight.

The syntax for the aset command is as follows:

```
/usr/aset/aset -l <level> -d <pathname>
```

Options to the aset command are described in Table 4.27.

TABLE 4.27 aset Command Options

Option	Description
<level>	Specifies the level of security. Valid values are low, medium, and high: **low**—This level ensures that attributes of system files are set to standard release values. At this level, ASET performs several checks and reports potential security weaknesses. At this level, ASET takes no action and does not affect system services. **medium**—This level provides adequate security control for most environments. At this level, ASET modifies some of the settings of system files and parameters, restricting system access to reduce the risks from security attacks. ASET reports security weaknesses and any modifications that it makes to restrict access. At this level, ASET does not affect system services. **high**—This level renders a highly secure system. At this level, ASET adjusts many system files and parameter settings to minimum access permissions. Most system applications and commands continue to function normally, but at this level, security considerations take precedence over other system behavior.
<pathname>	Specifies the working directory for ASET. The default is /usr/aset.

The following example runs ASET at low security, using the default working directory /usr/aset:

```
# /usr/aset/aset -l low
======= ASET Execution Log =======
ASET running at security level low
Machine = holl300s; Current time = 0530_14:03
aset: Using /usr/aset as working directory
Executing task list ...
        firewall
        env
        sysconf
        usrgrp
        tune
        cklist
        eeprom
All tasks executed. Some background tasks may still be running.
Run /usr/aset/util/taskstat to check their status:
     /usr/aset/util/taskstat     [aset_dir]
where aset_dir is ASET's operating directory,currently=/usr/aset.
When the tasks complete, the reports can be found in:
     /usr/aset/reports/latest/*.rpt
You can view them by:
     more /usr/aset/reports/latest/*.rpt
#
```

Common-Sense Security Techniques

A system administrator can have the best system security measures in place, but without the users' cooperation, system security may be compromised. The system administrator must teach common-sense rules regarding system security, such as the following:

- Use proper passwords. Countless sites use weak passwords such as `admin` or `supervisor` for their root accounts.
- Don't give your password to anyone, no matter who the person says he or she is. One of the best system crackers of our time said that he would simply pose as a system support person, ask a user for a password, and get free reign with the system.
- Only give out a password to a known, trusted person. Users should know that no one would ever email or call asking for the password.
- If you walk away from a system, log out or lock the screen.
- Don't connect modems to the system without approval from the system administrator.

Summary

This chapter describes how to add, modify, and remove user accounts using both the SMC and the command line. The GUI of the SMC makes managing user accounts much easier than using the command-line method.

This chapter also describes the user shell initialization files. It describes how to use these files to customize the user work environment. In addition, this chapter describes many of the default shell environment variables that control the user shell environment.

This chapter also discusses fundamental concepts in system security. When you're considering security, you need to begin by securing the hardware in a safe location. Remember that anyone who has physical access to a computer can access the operating system and data, regardless of how secure you've made everything else.

Keep your data secure by controlling the user logins on the system. You should make sure that users have secure passwords and are not making their logins and passwords public. You should implement password aging and restricted shells where they make sense.

You should set up file and directory permissions to ensure that users have access to only the data that they are authorized to see. You should utilize secure `umask` values and, if necessary, ACLs. You should monitor all user activities by using the Solaris utilities described in this chapter. Finally, you should not set `setuid` and `setgid` permissions unless absolutely necessary.

If your system is on a network, you should implement the network security measures that are described in this chapter. You should turn off unneeded services, using the "deny first, then allow" rule. In other words, you should turn off as many services and applications as possible, and then you should selectively turn on those that are essential. You should utilize trusted systems carefully. Also, you should keep your operating system security patches up-to-date. As new threats are discovered, you should quickly fix them by installing security patches as they become available. Chapter 2, "Installing the Solaris 10 Operating Environment," describes the process of obtaining and loading system patches.

In this chapter you have learned about securing the superuser password. You need to keep it under tight control and make sure that it is never made available to anyone except those who are authorized. You should limit using the superuser login unless the task to be performed requires root privileges. Chapter 11 describes RBAC, which is a great alternative to giving out the root password to system operators and junior-level administrators.

Key Terms

- ACL
- ASET
- Default shell
- Effective GID
- File access permissions
- GID
- Group
- High ASET security
- Home directory
- Login shell
- Low ASET security
- Medium ASET security
- Network service
- Password aging
- Password encryption
- Primary group
- Restricted shell
- Secondary group
- Secure Shell
- Set-user identification permission
- Set-group identification permission
- Shell variable
- Sticky bit
- Trusted host
- UID
- User initialization file
- User mask

Exercises

4.1 Managing User Accounts

In this exercise, you use the SMC to add new users to your system, lock user accounts, and set up password aging.

Estimated time: 20 minutes

1. After the SMC GUI appears, use the SMC to add the following list of users:

Login*	Password	UID	Pri GID	Secondary GID
`user3`	`trng`	1003	10	14
`user4`	`trng`	1004	10	14
`user5`	`trng`	1005	10	
`locked1`	(lock accnt)	1006	10	
`nopass1`	(no password)	1008	10	

2. Log out.
3. Try logging in as the user `locked1`.

4.2 User Initialization Files

In this exercise, you work with user initialization files.

Estimated time: 20 minutes

1. Use the `vi` editor to edit the `/etc/skel/local.profile` file by adding the following entries and setting the following variables:

   ```
   EDITOR=/usr/bin/vi; export EDITOR
   PATH=$PATH:/usr/lib/lp; export EDITOR
   ```

2. Use the SMC to create a new user called `user9` that uses the Korn shell. Log in as `user9` and verify that all the variables you set in `/etc/skel/local.profile` are set correctly in the user's environment by typing the following:

   ```
   env
   ```

3. Create a `.profile` file for `user9` that includes two aliases and sets the primary prompt to display the current working directory. Use the `vi` editor to add the following three lines to the `.profile` file that is located in `user9`'s home directory:

   ```
   alias del='rm -i'
   alias hi='echo hello'
   PS1=\$PWD' $'
   ```

4. Log out and log back in as the same user to verify that the `.profile` file works. Do you have a new shell prompt?
5. Verify that your new aliases are defined by typing the following:

   ```
   alias
   ```

6. Log out and log back in again as root.
7. Use `useradd` to create a new user named `user10`, specify the Korn shell as the default shell, and assign the password `trng`:

   ```
   # useradd -u 1010 -g 10 -d /export/home/user10 -m \
   -s /bin/ksh -c "Solaris Student" user10
   # passwd user10
    New Passwd:
    Re-enter new passwd:
   ```

8. Log out and log back in as `user10`. Record the list of initialization files in your home directory by issuing the `ls -la` command. Which of these files is the same as `/etc/skel/local.profile`?

9. Copy `/etc/skel/local.profile` to `.profile`.
10. Log out and log back in as `user10`. Verify that the variables set in the `.profile` file for `user9` are also set in `user10`'s login (`PATH` and `EDITOR`). Are they correct?

4.3 Monitoring Users

In this exercise, you use the various utilities to monitor users who are accessing your system.

Estimated time: 5 minutes

1. Log in as root.
2. Create a file called `loginlog` in the `/var/adm` directory and set the file permission to 600:

```
cd /var/adm
touch loginlog
chmod 600 loginlog
```

3. Log out and log back in. Do not log in using the CDE; log in using the command line.
4. Enter `root` after the login prompt and supply an incorrect password. Do this five times. After the fifth attempt, log in as root using the correct password and examine the `/var/adm/loginlog` file:

```
more /var/adm/loginlog
```

5. Use the `finger` command to display information about the user named `user9`:

```
finger user9
finger -m user9
```

6. User the `finger` command to display information about a user on another system:

```
finger user9@<hostname>
finger -m user9@<hostname>
```

7. Use the `last` command to display user and reboot activity.
8. Use the `logins` command to obtain information about the `user9` login account:

```
logins -x -l user9
```

4.4 File Access

In this exercise, you use Unix permissions to control file access by allowing/disallowing access to files and directories.

Estimated time: 20 minutes

1. Log in as user9.
2. Enter the umask command to determine your current umask value:

```
umask
```

   If the umask is not 002, change it by entering the following:

```
umask 002
```

3. Create a file called file1 in your home directory:

```
cd $HOME
touch file1
```

4. Enter ls -l to see the default permission that was assigned to the file1 file.
5. Set your umask to 022:

```
umask 022
```

6. Create a file named file2 and look at the default permission value:

```
touch file2
ls -l
```

7. Create a new user called newuser:

```
useradd -u 3001 -g 10 -d /export/home/user20 -m \
-s /bin/ksh -c "Temporary User" user20
```

8. Set the password for user20:

```
passwd user20
```

9. Log out and log back in as user9. You are placed in your home directory, /export/home/user9.
10. Create a new file named file10 and list the permissions:

```
touch file10
ls -l
```

11. Use chmod to set the UID permissions on file10 and list the permissions:

```
chmod 4555 file10
ls -l
```

12. Use chmod to set the UID and GID permissions on file10, and then display the permissions:

```
chmod 6555 file10
ls -l
```

   What changes?

13. Use chmod to remove all execute permissions from file10, and then display the new permissions:

```
chmod 6444 file10
ls -l
```

14. List the directory permissions on /tmp:

```
ls -ld /tmp
```

Note that the sticky bit is set on /tmp.

15. As user9, change to the /tmp directory and create a file called file1:

```
cd /tmp
touch file1
ls -l
```

Note the permissions on the file. They should be 644 (rw-r---r--).

16. Become user20, and in the /tmp directory, remove the file named file1:

```
su user20
cd /tmp
rm file1
```

What message do you receive?

17. Exit the current shell to return to being user9. Change to the user9 home directory and set the ACL on file10 so that user20 has read and write permissions on the file:

```
exit
cd $HOME
setfacl -m user:user20:6 file10
```

18. List the file permissions on file10 by issuing ls -l. Note the +, which indicates that an ACL is set on the file.

19. List the ACL entry on file10 as follows:

```
getfacl file10
```

20. Remove the ACL from file10 as follows:

```
setfacl -d u:user20 file10
```

4.5 Restricting Root Access

In this exercise, you make changes to the system to restrict root logins.

Estimated time: 10 minutes

1. Try to log in to your system as root from a remote system. If the `/etc/default/login` file has not been modified from its default settings, you should not be able to log in.
2. Log in to your system from the console as root.
3. Use `vi` to edit the file `/etc/default/login`, adding a pound sign (#) at the beginning of the following line:

   ```
   #CONSOLE=/dev/console
   ```

4. Try to log in to your system as root from a remote system. Does it work?
5. Now try to open an FTP connection from a remote system:

   ```
   ftp <hostname>
   ```

6. When you are prompted with a login name, try to get in as root. If the `/etc/ftpusers` file has not been modified from its default settings, you get a `Login Incorrect` message and are not able to log in.
7. Remove root from the `/etc/ftpusers` files. Does the FTP session work now?
8. Disallow all FTP connections using the `inetadm` command as follows:

   ```
   inetadm -d ftp
   ```

9. Try to connect from a remote system via FTP.

Exam Questions

1. What is the maximum length of a username?

   ❍ **A.** Eight characters

   ❍ **B.** Six characters

   ❍ **C.** Seven characters

   ❍ **D.** Unlimited

2. UID `0` is typically which of the following?

   ❍ **A.** root

   ❍ **B.** A daemon

   ❍ **C.** `adm`

   ❍ **D.** `lpr`

3. How many groups can a user belong to?

   ❍ **A.** 1

   ❍ **B.** 32

   ❍ **C.** Unlimited

   ❍ **D.** 16

4. When you add a new user account via the Add User Wizard, which of the following options are not available for setting the password? (Select the two best answers.)

   ❍ **A.** The password is cleared until first login.

   ❍ **B.** The account is locked.

   ❍ **C.** No password is assigned.

   ❍ **D.** Have the system generate a password.

5. What is the best way to delete a login but retain the user's files?

   ❍ **A.** Delete the login but deselect the Delete Home Directory check box.

   ❍ **B.** Change the password on the login.

   ❍ **C.** Change the UID of the login.

   ❍ **D.** Delete the login, but don't delete files by using the `rm` command.

6. Which of the following is not a default user initialization file?

   ❍ **A.** `.cshrc`

   ❍ **B.** `.login`

   ❍ **C.** `.profile`

   ❍ **D.** `.exrc`

7. Which directory contains the Solaris default initialization files?

   ❍ **A.** `/etc/default`

   ❍ **B.** `/etc/skel`

   ❍ **C.** `/etc/dfs`

   ❍ **D.** `/home`

8. What is the proper syntax to set the default path in the Korn shell?

- ❍ **A.** `PATH=</dirname1>:</dirname2>:</dirname3>:.; export PATH`
- ❍ **B.** `setenv path =(</dirname1> </dirname2> /dirname3> .)`
- ❍ **C.** `set path =(</dirname1> </dirname2> </dirname3> .)`
- ❍ **D.** `setenv PATH </dirname1>:</dirname2>:</dirname3>`

9. What is the proper syntax to set the default path in the C shell?

- ❍ **A.** `set path = (</dirname1> </dirname2> </dirname3> .)`
- ❍ **B.** `PATH=</dirname1:/dirname2>:</dirname3>:.; export PATH`
- ❍ **C.** `setenv path =(</dirname1> </dirname2> </dirname3> .)`
- ❍ **D.** `set path=</dirname1> </dirname2> </dirname3> .`

10. Which of the following files contains encrypted password information?

- ❍ **A.** `/etc/shadow`
- ❍ **B.** `/etc/passwd`
- ❍ **C.** `/etc/default/password`
- ❍ **D.** `/etc/password`

11. What is the sitewide initialization file for the Korn shell called?

- ❍ **A.** `/etc/profile`
- ❍ **B.** `$HOME/.profile`
- ❍ **C.** `/etc/.profile`
- ❍ **D.** `/etc/skel/local.profile`

12. What is the sitewide initialization file for the C shell called?

- ❍ **A.** `/etc/.login`
- ❍ **B.** `/etc/login`
- ❍ **C.** `$HOME/.login`
- ❍ **D.** `/etc/skel/local.login`

13. What is the maximum UID number in Solaris 10?

- ❍ **A.** `2,147,483,647`
- ❍ **B.** `60,000`
- ❍ **C.** `120,000`
- ❍ **D.** Unlimited

14. What can you do if `CONSOLE=` is included in the `/etc/default/login` file?

- ❍ **A.** Log in as root from the network and console.
- ❍ **B.** Log in as a regular user and then use `su` to become root.
- ❍ **C.** Log in as root from the console but not from the network.
- ❍ **D.** Log in as root from the network but not from the console.

15. Which of the following are functions of the `/etc/group` file? (Select the two best answers.)

- ❍ **A.** Assigns users to secondary groups
- ❍ **B.** Assigns a name to a group ID number
- ❍ **C.** Provides a special group for `su` privileges
- ❍ **D.** Specifies which users can access network resources, such as printers

16. You are a system administrator and suspect that one of your users has repeatedly tried to use `su` to gain root privileges. Which of the following files would you look at to see if your suspicion is correct?

- ❍ **A.** `/usr/adm/syslog`
- ❍ **B.** `/usr/adm/lastlog`
- ❍ **C.** `/usr/adm/utmpx`
- ❍ **D.** `/var/adm/sulog`

17. What effect does the sticky bit have if it is set on the `/tmp` directory as `drwxrwxrwt 2 sys sys 512 May 26 11:02 /tmp`?

- ❍ **A.** It permits superuser access only.
- ❍ **B.** It prohibits all read-write permissions.
- ❍ **C.** It allows only the owner to remove and rename his or her files.
- ❍ **D.** It is a security risk because any user can delete another user's files.

18. Which of the following files controls the default policy on password aging?

- ❍ **A.** `/etc/default/login`
- ❍ **B.** `/etc/default/passwd`
- ❍ **C.** `/etc/shadow`
- ❍ **D.** `/etc/passwd`

19. Which of the following do not make secure passwords?

- ❍ **A.** Phrases
- ❍ **B.** Nonsense words
- ❍ **C.** Words with numbers or symbols
- ❍ **D.** Employee numbers

20. Which of the following makes a secure password?

- ❍ **A.** A combination of six or more letters
- ❍ **B.** Your name forward, backward, or jumbled
- ❍ **C.** Keyboard patterns (such as `asdfgh`)
- ❍ **D.** Any word in the dictionary

21. Password aging and encryption are stored in which of the following files?

- ❍ **A.** `/etc/passwd`
- ❍ **B.** `/etc/shadow`
- ❍ **C.** `/etc/default/passwd`
- ❍ **D.** `/etc/default/login`

22. On file permissions, what does the w in the example `-rwxr-xr-x` mean?

- ❍ **A.** Write privileges for the owner
- ❍ **B.** Write privileges for the owner and group
- ❍ **C.** Write privileges for everyone
- ❍ **D.** Write privileges for root only

23. What command is used to change read, write, and execute permissions on a file?

❍ **A.** `chgrp`

❍ **B.** `chown`

❍ **C.** `chmod`

❍ **D.** `passwd`

24. When a user creates a file or directory, which of the following controls the default file permissions assigned to the file or directory?

❍ **A.** `chmod`

❍ **B.** Permissions assigned

❍ **C.** `umask`

❍ **D.** `chown`

25. To what does a `umask` value of `022` set the default permissions on a directory?

❍ **A.** `644`

❍ **B.** `755`

❍ **C.** `022`

❍ **D.** `533`

26. To what does a `umask` value of `022` set the default permissions on a file?

❍ **A.** `644`

❍ **B.** `755`

❍ **C.** `022`

❍ **D.** `533`

27. What do the permissions `dr-xr--r--` on a directory mean?

❍ **A.** Only the owner and group member can list files in this directory.

❍ **B.** Only the owner can open files in this directory.

❍ **C.** Neither read, write, nor execute privileges have been assigned.

❍ **D.** Only the owner can remove files in this directory.

28. What is the difference between `chmod` and `umask`?

- ❍ **A.** A `chmod` value can be set by individual users, whereas `umask` operates on the system level.
- ❍ **B.** `chmod` uses the sticky bit, and `umask` doesn't.
- ❍ **C.** `umask` permissions are stored in a directory rather than in files.
- ❍ **D.** `umask` changes the default permissions for every file and directory created in the future, whereas `chmod` works on a specific directory or file that already exists.

29. What does a restricted shell not allow the user to do?

- ❍ **A.** Change directories.
- ❍ **B.** Redirect output.
- ❍ **C.** Remove files.
- ❍ **D.** Execute scripts.

30. To what can `rsh` refer?

- ❍ **A.** The default system shell or the remote shell command
- ❍ **B.** A combination of the Bourne and C shell or a restricted shell
- ❍ **C.** The variable used to limit the number of login attempts or a restricted shell
- ❍ **D.** A restricted shell or the remote shell command

31. Which of the following commands displays users who don't have passwords?

- ❍ **A.** Use `more /etc/passwd`
- ❍ **B.** `logins -p`
- ❍ **C.** `passwd`
- ❍ **D.** `attributes`

32. Which of the following files contains a list of trusted hosts for a remote system?

- ❍ **A.** `/.rhosts`
- ❍ **B.** `/etc/hosts.equiv`
- ❍ **C.** `/etc/default/login`
- ❍ **D.** `/etc/hosts`

33. Which of the following files gives a specified user permission to log in remotely from the specified host without having to supply a password?

❍ **A.** `.rhosts`

❍ **B.** `/etc/hosts.equiv`

❍ **C.** `/etc/default/login`

❍ **D.** `/etc/hosts`

34. You can protect the superuser account on a system by restricting access to a specific device through what file?

❍ **A.** `/etc/hosts.equiv`

❍ **B.** `/etc/default/login`

❍ **C.** `/etc/default/passwd`

❍ **D.** `/etc/default/su`

35. Which of the following files lists all uses of the `su` command?

❍ **A.** `/var/adm/wtmpx`

❍ **B.** `/var/adm/messages`

❍ **C.** `/var/adm/lastlog`

❍ **D.** `/var/adm/sulog`

36. Which of the following makes specific checks and adjustments to system files and permissions to ensure system security?

❍ **A.** `chmod`

❍ **B.** `aset`

❍ **C.** An ACL

❍ **D.** The proper entry in the `/etc/default/login` file

37. Shell scripts that run `setuid` or `setgid` can be sufficiently secure.

❍ **A.** True

❍ **B.** False

38. Which of the following commands is used to set ACL entries on a file?

- ❍ **A.** `setfacl`
- ❍ **B.** `chmod`
- ❍ **C.** `chown`
- ❍ **D.** `getfacl`

39. What does the plus sign (+) to the right of the permission mode field indicate (`-rw-r-----+`)?

- ❍ **A.** The file has an ACL.
- ❍ **B.** The sticky bit is set.
- ❍ **C.** `setuid` permission has been set on the file.
- ❍ **D.** It sets group ID on execution.

40. Which of the following commands is used to delete an ACL?

- ❍ **A.** `setfacl -d` *<acl-entry-list>*
- ❍ **B.** `delfacl`
- ❍ **C.** `chown -acl`
- ❍ **D.** `setfacl -m`

41. Which of the following commands displays each user logged in and the active processes owned by each user?

- ❍ **A.** `whodo`
- ❍ **B.** `who`
- ❍ **C.** `w`
- ❍ **D.** `who -u`

42. Which of the following commands displays the time and date of the last reboot?

- ❍ **A.** `who -b`
- ❍ **B.** `who -i`
- ❍ **C.** `uptime`
- ❍ **D.** `uname`

Answers to Exam Questions

1. **B.** A user login name can contain two to eight uppercase characters (A–Z) or lowercase characters (a–z) or digits (0–9), but no underscores or spaces. The first character must be a letter, and at least one character must be a lowercase letter. For more information, see the section "Adding User Accounts with the SMC."

2. **A.** The UID for the root login is always `0`. For more information, see the section "Securing Superuser Access."

3. **D.** A user can belong to as many as 15 secondary groups. Added to the primary group, a user can belong to 16 total groups. For more information, see the section "Where User Account Information Is Stored."

4. **A, B, D.** The password is cleared until first login is no longer an option in Solaris 10. You cannot lock an account via the Add User Wizard in the SMC. The SMC cannot automatically generate a password for a user account. For more information, see the section "Adding User Accounts with the SMC."

5. **A.** When you delete a user account in the SMC, you deselect the Delete Home Directory check box to retain all the user's files. For more information, see the section "Deleting User Accounts with the SMC."

6. **D.** The following are default user initialization files that are put into a user's home directory when the user's account is created: `.cshrc`, `.login`, and `.profile`. For more information, see the section "Customizing User Initialization Files."

7. **B.** The `/etc/skel` directory contains the Solaris default initialization files. For more information, see the section "Customizing User Initialization Files."

8. **A.** To set the default path in the Korn shell, you issue the following command: `PATH=</dirname1>:</dirname2>:</dirname3>:.; export PATH`. For more information, see the section "Setting Up Shell Initialization Files."

9. **A.** To set the default path in the C shell, you issue the following command: `set path = (</dirname1> </dirname2> </dirname3>.)` For more information, see the section "Setting Up Shell Initialization Files."

10. **A.** The `/etc/shadow` file contains the encrypted password information for each user account. For more information, see the section "Where User Account Information Is Stored."

11. **A.** The sitewide initialization file for the Korn shell is `/etc/profile`. For more information, see the section "Setting Up Shell Initialization Files."

12. **A.** The sitewide initialization file for the C shell is `/etc/.login`. For more information, see the section "Setting Up Shell Initialization Files."

13. **A.** UID numbers for regular users should range from `100` to `60,000`, but they can be as high as `2,147,483,647`. For more information, see the section "Adding User Accounts with the SMC."

14. **B.** In the /etc/default/login file, with no value defined for the variable CONSOLE, root cannot log in from anywhere—not even the console. The only way to get in to the system as root is to first log in as a regular user and become root by issuing the su command. For more information, see the section "Restricting Root Access."

15. **A, B.** The /etc/group file assigns users to secondary groups and assigns a name to a group ID number. For more information, see the section "Where User Account Information Is Stored."

16. **D.** Whenever someone issues the su command to switch from a user and become root, this activity is logged in a file called /var/adm/sulog. The sulog file lists all uses of the su command, not only those used to switch from a user to superuser. The entries in this file show the date and time the command was entered, whether it was successful, the port from which the command was issued, and the name of the user and the switched identity. For more information, see the section "Monitoring Superuser Access."

17. **C.** If the sticky bit is set on the /tmp directory as rwxrwxrwx, only the owner can remove and rename his or her files. For more information, see the section "Sticky Bits."

18. **B.** The /etc/default/passwd file controls the default policy on password aging. For more information, see the section "Controlling System Access."

19. **D.** Employee numbers are not secure passwords. For more information, see the section "Controlling System Access."

20. **A.** You should ensure that passwords contain a combination of 6–8 letters, numbers, or special characters. For more information, see the section "Controlling System Access."

21. **B.** Password encryption and password aging details are stored in the /etc/shadow file. For more information, see the section "Where User Account Information Is Stored."

22. **A.** On files, the w in the first field of the permissions list designates write privileges for the owner. For more information, see the section "Controlling File Access."

23. **C.** The chmod command changes access permissions on a file. You can use either symbolic mode (letters and symbols) or absolute mode (octal numbers) to change permissions on a file. For more information, see the section "Controlling File Access."

24. **C.** When a user creates a file or directory, the umask value controls the default file permissions assigned to the file or directory. For more information, see the section "Controlling File Access."

25. **B.** A umask value of 022 sets the default permission on a directory to 755 (rwxr-xr-x). For more information, see the section "Controlling File Access."

26. **A.** A umask value of 022 sets the default permission on a file to 644 (rw-r--r--). For more information, see the section "Controlling File Access."

27. **B.** The permissions r-xr--r-- on a directory allow only the owner to open files in that directory. For more information, see the section "Controlling File Access."

28. **D.** `umask` changes the default permissions for every file and directory created in the future, whereas `chmod` works on a specific directory or file that already exists. For more information, see the section "Controlling File Access."

29. **A, B.** A restricted shell does not allow the user to change directories or redirect output. For more information, see the section "Restricted Shells."

30. **D.** `rsh` refers to either a restricted shell or the remote shell command. You should not confuse the restricted shell `/usr/lib/rsh` with the remote shell `/usr/bin/rsh`. When you specify a restricted shell, you should not include the following directories in the user's path—`/bin`, `/sbin`, or `/usr/bin`. If you do include the m in the user's path, you will allow the user to start another shell (a nonrestricted shell). For more information, see the section "Restricted Shells."

31. **B.** You use the `logins -p` command to display usernames that do not have passwords associated with them. For more information, see the section "Monitoring Users and System Usage."

32. **B.** The `/etc/hosts.equiv` file contains a list of trusted hosts for a remote system, one per line. For more information, see the section "Trusted Hosts."

33. **A.** The `.rhosts` file is the user equivalent of the `/etc/hosts.equiv` file. It contains a list of trusted hosts for a remote system, as well as a list of users. If a host/user combination is listed in this file, the specified user is granted permission to log in remotely from the specified host without having to supply a password. For more information, see the section "The `.rhosts` File."

34. **B.** You can protect the superuser account on a system by restricting access to a specific device through the CONSOLE variable located in the `/etc/default/login` file. For more information, see the section "Restricting Root Access."

35. **D.** The `sulog` file lists all uses of the `su` command, not only those that are used to switch a user to superuser. The entries in the `sulog` file show the date and time the command was entered, whether it was successful, the port from which the command was issued, and the name of the user and the switched identity. For more information, see the section "Monitoring Superuser Access."

36. **B.** The Solaris 10 system software includes ASET, which helps you monitor and control system security by automatically performing tasks you would otherwise do manually. ASET performs seven tasks, making specific checks and adjustments to system files and permissions to ensure system security. For more information, see the section "ASET."

37. **B.** Except for the executables that are shipped with the `setuid` bit set to root, you should disallow the use of `setuid` programs. For more information, see the section "The `setuid` and `setgid` Programs."

38. **A.** You use the `setfacl` command to set ACL entries on a file or directory. For more information, see the section "Setting ACL Entries."

39. **A.** The plus sign (+) to the right of the permission mode field (`-rw-r-----+`) indicates that the file has an ACL. For more information, see the section "Setting ACL Entries."

40. **A.** You use the `setacl -d` command to delete an ACL on a file or directory. For more information, see the section "Setting ACL Entries."

41. **A.** Use the `whodo` command to display each user logged in and the active processes owned by that user. For more information, see the section "The `whodo` Command."

42. **A.** The `who -b` command displays the time and date of the last reboot. For more information, see the section "Checking Who Is Logged In."

Suggested Reading and Resources

For more information on this topic, refer to the *Solaris 10 System Administration Guide: Security Services* by Sun Microsystems, Part number 816-4557-10. This guide is available at `http://docs.sun.com`.

CHAPTER FIVE

Managing System Processes

Objectives

The following test objectives for Exam CX-310-200 are covered in this chapter:

Explain how to view system processes and clear hung processes.

- Managing system processes is a common task for any system administrator. You should know how to use the commands that display information for all active processes on the system, and how to terminate an active or deadlocked process.

Explain how to schedule an automatic one-time execution of a command and the automatic recurring execution of a command.

- Many processes compete for execution time so scheduling jobs to run at off-peak hours can dramatically improve system performance. The system administrator needs to understand how to use the Solaris batch processor to schedule execution of commands.

Outline

Study Strategies

The following study strategies will help you prepare for the test:

- Understand each of the commands in this chapter enough so that you can match the command and option with a description. Practice them on a Solaris system so that you can become familiar with the output they produce.
- Know all the commands used to display information about a process. When viewing processes, understand each of the fields that are displayed in the output.
- Finally, understand how to schedule commands via the Solaris batch-processing facilities. Become familiar with all of the associated configuration files: what they do and how they are formatted.

EXAM ALERT

Managing System Processes As of this writing, the topic of managing system processes is covered lightly on the CX-310-200 exam. This could change in the future as Sun keeps updating and changing its exams. The best approach is to be prepared and learn the material thoroughly. After all, it's a topic every system administrator needs to know to effectively perform the job.

Introduction

This chapter covers Solaris processes—how to view processes, understand the effects signals have on processes, and how to manage processes.

Viewing a Process

Objective:

Explain how to view system processes.

Solaris is a multitasking environment in which a number of programs run at the same time. This means that many users can be active on the system at the same time, running many jobs (processes) simultaneously. Each Solaris program can start and stop multiple processes while it is running, but only one job is active per processor at any given time while the other jobs wait in a job queue. Because each process takes its turn running in very short time slices (much less than a second each), multitasking operating systems give the appearance that multiple processes are running at the same time. A parent process forks a child process, which, in turn, can fork other processes.

NOTE

Forks The term *fork* is used to describe a process started from another process. As with a fork in the road, one process turns into two. You'll also see the term *spawn* used—the two words are interchangeable for the purposes of this subject.

A program can be made up of many processes. A *process* is part of a program running in its own address space. A process under Solaris consists of an *address space* and a set of data structures in the *kernel* to keep track of that process. The address space is divided into various sections that include the instructions that the process may execute, memory allocated during the execution of the process, the *stack*, and memory-mapped files. The kernel must keep track of the following data for each process on the system:

- Address space
- Current status of the process
- Execution priority of the process
- Resource usage of the process
- Current signal mask
- Ownership of the process

A process is distinct from a job, command, or program that can be composed of many processes working together to perform a specific task. For example, a computer-aided design application is a single program. When this program starts, it spawns other processes as it runs. When a user logs in to the program, it spawns yet other processes. Each process has a process ID associated with it and is referred to as a *PID*. You can monitor processes that are currently executing by using one of the commands listed in Table 5.1.

TABLE 5.1 Commands to Display Processes

Command	Description
`ps`	Executed from the command line to display information about active processes.
`pgrep`	Executed from the command line to find processes by a specific name or attribute.
`prstat`	Executed from the command line to display information about active processes on the system.
`sdtprocess`	A GUI used to display and control processes on a system. This utility requires the X Window System (also known as X Windows).
`SMC process tool`	A GUI available in the Solaris Management Console used to monitor and manage processes on a system.
`pargs`	Executed from the command line to examine the arguments and environment variables of a process.
`svcs`	With the `-p` option, this Service Management Facility command will list processes associated with each service instance.

Before getting into the commands used to monitor processes, you first need to become familiar with process attributes. A process has certain attributes that directly affect execution. These are listed in Table 5.2.

TABLE 5.2 Process Attributes

Attribute	Description
`PID`	The process identification (a unique number that defines the process within the kernel)
`PPID`	The parent PID (the parent of the process)
`UID`	The user ID number of the user who owns the process
`EUID`	The effective user ID of the process
`GID`	The group ID of the user who owns the process
`EGID`	The effective group ID that owns the process
`Priority`	The priority at which the process runs

Use the `ps` command to view processes currently running on the system. Use the `ps` command when you're on a character-based terminal and don't have access to a graphical display. Adding the -l option to the ps command displays a variety of other information about the processes currently running, including the state of each process (listed under S). The codes used to show the various process states are listed in Table 5.3.

TABLE 5.3 Process States

Code	Process State	Description
O	Running	The process is running on a processor.
S	Sleeping	The process is waiting for an event to complete.
R	Runnable	The process is on the run queue.
Z	Zombie state	The process was terminated and the parent is not waiting.
T	Traced	The process was stopped by a signal because the parent is tracing it.

To see all the processes that are running on a system, type the following:

```
ps -el
```

The system responds with the following output:

```
# ps -el

 F S  UID   PID  PPID C PRI NI  ADDR SZ    WCHAN TTY  TIME CMD
19 T   0      0    0  0   0 SY   ?     0        ?   0:18 sched
 8 S   0      1    0  0  40 20   ?   150      ? ?   0:00 init
19 S   0      2    0  0   0 SY   ?     0      ? ?   0:00 pageout
19 S   0      3    0  0   0 SY   ?     0      ? ?   0:01 fsflush
 8 S   0    309    1  0  40 20   ?   217      ? ?   0:00 sac
 8 S   0    315    1  0  40 20   ?   331      ? ?   0:00 sshd
 8 S   0    143    1  0  40 20   ?   273      ? ?   0:00 rpcbind
 8 S   0     51    1  0  40 20   ?   268      ? ?   0:00 sysevent
 8 S   0     61    1  0  40 20   ?   343      ? ?   0:01 picld
 8 S   0    453  403  0  50 20   ?  1106      ? ?   0:00 dtfile
 8 S   0    189    1  0  40 20   ?   509      ? ?   0:00 automoun
 8 S   0    165    1  0  40 20   ?   292      ? ?   0:00 inetd
 8 S   0    200    1  0  40 20   ?   415      ? ?   0:00 syslogd
 8 S   0    180    1  0  40 20   ?   266      ? ?   0:00 lockd
 8 S   0    219    1  0  40 20   ?   391      ? ?   0:00 lpsched
 8 S   1    184    1  0  40 20   ?   306      ? ?   0:00 statd
 8 S   0    214    1  0  40 20   ?   365      ? ?   0:00 nscd
 8 S   0    204    1  0  40 20   ?   254      ? ?   0:00 cron
 8 S   0    232    1  0  40 20   ?   173      ? ?   0:00 powerd
 8 S   0    255  254  0  40 20   ?   215      ? ?   0:00 smcboot
 8 S   0    258    1  0  40 20   ?   356      ? ?   0:02 vold
```

The manual page for the ps command describes all the fields displayed with the ps command, as well as all the command options. Table 5.4 lists some important fields.

TABLE 5.4 Process Fields

Field	Description
F	Flags associated with the process.
S	The state of the process. The two most common values are S for sleeping and R for runnable. An important value to look for is X, which means that the process is waiting for memory to become available. When you frequently see this on your system, you are out of memory. Refer to Table 5.3 for a complete list of the process states.
UID	The user ID of the process owner. For many processes, this is `0` because they run `setuid`.
PID	The process ID of each process. This value should be unique. Generally, PIDs are allocated lowest to highest, but they wrap at some point. This value is necessary for you to send a signal, such as the `kill` signal, to a process.
PPID	The parent process ID. This identifies the parent process that started the process. Using the PPID enables you to trace the sequence of process creation that took place.
PRI	The priority of the process. Without the `-c` option, higher numbers mean lower priority. With the `-c` option, higher numbers mean higher priority.
NI	The `nice` value, used in priority computation. This is not printed when the `-c` option is used. The process's `nice` number contributes to its scheduling priority. Making a process nicer means lowering its priority.
ADDR	The memory address of the process.
SZ	The `SIZE` field. This is the total number of pages in the process. Page sizes are 8192 bytes on sun4u systems, but vary on different hardware platforms. Issue the `/usr/bin/pagesize` command to display the page size on your system.
WCHAN	The address of an event for which the process is sleeping (if it's -, the process is running).
STIME	The starting time of the process (in hours, minutes, and seconds).
TTY	The terminal assigned to your process.
TIME	The cumulative CPU time used by the process in minutes and seconds.
CMD	The command that generated the process.

You often want to look at all processes. You can do this using the command `ps -el`. A number of options available with the `ps` command control what information gets printed. A few of them are listed in Table 5.5.

TABLE 5.5 ps Command Options

Option	Description
-A	Lists information for all processes. Identical to the -e option.
-a	Lists information about all the most frequently requested processes. Processes not associated with a terminal will not be listed.
-e	Lists information about every process on the system.

(continues)

TABLE 5.5 *Continued*

Option	Description
`-f`	Generates a full listing.
`-l`	Generates a long listing.
`-P`	Prints the number of the processor to which the process is bound, if any, under an additional column header `PSR`. This is a useful option on systems that have multiple processors.
`-u` *<username>*	Lists only process data for a particular user. In the listing, the numerical user ID is printed unless you give the `-f` option, which prints the login name.

For a complete list of options to the `ps` command, refer to the Solaris online manual pages.

NOTE

`sort` Command The `sort` command is useful when you're looking at system processes. Use the `sort` command as the pipe output to sort by size or PID. For example, to sort by the `SZ` field, use the command `ps -el | sort +9` (remember, `sort` starts numbering fields with 0).

pgrep

The `pgrep` command replaces the combination of the `ps`, `grep`, `egrep`, and `awk` commands that were used to manage processes in earlier releases of Solaris. The `pgrep` command examines the active processes on the system and reports the process IDs of the processes whose attributes match the criteria you specify on the command line. The command syntax for the `pgrep` command is shown here:

```
pgrep <options> <pattern>
```

`pgrep` options are described in Table 5.6.

TABLE 5.6 **`pgrep` Options**

Option	Description
`-d` *<delim>*	Specifies the output delimiter string to be printed between each matching process ID. If no `-d` option is specified, the default is a newline character.
`-f`	The regular expression pattern should be matched against the full process argument string. If no `-f` option is specified, the expression is matched only against the name of the executable file.
`-g` *<pgrplist>*	Matches only processes whose process group ID is in the given list.
`-G` *<gidlist>*	Matches only processes whose real group ID is in the given list. Each group ID may be specified as either a group name or a numerical group ID.

TABLE 5.6 *Continued*

Option	Description
`-l`	Long output format. Prints the process name along with the process ID of each matching process.
`-n`	Matches only the newest (most recently created) process that meets all other specified matching criteria.
`-P` *<ppidlist>*	Matches only processes whose parent process ID is in the given list.
`-s` *<sidlist>*	Matches only processes whose process session ID is in the given list.
`-t` *<termlist>*	Matches only processes that are associated with a terminal in the given list. Each terminal is specified as the suffix following `/dev/` of the terminal's device pathname in `/dev` (for example, `term/a` or `pts/0`).
`-u` *<euidlist>*	Matches only processes whose effective user ID is in the given list. Each user ID may be specified as either a login name or a numerical user ID.
`-U` *<uidlist>*	Matches only processes whose real user ID is in the given list. Each user ID may be specified as either a login name or a numerical user ID.
`-v`	Matches all processes except those that meet the specified matching criteria.
`-x`	Considers only processes whose argument string or executable filename exactly matches the specified pattern.
<pattern>	A pattern to match against either the executable filename or full process argument string.

For example, the following `pgrep` command finds all processes that have `"dt"` in the process argument string:

```
pgrep -l -f "dt"
```

The system responds with this:

```
  500 /usr/dt/bin/dtlogin -daemon
16224 ./dtterm
  438 /usr/dt/bin/dtlogin -daemon
  448 /usr/openwin/bin/Xsun :0 -defdepth 24 -nobanner -auth /var/dt/A:0-p_aW2a
  520 dtgreet -display :0
```

To find the process ID for the `lpsched` process, issue this command:

```
pgrep -l lpsched
```

The system responds with this:

```
6899 lpsched
```

prstat

Use the prstat command from the command line to monitor system processes. Again, like the ps command, it provides information on active processes. The difference is that you can specify whether you want information on specific processes, UIDs, CPU IDs, or processor sets. By default, prstat displays information about all processes sorted by CPU usage. Another nice feature with prstat is that the information remains on the screen and is updated periodically. The information displayed by the prstat command is described in Table 5.7.

TABLE 5.7 Column Headings for the prstat Command

Column Heading	Description
PID	The process identification (a unique number that defines the process within the kernel)
USERNAME	The login ID name of the owner of the process
SIZE	The total virtual memory size of the process in kilobytes (K), megabytes (M), or gigabytes (G)
RSS	The resident set size of the process in kilobytes, megabytes, or gigabytes
STATE	The state of the process:
	cpu<*n*>—Process is running on CPU.
	sleep—Process is waiting for an event to complete.
	run—Process is in the run queue.
	zombie—Process has terminated and parent is not waiting.
	stop—Process is stopped.
PRI	The priority of the process
NICE	The value used in priority computation
TIME	The cumulative execution time for the process
CPU	The percentage of recent CPU time used by the process
PROCESS	The name of the process
NLWP	The number of lightweight processes (LWPs) in the process

This section will introduce some new terminology, so Table 5.8 defines a few terms related to processing in general.

TABLE 5.8 Process Terminology

Term	Description
Multitasking	A technique used in an operating system for sharing a single processor among several independent jobs. Multitasking introduces overhead because the processor spends some time choosing the next job to run and saving and restoring tasks' state. However, it reduces the worst-case time from job submission to completion compared with a simple batch system, in which each job must finish before the next one starts. Multitasking also means that while one task is waiting for some external event, the CPU is free to do useful work on other tasks. A multitasking operating system should provide some degree of protection of one task from another to prevent tasks from interacting in unexpected ways, such as accidentally modifying the contents of each other's memory areas. The jobs in a multitasking system may belong to one or many users. This is distinct from parallel processing, in which one user runs several tasks on several processors. Time sharing is almost synonymous with multitasking, but it implies that there is more than one user.
Parallel processing	The simultaneous use of more than one CPU to solve a problem. The processors either may communicate to cooperate in solving a problem or may run completely independently, possibly under the control of another processor that distributes work to the others and collects results from them.
Multithreaded	Multithreaded is a process that has multiple flows (threads) of control. The traditional Unix process contained, and still contains, a single thread of control. Multithreading (MT) separates a process into many execution threads, each of which runs independently. For more information, see the Multithreaded Programming Guide at `http://docs.sun.com/` Part number 816-5137-10.
Lightweight process (LWP)	A single-threaded subprocess. LWPs are scheduled by the kernel to use available CPU resources based on their scheduling class and priority. LWPs include a kernel thread, which contains information that must be in memory all the time, and a LWP, which contains information that is swappable. A process can consist of multiple LWPs and multiple application threads. A lightweight process is somewhere between a thread and a full process.
Application thread	A series of instructions with a separate stack that can execute independently in a user's address space. The threads can be multiplexed on top of LWPs.
Address space	The range of addresses that a processor or process can access, or at which a device can be accessed. The term may refer to either a physical address or a virtual address. The size of a processor's address space depends on the width of the processor's address bus and address registers. Processes running in 32-bit mode have a 4 gigabyte address space (2^{32} bytes) and processes running in 64-bit mode have a 16 terabyte (2^{64} bytes) address space.
Shared memory	Usually refers to RAM, which can be accessed by more than one process in a multitasking operating system with memory protection.

The syntax for the `prstat` command is as follows:

```
prstat [options] <count> <interval>
```

Table 5.9 describes a few of the `prstat` command options and arguments.

TABLE 5.9 `prstat` Options and Arguments

Option	Description
`prstat` Options	
`-a`	Displays separate reports about processes and users at the same time.
`-c`	Continuously prints new reports beneath previous reports instead of overwriting them.
`-j <projlist>`	Reports only processes or LWPs whose project ID is in the given list. Each project ID can be specified as either a project name or a numerical project ID.
`-J`	Reports information about processes and projects.
`-k <tasklist>`	Reports only processes or LWPs whose task ID is in *tasklist*.
`-m`	Reports microstate process accounting information. In addition to all fields listed in `-v` mode, this mode also includes the percentage of time the process has spent processing system traps, text page faults, and data page faults, and waiting for user locks and waiting for CPU (latency time).
`-n <nproc>`	Restricts the number of output lines. The `<nproc>` argument specifies how many lines of process or LWP statistics are reported.
`-p <pidlist>`	Reports only processes that have a PID in the given list.
`-P <cpulist>`	Reports only processes or LWPs that have most recently executed on a CPU in the given list. The `<cpulist>` argument identifies each CPU by an integer as reported by `psrinfo`.
`-S <key>`	Sorts output lines by `<key>` in descending order. Values for `<key>` can be `cpu`—Sorts by process CPU usage. This is the default. `time`—Sorts by process execution time. `size`—Sorts by size of process image. `rss`—Sorts by resident set size. `pri`—Sorts by process priority.
`-s <key>`	Sorts output lines by `<key>` in ascending order. See the `-S` option for a list of valid *`keys`* to use.
`-t`	Reports total usage summary for each user.
`-u <uidlist>`	Reports only processes whose effective user ID is in the given list. The value for `<uidlist>` may be specified as either a login name or a numerical user ID.
`-U <uidlist>`	Reports only processes whose real user ID is in the given list. The value for `<uidlist>` may be specified as either a login name or a numerical user ID.

TABLE 5.9 *Continued*

Option	Description
`prstat` Arguments	
`<count>`	Specifies the number of times that the statistics are repeated. By default, `prstat` reports statistics until a termination signal is received.
`<interval>`	Specifies the sampling interval in seconds; the default interval is 5 seconds.

NOTE

`psrinfo` Command `psrinfo` displays one line for each configured processor, displaying whether it is online, non-interruptible, offline, or powered off, as well as when that status last changed.

The following example uses the `prstat` command to view the four most active root processes running. The `-n` option is used here to restrict the output to the top four processes. The next number, `5`, specifies the sampling interval in seconds, and the last number, `3`, runs the command three times:

```
prstat -u root -n 4 5 3
```

The system displays the following output:

```
PID USERNAME  SIZE   RSS  STATE  PRI  NICE  TIME     CPU  PROCESS/NLWP
4375 root     4568K 4344K cpu0    59    0   0:00:00 0.4% prstat/1
4298 root     7088K 5144K sleep   59    0   0:00:02 0.2% dtterm/1
 304 root     2304K 1904K sleep   59    0   0:02:35 0.0% mibiisa/7
 427 root     1832K 1304K sleep   59    0   0:00:00 0.0% rpc.rstatd/1
Total: 53 processes, 111 lwps, load averages: 0.02, 0.01, 0.01
```

The output updates on your display five times every three seconds.

I described projects in Chapter 4, "User and Security Administration," where user accounts can be assigned to project groups. These projects can also be used to label workloads and separate projects and a project's related processes from one another.

The project provides a networkwide administrative identifier for related work. A project consists of tasks, which collect a group of processes into a manageable entity that represents a workload component.

You can use the `prstat` command with the `-J` option to monitor the CPU usage of projects and the `-k` option to monitor tasks across your system. Therefore, you can have `prstat` report on the processes related to a project rather than just list all system processes. In addition, the system administrator can set processing limits on the project, such as setting a limit on the total amount of physical memory, in bytes, that is available to processes in the project. For more information on projects and resource capping, read the man pages on the following commands: `rcapd(1M)`, `project(4)`, `rcapstat(1)`, and `rcapadm(1M)`.

Process Manager

In the Desktop Environment (CDE & JAVA Desktop) you have access to the Process Manager GUI, `sdtprocess`, a graphical tool that provides a process manager window for monitoring and controlling system processes.

EXAM ALERT

The exam will most likely ask you about the command-line tools used to manage system processes, such as `kill`, `pkill`, `pargs`, and `pgrep`. You only need to understand that GUI tools can be used to manage processes and you should be prepared to identify these GUI tools.

The advantage of using the Process Manager is that you can view and control processes without knowing all the complex options associated with the `ps` and `kill` commands. For example, you can display processes that contain specific character strings, and you can sort the process list alphabetically or numerically. You can initiate a search using the `find` command, or you can terminate a process simply by highlighting it and clicking `kill`.

To open the Process Manager, you need to log into the Desktop windowing environment. You can start the GUI by executing the command `sdtprocess`, as follows:

```
sdtprocess &
```

Or, you can click Find Process on the Tools subpanel, as shown in Figure 5.1.

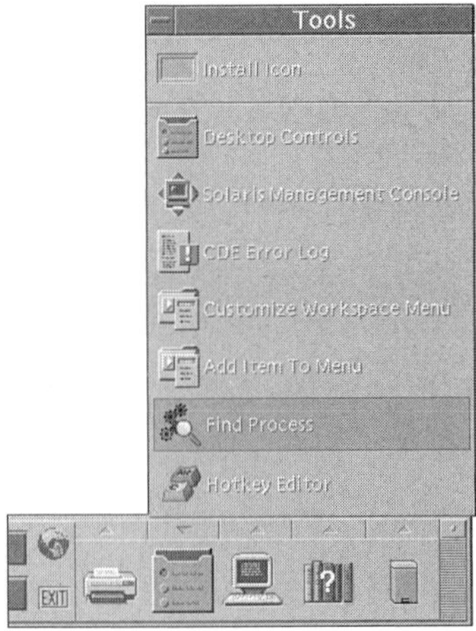

FIGURE 5.1 Front panel.

The Process Manager window opens, as shown in Figure 5.2.

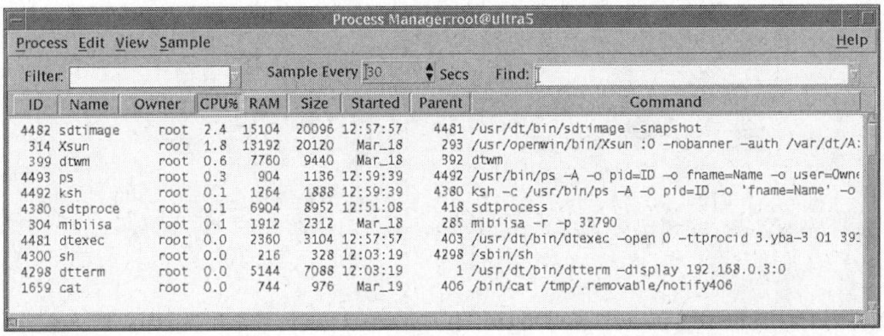

Figure 5.2 Process Manager window.

Each process attribute in the header of the Process Manager window provides detailed information about the process and is described in Table 5.10.

TABLE 5.10 Process Manager Window

Column Heading	Description
ID	Process ID
Name	Process name
Owner	Login ID name of the owner of the process
CPU%	Ratio of CPU time available in the same period, expressed as a percentage
RAM	Amount of RAM currently occupied by this process
Swap	Total swap size in virtual memory
Started	Actual start time (or date, if other than current)
Parent	Process ID of parent process, or PPID
Command	Actual Unix command (truncated) being executed

Click any of the column headings to sort the processes by that attribute. For example, click the `CPU` heading to sort all processes by their CPU usage. The list updates every 30 seconds, but you can enter a value in the `Sampling` field to update the list as frequently as you like. Finally, you can enter a text string that is common to the process entries of all the processes you want to display in the Find drop-down menu. In Figure 5.3, I entered "root" in the `Find` field to display all processes owned by root. I also changed the sampling rate to every 5 seconds and clicked the `CPU` heading to sort processes by their CPU usage.

Another nice feature of the Process Manager is the capability to display the ancestry of a process. When a Unix process initiates one or more processes, these are *child processes*, or children. Child and parent processes have the same user ID. To view a parent process and all the child processes that belong to it, highlight the process in the Process Manager window. Click Process from the toolbar at the top of the window and select Show Ancestry, as shown in Figure 5.4.

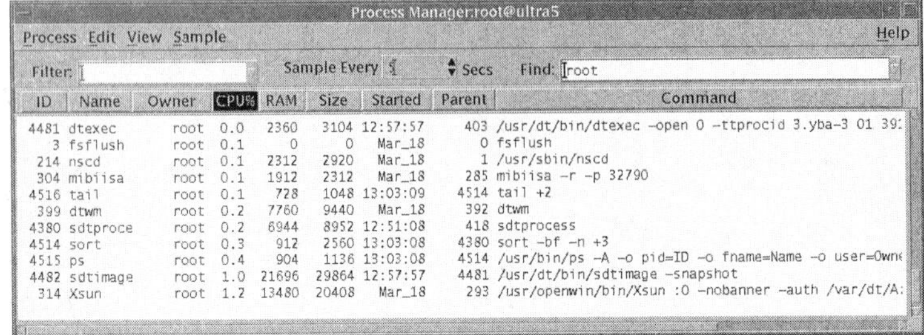

FIGURE 5.3 Sorted Process Manager window.

```
Process Manager:root@ultra5
Process  Edit  View  Sample                                                    Help
Look up Owner...               Sample Every      Secs   Find: root
Signal...
Debug...          Ctrl+G  PU%  RAM   Size  Started  Parent  Command
Trace System Calls...     .0   5144  7088 12:03:19     1 /usr/dt/bin/dtterm -display 192.168.0.3:0
Trace Children...         .0    216   328 12:03:19  4298 /sbin/sh
Show Stack...     Ctrl+t  .0   2360  3104 12:57:57   403 /usr/dt/bin/dtexec -open 0 -ttprocid 3.yba-3 01 39
Show Ancestry...          .1   1912  2312   Mar_18   285 mibiisa -r -p 32790
Kill              Ctrl+C  .1   7760  9440   Mar_18   392 dtwm
Exit                      .1   6944  8952 12:51:08   418 sdtprocess
                          .1    728  1048 13:04:09  4521 tail +2
                          .3    912  2528 13:04:08  4380 sort -bf -n +3
 4522 ps          root   0.5    904  1136 13:04:09  4521 /usr/bin/ps -A -o pid=ID -o fname=Name -o user=Own
  314 Xsun        root   0.6  13576 20504   Mar_18   293 /usr/openwin/bin/Xsun :0 -nobanner -auth /var/dt/A:
 4482 sdtimage    root   1.2  22144 31712 12:57:57  4481 /usr/dt/bin/sdtimage -snapshot
```

FIGURE 5.4 Selecting Show Ancestry.

The window shown in Figure 5.5 displays showing all the processes belonging to the parent.

```
Show Ancestry...
293   /usr/dt/bin/dtlogin -daemon
  316   /usr/dt/bin/dtlogin -daemon
    333   /bin/ksh /usr/dt/bin/Xsession
      376   /usr/dt/bin/sdt_shell -c      unset DT;      DISPLAY=:0;      /u
        379   -sh -c      unset DT;      DISPLAY=:0;      /usr/dt/bin/dtsess
          392   /usr/dt/bin/dtsession
            403   dtfile -session dtM7aGwj
              4481  /usr/dt/bin/dtexec -open 0 -ttprocid 3.yba-3 01 391 1289637
                4482  /usr/dt/bin/sdtimage -snapshot
```

Figure 5.5 Show Ancestry window.

The command-line equivalent to the Ancestry selection in the Process Manager is the `ptree` command. Use this command when you don't have a graphical display terminal. The `ptree` command displays the process ancestry trees containing the specified PIDs or users. The child processes are displayed indented from their respective parent processes. For example, here is the process tree for the -sh process, which has a PID of 293:

```
ptree 293
```

The system responds with this:

```
293   /usr/dt/bin/dtlogin -daemon
  316    /usr/dt/bin/dtlogin -daemon
    333    /bin/ksh /usr/dt/bin/Xsession
      376    /usr/dt/bin/sdt_shell -c  unset DT;DISPLAY=:0;/usr/dt/bin/dt
        379   -sh -c unset DT; DISPLAY=:0; usr/dt/bin/dtsession_res - \
              merge
          392    /usr/dt/bin/dtsession
            402    /usr/dt/bin/dtterm -session dthIaGth -C -ls
              418    -sh
```

SMC Process Tool

The Solaris Management Console (SMC) includes a GUI called the Process Tool, which is used for viewing and managing processes, similar to the Desktop Process Manager tool described in the previous section. You can use the job scheduler tool to

- Suspend a process
- Resume a suspended process
- Kill a process
- Display information about a process

To open the Process Tool, follow Step by Step 5.1.

STEP BY STEP

5.1 Opening the Process Tool

1. Start up the Solaris Management Console by typing

   ```
   smc
   ```

2. The SMC Welcome window appears as shown in Figure 5.6.
3. In the SMC navigation pane, open the Process Tool by clicking on the This Computer icon, then click on the System Status icon, then click on the Processes icon as shown in Figure 5.7.
4. The Process Tool displays as shown in Figure 5.8

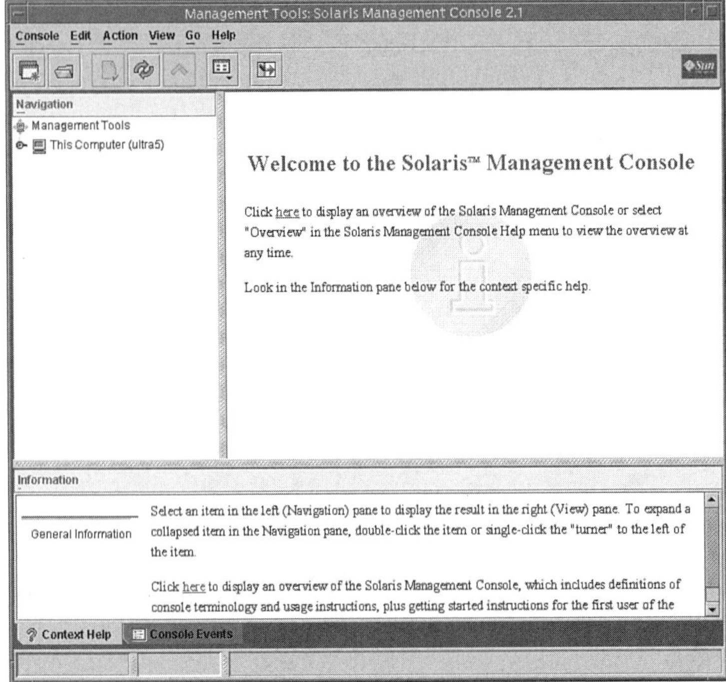

FIGURE 5.6 SMC Welcome Window.

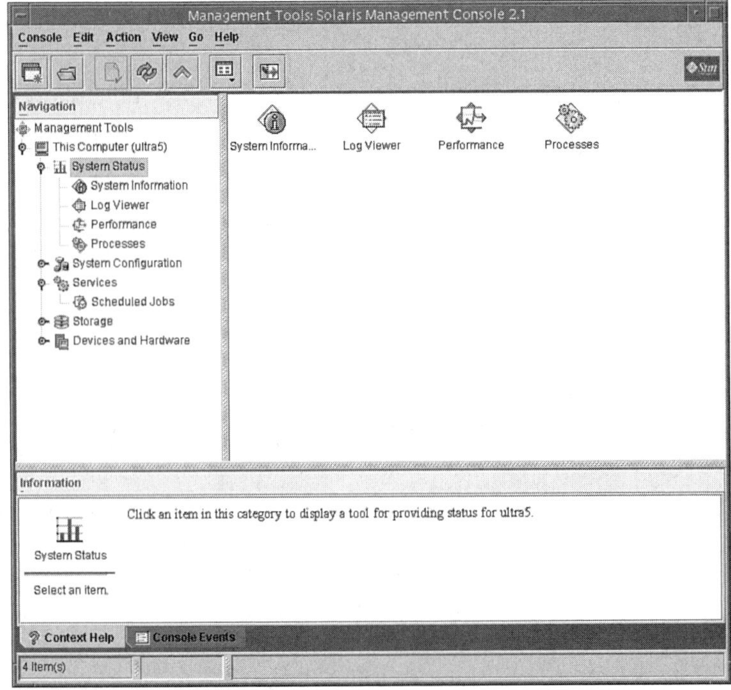

FIGURE 5.7 Opening the Job Scheduler.

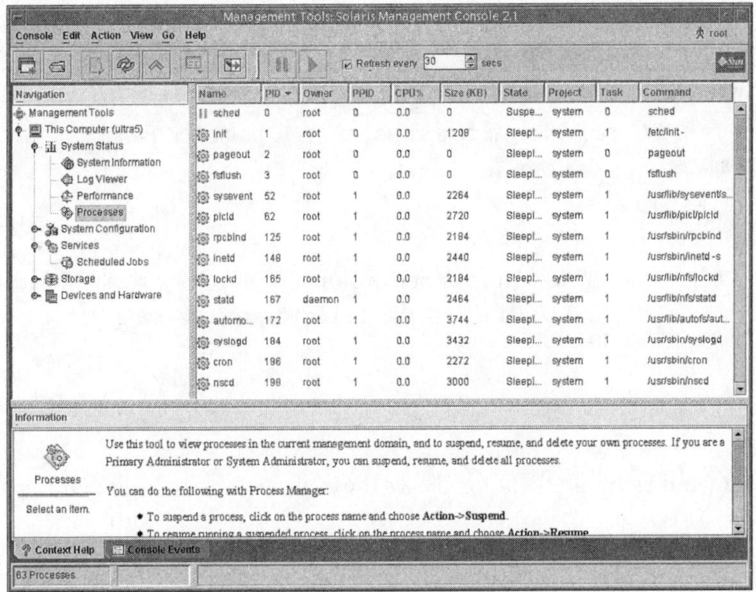

FIGURE 5.8 Process Tool.

The Process Tool works much the same way as the Process Manager tool described earlier.

pargs

The `pargs` command is used from the command line to examine the arguments and environment variables of a process (or number of processes). `pargs` can also be used to examine core files.

The syntax for the `pargs` command is as follows:

```
pargs [options] pid ¦ core
```

Table 5.11 describes the `pargs` command options and arguments.

TABLE 5.11 `pargs` Options and Arguments

Option/Arguments	Description
-a	Prints the process arguments.
-c	Treats strings in the target process as though they were encoded in 7-bit ASCII.
-e	Prints process environment variables and values.
-F	Force. Grabs the target process even if another process has control.

(continues)

TABLE 5.11 *Continued*

Option/Arguments	Description
-x	Prints process auxiliary vector.
<pid>	Process ID list. The PID list can be a single process ID or multiple PIDs separated by a space.
core	Processes a core file.

For example, use the pargs command to view all of the environment variables associated with the telnetd process, I first need to find the PID of the telnetd process using pgrep as follows:

```
# pgrep telnetd
16173
```

Next, I issue the pargs command using the PID for the telnetd process as an argument:

```
# pargs -e 16173
```

The system responds with

```
16173:  /usr/sbin/in.telnetd
envp[0]: SMF_RESTARTER=svc:/network/inetd:default
envp[1]: SMF_FMRI=svc:/network/telnet:default
envp[2]: SMF_METHOD=inetd_start
envp[3]: PATH=/usr/sbin:/usr/bin
envp[4]: TZ=US/Michigan
```

SVCS

The Service Management Facility (SMF) was described in Chapter 3, "Perform System Startup and Shutdown Procedures," so I won't be redundant by describing it again here. However, this is just a reminder that you can use the svcs command with the -p option to list all processes associated with each service instance.

Process Types

When sitting at a terminal and typing in commands, the user is typically executing *foreground processes*. Commands such as vi are foreground processes—they read input from the keyboard and display output to the terminal. Foreground processes maintain control of the terminal, and the user cannot do anything else in that terminal window until the execution of that command is complete.

Some processes are not interactive and don't need to run in the foreground. These are referred to as *background processes* or *jobs*. A background process gets detached from the terminal, freeing up the terminal while it is running. When a user decides to run a process in the background, you must arrange for the process to get its input from another source. In addition, you need to arrange for the process to output to a device other than the terminal, such as a file.

To run a process in the background, enter an `&` (ampersand) after the command:

```
find . -name core -print &
```

After typing in this command, you're returned to a command prompt. The `find` command executes in the background. One problem, however, is the standard output is still on your terminal. In other words, as the `find` command executes, the results still are displayed on your screen, which can become quite annoying. It's best to redirect the output to a file, as follows:

```
find . -name core -print  > /tmp/results &
```

After you put the `find` command in the background, the system displays two numbers associated with that process—the job number and the process ID number (PID) as follows:

```
    [1]    14919
```

You use this job number to control background processes.

NOTE

No Job Control in the `sh` shell The Bourne shell does not provide job control. Job control enables you to check and manage your background jobs. Thus, with the Bourne shell, you can submit jobs to the background, but you cannot manage them. Use `jsh` (job shell), which provides all the functionality of `sh` and enables job control. The Korn shell (`ksh`) and the C shell (`csh`) both allow for job control.

The shell maintains a table containing information about processes that are currently in the background. This is referred to as the *jobs table*. The jobs table is unique to the user, and each user has his own jobs table. Furthermore, the jobs table contains only entries for jobs that are running in your current shell. If you start a new shell, the jobs table for the new shell is empty. Each job in the table is assigned a number that is unique to that user only. In other words, two users can each have a job numbered 1. Don't confuse this job number with a process ID number; remember, process IDs are unique, and no two share the same number. Any jobs that the user has placed in the background are displayed here by typing in the `jobs` command, as follows:

```
jobs
```

The system responds with this:

```
[3] +  Running   find / -name bill -print > /tmp/results3 &
[2] -  Running   find / -name junk -print > /tmp/results2 &
[1]    Running   find / -name core -print > /tmp/results1 &
```

The jobs table contains the following information:

- A numeric value for each job
- A + (plus) symbol to designate the current job that user commands will operate on
- A - (minus) symbol to designate the next job that the user commands will operate on
- The status of the job
- The name of the job

Each job in the job table has one of the following states:

- `Running`—An active job
- `Stopped`—A job that has been suspended
- `Terminated`—A job that has been killed
- `Done`—A completed job

When the job finishes, the following is displayed on your terminal:

```
[1] +  Done      find / -name core -print > /tmp/results &
```

Note the job number of `1` and the status of `Done`.

If you want to terminate a job, use the `kill` command followed by a `%` (percent sign) and then the job number, as follows:

```
kill %1
```

CAUTION

Pay special attention to the use of the `%` (percent) symbol—it's absolutely required. Without it, you could kill the wrong process and potentially crash the system. Get familiar with the `kill` command in the next section of this chapter before you use it.

If you do not enter a number following the `%` sign, the command acts upon the current job entry listed in the jobs table. For this example, you are going to kill job number 1, as follows:

```
kill %1
```

The following message is displayed indicating successful termination:

```
[1] + Terminated   find / -name core -print > /tmp/results &
```

You can also bring a job back into the foreground with the `fg` command. Typing `fg` with no arguments brings the current job (the job with the + sign next to it in the jobs table) into the foreground. You can also specify the job by typing `fg %<job number>`, as follows:

```
fg %2
```

This brings job 2 back into the foreground on your terminal.

In a windowing environment such as Java Desktop System, placing jobs in the background is not an issue. Typically, you start a job in one window and open another window to continue working. Therefore, placing jobs into the background has all but disappeared unless you are working on a character-based terminal.

Using Signals

Objective:

Clearing hung processes.

Solaris supports the concept of sending software *signals* to a process. These signals are ways for other processes to interact with a running process outside the context of the hardware. The `kill` command is used to send a signal to a process. System administrators most often use the signals `SIGHUP`, `SIGKILL`, `SIGSTOP`, and `SIGTERM`. The `SIGHUP` signal is used by some utilities as a way to notify the process to do something, such as re-read its configuration file. The `SIGHUP` signal is also sent to a process if the remote connection is lost or hangs up. The `SIGKILL` signal is used to abort a process, and the `SIGSTOP` signal is used to pause a process. The SIGTERM signal is the default signal sent to processes by commands such as `k ill` and `pkill` when no signal is specified. Table 5.12 describes the most common signals an administrator is likely to use.

EXAM ALERT

Don't worry about remembering all of the signals listed; just be familiar with the more common signals, such as `SIGHUP`, `SIGKILL`, `SIGSTOP`, and `SIGTERM`.

TABLE 5.12 Signals Available Under Solaris

Signal	Number	Description
SIGHUP	1	Hangup. Usually means that the controlling terminal has been disconnected.
SIGINT	2	Interrupt. The user can generate this signal by pressing Ctrl+C or Delete.

(continues)

TABLE 5.12 *Continued*

Signal	Number	Description
SIGQUIT	3	Quits the process and produces a core dump.
SIGILL	4	Illegal instruction.
SIGTRAP	5	Trace or breakpoint trap.
SIGABRT	6	Abort.
SIGEMT	7	Emulation trap.
SIGFPE	8	Arithmetic exception. Informs a process of a floating-point error.
SIGKILL	9	Killed. Forces the process to terminate. This is a sure kill.
SIGBUS	10	Bus error.
SIGSEGV	11	Segmentation fault.
SIGSYS	12	Bad system call.
SIGPIPE	13	Broken pipe.
SIGALRM	14	Alarm clock.
SIGTERM	15	Terminated. A gentle kill that gives processes a chance to clean up.
SIGUSR1	16	User signal 1.
SIGUSR2	17	User signal 2.
SIGCHLD	18	Child status changed.
SIGPWR	19	Power fail or restart.
SIGWINCH	20	Window size change.
SIGURG	21	Urgent socket condition.
SIGPOLL	22	Pollable event.
SIGSTOP	23	Stopped (signal). Pauses a process.
SIGTSTP	24	Stopped (user).
SIGCONT	25	Continued.
SIGTTIN	26	Stopped (tty input).
SIGTTOU	27	Stopped (tty output).
SIGVTALRM	28	Virtual timer expired.
SIGPROF	29	Profiling timer expired.
SIGXCPU	30	CPU time limit exceeded.
SIGXFSZ	31	File size limit exceeded.
SIGWAITING	32	Concurrency signal reserved by threads library.
SIGLWP	33	Inter-LWP signal reserved by threads library.
SIGFREEZE	34	Checkpoint freeze.
SIGTHAW	35	Checkpoint thaw.
SIGCANCEL	36	Cancellation signal reserved by the threads library.

In addition, you can write a *signal handler*, or *trap*, in a program to respond to a signal being sent. For example, many system programs, such as the name server daemon, respond to the SIGHUP signal by re-reading their configuration files. This signal can then be used to update the process while running, without having to terminate and restart the process. Signal handlers cannot be installed for SIGSTOP (23) or SIGKILL (9). Because the process cannot install a signal handler for signal 9, an otherwise well-behaved process may leave temporary files around or not be able to finish out critical operations that it is in the middle of. Thus, kill -9 invites corruption of application data files and should only be used as a last resort.

Here's an example of how to trap a signal in a script:

```
trap '/bin/rm tmp$$;exit 1' 1 2 3 15
```

As the name suggests, trap traps system interrupt until some command can be executed. The previous example traps the signals 1, 2, 3, and 15, and executes the /bin/rm tmp$$ command before exiting the program. The example deletes all tmp files even if the program terminates abnormally.

The kill command sends a terminate signal (signal 15) to the process, and the process is terminated. Signal 15, which is the default when no options are used with the kill command, is a gentle kill that allows a process to perform cleanup work before terminating. Signal 9, on the other hand, is called a sure, unconditional kill because it cannot be caught or ignored by a process. If the process is still around after a kill -9, either it is hung up in the Unix kernel, waiting for an event such as disk I/O to complete, or you are not the owner of the process.

The kill command is routinely used to send signals to a process. You can kill any process you own, and the superuser can kill all processes in the system except those that have process IDs 0, 1, 2, 3, and 4. The kill command is poorly named because not every signal sent by it is used to kill a process. This command gets its name from its most common use—terminating a process with the kill -15 signal.

NOTE

Forking Problem A common problem occurs when a process continually starts up new copies of itself—this is referred to as *forking* or *spawning*. Users have a limit on the number of new processes they can fork. This limit is set in the kernel with the MAXUP (maximum number of user processes) value. Sometimes, through user error, a process keeps forking new copies of itself until the user hits the MAXUP limit. As a user reaches this limit, the system appears to be waiting. If you kill some of the user's processes, the system resumes creating new processes on behalf of the user. It can be a no-win situation. The best way to handle these runaway processes is to send the STOP signal to suspend all processes and then send a KILL signal to terminate the processes. Because the processes were first suspended, they can't create new ones as you kill them off.

You can send a signal to a process you own with the kill command. Many signals are available, as listed in Table 5.12. To send a signal to a process, first use the ps command to find the process ID (PID) number. For example, type `ps -ef` to list all processes and find the PID of the process you want to terminate:

```
ps -ef

UID     PID  PPID  C    STIME   TTY   TIME   CMD
root      0     0  0   Nov 27   ?     0:01   sched
root      1     0  0   Nov 27   ?     0:01   /etc/init -
root      2     0  0   Nov 27   ?     0:00   pageout
root      3     0  0   Nov 27   ?    12:52   fsflush
root    101     1  0   Nov 27   ?     0:00   /usr/sbin/in.routed -q
root    298     1  0   Nov 27   ?     0:00   /usr/lib/saf/sac -t 300
root    111     1  0   Nov 27   ?     0:02   /usr/sbin/rpcbind
root    164     1  0   Nov 27   ?     0:01   /usr/sbin/syslogd -n -z 12
root    160     1  0   Nov 27   ?     0:01   /usr/lib/autofs/automountd
.
.
.
root   5497   433  1 09:58:02  pts/4  0:00   script psef
```

To kill the process with a PID number of `5497`, type this:

```
kill 5497
```

Another way to kill a process is to use the `pkill` command. `pkill` functions identically to `pgrep`, which was described earlier, except that instead of displaying information about each process, the process is terminated. A signal name or number may be specified as the first command-line option to `pkill`. The value for the signal can be any value described in Table 5.12. For example, to kill the process named `psef` with a `SIGKILL` signal, issue the following command:

```
pkill -9 psef
```

NOTE

Killing a Process If no signal is specified, `SIGTERM (15)` is sent by default. This is the preferred signal to send when trying to kill a process. Only when a `SIGTERM` fails should you send a SIGKILL signal to a process. As stated earlier in this section, a process cannot install a signal handler for signal 9 and an otherwise well-behaved process might not shut down properly.

In addition, the Desktop Process Manager, which was described earlier, can be used to kill processes. In the Process Manager window, highlight the process that you want to terminate, click Process from the toolbar at the top of the window, and then select Kill from the pull-down menu, as shown in Figure 5.9.

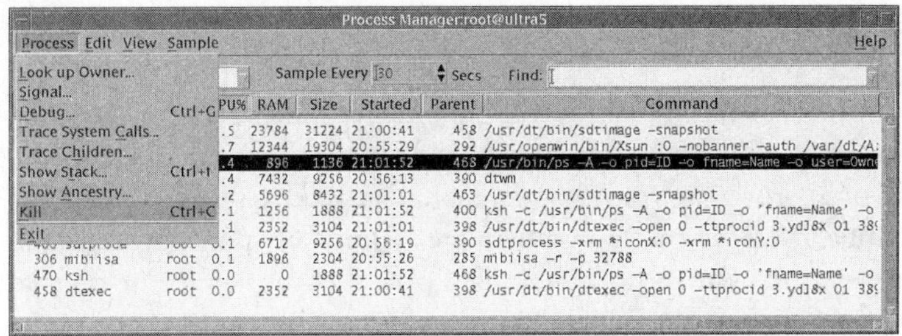

Figure 5.9 Killing processes.

The equivalent Unix command used by the Process Manager to terminate a process is shown here:

```
kill -9 <PID>
```

`<PID>` is the process ID of the selected process.

The `preap` command forces the killing of a defunct process, known as a *zombie*. In previous Solaris releases, zombie processes that could not be killed off remained until the next system reboot. Defunct processes do not normally impact system operation; however, they do consume a small amount of system memory. See the `preap` manual page for further details of this command.

Scheduling Processes

Processes compete for execution time. *Scheduling*, one of the key elements in a time-sharing system, determines which of the processes executes next. Although hundreds of processes might be present on the system, only one actually uses a given CPU at any given time. Time sharing on a CPU involves suspending a process and then restarting it later. Because the suspension and resumption of active processes occurs many times each second, it appears to the user that the system is performing many tasks simultaneously.

Unix attempts to manage the priorities of processes by giving a higher priority to those that have used the least amount of CPU time. In addition, processes that are waiting on an event, such as a keyboard press, get higher priority than processes that are purely CPU-driven.

On any large system with a number of competing user groups, the task of managing resources falls to the system administrator. This task is both technical and political. As a system administrator, you must understand your company goals to manage this task successfully. When you understand the political implications of who should get priority, you are ready to manage the technical details. As root, you can change the priority of any process on the system by using the `nice` or `priocntl` commands. Before you do this, you must understand how priorities work.

Scheduling Priorities

All processes have assigned to them an execution priority—an integer value that is dynamically computed and updated on the basis of several different factors. Whenever the CPU is free, the scheduler selects the most favored process to resume executing. The process selected is the one with the lowest-priority number because lower numbers are defined as more favored than higher ones. Multiple processes at the same priority level are placed in the run queue for that priority level. Whenever the CPU is free, the scheduler starts the processes at the head of the lowest-numbered nonempty run queue. When the process at the top of a run queue stops executing, it goes to the end of the line and the next process moves up to the front. After a process begins to run, it continues to execute until it needs to wait for an I/O operation to complete, receives an interrupt signal, or exhausts the maximum execution time slice defined on that system. A typical time slice is 10 milliseconds.

A Unix process has two priority numbers associated with it. One of the priority numbers is its requested execution priority with respect to other processes. This value (its `nice` number) is set by the process's owner and by root; it appears in the `NI` column in a `ps -l` listing. The other priority assigned to a process is the execution priority. This priority is computed and updated dynamically by the operating system, taking into account such factors as the process's `nice` number, how much CPU time it has had recently, and other processes that are running and their priorities. The execution priority value appears in the `PRI` column on a `ps -l` listing.

Although the CPU is the most-watched resource on a system, it is not the only one. Memory use, disk use, I/O activity, and the number of processes all tie together in determining the computer's throughput. For example, suppose you have two groups, A and B. Both groups require large amounts of memory—more than is available when both are running simultaneously. Raising the priority of Group A over Group B might not help if Group B does not fully relinquish the memory it is using. Although the paging system does this over time, the process of swapping a process out to disk can be intensive and can greatly reduce performance. A better alternative might be to completely stop Group B with a signal and then continue it later, when Group A has finished.

Changing the Priority of a Time-Sharing Process with `nice`

The `nice` command is supported only for backward compatibility with previous Solaris releases. The `priocntl` command provides more flexibility in managing processes. The priority of a process is determined by the policies of its scheduling class and by its `nice` number. Each time-sharing process has a global priority that is calculated by adding the user-supplied priority, which can be influenced by the `nice` or `priocntl` commands, and the system-calculated priority.

The execution priority number of a process is assigned by the operating system and is determined by several factors, including its schedule class, how much CPU time it has used, and its `nice` number. Each time-sharing process starts with a default `nice` number, which it inherits from its parent process. The `nice` number is shown in the `NI` column of the `ps` report.

A user can lower the priority of a process by increasing its user-supplied priority number. Only the superuser can increase the priority of a process by lowering its `nice` value. This prevents users from increasing the priorities of their own processes, thereby monopolizing a greater share of the CPU.

Two versions of the `nice` command are available: the standard version, `/usr/bin/nice`, and a version that is integrated into the C shell as a C shell built-in. `/usr/bin/nice` numbers range from `0` to `+39` and the default value is 20, while the C-shell built-in version of `nice` has values that range from –20 to +20. The lower the number, the higher the priority and the faster the process runs.

Use the `/usr/bin/nice` command as described in Table 5.13 when submitting a program or command.

TABLE 5.13 Setting Priorities with `nice`

Command	Description
Lowering the Priority of a Process Using `/usr/bin/nice`	
`nice` *<process_name>*	Increases the `nice` number by 4 units (the default)
`nice -4` *<process_name>*	Increases the `nice` number by 4 units
`nice -10` *<process_name>*	Increases the `nice` number by 10 units
Increasing the Priority of a Process	
`nice -n -10` *<process_name>*	Raises the priority of the command by lowering the `nice` number

NOTE

Root may run commands with a priority higher than normal by using a negative increment, such as -10. A negative increment assigned by an unprivileged user is ignored.

As a system administrator, you can use the `renice` command to change the priority of a process after it has been submitted. The `renice` command has the following form:

```
renice priority -n <value> -p <pid>
```

Use the `ps -el` command to find the PID of the process for which you want to change the priority. The process that you want to change in the following example is named `largejob`:

```
F S  UID   PID  PPID  C PRI  NI     ADDR    SZ    WCHAN TTY  TIME  CMD
9 S   0   8200  4100  0  84  20  f0274e38  193          ?    0:00 largejob
```

Issue the following command to increase the priority of PID `8200`:

```
renice -n -4 -p 8200
```

Issuing the `ps -el` command again shows the process with a higher priority:

```
F S  UID  PID  PPID  C PRI  NI     ADDR    SZ  WCHAN TTY   TIME   CMD
9 S   0  8200  4100  0  60  16  f0274e38  193         ?    0:00   largejob
```

Changing the Scheduling Priority of Processes with `priocntl`

The standard priority scheme has been improved since earlier versions of Solaris as part of its support for real-time processes. Real-time processes are designed to work in application areas in which a nearly immediate response to events is required. These processes are given nearly complete access to all system resources when they are running. Solaris uses time-sharing priority numbers ranging from `-20` to `20`. Solaris uses the `priocntl` command, intended as an improvement over the `nice` command, to modify process priorities. To use `priocntl` to change a priority on a process, type this:

```
priocntl -s -p <new-priority>  -i pid <process-id>
```

`new-priority` is the new priority for the process, and *`process-id`* is the PID of the process you want to change.

The following example sets the priority level for process `8200` to `-5`:

```
priocntl -s -p -5 -i pid 8200
```

The following example is used to set the priority (`nice` value) for every process created by a given parent process:

```
priocntl -s -p -5 -I ppid 8200
```

As a result of this command, all processes forked from process `8200` have a priority of `-5`.

The priority value assigned to a process can be displayed using the `ps` command, which was described earlier in this chapter.

The functionality of the `priocntl` command goes much further than what is described in this section. Consult the online manual pages for more information about the `priocntl` command.

Fair Share Scheduler (FSS) and the Fixed Scheduler (FX)

The *Fair Share Scheduler (FSS)* in Solaris 10 can be used to control the allocation of resources. The *Fixed Scheduler (FX)* is a fixed priority scheduler that provides an ensured priority for processes. Neither of these are objectives on the CX-310-200 exam and they are not covered in this chapter.

Using the Solaris Batch-Processing Facility

A way to divide processes on a busy system is to schedule jobs so that they run at different times. A large job, for example, could be scheduled to run at 2:00 a.m., when the system would normally be idle. Solaris supports two methods of batch processing: the `crontab` and `at` commands. The `crontab` command schedules multiple system events at regular intervals, and the `at` command schedules a single system event.

Configuring `crontab`

Objective:

Explain how to schedule the automatic recurring execution of a command.

`cron` is a Unix utility named after Chronos ("time"), the ancient Greek god of time. It enables you to execute commands automatically according to a schedule you define. The `cron` daemon schedules system events according to commands found in each `crontab` file. A `crontab` file consists of commands, one per line, that will be executed at regular intervals. The beginning of each line contains five date and time fields that tell the `cron` daemon when to execute the command. The sixth field is the full pathname of the program you want to run. These fields, described in Table 5.14, are separated by spaces.

TABLE 5.14 The `crontab` File

Field	Description	Values
1	Minute	`0` to `59`. A `*` in this field means every minute.
2	Hour	`0` to `23`. A `*` in this field means every hour.
3	Day of month	`1` to `31`. A `*` in this field means every day of the month.
4	Month	`1` to `12`. A `*` in this field means every month.
5	Day of week	`0` to `6` (`0` = `Sunday`). A `*` in this field means every day of the week.
6	Command	Enter the command to be run.

Follow these guidelines when making entries in the crontab file:

- Use a space to separate fields.
- Use a comma to separate multiple values in any of the date or time fields.
- Use a hyphen to designate a range of values in any of the date or time fields.
- Use an asterisk as a wildcard to include all possible values in any of the date or time fields. For example, an asterisk (*) can be used in the first five fields (time fields) to mean all legal values.
- Use a comment mark (#) at the beginning of a line to indicate a comment or a blank line.
- Each command within a crontab file must consist of one line, even if it is very long, because crontab does not recognize extra carriage returns.
- There can be no blank lines in the crontab file.

The following sample crontab command entry displays a reminder in the user's console window at 5:00 p.m. on the 1st and 15th of every month:

```
0 17 1,15 * * echo Hand in Timesheet > /dev/console
```

crontab files are found in the /var/spool/cron/crontabs directory. Several crontab files besides root are provided during the SunOS software installation process; they are also located in this directory. Other crontab files are named after the user accounts for which they are created, such as bill, glenda, miguel, or nicole. They also are located in the /var/spool/cron/crontabs directory. For example, a crontab file named root is supplied during software installation. Its contents include these command lines:

```
10 3 * * * /usr/sbin/logadm
15 3 * * 0 /usr/lib/fs/nfs/nfsfind
30 3 * * * [ -x /usr/lib/gss/gsscred_clean ] && /usr/lib/gss/gsscred_clean
#10 3 * * * /usr/lib/krb5/kprop_script ___slave_kdcs___
```

The first command line instructs the system to run logchecker at 3:10 a.m. on Sunday and Thursday. The second command line orders the system to execute nfsfind on Sunday at 3:15 a.m. The third command line runs each night at 3:30 a.m. and executes the gsscred command. The fourth command is commented out. The cron daemon never exits and is started via the svc:/system/cron:default service. The /etc/cron.d/FIFO file is used as a lock file to prevent running more than one instance of cron.

Creating and Editing a crontab File

Creating an entry in the crontab file is as easy as editing a text file using your favorite editor. Use the steps described next to edit this file; otherwise, your changes are not recognized until the next time the cron daemon starts up. cron examines crontab configuration files only during its own process-initialization phase or when the crontab command is run. This reduces the overhead of checking for new or changed files at regularly scheduled intervals.

Step by Step 5.2 tells you how to create or edit a crontab file.

STEP BY STEP

5.2 Creating or Editing a crontab File

1. (Optional) To create or edit a crontab file belonging to root or another user, become superuser.
2. Create a new crontab file or edit an existing one by typing the following:

   ```
   crontab -e
   ```

NOTE

crontab Default Editor The crontab command chooses the system default editor, which is ed, unless you've set the VISUAL or EDITOR variable to vi (or another editor), as follows:

```
EDITOR=vi;export EDITOR
```

3. Add command lines to the file, following the syntax described in Table 5.14. Because cron jobs do not inherit the users environment, such as PATH, you should specify the full pathname for commands.
4. Save the changes and exit the file. The crontab file is placed in /var/spool/cron/crontabs.
5. Verify the crontab file by typing the following:

   ```
   crontab -l
   ```

   The system responds by listing the contents of the crontab file.

Controlling Access to crontab

You can control access to crontab by modifying two files in the /etc/cron.d directory: cron.deny and cron.allow. These files permit only specified users to perform crontab tasks such as creating, editing, displaying, and removing their own crontab files. The cron.deny and cron.allow files consist of a list of usernames, one per line. These access control files work together in the following manner:

- If cron.allow exists, only the users listed in this file can create, edit, display, and remove crontab files.
- If cron.allow doesn't exist, all users may submit crontab files, except for users listed in cron.deny.
- If neither cron.allow nor cron.deny exists, superuser privileges are required to run crontab.

Superuser privileges are required to edit or create `cron.deny` and `cron.allow`.

During the Solaris software installation process, a default `/etc/cron.d/cron.deny` file is provided. It contains the following entries:

- `daemon`
- `bin`
- `nuucp`
- `listen`
- `nobody`
- `noaccess`

None of the users listed in the `cron.deny` file can access `crontab` commands. The system administrator can edit this file to add other users who are denied access to the `crontab` command. No default `cron.allow` file is supplied. This means that, after the Solaris software installation, all users (except the ones listed in the default `cron.deny` file) can access `crontab`. If you create a `cron.allow` file, only those users can access `crontab` commands.

Scheduling a Single System Event (`at`)

Objective:

Explain how to schedule an automatic one-time execution of a command.

The `at` command is used to schedule jobs for execution at a later time. Unlike `crontab`, which schedules a job to happen at regular intervals, a job submitted with `at` executes once, at the designated time.

To submit an `at` job, type `at`. Then specify an execution time and a program to run, as shown in the following example:

```
at 07:45am today
at> who > /tmp/log
at> <Press Control-d>
job 912687240.a at Thu Jun 6 07:14:00
```

When you submit an `at` job, it is assigned a job identification number, which becomes its filename along with the .a extension. The file is stored in the `/var/spool/cron/atjobs` directory. In much the same way as it schedules `crontab` jobs, the `cron` daemon controls the scheduling of `at` files.

The command syntax for at is shown here:

```
at -m <time> <date>
```

The at command is described in Table 5.15.

TABLE 5.15 at Command Syntax

Option	Description
-m	Sends you mail after the job is completed.
-l	Reports all jobs for the user.
-r	Removes a specified job.
<time>	The hour when you want to schedule the job. Add am or pm if you do not specify the hours according to a 24-hour clock. midnight, noon, and now are acceptable keywords. Minutes are optional.
<date>	The first three or more letters of a month, a day of the week, or the keywords today or tomorrow.

You can set up a file to control access to the at command, permitting only specified users to create, remove, or display queue information about their at jobs. The file that controls access to at is /etc/cron.d/at.deny. It consists of a list of usernames, one per line. The users listed in this file cannot access at commands. The default at.deny file, created during the SunOS software installation, contains the following usernames:

- daemon
- bin
- smtp
- nuucp
- listen
- nobody
- noaccess

With superuser privileges, you can edit this file to add other usernames whose at access you want to restrict.

Checking Jobs in Queue (atq and at -l)

To check your jobs that are waiting in the at queue, use the atq command. This command displays status information about the at jobs you created. Use the atq command to verify that you have created an at job. The atq command confirms that at jobs have been submitted to the queue, as shown in the following example:

```
atq
```

The system responds with this:

```
Rank  Execution Date Owner  Job          Queue  Job Name
1st   Jun  6, 08:00  root   912690000.a    a    stdin
2nd   Jun  6, 08:05  root   912690300.a    a    stdin
```

Another way to check an at job is to issue the at -l command. This command shows the status information on all jobs submitted by a user, as shown in this example:

```
at -l
```

The system responds with this:

```
user = root    912690000.a    Thu Jun  6 08:00:00
user = root    912690300.a    Thu Jun  6 08:05:00
```

Removing and Verifying Removal of at Jobs

To remove the at job from the queue before it is executed, type this:

```
at -r [job-id]
```

job-id is the identification number of the job you want to remove.

Verify that the at job has been removed by using the at -l (or atq) command to display the jobs remaining in the at queue. The job whose identification number you specified should not appear. In the following example, you'll remove an at job that was scheduled to execute at 8:00 a.m. on June 6. First, check the at queue to locate the job identification number:

```
at -l
```

The system responds with this:

```
user = root    912690000.a    Thu Jun  6 08:00:00
user = root    912690300.a    Thu Jun  6 08:05:00
```

Next, remove the job from the at queue:

```
at -r 912690000.a
```

Finally, verify that this job has been removed from the queue:

```
at -l
```

The system responds with this:

```
user = root    912690300.a    Thu Jun  6 08:05:00
```

Job Scheduler

The Solaris Management Console (SMC) includes a graphical tool to create and schedule jobs on your system. You can use the Job Scheduler Tool to

- View and modify job properties
- Delete a job
- Add a scheduled job
- Enable or disable job logging

To open the Job Scheduler, follow the steps described in the "SMC Process Tool" section to start up the SMC using the `smc` command.

1. In the Navigation pane of the SMC Welcome window, open the Job Scheduler by clicking on the This Computer icon, then click on the Services icon, and then click on the Scheduled Jobs icon as shown in Figure 5.10.

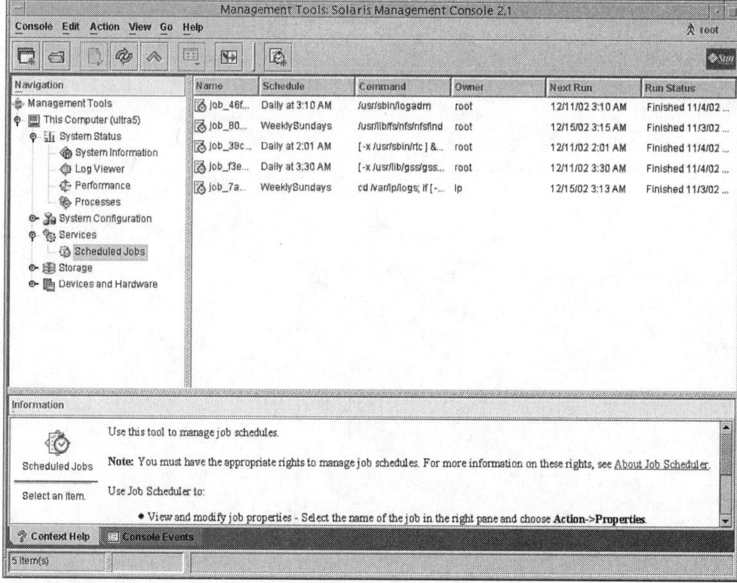

FIGURE 5.10 Opening the Job Scheduler.

2. You can add jobs to the `crontab` by selecting Action from the top toolbar as shown in Figure 5.11.

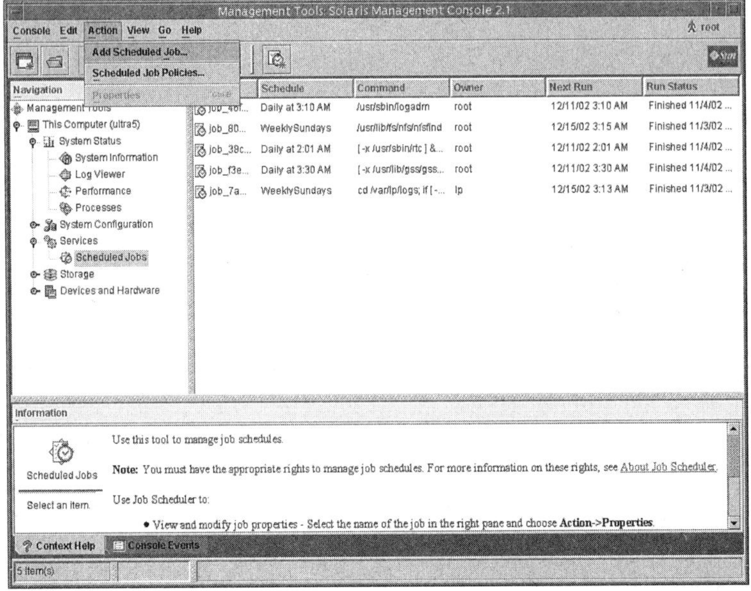

FIGURE 5.11 Adding a `cron` job.

3. Modify a `cron` job by double clicking on the job in the main window pane as shown in Figure 5.12.

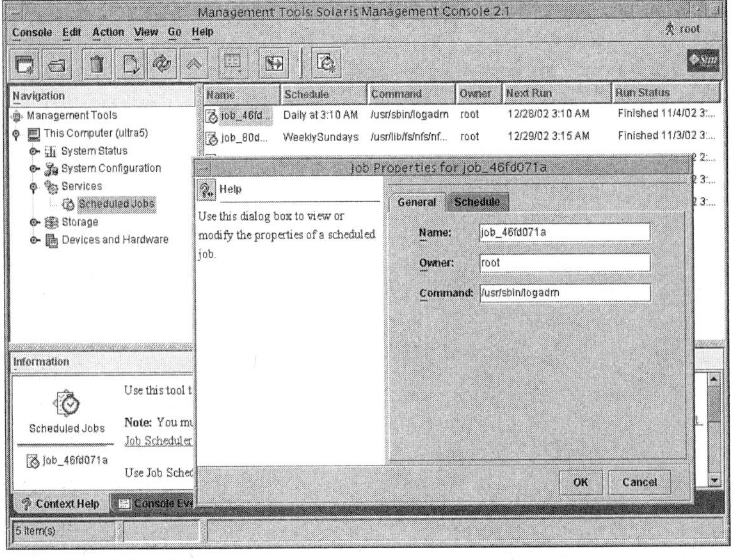

FIGURE 5.12 Modifiying a `cron` job.

Summary

This chapter described Solaris processes and the various Solaris utilities available to monitor them. Using commands such as `ps`, `prstat`, `pargs`, `sdtprocess`, and the SMC Process Tool, you can view all the attributes associated with a process. In addition, we described foreground and background jobs.

The concept of sending signals to a process was described. A signal is a message sent to a process to interrupt it and cause a response or action. You also learned how to send signals to processes to cause a response such as terminating a process.

Setting process priorities was described. We also described the concept of projects and tasks along with administrative commands used to administer them. The various commands, such as `nice` and `priocntl`, that are used to set and change process priorities were described. In addition, you learned how to use the `crontab` and `at` facilities. You can use these facilities to submit batch jobs and schedule processes to run when the system is less busy, to reduce the demand on resources such as the CPU and disks.

The system administrator needs to be aware of the processes that belong to each application. As users report problems, the system administrator can quickly locate the processes being used and look for irregularities. By keeping a close watch on system messages and processes, you'll become familiar with what is normal and what is abnormal. Don't wait for problems to happen—watch system messages and processes daily. Create shell scripts to watch processes for you and to look for irregularities in the system log files. By taking a proactive approach to system administration, you'll find problems before they affect the users.

In Chapter 6, "Managing the LP Print Service," we'll explore another topic that you'll need to become acquainted with—the LP Print Service, the facility responsible for printing within the Solaris environment.

Key Terms

- `at` command
- Process Manager GUI
- Child process
- `cron`
- `crontab`
- `crontab` file
- `nice` command
- Parent process
- `pgrep` command
- `preap` command
- `priocntl` command
- Process
- Project (as it relates to process management)
- `prstat` command
- `ps` command

- Signals
- SMC Job Scheduler
- SMC Process Tool
- Zombie process

Exercises

5.1 Displaying Process Information

In this exercise, you'll use the various utilities described in this chapter to display information about active processes.

Estimated time: 10 minutes

1. Log in as root into the Java Desktop Environment or CDE.
2. Open a new window and display the active processes using the ps command:

   ```
   ps -ef
   ```

3. Open another new window and display the active processes using the prstat command:

   ```
   prstat
   ```

   Notice how the ps command took a snapshot of the active processes, but the prstat command continues to update its display.
4. Type q to exit prstat.
5. Display the dtlogin process and all of its child processes. First obtain the PID of the dtlogin process with the pgrep command:

   ```
   pgrep dtlogin
   ```

   Now use the ptree command with the PID of the dtlogin process to display the ancestry tree:

   ```
   ptree <PID from dtlogin>
   ```

6. Now start the Process Manager.

   ```
   sdtprocess &
   ```

   Notice how the window updates periodically.
7. In the sample field at the top of the window, change the sample period from 30 to 5 seconds.
8. Sort the processes by ID by clicking on the ID button in the header.

5.2 Using the Batch Process

In this exercise, you'll use `crontab` to configure a process to execute everyday at a specified time.

Estimated time: 10 minutes

1. Log in as root into a Java Desktop or CDE session.
2. Make sure your default shell editor is set to `vi` (EDITOR=vi;export EDITOR) before beginning this exercise.
3. Open a new window and edit the `crontab` entry.

   ```
   crontab -e
   ```

4. Enter the following after the last line at the end of the file:

   ```
   0 11 * * * echo Hand in Timesheet > /dev/console
   ```

5. Save and close the file.

   Open a console window and at 11:00 a.m., you'll see the message `Hand in Timesheet` displayed.

Exam Questions

1. Which of the following commands finds all processes that have `dt` in the process argument string? Choose all that apply.

   ❍ **A.** `pgrep -l -f dt`

   ❍ **B.** `ps -ef dt`

   ❍ **C.** `ps -el dt`

   ❍ **D.** `ps -ef¦grep dt`

2. Which one of the following commands kills a process named `test`?

   ❍ **A.** `pkill test`

   ❍ **B.** `kill test`

   ❍ **C.** `ps -ef¦¦grep kill¦ kill -9`

   ❍ **D.** `kill test`

3. Which commands display active system processes and update at a specified interval? Choose all that apply.

   ❍ A. `ps`

   ❍ B. `prstat`

   ❍ C. `sdtprocess`

   ❍ D. `ptree`

4. In output from the `ps` command, what does an `R` stand for in the `S` field?

   ❍ A. The process is on the run queue.

   ❍ B. The process is receiving input.

   ❍ C. It is a regular process.

   ❍ D. The process is sleeping, so it must be restarted.

5. In output from the `ps` command, which of the following does the `UID` field display?

   ❍ A. The parent process

   ❍ B. The process id

   ❍ C. The process owner

   ❍ D. The priority of the process

6. Which one of the following options to the `ps` command lists only processes for a particular user?

   ❍ A. `-P`

   ❍ B. `-f`

   ❍ C. `-l`

   ❍ D. `-u`

7. Which one of the following commands lists all processes running on the local system?

   ❍ A. `ps -e`

   ❍ B. `ps -a`

   ❍ C. `ps -f`

   ❍ D. `ps -t`

8. Which one of the following sends a terminate signal (signal 15) to a process with a PID of 2930?

   ❍ **A.** `kill 2930`

   ❍ **B.** `stop 2930`

   ❍ **C.** Ctrl+C

   ❍ **D.** `cancel 2930`

9. Which one of the following signals kills a process unconditionally?

   ❍ **A.** 9

   ❍ **B.** 0

   ❍ **C.** 15

   ❍ **D.** 1

10. Which of the following commands is used to change the priority on a process? Choose all that apply.

   ❍ **A.** `renice`

   ❍ **B.** `priocntl`

   ❍ **C.** `ps`

   ❍ **D.** `hup`

11. Which one of the following commands is issued to increase the priority of PID 8200?

   ❍ **A.** `renice -n -4 -p 8200`

   ❍ **B.** `nice -n -4 -p 8200`

   ❍ **C.** `nice -i 8200`

   ❍ **D.** `renice -I -p 8200`

12. Which utilities can be used to show the process ancestry tree? Choose all that apply.

   ❍ **A.** `ps`

   ❍ **B.** `ptree`

   ❍ **C.** `sdtprocess`

   ❍ **D.** `prstat`

13. Which of the following commands schedules a command to run once at a given time?

❍ A. `crontab`

❍ B. `priocntl`

❍ C. `at`

❍ D. `cron`

14. Which of the following commands show(s) the jobs queued up by the `at` command? Choose all that apply.

❍ A. `atq`

❍ B. `at -l`

❍ C. `ps`

❍ D. `crontab`

15. Which one of the following `crontab` entries instructs the system to run `logchecker` at 3:10 on Sunday and Thursday nights?

❍ A. `0 4 * * 10,3 /etc/cron.d/logchecker`

❍ B. `10 3 * * 0,4 /etc/cron.d/logchecker`

❍ C. `* 10 3 0,4 /etc/cron.d/logchecker`

❍ D. `10 3 * * 0-4 /etc/cron.d/logchecker`

16. Which one of the following logs keeps a record of all `cron` activity?

❍ A. `/var/cron/log`

❍ B. `/var/spool/cron/log`

❍ C. `/var/adm/cron`

❍ D. `/var/adm/messages`

17. A user wants to execute a command later today, after leaving work. Which one of the following commands will allow him to do this?

❍ A. `runat`

❍ B. `at`

❍ C. `submit`

❍ D. None of the above

18. You've added the user name bcalkins to the /etc/cron.d/cron.allow file. You've removed the name bcalkins from the /etc/cron.d/cron.deny file. Which statement is true regarding crontab?

 - ❍ **A.** bcalkins cannot create crontab entries.
 - ❍ **B.** bcalkins can create crontab entries.
 - ❍ **C.** Only root can create crontab entries.
 - ❍ **D.** No one can create crontab entries.

Answers to Exam Questions

1. **A, D.** Use the pgrep and ps commands to view processes running on your system. The commands pgrep -l -f dt and ps -ef¦grep dt find all the processes that have dt in the process argument string and display them.
2. **A.** The command pkill test kills a process named test.
3. **B, C.** The prstat and sdtprocess commands display active system processes and can be configured to update at a specified interval.
4. **A.** In output from the ps command, the R in the S field means that the process is on the run queue.
5. **C.** In output from the ps command, the UID field displays the process owner.
6. **D.** The -u option to the ps command lists only processes for a particular user.
7. **A.** The -e option to the ps command lists all processes currently running on the system. The other options only list processes for the local user.
8. **A.** The command kill 2930 sends a terminate signal (signal 15) to a process with a PID of 2930.
9. **A.** Signal 9 stops a process unconditionally.
10. **A, B.** The commands renice and priocntl are used to change the priority on a process.
11. **A.** The renice -n -4 -p 8200 command is issued to increase the priority of a process with a PID of 8200.
12. **B, C.** The utilities ptree and sdtprocess are used to show the process ancestry tree.
13. **C.** The at command schedules a command to run once at a given time.
14. **A, B.** The atq and at -l commands show the jobs queued up by the at command.
15. **B.** The crontab entry 10 3 * * 0,4 /etc/cron.d/logchecker instructs the system to run logchecker at 3:10 on Sunday and Thursday nights.

16. **A.** The log file named `/var/cron/log` keeps a record of all `cron` activity.
17. **B.** Use the `at` command to execute a command or script at a later time.
18. **B.** Users can manage jobs if their name appears in the `/etc/cron.d/cron.allow` file and does not appear in the `/etc/cron.d/cron.deny` file.

Suggested Reading and Resources

1. Calkins, Bill. *Inside Solaris 9*. New Riders Publishing. November 2002.

CHAPTER SIX

Managing the LP Print Service

Objectives

The following test objectives for Exam CX-310-200 are covered in this chapter:

Configure and administer Solaris 10 OS print services, including client and server configuration, starting and stopping the LP print service, specifying a destination printer, and using the LP print service.

- **You need to be able to describe how printers function in the Solaris operating environment. You need to be familiar with the tools used to manage printer queues and the various files and directories that support the print function.**
- **Be prepared to explain how to configure printer classes, set the default printer, change the default printer class, remove a printer's configuration, start the LP print service, and stop the LP print service using the appropriate commands.**
- **Understand how to manage printer queues, how to send jobs to a printer, and how to manage those jobs.**

Outline

Study Strategies

The following study strategies will help you prepare for the test:

- This chapter does not show many lengthy step-by-step procedures, but it does introduce several commands that you use to manage printers, and it provides examples on how to use these commands. You should practice the step-by-step procedures as well as the commands to make sure that you understand where and when to use them.
- You should pay close attention to the differences between the System V Release 4 (SVR4) and the Berkeley Software Distribution (BSD) print services. You need to understand the basic functions of the Solaris print service.
- You need to make sure you understand the difference between a print server and a print client. You must understand the differences between local and networked printers, and you should pay close attention to the various configuration files that are used to define a printer.

The LP Print Service

Printers are standard peripherals for many computer systems. One of the first devices added to almost any new system is a printer. The multi-user nature of the Solaris operating environment means that the Solaris printer software is more complex than that of a single-user operating system. This means that adding a printer to a Solaris system requires more than just plugging it in.

This chapter describes how to set up local printers, set up access to remote printers, and perform some printer administration tasks by using the Print Manager graphical user interface (GUI) or the command line. Print Manager should meet most of a system administrator's needs for setting up printing services, adding printers to servers, or adding access from print clients to remote printers on print servers.

Setting up a printer from the command line can be a complex task. This chapter examines the hardware issues involved in connecting a printer to a Solaris system and then moves on to examine the more complex part of the process—configuring the software.

The Solaris Print Service

Objective:

Describe the purpose, features, and functionality of printer fundamentals, including print management tools, printer configuration types, Solaris LP print service, LP print service directory structure, and the Solaris operating environment printing process.

The Solaris print service is a default cluster that is installed when the operating system is initially installed. The function of the Solaris print service is described later in this chapter. To verify that the package is installed, you should look for the following software packages by using the `pkginfo` command as described in Chapter 2, "Installing the Solaris 10 Operating Environment":

Package	Description
`SUNWlpmsg`	ToolTalk programs for passing printer alerts.
`SUNWfdl`	Solaris Desktop Font Downloader for Adobe PostScript printers.
`SUNWscplp`	Solaris Print-Source Compatibility package. This package contains print utilities for user-interface and source-build compatibility with SunOS 4.x. These utilities are located in the `/usr` directory.
`SUNWslpr`	root (`/`) file system portion of the Service Location Protocol (SLP) framework. Includes the SLP configuration file and start scripts for the SLP daemon.

Package	Description
`SUNWslpu`	`/usr` file system portion of the SLP framework.
`SUNWmp`	MP (make pretty) print filter.
`SUNWpcr`	Solaris print client configuration files and utilities for the print service (root).
`SUNWpcu`	Solaris print client configuration files and utilities for the print service (usr).
`SUNWppm`	Solaris Print Manager.
`SUNWpsr`	Configuration and startup files for the print service.
`SUNWpsu`	Solaris Print-LP Server configuration files and utilities for the print service (usr).

NOTE

SLP SLP is an Internet Engineering Task Force (IETF) protocol for discovering shared resources (such as printers, file servers, and networked cameras) in an enterprise network. The Solaris 10 operating environment contains a full implementation of SLP, including application programming interfaces (APIs) that enable developers to write SLP-enabled applications. SLP also provides system administrators with a framework for ease of network extensibility.

Setting up a Solaris printer involves setting up the spooler, the print daemon, and the hardware (that is, the printer and the printer port). The system administrator needs to verify that the computer has at least 200MB of disk space available for `/var/spool/lp`. Print files will be sent to this location to be prepared for printing. Other configuration files are created, but Solaris takes care of that part for you. When you are setting up a printer, Solaris makes the required changes in the system's `/etc/printers.conf` file and the `/etc/lp` directory.

LP Print Service Directories

The LP print service includes the following directory structure, files, and logs:

- **`/usr/bin`**—This directory contains the LP print service user commands.
- **`/usr/sbin`**—This directory contains the LP print service administrative commands.
- **`/usr/share/lib/terminfo`**—This directory contains the `terminfo` database, which describes the capabilities of devices such as printers and terminals. The `terminfo` database is discussed later in this chapter.
- **`/usr/lib/lp`**—This directory contains the LP print service daemons, binary files used by the print service, PostScript filters, and default printer interface programs.

- `/usr/lib/lp/model`—This directory contains default printer interface programs (shell scripts) called `standard` and `netstandard`. The print service runs the `standard` interface script on local printers to do the following:

  - Initialize the printer port.
  - Initialize the printer.
  - Print a banner page.
  - Print the correct number of copies, as specified in the user's print request.

  The `netstandard` script is designed to support network printers. It collects the spooler and print database information and passes this information on to `/usr/lib/lp/bin/netpr`. `netpr` in turn opens the network connection and sends the data to the printer.

  When a print request is sent to a printer queue, the print service runs through the printer's standard script, which performs the following functions:

  - Initialize the printer port.
  - Initialize the actual printer, using the terminfo database to find the appropriate control sequences.
  - Print a banner page if configured to do so.
  - Print the specified number of copies.

  Printer interface file templates are located in the `/usr/lib/lp/model` directory. When a printer queue is created, this template file is copied to the `/etc/lp/interfaces` directory. The name of the interface file reflects the name of the printer. For example, a printer named `hplet1` would have an interface file named `/etc/lp/interfaces/hpljet1`. Printer interface files are scripts that can be modified as needed to change the behavior of the printer, such as turning off the banner page and enabling two-sided printing.

- `/usr/lib/lp/postscript`—This directory contains all the PostScript filter programs that the Solaris LP print service provides. Print filters are used to convert the content of the print request to a format that is accepted by the destination printer.

- `/etc/lp`—This directory contains the LP service configuration files. These files are edited by using the print service configuration tools described later in this chapter.

- `/etc/lp/fd`—This directory contains a set of print filter descriptor files. The files describe the characteristics of the filter and point to the actual filter program.

- `/etc/lp/interfaces`—This directory contains each printer interface program file which is copied from the `/usr/lib/lp/model` directory as described earlier. Entries in this directory are specific for each printer installed on the system.

- `/etc/lp/printers`—This directory contains subdirectories for each local printer attached to the system. Each subdirectory contains configuration information and alert files for each printer.
- `/var/spool/lp`—All current print requests are stored here until they are printed.
- `/var/lp/logs`—This directory contains a history log of print requests.

The Print Spooler

Spool stands for simultaneous peripheral operations online. The spooler is also referred to as the *queue*. Users execute the print spooler `lp` program when they want to print something. The print spooler then takes what the user wants to print and places it in the predefined `/var/spool/lp` print spooling directory.

Spooling space is the amount of disk space used to store and process requests in the print queue. The size of the `/var` directory depends on the size of the disk and how the disk is partitioned. If `/var` is not created as a separate partition, the `/var` directory uses some root partition space, which is likely to be quite small. A large spool directory could consume 600MB or more of disk space. To get a feel for this, you should look at the size and partitioning of the disks available on systems that could be designated as print servers.

When connecting printers, you need to first carefully evaluate the users' printing needs and usage patterns. If users typically print only short ASCII files, without sophisticated graphics or formatting requirements, a print server with 200MB to 300MB of disk space allocated to `/var` is probably sufficient. However, if many users are printing lengthy PostScript files, they will probably fill up the spooling space quite frequently. When `/var` fills up and users cannot queue their jobs for printing, workflow is interrupted. The size of `/var` is set when the operating system is loaded and disks are partitioned.

CAUTION

Running Out of Space in `/var` Some print jobs consume large amounts of disk space. In fact, one of my clients had a report that consumed more than 800MB when it was spooled to the printer. When `/var` runs out of disk space, many system functions cannot continue, such as printing, message logging, and mail. Make sure you provide adequate space in `/var` when setting up your system.

The SVR4 `lp` program is equivalent to the BSD `lpr` print program. In SunOS the print spooler is located in `/usr/spool`.

NOTE

BSD Print Systems Throughout this chapter, I make reference to the BSD print system for system administrators who might be familiar with it. The BSD printing protocol is an industry standard. It is widely used and provides compatibility between different types of systems from various manufacturers.

For sites that have a mix of BSD and SVR4 Unix, Sun has provided compatibility for both print systems in Solaris.

The LP Print Daemons

The `/usr/lib/lp/local/lpsched` daemon, also called the print scheduler, is the Unix utility that is responsible for scheduling and printing in Solaris 10. The `lpsched` daemon is started by the service management facility command, `svcadm`. For example, to start the `lpsched` print service, type

```
svcadm enable application/print/server
```

To shut down the `lp` print service, type

```
svcadm disable application/print/server
```

For compatibility, the `/usr/lib/lpsched` and `/usr/lib/lpshut` scripts are still available for starting and stopping the `lpsched` daemon, but these commands simply run the appropriate `svcadm enable` and `svcadm disable` commands.

Each print server has one `lpsched` daemon, which is started by the `svc:/application/print/server:default` service when the system is booted (provided a printer has been configured on this server). `lpsched` is also started automatically when a printer is added using the `lpadmin` command and disabled when the last printer has been removed.

The `lpsched` daemon starts or restarts the `lp` print service. Sometimes `lpsched` is referred to as the `lp` daemon. The `lpsched` print daemon takes output from the spooling directory and sends it to the correct printer. `lpsched` also tracks the status of printers and filters on the print server. `lpsched` is equivalent to the line printer daemon (`lpd`) in BSD Unix.

The service that handles the incoming print request from the network is `svc:/application/print/server:default`. You can check the status of this service using the `svcs` command described in Chapter 3 as follows:

```
svcs svc:/application/print/server
```

You can enable or disable the service using the `svcadm` command described earlier in this section.

The Internet services daemon, `/usr/sbin/inetd`, is started at bootup by the SMF, and it listens for service requests that are currently enabled. When a request arrives, the `inetd` daemon executes the server program that is associated with the service. The `inetd` daemon is described in Chapter 8, "The Solaris Network Environment." Print servers listen for print requests with the `inetd` daemon. When receiving a request, `inetd` starts the protocol adaptor `in.lpd` daemon, which is managed by the `svc:/application/print/rfc1179:default` service. The protocol adaptor translates the print request, communicates it to the print spooler, and returns the results to the requester. This protocol adaptor starts on demand and exits when it has serviced the network request, eliminating idle system overhead for printing.

Many methods can be used to define a printer on a Solaris system. Table 6.1 describes the tools Solaris provides for adding printers.

TABLE 6.1 Solaris Tools for Adding Printers

Utility	Description
Solaris Print Client	An interface that was previously available only with the Solstice AdminSuite set of administration tools. It is now available as part of the standard Solaris distribution software and is used to set up print clients.
Print Manager	A GUI that is used to manage printers in a name service environment. Print Manager is somewhat limited for advanced tasks.
LP print service commands	The command-line utilities that are used to set up and manage printers. These commands provide complete functionality.

Setting Up the Printer Hardware

Connecting printers to a Unix system is no one's favorite activity because it can quickly become a time-consuming task. Many printers are on the market, each with a unique interface.

When connecting a printer locally to a Sun system, you have four options:

- Use an Ethernet connection.
- Use a parallel connection.
- Use a serial connection.
- Use a universal serial bus (USB) connection.

The type of connection depends on the connectivity options available on the printer. Most modern printers have either an Ethernet or USB connection. If Ethernet or USB connectivity is not an option, a parallel connection is the preferred method. If no parallel option exists, the final choice is a serial connection.

Ethernet Connections

Most modern printers provide an option to add an Ethernet interface. A printer with an Ethernet connection is referred to as a *network printer*. A network printer is a hardware device that provides printing services to print clients without being directly cabled to a print server. It is a print server with its own system name and IP address, and it is connected directly to the network. The Ethernet interface might be internal or external to the printer. Using an Ethernet interface to install a printer is recommended in particular because of its speed (10Mbps or 100Mbps).

Parallel Connections

Most printers, with a few rare exceptions, have parallel interfaces. A parallel interface has a speed advantage over a serial interface, especially if it uses a Centronics interface.

If your system has a parallel port, you simply connect the printer to the Sun system by using a Centronics parallel cable. Some Sun systems do not have parallel interfaces at all, so you might have to add a parallel interface by purchasing a parallel interface from Sun.

Serial Connections

Some printers support both parallel and serial connections. Sometimes a printer is connected via the serial interface because the Sun system does not have an available parallel interface. Connecting a device by using a serial interface requires a thorough understanding of serial transmission. This method of connecting a printer is the most difficult because of the complexity in establishing the proper communications settings between the computer and the printer. It is also slower than other methods.

USB Connections

Most modern printers support USB connection, but some older Sun systems do not. If your Sun system has a USB port, this option provides a plug-n-play interface that is also hot-swappable, which allows devices to be plugged in and unplugged without the system being turned off. USB is intended to replace serial and parallel ports.

USB 1.0 has a maximum bandwidth of 12Mbps (which is equivalent to 1.5MBps) and up to 127 devices can be attached.

Setting Up a Network Printer

You use the vendor's software to configure the operating system of a network printer. After you have completed the vendor software installation, you don't need additional configuration. You must obtain this vendor software from the printer manufacturer and then install the printer on your system. Most network printers are easy to configure. The HP JetDirect print server is the most popular, but it is by no means the only print server available.

The first step in setting up the printer software is to connect the print server to the network and set its IP address and other network configuration settings. This process varies from one print server to another, so you need to follow the manufacturer's guidelines for information on how to do this. Next, you need to install the print server software and follow the manufacturer's guidelines for configuring the printer. The vendor's software configures everything; usually no additional software configuration is required.

CAUTION

Be Careful Using Print Manager to Add a Network Printer Unless a printer uses the `lpd` protocol, you should not use Print Manager to add, modify, or delete a network-based printer that is connected directly to a network with its own network interface card. You won't damage anything if you try this, but your printer will not be recognized by the system, even though the printer might appear in the printer tool window. You should always use the manufacturer-supplied software to manage the printer.

For printers that have parallel or serial connections, you must use the Solaris tools to configure the operating system to recognize the printer.

BSD Versus SVR4 Printing Software

The BSD Unix and SVR4 Unix are similar and yet different when it comes to the software that drives the Unix printing process. The two print systems are similar in that both are based on the concept of spooling. Both SVR4 and BSD print services support the concept of an interface program, which acts as a filter through which all output sent to the printer is passed. The following are examples of the uses of interface programs:

- **Adding a banner page**—Most Unix systems automatically add a banner page to the front of a print job. The purpose of the banner page is to identify the owner of the printer output in a shared printer setting.
- **Adding or removing a line-feed character**—Unix uses just the line-feed character to separate lines. The first problem you might encounter when testing a printer is that the text might come out in a stair-step manner. This problem can be overcome by installing the vendor's print software or interface file.

The differences between BSD and SVR4 are in the configuration files and the spooling directories, which the Solaris operating environment configures automatically. Differences also exist in the way the `lpsched` daemon handles print jobs as compared to the way the `lpd` daemon handles them in BSD.

SVR4 Print Service

In SVR4, one `lpsched` daemon services all printers. The `lpsched` daemon is continually running, and it provides the power for the print service. Only one instance of `lpsched` should be running at any time.

The LP print service performs the following functions:

- Administers files and schedules local print requests
- Receives and schedules network requests
- Filters files (if necessary) so that they print properly
- Starts programs that interface with the printers
- Tracks the status of jobs
- Tracks forms mounted on the printer
- Delivers alerts to mount new forms or different print wheels
- Delivers alerts about printing problems

Most of the `lp` configuration files are located in the `/var/spool/lp` directory, except for the interface files, which are located in the `/etc/lp/interfaces` directory. A `SCHEDLOCK` file should be in `/var/spool/lp`; it is responsible for ensuring that only one instance of `lpsched` runs. You use the `lpadmin` command to add, configure, and delete printers from the system.

Information about printers can be found in the `/etc/printers.conf` file and in files located in the `/etc/lp` directory. Solaris Print Manager provides a graphical interface to many of the `lp` commands listed in Table 6.2.

TABLE 6.2 Solaris Printing Commands

Command	Description
`accept/reject`	Enables or disables any further requests for a printer or class entering the spooling area.
`cancel`	Lets the user stop the printing of information.
`enable/disable`	Enables or disables more output from the spooler to the printer.
`lp`	Places information to be printed into the spooler.
`lpadmin`	Allows the configuration of the print service.
`lpmove`	Moves print requests between destinations.
`lpsched`	A script that runs the `svcadm` command to start the print service.
`lpshut`	A script that runs the `svcadm` command to stop the print service.
`lpstat`	Displays the status of the print service.

Although Solaris uses the SVR4 print model, it still supports BSD-style printing to provide interoperability. The widely used BSD printing protocol provides compatibility between different types of Unix and non-Unix systems from various manufacturers.

Print Servers Versus Print Clients

A *print server* is a system that has a local printer connected to it and makes the printer available to other systems on the network. A *print client* is a remote system that can send print requests to a print server. A system becomes a print client when you install the print client software and enable access to remote printers on the system. Any networked Solaris system with a printer can be a print server, as long as the system has adequate resources to manage the printing load.

The print client issues print commands that allow it to initiate print requests. The `print` command locates a printer and printer configuration information.

When a print job is sent from the print client, the user issues either the SVR4-style `lp` command or the BSD-style `lpr` command. Any one of the styles shown in Table 6.3 can be used to submit a print request.

TABLE 6.3 Valid Print Styles

Style	Description
Atomic	The `print` command and option followed by the printer name or class. Here's an example: `lp -d neptune filename`
POSIX	The `print` command and option followed by the server printer. Here's an example: `lpr -P galaxy:neptune` *`filename`*
Context	Context-based style as follows: `lpr -d thisdept/service/printer/`*`printer-name filename`*

If the user doesn't specify a printer name or class in a valid style, the command follows the search order defined in the `/etc/nsswitch.conf` file. By default, the command checks the user's `PRINTER` or `LPDEST` environment variable for a default printer name. These variables can be set in the user's startup file to specify a default printer to use. If neither environment variable for the default printer is defined, the command checks the `.printers` file in the user's home directory for the default printer alias. If the command does not find a default printer alias in the `.printers` file, it then checks the print client's `/etc/printers.conf` file for configuration information. If the printer is not found in the `/etc/printers.conf` file, the command checks the name service (NIS or NIS+), if any.

Configuring Software for a Solaris Printer

The print client software and the Print Manager application offer a graphical solution for setting up and managing printers in a networked environment. Print Manager provides a graphical interface to the `lp` commands listed in Table 6.2. The advantage of the Solaris Print Manager software is that it supports a name service (NIS or NIS+) that lets you centralize print administration for a network. If you're using a name service, Solaris Print Manager is the preferred method for managing printer configuration information. Using a name service for storing printer configuration information is desirable because it makes printer information available to all systems on the network, and that makes printing administration easier. The two tools are similar to one another and require the same type of information.

You can also use the `lpadmin` command at the command line to configure printers on individual systems. The next few sections describe how to set up a printer by using Print Manager and the command line.

Setting Up a Printer by Using Print Manager

Solaris Print Manager is a Java-based GUI that enables you to manage local and remote printer configuration. As with any Solaris GUI, your terminal must be able to display the X11 window environment in order to use this tool and you must be logged in as root.

You can follow the procedure in Step by Step 6.1 to set up a printer by using the Printer Manager.

STEP BY STEP

6.1 Setting Up a Printer by Using Print Manager

1. Log in as root on the system to which you want to connect the printer. The system on which you install the printer becomes the printer server.
2. Connect your printer to the server and turn on power to the printer.
3. Start up Print Manager by typing the following:

   ```
   /usr/sadm/admin/bin/printmgr &
   ```

   The windows shown in Figure 6.1 appear.
4. In the Select Naming Service window, select from the pull-down menu the name service you are using, as shown in Figure 6.2.
5. In the example in Figure 6.2, Files is selected from the pull-down menu because I am not using a name service at this time. After making your selection, click OK to continue. The Select Naming Service window closes.

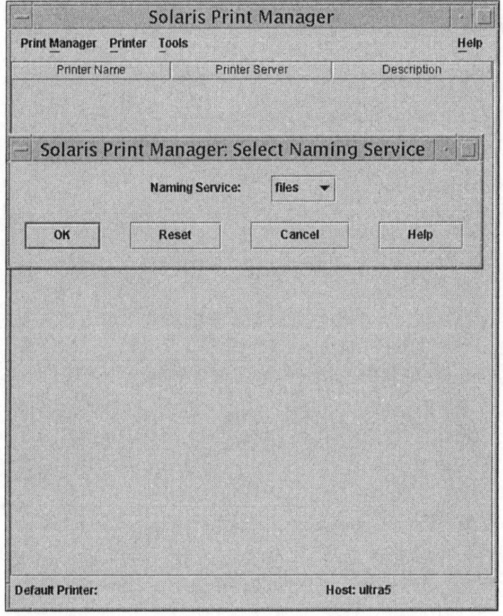

FIGURE 6.1 The Print Manager startup windows.

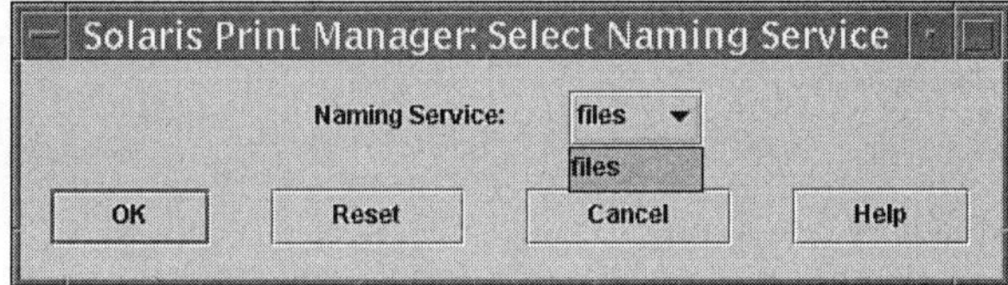

FIGURE 6.2 Selecting a name service.

6. From the main Solaris Print Manager window, click the Printer menu from the top toolbar and select New Attached Printer, as shown in Figure 6.3.

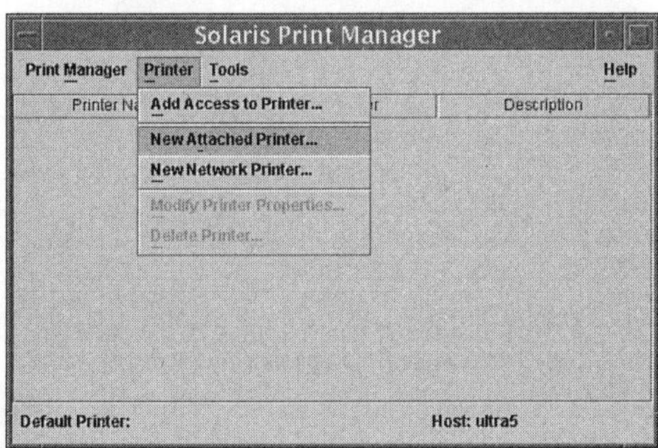

FIGURE 6.3 The Solaris Print Manager window.

The New Attached Printer window appears, as shown in Figure 6.4.

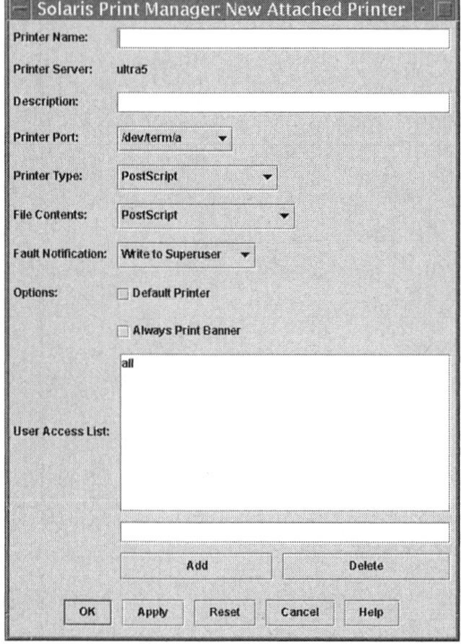

FIGURE 6.4 The New Attached Printer window.

7. Fill in the empty fields as follows:

   - **Printer Name**—Enter the name you want to give this printer.
   - **Description**—If you want to, enter a brief description of the printer.
   - **Printer Port**—Click the button and select the port to which the printer is connected:

     `/dev/term/a` is serial port A.

     `/dev/term/b` is serial port B.

     `/dev/bpp0` is the parallel port.

     `/dev/ecpp0` is the parallel port on Sun Ultra systems.

NOTE

Parallel Port on PCI-Based Systems On the PCI-based Sun systems (that is, AX machines and Ultra 30, 450, 5, 10, and 60), the parallel port is called `/dev/ecpp0` rather than `/dev/bpp0`, as on previous machines.

Select Other if you've connected an interface card with another device name.

- **Printer Type**—Click the button to select the printer type that matches your printer. The printer types here correspond to printers listed in the `/usr/share/lib/terminfo` directory. The printer type you select must correspond to an entry in the `terminfo` database. Unix works best with PostScript printers because page formatting of text and graphics from within the common desktop environment (CDE) is for a PostScript printer. If you want to set your printer type as a PostScript printer, your printer must be able to support PostScript. If you're using an HP LaserJet printer, you should choose `HPLaserJet` as the print type unless your LaserJet printer supports PostScript.
- **File Contents**—Click the button to select the format of the files that will be sent to the printer.
- **Fault Notification**—Click the button to select how to notify the superuser in case of a printer error.
- **Options**—Choose to print a banner or make this the default printer.

NOTE

Default Printers One printer can be identified as the default printer for the system. If a user does not specify a printer when printing, the job goes to the default printer.

- **User Access List**—If you want to, enter the names of the systems that are allowed to print to this printer. If nothing is entered, all clients are allowed access.

After you fill in all the fields, click the OK button. The window closes, and the new printer name appears in the Solaris Print Manager window, as shown in Figure 6.5.

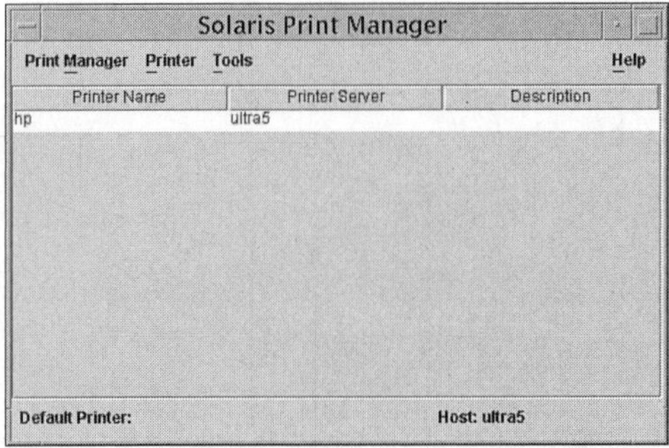

FIGURE 6.5 The new printer name in the Solaris Print Manager window.

Using a Printer Not Listed on the Printer Types Menu

Printer types listed in the Print Manager window correspond to printers listed in the `/usr/share/lib/terminfo` directory. If a printer type is not available for the type of printer you are adding, you might need to add an entry in the `/usr/share/lib/terminfo` database. Each printer is identified in the `terminfo` database by a short name; for example, an HP

LaserJet printer is listed under the `/usr/share/lib/terminfo/h` directory as `HPLaserJet`. The entries for PostScript printers are in `/usr/share/lib/terminfo/P`. The name found in the directory is the printer type you specify when setting up a printer.

If you cannot find a `terminfo` entry for your printer, you can try selecting a similar type of printer; however, you might have trouble keeping the printer set in the correct modes for each print request. If no `terminfo` entry exists for your type of printer and you want to keep the printer set in the correct modes, you can either customize the interface program used with the printer or add an entry to the `terminfo` database. You'll find the printer interface program located in the `/etc/lp/interfaces` directory. Editing an interface file or adding an entry to the `terminfo` database is beyond the scope of this book. A printer entry in the `terminfo` database contains and defines hundreds of items. Refer to the *Solaris System Administration Guide: Advanced Administration* at `http://docs.sun.com` for information on performing this task. Another good reference for this topic is John Strang and Tim O'Reilly's book *termcap & terminfo*, published by O'Reilly & Associates, Inc.

Setting Up a Printer by Using the `lpadmin` Command

If you are unable to use Print Manager, you can add a printer directly from the command line by using the `lpadmin` command. This method of setting up a printer provides the most flexibility, so if you're comfortable with using the command line, you should use it. The `lpadmin` command enables you to do the following:

- Define or remove printer devices and printer names.
- Specify printer interface programs and print options.
- Define printer types and file content types.
- Create and remove printer classes.
- Define, allow, and deny user lists.
- Specify fault recovery.
- Set or change the system default printer destination.

By using `lpadmin`, you can set all the print definitions, whereas Solaris Print Manager allows you to set only some of them when you install or modify a printer.

Before you use the `lpadmin` command to add a printer, you first need to gather the following information about the printer you are going to set up:

- Printer name
- Port device
- Printer type
- File content type

To set up a printer that is connected to the parallel port on a Sun Ultra system from the command line, you follow the procedure in Step by Step 6.2.

STEP BY STEP

6.2 Setting Up a Printer by Using `lpadmin`

1. Use the `lpadmin` command to define the printer name and the port device that the printer will use:

```
lpadmin -p ljet1 -v /dev/ecpp0
```

> **NOTE**
>
> **`lpadmin` Error Message** You might see an error such as this:
>
> ```
> UX:lpadmin: WARNING: "/dev/ecpp0" is accessible by others.
> TO FIX: If other users can access it you may get unwanted output. If this
> is not what you want change the owner to "lp" and change the mode to 0600.
> Processing continues.
> ```
>
> You can choose to modify permissions on this device file or leave them as is. If you modify permissions on `/dev/ecpp0`, when the print server and the print client are the same machine, the interface scripts run as the user that submitted the job. Therefore, if a user other than `lp` or root submits a job, the job will not have write access to `/dev/ecpp0`.

2. Set the printer type of the printer:

```
lpadmin -p ljet1 -T PS
```

3. Specify the file content types to which the printer can print directly:

```
lpadmin -p ljet1 -I postscript
```

4. Accept print requests for the printer:

```
accept ljet1
```

The system responds with the following:

```
destination "ljet1" now accepting requests
```

5. Enable the printer:

```
enable ljet1
```

The system responds with the following:

```
printer "ljet1" now enabled
```

6. Add a description for the printer:

```
lpadmin -p ljet1 -D "Engineering PS Printer"
```

7. Verify that the printer is ready:

```
lpstat -p ljet1
```

The system responds with the following:

```
printer ljet1 is idle. enabled since Dec 12 11:17 2005. available.
```

You now know how to set up a printer by using the command line. Next you'll learn how to manage printers by using the `lpadmin` command.

Administering Printers

Objective:

Explain how to configure printer classes, set the default printer, change the default printer class, remove a printer's configuration, start the LP print service, and stop the LP print service using the appropriate commands.

- Given a scenario, identify the appropriate commands to specify a destination printer, accept and reject print jobs, enable and disable printers, and move print jobs.

Managing the print system involves monitoring the `lp` system and uncovering reasons it might not be working properly. Other routine tasks involve cancelling print jobs and enabling or disabling a printer while it's being serviced. The following sections provide instructions for the daily tasks you will perform to manage printers and the print scheduler.

Note that the commands described in the following sections require superuser access.

Deleting Printers and Managing Printer Access

You can use Print Manager to delete a printer from the system. To do so, in the Print Manager main window, highlight the printer that you want to delete and, from the top toolbar, select Printer. From the pull-down menu, select Delete Printer, as shown in Figure 6.6. The printer queue is deleted from the system.

To delete a printer from the command line, you issue the following command on the system where the printer is connected:

```
lpadmin -x <printer-name>
```

The printer is deleted from the system.

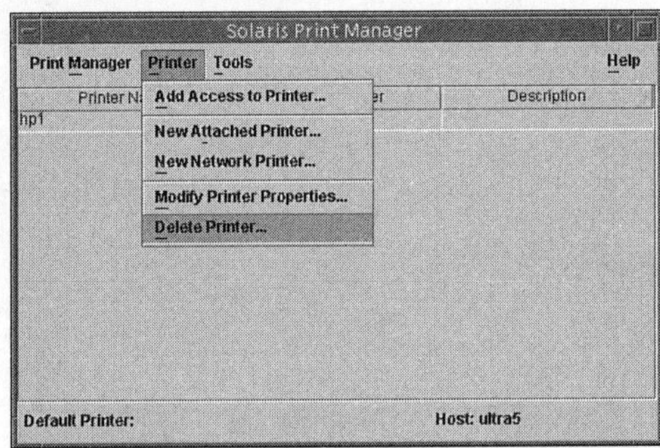

FIGURE 6.6 Deleting a printer.

Perhaps you do not want to remove the printer from the print server, but you want to keep a particular system from printing to the print server. In this case, you issue the following command on the print client from which you want to delete the printer:

```
lpsystem -r <print-server>
```

The print server is deleted from the print client's `/etc/lp/Systems` file.

To stop accepting print requests on a particular printer—perhaps because a printer will be going offline for repairs—you type the following command on the system where the printer is physically connected:

```
reject <printer-name>
```

This command prevents any new requests from entering the printer's queue while you are in the process of removing the printer. Use the `accept` command, described later in this section, to allow the queue to start accepting requests.

To allow a printer to keep taking requests but to stop the printer from printing the requests, you issue the following command on the system where the printer is physically connected:

```
disable <printer-name>
```

Printing will be halted on this system until you issue the following command:

```
enable <printer-name>
```

NOTE

Using `enable` in the bash Shell If you are using the `bash` shell, be aware that `enable` is a built-in shell command that conflicts with the LP system's `enable` command. When using `bash`, you must give the full path to `enable`, `/usr/bin/enable`.

When stopping or disabling a printer, you might need to move existing jobs that have been queued to that printer. To move print jobs from one printer to another, you use the `lpmove` command, as follows:

```
lpmove <printer1> <printer2>
```

The arguments for the `lpmove` command are described in Table 6.4.

TABLE 6.4 `lpmove` Arguments

Argument	Description
`<printer1>`	The name of the printer from which all print requests will be moved
`<printer2>`	The name of the printer to which all print requests will be moved

If you move all the print requests to another printer, the `lpmove` command automatically stops accepting print requests for `printer1`. The following command is necessary if you want to begin accepting new print requests for the printer:

```
accept printer1
```

In the following example, the `lpmove` command moves print requests from the printer `eps1` to the printer `eps2` (for example, when `eps1` is being taken down for maintenance). When the `eps1` printer is ready to start accepting print jobs again, you use the `accept` command to resume accepting print requests on `eps1`:

```
lpmove eps1 eps2
accept eps1
```

Creating Printer Classes

You can put several locally attached printers into a group called a *printer class*. This might be helpful if you have several printers sitting next to each other and it doesn't matter which printer your job goes to. After you have set up a printer class, users can specify the class (rather than individual printers) as the destination for a print request. The first printer in the class that is free to print is used. The result is faster turnaround because all printers are utilized. You create printer classes by issuing the `lpadmin` command with the `-c` option, as follows:

```
lpadmin -p <printer name> -c <class name>
```

No default printer classes are known to the print service; printer classes exist only if you define them. The following are three ways you can define printer classes:

- By printer type (for example, PostScript)
- By location (for example, 5th floor)
- By workgroup or department (for example, Accounting)

Alternatively, a class might contain several printers that are used in a particular order. The LP print service always checks for an available printer in the order in which printers were added to a class. Therefore, if you want a high-speed printer to be accessed first, you would add it to the class before you added a low-speed printer. As a result, the high-speed printer would handle as many print requests as possible. The low-speed printer would be used as a backup printer for when the high-speed printer was in use.

Printer class names must be unique and can contain a maximum of 14 alphanumeric characters and underscores. You are not obliged to define printer classes. You should add them only if you determine that using printer classes would benefit the users on the network.

Step by Step 6.3 describes how to define a printer class.

STEP BY STEP

6.3 Defining Printer Classes

1. Log in as superuser or issue the `lp` command on the print server.
2. Define a class of printers by using the `lpadmin` command:

   `lpadmin -p <printer-name> -c <printer-class>`

The arguments that are used with `lpadmin` to define printer classes are described in Table 6.5.

TABLE 6.5 `lpadmin` Arguments

Argument	Description
`-p <printer-name>`	This option allows you to specify the name of the printer you are adding to a class of printers.
`-c <printer-class>`	This option allows you to specify the printer class name.

The specified printer is added to the end of the class's list in the print server's `/etc/lp/classes/<printer-class>` file. If the printer class does not exist, it is created. You can verify what printers are in a printer class by using the `lpstat` command:

```
lpstat -c <printer-class>
```

The following example adds the printer `luna` to the class `roughdrafts`:

```
lpadmin -p luna -c roughdrafts
```

Checking Printer Status

You use the `lpstat` command to verify the status of a printer. You can use this command to determine which printers are available for use or to examine the characteristics of a particular printer. The `lpstat` command syntax is as follows:

```
lpstat [-a] [-d] [-p <printer-name> [-D] [-l]] [-t] [-u <logon_IDs>]
```

The `lpstat` command options are described in Table 6.6.

TABLE 6.6 `lpstat` Command Syntax and Options

Option	Description
`-a`	Reports whether printers are accepting requests. You can also specify a specific list of printers, as in `lpstat -a eps1 eps2 eps3`.
`-d`	Shows the system's default printer.
`-p` *<printer-name>*	Shows whether a printer is active or idle, when it was enabled or disabled, and whether it is accepting print requests. You can specify multiple printer names with this command. You use spaces or commas to separate printer names. If you use spaces, you need to enclose the list of printer names in quotes. If you don't specify the printer name, the status of all printers is displayed.
`-D`	Shows the description of the specified printer.
`-l`	Shows the characteristics of the specified printer.
`-t`	Shows status information about the LP print service, including the status of all printers—whether they are active and whether they are accepting print requests.
`-u` *<logon-IDs>*	Prints the status of output requests for users, in which *<logon-IDs>* can be one or all of the following: *<user>*—A user on the local system, as in `lpstat -u bcalkins`. *<host!user>*—A user on a system, as in `lpstat -u systema!bcalkins`. *<host!all>*—All users on a particular system, as in `lpstat -u systema!all`. *<all!user>*—A particular user on all systems, as in `lpstat -u all!bcalkins`. `all`—All users on all systems specified, as in `lpstat -u all`.

The following is an example of the `lpstat` command:

```
lpstat -p hplaser
```

The system responds with this:

```
printer hplaser is idle. enabled since Jun 16 10:09 2005.
available.
```

The following example requests a description of the printers `hplaser1` and `hplaser2`:

```
lpstat -p "hplaser1 hplaser2" -D
printer hplaser1 faulted. enabled since Jun 16 10:09 2005.
available.
unable to print: paper misfeed jam

Description: Printer by finance.
printer hplaser2 is idle. enabled since Jun 16 10:09 2005.
available.
Description: Printer in computer room.
```

The following example requests the characteristics of the printer `hplaser`:

```
lpstat -p hplaser -l
printer hplaser disabled since Tue Aug 30 20:25:34 2005. available.
        new printer
        Form mounted:
        Content types: simple
        Printer types: unknown
        Description:
        Connection: direct
        Interface: /usr/lib/lp/model/standard
        PPD: none
        On fault: write to root once
        After fault: continue
        Users allowed:
                (all)
        Forms allowed:
                (none)
        Banner required
        Character sets:
                (none)
        Default pitch:
        Default page size:
        Default port settings:
```

Managing Printer Queues

The routine task of managing printers involves managing their queues. Occasionally, large jobs are submitted that are not needed and can be aborted. Other times you might want to put a high-priority job ahead of other jobs that are waiting to be printed. The following sections outline some of the routine tasks you might want to perform on the printer queues.

Viewing a Print Job

To remove someone else's print job from the print queue, you first need to become root. Then you need to determine the request ID of the print request to cancel, by using the `lpstat` command as follows:

```
lpstat -u bcalkins
```

The system displays this:

```
eps1-1    bcalkins      1261    Mar 16 17:34
```

In this example, the user `bcalkins` has one request in the queue. The request ID is `eps1-1`.

Cancelling a Print Request

You can cancel a print request by using the `cancel` command, which has the following syntax:

```
cancel <request-ID> | <printer-name>
```

The arguments for the `cancel` command are described in Table 6.7.

TABLE 6.7 `cancel` Arguments

Argument	Description
<request-ID>	The request ID of a print request to be cancelled. You can specify multiple request IDs. You use spaces or commas to separate request IDs. If you use spaces, you need to enclose the list of request IDs in quotes.
<printer-name>	Specifies the printer for which you want to cancel the currently printing print request. You can specify multiple printer names with this command. You can use spaces or commas to separate printer names.

The following example cancels the `eps1-3` and `eps1-4` print requests:

```
cancel eps1-3 eps1-4
```

The system responds with this:

```
request "eps1-3" cancelled
request "eps1-4" cancelled
```

The following example cancels the print request that is currently printing on the printer `eps1`:

```
cancel eps1
```

The system responds with this:

```
request "eps1-9" cancelled
```

Sending a Print Job at a Higher Priority

The `lp` command with the `-q` option assigns the print request a priority in the print queue. You specify the priority level as an integer from `0` to `39`. You use `0` to indicate the highest priority and `39` to indicate the lowest. If no priority is specified, the system administrator assigns the default priority for a print service.

The following example illustrates how to send a print job to the printer `eps1`, with the highest priority:

```
lp -d eps1 -q 0 file1
```

Limiting User Access to a Printer

You can allow or deny users access to a printer by using the `lpadmin` command and adding usernames to an access list. The access list can be a list of specific users who are denied access (deny access list) or a list of users who are allowed access (allow access list). By default, all users are allowed access to a printer. This is the syntax for modifying access lists by using the `lpadmin` command:

```
lpadmin -p <printername> -u <lpadmin-argument>
```

The arguments for the `lpadmin` command that are used to control access to a printer are described in Table 6.8.

TABLE 6.8 `lpadmin` Arguments

Argument	Description
`-p <printer-name>`	This option allows you to specify the name of the printer to which the allow or deny user access list applies.
`-u allow:<user-list>`	This option allows you to specify the usernames to be added to the allow user access list. You can specify multiple usernames with this command. You use spaces or commas to separate names. If you use spaces, you need to enclose the list of names in quotes. Table 6.9 describes the valid values for *`user-list`*.
`-u deny:<user-list>`	This option allows you to specify the usernames to be added to the deny user access list. You can specify multiple usernames with this command. You use spaces or commas to separate names. If you use spaces, you need to enclose the list of names in quotes.

The specified users are added to the allow or deny user access list for the printer in one of the following files on the print server:

- `/etc/lp/printers/<printer-name>/users.allow`
- `/etc/lp/printers/<printer-name>/users.deny`

Table 6.9 provides the valid values for *user-list*.

TABLE 6.9 Values for Allow and Deny User Access Lists

Value for *user-list*	Description
user	A user on any system
all	All users on all systems
none	No user on any system
system!*user*	A user on the specified system only
!*user*	A user on the local system only
all!*user*	A user on any system
all!all	All users on all systems
system!all	All users on the specified system
!all	All users on the local system

NOTE

Specifying none in *user-list* If you specify none as the value for *user-list* in the allow user access list, the following files are not created for the print server:

/etc/lp/printers/<*printer-name*>/alert.sh
/etc/lp/printers/<*printer-name*>/alert.var
/etc/lp/printers/<*printer-name*>/users.allow
/etc/lp/printers/<*printer-name*>/users.deny

The following example gives only the users bcalkins and bholzgen access to the printer eps1:

```
lpadmin -p eps1 -u allow:bcalkins,bholzgen
```

The following example denies the users bcalkins and bholzgen access to the printer eps2:

```
lpadmin -p eps2 -u deny:"bcalkins bholzgen"
```

You can use the lpstat command to view access information about a particular printer. The following command displays access information for the printer named eps1:

```
lpstat -p eps1 -l
```

The system responds with this:

```
printer eps1 is idle. enabled since Mon Mar 20 14:39:48 EST 2002.
available.

        Form mounted:
        Content types: postscript
```

```
Printer types: PS
Description: epson
Connection: direct
Interface: /usr/lib/lp/model/standard
On fault: write to root once
After fault: continue
Users allowed:
bcalkins
bholzgen
Forms allowed:
       (none)
Banner not required
Character sets:

Default pitch:
Default page size: 80 wide 66 long
Default port settings:
```

Accepting or Rejecting Print Requests for a Printer

As root, you can stop accepting print requests for the printer by using the `reject` command. The command syntax is as follows:

```
reject [-r "reason"] <printer-name>
```

The arguments for the `reject` command are described in Table 6.10.

TABLE 6.10 `reject` Arguments

Argument	Description
`-r "reason"`	Tells the users why the printer is rejecting print requests. *reason* is stored and displayed whenever a user checks on the status of the printer by using `lpstat -p`.
<printer-name>	Specifies the name of the printer that will stop accepting print requests.

The following example stops the printer `eps1` from accepting print requests:

```
reject -r "eps1 is down for repairs" eps1
```

The system responds with this:

```
destination "eps1" will no longer accept requests
```

Any queued requests will continue printing as long as the printer is enabled. The following example sets the printer `eps1` to accept print requests again:

```
accept eps1
```

The system responds with this:

```
destination "eps1" now accepting requests
```

Cancelling a Print Request from a Specific User

You need to be the root or `lp` user if you want to cancel print requests of other users. You cancel a print request from a specific user with the `cancel` command. The syntax is as follows:

```
cancel -u <user-list> <printer-name>
```

The arguments for the `cancel` command are described in Table 6.11.

TABLE 6.11 `cancel` Arguments

Argument	Description
`-u` *<user-list>*	Cancels the print request for a specified user(s). *`user-list`* can be one or more usernames. You use spaces or commas to separate usernames. If you use spaces, you need to enclose the list of names in quotes.
<printer-name>	Specifies the printer(s) for which you want to cancel the specified user's print requests. You use spaces or commas to separate printer names. If you use spaces, you need to enclose the list of printer names in quotes. If you don't specify *`printer-name`*, the user's print requests will be cancelled on all printers.

The following example cancels all the print requests submitted by the user `bcalkins` on the printer `luna`:

```
cancel -u bcalkins  luna
```

The system responds with this:

```
request "luna-23" cancelled
```

The following example cancels all the print requests submitted by the user `bcalkins` on all printers:

```
cancel -u bcalkins
```

The system responds with this:

```
request "asteroid-3" cancelled
request "luna-8" cancelled
```

Changing the Priority of a Print Request

You can change the priority of a print request by using the following `lp` command:

```
lp -i <request-id> -H <change-priority> -q <priority-level>
```

The options for the `lp` command are described in Table 6.12.

TABLE 6.12 `lp` Options

Option	Description
`-i <request-id>`	Specifies the request ID(s) of a print request that you want to change. You use a space or a comma to separate request IDs. If you use spaces, you need to enclose the list of request IDs in quotation marks.
`-H <change-priority>`	Specifies one of the three ways to change the priority of a print request: `hold`—Places the print request on hold until you cancel it or instruct the LP print service to resume printing the request. `resume`—Places a print request that has been on hold in the queue. It will be printed according to its priority and placement in the queue. If you put a hold on a print job that is already printing, `resume` puts the print request at the head of the queue so that it becomes the next request printed. `immediate`—Places a print request at the head of the queue. If a request is already printing, you can put that request on hold to allow the next request to print immediately.
`-q <priority-level>`	Assigns the print request a priority in the print queue. You specify *`priority-level`* as an integer from `0` to `39`. `0` indicates the highest priority, and `39` indicates the lowest priority.

In the following example, the command changes a print request with the request ID `eps1-29` to priority level 1:

```
lp -i eps1-29 -q 1
```

Restarting the Print Scheduler

The Solaris print scheduler, `lpsched`, schedules all print requests on print servers. If printouts are not coming out of the printer, you might need to restart the print scheduler. To restart the print scheduler, you use the `svcadm restart scv:/application/print/server:default` command. If a print request was printing when the print scheduler stopped running, that request would be printed in its entirety when you restart the print scheduler. You first stop the scheduler by typing the following:

```
svcadm disable -t scv:/application/print/server:default
```

To restart the scheduler, you type the following:

```
svcadm enable -t scv:/application/print/server:default
```

Setting a User's Default Printer

When you add a printer, you are given the option of selecting that printer as the default printer for that particular system. You might want to set the default printer at the user level so that, on a particular system, users can specify their own default printers. If a user doesn't provide a printer name when sending a print job, the print command searches for the default printer in the following order:

1. LPDEST variable
2. PRINTER variable
3. System's default printer

These variables can be set in the user's `.profile` file. The `lp` command checks `LPDEST` and then `PRINTER`. If neither variable has been set, the print command searches for the variable named `_default` in the following file:

```
$HOME/.printers
```

An entry in this file that names `printer1` as the default printer looks like this:

```
default printer1
```

If the `$HOME/.printers` file does not exist, the `/etc/printers.conf` file is checked. An entry in this file would look like this:

```
_default¦lp:
        :use=system1:
        :bsdaddr=system1,printer1
```

If the `_default` variable is not set in the `/etc/printers.conf` file and if you're running a name service, the name service database is checked as described in Chapter 12, "Naming Services." If the destination printer name cannot be located in any of these files, the print request cannot be processed.

Modifying the Printer with Print Manager

You can use Solaris Print Manager to modify a printer after it has been added to the system. Modifications that can be made to a printer via Print Manager include the following:

- Giving the printer description
- Indicating the printer port
- Listing file contents
- Providing fault notification

- Selecting a default printer
- Printing a banner page
- Accepting and processing print requests
- Providing a user access list

To modify a printer via the Print Manager GUI, you select Printers from the top toolbar, and then you select Modify Printer Properties, as shown in Figure 6.7.

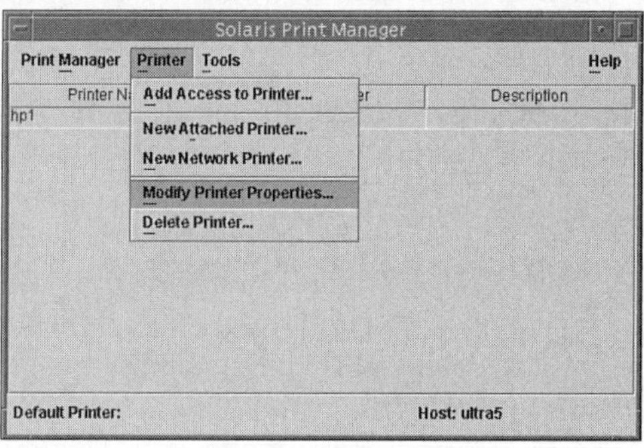

FIGURE 6.7 Modifying printers.

The Modify Printer Properties window appears, as shown in Figure 6.8.

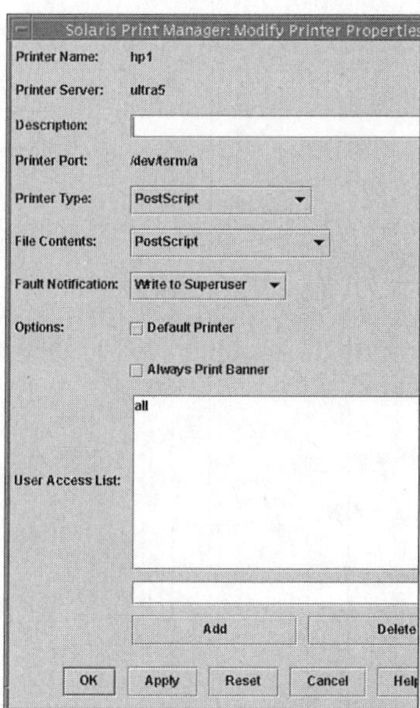

FIGURE 6.8 The Modify Printer Properties window.

You can modify the selected printer by selecting or filling in the appropriate fields in the Modify Printer Properties window.

Troubleshooting the Print Scheduler

The `lpsched` daemon keeps a log file of each print request that it processes and notes any errors that occur during the printing process. This log file is kept in the `/var/lp/logs/lpsched` file. By default, every Sunday at 3:13 a.m., the `lp cron` job renames the `/var/lp/logs/lpsched` file to a new `lpsched.n` file and starts a new log file. If errors occur or jobs disappear from the print queue, you can use the log files to determine what the `lpsched` daemon has done with a printing job.

Summary

As a system administrator, the majority of system problems I respond to are printer related. I could spend a great deal of time describing how to configure and troubleshoot the LP print service. I could explore a more in-depth discussion on configuring printer filters, creating `terminfo` databases, and troubleshooting printing problems, but that's beyond the scope of this book. To be prepared for the certification exam and basic system administration, you need to understand the basics of the LP print service, including the print spooler, print daemons, and printer configuration files. Also, you need to know where the printer related files and programs are stored in the Solaris 10 directory structure.

In addition to understanding the LP print service, you need to know how to use all the utilities and programs that are available to manage the LP print service. You need to know how to start and stop the print service and how to enable or disable it using all the methods described in this chapter.

You should also become familiar with third-party applications and how they prepare print jobs to be sent to the spooler. Many of the problems you may encounter are not with the Solaris print service but have to do with the way that the application formats the print job. This chapter introduces you to the Solaris print system and the `lpsched` daemon. For a more detailed discussion of the `lpsched` daemon, refer to *Solaris 10 System Administration Guide: Advanced Administration*, from Sun Microsystems.

Key Terms

- Default printer
- Local printer
- `lp`
- `lpd`
- `lpsched`
- Network printer
- Print client
- Print daemon
- Print queue
- Print Manager
- Print scheduler
- Print server
- Print service
- Printer class
- Spool
- `terminfo` database

Exercises

6.1 Configuring a Printer by Using `lpadmin` at the Command Line

This exercise shows you how to add and remove a local LaserJet 5M printer on a print server. The commands in this example must be executed on the print server where the printer is connected. The following information is available for the installation:

Printer name: hp1

Port device: /dev/ecpp0

System type: Ultra5

Printer type: HP LaserJet5M

File content type: PostScript/PCL

Estimated time: 10 minutes

1. As root, use the `lpadmin` command to add the printer named `hp1` to the parallel port (`/dev/ecpp0`), set the printer type as `hplaser`, and specify the file content type as `any`:

   ```
   lpadmin -p hp1 -v /dev/ecpp0 -T hplaser -I any
   ```

   Now, start accepting print requests for the printer and enable the printer:

   ```
   enable hp1
   accept hp1
   ```

2. Verify that the printer is set up and ready:

   ```
   lpstat -p hp1 -l
   ```

3. Send a print job to the printer to test it:

   ```
   lp -d hp1 /etc/hosts
   ```

4. Remove the printer:

   ```
   lpadmin -x hp1
   ```

5. Verify that the printer has been removed:

   ```
   lpstat -t
   ```

6.2 Configuring a Printer by Using the Print Manager GUI

In this exercise, you add a LaserJet 5M printer to the print server by using the Print Manager GUI.

Estimated time: 5 minutes

1. As root, start up Print Manager:

```
/usr/sadm/admin/bin/printmgr &
```

2. From the `Printer` button at the top of Print Manager window, select `New Attached Printer`. Fill in the fields as follows:

   Printer name: `hp1`

   Description: `Hplaser 5M`

   Printer port: `/dev/eccp0`

   Printer type: `HP Printer`

   File contents: `Any`

   Fault notification: `Mail to Superuser`

   Click OK when you're finished, and then exit Print Manager.

3. Verify that the printer is set up and ready by typing the following:

```
lpstat -p hp1 -l
```

6.3 Stopping and Starting the LP Print Service

In this exercise, you use the `svcadm disable` command to stop and start the LP print service.

Estimated time: 5 minutes

1. Halt the LP print service:

```
svcadm disable application/print/server
```

   Any printers that are currently printing when the command is invoked are stopped.

2. Use the `svcadm enable` command to start the LP print service:

```
svcadm enable application/print/server
```

   Printers that are restarted by using this command reprint all jobs that were interrupted with the `svcadm disable` command.

6.4 Setting Up a Network-Based Printer

This exercise illustrates how to configure a printer named `hplaser` that is connected directly to the network via its own network interface card that has the IP address `192.168.1.10`. In this example, the printer is utilizing an HP JetDirect interface, and you use Hewlett-Packard's JetAdmin software to configure the printer.

Estimated time: 15 minutes

1. Obtain the JetAdmin software from Hewlett-Packard's website (`www.hp.com`) and install it using the `pkgadd` command, as described in Chapter 2, "Installing the Solaris 10 Operating Environment." Make sure you get the correct version of JetAdmin. As of this writing, the current version is named `SOLd621.PKG`. Put the downloaded file in your `/tmp` directory.

2. Install the JetAdmin package into the `/opt/hpnp` directory by using the `pkgadd` command:

```
pkgadd -d /tmp/SOLd621.PKG
```

You should see the following output:

```
The following packages are available:
  1  HPNP     JetAdmin for Unix
              (sparc) D.06.21
Select package(s) you wish to process\
 (or 'all' to process all packages).
(default: all) [?,??,q]: 1
```

3. Type the following:

```
1 <return>
Processing package instance <HPNP> from </var/spool/pkg/SOLd621.PKG>
JetAdmin for Unix
(sparc) D.06.21
(c)Copyright Hewlett-Packard Company 1991, 1992,\
 1993. All Rights Reserved.
(c)Copyright 1983 Regents of the University of\
 California
(c)Copyright 1988, 1989 by Carnegie Mellon\
 University
              RESTRICTED RIGHTS LEGEND
Use, duplication, or disclosure by the U.S.\
 Government is subject to restrictions as set\
 forth in sub-paragraph (c)(1)(ii) of the Rights\
 in Technical Data and Computer Software clause\
 in DFARS 252.227-7013.
                  Hewlett-Packard Company
                  3000 Hanover Street
                  Palo Alto, CA 94304 U.S.A.
Where should HPNP be installed?
(<return> for /opt/hpnp) [?,q] <enter>
```

4. Keep all the default selections by pressing Enter `<return>` to install the JetAdmin package in the `/opt/hpnp` directory:

```
HPNP will be installed in /opt/hpnp.
Please configure the sub-packages you would like\
 to install.
-------------------------------------------
Done altering installation configuration
    1. [ N/A ]  JetPrint
```

```
    2. [ On  ]  JobMonitor
    3. [ On  ]  HPNPF
    4. [ On  ]  HPNPD
    5. [ On  ]  CONVERT
    ?.          Help
---------------------------------------------
Select a number to toggle an installation option.
When done select 0. Select ? for help information: 0
```

5. Enter 0 <return>, and the JetAdmin package is installed. You should see the following messages appear onscreen as the package is installing:

```
Select a number to toggle an installation option.
When done select 0. Select ? for help information: 0
Using </> as the package base directory.
## Processing package information.
## Processing system information.
## Verifying disk space requirements.
## Checking for conflicts with packages already\
 installed.
The following files are already installed on the\
 system and are being used by another package:
  /etc <attribute change only>
  /etc/init.d <attribute change only>
  /etc/rc1.d <attribute change only>
  /etc/rc2.d <attribute change only>
  /usr <attribute change only>
  /usr/bin <attribute change only>
Do you want to install these conflicting files\
 [y,n,?,q] y
```

6. Enter y <return> to install the conflicting packages.

```
This package contains scripts which will be\
 executed with super-user permission during\
 the process of installing this package.
Do you want to continue with the installation\
 of <HPNP> [y,n,?] y
```

7. Enter y <return> to continue the installation. You should see a list of files being installed, followed by this message:

```
Installation of <HPNP> was successful.
```

8. Configure the HP LaserJet printer by using the JetAdmin utility that you just installed:

```
/opt/hpnp/jetadmin
```

The following information is displayed:

```
*************************************************
*                   MAIN MENU                   *
*  HP JetAdmin Utility for UNIX (Rev. D.06.21)  *
*************************************************
   1) Configuration (super-user only):
     - configure printer, add printer to spooler
   2) Diagnostics:
     - diagnose printing problems
   3) Administration (super-user only):
     - manage HP printer, JetDirect
   4) Administration (super-user only):
     - manage JetAdmin
   5) Printer Status:
     - show printer status, location, and contact
                  ?) Help         q) Quit
Please enter a selection (q - quit):1
```

Enter 1 `<return>` to configure a new printer:

```
Printer Network Interface:
Create printer configuration in BOOTP/TFTP database
2) Remove printer configuration from BOOTP/TFTP
         Spooler:
Add printer to local spooler
Delete printer from local spooler
Modify existing spooler queue(s)
              ?) Help           q) Quit
Please enter a selection: 3
```

Enter 3 `<return>` to add your printer to the local spooler:

```
Enter the network printer name or IP address \
(q - quit): 192.168.1.10
```

Enter the IP address for your printer. In this example, I entered 192.168.1.10:

```
Following is a list of suggested parameter \
values for this queue. You can change any \
 settings by selecting the corresponding \
non-zero numbers. The values will be used to \
configure this queue when '0' is selected.
To abort the operation, press 'q'.
Configurable Parameters:           Current Settings
-----------------------            ----------------
   1) Lp destination (queue) name   [192_1]
   2) Status log                    [(No log)]
   3) Queue class                   [(not assigned)]
   4) JobMonitor                    [OFF]
   5) Default queue                 [NO]
```

```
    6) Additional printer configuration...
Select an item for change, or '0' to configure \
(q-quit):1
```

Enter 1 to change the name of the printer:

```
Currently used names:
hp1
Enter the lp destination name (default=192_1, q - quit): hplaser
```

Enter a name for the printer. In this example, I entered `hplaser`:

```
Following is a list of suggested parameter values \
for this queue. You can change any settings by \
selecting the corresponding non-zero numbers. \
The values will be used to configure this queue \
when '0' is selected.
To abort the operation, press 'q'.
Configurable Parameters:          Current Settings
-----------------------           ----------------
   1) Lp destination (queue) name   [hplaser]
   2) Status log                    [(No log)]
   3) Queue class                   [(not assigned)]
   4) JobMonitor                    [OFF]
   5) Default queue                 [NO]
   6) Additional printer configuration...
Select an item for change, or '0' to configure \
(q-quit):0
```

Enter 0 to configure the printer settings you've defined:

```
Ready to configure hplaser.
OK to continue? (y/n/q, default=y)y
```

Answer y to start the configuration process.

The system displays the following messages as the printer is being configured:

```
Finished adding "hplaser" to the spooler.
Press the return key to continue ...
```

Enter `<return>`, followed by q, and another q to exit the JetAdmin utility.

9. Verify that the printer is enabled and ready:

```
lpstat -p hplaser -l
```

The system displays information about the printer.

Exam Questions

1. Which of the following commands does the Unix utility use for printing in SRV4 Unix?

   ❍ **A.** `lpr`

   ❍ **B.** `lp`

   ❍ **C.** `lpd`

   ❍ **D.** `spool`

2. Where is the spool directory located in Solaris?

   ❍ **A.** `/var/spool/lpd`

   ❍ **B.** `/var/spool/lp`

   ❍ **C.** `/usr/spool/lp`

   ❍ **D.** `/usr/spool/lpd`

3. Which of the following commands prevents queuing of print requests?

   ❍ **A.** `disable`

   ❍ **B.** `cancel`

   ❍ **C.** `reject`

   ❍ **D.** `lpshut`

4. Which of the following can be used to add a local printer to a print server? (Select the two best answers.)

   ❍ **A.** SMC

   ❍ **B.** Print Manager

   ❍ **C.** `lpadmin`

   ❍ **D.** `lp`

5. Which of the following commands stops the print service?

   ❍ **A.** `lpsched`

   ❍ **B.** `lpshut`

   ❍ **C.** `cancel`

   ❍ **D.** `disable`

6. Which of the following commands submits the spooler information that is to be printed?

   - ❍ **A.** `lpd`
   - ❍ **B.** `print`
   - ❍ **C.** `lpsched`
   - ❍ **D.** `lp`

7. Which of the following statements is true of a print server?

   - ❍ **A.** It is a system that has a local printer connected to it.
   - ❍ **B.** It is a remote system that can send print requests to another system for printing.
   - ❍ **C.** It is a system that makes a printer available to other systems on the network.
   - ❍ **D.** Printing can be initiated from it.

8. If the user doesn't specify a printer name, which of the following environment variables tells the print service where to print?

   - ❍ **A.** $HOME
   - ❍ **B.** `$LPDEST`
   - ❍ **C.** `$PRINTER`
   - ❍ **D.** `$DEFAULT_DEST`

9. When adding a printer by using Print Manager, what is the Printer Server field used for?

   - ❍ **A.** It defines the name of the system to which the printer is connected.
   - ❍ **B.** It defines the system as a print server.
   - ❍ **C.** It selects a system from which to download the print software.
   - ❍ **D.** It defines a system that can spool to the local printers.

10. Which of the following is a serial port device?

   - ❍ **A.** `/dev/bpp0`
   - ❍ **B.** `/dev/term/ttya`
   - ❍ **C.** `/dev/term/a`
   - ❍ **D.** `/dev/fd`

11. Which of the following are valid printer ports?

❍ **A.** `/dev/terma`

❍ **B.** `/dev/term/a`

❍ **C.** `/dev/ecpp0`

❍ **D.** `/dev/term/ttya`

12. Which of the following commands cancels all print requests for the user `bcalkins` on the printer `jetprint`?

❍ **A.** `lprm -bcalkins jetprint`

❍ **B.** `cancel -Pjetprint bcalkins`

❍ **C.** `cancel -u bcalkins jetprint`

❍ **D.** `lpremove -Pjetprint bcalkins`

13. Which of the following can be used to delete a printer?

❍ **A.** `lpadmin -x`<*printer-name*>

❍ **B.** `lpshut` <*printer-name*>

❍ **C.** Print Manager

❍ **D.** `lpadmin -D` <*printer-name*>

14. Which of the following commands removes a job from the print queue?

❍ **A.** `lpmove`

❍ **B.** `cancel`

❍ **C.** `lpremove`

❍ **D.** `reject`

15. Which of the following daemons services all printers?

❍ **A.** `lpsched`

❍ **B.** `lpd`

❍ **C.** `lpr`

❍ **D.** `spoold`

16. Where is information on printers found?

 ❍ **A.** `/etc/printers.conf`

 ❍ **B.** `/etc/lp`

 ❍ **C.** `/var/spool/lp`

 ❍ **D.** `/etc/print`

17. Which of the following is a system that has a local printer connected to it and makes the printer available to other systems on the network?

 ❍ **A.** Print server

 ❍ **B.** Print client

 ❍ **C.** Client

 ❍ **D.** Server

18. Which of the following commands adds the printer `luna` to the class `roughdrafts`?

 ❍ **A.** `lpadmin -p luna -c roughdrafts`

 ❍ **B.** `lpadmin -class roughdrafts -p luna`

 ❍ **C.** `lpadmin luna -c roughdrafts`

 ❍ **D.** `lpadmin -cp roughdrafts luna`

19. Which of the following commands displays the characteristics of the printer `hplaser`?

 ❍ **A.** `lpstat -p hplaser -l`

 ❍ **B.** `lpstat -p hplaser`

 ❍ **C.** `lpadmin -p hplaser -l`

 ❍ **D.** `lpstat -a -p hplaser -l`

20. Which of the following commands changes a print request with the request ID `eps1-29` to priority level 1?

 ❍ **A.** `lp -i eps1-29 -q 1`

 ❍ **B.** `lpadmin -i eps1 -q 0`

 ❍ **C.** `lp -i eps1-29 -q 39`

 ❍ **D.** `lpadmin -i eps1 -q 39`

Answers to Exam Questions

1. **B.** The Unix utility responsible for printing in SVR4 Unix is called `lp`. For more information, see the section "The Solaris Print Service."

2. **B.** For Solaris, the spool directory is located in `/var/spool/lp`. For more information, see the section "The Print Spooler."

3. **C.** The `reject` command disables any further requests for a printer or class that is entering the spooling area. For more information, see the section "SVR4 Print Service."

4. **B, C.** You can use Print Manager or `lpadmin` to add a local printer to a print server. For more information, see the section "Setting Up a Printer by Using the `lpadmin` Command."

5. **B.** The `lpshut` command stops the print service. For more information, see the section "SVR4 Print Service."

6. **D.** The `lp` command places information to be printed into the spooler. For more information, see the section "The LP Print Daemons."

7. **A, C.** A print server is a system that has a local printer connected to it. A print server makes a printer available to other systems on the network. For more information, see the section "Print Servers Versus Print Clients."

8. **B, C.** If the user doesn't specify a printer name or class in a valid style, the print command checks the user's `PRINTER` or `LPDEST` environment variable for a default printer name. For more information, see the section "Setting a User's Default Printer."

9. **A.** When you use Print Manager to add a printer, the Printer Server field defines the name of the system (hostname) to which the printer is connected. For more information, see the section "Setting Up a Printer by Using Print Manager."

10. **C.** `/dev/term/a` is the serial port A device, the primary serial port on a Sun system. For more information, see the section "Setting Up a Printer by Using Print Manager."

11. **B, C.** Valid printer ports on a Solaris system include `/dev/term/a`, `/dev/term/b`, and `/dev/ecpp0`. For more information, see the section "Setting Up a Printer by Using Print Manager."

12. **C.** The following command cancels all print requests for the user `bcalkins` on the printer named `jetprint`:

    ```
    cancel -u bcalkins jetprint
    ```

    For more information, see the section "Cancelling a Print Request."

13. **A, C.** To delete a printer from the system, you can use either the `lpadmin -x` command or the Print Manager interface. For more information, see the section "Deleting Printers and Managing Printer Access."

14. **B.** You use the `cancel` command to remove a job from the print queue. For more information, see the section "Cancelling a Print Request."

15. **A.** The print scheduler, `lpsched`, handles print requests on print servers. For more information, see the section "Restarting the Print Scheduler."

16. **A, B.** When you set up a printer with Print Manager or `lpadmin`, Solaris makes the required changes in the system's `/etc/printers.conf` file and the `/etc/lp` directory. For more information, see the section "The Solaris Print Service."

17. **A.** The print server is a system that has a local printer connected to it and makes the printer available to other systems on the network. For more information, see the section "Print Servers Versus Print Clients."

18. **A.** To add a printer to a class, you use the following command syntax: `lpadmin -p` *`<printer-name>`* `-c` *`<printer-class>`*. For more information, see the section "Creating Printer Classes."

19. **A.** You use the `lpstat` command to display the characteristics of a particular printer: `lpstat -p` *`<printer-name>`* `-l`. For more information, see the section "Checking Printer Status."

20. **A.** You use the `lp` command to change the priority of a print job to priority level 1: `lp -i` *`<job name>`* `-q 1`. For more information, see the section "Changing the Priority of a Print Request."

Suggested Reading and Resources

For more information on this topic, refer to the *Managing Print Services* section of the *Solaris 10 Advanced System Administration Guide* by Sun Microsystems, part number 817-0403-10. This guide is available at `http://docs.sun.com`.

A good book on the topic of Unix printing in general is *Network Printing*, by Matthew Gast and Todd Radermacher.

7

CHAPTER SEVEN

Performing System Backups and Restorations

Objectives

The following test objectives for Exam CX-310-200 are covered in this chapter:

Given a backup requirement, develop a backup strategy that includes scheduled backups, number of tapes required, naming conventions, command protocols, and backup frequency/levels.

- Solaris 10 provides several utilities for copying data between disks, tapes, and other types of media. You need to understand the capabilities of each utility and determine which is best for a particular circumstance. This chapter describes all the utilities and commands used to back up and restore data on a Solaris system. When you're finished with this chapter, you should be able to develop a scheduled backup strategy and determine the number of tapes required, command protocols, and backup frequency/levels for any given scenario.

Back up a mounted file system by creating a UFS snapshot and performing a backup of the snapshot file.

- You need to understand how to create a read-only image of a mounted file system using the `fssnap` command. You also need to know how to backup the UFS snapshot to tape.

Restore data from a UFS snapshot and delete the UFS snapshot.

- You need to understand the methods of restoring an entire file system from a snapshot and removing a snapshot when it is no longer needed.

Explain how to perform UFS restores and special case recoveries.

- You need to understand all the steps required to restore a file or file system from tape for each of the various Solaris backup utilities.

Outline

Study Strategies

The following study strategies will help you prepare for the test:

- As you study this chapter, make sure that you thoroughly understand the various backup tools available in Solaris. On the exam, you'll need to match the correct tool to the task it can perform or the correct description. The exam questions are primarily on `ufsdump` and `ufsrestore`. For the exam you need to develop various backup strategies by using `ufsdump`. You also need to know how to restore the operating system from a backup by using the `ufsrestore` command.
- You should practice the commands and all the options on a live Solaris 10 system (SPARC or x86). You should try to memorize the examples that are provided in this chapter. They illustrate the commands and options that are most likely to appear on the exam. It's best if you have a tape drive with which to practice, but if you don't have one, you can practice using the commands for moving files between two partitions on a disk. You need to pay special attention to the `ufsdump` and `ufsrestore` commands.
- You should familiarize yourself with the exercises in this chapter. You should memorize them because the material they cover is on the exam.

Introduction

Backing up a system involves copying data from the system's hard disks onto removable media that can be safeguarded in a secure area. Backing up system data is one of the most crucial system administration functions and should be performed regularly. Backups are used to restore data if files become corrupted or if a system failure or another disaster destroys data. Having a fault-tolerant disk array is not enough. Disk mirroring and RAID 5 protect data in case of a hardware failure, but they do not protect against file corruption, natural disaster, or accidental deletion of a file. In other words, disk mirroring does not protect against flood damage or fire. In addition, if a program corrupts a particular file, the file will be just as corrupt on the mirrored copy as in the original. Therefore, you need to have in place some type of offline backup of your data. Backing up system data—the most important task you perform as a system administrator—must be done on a regular basis. Although even a comprehensive backup scheme can't guarantee that information will not be lost, you can use backups to make sure the loss will be minimal.

This chapter describes the methods available to perform backups, the types of backups, how to develop a solid backup strategy, and how to restore data if you encounter a loss. This chapter begins with a look at backup media and then an explanation of the `tar`, `dd`, `cpio`, and `pax` commands, which are used to copy data from disk to disk or from disk to tape. Then you'll learn about the `ufsdump` and `ufsrestore` utilities, the preferred methods of backing up data from a Solaris system to tape on a regular basis. This chapter also introduces a method of backing up live file systems, called `fssnap`. Finally, this chapter describes how to back up an entire Solaris operating environment by using the Solaris Flash Archive.

Many third-party backup applications are available for Solaris but are not covered on the exam. Therefore, this chapter describes only the methods that are available in the standard Solaris 10 distribution.

Backup Media

Selecting backup media is as critical as selecting the program to perform the backup. Your backup media should be removable so that the information can be taken to another site for safe storage in case of fire, flood, or other natural disaster. In some cases, the backup medium is simply another system on the network that's located in a different building from the primary data. Most backup systems, however, use tape media. Magnetic tape still provides the lowest cost per megabyte for storing data. Table 7.1 lists some typical tape devices that are used for storing backed-up data.

TABLE 7.1 Tape Device Types

Media Type	Capacity
1/2-inch reel tape	140MB (6250BPI)
1/4-inch cartridge tape (QIC)	8GB
8mm cartridge tape	40GB–70GB
4mm DAT cartridge tape (DDS-DDS4)	1GB–40GB
DLT (Digital Linear Tape) 1/2-inch cartridge tape	20GB–400GB
SDLT (Super Digital Linear Tape) cartridge tape	160GB–320GB
LTO (Linear Tape Open) cartridge tape	100GB–200GB

To achieve high capacity, one or more of these tape drives are often combined into cabinets called *tape libraries* or *tape silos*, which are capable of storing several terabytes of data, spread across tens or even hundreds of tapes. Robotic arms are used to locate, retrieve, and load tapes into a tape drive automatically to eliminate human intervention.

Tape Device Names

Chapter 1, "Managing File Systems," describes disk device names. Tape drives are also accessed through their logical device names. In fact, for each tape drive, you see 24 different logical device files assigned to each tape drive. These device files are located under the directory `/dev/rmt` and are comprised of numbers and letters:

```
/dev/rmt/#cn
```

The following are the numbers and letters in the device files:

- `#`—This number refers to the tape drive's logical device number. The first tape drive found by the system is given the designation `0`, the second is `1`, the third is `2`, and so forth. These numbers do not correspond to SCSI ID numbers.
- `c`—The letter following the device number is the tape density. This can be `l` (low), `m` (medium), `h` (high), `c` (compressed), or `u` (ultra compressed).
- `n`—If an `n` is present after the tape density letter, it means "no rewind." Sometimes after a tape drive is finished, you do not want the tape to automatically rewind. If the `n` is not present in the device name, the tape automatically rewinds when the backup is complete.

Table 7.2 describes 24 device files for a tape drive with a logical device number of `0`. Beside each device file listed is a description of what the letters mean. All these device files contain different attributes but refer to the same physical tape drive, `0`, and can be used at will.

TABLE 7.2 Tape Logical Device Files

Device Name	Description
0	SystemV (SysV)-style rewinding device with no compression. This is the standard tape device. When you use this device name, the tape rewinds when complete.
0b	Berkeley-style rewinding tape device with no compression.
0bn	Berkeley-style nonrewinding tape device with no compression.
0c	SysV-style rewinding tape device with compression.
0cb	Berkeley-style rewinding tape device with compression.
0cbn	Berkeley-style nonrewinding tape device with compression.
0cn	SysV-style nonrewinding tape device with compression.
0h	SysV-style rewinding tape device with high density.
0hb	Berkeley-style rewinding tape device with high density.
0hbn	Berkeley-style nonrewinding tape device with high density.
0hn	SysV-style nonrewinding tape device with high density.
0l	SysV-style rewinding tape device with low density.
0lb	Berkeley-style rewinding tape device with low density.
0lbn	Berkeley-style nonrewinding tape device with low density.
0ln	SysV-style nonrewinding tape device with low density.
0m	SysV-style rewinding tape device with medium density.
0mb	Berkeley-style rewinding tape device with medium density.
0mbn	Berkeley-style nonrewinding tape device with medium density.
0mn	SysV-style nonrewinding tape device with medium density.
0n	SysV-style nonrewinding tape device with no compression.
0u	SysV-style rewinding tape device with ultra compression.
0ub	Berkeley-style rewinding tape device with ultra compression.
0ubn	Berkeley-style nonrewinding tape device with ultra compression.
0un	SysV-style nonrewinding tape device with ultra compression.

NOTE

Compression Tape drives that support data compression contain internal hardware that performs the compression on the fly. You should check with your tape drive manufacturer to see if your tape drive supports compression.

Solaris Backup and Restoration Utilities

Objective:

Explain how to perform incremental, full, and remote backups to tape for an unmounted file system using the `ufsdump` command or explain how to back up a mounted file system using UFS snapshot.

Solaris provides the utilities listed in Table 7.3. These backup utilities can be used to copy data from disk to removable media and to restore it.

TABLE 7.3 Backup Utilities

Utility	Description
`tar`	Creates tape or file-based archives. This format is commonly used for transferring collections of files between systems.
`dd`	Converts and copies a file or raw device.
`cpio`	Copies data from one location to another.
`pax`	Copies files and directory subtrees to a single tape or file. This utility provides better portability than `tar` and `cpio`, so it can be used to transport files to other types of Unix systems.
`ufsdump`	Backs up all files in a file system.
`ufsrestore`	Restores some or all of the files archived with the `ufsdump` command.
`zip`	Packages and compresses archive files. This utility creates compressed archives that are portable across various platforms, including Unix, VMS, and Windows.
Flash Archive	Combines the use of Jumpstart and backup utilities to provide an easy mechanism for restoring a system to its initial state or cloning systems.
`jar`	Leverages the portability and flexibility of Java to provide capabilities similar to those of `tar`, `cpio`, and `zip`.

The `tar` Utility

The primary use of the `tar` (which stands for *tape archiver*) command is to copy file systems or individual files between a hard disk and tape or from one file system to another. You can also use `tar` to create a `tar` archive on a floppy disk and to extract files from a `tar` archive on a floppy disk. The `tar` command is popular because it's available on most Unix systems. If the data you are backing up requires more than one tape, you should use the `cpio`, `pax`, or `ufsdump` commands, which are described in the following sections. The `tar` command has the following syntax:

```
tar <options> <tar-filename> <file-list>
```

You can replace *`options`* with the list of command options in Table 7.4.

TABLE 7.4 Command Options for `tar`

Option	Description
`c`	Creates a `tar` file.
`t`	Lists the names of the specified files each time they occur in the `tar` filename. If no file argument is given, the names of all files in the `tar` file are listed. When `t` is used with the `v` function modifier, additional information displays for the specified files. `t` stands for *table of contents*.
`x`	Extracts or restores files from a `tar` filename.
`v`	Outputs information to the screen as `tar` reads or writes the archive. `v` stands for *verbose*.
`f`	Uses the `tar` filename argument as the name of the `tar` archive. If `f` is omitted, `tar` uses the device indicated by the `TAPE` environment variable (if it is set). If the `TAPE` variable is not set, `tar` uses the default values defined in `/etc/default/tar`. If the name of the `tar` file is `-`, `tar` writes to the standard output or reads from the standard input.

For a more complete listing of command options, see the Solaris online man pages.

`<tar-filename>` is used with the `f` option and can be any name you want. The filename can also be the name of a device, such as `/dev/rmt/0` or `/dev/rfd0`. *`<file-list>`* is a list of files you want to include in the archive.

`tar` Examples

The following examples illustrate the use of the `tar` command.

To create a tape archive of everything in the `/home/bcalkins` directory on tape device `/dev/rmt/0`, you type the following:

```
tar cvf /dev/rmt/0 /home/bcalkins
```

To list the files in the archive, you type the following:

```
tar tvf /dev/rmt/0
```

To restore the file `/home/bcalkins/.profile` from the archive, you type the following:

```
tar xvf /dev/rmt/0 /home/bcalkins/.profile
```

You use `tar` to create an archive file on disk instead of tape. The `tar` filename is `files.tar`, as follows:

```
tar cvf files.tar /home/bcalkins
```

To extract files that were created using the preceding example, you type the following:

```
tar xvf files.tar
```

Notice the use of the full pathname when creating an archive with `tar`. Using the full pathname to create an archive ensures that the files will be restored to their original locations in the directory hierarchy. You will not be able to restore them elsewhere.

If you want to be able to restore files with a relative pathname in the preceding example, you can change to the `/home/bcalkins` directory and specify files to be archived as `./*`. This puts the files into the archive, using a pathname that is relative to the current working directory rather than an absolute pathname (one beginning with a forward slash [/]). Files can then be restored into any directory. The use of relative pathnames is highly recommended so that you have the option of restoring an archive without overwriting files that exist but may be different from those in the archive.

The dd Utility

The main advantage of the `dd` command is that it quickly converts and copies files with different data formats, such as differences in block size, record length, or byte order.

The most common use of `dd` is to transfer a complete file system or partition image from a hard disk to a tape. You can also use it to copy files from one hard disk to another. When you're using it to copy data, the `dd` command makes an image copy (an exact byte-for-byte copy) of any medium, which can be either tape or disk. The syntax for the `dd` command is as follows:

```
dd if=<input-file> of=<output-file> <option=value>
```

The command arguments for `dd` are described in Table 7.5.

TABLE 7.5 dd Command Arguments

Argument	Description
`if`	Designates an input file. The input file can be a filename or a device name, such as `/dev/rmt/0`. If no input file is specified, input for `dd` is taken from the standard input.
`of`	Designates an output file. The output file can be a filename or a device name, such as `/dev/rmt/0`. If no output file is specified, output from `dd` is sent to the standard output.
`<option=value>`	Several other options can be used on the command line to specify buffer sizes, block sizes, and data conversions. See the Solaris online man page `dd` (1M) for a list of these options.

dd Examples

The next few examples illustrate the use of the `dd` command to copy data. The first example shows how the `dd` command is used to duplicate tapes:

```
dd if=/dev/rmt/0 of=/dev/rmt/1
```

This procedure requires two tape drives—a source tape and a destination tape.

The next example uses dd to copy one entire hard disk to another hard disk:

```
dd if=/dev/rdsk/c0t1d0s2 of=/dev/rdsk/c0t4d0s2 bs=128K
```

In this example, you need two disks, and both must have the same geometry. Disk geometry is discussed in Chapter 1.

CAUTION

Using dd to Copy Data Between Dissimilar Disk Drives Be careful when using dd to copy data between two different types of disk drives. We have used dd to move data from a 4GB disk to an 18GB disk, and the data transferred fine. We were able to access the data, and the option seemed to have completed correctly. Then we noticed that when we went into the `format` utility, the 18GB disk was labeled as a 4GB disk. This is because "everything" on the 4GB disk transferred to the 18GB disk—including the disk label! All of our work was wasted. We had to re-identify the disk type, relabel, and repartition the disk to get it to recognize the disk as an 18GB disk.

In this example, the option `bs=128K` specifies a block size. A large block size, such as 128KB or 4096KB, can decrease the time to copy by buffering large amounts of data. Notice in the example that the raw device is specified. For this technique to work properly, you must use the raw (character) device to avoid the buffered (block) input/output (I/O) system.

You can use the dd command with `tar` to create an archive on a remote tape drive. In the next example, `tar` is used to create an archive on a remote system by piping the output to a tape drive called `/dev/rmt/0` on a remote system named `xena`:

```
tar cvf - <files> ¦ rsh xena dd of=/dev/rmt/0 obs=128
```

Another example would be to read `tar` data coming from another Unix system such as older Silicon Graphics systems. The Silicon Graphics system swaps every pair of bytes, making a `tar` tape unreadable on a Solaris system. To read a `tar` tape from a Silicon Graphics system, you type the following:

```
dd if=/dev/rmt/0 conv=swab ¦ tar xvf -
```

Note that the argument for the `conv` option is swab ("swap bytes") and not swap. In a similar way, a Solaris system can create a `tar` tape that a Silicon Graphics system can read:

```
tar cvf - <files> ¦ dd of=/dev/rmt/0 conv=swab
```

The `cpio` Utility

The `cpio` command is used to copy data from one place to another. `cpio` stands for *copy input to output*. When copying files with `cpio`, you present a list of files to the system's standard input and write the file archive to the system's standard output. The principal advantage of `cpio` is its flexible syntax. The command acts as a filter program, taking input information from the standard input file and delivering its output to the standard output file. You can manipulate the input and output by using the shell to specify redirection and pipelines. The following are the advantages of `cpio` over other Unix utilities:

- `cpio` can back up and restore individual files, not just whole file systems. (`tar`, `pax`, and `ufsdump` also have this capability.)
- Backups made by `cpio` are slightly smaller than those created with `tar` because the `cpio` header is smaller.
- `cpio` can span multiple tapes; `tar` is limited to a single tape.

`cpio` has more options and is therefore perceived as a more complex command than `tar`.

The `cpio` utility operates in one of three modes: copy out (`cpio -o`), copy in (`cpio -i`), or pass (`cpio -p`). You use copy-out mode when creating a backup tape and copy-in mode when restoring or listing files from a tape. The pass mode is generally used to copy files from one location to another on disk. You must always specify one of these three modes. The command syntax for the `cpio` command is as follows:

```
cpio <mode> <option>
```

mode is `-i`, `-o`, or `-p`, and *option* is one of the options described in Table 7.6.

TABLE 7.6 Command Options for `cpio`

Option	Description
`-c`	Writes header information in ASCII format for portability.
`-d`	Creates directories as needed.
`-B`	Specifies that the input has a blocking factor of 5,120-byte records instead of the default 512-byte records. You must use the same blocking factor when you retrieve or copy files from the tape to the hard disk as you did when you copied files from the hard disk to the tape. You must use the `-B` option whenever you copy files or file systems to or from a tape drive.
`-v`	Reports the names of the files as they are processed. `-v` stands for *verbose*.
`-u`	Copies unconditionally. Without this option, an older file will not replace a newer file that has the same name.
`-m`	Retains the previous file modification time. This option is ineffective on directories that are being copied.
`-P`	With output, causes existing access control lists (ACLs) to be written along with other attributes, except for extended attributes, to the standard output. With input, causes existing ACLs to be extracted along with other attributes from standard input. `-P` stands for *preserve ACLs*.

`cpio` Examples

The following example shows how to copy the directory `/work` and its subdirectories to a tape drive with the device name `/dev/rmt/0`:

```
cd /work
-find . ¦ cpio -ocB > /dev/rmt/0
```

In this example, the `find` command locates all of the files in the current working directory and pipes them to the `cpio` command. The `-o` option specifies copy-out mode, `-c` outputs the header information in ASCII format, and `-B` increases the blocking factor to 5,120 bytes to improve the speed.

The following example shows how to copy the files located on a tape back into the directory named `/work` on a hard disk:

```
cd /work
cpio -icvdB < /dev/rmt/0
```

The `-i` option specifies copy-in mode, `-d` creates directories as needed to restore the data to the original location, and `-v` displays all the output.

Backing Up Files with Copy-Out Mode

To use copy-out mode to make backups, you send a list of files to the `cpio` command via the standard input of `cpio`. You use the Unix `find` command to generate the list of files to be backed up. You specify copy-out mode by using the `-o` option on the `cpio` command line. In the following example, a file named `list` contains a short list of files to be backed up to tape:

```
cpio -ovB < list > /dev/rmt/1
```

Normally, as indicated in Table 7.6, `cpio` writes files to the standard output in 512-byte records. By specifying the `-B` option, you can increase the record size to 5,120 bytes to significantly speed up the transfer rate, as shown in the previous example. You can use Unix commands to generate a list of files for `cpio` to back up in a number of other ways, as shown in the following examples.

You can back up files by entering filenames via the keyboard. You press Ctrl+D when you have finished typing filenames. For example, enter the following:

```
cpio -oB > /dev/rmt/1
File1.txt
File2.txt
Ctrl+d
```

You can use the `ls` command to generate the list of files to be backed up by `cpio`. You type the following to back up all the files in the current directory but not the files in subdirectories:

```
cd /home/bcalkins
ls -d * ¦ cpio -oB >/dev/rmt/1
```

You need to be careful when using `ls` to generate the list of files to back up. In particular, you should be sure that the `ls` command specifies the full path to the files that should be backed up. You will be dissatisfied with the results if you try to use `ls -R` or any other `ls` command on a directory unless you specify the `-d` option to `ls`.

In general, the best command to use for generating a file list is `find`. You can use the `find` command to generate a list of files that the user `bcalkins` created and modified in the past five days. The following is the list of files to be backed up:

```
find . -user bcalkins -mtime -5  -print ¦ cpio -oB > /dev/rmt/1
```

If the current tape fills up, the `cpio` program prompts you for another tape. You see a message such as the following:

```
If you want to go on, type device/file name when ready
```

You should then change the tape and enter the name of the backup device (for example, `/dev/rmt/1`).

Restoring Files with Copy-In Mode

You use the copy-in mode of `cpio` to restore files from tape to disk. The following examples describe methods used to restore files from a `cpio` archive.

The following example restores all files and directories from tape to disk:

```
cd /users
cpio -icvumB < /dev/rmt/1
```

The `cpio` options specified restore files unconditionally (`-u`) to the `/users` directory and retain previous file modification times (`-m`).

The following example selectively restores files that begin with `database`:

```
cpio -icvdumB 'database*' < /dev/rmt/1
```

The `-d` option in this example creates directories as needed.

NOTE

Using Wildcards with `cpio` You must use standard shell escapes to pass the wildcard argument (*) to `cpio`. For example, the wildcard argument can appear within single quotes.

To obtain a list of files that are on tape, you use the following code:

```
cpio -ictB < /dev/rmt/1
```

The list of files on `/dev/rmt/1` then appears onscreen.

Using Pass Mode

Pass mode is generally not used for backups. The destination must be a directory on a mounted file system, which means that pass mode cannot be used to transfer files to tape. However, you can use pass mode to copy files from one directory to another. The advantage of using cpio over cp is that with it, original modification times and ownership are preserved. You specify pass mode by using the -p option with cpio.

The following example copies all files from /users to /bkup:

```
cd /users
mkdir /bkup
find . ¦ cpio -pdumv /bkup
```

Files are listed onscreen as they are copied.

The pax Utility

The pax command has been included in Solaris since version 2.5. pax is a POSIX-conformant archive utility that can read and write tar and cpio archives. It is available on all Unix systems that are POSIX compliant, such as IBM's AIX, Hewlett-Packard's HP-UX, and some Linux distributions.

pax can read, write, and list the members of an archive file and copy directory hierarchies. The pax utility supports a wide variety of archive formats, including tar and cpio.

If pax finds an archive that is damaged or corrupted while it is processing, pax attempts to recover from media defects. It searches the archive to locate and process the largest possible number of archive members.

The action to be taken depends on the presence of the -r and -w options, which together form the four modes of operation: list, read, write, and copy (as described in Table 7.7). The syntax for the pax command is as follows:

```
pax <mode> <options>
```

TABLE 7.7 Four Modes of Operation for pax

Option	Operation Mode	Description
-r	Read mode	When -r is specified but -w is not, pax extracts the filenames and directories found in the archive file. The archive file is read from disk or tape. If an extracted file is a directory, the file hierarchy is extracted as well. The extracted files are created relative to the current file hierarchy.
None	List mode	When neither -r nor -w is specified, pax displays the filenames or directories found in the archive file. The archive file is read from disk, tape, or the standard input. The list is written to the standard output.

Table 7.7 *Continued*

Option	Operation Mode	Description
-w	Write mode	When -w is specified but -r is not, pax writes the contents of the file to the standard output in an archive format specified by the -x option. If no files are specified, a list of files to copy (one per line) is read from the standard input. A directory includes all the files in the file hierarchy whose root is at the file.
-rw	Copy mode	When both -r and -w are specified, pax copies the specified files to the destination directory.

In addition to selecting a mode of operation, you can select one or more options to pax from Table 7.8.

TABLE 7.8 Command Options for pax

Option	Description
-r	Reads an archive file from the standard input and extracts the specified files. If any intermediate directories are needed to extract an archive member, these directories are created.
-w	Writes files to the standard output in the specified archive format. When no file operands are specified, the standard input is read for a list of pathnames—one per line, without leading or trailing blanks.
-a	Appends files to the end of an archive that was previously written.
-b	Specifies the block size, which must be a multiple of 512 bytes with a maximum of 32,256 bytes. A block size can end with k or b to specify multiplication by 1,024 bytes (1KB) or 512 bytes, respectively. -b stands for *block size*.
-c	Matches all file or archive members except those specified by the `pattern` and `file` operands.
-f *<archive>*	Specifies *<archive>* as the pathname of the input or output archive. A single archive can span multiple files and different archive devices. When required, pax prompts for the pathname of the file or device in the next volume in the archive.
-i	Interactively renames files or archive members. For each archive member that matches a pattern operand or file that matches a file operand, a prompt is written to the terminal.
-n	Selects the first archive member that matches each pattern operand. No more than one archive member is matched for each pattern.

(continues)

Table 7.8 *Continued*

Option	Description
`-p <string>`	Specifies one or more file-characteristic options (privileges). *string* is a string that specifies file characteristics to be retained or discarded when the file is extracted. The string consists of the specification characters a, e, m, o, p, and v. Multiple characteristics can be concatenated within the same string, and multiple p options can be specified. The meanings of the specification characters are as follows: **a**—Does not preserve file access times **e**—Preserves everything: user ID, group ID, file mode bits, file access times, and file modification times **m**—Does not preserve file modification times **o**—Preserves the user ID and group ID **p**—Preserves the file mode bits **v**—Specifies verbose mode
`-x <format>`	Specifies the output archive format, with the default format being `ustar`. `pax` currently supports `cpio`, `tar`, `bcpio`, `ustar`, `sv4crc`, and `sv4cpio`.

For additional options to the `pax` command, see the Solaris man pages.

When you use `pax`, you can specify the `file` operand along with the options from Table 7.7. The `file` operand specifies a destination directory or file pathname. If you specify a directory operand that does not exist, that the user cannot write to, or that is not of type `directory`, `pax` exits with a nonzero exit status.

The `file` operand specifies the pathname of a file to be copied or archived. When the `file` operand does not select at least one archive member, `pax` writes the `file` operand pathnames in a diagnostic message to standard error and then exits with a nonzero exit status.

Another operand is the `pattern` operand, which is used to select one or more pathnames of archive members. Archive members are selected by using the filename pattern-matching notation described by `fnmatch`. The following are examples of `pattern` operands:

`pattern` Operand	Description
?	Matches any character
*	Matches multiple characters
[	Introduces a `pattern` bracket expression

When a `pattern` operand is not supplied, all members of the archive are selected. When a `pattern` operand matches a directory, the entire file hierarchy rooted at that directory is selected. When a `pattern` operand does not select at least one archive member, `pax` writes the `pattern` operand pathnames in a diagnostic message to standard error, and then exits with a nonzero exit status.

pax Examples

The following examples illustrate the use of the pax command.

To copy files to tape, you issue the following pax command, using -w to copy the current directory contents to tape and -f to specify the tape device:

```
pax -w -f /dev/rmt/0
```

To list a verbose table of contents for an archive stored on tape device /dev/rmt/0, you issue the following command:

```
pax -v -f /dev/rmt/0
```

The tape device in these two examples could have been a filename to specify an archive on disk.

You use the following command to interactively select the files to copy from the current directory to the destination directory:

```
pax -rw -i . <dest-dir>
```

Because pax understands tar and cpio formats, it is a very helpful tool when a tar or cpio archive contains absolute pathnames and the files should not be restored to their original locations. The key is the -s option, which allows files to be programmatically renamed. The following example uses the -s option to extract files from a tar archive, stripping the leading slash from any absolute pathname:

```
pax -r -s ',^/,,' -f file.tar
```

As you become more familiar with the pax utility, you might begin to use it in place of tar and cpio for the following reasons:

- It is portable to other Unix systems.
- It is capable of recovering damaged archives.
- It is capable of spanning multiple volumes.

The ufsdump Utility

Objective:

Explain how to perform incremental, full, and remote backups to tape for an unmounted file system using the ufsdump command, or explain how to back up a mounted file system using UFS snapshot.

Given a backup requirement, develop a backup strategy that includes scheduled backups, number of tapes required, naming conventions, command protocols, and backup frequency/levels.

Whereas the other Solaris utilities discussed in this chapter can be used to copy files from disk to tape, `ufsdump` is designed specifically for backups and is the recommended utility for backing up entire Solaris file systems. The `ufsdump` command copies files, directories, or entire file systems from a hard disk to tape or from disk to disk. The only drawback of using `ufsdump` is that the file systems must be inactive (that is, unmounted or read-only) before you can conduct a full backup. If the file system is still active, nothing in the memory buffers is copied to tape, and you could end up with a corrupt backup.

You should back up any file systems that are critical to users, including file systems that change frequently. Table 7.9 gives suggestions on the file systems to back up and the suggested frequency.

TABLE 7.9 File Systems to Back Up

File System	Frequency
root (/)	If you frequently add and remove clients and hardware on the network or you have to change important files in root (/), this file system should be backed up. You should do a full backup of the root file system between once a week and once a month. If `/var` is in the root file system and your site keeps user mail in the `/var/mail` directory on a mail server, you might want to back up root daily.
`/usr`	The contents of this file system are fairly static and need to be backed up only between once a week and once a month—and after new software or patches are installed.
`/export/home`	The `/export/home` file system usually contains the home directories and subdirectories of all users on the system; its files are volatile and should be backed up daily.

The `ufsdump` command has many built-in features that the other archive utilities don't have, including the following:

- The `ufsdump` command can be used to back up individual file systems to local or remote tape devices or disk drives. The device to which the files are being backed up can be on any system in the network. This command works quickly because it is aware of the structure of the Unix file system and it works directly through the raw device file.
- `ufsdump` has built-in options to create incremental backups that back up only the files that have been changed since a previous backup. This saves tape space and time.

- `ufsdump` has the capability to back up groups of systems over the network from a single system. You can run `ufsdump` on each remote system through a remote shell or remote login, and you can direct the output to the system on which the drive is located.
- With `ufsdump`, the system administrator can restrict user access to backup tables.
- The `ufsdump` command has a built-in option to verify data on tape against the source file system.

Backing up a file system with `ufsdump` is referred to as *dumping* a file system. When a file system is dumped, a level between 0 and 9 is specified. A level 0 dump is a full backup and contains everything on the file system. Levels 1 through 9 are incremental backups and contain only files that have changed since previous dumps at lower levels.

A recommended backup schedule involves a three-level dump strategy: a level 0 dump at the start of the month (manually), automated weekly level 5 dumps, and automated daily level 9 dumps. The automated dumps are performed at 4:30 a.m., for example—a time when most systems are typically idle. Automated daily dumps are performed Sunday through Friday mornings. Automated weekly dumps are performed on Saturday mornings. Backups are automated by creating a shell script and using `cron` to execute the script on a regular basis.

Table 7.10 shows the dump level performed on each day of a typical month. Note that the level 0 dump at the start of the month is performed manually because the entire system must be idle before you can back up the root file system. One way to ensure that the system is not being used is to put the system in single-user mode. The level 9 and 5 dumps are automated with `cron`, but also must be conducted when the file systems are not being used. See Chapter 5, "Managing System Processes," for more information on `cron`.

TABLE 7.10 File System Dump Schedule

Floating	Sun	Mon	Tues	Wed	Thurs	Fri	Sat
1st of month	0						
Week 1	9	9	9	9	9	9	5
Week 2	9	9	9	9	9	9	5
Week 3	9	9	9	9	9	9	5
Week 4	9	9	9	9	9	9	5

The backup schedule in Table 7.10 accomplishes the following:

- Each weekday tape accumulates all files changed since the end of the previous week or the initial level 0 backup for the first week. All files that have changed since the lower-level backup at the end of the previous week are saved each day.
- Each Saturday tape contains all files changed since the last level 0 backup.

This dump schedule requires at least four sets of seven tapes—one set for each week and one tape for the level 0 dump. Each set will be rotated each month. The level 0 tapes should not be overwritten and should be saved for at least a year, depending on your company's and jurisdiction's data-retention policy.

Even with the backup schedule outlined in Table 7.10, data can still be lost. For example, if a hard disk fails at 3 p.m., all modifications since the preceding 4:30 a.m. backup will be lost. Also, files that were deleted midweek will not appear on the level 5 tapes. Or a user may accidentally delete a file and not realize it for several weeks, but when the user wants to use the file, it is not there. If he asks you to restore the file from backup, the only tape it appears on is the level 0 backup, and it could be too far out of date to be useful. By not overwriting the daily level 9 tapes frequently, you can minimize this problem.

The syntax for the `ufsdump` command is as follows:

```
/usr/sbin/ufsdump <options> <arguments> <files-to-dump>
```

The options to the `ufsdump` command are described in Table 7.11.

TABLE 7.11 `ufsdump` Command Options

Option	Description
<options>	A single string of one-letter option names.
<arguments>	The argument that goes with each option. The option letters and the arguments that go with them must be entered in the same order.
<files-to-dump>	The files to back up. This argument must always come last. It specifies the source or contents of the backup. It usually identifies a file system, but it can also identify individual files or directories. For a file system, you specify the name of the file system or the raw device file for the disk slice where the file system is located.

Table 7.12 describes the options and arguments for the `ufsdump` command.

TABLE 7.12 Options for the `ufsdump` Command

Option	Description
`0` to `9`	Specifies the backup level. Level 0 is for a full backup of the entire file system. Levels 1 through 9 are for incremental backups of files that have changed since the last lower-level backup.
`a` *<archive-file>*	Instructs `ufsdump` to create an archive file. Stores a backup table of the tape contents in a specified file on the disk. The file can be understood only by `ufsrestore`, which uses the table to determine whether a file to be restored is present in a backup file and, if so, on which volume of the medium it resides.
`b` *<factor>*	Specifies the blocking factor: the number of 512-byte blocks to write to tape per operation.

Table 7.12 *Continued*

Option	Description
`c`	Instructs `ufsdump` to back up to cartridge tape. When end-of-media detection applies, this option sets the block size to 126.
`d <bpi>`	Specifies the tape density. You should use this option only when `ufsdump` cannot detect the end of the medium.
`D`	Backs up to floppy disk.
`f <dump-file>`	Specifies the destination of the backup. *`<dump-file>`* can be one of the following: A local tape drive or disk drive A remote tape drive or disk drive Standard output
	You use this argument when the destination is not the default local tape drive `/dev/rmt/0`. If you use the `f` option, you must specify a value for *`dump-file`*.
`l`	Specifies autoload. You use this option if you have an autoloading (stackloader) tape drive. When the end of a tape is reached, this option takes the drive offline and waits up to two minutes for the tape drive to be ready again. If the drive is ready within two minutes, it continues. If the drive is not ready after two minutes, autoload prompts the operator to load another tape.
`n`	Specifies notify. When intervention is needed, this option sends a message to all terminals of all users in the *`sys`* group.
`o`	Specifies offline. When `ufsdump` is finished with a tape or disk, it takes the drive offline, rewinds it (if it's a tape), and removes the medium, if possible. (For example, it ejects a disk or removes an 8mm autoloaded tape.)
`s <size>`	Specifies the length of tape, in feet, or the size of the disk, in the number of 1,024-byte blocks. You need to use this option only when `ufsdump` cannot detect the end of the medium.
`S`	Estimates the size of the backup. This option determines the amount of space needed to perform the backup (without actually doing it) and outputs a single number that indicates the estimated size of the backup, in bytes.
`t <tracks>`	Specifies the number of tracks for 1/4-inch cartridge tape. You need to use this option only when `ufsdump` cannot detect the end of the medium.
`u`	Updates the dump record. For a completed backup of a file system, this option adds an entry to the file `/etc/dumpdates`. The entry indicates the device name for the file system's disk slice, the backup level (0 to 9), and the date. No record is written when you do not use the `u` option or when you back up individual files or directories. If a record already exists for a backup at the same level, it is replaced.

(continues)

Table 7.12 *Continued*

Option	Description
v	Verifies the contents of the medium against the source file system after each tape or disk is written. If any discrepancies appear, this option prompts the operator to mount a new medium and then repeats the process. You use this option on an unmounted or snapshot file system only; any activity in the file system causes it to report discrepancies.
w	Lists the file systems appearing in `/etc/dumpdates` that have not been backed up within a day. When you use this option, all other options are ignored.
W	Shows all file systems that appear in `/etc/dumpdates` and highlights file systems that have not been backed up within a day. When you use this option, all other options are ignored.

The `ufsdump` command uses these options by default:

```
ufsdump 9uf /dev/rmt/0 <files-to-back-up>
```

`ufsdump` Examples

The following examples illustrate the use of the `ufsdump` command.

The following is an example of a full backup of the `/users` file system:

```
ufsdump 0ucf /dev/rmt/0 /users
  DUMP: Writing 63 Kilobyte records
  DUMP: Date of this level 0 dump: Thu Jul 25 10:43:25 2002
  DUMP: Date of last level 0 dump: the epoch
  DUMP: Dumping /dev/rdsk/c0t1d0s0 (pyramid1:/users) to /dev/rmt/0.
  DUMP: Mapping (Pass I) [regular files]
  DUMP: Mapping (Pass II) [directories]
  DUMP: Estimated 10168 blocks (4.96MB).
  DUMP: Dumping (Pass III) [directories]
  DUMP: Dumping (Pass IV) [regular files]
  DUMP: Tape rewinding
  DUMP: 10078 blocks (4.92MB) on 1 volume at 107 KB/sec
  DUMP: DUMP IS DONE
```

If you want to see how much space a backup is going to require, you issue the following command:

```
ufsdump S <filesystem>
```

The estimated number of bytes needed on tape to perform the level 0 backup is displayed.

In the following example, the local `/export/home` file system on a Solaris 10 system is backed up to a tape device on a remote Solaris 10 system called `sparc1`:

```
ufsdump 0ucf sparc1:/dev/rmt/0 /export/home
DUMP: Date of this level 0 dump: Thu Jul 25 10:43:25 2002
DUMP: Date of last level 0 dump: the epoch
DUMP: Dumping /dev/rdsk/c0t3d0s7 (/export/home) to /dev/rmt/0 \
 on host sparc1
DUMP: mapping (Pass I) [regular files]
DUMP: mapping (Pass II) [directories]
DUMP: estimated 19574 blocks (9.56MB)
DUMP: Writing 63 Kilobyte records
DUMP: dumping (Pass III) [directories]
DUMP: dumping (Pass IV) [regular files]
DUMP: level 0 dump on Thu Jul 25 10:43:25 2002
DUMP: Tape rewinding
DUMP: 19574 blocks (9.56MB) on 1 volume
DUMP: DUMP IS DONE
```

In this example, the `-u` option is used with the `ufsdump` command. This causes `ufsdump` to make an entry into the `/etc/dumpdates` file, which records the file system that was backed up, the level of the last backup, and the day, date, and time of the backup. Here's an example of looking into the `/etc/dumpdates` file:

```
more /etc/dumpdates
```

The system responds with the following:

```
/dev/rdsk/c0t0d0s7            0 Mon Mar 25 10:47:46 2005
/dev/rdsk/c0t0d0s6            0 Mon Mar 25 10:48:04 2005
```

When incremental backups are made by using `ufsdump`, the `ufsdump` command consults the `/etc/dumpdates` file to find the date of the most recent backup at the next lower level. `ufsdump` then copies all files modified or added since the date of that lower-level backup. You can also determine whether backups are being done by viewing the contents of the `/etc/dumpdates` file. If a backup fails, it is not recorded in `/etc/dumpdates`.

Another useful example is using `ufsdump` to copy the contents of one file system to another. In the section "The `dd` Utility," you learned how to copy data from one disk to another, but only when the disk geometry is exactly the same for each disk. In other words, `dd` works when you want to copy a 4GB disk to another 4GB disk. But if you want to replace an older 4GB disk with a new 18GB disk, you should not use `dd` to copy the data; a better option is to use `ufsdump`. Moving data from disk to tape and then back to disk again can be time consuming. Here's a way to move data directly to that file system by using `ufsdump` without going to tape:

```
ufsdump 0f - /export/home ¦ (cd /data; ufsrestore  -xf - )
```

In this example, all data in the `/export/home` file system is copied to the `/data` file system. Instead of specifying a tape device, this example specifies a `-` (hyphen). The hyphen dumps the data to standard output and restores the data from standard input rather than from a file or device. This creates and extracts the dump file in memory, speeding up the entire process.

The ufsrestore Utility

Objective:

Explain how to perform UFS restores and special case recoveries.

TIP

Restoring File Systems You need to understand each step described in Step by Step 7.1 and Step by Step 7.2, along with the order in which each step is performed. Also, you need to understand what the **restoresymtable** file is used for. These topics are likely to be on the exam.

The ufsrestore command copies files from backups created using the ufsdump command. As root, you can use ufsrestore to reload an entire file system from a level 0 dump and any incremental dumps that follow it, or to restore one or more single files from any dump tape. ufsrestore restores files with their original owner, last modification time, and mode (permissions).

The syntax for the ufsrestore command is as follows:

```
ufsrestore  <options>  <arguments> <filename(s)>
```

The options for the ufsrestore command are described in Table 7.13.

TABLE 7.13 ufsrestore Command Options

Option	Description
<options>	Gives you the choice of one and only one of these options: i, r, R, t, or x
<arguments>	Follows the *<options>* string with the arguments that match the options
<filename(s)>	Specifies files to be restored as arguments to the x or t options and must always come last

Table 7.14 describes some of the most common options and arguments for the ufsrestore command.

TABLE 7.14 Command Options for the `ufsrestore` Command

Option	Description
`i`	Runs `ufsrestore` in interactive mode. In this mode, you can use a limited set of shell commands to browse the contents of the medium and select individual files or directories to restore. See Table 7.15 for a list of available commands.
`r`	Restores the entire contents of the medium into the current working directory, which should be the top level of the file system. Information used to restore incremental dumps on top of the full dump is also included. To completely restore a file system, you use this option to restore the full (level 0) dump and then each incremental dump. This is intended for a new file system that was just created with the `newfs` command. `r` stands for *recursive*.
`x` *`<filename(s)>`*	Selectively restores the files you specify, using the *`<filename(s)>`* argument. *`<filename(s)>`* can be a list of files and directories. All files under a specified directory are restored unless you also use the `h` option. If you omit *`<filename(s)>`* or enter `.` for the root directory, all files on all volumes of the medium (or from standard input) are restored. Existing files are overwritten, and warnings are displayed. `x` stands for *extract*.
`t` *`<filename(s)>`*	Checks the files specified in the *`<filename(s)>`* argument against the medium. For each file, the full filename and the `inode` number (if the file is found) are listed. If the filename is not found, `ufsrestore` indicates that the file is not on the volume, meaning any volume in a multivolume dump. If you do not enter the *`<filename(s)>`* argument, all files on all volumes of the medium are listed, without distinction as to the volume on which the files are located. When you use the `h` option, only the directory files specified in *`<filename(s)>`*—not their contents—are checked and listed. The table of contents is read from the first volume of the medium or (if you use the `a` option) from the specified archive file. This option is mutually exclusive with the `x` and `r` options.
`b` *`<factor>`*	Specifies the number of 512-byte blocks to read from tape per operation. By default, `ufsrestore` tries to figure out the block size used in writing the tape. `b` stands for *blocking factor*.
`m`	Restores specified files into the current directory on the disk, regardless of where they are located in the backup hierarchy, and renames them with their `inode` numbers. For example, if the current working directory is `/files`, a file in the backup named `./database/test` with `inode` number 156 is restored as `/files/156`. This option is useful when you are extracting only a few files.
`s`*`<n>`*	Skips to the *n*th backup file on the medium. This option is useful when you put more than one backup on a single tape.
`v`	Displays the name and `inode` number of each file as it is restored. `v` stands for *verbose*.

For a full listing of options for the `ufsrestore` command, see the Solaris man pages.

Table 7.15 lists the commands that can be used with `ufsrestore` when you're using interactive mode (that is, `ufsrestore -i`).

TABLE 7.15 Commands for Interactive Restoration

Command	Description
`ls` *<directory-name>*	Lists the contents of either the current directory or the specified directory. Directories are suffixed with a forward slash (/). Entries in the current list to be restored (extracted) are marked by an asterisk (*) prefix. If the v option is in effect, `inode` numbers are also listed.
`cd` *<directory-name>*	Changes to the specified directory in the backup hierarchy.
`add` *<filename>*	Adds the current directory or the specified file or directory to the list of files to extract (restore). If you do not use the h option, all files in a specified directory and its subdirectories are added to the list. Note that it's possible that not all the files you want to restore to a directory will be on a single backup tape or disk. You might need to restore from multiple backups at different levels to get all the files.
`delete` *<filename>*	Deletes the current directory or the specified file or directory from the list of files to extract (restore). If you do not use the h option, all files in the specified directory and its subdirectories are deleted from the list. Note that the files and directories are deleted only from the extract list you are building. They are not deleted from the medium.
`extract`	Extracts the files in the list and restores them to the current working directory on the disk. You should specify 1 when asked for a volume number. If you are doing a multitape or multidisk restoration and are restoring a small number of files, you should start with the last tape or disk.
`help`	Displays a list of the commands you can use in interactive mode.
`pwd`	Displays the pathname of the current working directory in the backup hierarchy.
`q`	Quits interactive mode without restoring additional files.
`verbose`	Turns the `verbose` option on or off. You can also enter verbose mode by entering v on the command line outside interactive mode. When `verbose` is on, the interactive `ls` command lists `inode` numbers, and the `ufsrestore` command displays information about each file as it is extracted.

`ufsrestore` Examples

The following examples illustrate how to restore data from a tape by using `ufsrestore`.

You can use the `ufsrestore` command to display the contents of a tape:

```
ufsrestore tf /dev/rmt/0
     2       .
  4249       ./users
```

```
12400       ./users/bill
12401       ./users/bill/.login
12402       ./users/bill/.cshrc
12458       ./users/bill/admin
12459       ./users/bill/junk
```

You can use `ufsrestore` to restore a file from a backup that was created using `ufsdump`:

```
ufsrestore f /dev/rmt/0 filename
```

You can restore entire directories from a remote drive located on the system called `sparc1` by adding `sparc1:` to the front of the tape device name, as illustrated in the following example:

```
ufsrestore rf sparc1:/dev/rmt/0 filename
```

Occasionally, a file system becomes so damaged that you must completely restore it from a backup. If you have faithfully backed up file systems, you can restore them to the state of the last backup. The first step in recovering a file system is to delete everything in the damaged file system and re-create the file system by using the `newfs` command. To recover a damaged file system, follow the procedure described in Step by Step 7.1.

STEP BY STEP

7.1 Recovering and Restoring a Damaged File System

1. Unmount the corrupted file system /*<filesystem>*:

   ```
   umount  /<filesystem>
   ```

2. After you unmount the file system, issue the `newfs` command to create a new file system:

   ```
   newfs /dev/rdsk/<disk-partition-name>
   ```

   <disk-partition-name> is the name of the raw disk partition that contains the corrupted file system. Make sure you are using the correct device name; otherwise, you might destroy another file system.

3. Mount the file system to be restored and change to that directory:

   ```
   mount /dev/dsk/<c?t?d?s?> <directory>
   cd /<directory>
   ```

4. Load the tape and issue the following command:

   ```
   ufsrestore rf /dev/rmt/0
   ```

   The entire content of the tape is restored to the file system. All permissions, ownerships, and dates remain as they were when the last incremental tape was created.

   The next two steps are optional.

5. Remove the `restoresymtable` file created by the `ufsrestore` command. This is a temporary file that is created whenever you restore an entire file system from tape. The `restoresymtable` file is used only by `ufsrestore` for "check-pointing" when information is passed between incremental restorations. The `restoresymtable` file is not required after the file system has been successfully restored.

6. Unmount the file system and run `fsck` again to check the repaired file system.

Recovering the Root (/) or /usr File System

Sometimes a careless administrator with root access accidentally deletes part or all of the root or `/usr` file system. Other times the file system can become unusable because of a faulty disk drive or a corrupted file system. You can follow the procedure described in Step by Step 7.2 if you ever need to recover the root or `/usr` file system.

STEP BY STEP

7.2 Recovering the Root or /usr File System

1. Replace and partition the disk if it has failed.

2. Because the system cannot be booted from the boot disk, boot from the CD-ROM and re-create the failed file system by issuing the `newfs` command:

```
newfs /dev/rdsk/<disk-partition-name>
```

<disk-partition-name> is the name of the raw disk partition that contains the corrupted file system.

3. Check the new file system by using `fsck`:

```
fsck /dev/rdsk/<disk-partiton-name>
```

4. Mount the new file system on a temporary mount point:

```
mount /dev/dsk/<disk-partition-name> /mnt
```

5. Change to the `/mnt` directory:

```
cd /mnt
```

6. Write protect the tapes so that you don't accidentally overwrite them.

7. Load the tape and issue the following command:

```
ufsrestore rf /dev/rmt/0
```

The entire content of the tape is restored to the file system. All permissions, ownerships, and dates remain as they were when the last incremental tape was created.

8. Verify that the file system is restored:

```
ls
```

9. Remove the `restoresymtable` file that is created and used by `ufsrestore` to checkpoint the restoration:

```
rm restoresymtable
```

10. Change to the root (/) directory:

```
cd /
```

11. Unmount the newly created file system:

```
umount /mnt
```

12. Check the new file system with `fsck`:

```
fsck /dev/rdsk/<disk-partition-name>
```

The restored file system is checked for consistency.

13. If you are recovering the root (/) file system, create the boot blocks on the root partition by using the `installboot` command:

```
installboot  /usr/platform/'uname-I'/lib/fs/ufs/bootblk\
 /dev/rdsk/<disk-partition-name>
```

The `installboot` command installs the boot blocks onto the boot disk. Without the boot blocks, the disk cannot boot.

14. Insert a new tape into the tape drive and back up the new file system:

```
ufsdump 0uf /dev/rmt/n /dev/rdsk/<device-name>
```

A level 0 backup is performed. You should immediately make a backup of a newly created file system because `ufsrestore` repositions the files and changes the `inode` allocation.

15. Reboot the system with a reconfiguration reboot:

```
# shutdown -y -g0 -i0
ok boot -r
```

The system is rebooted.

The following example is an actual session that restores the root (/) file system from tape device `/dev/rmt/0` to Small Computer System Interface (SCSI) disk target `3`, slice `0`, on controller `0`:

```
# mount /dev/dsk/c0t3d0s0 /mnt
# cd /mnt
# devfsadm -c tape
# ufsrestore rf /dev/rmt/0
```

NOTE

devfsadm The devfsadm command with the -c tape option creates the /dev entries for the tape drive only. It creates links in /dev/rmt to the actual tape device special files. The devfsadm command is covered in Chapter 1.

Files are restored from tape. When this is complete, you are returned to a shell prompt. You can then remove the restoresymtable file, unmount the file system, and use fsck on the device:

```
# rm restoresymtable
# cd /
# umount /mnt
# fsck /dev/rdsk/c0t3d0s0
```

The system displays the fsck passes as the file system is checked:

```
# installboot
 /usr/platform/`uname -i`/lib/fs/ufs/bootblk /dev/rdsk/c0t3d0s0
# ufsdump 0uf /dev/rmt/0 /dev/rdsk/c0t3d0s0
# shutdown -y -g0 -i0
```

The system is halted. At the ok prompt, you perform a reconfiguration reboot as follows:

```
boot -r
```

Performing a reconfiguration reboot ensures that all devices connected to the system have been configured properly in the kernel and in the /dev and /devices directories.

Additional Notes About Restoring Files

When you restore files in a directory other than the root directory of the file system, ufsrestore re-creates the file hierarchy in the current directory. For example, if you restore to /home files that were backed up from /users/bcalkins/files, the files are restored in the directory /home/users/bcalkins/files.

When you restore individual files and directories, it's a good idea to restore them to a temporary directory such as /var/tmp. After you verify that you've retrieved the correct files, you can move them to their proper locations. You can restore individual files and directories to their original locations; however, if you do so, you should be sure that you do not overwrite newer files with older versions from the backup tape.

You should not forget to make regular backups of your operating system. Losing all the customization you do—such as adding user accounts, setting up printers, and installing application software—would be disastrous. Whenever you make modifications that affect the root (/),

/usr, /opt, or other operating system directories, you should bring down the system into single-user mode and perform a level 0 dump.

The fssnap Utility

Objective:

Explain how to perform incremental, full, and remote backups to tape for an unmounted file system using the ufsdump command, or explain how to back up a mounted file system using UFS snapshot.

You can use the fssnap command to create a read-only snapshot of a file system while the file system is mounted. A *snapshot* is a point-in-time image of a file system that provides a stable and unchanging device interface for backups. This snapshot uses the *backing-store file*. A few important points about the backing-store:

- The destination path of the backing store files must have enough free space to hold the file system data. The size of the backing store files vary with the amount of activity on the file system.
- The backing store file location must be different from the file system that is being captured in a snapshot.
- The backing-store files can reside on any type of file system, including another UFS file system or an NFS file system.
- Multiple backing-store files are created when you create a snapshot of a UFS file system that is larger than 512 Gbytes.

Unlike ufsdump, fssnap enables you to keep the file system mounted and the system in multiuser mode during backups. The snapshot is stored to disk, and then you can use Solaris backup commands such as ufsdump, tar, and cpio to back up the UFS snapshot. The result is a more reliable backup than you get with ufsdump alone.

When you use the fssnap command to create a file system snapshot, you should observe how much disk space the backing-store file consumes. The backing-store file itself uses no space initially, and then it grows quickly. As activity increases on the original file system, the backing-store file grows. This is because the size of the backing-store is activity related and is not related to the size of the original file system. It holds the original version of blocks that changed while the fssnap was active. If the file system has heavy use, the backing-store file increases in size quickly. On a heavily used file system, you need to make sure the backing-store file has enough space to grow.

NOTE

Disk Space for the Backing-Store File If the backing-store file runs out of disk space, the snapshot might delete itself, thus causing the backup to abort. If you are experiencing problems with the backup, you should examine the `/var/adm/messages` file for possible snapshot errors.

Step by Step 7.3 describes how to create snapshots.

STEP BY STEP

7.3 Creating Snapshots

1. Determine which file system you want to create the snapshot of. For this example, assume that you want to create a snapshot of `/export/home`.
2. Determine where you are going to store the backing-store file (that is, the snapshot). That file system should be large enough to hold an expanding backing-store file. In this example, you are going to use `/var/tmp` as a location to store the backing-store file.
3. Create the snapshot:

   ```
   fssnap -F ufs -o backing-store=/var/tmp /export/home
   ```

   `backing-store` can be abbreviated as `bs` (for example, `bs=/var/tmp`).

   The system responds with the name of the virtual device that is created:

   ```
   /dev/fssnap/0
   ```

4. Now you can back up the file system to tape (`/dev/rmt/0`) by specifying the virtual device (`/dev/fssnap/0`), as follows:

   ```
   ufsdump 0ucf /dev/rmt/0 /dev/fssnap/0
   ```

   The virtual device `/dev/fssnap/0` is described later in this section.

Here's what happens after you create the snapshot by using the `fssnap` command. A file, the backing-store file, is created in the `/var/tmp` file system. It's a normal file that can be listed just like any other file, by using the `ls` command:

```
ls -l /var/tmp
```

The following backing-store file is listed:

```
-rw-------    1 root     other     196665344 Mar 27 15:05 snapshot0
```

`snapshot0` is the name of the backing-store file. The backing-store file is a bitmapped file that contains copies of presnapshot data that has been modified since the snapshot was taken.

When you take the snapshot, the `snapshot0` file is created. As the original file system changes, the snapshot's backing-store file is updated, and the backing-store file grows.

NOTE

Limiting the Size of the Backing-Store File You can limit the size of the backing-store file by using the `maxsize` option, as follows:

```
fssnap -F ufs -o maxsize=600m,backing-store=/var/tmp /export/home
```

In this example, the size of the backing-store file is limited to 600MB; however, the backing-store file is a sparse file, which actually uses less disk space than the file system it represents

In addition, after you execute the `fssnap` command, two read-only virtual device files are created:

- **`/dev/fssnap/0`**—Block virtual device
- **`/dev/rfssnap/0`**—Raw virtual device

The virtual devices look and act like standard read-only devices, and you can use any of the existing Solaris commands with them. For example, you can mount the block virtual device by using the `mount` command, as follows:

```
mount -F ufs -o ro /dev/fssnap/0 /mnt
```

NOTE

Mounting the Snapshot Because the virtual devices are read-only, you need to mount the snapshot as read-only by using the `-o ro` option to the `mount` command.

You can go into the mount point and view the contents of the snapshot with the following:

```
ls -l /mnt
```

The contents of the snapshot are displayed:

```
total 3810
drwxr-xr-x   2 wcalkins staff        512 Mar 12 14:14 bcalkins
-rw-------   1 root     other    1933312 Mar 27 10:15 dump
drwx------   2 root     root        8192 Feb 26 15:33 lost+found
```

In this case, there wasn't much in the file system when the snapshot was created.

Now you can list the contents of the "real" file system named `/export/home`; remember that this is the live file system from which the snapshot was taken:

```
ls -l /export/home
total 3810
drwxr-xr-x   2 wcalkins staff        512 Mar 12 14:14 bcalkins
-rw-------   1 root     other    1933312 Mar 27 15:05 dump
-rw-r--r--   1 root     other         12 Mar 27 15:05 file1
drwx------   2 root     root        8192 Feb 26 15:33 lost+found
```

Notice in this example that things are changing. There is a new file named `file1`, and the dump file has a new time. The snapshot image, however, remains the way it was—none of the dates have changed, and none of the new files show up. When you back up the snapshot, you get a backup of the file system the way it was when you made the snapshot. Here's how you back up the snapshot by using the `ufsdump` command:

```
ufsdump 0ucf /dev/rmt/0 /dev/rfssnap/0
```

Notice that you're backing up the virtual device named `/dev/fssnap/0`. The backup that was created from the virtual device is a backup of the original file system and represents the state of the file system when the snapshot was taken. If you ever need to restore a file system from the backup, restore the data using `ufsrestore`, as if you had taken the backup directly from the original file system. For this recovery procedure, refer to the section titled "The `ufsrestore` Facility" earlier in this chapter.

To remove the snapshot, you issue the following command:

```
fssnap -d  /export/home
```

`/export/home` was the name of the file system you created the snapshot of. The system responds with the following:

```
Deleted snapshot 0
```

When you create a UFS snapshot, you can specify that the backing-store file be unlinked, which means the backing-store file is removed after the snapshot is deleted. Here's how you do this:

```
fssnap -F ufs -o unlink,backing-store=/var/tmp /export/home
```

When you use the `unlink` option, you cannot see the backing-store file. This might make administration more difficult because the file is not visible in the file system.

Earlier you did not specify the `-o unlink` option, so you have to delete the backing-store manually, as follows, after you run the `fssnap -d` command:

```
rm /var/tmp/snapshot0
```

The backing-store file occupies disk space until the snapshot is deleted, whether you use the `-o unlink` option to remove the backing-store file or you remove it manually.

Here are a few other facts about snapshots:

- The size of the backing-store file depends on how much data has changed since the snapshot was taken.
- A snapshot does not persist across system reboots.
- Snapshots are meant to be used on UFSs only.

For more information on options that can be used with the `fssnap` command to list and manage snapshots, refer to the man pages for `fssnap` and `fssnap_ufs`.

zip and unzip

`zip` is a compression and file-packaging utility that is now available on Solaris. `zip` is used on Unix, Microsoft Windows, Macintosh, and many other operating systems to compress files and then put those files into an archive file. The `zip` program is useful for combining a set of files for distribution or for saving disk space by temporarily compressing unused files or directories. You are likely to see Solaris patches distributed in `zip` format. The section "Installing a Patch" in Chapter 2, "Installing the Solaris 10 Operating Environment," provides information on patches.

You use the `unzip` command to extract the compressed files from an archive. Other than for installing patches, the `zip` and `unzip` commands are not covered on the exam. For more information, consult the online man pages.

Solaris Flash Archive

You can back up your Solaris operating environment (not the data) by creating a Flash archive. Previously in this chapter, you learned how to back up your operating system by using `ufsdump` and specifying a level 0 dump of the root (`/`), `/usr`, and other operating system–related file systems. The Flash archive feature can be used as a backup or to replicate an installation on a number of systems, called *clone systems*. (A description of the Flash archive is provided in Chapter 2. Installing a Flash Archive is also described in Chapter 14, "Advanced Installation Procedures.")

After the system has been set up and configured (but before it goes into production) is a good time to create the archive. While you're in single-user mode, you use the `flarcreate` command to create the Solaris Flash archive. The following is the syntax for this command:

```
flarcreate -n <name> <options> <path>/<filename>
```

The arguments for the command are described in Table 7.16.

TABLE 7.16 Arguments to the `flarcreate` Command

Argument	Description
<name>	Specifies the name that you give the archive.
<path>	Specifies the path to the directory in which you want to save the archive file. If you do not specify a path for saving the archive, `flarcreate` saves the archive file in the current directory.
<filename>	Specifies the name of the archive file.

Many options are available for the `flarcreate` command, and they are described in Chapter 13. The following example shows the options you use to create an archive of the entire operating environment on the local tape drive:

```
flarcreate -n osarchive -t /dev/rmt/0
```

The `-n` option allows you to identify the archive with a unique name. It is not the name with which the archive will be stored, however. The `-t` option specifies that the archive will be stored to tape.

If the archive creation is successful, the `flarcreate` command returns the exit code `0`. If the archive creation fails, the `flarcreate` command returns a nonzero exit code.

You can use the `flar` command to administer archives. The `flar` command includes subcommands for extracting information, splitting archives, and combining archives.

You can use the `flar` command with the `-i` option to get information about archives you have already created, as follows:

```
flar -i /data/vararchive
```

The system responds with the following:

```
files_archived_method=cpio
creation_date=20020327221216
creation_master=ultra5
content_name=vararchive
files_compressed_method=none
files_archived_size=34472960
content_architectures=sun4u
```

The `jar` Utility

The Java archive (JAR) file format enables you to bundle multiple files into a single archive file, much the same way you can bundle files by using the `tar` utility. Typically, a JAR file contains the class files and auxiliary resources associated with Java applets and applications.

The benefits of using the JAR file format include the following:

- **Security**—You can digitally sign the contents of a JAR file. Users who recognize your signature can then optionally grant your files security privileges that they wouldn't otherwise have.
- **Decreased download time**—If your applet is bundled in a JAR file, the applet's class files and associated resources can be downloaded to a browser in a single Hypertext Transfer Protocol (HTTP) transaction, without the need for opening a new connection for each file.
- **Compression**—The JAR format enables you to compress files for efficient storage.
- **Packaging for extensions**—The extensions framework provides a means by which you can add functionality to the Java core platform, and the JAR file format defines the packaging for extensions. Java 3D and JavaMail are examples of extensions developed by Sun. By using the JAR file format, you can turn your software into extensions as well.
- **Package sealing**—Packages stored in JAR files can optionally be sealed so that they can enforce version consistency. To seal a package within a JAR file means that all classes defined in that package must be found in the same JAR file.
- **Package versioning**—A JAR file can hold data about the files it contains, such as vendor and version information.
- **Portability**—The mechanism for handling JAR files is a standard part of the Java platform's core application programming interface (API).

The `jar` command is similar to the `tar` command in that it packages several files into a single file, but it also compresses the resulting file. It is a Java application that combines multiple files into a single JAR file. It is also a general-purpose archiving and compression tool that is based on Zip and the ZLIB compression format. The `jar` command was originally created so that Java programmers could download multiple files with one request rather than having to issue a download request for each separate file. `jar` is standard with the Solaris 10 operating system, and it is also available on any system that has a Java Virtual Machine (JVM) installed.

This is the syntax for the `jar` command:

```
jar cf <jar-file> <input-file(s)>
```

Table 7.17 describes the options and arguments used with the `jar` command.

TABLE 7.17 jar Command Options

Option	Description
c	Indicates that you want to create a JAR file.*
f	Indicates that you want the output to go to a file rather than to the system's standard output.*
i	Generates index information for the JAR file(s).
t	Lists the table of contents for the archive.
v	Produces verbose output on standard output while the JAR file is being built. The verbose output tells you the name of each file as it is added to the JAR file.
x	Extracts files from an archive.
0	Indicates that you don't want the JAR file to be compressed.
<jar-file>	Specifies the name that you want the resulting JAR file to have. You can use any filename for a JAR file. By convention, JAR filenames are given a `.jar` extension, although that is not required.
<input-file(s)>	Specifies a space-separated list of one or more files that you want to be placed in your JAR file. The *<input-file(s)>* argument can contain the wildcard asterisk (*) symbol. If *input-files* is a directory, the content of the directory is added to the JAR recursively.

*The c and f options can appear in either order, but there must not be any space between them.

You use the following to create a JAR file:

```
jar cf <jar-file> <input-file(s)>
```

You use the following to view the contents of a JAR file:

```
jar tf <jar-file>
```

You use the following to extract the contents of a JAR file:

```
jar xf <jar-file>
```

You use the following to extract specific files from a JAR file:

```
jar xf <jar-file> <archived-file(s)>
```

Here's an example of how to use `jar` to compress files located within two different directories. JAR files are packaged with the Zip file format, so you can use them for Zip-like tasks, such as lossless data compression, archiving, decompression, and archive unpacking. To package the audio and images directories into a single JAR file named `files.jar` in your default home directory, you would run the following command from inside the `/export/home/bcalkins` directory:

```
jar cvf ~/files.jar files.class audio images
```

The audio and images arguments represent directories, so the JAR tool recursively places them and their contents in the JAR file. The generated JAR file files.jar is placed in the user's home directory. Because the command used the v option for verbose output, you see something similar to this output when you run the command:

```
adding: files.class (in=3825) (out=2222) (deflated 41%)
adding: audio/ (in=0) (out=0) (stored 0%)
adding: audio/beep.au (in=4032) (out=3572) (deflated 11%)
adding: audio/ding.au (in=2566) (out=2055) (deflated 19%)
adding: audio/return.au (in=6558) (out=4401) (deflated 32%)
adding: audio/yahoo1.au (in=7834) (out=6985) (deflated 10%)
adding: audio/yahoo2.au (in=7463) (out=4607) (deflated 38%)
adding: images/ (in=0) (out=0) (stored 0%)
adding: images/cross.gif (in=157) (out=160) (deflated -1%)
adding: images/not.gif (in=158) (out=161) (deflated -1%)
```

You can see from this output that the JAR file files.jar is compressed. The JAR tool compresses files by default. You can turn off the compression feature by using the 0 option; in that case, the command looks like this:

```
jar cvf0 files.jar files.class audio images
```

Summary

This chapter described the standard copy and backup utilities available in Solaris. It also describes the various types of backup media available. It discussed `tar`, `dd`, `cpio`, and `pax`, and it described how to use these utilities to copy and restore files, directories, and entire file systems.

This chapter also described how to use `ufsdump` and `ufsrestore` to perform regular backups on a system. It described a recommended backup schedule that you can implement to safeguard any system from deliberate or accidental loss of data. This chapter described how to recover data from backup media. It described the procedures to restore single files and entire file systems. The chapter also described how to use `fssnap` and Solaris Flash archive as further methods to back up information.

Finally, the chapter described methods used to package and compress files (such as `zip` and `jar`).

As you're finding out with Solaris, there are often many ways to perform a task. You need to choose the method that best suits your environment. Although all the utilities described in this chapter do a good job of backing up your data, if your company has several servers and large storage pools, you might want to investigate some of the more robust backup packages available from third parties, such as Veritas and Legato. Sun also has a backup product, StorEdge Enterprise Backup, which is an optional package that can be purchased directly from Sun and added into your Solaris operating environment. Most of these add-on packages provide a comprehensive suite of utilities for conducting and managing backups in complex computing environments. In most cases, they allow single-point backups—not only for Solaris but for other operating systems as well.

Key Terms

- Block size
- File system dump
- Full backup
- Incremental backup
- Tape archive

Apply Your Knowledge

Exercises

These exercises utilize a tape drive connected as `/dev/rmt/0`. If your system does not have a tape drive attached to it, you should substitute the device `/dev/rmt/0n` for a filename such as `/tmp/foo`.

7.1 Using `tar`

In this exercise, you use the `tar` command to copy files from disk to tape.

Estimated time: 15 minutes (depending on the size of `/export/home`)

1. Log in as root and insert a tape in the tape drive. The tape will be erased, so you should use a blank tape and make sure the tape is not write protected.

2. Create a tape archive of everything in the `/export/home` directory on tape device `/dev/rmt/0`:

   ```
   tar cvf /dev/rmt/0 /export/home
   ```

3. List the contents of the archive:

   ```
   tar tvf /dev/rmt/0
   ```

4. Add another tape archive to the same tape. This is referred to as a *stacked tape*. To do this, you first need to advance the tape past the first archive by using the `mt` command:

   ```
   mt  -f /dev/rmt/0n fsf 1
   ```

   The `mt` utility sends commands to a magnetic tape drive. It can be used to rewind, retension, and fast forward a tape as well as many other operations. In the example, the `fsf` option will move the tape forward 1 record.

   Notice the use of the "no rewind" device (that is, `0n` rather than `0`).

5. Add the next archive of the `/var/adm` directory:

   ```
   tar cvf /dev/rmt/0n /var/adm
   ```

6. Rewind the tape:

   ```
   mt -f /dev/rmt/0 rew
   ```

7. List the first archive on the tape:

   ```
   tar tvf /dev/rmt/0n
   ```

8. List the contents of the second tape archive on the stacked tape:

```
tar tvf /dev/rmt/0
```

Note that it's important to make a notation on the tape label that this is a stacked tape and also to record the order of each archive on the tape.

7.2 Using `cpio` and `pax`

This exercise demonstrates how to copy user files that have been modified in the past 30 days to a tape drive with the device name `/dev/rmt/0`. You should specify a larger-than-default blocking factor to increase the transfer speed.

Estimated time: 15 minutes (depending on the size of `/export/home`)

1. Log in as root and insert a tape in the tape drive. The tape will be erased, so you should use a blank tape and make sure the tape is not write protected.

```
cd /export/home
```

2. Locate all files by using the `find` command and transfer them to tape by using `cpio`:

```
find . -mtime -30 -print | cpio -oB > /dev/rmt/0
```

3. List all the files that were backed up in step 2:

```
cpio -ict < /dev/rmt/0
```

4. Use the `pax` utility to list the contents of the tape that was created by using `cpio`:

```
pax -v -f /dev/rmt/0
```

7.3 Using `ufsdump` and `ufsrestore`

In this exercise, you use the `ufsdump` command to back up an entire file system. You then use the `ufsrestore` command to restore a file.

CAUTION

This Exercise Destroys Data This exercise removes and overwrites files in the `/var` file system. Therefore, you should not do this exercise on a production system.

Estimated time: 20 minutes

1. Log in as root and insert a tape in the tape drive. The tape will be erased, so you should use a blank tape and make sure the tape is not write protected.

2. Back up the entire /var file system to tape:

```
ufsdump 0ucf /dev/rmt/0 /var
```

3. Remove the /var/adm/messages file:

```
rm /var/adm/messages
```

4. Restore the /var/sadm/README file by using ufsrestore:

```
cd /var
ufsrestore -ivf /dev/rmt/0
```

5. At the ufsrestore> prompt, verify that the messages file is on the tape:

```
ls sadm/README
```

6. Mark the file for extraction, and then extract the file:

```
add sadm/README
extract
```

When the system asks you to specify the next volume, type **1**.

When the system says, set owner/mode for '.'?[yn], enter **y**.

Enter **q** to exit the ufsrestore utility.

7. Verify that the file has been restored to its proper location by using the ls -l command.

Exam Questions

1. What does the following command sequence do?

```
#cd /home/myjunk
#tar cvf /dev/rmt/0 .
```

❍ **A.** Take all the files in /home/myjunk, package them into a single tar archive on /dev/rmt/0, and print out a commentary of the process.

❍ **B.** Extract the contents of the tape at /dev/rmt/0 to /home/myjunk.

❍ **C.** tar all the files in /dev/rmt/0 to /home/myjunk, create a table of contents, and ignore checksum errors.

❍ **D.** tar all the files in the current directory into two separate archives—one for the contents of myjunk and one for the rest of /home.

2. Say you have the following backup schedule:

   - First Monday of the month—level 0 (tape 1)
   - All other Mondays—level 1 (tape 2)
   - Wednesdays—level 2 (tape 3)
   - Fridays—level 4 (tape 4)

   Which tapes would be needed to fully restore the system if it goes down the second Saturday of the month?

   - ❍ **A.** All four of them
   - ❍ **B.** Tapes 2–4
   - ❍ **C.** Tapes 1, 2, and 4
   - ❍ **D.** Tapes 1, 3, and 4

3. Which of the following commands can be used in conjunction with the `cpio` command to perform incremental archives?

   - ❍ **A.** `sort`
   - ❍ **B.** `find`
   - ❍ **C.** `grep`
   - ❍ **D.** `diff`

4. Which of the following utilities has a built-in function to perform incremental backups?

   - ❍ **A.** `tar`
   - ❍ **B.** `cpio`
   - ❍ **C.** `ufsdump`
   - ❍ **D.** `dd`

5. Which of the following commands lists the contents of a `tar` file without actually extracting the file?

   - ❍ **A.** `tar -cvf`
   - ❍ **B.** `tar -xvf`
   - ❍ **C.** `tar -tvf`
   - ❍ **D.** `tar -txf`

6. Which of the following is false regarding dd?

   ❍ **A.** It quickly converts and copies files with different data formats.

   ❍ **B.** It is a good backup tool.

   ❍ **C.** It is used to transfer a complete file system or partition from a hard disk to a tape.

   ❍ **D.** It is used to copy all data from one disk to another.

7. Which of the following is true regarding the `cpio` command?

   ❍ **A.** It is used to copy data from one place to another.

   ❍ **B.** It is not a good tool for backups.

   ❍ **C.** It can back up and restore individual files, not just entire file systems.

   ❍ **D.** Backups made by `cpio` are smaller than those created with `tar`.

8. Which of the following statements regarding the `pax` utility is false?

   ❍ **A.** It supports a wide variety of archive formats, including `tar` and `cpio`.

   ❍ **B.** It is a POSIX-conformant archive utility.

   ❍ **C.** It does not have a built-in function to perform incremental backups.

   ❍ **D.** It is old and not a recommended backup utility.

9. You need to perform a backup of the root file system without bringing the system to single-user mode or unmounting the root file system. Which is the best method of backing up an active, mounted file system?

   ❍ **A.** `fssnap`, then use `ufsdump` on the snapshot

   ❍ **B.** `fnssnap`, then use `ufsdump` on the snapshot

   ❍ **C.** `flarcreate`, then use `ufsdump` on the snapshot

   ❍ **D.** `ufsdump` alone can be used to back up an active file system

   ❍ E. `fssnapshot`, then use `ufsdump` on the snapshot

10. On an active file system, which command successfully backs up the root file system to the `/dev/rmt/0` tape device?

   ❍ **A.** `ufsdump -S0uf /dev/rmt/0  /`

   ❍ **B.** ``ufsdump 0uf /dev/rmt/0 `fssnap -o bs=/opt,raw` ``

   ❍ **C.** ``ufsdump 0uf /dev/rmt/0 `fssnap -o bs=/export,raw /` ``

   ❍ **D.** ``ufsdump 0uf /dev/rmt/0  `snapfs -o bs=/var/tmp,raw /` ``

11. Which statement about the `restoresymtable` file is true?

   ❍ **A.** The `restoresymtable` file manages the restoration of symbolic links to ensure that unnecessary copies of data are not restored.

   ❍ **B.** The `restoresymtable` file is used to coordinate the restoration of incremental dumps on top of a full dump. It can be deleted after the last incremental restoration.

   ❍ **C.** The `restoresymtable` file contains detailed information about the restored files. It's simply a log file that can be removed after the restoration of a full backup.

   ❍ **D.** The `restoresymtable` file is used for future full dumps of a file system that has been restored by using `ufsrestore`. It needs to be saved for when `ufsrestore` may be used to restore files to this file system later.

   ❍ **E.** You must not delete this binary file; it is needed by `ufsrestore` and `ufsdump`. You should put a backup copy of this file in another location.

Answers to Exam Questions

1. **A.** The first command changes your working directory, and the second creates the `tar` file. The commands shown in the example take all the files in the `/home/myjunk` directory, package them into a single `tar` archive on `/dev/rmt/0`, and print out a commentary of the process. For more information, see the section "The `tar` Utility."

2. **A.** To restore the data from backups, you first load the level 0 tape created the first Monday of the month, followed by the level 2 tape, followed by the level 3 tape, and finally the level 4 tape. For more information, see the section "The `ufsdump` Utility."

3. **B.** You use the `find` command with `cpio` to perform incremental archives. For more information, see the section "The `cpio` Utility."

4. **C.** `ufsdump` has built-in options for creating incremental backups that back up only those files that were changed since a previous backup. This saves tape space and time. For more information, see the section "The `ufsdump` Utility."

5. **C.** The `-t` option with the `tar` command lists the contents of a `tar` file. For more information, see the section "The `tar` Utility."

6. **B.** The main advantage of the `dd` command is that it can quickly convert and copy files with different data formats, such as differences in block size or record length. The most common use of this command is to transfer a complete file system or partition from your hard disk to a tape. You can also use it to copy files from one hard disk to another. `dd` does not make a good backup tool. For more information, see the section "The `dd` Utility."

7. **A, C, D.** `cpio` is used to copy data, back up and restore files and file systems, in a more compressed format than `tar`. For more information, see the section "The `cpio` Utility."

8. **D.** pax is a backup utility that has recently been added to Solaris. It works well as a backup utility. For more information, see the section "The pax Utility."

9. **A.** Unlike ufsdump, fssnap enables you to keep the file system mounted and the system in multi-user mode during backups. The snapshot is stored to disk, and then you can use Solaris backup commands such as ufsdump, tar, and cpio to back up the UFS snapshot. The result is a more reliable backup. For more information, see the section "The fssnap Utility."

10. **C.** The following example backs up the root (/) file system without requiring you to unmount the file system:

    ```
    # ufsdump 0uf /dev/rmt/0 `fssnap  -o bs=/export,raw  /`
    ```

    Because ufsdump requires the path to a raw device, the raw option is used. The command fssnap -o bs=/export,raw / is enclosed in backticks so that the file system snapshot is created in the /export file system and then backed up by ufsdump. After you use ufsdump, you need to ensure that you remove the snapshot to free up space on the backing store by using fssnap -d and by removing the temporary file created in /export. For more information, see the section "The fssnap Utility."

11. **B.** The restoresymtable file is created by the ufsrestore command when restoring an entire file system. This is a temporary file that is created whenever you restore an entire file system from tape. The restoresymtable file is used only by ufsrestore for "checkpointing," which involves information passed between incremental restorations. For example, if you perform an incremental restoration of data from backup tapes, the system uses information from the restoresymtable file to restore incremental backups on top of the latest full backup. The restoresymtable file is not required after the file system has been successfully restored, and it can be deleted by using the rm command. It is not removed automatically. For more information, see the section "The ufsrestore Utility."

Suggested Reading and Resources

Inside Solaris 9, by Bill Calkins, New Riders, 2002.

Unix Backup and Recovery, by W. Curtis Preston, O'Reilly, 1999.

CHAPTER EIGHT

The Solaris Network Environment

Objectives

The following test objectives for Exam CX-310-202 are covered in this chapter:

Control and monitor network interfaces including MAC addresses, IP addresses, network packets, and configure the IPv4 interfaces at boot time.

- This chapter describes the files that are used to configure IPv4 network interfaces, how to start and stop these network interfaces, and how to test whether the interfaces are working correctly. It also discusses two methods of changing the system hostname: editing a number of system files and using the `sys-unconfig` command.

Explain the client/server model; enable/disable server processes.

- The network services are started and managed by the Service Management Facility (SMF). This chapter describes how to manage network services as well as adding new ones to be managed by SMF. It also describes how the client/server model functions in the Solaris 10 environment.

Outline

Study Strategies

The following study strategies will help you prepare for the test:

- As you study this chapter, it's important that you practice using each command that is presented on a Solaris system. Practice is very important on these topics, and you should practice until you can repeat the procedure from memory.
- You should understand each command in this chapter and be prepared to match the command to the correct description.
- You should know all the terms listed in the "Key Terms" section at the end of this chapter. You should pay special attention to the section on network services, which has changed with the introduction of Solaris 10 and how to convert services to use the Service Management Facility (SMF). You should be prepared to match each term presented in this chapter with the correct definition.

Introduction

This chapter covers the basics of the Solaris network environment. It does not go into too much detail because Sun provides a separate certification track for Solaris network administrators, but it does provide you with the fundamental information you need to get started managing a Solaris system in a networked environment. The topics discussed here include some fundamental network terminology and information on setting up IPv4 network interfaces, managing network services, and configuring the services that are started automatically at boot time.

Network Fundamentals

Before you start managing a Solaris network, you need to know the definitions of some terms used in networking. There are numerous acronyms related to networking, and many of them are explained in the following sections. You'll first learn about the networking model that is deployed by Solaris 10, and then you'll learn about the types of networks that are available, including the various network protocols. Finally, you'll learn about the physical components of the network hardware, including the network interfaces and cables.

Network Topologies

The term *network topology* refers to the overall picture of the network and the arrangement in which the nodes on a network are connected to each other. The topology describes small and large networks, including local area networks (LANs) and wide area networks (WANs).

LANs

A *LAN* is a set of hosts, usually in the same building and on the same floor, connected by a high-speed medium such as Ethernet. A LAN might be a single Internet Protocol (IP) network or a collection of networks or subnets that are connected through high-speed switches and/or routers.

The network interface, and cable or wire, used for computer networks is referred to as *network media*. Normally a type of twisted-pair wire or fiber-optic cable connects nodes on a LAN. Twisted-pair cable has less bandwidth than optical fiber, but it is less costly and easier to install. With twisted-pair cable, the two individual wires are twisted around each other to minimize interference from the other twisted pairs in the cable. Twisted pair cable is available in two different categories:

- **Unshielded twisted pair (UTP)**—UTP is used in the majority of network environments where electromagnetic interference is not a problem.
- **Shielded twisted pair (STP)**—STP is used in noisy environments; the metal shield around the wires protects against excessive electromagnetic interference.

In addition, twisted-pair cable is available in stranded or solid wire (22 to 26 gauge). Stranded wire is used most commonly because it is very flexible and can be bent around corners. Solid wire cable suffers less attenuation (that is, signal loss) and can span longer distances, but it is less flexible than stranded wire and can break if it is repeatedly bent.

Furthermore, cable is grouped into seven categories, according to the Electronic Industries Alliance/Telecommunications Industry Association (EIA/TIA) standard EIA/TIA-568, based on its transmission capacity. The categories are listed in Table 8.1.

TABLE 8.1 Cable Categories

Category	Cable Type	Application
1	UTP	Analog voice
2	UTP	Digital voice and 1Mbps data
3	UTP, STP	16Mbps data
4	UTP, STP	20Mbps data
5	UTP, STP	10Mbps and 100Mbps data
5e	UTP, STP	1000Mbps (1Gbps) data
6	UTP, STP	155Mbps (ATM) and 1000Mbps (1Gbps) data

You can see from Table 8.1 that there are several variants of twisted-pair cable, each with different capacities. For example, Category 5 (Cat 5) UTP cable can support sustained data throughput of 100Mbps.

WANs

A wide area network (*WAN*) is a network that covers a potentially vast geographic area. An example of a WAN is the Internet. Another example is an enterprise network that links the separate offices of a single corporation into one network spanning an entire country or perhaps an entire continent. A WAN, unlike a LAN, usually makes use of third-party service providers for interconnection. It is a common misconception among newcomers to the world of networking that a WAN is simply a LAN but on a larger scale. This is not true because different technologies, equipment, and protocols are used in LANs and WANs. For example, Ethernet is a LAN technology that is not usually used in WANs (but this is changing with wider availability and lower cost of high-speed long-distance fiber connections).

Network Protocols and Network Models

A *network protocol* is the part of the network that you configure but cannot see. It's the "language" of the network, which controls data transmission between systems across the network. To understand protocols, you need to first understand network models.

A *network model* is an abstract common structure used to describe communication between systems. The two network models that provide the framework for network communication and that are the standards used in Solaris network environments are the International Standards Organization (ISO)/Open Systems Interconnection (OSI) reference model and the Transmission Control Protocol/Internet Protocol (TCP/IP) model. These models are discussed in the following sections.

The network models consist of different layers. You can think of the layers as steps that must be completed before the next step can be tackled, and before communication can occur between systems.

The ISO/OSI Model

The seven-layered ISO/OSI model was devised in the early 1980s. Although this model represents an ideal world and is somewhat meaningless in today's networking environment, it's quite helpful in identifying the distinct functions that are necessary for network communication to occur.

In the ISO/OSI model, individual services that are required for communication are arranged in seven layers that build on one another. Each layer describes a specific network function, as shown in Figure 8.1.

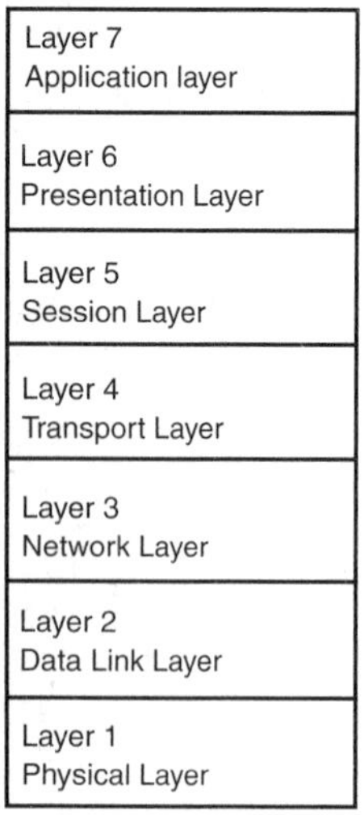

Layer 7 Application layer
Layer 6 Presentation Layer
Layer 5 Session Layer
Layer 4 Transport Layer
Layer 3 Network Layer
Layer 2 Data Link Layer
Layer 1 Physical Layer

Figure 8.1 The seven-layer ISO/OSI model.

Table 8.2 describes the function of each individual layer.

TABLE 8.2 The Seven Layers of the ISO/OSI Model

Layer Number	Layer Name	Function
1	Physical	Describes the network hardware, including electrical and mechanical connections to the network.
2	Data link	Splits data into frames for sending on the physical layer and receives acknowledgement frames. The data link layer performs error checking and retransmits frames that are not received correctly.
3	Network	Manages the delivery of data via the data link layer and is used by the transport layer. The most common network-layer protocol is IP.
4	Transport	Determines how to use the network layer to provide a virtually error-free, point-to-point connection so that Host A can send messages to Host B that arrive uncorrupted and in the correct order. TCP operates at this layer.
5	Session	Uses the transport layer to establish a connection between processes on different hosts. The session layer handles security and creation of the session.
6	Presentation	Performs functions such as text compression, code, or format conversion to try to smooth out differences between hosts. It allows incompatible processes in the application layer to communicate via the session layer.
7	Application	Is concerned with the user's view of the network (for example, formatting email messages). The presentation layer provides the application layer with a familiar, local representation of data that is independent of the format used on the network. Utilities such as `Telnet` and File Transfer Protocol (FTP) operate at this layer.

The TCP/IP Model

In order for a network to function properly, information must be delivered to the intended destination in an intelligible form. Because different types of networking software and hardware need to interact to perform the network function, designers developed the TCP/IP communications protocol suite (a collection of protocols), which is now recognized as a standard and is used throughout the world. Because it is a set of standards, TCP/IP runs on many different types of computers, making it easy for you to set up a heterogeneous network running any operating system that supports TCP/IP. The Solaris operating system includes the networking software to implement the TCP/IP communications protocol suite.

The TCP/IP model is a network communications protocol suite that consists of a set of formal rules that describe how software and hardware should interact within a network. The TCP/IP model has five layers:

- Hardware layer
- Network interface layer

- Internet layer
- Transport layer
- Application layer

EXAM ALERT

Four or Five Layers—Be careful on the exam because Sun has used both a four-layer and five-layer description of this model since Solaris 8. If a question describes a four-layer model then the hardware layer should be thought of as being integrated with the network interface layer.

Each of these is discussed in the following sections.

The Hardware Layer

The TCP/IP model hardware layer corresponds to the ISO/OSI model physical layer and describes the network hardware, including electrical and mechanical connections to the network. This layer regulates the transmission of unstructured bit streams over a transmission medium, which might be one of the following:

- Ethernet (described in Institute of Electrical and Electronics Engineers [IEEE] Standard 802.3)
- Token-passing bus (described in IEEE 802.4)
- Token Ring (described in IEEE 802.5)
- Metropolitan area networks (described in IEEE 802.6)
- Wireless LANs (described in IEEE 802.11)

NOTE

Support for Token Ring has been removed in Solaris 10, as it is now considered an obsolete technology.

For each medium, the IEEE has created an associated standard under project 802, which was named for the month (February) and year (1980) of its inception. Each medium has its own standard, which is named based on the 802 project. For example, Ethernet has its own standard: 802.3.

The Network Interface Layer

The TCP/IP model network interface layer corresponds to the ISO/OSI data link layer; it manages the delivery of data across the physical network. This layer provides error detection and packet framing. *Framing* is a process of assembling bits into manageable units of data. A *frame* is a series of bits with a well-defined beginning and end.

The network interface layer protocols include the following:

- Ethernet
- Fiber Distributed Data Interface (FDDI)
- Point-to-Point Protocol (PPP)
- Token Ring

These protocols are described later in this chapter.

The Internet Layer

The TCP/IP model Internet layer corresponds to the ISO/OSI network layer and manages data addressing and delivery between networks, as well as fragmenting data for the data link layer. The Internet layer uses the following protocols:

- **IP**—IP is the set of techniques for transferring data across a network. The majority of traffic across the Internet uses IP in conjunction with other protocols, such as Transmission Control Protocol (TCP) and User Datagram Protocol (UDP). IP determines the path a packet must take based on the destination host's IP address. Solaris 10 supports IP version 4 (IPv4) and IP version 6 (IPv6), which are discussed later in this chapter.
- **Internet Control Message Protocol (ICMP)**—ICMP allows for the generation of error messages, test packets, and informational messages related to IP.
- **Address Resolution Protocol (ARP)**—ARP defines the method that maps a 32-bit IP address to a 48-bit Ethernet address.
- **Reverse Address Resolution Protocol (RARP)**—RARP is the reverse of ARP. It maps a 48-bit Ethernet address to a 32-bit IP address.

The Transport Layer

The TCP/IP model transport layer corresponds to the ISO/OSI model transport layer and ensures that messages reach the correct application process by using Transmission Control Program (TCP) and User Datagram Protocol (UDP).

TCP uses a reliable, connection-oriented circuit for connecting to application processes. A connection-oriented virtual circuit allows a host to send data in a continuous stream to another host. It guarantees that all data is delivered to the other end in the same order as it was sent and without duplication. Communication proceeds through three well-defined phases: connection establishment, data transfer, and connection release.

UDP is a connectionless protocol. It has traditionally been faster than TCP because it does not have to establish a connection or handle acknowledgements. As a result, UDP does not guarantee delivery. UDP is lightweight and efficient, but the application program must take care of all error processing and retransmission. Considerable improvements in network technology, however, have virtually eliminated the performance gap between TCP and UDP, making TCP the protocol of choice.

The Application Layer

The TCP/IP model application layer corresponds to the session layer, presentation layer, and application layer of the ISO/OSI model. The TCP/IP model application layer manages user-accessed application programs and network services. This layer is responsible for defining the way in which cooperating networks represent data. The application layer protocols include the following:

- **Network File System (NFS)**—This client/server protocol and application is described in Chapter 9, "Virtual File Systems, Swap Space, and Core Dumps."
- **Network Information System (NIS), Network Information System Plus (NIS+), Domain Name System (DNS), and the Lightweight Directory Access Protocol (LDAP)**—These naming services are described in Chapter 12, "Naming Services."
- **`rlogin`, Telnet, and FTP**—These network services are described in the "Network Services" section, later in this chapter.
- **Hypertext Transfer Protocol (HTTP)**—HTTP is used by the World Wide Web to display text, pictures, and sound via a Web browser.
- **Simple Mail Transport Protocol (SMTP)**—SMTP provides delivery of email messages.
- **Remote Procedure Call (RPC)**—RPC is a protocol that one program can use to request services from another system on the network. RPC is described in the "Network Services" section, later in this chapter.
- **Routing Information Protocol (RIP)**—RIP provides for automated distribution of routing information between systems. Solaris 10 includes RIP version 2 (RIPv2), a significant update to RIP.
- **Simple Network Management Protocol (SNMP)**—SNMP is used to manage and monitor all types of networking equipment, including computers, hubs, and routers.

EXAM ALERT

Know Layers and Functions—For the exam, ensure that you are familiar with the layers of both the OSI seven-layer model and the TCP/IP model. You should be able to identify functions/protocols that operate at each layer and the order in which the layers are processed.

Encapsulation and Decapsulation

When you think of systems communicating via a network, you can imagine the data progressing through each layer down from the application layer to the hardware layer, across the network, and then flowing back up from the hardware layer to the application layer. A header is added to each segment that is received on the way down the layers (*encapsulation*), and a header is removed from each segment on the way up through the layers (*decapsulation*). Each header contains specific address information so that the layers on the remote system know how to forward the communication.

For example, in TCP/IP, a packet would contain a header from the physical layer, followed by a header from the network layer (IP), followed by a header from the transport layer (TCP), followed by the application protocol data.

Packets

A *packet* is the basic unit of information to be transferred over the network. A packet is organized much like a conventional letter. Each packet has a header that corresponds to an envelope. The header contains the addresses of the recipient and the sender, plus information on how to handle the packet as it travels through each layer of the protocol suite. The message part of the packet corresponds to the contents of the letter itself. A packet can contain only a finite number of bytes of data, depending on the network medium in use. Therefore, typical communications such as email messages are split into packets.

Ethernet

Ethernet is a standard that defines the physical components a machine uses to access the network and the speed at which the network runs. It includes specifications for cable, connectors, and computer interface components. Ethernet is a LAN technology that originally facilitated transmission of information between computers at speeds of up to 10Mbps. A later version of Ethernet, called 100BASE-T, or Fast Ethernet, pushed the speed up to 100Mbps, and Gigabit Ethernet supports data transfer rates of 1Gbps (1,000Mbps). Table 8.3 lists some common media names and their associated cable types.

TABLE 8.3 Ethernet Media

Ethernet Type	Medium
10BASE2	50-ohm ("thin") coaxial cable
10BASE5	75-ohm ("thick") coaxial cable
10BASE-T	Unshielded or shielded (UTP/STP) multistrand cable
100BASE-TX	Unshielded or shielded (UTP/STP) twisted pair cable
100BASE-FX	Fiber-optic cable
1000BASE-T	Unshielded or shielded (UTP/STP) twisted pair cable
1000BASE-CX	Copper cable used within wiring cabinets over short distances (<25 Meters)
1000BASE-LX	Fiber-optic cable

NOTE

10BASE2 and 10BASE5 media are now very rarely used; even 10BASE-T networks are becoming increasingly rare.

The 100BASE-T type of Ethernet is the most popular medium, but it is gradually being replaced by newer systems that support 1000BASE-T (gigabit) and a growing number of fiber-optic connected devices.

Ethernet uses a protocol called CSMA/CD, which stands for Carrier Sense Multiple Access with Collision Detection. *Multiple Access* means that every station can access the single cable to transmit data. *Carrier Sense* means that before transmitting data, a station checks the cable to determine whether any other station is already sending something. If the LAN appears to be idle, the station can begin to send data. When several computers connected to the same network need to send data, two computers might try to send at the same time, causing a collision of data. The Ethernet protocol senses this collision and notifies the computer to send the data again.

How can two computers send data at the same time? Isn't Ethernet supposed to check the network for other systems that might be transmitting before sending data across the network?

Here's what happens in a 10Mbps network: An Ethernet station sends data at a rate of 10Mbps. It allows 100 nanoseconds per bit of information that is transmitted. The signal travels about 0.3 meters (1 foot) in 1 nanosecond. After the electrical signal for the first bit has traveled about 30 meters (100 feet) down the wire, the station begins sending the second bit. An Ethernet cable can run for hundreds of feet. If two stations are located about 75 meters (250 feet) apart on the same cable and both begin transmitting at the same time, they will be in the middle of the third bit before the signal from each reaches the other station.

This explains the need for the *Collision Detection* part of CSMA/CD. If two stations begin sending data at the same time, their signals collide nanoseconds later. When such a collision occurs, the two stations stop transmitting and try again later, after a randomly chosen delay period.

This also explains why distances are an important consideration in planning Ethernet networks.

Although an Ethernet network can be built by using one common signal wire, such an arrangement is not flexible enough to wire most buildings. Unlike an ordinary telephone circuit, Ethernet wire cannot be spliced to connect one copper wire to another. Instead, Ethernet requires a *repeater*, a simple station that is connected to two wires. When the repeater receives data on one wire, it repeats the data bit-for-bit on the other wire. When collisions occur, the repeater repeats the collision as well. In buildings that have two or more types of Ethernet cable, a common practice is to use media converters, switches, or repeaters to convert the Ethernet signal from one type of wire to another. Network hardware is discussed in more detail later in the chapter.

NOTE

As of Solaris 10, the FDDI interface is no longer supported.

Network Hardware

The *network hardware* is the physical part of the network that you can actually see. The physical components connect the systems and include the network interface cards (NICs), hosts, cable, connectors, hubs, and routers, some of which are discussed in the following sections.

NICs

The computer hardware that allows you to connect a computer to a network is known as a network interface card (*NIC*), or network adapter. The network interface can support one or more communication protocols that specify how computers use the physical medium—the network cable or the radio spectrum—to exchange data. Most computer systems come with a preinstalled network interface.

Each LAN media type has its own associated network interface. For example, if you want to use Ethernet as your network medium, you must have an Ethernet interface installed in each host that is to be part of the network. The connectors on the board to which you attach the Ethernet cable are referred to as *Ethernet ports*.

Hosts

If you are an experienced Unix/Solaris user, you are no doubt familiar with the term *host*, which is often used as a synonym for *computer* or *machine*. From a TCP/IP perspective, only two types of entities exist on a network: routers and hosts. When a host initiates communication, it is called a *sending host*, or *sender*. For example, a host initiates communications when the user uses `ping` or sends an email message to another user. The host that is the target of the communication is called the *receiving host*, or *recipient*.

Each host has an Internet address and a hardware address that identify it to its peers on the network, and usually a hostname. These are described in Table 8.4.

TABLE 8.4 Host Information

Identity	Description
Hostname	Every system on the network usually has a unique hostname. Hostnames let users refer to any computer on the network by using a short, easily remembered name rather than the host's network IP address.
Internet address	Each machine on a TCP/IP network has a 32-bit Internet address (or IP address) that identifies the machine to its peers on the network. This address must be unique on the network.
Hardware address	Each host on a network has a unique Ethernet address, also referred to as the media access control (MAC) address. The manufacturer physically assigns this address to the machine's network interface card(s). This address is unique worldwide—not just for the network to which it is connected.

Hubs and Switches

Ethernet cable is run to each system from a hub or switch. A *hub* does nothing more than connect all the Ethernet cables so that the computers can connect to one another. It does not boost the signal or route packets from one network to another. When a packet arrives at one port, it is copied to the other ports so that all the computers on the LAN can see all the packets. Hubs can support from two to several hundred systems.

A *passive hub* serves as a conduit for the data, allowing it to go from one device, or segment, to another. *Intelligent hubs* include additional features that let you monitor the traffic passing through the hub and configure each port in the hub. Intelligent hubs are also called *manageable hubs*. A third type of hub, called a *packet-switching hub* (or *switch*), is a special type of hub that forwards packets to the appropriate port based on the packet's destination address.

A network that utilizes conventional hubs is a *shared network* because every node on the network competes for a fraction of the total bandwidth. In a shared network, data packets are broadcast to all stations until they discover their intended destinations; this wastes both time and network bandwidth. A switch remedies this problem by looking at the address for each data packet and delivering the packet directly to the correct destination, and this provides much better performance than the hub system. Most switches also support load balancing so that ports are dynamically reassigned to different LAN segments based on traffic patterns.

Most switches are autosensing, which means they support both Fast Ethernet (100Mbps) and Gigabit Ethernet (1000Mbps) ports. This lets the administrator establish a dedicated Ethernet channel for high-traffic devices such as servers.

In addition, some switches include a feature called *full-duplex data transfer*. With this feature, all computers on the switch can "talk" to the switch at the same time. Full-duplex data transfer also allows switches to send and receive data simultaneously to all connections, whereas a hub cannot. A hub simply works with one computer at a time and only sends or only receives data because it cannot handle simultaneous two-way communication.

Routers

A *router* is a machine that forwards packets from one network to another. In other words, whereas a hub connects computers, a router connects networks. To do this, a router must have at least two network interfaces. A machine with only one network interface cannot forward packets; it is considered a host. Most of the machines you set up on a network are likely to be hosts.

Routers use packet headers and a forwarding table, called a *routing table*, to determine where packets go. Routes can be either static (in which case they are preset by network/system administrator) or dynamic (in which case a route to a destination host is learned or calculated at the time that it is requested).

IPv4 Addressing

In IPv4, each host on a TCP/IP network has a 32-bit network address—referred to as the *IP address*—that must be unique for each host on the network. If the host will participate on the Internet, this address must also be unique to the Internet. For this reason, IP addresses are assigned by special organizations known as regional Internet registries (RIRs). The IPv4 address space is the responsibility of Internet Corporation for Assigned Names and Numbers (ICANN; see `www.icann.org`). The overall responsibility for IP addresses, including the responsibility for allocation of IP ranges, belongs to the Internet Assigned Numbers Authority (IANA; see `www.iana.org`).

An IP address is a sequence of 4 bytes and is written in the form of four decimal integers separated by periods (for example, `10.11.12.13`). Each integer is 8 bits long and ranges from 0 to 255. An IP address consists of two parts: a network ID, which is assigned by an RIR, and a host ID, which is assigned by the local administrator. The first integer of the address (`10.0.0.0`) determines the address type and is referred to as its *class*. Five classes of IP addresses exist: A, B, C, D, and E. The following sections briefly describe each class.

NOTE

IPv6 Due to limited address space and other considerations of the IPv4 scheme, a revised IP protocol is gradually being made available. The protocol, named IPv6, has been designed to overcome the major limitations of the current approach. IPv6 is compatible with IPv4, but IPv6 makes it possible to assign many more unique Internet addresses and offers support for improved security and performance. A brief section on IPv6 appears later in this chapter for background information, even though it is not a specific objective in the Solaris 10 Part II exam.

Class A Addresses

Class A addresses are used for very large networks with millions of hosts, such as the Internet. A Class A network number uses the first 8 bits of the IP address as its network ID. The remaining 24 bits make up the host part of the IP address. The value assigned to the first byte of a Class A network number falls within the range 0 to 127. For example, consider the IP address `75.4.10.4`. The value `75` in the first byte indicates that the host is on a Class A network. The remaining bytes, `4.10.4`, establish the host address. An RIR assigns only the first byte of a Class A number. Use of the remaining 3 bytes is left to the discretion of the owner of the network number. Only 126 Class A networks can exist because `0` is reserved for the network, and `127` is reserved for the loopback device, leaving `1` to `126` as usable addresses. Each Class A network can accommodate up to 16,777,214 hosts. The `10.x.x.x` network is reserved for use by private networks for hosts that are not connected to the Internet. If you want to assign a Class A network and you are not visible on the Internet, you can use one of these network addresses.

Class B Addresses

Class B addresses are used for medium-size networks, such as universities and large businesses with many hosts. A Class B address uses 16 bits for the network number and 16 bits for the host number. The first byte of a Class B network number is in the range 128 to 191. In the number `129.144.50.56`, the first 2 bytes, `129.144`, are assigned by an RIR and make up the network address. The last 2 bytes, `50.56`, make up the host address and are assigned at the discretion of the network's owner. A Class B network can accommodate a maximum of 65,534 hosts. Again, the first and last addresses on the network are reserved. The `0` host address is reserved for the network, and the `255` address is reserved as the IP broadcast address. Therefore, the actual number of hosts that can be assigned on a Class B network is 65,534, not 65,536. The network address ranges `172.16.x.x` through `172.31.x.x` are reserved for use by private networks that are not connected to the Internet. If you want to assign a Class B network and you are not visible on the Internet, you can use one of these network addresses.

Class C Addresses

Class C addresses are used for small networks with fewer than 254 hosts. A Class C address uses 24 bits for the network number and 8 bits for host number. A Class C network number occupies the first 3 bytes of an IP address; only the fourth byte is assigned at the discretion of the network's owner. The first byte of a Class C network number covers the range 192 to 223. The second and third bytes each cover the range 0 to 255. A typical Class C address might be `192.5.2.5`, with the first 3 bytes, `192.5.2`, forming the network number. The final byte in this example, 5, is the host number. A Class C network can accommodate a maximum of 254 hosts out of 256 addresses; again, this is because the first and last values are reserved. The `192.168.x.x` network ranges are specially reserved for private networks that are not connected to the Internet. If you want to assign a Class C network and you are not visible on the Internet, you can use one of these network addresses.

Class D and E Addresses

Class D addresses cover the range 224 to 239 and are used for IP multicasting, as defined in RFC 988. Class E addresses cover the range 240 to 255 and are reserved for experimental use.

Planning for IP Addressing

The first step in planning for IP addressing on a network is to determine how many IP addresses you need and whether the network is going to be connected to the Internet. If the network is not going to be connected to the Internet, you could choose addresses in the `10.x.x.x`, or `172.16.x.x–172.31.x.x`, or `192.168.x.x` range. For networks that are going to be connected to the Internet—and hence visible to the rest of the world—you need to obtain legal IP addresses; this is necessary because each host on a network must have a unique IP address. IP addresses can be obtained either through an Internet service provider (ISP) or an RIR, as mentioned earlier in this section. When you receive your network number, you can plan how you will assign the host parts of the IP address.

Your nearest RIR depends on where, geographically, your network is located. The current list of RIRs is as follows:

- **North and South America**—American Registry for Internet Numbers (ARIN; `www.arin.net`)
- **Europe**—RIPE network coordination center (`www.ripe.net`)
- **Asia-Pacific region**—Asia Pacific Network Information Center (APNIC; `www.apnic.org`)
- **Latin America and Caribbean**—Latin America and Caribbean Internet Addresses Registry (LACNIC; `www.lacnic.net`)
- **Africa**—Africa Network Information Center (AfriNIC; `www.afrinic.net`)

After you contact the correct RIR, you have to justify why you should be given global IP addresses. Normally, unless yours is a large organization, you would be expected to obtain IP addresses from your ISP.

NOTE

Being Careful with IP Addresses You should not arbitrarily assign network numbers to a network, even if you do not plan to attach your network to other existing TCP/IP networks. As your network grows, you might decide to connect it to other networks. Changing IP addresses at that time can be a great deal of work and can cause downtime. Instead, you might want to use the specially reserved IP networks `192.168.x.x`, or `172.16.x.x`–`172.31.x.x`, or `10.x.x.x` for networks that are not connected to the Internet.

IPv6

TIP

IPv6 No questions on the exam relate to IPv6. This section is included purely for background information.

As the Internet community continues to grow and use more IPv4 addresses, we have been running out of available IPv4 addresses. IPv6, also called IP Next Generation (IPng), improves Internet capability by using a simplified header format, longer addresses (128 instead of 32 bits), support for authentication and privacy, autoconfiguration of address assignments, and new Quality of Service (QoS) capabilities. Specifically, IPv6 provides these enhancements:

- **Expanded addressing capabilities**—Because IPv4 is a 32-bit protocol, it can accommodate approximately 4,300,000,000 addresses. It was estimated that IPv4 addresses would be exhausted in about the year 2008, but the implementation of Classless Internet Domain Routing (CIDR) has eased the shortage.

NOTE

CIDR—Classless Internet Domain Routing (CIDR) uses (typically) the first 18 bits of an IPv4 address as the network portion, leaving 14 bits to be used for the host. This implementation has meant that networks can be aggregated by routers for ease of delivery, in the same way as the telephone system uses area codes to route telephone calls. Note that CIDR is not a topic on the exam and is included only as background information.

IPv6 increases the IP address size from 32 bits to 128 bits, to support more levels of addressing hierarchy. Thus, the number of potential addresses is 4 billion × 4 billion × 4 billion times the size of the IPv4 address space.

Here's an example of an IPv6 address:

```
2001:0DB8:0000:0000:0000:FFFF:ACBC:19A1
```

The first 48 bits of the address represent the public topology. The next 16 bits represent the site topology.

- **Improved routing**—When the number of organizations connected to the Internet increases, the amount of memory and route information increases, too. This puts the burden on the router, which forwards the packet; it results in decreased look-up speed, which could be a fatal problem for a router with little capacity. Improvements in IPv6 addressing improve routing over what is available in IPv4.
- **Security**—The basic IPv6 specification includes security and privacy enhancements. The Internet has a number of security problems and lacks effective privacy and effective authentication mechanisms below the application layer. IPv6 remedies these shortcomings by having two integrated options that provide improved IP Security (IPsec) services:
  - Encapsulated Security Payload (ESP) (provides packet encryption)
  - Authentication Header (AH) (provides source authentication and integrity protection)
- **Real-time traffic support**—A new capability has been added to IPv6 to enable the labeling of packets that belong to particular traffic flows for which the sender requests special handling. For example, the sender can request nondefault quality of service or real-time service.

  To support real-time traffic such as videoconferencing, IPv6 has a concept of "flow label." Using flow label, a router can know which end-to-end flow a packet belongs to and then can find out what packet belongs to real-time traffic.

  In addition, a 4-bit priority field in the IPv6 header enables a source to identify the desired delivery priority of its packets, relative to other packets from the same source.
- **Header format simplification**—Some IPv4 header fields have been dropped or made optional in IPv6. This change reduces the common-case processing cost of packet handling. This change also keeps the bandwidth cost of the IPv6 header as low as possible, despite the increased size of the addresses. Even though the IPv6 addresses are four times longer than the IPv4 addresses, the IPv6 header is only twice the size of the IPv4 header.
- **Improved support for options**—Changes in the way IP header options are encoded allow for more efficient forwarding. Also, the length of options has less stringent limits with IPv6 than with IPv4. The changes also provide greater flexibility for introducing new options in the future.

Network Interfaces

A Sun system normally contains at least one network interface, to allow it to participate in a network environment. When you add a network interface to a system, a number of files need to be configured in order to create the connection between the hardware and the software address assigned to the interface. The following sections describe how to monitor, control, and configure an IPv4 network interface.

Controlling and Monitoring an IPv4 Network Interface

Objective:

- **Control and monitor network interfaces including MAC addresses, IP addresses, network packets, and configure the IPv4 interfaces at boot time.**

As root, you can use the `ifconfig -a` command to display both the system's IP and MAC addresses, as in this example:

```
ifconfig -a
lo0: flags=1000849<UP,LOOPBACK,RUNNING,MULTICAST,IPv4,VIRTUAL> mtu 8232 index 1
     inet 127.0.0.1 netmask ff000000
hme0: flags=1000843<UP,BROADCAST,RUNNING,MULTICAST,IPv4> mtu 1500 index 2
      inet 192.168.1.106 netmask ffffff00 broadcast 192.168.1.255
      ether 8:0:20:a2:63:82
```

You can also retrieve the MAC address from a system by using the `banner` command at the OpenBoot prompt, as described in Chapter 3, "Perform System Boot and Shutdown Procedures."

NOTE

Displaying a MAC Address If you enter the `ifconfig -a` command as a nonprivileged user, then only the IP address information is displayed. In order to display the MAC address as well as the IP address, the root user must enter `ifconfig -a` command.

You can mark an Ethernet interface as up or down by using the `ifconfig` command. Marking an interface as up allows it to communicate on the network. For example, to mark the `hme0` interface as `down`, you use the following command:

```
ifconfig hme0 down
ifconfig -a
lo0: flags=1000849<UP,LOOPBACK,RUNNING,MULTICAST,IPv4,VIRTUAL> mtu 8232 index 1
     inet 127.0.0.1 netmask ff000000
```

```
hme0: flags=1000842<BROADCAST,RUNNING,MULTICAST,IPv4> mtu 1500 index 2
      inet 192.168.1.106 netmask ffffff00 broadcast 192.168.1.255
      ether 8:0:20:a2:63:82
```

Notice that the up flags are no longer present for the `hme0` interface and also that the value of `flags` has changed to `1000842`.

To mark the interface as up, you use the following command:

```
ifconfig hme0 up
ifconfig -a
lo0: flags=1000849<UP,LOOPBACK,RUNNING,MULTICAST,IPv4,VIRTUAL> mtu 8232 index 1
     inet 127.0.0.1 netmask ff000000
hme0: flags=1000843<UP,BROADCAST,RUNNING,MULTICAST,IPv4> mtu 1500 index 2
      index 2 inet 192.168.1.106 netmask ffffff00 broadcast 192.168.1.255
      ether 8:0:20:a2:63:82
```

When the network interface is marked as up, the interface is ready to communicate with other systems on the network.

To determine whether another system can be contacted over the network, you use the `ping` command, as follows:

```
ping ultra10
```

If host `ultra10` is up, this message is displayed:

```
Ultra10 is alive
```

NOTE

Names to Addresses The `ultra10 is alive` command assumes that the host `ultra10` can be resolved either through an entry in the `/etc/hosts` file or by using DNS. If you do not know the hostname, you can use the `ping` command with the IP address instead of the hostname.

The message indicates that `ultra10` responded to the request and can be contacted. However, if `ultra10` is down or cannot receive the request, you receive the following response:

```
no answer from ultra10
```

In order for a `ping` request to be successful, the following conditions must be met:

- **The interface must be plumbed**—This is automatically carried out at boot time by the script `/lib/svc/method/net-physical`, as discussed in the section "Configuring an IPv4 Network Interface," later in this chapter.

- **The interface must be configured**—An address must be assigned to a network interface; this is carried out initially when you install the Solaris operating environment. Configuring the interface is discussed in the section "Configuring an IPv4 Network Interface," later in this chapter.
- **The interface must be up**—The network interface can communicate only when it is marked as `up`. This is done via the `ifconfig` command.
- **The interface must be physically connected**—The network interface must be connected to the network, using the appropriate cable.
- **The interface must have valid routes configured**—The routing provides the directions to the destination computer. This is an advanced networking topic that is not covered on the exam, but it is included here for completeness. A separate Solaris certification exam, "Solaris Network Administrator," deals with routing in detail.

Configuring an IPv4 Network Interface

When you install the Solaris operating environment, you configure a network interface as part of the installation program. You can configure additional interfaces at system boot time, or you can modify the original interface by having an understanding of only four files:

- `/lib/svc/method/net-physical`
- `/etc/hostname.<interface>`
- `/etc/inet/hosts`
- `/etc/inet/ipnodes`

Each of these is discussed in the following sections.

The `/lib/svc/method/net-physical` File

This script uses the `ifconfig` utility to configure each network interface that has an IP address assigned to it, by searching for files named `hostname.<interface>` in the `/etc` directory. An example of such a file is `/etc/hostname.hme0`, which refers to the configuration file for the first `hme` network interface (interface numbering starts with 0, not 1—hence `hme1` would be the second `hme` interface on the system).

For each `hostname.<interface>` file, the script runs the `ifconfig` command with the `plumb` option, which effectively installs the interface and enables the kernel to communicate with the named network interface.

NOTE

A New Startup Script The file `/lib/svc/method/net-physical` is new in the Solaris 10 operating environment. Those who are familiar with releases prior to Solaris 10 will recognize that this script carries out the same functions as the file `/etc/rcS.d/S30network.sh` in previous releases, but it is now part of the Service Management Facility (SMF).

The /etc/hostname.<interface> File

The files> files> `/etc/hostname.<interface>` file defines the network interfaces on the local host. At least one `/etc/hostname.<interface>` file should exist on the local machine. The Solaris installation program creates this file for you. In the filename, `<interface>` is replaced by the device name of the primary network interface.

This file contains only one entry: the hostname or IP address associated with the network interface. For example, suppose `hme0` is the primary network interface for a machine called `system1`. The file would be called `/etc/hostname.hme0`, and the file would contain the entry `system1` files> files>.

The /etc/inet/hosts File

The `hosts` database contains details of the machines on your network. This file contains the hostnames and IP addresses of the primary network interface and any other network addresses the machine must know about. You can use the `/etc/inet/hosts` file with other `hosts` databases, such as DNS, NIS, and NIS+. When a user enters a command such as `ping xena`, the system needs to know how to get to the `host` named `xena`. The `/etc/inet/hosts` file provides a cross-reference to look up and find `xena`'s network IP address. For compatibility with Berkeley Software Distribution (BSD)-based Unix operating systems, the file `/etc/hosts` is a symbolic link to `/etc/inet/hosts`.

Each line in the `/etc/inet/hosts` file uses the following format:

```
<address> <hostname> <nickname> [#comment]
```

Each field in this syntax is described in Table 8.5.

TABLE 8.5 The /etc/inet/hosts File Format

Field	Description
`<address>`	The IPv4 address for each interface the local host must know about.
`<hostname>`	The hostname assigned to the machine at setup and the hostnames assigned to additional network interfaces that the local host must know about.
`<nickname>`	An optional field that contains a nickname or an alias for the host. More than one nickname can exist.
`[# comment]`	An optional field in which you can include a comment.

When you run the Solaris installation program on a system, it sets up the initial `/etc/inet/hosts` file. This file contains the minimum entries that the local host requires: its loopback address, its IP address, and its hostname.

For example, the Solaris installation program might create the following entries in the `/etc/inet/hosts` file for a system called `xena`:

```
127.0.0.1        localhost              #loopback address
192.9.200.3      xena                loghost    #hostname
```

In the `/etc/inet/hosts` file for the machine `xena`, the IP address `127.0.0.1` is the loopback address, the reserved network interface used by the local machine to allow interprocess communication so that it sends packets to itself. The operating system, through the `ifconfig` command, uses the loopback address for configuration and testing. Every machine on a TCP/IP network must have an entry for the localhost and must use the IP address `127.0.0.1`.

The `/etc/inet/ipnodes` File

The `ipnodes` database contains details of the machines on your network. This file, like the `/etc/inet/hosts` file, contains the hostnames and IP addresses of the primary network interface and any other network addresses the machine must know about, but, unlike the `/etc/inet/hosts` file, the file can also contain IPv6 addresses. You can use the `/etc/inet/ipnodes` file with other hosts databases, such as DNS, NIS, and NIS+.

EXAM ALERT

No Compatibility `/etc` link—You should note that there is no `/etc/ipnodes` link to `/etc/inet/ipnodes`. This is a very common mistake to make in the exam when presented with `/etc/ipnodes` as an option.

Each line in the `/etc/inet/ipnodes` file uses the following format:

```
<address> <hostname> <nickname> [#comment]
```

Each field in this syntax is described in Table 8.6.

TABLE 8.6 The `/etc/inet/ipnodes` File Format

Field	Description
<address>	The IPv4 or IPv6 address for each host or interface the local host must know about.
<hostname>	The hostname assigned to the machine at setup and the hostnames assigned to additional network interfaces that the local host must know about.
<nickname>	An optional field that contains a nickname or an alias for the host. More than one nickname can exist.
[# *comment*]	An optional field in which you can include a comment.

When you run the Solaris installation program on a system, it sets up the initial /etc/inet/ipnodes file. This file contains the minimum entries that the local host requires: its loopback address, its IPv4 or IPv6 address, and its hostname.

For example, the Solaris installation program creates the following entries in the /etc/inet/ipnodes file for the system called xena used in the previous section:

```
::1        localhost
192.9.200.3      xena      loghost
```

The following step by step demonstrates how to configure a network interface from the command line. In this exercise, we'll configure the primary network interface (hme0) to achieve connectivity with other systems on the network. The hostname will be set to Achilles, with an IP Address of 192.168.0.111, and a network mask of 255.255.255.0, and the interface will be made operational as well.

STEP BY STEP

8.1 Configuring an IPv4 Network Interface

1. Display the current network interface configuration using the ifconfig command and make sure the interface is down as follows:

```
# ifconfig hme0 down
#ifconfig -a
lo0: flags=2001000849<UP,LOOPBACK,RUNNING,MULTICAST,IPv4,VIRTUAL> mtu 8232 index 1
        inet 127.0.0.1 netmask ff000000
hme0: flags=1000842<BROADCAST,RUNNING,MULTICAST,IPv4> mtu 1500 index 2
        inet 192.168.7.1 netmask ffffff00 broadcast 192.168.7.255
        ether 8:0:20:1e:86:90
```

2. Edit the files /etc/inet/hosts and /etc/inet/ipnodes and add the following entry:

```
192.168.0.111    achilles
```

3. Edit the file /etc/hostname.hme0 to contain the following entry:

```
achilles
```

4. Edit the file /etc/inet/netmasks and add the following entry:

```
192.168.0.0      255.255.255.0
```

5. The pre-configuration of the interface is now complete. We can now use the ifconfig command to initialize the interface and make it operational, as follows:

```
# ifconfig hme0 achilles netmask + broadcast + up
```

6. Verify that the interface is now operational and correctly configured, using the `ifconfig -a` command, as follows:

```
# ifconfig -a
lo0: flags=2001000849<UP,LOOPBACK,RUNNING,MULTICAST,IPv4,VIRTUAL> mtu 8232 index 1
        inet 127.0.0.1 netmask ff000000
hme0: flags=1000843<UP,BROADCAST,RUNNING,MULTICAST,IPv4> mtu 1500 index 2
        inet 192.168.0.111 netmask ffffff00 broadcast 192.168.0.255
        ether 8:0:20:1e:86:90
```

EXAM ALERT

Use the Plus (+)—Using the + option to the `ifconfig` command causes a lookup in the `/etc/inet/netmasks` file to determine the correct values, based on the network mask value that has been inserted for the relevant network. You must make sure the `/etc/inet/netmasks` file is accurate for this to work correctly. You can always specify the full values to the `ifconfig` command, but it requires that the broadcast address is calculated manually, which can be difficult when subnetworks are used.

Changing the System Hostname

There are two methods available for changing the system hostname: The first is to edit the necessary files manually and reboot the system, as described here.

The system's hostname is contained within four files on a Solaris system. It is necessary to modify all these files in order to successfully change the hostname of a system manually. These files need to be changed:

- **`/etc/nodename`**—This file contains the local source for a system name. In other words, it contains the hostname of the system. The only information contained within this file is the name of the system (for example, `ultra10`). This is the location where the system hostname is set. You can change the hostname by running the command `uname -S` and supplying a new hostname, but if you do so, the change does not persist across reboots. The command `uname -n`, which prints the node name of the system, looks in this file for the information.
- **`/etc/hostname.`*`<interface>`***—This file defines the network interfaces on the local host and is discussed earlier in this chapter, in the section "The `/etc/hostname.`*`<interface>`* File."
- **`/etc/inet/hosts`**—The `hosts` file contains details of the machines on your network and is discussed earlier in this chapter, in the section "The `/etc/inet/hosts` File."
- **`/etc/inet/ipnodes`**—This file contains details of the machines on your network and includes both IPv4 and IPv6 addresses. It is discussed in the previous section of this chapter, "The `/etc/inet/ipnodes` File."

Having changed the contents of the files listed above, the system needs to be rebooted to implement the new hostname.

The second method for changing the hostname is to use the `sys-unconfig` command. The result of running this command is the removal of the system identification details, similar to when you initiate a Solaris 10 installation.

When the command completes, the system automatically shuts down. To complete the process, boot the system. You will be presented with a number of configuration questions, such as hostname, IP address, subnet mask, default router, time zone, naming service configuration, and the root password—all very similar to when you perform an initial installation of the Solaris 10 Operating Environment.

Network Services

Objective:

- **Explain the client-server model and enable/disable server processes.**

In previous releases of Solaris, the `inetd` network daemon was responsible for running network services on demand and was configured by editing the file, `/etc/inetd.conf`. As of Solaris 10, this has all changed. The services that were previously configured using this file are now configured and managed by the Service Management Facility (SMF)—see chapter 3 for a full description of the Service Management Facility. A new command, `inetadm`, is used to carry out the management of these network services.

The default `/etc/inetd.conf` file now contains only a few entries, unlike in previous versions of Solaris where all of the network services were listed. The `/etc/inetd.conf` file may still be used as a mechanism for adding new (third-party additional software) services, but in order to make use of these services, they must be converted to run under SMF. This is carried out using the `inetconv` command. When you run this command with no options, it automatically reads the `/etc/inetd.conf` file and converts any entries to services that can run under SMF. The `inetd` daemon can no longer be run manually from the command line, nor can it be instructed to re-read its configuration file, as in previous releases of Solaris. Changes or modifications to the configuration of network services are done using the `inetadm` or `svccfg` commands.

NOTE

If you attempt to run `inetd` manually, outside of SMF, you will receive an error message.

To see the network services being managed by SMF, enter the `inetadm` command with no options:

```
# inetadm

ENABLED   STATE          FMRI
enabled   online         svc:/network/rpc/gss:default
enabled   online         svc:/network/rpc/mdcomm:default
enabled   online         svc:/network/rpc/meta:default
enabled   online         svc:/network/rpc/metamed:default
enabled   online         svc:/network/rpc/metamh:default
disabled  disabled       svc:/network/rpc/rex:default
enabled   online         svc:/network/rpc/rstat:default
enabled   online         svc:/network/rpc/rusers:default
disabled  disabled       svc:/network/rpc/spray:default
disabled  disabled       svc:/network/rpc/wall:default
disabled  disabled       svc:/network/tname:default
enabled   online         svc:/network/security/ktkt_warn:default
enabled   online         svc:/network/telnet:default
enabled   online         svc:/network/nfs/rquota:default
disabled  disabled       svc:/network/chargen:dgram
disabled  disabled       svc:/network/chargen:stream
disabled  disabled       svc:/network/daytime:dgram
disabled  disabled       svc:/network/daytime:stream
disabled  disabled       svc:/network/discard:dgram
disabled  disabled       svc:/network/discard:stream
disabled  disabled       svc:/network/echo:dgram
disabled  disabled       svc:/network/echo:stream
disabled  disabled       svc:/network/time:dgram
disabled  disabled       svc:/network/time:stream
enabled   online         svc:/network/ftp:default
disabled  disabled       svc:/network/comsat:default
enabled   online         svc:/network/finger:default
disabled  disabled       svc:/network/login:eklogin
disabled  disabled       svc:/network/login:klogin
enabled   online         svc:/network/login:rlogin
disabled  disabled       svc:/network/rexec:default
enabled   online         svc:/network/shell:default
disabled  disabled       svc:/network/shell:kshell
disabled  disabled       svc:/network/talk:default
enabled   online         svc:/application/font/stfsloader:default
enabled   online         svc:/application/x11/xfs:default
enabled   online         svc:/network/rpc/smserver:default
disabled  disabled       svc:/network/rpc/ocfserv:default
enabled   offline        svc:/application/print/rfc1179:default
disabled  disabled       svc:/platform/sun4u/dcs:default
disabled  disabled       svc:/network/uucp:default
disabled  disabled       svc:/network/security/krb5_prop:default
disabled  disabled       svc:/network/apocd/udp:default
```

```
enabled   online         svc:/network/rpc-100235_1/rpc_ticotsord:default
enabled   online         svc:/network/rpc-100083_1/rpc_tcp:default
enabled   online         svc:/network/rpc-100068_2-5/rpc_udp:default
enabled   online         svc:/network/tftp/udp6:default
```

The preceding code shows, for example, that the `spray` service is in the `disabled` state. To enable this service, use the `inetadm` command with the `-e` option:

```
# inetadm -e spray
```

Now you can see that the service has been enabled and is available for use:

```
# inetadm | grep spray

enabled   online         svc:/network/rpc/spray:default
```

To disable the `spray` service, use the `inetadm` command with the `-d` option:

```
# inetadm -d spray
```

Check again to verify that the service is now disabled:

```
# inetadm | grep spray

disabled  disabled       svc:/network/rpc/spray:default
```

NOTE

Other Commands Work Too—You are not limited to the `inetadm` command to view and control legacy network services. The `svcs -a` command can also be used to view the status, and the `svcadm` command can control legacy network services as well.

You can also list the properties and values of a selected network service, using the `-l` option to the `inetadm` command. The following code lists the properties of the `spray` service:

```
# inetadm -l spray

SCOPE     NAME=VALUE
          name="sprayd"
          endpoint_type="tli"
          proto="datagram_v"
          isrpc=TRUE
          rpc_low_version=1
          rpc_high_version=1
          wait=TRUE
          exec="/usr/lib/netsvc/spray/rpc.sprayd"
          user="root"
default   bind_addr=""
default   bind_fail_max=-1
```

```
default   bind_fail_interval=-1
default   max_con_rate=-1
default   max_copies=-1
default   con_rate_offline=-1
default   failrate_cnt=40
default   failrate_interval=60
default   inherit_env=TRUE
default   tcp_trace=FALSE
default   tcp_wrappers=FALSE
```

Each network service uses a port that represents an address space and is reserved for that service. Systems communicate with each other through these ports. Well-known ports are listed in the `/etc/services` file, which is a symbolic link to `/etc/inet/services`. The following are a few entries from the `/etc/services` file:

```
chargen          19/tcp          ttytst source
chargen          19/udp          ttytst source
ftp-data         20/tcp
ftp              21/tcp
```

From these entries, you can see that the `chargen` service uses port 19 and will use both TCP and UDP protocols. It also has aliases assigned.

Each network service uses a well-known port number that is used by all the hosts on the network. Keeping track of these ports can be difficult, especially on a network that supports several network services.

Solaris utilizes a client/server model known as *remote procedure calls* (*RPC*). With an RPC service, a client connects to a special server process, `rpcbind`, which is a "well-known service". `rpcbind` registers port numbers associated with each RPC service listed in the `/etc/rpc` file. The `rpcbind` process receives all RPC-based client application connection requests and sends the client the appropriate server port number. For example, `mountd` is listed in the `/etc/rpc` file as follows:

```
mountd           100005  mount showmount
```

The `mountd` daemon has a program number of `100005` and is also known as `mount` and `showmount`.

You use the `rpcinfo` utility with the `-p` option to list registered RPC programs running on a system. For example, you can check on processes on another system like this:

```
rpcinfo -p 192.168.1.21
```

The system responds with a list of all the registered RPC services found running on that system:

```
program      vers      proto    port     service
100005       1         udp      32784    mountd
```

The output displays the program number, version, protocol, port, and service name. One of them in this example is the `mountd` service.

You can also use `rpcinfo` to unregister an RPC program. When you use `rpcinfo` with the `-d` option, you can delete registration for a service. For example, if `sprayd` is running on the local system, you can unregister, and disable it as follows:

```
rpcinfo  -d sprayd 1
```

The `sprayd` service would be unregistered from RPC. You could restart the `sprayd` service by issuing a restart command using the `svcadm` command, as follows:

```
svcadm restart spray
```

This causes the `spray` service to restart and automatically re-register the RPC program associated with the `spray` service.

Network Maintenance

Solaris provides several network commands that you can use to check and troubleshoot a network:

- **`ping`**—`ping` stands for *packet Internet groper*. The `ping` command sends an ICMP packet to another host to test its network status. The remote system sends an ICMP packet back to the originating host if the `ping` command succeeds. If no packet is received from the remote system then it is deemed to be down and a message is returned to the calling host. The options to the command allow continuous packets or a specified number of packets to be sent as well as different sizes of packets.
- **`snoop`**—The `snoop` command captures and inspects network packets. Captured packets can be displayed as they are received or saved into a file to be analyzed later. `snoop` can produce large amounts of information, with each entry being displayed in single-line summary form or multiline verbose form.
- **`netstat`**—The `netstat` command displays network status information. You can see the status of the network interface, monitor how many packets are passing through the interface, and monitor how many errors are occurring. This command is used extensively in identifying overloaded networks where the packet collision rate would be much higher than expected.

Each of the commands listed here are demonstrated in Step by Step 8.2.

STEP BY STEP

8.2 Verifying That a Network Is Operational

1. Check the network connection to another system by typing the following:

```
ping <options> <ip-address>
```

For example, to check the network between `systemA` and `systemB`, type **`ping systemB`** from `systemA`. If the check is successful, the remote system replies with this:

```
systemB is alive
```

If the network is not active, you get this message:

```
no answer from systemB
```

If you get this negative response, check your cable and make sure that both the local system and the remote system are configured properly.

2. Use the `snoop` utility to determine what information is flowing between systems. The `snoop` utility can show what actually happens when one system sends a `ping` to another system. The following example shows network traffic being monitored between two hosts, namely `192.168.1.106` and `192.168.1.21`:

```
snoop 192.168.1.106 192.168.1.21
```

The system responds with the following:

```
Using device /dev/hme (promiscuous mode)
192.168.1.106 -> 192.168.1.21 ICMP Echo request (ID: 2677 Sequence number\
: 0)
192.168.1.21 -> 192.168.1.106 ICMP Echo reply (ID: 2677 Sequence number: \
0)
```

3. Check for network traffic by typing the following:

```
netstat -i 5
```

The system responds with this:

```
input   hme0   output  input   (Total)  output
packets errs   packets errs colls packets errs  packets errs colls
95218   49983  189     1    0     218706  49983 123677  1    0
0       0      0       0    0     3       0     3       0    0
0       0      0       0    0     4       0     4       0    0
1       1      0       0    0     144     1     143     0    0
0       0      0       0    0     256     0     256     0    0
0       0      0       0    0     95      0     95      0    0
0       0      0       0    0     1171    0     1171    0    0
```

The `netstat` command is used to monitor the system's TCP/IP network activity. `netstat` can provide some basic data about how much and what kind of network activity is happening. You should ignore the first line of output, as this shows the overall activity since the system was last booted. The `-i` option shows the state of the network interface used for TCP/IP traffic. The last option, `5`, reissues the `netstat` command every 5 seconds to get a good sampling of network activity, with each line showing the activity since the last display, in this case 5 seconds. You can press Ctrl+C to break out of the `netstat` command.

4. Look in the `colls` column to see if there is a large number of collisions. To calculate the network collision rate, divide the number of output collisions (`output colls`) by the number of output packets. A network wide collision rate greater than 10% can indicate an overloaded network, a poorly configured network, or hardware problems.

5. Examine the `errs` column to see if there is a large number of errors. To calculate the input packet error rate, divide the number of input errors by the total number of input packets. If the input error rate is high—more than 25%—the host might be dropping packets because of transmission problems. Transmission problems can be caused by other hardware on the network and by heavy traffic and low-level hardware problems. Routers can drop packets, forcing retransmissions and causing degraded performance.

6. Type **`ping -sRv`** ***`<hostname>`*** from the client to determine how long it takes a packet to make a round-trip on the network. If the round-trip takes more than a few milliseconds, the routers on the network are slow or the network is very busy. Issue the `ping` command twice and ignore the first set of results.

   The `ping -sRv` command also displays packet losses. If you suspect a physical problem, you can use `ping -sRv` to find the response times of several hosts on the network. If the response time (in milliseconds) from one host is not what you expect, you should investigate that host.

Summary

Although networking is a topic that could consume many chapters in this book, the fundamentals that you need to know to be able to manage a Solaris system on the network are described here. All the concepts that you need to know for the Sun Certified System Administrator for the Solaris 10 Operating Environment exam (CX-310-202) are described.

After reading this chapter, you should have an understanding of the two types of network models—ISO/OSI and TCP/IP—and the component layers of these two models.

The network hardware and software components are described in this chapter, along with the new method of configuring and managing network services. Some new commands were introduced, specifically `inetadm` and `inetconv`.

Finally, this chapter discussed some of the network-related commands and utilities that you can use for monitoring and maintaining the network. In a networked environment, system performance depends on how well you've maintained your network. An overloaded network can disguise itself as a slow system and can even cause downtime. You should monitor your network continuously. You need to know how the network looks when things are running well so that you know what to look for when the network is performing poorly. The network commands described in this chapter only report numbers. You're the one who decides whether these numbers are acceptable for your environment. As stated earlier, practice and experience will help you excel at system administration. The same holds true for network administration.

Chapter 9 describes how to manage swap space, configure core and crash dump files, and use NFS to share file systems across a network. You'll also learn how to configure the `automounter` for use with AutoFS.

Key Terms

- Decapsulation
- Encapsulation
- Ethernet
- Host
- Hostname
- Hub
- IP address
- ISO/OSI model
- LAN
- MAC address
- Network class
- Network interface
- Network protocol
- Network service
- Packet
- Router
- Remote Procedure Calls (RPC)
- Service Management Facility (SMF)
- TCP/IP
- WAN

Apply Your Knowledge

Exercises

The following exercises require that you have two hosts connected via an Ethernet network, one named hostA and the other named hostB.

8.1 Obtaining Network Information

In this exercise, you'll use the various network commands and utilities to obtain information about your system and network.

Estimated time: 15 minutes

1. Log in as root on hostA. Make sure you have an entry in your /etc/inet/hosts file for hostB.

2. As root, use the ifconfig command to display information about your network interface:

```
ifconfig -a
lo0: flags=1000849<UP,LOOPBACK,RUNNING,MULTICAST,IPv4>,VIRTUAL mtu 8232 index 1\
inet 127.0.0.1 netmask ff000000
hme0: flags=1000843<UP,BROADCAST,RUNNING,MULTICAST,DHCP,IPv4> mtu 1500 index 2\
inet 192.168.1.106 netmask ffffff00 broadcast 192.168.1.255
ether 8:0:20:a2:63:82
```

   The ifconfig utility shows that the Ethernet address of the hme0 interface is 8:0:20:a2:63:82. The first half of the address is generally specific to the manufacturer. In this case, 8:0:20 is Sun Microsystems. The last half of the address, in this case a2:63:82, is unique for every system.

3. Use ping to send ICMP echo requests from hostA to hostB:

```
ping hostB
```

   On hostA, use the rpcinfo utility with the -p option to list the registered RPC programs:

```
rpcinfo
```

4. Look for the sprayd service on your system:

```
rpcinfo ¦ grep sprayd
```

5. Stop the sprayd service on your local system, as follows:

```
rpcinfo -d sprayd 1
```

6. Verify that the sprayd service has been unregistered from RPC:

```
rpcinfo ¦ grep sprayd
```

7. Restart the sprayd service by issuing the `svcadm restart` command, as follows:

```
svcadm restart spray
```

8. Verify that the sprayd service now registered with RPC:

```
rpcinfo ¦ grep sprayd
```

8.2 Using snoop to Display Network Information

In this exercise, you'll use the snoop, spray, and ping commands to obtain information from your network.

Estimated time: 10 minutes

1. On hostA, log in to an X Window session (CDE, Gnome, or Java Desktop System [JDS]) as root. In one window, start up the snoop utility, as follows:

```
snoop hostA hostB
```

snoop shows what actually happens when hostA uses the ping command to communicate with hostB.

2. In a second window on hostA, type the following:

```
ping hostB
```

3. Watch the information that is displayed in the first window that is running snoop.
4. Issue the spray command to send a one-way stream of packets to hostB:

```
spray hostB
```

5. Watch the information that is displayed in the first window that is running snoop.

Exam Questions

1. Name and provide a brief description of each layer of the seven-layer OSI model.
2. Name and provide a brief description of each layer of the five-layer TCP/IP model.
3. In TCP/IP, a packet that contains a header from the physical layer, followed by a header from the network layer (IP), followed by a header from the transport layer (TCP), followed by the application protocol data would be referred to as what?

   ❍ **A.** Decapsulation

   ❍ **B.** Encapsulation

   ❍ **C.** Encryption

   ❍ **D.** Decryption

4. What other name refers to a host's unique Ethernet address?

 ❍ **A.** IP address

 ❍ **B.** MAC address

 ❍ **C.** Internet address

 ❍ **D.** Hostname

5. When you are setting up at least one network interface, which of the following network configuration files does the Solaris installation program always set up? (Choose all that apply.)

 ❍ **A.** `/etc/hostname.interface`

 ❍ **B.** `/etc/nodename`

 ❍ **C.** `/etc/inet/hosts`

 ❍ **D.** `/etc/defaultdomain`

6. Which command lists the network services and their current state?

 ❍ **A.** `inetadm`

 ❍ **B.** `inetd`

 ❍ **C.** `rpcinfo`

 ❍ **D.** `nfsd`

7. What is TCP/IP?

 ❍ **A.** A general name for a set of protocols that allow computers to share resources across the network

 ❍ **B.** A network security specification used widely on the Internet

 ❍ **C.** One of the services provided by DNS

 ❍ **D.** Transfer Control Protocol/Information Protocol

8. Which of the following statements about IP addresses are true? (Choose all that apply.)

 ❍ **A.** IP addresses are written as four sets of numbers separated by periods.

 ❍ **B.** IP addresses provide a means of identifying and locating network resources.

 ❍ **C.** IP addresses are divided into three unique numbers: network, class, and host.

 ❍ **D.** The IP address identifies the machine to its peers on the network.

9. Which of the following statements is true about the `/etc/hostname.xxy` file?

   ❍ **A.** It is a system script file.

   ❍ **B.** It is a Sparc executable file.

   ❍ **C.** It contains the hostname of the local host.

   ❍ **D.** It identifies the network interface on the local host.

10. Which of the following is a network component that forwards Ethernet packets from one network to another?

   ❍ **A.** Hub

   ❍ **B.** Switch

   ❍ **C.** Network interface

   ❍ **D.** Router

11. Which of the following contains the IP addresses and hostnames of machines on a network?

   ❍ **A.** `/etc/inet/hosts`

   ❍ **B.** `/etc/hostname.xxy`

   ❍ **C.** `/etc/defaultdomain`

   ❍ **D.** `/etc/nodename`

12. Which of the following address classes is for medium-sized networks such as campuses and large businesses with many hosts?

   ❍ **A.** Class A

   ❍ **B.** Class B

   ❍ **C.** Class C

   ❍ **D.** Class D

13. Which of the following are files that have to be edited when you manually change the hostname on a Solaris system? (Choose all that apply.)

   ❍ **A.** `/etc/nodename`

   ❍ **B.** `/etc/defaultdomain`

   ❍ **C.** `/etc/networks`

   ❍ **D.** `/etc/inet/hosts`

   ❍ **E.** `/etc/inetipnodes`

14. Which of the following commands is used to monitor the system's TCP/IP network activity?

 ❍ **A.** `iostat`

 ❍ **B.** `vmstat`

 ❍ **C.** `netstat`

 ❍ **D.** `ping`

15. Which command is used to determine the information that is flowing between systems across a network?

 ❍ **A.** `netstat`

 ❍ **B.** `snoop`

 ❍ **C.** `iostat`

 ❍ **D.** `ping`

Answers to Exam Questions

1. Layer 1, the physical layer, describes the network hardware, including electrical and mechanical connections to the network.

   Layer 2, the data link layer, splits data into frames for sending on the physical layer and receives acknowledgement frames. It performs error checking and retransmits frames that are not received correctly.

   Layer 3, the network layer, manages the delivery of data via the data link layer and is used by the transport layer. IP is the most common network-layer protocol.

   Layer 4, the transport layer, determines how to use the network layer to provide a virtually error-free, point-to-point connection so that Host A can send messages to Host B and they will arrive uncorrupted and in the correct order.

   Layer 5, the session layer, uses the transport layer to establish a connection between processes on different hosts. It handles security and the creation of the session.

   Layer 6, the presentation layer, performs functions such as text compression, code, or format conversion to try to smooth out differences between hosts. The presentation layer allows incompatible processes in the application layer to communicate via the session layer.

   Layer 7, the application layer, is concerned with the user's view of the network (for example, formatting email messages). The presentation layer provides the application layer with a familiar local representation of data that is independent of the format used on the network. For more information, see the section "The ISO/OSI Model."

2. The hardware layer corresponds to the ISO/OSI model physical layer and describes the network hardware, including electrical and mechanical connections to the network. This layer regulates the transmission of unstructured bit streams over a transmission medium.

   The network interface layer corresponds to the ISO/OSI model data link layer and manages the delivery of data across the physical network. This layer provides error detection and packet framing.

   The Internet layer corresponds to the ISO/OSI model network layer and manages data addressing and delivery between networks, as well as fragmenting data for the data link layer.

   The transport layer corresponds to the ISO/OSI model transport layer and ensures that messages reach the correct application process by using TCP and UDP.

   The application layer corresponds to the session layer, presentation layer, and application layer of the ISO/OSI model. The application layer manages user-accessed application programs and network services. This layer is responsible for defining the way in which cooperating networks represent data. For more information, see the section "The TCP/IP Model."

3. **B.** When you think of systems communicating via a network, you can imagine the data progressing through each layer down from the application layer to the hardware layer, across the network, and then flowing back up from the hardware layer to the application layer. A header is added to each segment received on the way down the layers. This is referred to as *encapsulation*. For more information, see the section "Encapsulation and Decapsulation."

4. **B.** A host's unique Ethernet address is also referred to as the MAC address. For more information, see the section "Network Hardware."

5. **A, B, C.** The network configuration files `/etc/hostname.interface`, `/etc/nodename`, and `/etc/inet/hosts` are initially set up by the Solaris installation program. For more information, see the section "Configuring an IPv4 Network Interface."

6. **A.** The `inetadm` command lists the network services and their current state. This is a new feature to Solaris 10. For more information, see the section "Network Services" and Chapter 3, "Perform System Boot and Shutdown Procedures" for a full description of the Service Management Facility (SMF).

7. **A.** TCP/IP is a general name for a set of protocols that allow computers to share resources across a network. For more information, see the section "The TCP/IP Model."

8. **A, B, D.** The following are true of IP addresses: IP addresses are written as four sets of numbers separated by periods, IP addresses provide a means of identifying and locating network resources, and IP addresses identify the machines to their peers on the network. For more information, see the section "IPv4 Addressing."

9. **D.** The `/etc/hostname.xxy` file identifies the network interface on the local host. For more information, see the section "Configuring an IPv4 Network Interface."

10. **D.** The router is a network component that forwards Ethernet packets from one network to another. For more information, see the section "Network Hardware."

11. **A.** The `/etc/inet/hosts` file contains the IP addresses and hostnames of machines on a network. For more information, see the section "Configuring an IPv4 Network Interface."

12. **B.** Class B addresses are for medium-sized networks, such as campuses and large businesses with many hosts. A Class B network can accommodate a maximum of 65,534 hosts. For more information, see the section "IPv4 Addressing."

13. **A, D, E.** The file `/etc/defaultdomain` sets the domain name and `/etc/networks` identifies the different networks. For more information, see the section "Changing the System Hostname."

14. **C.** The `netstat` command is used to monitor the system's TCP/IP network activity. `netstat` can provide some basic data about how much and what kind of network activity is happening. For more information, see the section "Network Maintenance."

15. **B.** The `snoop` command is used to determine what information is flowing between systems across a network. For more information, see the section "Network Maintenance."

Suggested Reading and Resources

Internetworking with TCP/IP: Principles, Protocols and Architecture. Douglas Comer. Prentice Hall, March 2000.

"IP Services" guide in the Solaris 10 documentation CD.

"IP Services" guide in the System Administration Collection of the Solaris 10 documentation set. See `http://docs.sun.com`.

"Managing Services" section in the "Basic System Administration" guide in the System Administration Collection of the Solaris 10 documentation set. See `http://docs.sun.com`.

"Managing Services" section in the "Basic System Administration" guide in the Solaris 10 documentation CD.

CHAPTER NINE

Virtual File Systems, Swap Space, and Core Dumps

Objectives

The following test objectives for exam 310-202 are covered in this chapter:

Explain virtual memory concepts and, given a scenario, configure and manage swap space.

- The Solaris operating environment can use disk space, called *swap areas* or *swap space*, for temporary memory storage when a system does not have enough physical memory to handle currently running processes. A system's memory requirements change, and you must be knowledgeable in swap space management in order to monitor these resources and make ongoing adjustments, as needed.

Manage crash dumps and core file behaviors.

- You can configure the creation and storage of crash dump and core files, depending on the requirement. You can create application core files on a global or per-process basis. You must be able to customize the configuration according to various circumstances.

Explain NFS fundamentals, and configure and manage the NFS server and client including daemons, files, and commands.

- Network File System (NFS) facilitates the sharing of data between networked systems. NFS servers share resources that are to be used by NFS clients. This chapter describes NFS and the tasks required to administer NFS servers and clients.

Troubleshoot various NFS errors.

- You must have a thorough understanding of the problems that can arise within the NFS client/server process and how to address them. This chapter describes a number of problem areas and what to do in order to rectify them.

Explain and manage AutoFS and use automount maps (master, direct, and indirect) to configure automounting.

- AutoFS allows NFS directories to be mounted and unmounted automatically. It also provides for centralized administration of NFS resources. This chapter describes AutoFS and how to configure the various automount maps.

Outline

Study Strategies

The following study strategies will help you prepare for the test:

- As you study this chapter, it's important that you practice on a Solaris system each Step by Step and each command that is presented. Practice is very important on these topics, so you should practice until you can repeat each procedure from memory.
- You need to understand each command in this chapter and be prepared to match the command to the correct description.
- You need to know all the terms listed in the "Key Terms" section at the end of this chapter.
- You must understand the concept of a virtual file system, including how it works, how to configure additional swap space, and how to use tools to monitor it.

Introduction

Swap space is used to supplement the use of physical memory when a running process requires more resources than are currently available. This chapter describes how to monitor the use of swap space as well as how to add more when necessary and how to delete additional swap space if it is no longer required. Swap space can be allocated either as a dedicated disk slice or in an existing file system as a normal file. The latter option is often only used as an emergency solution. Both of these methods for adding swap space are described in this chapter.

Core files are produced when a process encounters an unexpected error. When this happens, the memory contents of the process are dumped to a file for further analysis. This chapter describes the configuration of core files and how they can be managed effectively. This chapter also describes crash dump files and how to manage and configure them. Crash dump files are produced when a system encounters a failure that it cannot recover from. The contents of kernel memory is dumped to a temporary location (normally the swap device) before the system reboots and is moved to a permanent location to save it from being overwritten.

Network File System (NFS) is a means of sharing file systems across the network. NFS allows multiple systems to make use of the same physical file system without having to maintain numerous copies of the data, which could cause consistency problems. NFS is discussed in this chapter, as is AutoFS, a method of automatically mounting file systems on demand and unmounting them when a specified amount of time has elapsed during which no activity has occurred. This chapter describes how to configure automount maps and make use of this extremely useful feature.

The Swap File System

Objective:

Explain virtual memory concepts and, given a scenario, configure and manage swap space.

Physical memory is the random-access memory (RAM) installed in a computer. To view the amount of physical memory installed in your computer, type the following:

```
prtconf¦ grep "Memory size"
```

The system displays a message similar to the following:

```
Memory size: 384 Megabytes
```

Not all physical memory is available for Solaris processes. Some memory is reserved for kernel code and data structures. The remaining memory is referred to as *available memory*. Processes and applications on a system can use available memory.

Physical memory is supplemented by specially configured space on the physical disk that is known as *swap space*; together they are referred to as *virtual memory*. Swap space is configured either on a special disk partition known as a *swap partition* or on a swap file system (`swapfs`). In addition to swap partitions, special files called *swap files* can also be configured in existing Unix file systems (UFS) to provide additional swap space when needed.

Every process running on a Solaris system requires space in memory. Space is allocated to processes in units known as *pages*. Some of a process's pages are used to store the process executable, andand other pages are used to store the process's data.

Physical memory is a finite resource on any computer, and sometimes there are not enough pages in physical memory for all of a system's processes. When a physical memory shortfall is encountered, the virtual memory system begins moving data from physical memory out to the system's configured swap areas. When a process requests data that has been sent to a swap area, the virtual memory system brings that data back into physical memory. This process is known as *paging*.

The Solaris virtual memory system maps the files on disk to virtual addresses in memory—this is referred to as *virtual swap space*. As data in those files is needed, the virtual memory system maps the virtual addresses in memory to real physical addresses in memory. This mapping process greatly reduces the need for large amounts of physical swap space on systems with large amounts of available memory.

The virtual swap space provided by `swapfs` reduces the need for configuring large amounts of disk-based swap space on systems with large amounts of physical memory. This is because `swapfs` provides virtual swap space addresses rather than real physical swap space addresses in response to the requests to reserve swap space.

With the virtual swap space provided by `swapfs`, real disk-based swap space is required only with the onset of paging, because when paging occurs, processes are contending for memory. In this situation, `swapfs` must convert the virtual swap space addresses to physical swap space addresses in order for paging to actual disk-based swap space to occur.

Swap Space and TMPFS

The temporary file system (TMPFS) makes use of virtual memory for its storage—this can be either physical RAM or swap space; it is transparent to the user. `/tmp` is a good example of a TMPFS file system where temporary files and their associated information are stored in memory (in the `/tmp` directory) rather than on disk. This speeds up access to those files and results in a major performance enhancement for applications such as compilers and database management system (DBMS) products that use `/tmp` heavily.

TMPFS allocates space in the `/tmp` directory from the system's virtual memory resources. This means that as you use up space in `/tmp`, you are also using up virtual memory space. So if your applications use `/tmp` heavily and you do not monitor virtual memory usage, your system could run out of this resource.

Sizing Swap Space

The amount of swap space required on a system is based on the following criteria:

- Application programs need a minimum amount of swap space to operate properly. This information is usually contained in the documentation that comes with the application. You should follow the manufacturer's recommendation for swap space requirements.
- You need to determine whether large applications (such as compilers) will be using the `/tmp` directory. Then you need to allocate additional swap space to be used by TMPFS.
- To prevent any possible panic dumps resulting from fatal system failures, there must be sufficient swap space to hold the necessary kernel memory pages in RAM at the time of a failure. Kernel memory accounts for around 20% of total memory, so if you have 1GB of physical memory, you will need about 256MB of disk-based space for a worst-case crash dump.

NOTE

Movement of Swap Starting with the release of Solaris 9, the installation program allocates swap at the first available cylinder on the disk (this is normally cylinder 0). This practice allows the root file system the maximum space on the disk and allows for expansion of the file system during an upgrade.

The amount of disk-based swap space on a system must be large enough to be able to accommodate a kernel memory dump , plus the requirements of any concurrently running processes, including third-party applications and compilers. Many other factors also contribute to the amount of swap space you need to configure, such as the number of concurrent users and the naming service, Network Information System Plus (NIS+). It is quite rare nowadays to need more swap space than RAM, which used to be a recommendation with older versions of SunOS; in fact the opposite is often true—you now often need less swap space than physical RAM.

If you are prepared to keep track of your swap space and administer it regularly, you can run with much less swap space than in older versions of SunOS. (How to monitor swap space and how to add additional space to a running system are discussed in the next few sections.)

NOTE

Reducing Swap Space Problems If the amount of swap space is equal to the amount of physical RAM, you should generally experience no swap space problems, although the type of application being used on the system will be a major factor.

Monitoring Swap Resources

If you run into a swap shortfall due to heavy demand on memory, you get error messages on your system's console. The error might look something like this:

```
<application> is out of memory
 malloc error 0
 messages.1:SJul 18 15:12:47 ultra genunix: [ID 470503 kern.warning]
WARNING: Sorry, no swap space to grow stack for pid 100295 (myprog)
```

This error means that an application is trying to get more memory and there is no swap space available to back it.

You could fill up a TMPFS due to the lack of available swap and get the following error message:

```
<directory>: File system full, swap space limit exceeded
```

or this one:

```
<directory>: File system full, memory allocation failed
```

This type of message is displayed if a page cannot be allocated when a file is being written. This can occur, for example, when TMPFS tries to write more than it is allowed or when TMPFS runs out of physical memory while attempting to create a new file or directory.

You need to regularly monitor your swap space. This helps you determine whether you are running on the edge and need to increase the resource or maybe you have too much swap space allocated and are wasting disk space. Most commercial performance monitoring tools keep track of swap space or can be configured to generate warnings when it gets low. Besides these commercial tools, you can use the helpful tools that Solaris provides (see Table 9.1). System performance monitoring is not covered on the administrator certification exams, so this chapter describes only the `/usr/sbin/swap` command.

TABLE 9.1 Swap Monitoring Tools

Command	Description
`/usr/sbin/swap`	The `/usr/sbin/swap` utility provides a method for adding, deleting, and monitoring the system swap areas used by the memory manager.
`/usr/bin/ps`	You can use the `-al` options with the `/usr/bin/ps` command to report the total size of a process that is currently in virtual memory. The value includes all mapped files and devices, and it is reported in pages. These device mappings do not use swap space.

(continues)

TABLE 9.1 *Continued*

Command	Description
/usr/ucb/ps	You can use this Berkley version of the ps command with the -alx options to report the total size of a process that is currently in virtual memory. The value includes all mapped files and devices, and it is reported in kilobytes rather than pages.
/usr/bin/vmstat	This tool reports virtual memory statistics.
/usr/bin/sar	This is a system activity reporter.

You can use two options with the /usr/sbin/swap command to monitor swap space. You can use the -l option to list swap space and to determine the location of a system's swap areas:

```
swap -l
```

The system displays details of the system's physical swap space. This system has a 512MB swap slice allocated, as shown below:

```
swapfile             dev  swaplo blocks   free
/dev/dsk/c0t0d0s1   136,9     16 1049312  1049312
```

This output is described in Table 9.2.

TABLE 9.2 Output from the swap -l Command*

Keyword	Description
path	The pathname for the swap area (for example, /dev/dsk/c0t0d0s1).
dev	The major/minor device number for a block special device; this value is zeros other-wise.
swaplo	The swaplo value for the area, in 512-byte blocks. swaplo is a kernel parameter that you can modify, and it represents the offset, in 512-byte blocks, where usable swap space begins.
blocks	The swaplen value for the area, in 512-byte blocks. swaplen is a kernel parameter that you can modify, and it defines the size of the swap area, in 512-byte blocks.
free	The number of 512-byte blocks in this area that are not currently allocated.

*This table does not include swap space in the form of physical memory because that space is not associated with a particular swap area.

You use the -s option to list a summary of the system's virtual swap space:

```
swap -s
```

The system displays the following information, which shows the details of the system's physical swap space and includes physical memory too. This system has 384MB of physical memory and a 512MB swap slice:

```
total: 67648k bytes allocated + 19032k reserved = 86680k used, 724512k \
available
```

This output is described in Table 9.3

TABLE 9.3 Output from the swap -s Command

Keyword	Description
`bytes allocated`	The total amount of swap space, in 1,024-byte blocks, that is currently allocated as backing store (that is, disk-backed swap space).
`reserved`	The total amount of swap space, in 1,024-byte blocks, that is not currently allocated but is claimed by memory for possible future use.
`used`	The total amount of swap space, in 1,024-byte blocks, that is either allocated or reserved.
`available`	The total amount of swap space, in 1,024-byte blocks, that is currently available for future reservation and allocation.

You can use the amounts of swap space available and used (in the `swap -s` output) as a way to monitor swap space usage over time. If a system's performance is good, you can use `swap -s` to see how much swap space is available. When the performance of a system slows down, you can check the amount of swap space available to see if it has decreased. Then you can identify what changes to the system might have caused swap space usage to increase.

Keep in mind when using the `swap` command that the amount of physical memory available for swap usage changes dynamically as the kernel and user processes reserve and release physical memory.

NOTE

Swap Space Calculations The `swap -l` command displays swap space in 512-byte blocks, and the `swap -s` command displays swap space in 1,024-byte blocks. If you add up the blocks from `swap -l` and convert them to kilobytes, you'll see that it is less than the swap space used plus available (as shown in the `swap -s` output) because `swap -l` does not include physical memory in its calculation of swap space.

Setting Up Swap Space

Swap space is initially configured during software installation through the installation program. If you use the installation program's automatic layout of disk slices and do not manually change the size of the swap slice, the Solaris installation program allocates a default swap slice of 512MB.

NOTE

Crash Dumps As described later in this chapter, a *crash dump* is a disk copy of the kernel memory of the computer at the time of a fatal system error. When a fatal operating system error occurs, a message describing the error is printed to the console. The operating system then generates a crash dump by writing the contents of kernel memory to a predetermined dump device, which is typically a local disk partition. You can then analyze this crash dump to determine the cause of the system error. By default, the dump device is configured to be an appropriate swap partition. Therefore, it's necessary to make sure that your swap area is at least as large as about 25% of your physical RAM; otherwise, the system may not have enough room to store the crash dump. Crash dumps and core files are discussed later in this chapter, in the sections "Core File Configuration" and "Crash Dump Configuration."

The software installation program adds entries for swap slices and files in the `/etc/vfstab` file. These swap areas are activated each time the system is booted by `/sbin/swapadd`.

As system configurations change, more users are added, and new software packages are installed, you might need to add more swap space. There are two methods for adding more swap to a system:

- Create a secondary swap partition.
- Create a swap file in an existing UFS.

Creating a secondary swap partition requires additional, unused disk space. You use the `format` command as described in Chapter 1, "Managing File Systems," to create a new partition and file system on a disk. After you create the swap partition, you make an entry in the `/etc/vfstab` file so that the swap space is activated at bootup. The process is described in Step by Step 9.1.

STEP BY STEP

9.1 Creating a Secondary Swap File

1. Add an additional 512MB of swap space to your system. You don't have any more room on the disk for more swap space, but the `/data` directory (currently mounted on slice 4 of disk `c0t1d0`) is 512MB in size. Move all the data in `/data` to another server to free up the partition so that you can use it as a swap partition. You can use any one of the methods described in Chapter 7, "Performing System Backups and Restorations," to do this.
2. After freeing up the `/data` directory and unmounting `/dev/dsk/c0t1d0s4`, use the `format` utility to set the tag name to swap and the permission flag to wu (writable and unmountable), as follows:

```
partition> 4
Part      Tag         Flag  Cylinders     Size         Block
4     unassigned   wm    3400 - 4480  512.37MB (1041/0/0)    1049328
Enter partition id tag[unassigned]: swap
Enter partition permission flags[wm]: wu
Enter new starting cyl[3400]: <return>
Enter partition size[1049328b, 1041c, 1040e, 512.37mb, 0.50gb]: <return>
```

The bold text here identifies the keystrokes entered by the user during execution of the command.

Label the disk, as follows:

```
Partition> la
Ready to label disk? Y
```

3. Make an entry to the `/etc/vfstab` file, where the fields are as follows:

   Device to mount: *<name of swap block device or swap file>*

   Device to `fsck: --`

   `Mount point: --`

   FS-type: swap

   `fsck pass: --`

   Mount at boot: no

   Mount options: --

   Here's an example of an entry for the swap partition just added:

```
/dev/dsk/c0t1d0s4       -        -          swap - no       -
```

4. Run the swapadd script to add the swap to your system:

```
/sbin/swapadd
```

5. Verify that the swap has been added:

```
swap -l
```

   The system responds with this:

```
swapfile             dev  swaplo blocks   free
/dev/dsk/c0t0d0s1   136,9       16 1049312 1049312
/dev/dsk/c0t1d0s4   136,3       16 1052624 1052624
```

   `/dev/dsk/c0t1d0s4` has been added to the list of available swap areas.

EXAM ALERT

`/etc/vfstab` syntax **You should be familiar with the entry for swap files in `/etc/vfstab`. The syntax can be tricky, especially because of the hyphens.**

The following are additional notes that explain how to add swap partitions:

- On systems running the 32-bit version of Solaris, swap areas must not exceed 2GB. If you wanted to add a 9GB disk to a swap area, you should slice it up into 2GB chunks. Then, you need to put a separate entry in `/etc/vfstab` for each slice. On systems running the 64-bit version of Solaris 10, you can use a block device larger than 2GB.
- You get a large performance benefit from having swap partitions spread across separate disks. Swap space is allocated in a round-robin fashion from swap partition to swap partition, and it is not possible to prioritize usage of the various swap areas. Swap space is allocated 1MB at a time from each swap partition in turn, unless one is full.
- It is not worth making a striped metadevice to swap on; that would just add overhead and slow down paging.

The easiest way to add more swap space is to use the `mkfile` and `swap` commands to designate a part of an existing UFS as a supplementary swap area. You can do this as a temporary or semi-temporary solution for a swap shortage. Although you can do this for longer durations as well, it has a few disadvantages:

- A swap file is considered a file within a file system; therefore, when you back up a file system, a rather large swap file (empty file) is also backed up if you don't specifically exclude it.
- Because a swap file is simply a file in some file system, you are not able to unmount that file system while the swap file is in use.
- This method of creating a swap file has a negative effect on system performance because the swap file is slower than a dedicated swap slice.

Step by Step 9.2 explains how to add more swap space without repartitioning a disk.

STEP BY STEP

9.2 Adding Swap Space Without Repartitioning a Disk

1. As root, use the `df -h` command to locate a file system that has enough room to support a swap file that's the size that you want to add:

```
# df -h
Filesystem             size   used  avail capacity  Mounted on
```

```
/dev/dsk/c0t0d0s0      4.9G  3.7G  1.2G   77%   /
/devices                 0K    0K    0K    0%   /devices
ctfs                     0K    0K    0K    0%   /system/contract
proc                     0K    0K    0K    0%   /proc
mnttab                   0K    0K    0K    0%   /etc/mnttab
swap                   1.2G  1.0M  1.2G    1%   /etc/svc/volatile
objfs                    0K    0K    0K    0%   /system/object
fd                       0K    0K    0K    0%   /dev/fd
/dev/dsk/c0t0d0s7      4.0G  1.5G  2.4G   40%   /var
swap                   1.2G  304K  1.2G    1%   /tmp
swap                   1.2G   48K  1.2G    1%   /var/run
/dev/dsk/c0t1d0s0      3.9G  1.7G  2.2G   44%   /data1
/dev/dsk/c0t1d0s7      5.2G  7.1M  5.1G    1%   /data2
```

NOTE

Swap Permissions You can create a swap file without root permissions, but it is a good idea for root to be the owner of the swap file, to prevent someone from accidentally overwriting it.

2. Use the `mkfile` command to add a 512MB swap file named `swapfile` in the `/data2` partition:

   ```
   mkfile 512m /data2/swapfile
   ```

   Use the `ls -l /data2` command to verify that the file has been created:

   ```
   ls -l /data2/swapfile
   -rw------T   1 root   root 536870912 Aug 19 23:31 /data2/swapfile
   ```

   The system shows the file named `swapfile` along with the file size. Notice that the sticky bit (which is described in Chapter 4, "User and Security Administration") has automatically been set.

3. Activate the swap area by using the swap command:

   ```
   /usr/sbin/swap -a /data2/swapfile
   ```

   You must use the absolute pathname to specify the swap file. The swap file is added and available until the file system is unmounted, the system is rebooted, or the swap file is removed. Keep in mind that you can't unmount a file system while the swap file is still being used or a process is swapping to the swap file.

4. Verify that the new swap area was added:

   ```
   swap -l
   ```

   The system should respond with a message such as the following that shows the swap file:

   ```
   swapfile              dev  swaplo blocks   free
   /dev/dsk/c0t0d0s1    136,9      16 1049312 1049312
   /data2/swapfile         -       16 1048560 1048560
   ```

5. If this will be a permanent swap area, add to the /etc/vfstab file an entry for the swap file that specifies the full pathname of the swap file and designate swap as the file system type:

```
/data2/swapfile - - swap - no -
```

There is some disagreement as to which type of swap area provides the best performance: a swap partition or a swap file. There are factors in favor of both scenarios; however, these are two of the best reasons in favor of swap partitions:

- A partition provides contiguous space and can be positioned between the specific cylinders that will provide the best performance.
- A swap file has to work through the file system when updates are made, whereas a swap partition has data written to it at a lower level, bypassing the interaction with the file system; this makes a swap partition slightly faster than a swap file.

Sun's official statement, and the general consensus in the user community, is that there will be a performance impact if you go the swap file route rather than the partition route. Sun recommends that you use swap files only as a temporary solution, until you can add a swap partition.

NOTE

Swap Files on NFS In an emergency, when no other local space is available, it's possible to add a swap file to a networked file system by using NFS; this is described later in this chapter. Using NFS to access swap space on another host is not recommended, however, because it puts an increased load on your network and makes performance unacceptable. If you do need to use NFS for additional swap files, try using the -n option when you run `mkfile`, as this will only allocate disk blocks as they are written.

Swap files can be deleted as well as added. For example, you might determine that you have allocated too much swap space and that you need that disk space for other uses. Alternatively the additional swap space might have been temporarily added to accommodate a one-off large job. The steps involved in removing a swap file are outlined in Step by Step 9.3.

STEP BY STEP

9.3 Removing a Swap File

1. As root, use the swap -d command to remove the swap area:

```
swap -d /dev/dsk/c0t0d0s4   for a swap partition or,
swap -d /data2/swapfile            for a swap file.
```

2. Issue the swap -l command to ensure that the swap area is gone:

```
swap -l
swapfile             dev  swaplo blocks   free
/dev/dsk/c0t0d0s1   136,9      16 1049312 1049312
```

The swap file filename is removed from the list, so you know it is no longer available for swapping. The file itself is not deleted.

3. In the /etc/vfstab file, delete the entry for the swap file.

4. Remove the swap file to recover the disk space:

```
rm /data2/swapfile
```

If the swap area was in a partition, you can now allocate this disk space as you would a normal file system.

Core File Configuration

Objective

Manage crash dumps and core file behaviors.

Core files are created when a program or an application terminates abnormally. The default location for a core file to be written is the current working directory. However, as the system administrator, you might want to configure the system so that all core files are written to a central location. This would make administration and management of core files much easier because core files can sometimes take up a significant amount of disk space.

You manage core files by using the coreadm command:

```
coreadm  [-g pattern] [-G content] [-i pattern] [-I content] \
[-d option...]   [-e option...]

coreadm  [-p pattern] [-P content] [pid]
coreadm -u
```

The options for the coreadm command are described in Table 9.4.

TABLE 9.4 coreadm Command Options

Option	Description
-g *pattern*	Sets the global core file name pattern.
-G *content*	Sets the global core file content using one of the description tokens.
-i *pattern*	Sets the per-process core file name pattern.

(continues)

TABLE 9.4 *Continued*

Option	Description
`-I` *content*	Sets the per-process core file name to *content*.
`-d` *option*	Disables the specified core file option.
`-e` *option*	Enables the specified core file option.
`-p` *pattern*	Sets the per-process core file name pattern for each of the specified *pids*.
`-P` *content*	Sets the per-process core file content to *content*.
`-u`	Updates the systemwide core file options from the configuration file `/etc/coreadm.conf`.

Running `coreadm` with no options displays the current configuration, which you can determine by reading the file `/etc/coreadm.conf`.

A core file name pattern consists of a file system pathname, along with embedded variables. These variables are specified with a leading `%` character. The values are then expanded when a core file is created. Valid pattern variables are described in Table 9.5.

TABLE 9.5 `coreadm` Patterns

`coreadm` Pattern	Description
`%p`	Specifies the process ID (PID).
`%u`	Specifies the effective user ID.
`%g`	Specifies the effective group ID.
`%d`	Specifies the executable file directory name.
`%f`	Specifies the executable filename.
`%n`	Specifies the system node name. This is the same as running `uname -n`.
`%m`	Specifies the machine name. This is the same as running `uname -m`.
`%t`	Specifies the decimal value of time, as the number of seconds since 00:00:00 January 1, 1970.
`-z`	Specifies the name of the zone in which the process is executed (zonename).
`%%`	Specifies the a literal `%` character.

The `-d` and `-e` flags of the `coreadm` command can take several options. These are listed in Table 9.6.

TABLE 9.6 `coreadm` `-d` and `-e` Flag Options

Option	Description
`global`	Allows core dumps, using the global core pattern.
`process`	Allows core dumps, using the per-process core pattern.
`global-setid`	Allows `set-id` core dumps, using the global core pattern.
`proc-setid`	Allows `set-id` core dumps, using the per-process core pattern.
`log`	Produces a `syslog` message when an attempt is made to generate a global core file.

To modify the core file configuration so that all files are dumped into the directory `/cores` and named `core`, followed by the system name and then the name of the program being run, you can follow the procedure described in Step by Step 9.4.

STEP BY STEP

9.4 Configuring Core Files

1. As root, use the `coreadm` command to display the current `coreadm` configuration:

```
# coreadm
     global core file pattern:
     global core file content: default
       init core file pattern: core
         init core file content: default
            global core dumps: disabled
       per-process core dumps: enabled
      global setid core dumps: disabled
 per-process setid core dumps: disabled
     global core dump logging: disabled
```

2. As root, issue the following command to change the core file setup:

```
# coreadm -i /cores/core.%n.%f
```

3. Run `coreadm` again to verify that the change has been made permanent:

```
# coreadm
global core file pattern:
global core file content: default
       init core file pattern: /cores/core.%n.%f
       init core file content: default
            global core dumps: disabled
       per-process core dumps: enabled
      global setid core dumps: disabled
 per-process setid core dumps: disabled
     global core dump logging: disabled
```

The coreadm process is now configured by the Service Management Facility (SMF) at system boot time. Use the svcs command to check its status. The service name for this process is svc:/system/coreadm:default.

Crash Dump Configuration

Objective:

Manage crash dumps and core file behaviors.

When a serious error is encountered, the system displays an error message on the console, dumps the entire contents of physical memory to the disk, and then reboots the system. A *crash dump* is a snapshot of the physical memory, saved on disk, at the time that a fatal system error occurs.

Normally, crash dumps are configured to use the swap partition to write the contents of memory. The savecore program runs when the system reboots and saves the image in a predefined location, usually /var/crash/*<hostname>*, where *<hostname>* represents the name of the system.

You configure crash dump files by using the dumpadm command. Running this command with no options, as follows, displays the current configuration, which is obtained from the file /etc/dumpadm.conf:

```
# dumpadm
```

The system responds with this:

```
Dump content: kernel pages
Dump device: /dev/dsk/c0t0d0s1 (swap)
Savecore directory: /var/crash/ultra5
  Savecore enabled: yes
```

The following is the syntax of the dumpadm command:

```
/usr/sbin/dumpadm [-nuy] [-c content-type] [-d dump-device]\
[-m mink | minm  |  min%]  [-s savecore-dir] [-r root-dir]
```

The options for the dumpadm command are described in Table 9.7.

TABLE 9.7 dumpadm Command Syntax

Option	Description
-c *content-type*	Modifies crash dump content. Valid values are kernel (just kernel pages), all (all memory pages), and curproc (kernel pages and currently executing process pages).

TABLE 9.7 *Continued*

Option	Description
-d *dump-device*	Modifies the dump device. This can be specified either as an absolute pathname (such as /dev/dsk/c0t0d0s1) or the word swap, in which case the system identifies the best swap area to use.
-m*ink*¦*minm*¦*min%*	Maintains minimum free space in the current savecore directory, specified either in kilobytes, megabytes, or a percentage of the total current size of the directory.
-n	Disables savecore from running on reboot. This is not recommended because with it, any crash dumps would be lost.
-r *root-dir*	Specifies a different root directory. If this option is not used, the default / is used.
-s *savecore-dir*	Specifies a savecore directory other than the default /var/crash/hostname.
-y	Enables savecore to run on the next reboot. This setting is used by default.

To set up a dedicated disk slice named c0t2d0s2 for crash dumps, you issue the following command:

```
# dumpadm -d /dev/dsk/c0t2d0s2
```

The system responds with this:

```
Dump content: kernel pages
Dump device: /dev/dsk/c0t2d0s2 (dedicated)
Savecore directory: /var/crash/ultra5
  Savecore enabled: yes
```

The dumpadm process is now configured by the Service Management Facility (SMF) at system boot time. Use the svcs command to check its status. The service name for this process is svc:/system/dumpadm:default.

NFS

Objectives:

Explain NFS fundamentals, and configure and manage the NFS server and client including daemons, files, and commands.

- Troubleshoot various NFS errors.

The NFS service lets computers of different architectures, running different operating systems, share file systems across a network. Just as the `mount` command lets you mount a file system on a local disk, NFS lets you mount a file system that is located on another system anywhere on the network. Furthermore, NFS support has been implemented on many platforms, ranging from MS-DOS on personal computers to mainframe operating systems, such as Multiprogramming using Virtual Storage (MVS). Each operating system applies the NFS model to its file system semantics. For example, a Sun system can mount the file system from a Windows NT or Linux system. File system operations, such as reading and writing, function as though they are occurring on local files. Response time might be slower when a file system is physically located on a remote system, but the connection is transparent to the user regardless of the hardware or operating systems.

The NFS service provides the following benefits:

- Lets multiple computers use the same files so that everyone on the network can access the same data. This eliminates the need to have redundant data on several systems.
- Reduces storage costs by having computers share applications and data.
- Provides data consistency and reliability because all users access the same data.
- Makes mounting of file systems transparent to users.
- Makes accessing remote files transparent to users.
- Supports heterogeneous environments.
- Reduces system administration overhead.

The NFS service makes the physical location of the file system irrelevant to the user. You can use NFS to allow users to see all the data, regardless of location. With NFS, instead of placing copies of commonly used files on every system, you can place one copy on one computer's disk and have all other systems across the network access it. Under NFS operation, remote file systems are almost indistinguishable from local ones.

NFS Version 4

Solaris 10 introduced a new version of the NFS protocol, which has the following features:

- The User ID and Group ID are represented as strings. A new daemon process, `nfsmapid`, maps these IDs to local numeric IDs. The `nfsmapid` daemon is described later in this chapter, in the section "NFS Daemons."

- The default transport for NFS version 4 is the Remote Direct Memory Access (RDMA) protocol, a technology for memory-to-memory transfer over high speed data networks. RDMA improves performance by reducing load on the CPU and I/O. If RDMA is not available on both server and client then TCP is used as the transport.
- All state and lock information is destroyed when a file system is unshared. In previous versions of NFS, this information was retained.
- NFS version 4 provides a pseudo file system to give clients access to exported objects on the NFS server.
- NFS version 4 is a stateful protocol in that both the client and the server hold information about current locks and open files. When a crash or failure occurs, the client and the server work together to re-establish the open or locked files.
- NFS version 4 no longer uses the `mountd`, `statd`, or `nfslogd` daemons.
- NFS version 4 supports delegation, a technique where management responsibility of a file can be delegated by the server to the client. Delegation is supported in both the NFS server and the NFS client. A client can be granted a read delegation, which can be granted to multiple clients, or a write delegation, providing exclusive access to a file.

Servers and Clients

With NFS, systems have a client/server relationship. The NFS server is where the file system resides. Any system with a local file system can be an NFS server. As described later in this chapter, in the section "Setting Up NFS," you can configure the NFS server to make file systems available to other systems and users. The system administrator has complete control over which file systems can be mounted and who can mount them.

An *NFS client* is a system that mounts a remote file system from an NFS server. You'll learn later in this chapter, in the section "Mounting a Remote File System," how you can create a local directory and mount the file system. As you will see, a system can be both an NFS server and an NFS client.

NFS Daemons

NFS uses a number of daemons to handle its services. These services are initialized at startup from the `svc:/network/nfs/server:default` and `svc:/network/nfs/client:default` startup service management functions. The most important NFS daemons are described in Table 9.8.

TABLE 9.8 NFS Daemons

Daemon	Description
`nfsd`	An NFS server daemon that handles file system exporting and file access requests from remote systems. An NFS server runs multiple instances of this daemon. This daemon is usually invoked at the multi-user-server milestone and is started by the `svc:/network/nfs/server:default` service identifier.
`mountd`	An NFS server daemon that handles mount requests from NFS clients. This daemon provides information about which file systems are mounted by which clients. You use the `showmount` command, described later in this chapter, to view this information. This daemon is usually invoked at the multi-user-server milestone and is started by the `svc:/network/nfs/server:default` service identifier. This daemon is not used in NFS version 4.
`lockd`	A daemon that runs on the NFS server and NFS client and provides file-locking services in NFS. This daemon is started by the `svc:/network/nfs/client` service identifier at the multi-user milestone.
`statd`	A daemon that runs on the NFS server and NFS client and interacts with `lockd` to provide the crash and recovery functions for the locking services on NFS. This daemon is started by the `svc:/network/nfs/client` service identifier at the multi-user milestone. This daemon is not used in NFS version 4.
`rpcbind`	A daemon that facilitates the initial connection between the client and the server.
`nfsmapid`	A new daemon that maps to and from NFS v4 owner and group identification and UID and GID numbers. It uses entries in the `passwd` and `group` files to carry out the mapping, and also references `/etc/nsswitch.conf` to determine the order of access.
`nfs4cbd`	A new client side daemon that listens on each transport and manages the callback functions to the NFS server.
`nfslogd`	A daemon that provides operational logging to the Solaris NFS server. `nfslogd` is described later in this chapter, in the section "NFS Server Logging." The `nfslogd` daemon is not used in NFS version 4.

Setting Up NFS

Servers let other systems access their file systems by sharing them over the NFS environment. A shared file system is referred to as a *shared resource*. You specify which file systems are to be shared by entering the information in the file `/etc/dfs/dfstab`. Entries in this file are shared automatically whenever you start the NFS server operation. You should set up automatic sharing if you need to share the same set of file systems on a regular basis. Most file system sharing should be done automatically; the only time manual sharing should occur is during testing or troubleshooting.

The `/etc/dfs/dfstab` file lists all the file systems your NFS server shares with its NFS clients. It also controls which clients can mount a file system. If you want to modify `/etc/`

dfs/dfstab to add or delete a file system or to modify the way sharing is done, you edit the file with a text editor, such as vi. The next time the computer enters the multi-user-server milestone, the system reads the updated /etc/dfs/dfstab to determine which file systems should be shared automatically.

Each line in the dfstab file consists of a share command, as shown in the following example:

```
more /etc/dfs/dfstab
```

The system responds by displaying the contents of /etc/dfs/dfstab:

```
#       Place share(1M) commands here for automatic execution
#       on entering init state 3.
#
#       Issue the command 'svcadm enable network/nfs/server' to
#       run the NFS daemon processes and the share commands, after adding
#       the very first entry to this file.
#
#       share [-F fstype] [ -o options] [-d "<text>"] <pathname> \
[resource]
#       .e.g,
#       share  -F nfs  -o rw=engineering  -d "home dirs"  /export/home2
share -F nfs /export/install/sparc_10
share -F nfs /jumpstart
```

The /usr/sbin/share command exports a resource or makes a resource available for mounting. If it is invoked with no arguments, share displays all shared file systems. The share command can be run at the command line to achieve the same results as the /etc/dfs/dfstab file, but you should use this method only when testing.

This is the syntax for the share command:

```
share -F <FSType> -o <options> -d <description> <pathname>
```

where *<pathname>* is the name of the file system to be shared. Table 9.9 describes the options of the share command.

TABLE 9.9 share Command Syntax

Option	Description
-F *<FSType>*	Specifies the file system type, such as NFS. If the -F option is omitted, the first file system type listed in /etc/dfs/fstypes is used as the default (nfs).
-o *<options>*	Is one of the following options: rw—Makes *pathname* shared read-write to all clients. This is also the default behavior. rw=*client*[:*client*]...—Makes *pathname* shared read-write but only to the listed clients. No other systems can access *pathname*.

(continues)

TABLE 9.9 *Continued*

Option	Description
	`ro`—Makes *`pathname`* shared read-only to all clients.
	`ro=`*`client`*`[:`*`client`*`]...`—Makes *`pathname`* shared read-only, but only to the listed clients. No other systems can access *`pathname`*.
	`aclok`—Allows the NFS server to do access control for NFS version 2 clients (running Solaris 2.4 or earlier). When `aclok` is set on the server, maximum access is given to all clients. For example, with `aclok` set, if anyone has read permissions, everyone does. If `aclok` is not set, minimal access is given to all clients.
	`anon=`<*`uid`*>—Sets *`uid`* to be the effective user ID (UID) of unknown users. By default, unknown users are given the effective UID `nobody`. If *`uid`* is set to `-1`, access is denied.
	`index=`<*`file`*>—Loads a file rather than a listing of the directory containing this specific file when the directory is referenced by an NFS uniform resource locator (URL).
	`nosub`—Prevents clients from mounting subdirectories of shared directories. This only applies to NFS versions 2 and 3 because NFS version 4 does not use the Mount protocol.
	`nosuid`—Causes the server file system to silently ignore any attempt to enable the `setuid` or `setgid` mode bits. By default, clients can create files on the shared file system if the `setuid` or `setgid` mode is enabled. See Chapter 4 for a description of `setuid` and `setgid`.
	`public`—Enables NFS browsing of the file system by a WebNFS-enabled browser. Only one file system per server can use this option. The `-ro=`*`list`* and `-rw=`*`list`* options can be included with this option.
	`root=`*`host`*`[:` *`host`*`]...`—Specifies that only root users from the specified hosts have root access. By default, no host has root access, so root users are mapped to an anonymous user ID (see the description of the `anon=`<*`uid`*> option).
	`sec=`<*`mode`*>—Uses one or more of the security modes specified by <*`mode`*> to authenticate clients. The <*`mode`*> option establishes the security mode of NFS servers. If the NFS connection uses the NFS version 3 protocol, the NFS clients must query the server for the appropriate <*`mode`*> to use. If the NFS connection uses the NFS version 2 protocol, the NFS client uses the default security mode, which is currently `sys`. NFS clients can force the use of a specific security mode by specifying the `sec=`<*`mode`*> option on the command line. However, if the file system on the server is not shared with that security mode, the client may be denied access. The following are valid modes:
	`sys`—Use AUTH_SYS authentication. The user's Unix user ID and group IDs are passed in clear text on the network, unauthenticated by the NFS server.

TABLE 9.9 *Continued*

Option	Description
	dh—Use a Diffie-Hellman public key system. krb5—Use the Kerberos version 5 authentication. krb5i—Use the Kerberos version 5 authentication with integrity checking to verify that the data has not been compromised. krb5p—Use the Kerberos version 5 authentication with integrity checking and privacy protection (encryption). This is the most secure, but also incurs additional overhead. none—Use null authentication. log=<*tag*>—Enables NFS server logging for the specified file system. The optional <*tag*> determines the location of the related log files. The tag is defined in etc/nfs/nfslog.conf. If no tag is specified, the default values associated with the global tag in /etc/nfs/nfslog.conf are used. NFS logging is described later in this chapter, in the section "NFS Server Logging." Support for NFS logging is only available for NFS versions 2 and 3.
-d <*description*>	Provides a description of the resource being shared.

To share a file system as read-only every time the system is started up, you add this line to the /etc/dfs/dfstab file:

```
share -F nfs -o ro /data1
```

After you edit the /etc/dfs/dfstab file, restart the NFS server by either rebooting the system or by typing this:

```
svcadm restart nfs/server
```

You need to run the svcadm enable nfs/server command only after you make the first entry in the /etc/dfs/dfstab file. This is because at startup, when the system enters the multi-user-server milestone, mountd and nfsd are not started if the /etc/dfs/dfstab file is empty. After you have made an initial entry and have executed the svcadm enable nfs/server command, you can modify /etc/dfs/dfstab without restarting the daemons. You simply execute the shareall command, and any new entries in the /etc/dfs/dfstab file are shared.

NOTE

Sharing Even if you share a file system from the command line by typing the share command, mountd and nfsd still won't run until you make an entry into /etc/dfs/dfstab and run the svcadm enable nfs/server command.

When you have at least one entry in the /etc/dfs/dfstab file and when both mountd and nfsd are running, you can share additional file systems by typing the share command directly from the command line. Be aware, however, that if you don't add the entry to the /etc/dfs/dfstab file, the file system is not automatically shared the next time the system is restarted.

EXAM ALERT

File System Sharing There is often at least one question on the exam related to the sharing of file systems. Remember that the NFS server must be running in order for the share to take effect.

The dfshares command displays information about the shared resources that are available to the host from an NFS server. Here is the syntax for dfshares:

```
dfshares <servername>
```

You can view the shared file systems on a remote NFS server by using the dfshares command, like this:

```
dfshares apollo
```

If no *servername* is specified, all resources currently being shared on the local host are displayed. Another place to find information on shared resources is in the server's /etc/dfs/sharetab file. This file contains a list of the resources currently being shared.

Mounting a Remote File System

Chapter 1 describes how to mount a local file system by using the mount command. You can use the same mount command to mount a shared file system on a remote host using NFS. Here is the syntax for mounting NFS file systems:

```
mount -F NFS <options> <-o specific-options > <-O> \
<server>:<file-system> <mount-point>
```

In this syntax, *server* is the name of the NFS server in which the file system is located, *file-system* is the name of the shared file system on the NFS server, and *mount-point* is the name of the local directory that serves as the mount point. As you can see, this is similar to mounting a local file system. The options for the mount command are described in Table 9.10.

TABLE 9.10 NFS mount Command Syntax

Option	Description
-F NFS	Specifies the *FSType* on which to operate, in this case the value will be NFS.
-r	Mounts the specified file system as read-only.
-m	Does not append an entry to the /etc/mnttab table of the mounted file systems.

TABLE 9.10 *Continued*

Option	Description
-o <*specific-options*>	Can be any of the following options, separated by commas: rw ¦ ro—The resource is mounted read-write or read-only. The default is rw. acdirmax=n—The maximum time that cached attributes are held after directory update. The default is 60 seconds. acdirmin=n—The minimum time that cached attributes are held after directory update. The default is 30 seconds. acregmax=n—The maximum time that cached attributes are held after file modification. The default is 60 seconds. acregmin=n—The minimum time that cached attributes are held after file modification. The default is 3 seconds. actimeo=n—Set minimum and maximum times for directories and regular files, in seconds. forcedirectio ¦ noforcedirectio—If the file system is mounted with forcedirectio, then data is transferred directly between client and server, with no buffering on the client. Using noforcedirectio causes buffering to be done on the client. grpid—The GID of a new file is unconditionally inherited from that of the parent directory, overriding any set-GID options. noac—Suppress data and attribute caching. nocto—Do not perform the normal close-to-open consistency. This option can be used when only one client is accessing a specified file system. In this case, performance may be improved, but it should be used with caution. suid ¦ nosuid—setuid execution is enabled or disabled. The default is suid. remount—If a file system is mounted as read-only, this option remounts it as read-write. bg ¦ fg—If the first attempt to mount the remote file system fails, this option retries it in the background (bg) or in the foreground (fg). The default is fg. quota—This option checks whether the user is over the quota on this file system. If the file system has quotas enabled on the server, quotas are still checked for operations on this file system. noquota—This option prevents quota from checking whether the user has exceeded the quota on this file system. If the file system has quotas enabled on the server, quotas are still checked for operations on this file system.

(continues)

TABLE 9.10 *Continued*

Option	Description
	`retry=`*n*—This option specifies the number of times to retry the mount operation. The default is `10000`. `vers=`*<NFS-version-number>*—By default, the version of NFS protocol used between the client and the server is the highest one available on both systems. If the NFS server does not support the NFS 4 protocol, the NFS mount uses version 2 or 3. `port=`*n*—This option specifies the server IP port number. The default is `NFS_PORT`. `proto=netid ¦ rdma`—The default transport is the first rdma protocol supported by both client and server. If no rdma, then TCP is used and failing that, UDP. Note that NFS version 4 does not use UDP, so if you specify `proto=udp`, then NFS version 4 will not be used. `public`—Forces the use of the public file handle when connecting to the NFS server. `sec=mode`—Set the security mode for NFS transactions. NFS versions 3 and 4 mounts negotiate a security mode. Version 3 mounts pick the first mode supported, whereas version 4 mounts try each supported mode in turn, until one is successful. `rsize=`*<n>*—This option sets the read buffer size to *<n>* bytes. The default value is `32768` with version 3 or 4 of the NFS protocol. The default can be negotiated down if the server prefers a smaller transfer size. With NFS version 2, the default value is `8192`. `wsize=`*<n>*—This option sets the write buffer size to *<n>* bytes. The default value is `32768` with version 3 or 4 of the NFS protocol. The default can be negotiated down if the server prefers a smaller transfer size. With version 2, the default value is `8192`. `timeo=`*<n>*—This option sets the NFS timeout to *<n>* tenths of a second. The default value is 11 tenths of a second for connectionless transports and 600 tenths of a second for connection-oriented transports. `retrans=`*<n>*—This option sets the number of NFS retransmissions to *<n>*; the default value is `5`. For connection-oriented transports, this option has no effect because it is assumed that the transport will perform retransmissions on behalf of NFS. `soft ¦ hard`—This option returns an error if the server does not respond (`soft`), or it continues the retry request until the server responds (`hard`). If you're using `hard`, the system appears to hang until the NFS server responds. The default value is `hard`.

TABLE 9.10 *Continued*

Option	Description
	`intr` ¦ `nointr`—This option enables or does not enable keyboard interrupts to kill a process that hangs while waiting for a response on a hard-mounted file system. The default is `intr`, which makes it possible for clients to interrupt applications that might be waiting for an NFS server to respond.
	`xattr` ¦ `noxattr`—Allow or disallow the creation of extended attributes. The default is `xattr` (allow extended attributes).
	`-O`—The overlay mount lets the file system be mounted over an existing mount point, making the underlying file system inaccessible. If a mount is attempted on a preexisting mount point and this flag is not set, the mount fails, producing the "device busy" error.

File systems mounted with the `bg` option indicate that `mount` is to retry in the background if the server's mount daemon (`mountd`) does not respond when, for example, the NFS server is restarted. From the NFS client, `mount` retries the request up to the count specified in the `retry=<n>` option. After the file system is mounted, each NFS request made in the kernel waits a specified number of seconds for a response (specified with the `timeo=<n>` option). If no response arrives, the timeout is multiplied by 2, and the request is retransmitted. If the number of retransmissions has reached the number specified in the `retrans=<n>` option, a file system mounted with the `soft` option returns an error, and the file system mounted with the `hard` option prints a warning message and continues to retry the request. Sun recommends that file systems mounted as read-write or containing executable files should always be mounted with the `hard` option. If you use soft-mounted file systems, unexpected I/O errors can occur. For example, consider a write request: If the NFS server goes down, the pending write request simply gives up, resulting in a corrupted file on the remote file system. A read-write file system should always be mounted with the specified `hard` and `intr` options. This lets users make their own decisions about killing hung processes. You use the following to mount a file system named `/data` located on a host named `thor` with the `hard` and `intr` options:

```
mount -F nfs -o hard,intr thor:/data /data
```

If a file system is mounted `hard` and the `intr` option is not specified, the process hangs when the NFS server goes down or the network connection is lost. The process continues to hang until the NFS server or network connection becomes operational. For a terminal process, this can be annoying. If `intr` is specified, sending an interrupt signal to the process kills it. For a terminal process, you can do this by pressing Ctrl+C. For a background process, sending an `INT` or `QUIT` signal, as follows, usually works:

```
kill -QUIT 3421
```

NOTE

Overkill Won't Work Sending a KILL signal (-9) does not terminate a hung NFS process.

To mount a file system called /data that is located on an NFS server called thor, you issue the following command, as root, from the NFS client:

```
mount -F nfs -o ro thor:/data /thor_data
```

In this case, the /data file system from the server thor is mounted read-only on /thor_data on the local system. Mounting from the command line enables temporary viewing of the file system. If the umount command is issued or the client is restarted, the mount is lost. If you would like this file system to be mounted automatically at every startup, you can add the following line to the /etc/vfstab file:

```
thor:/data - /thor_data nfs - yes ro
```

NOTE

Mount Permissions The mount and umount commands require root access. The umount command and /etc/vfstab file are described in Chapter 1.

To view resources that can be mounted on the local or remote system, you use the dfmounts command, as follows:

```
dfmounts sparcserver
```

The system responds with a list of file systems currently mounted on sparcserver:

```
RESOURCE        SERVER PATHNAME             CLIENTS
   -            ultra5 /usr                 192.168.1.201
                ultra5 /usr/dt              192.168.1.201
```

Sometimes you rely on NFS mount points for critical information. If the NFS server were to go down unexpectedly, you would lose the information contained at that mount point. You can address this issue by using client-side failover. With *client-side failover*, you specify an alternative file system to use in case the primary file system fails. The primary and alternative file systems should contain equivalent directory structures and identical files. This option is available only on read-only file systems.

To set up client-side failover, on the NFS client, mount the file system by using the -ro option. You can do this from the command line or by adding an entry to the /etc/vfstab file that looks like the following:

```
zeus,thor:/data  -  /remote_data  nfs  -  no  -o ro
```

If multiple file systems are named and the first server in the list is down, failover uses the next alternative server to access files. To mount a replicated set of NFS file systems, which might have different paths to the file system, you use the following `mount` command:

```
mount -F nfs -o ro zeus:/usr/local/data,thor:/home/data /usr/local/data
```

Replication is discussed further in the “AutoFS” section, later in this chapter.

NFS Server Logging

A feature that first appeared in Solaris 8 is NFS server logging (refer to Chapter 1). NFS server logging provides event and audit logging functionality to networked file systems. The daemon `nfslogd` provides NFS logging, and you enable it by using the `log=`*<tag>* option in the `share` command, as described earlier in this chapter, in the section “Setting Up NFS.” When NFS logging is enabled, the kernel records all NFS operations on the file system in a buffer. The data recorded includes a timestamp, the client Internet Protocol (IP) address, the UID of the requestor, the file handle of the resource that is being accessed, and the type of operation that occurred. The `nfslogd` daemon converts this information into ASCII records that are stored in ASCII log files.

NOTE

No Logging in NFS Version 4 Remember that NFS logging is not supported in NFS version 4.

To enable NFS server logging, follow the procedure described in Step by Step 9.5.

STEP BY STEP

9.5 Enabling NFS Server Logging

1. As root, share the NFS by typing the following entry at the command prompt:

   ```
   share -F nfs -o ro,log=global <file-system-name>
   ```

   Add the entry above to your `/etc/dfs/dfstab` file if you want it to go into effect every time the server is booted.

2. If the `nfslogd` daemon is not already running, start it by entering this:

   ```
   /usr/lib/nfs/nfslogd
   ```

EXAM ALERT

NSF Server Logging Configuration You should be familiar with the concept of NFS server logging, especially the location of the configuration file (`/etc/nfs/nfslog.conf`). The `nfs` directory in the path can be easily forgotten, and you lose an exam point unnecessarily if you leave it out.

You can change the file configuration settings in the NFS server logging configuration file `/etc/nfs/nfslog.conf`. This file defines pathnames, filenames, and types of logging to be used by `nfslogd`. Each definition is associated with a tag. The `global` tag defines the default values, but you can create new tags and specify them for each file system you share. The NFS operations to be logged by `nfslogd` are defined in the `/etc/default/nfslogd` configuration file.

NOTE

Logging Pros and Cons NFS server logging is particularly useful for being able to audit operations carried out on a shared file system. The logging can also be extended to audit directory creations and deletions. With logging enabled, however, the logs can become large and consume huge amounts of disk space. It is necessary to configure NFS logging appropriately so that the logs are pruned at regular intervals.

AutoFS

Objective:

Explain how to configure AutoFS using automount maps.

When a network contains even a moderate number of systems, all trying to mount file systems from each other, managing NFS can quickly become a nightmare. The AutoFS facility, also called the *automounter*, is designed to handle such situations by providing a method by which remote directories are mounted automatically, only when they are being used. *AutoFS*, a client-side service, is a file system structure that provides automatic mounting.

When a user or an application accesses an NFS mount point, the mount is established. When the file system is no longer needed or has not been accessed for a certain period, the file system is automatically unmounted. As a result, network overhead is lower, the system boots faster because NFS mounts are done later, and systems can be shut down with fewer ill effects and hung processes.

File systems shared through the NFS service can be mounted via AutoFS. AutoFS is initialized by `automount`, which is run automatically when a system is started. The automount daemon, `automountd`, runs continuously, mounting and unmounting remote directories on an as-needed basis.

Mounting does not need to be done at system startup, and the user does not need to know the superuser password to mount a directory (normally file system mounts require superuser privilege). With AutoFS, users do not use the `mount` and `umount` commands. The AutoFS service mounts file systems as the user accesses them and unmounts file systems when they are no longer required, without any intervention on the part of the user.

However, some file systems still need to be mounted by using the `mount` command with root privileges. For example, on a diskless computer you must mount `/` (root), `/usr`, and `/usr/kvm` by using the `mount` command, and you cannot take advantage of AutoFS.

Two programs support the AutoFS service: `automount` and `automountd`. Both are run when a system is started by the `svc:/system/filesystem/autofs:default` service identifier.

The `automount` service sets up the AutoFS mount points and associates the information in the `/etc/auto_master` files with each mount point. The `automount` command, which is called at system startup time, reads the master map file `/etc/auto_master` to create the initial set of AutoFS mounts. These mounts are not automatically mounted at startup time. They are *trigger points*, also called *trigger nodes*, under which file systems are mounted in the future. The following is the syntax for `automount`:

```
automount -t <duration> -v
```

Table 9.11 describes the syntax options for the `automount` command.

TABLE 9.11 `automount` Command Syntax

Option	Description
`-t <duration>`	Sets the time, in seconds, that a file system is to remain mounted if it is not being used. The default value is 600 seconds.
`-v`	Selects verbose mode. Running the `automount` command in verbose mode allows easier troubleshooting.

If it is not specifically set, the value for *`duration`* of an unused mount is set to 10 minutes. In most circumstances, this value is good; however, on systems that have many automounted file systems, you might need to decrease the *`duration`* value. In particular, if a server has many users, active checking of the automounted file systems every 10 minutes can be inefficient. Checking AutoFS every 300 seconds (5 minutes) might be better. You can edit the `/etc/default/autofs` script to change the default values.

If AutoFS receives a request to access a file system that is not currently mounted, AutoFS calls `automountd`, which mounts the requested file system under the trigger node.

The `automountd` daemon handles the mount and unmount requests from the AutoFS service. The syntax of this command is as follows:

```
automountd < -Tnv > < -D name=value >
```

Table 9.12 describes the syntax options for the `automountd` command.

TABLE 9.12 `automountd` Command Syntax

Option	Description
`-T`	Displays each remote procedure call (RPC) to standard output. You use this option for troubleshooting.
`-n`	Disables browsing on all AutoFS nodes.
`-v`	Logs all status messages to the console.
`-D` <*name*>=<*value*>	Substitutes *value* for the automount map variable indicated by *name*. The default value for the automount map is `/etc/auto_master`.

The `automountd` daemon is completely independent from the `automount` command. Because of this separation, it is possible to add, delete, or change map information without first having to stop and start the `automountd` daemon process.

When AutoFS runs, `automount` and `automountd` initiate at startup time from the `svc:/system/filesystem/autofs` service identifier. If a request is made to access a file system at an AutoFS mount point, the system goes through the following steps:

1. AutoFS intercepts the request.
2. AutoFS sends to the `automountd` daemon a message for the requested file system to be mounted.
3. `automountd` locates the file system information in a map and performs the mount.
4. AutoFS allows the intercepted request to proceed.
5. AutoFS unmounts the file system after a period of inactivity.

NOTE

Automatic, Not Manual, Mounts Mounts managed through the AutoFS service should not be manually mounted or unmounted. Even if the operation is successful, the AutoFS service does not check that the object has been unmounted, and this can result in possible inconsistency. A restart clears all AutoFS mount points.

To see who might be using a particular NFS mount, you use the `showmount` command. The syntax for `showmount` is shown here:

```
showmount <options>
```

The options for the `showmount` command are described in Table 9.13.

TABLE 9.13 showmount Command Syntax

Option	Description
-a	Prints all the remote mounts in the format *hostname : directory*. *hostname* is the name of the client, and *directory* is the root of the file system that has been mounted.
-d	Lists directories that have been remotely mounted by clients.
-e	Prints the list of shared file systems.

The following example illustrates the use of showmount to display file systems currently mounted from remote systems. On the NFS server named neptune, you could enter the following command:

```
showmount -a
```

The system would display the following information:

```
apollo:/export/home/neil
```

showmount says that the remote host, apollo, is currently mounting /export/home/neil on this server.

AutoFS Maps

The behavior of the automounter is governed by its configuration files, called *maps*. AutoFS searches maps to navigate its way through the network. Map files contain information, such as the location of other maps to be searched or the location of a user's home directory, for example.

There are three types of automount maps: the master map, the direct map, and the indirect map. Each of these is described in the following sections.

Master Maps

To start the navigation process, the automount command reads the master map at system startup. This map is what tells the automounter about map files and mount points. The master map lists all direct and indirect maps and their associated directories.

The master map, which is in the /etc/auto_master file, associates a directory with a map. The master map is a list that specifies all the maps that AutoFS should check. The following example shows what an auto_master file could contain:

```
# Master map for automounter
#
 +auto_master
 /net    -hosts     -nosuid,nobrowse
 /home   auto_home  -nobrowse
```

This example shows the default `auto_master` file. The lines that begin with # are comments. The line that contains `+auto_master` specifies the AutoFS NIS table map, which is explained in Chapter 12, "Naming Services." Each line thereafter in the master map, `/etc/auto_master`, has the following syntax:

```
<mount-point> <map-name> <mount-options>
```

Each of these fields is described in Table 9.14.

TABLE 9.14 `/etc/auto_master` Fields

Field	Description
mount-point	The full (absolute) pathname of a directory that is used as the mount point. If the directory does not exist, AutoFS creates it, if possible. If the directory does exist and is not empty, mounting it hides its contents. In that case, AutoFS issues a warning. Using the notation `/-` as a mount point indicates that a direct map with no particular mount point is associated with the map.
map-name	The map that AutoFS uses to find directions to locations or mount information. If the name is preceded by a slash (/), AutoFS interprets the name as a local file. Otherwise, AutoFS searches for the mount information by using the search specified in the name service switch configuration file (`/etc/nsswitch.conf`). Name service switches are described in Chapter 12.
mount-options	An optional comma-separated list of options that apply to the mounting of the entries specified in *map-name*, unless the entries list other options. Options for each specific type of file system are listed in Table 9.10. For NFS-specific mount points, the `bg` (background) and `fg` (foreground) options do not apply.

NOTE

Map Format A line that begins with a pound sign (#) is a comment, and everything that follows it until the end of the line is ignored. To split long lines into shorter ones, you can put a backslash (\) at the end of the line. The maximum number of characters in an entry is 1,024.

Every Solaris installation comes with a master map, called `/etc/auto_master`, that has the default entries shown in Table 9.14. Without any changes to the generic system setup, clients should be capable of accessing remote file systems through the `/net` mount point. The following entry in `/etc/auto_master` allows this to happen:

```
/net    -hosts    -nosuid,nobrowse
```

For example, let's say that you have an NFS server named `apollo` that has the `/export` file system exported. Another system, named `zeus`, exists on the network. This system has the default

`/etc/auto_master` file; by default, it has a directory named `/net`. If you type the following, the command comes back showing that the directory is empty—nothing is in it:

```
ls /net
```

Now type this:

```
ls /net/apollo
```

The system responds with this:

```
export
```

Why was the `/net` directory empty the first time you issued the `ls` command? When you issued `ls /net/apollo`, why did it find a subdirectory? This is the automounter in action. When you specified `/net` with a hostname, `automountd` looked at the map file—in this case, `/etc/hosts`—and found `apollo` and its IP address. It then went to `apollo`, found the exported file system, and created a local mount point for `/net/apollo/export`. It also added this entry to the `/etc/mnttab` table:

```
-hosts  /net/apollo/export  autofs  nosuid,nobrowse,ignore,nest,\
dev=2b80005 941812769
```

This entry in the `/etc/mnttab` table is referred to as a *trigger node* (because changing to the specified directory, the mount of the file system is "triggered").

If you enter `mount`, as follows, you won't see anything mounted at this point:

```
mount
```

The system responds with this:

```
/ on /dev/dsk/c0t3d0s0 read/write/setuid/largefiles on \
Mon Aug  8 09:45:21 2005
/usr on /dev/dsk/c0t3d0s6 read/write/setuid/largefiles on \
Mon Aug  8 09:45:21 2005
/proc on /proc read/write/setuid on Mon Aug  8 09:45:21 2005
/dev/fd on fd read/write/setuid on Mon Aug  8 09:45:21 2005
/export on /dev/dsk/c0t3d0s3 setuid/read/write/largefiles on \
Mon Aug  8 09:45:24 2005
/export/swap on /dev/dsk/c0t3d0s4 setuid/read/write/largefiles on \
Mon Aug  8 09:45:24 \ 2005
/tmp on swap read/write on Mon Aug  8 09:45:24 2005
```

Now type this:

```
ls /net/apollo/export
```

You should have a bit of a delay while automountd mounts the file system. The system then responds with this:

```
files   lost+found
```

The files listed are files located on apollo, in the /export directory. If you enter mount, you see a file system mounted on apollo that wasn't listed before:

```
mount
/ on /dev/dsk/c0t3d0s0 read/write/setuid/largefiles on \
Mon Aug  8 09:45:21 2005
/usr on /dev/dsk/c0t3d0s6 read/write/setuid/largefiles on \
Mon Aug  8 09:45:21 2005
/proc on /proc read/write/setuid on Mon Aug  8 09:45:21 2005
/dev/fd on fd read/write/setuid on Mon Aug  8 09:45:21 2005
/export on /dev/dsk/c0t3d0s3 setuid/read/write/largefiles on \
Mon Aug  8 09:45:24 2005
/export/swap on /dev/dsk/c0t3d0s4 setuid/read/write/largefiles on \
Mon Aug  8 09:45:24 \ 2005
/tmp on swap read/write on Mon Aug  8 09:45:24 2005
/net/apollo/export on apollo:/export nosuid/remote on \
Fri Aug 12 09:48:03 2005
```

The automounter automatically mounted the /export file system that was located on apollo. Now look at the /etc/mnttab file again, and you will see additional entries:

```
more /etc/mnttab
/dev/dsk/c0t3d0s0   /       ufs  rw,suid,dev=800018,largefiles  941454346
/dev/dsk/c0t3d0s6   /usr    ufs  rw,suid,dev=80001e,largefiles  941454346
/proc    /proc   proc    rw,suid,dev=2940000     941454346
fd       /dev/fd fd      rw,suid,dev=2a00000     941454346
/dev/dsk/c0t3d0s3   /export ufs  suid,rw,largefiles,dev=80001b  941454349
/dev/dsk/c0t3d0s4       /export/swap    ufs     suid,rw,largefiles,\
dev=80001c 941454349
swap     /tmp    tmpfs   dev=1   941454349
-hosts   /net    autofs  ignore,indirect,nosuid,nobrowse,dev=2b80001  \
   941454394
auto_home        /home   autofs  ignore,indirect,nobrowse,dev=2b80002  \
  941454394
-xfn     /xfn    autofs  ignore,indirect,dev=2b80003     941454394
sparcserver:vold(pid246)       /vol    nfs     ignore,noquota,dev=2b40001\
 941454409
-hosts   /net/apollo/export     autofs  nosuid,nobrowse,ignore,nest,\
dev=2b80005  941812769
apollo:/export /net/apollo/export     nfs     nosuid,dev=2b40003 \
941813283
```

If the /net/apollo/export directory is accessed, the AutoFS service completes the process, with these steps:

1. It pings the server's mount service to see if it's alive.
2. It mounts the requested file system under /net/apollo/export. Now the /etc/mnttab file contains the following entries:

```
-hosts  /net/apollo/export    autofs nosuid,nobrowse,ignore,nest,\
dev=2b80005  941812769
apollo:/export /net/apollo/export     nfs     nosuid,dev=2b40003 \
941813283
```

Because the automounter lets all users mount file systems, root access is not required. AutoFS also provides for automatic unmounting of file systems, so there is no need to unmount them when you are done.

Direct Maps

A *direct map* lists a set of unrelated mount points that might be spread out across the file system. A complete path (for example, /usr/local/bin, /usr/man) is listed in the map as a mount point. A good example of where to use a direct mount point is for /usr/man. The /usr directory contains many other directories, such as /usr/bin and /usr/local; therefore, it cannot be an indirect mount point. If you used an indirect map for /usr/man, the local /usr file system would be the mount point, and you would cover up the local /usr/bin and /usr/etc directories when you established the mount. A direct map lets the automounter complete mounts on a single directory entry such as /usr/man, and these mounts appear as links with the name of the direct mount point.

A direct map is specified in a configuration file called /etc/auto_direct. With a direct map, there is a direct association between a mount point on the client and a directory on the server. A direct map has a full pathname and indicates the relationship explicitly. This is a typical /etc/auto_direct map:

```
/usr/local     -ro
/share ivy:/export/local/share
/src   ivy:/export/local/src
/usr/man      -ro        apollo:/usr/man zeus:/usr/man neptune:/usr/man
/usr/game     -ro        peach:/usr/games
/usr/spool/news     -ro        jupiter:/usr/spool/news saturn:/var/spool/news
```

> **NOTE**
>
> **Map Naming** The direct map name /etc/auto_direct is not a mandatory name; it is used here as an example of a direct map. The name of a direct map must be added to the /etc/auto_master file, but it can be any name you choose, although it should be meaningful to the system administrator.

Lines in direct maps have the following syntax:

```
<key> <mount-options> <location>
```

The fields of this syntax are described in Table 9.15.

TABLE 9.15 Direct Map Fields

Field	Description
key	Indicates the pathname of the mount point in a direct map. This pathname specifies the local directory on which to mount the NFS.
mount-options	Indicates the options you want to apply to this particular mount. These options, which are listed in Table 9.10, are required only if they differ from the map default options specified in the `/etc/auto_master` file. There is no concatenation of options between the automounter maps. Any options added to an automounter map override all the options listed in previously searched maps. For instance, options included in the `auto_master` map would be overwritten by corresponding entries in any other map.
location	Indicates the remote location of the file system, specified as *server:pathname*. More than one location can be specified. *pathname* should not include an automounted mount point; it should be the actual absolute path to the file system. For instance, the location of a home directory should be listed as `server:/export/home/username`, not as `server:/home/username`.

In the previous example of the `/etc/auto_direct` map file, the mount points, `/usr/man` and `/usr/spool/news`, list more than one location:

```
/usr/man        -ro    apollo:/usr/man zeus:/usr/man neptune:/usr/man
/usr/spool/news        -ro    jupiter:/usr/spool/news saturn:/var/spool/news
```

Multiple locations, such as those shown here, are used for replication, or failover. For the purposes of failover, a file system can be called a *replica* if each file is the same size and it is the same type of file system. Permissions, creation dates, and other file attributes are not a consideration. If the file size or the file system types are different, the remap fails and the process hangs until the old server becomes available.

Replication makes sense only if you mount a file system that is read-only because you must have some control over the locations of files that you write or modify. You don't want to modify one server's files on one occasion and, minutes later, modify the "same" file on another server. The benefit of replication is that the best available server is used automatically, without any effort required by the user.

If the file systems are configured as replicas, the clients have the advantage of using failover. Not only is the best server automatically determined, but, if that server becomes unavailable, the client automatically uses the next-best server.

An example of a good file system to configure as a replica is the manual (man) pages. In a large network, more than one server can export the current set of man pages. Which server you mount them from doesn't matter, as long as the server is running and exporting its file systems.

In the previous example, multiple mount locations are expressed as a list of mount locations in the map entry. With multiple mount locations specified, you could mount the man pages from the `apollo`, `zeus`, or `neptune` servers. The best server depends on a number of factors, including the number of servers supporting a particular NFS protocol level, the proximity of the server, and weighting. The process of selecting a server goes like this:

1. During the sorting process, a count of the number of servers supporting the NFS version 2, 3, and 4 protocols is done. The protocol supported on the most servers is the protocol that is supported by default. This provides the client with the maximum number of servers to depend on. If version 3 servers are most abundant, the sorting process becomes more complex because they will be chosen as long as a version 2 server on the local subnet is not being ignored. Normally servers on the local subnet are given preference over servers on a remote subnet. A version 2 server on the local subnet can complicate matters because it could be closer than the nearest version 3 server. If there is a version 2 server on the local subnet, and the closest version 3 server is on a remote subnet, the version 2 server is given preference. This is checked only if there are more version 3 servers than version 2 servers. If there are more version 2 servers than version 3 servers, only a version 2 server is selected.
2. After the largest subset of servers that have the same protocol version is found, that server list is sorted by proximity. Servers on the local subnet are given preference over servers on a remote subnet. The closest server is given preference, which reduces latency and network traffic. If several servers are supporting the same protocol on the local subnet, the time to connect to each server is determined, and the fastest time is used.

   You can influence the selection of servers at the same proximity level by adding a numeric weighting value in parentheses after the server name in the AutoFS map. Here's an example:

   ```
   /usr/man -ro apollo,zeus(1),neptune(2):/usr/man
   ```

   Servers without a weighting have a value of `0`, which makes them the most likely servers to be selected. The higher the weighting value is, the less chance the server has of being selected. All other server-selection factors are more important than weighting. Weighting is considered only in selections between servers with the same network proximity.

With failover, the sorting is checked once at mount time, to select one server from which to mount, and again if the mounted server becomes unavailable. Failover is particularly useful in a large network with many subnets. AutoFS chooses the nearest server and therefore confines NFS network traffic to a local network segment. In servers with multiple network interfaces, AutoFS lists the hostname associated with each network interface as if it were a separate server. It then selects the nearest interface to the client.

In the following example, you set up a direct map for /usr/local on zeus. Currently, zeus has a directory called /usr/local with the following directories:

```
ls /usr/local
```

The following local directories are displayed:

```
bin    etc    files    programs
```

If you set up the automount direct map, you can see how the /usr/local directory is overwritten by the NFS mount. Follow the procedure shown in Step by Step 9.6.

STEP BY STEP

9.6 Creating a Direct Map

1. Add the following entry in the master map file called /etc/auto_master:

   ```
   /-    /etc/auto_direct
   ```

2. Create the direct map file called /etc/auto_direct with the following entry:

   ```
   /usr/local    zeus:/usr/local
   ```

3. Because you're modifying a direct map, run automount to reload the AutoFS tables, as follows:

   ```
   # automount
   ```

   If you have access to the /usr/local directory, the NFS mount point is established by using the direct map you have set up. The contents of /usr/local have changed because the direct map has covered up the local copy of /usr/local:

   ```
   ls /usr/local
   ```

   You should see the following directories listed:

   ```
   fasttrack    answerbook
   ```

NOTE

Overlay Mounting The local contents of /usr/local have not been overwritten. After the NFS mount point is unmounted, the original contents of /usr/local are redisplayed.

If you enter the mount command, you see that /usr/local is now mounted remotely from zeus:

```
mount
/ on /dev/dsk/c0t3d0s0 read/write/setuid/largefiles on \
Mon Aug 8 09:45:21 2005
```

```
/usr on /dev/dsk/c0t3d0s6 read/write/setuid/largefiles on \
Mon Aug 8 09:45:21 2005
/proc on /proc read/write/setuid on Mon Aug 8 09:45:21 2005
/dev/fd on fd read/write/setuid on Mon Aug 8 09:45:21 2005
/export on /dev/dsk/c0t3d0s3 setuid/read/write/largefiles on \
Mon Aug 8 09:45:24 2005
/export/swap on /dev/dsk/c0t3d0s4 setuid/read/write/largefiles on \
Mon Aug 8 09:45:24 2005
/tmp on swap read/write on Mon Aug 8 09:45:24 2005
/usr/local on zeus:/usr/local read/write/remote on \
Sat Aug 13 08:06:40 2005
```

Indirect Maps

Indirect maps are the simplest and most useful AutoFS maps. An *indirect map* uses a key's substitution value to establish the association between a mount point on the client and a directory on the server. Indirect maps are useful for accessing specific file systems, such as home directories, from anywhere on the network. The following entry in the `/etc/auto_master` file is an example of an indirect map:

```
/share        /etc/auto_share
```

With this entry in the `/etc/auto_master` file, `/etc/auto_share` is the name of the indirect map file for the mount point `/share`. For this entry, you need to create an indirect map file named `/etc/auto_share`, which would look like this:

```
# share directory map for automounter
 #
 ws            neptune:/export/share/ws
```

If the `/share` directory is accessed, the AutoFS service creates a trigger node for `/share/ws`, and the following entry is made in the `/etc/mnttab` file:

```
-hosts  /share/ws     autofs  nosuid,nobrowse,ignore,nest,dev=###
```

If the `/share/ws` directory is accessed, the AutoFS service completes the process with these steps:

1. It pings the server's `mount` service to see if it's alive.
2. It mounts the requested file system under `/share`. Now the `/etc/mnttab` file contains the following entries:

   ```
   -hosts  /share/ws     autofs  nosuid,nobrowse,ignore,nest,dev=###
   neptune:/export/share/ws /share/ws    nfs    nosuid,dev=####  #####
   ```

Lines in indirect maps have the following syntax:

```
<key>  <mount-options>  <location>
```

The fields in this syntax are described in Table 9.16.

TABLE 9.16 Indirect Map Field Syntax

Field	Description
key	A simple name (with no slashes) in an indirect map.
mount-options	The options you want to apply to this particular mount. These options, which are described in Table 9.10, are required only if they differ from the map default options specified in the /etc/auto_master file.
location	The remote location of the file system, specified as *server:pathname*. More than one location can be specified. *pathname* should not include an automounted mount point; it should be the actual absolute path to the file system. For instance, the location of a directory should be listed as server:/usr/local, not as server:/net/server/usr/local.

For example, say an indirect map is being used with user home directories. As users log in to several different systems, their home directories are not always local to the system. It's convenient for the users to use the automounter to access their home directories, regardless of what system they're logged in to. To accomplish this, the default /etc/auto_master map file needs to contain the following entry:

```
/home       /etc/auto_home          -nobrowse
```

/etc/auto_home is the name of the indirect map file that contains the entries to be mounted under /home. A typical /etc/auto_home map file might look like this:

```
more /etc/auto_home
 dean                     willow:/export/home/dean
 william                  cypress:/export/home/william
 nicole                   poplar:/export/home/nicole
 glenda                   pine:/export/home/glenda
 steve                    apple:/export/home/steve
 burk                     ivy:/export/home/burk
 neil     -rw,nosuid      peach:/export/home/neil
```

NOTE

Indirect Map Names As with direct maps, the actual name of an indirect map is up to the system administrator, but a corresponding entry must be placed in the /etc/auto_master file, and the name should be meaningful to the system administrator.

Now assume that the /etc/auto_home map is on the host oak. If user neil has an entry in the password database that specifies his home directory as /home/neil, whenever he logs in to computer oak, AutoFS mounts the directory /export/home/neil, which resides on the computer peach. Neil's home directory is mounted read-write, nosuid. Anyone, including Neil, has access to this path from any computer set up with the master map referring to the /etc/auto_home map in this example. Under these conditions, user neil can run login, or rlogin, on any computer that has the /etc/auto_home map set up, and his home directory is mounted in place for him.

Another example of when to use an indirect map is when you want to make all project-related files available under a directory called /data that is to be common across all workstations at the site. Step by Step 9.7 shows how to do this.

STEP BY STEP

9.7 Setting Up an Indirect Map

1. Add an entry for the /data directory to the /etc/auto_master map file:

```
/data      /etc/auto_data     -nosuid
```

   The auto_data map file, named /etc/auto_data, determines the contents of the /data directory.

2. Add the -nosuid option as a precaution. The -nosuid option prevents users from creating files with the setuid or setgid bit set.

3. Create the /etc/auto_data file and add entries to the auto_data map. The auto_data map is organized so that each entry describes a subproject. Edit /etc/auto_data to create a map that looks like the following:

```
compiler    apollo:/export/data/&
window      apollo:/export/data/&
files       zeus:/export/data/&
drivers     apollo:/export/data/&
man         zeus:/export/data/&
tools       zeus:/export/data/&
```

NOTE

Using the Entry Key The ampersand (&) at the end of each entry is an abbreviation for the entry key. For instance, the first entry is equivalent to the compiler apollo:/export/data/compiler.

Because the servers apollo and zeus view similar AutoFS maps locally, any users who log in to these computers find the /data file system as expected. These users are provided direct access to local files through loopback mounts instead of NFS mounts.

4. Because you changed the /etc/auto_master map, the final step is to reload the AutoFS tables, as follows:

```
# automount
```

Now, if a user changes to the /data/compiler directory, the mount point to apollo:/export/data/compiler is created:

```
cd /data/compiler
```

5. Type mount to see the mount point that was established:

```
mount
```

The system shows that /data/compiler is mapped to apollo:/export/data/compiler:

```
/data/compiler on apollo:/export/data/compiler read/write/remote \
on Fri Aug  12 17:17:02 2005
```

If the user changes to /data/tools, the mount point to zeus:/export/data/tools is created under the mount point /data/tools.

NOTE

Directory Creation There is no need to create the directory /data/compiler to be used as the mount point. AutoFS creates all the necessary directories before establishing the mount.

You can modify, delete, or add entries to maps to meet the needs of the environment. As applications (and other file systems that users require) change location, the maps must reflect those changes. You can modify AutoFS maps at any time. However, changes do not take place until the file system is unmounted and remounted. If a change is made to the auto_master map or to a direct map, those changes do not take place until the AutoFS tables are reloaded, as follows:

```
# automount
```

EXAM ALERT

Direct Versus Indirect Maps Remember the difference between direct and indirect maps. The /- entry in /etc/auto_master signifies a direct map because there is no mount point specified. This means that an absolute pathname is specified in the map. Indirect maps contain relative addresses, so the starting mount point, such as /home, appears in the /etc/auto_master entry for an indirect map.

When to Use automount

The most common and most advantageous use of automount is for mounting infrequently used file systems on an NFS client, such as online reference man pages. Another common use is accessing user home directories anywhere on the network. This works well for users who do not have a dedicated system and who tend to log in from different locations. Without the AutoFS service, to permit access, a system administrator has to create home directories on every system that the user logs in to. Data has to be duplicated everywhere, and it can easily become out of sync. You certainly don't want to create permanent NFS mounts for all user home directories on each system, so mounting infrequently used file systems on an NFS client is an excellent use for automount.

You also use automount if a read-only file system exists on more than one server. By using automount instead of conventional NFS mounting, you can configure the NFS client to query all the servers on which the file system exists and mount from the server that responds first.

You should avoid using automount to mount frequently used file systems, such as those that contain user commands or frequently used applications; conventional NFS mounting is more efficient in this situation. It is quite practical and typical to combine the use of automount with conventional NFS mounting on the same NFS client.

Summary

In this chapter, you have learned how a Solaris system utilizes the `swapfs` file system as virtual memory storage when the system does not have enough physical memory to handle the needs of the currently running processes. You have learned how to add, monitor, and delete swap files and partitions. You have also learned how to manage core files and crash dumps.

This chapter also described what NFS is and how to share resources on an NFS server. Accessing resources on the NFS client from a server was discussed, as was configuring NFS to record all activity via the NFS logging daemon, `nfslogd`.

Finally, this chapter described AutoFS and the many options that are available when you're mounting NFS resources so that user downtime is minimized by unplanned system outages and unavailable resources.

Key Terms

- automount
- Core file
- Crash dump
- Direct map
- Dynamic failover
- Hard mount
- Indirect map
- lockd
- mountd
- nfsd
- nfsmapid
- nfs4cbd
- NFS
- NFS client
- NFS logging
- NFS server
- NFS Version 4
- Replication
- Secondary swap partition
- Shared resource
- Soft mount
- Swap file
- Trigger point
- Virtual file system

Exercises

9.1 Adding Temporary Swap Space

In this exercise, you'll create a swap file to add additional, temporary swap space on your system.

Estimated time: 15 minutes

1. As root, use the `df -h` command to locate a file system that has enough room to support a 512MB swap file.
2. Use the `mkfile` command to add a 512MB swap file named `swapfile` in a directory, as follows:

   ```
   mkfile 512m /<directory>/swapfile
   ```

3. Use the `ls -l /<directory>` command to verify that the file has been created.
4. Activate the swap area with the `swap` command:

   ```
   /usr/sbin/swap -a /<directory>/swapfile
   ```

5. Use the `swap -l` command to verify that the new swap area was added:

   ```
   swap -l
   ```

6. Use the `swap -d` command to remove the swap area:

   ```
   swap -d /<directory>/swapfile
   ```

7. Issue the `swap -l` command to verify that the swap area is gone:

   ```
   swap -l
   ```

8. Remove the swapfile that was created:

   ```
   rm /<directory>/swapfile
   ```

The following two exercises require a minimum of two networked Solaris systems. You need to determine in advance which system will serve as the NFS server and which system will be the NFS client. The NFS server must have man pages installed in the `/usr/share/man` directory.

9.2 NFS Server Setup

In this exercise, you'll set up an NFS server to share the contents of the `/usr/share/man` directory for read-only access.

Estimated time: 30 minutes

1. Make the following entry in the `/etc/dfs/dfstab` file:

   ```
   share -F nfs -o ro /usr/share/man
   ```

2. Restart the NFS server service to start the `nfsd` and `mountd` daemons:

   ```
   svcadm restart nfs/server
   ```

3. Verify that the NFS server service is online by typing this:

   ```
   svcs nfs/server
   ```

4. Verify that the resource is shared by typing this:

```
share
```

The system displays this:

```
-      /usr/share/man    ro    ""
```

5. On the NFS client, rename the `/usr/share/man` directory so that man pages are no longer accessible:

```
cd /usr/share
mv man man.bkup
```

6. Verify that the manual pages are no longer accessible by typing this:

```
man tar
```

7. Create a new `man` directory to be used as a mount point:

```
mkdir man
```

8. Verify that you are able to see the shared resource on the NFS server by typing this:

```
dfshares <nfs-server-name>
```

The system should display a message similar to the following:

```
RESOURCE                        SERVER  ACCESS     TRANSPORT
192.168.0.4:/usr/share/man      192.168.0.4           -
```

9. Mount the `/usr/share/man` directory located on the NFS server to the directory you created in step 8:

```
mount <nfs-server-name>:/usr/share/man \
/usr/share/man
```

10. Now see if the man pages are accessible by typing this:

```
man tar
```

11. Verify the list of mounts that the server is providing by typing this:

```
dfmounts <nfs-server-name>
```

The system should display something like this:

```
RESOURCE   SERVER  PATHNAME                  CLIENTS
  -         192.168.0.4 /usr/share/man      192.168.0.21
```

12. Unmount the directory on the NFS client:

```
umountall -r
```

The `-r` option specifies that only remote file system types are to be unmounted.

13. Verify that the file system is no longer mounted by typing this:

```
dfmounts <nfs-server-name>
```

14. On the NFS server, unshare the /usr/share/man directory:

```
unshare /usr/share/man
```

15. On the NFS client, try to mount the /usr/share/man directory from the NFS server, as follows:

```
mount <nfs-server-name>:/usr/share/man \
/usr/share/man
```

The NFS server should not allow you to mount the file system.

16. Check the shared resources on the NFS server by typing this:

```
dfshares <nfs-server-name>
```

The file system can no longer be mounted because it is no longer shared.

9.3 Using AutoFS

This exercise demonstrates the use of AutoFS.

Estimated time: 30 minutes

1. The NFS server should already have an entry in the /etc/dfs/dfstab file from the previous exercise. It looks like this:

```
share -F nfs -o ro /usr/share/man
```

The nfsd and mountd daemons should also be running on this server. On the NFS client, verify that the man pages are not working by typing this:

```
man tar
```

2. On the NFS client, remove the directory you created in Exercise 9.2:

```
rmdir /usr/share/man
```

3. On the NFS client, edit the /etc/auto_master file to add the following line for a direct map:

```
/-      auto_direct
```

4. On the NFS client, use vi to create a new file named /etc/auto_direct. Add the following line to the new file:

```
/usr/share/man     <nfs-server-name>:/usr/share/man
```

5. Run the automount command to update the list of directories managed by AutoFS:

```
automount -v
```

6. Now see if man pages are working on the NFS client by typing this:

```
man tar
```

7. On the NFS client, use `mount` to see whether AutoFS automatically mounted the remote directory on the NFS server:

```
mount
```

8. On the NFS server, unshare the shared directory by typing this:

```
unshareall
```

9. On the NFS server, shut down the NFS server daemons:

```
svcadm disable nfs/server
```

10. On the NFS client, edit the `/etc/auto_master` file and remove this line:

```
/-    auto_direct
```

11. On the NFS client, remove the file named `/etc/auto_direct`:

```
rm /etc/auto_direct
```

12. On the NFS client, run the `automount` command to update the list of directories managed by AutoFS:

```
automount -v
```

13. On the NFS client, return `/usr/share/man` to its original state, like this:

```
cd /usr/share
rmdir man
mv man.bkup man
```

Exam Questions

1. After you create and add additional swap space, what is the correct method to ensure the swap space is available following subsequent reboots?

   ❍ **A.** You can add an entry to the `/etc/vfstab` file.

   ❍ **B.** You can modify the startup scripts to include a `swapadd` command.

   ❍ **C.** Swap cannot be added; therefore, you must adjust the size of the swap partition.

   ❍ **D.** Additional steps are required because the necessary changes are made to the startup file when the swap space is added.

2. Which command is used to create a swap file?

   ❍ **A.** `cat`

   ❍ **B.** `touch`

   ❍ **C.** `mkfile`

   ❍ **D.** `swapadd`

   ❍ **E.** `newfs`

3. Which command is used to show the available swap space?

   ❍ **A.** `prtconf`

   ❍ **B.** `iostat`

   ❍ **C.** `swap -s`

   ❍ **D.** `vmstat`

   ❍ **E.** `/usr/bin/ps`

4. How are swap areas activated each time the system boots?

   ❍ **A.** The entry in the `/etc/vfstab` file activates them.

   ❍ **B.** The `/sbin/swapadd` script activates them.

   ❍ **C.** The `/usr/sbin/swap -a` command activates them.

   ❍ **D.** The swapon command activates them.

5. Which statements are true about swap areas? (Choose three.)

   ❍ **A.** An NFS file system can be used for a swap area.

   ❍ **B.** A swap file is the preferred method of adding swap space on a permanent basis.

   ❍ **C.** A swap file is created in any ordinary file system.

   ❍ **D.** You cannot unmount a file system while a swap file is in use.

   ❍ **E.** A swap area must not exceed 2GB on a Solaris 10 system.

   ❍ **F.** Using a striped metadevice for swap space is very advantageous and improves performance.

6. If you add resources to a particular file, you can then make the resources available and unavailable by using the `shareall` and `unshareall` commands. Which of the following files is that particular file?

❍ **A.** `/etc/dfs/dfstab`

❍ **B.** `/etc/dfs/sharetab`

❍ **C.** `/etc/vfstab`

❍ **D.** `/etc/mnttab`

7. To stop and restart NFS to enable a new share, which of the following do you use?

❍ **A.** `svcadm restart autofs`

❍ **B.** `svcadm restart nfs/client`

❍ **C.** `svcadm restart nfs/server`

❍ **D.** `automount -v`

8. In AutoFS, which of the following associates a directory with a map?

❍ **A.** `indirect`

❍ **B.** `direct`

❍ **C.** `automount`

❍ **D.** `automountd`

9. Which of the following maps has a full pathname and indicates the relationship explicitly?

❍ **A.** `NIS`

❍ **B.** `auto_master`

❍ **C.** `indirect`

❍ **D.** `direct`

10. NFS daemons are started at bootup from which of the following services or files? (Choose two.)

❍ **A.** `svc:/network/nfs/server`

❍ **B.** `svd:/network/nfs/client`

❍ **C.** `svc:/system/filesystem/autofs`

❍ **D.** `/etc/inittab`

11. Which of the following is not an NFS daemon?

   ❍ **A.** `rpcd`

   ❍ **B.** `mountd`

   ❍ **C.** `lockd`

   ❍ **D.** `statd`

12. Which NFS daemons are found only on the NFS server? (Choose three.)

   ❍ **A.** `nfsd`

   ❍ **B.** `lockd`

   ❍ **C.** `mountd`

   ❍ **D.** `nfslogd`

13. Which file do you use to specify the file systems that are to be shared?

   ❍ **A.** `/etc/dfs/sharetab`

   ❍ **B.** `/etc/dfs/dfstab`

   ❍ **C.** `/etc/vfstab`

   ❍ **D.** `/etc/mnttab`

14. Which command makes a resource available for mounting?

   ❍ **A.** `export`

   ❍ **B.** `share`

   ❍ **C.** `exportfs`

   ❍ **D.** `mount`

15. Which command displays information about shared resources that are available to the host from an NFS server?

   ❍ **A.** `shareall`

   ❍ **B.** `share`

   ❍ **C.** `dfshares`

   ❍ **D.** `dfinfo`

16. File systems mounted with which of the following options indicate that `mount` is to retry in the background if the server's mount daemon (`mountd`) does not respond?

❍ **A.** `intr`

❍ **B.** `fg`

❍ **C.** `bg`

❍ **D.** `soft`

17. Which of the following options to the `mount` command specifies how long (in seconds) each NFS request made in the kernel should wait for a response?

❍ **A.** `retrans`

❍ **B.** `timeo`

❍ **C.** `retry`

❍ **D.** `remount`

18. File systems that are mounted read-write or that contain executable files should always be mounted with which option?

❍ **A.** `hard`

❍ **B.** `intr`

❍ **C.** `soft`

❍ **D.** `nointr`

19. From the NFS client, which of the following options makes `mount` retry the request up to a specified number of times when the NFS server becomes unavailable?

❍ **A.** `retry`

❍ **B.** `retrans`

❍ **C.** `remount`

❍ **D.** `timeo`

20. When an NFS server goes down, which of the following options to the `mount` command allows you to send a kill signal to a hung NFS process?

❍ **A.** `bg`

❍ **B.** `nointr`

❍ **C.** `intr`

❍ **D.** `timeo`

21. Which of the following programs support the AutoFS service? (Choose two.)

❍ **A.** `automount`

❍ **B.** `automountd`

❍ **C.** `mount`

❍ **D.** `share`

22. From which of the following files does `automountd` start?

❍ **A.** `/etc/init.d/volmgt`

❍ **B.** `svc:/system/filesystem/autofs`

❍ **C.** `svc:/network/nfs/server`

❍ **D.** `svc:/network/nfs/client`

23. Which of the following commands do you use to see who is using a particular NFS mount?

❍ **A.** `nfsstat`

❍ **B.** `dfshares`

❍ **C.** `showmount`

❍ **D.** `ps`

24. Which of the following files lists all direct and indirect maps for AutoFS?

❍ **A.** `/etc/auto_master`

❍ **B.** `/etc/auto_direct`

❍ **C.** `/etc/auto_share`

❍ **D.** `/lib/svc/method/svc-autofs`

25. Every Solaris installation comes with a default master map with default entries. Without any changes to the generic system setup, clients should be able to access remote file systems through which of the following mount points?

❍ **A.** `/tmp_mnt`

❍ **B.** `/net`

❍ **C.** `/export`

❍ **D.** `/export/home`

26. Which of the following is the simplest and most useful AutoFS map?

- ❍ **A.** Direct map
- ❍ **B.** Indirect map
- ❍ **C.** Master map
- ❍ **D.** All are equal

27. What is the default time for `automountd` to unmount a file system that is not in use?

- ❍ **A.** 600 seconds
- ❍ **B.** 60 seconds
- ❍ **C.** 120 seconds
- ❍ **D.** 180 seconds

28. What types of maps are available in AutoFS?

- ❍ **A.** Direct and indirect
- ❍ **B.** Master, direct, and indirect
- ❍ **C.** Master and direct
- ❍ **D.** Master and indirect

29. Which of the following commands is used to cause a disk resource to be made available to other systems via NFS?

- ❍ **A.** `mount`
- ❍ **B.** `share`
- ❍ **C.** `export`
- ❍ **D.** `dfshares`

30. Which of the following scripts or services starts up the NFS log daemon?

- ❍ **A.** `/usr/lib/nfs/nfslogd`
- ❍ **B.** `/etc/nfs/nfslog.conf`
- ❍ **C.** `/etc/dfs/dfstab`
- ❍ **D.** `/etc/default/nfs`

31. Which of the following daemons provides NFS logging?

   ❍ **A.** `syslogd`

   ❍ **B.** `nfsd`

   ❍ **C.** `statd`

   ❍ **D.** `nfslogd`

Answers to Exam Questions

1. **A.** After you create and add additional swap space, you can add an entry for that swap space in the `/etc/vfstab` file to ensure that the swap space is available following subsequent reboots. For more information, see the section "Setting Up Swap Space."
2. **C.** You use the `mkfile` and `swap` commands to designate a part of an existing UFS as a supplementary swap area. For more information, see the section "Setting Up Swap Space."
3. **C.** The `swap -s` command is used to display the available swap space on a system. For more information, see the section "Setting Up Swap Space."
4. **B.** Swap areas are activated by the `/sbin/swapadd` script each time the system boots. For more information, see the section "Setting Up Swap Space."
5. **A, C, D.** These statements are all true of a swap area: An NFS file system can be used for a swap area; a swap file is created in any ordinary file system; and you cannot unmount a file system while a swap file is in use. For more information, see the section "Setting Up Swap Space."
6. **A.** If you execute the `shareall` command, any new entries in the `/etc/dfs/dfstab` file are shared. If you execute the `unshareall` command, any entries in the `/etc/dfs/dfstab` file are unshared. For more information, see the section "Setting Up NFS."
7. **C.** To restart NFS to enable a new share, you type `svcadm restart nfs/server`. For more information, see the section "NFS Daemons."
8. **C.** The `automount` command, which is called at system startup time, reads the master map file named `auto_master` to create the initial set of AutoFS mounts. For more information, see the section "AutoFS."
9. **D.** With a `direct` map, there is a direct association between a mount point on the client and a directory on the server. A `direct` map has a full pathname and indicates the relationship explicitly. For more information, see the section "AutoFS Maps."
10. **A, B.** NFS uses a number of daemons to handle its services. These services are initialized at startup from the `svc:/network/nfs/server` and `svc:/network/nfs/client` service identifiers. For more information, see the section "NFS Daemons."
11. **A.** `mountd`, `lockd`, and `statd` are all NFS daemons. `rpcd` is not an NFS daemon. For more information, see the section "NFS Daemons."

12. **A, B, D.** The NFS daemons found only on the NFS server are `nfsd`, `lockd`, and `nfslogd`. For more information, see the section "NFS Daemons."

13. **B.** A shared file system is referred to as a shared resource. You specify which file systems are to be shared by entering the information in the file `/etc/dfs/dfstab`. For more information, see the section "Setting Up NFS."

14. **B.** The `share` command exports a resource and makes a resource available for mounting. For more information, see the section "Setting Up NFS."

15. **C.** The `dfshares` command displays information about the shared resources that are available to the host from an NFS server. For more information, see the section "Setting Up NFS."

16. **C.** File systems mounted with the `bg` option indicate that `mount` is to retry in the background if the server's mount daemon (`mountd`) does not respond when, for example, the NFS server is restarted. For more information, see the section "Mounting a Remote File System."

17. **B.** After the file system is mounted, each NFS request made in the kernel waits a specified number of seconds for a response (which is specified with the `timeo=`<*n*> option). For more information, see the section "Mounting a Remote File System."

18. **A.** Sun recommends that file systems that are mounted as read-write or that contain executable files should always be mounted with the `hard` option. For more information, see the section "Mounting a Remote File System."

19. **A.** From the NFS client, `mount` retries the request up to the count specified in the `retry=`<*n*> option. After the file system is mounted, each NFS request that is made in the kernel waits a specified number of seconds for a response. For more information, see the section "Mounting a Remote File System."

20. **C.** If a file system is mounted hard and the `intr` option is not specified, the process hangs until the remote file system reappears if the NFS server goes down. If `intr` is specified, sending an interrupt signal to the process kills it. For more information, see the section "Mounting a Remote File System."

21. **A, B.** File systems that are shared through the NFS service can be mounted by using AutoFS. AutoFS, a client-side service, is a file system structure that provides automatic mounting. AutoFS is initialized by `automount`, which is run automatically when a system is started. The automount daemon, named `automountd`, runs continuously, mounting and unmounting remote directories on an as-needed basis. For more information, see the section "AutoFS."

22. **B.** Two programs support the AutoFS service: `automount` and `automountd`. Both are run when a system is started by the `svc:/system/filesystem/autofs` service identifier. For more information, see the section "AutoFS."

23. **C.** To see who is using a particular NFS mount, you use the `showmount` command. For more information, see the section "AutoFS."

24. **A.** A master map, which is in the `/etc/auto_master` file, associates a directory with a map. A master map is a list that specifies all the maps that AutoFS should check. For more information, see the section "AutoFS Maps."

25. **B.** Without any changes to the generic system setup, clients should be able to access remote file systems through the `/net` mount point. For more information, see the section "AutoFS Maps."

26. **B.** Indirect maps are the simplest and most useful maps. Indirect maps are useful for accessing specific file systems, such as home directories, from anywhere on the network. For more information, see the section "AutoFS Maps."

27. **A.** The `-t` option to the `automount` command sets the time, in seconds, that a file system is to remain mounted if it is not being used. The default is 600 seconds. For more information, see the section "AutoFS."

28. **B.** The three types of AutoFS maps are master, direct, and indirect maps. For more information, see the section "AutoFS Maps."

29. **B.** The `share` command is used to specify a disk resource that is to be made available to other systems via NFS. `share` exports a resource or makes a resource available for mounting. For more information, see the section "Setting Up NFS."

30. **A.** The `/usr/lib/nfs/nfslogd` script starts up the NFS log daemon (`nfslogd`). For more information, see the section "NFS Server Logging."

31. **D.** The `nfslogd` daemon provides NFS logging and is enabled by using the `log=<tag>` option in the `share` command. When NFS logging is enabled, all NFS operations on the file system are recorded in a buffer by the kernel. For more information, see the section "NFS Server Logging."

Suggested Reading and Resources

"System Administration Guide: Advanced Administration," and "System Administration Guide: Network Services" manuals from the Solaris 10 documentation CD.

"System Administration Guide: Network Services," and "System Administration Guide: Advanced Administration" books in the System Administration Collection of the Solaris 10 documentation set. See `http://docs.sun.com`.

CHAPTER TEN

Managing Storage Volumes

Objectives

The following test objectives for Exam CX-310-202 are covered in this chapter:

Analyze and explain RAID (0, 1, 5) and SVM concepts (logical volumes, soft partitions, state databases, hot spares, and hot spare pools).

- A thorough understanding of the most popular RAID levels is essential to any system administrator managing disk storage. This chapter covers all the basic Solaris Volume Manager (SVM) concepts that the system administrator needs to know for the exam.

Create the state database, build a mirror, and unmirror the root file system.

- The system administrator needs to be able to manipulate the state database replicas and create logical volumes, such as mirrors (RAID 1). This chapter details the procedure for creating the state databases as well as mirroring and unmirroring the root file system.

Outline

Study Strategies

The following strategies will help you prepare for the test:

- As you study this chapter, the main objective is to become comfortable with the terms and concepts that are introduced.
- For this chapter it's important that you practice, on a Solaris system (ideally with more than one disk), each step-by-step and each command that is presented. Practice is very important on these topics, so you should practice until you can repeat each procedure from memory.
- Be sure that you understand the levels of RAID discussed and the differences between them.
- Be sure that you know all of the terms listed in the "Key Terms" section at the end of this chapter. Pay special attention to metadevices and the different types that are available.

Introduction

With standard disk devices, each disk slice has its own physical and logical device. In addition, with standard Solaris file systems, a file system cannot span more than one disk slice. In other words, the maximum size of a file system is limited to the size of a single disk. On a large server with many disk drives, standard methods of disk slicing are inadequate and inefficient. This was a limitation in all Unix systems until the introduction of virtual disks, also called *virtual volumes*. To eliminate the limitation of one slice per file system, there are virtual volume management packages that are able to create virtual volume structures in which a single file system can consist of nearly an unlimited number of disks or partitions. The key feature of these virtual volume management packages is that they transparently provide a virtual volume that can consist of many physical disk partitions. In other words, disk partitions are grouped across several disks to appear as one single volume to the operating system.

Each flavor of Unix has its own method of creating virtual volumes, and Sun has addressed virtual volume management with their Solaris Volume Manager product called SVM, which is included as part of the standard Solaris 10 release.

The objectives in the Part II exam have changed so that you are now required to be able to set up virtual disk volumes. This chapter introduces you to SVM and describes SVM in enough depth to meet the objectives of the certification exam. It is by no means a complete reference for SVM.

Also in this chapter, we have included a brief introduction of Veritas Volume Manager, an unbundled product that is purchased separately. Even though this product is not specifically included in the objectives for the exam, it provides some useful background information.

RAID

Objective:

Analyze and explain RAID 0, 1, 5.

When describing SVM volumes, it's common to describe which level of RAID the volume conforms to. RAID is an acronym for *Redundant Array of Inexpensive (or Independent) Disks*. Usually these disks are housed together in a cabinet and referred to as an *array*. There are several RAID levels, each referring to a method of organizing data while ensuring data resilience or performance. These levels are not ratings, but rather classifications of functionality. Different RAID levels offer dramatic differences in performance, data availability, and data integrity depending on the specific I/O environment. Table 10.1 describes the various levels of RAID.

TABLE 10.1 RAID Levels

RAID Level	Description
0	Striped disk array without fault tolerance.
1	Maintains duplicate sets of all data on separate disk drives (mirroring).
2	Data striping and bit interleave. Data is written across each drive in succession one bit at a time. Checksum data is recorded in a separate drive. This method is very slow for disk writes and is seldom used today since Error Checking and Correction (ECC) is embedded in almost all modern disk drives.
3	Data striping with bit interleave and parity checking. Data is striped across a set of disks one byte at a time, and parity is generated and stored on a dedicated disk. The parity information is used to re-create data in the event of a disk failure.
4	This is the same as level 3 RAID except data is striped across a set of disks at a block level. Parity is generated and stored on a dedicated disk.
5	Unlike RAID 3 and 4, where parity is stored on one disk, both parity and data are striped across a set of disks.
6	Similar to RAID 5, but with additional parity information written to recover data if two drives fail.
1+0	Combination of RAID 1 mirrors that are then striped.

RAID level 0 does not provide data redundancy, but is usually included as a RAID classification because it is the basis for the majority of RAID configurations in use. Table 10.1 described some of the more popular RAID levels; however, many are not provided in SVM. The following is a more in-depth description of the RAID levels provided in SVM.

EXAM ALERT

RAID Levels For the exam, you should be familiar with RAID levels 0, 1, 5, and 1+0. These are the only levels that can be used with Solaris Volume Manager.

RAID 0

Although they do not provide redundancy, stripes and concatenations are often referred to as RAID 0. With striping, data is spread across relatively small, equally sized fragments that are allocated alternately and evenly across multiple physical disks. Any single drive failure can cause the volume to fail and could result in data loss. RAID 0, especially true with stripes, offers a high data transfer rate and high I/O throughput, but suffers lower reliability and availability than a single disk.

RAID 1

RAID 1 employs data mirroring to achieve redundancy. Two copies of the data are created and maintained on separate disks, each containing a mirror image of the other. RAID 1 provides an opportunity to improve performance for reads because read requests will be directed to the mirrored copy if the primary copy is busy. RAID 1 is the most expensive of the array implementations because the data is duplicated. In the event of a disk failure, RAID 1 provides the highest performance because the system can switch automatically to the mirrored disk with minimal impact on performance and no need to rebuild lost data.

RAID 5

RAID 5 provides data striping with distributed parity. RAID 5 does not have a dedicated parity disk, but instead interleaves both data and parity on all disks. In RAID 5, the disk access arms can move independently of one another. This enables multiple concurrent accesses to the multiple physical disks, thereby satisfying multiple concurrent I/O requests and providing higher transaction throughput. RAID 5 is best suited for random access data in small blocks. There is a "write penalty" associated with RAID 5. Every write I/O will result in four actual I/O operations, two to read the old data and parity and two to write the new data and parity.

RAID 1+0

SVM supports both RAID 1+0 (mirrors that are then striped). This combines the benefits of RAID 1 for redundancy and RAID 0 for performance. If a device fails, the entire stripe or concatenation is not taken offline, only the failed device—a characteristic of 1+0.

Solaris Volume Manager (SVM)

Objective:

Analyze and explain SVM concepts (logical volumes, soft partitions, state databases, hot spares, and hot spare pools).

- Create the state database, build a mirror, and unmirror the root file system.

SVM, formerly called Solstice DiskSuite, comes bundled with the Solaris 10 operating system and uses virtual disks, called volumes, to manage physical disks and their associated data. A *volume* is functionally identical to a physical disk from the point of view of an application. You may also hear volumes referred to as virtual or pseudo devices.

A recent feature of SVM is soft partitions. This breaks the traditional eight-slices-per-disk barrier by allowing disks, or logical volumes, to be subdivided into many more partitions. One reason for doing this might be to create more manageable file systems, given the ever-increasing capacity of disks.

NOTE

SVM Terminology If you are familiar with Solstice DiskSuite, you'll remember that virtual disks were called *metadevices*. SVM uses a special driver, called the metadisk driver, to coordinate I/O to and from physical devices and volumes, enabling applications to treat a volume like a physical device. This type of driver is also called a *logical*, or *pseudo* driver.

In SVM, volumes are built from standard disk slices that have been created using the `format` utility. Using either the SVM command-line utilities or the graphical user interface of the Solaris Management Console (SMC), the system administrator creates each device by executing commands or dragging slices onto one of four types of SVM objects: volumes, disk sets, state database replicas, and hot spare pools. These elements are described in Table 10.2.

TABLE 10.2 SVM Elements

Object	Description
Volume	A *volume*, or *metadevice*, is a group of physical slices that appear to the system as a single, logical device. A volume is used to increase storage capacity and increase data availability. Solaris 10 SVM can support up to 8,192 logical volumes per disk set (see below), but the default is to support 128 logical volumes, namely `d0` thru `d127`. The various types of volumes are described in the next section of this chapter.
State database	A *state database* is a database that stores information about the state of the SVM configuration. Each state database is a collection of multiple, replicated database copies. Each copy is referred to as a state database replica. SVM cannot operate until you have created the state database and its replicas. You should create at least three state database replicas when using SVM because the validation process requires a majority (half + 1) of the state databases to be consistent with each other before the system will start up correctly. Each state database replica should ideally be physically located on a separate disk (and preferably a separate disk controller for added resilience).
Soft partition	A *soft partition* is a means of dividing a disk or volume into as many partitions as needed, overcoming the current limitation of eight. This is done by creating logical partitions within physical disk slices or logical volumes.
Disk set	A *disk set* is a set of disk drives containing state database replicas, volumes, and hot spares that can be shared exclusively, but not at the same time, by multiple hosts. If one host fails, another host can take over the failed host's disk set. This type of failover configuration is referred to as a *clustered environment*.
Hot spare	A *hot spare* is a slice that is reserved for use in case of a slice failure in another volume, such as a submirror or a RAID 5 metadevice. It is used to increase data availability.
Hot spare pool	A *hot spare pool* is a collection of *hot spares*. A *hot spare pool* can be used to provide a number of *hot spares* for specific volumes or metadevices. For example, a pool may be used to provide resilience for the rootdisk, while another pool provides resilience for data disks.

SVM Volumes

The types of SVM volumes you can create using Solaris Management Console or the SVM command-line utilities are concatenations, stripes, concatenated stripes, mirrors, and RAID 5 volumes. All of the SVM volumes are described in the following sections.

NOTE

No more Transactional Volumes As of Solaris 10, you should note that transactional volumes are no longer available with the Solaris Volume Manager (SVM). Use UFS logging to achieve the same functionality.

Concatenations

Concatenations work much the same way the Unix `cat` command is used to concatenate two or more files to create one larger file. If partitions are *concatenated*, the addressing of the component blocks is done on the components sequentially, which means that data is written to the first available slice until it is full, then moves to the next available slice. The file system can use the entire concatenation, even though it spreads across multiple disk drives. This type of volume provides no data redundancy, and the entire volume fails if a single slice fails. A concatenation can contain disk slices of different sizes because they are merely joined together.

Stripes

A *stripe* is similar to a concatenation, except that the addressing of the component blocks is interlaced on all of the slices comprising the stripe rather than sequentially. In other words, all disks are accessed at the same time in parallel. Striping is used to gain performance. When data is striped across disks, multiple controllers can access data simultaneously. An *interlace* refers to a grouped segment of blocks on a particular slice, the default value being 16K. Different interlace values can increase performance. For example, with a stripe containing five physical disks, if an I/O request is, say, 64K, then four chunks of data (16K each because of the interlace size) will be read simultaneously due to each sequential chunk residing on a separate slice.

The size of the interlace can be configured when the slice is created and cannot be modified afterward without destroying and recreating the stripe. In determining the size of the interlace, the specific application must be taken into account. If, for example, most of the I/O requests are for large amounts of data, say 10 Megabytes, then an interlace size of 2 Megabytes produces a significant performance increase when using a five disk stripe. You should note that, unlike a concatenation, the components making up a stripe must all be the same size.

Concatenated Stripes

A *concatenated stripe* is a stripe that has been expanded by concatenating additional striped slices.

Mirrors

A *mirror* is composed of one or more stripes or concatenations. The volumes that are mirrored are called *submirrors*. SVM makes duplicate copies of the data located on multiple physical disks, and presents one virtual disk to the application. All disk writes are duplicated; disk reads come from one of the underlying submirrors. A mirror replicates all writes to a single logical device (the mirror) and then to multiple devices (the submirrors) while distributing read operations. This provides redundancy of data in the event of a disk or hardware failure.

There are some mirror options that can be defined when the mirror is initially created, or following the setup. The options allow, for example, all reads to be distributed across the submirror components, improving the read performance. Table 10.3 describes the mirror read policies that can be configured.

TABLE 10.3 Mirror Read Policies

Read Policy	Description
Round Robin	This is the default policy and distributes the reads across submirrors.
Geometric	Reads are divided between the submirrors based on a logical disk block address.
First	This directs all reads to use the first submirror only.

Write performance can also be improved by configuring writes to all submirrors simultaneously. The trade-off with this option, however, is that all submirrors will be in an unknown state if a failure occurs. Table 10.4 describes the write policies that can be configured for mirror volumes.

TABLE 10.4 Mirror Write Policies

Write Policy	Description
Parallel	This is the default policy and directs the write operation to all submirrors simultaneously.
Serial	This policy specifies that writes to one submirror must complete before writes to the next submirror are started.

If a submirror goes offline, it must be resynchronized when the fault is resolved and it returns to service.

EXAM ALERT

Read and Write Policies Make sure you are familiar with the policies for both read and write as there have been exam questions that ask for the valid mirror policies.

RAID 5 Volumes

A RAID 5 volume stripes the data, as described in the "Stripes" section earlier, but in addition to striping, RAID 5 replicates data by using parity information. In the case of missing data, the data can be regenerated using available data and the parity information. A RAID 5 metadevice is composed of multiple slices. Some space is allocated to parity information and is distributed across all slices in the RAID 5 metadevice. The striped metadevice performance is better than the RAID 5 metadevice because the RAID 5 metadevice has a parity overhead, but merely striping doesn't provide data protection (redundancy).

Planning Your SVM Configuration

When designing your storage configuration, keep the following guidelines in mind:

- Striping generally has the best performance, but it offers no data protection. For write-intensive applications, RAID 1 generally has better performance than RAID 5.
- RAID 1 and RAID 5 volumes both increase data availability, but they both generally result in lower performance, especially for write operations. Mirroring does improve random read performance.
- RAID 5 requires less disk space, therefore RAID 5 volumes have a lower hardware cost than RAID 1 volumes. RAID 0 volumes have the lowest hardware cost.
- Identify the most frequently accessed data, and increase access bandwidth to that data with mirroring or striping.
- Both stripes and RAID 5 volumes distribute data across multiple disk drives and help balance the I/O load.
- Use available performance monitoring capabilities and generic tools such as the `iostat` command to identify the most frequently accessed data. Once identified, the "access bandwidth" to this data can be increased using striping.
- A RAID 0 stripe's performance is better than that of a RAID 5 volume, but RAID 0 stripes do not provide data protection (redundancy).
- RAID 5 volume performance is lower than stripe performance for write operations because the RAID 5 volume requires multiple I/O operations to calculate and store the parity.
- For raw random I/O reads, the RAID 0 stripe and the RAID 5 volume are comparable. Both the stripe and RAID 5 volume split the data across multiple disks, and the RAID 5 volume parity calculations aren't a factor in reads except after a slice failure.
- For raw random I/O writes, a stripe is superior to RAID 5 volumes.

EXAM ALERT

RAID Solutions You might get an exam question that describes an application and then asks which RAID solution would be best suited for it. For example, a financial application with mission-critical data would require mirroring to provide the best protection for the data, whereas a video editing application would require striping for the pure performance gain. Make sure you are familiar with the pros and cons of each RAID solution.

Using SVM, you can utilize volumes to provide increased capacity, higher availability, and better performance. In addition, the hot spare capability provided by SVM can provide another level of data availability for mirrors and RAID 5 volumes. *Hot spares* were described earlier in this chapter.

After you have set up your configuration, you can use Solaris utilities such as `iostat`, `metastat`, and `metadb` to report on its operation. The `iostat` utility is used to provide information on disk usage and will show you which metadevices are being heavily utilized, while the `metastat` and `metadb` utilities provide status information on the metadevices and state databases, respectively. As an example, the output shown below provides information from the `metastat` utility whilst two mirror metadevices are being synchronized:

```
# metastat -i
d60: Mirror
    Submirror 0: d61
      State: Okay
    Submirror 1: d62
      State: Resyncing
    Resync in progress: 15 % done
    Pass: 1
    Read option: roundrobin (default)
    Write option: parallel (default)
    Size: 10462032 blocks (5.0 GB)d61: Submirror of d60
    State: Okay
    Size: 10462032 blocks (5.0 GB)
    Stripe 0:
        Device     Start Block  Dbase        State Reloc Hot Spare
        c0t3d0s4           0     No           Okay   Yes
d62: Submirror of d60
    State: Resyncing
    Size: 10462032 blocks (5.0 GB)
    Stripe 0:
        Device     Start Block  Dbase        State Reloc Hot Spare
        c0t1d0s5           0     No           Okay   Yes
d50: Mirror
    Submirror 0: d51
      State: Okay
    Submirror 1: d52
      State: Resyncing
```

```
    Resync in progress: 26 % done
    Pass: 1
    Read option: roundrobin (default)
    Write option: parallel (default)
    Size: 4195296 blocks (2.0 GB)
d51: Submirror of d50
    State: Okay
    Size: 4195296 blocks (2.0 GB)
    Stripe 0:
        Device      Start Block  Dbase        State Reloc Hot Spare
        c0t3d0s3           0     No            Okay   Yes
d52: Submirror of d50
    State: Resyncing
    Size: 4195296 blocks (2.0 GB)
    Stripe 0:
        Device      Start Block  Dbase        State Reloc Hot Spare
        c0t1d0s4           0     No            Okay   Yes
Device Relocation Information:
Device   Reloc  Device ID
c0t1d0   Yes    id1,dad@ASAMSUNG_SP0411N=S01JJ60X901935
c0t0d0   Yes    id1,dad@AWDC_AC310200R=WD-WT6750311269
#
```

Notice from the preceding output that there are two mirror metadevices, each containing two submirror component metadevices—`d60` contains submirrors `d61` and `d62`, and `d50` contains submirrors `d51` and `d52`. It can be seen that the metadevices `d52` and `d62` are in the process of resynchronization. Use of this utility is important as there could be a noticeable degradation of service during the resynchronization operation on these volumes, which can be closely monitored as `metastat` also displays the progress of the operation, in percentage complete terms. Further information on these utilities is available from the online manual pages.

You can also use SVM's Simple Network Management Protocol (SNMP) trap generating daemon to work with a network monitoring console to automatically receive SVM error messages. Configure SVM's SNMP trap to trap the following instances:

- A RAID 1 or RAID 5 subcomponent goes into "needs maintenance" state. A disk failure or too many errors would cause the software to mark the component as "needs maintenance."
- A hot spare volume is swapped into service.
- A hot spare volume starts to resynchronize.
- A hot spare volume completes resynchronization.
- A mirror is taken offline.
- A disk set is taken by another host and the current host panics.

The system administrator is now able to receive, and monitor, messages from SVM when an error condition or notable event occurs. All operations that affect SVM volumes are managed by the metadisk driver, which is described in the next section.

Metadisk Driver

The metadisk driver, the driver used to manage SVM volumes, is implemented as a set of loadable pseudo device drivers. It uses other physical device drivers to pass I/O requests to and from the underlying devices. The metadisk driver operates between the file system and application interfaces and the device driver interface. It interprets information from both the UFS or applications and the physical device drivers. After passing through the metadevice driver, information is received in the expected form by both the file system and the device drivers. The metadevice is a loadable device driver, and it has all the same characteristics as any other disk device driver.

The volume name begins with "d" and is followed by a number. By default, there are 128 unique metadisk devices in the range of 0 to 127. Additional volumes, up to 8192, can be added to the kernel by editing the `/kernel/drv/md.conf` file. The meta block device accesses the disk using the system's normal buffering mechanism. There is also a character (or raw) device that provides for direct transmission between the disk and the user's read or write buffer. The names of the block devices are found in the `/dev/md/dsk` directory, and the names of the raw devices are found in the `/dev/md/rdsk` directory. The following is an example of a block and raw logical device name for metadevice `d0`:

```
/dev/md/dsk/d0    - block metadevice d0
/dev/md/rdsk/d0   - raw metadevice d0
```

You must have root access to administer SVM or have equivalent privileges granted through RBAC. (RBAC is described in Chapter 11, "Controlling Access and Configuring System Messaging.")

SVM Commands

There are a number of SVM commands that will help you create, monitor, maintain and remove metadevices. All the commands are delivered with the standard Solaris 10 Operating Environment distribution. Table 10.5 briefly describes the function of the more frequently used commands that are available to the system administrator.

NOTE

Where They Live The majority of the SVM commands reside in the `/usr/sbin` directory, although you should be aware that `metainit`, `metadb`, `metastat`, `metadevadm`, and `metarecover` reside in `/sbin`—there are links to these commands in `/usr/sbin` as well.

TABLE 10.5 Solaris Volume Manager Commands

Command	Description
`metaclear`	Used to delete metadevices and can also be used to delete hot spare pools.
`metadb`	Used to create and delete the state database and its replicas.
`metadetach`	Used to detach a metadevice, typically removing one half of a mirror.
`metadevadm`	Used to update the metadevice information, an example being if a disk device changes its target address (ID).
`metahs`	Used to manage hot spare devices and hot spare pools.
`metainit`	Used to configure metadevices. You would use `metainit` to create concatenations or striped metadevices.
`metattach`	Used to attach a metadevice, typically used when creating a mirror or adding additional mirrors.
`metaoffline`	Used to place submirrors in an offline state.
`metaonline`	Used to place submirrors in an online state.
`metareplace`	Used to replace components of submirrors or RAID5 metadevices. You would use `metareplace` when replacing a failed disk drive.
`metarecover`	Used to recover soft partition information.
`metaroot`	Used to set up the system files for the root metadevice. `metaroot` adds an entry to `/etc/system` and also updates `/etc/vfstab` to reflect the new device to use to mount the root (`/`) file system.
`metastat`	Used to display the status of a metadevice, all metadevices, or hot spare pools.

NOTE

No More `metatool` You should note that the `metatool` command is no longer available in Solaris 10. Similar functionality—managing metadevices through a graphical utility—can be achieved using the Solaris Management Console (SMC), specifically the Enhanced Storage section.

Creating the State Database

The SVM state database contains vital information on the configuration and status of all volumes, hot spares, and disk sets. There are normally multiple copies of the state database, called *replicas*, and it is recommended that state database replicas be located on different physical disks, or even different controllers if possible, to provide added resilience.

The state database, together with its replicas, guarantees the integrity of the state database by using a *majority consensus algorithm*. The algorithm used by SVM for database replicas is as follows:

- The system will continue to run if at least half of the state database replicas are available.
- The system will panic if fewer than half of the state database replicas are available.
- The system cannot reboot into multi-user mode unless a majority (half+1) of the total number of state database replicas are available.

NOTE

No Automatic Problem Detection The SVM software does not detect problems with state database replicas until there is a change to an existing SVM configuration and an update to the database replicas is required. If insufficient state database replicas are available, you'll need to boot to single-user mode, and delete or replace enough of the corrupted or missing database replicas to achieve a quorum.

If a system crashes and corrupts a state database replica then the majority of the remaining replicas must be available and consistent; that is, half + 1. This is why at least three state database replicas must be created initially to allow for the majority algorithm to work correctly.

You also need to put some thought into the placement of your state database replicas. The following are some guidelines:

- When possible, create state database replicas on a dedicated slice that is at least 4MB in size for each database replica that it will store.
- You cannot create state database replicas on slices containing existing file systems or data.
- When possible, place state database replicas on slices that are on separate disk drives. If possible, use drives that are on different host bus adapters.
- When distributing your state database replicas, follow these rules:
  - Create three replicas on one slice for a system with a single disk drive. Realize, however, if the drive fails, all your database replicas will be unavailable and your system will crash.
  - Create two replicas on each drive for a system with two to four disk drives.
  - Create one replica on each drive for a system with five or more drives.

The state database and its replicas are managed using the `metadb` command. The syntax of this command is

```
/sbin/metadb -h
     /sbin/metadb [-s setname]
     /sbin/metadb [-s setname] -a [-f] [-k system-file] mddbnn
```

```
/sbin/metadb [-s setname] -a [-f] [-k system-file] [- c number]\
➥[-l length] slice...
/sbin/metadb [-s setname] -d [-f] [-k system-file] mddbnn
/sbin/metadb [-s setname] -d [-f] [-k system-file] slice...
/sbin/metadb [-s setname] -i
/sbin/metadb [-s setname] -p [-k system-file] [mddb.cf-file]
```

Table 10.6 describes the options available for the `metadb` command.

TABLE 10.6 `metadb` Command Options

Option	Description
`-a`	Specifies the creation of a new database replica.
`-c` *<number>*	Specifies the number of replicas to be created on each device. The default is 1.
`-d`	Deletes all the replicas that are present in the specified `slice`.
`-f`	Forces the creation of the first database replica (when used in conjunction with the `-a` option) and the deletion of the last remaining database replica (when used in conjunction with the `-d` option).
`-h`	Displays the usage message.
`-i`	Displays status information about all database replicas.
`-k` *<system-file>*	Specifies the name of the kernel file where the replica information should be written; by default, this is `/kernel/drv/md.conf`.
`-l` *<length>*	Specifies the size (in blocks) of each replica. The default length is 8,192 blocks.
`-p`	Specifies that the system file (default is `/kernel/drv/md.conf`) should be updated with entries from `/etc/lvm/mddb.cf`.
`-s` *<setname>*	Specifies the name of the diskset on which `metadb` should run.
`slice`	Specifies the disk slice to use; for example, `/dev/dsk/c0t0d0s6`.

In the following example, I have reserved a slice (slice 4) on each of two disks to hold the copies of the state database, and I'll create two copies in each reserved disk slice, giving a total of four state database replicas. In this scenario, the failure of one disk drive will result in a loss of more than half of the operational state database replicas, but the system will continue to function. The system will panic only when more than half of the database replicas are lost. For example, if I had created only three database replicas and the drive containing two of the replicas fails, the system will panic.

To create the state database and its replicas, using the reserved disk slices, enter the following command:

```
# metadb -a -f -c2 c0t0d0s4 c0t1d0s4
```

Here, `-a` indicates a new database is being added, `-f` forces the creation of the initial database, `-c2` indicates that two copies of the database are to be created, and the two `cxtxdxsx` entries describe where the state databases are to be physically located. The system returns the prompt; there is no confirmation that the database has been created.

The following example demonstrates how to remove the state database replicas from two disk slices, namely `c0t0d0s4` and `c0t1d0s4`:

```
# metadb -d c0t0d0s4 c0t1d0s4
```

The next section shows how to verify the status of the state database.

Monitoring the Status of the State Database

When the state database and its replicas have been created, you can use the `metadb` command, with no options, to see the current status. If you use the `-i` flag then you will also see a description of the status flags.

Examine the state database as shown here:

```
# metadb -i
        flags           first blk       block count
     a m  p  luo        16              8192            /dev/dsk/c0t0d0s4
     a    p  luo        8208            8192            /dev/dsk/c0t0d0s4
     a    p  luo        16              8192            /dev/dsk/c0t1d0s4
     a    p  luo        8208            8192            /dev/dsk/c0t1d0s4
 r - replica does not have device relocation information
 o - replica active prior to last mddb configuration change
 u - replica is up to date
 l - locator for this replica was read successfully
 c - replica's location was in /etc/lvm/mddb.cf
 p - replica's location was patched in kernel
 m - replica is master, this is replica selected as input
 W - replica has device write errors
 a - replica is active, commits are occurring to this replica
 M - replica had problem with master blocks
 D - replica had problem with data blocks
 F - replica had format problems
 S - replica is too small to hold current data base
 R - replica had device read errors
```

Each line of output is divided into the following fields:

- `flags`—This field will contain one or more state database status letters. A normal status is a "u" and indicates that the database is up-to-date and active. Uppercase status letters indicate a problem and lowercase letters are informational only.
- `first blk`—The starting block number of the state database replica in its partition. Multiple state database replicas in the same partition will show different starting blocks.

- `block count`—The size of the replica in disk blocks. The default length is 8192 blocks (4MB), but the size could be increased if you anticipate creating more than 128 metadevices, in which case, you would need to increase the size of all state databases.

The last field in each state database listing is the path to the location of the state database replica.

As the code shows, there is one master replica; all four replicas are active and up to date and have been read successfully.

Recovering from State Database Problems

SVM requires that at least half of the state database replicas must be available for the system to function correctly. When a disk fails or some of the state database replicas become corrupt, they must be removed with the system at the Single User state, to allow the system to boot correctly. When the system is operational again (albeit with fewer state database replicas), additional replicas can again be created.

The following example shows a system with two disks, each with two state database replicas on slices `c0t0d0s7` and `c0t1d0s7`.

If we run `metadb -i`, we can see that the state database replicas are all present and working correctly:

```
# metadb -i
        flags           first blk       block count
     a m  p  luo        16              8192            /dev/dsk/c0t0d0s7
     a    p  luo        8208            8192            /dev/dsk/c0t0d0s7
     a    p  luo        16              8192            /dev/dsk/c0t1d0s7
     a    p  luo        8208            8192            /dev/dsk/c0t1d0s7
 r - replica does not have device relocation information
 o - replica active prior to last mddb configuration change
 u - replica is up to date
 l - locator for this replica was read successfully
 c - replica's location was in /etc/lvm/mddb.cf
 p - replica's location was patched in kernel
 m - replica is master, this is replica selected as input
 W - replica has device write errors
 a - replica is active, commits are occurring to this replica
 M - replica had problem with master blocks
 D - replica had problem with data blocks
 F - replica had format problems
 S - replica is too small to hold current data base
 R - replica had device read errors
```

Subsequently, a disk failure or corruption occurs on the disk `c0t1d0` and renders the two replicas unusable. The `metadb -i` command shows that there are write errors on the two replicas on `c0t1d0s7`:

```
metadb -i
        flags           first blk       block count
     a m  p  luo        16              8192            /dev/dsk/c0t0d0s7
     a    p  luo        8208            8192            /dev/dsk/c0t0d0s7
     M    p             16              unknown         /dev/dsk/c0t1d0s7
     M    p             8208            unknown         /dev/dsk/c0t1d0s7
 r - replica does not have device relocation information
 o - replica active prior to last mddb configuration change
 u - replica is up to date
 l - locator for this replica was read successfully
 c - replica's location was in /etc/lvm/mddb.cf
 p - replica's location was patched in kernel
 m - replica is master, this is replica selected as input
 W - replica has device write errors
 a - replica is active, commits are occurring to this replica
 M - replica had problem with master blocks
 D - replica had problem with data blocks
 F - replica had format problems
 S - replica is too small to hold current data base
 R - replica had device read errors
```

When the system is rebooted, the following messages appear:

```
Insufficient metadevice database replicas located.
Use metadb to delete databases which are broken.
Ignore any Read-only file system error messages.
Reboot the system when finished to reload the metadevice database.
After reboot, repair any broken database replicas which were deleted.
```

To repair the situation, you will need to be in single-user mode, so boot the system with `-s` and then remove the failed state database replicas on `c0t1d0s7`.

```
# metadb -d c0t1d0s7
```

Now reboot the system again—it will boot with no problems, although you now have fewer state database replicas. This will enable you to repair the failed disk and re-create the metadevice state database replicas.

Creating a Concatenated Volume

You create a simple volume when you want to place an existing file system under SVM control. The command to create a simple volume is `metainit`. Here is the syntax for `metainit`:

```
/sbin/metainit -h
/sbin/metainit [generic options]  concat/stripe  numstripes
/sbin/metainit [generic options]  mirror   -m submirror
/sbin/metainit [generic options]  RAID  -r component... [-i interlace]
/sbin/metainit [generic options]  -a
/sbin/metainit [generic options]  softpart -p [-e]  component size
/sbin/metainit -r
```

Table 10.7 describes the options available for the `metainit` command.

TABLE 10.7 `metainit` Command Options

Option	Description
`-f`	A generic option that forces the `metainit` command to continue even if one of the slices contains a mounted file system or is being used as swap. This option is necessary if you are configuring mirrors on root (`/`), swap, or `/usr`.
`-h`	A generic option that displays a usage message.
`-n`	A generic option that checks the syntax of the command without actually executing it.
`-r`	A generic option that is used in shell scripts to set up all metadevices that were previously enabled before the system either crashed or was shut down. Information about previously configured metadevices is obtained from the state database.
`concat/stripe`	Specifies the name (`dxxx`) of the concatenation, stripe, or concat/stripe being defined.
`numstripes`	Specifies the number of stripes in the metadevice. For a simple stripe, this will be `1`.
`component`	Specifies the logical name of the physical disk slice being configured, such as `/dev/dsk/c0t0d0s0`. For a RAID5 stripe, there must be a minimum of three slices.
`mirror -m submirror`	Specifies the metadevice name of the mirror. The `-m` indicates that a mirror is being configured, and `submirror` identifies the metadevice that creates the initial one-way mirror.
`RAID -r`	Specifies the name of the RAID5 metadevice. The `-r` indicates that the configuration is a RAID5 metadevice.
`-i` *<interlace>*	Specifies the interlace parameter. This tells SVM how much data to write to a stripe or RAID5 metadevice before moving on to the next component in the stripe or RAID5 metadevice. The default is 16k.
`-a`	Activates all the metadevices specified in the `/etc/lvm/md.tab` file.

In the following example, a simple concatenation metadevice will be created using the disk slice `/dev/dsk/c0t0d0s5`. The metadevice will be named `d100`:

```
# metainit -f d100 1 1 c0t0d0s5
d100: Concat/Stripe is setup
```

Monitoring the Status of a Volume

Solaris Volume Manager provides the `metastat` command to monitor the status of all volumes. The syntax of this command is as follows:

```
/usr/sbin/metastat -h
/usr/sbin/metastat [-a] [-B] [-c] [-i] [-p] [-q] [-s setname] component
```

Table 10.8 describes the options for the `metastat` command.

TABLE 10.8 `metastat` Command Options

Option	Description
`-a`	Displays the metadevices for all disksets owned by the current host.
`-B`	Displays the status of all 64-bit metadevices and hot spares.
`-c`	Displays concise output, only one line per metadevice.
`-h`	Displays a usage message.
`-i`	Checks the status of RAID1 (mirror) volumes as well as RAID5 and hot spares.
`-p`	Displays the list of active metadevices and hot spare pools. The output is displayed in the same format as the configuration file `md.tab`.
`-q`	Displays the status of metadevices, but without the device relocation information.
`-s` <*diskset*>	Restricts the status to that of the specified *diskset*.
`-t`	Displays the status and timestamp of the metadevices and hot spares. The timestamp shows the date and time of the last state change.
`component`	Specifies the component or metadevice to restrict the output. If this option is omitted, the status of all metadevices is displayed.

In the following example, the `metastat` command is used to display the status of a single metadevice, `d100`:

```
# metastat d100
d100: Concat/Stripe
    Size: 10489680 blocks (5.0 GB)
    Stripe 0:
        Device      Start Block  Dbase        State Reloc Hot Spare
        c0t0d0s5           0     No            Okay   Yes

Device Relocation Information:
Device   Reloc  Device ID
c0t1d0   Yes    id1,dad@ASAMSUNG_SP0411N=S01JJ60X901935
```

In the next example, the `metastat -c` command displays the status for the same metadevice (`d100`), but this time in concise format:

```
# metastat -c d100
d100             s  5.0GB c0t0d0s5
```

Creating a Soft Partition

Soft partitions are used to divide large partitions into smaller areas, or *extents*, without the limitations imposed by hard slices. The soft partition is created by specifying a start block and a block size. Soft partitions differ from hard slices created using the `format` command because soft partitions can be non-contiguous, whereas a hard slice is contiguous. Therefore, soft partitions can cause I/O performance degradation.

A soft partition can be built on a disk slice or another SVM volume, such as a concatenated device. You'll create soft partitions using the SVM command `metainit`. For example, let's say that we have a hard slice named `c2t1d0s1` that is 10GB in size and was created using the `format` command. To create a soft partition named `d10` which is 1GB in size, and assuming that you've already created the required database replicas, issue the following command:

```
# metainit d10 -p c2t1d0s1 1g
```

The system responds with

```
d10: Soft Partition is setup
```

View the soft partition using the `metastat` command:

```
# metastat d10
d10: Soft Partition
    Device: c2t1d0s1
    State: Okay
    Size: 2097152 blocks (1.0 GB)
        Device      Start Block  Dbase Reloc
        c2t1d0s1       25920      Yes   Yes

        Extent              Start Block              Block count
             0                    25921                  2097152

Device Relocation Information:
Device   Reloc  Device ID
c2t1d0   Yes    id1,sd@SIBM_____DDRS34560SUN4.2G564442__________
```

Create a file system on the soft partition using the `newfs` command as follows:

```
# newfs /dev/md/rdsk/d10
```

Now you can mount a directory named `/data` onto the soft partition as follows:

```
# mount /dev/md/dsk/d10 /data
```

To remove the soft partition named `d10`, unmount the file system that is mounted to the soft partition and issue the `metaclear` command as follows:

```
# metaclear d10
```

CAUTION

Removing the soft partition destroys all data that is currently stored on that partition.

The system responds with

```
d10: Soft Partition is cleared
```

Expanding an SVM Volume

With SVM, you can increase the size of a file system while it is active and without unmounting the file system. The process of expanding a file system consists of first increasing the size of the SVM volume, and then growing the file system that has been created on the partition. In Step by Step 10.1, I'll increase the size of a soft partition and the file system mounted on it.

STEP BY STEP

10.1 Increasing the Size of a Mounted File System

1. Check the current size of the `/data` file system, as follows:

   ```
   # df -h /data
   Filesystem            size   used  avail capacity  Mounted on
   /dev/md/dsk/d10       960M   1.0M   901M     1%    /data
   ```

   Note that the size of `/data` is currently 960MB.

   A `metastat -c` shows the size as 12GB:

   ```
   # metastat -c d10
   d10              p  1.0GB c2t1d0s1
   ```

2. Use the `metattach` command to increase the SVM volume named `d10` from 1GB to 2GB as follows:

   ```
   # metattach d10 1gb
   ```

   Another `metastat -c` shows that the soft partition is now 2GB, as follows:

   ```
   # metastat -c d10
   d10              p  2.0GB c2t1d0s1
   ```

   Check the size of `/data` again, and note that the size did not change:

   ```
   # df -h /data
   Filesystem            size   used  avail capacity  Mounted on
   /dev/md/dsk/d10       960M   1.0M   901M     1%    /data
   ```

3. To increase the mounted file system /data, use the growfs command as follows:

```
# growfs -M /data /dev/md/rdsk/d10
Warning: 416 sector(s) in last cylinder unallocated
/dev/md/rdsk/d10:       4194304 sectors in 1942 cylinders of 16 tracks,
135 sectors
        2048.0MB in 61 cyl groups (32 c/g, 33.75MB/g, 16768 i/g)
super-block backups (for fsck -F ufs -o b=#) at:
 32, 69296, 138560, 207824, 277088, 346352, 415616, 484880, 554144, 623408,
 3525584, 3594848, 3664112, 3733376, 3802640, 3871904, 3941168, 4010432,
 4079696, 4148960,
```

Another df -h /data command shows that the /data file system has been increased as follows:

```
# df -h /data
Filesystem            size   used  avail capacity  Mounted on
/dev/md/dsk/d10       1.9G   2.0M   1.9G     1%    /data
```

Soft partitions can be built on top of concatenated devices, and you can increase a soft partition as long as there is room on the underlying metadevice. For example, you can't increase a 1GB soft partition if the metadevice on which it is currently built is only 1GB in size. However, you could add another slice to the underlying metadevice d9.

In Step by Step 10.2 we will create an SVM device on c2t1d0s1 named d9 that is 4GB in size. We then will create a 3GB soft partition named d10 built on this device. To add more space to d10, we first need to increase the size of d9, and the only way to accomplish this is to add more space to d9, as described in the Step by Step.

STEP BY STEP

10.2 Concatenate a New Slice to an Existing Slice

1. Log in as root and create metadbs as described earlier in this chapter.
2. Use the metainit command to create a simple SVM volume on c2t1d0s1 as follows:

```
# metainit d9 1 1 c2t1d0s1
d9: Concat/Stripe is setup
```

Use the metastat command to view the simple metadevice named d9 as follows:

```
# metastat d9
d9: Concat/Stripe
    Size: 8311680 blocks (4.0 GB)
    Stripe 0:
        Device     Start Block  Dbase        State Reloc Hot Spare
        c2t1d0s1      25920     Yes           Okay   Yes
```

```
Device Relocation Information:
Device   Reloc  Device ID
c2t1d0   Yes    id1,sd@SIBM_____DDRS34560SUN4.2G564442__________
```

3. Create a 3GB soft partition on top of the simple device as follows:

```
#  metainit d10 -p d9 3g
d10: Soft Partition is setup
```

4. Before we can add more space to d10, we first need to add more space to the simple volume by concatenating another 3.9GB slice (c2t2d0s1) to d9 as follows:

```
# metattach d9 c2t2d0s1
d9: component is attached
```

The metastat command shows the following information about d9:

```
# metastat d9
d9: Concat/Stripe
    Size: 16670880 blocks (7.9 GB)
    Stripe 0:
        Device      Start Block  Dbase         State Reloc Hot Spare
        c2t1d0s1       25920     Yes            Okay   Yes
    Stripe 1:
        Device      Start Block  Dbase         State Reloc Hot Spare
        c2t2d0s1           0     No             Okay   Yes

Device Relocation Information:
Device   Reloc  Device ID
c2t1d0   Yes    id1,sd@SIBM_____DDRS34560SUN4.2G564442__________
c2t2d0   Yes    id1,sd@SIBM_____DDRS34560SUN4.2G3Z1411__________
```

Notice that the metadevice d9 is made up of two disk slices (c2t1d0s1 and c2t2d0s1) and that the total size of d9 is now 7.9GB.

5. Now we can increase the size of the metadevice d10 using the metattach command described in Step by Step 10.1.

Creating a Mirror

A *mirror* is a logical volume that consists of more than one metadevice, also called a *submirror*. In this example, there are two physical disks: c0t0d0 and c0t1d0. Slice 5 is free on both disks, which will comprise the two submirrors, d12 and d22. The logical mirror will be named d2; it is this device that will be used when a file system is created. Step by Step 10.3 details the whole process:

STEP BY STEP

10.3 Creating a Mirror

1. Create the two simple metadevices that will be used as submirrors first.

```
# metainit d12 1 1 c0t0d0s5
d12: Concat/Stripe is setup
# metainit d22 1 1 c0t1d0s5
d22: Concat/Stripe is setup
```

2. Having created the submirrors, now create the actual mirror device, d2, but only attach one of the submirrors—the second submirror will be attached manually.

```
# metainit d2 -m d12
d2: Mirror is setup
```

   At this point, a one-way mirror has been created.

3. Now attach the second submirror to the mirror device, d2.

```
# metattach d2 d22
d2: Submirror d22 is attached
```

   At this point, a two-way mirror has been created and the second submirror will be synchronized with the first submirror to ensure they are both identical.

CAUTION

It is not recommended to create a mirror device and specify both submirrors on the command line, because even though it will work, there will not be a resynchronization between the two submirrors, which could lead to data corruption.

4. Verify that the mirror has been created successfully and that the two submirrors are being synchronized.

```
# metastat
d2: Mirror
    Submirror 0: d12
      State: Okay
    Submirror 1: d22
      State: Resyncing
    Resync in progress: 27 % done
    Pass: 1
    Read option: roundrobin (default)
    Write option: parallel (default)
    Size: 4194828 blocks (2.0 GB)
```

```
d12: Submirror of d2
    State: Okay
    Size: 4194828 blocks (2.0 GB)
    Stripe 0:
        Device      Start Block  Dbase        State Reloc Hot Spare
        c0t0d0s5          0      No            Okay   Yes

d22: Submirror of d2
    State: Resyncing
    Size: 4194828 blocks (2.0 GB)
    Stripe 0:
        Device      Start Block  Dbase        State Reloc Hot Spare
        c0t1d0s5          0      No            Okay   Yes
```

Notice that the status of d12, the first submirror, is *Okay*, and that the second submirror, d22, is currently *resyncing*, and is 27% complete. The mirror is now ready for use as a file system.

5. Create a UFS file system on the mirrored device:

```
# newfs /dev/md/rdsk/d2
newfs: construct a new file system /dev/md/rdsk/d2: (y/n)? y
Warning: 4016 sector(s) in last cylinder unallocated
/dev/md/rdsk/d2:        4194304 sectors in 1029 cylinders of 16 tracks, 255
sectors
        2048.0MB in 45 cyl groups (23 c/g, 45.82MB/g, 11264 i/g)
super-block backups (for fsck -F ufs -o b=#) at:
 32, 94128, 188224, 282320, 376416, 470512, 564608, 658704, 752800, 846896,
 3285200, 3379296, 3473392, 3567488, 3661584, 3755680, 3849776, 3943872,
 4037968, 4132064,
```

Note that it is the d2 metadevice that has the file system created on it.

6. Run `fsck` on the newly created file system before attempting to mount it. This step is not absolutely necessary, but is good practice because it verifies the state of a file system before it is mounted for the first time:

```
# fsck /dev/md/rdsk/d2
** /dev/md/rdsk/d2
** Last Mounted on
** Phase 1 - Check Blocks and Sizes
** Phase 2 - Check Pathnames
** Phase 3 - Check Connectivity
** Phase 4 - Check Reference Counts
** Phase 5 - Check Cyl groups
2 files, 9 used, 2033046 free (14 frags, 254129 blocks, 0.0% fragmentation)
```

The file system can now be mounted in the normal way. Remember to edit `/etc/vfstab` to make the mount permanent. Remember to use the md device and for this example, we'll mount the file system on `/mnt`.

```
# mount /dev/md/dsk/d2 /mnt
#
```

Unmirroring a Non-Critical File System

This section details the procedure for removing a mirror on a file system that can be removed and remounted without having to reboot the system. Step by Step 10.4 shows how to achieve this. This example uses a file system, /test, that is currently mirrored using the metadevice, d2; a mirror that consists of d12 and d22. The underlying disk slice for this file system is /dev/dsk/c0t0d0s5:

STEP BY STEP

10.4 Unmirror a Non-Critical File System

1. Unmount the /test file system.

```
# umount /test
```

2. Detach the submirror, d12, that is going to be used as a UFS file system.

```
# metadetach d2  d12
d2: submirror d12 is detached
```

3. Delete the mirror (d2) and the remaining submirror (d22).

```
# metaclear -r d2
d2: Mirror is cleared
d22: Concat/Stripe is cleared
```

At this point, the file system is no longer mirrored. It is worth noting that the metadevice, d12, still exists and can be used as the device to mount the file system. Alternatively, the full device name, /dev/dsk/c0t0d0s5, can be used if you do not want the disk device to support a volume. For this example, we will mount the full device name (as you would a normal UFS file system), so we will delete the d12 metadevice first.

4. Delete the d12 metadevice:

```
# metaclear d12
d22: Concat/Stripe is cleared
```

5. Edit /etc/vfstab to change the entry:

```
/dev/md/dsk/d2     /dev/md/rdsk/d2     /test  ufs  2  yes  -
```

to

```
/dev/dsk/c0t0d0s5 /dev/rdsk/c0t0d0s5 /test  ufs  2  yes  -
```

6. Remount the /test file system:

```
# mount /test
```

Mirroring the Root File System

In this section we will create another mirror, but this time it will be the root file system. This is different from Step by Step 10.3 because we are mirroring an existing file system that cannot be unmounted. We can't do this while the file system is mounted, so we'll configure the metadevice and a reboot will be necessary to implement the logical volume and to update the system configuration file. The objective is to create a two-way mirror of the root file system, currently residing on /dev/dsk/c0t0d0s0. We will use a spare disk slice of the same size, /dev/dsk/c0t1d0s0, for the second submirror. The mirror will be named d0, and the submirrors will be d10 and d20. Additionally, because this is the root (/) file system, we'll also configure the second submirror as an alternate boot device, so that this second slice can be used to boot the system if the primary slice becomes unavailable. Step by Step 10.5 shows the procedure to follow:

STEP BY STEP

10.5 Mirror the root File System

1. Verify that the current root file system is mounted from /dev/dsk/c0t0d0s0.

```
# df -h /
Filesystem             size   used  avail capacity  Mounted on
/dev/dsk/c0t0d0s0      4.9G   3.7G   1.2G    77%    /
```

2. Create the state database replicas, specifying the disk slices c0t0d0s4 and c0t0d0s5. We will be creating two replicas on each slice.

```
# metadb -a -f -c2 c0t0d0s4 c0t1d0s4
```

3. Create the two submirrors, d10 and d20.

```
# metainit -f d10 1 1 c0t0d0s0
d10: Concat/Stripe is setup
# metainit d20 1 1 c0t1d0s0
d20: Concat/Stripe is setup
```

   Note that the -f option was used in the first metainit command. This is the option to *force* the execution of the command, because we are creating a metadevice on an existing, mounted file system. The -f option was not necessary in the second metainit command because the slice is currently unused.

4. Create a one-way mirror, d0, specifying d10 as the submirror to attach.

```
# metainit d0 -m d10
d0: Mirror is setup
```

5. Set up the system files to support the new metadevice, after taking a backup copy of the files that will be affected. It is a good idea to name the copies with a relevant extension, so that they can be easily identified if you later have to revert to the original files, if problems are encountered. We will use the `.nosvm` extension in this step by step.

```
# cp /etc/system /etc/system.nosvm
# cp /etc/vfstab /etc/vfstab.nosvm
# metaroot d0
```

   The `metaroot` command has added the following lines to the system configuration file, `/etc/system`, to allow the system to boot with the / file system residing on a logical volume. This command is only necessary for the `root` device.

```
* Begin MDD root info (do not edit)
rootdev:/pseudo/md@0:0,0,blk
* End MDD root info (do not edit)
```

   It has also modified the `/etc/vfstab` entry for the / file system. It now reflects the metadevice to use to mount the file system at boot time:

```
/dev/md/dsk/d0  /dev/md/rdsk/d0 /       ufs     1       no      -
```

6. Synchronize file systems prior to rebooting the system.

```
# lockfs -fa
```

   The `lockfs` command is used to flush all buffers so that when the system is rebooted, the file systems are all up to date. This step is not compulsory, but is good practice.

7. Reboot the system.

```
# init 6
```

8. Verify that the `root` file system is now being mounted from the metadevice `/dev/md/dsk/d0`.

```
# df -h /
Filesystem             size   used  avail capacity  Mounted on
/dev/md/dsk/d0         4.9G   3.7G   1.2G    77%    /
```

9. The next step is to attach the second submirror and verify that a resynchronization operation is carried out.

```
# metattach d0 d20
d0: Submirror d20 is attached
# metastat
d0: Mirror
    Submirror 0: d10
      State: Okay
    Submirror 1: d20
      State: Resyncing
    Resync in progress: 62 % done
    Pass: 1
```

```
    Read option: roundrobin (default)
    Write option: parallel (default)
    Size: 10462032 blocks (5.0 GB)

d10: Submirror of d0
    State: Okay
    Size: 10462032 blocks (5.0 GB)
    Stripe 0:
        Device     Start Block  Dbase        State Reloc Hot Spare
        c0t0d0s0          0     No            Okay   Yes

d20: Submirror of d0
    State: Resyncing
    Size: 10462032 blocks (5.0 GB)
    Stripe 0:
        Device     Start Block  Dbase        State Reloc Hot Spare
        c0t1d0s0          0     No            Okay   Yes
```

10. Install a boot block on the second submirror to make this slice bootable. This step is necessary because it is the root (/) file system that is being mirrored.

```
# installboot /usr/platform/`uname -i`/lib/fs/ufs/bootblk /dev/rdsk/c0t1d0s0
#
```

The `uname -I` command substitutes the system's platform name.

11. Identify the physical device name of the second submirror. This will be required to assign an OpenBoot alias for a backup boot device.

```
# ls -l /dev/dsk/c0t1d0s0
lrwxrwxrwx   1 root     root          46 Mar 12  2005 /dev/dsk/c0t1d0s0 ->\
 ../../devices/pci@1f,0/pci@1,1/ide@3/dad@1,0:a
#
```

Record the address starting with `/pci...` and change the `dad` string to `disk`, leaving you, in this case, with `/pci@1f,0/pci@1,1/ide@3/disk@1,0:a`.

12. For this step you need to be at the ok prompt, so enter `init 0` to shut down the system.

```
# init 0
# svc.startd: The system is coming down.  Please wait.
svc.startd: 74 system services are now being stopped.
[ output truncated ]
ok
```

Enter the `nvalias` command to create an alias named `backup-root`, which points to the address recorded in step 11.

```
ok nvalias backup-root /pci@1f,0/pci@1,1/ide@3/disk@1,0:a
```

Now inspect the current setting of the boot-device variable and add the name backup-root as the secondary boot path, so that this device is used before going to the network. When this has been done, enter the nvstore command to save the alias created.

```
ok printenv boot-device
boot-device = disk net
ok setenv boot-device disk backup-root net
boot-device = disk backup-root net
ok nvstore
```

13. The final step is to boot the system from the second submirror to prove that it works. This can be done manually from the ok prompt, as follows:

```
ok boot backup-root
Resetting ...
[… output truncated]

Rebooting with command: boot backup-root
Boot device: /pci@1f,0/pci@1,1/ide@3/disk@1,0  File and args:
SunOS Release 5.10 Version Generic 64-bit
Copyright 1983-2005 Sun Microsystems, Inc.  All rights reserved.
Use is subject to license terms.
[… output truncated]
<hostname> console login:
```

Unmirroring the Root File System

Unlike Step by Step 10.4, where a file system was unmirrored and remounted without affecting the operation of the system, unmirroring a root file system is different because it cannot be unmounted while the system is running. In this case, it is necessary to perform a reboot to implement the change. Step by Step 10.6 shows how to unmirror the root file system that was successfully mirrored in Step by Step 10.5. This example comprises a mirror, d0, consisting of two submirrors, d10 and d20. The objective is to remount the / file system using its full disk device name, /dev/dsk/c0t0d0s0, instead of using /dev/md/dsk/d0:

STEP BY STEP

10.6 Unmirror the root File System

1. Verify that the current root file system is mounted from the metadevice /dev/md/dsk/d0.

```
# df -h /
Filesystem             size   used  avail capacity  Mounted on
/dev/md/dsk/d0         4.9G   3.7G   1.2G    77%    /
```

2. Detach the submirror that is to be used as the / file system.

```
# metadetach d0 d10
d0: Submirror d10 is detached
```

3. Set up the /etc/system file and /etc/vfstab to revert to the full disk device name, /dev/dsk/c0t0d0s0.

```
# metaroot /dev/dsk/c0t0d0s0
```

Notice that the entry that was added to /etc/system when the file system was mirrored has been removed, and that the /etc/vfstab entry for / has reverted back to /dev/dsk/c0t0d0s0.

4. Reboot the system to make the change take effect.

```
# init 6
```

5. Verify that the root file system is now being mounted from the full disk device, /dev/dsk/c0t0d0s0.

```
# df -h /
Filesystem             size   used  avail capacity  Mounted on
/dev/dsk/c0t0d0s0      4.9G   3.7G   1.2G    77%    /
```

6. Remove the mirror, d0, and its remaining submirror, d20.

```
# metaclear -r d0
d0: Mirror is cleared
d20: Concat/Stripe is cleared
```

7. Finally, remove the submirror, d10, that was detached earlier in step 2.

```
# metaclear d10
d10: Concat/Stripe is cleared
```

Troubleshooting Root File System Mirrors

Occasionally, a root mirror fails and recovery action has to be taken. Often, only one side of the mirror fails, in which case it can be detached using the metadetach command. You then replace the faulty disk and reattach it. Sometimes though, a more serious problem occurs prohibiting you from booting the system with SVM present. In this case, you have two options available to you. First, temporarily remove the SVM configuration so that you boot from the original c0t0d0s0 device, or second, you boot from a CD-ROM and recover the root file system manually, by carrying out an fsck.

To disable SVM, you must reinstate pre-SVM copies of the files /etc/system and /etc/vfstab. In Step by Step 10.5 we took a copy of these files (step 5). This is good practice and should always be done when editing important system files. Copy these files again, to take a current backup, and then copy the originals back to make them operational, as shown here:

```
# cp /etc/system /etc/system.svm
# cp /etc/vfstab /etc/vfstab.svm
# cp /etc/system.nosvm /etc/system
# cp /etc/vfstab.nosvm /etc/vfstab
```

You should now be able to reboot the system to single-user without SVM and recover any failed file systems.

If the preceding does not work, it might be necessary to repair the root file system manually, requiring you to boot from a CD-ROM. Insert the Solaris 10 CD 1 disk (or the Solaris 10 DVD) and shut down the system if it is not already shut down.

Boot to single-user from the CD-ROM as follows:

```
ok boot cdrom -s
```

When the system prompt is displayed, you can manually run `fsck` on the root file system. In this example, I am assuming a root file system exists on `/dev/rdsk/c0t0d0s0`:

```
# fsck /dev/rdsk/c0t0d0s0
** /dev/rdsk/c0t0d0s0
** Last Mounted on /
** Phase 1 - Check Blocks and Sizes
** Phase 2 - Check Pathnames
** Phase 3 - Check Connectivity
** Phase 4 - Check Reference Counts
** Phase 5 - Check Cyl groups
FREE BLK COUNT(S) WRONG IN SUPERBLK
SALVAGE? y
136955 files, 3732764 used, 1404922 free (201802 frags, 150390 blocks, \
3.9% fragmentation)
***** FILE SYSTEM WAS MODIFIED *****
```

You should now be able to reboot the system using SVM and you should resynchronize the root mirror as soon as the system is available. This can be achieved easily by detaching the second submirror and then reattaching it. The following example shows a mirror `d0` consisting of `d10` and `d20`:

```
# metadetach d0 d20
d0: submirror d20 is detached
# metattach d0 d20
d0: submirror d20 is attached
```

To demonstrate that the mirror is performing a resynchronization operation, you can issue the `metastat` command as follows, which will show the progress as a percentage:

```
# metastat d0
d0: Mirror
    Submirror 0: d10
```

```
      State: Okay
    Submirror 1: d20
      State: Resyncing
    Resync in progress: 37 % done
    Pass: 1
    Read option: roundrobin (default)
    Write option: parallel (default)
    Size: 10462032 blocks (5.0 GB)

d10: Submirror of d0
    State: Okay
    Size: 10462032 blocks (5.0 GB)
    Stripe 0:
        Device     Start Block  Dbase        State Reloc Hot Spare
        c0t0d0s0          0     No            Okay   Yes

d20: Submirror of d0
    State: Resyncing
    Size: 10489680 blocks (5.0 GB)
    Stripe 0:
        Device     Start Block  Dbase        State Reloc Hot Spare
        c0t1d0s0          0     No            Okay   Yes

Device Relocation Information:
Device   Reloc  Device ID
c0t0d0   Yes    id1,dad@AWDC_AC310200R=WD-WT6750311269
c0t1d0   Yes    id1,dad@ASAMSUNG_SP0411N=S01JJ60X901935
```

Veritas Volume Manager

EXAM ALERT

Veritas Volume Manager There are no questions on the Veritas Volume Manager in the exam. This section has been included solely to provide some additional information for system administrators and to allow comparison between this product and the Solaris Volume Manager. A course is run by Sun Microsystems for administrators using Veritas Volume Manager.

Veritas Volume Manager is an unbundled software package that can be purchased separately via Sun, or direct from Veritas, and does not come as part of the standard Solaris 10 release. This product has traditionally been used for managing Sun's larger StorEdge disk arrays. It is widely used for performing Virtual Volume Management functions on large scale systems such as Sun, Sequent, and HP. Although Veritas Volume Manager also provides the capability to mirror the OS drive, in actual industry practice, you'll still see SVM used to mirror the OS drive, even on large Sun servers that use Veritas Volume Manager to manage the remaining data. It used to be much more robust than the older Solstice DiskSuite product—the predecessor to the Solaris Volume Manager, providing tools that identify and analyze storage access patterns so that I/O loads can be balanced across complex disk configurations. SVM is now a much more robust product but the difference is negligible.

Veritas Volume Manager is a complex product that would take much more than this chapter to describe in detail. This chapter will, however, introduce you to the Veritas Volume Manager and some of the terms you will find useful.

The Volume Manager builds virtual devices called *volumes* on top of physical disks. A *physical disk* is the underlying storage device (media), which may or may not be under Volume Manager control. A physical disk can be accessed using a device name such as `/dev/rdsk/c#t#d`. The physical disk, as explained in Chapter 1, can be divided into one or more slices.

Volumes are accessed by the Solaris file system, a database, or other applications in the same way physical disk partitions would be accessed. Volumes and their virtual components are referred to as *Volume Manager objects*.

There are several Volume Manager objects that the Volume Manager uses to perform disk management tasks (see Table 10.9).

TABLE 10.9 Volume Manager Objects

Object Name	Description
VM Disk	A contiguous area of disk space from which the Volume Manager allocates storage. Each VM disk corresponds to at least one partition. A VM disk usually refers to a physical disk in the array.
Disk Group	A collection of VM disks that share a common configuration. The default disk group used to be `rootdg` (the root disk group) in versions prior to version 4, but there is now no default disk group assigned. Additional disk groups can be created, as necessary. Volumes are created within a disk group; a given volume must be configured from disks belonging to the same disk group. Disk groups allow the administrator to group disks into logical collections for administrative convenience.
Subdisk	A set of contiguous disk blocks; subdisks are the basic units in which the Volume Manager allocates disk space. A VM disk can be divided into one or more subdisks.
Plex	Often referred to as mirrors; a plex consists of one or more subdisks located on one or more disks, forming one side of a mirror configuration. The use of two or more plexes forms a functional mirror.
Volume	A virtual disk device that appears to be a physical disk partition to applications, databases, and file systems, but does not have the physical limitations of a physical disk partition. Volumes are created within a disk group; a given volume must be configured from disks belonging to the same disk group.

NOTE

Plex Configuration A number of plexes (usually two) are associated with a volume to form a working mirror. Also, stripes and concatenations are normally achieved during the creation of the plex.

Volume Manager objects can be manipulated in a variety of ways to optimize performance, provide redundancy of data, and perform backups or other administrative tasks on one or more physical disks without interrupting applications. As a result, data availability and disk subsystem throughput are improved.

Veritas Volume Manager manages disk space by using contiguous sectors. The application formats the disks into only two slices: Slice 3 and Slice 4. Slice 3 is called a *private area* and Slice 4 is the *public area*. Slice 3 maintains information about the virtual to physical device mappings, while Slice 4 provides space to build the virtual devices. The advantage to this approach is that there is almost no limit to the number of subdisks you can create on a single drive. In a standard Solaris disk partitioning environment, there is an eight-partition limit per disk.

The names of the block devices for virtual volumes created using Veritas Volume Manager are found in the `/dev/vx/dsk/<disk_group>/<volume_name>` directory, and the names of the raw devices are found in the `/dev/vx/rdsk/<disk_group>/<volume_name>` directory. The following is an example of a block and raw logical device name:

```
/dev/vx/dsk/apps/vol01 - block device /dev/vx/rdsk/apps/vol01 - \raw device
```

Summary

This chapter described the basic concepts behind RAID and the Solaris Volume Manager (SVM). This chapter described the various levels of RAID along with the differences between them, as well as the elements of SVM and how they can be used to provide a reliable data storage solution. We also covered the creation and monitoring of the state database replicas and how to mirror and unmirror file systems. Finally, you learned about Veritas Volume Manager, a third-party product used predominantly in larger systems with disk arrays.

Key Terms

- Virtual volume
- Metadevice
- RAID (0, 1, 5, and 1+0)
- Metadisk
- Soft partition
- Volume
- Concatenation
- Stripe
- Mirror
- Submirror
- Meta state database
- Hot spare pool
- Veritas Volume Manager objects
- Hot-pluggable
- Hot-swappable

Exercises

10.1 Monitoring Disk Usage

In this exercise, you'll see how to use the `iostat` utility to monitor disk usage. You will need a Solaris 10 workstation with local disk storage and a file system with at least 50 Megabytes of free space. You will also need CDE window sessions. For this exercise, you do not have to make use of metadevices because the utility will display information on standard disks as well as metadevices. The commands are identical whether or not you are running Solaris Volume Manager. Make sure you have write permission to the file system.

Estimated Time: 5 minutes

1. In the first window, start the `iostat` utility so that extended information about each disk or metadevice can be displayed. Also, you will enter a parameter to produce output every 3 seconds. Enter the following command at the command prompt:

```
iostat -xn 3
```

2. The output will be displayed and will be updated every 3 seconds. Watch the %b column, which tells you how busy the disk, or metadevice, is at the moment.

3. In the second window, change to the directory where you have at least 50 Megabytes of free disk space and create an empty file of this size, as shown in the following code. My example directory is `/data`. The file to be created is called `testfile`.

```
cd /data
mkfile 50M testfile
```

4. The file will take several seconds to be created, but watch the output being displayed in the first window and notice the increase in the %b column of output. You should see the affected file system suddenly become a lot busier. Continue to monitor the output when the command has completed and notice that the disk returns to its normal usage level.

5. Press Ctrl+C to stop the `iostat` output in the first window and delete the file created when you have finished, as shown here:

```
rm testfile
```

Exam Questions

1. Which of the following is a device that represents several disks or disk slices?

   ❍ **A.** Physical device

   ❍ **B.** Volume

   ❍ **C.** Pseudo device

   ❍ **D.** Instance

2. Which of the following provides redundancy of data in the event of a disk or hardware failure?

   ❍ **A.** Mirror

   ❍ **B.** Concatenated stripe

   ❍ **C.** Stripe

   ❍ **D.** Metadevice

3. Which of the following types of addressing interlaces component blocks across all of the slices?

   ❍ **A.** Metadevice

   ❍ **B.** Concatenated stripe

   ❍ **C.** Mirror

   ❍ **D.** Stripe

4. Which of the following volumes organizes the data sequentially across slices?

❍ **A.** Mirror

❍ **B.** Stripe

❍ **C.** Concatenation

❍ **D.** Metadevice

5. Which of the following devices was created using Veritas Volume Manager?

❍ **A.** `/dev/vx/dsk/apps/vol01`

❍ **B.** `/dev/md/dsk/d0`

❍ **C.** `/dev/dsk/vx/apps/vol01`

❍ **D.** `/dev/dsk/md/d0`

6. In Veritas Volume Manager, which of the following is a group of physical slices that appear to the system as a single, logical device?

❍ **A.** Metadevice

❍ **B.** Volume

❍ **C.** Virtual disk

❍ **D.** Plex

7. Which of the following is a collection of slices reserved to be automatically substituted in case of slice failure in either a submirror or RAID 5 metadevice?

❍ **A.** Hot spare pool

❍ **B.** Subdisks

❍ **C.** Plexes

❍ **D.** Disk group

8. Which of the following is a set of contiguous disk blocks; these are the basic units in which the Veritas Volume Manager allocates disk space?

❍ **A.** Disk group

❍ **B.** Plexes

❍ **C.** Subdisks

❍ **D.** Metadevice

9. Which of the following replicates data by using parity information, so that in the case of missing data, the missing data can be regenerated using available data and the parity information?

   ❍ **A.** Hot spare pool

   ❍ **B.** Mirroring

   ❍ **C.** Trans

   ❍ **D.** RAID 5

10. Which of the following has an eight-partition limit per disk?

   ❍ **A.** Solaris Volume Manager

   ❍ **B.** Veritas Volume Manager

   ❍ **C.** VM disk

   ❍ **D.** Standard Solaris SPARC disk

   ❍ **E.** Plex

11. Which of the following commands would create 3-state database replicas on slice `c0t0d0s3`?

   ❍ **A.** `metadb -i`

   ❍ **B.** `metainit -a -f -c3 c0t0d0s3`

   ❍ **C.** `metadb -a -f -c3 c0t0d0s3`

   ❍ **D.** `metaclear`

12. Which of the following commands would create a one-way mirror (`d1`), using metadevice `d14` as the submirror?

   ❍ **A.** `metaclear -r d1`

   ❍ **B.** `metainit d1 -m d14`

   ❍ **C.** `metainit d1 1 1 d14`

   ❍ **D.** `metadb -i`

Answers to Exam Questions

1. **B.** A volume (often called a `metadevice`) is a group of physical slices that appear to the system as a single, logical device. A volume is used to increase storage capacity and increase data availability. For more information, see the "Solaris SVM" section.

2. **A.** A mirror is composed of one or more simple metadevices called submirrors. A mirror replicates all writes to a single logical device (the mirror) and then to multiple devices (the submirrors) while distributing read operations. This provides redundancy of data in the event of a disk or hardware failure. For more information, see the "Solaris SVM" section.

3. **D.** A stripe is similar to concatenation, except that the addressing of the component blocks is interlaced on all of the slices rather than sequentially. For more information, see the "SVM Volumes" section.

4. **C.** Concatenations work in much the same way as the Unix `cat` command is used to concatenate two or more files to create one larger file. If partitions are concatenated, the addressing of the component blocks is done on the components sequentially. The file system can use the entire concatenation. For more information, see the "SVM Volumes" section.

5. **A.** The names of the block devices for virtual volumes created using Veritas Volume Manager are found in the `/dev/vx/dsk/`*`<disk_group>`*`/`*`<volume_name>`* directory. For more information, see the "Veritas Volume Manager" section.

6. **B.** A volume is a virtual disk device that appears to applications, databases, and file systems like a physical logical device, but does not have the physical limitations of a physical disk partition. For more information, see the "Veritas Volume Manager" section.

7. **A.** A hot spare pool is a collection of slices (hot spares) reserved to be automatically substituted in case of slice failure in either a submirror or RAID 5 metadevice. For more information, see the "Solaris SVM" section.

8. **C.** A set of contiguous disk blocks, subdisks are the basic units in which the Volume Manager allocates disk space. For more information, see the "Veritas Volume Manager" section.

9. **D.** RAID 5 replicates data by using parity information. In the case of missing data, the data can be regenerated using available data and the parity information. For more information, see the "RAID" section.

10. **D.** In a standard Solaris SPARC disk-partitioned environment, there is an eight-partition limit per disk. For more information, see the "Solaris SVM" section.

11. **C.** The command `metadb -a -f -c3 c0t0d0s3` would create the required state database replicas; see the "Creating the State Database" section.

12. **B.** The command `metainit d1 -m d14` would create a one-way mirror; see the "Creating a Mirror" section.

Suggested Reading and Resources

1. Solaris 10 Documentation CD—"Solaris Volume Manager Administration Guide" manual.

2. `http://docs.sun.com`. Solaris 10 documentation set. *Solaris Volume Manager Administration Guide* book in the System Administration collection.

CHAPTER ELEVEN

Controlling Access and Configuring System Messaging

Objectives

The following test objectives for Exam CX-310-202 are covered in this chapter:

Configure Role-Based Access Control (RBAC), including assigning rights, profiles, roles, and authorizations to users.

- This chapter describes Role-Based Access Control (RBAC), and identifies the four main databases involved with RBAC. The system administrator needs to understand the function and structure of each of these databases and how to apply the RBAC functionality in real-world situations.

Analyze RBAC configuration file summaries and manage RBAC using the command line.

- You will see how to assign a role to a user and use rights profiles by using commands that are described in this chapter. These can greatly assist the system administrator when managing a large number of rights that are to be assigned to a number of users.

Explain `syslog()` function fundamentals, and configure and manage the `/etc/syslog.conf` file and `syslog` messaging.

- This chapter describes the basics of system messaging in the Solaris operating environment, introduces the daemon responsible for managing the messaging, and describes the configuration file that determines what information is logged and where it is stored. It also describes the new method of restarting/refreshing the `syslog` process when changes are made to its configuration file.

Outline

Study Strategies

The following strategies will help you prepare for the test:

- As you study this chapter, it's important that you practice each exercise and each command that is presented on a Solaris system. Hands-on experience is important when learning these topics, so practice until you can repeat the procedures from memory.
- Be sure you understand each command and be prepared to match the command to the correct description.
- Be sure you know all of the terms listed in the "Key Terms" section at the end of this chapter. Pay special attention to the databases used in Role-Based Access Control (RBAC) and the uses and format of each. Be prepared to match the terms presented in this chapter with the correct description.
- Finally, you must understand the concept of system messaging—its purpose, how it works, and how to configure and manage it.

Introduction

This chapter covers two main topics—Role-Based Access Control (RBAC) and system messaging (`syslog`). These are both related in that they participate in the securing and monitoring of systems in a Solaris environment. The use of Role-Based Access Control makes the delegation of authorizations much easier for the system administrator to manage, as groups of privileges can easily be given to a role through the use of profiles. Also, the use of roles means that a user has to first log in using his or her normal ID, then use the `su` command to gain access to the role (and therefore assigned privileges). This has the advantage of being logged and so helps to establish accountability. The system messaging service (`syslog`) stores important system and security messages and is fully configurable. The system administrator can tune the service so that certain messages are delivered to several places (such as a log file, a message, and the system console), greatly increasing the chances of it being noticed quickly.

Role-Based Access Control (RBAC)

Objectives:

Configure Role-Based Access Control (RBAC) including assigning rights, profiles, roles, and authorizations to users.

- Analyze RBAC configuration file summaries and manage RBAC using the command line.

Granting superuser access to non-root users has always been an issue in Unix systems. In the past, you had to rely on a third-party package, such as `sudo`, to provide this functionality. The problem was that `sudo` was an unsupported piece of freeware that had to be downloaded from the Internet and installed onto your system. In extreme cases, the system administrator had to set the `setuid` permission bit on the file so that a user could execute the command as root.

With Role-Based Access Control (RBAC) in the Solaris 10 operating environment, administrators can not only assign limited administrative capabilities to non-root users, they can also provide the mechanism where a user can carry out a specific function as another user (if required). This is achieved through three features:

- **Authorizations**—User rights that grant access to a restricted function.
- **Execution profiles**—Bundling mechanisms for grouping authorizations and commands with special attributes; for example, user and group IDs or superuser ID.
- **Roles**—Special type of user accounts intended for performing a set of administrative tasks.

CAUTION

Assigning Superuser Access Using RBAC Most often, you will probably use RBAC to provide superuser access to administrative tasks within the system. Be careful to exercise caution and avoid creating security lapses by providing access to administrative functions by unauthorized users.

Using RBAC

To better describe RBAC, it's easier to first describe how a system administrator would utilize RBAC to delegate an administrative task to a non-root user in a fictional setting at Acme Corp.

At Acme Corp., the system administrator is overwhelmed with tasks. He is going to delegate some of his responsibility to Neil, a user from the engineering department who helps out sometimes with system administration tasks.

The system administrator first needs to define which tasks he wants Neil to help out with. He has identified three tasks:

- Change user passwords, but do not add or remove accounts.
- Mount and share file systems.
- Shut down the system.

In RBAC, when we speak of delegating administrative tasks, it is referred to as a role account. A *role account* is a special type of user account that is intended for performing a set of administrative tasks. It is like a normal user account in most respects except that users can gain access to it only through the `su` command after they have logged in to the system with their normal login account. A role account is not accessible for normal logins, for example, through the CDE login window. From a role account, a user can access commands with special attributes, typically the superuser privilege, which are not available to users in normal accounts.

At Acme Corp, the system administrator needs to define a role username for the tasks he wants to delegate. Let's use the role username "adminusr." After Neil logs in with his normal login name of `ncalkins`, he then needs to issue the `su` command and switch to `adminusr` whenever he wants to perform administrative tasks. In this chapter, you learn how to create a role account using the command line interface, although you should note that the Solaris Management Console can also be used.

So far we have determined that we want to name the role account `adminusr`. The system administrator creates the role account using the `roleadd` command. The `roleadd` command adds a role account to the `/etc/passwd`, `etc/shadow`, and `/etc/user_attr` files. The syntax for the `roleadd` command is as follows:

```
roleadd [-c comment] [-d dir] [-e expire] [-f inactive] [-g group]\
 [-G group] [-m] [-k skel_dir] [-u uid] [-s shell] \
[-A authorization] <role username>
```

You'll notice that roleadd looks a great deal like the useradd command described in Chapter 4, "User and Security Administration." Table 11.1 describes the options for the roleadd command.

TABLE 11.1 roleadd Options

Option	Description
-c <*comment*>	Any text string to provide a brief description of the role.
-d <*dir*>	The home directory of the new role account.
-m	Creates the new role's home directory if it does not already exist.
-e <*expire*>	Specifies the expiration date for a role. After this date, no user can access this role. The <*expire*> option argument is a date entered using one of the date formats included in the template file /etc/datemsk. For example, you can enter 10/30/02 or October 30, 2002. A value of " " defeats the status of the expired date.
-f <*inactive*>	Specifies the maximum number of days allowed between uses of a login ID before that login ID is declared invalid. Normal values are positive integers.
-g <*group*>	Specifies an existing group's integer ID or character-string name. It redefines the role's primary group membership.
-G <*group*>	Specifies an existing group's integer ID, or character string name. It redefines the role's supplementary group membership. Duplicates between groups with the -g and -G options are ignored.
-s <*shell*>	Specifies the user's shell on login. The default is /bin/pfsh.
-A <*authorization*>	Both of these options respectively assign authorizations and profiles to the role.
-P <*profile*>	Authorizations and profiles are described later in this section.
-u <*uid*>	Specifies a UID for the new role. It must be a non-negative decimal integer. The UID associated with the role's home directory is not modified with this option; a role does not have access to its home directory until the UID is manually reassigned using the chown command.

The other options are the same options that were described for the useradd command, outlined in Chapter 4.

When creating a role account with the roleadd command, you need to specify an authorization and profile to the role. An *authorization* is a user right that grants access to a restricted function. It is a unique string that identifies what is being authorized as well as who created the authorization.

Certain privileged programs check the authorizations to determine whether users can execute restricted functionality. Following are the predefined authorizations from the /etc/security/auth_attr file that apply to the tasks to be delegated:

```
solaris.admin.usermgr.pswd:::Change Password::help=AuthUserMgrPswd.html
solaris.system.shutdown:::Shutdown the System::help=SysShutdown.html
solaris.admin.fsmgr.write:::Mount and Share File Systems::\
help=AuthFsMgrWrite.html
```

All authorizations are stored in the `auth_attr` database, so the system administrator needs to use one or more of the authorizations that are stored in that file. For the Acme Corp. example, the system administrator needs to specify the authorizations shown here:

```
solaris.admin.usermgr.pswd
solaris.system.shutdown
solaris.admin.fsmgr.write
```

The system administrator would therefore issue the `roleadd` command as follows:

```
roleadd -m -d /export/home/adminusr -c "Admin Assistant" \
-A solaris.admin.usermgr.pswd,solaris.system.shutdown,\
solaris.admin.fsmgr.write adminusr
```

A role account named `adminusr` with the required directory structures has been created. The next step is to set the password for the `adminusr` role account by typing the following:

```
passwd adminusr
```

You are prompted to type the new password twice.

Now we need to set up Neil's account so he can access the new role account named `adminusr`. With the `usermod` command, we assign the role to the user account using the `-R` option as follows:

```
usermod -R adminusr neil
```

NOTE

No Need to Be Logged Out Previously, you needed to ensure that the user was not logged in at the time of assigning a role; otherwise you received an error message and the role was not assigned. This is no longer the case and a role can be assigned to a user whilst the user is still logged in.

To access the administrative functions, Neil needs to first log in using his regular user account named `neil`. Neil can check which roles he has been granted by typing the following at the command line:

```
roles
```

The system responds with the roles that have been granted to the user account `neil` as follows:

```
adminusr
```

Neil then needs to su to the adminusr account by typing the following:

```
su adminusr
```

Neil is prompted to type the password for the role account.

Now Neil can modify user passwords, shut down the system, and mount and share file systems. Any other user trying to su to the adminusr account gets this message:

```
$ su adminusr
Password:
Roles can only be assumed by authorized users
su: Sorry
$
```

If later on, the system administrator wants to assign additional authorizations to the role account named adminusr, he would do so using the rolemod command. The rolemod command modifies a role's login information on the system. The syntax for the rolemod command is as follows:

```
rolemod [-u uid] [-o] [-g group] [-G group] [-d dir] [-m] [-s shell]\
[-c comment] [-l new_name] [-f inactive] [-e expire] [-A Authorization]\
[-P profile] <role account>
```

Options for the rolemod command where they differ from the roleadd command are described in Table 11.2.

TABLE 11.2 rolemod Options

Option	Description
-A <authorization>	One or more comma-separated authorizations as defined in the auth_attr database. This replaces any existing authorization setting.
-d *<dir>*	Specifies the new home directory of the role. It defaults to *<base_dir>*/login, in which *<base_dir>* is the base directory for new login home directories, and login is the new login.
-l *<new_logname>*	Specifies the new login name for the role. The *<new_logname>* argument is a string no more than eight bytes consisting of characters from the set of alphabetic characters, numeric characters, period (.), underline (_), and hyphen (-). The first character should be alphabetic and the field should contain at least one lowercase alphabetic character. A warning message is written if these restrictions are not met. A future Solaris release might refuse to accept login fields that do not meet these requirements. The *<new_logname>* argument must contain at least one character and must not contain a colon (:) or NEWLINE (\n).
-m	Moves the role's home directory to the new directory specified with the -d option. If the directory already exists, it must have permissions read/write/execute by group, in which group is the role's primary group.

TABLE 11.2 *Continued*

Option	Description
`-o`	Allows the specified UID to be duplicated (nonunique).
`-P <profile>`	Replaces any existing profile setting. One or more comma-separated execution profiles are defined in the `auth_attr` database.
`-u <uid>`	Specifies a new UID for the role. It must be a non-negative decimal integer. The UID associated with the role's home directory is not modified with this option; a role does not have access to its home directory until the UID is manually reassigned using the `chown` command.

To add the ability to purge log files, you need to add `solaris.admin.logsvc.purge` to the list of authorizations for `adminusr`. To do this, issue the `rolemod` command as follows:

```
rolemod -A solaris.admin.usermgr.pswd,solaris.system.shutdown,\
solaris.admin.fsmgr.write,solaris.admin.logsvc.purge  adminusr
```

You can verify that the new authorizations have been added to the role by typing the `auths` command at the command line as shown below:

```
auths adminusr
solaris.admin.usermgr.pswd,solaris.system.shutdown,solaris.admin.fsmgr.\
write,solaris.admin.logsvc.purge,…
[ output has been truncated]
```

CAUTION

`rolemod` Warning The `rolemod` command does not add to the existing authorizations; it replaces any existing authorization setting.

If you want to remove a role account, use the `roledel` command as follows:

```
roledel [-r] <role account name>
```

The `-r` option removes the role's home directory from the system. For example, to remove the `adminusr` role account, issue the following command:

```
roledel -r adminusr
```

The next section discusses each of the RBAC databases in detail, describing the entries made when we executed the `roleadd` and `usermod` commands.

RBAC Components

RBAC relies on the following four databases to provide users access to privileged operations:

- **/etc/user_attr (extended user attributes database)**—Associates users and roles with authorizations and profiles.
- **/etc/security/auth_attr (authorization attributes database)**—Defines authorizations and their attributes and identifies the associated help file.
- **/etc/security/prof_attr (rights profile attributes database)**—Defines profiles, lists the profile's assigned authorizations, and identifies the associated help file.
- **/etc/security/exec_attr (profile attributes database)**—Defines the privileged operations assigned to a profile.

These four databases are logically interconnected.

EXAM ALERT

RBAC Database Functions You need to be able to correctly identify the function and location of each RBAC database. A common exam question is to match the description with the relevant RBAC database. Remember that the user_attr database resides in the /etc directory and not in the /etc/security directory.

Extended User Attributes (user_attr) Database

The /etc/user_attr database supplements the passwd and shadow databases. It contains extended user attributes, such as authorizations and profiles. It also allows roles to be assigned to a user. Following is an example of the /etc/user_attr database:

```
more /etc/user_attr
# Copyright (c) 2003 by Sun Microsystems, Inc. All rights reserved.
#
# /etc/user_attr
#
# user attributes. see user_attr(4)
#
#pragma ident   "@(#)user_attr  1.1     03/07/09 SMI"
#
adm::::profiles=Log Management
lp::::profiles=Printer Management
root::::auths=solaris.*,solaris.grant;profiles=All
adminusr::::type=role;auths=solaris.admin.usermgr.pswd,/
solaris.system.shutdown,solaris.admin.fsmgr.write;profiles=All
neil::::type=normal;roles=adminusr
```

The following fields in the `user_attr` database are separated by colons:

```
user:qualifier:res1:res2:attr
```

Each field is described in Table 11.3.

TABLE 11.3 `user_attr` Fields

Field Name	Description
`user`	Describes the name of the user or role, as specified in the `passwd` database.
`qualifier`	Reserved for future use.
`res1`	Reserved for future use.
`res2`	Reserved for future use.
`attr`	Contains an optional list of semicolon-separated (;) key-value pairs that describe the security attributes to be applied when the user runs commands. Eight valid keys exist: `auths`, `profiles`, `roles`, `type`, `project`, `defaultpriv`, `limitpriv`, and `lock_after_retries`. `auths`—Specifies a comma-separated list of authorization names chosen from names defined in the `auth_attr` database. Authorization names can include the asterisk (*) character as a wildcard. For example, `solaris.device.*` means all of the Solaris device authorizations. `profiles`—Contains an ordered, comma-separated list of profile names chosen from `prof_attr`. A profile determines which commands a user can execute and with which command attributes. At minimum, each user in `user_attr` should have the `All` profile, which makes all commands available but without attributes. The order of profiles is important; it works similarly to Unix search paths. The first profile in the list that contains the command to be executed defines which (if any) attributes are to be applied to the command. Profiles are described in the section titled "Authorizations (`auth_attr`) Database." `roles`—Can be assigned to the user using a comma-separated list of role names. Note that roles are defined in the same `user_attr` database. They are indicated by setting the *type* value to role. Roles cannot be assigned to other roles. `type`—Can be set to normal, if this account is for a normal user, or to role, if this account is for a role. A normal user assumes a role after he has logged in. `project`—Can be set to a project from the projects database, so that the user is placed in a default project at login time. `defaultpriv`—The list of default privileges the user is assigned. `limitpriv`—The system administrator can limit the set of privileges allowed, and this attribute contains the maximum set of privileges the user can be allowed. Care must be taken when limiting privileges so as to not affect other applications the user might execute. `Lock_after_retries`—Specifies whether an account is locked out following a number of failed logins. The number of failed logins is taken from the `RETRIES` option in `/etc/default/login`. The default is no.

In the previous section, we issued the following `roleadd` command to add a role named `adminusr`:

```
roleadd -m -d /export/home/adminusr -c "Admin Assistant"\
 -A solaris.admin.usermgr.pswd,solaris.system.shutdown,\
solaris.admin.fsmgr.write adminusr
```

The `roleadd` command made the following entry in the `user_attr` database:

```
adminusr::::type=role;auths=solaris.admin.usermgr.pswd,\
solaris.system.shutdown,solaris.admin.fsmgr.write;profiles=All
```

We can then issue the following `usermod` command to assign the new role to the user `neil`:

```
usermod -R useradmin neil
```

and then make the following entry to the `user_attr` database:

```
neil::::type=normal;roles=adminusr
```

Authorizations (auth_attr) Database

An authorization is a user right that grants access to a restricted function. In the previous section, the system administrator wanted to delegate some of the system administrative tasks to Neil. Assigning authorizations to the role named `adminusr` did this. An authorization is a unique string that identifies what is being authorized as well as who created the authorization. Remember that we used the following authorizations to give Neil the ability to modify user passwords, shut down the system, and mount and share file systems:

```
solaris.admin.usermgr.pswd
solaris.system.shutdown
solaris.admin.fsmgr.write
```

Certain privileged programs check the authorizations to determine whether users can execute restricted functionality. For example, the `solaris.jobs.admin` authorization is required for one user to edit another user's `crontab` file.

All authorizations are stored in the `auth_attr` database. If no name service is used, the database is located in a file named `/etc/security/auth_attr`. Authorizations can be assigned directly to users (or roles), in which case they are entered in the `user_attr` database. Authorizations can also be assigned to profiles, which in turn are assigned to users. They are described in the "Rights Profiles (`prof_attr`) Database" section, later in this chapter.

The fields in the `auth_attr` database are separated by colons, as shown here:

```
authname:res1:res2:short_desc:long_desc:attr
```

Each field is described in Table 11.4.

TABLE 11.4 `auth_attr` Fields

Field Name	Description
`authname`	A unique character string used to identify the authorization in the format *`prefix.[suffix]`*. Authorizations for the Solaris operating environment use *`solaris`* as a prefix. All other authorizations should use a prefix that begins with the reverse-order Internet domain name of the organization that creates the authorization (for example, `com.xyzcompany`). The suffix indicates what is being authorized, typically the functional area and operation. When no suffix exists (that is, the `authname` consists of a prefix and functional area and ends with a period), the `authname` serves as a heading for use by applications in their GUIs rather than as an authorization. The `authname solaris.printmgr` is an example of a heading. When the `authname` ends with the word *grant*, the `authname` serves as a grant authorization and allows the user to delegate related authorizations (that is, authorizations with the same prefix and functional area) to other users. The `authname solaris.printmgr.grant` is an example of a grant authorization; it gives the user the right to delegate such authorizations as `solaris.printmgr.admin` and `solaris.printmgr.nobanner` to other users.
`res1`	Reserved for future use.
`res2`	Reserved for future use.
`short_desc`	A shortened name for the authorization suitable for displaying in user interfaces, such as in a scrolling list in a GUI.
`long_desc`	A long description. This field identifies the purpose of the authorization, the applications in which it is used, and the type of user interested in using it. The long description can be displayed in the help text of an application.
`attr`	An optional list of semicolon-separated (;) key-value pairs that describe the attributes of an authorization. Zero or more keys can be specified. The keyword *`help`* identifies a help file in HTML. Help files can be accessed from the `index.html` file in the `/usr/lib/help/auths/locale/C` directory.

The following are some typical values found in the default `auth_attr` database:

```
solaris.admin.usermgr.pswd:::Change Password::help=AuthUserMgrPswd.html
solaris.system.shutdown:::Shutdown the System::help=SysShutdown.html
solaris.admin.fsmgr.write:::Mount and Share File Systems::\
help=AuthFsMgrWrite.html
```

Look at the relationship between the `auth_attr` and the `user_attr` databases for the `adminusr` role we added earlier:

```
adminusr::::type=role;auths=solaris.admin.usermgr.pswd,\
solaris.system.shutdown,solaris.admin.fsmgr.write;profiles=All
```

Notice the authorization entries that are **bold**. These authorization entries came out of the auth_attr database, shown previously. The solaris.system.shutdown authorization, which is defined in the auth_attr database, gives the role the right to shut down the system.

Rights Profiles (prof_attr) Database

We referred to rights profiles, or simply profiles, earlier in this chapter. Up until now, we assigned authorization rights to the role account. Defining a role account that has several authorizations can be tedious. In this case, it's better to define a profile, which is several authorizations bundled together under one name called a *profile name*. The definition of the profile is stored in the prof_attr database. Following is an example of a profile named Operator, which is in the default prof_attr database. Again, if you are not using a name service, the prof_attr file is located in the /etc/security directory.

```
Operator:::Can perform simple administrative tasks:profiles=Printer
Management,Media Backup,All;help=RtOperator.html
```

Several other profiles are defined in the prof_attr database. Colons separate the fields in the prof_attr database, as follows:

```
profname:res1:res2:desc:attr
```

The fields are defined in Table 11.5.

TABLE 11.5 prof_attr Fields

Field Name	Description
profname	The name of the profile. Profile names are case sensitive.
res1	A field reserved for future use.
res2	A field reserved for future use.
desc	A long description. This field should explain the purpose of the profile, including what type of user would be interested in using it. The long description should be suitable for displaying in the help text of an application.
attr	An optional list of key-value pairs separated by semicolons (;) that describe the security attributes to apply to the object upon execution. Zero or more keys can be specified. The two valid keys are *help* and *auths*. The keyword *help* identifies a help file in HTML. Help files can be accessed from the index.html file in the /usr/lib/help/auths/locale/C directory. *auths* specifies a comma-separated list of authorization names chosen from those names defined in the auth_attr database. Authorization names can be specified using the asterisk (*) character as a wildcard.

Perhaps the system administrator wants to create a new role account and delegate the task of printer management and backups. He could look through the user_attr file for each authorization and assign each one to the new role account using the `roleadd` command, or he could use the `Operator` profile currently defined in the `prof_attr` database, which looks like this:

The Operator profile consists of three other profiles:

- `Printer Management`
- `Media Backup`
- `All`

Let's look at each of these profiles as defined in the `prof_attr` database:

```
Printer Management:::Manage printers, daemons, spooling:help=RtPrntAdmin.\
html;auths=solaris.admin.printer.read,solaris.admin.printer.modify,\
solaris.admin.printer.delete
Media Backup:::Backup files and file systems:help=RtMediaBkup.html
All:::Execute any command as the user or role:help=RtAll.html
```

`Printer Management` has the following authorizations assigned to it:

- `solaris.admin.printer.read`
- `solaris.admin.printer.modify`
- `solaris.admin.printer.delete`

When you look at these three authorizations in the `auth_attr` database, you see the following entries:

```
solaris.admin.printer.read:::View Printer Information::
help=AuthPrinterRead.html
solaris.admin.printer.modify:::Update Printer Information::
help=AuthPrinterModify.html
solaris.admin.printer.delete:::Delete Printer Information::
help=AuthPrinterDelete.html
```

Assigning the `Printer Management` profile is the same as assigning the three authorizations for viewing, updating, and deleting printer information.

The `Media Backup` profile provides authorization for backing up data, but not restoring data. The `Media Backup` profile does not have authorizations associated with it like the `Printer Management` profile has. I'll describe how this profile is defined in the next section when I describe execution attributes.

The `All` profile grants the right for a role account to use any command when working in an administrator's shell. These shells can only execute commands that have been explicitly assigned to a role account through granted rights. We'll explore this concept further when I describe execution attributes in the next section.

To create a new role account named admin2 specifying the Operator profile, use the roleadd command with the -P option, as follows:

```
roleadd -m -d /export/home/admin2 -c "Admin Assistant" -P Operator admin2
```

The following entry is added to the user_attr database:

```
admin2::::type=role;profiles=Operator
```

At any time, users can check which profiles have been granted to them with the profiles command, as follows:

```
profiles
```

The system lists the profiles that have been granted to that particular user account.

Execution Attributes (exec_attr) Database

An execution attribute associated with a profile is a command (with any special security attributes) that can be run by those users or roles to which the profile is assigned. For example, in the previous section, we looked at the profile named Media Backup in the prof_attr database. Although no authorizations were assigned to this profile, the Media Backup profile was defined in the exec_attr database as follows:

```
Media Backup:suser:cmd:::/usr/bin/mt:euid=0
Media Backup:suser:cmd:::/usr/sbin/tar:euid=0
Media Backup:suser:cmd:::/usr/lib/fs/ufs/ufsdump:euid=0;gid=sys
```

The fields in the exec_attr database are as follows and are separated by colons:

```
name:policy:type:res1:res2:id:attr
```

The fields are defined in Table 11.6.

TABLE 11.6 exec_attr Fields

Field Name	Description
Name	The name of the profile. Profile names are case sensitive.
policy	The security policy associated with this entry. Currently, suser (the superuser policy model) is the only valid policy entry.
type	The type of entity whose attributes are specified. Currently, the only valid type is cmd (command).
res1	This field is reserved for future use.
res2	This field is reserved for future use.

TABLE 11.6 *Continued*

Field Name	Description
`id`	A string identifying the entity; the asterisk (*) wildcard can be used. Commands should have the full path or a path with a wildcard. To specify arguments, write a script with the arguments and point the id to the script.
`attr`	An optional list of semicolon (;) separated key-value pairs that describe the security attributes to apply to the entity upon execution. Zero or more keys can be specified. The list of valid keywords depends on the policy being enforced. Four valid keys exist: `euid`, `uid`, `egid`, and `gid`. `euid` and `uid` contain a single username or numeric user ID. Commands designated with `euid` run with the effective UID indicated, which is similar to setting the `setuid` bit on an executable file. Commands designated with `uid` run with both the real and effective UIDs. `egid` and `gid` contain a single group name or numeric group ID. Commands designated with `egid` run with the effective GID indicated, which is similar to setting the `setgid` bit on an executable file. Commands designated with `gid` run with both the real and effective GIDs.

NOTE

Trusted Solaris You will see an additional security policy if you are running Trusted Solaris, a special security-enhanced version of the operating environment. The policy `tsol` is the trusted solaris policy model.

Looking back to the `Media Backup` profile as defined in the `exec_attr` database, we see that the following commands have an effective UID of 0 (superuser):

```
/usr/bin/mt
/usr/sbin/tar
/usr/lib/fs/ufs/ufsdump
```

Therefore, any user that has been granted the `Media Backup` profile can execute the previous backup commands with an effective user ID of 0 (superuser).

In the `prof_attr` database, we also saw that the `Operator` profile consisted of a profile named `All`. Again, `All` did not have authorizations associated with it. When we look at the `exec_attr` database for a definition of the `All` profile, we get the following entry:

```
All:suser:cmd:::*:
```

Examining each field, we see that `All` is the profile name, the security policy is `suser`, and the type of entity is `cmd`. The attribute field has an `*`.

It's common to grant all users the `All` profile. The `*` is a wildcard entry that matches every command. In other words, the user has access to any command while working in the shell.

Without the All profile, a user would have access to the privileged commands, but no access to normal commands such as ls and cd. Notice that no special process attributes are associated with the wildcard, so the effect is that all commands matching the wildcard run with the UID and GID of the current user (or role).

NOTE

The All Profile Always assign the All profile last in the list of profiles. If it is listed first, no other rights are consulted when you look up command attributes.

syslog

Objective:

Explain syslog function fundamentals and configure and manage the /etc/syslog.conf file and syslog messaging.

A critical part of the system administrator's job is monitoring the system. Solaris uses the syslog message facility to do this. syslogd is the daemon responsible for capturing system messages. The messages can be warnings, alerts, or simply informational messages. As the system administrator, you customize syslog to specify where and how system messages are to be saved.

The syslogd daemon receives messages from applications on the local host or from remote hosts and then directs messages to a specified log file. To each message that syslog captures, it adds a timestamp, the message type keyword at the beginning of the message, and a newline at the end of the message. For example, the following messages were logged in the /var/adm/messages file:

```
July 15 23:06:39 ultra10 ufs: [ID 845546 kern.notice] NOTICE: alloc: /var: \
 file system full

Sep  1 04:57:06 docbert nfs: [ID 563706 kern.notice] NFS server saturn.east ok
```

syslog enables you to capture messages by facility (the part of the system that generated the message) and by level of importance. Facility is considered to be the service area generating the message or error (such as printing, email, or network), whereas the level can be considered the level of severity (such as notice, warning, error, or emergency). syslog also enables you to forward messages to another machine so that all your messages can be logged in one location. The syslogd daemon reads and logs messages into a set of files described by the configuration file /etc/syslog.conf. When the syslogd daemon starts up, it preprocesses the /etc/syslog.conf file through the m4 macro processor to get the correct information for specific log files. syslogd does not read the /etc/syslog.conf file directly. syslogd starts m4, which parses the /etc/syslog.conf file for ifdef statements that can be interpreted by m4. The function `ifdef` is an integral part of `m4` and identifies the system designated as `LOGHOST`. The macro is then able to evaluate whether log files are to be held locally or on a remote system, or a combination of both.

If m4 doesn't recognize any m4 commands in the `syslog.conf` file, output is passed back to `syslogd`. `syslogd` then uses this output to route messages to appropriate destinations. When m4 encounters `ifdef` statements that it can process, the statement is evaluated for a true or false condition and the message is routed relative to the output of the test.

EXAM ALERT

`/etc/syslog.conf` and `ifdef` statements Make sure you become familiar with the facilities and values listed in the tables in this section. An exam question might provide a sample file and ask where a specific type of message, such as a failed login, will be logged. Also watch out for the `ifdef` statements to see if the logging is being carried out on a remote system.

An entry in the `/etc/syslog.conf` file is composed of two fields:

```
selector      action
```

The `selector` field contains a semicolon-separated list of priority specifications of this form:

```
facility.level [ ; facility.level ]
```

The `action` field indicates where to forward the message. Many defined facilities exist.

EXAM ALERT

Separate with Tabs The separator between the two fields must be a tab character. Spaces will not work and will give unexpected results. This is a very common mistake to make.

The facilities are described in Table 11.7.

TABLE 11.7 Recognized Values for Facilities

Value	Description
`user`	Messages generated by user processes. This is the default priority for messages from programs or facilities not listed in this file.
`kern`	Messages generated by the kernel.
`mail`	The mail system.
`daemon`	System daemons, such as `in.ftpd`.
`auth`	The authorization system, such as `login`, `su`, `getty`, and others.

(continues)

TABLE 11.7 *Continued*

Value	Description
lpr	lpr is the syslogd facility responsible for generating messages from the line printer spooling system—lpr and lpc.
news	Reserved for the Usenet network news system.
uucp	Reserved for the UUCP system. It does not currently use the syslog mechanism.
cron	The cron/at facility, such as crontab, at, cron, and others.
audit	The audit facility, such as auditd.
local0-7	Reserved for local use.
mark	For timestamp messages produced internally by syslogd.
*	Indicates all facilities except the mark facility.

Table 11.8 lists recognized values for the syslog level field. They are listed in descending order of severity.

TABLE 11.8 Recognized Values for level

Value	Description
emerg	Panic conditions that would normally be broadcast to all users.
alert	Conditions that should be corrected immediately, such as a corrupted system database.
crit	Warnings about critical conditions, such as hard device errors.
err	Other errors.
warning	Warning messages.
notice	Conditions that are not error conditions but that might require special handling, such as a failed login attempt. A failed login attempt is considered a notice and not an error.
info	Informational messages.
debug	Messages that are normally used only when debugging a program.
none	Does not send messages from the indicated facility to the selected file. For example, the entry *.debug;mail.none in /etc/syslog.conf sends all messages except mail messages to the selected file.

NOTE

Levels Include All Higher Levels Too When you specify a syslog level, it means that the specified level *and all higher levels*. For example, if you specify the err level, then this will include crit, alert and emerg levels as well.

Values for the `action` field can have one of four forms:

- A filename, beginning with a leading slash. This indicates that messages specified by the selector are to be written to the specified file. The file is opened in append mode and must already exist. `syslog` will not create the file if it doesn't already exist.
- The name of a remote host, prefixed with a `@`. An example is `@server`, which indicates that messages specified by the selector are to be forwarded to `syslogd` on the named host. The hostname `loghost` is the hostname given to the machine that will log `syslogd` messages. Every machine is its own `loghost` by default. This is specified in the local `/etc/hosts` file. It is also possible to specify one machine on a network to be `loghost` by making the appropriate host table entries. If the local machine is designated as `loghost`, `syslogd` messages are written to the appropriate files. Otherwise, they are sent to the machine `loghost` on the network.
- A comma-separated list of usernames, which indicates that messages specified by the selector are to be written to the named users if they are logged in.
- An asterisk, which indicates that messages specified by the selector are to be written to all logged-in users.

Blank lines are ignored. Lines in which the first nonwhitespace character is a `#` are treated as comments.

All of this becomes much clearer when you look at sample entries from an `/etc/syslog.conf` file:

```
*.err     /dev/console
*.err;daemon,auth.notice;mail.crit     /var/adm/messages
mail.debug    /var/log/syslog
*.alert     root
*.emerg    *
kern.err    @server
*.alert;auth.warning     /var/log/auth
```

In this example, the first line prints all errors on the console.

The second line sends all errors, daemon and authentication system notices, and critical errors from the mail system to the file `/var/adm/messages`.

The third line sends mail system debug messages to `/var/log/syslog`.

The fourth line sends all alert messages to user root.

The fifth line sends all emergency messages to all users.

The sixth line forwards kernel messages of `err` (error) severity or higher to the machine named server.

The last line logs all alert messages and messages of `warning` level or higher from the authorization system to the file `/var/log/auth`.

The level `none` may be used to disable a facility. This is usually done in the context of eliminating messages. For example:

```
*.debug;mail.none /var/adm/messages
```

This selects debug messages and above from all facilities except those from mail. In other words, mail messages are disabled. The mail system, sendmail, logs a number of messages. The mail system can produce a large amount of information, so some system administrators disable mail messages or send them to another file that they clean out frequently. Before disabling mail messages, however, remember that sendmail messages come in very handy when you're diagnosing mail problems or tracking mail forgeries.

As of Solaris 10, the mechanism for stopping, starting, and refreshing `syslogd` has changed. The `syslog` function is now under the control of the Service Management Facility (SMF), which is described in detail in Chapter 3.

To stop or start `syslogd`, use the `svcadm` command with the appropriate parameter, `enable` or `disable` as follows:

```
# svcadm enable -t system-log
# svcadm disable -t system-log
```

The `syslog` facility reads its configuration information from `/etc/syslog.conf` whenever it receives a refresh command from the service administration command, `svcadm`, and when the system is booted. You can make your changes to `/etc/syslog.conf`, then run the following command to cause the file to be re-read by the `syslogd` daemon:

```
# svcadm refresh system-log
```

EXAM ALERT

No More `kill -HUP` Make sure you remember that the `kill -HUP` facility should no longer be used to try to cause a daemon process to re-read its configuration file, even though it still works. The `svcadm refresh` command is now the recommended way of achieving this.

The first message in the logfile is logged by the `syslog` daemon itself to show when the process was started.

`syslog` logs are automatically rotated on a regular basis. In previous Solaris releases, this was achieved by the program `newsyslog`. A new method of log rotation was introduced with Solaris 9—`logadm`, a program normally run as a root-owned cron job. A configuration file `/etc/logadm.conf` is now used to manage log rotation and allows a number of criteria to be specified. See the `logadm` and `logadm.conf` manual pages for further details.

Using the `logger` Command

The `logger` command provides the means of manually adding one-line entries to the system logs from the command line. This is especially useful in shell scripts.

The syntax for the `logger` command is as follows:

```
logger [-i] [-f file] [-p priority] [-t tag] [message] ...
```

Options to the `logger` command are described in Table 11.9.

TABLE 11.9 `logger` Options

Option	Description
`-i`	Logs the Process ID (PID) of the `logger` process with each line written to a log file.
`-f <file>`	Use the contents of *`file`* as the message to be logged.
`-P <priority>`	The message priority. This can be defined as a numeric value or as a `facility.level` pair as described in Tables 11.7 and 11.8 of this chapter. The default priority is `user.notice`.
`-t <tag>`	Marks each line with the specified tag.
`message`	One or more string arguments, separated by a single space character comprising the text of the message to be logged.

As an example, to log a message to the default system log file stating that the backups have completed successfully, enter the following:

```
logger "Backups Completed Successfully"
```

Summary

In this chapter you learned about Role-Based Access Control (RBAC), which allows the system administrator to delegate administrative responsibilities to users without having to divulge the root password. A number of profiles allow privileges to be grouped together so that a user can easily be granted a restricted set of additional privileges. There are four main RBAC databases that interact with each other to provide users with access to privileged operations:

- **/etc/security/auth_attr**—Defines authorizations and their attributes and identifies the associated help file.
- **/etc/security/exec_attr**—Defines the privileged operations assigned to a profile.
- **/etc/security/prof_attr**—Defines the profiles, lists the profile's assigned authorizations, and identifies the associated help file.
- **/etc/user_attr**—Associates users and roles with authorizations and execution profiles.

Also in this chapter, you learned about the system logging facility (`syslog`) and the configuration that facilitates routing of system messages according to specific criteria, as well as determining where the messages are logged. The `logger` command was covered, which allows the system administrator to enter ad-hoc messages into the system log files.

Key Terms

- Authorization
- Execution profile
- `logger`
- RBAC
- RBAC databases (know about all four)
- Rights profile
- Role
- `syslog`
- `svcadm` command

Review Exercises

11.1 Creating a User and a Role

In this exercise, you'll create a new role named `admin1` and a profile called `Shutdown`. The `Shutdown` profile will be added to the role. A user account trng1 will be created and have the `admin1` role assigned to it. The user will then assume the role and execute a privileged command to shut down the system.

Estimated time: 20 minutes

To create a user and a role, perform the following steps:

1. Create the role named `admin1`, as shown here:

   ```
   roleadd -u 2000 -g 10 -d /export/home/admin1 -m admin1
   passwd admin1
   ```

   You will be prompted to enter the password twice.

2. Create a profile to allow the user to shut down a system.

   Edit the `/etc/security/prof_attr` file and enter the following line:

   ```
   Shutdown:::Permit system shutdown:
   ```

   Save and exit the file.

3. Add the `Shutdown` and `All` profiles to the role as follows:

   ```
   rolemod -P Shutdown,All admin1
   ```

4. Verify that the changes have been made to the `user_attr` database:

   ```
   more /etc/user_attr
   ```

5. Create the user account and assign it access to the admin1 role:

   ```
   useradd -u 3000 -g 10 -d /export/home/trng1 -m -s /bin/ksh -R admin1\
    trng1
   ```

6. Assign a password to the new user account as follows:

   ```
   passwd trng1
   ```

   You will be prompted to enter the password twice.

7. Verify that the entry has been made to the passwd, shadow, and `user_attr` files as follows:

   ```
   more /etc/passwd
   more /etc/shadow
   more /etc/user_attr
   ```

8. Assign commands to the `Shutdown` profile:

   Edit the `/etc/security/exec_attr` file and add the following line:

   ```
   Shutdown:suser:cmd:::/usr/sbin/shutdown:uid=0
   ```

   Save and exit the file.

9. Test the new role and user account as follows:

   a. Log in as trng1.

   b. List the roles that are granted to you by typing the following:

   ```
   roles
   ```

   c. Use the `su` command to assume the role admin1:

   ```
   su admin1
   ```

   You will be prompted to enter the password for the role.

   d. List the profiles that are granted to you by typing the following:

   ```
   profiles
   ```

   e. Shut down the system:

   ```
   /usr/sbin/shutdown -i 0 -g 0
   ```

Exam Questions

1. Which of the following commands is used to create a role?

   ❍ **A.** `useradd`

   ❍ **B.** `makerole`

   ❍ **C.** `roleadd`

   ❍ **D.** `addrole`

2. In Role-Based Access Control, which file contains details of the user attributes?

   ❍ **A.** `/etc/security/prof_attr`

   ❍ **B.** `/etc/user_attr`

   ❍ **C.** `/etc/security/user_attr`

   ❍ **D.** `/etc/shadow`

3. Which two statements about the `roleadd` command are true? (Choose two.)

   ❍ **A.** `roleadd` looks similar to the `useradd` command.

   ❍ **B.** `roleadd` uses the profile shell (`pfsh`) as the default shell.

   ❍ **C.** The `-A` option associates an account with a profile.

   ❍ **D.** An account created with `roleadd` is the same as a normal login account.

4. Which component of RBAC associates users and roles with authorizations and profiles?

   ❍ **A.** `user_attr`

   ❍ **B.** `prof_attr`

   ❍ **C.** `auth_attr`

   ❍ **D.** `exec_attr`

5. Which component of RBAC defines the privileged operations assigned to a profile?

   ❍ **A.** `user_attr`

   ❍ **B.** `prof_attr`

   ❍ **C.** `auth_attr`

   ❍ **D.** `exec_attr`

6. In the execution attributes database, which of the following is not a valid value for the `attr` field?

   ❍ **A.** `euid`

   ❍ **B.** `uid`

   ❍ **C.** `egid`

   ❍ **D.** `suid`

7. After creating an RBAC role, you find that the only commands that can be executed within the role are the privileged commands that you have set up. Ordinary nonprivileged commands are not available. The RBAC setup has a problem. What is the cause of this problem?

   ❍ **A.** The role is not associated with a correct profile.

   ❍ **B.** The access mechanism to the role is not initializing properly.

   ❍ **C.** The role's profile is not associated with the correct commands.

   ❍ **D.** The file identifying the privileged commands has missing entries.

   ❍ **E.** The role's profile is not associated with the correct authorizations.

8. Which of the following are valid RBAC databases? (Choose three)

- ❍ **A.** `/etc/usr_attr`
- ❍ **B.** `/etc/user_attr`
- ❍ **C.** `/etc/security/exec_attr`
- ❍ **D.** `/etc/security/prof_attr`

9. You want to enable a user to administer all user `cron` tables. This includes amending entries in any user's `crontab`. Given due care to system security, what should you do to enable the user to carry out this duty?

- ❍ **A.** Give the user the root password.
- ❍ **B.** Set the `suid` on the `crontab` command.
- ❍ **C.** Use RBAC to authorize the user to administer `cron` tables.
- ❍ **D.** Use RBAC to give the user an ID of root when executing the `crontab` command.
- ❍ **E.** Use the ACL mechanism to give the user RW access to each `crontab` table.

10. Which command(s) grant a user access to a role account? Choose all that apply.

- ❍ **A.** `roleadd`
- ❍ **B.** `rolemod`
- ❍ **C.** `useradd`
- ❍ **D.** `usermod`

11. Which option to the `rolemod` command appends an authorization to an exiting list of authorizations?

- ❍ **A.** `-A`
- ❍ **B.** `-P`
- ❍ **C.** `-a`
- ❍ **D.** `-o`
- ❍ **E.** None

12. In which files are profiles defined? Choose all that apply.

   ❍ **A.** `/etc/security/prof_attr`

   ❍ **B.** `/etc/user_attr`

   ❍ **C.** `/etc/security/exec_attr`

   ❍ **D.** `/etc/security/auth_attr`

13. Which statements are true regarding the following line? Choose all that apply.

```
Media Restore:suser:cmd:::/usr/lib/fs/ufs/ufsrestore:euid=0
```

   ❍ **A.** It represents a profile in the `exec_attr` database.

   ❍ **B.** Any role that has Media Restore as a profile is able to execute the `ufsrestore` command with an effective UID of root.

   ❍ **C.** It represents a profile in the `prof_attr` database.

   ❍ **D.** It represents a role definition in the `user_attr` database.

14. In RBAC, which of the following is a bundling mechanism for grouping authorizations and commands with special attributes?

   ❍ **A.** Profile

   ❍ **B.** Role

   ❍ **C.** Authorization

   ❍ **D.** Group

Answers to Exam Questions

1. **C.** Use the `roleadd` command to create a role account. For more information, see the "Using RBAC" section.

2. **B.** `/etc/user_attr` contains details of the extended user attributes. For more information, see the "RBAC Components" section.

3. **A, B.** The `roleadd` command looks very similar to the `useradd` command, but it uses the profile shell as the default shell. For more information, see the "Using RBAC" section.

4. **A.** `user_attr` (extended user attributes database) associates users and roles with authorizations and profiles. For more information, see the "RBAC Components" section.

5. **D.** `exec_attr` (profile attributes database) defines the privileged operations assigned to a profile. For more information, see the "RBAC Components" section.

6. **D.** Four valid keys exist: `euid`, `uid`, `egid`, and `gid`. For more information, see the "RBAC Components" section.

7. **A.** If a role is not associated with a correct profile, the only commands that can be executed within the role are the privileged commands that you have set up. Ordinary non-privileged commands are unavailable. For more information, see the "RBAC Components" section.

8. **B, C, D.** The three valid RBAC databases are `/etc/user_attr`, `/etc/security/exec_attr`, and `/etc/security/prof_attr`. For more information, see the "RBAC Components" section.

9. **C.** To enable a user to administer all user `cron` tables, configure RBAC to authorize the user to administer `cron` tables. For more information, see the "Using RBAC" section.

10. **C, D.** Use the `roleadd` command to create a role account. Then, with the `usermod` command, assign the role to an existing user account using the `-R` option. If you are creating a new user account, use the `useradd` command with the `-R` option to assign the role to the new user account. For more information, see the "Using RBAC" section.

11. **E.** The `rolemod` command does not add to the existing authorizations; it replaces any existing authorization setting. For more information, see the "Using RBAC" section.

12. **A, C.** `/etc/security/prof_attr` (rights profile attributes database) defines profiles, lists the profile's assigned authorizations, and identifies the associated help file. `/etc/security/exec_attr` (profile attributes database) defines the privileged operations assigned to a profile. For more information, see the "RBAC Components" section.

13. **A, B.** The following entry in the `exec_attr` database represents a profile named Media Restore:

    ```
    Media Restore:suser:cmd:::/usr/lib/fs/ufs/ufsrestore:euid=0
    ```

    Any role that has Media Restore as a profile can execute the `ufsrestore` command with an effective UID of root. For more information, see the "RBAC Components" section.

14. **A.** Execution profiles are bundling mechanisms for grouping authorizations and commands with special attributes. For more information, see the "RBAC Components" section.

Suggested Readings and Resources

1. Solaris 10 Documentation CD—"Security Services" and "System Administration Guide: Advanced Administration" manuals.

2. `http://docs.sun.com`. Solaris 10 documentation set—"Security Services" and "System Administration Guide: Advanced Administration" books in the System Administration collection.

CHAPTER TWELVE

Naming Services

Objectives

The following test objectives for exam 310-202 are covered in this chapter:

Explain naming services (DNS, NIS, NIS+, and LDAP) and the naming service switch file (database sources, status codes, and actions).

- ▶ The name services in Solaris help to centralize the shared information on your network. This chapter describes the name services available in Solaris 10 so that you can identify the appropriate name service to use for your network. The name service switch file `/etc/nsswitch.conf` is used to direct requests to the correct name service in use on the system or network. This chapter describes how to select and configure the correct file for use with the available naming services.

Configure, stop and start the Name Service Cache Daemon (`nscd`) and retrieve naming service information using the `getent` command.

- ▶ This chapter describes the use of the Name Service Cache Daemon (`nscd`), which speeds up queries of the most common data and the `getent` command to retrieve naming service information from specified databases.

Configure name service clients during install, configure the DNS client, and set up the LDAP client (client authentication, client profiles, proxy accounts, and LDAP configurations) after installation.

- ▶ This chapter describes how to configure a DNS client and an LDAP client. It assumes, however, that a DNS server and an LDAP server have already been configured elsewhere.

Explain NIS and NIS security including NIS namespace information, domains, processes, `securenets`, and password.adjunct.

- ▶ The NIS name service is covered along with what a domain is and which processes run to manage the domain from a master server, slave server, and client perspective. This chapter also discusses NIS security.

Configure the NIS domain: Build and update NIS maps, manage the NIS master and slave server, configure the NIS client, and troubleshoot NIS for server and client failure messages.

- ▶ This chapter describes how to configure and manage an NIS domain, including setting up an NIS master server, an NIS slave server, and an NIS client. NIS provides a number of default *maps*, which will also be examined, along with the failure messages that can be encountered both on a server and a client.

Outline

Study Strategies

The following strategies will help you prepare for the test:

- As you study this chapter, be prepared to state the purpose of a name service and the type of information it manages. You'll need at least two networked Solaris systems to practice the examples and step-by-step exercises. We highly recommend that you practice the tasks until you can perform them from memory.
- NIS is covered in-depth as the main naming service, although you will have to know how to configure LDAP and DNS clients. See if you can make use of an existing LDAP or DNS server to practice client commands. The exam focuses mainly on NIS with only a few questions on the other name services. Be sure that you understand how to configure NIS master servers, slave servers, and clients. You'll need to understand entries in the NIS name service switch file.
- Be prepared to describe the characteristics of each naming service, compare their functionality, and identify the correct name service switch file associated with a naming service.
- Finally, study the terms provided at the end of this chapter in the "Key Terms" section. Also, be sure you can describe each command we've covered in this chapter, specifically the ones we've used as examples. On the exam you will be asked to match a command or term with the appropriate description.

Introduction

This chapter concentrates mainly on how to configure and administer the servers and clients in an NIS (Network Information Service) domain. NIS is a huge topic that could potentially span several volumes. The purpose of this chapter is to prepare you for questions regarding NIS that might appear on the exam. We also want to provide an overview of NIS, complete enough so that you are equipped to set up a basic NIS network and understand its use. A brief overview of NIS+, originally designed as a replacement for NIS, is included in this chapter, but you should note that Sun does not intend to support this name service in future releases of the Solaris operating environment. It is included here for background information and comprehensiveness, as it is not specifically tested in the exam other than to explain what it is.

DNS and LDAP are also introduced in this chapter (LDAP is expected to replace NIS and NIS+ in the future). This chapter shows how to set up a client using the LDAP and DNS Naming Services.

Name Services Overview

Name services store information in a central location that users, systems, and applications must be able to access to communicate across the network. Information is stored in files, maps, or database tables. Without a central name service, each system would have to maintain its own copy of this information. Therefore, centrally locating this data makes it easier to administer large networks.

NOTE

DNS Exception The DNS name service can be thought of as an exception when considering its global nature because information is stored in hierarchical root servers and in many other servers around the world. The examples provided in this book relate to Local Area Networks, where a DNS server would contain host information relating to the local environment, and is therefore centrally located. The exception applies when the DNS server is connected to the Internet and is part of the global DNS name space.

The information handled by a name service includes, but is not limited to, the following:

- System (host) names and addresses
- User names
- Passwords
- Groups
- Automounter configuration files (`auto.master`, `auto.home`)
- Access permissions and RBAC database files

The Solaris 10 release provides the name services listed in Table 12.1.

TABLE 12.1 Name Services

Name Service	Description
/etc files	The original Unix naming system
NIS	The Network Information Service
NIS+	The Network Information Service Plus (NIS+ is being dropped from future Solaris releases; NIS+ users are recommended to migrate to LDAP)
DNS	The Domain Name System
LDAP	Lightweight Directory Access Protocol

A name service enables centralized management of host files so that systems can be identified by common names instead of by numerical addresses. This simplifies communication because users do not have to remember to enter cumbersome numerical addresses such as 129.44.3.1.

Addresses are not the only network information that systems need to store. They also need to store security information, email addresses, information about their Ethernet interfaces, network services, groups of users allowed to use the network, services offered on the network, and so on. As networks offer more services, the list grows. As a result, each system might need to keep an entire set of files similar to `/etc/hosts`.

As this information changes, without a name service, administrators must keep it current on every system in the network. In a small network, this is simply tedious, but on a medium or large network, the job becomes not only time consuming but also nearly unmanageable.

A name service solves this problem. It stores network information on servers and provides the information to clients that ask for it.

The Name Service Switch File

The name service switch file controls how a client workstation or application obtains network information. The name service switch is often simply referred to as "the switch." The switch determines which naming services an application uses to obtain naming information, and in what order. It is a file called `nsswitch.conf`, which is stored in each system's `/etc` directory. Also in every system's `/etc` directory, you'll find templates that can be used as the `nsswitch.conf` file, as described in Table 12.2. Whatever name service you choose, select the appropriate name service switch template, copy it to `nsswitch.conf`, and customize it as required.

TABLE 12.2 Name Service Switch Template Files

Name	Description
`nsswitch.files`	Use this template when local files in the `/etc` directory are to be used and no name service exists.
`nsswitch.nis`	Uses the NIS database as the primary source of all information except the `passwd`, `group`, `automount`, and `aliases` maps. These are directed to use the local `/etc` files first and then the NIS databases.
`nsswitch.nisplus`	Uses the NIS+ database as the primary source of all information except the `passwd`, `group`, `automount`, and `aliases` tables. These are directed to use the local `/etc` files first and then the NIS+ databases.
`nsswitch.dns`	Sets up the name service to search the local `/etc` files for all entries except the `hosts` entry. The `hosts` entry is directed to use DNS for lookup.
`nsswitch.ldap`	Uses LDAP as the primary source of all information except the `passwd`, `group`, `automount`, and `aliases` tables. These are directed to use the local `/etc` files first and then the LDAP databases.

When you install Solaris 10, the correct template file is copied to `/etc/nsswitch.conf`. This template file contains the default switch configurations used by the chosen naming service. If during software installation you select "none" as the default name service, then the local `/etc` files will be used. In this case, `/etc/nsswitch.conf` is created from `nsswitch.files`, which looks like this:

```
# /etc/nsswitch.files:
#
# An example file that could be copied over to /etc/nsswitch.conf; it
# does not use any naming service.
#
# "hosts:" and "services:" in this file are used only if the
# /etc/netconfig file has a "-" for nametoaddr_libs of "inet" transports.

passwd:     files
group:      files
hosts:      files
ipnodes:    files
networks:   files
protocols:  files
rpc:        files
ethers:     files
netmasks:   files
bootparams: files
publickey:  files
# At present there isn't a 'files' backend for netgroup;  the system will
#   figure it out pretty quickly, and won't use netgroups at all.
netgroup:   files
automount:  files
aliases:    files
```

```
services:   files
sendmailvars:   files
printers:       user files
auth_attr:  files
prof_attr:  files
project:    files
```

If you decide to use a different name service after software installation, you can move the correct switch file into place manually. For example, if you start using NIS then copy `/etc/nsswitch.nis` as follows:

```
cp /etc/nsswitch.nis /etc/nsswitch.conf
```

The default `/etc/nsswitch.nis` file looks like this:

```
# /etc/nsswitch.nis:
#
# An example file that could be copied over to /etc/nsswitch.conf; it
# uses NIS (YP) in conjunction with files.
#
# "hosts:" and "services:" in this file are used only if the
# /etc/netconfig file has a "-" for nametoaddr_libs of "inet" transports.

# NIS service requires that svc:/network/nis/client:default be enabled
# and online.

# the following two lines obviate the "+" entry in /etc/passwd and /etc/group.
passwd:     files nis
group:      files nis

# consult /etc "files" only if nis is down.
hosts:      nis [NOTFOUND=return] files

# Note that IPv4 addresses are searched for in all of the ipnodes databases
# before searching the hosts databases.
ipnodes:    nis [NOTFOUND=return] files

networks:   nis [NOTFOUND=return] files
protocols:  nis [NOTFOUND=return] files
rpc:        nis [NOTFOUND=return] files
ethers:     nis [NOTFOUND=return] files
netmasks:   nis [NOTFOUND=return] files
bootparams: nis [NOTFOUND=return] files
publickey:  nis [NOTFOUND=return] files

netgroup:   nis

automount:  files nis
aliases:    files nis
```

```
# for efficient getservbyname() avoid nis
services:   files nis
printers:   user files nis

auth_attr:  files nis
prof_attr:  files nis
project:    files nis
```

Each line of the /etc/nsswitch.nis file identifies a particular type of network information, such as host, password, and group, followed by one or more sources, such as NIS maps, the DNS hosts table, or the local /etc files. The source is where the client looks for the network information. For example, the system should first look for the passwd information in the /etc/passwd file. Then, if it does not find the login name there, it needs to query the NIS server.

The name service switch file lists many types of network information, called databases, with their name service sources for resolution, and the order in which the sources are to be searched. Table 12.3 lists valid sources that can be specified in this file.

TABLE 12.3 Database Sources

Source	Description
files	Refers to the client's local /etc files
nisplus	Refers to an NIS+ table
nis	Refers to an NIS table
user	Refers to the ${HOME}/.printers file
dns	Applies only to the hosts entry
ldap	Refers to the LDAP directory
compat	Supports an old-style + syntax that used to be used in the passwd and group information

As shown in the previous nsswitch.nis template file, the name service switch file can contain action values for several of the entries. When the naming service searches a specified source, such as local files or NIS, the source returns a status code. These status codes are described in Table 12.4.

TABLE 12.4 Name Service Search Status Codes

Source	Description
SUCCESS	Requested entry was found.
UNAVAIL	Source was unavailable.
NOTFOUND	Source contains no such entry.
TRYAGAIN	Source returned an "I am busy, try later" message.

For each status code, two actions are possible:

- **Continue**—Try the next source.
- **Return**—Stop looking for an entry.

The default actions are as follows:

SUCCESS = return

UNAVAIL = continue

NOTFOUND = continue

TRYAGAIN = continue

Normally, a success indicates that the search is over and an unsuccessful result indicates that the next source should be queried. There are occasions, however, when you want to stop searching when an unsuccessful search result is returned. For example, the following entry in the `nsswitch.nis` template states that only the NIS hosts table in the NIS map is searched:

```
hosts: nis [NOTFOUND=return] files
```

If the NIS map has no entry for the host lookup, the system would not reference the local `/etc/hosts` file. Remove the `[NOTFOUND=return]` entry if you want to search the NIS hosts table and the local `/etc/hosts` file.

NOTE

`NOTFOUND=return` The next source in the list will only be searched if NIS is down, or has been disabled.

/etc Files

`/etc` files are the traditional Unix way of maintaining information about hosts, users, passwords, groups, and automount maps, to name just a few. These files are text files located on each individual system that can be edited using the `vi` editor or the text editor within CDE.

Each file needs to be individually maintained and on a large network, this can be a difficult task. As IP addresses change, and users' accounts are added and deleted, it can become difficult to maintain all these files and keep them in sync between each system. On a large changing network, the traditional approach to maintaining this information had to change; therefore, the following name services were introduced.

NIS

NIS, formerly called the Yellow Pages (YP), is a distributed database system that lets the system administrator administer the configuration of many hosts from a central location. Common configuration information, which would have to be maintained separately on each host in a network without NIS, can be stored and maintained in a central location and then propagated to all the nodes in the network. NIS stores information about workstation names and addresses, users, the network itself, and network services. This collection of network information is referred to as the *NIS namespace*.

NOTE

YP to NIS As stated, NIS was formerly known as Sun Yellow Pages (YP). The functionality of the two remains the same; only the name has changed.

Before beginning the discussion of the structure of NIS, you need to be aware that the NIS administration databases are called *maps*. An NIS domain is a collection of systems that share a common set of NIS maps.

The Structure of the NIS Network

The systems within an NIS network are configured in the following ways:

- Master server
- Slave servers
- Clients of NIS servers

The center of the NIS network is the *NIS master server*. The system designated as master server contains the set of maps that you, the NIS administrator, create and update as necessary. After the NIS network is set up, any changes to the maps must be made on the master server. Each NIS domain must have one, and only one, master server. The master server should be a system that can handle the additional load of propagating NIS updates with minimal performance degradation.

In addition to the master server, you can create backup servers, called *NIS slave servers*, to take some of the load off the master server and to substitute for the master server if it goes down. If you create an NIS slave server, the maps on the master server are transferred to the slave server. A slave server has a complete copy of the master set of NIS maps. If a change is made to a map on the master server, the updates are propagated among the slave servers. The existence of slave servers lets the system administrator evenly distribute the load that results from answering NIS requests. It also minimizes the impact of a server becoming unavailable.

Typically, all the hosts in the network, including the master and slave servers, are *NIS clients*. If a process on an NIS client requests configuration information, it calls NIS instead of looking in its local configuration files. For group and password information and mail aliases, the `/etc` files might be consulted first, and then NIS might be consulted if the requested information is not found in the `/etc` files. Doing this, for example, allows each physical system to have a separate root account password.

Any system can be an NIS client, but only systems with disks should be NIS servers, whether master or slave. Servers are also clients of themselves.

As mentioned earlier, the set of maps shared by the servers and clients is called the *NIS domain*. The master copies of the maps are located on the NIS master server, in the directory `/var/yp/<domainname>`, in which `<domainname>` is the chosen name for your own domain. Under the `<domainname>` directory, each map is stored as two files: `<mapname>.dir` and `<mapname>.pag`. Each slave server has an identical directory containing the same set of maps.

When a client starts up, it broadcasts a request for a server that serves its domain. Any server that has the set of maps for the client's domain, whether it's a master or a slave server, can answer the request. The client "binds" to the first server that answers its request, and that server then answers all its NIS queries.

A host cannot be the master server for more than one NIS domain. However, a master server for one domain might be a slave server for another domain. A host can be a slave server for multiple domains. A client, however, belongs to only one domain.

Determining How Many NIS Servers You Need

The following guidelines can be used to determine how many NIS servers you need in your domain:

- You should put at least one server on each subnet in your domain, depending on the total number of clients. When a client starts up, it broadcasts a message to find the nearest server. Solaris 10 does not require the server to be on the same subnet, but it is faster and more resilient to do so.
- In general, the number of NIS clients a server can handle is limited by the physical hardware specification and current load of the server. A fast, lightly loaded server can easily support hundreds of NIS clients, while a slower, heavily loaded database server, for example, would struggle to support 50 clients.

Determining Which Hosts Will Be NIS Servers

Determine which systems on your network will be NIS servers as follows:

- Choose servers that are reliable and highly available.
- Choose fast servers that are not used for CPU-intensive applications. Do not use gateways or terminal servers as NIS servers.
- Although it isn't a requirement, it's a good idea to distribute servers appropriately among client networks. In other words, each subnet should have enough servers to accommodate the clients on that subnet.

Information Managed by NIS

As discussed, NIS stores information in a set of files called maps. Maps were designed to replace Unix `/etc` files, as well as other configuration files.

NIS maps are two-column tables. One column is the key, and the other column is the information value related to the key. NIS finds information for a client by searching through the keys. Some information is stored in several maps because each map uses a different key. For example, the names and addresses of systems are stored in two maps: `hosts.byname` and `hosts.byaddr`. If a server has a system's name and needs to find its address, it looks in the `hosts.byname` map. If it has the address and needs to find the name, it looks in the `hosts.byaddr` map.

Maps for a domain are located in each server's `/var/yp/`*<domainname>* directory. For example, the maps that belong to the domain pyramid.com are located in each server's `/var/yp/pyramid.com` directory.

An NIS Makefile is stored in the `/var/yp` directory of the NIS server at installation time. If you run the `/usr/ccs/bin/make` command in that directory, `makedbm` creates or modifies the default NIS maps from the input files. For example, an input file might be `/etc/hosts`. Issue the following command to create the NIS map files:

```
cd /var/yp
/usr/ccs/bin/make
```

NOTE

Generate Maps on the Master Server Only Always make the maps on the master server and never on a slave server. If you run `make` on a slave server, the maps will be generated from data in the slave server's local files and will be inconsistent with the rest of the domain. Additionally, NIS clients that are bound to the slave server will be querying inconsistent data and receiving unexpected results.

Creating NIS maps is described in more detail later in this chapter in the "Configuring an NIS Master Server" section.

Solaris provides a default set of NIS maps. They are described in Table 12.5, including the corresponding file that is used to create each of them. You might want to use all or only some of these maps. NIS can also use whatever maps you create or add, if you install other software products.

TABLE 12.5 Default NIS Maps

Map Name	Corresponding NIS Admin File	Description
ageing.byname	/etc/shadow	Contains password aging information.
audit_user	/etc/security/audit_user	Contains per user auditing preselection data.
auth_attr	/etc/security/auth_attr	Contains the authorization description database, part of RBAC.
auto.home	/etc/auto_home	Automounter file for home directories.
auto.master	/etc/auto_master	Master automounter map.
bootparams	/etc/bootparams	Contains the pathnames that clients need during startup: root, swap, and possibly others.
ethers.byaddr	/etc/ethers	Contains system names and Ethernet addresses. The Ethernet address is the key in the map.
ethers.byname	/etc/ethers	Contains system names and Ethernet addresses. The system name is the key.
exec_attr	/etc/security/exec_attr	Contains execution profiles, part of RBAC.
group.adjunct.byname	/etc/group	C2 security option for group files that use passwords.
group.bygid	/etc/group	Contains group security information. The GID (group ID) is the key.
group.byname	/etc/group	Contains group security information. The group name is the key.
hosts.byaddr	/etc/hosts	Contains the system name and IP address. The IP address is the key.
hosts.byname	/etc/hosts	Contains the system name and IP address. The system (host) name is the key.
ipnodes.byaddr	/etc/inet/ipnodes	Contains the system name and IP address. The IP address is the key.

(continues)

Map Name	Corresponding NIS Admin File	Description
ipnodes.byaddr	/etc/inet/ipnodes	Contains the system name and IP address. The system (host) name is the key.
mail.aliases	/etc/mail/aliases	Contains aliases and mail addresses. The alias is the key.
mail.byaddr	/etc/mail/aliases	Contains mail addresses and aliases. The mail address is the key.
netgroup	/etc/netgroup	Contains the group name, username, and system name. The group name is the key.
netgroup.byhost	/etc/netgroup	Contains the group name, username, and system name. The system name is the key.
netgroup.byuser	/etc/netgroup	Contains the group name, username, and system name. The username is the key.
netid.byname	/etc/passwd	Used for Unix-style hosts and group authentication. It contains the system name and mail address (including domain name). If a `netid` file is available, it is consulted in addition to the data available through the other files.
netmasks.byaddr	/etc/netmasks	Contains the network masks to be used with IP subnetting. The address is the key.
networks.byaddr	/etc/networks	Contains names of networks known to your system and their IP addresses. The address is the key.
networks.byname	/etc/networks	Contains names of networks known to your system and their IP addresses. The name of the network is the key.
passwd.adjunct.byname	/etc/passwd and /etc/shadow	Contains auditing shadow information and the hidden password information for C2 clients.
passwd.byname	/etc/passwd and /etc/shadow	Contains password and shadow information. The username is the key.
passwd.byuid	/etc/passwd and /etc/shadow	Contains password and shadow information. The user ID is the key.
prof_attr	/etc/security/prof_attr	Contains profile descriptions, part of RBAC.
project.byname	/etc/project	Contains the projects in use on the network. The project name is the key.

Map Name	Corresponding NIS Admin File	Description
project.bynumber	/etc/project	Contains the projects in use on the network. The project number (ID) is the key.
protocols.byname	/etc/protocols	Contains the network protocols known to your network. The protocol is the key.
protocols.bynumber	/etc/protocols	Contains the network protocols known to your network. The protocol number is the key.
publickey.byname	/etc/publickey	Contains public or secret keys. The username is the key.
rpc.bynumber	/etc/rpc	Contains the program number and the name of Remote Procedure Calls (RPCs) known to your system. The program number is the key.
services.byname	/etc/services	Lists Internet services known to your network. The key port or protocol is the key.
services.byservicename	/etc/services	Lists Internet services known to your network. The service name is the key.
timezone.byname	/etc/timezone	Contains the default timezone database. The timezone name is the key.
user_attr	/etc/user_attr	Contains the extended user attributes database, part of RBAC.
ypservers	N/A	Lists the NIS servers known to your network. It's a single-column table with the system name as the key.

The information in these files is put into NIS databases automatically when you create an NIS master server. Other system files can also be managed by NIS if you want to customize your configuration.

NIS makes updating network databases much simpler than with the /etc file system. You no longer have to change the administrative /etc files on every system each time you modify the network environment. For example, if you add a new system to a network running NIS, you only have to update the input file on the master server and run /usr/ccs/bin/make from the /var/yp directory. This process automatically updates the hosts.byname and hosts.byaddr maps. These maps are then transferred to any slave servers and made available to all the domain's client systems and their programs.

Just as you use the cat command to display the contents of a text file, you can use the ypcat command to display the values in a map. Here is the basic ypcat syntax:

```
ypcat [-k] <mapname>
```

If a map is composed only of keys, as in the case of `ypservers`, use `ypcat -k`—otherwise, `ypcat` prints blank lines.

In this case, `mapname` is the name of the map you want to examine.

You can use the `ypwhich` command to determine which server is the master of a particular map:

```
ypwhich -m <mapname>
```

In this case, `mapname` is the name of the map whose master you want to find. `ypwhich` responds by displaying the name of the master server.

These and other NIS commands are covered in the following sections.

Planning Your NIS Domain

Before you configure systems as NIS servers or clients, you must plan the NIS domain. Each domain has a domain name, and each system shares the common set of maps belonging to that domain. Step by Step 12.1 outlines the steps for planning an NIS domain.

STEP BY STEP

12.1 Planning Your NIS Domain

1. Decide which systems will be in your NIS domain.
2. Choose an NIS domain name. AN NIS domain name can be up to 256 characters long, although much shorter names are more practical. A good practice is to limit domain names to no more than 32 characters. Domain names are case sensitive. For convenience, you can use your Internet domain name as the basis for your NIS domain name. For example, if your Internet domain name is `pdesigninc.com`, you can name your NIS domain `pdesigninc.com`.
3. Before a system can use NIS, the correct NIS domain name and system name must be set. This must be done on the NIS servers as well as the clients. A system's host name is set by the system's `/etc/nodename` file, and the system's domain name is set by the system's `/etc/defaultdomain` file. These files are read at startup, and the contents are used by the `uname -s` and `domainname` commands, respectively. A sample `/etc/nodename` file would look like this:

   ```
   more /etc/nodename
   ```

   The system responds with this:

   ```
   sparcserver
   ```

   A sample `/etc/defaultdomain` file would look like this:

   ```
   more /etc/defaultdomain
   ```

The system responds with this:

```
pdesigninc.com
```

In order to set the domain name, you would either have to run the `domainname` command, entering your domain name as the argument to the command, or reboot if you have edited `/etc/defaultdomain`. Whichever way you choose, you are now ready to configure your NIS master server.

Configuring an NIS Master Server

Before configuring an NIS master server, be sure the NIS software cluster is installed. The package names are SUNWypu and SUNWypr. Use the `pkginfo` command to check for these packages. Both packages are part of the standard Solaris 10 release. The daemons that support the NIS are described in Table 12.6.

TABLE 12.6 NIS Daemons

Daemon	Function
`ypserv`	This daemon is the NIS database lookup server. The `ypserv` daemon's primary function is to look up information in its local database of NIS maps. If the `/var/yp/ypserv.log` file exists when `ypserv` starts up, log information is written to it (if error conditions arise). At least one `ypserv` daemon must be present on the network for the NIS service to function.
`ypbind`	This daemon is the NIS binding process that runs on all client systems that are set up to use NIS. The function of `ypbind` is to remember information that lets all NIS client processes on a node communicate with some NIS server process.
`ypxfrd`	This daemon provides the high-speed map transfer. `ypxfrd` moves an NIS map in the default domain to the local host. It creates a temporary map in the directory `/var/yp/ypdomain`.
`rpc.yppasswdd`	This daemon handles password change requests from the `yppasswd` command. It changes a password entry in the `passwd`, shadow, and `security/passwd.adjunct` files.
`rpc.ypupdated`	This daemon updates NIS information. `ypupdated` consults the updaters file in the `/var/yp` directory to determine which NIS maps should be updated and how to change them.

The commands that you use to manage NIS are shown in Table 12.7. We describe some of these commands in more detail later when we show examples of setting up NIS.

TABLE 12.7 NIS Commands

Utility	Function
`make`	This command updates NIS maps by reading the Makefile (if run in the `/var/yp` directory). You can use `make` to update all maps based on the input files or to update individual maps.
`makedbm`	This command creates a dbm file for an NIS map. The `makedbm` command takes an input file and converts it to a pair of files in ndbm format. When you run `make` in the `/var/yp` directory, `makedbm` creates or modifies the default NIS maps from the input files.
`ypcat`	This command lists data in an NIS map.
`ypinit`	This command builds and installs an NIS database and initializes the NIS client's (and server's) `ypservers` list. `ypinit` is used to set up an NIS client system. You must be the superuser to run this command.
`yppoll`	This command gets a map order number from a server. The `yppoll` command asks a `ypserv` process what the order number is and which host is the master NIS server for the named map.
`yppush`	This command propagates a new version of an NIS map from the NIS master server to NIS slave servers.
`ypset`	This command sets binding to a particular server. `ypset` is useful for binding a client node that is on a different broadcast network.
`ypstart`	This command is used to start NIS. After the host has been configured using the `ypinit` command, `ypstart` automatically determines the machine's NIS status and starts the appropriate daemons. This command, although still available, is not the recommended way to start NIS and might even have unpredictable results. NIS should be started via the Service Management Facility (SMF).
`ypstop`	This command is used to stop the NIS processes. This command, although still available, is not the recommended way to stop the NIS processes and might even have unpredictable results. NIS should be stopped via the Service Management Facility (SMF).
`ypwhich`	This command returns the name of the NIS server that supplies the NIS name services to an NIS client, or it returns the name of the master for a map.

EXAM ALERT

Identifying Daemons Versus Commands Make sure you are familiar with what each daemon and command does. Exam questions are frequently presented by describing the daemon or command and asking you to identify it correctly.

An NIS master server holds the source files for all the NIS maps in the domain. Any changes to the NIS maps must be made on the NIS master server. The NIS master server delivers information to NIS clients and supplies the NIS slave servers with up-to-date maps. Before the NIS master server is started, some of the NIS source files need to be created.

The basic steps for setting up an NIS master server are as follows:

- Creating the master passwd file
- Creating the master group file
- Creating the master hosts file
- Creating other master files
- Preparing the Makefile
- Setting up the master server with ypinit
- Starting and stopping NIS on the master server
- Setting up the name service switch

Each of these tasks is described in the following subsections.

Creating the Master passwd File

The first task in setting up an NIS master server is to prepare the source file for the passwd map. However, be careful with this source file. The source files can be located either in the /etc directory on the master server or in some other directory. Locating the source files in /etc is undesirable because the contents of the maps are then the same as the contents of the local files on the master server. This is a special problem for passwd and shadow files because all users would have access to the master server maps, and because the root password would be passed to all YP clients through the passwd map.

Sun recommends that for security reasons, and to prevent unauthorized root access, the files used to build the NIS password maps should not contain an entry for root. Therefore, the password maps should not be built from the files located in the master server's /etc directory. The password files used to build the passwd maps should have the root entry removed from them, and they should be located in a directory that can be protected from unauthorized access.

For this exercise, copy all the source files from the /etc directory into the /var/yp directory. Because the source files are located in a directory other than /etc, modify the Makefile in /var/yp by changing the DIR=/etc line to DIR=/var/yp. Also, modify the PWDIR password macro in the Makefile to refer to the directory in which the passwd and shadow files reside by changing the line PWDIR=/etc to PWDIR=/var/yp.

Now, to create the passwd source file, use a copy of the /etc/passwd file on the system that becomes the master NIS server. Create a passwd file that has all the logins in it. This file is used to create the NIS map. Step by Step 12.2 shows you how to create the passwd source file.

STEP BY STEP

12.2 Creating the Password Source File

1. Copy the `/etc/passwd` file from each host in your network to the `/var/yp` directory on the host that will be the master server. Name each copy `/var/yp/passwd.`*<hostname>*, in which *<hostname>* is the name of the host it came from.

2. Concatenate all the `passwd` files into a temporary `passwd` file, as follows:

```
cd /var/yp
cat passwd passwd.hostname1 passwd.hostname2 ... > passwd.temp
```

3. Issue the `sort` command to sort the temporary `passwd` file by username, and then pipe it to the `uniq` command to remove duplicate entries:

```
sort -t : -k 1,1 /var/yp/passwd.temp | uniq > /var/yp/passwd.temp
```

NOTE

Sorting the `passwd` File NIS does not require that the `passwd` file be sorted in any particular way. Sorting the `passwd` file simply makes it easier to find duplicate entries.

4. Examine `/var/yp/passwd.temp` for duplicate usernames that were not caught by the previous `uniq` command. This could happen if a user login occurs twice, but the lines are not exactly the same. If you find multiple entries for the same user, edit the file to remove redundant ones. Be sure each user in your network has a unique username and UID (user ID).

5. Issue the following command to sort the temporary `passwd` file by UID:

```
sort -o /var/yp/passwd.temp -t: -k 3n,3 /var/yp/passwd.temp
```

6. Examine `/var/yp/passwd.temp` for duplicate UIDs once more. If you find multiple entries with the same UID, edit the file to change the UIDs so that no two users have the same UID.

NOTE

Duplicate UIDs and Usernames You will have to resolve duplicate UIDs (where the same UID has been used on more than one system) and usernames (where a user has previously had home directories on each system). The NIS-managed UID will have ownership of any duplicated UID's files unless they are changed accordingly to match modifications made to this file.

7. Remove the root login from the `/var/yp/passwd.temp` file. If you notice that the root login occurs more than once, remove all entries.

8. After you have a complete `passwd` file with no duplicates, move `/var/yp/passwd.temp` (the sorted, edited file) to `/var/yp/passwd`. This file is used to generate the `passwd` map for your NIS domain. Remove all the `/var/yp/passwd.`*<hostname>* files from the master server.

Creating the Master Group File

Just like creating a master `/var/yp/passwd` file, the next task is to prepare one master `/var/yp/group` file to be used to create an NIS map. To create the master group file, follow Step by Step 12.3.

STEP BY STEP

12.3 Creating the Master Group File

1. Copy the `/etc/group` file from each host in your NIS domain to the `/var/yp` directory on the host that will be the master server. Name each copy `/var/yp/group.`*<hostname>*, in which *<hostname>* is the name of the host it came from.
2. Concatenate all the group files, including the master server's group file, into a temporary group file:

```
cd /var/yp
cat group group.hostname1 group.hostname2 ... > group.temp
```

3. Issue the following command to sort the temporary group file by group name:

```
sort -o /var/yp/group.temp -t: -k1,1 /var/yp/group.temp
```

   NIS does not require that the group file be sorted in any particular way. Sorting the group file simply makes it easier to find duplicate entries.
4. Examine `/var/yp/group.temp` for duplicate group names. If a group name appears more than once, merge the groups that have the same name into one group and remove the duplicate entries.
5. Issue the following command to sort the temporary group file by GID:

```
sort -o /var/yp/group.temp -t: -k 3n,3 /var/yp/group.temp
```

6. Examine `/var/yp/group.temp` for duplicate GIDs. If you find multiple entries with the same GID, edit the file to change the GIDs so that no two groups have the same GID.

NOTE

Duplicate GIDs You will have to resolve duplicate GIDs (where the same GID has been used on more than one system) and group names (where a group has previously existed on each system). The NIS-managed GID will have group ownership of any duplicated GID's files unless they are changed accordingly to match modifications made to this file.

7. Move /var/yp/group.temp (the sorted, edited file) to /var/yp/group. This file is used to generate the group map for your NIS domain. Remove the /var/yp/group.*<hostname>* files from the master server.

Creating the Master hosts File

Now create the master /etc/hosts file the same way you created the master /var/yp/passwd and /var/yp/group files (see Step by Step 12.4).

STEP BY STEP

12.4 Creating the Master hosts File

1. Copy the /etc/hosts file from each host in your NIS domain to the /var/yp directory on the host that will be the master server. Name each copy /var/yp/hosts.*<hostname>*, in which *<hostname>* is the name of the host from which it came.
2. Concatenate all the host files, including the master server's host file, into a temporary hosts file, as follows:

```
cd /var/yp
cat hosts hosts.hostname1 hosts.hostname2 ... > hosts.temp
```

3. Issue the following command to sort the temporary hosts file so that duplicate IP addresses are on adjacent lines:

```
sort -o /var/yp/hosts.temp /var/yp/hosts.temp
```

4. Examine /var/yp/hosts.temp for duplicate IP addresses. If you need to map an IP address to multiple hostnames, include them as aliases in a single entry.
5. Issue the following command to sort the temporary hosts file by hostname:

```
sort -o /var/yp/hosts.temp -b -k 2,2 /var/yp/hosts.temp
```

6. Examine /var/yp/hosts.temp for duplicate hostnames. A hostname can be mapped to multiple IP addresses only if the IP addresses belong to different LAN cards on the same host. If a hostname appears in multiple entries that are mapped to IP addresses on different hosts, remove all the entries but one.
7. Examine the /var/yp/hosts.temp file for duplicate aliases. No alias should appear in more than one entry.
8. Move /var/yp/hosts.temp (the sorted, edited file) to /var/yp/hosts. This file is used to generate the host's map for your NIS domain. Remove the /var/yp/hosts.*<hostname>* files from the master server.

Creating Other Master Files

The following files, which were described in Table 12.2, can also be copied to the /var/yp directory to be used as source files for NIS maps, but first be sure that they reflect an up-to-date picture of your system environment:

- /etc/security/audit_user
- /etc/security/auth_attr
- /etc/auto_home
- /etc/auto_master
- /etc/bootparams
- /etc/ethers
- /etc/security/exec_attr
- /etc/inet/ipnodes
- /etc/netgroup
- /etc/netmasks
- /etc/networks
- /etc/security/prof_attr
- /etc/project
- /etc/protocols
- /etc/publickey
- /etc/rpc
- /etc/services
- /etc/shadow
- /etc/timezone
- /etc/user_attr

Unlike other source files, the /etc/mail/aliases file cannot be moved to another directory. This file must reside in the /etc/mail directory. Be sure that the /etc/mail/aliases source file is complete by verifying that it contains all the mail aliases that you want to have available throughout the domain.

Preparing the Makefile

After checking the source files and copying them into the source file directory, you need to convert those source files into the ndbm format maps that NIS uses. This is done automatically for you by ypinit. We describe how to use ypinit in the next section.

The ypinit script calls the program make, which uses the file Makefile located in the /var/yp directory. A default Makefile is provided for you in this directory. It contains the commands needed to transform the source files into the desired ndbm format maps.

The function of the Makefile is to create the appropriate NIS maps for each of the databases listed under "all." After passing through makedbm, the data is collected in two files, mapname.dir and mapname.pag. Both files are located in the /var/yp/*<domainname>* directory on the master server.

The Makefile builds passwd maps from the $PWDIR/passwd, $PWDIR/shadow, and $PWDIR/security/passwd.adjunct files, as appropriate.

Setting Up the Master Server with `ypinit`

The `/usr/sbin/ypinit` shell script sets up master and slave servers and clients to use NIS. It also initially runs `make` to create the maps on the master server. See Step by Step 12.5 to set up a master server using `ypinit`.

STEP BY STEP

12.5 Using `ypinit` to Set Up the Master Server

1. Become root on the master server and ensure that the name service receives its information from the `/etc` files, not from NIS, by typing the following:

   ```
   cp /etc/nsswitch.files /etc/nsswitch.conf
   ```

2. Edit the `/etc/hosts` file to add the name and IP address of each of the NIS servers.

3. To build new maps on the master server, type

   ```
   /usr/sbin/ypinit -m
   ```

   `ypinit` prompts you for a list of other systems to become NIS slave servers. Type the name of the server you are working on, along with the names of your NIS slave servers. Enter the server name, and then press Enter. Do this for each server. Enter each server on a separate line. Press Ctrl+D when you're finished. At this point, the entered list of servers is displayed and you are asked if it is correct. Type **y** if it is correct. If the list is not correct, then type **n** and you will be returned to the list of servers to add extra entries.

4. `ypinit` asks whether you want the procedure to terminate at the first nonfatal error or to continue despite nonfatal errors. Type **y**.

   If you typed y, `ypinit` exits upon encountering the first problem; you can then fix the problem and restart `ypinit`. This procedure is recommended if you are running `ypinit` for the first time. If you prefer to continue, you can manually try to fix all the problems that might occur, and then restart `ypinit`.

> **NOTE**
>
> **Nonfatal Errors** A nonfatal error might be displayed if some of the map files are not present. These errors do not affect the functionality of NIS.

5. `ypinit` asks whether the existing files in the `/var/yp/`*<domainname>* directory can be destroyed.

   This message is displayed only if NIS was previously installed. You must answer yes to install the new version of NIS.

6. After `ypinit` has constructed the list of servers, it invokes `make`.

   The `make` command uses the instructions contained in the Makefile located in `/var/yp`. It cleans any remaining comment lines from the files you designated and then runs `makedbm` on them, creating the appropriate maps and establishing the name of the master server for each map.

7. To enable NIS as the naming service, type

   ```
   cp /etc/nsswitch.nis /etc/nsswitch.conf
   ```

   This command replaces the current switch file with the default NIS-oriented one. You can edit this file as necessary. The name service switch file `/etc/nsswitch.conf` is described later in this chapter.

Now that the master maps are created, you can start the NIS daemons on the master server.

EXAM ALERT

Selecting the Correct Command Option Exam questions are often based on the syntax of the `ypinit` command. You might be given a scenario where you are asked to select the correct command option to initialize either a master server, a slave server, or a client. Ensure that you are completely familiar with what each command option achieves.

Starting and Stopping NIS on the Master Server

To start up NIS on the master server, you need to start the `ypserv` process on the server and run `ypbind`. The daemon `ypserv` answers information requests from clients after looking them up in the NIS maps. You can start up NIS manually on the server by running the `svcadm enable nis/server` command from the command line, followed by `svcadm enable nis/client`. After you configure the NIS master server by running `ypinit`, the NIS server is is automatically invoked to start up `ypserv` whenever the system is started up. This is actioned via SMF.

To manually stop the NIS server processes, run the `svcadm disable nis/server` command on the server as follows:

```
svcadm disable nis/server
svcadm disable nis/client
```

NOTE

NIS and SMF You should note that the NIS service is now managed via the Service Management Facility (SMF) and can be stopped and started using the `svcadm` command. You can still use the `ypstop` and `ypstart` commands, but you might get unexpected results, especially as SMF could automatically restart the service if you stop it manually. The recommended way to start and stop NIS is via SMF.

Setting Up NIS Clients

As root, you must perform four tasks to set up a system as an NIS client:

- Ensure that user account information from the /etc/passwd and /etc/group files on the client has already been taken into account in the master passwd and group files. If not, then refer back to the previous section "Setting Up the Master passwd File" and "Creating the Master Group File" for details on how to merge existing account information into the NIS-managed maps.

NOTE

Client Home Directories Home directories that have previously existed on separate systems need to be taken into account when NIS is introduced. Without correct handling, a user's files might come under the ownership of another user, unless they are dealt with at the time of any passwd and group modifications.

- Set the domain name on the client.
- Set up the nsswitch.conf file on the client, as described earlier in this chapter.
- Configure the client to use NIS, as explained next.

The first step is to remove from the /etc/passwd file all the user entries that are managed by the NIS server. Don't forget to update the /etc/shadow file. Also, remove entries from /etc/group, /etc/hosts, and any other network files that are now managed by NIS.

After setting up the nsswitch.conf file and setting your domain name as described in the section titled "Planning Your NIS Domain," you configure each client system to use NIS by logging in as root and running the /usr/sbin/ypinit command, as follows:

```
ypinit -c
```

You are asked to identify the NIS servers from which the client can obtain name service information. Enter each server name, followed by a carriage return. You can list one master and as many slave servers as you want. The servers that you list can be located anywhere in the domain. It is good practice to first list the servers closest (in network terms) to the system, followed by the more distant servers on the network because the client attempts to bind to the first server on the list.

When you enter a server name during the client setup, the file /var/yp/<domainname>/ypservers is populated with the list of servers you enter. This list is used each time the client is rebooted, to establish a "binding" with an NIS server. An alternative method is to rename the previously mentioned file and restart NIS. This causes the client to "broadcast" over the local subnet to try to find an NIS server to bind to. If no server responds, then the client will be unable to use the name service until either an NIS slave server is configured on the same subnet, or the list of servers is re-instated.

Test the NIS client by logging out and logging back in using a login name that is no longer in the `/etc/passwd` file and is managed by NIS. Test the host's map by pinging a system that is not identified in the local `/etc/hosts` file.

Setting Up NIS Slave Servers

Before setting up the NIS slave server, you must set it up as an NIS client. After you've verified that the NIS master server is functioning properly by testing the NIS on this system, you can set up the system as a slave server. Your network can have one or more slave servers. Having slave servers ensures the continuity of NIS if the master server is unavailable. Before actually running `ypinit` to create the slave servers, you should run the `domainname` command on each NIS slave to be sure that the domain name is consistent with the master server. Remember, the domain name is set by adding the domain name to the `/etc/defaultdomain` file.

To set up an NIS slaver server, see Step by Step 12.6.

STEP BY STEP

12.6 Setting Up the NIS Slave Server

1. As root, edit the `/etc/hosts` file on the slave server to add the name and IP address of the NIS master server. At this point, we are assuming that you're not using DNS to manage hostnames (DNS is covered later in this chapter). Step 3 prompts you for the hostname of the NIS master server. You need an entry for this hostname in the local `/etc/hosts` file; otherwise, you need to specify the IP address of the NIS server.
2. Change directories to `/var/yp` on the slave server.
3. To initialize the slave server as a client, type the following:

   ```
   /usr/sbin/ypinit -c
   ```

   The `ypinit` command prompts you for a list of NIS servers. Enter the name of the local slave you are working on first and then the master server, followed by the other NIS slave servers in your domain, in order, from the physically closest to the farthest (in network terms).
4. Next, you need to determine whether `ypbind` is already running. If it is running, you need to stop and restart it. Check to see if `ypbind` is running by typing this:

   ```
   pgrep -l ypbind
   ```

   If a listing is displayed, `ypbind` is running. If `ypbind` is running, stop it by typing this:

   ```
   svcadm disable nis/client
   ```

5. Type the following to restart `ypbind`:

```
svcadm enable nis/client
```

6. To initialize this system as a slave, type the following:

```
/usr/sbin/ypinit -s master
```

   In this example, *`master`* is the system name of the existing NIS master server.

   Repeat the procedures described in these steps for each system that you want configured as an NIS slave server.

7. Now you can start daemons on the slave server and begin the NIS. First, you must stop all existing `yp` processes by typing the following:

```
svcadm disable nis/server
```

   To start `ypserv` on the slave server and run `ypbind`, you can either reboot the server or type the following:

```
svcadm enable nis/server
```

Creating Custom NIS Maps

NIS provides a number of default maps, as we have already seen earlier in this chapter. You can also add your own map to be managed by NIS. This is a simple process where you first create the file with a normal text editor such as `vi` and then create the map. The following example shows how to create a fictional address book map called abook from the text file `/etc/abook`. We assume here that the domain being used is `pdesigninc.com`:

```
cd /var/yp
makedbm /etc/abook pdesigninc.com/abook
```

The map is now created and exists in the master server's directory. You can now run such commands as `ypcat` to list the contents of the map. To distribute it to other slave servers, use the `ypxfr` command.

If you want to verify the contents of an NIS map, you can use the `makedbm` command with the `-u` flag. This will write the contents of the map to the screen, so redirect the output to another file if it's going to produce a large amount of text.

To make a new NIS map permanent, you will have to add the details of the new map to the Makefile in `/var/yp`. Have a look at the Makefile to see how to modify it to add a new entry. When this has been done, any further changes to the new map will automatically be propagated to all other NIS servers when the `make` command is run.

NIS Security

NIS has been traditionally insecure because the passwd map contains the encrypted passwords for all user accounts. Any user can list the contents of the passwd map, so a potential attacker could easily gather the encrypted passwords for use with a password cracking program. This issue is partially addressed in two ways: by using the passwd.adjunct file to remove encrypted passwords from the passwd map, and using the securenets file to restrict the hosts, or networks, that can access the NIS maps.

The passwd.adjunct Map

If you copy the contents of your shadow file to passwd.adjunct in the same directory as your passwd and shadow files (/var/yp in the examples used in this chapter) then a separate map, passwd.adjunct.byname, will be created. This map is only accessible by the root user and protects the encrypted passwords from unauthorized users. In addition to creating the file, you will also have to modify the NIS Makefile (held in /var/yp) to add the passwd.adjunct entry to the "all" section. This ensures that the map is updated when changes are made.

NOTE

Extra Editing The only downside of using this option is that when a new user is created or an existing user modified, the passwd.adjunct file must be amended to correctly reflect the current shadow file. This is an overhead for the system administrator, but should be offset against the increased security that is achieved by doing this.

The securenets File

A further enhancement to NIS security is to restrict the hosts, or networks, that can access the NIS namespace. The file /var/yp/securenets achieves this.

Entries in this file consist of two fields, a netmask and a network.

An example securenets file is shown here:

```
255.255.255.0 210.100.35.0
255.255.255.0 210.100.36.0
255.255.255.0 210.100.37.0
```

This code shows that only hosts with IP addresses in the specified networks can access the NIS namespace.

You can also add entries for specific hosts. A modified securenets file is shown below adding two individual hosts:

```
host 10.48.76.3
host 10.48.76.4
```

```
255.255.255.0 210.100.35.0
255.255.255.0 210.100.36.0
255.255.255.0 210.100.37.0
```

NOTE

`securenets` Warning Don't fall into the trap of not allowing your own NIS servers to access the NIS namespace. You should make sure that all NIS servers are covered by the network entries in the `securenets` file; otherwise they might not be authorized. If any servers are not on these networks then you will need to add individual host entries.

The `securenets` file is read by the `ypserv` and `ypxfrd` processes on startup. If you make any modifications to the `securenets` file then you must also restart the NIS daemons to allow the changes to take effect.

Troubleshooting NIS

This section provides some details of how to troubleshoot NIS when problems occur, and the actions to take. It looks briefly at some of the errors seen on the server as well as some of the errors seen on a client.

Binding Problems

Normally, when a client fails to bind with an NIS server, one of the following has occurred:

- `ypbind` isn't running on the client: In this case enter `svcadm enable network/nis/client` to start the process.
- The domain name is set incorrectly or not set at all: Check the contents of `/etc/defaultdomain` or run the `domainname` command. Frequently, this problem occurs because the domain name has been set manually, but not entered into the file `/etc/defaultdomain`, so when the system is rebooted, the domain name is lost.
- No NIS server is available: This would point to a possible network problem, particularly if you have several NIS servers configured in the domain. Check that the client has network connectivity. If only a single NIS server is present, then you should check that the `ypserv` daemon is running. Also, check that the client's `/etc/nsswitch.conf` is configured correctly.

Server Problems

Problems encountered in an NIS environment normally point to network or hardware problems, especially when there are several NIS servers available. If you find that you cannot connect to an NIS server, or if you are not getting any response to NIS commands, try the following:

- `ping` the server to make sure it is accessible across the network.
- Run `ypwhich` to verify which server you are meant to be bound to.
- Check that the NIS daemons are running on the server and restart the service if necessary. You can restart the NIS server by executing `svcadm restart network/nis/server`.
- Check that the server isn't busy or overloaded. Use commands such as `vmstat`, `iostat`, and `netstat` to monitor the server for possible performance issues.

NIS+

NIS+ is similar to NIS, but with more features. NIS+ is not an extension of NIS, but a new system. It was designed to replace NIS.

NOTE

End of Life for NIS+ It is important to note that Sun Microsystems issued an end of support notice for NIS+ with the release of Solaris 9, and again with the release of Solaris 10. It is likely that Solaris 10 will be the last release to contain NIS+ as a naming service. Sun recommends that users of NIS+ migrate to LDAP—using the Sun Java System Directory Server. To this end, and because NIS+ is not mentioned as an objective for this exam, it is only briefly covered in this chapter.

NIS addresses the administrative requirements of small-to-medium client/server computing networks—those with less than a few hundred clients. Some sites with thousands of users find NIS adequate as well. NIS+ is designed for the now-prevalent larger networks in which systems are spread across remote sites in various time zones and in which clients number in the thousands. In addition, the information stored in networks today changes much more frequently, and NIS had to be updated to handle this environment. Last but not least, systems today require a higher level of security than provided by NIS, and NIS+ addresses many security issues that NIS did not.

Hierarchical Namespace

NIS+ lets you store information about workstation addresses, security, mail, Ethernet interfaces, and network services in central locations where all workstations on a network can access it. This configuration of network information is referred to as the NIS+ namespace.

The NIS+ namespace is the arrangement of information stored by NIS+. The namespace can be arranged in a variety of ways to fit an organization's needs. NIS+ can be arranged to manage large networks with more than one domain. Although the arrangement of an NIS+ namespace can vary from site to site, all sites use the same structural components: directories, tables, and groups. These components are called *objects*, and they can be arranged into a hierarchy that resembles a Unix file system.

Directory objects form the skeleton of the namespace. When arranged in a treelike structure, they divide the namespace into separate parts, much like Unix directories and subdirectories. The topmost directory in a namespace is the root directory. If a namespace is flat, it has only one directory: the root directory. The directory objects beneath the root directory are called *directories*.

A namespace can have several levels of directories. When identifying the relation of one directory to another, the directory beneath is called the *child directory*, and the directory above is the *parent*.

Although Unix directories are designed to hold Unix files, NIS+ directories are designed to hold NIS+ objects: other directories, tables, and groups. Any NIS+ directory that stores NIS+ groups is named `groups_dir`, and any directory that stores NIS+ system tables is named `org_dir`.

NIS+ Security

NIS+ security is enhanced in two ways. First, it can authenticate access to the service, so it can discriminate between access that is enabled to members of the community and other network entities. Second, it includes an authorization model that allows specific rights to be granted or denied based on this authentication.

Authentication

Authentication is used to identify *NIS+ principals*. An NIS+ principal might be someone who is logged in to a client system as a regular user, someone who is logged in as superuser, or any process that runs with superuser permission on an NIS+ client system. Thus, an NIS+ principal can be a client user or a client workstation. Every time a principal (user or system) tries to access an NIS+ object, the user's identity and password are confirmed and validated.

Authorization

Authorization is used to specify access rights. Every time NIS+ principals try to access NIS+ objects, they are placed in one of four authorization classes, or categories:

- **Owner**—A single NIS+ principal
- **Group**—A collection of NIS+ principals
- **World**—All principals authenticated by NIS+
- **Nobody**—Unauthenticated principals

The NIS+ server finds out what access rights are assigned to that principal by that particular object. If the access rights match, the server answers the request. If they do not match, the server denies the request and returns an error message.

NIS+ authorization is the process of granting NIS+ principals access rights to an NIS+ object. Access rights are similar to file permissions. Four types of access rights exist:

- **Read**—The principal can read the contents of the object.
- **Modify**—The principal can modify the contents of the object.
- **Create**—The principal can create new objects in a table or directory.
- **Destroy**—The principal can destroy objects in a table or directory.

Access rights are displayed as 16 characters. They can be displayed with the command `nisls -l` and can be changed with the command `nischmod`.

The NIS+ security system lets NIS+ administrators specify different read, modify, create, and destroy rights to NIS+ objects for each class. For example, a given class could be permitted to modify a particular column in the `passwd` table but not read that column, or a different class could be allowed to read some entries of a table but not others.

The implementation of the authorization scheme just described is determined by the domain's level of security. An NIS+ server can operate at one of three security levels, summarized in Table 12.8.

TABLE 12.8 NIS+ Security Levels

Security Level	Description
0	Security level 0 is designed for testing and setting up the initial NIS+ namespace. An NIS+ server running at security level 0 grants any NIS+ principal full access rights to all NIS+ objects in the domain. Level 0 is for setup purposes only, and administrators should use it only for that purpose. Regular users should not use level 0 on networks in normal operation.
1	Security level 1 uses `AUTH_SYS` security. This level is not supported by NIS+, and it should not be used.
2	Security level 2 is the default. It is the highest level of security currently provided by NIS+ and is the default level assigned to an NIS+ server. It authenticates only requests that use Data Encryption Standard (DES) credentials. Requests with no credentials are assigned to the nobody class and have whatever access rights have been granted to that class. Requests that use invalid DES credentials are retried. After repeated failures to obtain a valid DES credential, requests with invalid credentials fail with an authentication error. (A credential might be invalid for a variety of reasons—the principal making the request might not be logged in on that system, the clocks might be out of sync, there might be a key mismatch, and so forth.)

DNS

DNS is the name service used by the Internet and other Transmission Control Protocol/ Internet Protocol (TCP/IP) networks. It was developed so that workstations on the network can be identified by common names instead of Internet addresses. DNS is a system that converts domain names to their IP addresses and vice versa. Without it, users would have to remember numbers instead of words to get around the Internet. The process of finding a computer's IP address by using its hostname as an index is referred to as *name-to-address resolution*, or *mapping*. DNS duplicates some of the information stored in the NIS or NIS+ tables, but DNS information is available to all hosts on the network.

The collection of networked systems that use DNS is referred to as the *DNS namespace*. The DNS namespace can be divided into a hierarchy of domains. A DNS domain is simply a group of systems. Two or more name servers support each domain: the primary, secondary, or cache-only server. Each domain must have one primary server and should have at least one secondary server to provide backup.

Configuring the DNS Client

On the client side, DNS is implemented through a set of dynamic library routines, collectively called the *resolver*. The resolver's function is to resolve users' queries. The resolver is neither a daemon nor a single program; instead, it is a set of dynamic library routines used by applications that need to find IP addresses given the domain names.

The resolver library uses the file `/etc/resolv.conf`, which lists the addresses of DNS servers where it can obtain its information. The resolver reads this `/etc/resolv.conf` file to find the name of the local domain and the location of domain name servers. It sets the local domain name and instructs the resolver routines to query the listed name servers for information. Normally, each DNS client system on your network has a `resolv.conf` file in its `/etc` directory. (If a client does not have a `resolv.conf` file, it defaults to using a server at IP address 127.0.0.1, which is the local host.) Here's an example of the `/etc/resolv.conf` file:

```
; Sample resolv.conf file for the machine server1
domain example.com
; try local name server
nameserver 127.0.0.1
; if local name server down, try these servers
nameserver 123.45.6.1
nameserver 111.22.3.5
```

The first line of the `/etc/resolv.conf` file lists the domain name in this form:

```
domain <domainname>
```

<domainname> is the name registered with the Internet's domain name servers.

NOTE

Domain Name Format No spaces or tabs are permitted at the end of the domain name. Make sure that you enter a hard carriage return immediately after the last character of the domain name.

The second line identifies the loopback name server in the following form:

```
nameserver 127.0.0.1
```

The remaining lines list the IP addresses of up to three DNS master, secondary, or cache-only name servers that the resolver should consult to resolve queries. (Do not list more than three primary or secondary servers.) Name server entries have the following form:

```
nameserver <IP_address>
```

<*IP_address*> is the IP address of a DNS name server. The resolver queries these name servers in the order they are listed until it obtains the information it needs.

Whenever the resolver must find the IP address of a host (or the hostname corresponding to an address), it builds a query package and sends it to the name servers listed in /etc/resolv.conf. The servers either answer the query locally or contact other servers known to them, ultimately returning the answer to the resolver.

After the resolver is configured, a system can request DNS service from a name server. If a system's /etc/nsswitch.conf file specifies hosts: dns, the resolver libraries are automatically used. If the nsswitch.conf file specifies some other name service before DNS, such as NIS, that name service is consulted first for host information. Only if that name service does not find the host in question are the resolver libraries used.

For example, if the hosts line in the nsswitch.conf file specifies hosts: nis dns, the NIS name service is first searched for host information. If the information is not found in NIS, the DNS resolver is used. Because name services such as NIS and NIS+ contain only information about hosts in their own network, the effect of a hosts: nis dns line in a switch file is to specify the use of NIS for local host information and DNS for information on remote hosts on the Internet. If the resolver queries a name server, the server returns either the requested information or a referral to another server.

Name-to-address mapping occurs if a program running on your local system needs to contact a remote computer. The program most likely knows the hostname of the remote computer but might not know how to locate it, particularly if the remote system is in another network. To obtain the remote system's address, the program requests assistance from the DNS software running on your local system, which is considered a DNS client.

The DNS client sends a request to a DNS name server, which maintains the distributed DNS database. Each DNS server implements DNS by running a daemon called in.named. When run without any arguments, `in.named` reads the default configuration file `/etc/named.conf`, loads DNS zones it is responsible for, and listens for queries from the DNS clients.

The files in the DNS database bear little resemblance to the NIS+ host table or even to the local `/etc/hosts` file, although they maintain similar information: the hostnames, IP addresses, and other information about a particular group of computers. The name server uses the hostname that your system sent as part of its request to find or "resolve" the IP address of the remote system. It then returns this IP address to your local system if the hostname is in its DNS database.

If the hostname is not in that name server's DNS database, this indicates that the system is outside its authority—or, to use DNS terminology, outside the local administrative domain. If your network is connected to the Internet, then external servers will be consulted to try and resolve the hostname.

Because maintaining a central list of domain name/IP address correspondences would be impractical, the lists of domain names and IP addresses are distributed throughout the Internet in a hierarchy of authority. A DNS server that maps the domain names in your Internet requests or forwards them to other servers the Internet. It is probably provided by your Internet access provider.

Lightweight Directory Access Protocol (LDAP)

LDAP is the latest name-lookup service to be added to Solaris. It can be used in conjunction with or in place of NIS+ or DNS. Specifically, LDAP is a directory service. A directory service is like a database, but it contains more descriptive, attribute-based information. The information in a directory is generally read, not written.

LDAP is used as a resource locator, but it is practical only in read intensive environments in which you do not need frequent updates. LDAP can be used to store the same information that is stored in NIS or NIS+. Use LDAP as a resource locator for an online phone directory to eliminate the need for a printed phone directory. This application is mainly read-intensive, but authorized users can update the contents to maintain its accuracy.

LDAP provides a hierarchical structure that more closely resembles the internal structure of an organization and can access multiple domains, similar to DNS or NIS+. NIS provides only a flat structure and is accessible by only one domain. In LDAP, directory entries are arranged in a hierarchical, tree-like structure that reflects political, geographic, or organizational boundaries. Entries representing countries appear at the top of the tree. Below them are entries representing states or national organizations. Below them might be entries representing people, organizational units, printers, documents, or just about anything else you can think of.

LDAP has provisions for adding and deleting an entry from the directory, changing an existing entry, and changing the name of an entry. Most of the time, though, LDAP is used to search for information in the directory.

NOTE

LDAP Information LDAP is a protocol that email programs can use to look up contact information from a server. For instance, every email program has a personal address book, but how do you look up an address for someone who has never sent you email? Client programs can ask LDAP servers to look up entries in a variety of ways. The LDAP search operation allows some portion of the directory to be searched for entries that match some criteria specified by a search filter.

LDAP servers index all the data in their entries, and *filters* may be used to select just the person or group you want and return just the information you want to see. Information can be requested from each entry that matches the criteria. For example, here's an LDAP search translated into plain English: "Search people located in Hudsonville whose names contain 'Bill' and who have an email address. Return their full name and email address."

Perhaps you want to search the entire directory subtree below the University of Michigan for people with the name Bill Calkins, retrieving the email address of each entry found. LDAP lets you do this easily. Or, you might want to search the entries directly below the U.S. entry for organizations with the string "Pyramid" in their names and that have a fax number. LDAP lets you do this.

Some directory services provide no protection, allowing anyone to see the information. LDAP provides a method for a client to authenticate, or prove, its identity to a directory server, paving the way for rich access control to protect the information the server contains.

LDAP was designed at the University of Michigan to adapt a complex enterprise directory system, called X.500, to the modern Internet. A directory server runs on a host computer on the Internet, and various client programs that understand the protocol can log in to the server and look up entries. X.500 is too complex to support on desktops and over the Internet, so LDAP was created to provide this service to general users.

Sun Java System Directory Server

Sun Java System Directory Server is a Sun product that provides a centralized directory service for your network and is used to manage an enterprise-wide directory of information, including the following:

- Physical device information, such as data about the printers in your organization. This could include information on where they are located, whether they support color or duplexing, the manufacturer and serial number, company asset tag information, and so on.

- Public employee information, such as name, phone number, email address, and department.
- Logins and passwords.
- Private employee information, such as salary, employee identification numbers, phone numbers, emergency contact information, and pay grade.
- Customer information, such as the name of a client, bidding information, contract numbers, and project dates.

Sun Java System Directory Server meets the needs of many applications. It provides a standard protocol and a common application programming interface (API) that client applications and servers need to communicate with each another.

As discussed earlier, Java System Directory Server provides a hierarchical namespace that can be used to manage anything that has previously been managed by the NIS and NIS+ name services. The advantages of the Java System Directory Server over NIS and NIS+ are listed here:

- It gives you the capability to consolidate information by replacing application-specific databases. It also reduces the number of distinct databases to be managed.
- It allows for more frequent data synchronization between masters and replicas.
- It is compatible with multiple platforms and vendors.
- It is more secure.

Because LDAP is platform independent, it very likely will eventually replace NIS and NIS+, providing all the functionality once provided by these name services.

The Java System Directory Server runs as the `ns-slapd` process on your directory server. The server manages the directory databases and responds to all client requests. Each host in the domain that uses resources from the LDAP server is referred to as an LDAP client.

Setting Up the LDAP Client

It's not within the scope of this chapter to describe how to set up an LDAP server; this requires an in-depth working knowledge of LDAP. For background information on LDAP and Java System Directory Server, refer to the System Administration Guide: Naming and Directory Services (DNS, NIS, and LDAP) Guide available at `http://docs.sun.com`.

It's assumed that the LDAP server has already been configured as a naming service with the appropriate client profiles in place. The scope of this chapter is to describe how to set up the LDAP client.

Before setting up the LDAP client, a few things must already be in place:

- ▶ The client's domain name must be served by the LDAP server.
- ▶ The nsswitch.conf file must point to LDAP for the required services. This would be achieved by copying the file /etc/nsswitch.ldap to /etc/nsswitch.conf.
- ▶ At least one server for which a client is configured must be up and running.

The ldapclient utility is used to set up LDAP client. ldapclient assumes that the server has already been configured with the appropriate client profiles. The LDAP client profile consists of configuration information that the client uses to access the LDAP information on the LDAP server. You must install and configure the LDAP server with the appropriate profiles before you can set up any clients.

To initialize a client using a profile, log in as root.

Run the ldapclient command as follows:

```
ldapclient init -a profileName=new -a domainName=east.example.com \
192.168.0.1
```

Where init initializes the host as an LDAP client, profileName refers to an existing profile on the LDAP server. domainName refers to the domain for which the LDAP server is configured.

The system responds with this:

```
System successfully configured
```

To initialize a client using a proxy account, run the ldapclient command as follows:

```
ldapclient init -a proxyDN=proxyagent \
-a profileName=New \
-a domainName=east.example.com \
-a proxyPassword=test0000 \
192.168.0.1
```

The proxyDN and proxyPassword parameters are necessary if the profile is to be used as a proxy. The proxy information is stored in the file /var/ldap_client_cred. The remaining LDAP client information is stored in the file /var/ldap_client_file.

Modifying the LDAP Client

After the LDAP client has been set up, it can be modified using the ldapclient mod command. One of the things you can change here is the authentication mechanism used by the client. If there is no particular encryption service being used then set this to *simple* as shown here:

```
ldapclient mod -a authenticationMethod=simple
```

Listing the LDAP Client Properties

To list the properties of the LDAP client, use the `ldapclient list` command as shown here:

```
ldapclient list
NS_LDAP_FILE_VERSION= 2.0
NS_LDAP_BINDDN= cn=proxyagent
NS_LDAP_BINDPASSWD= <encrypted password>
NS_LDAP_SERVERS= 192.168.0.1
NS_LDAP_AUTH= simple
```

Uninitializing the LDAP Client

To remove an LDAP client and restore the name service that was in use prior to initializing this client, use the `ldapclient uninit` command as follows:

```
ldapclient uninit
```

The system responds with this:

```
System successfully recovered
```

Name Service Cache Daemon (nscd)

`nscd` is a daemon that runs on a Solaris system and provides a caching mechanism for the most common name service requests. It is automatically started when the system boots to a multi-user state. `nscd` provides caching for the following name service databases:

- `passwd`
- `group`
- `hosts`
- `ipnodes`
- `exec_attr`
- `prof_attr`
- `user_attr`

Because `nscd` is running all the time as a daemon, any `nscd` commands that are entered are passed to the already running daemon transparently. The behavior of `nscd` is managed via a configuration file `/etc/nscd.conf`. This file lists a number of tunable parameters for each of the supported databases listed above.

The syntax for the nscd command is shown as follows:

```
nscd  [-f  configuration-file]  [-g] [-e  cachename , yes ¦ no] \
 [-i  cachename]
```

The options for the nscd command are described in Table 12.9.

TABLE 12.9 nscd Syntax

Option	Description
-f configuration-file	Causes nscd to read its configuration data from the specified file.
-g	Displays current configuration and statistical data.
-e cachename, yes¦no	Enables or disables the specified cache.
-i cachename	Invalidates the specified cache.

Whenever a change is made to the name service switch file, /etc/nsswitch.conf, the nscd daemon must be stopped and started so that the changes take effect. The commands to stop and start nscd have changed because the cache daemon is now managed by the Service Management Facility (SMF). The commands to use are as follows:

```
svcadm restart system/name-service-cache
```

Statistics can be obtained from nscd by running the command with the -g flag. This is the only option that can be run by a nonprivileged user. The truncated output that follows shows the results of the cache statistics for the hosts database:

```
#nscd -g
[…output truncated…]
hosts cache:
       Yes  cache is enabled
         44  cache hits on positive entries
         0  cache hits on negative entries
         3  cache misses on positive entries
         1  cache misses on negative entries
      91.7% cache hit rate
         0  queries deferred
         4  total entries
       211  suggested size
      3600  seconds time to live for positive entries
         5  seconds time to live for negative entries
        20  most active entries to be kept valid
      Yes check /etc/{passwd, group, hosts, inet/ipnodes} file for changes
        No  use possibly stale data rather than waiting for refresh
[...output truncated...]
```

The getent Command

The getent command is used to get a list of entries from a name service database. The information comes from one of the sources pointed to by the /etc/nsswitch.conf file.

The syntax for the getent command is shown in the following code:

```
getent database [key...]
```

The options for the getent command are described in Table 12.10.

TABLE 12.10 getent Syntax

Option	Description
database	The name of the database to be examined. This can be hosts, group, passwd, ipnodes, services, protocols, ethers, networks, or netmasks.
Key ...	An appropriate key for the specified database. For example, hostname or IP address for the hosts database. Multiple keys can be specified.

The getent command displays the entries of the specified database that match each of the keys. If no key is specified, then all entries are printed. The following example looks at the root entry of the passwd database:

```
# getent passwd root
root:x:0:1:Super-User:/:/sbin/sh
```

Summary

This chapter covered all the name service topics that are included in the Solaris 10 System Administrator exams. This includes the local files in the `/etc` directory, NIS, NIS+, DNS, and LDAP.

This chapter described how to configure the master server, slave servers, and clients for the most commonly used name service, NIS. Configuring clients for DNS and LDAP were also covered briefly. The name service switch file used by the operating system for any network information lookups was covered.

In addition, this chapter described the Sun Java System Directory Server that could soon replace NIS+, and eventually NIS. If you will be migrating from NIS+, you can refer to the section titled "Transitioning from NIS+ to LDAP" in the *Solaris 10 System Administration Guide: Naming and Directory Services (NIS+)*, which is available on the Solaris Documentation CD and the online documentation site `http://docs.sun.com`.

Finally in this chapter, we described the Name Service Cache Daemon used to speed up requests for the most common name service requests, and also the `getent` command, which is used to retrieve entries from specified name service databases.

Of course, better understanding of the naming services will come as you use the systems described and become experienced over time. Many large networks that use a name service are heterogeneous, meaning that they have more than just Solaris systems connected to the network. Refer to the vendor's documentation for each particular system to understand how each different operating system implements name services. You will see that most are similar in their implementation, with only subtle differences.

Key Terms

- DNS
- DNS resolver
- Hierarchical namespace
- LDAP
- Makefile
- Master NIS server
- Name service
- Name service switch
- NIS
- NIS client
- NIS map
- NIS security (`passwd.adjunct`)
- NIS source file
- NIS+
- NIS+ authorization (four classes and four types of access rights)

- NIS+ objects
- NIS+ security levels (three levels)
- nscd (Name Service Cache Daemon)
- /var/yp/securenets file
- Slave NIS server

Exercises

For these exercises, you'll need two Solaris systems attached to a network. One system will be configured as the NIS master server, and the other will be the NIS client.

12.1 Setting Up the NIS Master Server

In this exercise, you'll go through the steps to set up your NIS master server.

Estimated Time: 20 minutes

1. Login as root.
2. Set your domain name if it is not already set:

   ```
   domainname <yourname>.com
   ```

   Populate the /etc/defaultdomain file with your domain name.

   ```
   domainname > /etc/defaultdomain
   ```

3. On the system that will become your master NIS server, create the master /var/yp/passwd, /var/yp/group, and /var/yp/hosts files. Follow the instructions described in this chapter to create these files.
4. Change entries for /etc to /var/yp in /var/yp/makefile as follows:

   Change the following:

   ```
   DIR = /etc
   PWDIR = /etc
   ```

   into the following:

   ```
   DIR = /var/yp
   PWDIR = /var/yp
   ```

5. Create the name service switch file by copying the NIS template file as follows:

   ```
   cp /etc/nsswitch.nis /etc/nsswitch.conf
   ```

6. Run the ypinit command as follows to set up this system as the NIS master:

   ```
   ypinit -m
   ```

   When asked for the next host to add as an NIS slave server, enter CTRL+D. For this exercise, we will not be adding an NIS slave server.

Indicate you do not want `ypinit` to quit on nonfatal errors by typing **N** when asked.

You'll know the process was successful when you get the message indicating that the current system was set up as a master server without any errors.

7. Start up the NIS service on the master server by running

```
svcadm enable network/nis/server
```

8. Verify that the NIS master server is up by typing

```
ypwhich -m
```

12.2 Setting Up the NIS Client

In this exercise, you'll go through the steps to set up your NIS client.

Estimated time: 10 minutes

1. Login as root.
2. Set your domain name if it is not already set:

```
domainname <yourname>.com
```

Populate the `/etc/defaultdomain` file with your domain name:

```
domainname > /etc/defaultdomain
```

3. Create the name service switch file by copying the NIS template file as follows:

```
cp /etc/nsswitch.nis /etc/nsswitch.conf
```

4. Configure the client system to use NIS by running the `ypinit` command as follows:

```
ypinit -c
```

You will be asked to identify the NIS server from which the client can obtain name service information. Type the NIS master server name, followed by a carriage return.

When asked for the next host to add, press Ctrl+D.

5. Start the NIS daemons by executing the following script:

```
svcadm enable network/nis/server
```

6. Verify that the NIS client is bound to the NIS master by typing

```
ypwhich
```

The master server name should be displayed.

7. Test the NIS client by logging out and logging back in using a login name that is no longer in the local `/etc/passwd` file and is managed by NIS.

Exam Questions

1. Which of the following services stores information that users, systems, and applications must have access to in order to communicate across the network, in a central location?

   ❍ **A.** NIS

   ❍ **B.** NFS service

   ❍ **C.** Automount

   ❍ **D.** AutoFS

2. Which of the following is *not* a Solaris name service?

   ❍ **A.** DES

   ❍ **B.** `/etc`

   ❍ **C.** NIS+

   ❍ **D.** DNS

3. Which of the following is the traditional Unix way of maintaining information about hosts, users, passwords, groups, and automount maps?

   ❍ **A.** DNS

   ❍ **B.** NIS

   ❍ **C.** NIS+

   ❍ **D.** `/etc`

4. What are the NIS administration databases called?

   ❍ **A.** Files

   ❍ **B.** Tables

   ❍ **C.** Maps

   ❍ **D.** Objects

5. What is the set of maps shared by the servers and clients called?

   ❍ **A.** A table

   ❍ **B.** An object

   ❍ **C.** The NIS domain

   ❍ **D.** None of the above

6. When you add a new system to a network running NIS, you have to update the input file in the master server and run which of the following?

   ❍ **A.** `makedbm`

   ❍ **B.** `make`

   ❍ **C.** `yppush`

   ❍ **D.** `ypinit`

7. Which of the following commands is used to display the values in an NIS map?

   ❍ **A.** `ypcat`

   ❍ **B.** `ypwhich`

   ❍ **C.** `ypserv`

   ❍ **D.** `ypbind`

8. Which of the following commands can be used to determine which server is the master of a particular map?

   ❍ **A.** `ypbind`

   ❍ **B.** `ypcat`

   ❍ **C.** `ypserv`

   ❍ **D.** `ypwhich -m`

9. Which of the following propagates a new version of an NIS map from the NIS master server to NIS slave servers?

   ❍ **A.** `ypinit`

   ❍ **B.** `yppush`

   ❍ **C.** `make`

   ❍ **D.** `yppoll`

10. Which of the following sets up master and slave servers and clients to use NIS?

   ❍ **A.** `makedbm`

   ❍ **B.** `make`

   ❍ **C.** `ypinit`

   ❍ **D.** `yppush`

11. Which of the following is the configuration file for the name service switch?

❍ **A.** `nsswitch.conf`

❍ **B.** `resolve.conf`

❍ **C.** `/etc/netconfig`

❍ **D.** `nsswitch.nis`

12. Each line of which of the following files identifies a particular type of network information, such as host, password, and group, followed by one or more sources, such as NIS+ tables, NIS maps, the DNS hosts table, or local `/etc`?

❍ **A.** `resolve.conf`

❍ **B.** `nsswitch.conf`

❍ **C.** `/etc/netconfig`

❍ **D.** `nsswitch.nis`

13. In the name service switch file, what does the following entry mean if the NIS naming service is being used?

```
hosts: nis [NOTFOUND=return] files
```

❍ **A.** Search the NIS map and then the local `/etc/hosts` file.

❍ **B.** Search only the NIS hosts table in the NIS map.

❍ **C.** Search only the `/etc/hosts` file.

❍ **D.** Do not search the NIS hosts table or the local `/etc/hosts` file.

14. Which name service switch template files are found in Solaris 10? Choose all that apply.

❍ **A.** `nsswitch.files`

❍ **B.** `nsswitch.nis+`

❍ **C.** `nsswitch.nisplus`

❍ **D.** `nsswitch.fns`

15. What are the four types of NIS+ access rights?

❍ **A.** Read, write, create, modify

❍ **B.** Read, write, execute, no access

❍ **C.** Read, write, delete, modify

❍ **D.** Read, modify, create, destroy

16. Which of the following is the name service provided by the Internet for TCP/IP networks?

❍ **A.** DNS

❍ **B.** NIS

❍ **C.** NIS+

❍ **D.** None of the above

17. Each server implements DNS by running a daemon called

❍ **A.** `named`

❍ **B.** `in.named`

❍ **C.** `nfsd`

❍ **D.** `dnsd`

18. The primary task of DNS is to provide

❍ **A.** Security service

❍ **B.** Name-to-address resolution

❍ **C.** Name service

❍ **D.** Namespace services

19. Which of the following describes the difference between NIS+ authentication and authorization?

❍ **A.** Authentication is checking whether the information requester is a valid user on the network, and authorization determines whether the particular user is allowed to have or modify the information.

❍ **B.** Authorization is checking whether the information requester is a valid user on the network, and authentication determines whether the particular user is allowed to have or modify the information.

20. This file determines how a particular type of information is obtained and in which order the naming services should be queried. Which file is being described?

❍ **A.** `/etc/nsswitch.conf`

❍ **B.** `/etc/resolve.conf`

❍ **C.** `/etc/nsswitch.nis`

❍ **D.** `/etc/nsswitch.nisplus`

21. How many name services does Solaris 10 support?

 ❍ **A.** 3

 ❍ **B.** 4

 ❍ **C.** 5

 ❍ **D.** 6

22. Which of the following is the name service used by the Internet?

 ❍ **A.** DNS

 ❍ **B.** NIS

 ❍ **C.** NIS+

 ❍ **D.** DES

23. Which of the following commands is used to set up an NIS master server?

 ❍ **A.** `ypserver -m`

 ❍ **B.** `nisinit -m`

 ❍ **C.** `nisserver -m`

 ❍ **D.** `ypinit -m`

Answers to Exam Questions

1. **A.** NIS stores information about workstation names, addresses, users, the network itself, and network services. For more information, see the "Name Services Overview" section.

2. **A.** DES is not a Solaris name service. For more information, see the "Name Services Overview" section.

3. **D.** `/etc` files are the traditional Unix way of maintaining information about hosts, users, passwords, groups, and automount maps. For more information, see the "Name Services Overview" section.

4. **C.** The NIS administration databases are called maps. For more information, see the "Name Services Overview" section.

5. **C.** The set of maps shared by the servers and clients is called the *NIS domain*. For more information, see the "Name Services Overview" section.

6. **B.** To update the input file in the master server with a new system name, you'll execute the `/usr/ccs/bin/make` command. For more information, see the "Configuring an NIS Master Server" section.

7. **A.** Just as you use the `cat` command to display the contents of a text file, you can use the `ypcat` command to display the values in a map. For more information, see the "Configuring an NIS Master Server" section.

8. **D.** You can use the `ypwhich -m` command to determine which server is the master of a particular map. For more information, see the "Configuring an NIS Master Server" section.

9. **B.** The command `yppush` propagates a new version of an NIS map from the NIS master server to NIS slave servers. For more information, see the "Configuring an NIS Master Server" section.

10. **C.** The `ypinit` command builds and installs an NIS database and initializes the NIS client's (and server's) ypservers list. For more information, see the "Configuring an NIS Master Server" section.

11. **A.** In setting up the NIS, set up the name service switch, which involves editing the `/etc/nsswitch.conf` file. For more information, see the "The Name Service Switch" section.

12. **B.** Each line of the `/etc/nsswitch.conf` file identifies a particular type of network information, such as host, password, and group, followed by one or more sources, such as NIS+ tables, NIS maps, the DNS hosts table, or the local `/etc`. For more information, see the "Setting Up the Name Service Switch" section.

13. **B.** The following entry in the `nsswitch.nis` template states that only the NIS hosts table in the NIS map is searched:

    ```
    hosts: nis [NOTFOUND=return] files
    ```

    For more information, see the "Setting Up the Name Service Switch" section.

14. **A, C.** The following template files are available: nsswitch.files, `nsswitch.nisplus`, `nsswitch.nis`, `nsswitch.dns`, and `nsswitch.ldap`. For more information, see the "The Name Service Switch" section.

15. **D.** Access rights are similar to file permissions. There are four types of access rights: `read`, `modify`, `create`, and `destroy`. For more information, see the "NIS+ Security" section.

16. **A.** DNS is the name service provided by the Internet for Transmission Control Protocol/Internet Protocol (TCP/IP) networks. For more information, see the "DNS" section.

17. **B.** Each server implements DNS by running a daemon called `in.named`. For more information, see the "DNS" section.

18. **B.** The process of finding a computer's IP address by using its hostname as an index is referred to as name-to-address resolution, or mapping. The primary task of DNS is to provide name-to-address resolution. For more information, see the "DNS" section.

19. **A.** Authentication is used to identify NIS+ principals. An NIS+ principal can be a client user or a client workstation. Every time a principal (user or system) tries to access an NIS+ object, the user's identity and secure RPC password are confirmed and validated. Authorization is used to specify access rights. For more information, see the "NIS+ Security" section.

20. **A.** The `/etc/nsswitch.conf` file determines how a particular type of information is obtained and in which order the naming services should be queried. For more information, see the "The Name Service Switch" section.

21. **C.** There are five name services that Solaris 10 supports: `/etc` files, NIS, NIS+, DNS, and LDAP. For more information, see the "Name Services Overview" section.

22. **A.** DNS is the name service used by the Internet. For more information, see the "DNS" section.

23. **D.** To build new maps on the master server, type **`/usr/sbin/ypinit -m`**. For more information, see the "Configuring an NIS Master Server" section.

Suggested Reading and Resources

Solaris 10 Documentation CD—*System Administration Guide: Advanced Administration and System Administration Guide: Naming and Directory Services* manuals.

`http://docs.sun.com`. Solaris 10 documentation set. *System Administration Guide: Advanced Administration and System Administration Guide: Naming and Directory Services* books in the System Administration collection.

CHAPTER THIRTEEN

Solaris Zones

Objectives

The following test objectives for exam 310-202 are covered in this chapter:

Explain consolidation issues, features of Solaris zones, and decipher between the different zone concepts, including zone types, daemons, networking, command scope and, given a scenario, create a Solaris zone.

- This chapter helps you understand the components of the new zones feature, first introduced in Solaris 10. It describes the zone concepts and how they fit into the overall container structure.

Given a zone configuration scenario, identify zone components and `zonecfg` resource parameters, allocate file system space, use the `zonecfg` command, describe the interactive configuration of a zone, and view the zone configuration file.

- This chapter explains the different components of a zone and how to carry out zone configuration. It also displays the zone configuration and the mechanism to verify that a zone has been configured correctly.

Given a scenario, use the `zoneadm` command to view, install, boot, halt, reboot, and delete a zone.

- In this chapter, we create a zone. We'll see how to install zones, check the status of installed zones, boot and reboot, as well as uninstall and remove zones. We also show how zones are viewed from a global zone.

Outline

Study Strategies

The following strategies will help you prepare for the test:

- Make sure you are familiar with all of the concepts introduced in this chapter, particularly the types of zones and the commands used to create, manipulate, and manage them.
- Practice the step-by-step examples provided in this chapter on a Solaris system. Be sure that you understand each step and can describe the process of setting up a zone, installing and booting a zone, as well as uninstalling and deleting a zone.
- You need to know all the terms listed in the "Key Terms" section at the end of this chapter.
- Understand each of the commands described in this chapter. Get familiar with all of the options, especially the ones used in the examples. You'll see questions on the exam related to the `zonecfg`, `zoneadm`, and `zlogin` commands.

Introduction

Solaris zones is a major new feature of Solaris 10 and provides additional facilities that were not available in previous releases of the Operating Environment. Zones allow virtual environments to run on the same physical system. Previously, the only way of compartmenting an environment was to purchase a separate server, or use an expensive high-end server, capable of physical partitioning, such as the E10K or E15K. Now you can create virtual environments on any machine capable of running the Solaris 10 Operating Environment.

Zones provide a virtual operating system environment within a single physical instance of Solaris 10. Applications can run in an isolated, and secure environment. This isolation prevents an application running in one zone from monitoring or affecting an application running in a different zone. A further important aspect of zones is that a failing application, such as one that would traditionally have leaked all available memory, or exhausted all CPU resources, can be limited to only affect the zone in which it is running. This is achieved by limiting the amount of physical resources on the system that the zone can use.

This chapter looks at the whole concept of Solaris zones and how to configure and create a zone, make it operational, and then remove it. Resource management is not an objective for exam 310-202, but a brief introduction is included in this chapter to help put the zones feature in the correct context.

CAUTION

Zones and Containers Some refer to zones and containers interchangeably as if they mean exactly the same thing. This is incorrect because containers is a technology that comprises the resource management features, such as resource pools and Solaris zones. Solaris zones is a subset of containers, so the two terms should not be used interchangeably.

Consolidation and Resource Management

Resource management is one of the components of the Solaris 10 containers technology. It allows you to do the following:

- Allocate specific computer resources, such as CPU time and memory.
- Monitor how resource allocations are being used, and adjust the allocations when required.
- Generate more detailed accounting information—the extended accounting feature of Solaris 10 provides this facility.
- A new resource capping daemon (`rcapd`) allows you to regulate how much physical memory is used by a project, by "capping" the overall amount that can be used. Remember that a project can be a number of processes or users, so it provides a useful control mechanism for a number of functions.

Consolidation

The resource management feature of Solaris containers is extremely useful when you want to consolidate a number of applications to run on a single server.

Consolidation has become more popular in recent years because it reduces the cost and complexity of having to manage numerous separate systems. You can consolidate applications onto fewer, larger, more scalable servers, and also segregate the workload to restrict the resources that each can use.

Previously, a number of applications would run on separate servers, with each application having full access to the system on which it is running. Using the resource management feature, multiple workloads can now be run on a single server, providing an isolated environment for each, so that one workload cannot affect the performance of another.

Resource pools can be utilized to group applications, or functions, together and control their resource usage globally, such as the maximum amount of CPU resource or memory. Additionally, the resource management feature can tailor the behavior of the Fair Share Scheduler (FSS) to give priority to specific applications. This is very useful if you need to allocate additional resources to a group of resources for a limited period of time. An example of this would be when a company runs end-of-month reports. Before resource management was introduced, this would have meant that a larger server would be needed to accommodate the resource requirement, even though it only would be used to its capacity once a month. Now the resources can be allocated according to priority, allowing the server to be more efficiently utilized.

Solaris Zones

Objectives:

Explain consolidation issues and features of Solaris zones, and decipher between the different zone concepts including zone types, daemons, networking, command scope, and given a scenario, create a Solaris zone.

- Given a zone configuration scenario, identify zone components and `zonecfg` resource parameters, allocate file system space, use the `zonecfg` command, describe the interactive configuration of a zone, and view the zone configuration file.
- Given a scenario, use the `zoneadm` command to view, install, boot, halt, reboot, and delete a zone.

The zones technology provides virtual operating system services to allow applications to run in an isolated and secure environment. A zone is a virtual environment that is created within a single running instance of the Solaris Operating Environment. Applications running in a zone environment cannot affect applications running in a different zone, even though they exist and run on the same physical server. Even a privileged user in a zone cannot monitor or access processes running in a different zone.

Types of Zones

There are two types of zones, *global* and *non-global*. Think of a global zone as the server itself, the traditional view of a Solaris system as we all know it, where you can login as `root` and have full control of the entire system. The global zone is the default zone and is used for system-wide configuration and control. Every system contains a global zone and there can only be one global zone on a physical Solaris server.

A non-global zone is created from the global zone and also managed by it. You can have up to 8192 non-global zones on a single physical system—the only real limitation is the capability of the server itself. Applications that run in a non-global zone are isolated from applications running in a separate non-global zone, allowing multiple versions of the same application to run on the same physical server.

Zone States

Non-global zones are referred to simply as *zones* and can be in a number of states depending on the current state of configuration or readiness for operation. You should note that zone states only refer to non-global zones because the global zone is always running and represents the system itself. The only time the global zone is not running is when the server has been shut down.

Table 13.1 describes the six states that a zone can be in:

TABLE 13.1 Zone States

State	Description
Configured	A zone is in this state when the configuration has been completed and storage has been committed. Additional configuration that must be done after the initial reboot has yet to be done.
Incomplete	A zone is set to this state during an install or uninstall operation. Upon completion of the operation, it changes to the correct state.
Installed	A zone in this state has a confirmed configuration. The `zoneadm` command is used to verify that the zone will run on the designated Solaris system. Packages have been installed under the zone's `root` path. Even though the zone is installed, it still has no virtual platform associated with it.
Ready	The zone's virtual platform is established. The kernel creates the `zsched` process, the network interfaces are plumbed and file systems are mounted. The system also assigns a zone ID at this state, but there are no processes associated with this zone.

TABLE 13.1 *Continued*

State	Description
Running	A zone enters this state when the first user process is created. This is the normal state for an operational zone.
Shutting Down + Down	Transitional states that are only visible while a zone is in the process of being halted. If a zone cannot shut down for any reason, then it will also display this state.

EXAM ALERT

Know Your Zone States There is often at least one question in the exam relating to different zone states. Pay particular attention to the differences between the *configured*, *installed*, *ready*, and *running* states. You may get a question that asks you to match the correct state to the correct description.

Zone Features

This section describes the features of both the global zone and non-global zones.

The global zone has the following features:

- The global zone is assigned zone ID 0 by the system.
- It provides the single bootable instance of the Solaris Operating Environment that runs on the system.
- It contains a full installation of Solaris system packages.
- It can contain additional software, packages, file, or data that was not installed through the packages mechanism.
- Contains a complete product database of all installed software components.
- It holds configuration information specific to the global zone, such as the global zone hostname and the file system table.
- It is the only zone that is aware of all file systems and devices on the system.
- It is the only zone that is aware of non-global zones and their configuration.
- It is the only zone from which a non-global zone can be configured, installed, managed, and uninstalled.

Non-global zones have the following features:

- The non-global zone is assigned a zone ID by the system when it is booted.
- It shares the Solaris kernel that is booted from the global zone.

- It contains a subset of the installed Solaris system packages.
- It can contain additional software packages, shared from the global zone.
- It can contain additional software packages that are not shared from the global zone.
- It can contain additional software, files, or data that was not installed using the package mechanism, or shared from the global zone.
- It contains a complete product database of all software components that are installed in the zone. This includes software that was installed independently of the global zone as well as software shared from the global zone.
- It is not aware of the existence of other zones.
- It cannot install, manage, or uninstall other zones, including itself.
- It contains configuration information specific to itself, the non-global zone, such as the non-global zone hostname and file system table.

Non-Global Zone Root File System Models

A non-global zone contains its own `root` (/) file system. The size and contents of this file system depend on how you configure the global zone and the amount of configuration flexibility that is required.

There is no limit on how much disk space a zone can use, but the zone administrator, normally the system administrator, must ensure that sufficient local storage exists to accommodate the requirements of all non-global zones being created on the system.

The system administrator can restrict the overall size of the non-global zone file system by using any of the following:

- Standard disk partitions on a disk can be used to provide a separate file system for each non-global zone
- Soft partitions can be used to divide disk slices or logical volumes into a number of partitions. Soft partitions were covered in Chapter 9, "Virtual File Systems, Swap Space, and Core Dumps."
- Use a `lofi`-mounted file system to place the zone on. For further information on the loopback device driver see the manual pages for `lofi` and `lofiadm`.

Sparse Root Zones

When you create a non-global zone, you have to decide how much of the global zone file system you want to be inherited from the global zone. A *sparse root* zone optimizes sharing by implementing read-only loopback file systems from the global zone and only installing a subset of the system root packages locally. The majority of the root file system is shared (inherited) from the global zone. Generally this model would require about 100 Megabytes of disk space when the global zone has all of the standard Solaris packages installed. A *sparse root* zone uses the `inherit-pkg-dir` resource, where a list of inherited directories from the global zone are specified.

Whole Root Zones

This model provides the greatest configuration flexibility because all of the required (and any other selected) Solaris packages are copied to the zone's private file system, unlike the *sparse root* model where loopback file systems are used. The disk space requirement for this model is considerably greater and is determined by evaluating the space used by the packages currently installed in the global zone.

Networking in a Zone Environment

On a system supporting zones the zones can communicate with each other over the network, but even though the zones reside on the same physical system, network traffic is restricted so that applications running on a specified zone cannot interfere with applications running on a different zone.

Each zone has its own set of bindings and zones can all run their own network daemons. As an example, consider three zones all providing web server facilities using the `apache` package. Using zones, all three zones can host websites on port 80, the default port for `http` traffic, without any interference between them. This is because the IP stack on a system supporting zones implements the separation of network traffic between zones.

The only interaction allowed is for ICMP traffic to resolve problems, so that commands such as `ping` can be used to check connectivity.

Of course, when a zone is running, it behaves like any other Solaris system on the network in that you can `telnet` or `ftp` to the zone as if it was any other system, assuming the zone has configured these network services for use.

When a zone is created, a dedicated IP address is configured that identifies the host associated with the zone. In reality though, the zone's IP address is configured as a logical interface on the network interface specified in the zone's configuration parameters. Only the global zone has visibility of all zones on the system and can also inspect network traffic, using for example, `snoop`.

Zone Daemons

The zone management service is managed through the Service Management Facility (SMF), the service identifier is called: `svc:/system/zones:default`

There are two daemon processes associated with zones, `zoneadmd` and `zsched`.

The `zoneadmd` daemon starts when a zone needs to be managed. An instance of `zoneadmd` will be started for each zone, so it is not uncommon to have multiple instances of this daemon running on a single server. It is started automatically by SMF and is also shut down automatically when no longer required. The `zoneadmd` daemon carries out the following actions:

- Allocates the zone ID and starts the `zsched` process
- Sets system-wide resource controls
- Prepares the zone's devices if any are specified in the zone configuration
- Plumbs the virtual network interface
- Mounts any loopback or conventional file systems

The `zsched` process is started by `zoneadmd` and exists for each active zone (a zone is said to be active when in the *ready*, *running*, or *shutting down* state. The job of `zsched` is to keep track of kernel threads running within the zone. It is also known as the *zone scheduler*.

Configuring a Zone

Before a zone can be installed and booted it has to be created and configured. This section deals with the initial configuration of a zone and describes the zone components.

A zone is configured using the `zonecfg` command. The `zonecfg` command is also used to verify that the resources and properties that are specified during configuration are valid for use on a Solaris system. `zonecfg` checks that a zone path has been specified and that for each resource, all of the required properties have been specified.

The `zonecfg` Command

The `zonecfg` command is used to configure a zone. It can run interactively, on the command-line, or using a command-file. A command-file is created by using the `export` subcommand of `zonecfg`. `zonecfg` carries out the following operations:

- Create, or delete, a zone configuration
- Add, or remove, resources in a configuration
- Set the properties for a resource in the configuration
- Query and verify a configuration
- Commit (save) a configuration
- Revert to a previous configuration
- Exit from a `zonecfg` session

When you enter `zonecfg` in interactive mode, the prompt changes to show that you are in a `zonecfg` session. If you are configuring a zone called *apps*, then the prompt changes as follows:

```
# zonecfg -z apps
zonecfg:apps>
```

This is known as the *global* scope of `zonecfg`. When you configure a specific resource, the prompt changes to include the resource being configured. The command scope also changes so that you are limited to entering commands relevant to the current scope. You have to enter an `end` command to return to the *global* scope.

Table 13.2 describes the subcommands that are available with the interactive mode of `zonecfg`:

TABLE 13.2 `zonecfg` Subcommands

Subcommand	Description
`help`	Print general help, or help about a specific resource.
`create`	Begin configuring a zone. This starts a configuration in memory for a new zone.
`export`	Print the configuration to `stdout`, or to a specified file name, which can be used as a command file.
`add`	In the *global* scope, this command takes you to the specified resource scope. In the *resource* scope, it adds the specified property to the resource type.
`set`	Set a specified property name to a specified property value.
`select`	This is applicable only in the *global* scope and selects the resource of the specified type. The scope changes to the resource, but you have to enter sufficient property *name-value* pairs to uniquely identify the required resource.
`remove`	In the *global* scope, remove the specified resource type. You have to enter sufficient property *name-value* pairs to uniquely identify the required resource.
`end`	This is only available in the *resource* scope and ends the current resource specification.
`cancel`	This is only available in the *resource* scope. It ends the resource specification and returns to the *global* scope. Any partially specified resources are discarded.
`delete`	Destroy the specified configuration. You need to use the `-F` option to force deletion with this option.
`info`	Display information about the current configuration. If a resource type is specified, then display information about the resource type.
`verify`	Verify the current configuration to ensure all resources have the required properties specified.
`commit`	Commit the current configuration from memory to disk. A configuration must be committed before it can be used by the `zoneadm` command, described later in this chapter.
`revert`	Revert the configuration to the last committed state.
`exit -F`	Exit the `zonecfg` session. You can use the `-F` option with this subcommand to force the command to execute.

Table 13.3 lists the resource types that are applicable to the `zonecfg` command:

TABLE 13.3 `zonecfg` Resource Types

Resource Type	Description
`zonename`	The *zonename* identifies the zone and must be unique. It can't be longer than 64 characters. It's case-sensitive and must begin with an alpha-numeric character. It can also contain underbars (_), hyphens (-), and periods (.). The name *global* and all names beginning with *SUNW* are reserved and not allowed.
`zonepath`	This is the path to the zone `root` in relation to the global zone's `root` directory (`/`). To restrict visibility to non-privileged users in the global zone, the permissions on the zonepath directory should be set to 700.
`fs`	Each zone can mount file systems. This resource specifies the path to the file system mount point.
`inherit-pkg-dir`	This type specifies directories that contain software packages that are shared with the global zone, or inherited from the global zone. The non-global zone only inherits read-only access. There are four default `inherit-pkg-dir` resources included in the configuration, namely `/lib`, `/sbin`, `/platform` and `/usr`. The packages associated with these directories are inherited (in a read-only loopback file system mount) by the non-global zone.
`net`	Each zone can have network interfaces that are plumbed when the zone transitions from the *installed* state to the *ready* state. Network interfaces are implemented as virtual interfaces.
`device`	Each zone can have devices that are configured when the zone transitions from the *installed* state to the *ready* state.
`rctl`	This type is used for zone-wide resource controls. The controls are enabled when the zone transitions from the *installed* state to the *ready* state. The zone-wide resource controls implemented in Solaris 10 are *zone.cpu-shares* and zone.max-lwps.
`attr`	This is a generic type and is most often used for comments.

Some of the resource types described in Table 13.3 also have properties that need to be configured if the resource type is to be used. The following list describes the properties and the parameters, along with examples of usage:

- `fs` `dir`, `special`, `raw`, `type`, `options`

  The following code gives an example of how these properties are used. The **bold** type indicates the keystrokes entered at the keyboard.

  ```
  zonecfg:apps> add fs
  zonecfg:apps:fs> set dir=/testmount
  zonecfg:apps:fs> set special=/dev/dsk/c0t1d0s0
  zonecfg:apps:fs> set raw=/dev/rdsk/c0t1d0s0
  ```

```
zonecfg:apps:fs> set type=ufs
zonecfg:apps:fs> add options [logging, nosuid]
zonecfg:apps:fs> end
```

This code example specifies that /dev/dsk/c0t1d0s0 in the global zone is to be mounted on directory /testmount in the non-global zone and the raw device /dev/rdsk/c0t1d0s0 is the device to fsck before attempting the mount. The file system is of type ufs and a couple of mount options have been added too.

- inherit-pkg-dir dir

  This specifies the directory that is to be loopback mounted from the global zone. The following example shows that /opt/sfw is to be mounted:

  ```
  zonecfg:apps> add inherit-pkg-dir
  zonecfg:apps:inherit-pkg-dir> set dir=/opt/sfw
  zonecfg:apps:inherit-pkg-dir> end
  ```

- net address, physical

  This specifies the setup of the network interface for the zone. The following code example specifies an IP address of 192.168.0.42 and that the physical interface to be used is hme0:

  ```
  zonecfg:apps> add net
  zonecfg:apps:net> set physical=hme0
  zonecfg:apps:net> set address=192.168.0.42
  zonecfg:apps:net> end
  ```

- device match

  This specifies a device to be included in the zone. The following code example includes a tape drive, /dev/rmt/0:

  ```
  zonecfg:apps> add device
  zonecfg:apps:device> set match=/dev/rmt/0
  zonecfg:apps:device> end
  ```

- rctl name, value

  There are two zone-wide resource controls, namely zone.cpu-shares and zone.max-lwps. The *zone.cpu-shares* limits the zone's share of the CPU resources, and the *zone.max-lwps* limits the number of Lightweight Processes that the zone can run. These two controls prevent the zone from exhausting resources that could affect the performance or operation of other zones.

  The following example sets the number of CPU shares to 20:

  ```
  zonecfg:apps> add rctl
  zonecfg:apps:rctl> set name=zone.cpu-shares
  ```

```
zonecfg:apps:rctl> set value=(priv=privileged,limit=20,action=none)
zonecfg:apps:rctl> end
```

- `attr` name, type, value

  The `attr` resource type is mainly used for adding a comment to a zone. The following example adds a comment for the zone `apps`:

```
zonecfg:apps> add attr
zonecfg:apps:attr> set name=comment
zonecfg:apps:attr> set type=string
zonecfg:apps:attr> set value="The Application Zone"
zonecfg:apps:attr> end
```

Viewing the Zone Configuration

The zone configuration data can be viewed in two ways:

- Viewing a file
- Using the `export` option of `zonecfg`

Both of these are described here:

The zone configuration file is held in the `/etc/zones` directory and is stored as an `xml` file. To view the configuration for a zone named *testzone*, you would enter:

```
# cat /etc/zones/testzone.xml
```

The alternative method of viewing the configuration is to use the `zonecfg` command with the `export` option. The following example shows how to `export` the configuration data for zone `testzone`:

```
# zonecfg -z testzone export
```

By default, the output goes to `stdout`, but this can be changed by entering a filename instead. If you save the configuration to a file, then it can be used at a later date, if required, as a command file input to the `zonecfg` command. This option is useful if you have to recreate the zone for any reason.

Installing a Zone

When a zone has been configured, the next step in its creation is to install it. This has the effect of copying the necessary files from the global zone and populating the product database for the zone. You should verify a configuration before it is installed to ensure that everything is set up correctly.

To verify the zone configuration for a zone named `testzone` enter the following command:

```
zoneadm -z testzone verify
```

If, for example, the `zonepath` does not exist, or it has not had the correct permissions set, then the `verify` operation will generate a suitable error message.

When the zone has been successfully verified it can be installed, as follows:

```
zoneadm -z testzone install
```

A number of status and progress messages are displayed on the screen as the files are copied and the package database is updated.

Notice that whilst the zone is installing, its state will change from *configured* to *incomplete*. The state will change to *installed* when the `install` operation has completed.

Booting a Zone

Before issuing the `boot` command, a zone needs to be transitioned to the `ready` state. This can be done using the `zoneadm` command as follows:

```
zoneadm -z testzone ready
```

The effect of the `ready` command is to establish the virtual platform, plumb the network interface and mount any file systems. At this point though, there are no processes running.

To boot the zone `testzone`, issue the following command:

```
zoneadm -z testzone boot
```

Confirm that the zone has booted successfully by listing the zone using the `zoneadm` command as follows:

```
zoneadm -z testzone list -v
```

The state of the zone will have changed to `running` if the `boot` operation was successful.

NOTE

No Need to Ready If you want to boot a zone, then there is no need to transition to the `ready` state. The `boot` operation does this automatically prior to booting the zone.

Halting a Zone

To shut down a zone, issue the `halt` option of the `zoneadm` command as shown in the following:

```
zoneadm -z testzone halt
```

The zone state changes from `running` to `installed` when a zone is halted.

Rebooting a Zone

A zone can be rebooted at any time without affecting any other zone on the system. The `reboot` option of the `zoneadm` command is used to reboot a zone as shown here to reboot the zone *testzone*:

```
zoneadm -z testzone reboot
```

The state of the zone should be `running` when the reboot operation has completed.

Uninstalling a Zone

When a zone is no longer required, it should be uninstalled before it is deleted. In order to uninstall a zone, it must first be halted. When this has been done, issue the uninstall command as shown here to uninstall the zone `testzone`:

```
zoneadm -z testzone uninstall -F
```

The `-F` option forces the command to execute without confirmation. If you omit this option, then you will be asked to confirm that you wish to uninstall the zone.

Deleting a Zone

When a zone has been successfully uninstalled, its configuration can be deleted from the system. Enter the `zonecfg` command as shown here to delete the zone `testzone` from the system:

```
zonecfg -z testzone delete -F
```

The `-F` option forces the command to execute without confirmation. If you omit this option, then you will be asked to confirm that you wish to delete the zone configuration.

EXAM ALERT

Remember the Force Unlike most other Unix commands, `zoneadm` and `zonecfg` use an uppercase letter `F` to force the command to be executed without prompting you for confirmation. All other commands, such as `mv`, `rm`, and `umount`, for example, always use a lowercase letter `f`. Make sure you are aware of this anomaly when you sit for the exam.

Zone Login

When a zone is operational and running, the normal network access commands can be used to access a zone, such as `telnet`, `rlogin`, and `ssh`, but a non-global zone can also be accessed from the global zone using `zlogin` command. This is necessary for administration purposes and to be able to access the console session for a zone. Only the Superuser (`root`), or a role with the RBAC profile "*Zone Management*" can use the `zlogin` command from the global zone.

The syntax for the `zlogin` command is as follows:

```
zlogin [-CE] [-e c] [-l username] zonename
zlogin [-ES] [-e c] [-l username]  zonename  utility  [argument...]
```

`zlogin` works in three modes:

- Interactive—where a login session is established from the global zone.
- Non-interactive—where a single command or utility can be executed. Upon completion of the command (or utility), the session is automatically closed.
- Console—where a console session is established for administration purposes.

Table 13.4 describes the various options for `zlogin`:

TABLE 13.4 `zlogin` Options

Option	Description
`-C`	A connection is made to the zone's console device and `zlogin` operates in console mode.
`-e c`	Changes the Escape sequence to exit from the console session, the default is the *tilde* (~).
`-E`	Disables the use of extended functions and also prohibits the use of the Escape sequence to disconnect from the session.
`-l username`	Specifies a different user for the zone login. User `root` is used when this option is omitted. This option cannot be used when using `zlogin` in console mode.
`-S`	"Safe" login mode. This option is used to recover a damaged zone when other login forms do not work. This option cannot be used in console mode.
`zonename`	Specifies the zone to connect to.
`utility`	Specifies the utility, or command, to run in the zone.
`argument`	This option allows arguments to be specified and passed to the utility or command being executed.

Initial Zone Login

When a zone has been installed and is booted for the first time, it is still not fully operational because the internal zone configuration needs to be completed. This includes setting the following:

- Language
- Terminal Type
- Host name
- Security Policy
- Name Service
- Time Zone
- Root Password

These settings are configured interactively the first time you use `zlogin` to connect to the zone console, similar to when you first install the Solaris 10 Operating Environment. The zone then reboots to implement the changes. When this reboot completes, the zone is fully operational.

NOTE

Initial Console Login You **must** complete the configuration by establishing a console connection. If this is not completed, the zone will not be operational and users will be unable to connect to the zone across the network.

Using a `sysidcfg` File

Instead of completing the zone configuration interactively, you can pre-configure the required options in a `sysidcfg` file. This enables the zone configuration to be completed without intervention. The `sysidcfg` file needs to be placed in the `/etc` directory of the zone's `root`. For a zone named `testzone` with a `zonepath` of `/export/zones/testzone`, the `sysidcfg` file would be placed in `/export/zones/testzone/root/etc`.

The following example of a `sysidcfg` file sets the required parameters, but doesn't use a naming service, or a security policy. Note that the `root` password entry needs to include the encrypted password:

```
lang=C
system_locale=en_GB
terminal=vt100
network_interface=primary {
     hostname=testzone
}
```

```
security_policy=NONE
name_service=NONE
timezone=GB
root_password=dKsw26jNk2CCE
```

There is one other question that is asked by the zone configuration utility, relating to NFS version 4 domain parameter. To complete a hands-off configuration, create the following file in the zone's `root/etc` directory:

```
# touch /export/zones/testzone/root/etc/.NFS4inst_state.domain
```

This file indicates that the NFSv4 domain has been set, so you don't get asked to confirm it.

> **NOTE**
>
> **Install `sysidcfg` Before Boot** You need to install the `sysidcfg` file and create the `.NFS4inst_state.domain` file **before** the initial boot of the zone, otherwise the files will be ignored and you will have to complete the zone setup interactively.

Logging in to the Zone Console

You can access the console of a zone by using the `zlogin -C <zonename>` command. If you are completing a hands-off configuration, connect to the console before the initial boot and you will see the boot messages appear in the console as well as the reboot after the `sysidcfg` file has been referenced.

The following session shows what happens when the zone `testzone` is booted for the first time, using a `sysidcfg` file:

```
# zlogin -C testzone

[NOTICE: Zone readied]

[NOTICE: Zone booting up]


SunOS Release 5.10 Version Generic 64-bit
Copyright 1983-2005 Sun Microsystems, Inc.  All rights reserved.
Use is subject to license terms.
Hostname: testzone
Loading smf(5) service descriptions: 100/100
Creating new rsa public/private host key pair
Creating new dsa public/private host key pair

rebooting system due to change(s) in /etc/default/init
```

```
[NOTICE: Zone rebooting]


SunOS Release 5.10 Version Generic 64-bit
Copyright 1983-2005 Sun Microsystems, Inc.  All rights reserved.
Use is subject to license terms.
Hostname: testzone

testzone console login:
```

Logging in to a Zone

The Superuser (`root`), or a role with the RBAC profile "*Zone Management*", can log directly into a zone from the global zone, without having to supply a password. The system administrator uses the `zlogin` command; the following example shows a zone login to the `testzone` zone, the command `zonename` is run and then the connection is closed:

```
# zlogin testzone
[Connected to zone 'testzone' pts/6]
Sun Microsystems Inc.    SunOS 5.10      Generic January 2005
# zonename
testzone
# exit

[Connection to zone 'testzone' pts/6 closed]
```

Running a Command in a Zone

In the previous section an interactive login to a zone was achieved. Here, a non-interactive login is actioned and a single command is executed. The connection is automatically disconnected as soon as the command has completed. The following example shows how this works. First, the `hostname` command is run, demonstrating that we are on the host called *global*, then a non-interactive login to the `testzone` zone runs, which runs the `zonename` command and then exits automatically. Finally, the same `hostname` command is run, which shows we are back on the host called `global`:

```
# hostname
global
# zlogin testzone zonename
testzone
# hostname
global
```

EXAM ALERT

No `-z` in `zlogin` Be careful not to include the `-z` option when answering questions on `zlogin` in the exam. It's easy to get confused with the `zoneadm` command, where the `-z` option IS used.

Creating a Zone

Now that we have seen the technicalities of configuring a zone, let's put it all together and create a zone. Step by Step 13.1 configures the zone named `testzone`, installs it and boots it. Finally, we will list the zone configuration data.

STEP BY STEP

13.1 Creating a zone

1. Perform the initial configuration on a zone named `testzone`. The zonepath will be `/export/zones/testzone` and the IP address will be `192.168.0.43`. This zone will be a *sparse root* zone with no additional file systems being mounted from the global zone. Create the zonepath and assign the correct permission (`700`) to the directory. The **bold** text identifies the keystrokes to be entered at the keyboard:

```
# mkdir -p /export/zones/testzone
# chmod 700 /export/zones/testzone
```

2. Enter the `zonecfg` command to configure the new zone.

```
# zonecfg -z testzone
testzone: No such zone configured
Use 'create' to begin configuring a new zone.
zonecfg:testzone>create
zonecfg:testzone>set zonepath=/export/zones/testzone
zonecfg:testzone>set autoboot=true
zonecfg:testzone>add net
zonecfg:testzone:net>set physical=hme0
zonecfg:testzone:net> zonecfg:testzone:net>set address=192.168.0.43
zonecfg:testzone:net>end
zonecfg:testzone> add rctl
zonecfg:testzone:rctl> set name=zone.cpu-shares
zonecfg:testzone:rctl> add value (priv=privileged,limit=20,action=none)
zonecfg:testzone:rctl> end
zonecfg:testzone> add attr
zonecfg:testzone:attr> set name=comment
zonecfg:testzone:attr> set type=string
zonecfg:testzone:attr> set value="First zone - Testzone"
zonecfg:testzone:attr> end
```

3. Having entered the initial configuration information, use a separate login session to check to see if the zone exists using the `zoneadm` command.

```
# zoneadm -z testzone list -v
zoneadm: testzone: No such zone configured
```

At this point the zone configuration has not been committed and saved to disk, so it only exists in memory.

4. Verify and save the zone configuration. Exit `zonecfg` and then check to see if the zone exists using the `zoneadm` command.

```
zonecfg:testzone> verify
zonecfg:testzone> commit
zonecfg:testzone> exit
# zoneadm -z testzone list -v
ID NAME             STATUS         PATH
   - testzone       configured     /export/zones/testzone
```

Notice that the zone now exists and that it has been placed in the *configured* state.

5. Use the `zoneadm` command to verify that the zone is correctly configured and ready to be installed:

```
# zoneadm -z testzone verify
```

6. Install the zone:

```
# zoneadm -z testzone install
Preparing to install zone <testzone>.
Creating list of files to copy from the global zone.
Copying <77108> files to the zone.
Initializing zone product registry.
Determining zone package initialization order.
Preparing to initialize <1141> packages on the zone.
Initialized <1141> packages on zone.
Zone <testzone> is initialized.
The file </export/zones/testzone/root/var/sadm/system/logs/install_log> contains\
a log of the zone installation.
```

7. The zone is now ready to be used operationally. Change the state to `ready` and verify that it has changed, then boot the zone and check that the state has changed to `running`.

```
# zoneadm -z testzone ready
# zoneadm -z testzone list -v
ID NAME             STATUS         PATH
   7 testzone       ready          /export/zones/testzone
# zoneadm -z testzone boot
# zoneadm -z testzone list -v
ID NAME             STATUS         PATH
   7 testzone       running        /export/zones/testzone
```

8. View the configuration data by exporting the configuration to `stdout`.

```
# zonecfg -z testzone export
create -b
set zonepath=/export/zones/testzone
set autoboot=true
```

```
add inherit-pkg-dir
set dir=/lib
end
add inherit-pkg-dir
set dir=/platform
end
add inherit-pkg-dir
set dir=/sbin
end
add inherit-pkg-dir
set dir=/usr
end
add net
set address=192.168.0.43
set physical=hme0
end
add rctl
set name=zone.cpu-shares
add value (priv=privileged,limit=20,action=none)
end
add attr
set name=comment
set type=string
set value="First zone - Testzone"
end
```

Notice the four default `inherit-pkg-dir` entries showing that this is a *sparse root zone.*

EXAM ALERT

Zone Configuration File You can also view the configuration file directly by viewing `/etc/zones/<zonename>.xml`. This file is created when you save the configuration using `zonecfg`. You might be asked this location in the exam.

Summary

The Solaris zones facility is a major step forward in the Solaris Operating Environment. It allows virtualization of Operating System services so that applications can run in an isolated and secure environment. Previously, this functionality has only been available on high-end, extremely expensive servers. One of the advantages of zones is that multiple versions of the same application can be run on the same physical system, but independently of each other. Solaris zones also protects the user from having a single application able to exhaust the CPU or memory resources when it encounters an error.

This chapter has described the concepts of Solaris zones and the zone components as well as the types of zone that can be configured.

You have seen how to configure a zone from scratch, and install and boot a zone. You also learned how to access the zone console, and login to a zone for system administration purposes.

Key Terms

- Consolidation
- Global zone
- Non-global zone
- Resource management
- Sparse root zone
- Virtualization
- Whole root zone
- `zlogin`
- `zonecfg`
- `zoneadm`
- `zoneadmd`
- `zone`

Review Exercises

13.1 Creating a Whole Root Zone

In this exercise, you'll see how to create a non-global zone, which copies the Solaris packages to the zone's private file system. You will need a Solaris 10 workstation with approximately 3.5 Gigabytes of free disk space. Make sure you are logged in as `root` and are running a window system (either CDE or Gnome). The zone you are going to create will be called `zone1` and its IP address will be `192.168.0.28`.

Estimated Time: 1 hour

1. Open a terminal window and identify a file system with at least 3.5 Gigabytes of free disk space. For this example, we have used the `/export` file system. Create the zone directory. You also need to set the permissions on the directory. Enter the following commands at the command prompt:

```
# mkdir -p /export/zones/zone1
# chmod 700 /export/zones/zone1
```

2. Now start creating the zone, using the `zonecfg` command. In this exercise, only the basic setup is required, but in order to create a *whole root* zone, the default inherited file systems must be removed. This is necessary to ensure the entire Solaris package collection is copied to the zone. Enter the commands as shown here in **bold**:

```
# zonecfg -z zone1

zone1: No such zone configured
Use 'create' to begin configuring a new zone.
zonecfg:zone1> create
zonecfg:zone1> set zonepath=/export/zones/zone1
zonecfg:zone1> set autoboot=true
zonecfg:zone1> add net
zonecfg:zone1:net> set address=192.168.0.28
zonecfg:zone1:net> set physical=hme0
zonecfg:zone1:net> end
zonecfg:zone1> add rctl
zonecfg:zone1:rctl> set name=zone.cpu-shares
zonecfg:zone1:rctl> add value (priv=privileged,limit=20,action=none)
zonecfg:zone1:rctl> end
zonecfg:zone1> add attr
zonecfg:zone1:attr> set name=comment
zonecfg:zone1:attr> set type=string
zonecfg:zone1:attr> set value="This is a whole root zone"
zonecfg:zone1:attr> end
zonecfg:zone1> remove inherit-pkg-dir dir=/lib
zonecfg:zone1> remove inherit-pkg-dir dir=/platform
zonecfg:zone1> remove inherit-pkg-dir dir=/sbin
```

```
zonecfg:zone1> remove inherit-pkg-dir dir=/usr
zonecfg:zone1> verify
zonecfg:zone1> commit
zonecfg:zone1> exit
```

3. The zone has now been created and should be in the `configured` state. You can view the state by entering the following command:

```
# zoneadm -z zone1 list -v
```

4. Verify the zone and then enter the command to install the files from the global zone as follows:

```
# zoneadm -z zone1 verify
# zoneadm -z zone1 install
```

5. Several messages inform you of the progress of the installation. When it has completed, verify that the zone state has now changed to `installed` by re-entering the following command:

```
# zoneadm -z zone1 list -v
```

6. The next thing to do is to make the zone ready and boot it so that it is running:

```
# zoneadm -z zone1 ready
# zoneadm -z zone1 boot
```

7. Add an entry to the global zone `/etc/hosts` file and try to connect to the hostname for the zone, using `telnet`. This will fail because the internal configuration of the zone has yet to be completed. Complete the installation by logging in to the console of the newly created zone:

```
# zlogin -C zone1
```

8. A console session will be established with the new zone. A number of questions need to be answered before the zone is fully operational. Enter the language, locale, terminal, the hostname for the zone, a security policy (if required), a naming service (choose "none" if a naming service is not being used), and a time zone. Finally, you will be asked to enter a `root` password.
9. When you have entered all of the required information, a final prompt appears concerning the NFSv4 domain name. Answer this question ("no" is the default).
10. The zone reboots to implement the configuration you have just specified. The reboot only takes a few seconds, when complete, you will be able to `telnet` to the zone as if it was any other remote system.

Exam Questions

1. Which of the following is the correct command to install the zone called appzone1?

   ❍ **A.** `zonecfg -z appzone1 install`

   ❍ **B.** `zoneadm appzone1 install`

   ❍ **C.** `zoneadm -z appzone1 install`

   ❍ **D.** `zonecfg appzone1 install`

2. Which of the following would uninstall the zone called appzone1 automatically, without requesting confirmation from the system administrator?

   ❍ **A.** `zonecfg appzone1 uninstall`

   ❍ **B.** `zoneadm -z appzone1 uninstall -F`

   ❍ **C.** `zoneadm -z appzone1 install -U`

   ❍ **D.** `zoneadm -z appzone1 uninstall`

3. Which of the following are valid types of Root File System types for a non-global zone? (Choose 2.)

   ❍ **A.** Whole Root

   ❍ **B.** Zone Root

   ❍ **C.** Part Root

   ❍ **D.** Sparse Root

4. You are the system administrator and you need to administer a zone called testzone. Which command will perform an interactive administration login to the zone directly from the global zone?

   ❍ **A.** `zlogin -z testzone`

   ❍ **B.** `zlogin testzone`

   ❍ **C.** `zoneadm testzone`

   ❍ **D.** `zoneadm -z testzone`

5. You are the system administrator and you need to see if the user account `testuser` has been created in the zone `testzone`. Which command from the global zone will achieve this using a non-interactive login to the zone?

- ❍ **A.** `zoneadm testzone grep testuser /etc/passwd`
- ❍ **B.** `zlogin -z testzone grep testuser /etc/passwd`
- ❍ **C.** `grep testuser /etc/passwd`
- ❍ **D.** `zlogin testzone grep testuser /etc/passwd`

6. You are creating a new non-global zone. Which of the following zone names is invalid?

- ❍ **A.** `zone1`
- ❍ **B.** `sunzone`
- ❍ **C.** `SUNWzone`
- ❍ **D.** `sun-zone`

7. Which of the following are features of the global zone? (Choose 3.)

- ❍ **A.** The global zone is not aware of the existence of other zones.
- ❍ **B.** The global zone is always assigned Zone ID 0.
- ❍ **C.** It contains a full installation of Solaris system packages.
- ❍ **D.** It contains a subset of the installed Solaris system packages.
- ❍ **E.** It provides the single bootable instance of the Solaris Operating Environment that runs on the system.

8. Which of the following describes how networking in a non-global zone is implemented in Solaris zones?

- ❍ **A.** Each non-global zone requires its own physical network interface
- ❍ **B.** All non-global zones must use the same IP address
- ❍ **C.** Each non-global zone uses a logical interface and is assigned a unique IP address
- ❍ **D.** Non-global zones must use unique port numbers to avoid conflict

9. Which command displays the current state of the zone `testzone`?

- ❍ **A.** `zoneadm list`
- ❍ **B.** `zoneadm -z testzone list -v`
- ❍ **C.** `zonecfg -z testzone list`
- ❍ **D.** `zlogin testzone zonename`

10. This daemon process allocates the zone ID for a non-global zone, plumbs the virtual network interface, and mounts any loopback or conventional file systems. Which daemon process is being described?

❍ **A.** `zoneadmd`

❍ **B.** `zsched`

❍ **C.** `init`

❍ **D.** `inetd`

11. You are configuring a non-global zone called `zone1`, which has a zonepath of `/export/zones/zone1`. You have pre-configured the zone configuration by creating a `sysidcfg` file, and you need to install it in the correct location so that when you login following the initial boot of the zone, the configuration will complete automatically. Where are you going to install the `sysidcfg` file?

❍ **A.** `/export/zones/zone1`

❍ **B.** `/etc`

❍ **C.** `/export/zones/zone1/etc`

❍ **D.** `/export/zones/zone1/root/etc`

12. This transitional zone state can be seen when a non-global zone is being installed or uninstalled. Which zone state is being described?

❍ **A.** `ready`

❍ **B.** `incomplete`

❍ **C.** `configured`

❍ **D.** `installed`

13. You have a non-global zone called *tempzone* which is no longer required. The zone has already been halted and uninstalled. Which command will actually delete the zone configuration for this zone without asking for confirmation?

❍ **A.** `zonecfg delete tempzone`

❍ **B.** `zoneadm -z tempzone delete -F`

❍ **C.** `zonecfg -z tempzone delete -F`

❍ **D.** `zoneadm delete tempzone`

14. Which option of the `zlogin` command would be used to gain access to a damaged zone for recovery purposes when other forms of login are not working?

❍ **A.** `-C`

❍ **B.** `-S`

❍ **C.** `-l`

❍ **D.** `-E`

15. Which of the following are valid states for a non-global zone? (Choose 3.)

❍ **A.** `configured`

❍ **B.** `prepared`

❍ **C.** `uninstalled`

❍ **D.** `ready`

❍ **E.** `booting`

❍ **F.** `running`

16. Which of the following are features of a non-global zone? (Choose 2)

❍ **A.** It provides the single bootable instance of the Solaris Operating Environment that runs on a system.

❍ **B.** It contains a full installation of Solaris system packages.

❍ **C.** It contains a subset of the installed Solaris system packages.

❍ **D.** Its zone ID is assigned when it is booted.

❍ **E.** It is always assigned Zone ID 0.

17. You have created a new non-global zone called `newzone` and want to view the zone configuration data. Which of the following will display the required information? (Choose 2.)

❍ **A.** `cat /etc/zones/newzone.xml`

❍ **B.** `cat /export/zones/newzone/root/etc/zones/newzone.xml`

❍ **C.** `zoneadm -z newzone list -v`

❍ **D.** `zonecfg -z newzone export`

Answers to Exam Questions

1. **C.** The command `zoneadm -z appzone1 install` will successfully install the zone called `appzone1`. For more information, see the section "Installing a Zone."
2. **B.** The command `zoneadm -z appzone1 uninstall -F` will successfully uninstall the zone called `appzone1` without asking the administrator for confirmation. For more information, see the section "Uninstalling a Zone."
3. **A and D.** *Whole Root* and *Sparse Root* are valid types of Root File System in the non-global zone. For more information, see the section "Non-global Zone Root File System Models."
4. **B.** The command `zlogin testzone` will initiate an interactive login to the zone from the global zone. For more information, see the section "Logging in to a Zone."
5. **D.** The command `zlogin testzone grep testuser /etc/passwd` will run the command `grep testuser /etc/passwd` in the `testzone` zone, in a non-interactive login from the global zone. For more information, see the section "Running a Command in a Zone."
6. **C.** The zone name "SUNWzone" is invalid because all zonenames beginning with "SUNW" are reserved. For more information, see the section "The `zonecfg` Command."
7. **B, C and E.** The global zone is always assigned Zone ID 0, it contains a full installation of Solaris system packages, and it also provides the single bootable instance of the Solaris Operating Environment that runs on the system. For more information, see the section "Zone Features."
8. **C.** Networking in non-global zones is implemented by using a logical network interface and the zone is assigned a unique IP address. For more information, see the section "Networking in a Zone Environment."
9. **B.** The command `zoneadm -z testzone list -v` will display the current state of the zone called `testzone`. For more information, see the section "Booting a Zone."
10. **A.** The `zoneadmd` daemon process assigns the zone ID to a non-global zone; it also plumbs the virtual network interface and mounts any loopback or conventional file systems. For more information, see the section "Zone Daemons."
11. **D.** In order to get the non-global zone `zone1` to automatically complete the zone configuration, the `sysidcfg` would be installed in the `/export/zones/zone1/root/etc` directory. For more information, see the section "Using a `sysidcfg` File."
12. **B.** The zone state being described is `incomplete`, because it is a transitional state that is displayed when a non-global zone is being installed or uninstalled.
13. **C.** The command `zonecfg -z tempzone delete -F` will successfully delete the configuration for zone `tempzone`.
14. **B.** The `zlogin -S` command is used to gain access to a damaged zone for recovery purposes when other forms of login are not working. For more information, see the section "Zone Login."

15. **A, D, and F.** The valid zone states are `configured`, `ready` and `running`. For more information, see the section "Zone States."

16. **C and D.** The non-global zone contains a subset of the installed Solaris system packages and its zone ID is assigned by the system when it boots.

17. **A and D.** The two ways of displaying the zone configuration data for the zone `newzone` are `cat /etc/zones/newzone.xml` and `zonecfg -z newzone export`. For more information, see the section "Viewing the Zone Configuration."

Suggested Reading and Resources

1. "System Administration Guide: Solaris Containers—Resource Management and Solaris Zones " manual from the Solaris 10 Documentation CD.

2. "System Administration Guide: Solaris Containers—Resource Management and Solaris Zones" book in the System Administration Collection of the Solaris 10 documentation set. See `http://docs.sun.com`.

CHAPTER FOURTEEN

Advanced Installation Procedures

Objectives

The following test objectives for exam 310-202 are covered in this chapter:

Explain custom JumpStart configuration, including the boot, identification, configuration, and installation services.

- ▶ This chapter helps you understand the components of a JumpStart network installation. You'll learn about setting up servers and clients to support a JumpStart installation including JumpStart related commands, configuration files, and services.

Configure a JumpStart including implementing a JumpStart server; editing the `sysidcfg`, rules, and profile files; and establishing JumpStart software alternatives (setup, establishing alternatives, troubleshooting, and resolving problems).

- ▶ This chapter shows you how to implement a JumpStart installation as well as the files and scripts that are modified and used.

Explain Flash, create and manipulate the Flash archive, and use it for installation.

- ▶ The Solaris Flash feature takes a snapshot of a Solaris operating environment, complete with patches and applications, if desired. It can only be used in initial installations, however, not upgrades.

Given a Preboot Execution Environment (PXE) installation scenario, identify requirements and install methods, configure both the install and DHCP server, and boot the x86 client.

- ▶ This chapter shows how to use the Preboot Execution Environment (PXE) to boot and install an x86 client across the network.

Outline

Study Strategies

The following strategies will help you prepare for the test:

- Practice the step-by-step examples provided in this chapter on a Solaris system. Be sure that you understand each step and can describe the process of setting up a boot server, an install server, and a configuration server. You should also be able to identify the events that occur during the JumpStart client boot sequence.
- Understand each of the commands described in this chapter. Get familiar with all of the options, especially the ones used in the examples. You'll see questions on the exam related to the `add_install_client` and `add_to_install_server` scripts.
- State the purpose of the `sysidcfg` file, the class file, and the rules file. Given the appropriate software source, be prepared to explain how to create a configuration server with a customized rules file and class files.
- State the purpose of the JumpStart server and identify the main components of each type of server. Learn the terms listed in the "Key Terms" section of this chapter. Be prepared to provide a description of each term.
- State the features and limitations of Solaris Flash and be able to implement a Flash Archive. Practice the Flash Archive example in this chapter using two Solaris systems. Make sure you are comfortable with the concepts being introduced as well as the procedures to successfully use this powerful feature.
- Become familiar with the Preboot Execution Environment (PXE) features, the requirements, and the procedures to follow in order to get an x86 client to successfully boot across the network. Also, make sure you understand what the DHCP symbols represent, and be prepared for a question in the exam that asks you to match a symbol with its corresponding description.

Introduction

There are seven ways to install the Solaris software on a system: interactive installation, both GUI and command-line, JumpStart, WAN Boot (described in Chapter 2, "Installing the Solaris 10 Operating Environment"), custom JumpStart, Solaris Flash (described in this chapter), and installation over the network (also described in Chapter 2). This chapter focuses on how to install the Solaris operating environment on clients using the custom JumpStart method. This method allows identical installations to be applied to many clients.

Another method of replicating installations is to use the Solaris Flash feature, which involves taking a complete snapshot of the Solaris operating environment, including patches and applications if you wish, and creating an archive that can be used to install other systems. This method effectively creates a clone.

This chapter looks at both the Custom JumpStart utility and the Solaris Flash feature of Solaris, showing how to use both to install the Solaris software.

Finally, this chapter introduces a new method of installing x86-based clients, namely the Preboot Execution Environment (PXE), which allows a full installation over the network using DHCP.

CAUTION

Terminology Warning You'll see the class file referred to as the profile in many Sun documents, scripts, and programs that relate to JumpStart. In the Sun System Administration training classes, however, it is referred to as a class file. That's how we refer to it throughout this chapter. On the exams, it is also referred to as a class file. The same is true for the configuration server. Sometimes Sun will refer to this server as a profile server.

JumpStart

Objectives:

Explain custom JumpStart configuration, including the boot, identification, configuration, and installation services.

- Configure a JumpStart including implementing a JumpStart server; editing the `sysidcfg`, rules, and profile files; and establishing JumpStart software alternatives (setup, establishing alternatives, troubleshooting, and resolving problems).

There are two versions of JumpStart: JumpStart and custom JumpStart. JumpStart lets you automatically install the Solaris software on a SPARC-based system just by inserting the Solaris CD and powering on the system. You do not need to specify the `boot` command at the `ok` prompt. The software that is installed is specified by a default class file that is chosen based on the system's model and the size of its disks; you can't choose the software that is installed.

For new SPARC systems shipped from Sun, this is the default method of installing the operating system when you first power on the system.

The custom JumpStart method of installing the operating system provides a way to install groups of similar systems automatically and identically. If you use the interactive method to install the operating system, you must interact with the installation program by answering various questions. At a large site with several systems that are to be configured exactly the same, this task can be monotonous and time consuming. In addition, there is no guarantee that each system is set up the same. Custom JumpStart solves this problem by providing a method to create sets of configuration files beforehand so that the installation process can use them to configure each system automatically.

Custom JumpStart requires up-front work, creating custom configuration files before the systems can be installed, but it's the most efficient way to centralize and automate the operating system installation at large enterprise sites. Custom JumpStart can be set up to be completely hands off.

The custom configuration files that need to be created for JumpStart are the rules and class files. Both of these files consist of several keywords and values and are described in this chapter.

Another file that is introduced in this chapter is the `sysidcfg` file, which can be used to preconfigure the system identification information and achieve a fully hands-off installation.

Table 14.1 lists the various commands that are introduced in this chapter.

TABLE 14.1 JumpStart Commands

Command	Description
`setup_install_server`	Sets up an install server to provide the operating system to the client during a JumpStart installation. This command is also used to set up a boot-only server when the `-b` option is specified.
`add_to_install_server`	A script that copies additional packages within a product tree on the Solaris 10 Software and Solaris 10 Languages CDs to the local disk on an existing install server.
`add_install_client`	A command that adds network installation information about a system to an install or boot server's `/etc` files so that the system can install over the network.
`rm_install_client`	Removes JumpStart clients that were previously set up for network installation.
`check`	Validates the information in the rules file.
`pfinstall`	Performs a dry run installation to test the class file.
`patchadd -C`	A command to add patches to the files in the miniroot (located in the `Solaris_10/Tools/Boot` directory) of an installation CD image created by `setup_install_server`. This facility enables you to patch Solaris installation commands and other miniroot-specific commands.

There are three main components to JumpStart:

- **Boot and Client Identification Services**—These services are provided by a networked boot server and provide the information that a JumpStart client needs to boot using the network.
- **Installation Services**—These are provided by a networked install server, which provides an image of the Solaris operating environment the JumpStart client uses as its source of data to install.
- **Configuration Services**—These are provided by a networked configuration server and provide information that a JumpStart client uses to partition disks and create file systems, add or remove Solaris packages, and perform other configuration tasks.

NOTE

Server Configurations At times we describe the boot server, the install server, and the configuration server as though they are three separate systems. The reality, however, is that most sites will have one system that performs all three functions. This is described in more detail in the section "The Install Server," later in this chapter.

Each of these components is described in this chapter. If any of these three components is improperly configured, the JumpStart clients can

- Fail to boot.
- Fail to find a Solaris Operating Environment to load.
- Ask questions interactively for configuration.
- Fail to partition disks, create file systems, and load the operating environment.

Preparing for a Custom JumpStart Installation

The first step in preparing a custom JumpStart installation is to decide how you want the systems at your site to be installed. Here are some questions that need to be answered before you begin:

- Will the installation be an initial installation or an upgrade?
- What applications will the system support?
- Who will use the system?
- How much swap space is required?

These questions will help you group the systems when you create the class and rules files later in this chapter.

Additional concerns to be addressed include what software packages need to be installed and what size the disk partitions need to be in order to accommodate the software. After you answer these questions, group systems according to their configuration (as shown in the example of a custom JumpStart near the end of this chapter).

The next step in preparing a custom JumpStart installation is to create the configuration files that will be used during the installation: the `rules.ok` file (a validated rules file) and a class file for each group of systems. The `rules.ok` file is a file that should contain a rule for each group of systems you want to install. Each rule distinguishes a group of systems based on one or more system attributes. The rule links each group to a class file, which is a text file that defines how the Solaris software is to be installed on each system in the group. Both the `rules.ok` file and the class files must be located in a JumpStart directory that you define.

The custom JumpStart configuration files that you need to set up can be located on either a diskette (called a *configuration diskette*) or a server (called a *configuration server*). Use a configuration diskette when you want to perform custom JumpStart installations on non-networked standalone systems. Use a configuration server when you want to perform custom JumpStart installations on networked systems that have access to the server. This chapter covers both procedures.

What Happens During a Custom JumpStart Installation?

This section provides a quick overview of what takes place during a custom JumpStart installation. Each step is described in detail in this chapter.

To prepare for the installation, you create a set of JumpStart configuration files, the rules and class files, on a server that is located on the same network as the client you are installing. Next, you set up the server to provide a startup kernel that is passed to the client across the network. This is called the *boot server* (or sometimes it is referred to as the *startup server*).

After the client starts up, the boot server directs the client to the JumpStart directory, which is usually located on the boot server. The configuration files in the JumpStart directory direct and automate the entire Solaris installation on the client.

To be able to start up and install the operating system on a client, you need to set up three servers: a boot server, an install server, and a configuration server. These can be three separate servers; however, in most cases, one server provides all of these services.

The Boot Server

The boot server, also called the startup server, is where the client systems access the startup files. This server must be on the local subnet (not across routers). Though it is possible to install systems over the network that are not on the same subnet as the install server, there must be a boot server that resides on the same subnet as the client.

When a client is first turned on, it does not have an operating system installed or an IP address assigned; therefore, when the client is first started, the boot server provides this information. The boot server running the RARP (Reverse Address Resolution Protocol) daemon, `in.rarpd`, looks up the Ethernet address in the `/etc/ethers` file, checks for a corresponding name in its `/etc/hosts` file, and passes the Internet address back to the client.

> **NOTE**
>
> **Check rarpd Daemon** `rarpd` is a daemon that is not always running. The `inetd` daemon is the network listener that starts `rarpd` automatically whenever a request is made. A corresponding entry for `rarpd` should exist in inetd.conf.

RARP is a method by which a client is assigned an IP address based on a lookup of its Ethernet address. After supplying an IP address, the server searches the `/tftpboot` directory for a symbolic link named for the client's IP address expressed in hexadecimal format. This link points to a boot program for a particular Solaris release and client architecture. For SPARC systems, the file name is `<hex-IP address.architecture>`, for example:

```
C009C864.SUN4U -> inetboot.sun4u.Solaris_10-1
```

The boot server uses the `in.tftpd` daemon to transmit the boot program to the client via trivial file transfer protocol (TFTP). The client runs this boot program to start up.

The boot program tries to mount the root file system. To do so, it issues the `whoami` request to discover the client's hostname. The boot server running the boot parameter daemon, `rpc.bootparamd`, looks up the hostname and responds to the client. The boot program then issues a `getfile` request to obtain the location of the client's root and swap space. The boot server responds with the information obtained from the `/etc/bootparams` file.

Once the client has its boot parameters, the boot program on the client mounts the `/` (root) file system from the boot server. The client loads its kernel and starts the `init` program. When the boot server is finished bootstrapping the client, it redirects the client to the configuration server.

The client searches for the configuration server using the `bootparams` information. The client mounts the configuration directory and runs `sysidtool`. The client then uses the `bootparams` information to locate and mount the installation directory where the Solaris image resides. The client then runs the `suninstall` program and installs the operating system.

For boot operations to proceed, the following files and directories must be properly configured on the boot server:

- `/etc/ethers`
- `/etc/hosts`
- `/etc/bootparams`
- `/etc/dfs/dfstab`
- `/tftpboot`

The following sections describe each file.

/etc/ethers

When the JumpStart client boots, it has no IP address, so it broadcasts its Ethernet address to the network using RARP. The boot server receives this request and attempts to match the client's Ethernet address with an entry in the local `/etc/ethers` file.

If a match is found, the client name is matched to an entry in the `/etc/hosts` file. In response to the RARP request from the client, the boot server sends the IP address from the `/etc/hosts` file back to the client. The client continues the boot process using the assigned IP address.

An entry for the JumpStart client must be created by editing the `/etc/ethers` file or using the `add_install_client` script described later in this chapter in the section titled "Setting Up Clients."

/etc/hosts

The `/etc/hosts` file was described in Chapter 8, "The Solaris Network Environment." The `/etc/hosts` file is the local file that associates the names of hosts with their IP addresses. The boot server references this file when trying to match an entry from the local `/etc/ethers` file in response to a RARP request from a client. In a name service environment, this file would be controlled by NIS. See Chapter 12, "Naming Services," for more information on how this file can be managed by NIS.

/etc/dfs/dfstab

The `/etc/dfs/dfstab` file lists local file systems to be shared to the network. This file is described in detail in Chapter 9, "Virtual File Systems, Swap, and Core Dumps."

/etc/bootparams

The /etc/bootparams file contains entries that network clients use for booting. JumpStart clients retrieve the information from this file by issuing requests to a server running the rpc.bootparamd program. See the section titled "Setting Up Clients" later in this chapter for more information on how this file is configured.

/tftpboot

/tftpboot is a directory that contains the inetboot.SUN4x.Solaris_10-1 file that is created for each JumpStart client when the add_install_client script is run.

The client's IP address is expressed in hexadecimal format. This link points to a boot program for a particular Solaris release and client architecture.

When booting over the network, the JumpStart client's boot PROM makes a RARP request, and when it receives a reply, the PROM broadcasts a TFTP request to fetch the inetboot file from any server that responds and executes it. See how this directory is configured in the section titled "Setting Up Clients."

Setting Up the Boot Server

The boot server is set up to answer RARP requests from clients using the add_install_client command. Before a client can start up from a boot server, the setup_install_server command is used to set up the boot server. If the same server is going to be used as a boot server and an install server, proceed to the next section titled "The Install Server."

To setup the boot server, follow the steps in Step by Step 14.1.

NOTE

Booting on a Separate Subnet Normally, the install server also provides the boot program for booting clients. However, the Solaris network booting architecture requires you to set up a separate boot server when the install client is on a different subnet than the install server. Here's the reason: SPARC install clients require a boot server when they exist on different subnets because the network booting architecture uses the reverse address resolution protocol (RARP). When a client boots, it issues a RARP request to obtain its IP address. RARP, however does not acquire the netmask number, which is required to communicate across a router on a network. If the boot server exists across a router, the boot will fail because the network traffic cannot be routed correctly without a netmask.

STEP BY STEP

14.1 Setting Up the Boot Server

1. On the system that is the boot server, log in as root. Ensure the system has an empty directory with approximately 350MB of available disk space.

2. Insert the Solaris 10 Software CD 1 into the CD-ROM drive, allowing `vold` to automatically mount the CD. Change the directory to the mounted CD. Following is an example:

```
cd /cdrom/cdrom0/s0/Solaris_10/Tools
```

3. Use the `setup_install_server` command to set up the boot server. The `-b` option copies just the startup software from the Solaris CD to the local disk. Enter this command:

```
./setup_install_server -b <boot_dir_path>
```

where `-b` specifies that the system is set up as a boot server and *<boot_dir_path>* specifies the directory where the CD image is to be copied. You can substitute any directory path, as long as that path is shared across the network.

For example, the following command copies the kernel architecture information into the `/export/jumpstart` directory:

```
./setup_install_server -b /export/jumpstart
```

The system responds with this:

```
Verifying target directory...
Calculating space required for the installation boot image
Copying Solaris_10 Tools hierarchy...
Copying Install Boot Image hierarchy...
Install Server setup complete
```

NOTE

Insufficient Disk Space The following error indicates that there is not enough room in the directory to install the necessary files. You'll need to either clean up files in that file system to make more room or choose a different file system:

```
ERROR: Insufficient space to copy Install Boot image
 362978 necessary -69372 available.
```

NOTE

Destination Must Be Empty The location in which you are trying to create the boot server must be empty. You'll see the following error if the target directory is not empty:

```
The target directory /export/jumpstart is not empty. Please choose\
 an empty directory or remove all files from the specified\
directory and run this program again.
```

If no errors are displayed, the boot server is now set up. This boot server will handle all boot requests on this subnet. A client can only boot to a boot server located on its subnet. If you have JumpStart clients on other subnets, you'll need to create a boot server for each of those subnets. The installation program will create a subdirectory named `Solaris_10` in the `<boot_dir_path>` directory.

The Install Server

As explained in the previous section, the boot server and the install server are typically the same system. The exception is when the client on which Solaris 10 is to be installed is located on a different subnet than the install server. Then a boot server is required on that subnet.

The install server is a networked system that provides Solaris 10 CD images (or a single DVD image) from which you can install Solaris 10 on another system on the network. You can create an install server by copying the images on the Solaris installation media onto the server's hard disk. This chapter focuses on using CD images, but you should be aware that Solaris 10 is also available on a single DVD.

By copying these CD images to the server's hard disk, you enable a single install server to provide Solaris 10 CD images for multiple releases, including Solaris 10 CD images for different platforms. For example, a SPARC install server could provide the following:

- Solaris 10 Software CD 1 CD image
- Solaris 10 Software CD 2 CD image
- Solaris 10 Software CD 3 CD image
- Solaris 10 Software CD 4 CD image
- Solaris 10 Languages CD image (this CD is optional)

To set up a server as a boot and installer server, complete Step by Step 14.2. This Step by Step assumes that all systems are on the same subnet, and the boot and install server are to be on the same system.

STEP BY STEP

14.2 Setting Up a Server As a Boot and Install Server

1. The first step is to copy the Solaris 10 Software CD images to the server by performing the following steps:

   Insert the CD labeled "Solaris 10 Software CD 1" into the CD-ROM and allow `vold` to automatically mount the CD. Change to the `Tools` directory on the CD as follows:

   ```
   cd /cdrom/cdrom0/s0/Solaris_10/Tools
   ```

2. Use the `setup_install_server` command to install the software onto the hard drive. The syntax for the `setup_install_server` command is as follows:

```
./setup_install_server <install_dir_path>
```

<install_dir_path> is the path to which the CD images will be copied. This directory must be empty, and must be shared so that the JumpStart client can access it across the network during the JumpStart installation. Many system administrators like to put the CD images for the boot server and install server into `/export/install` and create a directory for each architecture being installed, such as *sparc_10*, or *x86_10*. This is because the install server could be used to hold multiple versions and multiple architectures. It's a personal preference; just be sure that the target directory is empty, shared, and has approximately 3GB of space available, if all four CD images and the Language CD image are to be copied.

To install the operating environment software into the `/export/install/sparc_10` directory, issue the following command:

```
./setup_install_server /export/install/sparc_10
```

The system responds with:

```
Verifying target directory…
Calculating the required disk space for the Solaris_10 Product
Calculating space required for the installation boot image
Copying the CD image to disk...
Copying Install boot image hierarchy...
Install Server setup complete
```

3. Eject the CD and insert the CD labeled "Solaris 10 Software CD 2" into the CD-ROM, allowing `vold` to automatically mount the CD.

Change to the `Tools` directory on the mounted CD as follows:

```
cd /cdrom/cdrom0/Solaris_10/Tools
```

4. Run the `add_to_install_server` script to install the additional software into the *<install_dir_path>* directory as follows:

```
./add_to_install_server <install_dir_path>
```

For example, to copy the software into the `/export/install/sparc_10` directory, issue the following command:

```
./add_to_install_server /export/install/sparc_10
```

The system will respond with the following messages:

```
The following Products will be copied to /export/install/sparc_10/\
Solaris_10/Product:

Solaris_2
```

```
If only a subset of products is needed enter Control-C \
and invoke ./add_to_install_server with the -s option.

Checking required disk space...

Copying Top Level Installer...
131008 blocks

Copying Tools Directory...
4256 blocks

Processing completed successfully.
```

After checking for the required disk space, the image is copied from CD to disk. When it's finished installing, repeat the process with the remaining CDs and then with the Solaris 10 Languages CD, if you are planning to support multiple languages.

After copying the Solaris CDs, you can use the `patchadd -C` command to patch the Solaris miniroot image on the install server's hard disk. This option only patches the miniroot. Systems that are installed will still have to apply recommended patches if they are required.

The Configuration Server

If you are setting up custom JumpStart installations for systems on the network, you have to create a directory on a server called a *configuration directory*. This directory contains all the essential custom JumpStart configuration files, such as the rules file, the `rules.ok` file, the class file, the check script, and the optional `begin` and `finish` scripts.

The server that contains a JumpStart configuration directory is called a *configuration server*. It is usually the same system as the install and boot server, although it can be a completely different server. The configuration directory on the configuration server should be owned by root and should have permissions set to 755.

To set up the configuration server, follow Step by Step 14.3.

STEP BY STEP

14.3 Setting Up a Configuration Server

1. Choose the system that acts as the server, and log in as root.
2. Create the configuration directory anywhere on the server (such as `/jumpstart`).

3. To be certain that this directory is shared across the network, edit the `/etc/dfs/dfstab` file and add the following entry:

```
share -F nfs -o ro,anon=0 /jumpstart
```

4. Execute the `svcadm enable network/nfs/server` command. If the system is already an NFS server, you need only to type **`shareall`** and press Enter.

5. Place the JumpStart files (that is, rules, `rules.ok`, and class files) in the `/jumpstart` directory. The rules, `rules.ok`, and class files are covered later in this section. Sample copies of these files can be found in the `Misc/jumpstart_sample` subdirectory of the location where you installed the JumpStart install server.

You can also use the `add_install_client` script, which makes an entry into the `/etc/dfs/dfstab` file as part of the script. The `add_install_client` script is described in the section titled "Setting Up Clients."

Setting Up a Configuration Diskette

An alternative to setting up a configuration server is to create a configuration diskette (provided that the systems that are to be installed have diskette drives). If you use a diskette for custom JumpStart installations, the essential custom JumpStart files (the rules file, the `rules.ok` file, and the class files) must reside in the root directory on the diskette. The diskette that contains JumpStart files is called a configuration diskette. The custom JumpStart files on the diskette should be owned by root and should have permissions set to 755. See Step by Step 14.4 to set up a configuration disk.

STEP BY STEP

14.4 Setting Up a Configuration Disk

1. Format the disk by typing the following:

```
fdformat -U
```

2. If your system uses Volume Manager, insert the disk, and it will be mounted automatically.

3. Create a file system on the disk by issuing the `newfs` command:

```
newfs /vol/dev/aliases/floppy0
```

(The `newfs` command is covered in Chapter 1, "Managing File Systems.")

4. Eject the disk by typing the following:

```
eject floppy
```

5. Insert the formatted disk into the disk drive.

You have completed the creation of a disk that can be used as a configuration disk. Now you can create the rules file and create class files on the configuration disk to perform custom JumpStart installations.

The Rules File

The *rules file* is a text file that should contain a rule for each group of systems you want to install automatically. Each rule distinguishes a group of systems based on one or more system attributes and links each group to a class file, which is a text file that defines how the Solaris software is installed on each system in the group.

After deciding how you want each group of systems at your site to be installed, you need to create a rules file for each specific group of systems to be installed. The `rules.ok` file is a validated version of the rules file that the Solaris installation program uses to perform a custom JumpStart installation.

After you create the rules file, validate it with the check script by changing to the `/export/jumpstart` directory and issuing the `check` command. If the check script runs successfully, it creates the `rules.ok` file. During a custom JumpStart installation, the Solaris installation program reads the `rules.ok` file and tries to find the first rule that has a system attribute matching the system being installed. If a match occurs, the installation program uses the class file specified in the rule to install the system.

A sample rules file for a Sun Ultra is shown next. You'll find a sample rules file on the install server located in the `<install_dir_path>/Solaris_10/Misc/jumpstart_sample` directory, where `<install_dir_path>` is the directory that was specified using the `setup_install_server` script when the install server was set up. For the examples in this chapter, the install directory is `/export/install/sparc_10`.

Notice that almost all the lines in the file are commented out. These are simply instructions and sample entries to help the system administrator make the correct entry. The last, uncommented line is the rule we added for the example. The syntax is discussed later in this chapter. Each line in the code table has a rule keyword and a valid value for that keyword. The Solaris installation program scans the rules file from top to bottom. If the program matches an uncommented rule keyword and value with a known system, it installs the Solaris software specified by the class file listed in the class file field. Following is the sample rules file:

```
#
#       @(#)rules 1.12 94/07/27 SMI
#
# The rules file is a text file used to create the rules.ok file for
# a custom JumpStart installation. The rules file is a lookup table
# consisting of one or more rules that define matches between system
# attributes and profiles.
#
```

```
# This example rules file contains:
#   o syntax of a rule used in the rules file
#   o rule_keyword and rule_value descriptions
#   o rule examples
#
# See the installation manual for a complete description of the rules file
#
#
##########################################################################
#
# RULE SYNTAX:
#
# [!]rule_keyword rule_value [&& [!]rule_keyword rule_value]... \
begin profile finish
#
#     "[ ]"  indicates an optional expression or field
#     "..."  indicates the preceding expression may be repeated
#      "&&"  used to "logically AND" rule_keyword and rule_value pairs \
together
#       "!"  indicates negation of the following rule_keyword
#
#  rule_keyword       a predefined keyword that describes a general system
#                     attribute. It is used with the rule_value to match a
#                     system with the same attribute to a profile.
#
#  rule_value  a value that provides the specific system attribute
#                     for the corresponding rule_keyword. A rule_value can
#                     be text or a range of values (NN-MM).
#                     To match a range of values, a system's value must be
#                     greater than or equal to NN and less than or equal \
to MM.
#
#  begin       a file name of an optional Bourne shell script
#              that will be executed before the installation begins.
#              If no begin script exists, you must enter a minus sign(-)
#              in this field.
#
#  profile     a file name of a text file used as a template by the
#              custom JumpStart installation software that defines how
#              to install Solaris on a system.
#
#  finish      a file name of an optional Bourne shell script
#              that will be executed after the installation completes.
#              If no finish script exists, you must enter a minus sign (-)
#              in this field.
#
# Notes:
# 1.        You can add comments after the pound sign (#) anywhere on a \
line.
```

```
# 2.        Rules are matched in descending order: first rule through \
the last rule.
# 3.        Rules can be continued to a new line by using the backslash\
 (\) before
#           the carriage return.
# 4.        Don't use the "*" character or other shell wildcards, \
because the rules
#           file is interpreted by a Bourne shell script.
#
#
###########################################################################
#
# RULE_KEYWORD AND RULE_VALUE DESCRIPTIONS
#
#
#        rule_keyword   rule_value Type     rule_value Description
# ------------    --------------       ---------------------
#        any   minus sign (-) always matches
#        arch   text   system's architecture type
#        domainname    text   system's domain name
#        disksize      text range    system's disk size
#                      disk device name (text)
#                      disk size (MBytes range)
#        hostname      text   system's host name
#        installed     text text     system's insta lled version of Solaris
#                      disk device name (text)
#                      OS release (text)
#        karch text    system's kernel architecture
#        memsize       range  system's memory size (MBytes range)
#        model text    system's model number
#        network       text   system's IP address
#        totaldisk     range  system's total disk size (MBytes range)
#
#
###########################################################################
#
# RULE EXAMPLES
#
# The following rule matches only one system:
#

#hostname sample_host    -       host_class      set_root_pw

# The following rule matches any system that is on the 924.222.43.0 \
network
# and has the sun4u kernel architecture:
#    Note: The backslash (\) is used to continue the rule to a new line.

#network 924.222.43.0 && \
```

```
#       karch sun4c     -       net924_sun4u     -

# The following rule matches any sparc system with a c0t3d0 disk that is
# between 400 to 600 MBytes and has Solaris 2.1 installed on it:

#arch sparc && \
#               disksize c0t3d0 400-600 && \
#               installed c0t3d0s0 solaris_2.1 - upgrade   -

#
# The following rule matches all x86 systems:

#arch i386   x86-begin   x86-class   -

#
# The following rule matches any system:

#any -    -   any_machine   -
#
# END RULE EXAMPLES
#
#
karch sun4u     -    basic_prof    -
```

Table 14.2 describes the syntax that the rules file must follow.

TABLE 14.2 Rule Syntax

Field	Description
!	Use this before a rule keyword to indicate negation.
[ ]	Use this to indicate an optional expression or field.
...	Use this to indicate that the preceding expression might be repeated.
`rule_keyword`	A predefined keyword that describes a general system attribute, such as a hostname (`hostname`) or the memory size (`memsize`). It is used with `rule_value` to match a system with the same attribute to a profile. The complete list of `rule_keywords` is described in Table 14.3.
`rule_value`	Provides the specific system attribute value for the corresponding `rule_keyword`. See Table 14.3 for the list of `rule_values`.
&&	Use this to join rule keyword and rule value pairs in the same rule (a logical AND). During a custom JumpStart installation, a system must match every pair in the rule before the rule matches.
`<begin>`	A name of an optional Bourne shell script that can be executed before the installation begins. If no `begin` script exists, you must enter a minus sign (`-`) in this field. All `begin` scripts must reside in the JumpStart directory. See the section "`begin` and `finish` Scripts" for more information.

(continues)

TABLE 14.2 *Continued*

Field	Description
`<profile>`	The name of the class file, a text file that defines how the Solaris software is installed on the system if a system matches the rule. The information in a class file consists of class file keywords and their corresponding class file values. All class files must reside in the JumpStart directory. Class files are described in the section "Creating Class Files."
`<finish>`	The name of an optional Bourne shell script that can be executed after the installation completes. If no `finish` script exists, you must enter a minus sign (`-`) in this field. All `finish` scripts must reside in the JumpStart directory. See the section "`begin` and `finish` Scripts" for more information.

Rules File Requirements

The rules file must have the following:

- At least one rule
- The name "rules"
- At least a rule keyword, a rule value, and a corresponding profile
- A minus sign (`-`) in the `begin` and `finish` fields if there is no entry

The rules file should be saved in the JumpStart directory, should be owned by root, and should have permissions set to 644.

The rules file can contain any of the following:

- A comment after the pound sign (#) anywhere on a line. If a line begins with a `#`, the entire line is a comment. If a `#` is specified in the middle of a line, everything after the `#` is considered a comment.
- Blank lines.
- Rules that span multiple lines. You can let a rule wrap to a new line, or you can continue a rule on a new line by using a backslash (\) before pressing Enter.

Table 14.3 describes the `rule_keywords` and `rule_values` that were introduced earlier.

TABLE 14.3 `rule` keyword and `rule value` Descriptions

Rule Keyword	Rule Value	Description
`any`	Minus sign (-)	The match always succeeds.
`arch`	*<processor_type>*	See the "Platform" keyword for the valid values for `processor_type`.
`platform` SPARC x86	*<processor_type>* `sparc i386`	Matches a system's processor type. The `uname -p` command reports the system's processor type.
`domainname`	*<domain_name>*	Matches a system's domain name, which controls how a name service determines information. If you have a system already installed, the `domainname` command reports the system's domain name.
`disksize`	*<disk_name> <size_range> <disk_name>*. A disk name in the form c?t?d?, such as `c0t0d0`, or the special word `rootdisk`. If `rootdisk` is used, the disk to be matched is determined in the following order: 1. The disk that contains the preinstalled boot image (a new SPARC-based system with factory JumpStart installed). 2. The `c0t0d0s0` disk, if it exists. 3. The first available disk (searched in kernel probe order). 4. *<size_range>* The size of disk, which must be specified as a range of MB (xx–xx).	Matches a system's disk (in MB), such as disksize `c0t0d0` 32768–65536. This example tries to match a system with a `c0t0d0` disk that is between 32768 and 65536MB (32–64GB). Note: When calculating `size_range`, remember that a megabyte equals 1,048,576 bytes.
`hostaddress`	*<IP_address>*	Matches a system's IP address.
`hostname`	*<host_name>*	Matches a system's host name. If you have a system already installed, the `uname -n` command reports the system's host name.

(continues)

TABLE 14.3 *Continued*

Rule Keyword	Rule Value	Description
`installed`	*<slice>* *<version>* *<slice>* A disk slice name in the form c?t?d?s?, such as `c0t0d0s5`, or the special words any or `rootdisk`. If any is used, all the system's disks will try to be matched (in kernel probe order). If `rootdisk` is used, the disk to be matched is determined in the following order: 1. The disk that contains the preinstalled boot image (a new SPARC-based system with factory JumpStart installed). 2. The disk `c0t0d0s0`, if it exists. 3. The first available disk (searched in kernel probe order). 4. *<version>* A version name, Solaris_2.x, or the special words `any` or `upgrade`. If `any` is used, any Solaris or SunOS release is matched. If `upgrade` is used, any upgradeable Solaris 2.1 or greater release is matched.	Matches a disk that has a root file system corresponding to a particular version of Solaris software. Example: `installed c0t0d0s0 Solaris_9`. This example tries to match a system that has a Solaris 9 root file system on `c0t0d0s0`.
`karch`	*<platform_group>*. Valid values are `sun4m`, `sun4u`, `i86pc`, and `prep` (the name for PowerPC systems).	Matches a system's platform group. If you have a system already installed, the `arch -k` command or the `uname -m` command reports the system's platform group.
`memsize`	*<physical_mem>* The value must be a range of MB (xx–xx) or a single MB value.	Matches a system's physical memory size (in MB). Example: `memsize 256-1024` The example tries to match a system with a physical memory size between 256 and 1GB. If you have a system already installed, the output of the `prtconf` command (line 2) reports the system's physical memory size.
`model`	*<platform_name>*	Matches a system's platform name. Any valid platform name will work. To find the platform name of an installed system, use the `uname -i` command or the output of the `prtconf` command (line 5). Note: If the *<platform_name>* contains spaces, you must enclose it in single quotes ('). Example: `'SUNW, Ultra-5_10'`.

TABLE 14.3 *Continued*

Rule Keyword	Rule Value	Description
`network`	*<network_num>*	Matches a system's network number, which the Solaris installation program determines by performing a logical AND between the system's IP address and the subnet mask. Example: `network 193.144.2.1`. This example tries to match a system with a 193.144.2.0 IP address (if the subnet mask were 255.255.255.0).
`osname`	*<solaris_2.x>*	Matches a version of Solaris software already installed on a system. Example: `osname Solaris_9`. This example tries to match a system with Solaris 9 already installed.
`totaldisk`	*<size_range>*. The value must be specified as a range of MB (xx–xx).	Matches the total disk space on a system (in MB). The total disk space includes all the operational disks attached to a system. Example: `totaldisk 32768-65536`. This example tries to match a system with a total disk space between 32GB and 64GB.

During a custom JumpStart installation, the Solaris installation program attempts to match the system being installed to the rules in the `rules.ok` file in order—the first rule through the last rule.

Rules File Matches

A rule match occurs when the system being installed matches all the system attributes defined in the rule. As soon as a system matches a rule, the Solaris installation program stops reading the `rules.ok` file and begins installing the software based on the matched rule's class file.

Here are a few sample rules:

```
karch sun4u  -  basic_prof  -
```

The previous example specifies that the Solaris installation program should automatically install any system with the `sun4u` platform group based on the information in the `basic_prof` class file. There is no `begin` or `finish` script.

```
hostname pyramid2   -   ultra_class   -
```

The rule matches a system on the network called pyramid2. The class file to be used is named ultra_class. No begin or finish script is specified:

```
network 192.168.0.0 && !model 'SUNW,Ultra-5_10' - net_class set_root_passwd
```

The third rule matches any system on the network that is not an Ultra 5 or Ultra 10. The class file to be used is named net_class, and the finish script to be run is named set_root_passwd.

```
any - - generic_class -
```

The last example matches any system. The class file to be used is named generic_class and there is no begin or finish script.

Validating the Rules File

Before the rules file can be used, you must run the check script to validate that this file is set up correctly. If all the rules are valid, the rules.ok file is created.

To validate the rules file, use the check script provided in the *<install_dir_path>*/Solaris_10/Misc/jumpstart_sample directory on the install server.

Copy the check script to the directory containing your rules file and run the check script to validate the rules file:

```
cd /jumpstart
./check [-p path] [-r file_name]
```

<install_dir_path> is the directory that was specified using the setup_install_server script when the install server was set up.

The check script options are described in Table 14.4.

TABLE 14.4 Check Script Options

Option	Description
-p *<path>*	Validates the rules file by using the check script from a specified Solaris 10 CD image, instead of the check script from the system you are using. *<path>* is the pathname to a Solaris installation image on a local disk or a mounted Solaris CD. Use this option to run the most recent version of check if your system is running a previous version of Solaris.
-r *<file_name>*	Specifies a rules file other than a file named "rules." Using this option, you can test the validity of a rule before integrating it into the rules file. With this option, a rules.ok file is not created.

When you use check to validate a rules file, the following things happen:

1. The rules file is checked for syntax. check makes sure that the rule keywords are legitimate, and the <begin>, <class>, and <finish> fields are specified for each rule.

2. If no errors are found in the rules file, each class file specified in the rules file is checked for syntax. The class file must exist in the JumpStart installation directory and is covered in the next section.

3. If no errors are found, check creates the rules.ok file from the rules file, removing all comments and blank lines, retaining all the rules, and adding the following comment line to the end:

   ```
   version=2 checksum=<num>
   ```

   As the check script runs, it reports that it is checking the validity of the rules file and the validity of each class file. If no errors are encountered, it reports the following:

   ```
   The custom JumpStart configuration is ok.
   ```

The following is a sample session that uses check to validate a rules and class file. I named the rules file "rulestest" temporarily, the class file is named "basic_prof" and I am using the -r option. With -r, the rules.ok file is not created, and only the rulestest file is checked.

```
# /export/jumpstart/install/Solaris_10/Misc/jumpstart_sample/check -r \
/tmp/rulestest
Validating /tmp/rulestest...
Validating profile basic_prof...

Error in file "/tmp/rulestest", line 113
              any - - any_maine -
ERROR: Profile missing: any_maine
```

In this example, the check script found a bad option. "any_machine" had been incorrectly entered as "any_maine." The check script reported this error.

In the next example, the error has been fixed, we copied the file from rulestest to /export/jumpstart/rules, and reran the check script:

```
#cp rulestest /export/jumpstart/rules
#/export/jumpstart/install/Solaris_10/Misc/jumpstart_sample/check
Validating rules...
Validating profile basic_prof...
Validating profile any_machine...
The custom JumpStart configuration is ok.
```

As the check script runs, it reports that it is checking the validity of the rules file and the validity of each class file. If no errors are encountered, it reports The custom JumpStart configuration is ok. The rules file is now validated.

After the rules.ok file is created, verify that it is owned by root and that it has permissions set to 644.

`begin` and `finish` Scripts

A *`begin`* script is a user-defined Bourne shell script, located in the JumpStart configuration directory on the configuration server, specified within the rules file, that performs tasks before the Solaris software is installed on the system. You can set up *`begin`* scripts to perform the following tasks:

- Backing up a file system before upgrading
- Saving files to a safe location
- Loading other applications

Output from the *`begin`* script goes to `/var/sadm/system/logs/begin.log`.

CAUTION

Beware of `/a` Be careful not to specify something in the script that would prevent the mounting of file systems to the `/a` directory during an initial or upgrade installation. If the Solaris installation program cannot mount the file systems to `/a`, an error occurs, and the installation fails.

`begin` scripts should be owned by root and should have permissions set to 744.

In addition to *`begin`* scripts, you can also have *`finish`* scripts. A *`finish`* script is a user-defined Bourne shell script, specified within the rules file, that performs tasks after the Solaris software is installed on the system but before the system restarts. *`finish`* scripts can be used only with custom JumpStart installations. You can set up *`finish`* scripts to perform the following tasks:

- Move saved files back into place.
- Add packages or patches.
- Set the system's root password.

Output from the *`finish`* script goes to `/var/sadm/system/logs/finish.log`.

When used to add patches and software packages, `begin` and `finish` scripts can ensure that the installation is consistent between all systems.

Creating `class` Files

A *`class`* file is a text file that defines how to install the Solaris software on a system. Every rule in the rules file specifies a *`class`* file that defines how a system is installed when the rule is matched. You usually create a different *`class`* file for every rule; however, the same *`class`* file can be used in more than one rule.

A *class* file consists of one or more `class` file keywords (they are described in the following sections). Each `class` file keyword is a command that controls one aspect of how the Solaris installation program installs the Solaris software on a system. Use the vi editor (or any other text editor) to create a *class* file in the JumpStart configuration directory on the configuration server. You can create a new *class* file or edit one of the sample profiles located in `/cdrom/cdrom0/s0/Solaris_10/Misc/jumpstart_sample` on the Solaris 10 Software CD 1. The *class* file can be named anything, but it should reflect the way in which it installs the Solaris software on a system. Sample names are `basic_install`, `eng_profile`, and `accntg_profile`.

A `class` file must have the following:

- The `install_type` keyword as the first entry
- Only one keyword on a line
- The `root_device` keyword if the systems being upgraded by the `class` file have more than one root file system that can be upgraded

A `class` file can contain either of the following:

- A comment after the pound sign (#) anywhere on a line. If a line begins with a #, the entire line is a comment. If a # is specified in the middle of a line, everything after the # is considered a comment.
- Blank lines.

The `class` file is made up of keywords and their values. The `class` file keywords and their respective values are described in the following sections.

archive_location

This keyword is used when installing a Solaris Flash Archive and specifies the source of the Flash Archive. The syntax for this option is shown here:

```
archive_location retrieval type location
```

The *retrieval_type* parameter can be one of the following:

- NFS
- HTTP or HTTPS
- FTP
- Local Tape
- Local Device
- Local File

The syntax for a Flash Archive located on an NFS server is as follows:

```
archive_location nfs server_name:/path/filename retry n
```

Where *retry n* specifies the maximum number of attempts to mount the archive.

The syntax for a Flash Archive located on an HTTP or HTTPS server is as follows:

```
archive_location http://server_name:port/path/filename <optional keywords>

archive_location https://server_name:port/path/filename <optional keywords>
```

Table 14.5 lists the optional keywords that can be used with this option:

TABLE 14.5 `HTTP Server Optional` Keywords

Keyword	Description
`auth basic` *`user password`*	If the HTTP server is password protected then a username and password must be supplied to access the archive.
`timeout` *`min`*	Specifies the maximum time, in minutes, that is allowed to elapse without receiving data from the HTTP server.
`proxy` *`host:port`*	Specifies a proxy host and port. The `proxy` option can be used when you need to access an archive from the other side of a firewall. The *`port`* value must be supplied.

The syntax for a Flash Archive located on an FTP server is as follows:

```
archive_location ftp://username:password@server_name:port/path/filename <optional
keywords>
```

Table 14.6 lists the optional keywords that can be used with this option:

TABLE 14.6 `FTP Server Optional` Keywords

Keyword	Description
`timeout` *`min`*	Specifies the maximum time, in minutes, that is allowed to elapse without receiving data from the FTP server.
`proxy` *`host:port`*	Specifies a proxy host and port. The `proxy` option can be used when you need to access an archive from the other side of a firewall. The *`port`* value must be supplied.

The syntax for a Flash Archive located on local tape is as follows:

```
archive_location local_tape device position
```

where *`device`* specifies the device path of the tape drive and *`position`* specifies the file number on the tape where the archive is located. The *`position`* parameter is useful because you can store a `begin` script or a `sysidcfg` file on the tape prior to the actual archive.

The syntax for a Flash Archive located on a local device is as follows:

```
archive_location local_device device path/filename file_system_type
```

The syntax for a Flash Archive located in a local file is as follows:

```
archive_location local_file path/filename
```

All that is needed for this option is to specify the full pathname to the Flash Archive file.

backup_media

backup_media defines the medium that is used to back up file systems if they need to be reallocated during an upgrade because of space problems. If multiple tapes or disks are required for the backup, you are prompted to insert these during the upgrade. Here is the backup_media syntax:

```
backup_media <type> <path>
```

type can be one of the keywords listed in Table 14.7.

TABLE 14.7 backup_media Keywords

Keyword	Description
local_tape	Specifies a local tape drive on the system being upgraded. The *<path>* must be the character (raw) device path for the tape drive, such as /dev/rmt/0.
local_diskette	Specifies a local diskette drive on the system being upgraded. The *<path>* is the local diskette, such as /dev/rdiskette0. The diskette must be formatted.
local_filesystem	Specifies a local file system on the system being upgraded. The *<path>* can be a block device path for a disk slice or the absolute *<path>* to a file system mounted by the /etc/vfstab file. Examples of *<path>* are /dev/dsk/c0t0d0s7 and /home.
remote_filesystem	Specifies an NFS file system on a remote system. The *<path>* must include the name or IP address of the remote system (host) and the absolute *<path>* to the file system. The file system must have read/write access. A sample *<path>* is sparc1:/home.
remote_system	Specifies a directory on a remote system that can be reached by a remote shell (rsh). The system being upgraded must have access to the remote system. The *<path>* must include the name of the remote system and the absolute path to the directory. If a user login is not specified, the login is tried as root. A sample *<path>* is bcalkins@sparcl:/home.

Here are some examples of class file keywords being used:

```
backup_media local_tape /dev/rmt/0
backup_media local_diskette /dev/rdiskette0
```

```
backup_media local_filesystem /dev/dsk/c0t3d0s7
backup_media local_filesystem /export
backup_media remote_filesystem sparc1:/export/temp
backup_media remote_system bcalkins@sparc1:/export/temp
```

`backup_media` must be used with the `upgrade` option only when disk space re-allocation is necessary.

boot_device

`boot_device` designates the device where the installation program installs the root file system and consequently what the system's startup device is. The `eeprom` value also lets you update the system's EEPROM if you change its current startup device so that the system can automatically start up from the new startup device.

Here's the `boot_device` syntax:

```
boot_device <device> <eeprom>
```

The `device` and `eeprom` values are described in Table 14.8.

TABLE 14.8 `boot_device` Keywords

Keyword	Description
<device>	Specifies the startup device by specifying a disk slice, such as `c0t1d0s0` (`c0d1` for x86 systems). It can be the keyword `existing`, which places the root file system on the existing startup device, or the keyword `any`, which lets the installation program choose where to put the root file system.
<eeprom>	Specifies whether you want to update the system's EEPROM to the specified startup device. *<eeprom>* specifies the value `update`, which tells the installation program to update the system's EEPROM to the specified startup device, or `preserve`, which leaves the startup device value in the system's EEPROM unchanged. An example for a Sparc system is `boot_device c0t1d0s0 update`.

NOTE

X86 Preserve Only For x86 systems, the *<eeprom>* parameter must be *`preserve`*.

The installation program installs the root file system on `c0t1d0s0` and updates the EEPROM to start up automatically from the new startup device. For more information on the `boot device`, see Chapter 3, "Perform System Boot and Shutdown Procedures."

bootenv_createbe

bootenv_createbe enables an empty, inactive boot environment to be created at the same time as installing the Solaris OS. You only need to create a / file system; other file system slices are reserved, but not populated. This kind of boot environment is installed with a Solaris flash archive, at which time the other reserved file system slices are created.

Here's the bootenv createbe syntax:

```
bootenv createbe bename new_BE_name filesystem mountpoint:device:fs_options
```

The bename and filesystem values are described in Table 14.9.

TABLE 14.9 bootenv createbe Keywords

Keyword	Description
bename	Specifies the name of the new boot environment to be created. It can be no longer than 30 characters, all alphanumeric, and must be unique on the system.
filesystem	Specifies the type and number of filesystems to be created in the new boot environment. The *mountpoint* can be any valid mount point, or a hyphen (-) for *swap*, and *fs_options* can be *swap* or *ufs*. You cannot use Solaris Volume Manager volumes or Veritas Volume Manager objects—the device must be in the form */dev/dsk/cwtxdysz*.

client_arch

client_arch indicates that the operating system server supports a platform group other than its own. If you do not specify client_arch, any diskless client that uses the operating system server must have the same platform group as the server. client_arch can be used only when system_type is specified as *server*. You must specify each platform group that you want the operating system server to support.

Here's the client_arch syntax:

```
client_arch karch_value [karch_value...]
```

Valid values for <*karch_value*> are sun4u and i86pc.

Here's an example:

```
client_arch sun4u
```

client_root

client_root defines the amount of root space, in MB, to allocate for each diskless client. If you do not specify client_root in a server's profile, the installation software automatically allocates 15MB of root space per client. The size of the client root area is used in combination with the `num_clients` keyword to determine how much space to reserve for the `/export/root` file system. You can only use the `client_root` keyword when `system_type` is specified as *server*.

Here's the syntax:

```
client_root <root_size>
```

`<root_size>` is specified in MB. Here's an example:

```
client_root 20
```

NOTE

Don't Waste Space When allocating root space, 20MB is an adequate size. 15MB is the minimum size required. Any more than 20MB is just wasting disk space.

client_swap

`client_swap` defines the amount of swap space, in MB, to allocate for each diskless client. If you do not specify `client_swap`, 32MB of swap space is allocated. Physical memory plus swap space must be a minimum of 32MB. If a class file does not explicitly specify the size of swap, the Solaris installation program determines the maximum size that the swap file can be, based on the system's physical memory. The Solaris installation program makes the size of swap no more than 20 percent of the disk where it resides, unless there is free space left on the disk after the other file systems are laid out.

Here's the syntax:

```
client_swap <swap_size>
```

`<swap_size>` is specified in MB.

Here's an example:

```
client_swap 64
```

This example specifies that each diskless client has a swap space of 64MB.

cluster

`cluster` designates which software group to add to the system. The software groups are listed in Table 14.10.

TABLE 14.10 Software Groups

Software Group	group_name
Reduced network support	SUNWCrnet
Core	SUNWCreq
End-user system support	SUNWCuser
Developer system support	SUNWCprog
Entire distribution	SUNWCall
Entire distribution plus OEM support	SUNWCXall

You can specify only one software group in a profile, and it must be specified before other cluster and package entries. If you do not specify a software group with `cluster`, the end-user software group, `SUNWCuser`, is installed on the system by default.

Here is `cluster`'s syntax:

```
cluster <group_name>
```

Here's an example:

```
cluster SUNWCall
```

This example specifies that the Entire Distribution group should be installed.

The `cluster` keyword can also be used to designate whether a `cluster` should be added to or deleted from the software group that was installed on the system. `add` and `delete` indicate whether the cluster should be added or deleted. If you do not specify `add` or `delete`, `add` is set by default.

Here's the syntax:

```
cluster <cluster_name> [add ¦ delete]
```

<cluster_name> must be in the form `SUNWCname`.

dontuse

`dontuse` designates one or more disks that you don't want the Solaris installation program to use. By default, the installation program uses all the operational disks on the system. *<disk_name>* must be specified in the form `c?t?d?` or `c?d?`, such as `c0t0d0`.

Here's the syntax:

```
dontuse disk_name [disk_name...]
```

Here's an example:

```
dontuse c0t0d0 c0t1d0
```

NOTE

dontuse and usedisk You cannot specify the `usedisk` keyword and the `dontuse` keyword in the same class file because they are mutually exclusive.

filesys

`filesys` can be used to create local file systems during the installation by using this syntax:

```
filesys <slice> <size> [file_system] [optional_parameters]
```

The values listed in Table 14.11 can be used for *<slice>*.

TABLE 14.11 <slice> Values

Value	Description
`any`	This variable tells the installation program to place the file system on any disk.
`c?t?d?s?` or `c?d??z`	The disk slice where the Solaris installation program places the file system, such as `c0t0d0s0`.
`rootdisk.sn`	The variable that contains the value for the system's root disk, which is determined by the Solaris installation program. The `sn` suffix indicates a specific slice on the disk.

The values listed in Table 14.12 can be used for *<size>*.

TABLE 14.12 <size> Values

Value	Description
`num`	The size of the file system in MB.
`existing`	The current size of the existing file system.
`auto`	The size of the file system is determined automatically, depending on the selected software.
`all`	The specified slice uses the entire disk for the file system. When you specify this value, no other file systems can reside on the specified disk.
`free`	The remaining unused space on the disk is used for the file system.
<start>:*<size>*	The file system is explicitly partitioned. *<start>* is the cylinder where the slice begins, and *<size>* is the number of cylinders for the slice.

`file_system` is an optional field when `slice` is specified as `any` or `c?t?d?s?`. If `file_system` is not specified, `unnamed` is set by default, but you can't specify the `optional_parameters` value.

The values listed in Table 14.13 can be used for `file_system`.

TABLE 14.13 file_system Values

Value	Description
<mount_pt_name>	The file system's mount point name, such as /opt.
<swap>	The specified slice is used as swap.
<overlap>	The specified slice is defined as a representation of the whole disk. overlap can be specified only when <size> is existing, all, or start:size.
<unnamed>	The specified slice is defined as a raw slice, so the slice does not have a mount point name. If file_system is not specified, unnamed is set by default.
<ignore>	The specified slice is not used or recognized by the Solaris installation program. This can be used to ignore a file system on a disk during an installation so that the Solaris installation program can create a new file system on the same disk with the same name. ignore can be used only when existing partitioning is specified.

In the following example, the size of swap is set to 512MB, and it is installed on c0t0d0s1:

```
filesys                    c0t0d0s1 512 swap
```

In the next example, /usr is based on the selected software, and the installation program determines what disk to put it on when you specify the any value:

```
filesys                    any auto /usr
```

The optional_parameters field can be one of the options listed in Table 14.14.

TABLE 14.14 optional_parameters Options

Option	Description
preserve	The file system on the specified slice is preserved. preserve can be specified only when size is existing and slice is c?t?d?s?.
<mount_options>	One or more mount options that are added to the /etc/vfstab entry for the specified *<mount_pt_name>*.

A new option to the filesys keyword in Solaris 10 is mirror, which facilitates the creation of RAID-1 volumes as part of the custom JumpStart installation. This facility allows the creation of mirrored filesystems. You can issue this keyword more than once to create mirrors for different file systems.

NOTE

Only on Initial Install The filesys mirror keyword is only supported for initial installations.

The syntax for the `filesys mirror` keyword is as follows:

```
Filesys mirror [:name]slice [slice] size file_system optional_parameters
```

Table 14.15 details the available options for the `filesys mirror` keyword.

TABLE 14.15 `filesys mirror` Options

Option	Description
`name`	An optional keyword allowing you to name the mirror. The naming convention follows metadevices in Solaris Volume Manager, in the format dxxx (where *xxx* is a number between 0 and 127); for example `d50`. If a name is not specified then the custom JumpStart program assigns one for you.
`slice`	Specifies the disk slice where the custom JumpStart program places the file system you want to duplicate with the mirror.
`size`	The size of the file system in Megabytes.
`file_system`	Specifies the file system you are mirroring. This can be any file system, including root (`/`) or `swap`.
`optional parameters`	One or more mount options that are added to the `/etc/vfstab` entry for the specified *<mount_pt_name>*.

`filesys` can also be used to set up the installed system to mount remote file systems automatically when it starts up. You can specify `filesys` more than once. The following syntax describes using `filesys` to set up mounts to remote systems:

```
filesys <server>:<path> <server_address> <mount_pt_name> [mount_options]
```

The `filesys` keywords are described in Table 14.16.

TABLE 14.16 `filesys` Remote Mount Keywords

Keyword	Description
<server>:	The name of the server where the remote file system resides. Don't forget to include the colon (:).
<path>	The remote file system's mount point name.
<server_address>	The IP address of the server specified in *<server>*:*<path>*. If you don't have a name service running on the network, this value can be used to populate the `/etc/hosts` file with the server's IP address, but you must specify a minus sign (-).
<mount_pt_name>	The name of the mount point where the remote file system will be mounted.
[*mount_options*]	One or more mount options that are added to the `/etc/vfstab` entry for the specified *<mount_pt_name>*. If you need to specify more than one mount option, the mount options must be separated by commas and no spaces. An example is `ro,quota`.

Here's an example:

```
filesys zeus:/export/home/user1 192.9.200.1 /home ro,bg,intr
```

forced_deployment

This keyword forces a Solaris Flash differential archive to be installed on a clone system even though the clone system is different than what the software expects. This option deletes files to bring the clone system to an expected state, so it should be used with caution.

install_type

`install_type` specifies whether to perform the initial installation option or the upgrade option on the system. `install_type` must be the first class file keyword in every profile.

Following is the syntax:

```
install_type [initial_install ¦ upgrade]
```

Select one of `initial_install`, `upgrade`, `flash_install` or `flash_update`.

Here's an example:

```
install_type initial_install
```

geo

The `geo` keyword followed by a *`locale`* designates the regional locale or locales you want to install on a system (or to add when upgrading a system). The syntax is

```
geo <locale>
```

Values you can specify for `locale` are listed in Table 14.17.

TABLE 14.17 `locale` Values

Value	Description
`N_Africa`	Northern Africa, including Egypt
`C_America`	Central America, including Costa Rica, El Salvador, Guatemala, Mexico, Nicaragua, and Panama
`N_America`	North America, including Canada and the United States
`S_America`	South America, including Argentina, Bolivia, Brazil, Chile, Colombia, Ecuador, Paraguay, Peru, Uruguay, and Venezuela
`Asia`	Asia, including Japan, Republic of Korea, Republic of China, Taiwan, and Thailand
`Ausi`	Australasia, including Australia and New Zealand
`C_Europe`	Central Europe, including Austria, Czech Republic, Germany, Hungary, Poland, Slovakia, and Switzerland

(continues)

TABLE 14.17 *Continued*

Value	Description
`E_Europe`	Eastern Europe, including Albania, Bosnia, Bulgaria, Croatia, Estonia, Latvia, Lithuania, Macedonia, Romania, Russia, Serbia, Slovenia, and Turkey
`N_Europe`	Northern Europe, including Denmark, Finland, Iceland, Norway, and Sweden
`S_Europe`	Southern Europe, including Greece, Italy, Portugal, and Spain
`W_Europe`	Western Europe, including Belgium, France, Great Britain, Ireland, and the Netherlands
`M_East`	Middle East, including Israel

Refer to the "International Language Environments Guide" in the "Solaris 10 International Language Support Collection" for a complete listing of `locale` values. This guide is available on the Solaris 10 documentation CD, or online at `http://docs.sun.com`.

Here's an example where the locale specified is `S_America`:

```
geo S_America
```

layout_constraint

`layout_constraint` designates the constraint that auto-layout has on a file system if it needs to be re-allocated during an upgrade because of space problems. `layout_constraint` can be used only for the `upgrade` option when disk space re-allocation is required.

With `layout_constraint`, you specify the file system and the constraint you want to put on it.

Here's the syntax:

```
layout_constraint <slice> <constraint> [minimum_size]
```

The `<slice>` field specifies the file system disk slice on which to specify the constraint. It must be specified in the form `c?t?d?s?` or `c?d?s?`.

Table 14.18 describes the options for `layout_constraint`.

TABLE 14.18 `layout_constraint` **Options**

Option	Description
`changeable`	Auto-layout can move the file system to another location and can change its size. You can change the file system's size by specifying the `minimum_size` value. When you mark a file system as `changeable` and `minimum_size` is not specified, the file system's minimum size is set to 10 percent greater than the minimum size required. For example, if the minimum size for a file system is 1000MB, the changed size would be 1010MB. If `minimum_size` is specified, any free space left over (the original size minus the minimum size) is used for other file systems.

TABLE 14.18 *Continued*

Option	Description
`movable`	Auto-layout can move the file system to another slice on the same disk or on a different disk, and its size stays the same.
`available`	Auto-layout can use all the space on the file system to re-allocate space. All the data in the file system is then lost. This constraint can be specified only on file systems that are not mounted by the `/etc/vfstab` file.
`collapse`	Auto-layout moves (collapses) the specified file system into its parent file system. You can use this option to reduce the number of file systems on a system as part of the upgrade. For example, if the system has the `/usr` and `/usr/openwin` file systems, collapsing the `/usr/openwin` file system would move it into `/usr` (its parent).
`minimum_size`	This value lets you change the size of a file system by specifying the size you want it to be after auto-layout re-allocates. The size of the file system might end up being more if unallocated space is added to it, but the size is never less than the value you specify. You can use this optional value only if you have marked a file system as `changeable`. The `minimum size` cannot be less than the file system needs for its existing contents.

The following are some examples:

```
layout_constraint c0t0d0s3 changeable 1200
```

The file system `c0t0d0s3` can be moved to another location, and its size can be changed to more than 1200MB but no less than 1200MB.

```
layout_constraint c0t0d0s4 movable
```

The file system on slice `c0t0d0s4` can move to another disk slice, but its size stays the same:

```
layout_constraint c0t2d0s1 collapse
```

`c0t2d0s1` is moved into its parent directory to reduce the number of file systems.

local_customization

This keyword is used when installing Solaris Flash archives and can be used to create custom scripts to preserve local configurations on a clone system before installing a Solaris Flash Archive. The syntax for this option is

```
local_customization local_directory
```

The *`local_directory`* parameter specifies the directory on the clone system where any scripts are held.

locale

locale designates which language or locale packages should be installed for the specified locale_name. A locale determines how online information is displayed for a specific language or region, such as date, time, spelling, and monetary value. Therefore, if you want English as your language but you also want to use the monetary values for Australia, you would choose the Australia locale value (en_AU) instead of the English language value (C).

The English language packages are installed by default. You can specify a locale keyword for each language or locale you need to add to a system.

Following is the locale syntax:

```
locale locale_name
```

Here's an example:

```
locale es
```

This example specifies Spanish as the language package you want installed.

metadb

The metadb keyword allows you to create Solaris Volume Manager state database replicas as part of the custom JumpStart installation. You can use this keyword more than once to create state database replicas on several disk slices.

The syntax for this keyword is shown here:

```
metadb slice [size size-in-blocks] [count number-of-replicas]
```

Table 14.19 describes the options for metadb.

TABLE 14.19 metadb Options

Option	Description
slice	The disk slice on which you want to place the state database replica. It must be in the format *cwtxdysz*.
size size-in-blocks	The number of blocks specifying the size of the replica. If this option is omitted, a default size of 8192 is allocated.
count number-of-replicas	The number of replicas to create. If this option is omitted, then 3 replicas are created by default.

no_content_check

This keyword is used when installing Solaris Flash Archives. When specified, it ignores file-by-file validation, which is used to ensure that a clone system is a duplicate of the master system. Only use this option if you are sure the clone is a duplicate of the master system, because files are deleted to bring the clone to an expected state if discrepancies are found.

no_master_check

This keyword is used when installing Solaris Flash Archives. When specified, it ignores the check to verify that a clone system was built from the original master system. Only use this option if you are sure the clone is a duplicate of the original master system.

num_clients

When a server is installed, space is allocated for each diskless client's root (/) and swap file systems. `num_clients` defines the number of diskless clients that a server supports. If you do not specify `num_clients`, five diskless clients are allocated. You can only use this option when `system_type` is set to *server*.

Following is the syntax:

```
num_clients client_num
```

Here's an example:

```
num_clients 10
```

In this example, space is allocated for 10 diskless clients.

package

`package` designates whether a package should be added to or deleted from the software group that is installed on the system. `add` or `delete` indicates the action required. If you do not specify `add` or `delete`, `add` is set by default.

Following is the syntax:

```
package package_name [add [retrieval_type location] ¦ delete]
```

The `package_name` must be in the form `SUNW`*name*.

The *retrieval_type* parameter can be one of the following:

- NFS
- HTTP or HTTPS
- Local Device
- Local File

The syntax for a package located on an NFS server is as follows:

```
package package_name add nfs server_name:/path retry n
```

where `retry n` specifies the maximum number of attempts to mount the directory.

The syntax for a package located on an HTTP or HTTPS server is as follows:

```
package package_name add http://server_name:port/path <optional keywords>
package package_name add https://server_name:port/path <optional keywords>
```

Table 14.20 lists the optional keywords that can be used with this option.

TABLE 14.20 HTTP package Optional Keywords

Keyword	Description
`timeout` *min*	Specifies the maximum time, in minutes, that is allowed to elapse without receiving data from the HTTP server.
`proxy` *host:port*	Specifies a proxy host and port. The `proxy` option can be used when you need to access a package from the other side of a firewall. The *port* value must be supplied.

The syntax for a package located on a local device is as follows:

```
package package_name add local_device device path file_system_type
```

The syntax for a package located in a local file is as follows:

```
package package_name add local_file path
```

All that is needed for this option is to specify the full pathname to the directory containing the package.

Here's an example:

```
package SUNWxwman add nfs server1:/var/spool/packages retry 5
```

In this example, `SUNWxwman` (X Window online man pages) is being installed on the system from a location on a remote NFS server.

partitioning

`partitioning` defines how the disks are divided into slices for file systems during the installation. If you do not specify `partitioning`, the default is set.

Following is the syntax:

```
partitioning default|existing|explicit
```

The `partitioning` options are described in Table 14.21.

TABLE 14.21 partitioning Options

Option	Description
default	The Solaris installation program selects the disks and creates the file systems where the specified software is installed. Except for any file systems specified by the `filesys` keyword, `rootdisk` is selected first. Additional disks are used if the specified software does not fit on `rootdisk`.
existing	The Solaris installation program uses the existing file systems on the system's disks. All file systems except `/`, `/usr`, `/usr/openwin`, `/opt`, and `/var` are preserved. The installation program uses the last mount point field from the file system superblock to determine which file system mount point the slice represents. When you specify the `filesys` class file keyword with `partitioning`, `existing` must be specified.
explicit	The Solaris installation program uses the disks and creates the file systems specified by the `filesys` keywords. If you specify only the root (`/`) file system with the `filesys` keyword, all the Solaris software is installed in the root file system. When you use the `explicit` class file value, you must use the `filesys` class file keyword to specify which disks to use and what file systems to create.

root_device

`root_device` designates the system's root disk.

Following is the syntax:

```
root_device slice
```

Here's an example:

```
root_device c0t0d0s0
```

NOTE

Specifying Mirrors If you are upgrading a RAID-1 (`mirror`) volume then the slice you specify should be one side of the `mirror`. The other side will be upgraded automatically.

system_type

`system_type` defines the type of system being installed. If you do not specify `system_type` in a class file, `standalone` is set by default.

Following is the syntax:

```
system_type [standalone ¦ server]
```

Here's an example:

```
system_type server
```

usedisk

`usedisk` designates one or more disks that you want the Solaris installation program to use when the `partitioning` default is specified. By default, the installation program uses all the operational disks on the system. `disk_name` must be specified in the form `c?t?d?` or `c?d?`, such as `c0t0d0`. If you specify the `usedisk` class file keyword in a class file, the Solaris installation program uses only the disks that you specify.

Following is the syntax:

```
usedisk disk_name [disk_name]
```

Here's an example:

```
usedisk c0t0d0 c0t1d0
```

NOTE

dontuse and usedisk You cannot specify the `usedisk` keyword and the `dontuse` keyword in the same class file because they are mutually exclusive.

Testing Class Files

After you create a class file, you can use the `pfinstall` command to test it. Testing a class file is sometimes called a *dry run* installation. By looking at the installation output generated by `pfinstall`, you can quickly determine whether a class file will do what you expect. For example, you can determine whether a system has enough disk space to upgrade to a new release of Solaris before you actually perform the upgrade.

To test a class file for a particular Solaris release, you must test it within the Solaris environment of the same release. For example, if you want to test a class file for Solaris 10, you have to run the `pfinstall` command on a system running Solaris 10.

To test the class file, change to the JumpStart directory that contains the class file and type the following:

```
/usr/sbin/install.d/pfinstall -d
```

or type the following:

```
/usr/sbin/install.d/pfinstall -D
```

CAUTION

Install or Test? Without the `-d` or `-D` option, `pfinstall` actually installs the Solaris software on the system by using the specified class file, and the data on the system is overwritten.

Following is the syntax for `pfinstall`:

```
/usr/sbin/install.d/pfinstall [-D|-d] <disk_config> [-c <path>] <profile>
```

The `pfinstall` options are described in Table 14.22.

TABLE 14.22 `pfinstall` Options

Option	Description
`-D`	Tells `pfinstall` to use the current system's disk configuration to test the class file against.
`-d` *`<disk_config>`*	Tells `pfinstall` to use a disk configuration file, *`<disk_config>`*, to test the class file against. If the *`<disk_config>`* file is not in the directory where `pfinstall` is run, you must specify the path. This option cannot be used with an upgrade class file (an install-type upgrade). You must always test an upgrade class file against a system's disk configuration using the `-D` option. A disk configuration file represents a disk's structure. It describes a disk's bytes per sector, flags, and slices. See the example following this table of how to create the *`<disk_config>`* file.
`-c` *`<path>`*	Specifies the path to the Solaris CD image. This is required if the Solaris CD is not mounted on `/cdrom`. For example, use this option if the system is using Volume Manager to mount the Solaris CD.
`<profile>`	Specifies the name of the class file to test. If class file is not in the directory where `pfinstall` is being run, you must specify the path.

You can create a *`<disk_config>`* file by issuing the following command:

```
prtvtoc /dev/rdsk/<device_name> > <disk_config>
```

`/dev/rdsk/`*`<device_name>`* is the device name of the system's disk. *`<device_name>`* must be in the form `c?t?d?s2` or `c?d?s2`. *`<disk_config>`* is the name of the disk configuration file to contain the redirected output.

NOTE

Identifying Disks `c?t?d?s2` designates a specific target for a SCSI disk, and `c?d?s2` designates a non-SCSI disk.

Here's an example:

```
prtvtoc /dev/rdsk/c0t0d0s2 > test
```

The file named "test" created by this example would be your *<disk_config>* file, and it would look like this:

```
* /dev/rdsk/c0t0d0s2 partition map
*
* Dimensions:
*      512 bytes/sector
*      126 sectors/track
*        4 tracks/cylinder
*      504 sectors/cylinder
*     4106 cylinders
*     4104 accessible cylinders
*
* Flags:
*     1: unmountable
*    10: read-only
*
*                          First    Sector Last
*Partition  Tag   Flags  Sector    Count     Sector    Mount Directory
     0       2     00     0         268632    268631    /
     1       3     01     268632    193032    461663
     2       5     00     0         2068416   2068415
     3       0     00     461664    152712     614375   /export
     4       0     00     614376    141624     755999   /export/swap
     6       4     00     756000    1312416    068415   /usr
```

> **NOTE**
>
> **Multiple Disks** If you want to test installing Solaris software on multiple disks, concatenate single disk configuration files and save the output to a new file.

The following example tests the `ultra_class` class file against the disk configuration on a Solaris 10 system on which `pfinstall` is being run. The `ultra_class` class file is located in the `/export/jumpstart` directory, and the path to the Solaris CD image is specified because Volume Management is being used.

In addition, if you want to test the class file for a system with a specific system memory size, set `SYS_MEMSIZE` to the specific memory size in MB as follows:

```
SYS_MEMSIZE=memory_size
export SYS_MEMSIZE
cd /export/jumpstart
/usr/sbin/install.d/pfinstall -D -c /cdrom/cdrom0/s0 ultra_class
```

The system tests the class file and displays several pages of results. Look for the following message, which indicates that the test was successful:

```
Installation complete
Test run complete. Exit status 0.
```

sysidcfg File

When a JumpStart client boots for the first time, the booting software first tries to obtain system identification information (such as the system's hostname, IP address, locale, timezone, and root password) from a file named sysidcfg and then from the name service database. If you're not using a name service, you'll use this file to answer system identification questions during the initial part of the installation. If you're using a name service, you'll want to look over the section titled "Setting Up JumpStart in a Name Service Environment."

You'll use the sysidcfg file to answer system identification questions during the initial part of the installation. If the JumpStart server provides this information, the client bypasses the initial system identification portion of the Solaris 10 installation process. Without the sysidcfg file, the client displays the appropriate interactive dialog to request system identification information. You must create a unique sysidcfg file for every system that requires different configuration information.

The sysidcfg file can reside on a shared NFS directory or the root (/) directory on a UFS file system. It can also reside on a PCFS file system located on a diskette. Only one sysidcfg file can reside in a directory or on a diskette. The location of the sysidcfg file is specified by the -p argument to the add_install_client script used to create a JumpStart client information file.

Creating a sysidcfg file requires the system administrator to specify a set of keywords in the sysidcfg file to preconfigure a system. There are two types of keywords you use in the sysidcfg file: independent and dependent. Here's an example illustrating independent and dependent keywords:

```
name_service=NIS {domain_name=pyramid.com name_server=server(192.168.0.1)}
```

In this example, name_service is the independent keyword, while domain_name and name_server are the dependent keywords.

NOTE

Dependent Keywords Enclose all dependent keywords in curly braces {} to tie them to their associated independent keyword. Values can optionally be enclosed in single (') or double quotes (").

To help explain sysidcfg keywords, we'll group them in categories and describe each of them in detail.

Name Service, Domain Name, and Name Server Keywords

The following keywords are related to the name service you will be using.

The `name_service=<value>` keyword is assigned one of five values which specify the name service to be used: NIS, NIS+, LDAP, DNS, and NONE. These are described below:

- **NIS or NIS+**—If you are using NIS as your name service, for example, then specify the following:

  ```
  name_service=NIS
  ```

  For the NIS and NIS+ values, additional keywords are specified, which are

  ```
  domain_name=<value>
  ```

  The domain `<value>` in the previous line is the domain name such as `pyramid.com`.

  ```
  name_server=<value>
  ```

  The `name_server <value>` is the hostname or IP address for the name server. For the `name_server <value>`, you can specify up to three IP addresses for the name_server. For example:

  ```
  name_server=192.168.0.1,192.168.0.2,192.168.0.3
  ```

- **DNS**—If you are using DNS for the `name_service <value>`, specify the following:

  ```
  name_service=DNS
  ```

  Then you'll need to specify the following additional dependent keywords:

  ```
  domain_name=<value>
  ```

  Enter the domain name for the `domain_name <value>`. For example, if the domain name is `pyramid.com`, specify it as follows:

  ```
  domain_name=pyramid.com
  ```

  For the `name_server <value>`, you can specify up to three IP addresses for the `name_server`. For example:

  ```
  name_server=192.168.0.1,192.168.0.2,192.168.0.3
  ```

  The search option adds the values to the search path to use for DNS queries. Specify the following:

  ```
  search=<value>
  ```

  where `<value>` is the search entry, which cannot exceed 250 characters. Here's a sample DNS search entry:

  ```
  search=pyramid.com,east.pyramid.com,west.pyramid.com
  ```

- **LDAP**—If you are using LDAP for the name_service *<value>*, specify the following:

  ```
  name_service=LDAP
  ```

  Then you'll need to specify the following additional dependent keywords:

  ```
  domain_name=<value>
  ```

  Enter the domain name for the domain_name *<value>*. For example, if the domain name is pyramid.com, specify it as follows:

  ```
  domain_name=pyramid.com
  ```

  The profile parameter can also be specified to identify an LDAP profile to use. Specify this as follows:

  ```
  profile=<value>
  ```

  where *<value>* is the profile name.

  The profile server identifies the IP address of the profile server from which the LDAP profile can be obtained. Specify this as follows:

  ```
  profile_server=<value>
  ```

  where *<value>* is the IP address of the profile server.

  Here's an example LDAP entry with its dependent keywords:

  ```
  name_service_LDAP
  {domain_name=west.pyramid.com
  profile=default
  profile_server=192.168.0.100}
  ```

Network Related Keywords

Network related keywords relate to the network interface to be used. Specify this item as follows:

```
network_interface=<value>
```

Specify a *<value>* for the interface to be configured. You can enter a specific interface, such as hme0, or you can enter NONE (if there are no interfaces to configure) or PRIMARY (to select the primary interface) as follows:

```
network_interface=hme0
```

If you are not using DHCP, the dependent keywords for a PRIMARY interface are as follows:

```
hostname=<hostname>
ip_address=<ip_address>
```

```
netmask=<netmask value>
default_route=<ip_address>
protocol_ipv6=<yes or no>
```

For example, if your primary network interface is named `hme0`, here's a sample `sysidcfg` file:

```
network_interface=hme0
{primary hostname=client1
ip_address=192.168.0.10
netmask=255.255.255.0
default_route=192.168.0.1
protocol_ipv6=no}
```

If you are using DHCP, the only keywords available are the following:

```
dhcp protocol_ipv6=<yes or no>
```

For example, here's a sample entry:

```
network_interface=hme0
{primary dhcp protocol_ipv6=no}
```

Whether using DHCP or not, the `protocol_ipv6` keyword is optional.

NOTE

Multiple Interfaces Allowed You can now enter multiple network interfaces into the `sysidcfg` file; just specify a separate `network_interface` entry for each one to be included.

Setting the Root Password

The root password keyword is

```
root_password=<encrypted passwd>
```

The value for `<encrypted passwd>` is taken from the `/etc/shadow` file. For example, an entry might look like this:

```
root_password=XbcjeAgl8jLeI
```

The following is the security related keyword:

```
security_policy=<value>
```

Where `<value>` is either `KERBEROS` or `NONE`.

When specifying the KERBEROS value, you'll need to also specify the following dependent keywords:

```
default_realm=<fully qualified domain name>
admin_server=<fully qualified domain name>
kdc=<value>
```

<value> can list a maximum of three key distribution centers (KDCs) for a `security_policy` keyword. At least one is required. Here's an example using the `security_policy` keyword:

```
security_policy=kerberos
{default_realm=pyramid.com
admin_server=krbadmin.pyramid.com
kdc=kdc1.pyramid.com,kdc2.pyramid.com}
```

Setting the System Locale, Terminal, Time Zone, and Time Server

The keyword used to set the system locale is

```
system_locale=<value>
```

<value> is an entry from the `/usr/lib/locale` directory. The following example sets the value to English:

```
system_locale=en_US
```

The keyword to set the terminal type is as follows:

```
terminal=<terminal_type>
```

<terminal_type> is an entry from the `/usr/share/lib/terminfo` database. The following example sets the terminal type to vt100:

```
terminal=vt100
```

The keyword to set the time zone is as follows:

```
timezone=<timezone>
```

<timezone> is an entry from the `/usr/share/lib/zoneinfo` directory. The following entry sets the time zone to Eastern Standard Time:

```
timezone=EST
```

The keyword to set the time server is as follows:

```
timeserver=<value>
```

<value> can be `LOCALHOST`, `HOSTNAME`, or `IP_ADDRESS`. The following example sets the time server to be the `localhost`:

```
timeserver=localhost
```

The following rules apply to keywords in the sysidcfg file:

- Keywords can be in any order.
- Keywords are not case sensitive.
- Keyword values can be optionally enclosed in single quotes (').
- Only the first instance of a keyword is valid; if you specify the same keyword more than once, the first keyword specified will be used.

The following is a sample sysidcfg file, located in the configuration directory named /export/jumpstart:

```
system_locale=en_US
timezone=EST
timeserver=localhost
terminal=vt100
name_service=NONE
security_policy=none
root_password=XbcjeAgl8jLeI
network_interface=hme0 {primary protocol_ipv6=no netmask=255.255.255.0}
```

Setting Up JumpStart in a Name Service Environment

As stated in the previous section, you can use the sysidcfg file to answer system identification questions during the initial part of installation regardless of whether a name service is used. When the sysidcfg file is used with the NIS naming service, identification parameters such as locale and time zone can be provided from the name service. The sysidcfg file necessary for installing a JumpStart client on a network running the NIS name service is typically much shorter, and a separate sysidcfg file for each client is unnecessary.

You'll use the /etc/locale, /etc/timezone, /etc/hosts, /etc/ethers, and /etc/netmasks files as the source for creating NIS databases to support JumpStart client installations. See Chapter 12, "Naming Services," for more information on NIS and how to create NIS maps.

Setting Up Clients

Now you need to set up the clients to install over the network. After setting up the /export/jumpstart directory and the appropriate files, use the add_install_client command on the install server to set up remote workstations to install Solaris from the install server. The command syntax for the add_install_client command is as follows:

```
add_install_client [-e <ethernet_addr>] [-i <ip_addr>] \
[-s <install_svr:/dist>] [-c <config_svr:/config_dir>] \
[-p <sysidcfg_svr/sysid_config_dir>] <host_name> <platform group>

add_install_client -d [-s <install_svr:/dist>] [-c <config_svr:/config_dir>] \
[-p <sysidcfg_svr/sysid_config_dir>] [-t install_boot_image_path] \
<platform_name> <platform group>
```

The `add_install_client` options are described in Table 14.23.

TABLE 14.23 `add_install_client` Options

Option	Description
`-d`	Specifies that the client is to use DHCP to obtain the network install parameters. This option must be used for PXE clients to boot from the network.
`-e <ethernet_addr>`	Specifies the Ethernet address of the install client and is necessary if the client is not defined in the name service.
`-i <ip_addr>`	Specifies the IP address of the install client and is necessary if the client is not defined in the name service.
`-s <install_svr:/dist>`	Specifies the name of the install server (*install_svr*) and the path to the Solaris 10 operating environment distribution (*/dist*). This option is necessary if the client is being added to a boot server.
`-p < sysidcfg_svr/ sysid_config_dir>`	Specifies the configuration server (*sysidcfg_svr*) and the path to the `sysidcfg` file (*sysid_config_dir*).
`-t < install_boot_image_path>`	This option allows you to specify an alternate miniroot.
`<host_name>`	The hostname for the install client.
`-c <config_svr:/config_dir>`	Specifies the configuration server (*config_svr*) and path (*/config_dir*) to the configuration directory.
`<platform_name>`	Specifies the platform group to be used. Determine the platform group of the client by running `uname -i`. For an ultra10 box, this would be set to `SUNW,Ultra-5_10`.
`<platform_group>`	Specifies the client's architecture of the systems that use *<servername>* as an install server.

For additional options to the `add_install_client` command, see the Solaris online manual pages.

In Step by Step 14.5, you'll create a JumpStart client that will boot from a system that is configured as both the boot and install server. In addition, the entire Solaris 10 media is copied to the local disk.

STEP BY STEP

14.5 Creating a JumpStart Client

NOTE

Example Setup In the following steps, the following associations have been made in the examples:

Install server name—`ultra5`

Distribution directory—`/export/jumpstart/install`

Configuration server name—`ultra5`

Configuration directory—`/export/jumpstart/config`

Boot server name—`ultra5`

Install client—`client1`

Install client's MAC address—`8:0:20:21:49:25`

Client architecture—`sun4u`

1. On the install server, change to the directory that contains the installed Solaris 10 Operating Environment image as follows:

```
cd /export/jumpstart/install/Solaris_10/Tools
```

2. Create the JumpStart client using the `add_install_client` script found in the local directory as follows:

```
./add_install_client -s ultra5:/export/jumpstart/install -c ultra5:
/export/jumpstart/config -p ultra5:/jumpstart -e 8:0:20:21:49:25 \
-i 192.168.1.106 client1 sun4u
```

The system responds with

```
Adding Ethernet number for client1 to /etc/ethers
Adding "share -F nfs -o ro,anon=0 /export/jumpstart/install" to \
/etc/dfs/dfstab
making /tftpboot
enabling tftp in /etc/inetd.conf
updating /etc/bootparams
copying inetboot to /tftpboot
```

The `add_install_client` script automatically made entries into the following files and directory:

`/etc/ethers`

```
8:0:20:21:49:25  client1
```

`/etc/dfs/dfstab`

```
share -F nfs -o ro,anon=0 /export/jumpstart/install
```

/etc/bootparams

```
client1  root=ultra5:/export/jumpstart/Solaris_10/Tools/Boot \
install=ultra5:
/export/jumpstart/install boottype=:in sysid_\
config=ultra5:/export/jumpstart/config
install_config=ultra5:/export/jumpstart rootopts=:rsize=32768
```

/tftpboot directory

```
lrwxrwxrwx   1 root     other    26 Jun 19 16:11 C0A8016A -> \
inetboot.SUN4U.Solaris_10-1
lrwxrwxrwx   1 root     other    26 Jun 19 16:11 C0A8016A.SUN4U ->\
inetboot.SUN4U.Solaris_10-1
-rwxr-xr-x   1 root     other     158592 Jun 19 16:11 \
inetboot.SUN4U.Solaris_10-1
-rw-r--r--   1 root     other   317 Jun 19 16:11 rm.192.168.1.106\
lrwxrwxrwx   1 root     other     1 Jun 19 16:11  tftpboot -> .
```

3. Use the `rm_install_client` command to remove a JumpStart client's entries and configuration information from the boot server as follows:

   ```
   ./rm_install_client client1
   ```

   The system responds with

   ```
   removing client1 from bootparams
   removing /etc/bootparams, since it is empty
   removing /tftpboot/inetboot.SUN4U.Solaris_10-1
   removing /tftpboot
   disabling tftp in /etc/inetd.conf
   ```

TIP

Know your `config` files Make sure you are familiar with the differences between the rules file, a class file, and the `sysidcfg` file. It is quite common to get an exam question that displays the contents of one of them and asks the candidate to identify which one it is.

Troubleshooting JumpStart

The most common problems encountered with custom JumpStart involve the setting up of the network installation, or booting the client. This section describes briefly some of the more popular errors and what to do if you are faced with them.

Installation Setup

When running the `add_install_client` command to set up a new JumpStart client, you might get the following message:

```
Unknown client "hostname"
```

The probable cause of this error message is that the client does not have an entry in the `hosts` file (or table if using a name service).

Make sure the client has an entry in the `hosts` file, or table, and rerun the `add_install_client` command.

When you have setup the JumpStart Install server, make sure the relevant directories are shared correctly. It is a common problem to share the file systems at the wrong level, so that the table of contents file cannot be found when the client tries to mount the remote file system.

Client Boot Problems

The following error message can appear if the Ethernet address of the JumpStart client has been specified incorrectly:

```
Timeout waiting for ARP/RARP packet…
```

Check the `/etc/ethers` file on the JumpStart server and verify that the client's Ethernet address has been specified correctly.

When booting the client from the network, to initiate a custom JumpStart installation, you might get the following error message if more than one server attempts to respond to the boot request:

```
WARNING: getfile: RPC failed: error 5 (RPC Timed out).
```

This error indicates that more than one server has an entry for the client in its `/etc/bootparams` file. To rectify this problem, you will need to check the servers on the subnet to find any duplicate entries and remove them, leaving only the entry required on the JumpStart server.

When booting the client from the network, you could get the following error message if the system cannot find the correct media required for booting:

```
The file just loaded does not appear to be executable
```

You will need to verify that the custom JumpStart server has been correctly set up as a boot and install server. Additionally, make sure you specified the correct platform group for the client when you ran `add_install_client` to set up the client to be able to use JumpStart.

A Sample JumpStart Installation

The following example shows how you would set up a custom JumpStart installation for a fictitious site. The network consists of an Enterprise 3000 server and five Ultra1 workstations. The next section details how to start the JumpStart installation process by creating the install server.

Setting Up the Install Server

The first step is to set up the install server (see Step by step 14.6). You'll choose the Enterprise server. This is where the contents of the Solaris CD are located. The contents of the CD can be made available by either loading the CD in the CD-ROM drive or copying the CD to the server's local hard drive. For this example, you will copy the files to the local hard drive. Use the `setup_install_server` command to copy the contents of the Solaris CD to the server's local disk. Files are copied to the `/export/install` directory.

STEP BY STEP

14.6 Setting Up the Install Server

1. Insert the Solaris Software CD 1 into the server's CD-ROM drive.
2. Type the following:

   ```
   cd /cdrom/cdrom0/s0/Solaris_10/Tools
   ./setup_install_server /export/install
   ```

   The system responds with this:

   ```
   Verifying target directory...
   Calculating the required disk space for the Solaris_10 Product
   Calculating space required for the installation boot image
   Copying the CD image to disk...
   Copying Install boot image hierarchy...
   Install Server setup complete
   ```

3. Eject the Solaris 10 Software CD 1 and put in the Solaris 10 Software CD 2. Let `vold` automatically mount the CD.
4. Change to the Tools directory on the CD as follows:

   ```
   cd /cdrom/cdrom0/Solaris_10/Tools
   ```

5. Execute the `add_to_install_server` script as follows to copy the images from the CD to the `/export/install` directory:

   ```
   ./add_to_install_server /export/install
   ```

6. Repeat steps 3, 4, and 5 for the remaining CDs.

Creating the JumpStart Directory

After you install the install server, you need to set up a JumpStart configuration directory on the server. This directory holds the files necessary for a custom JumpStart installation of the

Solaris software. You set up this directory by copying the sample directory from one of the Solaris CD images that has been put in `/export/install`. Do this by typing the following:

```
mkdir /jumpstart
cp -r /export/install/Solaris_10/Misc/jumpstart_sample /jumpstart
```

Any directory name can be used. You'll use `/jumpstart` for this example.

Setting Up a Configuration Server

Follow the procedure in Step by Step 14.7 to set up a configuration server.

STEP BY STEP

14.7 Setting Up a Configuration Server

1. Log in as root on the server where you want the JumpStart configuration directory to reside.
2. Edit the `/etc/dfs/dfstab` file. Add the following entry:

   ```
   share -F nfs -o ro,anon=0 /jumpstart
   ```

> **NOTE**
>
> **NFS Server** It may be necessary to run the `svcadm enable nfs/server` command if the NFS server daemons are not running. See Chapter 9, "Virtual File Systems, Swap Space, and Core Dumps," for more information.

3. Type **`shareall`** and press Enter. This makes the contents of the `/jumpstart` directory accessible to systems on the network.
4. Working with the sample class file and rules files that were copied into the JumpStart directory earlier, use them to create configuration files that represent your network. For this example, I create a class file named `engrg_prof`. It looks like this:

   ```
   #Specifies that the installation will be treated as an initial
   #installation, as opposed to an upgrade.
   install_type initial_install
   #Specifies that the engineering systems are standalone systems.
   system_type standalone
   #Specifies that the JumpStart software uses default disk
   #partitioning for installing Solaris software on the engineering
   #systems.
   partitioning default
   #Specifies that the developer's software group will be
   #installed.
   Cluster     SUNWCprog
   ```

```
#Specifies that each system in the engineering group will have 512
#Mbytes of swap space.
filesys any 512 swap
```

The rules file contains the following rule:

```
network 192.9.200.0 - engrg_prof -
```

This rules file states that systems on the `192.9.200.0` network are installed using the `engrg_prof` class file.

5. Validate the rules and class files as follows:

```
cd /jumpstart
./check
/usr/sbin/install.d/pfinstall -d -c /export/install engrg_prof
```

If `check` doesn't find any errors, it creates the `rules.ok` file. Look for the following message, which indicates that the `pfinstall` test was successful:

```
Installation complete
Test run complete. Exit status 0.
```

You are finished creating the configuration server.

Setting Up Clients

Now, on the install server, set up each client as follows:

```
cd /export/install/Solaris_10/Tools

./add_install_client -s sparcserver:/export/install -c sparcserver:/jumpstart\
-p sparcserver:/jumpstart -e 8:0:20:21:49:25 -i 192.9.200.106 sun1 sun4u


./add_install_client -s sparcserver:/export/install -c sparcserver:/jumpstart \
-p sparcserver:/jumpstart -e 8:0:20:21:49:24 -i 192.9.200.107 sun2 sun4u
```

This example sets up two engineering workstations, `sun1` and `sun2`, so that they can be installed over the network from the install server named `sparcserver`.

Starting Up the Clients

After the setup is complete, you can start up the engineering systems by using the following startup command at the `OK` (PROM) prompt of each system:

```
boot net  -  install
```

You'll see the following displayed on the screen:

```
Rebooting with command: net - install
Boot device: /pci@1f,0/pci@1,1/network@1,1  File and args: - \
install
20800
SunOS Release 5.10 Version Generic_64-bit
Copyright 1983-2005 Sun Microsystems, Inc.  All rights reserved.
whoami: no domain name
Configuring /dev and /devices
Using RPC Bootparams for network configuration information.
Configured interface hme0
Using sysid configuration file 192.9.200.101:/jumpstart/sysidcfg
The system is coming up.  Please wait.
Starting remote procedure call (RPC) services: sysidns done.
Starting Solaris installation program...
Searching for JumpStart directory...
Using rules.ok from 192.9.200.101:/jumpstart.
Checking rules.ok file...
Using profile: engrg_prof
Executing JumpStart preinstall phase...
Searching for SolStart directory...
Checking rules.ok file...
Using begin script: install_begin
Using finish script: patch_finish
Executing SolStart preinstall phase...
Executing begin script "install_begin"...
Begin script install_begin execution completed.
Processing default locales
        - Specifying default locale (en_US)
Processing profile
        - Selecting cluster (SUNWCprog)

WARNING: Unknown cluster ignored (SUNWCxgl)
        - Selecting package (SUNWaudmo)
        - Selecting locale (en_US)

Installing 64 Bit Solaris Packages
- Selecting all disks
- Configuring boot device
- Configuring swap (any)
- Configuring /opt (any)
- Automatically configuring disks for Solaris operating environment

Verifying disk configuration
Verifying space allocation
        - Total software size:  2401.60 Mbytes
Preparing system for Solaris install
```

```
Configuring disk (c0t0d0)
        - Creating Solaris disk label (VTOC)

Creating and checking UFS file systems
- Creating / (c0t0d0s0)
- Creating /opt (c0t0d0s5)

Beginning Solaris software installation
Starting software installation
SUNWxwrtl...done.  2401.55 Mbytes remaining.
SUNWulcf....done.  2397.28 Mbytes remaining.
SUNWuium....done.  2397.25 Mbytes remaining.
SUNWuiu8....done.  2390.46 Mbytes remaining.
  <output truncated>

Completed software installation

Solaris 10 software installation succeeded

Customizing system files
        - Mount points table (/etc/vfstab)
        - Network host addresses (/etc/hosts)

Customizing system devices
        - Physical devices (/devices)
        - Logical devices (/dev)

Installing boot information
        - Installing boot blocks (c0t0d0s0)

Installation log location
        - /a/var/sadm/system/logs/install_log (before reboot)
        - /var/sadm/system/logs/install_log (after reboot)

Installation complete
Executing SolStart postinstall phase...
Executing finish script "patch_finish"...

Finish script patch_finish execution completed.
Executing JumpStart postinstall phase...

The begin script log 'begin.log'
is located in /var/sadm/system/logs after reboot.

The finish script log 'finish.log'
is located in /var/sadm/system/logs after reboot.

syncing file systems... done
rebooting...
```

The client reads the `sysidcfg` file, then the class file, and then the `rules.ok` file on the server. If any system identification information is missing in the `sysidcfg` file, the client will display the appropriate dialog requesting identification information. The system then automatically installs the Solaris operating environment.

This completes the JumpStart configuration.

Solaris Flash

Objective:

Explain Flash, create and manipulate the Flash archive, and use it for installation.

The main feature of Solaris Flash is to provide a method to store a snapshot of the Solaris operating environment, complete with all installed patches and applications. This snapshot is referred to as the *Flash archive* and the system that the archive is taken from is referred to as the master machine. This archive can be stored on disk, CD-ROM, or tape media. You can use this archive for disaster recovery purposes or to replicate (clone) an environment on one or more other systems. When using a Flash archive to install the Solaris environment onto a system, the target system we are installing the environment on is referred to as the installation client.

When you're ready to install the Solaris environment using the Flash archive, you can access the archive on either local media or across the network. Furthermore, when installing from a Flash archive onto the installation client, the install can be modified from the original archive to accommodate things such as kernel architecture, device differences, or partitioning schemes between the master machine and the installation client.

In this section, we describe how to create the Flash archive and how to install the operating system on an installation client from a Flash archive.

NOTE

Flash Install Enhancement A Flash installation can now be used to update a system, using a differential Flash Archive. Previously, a Flash Install could only be used to perform an initial installation. A new *`install_type`* of *`flash_update`* is available with Solaris 10.

Creating a Flash Archive

The first step is to identify the master machine. This system will serve as the template for the archive and all software and data on the master machine, unless specifically excluded, will become part of the Flash archive that will be installed on the installation client.

Next, make sure that the master machine is completely installed, patched, and has all of its applications installed. Depending on the application, you may want to create the archive before the application is configured however. This will allow you to configure the application specifically for each system it is running on. To ensure that the archive is clean, it's recommended that the archive be created before the master machine has ever gone into production and while the system is in a quiescent state.

Finally, determine where the archive will be stored. You can store the archive onto a disk, a CD-ROM, or a tape. Once the archive has been stored, you can even compress it so that it takes up less space. Because these archives can be used for disaster recovery, store the archive somewhere offsite.

You'll use the `flarcreate` command to create the archive. The syntax for the command is as follows:

```
flarcreate -n name [-R root] [-A system_image] [-H] [-I]  [-M]  [-S]  [-c] \
[-t  [-p posn] [-b blocksize]] [-i date] [-u section...] [-m  master] \
[-f   [filelist ¦ -] [-F]] [-a author] [-e  descr ¦ -E  descr_file] \
[-T  type] [-U key=value...] [-x exclude...] [-y  include...]\
[-z  filelist...] [-X filelist...] archive
```

The options to the `flarcreate` command are described in Table 14.24. In the previous command syntax, <*archive*> is the name of the archive file to be created. If you do not specify a path, `flarcreate` saves the archive file in the current directory.

TABLE 14.24 Command Line Options for `flarcreate`

The Following Option Is Required

Option	Description
`-n <name>`	The value of this flag is the name of the archive. This is a name stored internally in the archive and should not be confused with the filename used when storing the archive.
The Following General Options Are Available	
`-A <system_image>`	Create a differential Flash Archive by comparing a new system image with the image specified by *`system_image`*.
`-f <filelist>`	Use the contents of *`filelist`* as a list of files to include in the archive.
`-F`	Use ONLY files listed in *`filelist`*, making this an absolute list of files, instead of an addition to the normal file list.
`-c`	Compresses the archive by using the `compress` command.
`-H`	Do not generate a hash identifier.
`-I`	Ignore the integrity check.

(continues)

TABLE 14.24 *Continued*

Option	Description
-M	Only used for a differential archive, and is generally not recommended. This option bypasses the integrity check of a clone system.
-R *<root>*	Creates the archive from the file system tree that is rooted at root. If you do not specify this option, `flarcreate` creates an archive from a file system that is rooted at /.
-S	Skips the disk space check and doesn't write archive size data to the archive.
-x *<exclude>*	Excludes the file or directory from the archive. If you specify a file system with -R root, the path to the directory to exclude is assumed to be relative to root.
-y *<include>*	Includes the file or directory in the archive. This option can be used in conjunction with the x option to include a specific file or directory within an excluded directory.
-X *<filelist>*	Uses the contents of *filelist* as a list of files or directories to exclude from the archive.
-z *<filelist>*	The *filelist* argument contains filenames, or directory names, prefixed with either a plus (+), to include in the archive, or minus (-) to exclude from the archive.
Options for Archive Identification	
-i *<date>*	If you do not specify a date, `flarcreate` uses the current system time and date.
-m *<master>*	If you do not specify a master, `flarcreate` uses the system name that is reported by `uname -n`.
-e *<descr>*	Specifies a description.
-E *<descr_file>*	Specifies a description is contained in file *descr_file*.
-T *<type>*	Specifies the content type of the archive.
-a *<author>*	Allows you to specify the author of the archive.

Additional options are available, such as for creating the archive on tape and adding some user-defined options. Information on these options is found in the online manual pages and in the Solaris 10 Installation Guide in the Solaris 10 Release and Installation Collection.

The following example shows how to use the `flarcreate` command to create the Flash archive:

```
flarcreate -n "Solaris 10 Ultra Archive" -a "WS Calkins" \
-R / -x /var/tmp /u01/ultra.flar
```

In the previous example, we are creating a Flash archive named "Solaris 10 Ultra Archive." We are specifying the author (creator) to be labeled as "WS Calkins." The -R option specifies to recursively descend from the specified directory. We also specify the -x option to exclude /var/tmp. The last part of the command specifies which directory to store the archive in and what to name the archive.

After entering the command and pressing the Return key, the flarcreate command will display the status of the operation as follows:

```
Full Flash
Checking integrity...
Integrity OK.
Running precreation scripts...
Precreation scripts done.
Determining the size of the archive...
7462766 blocks
The archive will be approximately 3.55GB.
Creating the archive...
7462766 blocks
Archive creation complete.
```

When the operation is complete, I can see the archive file by issuing the ls command as follows:

```
ls -l /u01/ultra.flar
-rw-r--r--   1 root    other   3820943938  Sep 3 11:12 \ ultra.flar
```

The flar command is used to administer Flash archives. With the flar command, you can

- Extract information from an archive
- Split archives
- Combine archives

To use the flar command to extract information from an archive, use the following command:

```
flar -i /u01/ultra.flar
```

The system displays the following information about the Flash archive:

```
archive_id=fb2cfa3c51d3af4a10ce6e804243fe19
files_archived_method=cpio
creation_date=20050903111231
creation_master=ultra10
content_name=Solaris 10 Ultra Archive
creation_node=ultra10
creation_hardware_class=sun4u
creation_platform=SUNW,Ultra-5_10
creation_processor=sparc
creation_release=5.10
creation_os_name=SunOS
```

```
creation_os_version=Generic
files_compressed_method=none
files_archived_size=3820943929
content_author=WS Calkins
content_architectures=sun4u
type=FULL
```

For additional information on the `flarcreate` or `flar` commands, refer to the online manual pages or the Solaris 10 Installation Guide in the Solaris 10 Release and Installation Collection.

Using the Solaris Installation Program to Install a Flash Archive

In the previous section we described how to create a Flash archive. In this section, you learn how to install this archive on an installation client using the GUI-based Solaris installation program.

The Flash archive was created on a system named `ultra10` with the IP address of `192.168.0.110` and placed into a file system named `/u01`. On `ultra10` we need to share the `/u01` file system so that the archive is available to other systems on the network via NFS. You use the `share` command to do this. NFS and the `share` command are described in Chapter 9.

Initiate a Solaris installation from CD-ROM. When prompted to select the Installation Media as shown in Figure 14.1, select Network File System.

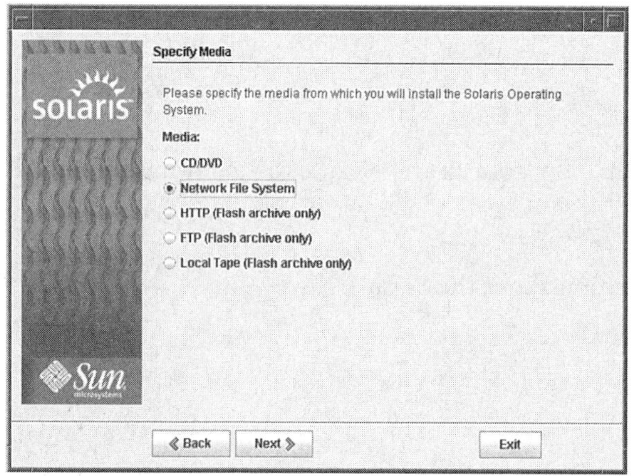

FIGURE 14.1 Specify Media window.

Click on the Next button and you'll be prompted to enter the path to the network file system that contains the Flash archive as shown in Figure 14.2.

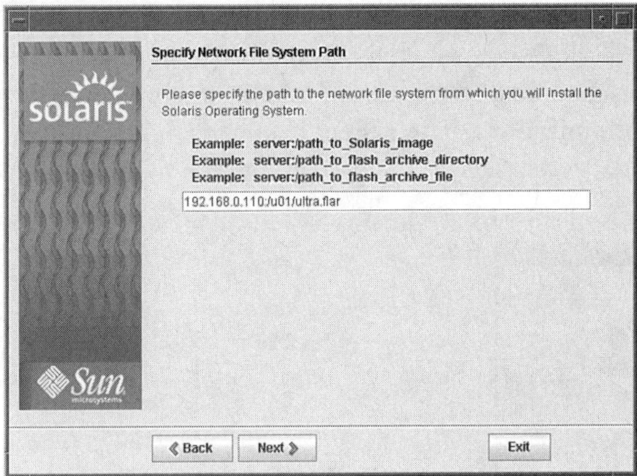

FIGURE 14.2 Specify Network file system path window.

After entering the path, click on the Next button and the Flash Archive Summary window will appear as shown in Figure 14.3.

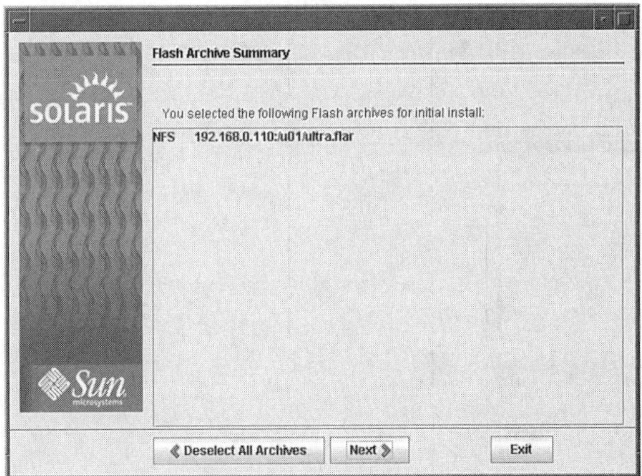

FIGURE 14.3 Flash Archive Summary window.

The selected archive will be listed. Verify that it is correct and then click on the Next button to continue. You'll be prompted to enter any additional archives that you would like to install, as shown in Figure 14.4.

We have no additional archives to install, so you'll click on the Next button and the system is initialized as shown in Figure 14.5.

After the system initialization is finished, you'll see the Disk Selection window displayed as with a normal GUI-based installation. From this point forward, the installation will continue as a normal GUI-based installation. The difference is that you will not be asked to select the software that you want to install. Instead, the entire Flash archive will be installed. When the installation is complete, the system will reboot (if you selected this option during the earlier dialog), and the login message will appear. The final step is to log in as root, configure your applications, and make system-specific customizations. The system is now ready for production use.

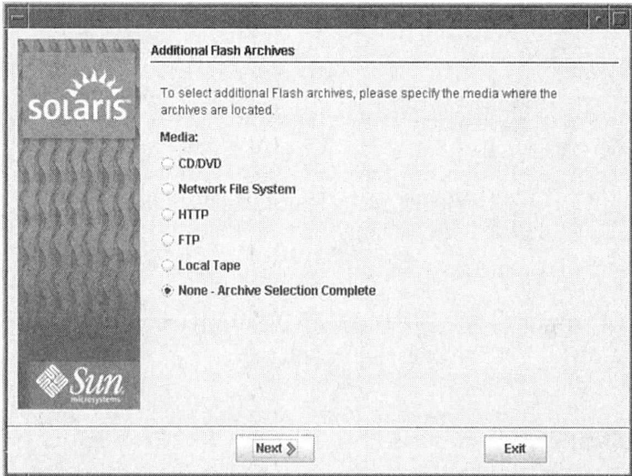

FIGURE 14.4 Additional Flash Archives window.

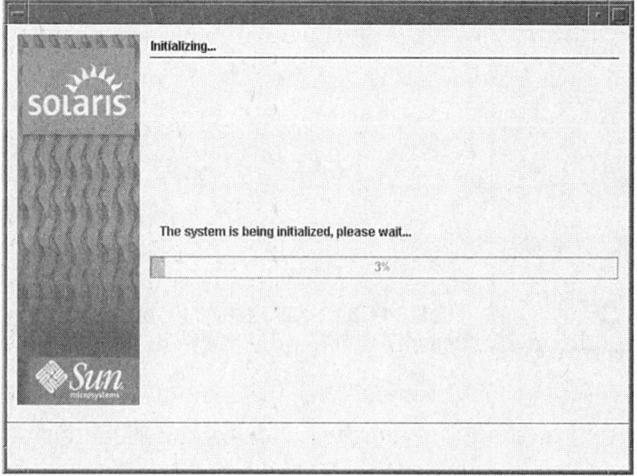

FIGURE 14.5 Initialization window.

Solaris Flash and JumpStart

Earlier in this chapter, we described how to set up a JumpStart installation. If you recall, we set up a boot server, which provided the information that a JumpStart client needed to boot across the network. We also set up an install server, which supplied the Solaris image, and we created the profile and rules configuration files which provided additional setup information such as disk partitions and software packages.

You can utilize a Solaris Flash archive in a JumpStart installation, but first you need to add the installation client to the JumpStart boot server as described earlier in this chapter.

The next step is to create a profile for the installation client. This was also described earlier in this chapter. However, when using JumpStart to install from a Flash archive, only the following keywords can be used in the profile:

- `archive_location`
- `install_type`—For a full flash archive install, specify this option as flash_install. For a differential flash archive, specify `flash_update`.
- `partitioning`—Only the keyword values of `explicit` or `existing` must be used.
- `filesys`—The keyword value `auto` must not be used.
- `forced_deployment`
- `local_customization`
- `no_content_check`—Used only for a differential flash archive.
- `no_master_check`—Used only for a differential flash archive.
- `package`—Only used for a full flash installation; cannot be used with a differential flash archive.
- `root_device`

Here's an example profile for an installation client using a Flash archive:

```
install_type     flash_install
archive_location nfs://192.168.0.110/u01/ultra.flar
partitioning explicit
#
#8 GB / and 1GB swap on a 9GB Disk
#
filesys     rootdisk.s0    free        /
filesys     rootdisk.s1    1:449    swap
```

The rules and `sysidcfg` files for the Flash installation client would be the same as described earlier in this chapter.

When finished configuring the profile, rules, and `sysidcfg` files, and assuming the Flash archive is available on the install server in a shared file system, you can boot the installation client using

```
boot net - install
```

The automated installation will proceed without further intervention and the system will be installed using the Flash archive.

Preboot Execution Environment (PXE)

The Preboot Execution Environment, or PXE, is a direct form of network boot that can be used to install the Solaris Operating Environment over the network using DHCP. It does not require the client to have any form of local boot media.

PXE is only available to x86 systems that implement the Intel Preboot Execution Environment specification. You will need to consult the hardware documentation for your system to determine whether or not it supports the PXE network boot.

To use PXE, you need three systems. These are as follows:

- A configured install server containing the Solaris boot image and images of the Solaris CDs
- A configured DHCP server from which to boot successfully
- An x86 client that supports the PXE network boot

NOTE

Only One DHCP Server—You must make sure that there is only *one* DHCP server on the same subnet as the PXE client because the PXE network boot does not work properly on a subnet containing multiple DHCP servers.

Preparing for a PXE Boot Client

As you saw in the previous section, three systems are required in order to be able to make use of the PXE network boot. The first of these is the `install server`. Setting up the `install server` is described earlier in this chapter in the section "The Install Server." The procedure for an x86 install server is the same, but you will be storing x86 CD images instead of SPARC.

NOTE

You Can Still Use SPARC—Even though you are setting up an x86 installation, you can still use a SPARC system as your install server if you wish. All it does is share the CD images over the network, and a single install server can serve both SPARC and x86 clients. Remember that you cannot run `setup install server` on a SPARC system using an x86 CD, or vice versa, but you can from a DVD.

The third system is also very straightforward because you have to consult your hardware documentation to verify whether PXE network boot is supported by the BIOS. It is worth investigating whether an upgrade to the BIOS firmware is necessary as well.

It is the second of these systems that requires the most work. Configuring a DHCP server is beyond the scope of this exam and is covered completely in the Solaris 10 Network Administrator Exam (Exam 310-302). It is necessary, however, to create some vendor class macros so that the correct configuration information is passed to the client when booting across the network.

NOTE

DHCP Already Configured—You should note that a working DHCP server should already be configured. The details described in this section merely configure some parameters within the DHCP server.

Configuring the DHCP Server

There are a few parameters that need to be configured to ensure that the client, when booted, has all the information it requires in order to boot successfully, and then access the install server containing the correct CD images, required for the installation of the Solaris Operating Environment. Table 14.25 lists some of the most common parameters.

TABLE 14.25 Vendor Client Class Options

Symbol Name	Code	Type	Granularity	Max	Description
`SrootIP4`	2	IP Address	1	1	The *root* server's IP address
`SrootNM`	3	ASCII Text	1	0	The *root* server's hostname
`SrootPTH`	4	ASCII Text	1	0	The path to the client's *root* directory on the root server
`SinstIP4`	10	IP Address	1	1	The JumpStart install server's IP address
`SinstNM`	11	ASCII Text	1	0	The JumpStart install server's hostname
`SinstPTH`	12	ASCII Text	1	0	The path to the installation image on the JumpStart install server

The fields are described here:

- **Symbol Name**—The name of the symbol.
- **Code**—A unique code number.
- **Type**—The data type of the entry.
- **Granularity**—The number of instances. For example, a symbol with a data type of `IP Address` and a `Granularity` of 2 means that the entry must contain two IP addresses.

- **Max**—The maximum number of values. For example, a symbol with a data type of `IP Address`, `Granularity` of 2, and `Maximum` of 2 means that the symbol can contain a maximum of two pairs of IP addresses.
- **Description**—A textual description of the symbol.

You can add these symbols to the DHCP server using either the command `dhtadm` or the GUI-based `dhcpmgr` commands. The example here shows how to add a symbol (*`SrootIP4`*) and Vendor Client Class (*`SUNW.i86pc`*) to the `achilles` macro using the GUI-based `dhcpmgr`.

1. Start `dhcpmgr` by entering **`/usr/sadm/admin/bin/dhcpmgr&`** from any CDE window. The DHCP manager window appears as shown in Figure 14.6

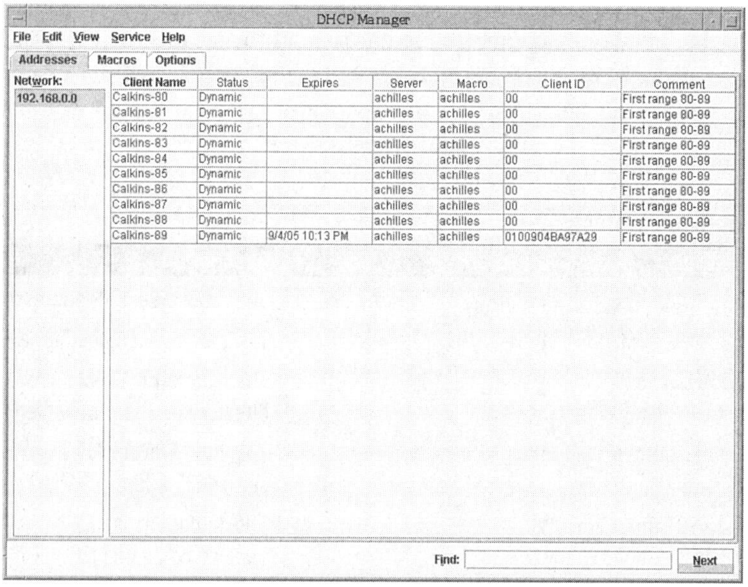

DHCP Manager

File Edit View Service Help

Addresses | Macros | Options

Network: 192.168.0.0

Client Name	Status	Expires	Server	Macro	Client ID	Comment
Calkins-80	Dynamic		achilles	achilles	00	First range 80-89
Calkins-81	Dynamic		achilles	achilles	00	First range 80-89
Calkins-82	Dynamic		achilles	achilles	00	First range 80-89
Calkins-83	Dynamic		achilles	achilles	00	First range 80-89
Calkins-84	Dynamic		achilles	achilles	00	First range 80-89
Calkins-85	Dynamic		achilles	achilles	00	First range 80-89
Calkins-86	Dynamic		achilles	achilles	00	First range 80-89
Calkins-87	Dynamic		achilles	achilles	00	First range 80-89
Calkins-88	Dynamic		achilles	achilles	00	First range 80-89
Calkins-89	Dynamic	9/4/05 10:13 PM	achilles	achilles	0100904BA97A29	First range 80-89

Find: Next

FIGURE 14.6 DHCP Manager window.

Note that the DHCP server is already configured to support 10 IP addresses and that the DHCP server name is *`achilles`*.

2. Select the `Options` tab and the Options window appears. From the `Edit` menu, select `Create` as shown in Figure 14.7

3. A sub window appears to create the option. Enter the name `SrootIP4` in the `Name` field. The next field is a pull-down menu; select `Vendor` from this menu as shown in Figure 14.8.

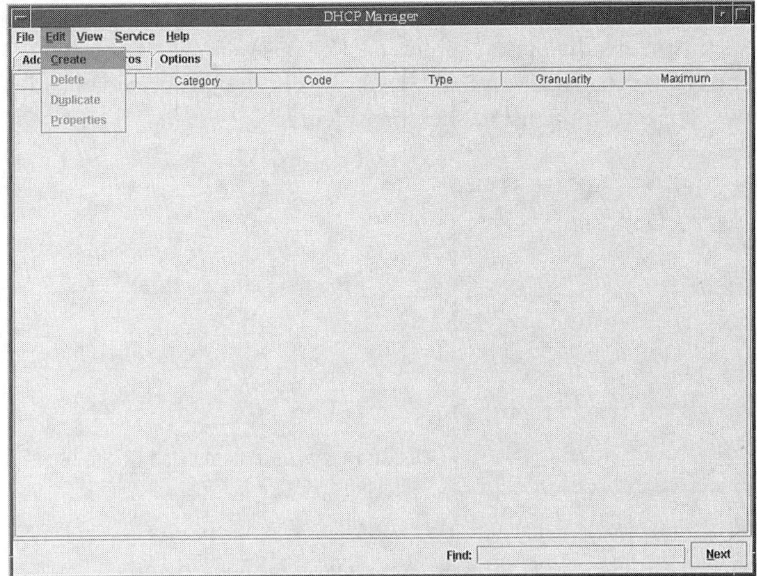

FIGURE 14.7 DHCP Options window.

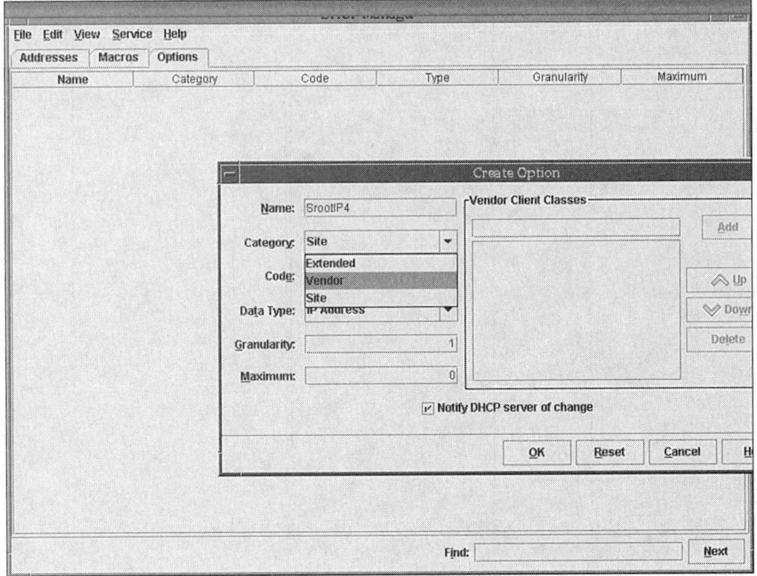

FIGURE 14.8 DHCP Create Options window.

4. Refer back to Table 14.25, which lists the valid values for the symbols to be added. In this case, the code value for the symbol `SrootIP4` is `2`. The type is currently set to `IP Address`, which is correct. Table 14.25 also states the values for `Granularity` and `Maximum`; enter these accordingly into their correct locations.

5. On the right side of the window is the `Vendor Client Classes` box. This is where you specify which class of systems the option applies to. For this example, if an x86 client is being used, the client class is `SUNW.i86pc`. Enter this in the box provided and click `Add`. The class now appears in the list as shown in Figure 14.9.

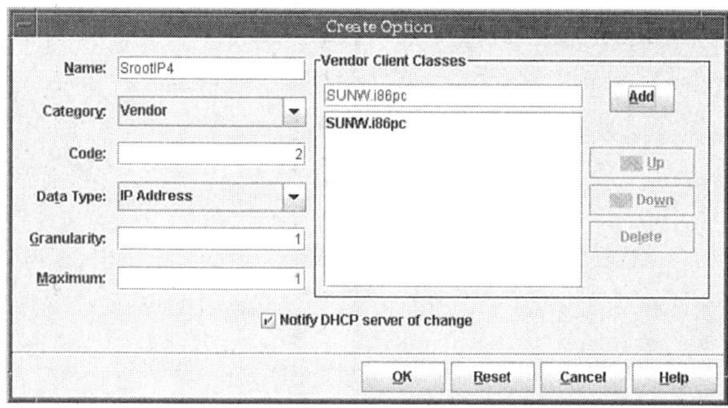

FIGURE 14.9 DHCP completed Create Options window.

6. Make sure the box marked `Notify DHCP server of change` is checked and click `OK` to complete the operation.

7. You are returned to the `Options` window, which now includes the symbol just created. Figure 14.10 shows this.

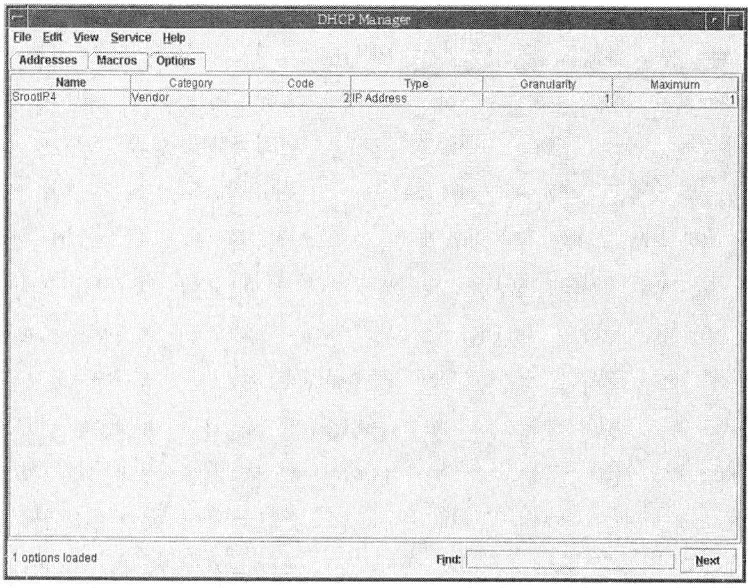

FIGURE 14.10 DHCP Options window with a symbol defined.

8. The remaining symbols can be added by repeating the previous steps.

9. To add the symbol `SrootIP4` to the `achilles` macro, select the `Macro` tab and the `achilles` macro from the list on the left. Figure 14.11 shows the current contents of this macro.

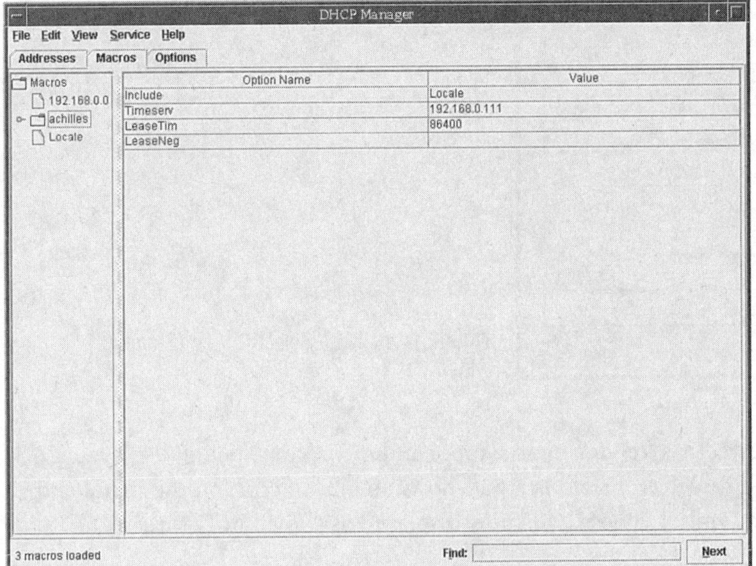

FIGURE 14.11 The `achilles` macro.

10. From the `Edit` menu, select `Properties`. Figure 14.12 shows the Properties window.

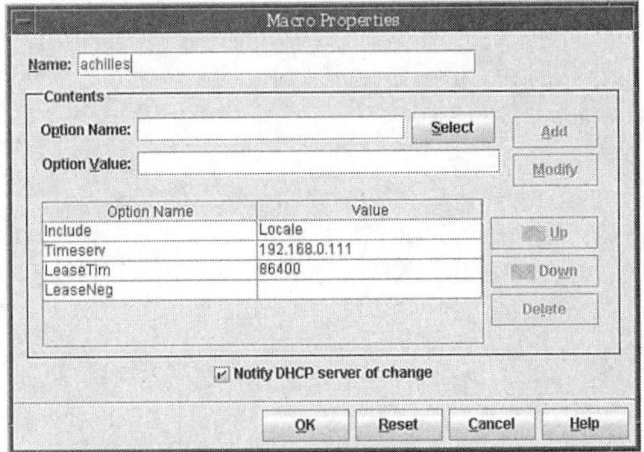

FIGURE 14.12 The Properties window.

11. You need to locate the symbol that you want to add, so click on `Select` to the right of the `Option Name` field. The `Select Option` window appears as shown in Figure 14.13.

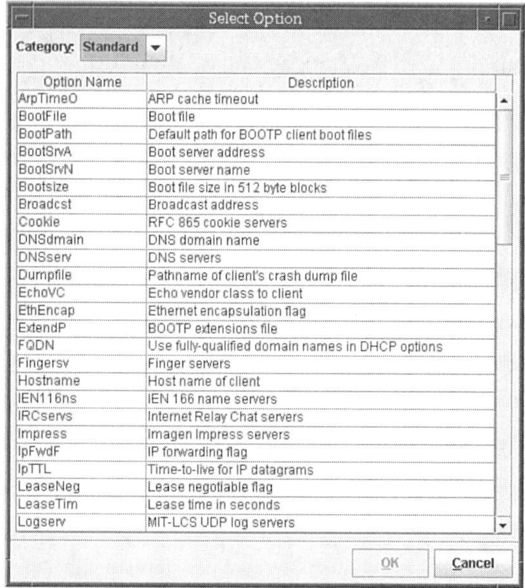

FIGURE 14.13 The Select Option (Standard) window.

12. The symbol just created is a `Vendor` class symbol and the options being displayed are `standard` symbols. The selector field is a pull-down menu, so click on the menu and choose `Vendor`. The symbol `SrootIP4` is now displayed as shown in Figure 14.14.

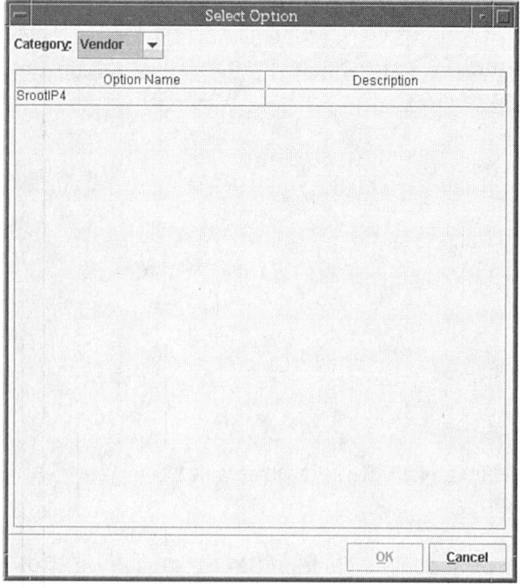

FIGURE 14.14 The Select Option (Vendor) window.

13. Click on the symbol `SrootIP4` and then click `OK` to display the Macro Properties window. This symbol identifies the IP Address of the JumpStart root server, which is `192.168.0.110` for this example. Enter this in the `Option Value` field as shown in Figure 14.15.

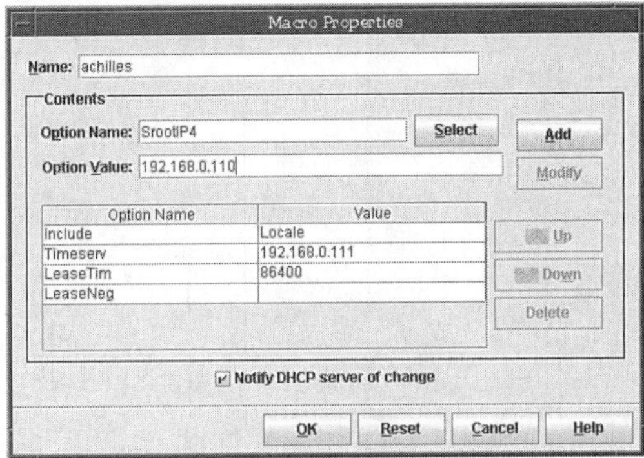

FIGURE 14.15 The Macro Properties window.

14. Click `Add` to insert the symbol and value into the macro properties. Figure 14.16 demonstrates that the symbol `SrootIP4` has been added to the macro.

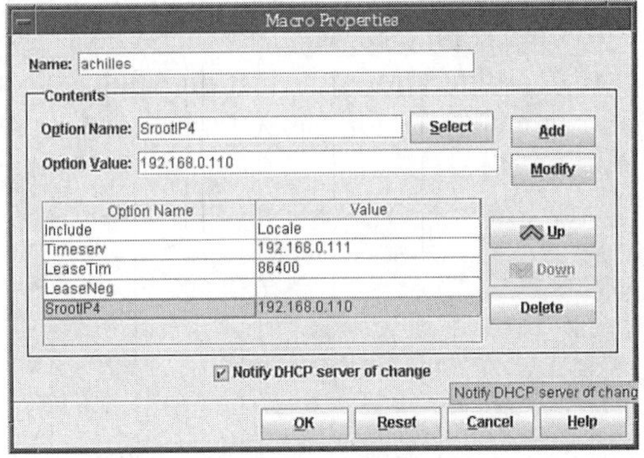

FIGURE 14.16 The Macro Properties window with symbol added.

15. When you click `OK` to complete the operation, you are returned to the macro window, showing the contents of the `achilles` macro. Figure 14.17 shows the completed operation.

16. Repeat this operation for the other symbols that the DHCP server requires to properly support the PXE network boot.

When the macro and symbols have been configured, the DHCP server is ready to handle the client correctly when it boots across the network.

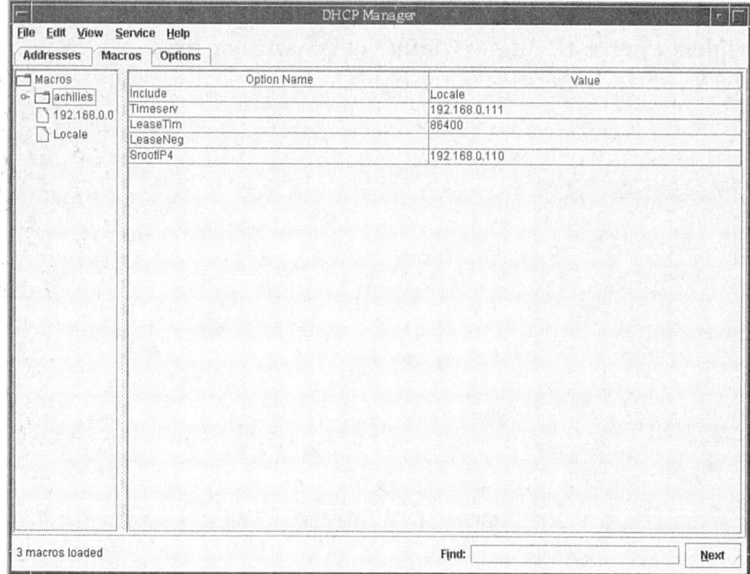

FIGURE 14.17 The `achilles` macro with symbol added.

Adding an x86 Client to Use DHCP

Having configured the DHCP server, the only remaining task is to add the client to the install server. This is carried out using the `add_install_client` command, virtually the same as for a custom JumpStart, but this time the majority of the configuration information will be supplied by the DHCP server. The following command adds support for the `SUNW.i86pc` class of system:

```
# cd /export/install/x86pc/Tools
# ./add_install_client -d SUNW.i86pc i86pc
```

Booting the x86 Client

When the install server and the DHCP server have been configured correctly and the x86 client has been added, the only remaining thing to do is to boot the x86 client to install over the network. The way in which this is done depends on the hardware that you have, but usually one of the following will have the desired effect:

- Enter the system BIOS by typing the appropriate keystrokes
- Configure the BIOS to boot from the network
- Adjust the boot device priority list, if present, so that a network boot is attempted first
- Exit the system BIOS

The system should start booting from the network and should prompt you for the type of installation you want to run. The remainder of the installation process depends on which installation type you choose.

NOTE

Set Boot Options Back—Remember when the installation finishes and the system reboots, to re-enter the system BIOS and restore the original boot configuration.

Summary

It's been my experience that JumpStart is not widely used, mainly because of its complexity. Many system administrators would rather go through an interactive installation for each system than automate the process. Many of the popular Unix systems have installation programs similar to JumpStart, and most are underutilized. System administrators could save a great deal of time if they would only learn more about this type of installation.

The key to using JumpStart is whether or not it will benefit you to spend the time learning and understanding what is required; and then creating the necessary class files, an install server, a configuration server; and editing a rules file to ensure all systems are accommodated. For system administrators managing large numbers of systems, say 100+, it is probably worth the effort, especially if the JumpStart installation is to be used more than once. A good example of this is in a test environment, where systems might have to be regularly reinstalled to a particular specification. If, on the other hand, the system administrator only manages three or four systems, and they only need to be installed once, then it is questionable as to whether the time will be worth investing. It might be more efficient to carry out interactive installations.

We've described the entire process of installing a networked system via JumpStart, including how to set up the boot server, the install server, and the configuration files located on the configuration server. We also described the necessary procedures that need to be performed for each client that you plan to install.

You also learned how to use the Solaris Flash archive feature to create an exact image of a particular Solaris environment and replicate this environment across many systems, or simply store it away in case you need to rebuild the system as a result of a system failure. You learned how the Flash archive can be used in a JumpStart session for a completely automated installation.

Finally in this chapter, you learned about a new facility, the Preboot Execution Environment (PXE), which facilitates the installing of x86 clients across the network using a DHCP server to provide the boot configuration information. You also learned how to configure a DHCP server to add the required symbols to properly support a booting x86 client.

This concludes the study material for the second exam. We encourage you to use the test exams on the enclosed CD-ROM to test your knowledge of the chapters you've read. If you fully understand all the material covered in this book, you should have no problem passing both exams. If you don't score well on the enclosed CD-ROM, go back and review the topics you are weak in.

Before taking the exam however, visit `www.pdesigninc.com` and read up-to-date information about the exams, comments from others that have taken the exams, test-taking tips, and links to additional study materials to be sure you are adequately prepared before spending $150 for every exam.

When you're confident that you understand all the material covered in this section, you are ready to take the real exam. Good luck!

KEY TERMS

- Boot server
- Class file
- Custom JumpStart
- DHCP Server
- Flash Installation
- Flash archive
- Install server
- JumpStart server
- JumpStart client
- Preboot Execution Environment
- Profile
- RARP
- Rules files
- Solaris Flash

Exercises

14.1 Creating JumpStart Servers

In this exercise, you'll create a JumpStart boot server, install server, configuration server, configuration files, and configure a JumpStart client to automatically install the Solaris 10 operating environment across the network.

For this exercise, you'll need two systems connected on a network. One system will serve as the `boot/install/configuration` server, so it needs about 2.5GB of free disk space. The second system will be the client and will have the entire disk destroyed and the operating system reloaded.

CAUTION

Destructive Process This procedure destroys data on the disk. Be sure you have proper backups if you want to save any data on these systems.

Estimated time: 1 hour

1. On the system that will be used as the boot and install server, log in as root.
2. Edit the `/etc/hosts` file and make an entry for the JumpStart client.
3. Create the boot server as follows:
   a) Insert the CD labeled Solaris 10 CD 1 and let `vold` automatically mount the CD.
   b) Change to the Tools directory on the CD as follows:

```
cd /cdrom/cdrom0/s0/Solaris_10/Tools
```

c) Run the setup_install_server script and specify the location for the CD image. Be sure you have about 2.5GB of free space and the target directory is empty. In the following example, I'm using /export/install as the install directory:

```
./setup_install_server /export/install
```

4. Add the additional software as follows:

a) Eject the Solaris 10 CD 1 and put in the Solaris 10 CD 2. Let vold automatically mount the CD.

b) Change to the Tools directory on the CD as follows:

```
cd /cdrom/cdrom0/Solaris_10/Tools
```

c) Execute the add_to_install_server script as follows to copy the images from the CD to the /export/install directory:

```
./add_to_install_server /export/install
```

d) Repeat the procedure with the remaining CDs.

5. Now create the JumpStart configuration directory as follows:

```
mkdir /jumpstart
```

6. Add the following entry in the /etc/dfs/dfstab file for this directory to share it across the network:

```
share -F nfs -o ro,anon=0 /jumpstart
```

7. Start the NFS server as follows if the nfsd daemon is not already running:

```
svcadm enable nfs/server
```

8. In the /jumpstart directory, use the vi editor to create a class file named basic_class with the following entries:

```
#Specifies that the installation will be treated as \
an initial
#installation, as opposed to an upgrade.
install_type initial_install
#Specifies that the engineering systems are \
standalone systems.
system_type standalone
#Specifies that the JumpStart software uses default \
disk
#partitioning for installing Solaris software on the \
engineering
#systems.
```

```
partitioning default
#Specifies that the developer's software group will \
be
#installed
cluster SUNWCprog
#Specifies that each system in the engineering group\
 will have 512
#Mbytes of swap space.
filesys any 512 swap
```

9. In the `/jumpstart` directory, use the `vi` editor to create a rules file named rules with the following entry:

```
hostname sun1 - basic_class -
```

10. Validate the class and rules files with the `check` and `pfinstall` commands as follows:

```
cd /jumpstart

/export/install/Solaris_10/Misc/jumpstart_sample/check

/usr/sbin/install.d/pfinstall -d -c /export/install basic_class
```

11. Now set up the JumpStart client as follows:

```
cd /export/install/Solaris_10/Tools
./add_install_client -s <SERVERNAME>:/export/install \
-c <SERVERNAME>:/jumpstart -p <SERVERNAME>:/jumpstart -e <MAC ADDRESS>\
 <CLIENTNAME>  <PLATFORM>
```

Where `SERVERNAME` is the hostname of your boot/install server, `MAC ADDRESS` is your client's Ethernet address, `CLIENTNAME` is your client's hostname, and `PLATFORM` is your client's architecture (such as `sun4u`).

For example:

```
./add_install_client -s \ sparcserver:/export/install\
-c sparcserver:/jumpstart -p sparcserver:/jumpstart \
-e 8:0:20:21:49:24  sun1 sun4u
```

12. Go to the client, turn on the power, and at the boot PROM, issue the following command:

```
boot net - install
```

The JumpStart installation executes.

Exam Questions

1. Which of the following is a method to automatically install Solaris on a new SPARC system by inserting the Solaris Operating System CD-ROM in the drive and powering on the system?

   ❍ **A.** JumpStart

   ❍ **B.** Wan Boot Installation

   ❍ **C.** Interactive installation

   ❍ **D.** Custom JumpStart

2. Which of the following is a method to automatically install groups of identical systems?

   ❍ **A.** Custom JumpStart

   ❍ **B.** JumpStart

   ❍ **C.** Network Installation

   ❍ **D.** Interactive installation

3. Which of the following sets up an install server to provide the operating system to the client during a JumpStart installation?

   ❍ **A.** `add_install_client`

   ❍ **B.** `add_install_server`

   ❍ **C.** `pfinstall`

   ❍ **D.** `setup_install_server`

4. For a JumpStart installation, which of the following files should contain a rule for each group of systems that you want to install?

   ❍ **A.** `sysidcfg`

   ❍ **B.** `rules.ok`

   ❍ **C.** `profile`

   ❍ **D.** `check`

5. For a JumpStart installation, which of the following servers is set up to answer RARP requests from clients?

   ❍ **A.** Boot server

   ❍ **B.** Install server

   ❍ **C.** Configuration server

   ❍ **D.** JumpStart server

6. Which of the following is used as an alternative to setting up a configuration directory ?

   - ❍ **A.** Boot server
   - ❍ **B.** Install server
   - ❍ **C.** Configuration diskette
   - ❍ **D.** `rules.ok` file

7. For a JumpStart installation, which of the following files contains the name of a `finish` script?

   - ❍ **A.** `check`
   - ❍ **B.** `profile`
   - ❍ **C.** `rules.ok`
   - ❍ **D.** `profile diskette`

8. Which of the following is a user-defined Bourne shell script, specified within the rules file?

   - ❍ **A.** `add_install_client` script
   - ❍ **B.** `class` file
   - ❍ **C.** `check` script
   - ❍ **D.** `begin` script

9. In JumpStart, which of the following files defines how to install the Solaris software on a system?

   - ❍ **A.** `class` file
   - ❍ **B.** `rules`
   - ❍ **C.** `rules.ok`
   - ❍ **D.** `install.log`

10. Which of the following is used to test a JumpStart class file?

    - ❍ **A.** `check`
    - ❍ **B.** `pfinstall`
    - ❍ **C.** `rules`
    - ❍ **D.** `add_install_client`

11. When working with JumpStart, which of the following files is *not* used to provide information about clients?

  ❍ **A.** `rules`

  ❍ **B.** `sysidcfg`

  ❍ **C.** `check`

  ❍ **D.** `class`

12. Which of the following is not a valid entry in the first field in the rules file ?

  ❍ **A.** `karch`

  ❍ **B.** `any`

  ❍ **C.** `hostname`

  ❍ **D.** `ip_address`

13. Which of the following files is the JumpStart file that can use any name and still work properly?

  ❍ **A.** `class`

  ❍ **B.** `rules`

  ❍ **C.** `sysidcfg`

  ❍ **D.** `pfinstall`

14. Which of the following scripts will update or create the `rules.ok` file?

  ❍ **A.** `pfinstall`

  ❍ **B.** `check`

  ❍ **C.** `setup_install_server`

  ❍ **D.** `install_type`

15. Which of the following supplies the operating system during a JumpStart installation?

  ❍ **A.** Setup server

  ❍ **B.** Install server

  ❍ **C.** Profile server

  ❍ **D.** `/jumpstart` directory

16. Which of the following contains the JumpStart directory and configuration files such as the `class` file and the `rules` file?

❍ **A.** Profile diskette

❍ **B.** Setup server

❍ **C.** Install server

❍ **D.** Configuration server

17. Which of the following commands is issued on the install server to set up remote workstations to install Solaris from the install server?

❍ **A.** `add_install_client`

❍ **B.** `add_install_server`

❍ **C.** `setup_install_client`

❍ **D.** `setup_client`

18. Which of the following commands sets up a system as a boot server only?

❍ **A.** `setup_install_server`

❍ **B.** `add_install_server -b`

❍ **C.** `setup_install_server -b`

❍ **D.** `setup_boot_server`

19. Which of the following commands is used on a JumpStart client to start the installation?

❍ **A.** `boot net - install`

❍ **B.** `boot net`

❍ **C.** `boot - jumpstart`

❍ **D.** `boot net - jumpstart`

20. Which script copies additional packages within a product tree to the local disk on an existing install server?

❍ **A.** `add_install_server -a`

❍ **B.** `add_to_install_server`

❍ **C.** `setup_install_server`

❍ **D.** `_server -a`

21. Which of the following class file keywords is valid ONLY for a Solaris Flash Install using JumpStart?

 ❍ **A.** `archive_location`

 ❍ **B.** `install_type`

 ❍ **C.** `locale`

 ❍ **D.** `system_type`

22. Which of the following are required to be able to boot an x86 client using the PXE network boot and install method? (Choose 3)

 ❍ **A.** A system with more than 1 GB of physical memory

 ❍ **B.** An x86 client with a system BIOS that supports the Intel Preboot Execution Environment specification

 ❍ **C.** A configured DHCP server

 ❍ **D.** A server running either NIS or NIS+ naming service

 ❍ **E.** An install server

23. Which of the following symbols would you configure in a DHCP server to correctly specify the Hostname of the JumpStart Install server so that a PXE network client would be passed the correct configuration information at boot time?

 ❍ **A.** `SinstIP4`

 ❍ **B.** `SinstNM`

 ❍ **C.** `SrootNM`

 ❍ **D.** `SrootIP4`

Answers to Exam Questions

1. **A**. JumpStart lets you automatically install the Solaris software on a SPARC-based system just by inserting the Solaris CD and powering on the system. You do not need to specify the `boot` command at the `ok` prompt. For more information, see the section "JumpStart."

2. **A.** The custom JumpStart method of installing the operating system provides a way to install groups of similar systems automatically and identically. For more information, see the section "JumpStart."

3. **D.** The `setup_install_server` script sets up an install server to provide the operating system to the client during a JumpStart installation. For more information, see the section "The Install Server."

4. **B.** The `rules.ok` file is a file that should contain a rule for each group of systems you want to install. For more information, see the section "The Rules File."

5. **A.** The boot server is set up to answer RARP requests from a JumpStart client. For more information, see the section "Setting Up the Boot Server."

6. **C.** A configuration disk is used as an alternate to setting up a configuration directory. For more information, see the section "Setting Up a Configuration Diskette."

7. **C.** The `rules.ok` file contains the name of a `finish` script. For more information, see the section "The Rules File."

8. **D.** A `begin` script is a user-defined Bourne shell script, located in the JumpStart configuration directory on the configuration server, specified within the rules file, that performs tasks before the Solaris software is installed on the system. For more information, see the section "`begin` and `finish` Scripts."

9. **A.** A `class` file is a text file that defines how to install the Solaris software on a system. For more information, see the section "Creating Class Files."

10. **B.** After you create a class file, you can use the `pfinstall` command to test it. For more information, see the section "Testing Class Files."

11. **C.** The `sysidcfg`, `rules`, and `class` files all provide information about the JumpStart client. The `check` script is used to validate the rules file. For more information, see the section "JumpStart."

12. **D.** `any`, `hostname`, and `karch` are all valid keywords that can be used in the rules file. For more information, see the section "The Rules File."

13. **A.** The `class` file can be named anything, but it should reflect the way in which it installs the Solaris software on a system. For more information, see the section "Creating Class Files."

14. **B.** The `check` script will update or create the `rules.ok` file. For more information, see the section "Validating the Rules File ."

15. **B.** The install server supplies the operating system during a JumpStart installation. For more information, see the section "The Install Server."

16. **D.** The configuration server contains all the essential custom JumpStart configuration files, such as the `rules` file, the `rules.ok` file, the `class` file, the `check` script, and the optional `begin` and `finish` scripts. For more information, see the section "Configuration Server."

17. **A.** Use the `add_install_client` command on the install server to set up remote workstations to install Solaris from the install server. For more information, see the section "Setting Up Clients."

18. **C.** `setup_install_server -b` sets up a system as a boot server only. For more information, see the section "Setting Up the Boot Server."

19. **A.** `boot net - install` is used on a JumpStart client to start the installation. For more information, see the section "Starting Up the Clients."

20. **B.** The `add_to_install_server` script copies additional packages within a product tree to the local disk on an existing install server. For more information, see the section "The Install Server."

21. **A.** The `archive_location` option is a valid class file keyword that is only used when installing a Flash Archive using JumpStart. For more information, see the section "Creating Class Files."

22. **B, C, and E.** The requirements for a PXE network boot are that there is an install server, a configure DHCP server, and an x86 client that supports the Intel Preboot Execution Environment specification. For more information, see the section "Preboot Execution Environment."

22. **B.** The DHCP symbol `SinstNM` specifies the hostname of the JumpStart Install server. For more information, see the section "Configuring the DHCP Server ."

Suggested Reading and Resources

1. Solaris 10 Documentation CD. "Solaris 10 Installation Guide: Custom JumpStart and Advanced Installations" manual.
2. `http://docs.sun.com`. Solaris 10 documentation set. "Solaris 10 Installation Guide: Custom JumpStart and Advanced Installations" book in the Solaris 10 Release and Installation collection.
3. Solaris 10 Documentation CD. "Solaris 10 Installation Guide: Solaris Flash Archives (Creation and Installation)" manual.
4. `http://docs.sun.com`. Solaris 10 documentation set. "Solaris 10 Installation Guide: Solaris Flash Archives (Creation and Installation)" book in the Solaris 10 Release and Installation collection.
5. Solaris 10 Documentation CD. "Solaris 10 Installation Guide: Network Based Installations" manual.
6. `http://docs.sun.com`. Solaris 10 documentation set. "Solaris 10 Installation Guide: Network Based Installations" book in the Solaris 10 Release and Installation collection.

PART II
Final Review

Fast Facts

The Fast Facts listed in this chapter are designed as a refresher of key points, topics, and knowledge that are required to be successful on the Solaris System Administrator Certification exam. By using these summaries of key points, you can spend an hour prior to your exam to refresh your understanding of key topics and ensure that you have a solid understanding of the objectives and the information required for you to succeed in each major area of the exam.

This chapter is divided into two parts: Section 1 covers Exam CX-310-200, and Section 2 covers Exam CX-310-202. Therefore, you only need to study the section applicable to the exam you are preparing for. If you have a thorough understanding of the key points here, chances are good that you will pass the exam.

This chapter is designed as a quick study aid that you can use just prior to taking the exam. You should be able to review the Fast Facts for each exam in less than an hour. It cannot serve as a substitute for knowing the material supplied in these chapters. However, its key points should refresh your memory on critical topics. In addition to the information located in this chapter, remember to review the Glossary terms because they are intentionally not covered here.

Section 1—Exam CX-310-200

Study these Fast Facts only when preparing for the Sun Certified System Administrator for the Solaris 10 Operating Environment—Part I exam (CX-310-200).

Managing File Systems

A file system is a structure of files and directories used to organize and store files on disks and other storage media. All disk-based computer systems have a file system. In Unix, file systems have two basic components: files and directories. A *file* is the actual information as it is stored on the disk, and a *directory* is a listing of the filenames. In addition to keeping track of filenames, the file system must also keep track of files' access dates, permissions, and ownership.

A *hard disk* consists of several separate disk platters mounted on a common spindle. Data stored on each platter surface is written and read by disk heads. The circular path a disk head traces over a spinning disk platter is called a *track*.

Each track is made up of a number of sectors laid end to end. A *sector* consists of a header, a trailer, and 512 bytes of data. The header and trailer contain error-checking information to help ensure the accuracy of the data. Taken together, the set of tracks traced across all of the individual disk platter surfaces for a single position of the heads is called a *cylinder*.

Devices and Drivers

In Solaris, each disk device is described in three ways, using three distinct naming conventions:

- **Physical device name**—Represents the full device pathname in the device information hierarchy.
- **Instance name**—Represents the kernel's abbreviation name for every possible device on the system.
- **Logical device name**—Used by system administrators with most system commands to refer to devices.

The system commands used to provide information about physical devices are described in Table 1.

TABLE 1 Device Information Commands

Command	Description
`prtconf`	Displays system configuration information, including the total amount of memory and the device configuration, as described by the system's hierarchy. This useful tool verifies whether a device has been seen by the system.
`sysdef`	Displays device configuration information, including system hardware, pseudo devices, loadable modules, and selected kernel parameters.
`dmesg`	Displays system diagnostic messages as well as a list of devices attached to the system since the most recent restart.

You can add new devices to a system without requiring a reboot if your system supports hot-plug devices. It's all handled by the `devfsadmd` daemon that transparently builds the necessary configuration entries. Older commands such as `drvconfig`, `disks`, `tapes`, `ports`, and `devlinks` have been replaced by the `devfsadm` utility. The `devfsadm` command should now be used in place of all these commands; however, `devfsadmd`, the `devfsadm` daemon, automatically detects device configuration changes, so there should be no need to run this command interactively.

During the process of building the `/devices` directory, the `devfsadmd` daemon assigns each device a major device number by using the name-to-number mappings held in the `/etc/name_to_major` file. This file is maintained by the system. The major device number indicates the general device class, such as `disk`, `tape`, or `serial line`. The minor device number indicates the specific member within that class.

The `/dev/dsk` directory refers to the block or buffered device file, and the `/dev/rdsk` directory refers to the character or raw device file. The "r" in `rdsk` stands for "raw."

Instance Names

The instance name represents the kernel's abbreviated name for every possible device on the system. For example, on an Ultra system, `dad0` represents the instance name of the IDE disk drive, and `hme0` is the instance name for the network interface. Instance names are mapped to a physical device name in the `/etc/path_to_inst` file.

File Systems

Following are the four types of disk-based file systems used by Solaris 10:

- **UFS**—The Unix file system, which is based on the BSD Fast file system (the traditional Unix file system). The UFS is the default disk-based file system used in Solaris.
- **HSFS**—The High Sierra and ISO 9660 file system. The HSFS is used on CD-ROMs and is a read-only file system.
- **PCFS**—The PC file system, which allows read/write access to data and programs on DOS-formatted disks.
- **UDF (Universal Disk Format) file system**—UDF is the industry-standard format for storing information on the optical media technology called DVD (Digital Versatile Disc).

Virtual file systems, previously called pseudo file systems, are virtual or memory-based file systems that create duplicate paths to other disk-based file systems or provide access to special kernel information and facilities. Most virtual file systems do not use file system disk space, although a few exceptions exist. The following is a list of some of the more common types of virtual file systems:

- **Cachefs**—The cache file system.
- **TMPFS**—The temporary file system uses local memory for file system reads and writes.
- **`/var/run`**—`/var/run` is the repository for temporary system files that are not needed across systems.

- **MNTFS**—The MNTFS type maintains information about currently mounted file systems.
- **DEVFS**—The DEVFS is used to manage the namespace of all devices on the system. This file system is used for the `/devices` directory.

Disks are divided into regions called disk slices or disk partitions using the `format` utility or the Solaris Management Console. Make sure you understand all of the Format menu options and what tasks they perform. The following displays the main menu options in the `format` utility:

```
disk - select a disk
    type - select (define) a disk type
    partition - select (define) a partition table
    current - describe the current disk
    format - format and analyze the disk
    repair - repair a defective sector
    label - write label to the disk
    analyze - surface analysis
    defect - defect list management
    backup - search for backup labels
    verify - read and display labels
    save - save new disk/partition definitions
    inquiry - show vendor, product and revision
    volname - set 8-character volume name
    !<cmd> - execute <cmd>, then return
    quit   -  Quit the format utility
```

Here are the menu options available in the partition section of the `format` utility:

```
PARTITION MENU:
  0 - change '0' partition
  1 - change '1' partition
  2 - change '2' partition
  3 - change '3' partition
  4 - change '4' partition
  5 - change '5' partition
  6 - change '6' partition
  7 - change '7' partition
  select - select a predefined table
  modify - modify a predefined partition table
  name - name the current table
  print - display the current table
  label - write partition map and label to the disk
  !<cmd> - execute <cmd>, then return
  quit   -  Quit the format utility
```

When you create a UFS, the disk slice is divided into cylinder groups. Disk configuration information is stored in the disk label. If you know the disk and slice number, you can display information for a disk by using the print volume table of contents (`prtvtoc`) command.

The slice is then divided into blocks to control and organize the structure of the files within the cylinder group. A UFS has the following four types of blocks. Each performs a specific function in the file system:

- **Bootblock**—Stores information used when booting the system
- **Superblock**—Stores much of the information about the file system
- **Inode**—Stores all information about a file except its name
- **Storage or data block**—Stores data for each file

File systems can be mounted from the command line by using the `mount` command. The commands in Table 2 are used from the command line to mount and unmount file systems.

TABLE 2 File System Commands

Command	Description
`mount`	Mounts specified file systems and remote resources
`mountall`	Mounts all file systems specified in a file system table (`vfstab`)
`umount`	Unmounts specified file systems and remote resources
`umountall`	Unmounts all file systems specified in a file system table

Common options used when mounting file systems are listed in Table 3.

TABLE 3 UFS Mount Options

Option	Description
`-rw|ro`	Specifies read/write or read-only. The default is read/write.
`-nosuid`	Disallows `setuid` execution and prevents devices on the file system from being opened. The default is to enable `setuid` execution and to allow devices to be opened.
`-f`	Fakes an entry in `/etc/mnttab` but doesn't really mount any file systems.
`-n`	Mounts the file system without making an entry in `/etc/mnttab`.
`-largefiles`	Specifies that a file system might contain one or more files larger than 2GB. It is not required that a file system mounted with this option contain files larger than 2GB, but this option allows such files within the file system. `largefiles` is the default.

(continues)

TABLE 3 *Continued*

Option	Description
`-nolargefiles`	Provides total compatibility with previous file system behavior, enforcing the 2GB maximum file size limit.
`-logging/nologging`	Enables/disables UFS logging on a file system; `logging` is the default in Solaris 10.

Use the `df` command and its options to see the capacity of each file system mounted on a system, the amount of space available, and the percentage of space already in use. Use the `du` (directory usage) command to report the number of free disk blocks and files.

Creating a UFS

`mkfs` constructs a file system on the character (or raw) device found in the `/dev/rdsk` directory. Again, it is highly recommended that you do not run the `mkfs` command directly, but instead use the friendlier `newfs` command, which automatically determines all the necessary parameters required by `mkfs` to construct the file system.

The `/etc/vfstab` (virtual file system table) file contains a list of file systems to be automatically mounted when the system is booted to the multi-user state. Each column of information follows this format:

- **`device to mount`**—The buffered device that corresponds to the file system being mounted.
- **`device to fsck`**—The raw (character) special device that corresponds to the file system being mounted. This determines the raw interface used by `fsck`. Use a dash (`-`) when there is no applicable device, such as for `swap`, `/proc`, `tmp`, or a network-based file system.
- **`mount point`**—The default mount point directory.
- **`FS type`**—The type of file system.
- **`fsck pass`**—The pass number used by `fsck` to decide whether to check a file. When the field contains a dash (`-`), the file system is not checked. When the field contains a value of `1` or greater, the file system is checked sequentially. File systems are checked sequentially in the order that they appear in the `/etc/vfstab` file. The value of the pass number has no effect on the sequence of file system checking.
- **`mount at boot`**—Specifies whether the file system should be automatically mounted when the system is booted. The RC scripts located in the `/etc` directory specify which file system gets mounted at each run level.

- **mount options**—A list of comma-separated options (with no spaces) used when mounting the file system. Use a dash (-) to show no options.

Use the `fsck` command to repair file systems. `fsck` is a multipass file system check program that performs successive passes over each file system, checking blocks and sizes, pathnames, connectivity, reference counts, and the map of free blocks (possibly rebuilding it). `fsck` also performs file system cleanup.

Volume Management

Volume management, with the `vold` daemon, is the mechanism that automatically mounts CD-ROMs and file systems when removable media containing recognizable file systems are inserted into the devices. The `vold` daemon is the workhorse behind volume manager. It is automatically started by the `/etc/init.d/volmgt` script. `vold` reads the `/etc/vold.conf` configuration file at startup. The `vold.conf` file contains the volume manager configuration information that `vold` uses.

Several other commands help you administer the volume manager on your system. They are described in Table 4.

TABLE 4 Volume Manager Commands

Command	Description
`rmmount`	Removable media mounter. Used by `vold` to automatically mount a `/cdrom`, `/floppy`, Jaz, or Zip drive if one of these media types is installed.
`volcancel`	Cancels a user's request to access a particular CD-ROM or floppy file system. This command, issued by the system administrator, is useful if the removable medium containing the file system is not currently in the drive.
`volcheck`	Checks the drive for installed media. By default, it checks the drive pointed to by `/dev/diskette`.
`volmissing`	Specified in `vold.conf` and notifies the user if an attempt is made to access a removable media type that is no longer in the drive.
`vold`	The volume manager daemon, controlled by `/etc/vold.conf`.
`volrmmount`	Simulates an insertion so that `rmmount` will mount the media, or simulates an ejection so that `rmmount` will unmount the media.

File systems are checked and repaired with the `fsck` (file system check) command. `fsck` is a multipass file system check program that performs successive passes over each file system, checking blocks and sizes, pathnames, connectivity, reference counts, and the map of free blocks (possibly rebuilding it). `fsck` also performs cleanup.

Installing the Solaris 10 Operating Environment

The computer must meet the following requirements before you can install Solaris 10 using the interactive installation method:

- The system must have a minimum of 128MB of RAM (256MB is recommended). Sufficient memory requirements are determined by several factors, including the number of active users and applications you plan to run.
- The media is distributed on CD-ROM and DVD only, so a CD-ROM or DVD-ROM is required either locally or on the network. You can use all of the Solaris installation methods to install the system from a networked CD-ROM or DVD-ROM.
- A minimum of 2GB of disk space is required. See the next section for disk space requirements for the specific Solaris software you plan to install. Also, remember to add disk space to support your environment's swap space requirements.
- When upgrading the operating system, you must have an empty 512MB slice on the disk. The swap slice is preferred, but you can use any slice that will not be used in the upgrade such as root (`/`), `user`, `var`, and `opt`.
- The system must be a SPARC (`sun4u` or `sun4m`) or supported x86/x64-based system.

Be familiar with the following software terms:

- **Software Package**—A collection of files and directories in a defined format.
- **Software Group**—Software packages are grouped into software groups, which are logical collections of software packages. Sometimes these groups are referred to as *clusters*.

For SPARC systems, software groups are grouped into six configuration groups to make the software installation process easier. These five configuration groups are reduced networking support, core system support, end-user support, developer system support, entire distribution, and entire distribution plus OEM system support.

You can use one of seven methods to install the Solaris software: interactive using a GUI, interactive using the command line, JumpStart, custom JumpStart, Flash Archive, WAN Boot, or Solaris Upgrade.

You have two upgrade options available. One upgrade option is available in the interactive installation if you are currently running Solaris 2.6, 7, 8, or 9 and you want to upgrade to Solaris 10. The other upgrade option is the Solaris Live upgrade, which enables an upgrade to be installed while the operating system is running and can significantly reduce the downtime associated with an upgrade. As described in Chapter 2, both upgrade options preserve most customizations you made in the previous version of Solaris.

During the installation, Solaris allocates disk space into separate file systems. By default, the interactive installation program (`suninstall`) sets up the root (`/`) and swap partitions. It's typical to add additional file systems. The following is a typical partitioning scheme for a system with a single disk drive:

- **root (`/`) and `/usr`**—Solaris normally creates two partitions for itself: root (`/`) and `/usr`. The installation program determines how much space you need. Most of the files in these two partitions are static. If the root (`/`) file system fills up, the system will not operate properly.
- **swap**—This area on the disk doesn't have files in it. In Unix you're allowed to have more programs running than will fit into the physical memory. The pieces that aren't currently needed in memory are transferred into swap to free up physical memory for other active processes.
- **`/export/home`**—On a single-disk system, everything not in root (`/`), `/usr`, or swap should go into a separate partition. `/export/home` is where you would put user home directories and user-created files.
- **`/var` (optional)**—Solaris uses this area for system log files, print spoolers, and email.
- **`/opt` (optional)**—By default, the Solaris installation program loads optional software packages here. Also, third-party applications are usually loaded into `/opt`.

Tools for Managing Software

Solaris provides tools for adding and removing software from a system. Those tools are described in Table 5.

TABLE 5 Tools for Managing Software

Command	Description
Managing Software from the Command Line	
`pkgadd`	Adds software packages to the system.
`pkgrm`	Removes software packages from the system.
`pkgchk`	Checks the accuracy of a software package installation.
`pkginfo`	Displays software package information.
`pkgask`	Stores answers in a response file so that they can be supplied automatically during an installation.
`pkgparam`	Displays package parameter values.

(continues)

TABLE 5 *Continued*

Command	Description
Managing Software from the Graphical User Interface	
Solaris Product Registry	Manages all of your Solaris software.
Web Start installer	Invokes a Web Start install wizard.

Software Patches

Another system administration task is managing system software patches. A *patch* is a fix to a reported software problem. Sun will ship several software patches to customers so that problems can be resolved before the next release of software. The existing software is derived from a specified package format that conforms to the ABI.

Patches are identified by unique alphanumeric strings. The patch base code comes first, then a hyphen, and then a number that represents the patch revision number. For example, patch `110453-01` is a Solaris patch to correct a known problem.

You might want to know more about patches that have previously been installed. Table 6 shows commands that provide useful information about patches already installed on a system.

TABLE 6 Helpful Commands for Patch Administration

Command	Function
`showrev -p`	Shows all patches applied to a system.
`pkgparam` *<pkgid>* `PATCHLIST`	Shows all patches applied to the package identified by *<pkgid>*.
`pkgparam` *<pkgid>* `PATCH INFO` *<patch-number>*	Shows the installation date and name of the host from which the patch was applied. *<pkgid>* is the name of the package (for example, `SUNWadmap`), and *<patch-number>* is the specific patch number.
`patchadd -R` *<client_root_path>* `-p`	Shows all patches applied to a client, from the server's console.
`patchadd -p`	Shows all patches applied to a system.
`patchrm` *<patchname>*	Removes a specified patch. *<patchname>* is the name of the patch to be removed.
`smpatch`	A tool for managing patches.
`Patch Tool`	Solaris Management Console Tool for managing patches.

System Startup and Shutdown

During system startup, or bootup, the boot process goes through the following phases:

1. **Boot PROM phase**—After you turn on power to the system, the PROM displays system identification information and runs self-test diagnostics to verify the system's hardware and memory. It then loads the primary boot program, called `bootblk`.

2. **Boot program phase**—The `bootblk` program finds and executes the secondary boot program (called `ufsboot`) from the UFS and loads it into memory. After the `ufsboot` program is loaded, it loads the two-part kernel.

3. **Kernel initialization phase**—The kernel initializes itself and begins loading modules, using `ufsboot` to read the files. When the kernel has loaded enough modules to mount the root file system, it unmaps the `ufsboot` program and continues, using its own resources.

4. **`init` phase**—The kernel starts the Unix operating system, mounts the necessary file systems, and runs `/sbin/init` to bring the system to the `initdefault` state specified in `/etc/inittab`.

   The kernel creates a user process and starts the `/sbin/init` process, which starts other processes by reading the `/etc/inittab` file.

   The `/sbin/init` process starts the run control (rc) scripts, which execute a series of other scripts. These scripts (`/sbin/rc*`) check and mount file systems, start various processes, and perform system maintenance tasks.

5. **`svc.startd` phase**—The `svc.startd` daemon starts the system services and boots the system to the appropriate milestone.

OpenBoot Environment

The hardware-level user interface that you see before the operating system starts is called the OpenBoot PROM (OBP). The primary tasks of the OpenBoot firmware are as follows:

- Test and initialize the system hardware.
- Determine the hardware configuration.
- Start the operating system from either a mass storage device or a network.
- Provide interactive debugging facilities for testing hardware and software.
- Allow modification and management of system startup configuration, such as NVRAM parameters.

Specifically, the following tasks are necessary to initialize the operating system kernel:

1. OpenBoot displays system identification information and then runs self-test diagnostics to verify the system's hardware and memory. These checks are known as a POST.
2. OpenBoot loads the primary startup program, `bootblk`, from the default startup device.
3. The `bootblk` program finds and executes the secondary startup program, `ufsboot`, and loads it into memory. The `ufsboot` program loads the operating system kernel.

A *device tree* is a series of node names separated by slashes (/). The top of the device tree is the root device node. Following the root device node, and separated by a leading slash (/), is a bus nexus node. Connected to a bus nexus node is a leaf node, which is typically a controller for the attached device. Each device pathname has this form:

```
driver-name@unit-address:device-arguments
```

Nodes are attached to a host computer through a hierarchy of interconnected buses on the device tree. OpenBoot deals directly with the hardware devices in the system. Each device has a unique name that represents both the type of device and the location of that device in the device tree. The OpenBoot firmware builds a device tree for all devices from information gathered at the POST. Sun uses the device tree to organize devices that are attached to the system.

Device pathnames tend to get very long; therefore, the OpenBoot environment utilizes a method that allows you to assign shorter names to the long device pathnames. These shortened names are called *device aliases* and they are assigned using the `devalias` command. Table 7 describes the `devalias` command, which is used to examine, create, and change OpenBoot aliases.

TABLE 7 `devalias` Commands

Command	Description
`devalias`	Displays all current device aliases.
`devalias_<alias>`	Displays the device pathname corresponding to `alias`.
`devalias_<alias> <device-path>`	Defines an `alias` representing `device-path`.

When the kernel is loading, it reads the `/etc/system` file where system configuration information is stored. This file modifies the kernel's parameters and treatment of loadable modules. It specifically controls the following:

- The search path for default modules to be loaded at boot time as well as the modules not to be loaded at boot time
- The modules to be forcibly loaded at boot time rather than at first access

- The root type and device
- The new values to override the default kernel parameter values

Various parameters are used to control the OpenBoot environment. Any user can view the OpenBoot configuration variables from a Unix prompt by typing the following:

```
/usr/sbin/eeprom
```

OpenBoot can be used to gather and display information about your system with the commands described in Table 8.

TABLE 8 OpenBoot Commands

Command	Description
`banner`	Displays the power-on banner
`show-sbus`	Displays a list of installed and probed SBus devices
`.enet-addr`	Displays the current Ethernet address
`.idprom`	Displays ID PROM contents, formatted
`.traps`	Displays a list of SPARC trap types
`.version`	Displays the version and date of the startup PROM
`.speed`	Displays CPU and bus speeds
`show-devs`	Displays all installed and probed devices

In addition, various hardware diagnostics can be run in OpenBoot to troubleshoot hardware and network problems.

The operating system is booted from the OpenBoot prompt using the `boot` command. You can supply several options to the OpenBoot `boot` command at the `ok` prompt. Table 9 describes each of these.

TABLE 9 `boot` Command Options

Option	Description
`-a`	An interactive boot
`-r`	A reconfiguration boot
`-s`	A single-user boot
`-v`	A verbose-mode boot

The following list describes the steps for booting interactively:

1. At the `ok` prompt, type **`boot -a`** and press Enter. The boot program prompts you interactively.

2. Press Enter to use the default kernel (/kernel/unix) as prompted, or type the name of the kernel to use for booting and press Enter.
3. Press Enter to use the default modules directory path as prompted, or type the path for the modules directory and press Enter.
4. Press Enter to use the default /etc/system file as prompted, or type the name of the system file and press Enter.
5. Press Enter to use the default root file system type as prompted (UFS for local disk booting, or NFS for diskless clients).
6. Press Enter to use the default physical name of the root device as prompted, or type the device name.

The Kernel

After the boot command initiates the kernel, the kernel begins several phases of the startup process. The first task is for OpenBoot to load the two-part kernel. The secondary startup program, ufsboot, which is described in the preceding section, loads the operating system kernel. The core of the kernel is two pieces of static code called genunix and unix. genunix is the platform-independent generic kernel file, and unix is the platform-specific kernel file. When the system boots, ufsboot combines these two files into memory to form the running kernel.

The kernel initializes itself and begins loading modules, using ufsboot to read the files. After the kernel has loaded enough modules to mount the root file system, it unmaps the ufsboot program and continues, using its own resources. The kernel creates a user process and starts the /sbin/init process.

During the init phase of the boot process, the init daemon (/sbin/init) reads the /etc/default/init file to set any environment variables. By default, only the TIMEZONE variable is set. Then, init reads the /etc/inittab file and executes any process entries that have sysinit in the action field, so that any special initializations can take place before users login.

After reading the /etc/inittab file, init starts the svc.startd daemon, which is responsible for starting and stopping other system services such as mounting file systems and configuring network devices. In addition, svc.startd will execute legacy run control (rc) scripts, which are described later in this section.

The kernel is dynamically configured in Solaris 10. The kernel consists of a small static core and many dynamically loadable kernel modules. Many kernel modules are loaded automatically at boot time, but for efficiency, others—such as device drivers—are loaded from the disk as needed by the kernel.

When the kernel is loading, it reads the /etc/system file where system configuration information is stored. This file modifies the kernel's parameters and treatment of loadable modules.

After control of the system is passed to the kernel, the system begins initialization and starts the `svc.startd` daemon. In Solaris 10, the `svc.startd` daemon replaces the init process as the master process starter and restarter. Where in previous version of Solaris, `init` would start all processes and bring the system to the appropriate "run level" or "init state," now SMF, or more specifically, the `svc.startd` daemon, assumes the role of starting system services.

The service instance is the fundamental unit of administration in the SMF framework and each SMF service has the potential to have multiple versions of it configured. An instance is a specific configuration of a service and multiple instances of the same version can run in the Solaris operating environment.

The services started by `svc.startd` are referred to as milestones. The milestone concept replaces the traditional run levels that were used in previous versions of Solaris. A milestone is a special type of service which represents a group of services. A milestone is made up of several SMF services. For example, the services which constituted run levels S, 2, and 3 in previous versions of Solaris are now represented by milestone services named.

`milestone/single-user` (equivalent to run level S)

`milestone/multi-user` (equivalent to run level 2)

`milestone/multi-user-server` (equivalent to run level 3)

Other milestones that are available in the Solaris 10 OE are

`milestone/name-services`

`milestone/devices`

`milestone/network`

`milestone/sysconfig`

An SMF manifest is an XML (Extensible Markup Language) file that contains a complete set of properties that are associated with a service or a service instance. The properties are stored in files and subdirectories located in `/var/svc/manifest`.

The SMF provides a set of command-line utilities used to administer and configure the SMF that are described in Chapter 3.

A run level is a system state (run state), represented by a number or letter, that identifies the services and resources that are currently available to users. The `who -r` command can still be used to identify a systems run state as follows:

```
who -r
```

The system responds with the following, indicating that run-level 3 is the current run state:

```
.       run-level 3  Aug  4 09:38     3      1  1
```

Since the introduction of SMF in Solaris 10, we now refer to these run states as milestones and Chapter 3 describes how the legacy run states coincide with the Solaris 10 milestones.

Commands to Shut Down the System

When preparing to shut down a system, you need to determine which of the following commands is appropriate for the system and the task at hand:

`/usr/sbin/shutdown`

`/sbin/init`

`/usr/sbin/halt`

`/usr/sbin/reboot`

`/usr/sbin/poweroff`

Stop+A or L1+A (to be used as a last resort)

User and Security Administration

Use the Solaris Management Console (SMC) GUI or the command line to create and manage user accounts.

Table 10 describes field entries you'll need to know when setting up a new user account using SMC.

TABLE 10 Add User Fields

Item	Description
User Name	Enter a unique login name that will be entered at the Solaris login prompt.
User ID	Enter the unique user ID (UID). SMC automatically assigns the next available UID; however, in a networked environment, make sure this number is not duplicated by another user on another system.
Primary Group	Enter the primary group name or GID (group ID) number for the group to which the user will belong.
Full Name/Description	These two fields are comment fields and are optional. Enter any comments such as the full username or phone number.
Password	Click this button to specify the password status. Selectable options are as follows: **User Must Set Password at First Login**—This is the default. The account does not have a password assigned. The user is prompted for a password on first login, unless `passreq=no` is set in `/etc/default/login`.

TABLE 10 *Continued*

Item	Description
	User Must Use This Password at First Login—The account will have a password that you set in advance.
Path	This will be the location of the user's home directory and where his or her personal files will be stored.

Another way to manage user accounts is from the command line. Although using the command line is more complex than using the SMC GUI, the command line provides a little more flexibility. Solaris supplies the user administration commands described in Table 11 for setting up and managing user accounts.

TABLE 11 Account Administration Commands

Command	Description
`useradd`	Adds a new user account
`userdel`	Deletes a user account
`usermod`	Modifies a user account
`groupadd`	Adds a new group
`groupmod`	Modifies a group (for example, changes the group ID or name)
`groupdel`	Deletes a group
`smuser`	The command line equivalent of the SMC GUI tool that manages one or more user entries in the local `/etc` files, NIS, or NIS+ name service
`smgroup`	The command line equivalent of the SMC GUI tool that manages one or more group definitions in the group database for the local `/etc` files, NIS, or NIS+ name service

Shells and Initialization Files

The Solaris 10 operating environment offers five commonly used shells:

- **The Bourne shell (`/sbin/sh`)**—The default shell. It is a command programming language that executes commands read from a terminal or a file.
- **The C shell (`/bin/csh`)**—A command interpreter with a C-like syntax. The C-shell provides a number of convenient features for interactive use that are not available with the Bourne shell, including filename completion, command aliasing, and history substitution.
- **The TENEX C shell (`/bin/tcsh`)**—An enhanced version of the C shell with complete backward compatibility. The enhancements are mostly related to interactive use, including the ability to use arrow keys for command history retrieval and command-line editing.

- **The Korn shell (/bin/ksh)**—A command programming language that executes commands read from a terminal or a file.
- **The Bourne Again shell (/bin/bash)**—Bash is a sh-compatible command language interpreter that executes commands read from the standard input or from a file. Bash also incorporates useful features from the Korn and C shells (ksh and csh).

The login shell is the command interpreter that runs when you log in. The Solaris 10 operating environment offers the three most commonly used shells, as described in Table 12.

TABLE 12 Basic Features of the Bourne, C, and Korn Shells

Feature	sh	csh	tcsh	ksh	bash
Syntax compatible with sh	Yes	No	No	Yes	Yes
Job control	Yes	Yes	Yes	Yes	Yes
History list	No	Yes	Yes	Yes	Yes
Command-line editing	No	Yes	Yes	Yes	Yes
Aliases	No	Yes	Yes	Yes	Yes
Protect files from overwriting	No	Yes	Yes	Yes	Yes
Ignore Ctrl+D (ignoreeof)	No	Yes	Yes	Yes	Yes
Enhanced cd	No	Yes	Yes	Yes	Yes
Initialization file separate	No	Yes	Yes	Yes	Yes
Logout file	No	Yes	Yes	No	Yes
Functions	Yes	No	No	Yes	Yes
Arrow keys for command edits	No	No	Yes	No	Yes

The logout file functionality can be implemented with the use of a trap statement in /etc/profile:

```
trap 'test -f $HOME/.shlogout && . $HOME/.shlogout' EXIT
```

A shell initialization file is a shell script that runs automatically each time the user logs in. The initialization file will set up the work environment and customize the shell environment for the user.

C shell initialization files run in a particular sequence after the user logs in to the system. For the C shell and tcsh, initialization files are run in the following sequence:

1. Commands in /etc/.login are executed.
2. Commands from the $HOME/.cshrc file (located in your home directory) are executed. In addition, each time you start a new shell or open a new window in CDE, commands

from the `$HOME/.cshrc` are run. In `tcsh`, if `$HOME/.tcshrc` exists, it is used instead of `$HOME/.cshrc`.

3. The shell executes commands from the `$HOME/.login` file (located in your home directory). Typically, the `$HOME/.login` file contains commands to specify the terminal type and environment.
4. Finally, when startup processing is complete, the C shell begins reading commands from the default input device, the terminal.
5. When the shell terminates, it performs commands from the `$HOME/.logout` file (if it exists in your home directory).

Bourne shell initialization files run in a particular sequence after the user logs in to the system. For the Bourne shell, initialization files are run in the following sequence:

1. Commands in `/etc/profile` are executed.
2. Commands from the `$HOME/.profile` file (located in your home directory) are executed. Typically, the `$HOME/.profile` file contains commands to specify the terminal type and environment.
3. Finally, when startup processing is complete, the Bourne shell begins reading commands from the default input device, the terminal.

Korn shell initialization files run in a particular sequence after the user logs in to the system. For the Korn shell, initialization files are run in the following sequence:

1. Commands in `/etc/profile` are executed.
2. Commands from the `$HOME/.profile` file (located in your home directory) are executed. Typically, the `$HOME/.profile` file contains commands to specify the terminal type and environment.
3. If the environment variable `$ENV` is set to the name of a file and that file is present, commands located in this file are executed. In addition, this initialization file gets read (and the commands get executed) every time a new Korn shell is started after login.
4. Finally, when startup processing is complete, the Korn shell begins reading commands from the default input device, the terminal.

Bash initialization files run in a particular sequence after the user logs in to the system. For the Bash shell, initialization files are run in the following sequence:

1. Commands in `/etc/profile` are executed.
2. Commands in `$HOME/.bash_profile` are executed. This file serves the same purpose as `$HOME/.profile` in the Bourne and Korn shells.

3. Commands in `$HOME/.bashrc` are executed, but only if this is not a login shell.
4. When startup processing is complete, `bash` begins reading commands from the default input device, the terminal.
5. As a login session exits, `$HOME/.bash_logout` is processed.

The Solaris 10 system software provides default user initialization files for each shell in the `/etc/skel` directory on each system. These files are listed in Table 13.

TABLE 13 Default Initialization Files

Name	Description
`local.cshrc`	The default `.cshrc` file for the C shell
`local.login`	The default `.login` file for the C shell
`local.profile`	The default `.profile` file for the Bourne and Korn shells

System Security

Protecting your system against unauthorized access or modification begins with controlling access to your system. Several files that control default system access are stored in the `/etc/default` directory. Table 14 summarizes the files in the `/etc/default directory`.

TABLE 14 Files in the `/etc/default` Directory

Filename	Description
`/etc/default/passwd`	Controls default policy on password aging.
`/etc/default/login`	Controls system login policies, including root access. The default is to limit root access to the console.
`/etc/default/su`	Specifies where attempts to `su` to root are logged and where these log files are located. The file also specifies whether attempts to `su` to root are displayed on a named device (such as a system console).

Controlling access to systems also involves using passwords and appropriate file permissions. Enforce the following guidelines on passwords:

- Passwords should contain a combination of six to eight letters, numbers, or special characters. Don't use fewer than six characters.
- Mix upper- and lowercase characters.
- Use a password with nonalphabetic characters, such as numerals or punctuation.
- Do not use words from a dictionary or easy-to-guess words.

Most of the user account information is stored in the /etc/passwd file; however, password encryption and password aging details are stored in the /etc/shadow file. Group information is stored in the /etc/group file.

Protecting Data

System security also involves protecting your data using standard Unix file permissions. File access permissions are shown by the `ls -la` command. The first column returned describes the type of file and its access permissions for the user, group, and others using letters. The r, w, and x are described in Table 15.

TABLE 15 File Access Permissions

Symbol	Permission	Means That Designated Users...
r	Read	Can open and read the contents of a file.
w	Write	Can write to the file (modify its contents), add to it, or delete it.
x	Execute	Can execute the file (if it is a program or shell script).
-	Denied	Cannot read, write to, or execute the file.

When listing the permissions on a directory, all columns of information are the same as for a file, with one exception. The r, w, and x found in the first column are treated slightly differently than for a file. These are described in Table 16.

TABLE 16 Directory Access Permissions

Symbol	Permission	Means That Designated Users...
r	Read	Can list files in the directory.
w	Write	Can add or remove files or links in the directory.
x	Execute	Can open or execute files in the directory. Also can make the directory and the directories beneath it current.
-	Denied	Do not have read, write, or execute privileges.

Use the commands listed in Table 17 to modify file access permissions and ownership, but remember that only the owner of the file or root can assign or modify these values.

TABLE 17 File Access Commands

Command	Description
chmod	Changes access permissions on a file. You can use either symbolic mode (letters and symbols) or absolute mode (octal numbers) to change permissions on a file.
chown	Changes the ownership of a file.
chgrp	Changes the group ownership of a file.

When a user creates a file or directory, the user mask controls the default file permissions assigned to the file or directory and is set using the `umask` command.

Access Control Lists (ACLs)

ACLs (pronounced *ackls*) can provide greater control over file permissions when the traditional Unix file protection in the Solaris operating system is not enough. An ACL provides better file security by enabling you to define file permissions for the owner, owner's group, others, specific users and groups, and default permissions for each of these categories. The following are commands used to set and modify ACL entries:

- **`setfacl`**—Set, modify, or delete ACL entries on a file
- **`getfacl`**—Display or copy the ACL entry on a file

Monitoring Users

As the system administrator, you'll need to monitor system resources and watch for unusual activity. Having a method to monitor the system is useful when you suspect a breach in security. The following commands are used to monitor users and system activity:

`logins`	A command to monitor a particular user's activities.
`loginlog`	A file that contains one entry for each failed login attempt.
`who`	Shows who is logged into the system. `who` lists the login account name, terminal device, login date and time, and where the user logged in.
`whodo`	Displays each user logged in and the active processes owned by that user. The output shows the date, time, and machine name. For each user logged in, the system displays the device name, UID, and login time, followed by a list of active processes associated with the UID.
`last`	Displays the sessions of the specified users and terminals in chronological order. For each user, `last` displays the time when the session began, the duration of the session, and the terminal where the session took place.

Network Security

It is critical to turn off all unneeded network services because many of the services run by `inetd`, such as `rexd`, pose serious security threats. `rexd` is the daemon responsible for remote program execution. On a system connected to the rest of the world via the Internet or other public network, this could create a potential entry point for a hacker. TFTP should absolutely be disabled if you don't have diskless clients using it. Most sites will also disable `Finger` so that external users can't figure out the usernames of your internal users. Everything else depends on the needs of your site.

Solaris 10's File Transfer Protocol (FTP) is a common tool for transferring files across the network. Although most sites leave FTP enabled, you need to limit who can use it. Solaris 10 contains a file named `/etc/ftpd/ftpusers` that is used to restrict access via FTP. The `/etc/ftpd/ftpusers` file contains a list of login names that are prohibited from running an FTP login on the system.

The `/etc/hosts.equiv` file contains a list of trusted hosts for a remote system and can present a potential security risk. When an entry for a host is made in `/etc/hosts.equiv`, such as the sample entry for `system1`, this means that the host is trusted and so is any user at that machine. If the username is also mentioned, as in the second entry in the same file, the host is trusted only if the specified user is attempting access. A single line of `+` in the `/etc/hosts.equiv` file indicates that every known host is trusted—this should never be used.

The `$HOME/.rhosts` file is the user equivalent of the `/etc/hosts.equiv` file, except any user can create an `$HOME/.rhosts` file granting access to whomever the user chooses—without the system administrator's knowledge. The system administrator should disallow the use of `.rhosts` files—or even better, disable all `R` services.

It is recommended that you use the secure shell (`ssh`) when establishing communication between two hosts over insecure networks such as the Internet. The secure shell is much safer than previous methods used to access remote systems such as `rlogin`, `rsh`, and `rcp`. The secure shell daemon (`sshd`) listens for connections and handles the encrypted authentication exchange between two hosts. When authentication is complete, the user can execute commands and copy files remotely and securely.

Restricting Root Access

Root access needs to be safeguarded against unauthorized use. You should assume that any intruder is looking for root access. You can protect the superuser account on a system by restricting access to a specific device through the `/etc/default/login` file. In the `/etc/default/login` file, you can control where root is able to log in by assigning one of the following values to the variable named `CONSOLE`:

`CONSOLE=/dev/console`	Root is only allowed to login from the console device.
`CONSOLE=`	With no value defined, root cannot log in from anywhere, not even from the console.

Users can still log in using a non-root login and issue the `su` command to switch from being a user to being root, but this activity is logged in the file `/var/adm/sulog`. The `sulog` file lists all uses of the `su` command—not only those used to switch from being a user to being superuser.

Managing Processes

A process is distinct from a job or command, which can be composed of many processes working together to perform a specific task. Each process has a process ID associated with it and is referred to as a pid. You can monitor processes that are currently executing by using one of the commands listed in Table 18.

TABLE 18 Commands to Display Processes

Command	Description
`ps`	Executed from the command line to display information about active processes.
`pgrep`	Executed from the command line to find processes by a specific name or attribute.
`prstat`	Executed from the command line to display information about active processes on the system.
`psrinfo`	Displays one line for each configured processor, displaying whether it is online, noninterruptible, offline, or powered off, as well as when that status last changed.
`pargs`	Used from the command line to examine the arguments and environment variables of a process (or number of processes). `pargs` can also be used to examine core files.
`sdtprocess`	A GUI used to display and control processes on a system. This utility requires a terminal capable of displaying graphics.
SMC	The Solaris Management Console Processes Tool to view, suspend, resume, and delete processes.

A process has certain attributes that directly affect execution. These are listed in Table 19.

TABLE 19 Process Attributes

Attribute	Description
`PID`	The process identification (a unique number that defines the process within the kernel).
`PPID`	The parent `PID` (the creator of the process).
`UID`	The user ID number of the user who owns the process.
`EUID`	The effective user ID of the process.
`GID`	The group ID of the user who owns the process.
`EGID`	The effective group ID that owns the process.
`Priority`	The priority at which the process runs.

Using the `kill` Command

The `kill` command sends a terminate signal (signal 15) to the process, and the process is terminated. Signal 15, which is the default when no options are used with the `kill` command, is a gentle kill that allows a process to perform cleanup work before terminating. Signal 9, on the other hand, is called a sure, unconditional kill because it cannot be caught or ignored by a process. If the process is still around after a `kill -9`, it is either hung up in the Unix kernel, waiting for an event such as disk I/O to complete, or you are not the owner of the process.

Another way to kill a process is to use the `pkill` command. A signal name or number may be specified as the first command-line option to `pkill`. For example, to kill the process named `psef`, issue the following command:

```
pkill -9 psef
```

A way to divide processes on a busy system is to schedule jobs so that they run at different times. A large job, for example, could be scheduled to run at 2 a.m., when the system would normally be idle. Solaris supports three methods of batch processing: the `crontab` command, `at` command, and SMC Job Scheduler tool. The `crontab` command schedules multiple system events at regular intervals, and the `at` command schedules a single system event for execution at a later time.

The `cron` daemon handles the automatic scheduling of `crontab` commands. Its function is to check the `/var/spool/cron/crontab` directory every 15 minutes for the presence of `crontab` files. It checks for new `crontab` files or changes to existing ones, reads the execution times listed within the files, and submits the commands for execution at the proper times.

Table 20 describes the fields in the `crontab` file for scheduling jobs to run on a regular basis.

TABLE 20 The `crontab` File

Field	Description	Values
1	Minute	0–59. An * in this field means every minute.
2	Hour	0–23. An * in this field means every hour.
3	Day of month	1–31. An * in this field means every day of the month.
4	Month	1–12. An * in this field means every month.
5	Day of week	0–6 (0 = Sunday). An * in this field means every day of the week.
6	Command	Enter the command to be run.

Control who can access the `crontab` by configuring `/etc/cron.d/cron.deny` and `/etc/cron.d/cron.allow`. These access control files work together in the following manner:

- If `cron.allow` exists, only the users listed in this file can create, edit, display, and remove `crontab` files.
- If `cron.allow` doesn't exist, all users may submit `crontab` files, except for users listed in `cron.deny`.

- If neither cron.allow nor cron.deny exists, superuser privileges are required to run crontab.

The Solaris Management Console (SMC) includes a graphical tool to create and schedule cron jobs on your system. You can use the Job Scheduler Tool to

- View and modify job properties.
- Delete a job.
- Add a scheduled job.
- Enable or disable job logging.

The Job Scheduler tool is really just a GUI for managing crontab entries.

Projects and Tasks

Projects and tasks are used to identify what is called a *workload*. For projects, this means some related work, such as payroll development. For tasks, it means a group of processes that represent a component of a workload, such as calculation of pay.

The concept behind projects is to be able to identify the separate workloads that are running on the system, and then to administer and report on them individually. Projects are useful when using a chargeback method to "bill" each project for resource usage. This allows the extended accounting software to identify how much resource a particular project has used.

A user or group can belong to one or more projects and also can be assigned a default project, very similar to the standard Solaris group membership mechanism. Project administration is carried out using the file /etc/project.

Table 21 lists a number of commands that are used to administer projects and tasks.

TABLE 21 Project and Task Administration Commands

Command	Description
projects	Prints the project membership of a user.
newtask	Executes the user's default shell or specified command, placing the command in a new task that is owned by the specified project.
projadd	Adds a new project entry to the /etc/project file.
projmod	Modifies a project's information held in the /etc/project file.
projdel	Deletes a project entry from the /etc/project file.
id	Used with the -p option, prints the current project ID in addition to the user and group IDs.

Managing the LP Print Service

Many methods can be used to define a printer on a Solaris system. The following tools are available in Solaris 10 to set up and administer printers:

- **Solaris Print Manager**—A GUI that provides the ability to configure and manage printers.
- **LP print service commands**—The various LP commands available from the command line to configure and manage printers.

Although the GUI is an easy tool to use, the LP commands used from the command line offer more functionality. Table 22 lists the `lp` commands, which are the command-line means for controlling printers and print queues.

TABLE 22 Solaris `lp` Commands

Command	Description
`accept/reject`	Enables or disables any further requests for a printer or class entering the spooling area.
`cancel`	Lets the user stop the printing of information.
`enable/disable`	Enables or disables any more output from the spooler to the printer.
`lp`	The user's print command. Places information to be printed into the spooler.
`lpadmin`	Allows the configuration of the print service.
`lpmove`	Moves print requests between destinations.
`lpsched`	Starts the print service.
`lpshut`	Stops the print service.
`lpstat`	Displays the status of the print service.

There are three types of printer configurations that you need to understand:

- **Local printer**—A printer physically connected to a system and accessed from that local system.
- **Network printer**—A printer physically attached to the network with its own hostname and IP address. A network printer provides print services to clients, but is not directly connected to a print server.
- **Remote printer**—A printer that users access over the network. This printer is either physically attached to a remote system or is physically attached to the network.

A *print server* is a system that has a local printer connected to it and makes the printer available to other systems on the network. A *print client* is a remote system that can send print requests to a print server. A system becomes a print client when you install the print client software and enable access to remote printers on the system. Any networked Solaris system with a printer can be a print server, as long as the system has adequate resources to manage the printing load.

The LP Print Daemons

The `/usr/lib/lpsched`, also referred to as the scheduler daemon, is the Unix utility that is responsible for scheduling and printing in Solaris 10. Sometimes it is referred to as the `lp` daemon. The `lpsched` print daemon takes output from the spooling directory and sends it to the correct printer. `lpsched` also tracks the status of printers and filters on the print server.

The `/usr/sbin/inetd` daemon is started at bootup, and it listens for service requests on all the ports associated with each of the services listed in its configuration file. When `inetd` receives a print request, `in.lpd` is started to service the connection. The `in.lpd` daemon exits after the request has been serviced.

The Solaris LP print service performs the following functions:

- **Initialization**—Initializes a printer prior to sending it a print request to ensure that the printer is in a known state.
- **Queuing**—Schedules the print requests that are waiting to be sent to the printer.
- **Tracking**—Tracks the status of every print request. It enables the system administrator to manage all of the requests and allows users to view or cancel their own requests. It also logs errors that may have occurred during the printing process.
- **Fault notification**—This function prints the error message on the console or sends the message via email to the user.
- **Filtering**—Converts the print jobs to the appropriate type of file for the destination printer.

Most of the `lp` configuration files are located in the `/var/spool/lp` directory, except for the interface files, which are located in the `/etc/lp/interfaces` directory. A `SCHEDLOCK` file should be in `/var/spool/lp`; it is responsible for ensuring that only one instance of `lpsched` runs. You use the `lpadmin` command to add, configure, and delete printers from the system.

You can put several locally attached printers into a group called a *printer class*. When you have set up a printer class, users can then specify the class (rather than individual printers) as the destination for a print request. The first printer in the class that is free to print is used. You create printer classes with the `lpadmin` command as follows:

```
lpadmin -p <printer-name> -c <printer-class>
```

Performing System Backups and Restorations

Solaris provides the utilities listed in Table 23. They can be used to back up data from disk to removable media and restore it.

TABLE 23 Backup Utilities

Utility	Description
`tar`	Archives data to another directory, system, or medium.
`dd`	Copies data quickly.
`cpio`	Copies data from one location to another.
`pax`	Copies files and directory subtrees to a single tape. This command provides better portability than `tar` or `cpio`, so it can be used to transport files to other types of Unix systems.
`ufsdump`	Backs up all files in a file system.
`ufsrestore`	Restores some or all of the files archived with the `ufsdump` command.
`zip`	This utility creates compressed archives that are portable across various platforms, including Unix, VMS, and Windows.
Web Start flash	Combines the use of JumpStart and backup utilities to provide an easy mechanism for restoring a system to its initial state or cloning systems.
`jar`	Uses Java to provide capabilities similar to those of `tar`, `cpio`, and `zip`.

You can use the `fssnap` command to create a read-only snapshot of a file system while the file system is mounted. A *snapshot* is a point-in-time image of a file system that provides a stable and unchanging device interface for backups. Unlike `ufsdump`, a UFS snapshot enables you to keep the file system mounted and the system in multiuser mode during backups. The snapshot is stored to disk, and then you can use Solaris backup commands like `ufsdump`, `tar`, and `cpio` to back up the UFS snapshot.

Create the snapshot using the `fssnap` command as follows:

```
fssnap -F ufs -o bs=/var/tmp /export/home
```

Another way to back up your Solaris operating environment (not the data) is to create a Web Start archive. The Web Start flash archive feature can be used to back up your Solaris operating environment or to replicate an installation on a number of systems, called clone systems. While in single-user mode, you can use the `flarcreate` command to create the Web Start archive.

Section 2—Exam CX-310-202

Study these fast facts only when preparing for the Sun Certified System Administrator for the Solaris 10 Operating Environment—Part II exam (CX-310-202).

The Solaris Network Environment

In the ISO/OSI model, services that are required for communication are arranged in seven layers that build on one another. Think of the layers as steps that must be completed before you can move on to the next step and ultimately communicate between systems. Table 24 describes the function of each individual layer.

TABLE 24 Network Layers

ISO/OSI Layer	Function
Physical	Layer 1 describes the network hardware, including electrical and mechanical connections to the network.
Data link	Layer 2 splits data into frames for sending on to the physical layer and receives acknowledgement frames. It performs error checking and re-transmits frames not received correctly.
Network	Layer 3 manages the delivery of data via the data link layer and is used by the transport layer. The most common network layer protocol is IP.
Transport	Layer 4 determines how to use the network layer to provide a virtual, error-free, point-to-point connection so that host A can send data to host B and it will arrive uncorrupted and in the correct order.
Session	Layer 5 uses the transport layer to establish a connection between processes on different hosts. It handles security and creation of the session.
Presentation	Layer 6 performs functions such as text compression and code or format conversion to try to smooth out differences between hosts. It allows incompatible processes in the Application layer to communicate via the Session layer.
Application	Layer 7 is concerned with the user's and applications' view of the network. The presentation layer provides the application layer with a familiar local representation of data independent of the format used on the network.

Network Definitions and Hardware

Following are some network definitions and descriptions of networking hardware components:

- **Packet**—A packet is the unit of data to be transferred over the network, typically 1500 bytes for Ethernet.

- **Ethernet**—Ethernet is a set of standards that define the physical components and protocol that a machine uses to access the network, and the speed at which the network runs. It includes specifications for cabling, connectors, and computer interface components. Furthermore, the Ethernet standards include data link layer protocols that run on Ethernet hardware.
- **NIC**—The computer hardware that lets you connect the computer to a network is known as a *Network Interface Card (NIC)* or network adapter. Most computers nowadays come with a NIC already installed.
- **Host**—If you are an experienced Solaris user, you are no doubt familiar with the term *host*, often used as a synonym for computer or machine. From a TCP/IP perspective, only two types of entities exist on a network: routers and hosts.
- **Switch**—A multiport device that connects a number of systems on a network. Unlike the hub, the switch reduces network collisions by only sending packets to the intended destination, instead of sending them to all connected systems. Switches are now used more commonly than hubs.
- **Hubs and cabling**—Ethernet cabling is run to each system from a hub or switch. The hub does nothing more than connect all the Ethernet cables so that the computers can connect to one another. It does not boost the signal or route packets from one network to another.
- **Router**—A router is a machine that forwards packets from one network to another. In other words, the router connects networks, and the hub connects hosts.

Network Classes

There are five classes of IP addresses: A, B, C, D, and E. The following is a brief description of each class.

Class A Networks

Class A networks are used for large networks with millions of hosts, such as large multinational businesses with offices around the world. A class A network number uses the first 8 bits of the IP address as its network ID. The remaining 24 bits comprise the host part of the IP address. The values assigned to the first byte of class A network numbers fall within the range 0–127. For example, consider the IP address `75.4.10.4`. The value `75` in the first byte indicates that the host is on a class A network. The remaining bytes, `4.10.4`, establish the host address. The Internet registries assign only the first byte of a class A number. Use of the remaining three bytes is left to the discretion of the owner of the network number. Only 127 class A networks can exist; each of these networks can accommodate up to 16,777,214 hosts.

Class B Networks

Class B networks are medium-sized networks, such as universities and large businesses with many hosts. A class B network number uses 16 bits for the network number and 16 bits for host numbers. The first byte of a class B network number is in the range 128–191. In the number `129.144.50.56`, the first two bytes, `129.144`, are assigned by the Internet registries and comprise the network address. The last two bytes, `50.56`, make up the host address and are assigned at the discretion of the network's owner. A class B network can accommodate a maximum of 65,534 hosts.

Class C Networks

Class C networks are used for small networks containing fewer than 254 hosts. Class C network numbers use 24 bits for the network number and 8 bits for host numbers. A class C network number occupies the first three bytes of an IP address; only the fourth byte is assigned at the discretion of the network's owner. The first byte of a class C network number covers the range 192–223. The second and third bytes each cover the range 0–255. A typical class C address might be `192.5.2.5`, with the first three bytes, `192.5.2`, forming the network number. The final byte in this example, `5`, is the host number. A class C network can accommodate a maximum of 254 hosts.

Class D and E Networks

Class D addresses cover the range 224–239 and are used for IP multicasting as defined in RFC 988. Class E addresses cover the range 240–255 and are reserved for experimental use.

Classless Internet and Classless Inter Domain Routing (CIDR)

CIDR, also called *supernetting*, uses (typically) the first 18 bits of an IPv4 address as the network portion, leaving 14 bits to be used for the host. This implementation has meant that networks can be aggregated by routers for ease of delivery, in the same way as the telephone system uses area codes to route telephone calls. The Internet now operates in a classless mode, and has greatly increased the number of IPv4 addresses that are available. There will not be any questions in the exam on CIDR. This is included for information only.

Configuring Network Interfaces

You can configure additional interfaces at system boot or modify the original interface by having an understanding of only three files: `/etc/hostname.<interface>`, `/etc/inet/hosts`, and `/etc/inet/ipnodes`.

`/etc/hostname.<interface>`

This file defines the network interfaces on the local host. At least one `/etc/hostname.<interface>` file should exist on the local machine. The Solaris installation program creates this file for you. In the filename, `<interface>` is replaced by the device name of the primary network interface.

The file contains only one entry: the hostname or IP address associated with the network interface. For example, suppose `hme0` is the primary network interface for a machine called `system1`. The file would be called `/etc/hostname.hme0`, and the file would contain the entry `system1`. An entry for `system1` should also exist in the `/etc/inet/hosts` file.

/etc/inet/hosts

The hosts database contains details of the machines on your network. This file contains the hostnames and IPv4 addresses of the primary network interface and any other network addresses the machine must know about. When a user enters a command such as `ping xena`, the system needs to know how to get to the host named xena. The `/etc/inet/hosts` file provides a cross-reference to look up and find xena's network IP address. For compatibility with BSD-based operating systems, the file `/etc/hosts` is a symbolic link to `/etc/inet/hosts`.

Each line in the `/etc/inet/hosts` file uses the following format:

```
<address> <hostname> [nickname] [#comment]
```

Each field in this syntax is described in Table 25.

TABLE 25 `/etc/inet/hosts` File Format Fields

Field	Description
<address>	The IP address for each interface the local host must know about.
<hostname>	The hostname assigned to the machine at setup and the hostnames assigned to additional network interfaces that the local host must know about.
[*nickname*]	An optional field containing a nickname or alias for the host. More than one nickname can exist.
[# comment]	An optional field where you can include a comment.

/etc/inet/ipnodes

The `ipnodes` database also contains details of the machines on your network. This file contains the hostnames and IPv4 or IPv6 addresses of the primary network interface and any other network addresses the machine must know about. You should note that, unlike the `/etc/hosts` file, which is a link to `/etc/inet/hosts`, there is no `/etc/ipnodes` link. The syntax for the `ipnodes` file is the same as the `hosts` file.

Changing the System Hostname

To manually change the hostname of a system, modify the following four files and reboot:

- **`/etc/nodename`**—This file contains the official name when referring to a system; this is the hostname of the system.

- **/etc/hostname.<*interface*>**—This file defines the network interfaces on the local host.
- **/etc/inet/hosts**—The hosts file contains details of the machines on your network. This file contains only the IPv4 address for a host.
- **/etc/inet/ipnodes**—This file is similar to the `hosts` file, but contains IPv6 or IPv4 addresses for hosts. It is automatically populated when the Operating Environment is installed and any changes to the `/etc/inet/hosts` file should be replicated here.

You can also use the `sys-unconfig` command to change the system hostname. This method actually requires you to re-enter most of the system identification that was entered when the Solaris Operating Environment was initially installed. When you run `sys-unconfig`, the system automatically shuts down. When it is next started, you are prompted to enter the information for IP address, hostname, network mask, time zone, name service, and the root password.

Virtual File Systems, Swap Space, and Core Dumps

Physical memory is supplemented by specially configured space on the physical disk known as *swap*. Swap is configured either on a special disk partition known as a swap partition or on a swap file system. In addition to swap partitions, special files called *swap files* can also be configured in existing UFSs to provide additional swap space when needed. The Solaris virtual memory system provides transparent access to physical memory, swap, and memory-mapped objects.

Swap Space

The `swap` command is used to add, delete, and monitor swap files. The options for `swap` are shown in Table 26.

TABLE 26 swap Command Options

Option	Description
-a	Adds a specified swap area. You can also use the script `/sbin/swapadd` to add a new swap file.
-d	Deletes a specified swap area.
-l	Displays the location of your systems' swap areas.
-s	Displays a summary of the system's swap space.

The Solaris installation program automatically allocates 512 Megabytes of swap if a specific value is not specified.

Core File and Crash Dump Configuration

Core files are created when a program, or application, terminates abnormally. The default location for a core file to be written is the current working directory.

Core files are managed using the `coreadm` command. When entered with no options, `coreadm` displays the current configuration, as specified by `/etc/coreadm.conf`. The options are shown in Table 27.

TABLE 27 `coreadm` Syntax

Option	Description
`-g pattern`	Set the global core file name pattern.
`-G content`	Set the global core file content using one of the description tokens.
`-i pattern`	Set the per-process core file name pattern.
`-I content`	Set the per-process core file name to `content`.
`-d option`	Disable the specified core file option.
`-e option`	Enable the specified core file option.
`-p` *`pattern`*	Sets the per-process core file name pattern for each of the specified `pids`.
`-P` *`content`*	Sets the per-process core file content to `content`.
`-u`	Update the systemwide core file options from the configuration file `/etc/coreadm.conf`.

Core file names can be customized using a number of embedded variables. Table 28 lists the possible patterns:

TABLE 28 `coreadm` Patterns

`coreadm` Pattern	Description
`%p`	The Process ID (PID)
`%u`	Effective User ID
`%g`	Effective Group ID
`%d`	Specifies the executable file directory name.
`%f`	Executable filename
`%n`	System node name (same as running `uname -n`)
`%m`	Machine name (same as running `uname -m`)

(continues)

TABLE 28 *Continued*

coreadm Pattern	Description
%t	Decimal value of time (number of seconds since 00:00:00 January 1 1970)
-z	Specifies the name of the zone in which the process executed (zonename)
%%	A literal '%' character

A crash dump is a snapshot of the kernel memory, saved on disk, at the time a fatal system error occurred. When a serious error is encountered, the system displays an error message on the console, dumps the contents of kernel memory by default, and then reboots the system.

Normally, crash dumps are configured to use the swap partition to write the contents of memory. The `savecore` program runs when the system reboots and saves the image in a predefined location, usually `/var/crash/<hostname>` where *<hostname>* represents the name of your system.

Configuration of crash dump files is carried out with the `dumpadm` command. Running this command with no options will display the current configuration by reading the file `/etc/dumpadm.conf`.

`dumpadm` options are shown in Table 29.

TABLE 29 dumpadm Options

Option	Description
-c content-type	Modify crash dump content; valid values are `kernel` (just kernel pages), `all` (all memory pages), and `curproc` (kernel pages and currently executing process pages).
-d dump-device	Modify the dump device. This can be specified either as an absolute pathname (such as `/dev/dsk/c0t0d0s3`) or the word swap when the system will identify the best swap area to use.
-mink¦minm¦min%	Maintain minimum free space in the current savecore directory, specified either in kilobytes, megabytes, or a percentage of the total current size of the directory.
-n	Disable `savecore` from running on reboot. This is not recommended as any crash dumps would be lost.
-r root-dir	Specify a different root directory. If this option is not used, the default "/" is used.
-s savecore-dir	Specify a different savecore directory, instead of the default `/var/crash/hostname`.
-y	Enable `savecore` to run on the next reboot. This setting is used by default.

The `gcore` command can be used to create a core image of a specified running process. By default, the resulting file will be named `core.<pid>`, where *<pid>* is the `pid` of the running process.

gcore options are shown in Table 30.

TABLE 30 gcore Options

Option	Description
-c content-type	Produces image files with the specified content. This uses the same tokens as coreadm, but cannot be used with the -p or -g options.
-F	Force. This option grabs the specified process even if another process has control.
-g	Produces core image files in the global core file repository, using the global content that was configured with coreadm.
-o filename	Specify filename to be used instead of core as the first part of the name of the core image files.
-p	Produces process-specific core image files, with process-specific content, as specified by coreadm.

Network File System (NFS)

The NFS service allows computers of different architectures, running different operating systems, to share file systems across a network. Just as the mount command lets you mount a file system on a local disk, NFS lets you mount a file system that is located on another system anywhere on the network. The NFS service provides the following benefits:

- Lets multiple computers use the same files so that everyone on the network can access the same data. This eliminates the need to have redundant data on several systems.
- Reduces storage costs by having computers share applications and data.
- Provides data consistency and reliability because all users can read the same set of files.
- Makes mounting of file systems transparent to users.
- Makes accessing remote files transparent to users.
- Supports heterogeneous environments.
- Reduces system administration overhead.

Solaris 10 introduced NFS version 4, which has the following features:

- The UID and GID are represented as strings, and a new daemon, nfs4mapid, provides the mapping to numeric IDs.
- The default transport for NFS version 4 is the Remote Direct Memory Access (RDMA) protocol, a technology for memory-to-memory transfer over high speed data networks.

- All state and lock information is destroyed when a file system is unshared. In previous versions of NFS, this information was retained.
- NFS4 provides a pseudo file system to give clients access to exported objects on the NFS server.
- NFS4 is a stateful protocol where both the client and server hold information about current locks and open files. When a failure occurs, the two work together to re-establish the open, or locked files.
- NFS4 no longer uses the `mountd`, `statd`, or `nfslogd` daemons.
- NFS4 supports delegation, which allows the management responsibility of a file to be delegated to the client. Both the server and client support delegation. A client can be granted a read delegation, which can be granted to multiple clients, or a write delegation, providing exclusive access to a file.

NFS uses a number of daemons to handle its services. These services are initialized at startup from the `svc:/network/nfs/server:default` and `svc:/network/nfs/client:default` startup service management functions. The most important NFS daemons are outlined in Table 31.

TABLE 31 NFS Daemons

Daemon	Description
`nfsd`	This daemon handles file system exporting and file access requests from remote systems. An NFS server runs multiple instances of this daemon. This daemon is usually invoked at the `multi-user-server` milestone and is started by the `svc:/network/nfs/server:default` service identifier.
`mountd`	This daemon handles mount requests from NFS clients. This daemon also provides information about which file systems are mounted by which clients. Use the `showmount` command to view this information. This daemon is usually invoked at the `multi-user-server` milestone and is started by the `svc:/network/nfs/server:default` service identifier. This daemon is not used in NFS version 4.
`lockd`	This daemon runs on the NFS server and NFS client, and provides file-locking services in NFS. This daemon is started by the `svc:/network/nfs/client` service identifier at the `multi-user` milestone.
`statd`	This daemon runs on the NFS server and NFS client, and interacts with `lockd` to provide the crash and recovery functions for the locking services on NFS. This daemon is started by the `svc:/network/nfs/client` service identifier at the `multi-user` milestone. This daemon is not used in NFS version 4.
`rpcbind`	This daemon facilitates the initial connection between the client and the server.

TABLE 31 *Continued*

Daemon	Description
`nfsmapid`	A new daemon that maps to and from NFS v4 owner and group identification and UID and GID numbers. It uses entries in the `passwd` and `group` files to carry out the mapping, and also references `/etc/nsswitch.conf` to determine the order of access.
`nfs4cbd`	A new client side daemon that listens on each transport and manages the callback functions to the NFS server.
`nfslogd`	This daemon provides operational logging to the Solaris NFS server. NFS logging uses the configuration file `/etc/nfs/nfslog.conf`. The `nfslogd` daemon is not used in NFS version 4.

Autofs

When a network contains even a moderate number of systems, all trying to mount file systems from each other, managing NFS can quickly become a nightmare. The `Autofs` facility, also called the automounter, is designed to handle such situations by providing a method in which remote directories are mounted only when they are being used.

When a request is made to access a file system at an `Autofs` mount point, the system goes through the following steps:

1. `Autofs` intercepts the request.
2. `Autofs` sends a message to the `automountd` daemon for the requested file system to be mounted.
3. `automountd` locates the file system information in a map and performs the mount.
4. `Autofs` allows the intercepted request to proceed.
5. `Autofs` unmounts the file system after a period of inactivity.

Managing Storage Volumes

Solaris Volume Manager (SVM), formally called Solstice DiskSuite, comes bundled with the Solaris 10 operating system and uses virtual disks, called *volumes*, to manage physical disks and their associated data. A volume is functionally identical to a physical disk in the view of an application. You may also hear volumes referred to as virtual or pseudo devices. SVM uses metadevice objects, of which there are four main types: metadevices, state database replicas, disk sets, and hot spare pools. These are described in Table 32.

TABLE 32 SVM Objects

Object	Description
Volume	A volume is a group of physical slices that appear to the system as a single, logical device. A volume is used to increase storage capacity and increase data availability. The various types of volumes are described next.
State database	A database that stores information about the state of the SVM configuration. Each state database is a collection of multiple, replicated database copies. Each copy is referred to as a state database replica. SVM cannot operate until you have created the state database and its replicas.
Disk sets	A set of disk drives containing state database replicas, volumes, and hot spares that can be shared exclusively, but not at the same time, by multiple hosts. If one host fails, another host can take over the failed host's disk set. This type of fail-over configuration is referred to as a clustered environment.
Hot spare pool	A collection of slices (hot spares) reserved for automatic substitution in case of slice failure in either a submirror or RAID 5 metadevice. Hot spares are used to increase data availability.

The types of SVM volumes you can create using Solaris Management Console or the SVM command-line utilities are concatenations, stripes, concatenated stripes, mirrors, and RAID5 volumes. SVM volumes can be any of the following:

- **Concatenation**—Concatenations work much the way the Unix `cat` command is used to concatenate two or more files to create one larger file. If partitions are concatenated, the addressing of the component blocks is done on the components sequentially, which means that data is written to the first available stripe until it is full, then moves to the next available stripe. The file system can use the entire concatenation, even though it spreads across multiple disk drives. This type of volume provides no data redundancy and the entire volume fails if a single slice fails.
- **Stripe**—A stripe is similar to a concatenation, except that the addressing of the component blocks is interlaced on the slices rather than sequentially. In other words, all disks are accessed at the same time in parallel. Striping is used to gain performance. When data is striped across disks, multiple disk heads and possibly multiple controllers can access data simultaneously. *Interlace* refers to the size of the logical data chunks on a stripe. Different interlace values can increase performance.
- **Concatenated stripe**—A concatenated stripe is a stripe that has been expanded by concatenating additional striped slices.
- **Mirror**—A mirror is composed of one or more stripes or concatenations. The volumes that are mirrored are called submirrors. SVM makes duplicate copies of the data located on multiple physical disks, and presents one virtual disk to the application. All disk writes are duplicated; disk reads come from one of the underlying submirrors. A mirror replicates all writes to a single logical device (the mirror) and then to multiple

devices (the submirrors) while distributing read operations. This provides redundancy of data in the event of a disk or hardware failure.

- **RAID 5**—Stripes the data across multiple disks to achieve better performance. In addition to striping, RAID 5 replicates data by using parity information. In the case of missing data, the data can be regenerated using available data and the parity information. A RAID 5 metadevice is composed of multiple slices. Some space is allocated to parity information and is distributed across all slices in the RAID5 metadevice. The striped metadevice performance is better than the RAID 5 metadevice, but it doesn't provide data protection (redundancy).

RAID (Redundant Array of Inexpensive Disks)

When describing SVM volumes, it's common to describe which level of RAID the volume conforms to. Usually these disks are housed together in a cabinet and referred to as an array. There are several RAID levels, each referring to a method of distributing data while ensuring data redundancy. These levels are not ratings, but rather classifications of functionality. Different RAID levels offer dramatic differences in performance, data availability, and data integrity depending on the specific I/O environment. Table 33 describes the various levels of RAID.

TABLE 33 RAID Levels

RAID Level	Description
0	Striped Disk Array without Fault Tolerance.
1	Maintains duplicate sets of all data on separate disk drives. Commonly referred to as mirroring.
2	Data striping and bit interleave. Data is written across each drive in succession one bit at a time. Checksum data is recorded in a separate drive. This method is very slow for disk writes and is seldom used today because ECC is embedded in almost all modern disk drives.
3	Data striping with bit interleave and parity checking. Data is striped across a set of disks one byte at a time, and parity is generated and stored on a dedicated disk. The parity information is used to re-create data in the event of a disk failure.
4	Same as level 3 except data is striped across a set of disks at a block level. Parity is generated and stored on a dedicated disk.
5	Unlike RAID 3 and 4 where parity is stored on one disk, both parity and data are striped across a set of disks.
6	Similar to RAID 5, but with additional parity information written to recover data if two drives fail.
1+0	Combination of RAID 1 (mirror) for resilience and RAID 0 for performance. The benefit of this RAID level is that a failed disk will only render the unit unavailable, and not the entire stripe.

The State Database

The SVM state database contains vital information on the configuration and status of all volumes, hot spares, and disk sets. There are normally multiple copies of the state database, called replicas, and it is recommended that state database replicas be located on different physical disks, or even controllers if possible, to provide added resilience.

The state database, together with its replicas, guarantees the integrity of the state database by using a *majority consensus algorithm*.

The state database is created and managed using the `metadb` command. Table 34 shows the `metadb` options.

TABLE 34 `metadb` Options

Option	Description
`-a`	Attach a new database device.
`-c number`	Specifies the number of state database replicas to be placed on each device. The default is 1.
`-d`	Delete all replicas on the specified disk slice.
`-f`	Used to create the initial state database. It is also used to force the deletion of the last replica.
`-h`	Displays a usage message.
`-i`	Inquire about the status of the replicas.
`-k system-file`	Specifies a different file where replica information should be written. The default is `/kernel/drv/md.conf`.
`-l length`	Specifies the length of each replica. The default is `8192` blocks.
`-p`	Specifies that the system file (default `/kernel/drv/md.conf`) is updated with entries from `/etc/lvm/mddb.cf`.
`-s setname`	Specifies the name of the diskset to which the `metadb` command applies.

Controlling Access and Configuring System Messaging

Role-Based Access Control (RBAC) and system logging are related in that they are involved in the securing and monitoring of systems in a Solaris environment.

Role-Based Access Control (RBAC)

With role-based access control (RBAC) in the Solaris 10 operating environment, administrators can assign limited administrative capabilities to non-root users. This is achieved through three features:

- **Authorizations**—User rights that grant access to a restricted function
- **Execution profiles**—Bundling mechanisms for grouping authorizations and commands with special attributes; for example, user and group IDs or superuser ID
- **Roles**—Special types of user accounts intended for performing a set of administrative tasks

RBAC relies on the following four databases to provide users access to privileged operations:

- **`user_attr` (extended user attributes database)**—Associates users and roles with authorizations and profiles
- **`auth_attr` (authorization attributes database)**—Defines authorizations and their attributes and identifies the associated help file
- **`prof_attr` (rights profile attributes database)**—Defines profiles, lists the profile's assigned authorizations, and identifies the associated help file
- **`exec_attr` (profile attributes database)**—Defines the privileged operations assigned to a profile

Naming Services

The information handled by a name service includes the following:

- System (host) names and addresses
- Usernames
- Passwords
- Access permissions

Table 35 describes the name services available in Solaris 10.

TABLE 35 Name Services

Name Service	Description
/etc files	The original Unix naming system.
NIS	The Network Information Service.
NIS+	The Network Information Service Plus.
DNS	The Domain Name System.
LDAP	Lightweight Directory Access Protocol.

/etc Files

/etc files are the traditional Unix way of maintaining information about hosts, users, passwords, groups, and automount maps, to name just a few. These files are text files located on each individual system that can be edited using the vi editor or the text editor within CDE.

NIS

The NIS, formerly called the Yellow Pages (YP), is a distributed database system that allows the system administrator to administer the configuration of many hosts from a central location. Common configuration information, which would have to be maintained separately on each host in a network without NIS, can be stored and maintained in a central location, and then propagated to all the nodes in the network. NIS stores information about workstation names and addresses, users, the network itself, and network services.

The systems within an NIS network are configured in the following ways:

- Master server
- Slave servers
- Clients of NIS servers

The name service switch controls how a client workstation or application obtains network information. Each workstation has a name service switch file in its /etc directory. In every system's /etc directory, you'll find templates for the nsswitch.conf file. These templates are described in Table 36.

TABLE 36 Name Service Switch Template Files

Name	Description
nsswitch.files	This template file is used when local files in the /etc directory are to be used and no name service exists.
nsswitch.nis	This template file uses the NIS database as the primary source of all information except the passwd, group, automount, and aliases maps. These are directed to use the local /etc files first, and then the NIS databases.
nsswitch.nisplus	This template file uses the NIS+ database as the primary source of all information except the passwd, group, automount, and aliases tables. These are directed to use the local /etc files first, and then the NIS+ databases.
nsswitch.dns	This template file searches the local /etc files for all entries except the hosts entry. The hosts entry is directed to use DNS for lookup.
nsswitch.ldap	This template file uses LDAP as the primary source of all information except the passwd, group, automount, and aliases tables. These are directed to use the local /etc files first, and then the LDAP databases.

The name service switch file contains a list of more than 19 types of network information, called databases, with their name service sources for resolution and the order in which the sources are to be searched. Table 37 lists valid sources that can be specified in this file.

TABLE 37 Database Sources for Services in /etc/nsswitch.conf

Source	Description
files	Refers to the client's local /etc files
nisplus	Refers to an NIS+ table
nis	Refers to an NIS table
user	Applies to printers only and specifies that printer information be obtained from the ${HOME}/.printers file
dns	Applies only to the hosts entry
ldap	Refers to a dictionary information tree (DIT)
compat	Supports an old style [+] syntax that was used in the passwd and group information

NIS+

NIS+ is similar to NIS, but with more features. NIS+ is not an extension of NIS, but a new system. It was designed to replace NIS.

NIS addresses the administrative requirements of small-to-medium client/server computing networks—those with less than a few hundred clients. Some sites with thousands of users find

NIS adequate as well. NIS+ is designed for the now-prevalent larger networks in which systems are spread across remote sites in various time zones and in which clients number in the thousands. In addition, the information stored in networks today changes much more frequently, and NIS had to be updated to handle this environment. Lastly, systems today require a high level of security, and NIS+ addresses many security issues that NIS did not.

Remember that NIS+ is being discontinued and will not be part of a future Solaris release.

DNS

DNS is the name service used by the Internet and other Transmission Control Protocol/ Internet Protocol (TCP/IP) networks. It was developed so that workstations on the network could be identified by common names instead of numerical Internet addresses. DNS is a program that converts domain names to their IP addresses. Without it, users have to remember numbers instead of words to get around the Internet. The process of finding a computer's IP address by using its hostname as an index is referred to as name-to-address resolution, or mapping.

Lightweight Directory Access Protocol (LDAP)

LDAP is the latest name-lookup service to be added to Solaris and is expected to replace NIS and NIS+ in the future. Specifically, LDAP is a directory service. A directory service is like a database, but tends to contain more descriptive, attribute-based information. The information in a directory is generally read, not written.

Solaris Zones

Zones provide a virtual operating system environment within a single physical instance of Solaris 10. Applications can run in an isolated and secure environment. This isolation prevents an application running in one zone from monitoring or affecting an application running in a different zone.

There are two types of zones, *global* and *non-global*. Think of a global zone as the server itself, the traditional view of a Solaris system as we all know it, whereas a non-global zone is created from the global zone and also managed by it. You can have up to 8,192 non-global zones on a single physical system, Applications running in a non-global zone are isolated from applications running in a different non-global zone, allowing multiple versions of the same application to run on the same physical server.

A zone is created using the `zonecfg` command. With this command you can do the following:

- Create or delete a zone configuration
- Add or remove resources in a configuration

- Set the properties for a resource in the configuration
- Query and verify a configuration
- Commit (save) a configuration
- Revert to a previous configuration
- Exit from a `zonecfg` session

Advanced Installation Procedures

This section concentrates on two facilities to make it easier to install the Solaris operating environment on multiple systems. JumpStart and Solaris Flash allow identical systems to be installed automatically without the need for manual intervention. Each of these is covered in the following sections.

JumpStart

JumpStart has three main components:

- **Boot and Client Identification Services**—Provided by a networked boot server, these services provide the information that a JumpStart client needs to boot using the network.
- **Installation Services**—Provided by a networked install server, Installation Services provide an image of the Solaris operating environment that a JumpStart client uses as its media source. The image is normally a disk file located on the install server.
- **Configuration Services**—Provided by a networked configuration server, these services provide information that a JumpStart client uses to partition disks and create file systems, add or remove Solaris packages, and perform other configuration tasks.

Table 38 lists and describes some JumpStart commands.

TABLE 38 JumpStart Commands

Command	Description
`setup_install_server`	Sets up an install server to provide the operating system to the client during a JumpStart installation.
`add_to_install_server`	Copies additional packages within a product tree on the Solaris 10 Software and Solaris 10 Languages CDs to the local disk on an existing install server.

(continues)

TABLE 38 *Continued*

Command	Description
`add_install_client`	Adds network installation information about a system to an install or boot server's `/etc` files so that the system can install over the network.
`rm_install_client`	Removes JumpStart clients that were previously set up for network installation.
`check`	Validates the information in the rules file.
`pfinstall`	Performs a "dry run" installation to test the profile.
`patchadd -C`	Adds patches to the files located in the miniroot (that is, `Solaris_10/Tools/Boot`) on an image of an installation CD image created by `setup_install_server`. This facility enables you to patch Solaris installation commands and other miniroot-specific commands.

Solaris Flash

The main feature of Solaris Flash is to provide a method to store a snapshot of the Solaris operating environment complete with all installed patches and applications. This snapshot is referred to as the Flash archive and the system that the archive is taken from is referred to as the master machine.

A Flash installation can be used to perform an initial installation or to update an existing installation.

A Flash archive is created with the `flarcreate` command. You can create a Flash archive that contains a full snapshot of the system, or a differential archive containing only the changes that have been applied when compared to an existing Flash archive. Flash archives are administered with the `flar` command.

With the `flar` command, you can

- Extract information from an archive.
- Split archives.
- Combine archives.

When using JumpStart to install from a Flash archive, only the following keywords can be used in the profile:

- **`archive_location`**
- **`install_type`**—For a full flash archive install, specify this option as `Flash_install`. For a differential Flash archive, specify `flash_update`.

- **partitioning**—Only the keyword values of `explicit` or `existing` must be used.
- **filesys**—The keyword value `auto` must not be used.
- **forced_deployment**
- **local_customization**
- **no_content_check**—Used only for a differential flash archive.
- **no_master_check**—Used only for a differential flash archive.
- **package**—Only used for a full flash installation; cannot be used with a differential flash archive.
- **root_device**

Chapter Practice Exam

This exam consists of 60 questions reflecting the material covered in the chapters. The questions are representative of the types of questions you should expect to see on the Solaris exam; however, they are not intended to match exactly what is on the exam. Questions 1–33 pertain to exam CX-310-200 and questions 34–56 pertain to the CX-310-202 exam.

Some of the questions require that you choose the best possible answer. Often, you are asked to identify the best course of action to take in a given situation. The questions require that you read them carefully and thoroughly before you attempt to answer them. It is strongly recommended that you treat this practice exam as if you were taking the actual exam. Time yourself, read carefully, and answer all of the questions to the best of your ability.

The answers to all of the questions appear in the section following the exam. Check your answers against those in the answer section, and then read the explanations provided. You may also want to return to the chapters in the book to review the material associated with your incorrect answers.

Practice Exam Questions

1. The kernel consists of which of the following?

   ❍ **A.** The shell and environment variables

   ❍ **B.** A small static core and many dynamically loadable modules

   ❍ **C.** Boot PROM and the operating system

   ❍ **D.** System milestones

2. What are the characteristics of changing to the single user run level? Choose all that apply.

   ❍ **A.** Equivalent to run level S.

   ❍ **B.** Shutdown state.

   ❍ **C.** All users are logged out.

   ❍ **D.** File systems remain mounted.

3. Which daemon is responsible for maintaining system services?

   ❍ **A.** `init`

   ❍ **B.** `inetd`

   ❍ **C.** `startd`

   ❍ **D.** `svc.startd`

4. Which of the following is a service identifier used to identify a specific service within the Solaris Management Facility?

   ❍ **A.** milestone

   ❍ **B.** `lrc:/etc/rc3.d/S90samba`

   ❍ **C.** `svc:/system/filesystem/local:default`

   ❍ **D.** `/var/svc/manifest/milestone/multi-user.xml`

5. Which service state indicates that a service is not configured to startup and run?

   ❍ **A.** uninitialized

   ❍ **B.** offline

   ❍ **C.** disabled

   ❍ **D.** degraded

6. Which of the following restricts the set of operations that users are allowed to perform at the OpenBoot prompt?

❍ **A.** security-password

❍ **B.** set-security

❍ **C.** set-secure

❍ **D.** security-mode

7. The bootstrap procedure consists of which of the following basic phases? Choose all that apply.

❍ **A.** Load the kernel.

❍ **B.** Automatically boot the system if the auto-boot? parameter is set to true.

❍ **C.** Hardware power-up.

❍ **D.** Execute power-on self-test (POST).

8. What is the best command to find your hardware platform and current operating system release?

❍ **A.** `init -q`

❍ **B.** `sysdef`

❍ **C.** `uname -a`

❍ **D.** `arch`

9. What information will you need during the installation process? Choose all that apply.

❍ **A.** IP address

❍ **B.** Product code

❍ **C.** Timezone

❍ **D.** Root password

10. Which of the following conditions will prevent a patch from being installed? Choose all that apply.

❍ **A.** The patch being installed requires another patch that is not installed.

❍ **B.** The patch is incompatible with another, already installed patch.

❍ **C.** The patch was removed.

❍ **D.** The patch version is not the most up-to-date version.

11. What does the `pkgchk` command do?

❍ **A.** Displays information about software packages installed on the system

❍ **B.** Stores answers in a response file so that they can be supplied automatically during an installation

❍ **C.** Determines the accuracy of a software package installation

❍ **D.** Used to determine whether the contents or attributes of a file have changed since it was installed with the package

12. In the Solaris Management Console, what is the field that corresponds to the maximum number of days an account can go without being accessed before it is automatically locked?

❍ **A.** User Must Keep for:

❍ **B.** Max Inactive

❍ **C.** User Must Change Within:

❍ **D.** Expires if Not Used for:

13. Respectively, what are the user initialization files for the Bourne, Korn, and C shell?

❍ **A.** `.bshrc`, `.kshrc`, `.cshrc`.

❍ **B.** `.exrc`, `.profile`, `.login`.

❍ **C.** `.profile`, `.profile`, `.login`.

❍ **D.** `.profile` works for all shells.

14. Which of the following file systems can reside on a local physical disk? Choose all that apply.

❍ **A.** HSFS

❍ **B.** TMPFS

❍ **C.** UFS

❍ **D.** NFS

15. Which file system block contains information about the file system?

❍ **A.** Boot block

❍ **B.** Superblock

❍ **C.** Inode

❍ **D.** Data block

16. To view the capacity of all file systems mounted on a system, which command should you use?

 - ❍ **A.** `du -a`
 - ❍ **B.** `ls`
 - ❍ **C.** `df`
 - ❍ **D.** `mountall`

17. Which command is a friendlier way to create a file system?

 - ❍ **A.** `mkfs`
 - ❍ **B.** `newfs`
 - ❍ **C.** `fsck`
 - ❍ **D.** `mknod`

18. Which of the following commands cannot be used to copy file systems?

 - ❍ **A.** `dd`
 - ❍ **B.** `ufsdump`
 - ❍ **C.** `fsck`
 - ❍ **D.** `volcopy`

19. Which command might you use to see which process is preventing a file system from being unmounted?

 - ❍ **A.** `ps`
 - ❍ **B.** `mountall`
 - ❍ **C.** `fsck`
 - ❍ **D.** `fuser`

20. Which of the following is an easily guessed password? Choose all that apply.

 - ❍ **A.** Britney
 - ❍ **B.** TnKOTb!
 - ❍ **C.** Dietcoke
 - ❍ **D.** ZunSp0ts

21. What would a default umask of 023 set as default permissions on new files?

❍ **A.** Owner no rights; Group write only; World write and execute only

❍ **B.** Owner read, write, execute; Group read only; World execute only

❍ **C.** Owner read, write; Group read only; World read only

❍ **D.** Owner no rights; Group read and execute only; World read only

22. The second field of the `/etc/group` file is used to store the group password. What is the effect of a group password?

❍ **A.** Access to each group is granted only to users in a group.

❍ **B.** Users who are not members of the group can access it if they know the password.

❍ **C.** Users who are primary members of the group are required to use the group password to gain access to the group.

❍ **D.** Users who are secondary members of the group are required to use the group password to gain access to the group.

23. What would you use the `prstat` command to do? Choose all that apply.

❍ **A.** Get information on all the processes for a particular user.

❍ **B.** Determine disk usage.

❍ **C.** Determine which processes are consuming the most CPU cycles.

❍ **D.** Change system run levels.

24. Which of the following signals kills a process unconditionally?

❍ **A.** `SIGHUP`

❍ **B.** `SIGKILL`

❍ **C.** `SIGTERM`

❍ **D.** `SIGQUIT`

25. What does the `at` command do?

❍ **A.** Stands for "all terminate"; kills all nonroot processes.

❍ **B.** Runs a batch job once at a specific time in the future.

❍ **C.** Sets a repeating batch job to run at a specific time of day.

❍ **D.** Displays the time of last login for a user.

26. If a nonroot user does not want to use the system default printer, how can that user select another printer to be the default? Choose all that apply.

- ❍ **A.** `lpadmin`
- ❍ **B.** Specify the printer in the `$HOME/.printers` file
- ❍ **C.** `lpstat -d` *`<printername>`*
- ❍ **D.** Set the `LPDEST` variable
- ❍ **E.** `/usr/sadm/admin/bin.printmgr`

27. Which command(s) could tell you if a print queue is down? Choose all that apply.

- ❍ **A.** `lpadmin`
- ❍ **B.** `lpstat`
- ❍ **C.** `admintool`
- ❍ **D.** `Print Manager`

28. What does the command `tar xvf /tmp/backup.tar` do? Choose all that apply.

- ❍ **A.** Extracts the absolute paths of the archives in `/tmp/backup.tar`, creating new directories and overwriting files if necessary
- ❍ **B.** Prints a verbose listing of the files and directories in `/tmp/backup.tar`
- ❍ **C.** Compresses `/tmp/backup.tar`
- ❍ **D.** Archives the current directory and its contents to `/tmp/backup.tar`

29. Which of the following statements about the `dd` command is false?

- ❍ **A.** It quickly converts and copies files with different data formats.
- ❍ **B.** It can be used to copy an entire file system or partition to tape.
- ❍ **C.** It can compress files quickly and efficiently.
- ❍ **D.** It can be used to read standard input from another program to write to tape.

30. To what do the directories in `/proc` correspond?

- ❍ **A.** File systems
- ❍ **B.** Physical and virtual devices attached to the system
- ❍ **C.** Active process IDs
- ❍ **D.** Active UIDs

31. In Solaris, each disk device is described by which naming conventions? Choose all that apply.

- ❍ **A.** Instance name
- ❍ **B.** Physical device name
- ❍ **C.** Virtual name
- ❍ **D.** Logical device name

32. Which statements about Solaris Management Console are false?

- ❍ **A.** It provides single console, single login administration of multiple Solaris systems.
- ❍ **B.** It provides an easy-to-navigate GUI console.
- ❍ **C.** It has a command-line interface in addition to the GUI controls.
- ❍ **D.** It uses Role-Based Access Control.

33. What can the SMC Toolbox Editor do? Choose all that apply.

- ❍ **A.** Suspend, resume, monitor, and control processes.
- ❍ **B.** Install software packages and patches.
- ❍ **C.** Schedule, start, and manage jobs.
- ❍ **D.** View and manage mounts, shares, and usage information.

34. Which of the following is a hands-off method to automatically install groups of identical systems?

- ❍ **A.** JumpStart
- ❍ **B.** Custom JumpStart
- ❍ **C.** Interactive Installation
- ❍ **D.** Network Install
- ❍ **E.** Solaris Flash

35. In the ISO/OSI network reference model, what is the Presentation layer described as?

- ❍ **A.** It manages the delivery of data via the data link layer and is used by the transport layer. The most common network layer protocol is IP.
- ❍ **B.** It determines how to use the network layer to provide a virtual, error-free, point-to-point connection so that host A can send messages to host B and they will arrive uncorrupted and in the correct order.
- ❍ **C.** It uses the transport layer to establish a connection between processes on different hosts. It handles security and creation of the session.
- ❍ **D.** It performs functions such as text compression and code or format conversion to try to smooth out differences between hosts.

36. Which of the following usually spans more than one network?

- ❍ **A.** Switch
- ❍ **B.** Router
- ❍ **C.** NIC
- ❍ **D.** Host

37. How many IP addresses are available to be assigned within a Class C network?

- ❍ **A.** 254
- ❍ **B.** 24
- ❍ **C.** 65,534
- ❍ **D.** None

38. Which pseudo file system resides on a physical disk?

- ❍ **A.** procfs
- ❍ **B.** swapfs
- ❍ **C.** tmpfs
- ❍ **D.** fdfs

39. Which command is used to create an install server for use with a custom JumpStart installation?

- ❍ **A.** `check`
- ❍ **B.** `setup_install_server`
- ❍ **C.** `add_install_client`
- ❍ **D.** `setup_install_server -b`

40. Network File systems that are mounted read-write or that contain executable files should always be mounted with which of the following options? Choose all that apply.

- ❍ **A.** `hard`
- ❍ **B.** `intr`
- ❍ **C.** `soft`
- ❍ **D.** `nointr`

41. When you share a file system across the network for the first time, the NFS server must be started. Which command will achieve this?

❍ **A.** `share`

❍ **B.** `svcadm enable nfs/server`

❍ **C.** `mountall`

❍ **D.** `svcs -l nfs/server`

42. Which of the following provides a means for selective access to administrative capabilities? Choose all that apply.

❍ **A.** Giving a user the root password

❍ **B.** Use of the `sudo` command

❍ **C.** RBAC

❍ **D.** usermod

43. You have created a metadevice, `d30`, which is a mirror of the root filesystem. Which command carries out the necessary setup to complete the operation, by editing `/etc/vfstab` and `/etc/system`?

❍ **A.** `metadb`

❍ **B.** `metainit`

❍ **C.** `metaroot`

❍ **D.** `metaclear`

44. How would you determine the NIS server used by a given machine?

❍ **A.** Use `ypwhich`.

❍ **B.** Use `ypcat`.

❍ **C.** Look in the `/etc/nsswitch.conf` file.

❍ **D.** Use `nisls`.

45. What file would you edit to make the local `/etc/hosts` file take precedence over DNS or NIS host lookups?

❍ **A.** `/etc/inetd.conf`

❍ **B.** `/etc/resolv.conf`

❍ **C.** `/etc/defaultrouter`

❍ **D.** `/etc/nsswitch.conf`

46. Which of the following is the method of automatically installing groups of identical systems without any manual intervention?

- ❍ **A.** JumpStart
- ❍ **B.** Custom JumpStart
- ❍ **C.** Interactive Installation
- ❍ **D.** WAN Boot Install

47. What command would you use to do a dry run installation to test a JumpStart profile?

- ❍ **A.** `check`
- ❍ **B.** `patchadd -C`
- ❍ **C.** `fsck`
- ❍ **D.** `pfinstall`

48. Which of the following files would *not* be used to manually change the hostname of a Solaris system?

- ❍ **A.** `/etc/inet/hosts`
- ❍ **B.** `/etc/defaultrouter`
- ❍ **C.** `/etc/nodename`
- ❍ **D.** `/etc/net/ticlts/hosts`

49. Which command would you use to configure the behavior of core files?

- ❍ **A.** `savecore`
- ❍ **B.** `svcadm restart svc:/system/coreadm:default`
- ❍ **C.** `coreadm`
- ❍ **D.** `admcore`

50. Which command would you use to modify the default crash dump device?

- ❍ **A.** `crashadm`
- ❍ **B.** `dumpadm`
- ❍ **C.** `/var/crash`
- ❍ **D.** `gcore`

51. Which of the following would assign the role adminusr to the user bill?

❍ **A.** `rolemod adminusr -u bill`

❍ **B.** `moduser bill -R adminusr`

❍ **C.** `usermod -R adminusr bill`

❍ **D.** `modrole -u bill -r adminusr`

52. You have created a new zone called `apps` and need to check on its current state. Which command will display the state of this zone?

❍ **A.** `zoneadm -z apps list -v`

❍ **B.** `zlogin apps`

❍ **C.** `zlogin -C apps`

❍ **D.** `zoneadm -z apps install`

53. Which of the following is not a RBAC database?

❍ **A.** `/etc/security/prof_attr`

❍ **B.** `/etc/security/exec_attr`

❍ **C.** `/etc/security/user_attr`

❍ **D.** `/etc/security/auth_attr`

54. Where does the configuration file reside that handles NFS logging?

❍ **A.** `/etc/nfslog`

❍ **B.** `/etc/nfs/nfslog.conf`

❍ **C.** `/etc/inetd.conf`

❍ **D.** `/etc/default/nfs`

55. This RAID configuration maintains duplicate sets of all data on separate disk drives.

❍ **A.** RAID 0

❍ **B.** RAID 1

❍ **C.** RAID 5

❍ **D.** RAID 53

56. This RAID configuration is where data and parity are striped across a set of disks.

- ❍ **A.** RAID 0
- ❍ **B.** RAID 1
- ❍ **C.** RAID 5
- ❍ **D.** RAID 10

57. This command is used to add a client to the LDAP naming service.

- ❍ **A.** `add_ldap`
- ❍ **B.** `ldapclient`
- ❍ **C.** `add_client ldap`
- ❍ **D.** `ldapinstall`

58. You have made a modification to your `syslog` configuration to allow extra messages to be logged. Which command will force the `syslogd` daemon to re-read the configuration file and make the change active?

- ❍ **A.** `svcs -l system/system-log`
- ❍ **B.** `svcadm disable system/system-log`
- ❍ **C.** `svcadm refresh system/system-log`
- ❍ **D.** `syslogd -HUP`

59. You have inherited a system and you are examining the custom JumpStart file to provide a hands-off installation. One of the parameters specifies `archive_location` and lists an NFS mount as its parameter. What would this tell you about the custom JumpStart process?

- ❍ **A.** The system being installed is being used as a file server and will share the specified file system
- ❍ **B.** The installation will be making use of a Solaris Flash Archive and the location of the Flash Archive is contained in the parameter
- ❍ **C.** The system being installed will use this location to backup its existing file system before the installation commences
- ❍ **D.** This points to the install server where the Solaris CD images can be found

60. Your system currently has four state database replicas installed, two on each disk. What happens to a running system if one of the disk drives fails and you lose two of the state database replicas?

 - ❍ **A.** The system remains running
 - ❍ **B.** The system panics
 - ❍ **C.** The system will not start SVM the next time it boots and must be booted into single user mode.
 - ❍ **D.** The system hangs

Practice Exam Answers

1. **B.** The kernel consists of a small static core and many dynamically loadable kernel modules. Many kernel modules are loaded automatically at boot time, but for efficiency, others—such as device drivers—are loaded from the disk as needed by the kernel. The shell and environmental variables are user specific and are loaded when each user logs in. The boot PROM is firmware and is considered part of the hardware. The system milestones are part of the operating system, not the kernel. For more information, see Chapter 3, "Perform System Boot and Shutdown Procedures."

2. **A, C, D.** The single-user milestone, also called run level s, is the single-user (system administrator) state. Only root is allowed to log in at the console, and any users logged in are logged out when entering this run level. All file systems previously mounted remain mounted and accessible. All services except the most basic operating system services are shut down in an orderly manner. The shutdown state is referred to as run level 0. For more information, see Chapter 3, "System Startup and Shutdown."

3. **D.** The `svc.startd` daemon is responsible for maintaining the system services and ensures that the system boots to the correct milestone.

4. **B, C.** `lrc:/etc/rc3.d/S90samba` is the FRMI for a legacy service. `svc:/system/filesystem/local:default` is an example of service identifier within the SMF. A milestone is a special type of service made up of a defined set of other services, but does not define a specific service. `/var/svc/manifest/milestone/multi-user.xml` describes the dependencies for a milestone.

5. **B.** Disabled indicates that the service is not configured to start up and is not running. Uninitialized is the state of a service before the configuration has been read. Offline indicates that the service is not yet running, but is configured to run. Degraded indicates the service is enabled, but is running at a limited capacity.

6. **D.** `security-mode` restricts the set of operations that users are allowed to perform at the OpenBoot prompt. `security-password` sets the password, but does not set the security mode that restricts users. `set-security` and `set-secure` are not OpenBoot NVRAM variables. For more information, see Chapter 3.

7. **B, C, D.** On most Ultra-based systems, the bootstrap procedure consists of some basic phases. First, the system hardware is powered on and the system firmware (PROM) executes a power-on self-test (POST). After the tests have been completed successfully, the firmware attempts to autoboot if the appropriate OpenBoot configuration variable (auto-boot?) has been set to true. Otherwise it enters interactive OpenBoot command mode. The bootstrap procedure does not include loading the kernel. For more information, see Chapter 3.

8. **C.** The `uname` command, with the `-a` flag set, displays basic information currently available from the system, including hardware platform and current operating system release. The `sysdef` command outputs the current system definition such as hardware devices, loadable modules, and kernel parameters. The `init` command is used to start processes from information in the `inittab` file. The `arch` command displays the system's application architecture. For more information, see Chapter 2, "Installing the Solaris 10 Operating Environment."

9. **A, C, D.** The Solaris Installation program prompts you for the following: hostname, IP address, Subnet mask, whether to install Ipv6, name service, whether to use Kerberos network authentication system, timezone, root password, and language. For more information, see Chapter 2.

10. **A, B.** A patch might not be installed if it requires another patch that is not installed or if the patch is incompatible with another, previously installed patch. For more information, see Chapter 2.

11. **C, D.** The `pkgchk` command checks the accuracy of a software package installation and can be used to determine whether the contents or attributes of a file have changed since it was installed with the package. Use the `pkginfo` command to display software package information and use `pkgask` to store answers for an interactive installation. For more information, see Chapter 2.

12. **D.** "Expires if Not Used for:" is the correct option. Select the number of days that can elapse before the user's password expires if the user does not log in to this account. The "User Must Keep for:" field specifies the minimum number of days a user must wait before changing a password or reusing a previous password. The "User Must Change Within:" field allows you to set the maximum number of days that can elapse before a user must change his password. Max Inactive is an invalid field and does not appear in the SMC. For more information, see Chapter 4, "User and Security Administration."

13. **C.** Bourne and Korn shells initialize with a `.profile`, whereas the C shell uses `.login` and `.cshrc`. For more information, see Chapter 4.

14. **A, C.** The High Sierra file system (HSFS) is a read-only file system used on CD-ROMs, and the Unix file system (UFS) is the default disk-based file system used by Solaris. TMPFS resides in memory. Data in this type of file system is destroyed upon reboot. NFS is the Network File System, which is remotely mounted over the network. For more information, see Chapter 1, "Managing File Systems."

15. **B.** The superblock stores much of the information about the file system. The boot block stores information used to boot the system and does not store information about file systems. An inode stores all the information about a file except its name. A storage or data block stores the actual data for each file. For more information, see Chapter 1.

16. **C.** The `df` command and its options can be used to see the capacity of each file system mounted on a system, the amount of space available, and the percentage of space already in use. The `ls` command is used to list information about files and directories. The `du` command summarizes disk usage, but does not provide file system capacity information. The `mountall` command is used to mount all file systems listed in the `/etc/vfstab` file. For more information, see Chapter 1.

17. **B.** The `newfs` command automatically determines all the necessary parameters to pass to `mkfs` to construct new file systems. `newfs` was added in Solaris as a friendly front-end to the `mkfs` command to make the creation of new file systems easier. The `fsck` command is used to check and repair file systems. The `mknod` command is used to create special device files. For more information, see Chapter 1.

18. **C.** The `fsck` command checks and repairs file systems. Any of the others could be used to copy one file system to another. `dd` is used to convert and copy files reading input, one block at a time. `ufsdump` is used to perform file system dumps that can be used to copy file systems from one disk slice to another. `volcopy` is used to make an image copy of a file system. For more information, see Chapter 1.

19. **D.** The `fuser` command can be used to display which processes are using a particular file system. The following example uses the `fuser` command to find out why `/cdrom` is busy:

    fuser –c -u /cdrom

    The `fsck` command is used to check and repair file systems. The `mountall` command is used to mount all file systems listed in the `/etc/vfstab` file. The `ps` command is used to list system processes and report their status, but it does not identify which file system a process may be accessing. For more information, see Chapter 1.

20. **A, C.** Although it is debatable what a "good" password might be, a proper name (Britney) is easy for a password guesser to guess. A password should contain a combination of letters, numbers, and symbols (such as space, comma, period, and so on). Varying case and mixing words can also help expand the number of possibilities that must be covered by a password-guessing program before finding the password. For more information, see Chapter 4.

21. **C.** A umask of 023 makes a mask, automatically unsetting those permission bits from otherwise full permissions. Because each digit represents an octal number corresponding respectively to Owner, Group, and World, the permissions displayed by the `ls` command would be displayed as `rw-r--r--`. The first three permission bits are `rw-` (read, write) for Owner, followed by `r--` (read only) for Group, and finally `r--` (read only) for World. For more information, see Chapter 4.

22. **B.** When using the `newgrp` command to switch your effective group ID, a password is demanded if the group has a password (second field of the `/etc/group` file) and the user is not listed in `/etc/group` as being a member of that group. For more information, see Chapter 4.

23. **A, C.** The `prstat` command is used from the command line to monitor system processes. Like the `ps` command, it provides information on active processes. The difference is that you can specify whether you want information on specific processes, UIDs, CPU IDs, or processor sets. By default, `prstat` displays information about all processes sorted by CPU usage. For more information, see Chapter 5, "Managing System Processes."

24. **B.** The SIGKILL signal can be sent to a process with `kill -9` or `kill -SIGKILL`. Signal 9 is called a sure, unconditional kill because it cannot be caught or ignored by a process. If the process is still around after a `kill -9`, it is either hung up in the Unix kernel, waiting for an event such as disk I/O to complete, or you are not the owner of the process. For more information, see Chapter 5.

25. **B.** The `at` command is used to schedule jobs for execution at a later time. Unlike `crontab`, which schedules a job to happen at regular intervals, a job submitted with `at` executes once, at the designated time. For more information, see Chapter 5.

26. **B, D.** The Print Manager allows the system administrator to set the default printer. If the user doesn't specify a printer name or class in a valid style, the command checks the `printers` entry in the `/etc/nsswitch.conf` file for the search order. By default, the `/etc/nsswitch.conf` file instructs the command to search the user's PRINTER or LPDEST environment variable for a default printer name. These variables can be set by the user. If neither environment variable for the default printer is defined, the command checks the `.printers` file in the user's home directory for the default printer alias; again, this file can be set up by the user. If the command does not find a default printer alias in the `.printers` file, it then checks the print client's `/etc/printers.conf` file for configuration information. If the printer is not found in the `/etc/printers.conf` file, the command checks the name service (NIS or NIS+), if any. You must be root or a member of group 14 in order to user the Print Manager or the `lpadmin` command to set a system default printer. For more information, see Chapter 6.

27. **B.** The `lpstat -p <printer>` command will tell you whether a printer is active or idle, when it was enabled or disabled, and whether it is accepting print requests. The `lpadmin` command is used to configure the LP print service such as adding printers. Admintool and Print Manager can be used to create and remove printers, but they do not display information about printers. For more information, see Chapter 6.

28. **A, B.** This command uses the flags `x` (extract archive), `v` (verbose, lists all files and directories extracted), and `f` (archive is in the file following this argument). If `backup.tar` has files that specify absolute paths (for example, `/etc/shadow`), the files will be extracted to disk using the absolute paths. New directories will get created and files will get overwritten, so be careful and be very sure that you trust the creator of a tar file before you extract it as root. For more information, see Chapter 7, "Perform System Backups and Restorations."

29. **C.** The `dd` command quickly converts and copies files with different data formats, such as differences in block size or record length. `dd` can be used to copy an entire file system or partition to tape, and can take input from other programs through standard input. It cannot, however, compress files as it copies because it is a byte-by-byte image copy. For more information, see Chapter 7.

30. **C.** Each entry in the `/proc` directory is a decimal number corresponding to a process ID. Each directory in `/proc` has files that contain more detailed information about that process. For more information, see Chapter 5.

31. **A, B, D.** In Solaris, each disk device is described in three ways, using three distinct naming conventions:

    - **Physical device name**—Represents the full device pathname in the device information hierarchy.
    - **Instance name**—Represents the kernel's abbreviation name for every possible device on the system.
    - **Logical device name**—Used by system administrators with most file system commands to refer to devices.

    For more information, see Chapter 1.

32. **C.** Although you can find command-line equivalents to SMC tools such as `smuser` and `smgroup`, no command-line interface exists for the Solaris Management Console. For more information, see Chapter 4.

33. **A, C, D.** The SMC Toolbox Editor manages processes, users, file system mounts and shares, disks, and serial ports; schedules jobs; and has a log viewer. You can also use SMC to install patches, but not to install software. For more information, see Chapter 4.

34. **B, E.** The custom JumpStart method of installing the operating system provides a hands-off method to install groups of similar systems automatically and identically. If you use an interactive method to install the operating system (such as JumpStart, Network Install, or an Interactive Installation), you must carry on a dialog with the installation program by answering various questions. Solaris Flash is also a hands-off installation method that enables you to replicate, or clone, a Solaris environment across many similar systems. The master system and the clone systems must have the same kernel architectures. For example, you can use a Solaris Flash archive that was created from a master system that has a sun4u architecture only to install other systems with a sun4u architecture. For more information, see Chapter 2.

35. **D.** Answer A describes the Network layer, Answer B describes the Transport layer, and Answer C describes the Session layer. For more information, see Chapter 8, "The Solaris Network Environment."

36. **B.** A router is a machine that forwards packets from one network to another. In other words, the router connects networks, whereas the switch connects computers on the same network. A host *can* be a router, but this is not usually the case. An NIC (network interface card) is the hardware in a host that allows it to connect to a network. For more information, see Chapter 8.

37. **A.** Class C network numbers use 24 bits for the network number and 8 bits for host numbers. A Class C network number occupies the first three bytes of an IP address; only the fourth byte is assigned at the discretion of the network's owner. The first and last addresses on a network are reserved for the network number and the broadcast address. As such, a Class C network can accommodate a maximum of 254 hosts. For more information, see Chapter 8.

38. **B.** The swapfs pseudo file system is either a swap partition on a disk, or a swap file residing in another file system on a disk. The procfs, tmpfs, and fdfs all reside in memory. For more information, see Chapter 9, "Virtual File Systems, Swap Space, and Core Dumps."

39. **B.** The `setup_install_server` command is used to create an install server for use within a custom JumpStart environment. Answer A is the command to verify the `rules` file and create the `rules.ok` file; Answer C is used to set up a client to be able to boot across the network and install using custom JumpStart; and Answer D is the command to set up a boot-only server, which would not contain the Solaris images. For more information, see Chapter 14, "Advanced Installation Procedures."

40. **A, B.** Sun recommends that file systems mounted as read-write, or containing executable files, should always be mounted with the hard option. If you use soft-mounted file systems, unexpected I/O errors can occur. For example, consider a write request. If the NFS server goes down, the pending write request simply gives up, resulting in a corrupted file on the remote file system. A read-write file system should always be mounted with the specified `hard` and `intr` options. This lets users make their own decisions about killing hung processes. For more information, see Chapter 9.

41. **B.** The correct command to start the NFS server service after the initial share has been configured is `svcadm enable nfs/server`. Answer A is the command that is entered into `/etc/dfs/dfstab` to define the share, Answer C is the command to mount all file systems listed in `/etc/vfstab`, and Answer D is the command to list the details and dependencies of the NFS server service. For more information, see Chapter 9.

42. **B, C.** Both `sudo` and Role-Based Access Control (RBAC) allow the system administrator to assign limited administrative capabilities to non-root users—albeit in different ways. Giving out the root password allows a user full access to all the powers of root, making for very poor security. For more information, see Chapter 11, "Controlling Access and Configuring System Messaging."

43. **C.** The `metaroot` command is used to carry out the necessary setup for putting a root file system under SVM control. Answer A is the command for creating and managing the state database, Answer B is the command for creating new metadevices, and Answer D is the command for clearing or removing metadevices. For more information, see Chapter 10, "Managing Storage Volumes."

44. **A.** With no arguments, the `ypwhich` command displays the server currently providing NIS services; that is, the server that the client is bound to. The current NIS master server is determined by running `ypwhich -m`, which lists all of the maps and the master server for each map. The `ypcat` command is used to display the contents of a NIS map. `/etc/nsswitch.conf` is used to determine the order in which data is obtained, and the `nisls` command is used in NIS+ to display the contents of an object. For more information, see Chapter 12, "Naming Services."

45. **D.** The name service switch, `/etc/nsswitch.conf`, controls how a client workstation or application obtains network information. In this case, you would edit the `/etc/nsswitch.conf` file and change the hosts line to read `hosts: files dns nis`. The file `/etc/inetd.conf` is used to configure legacy network services, `/etc/resolv.conf` is used by DNS to identify the DNS lookup servers, and `/etc/defaultrouter` is used to identify the default route address. For more information, see Chapter 12.

46. **B, D.** The Custom JumpStart and WAN Boot (with a Flash Archive) methods of installing the operating system provides a way to install groups of similar systems automatically and identically. If you use the Jump Start or Interactive Install method to install the operating system, you must carry on a dialog with the installation program by answering various questions. For more information, see Chapter 14, "Advanced Installation Procedures."

47. **D.** After you create a profile, you can use the `pfinstall` command to test it. Testing a class file is sometimes called a dry run installation. By looking at the installation output generated by `pfinstall`, you can quickly determine whether a class file will do what you expect. The `check` command is used to verify the rules file, `patchadd` is used to install operating environment patches to the system, and `fsck` is the command to use to check the consistency of file systems. For more information, see Chapter 14.

48. **B.** The file `/etc/defaultrouter` is not used in changing the hostname of a Solaris system. For more information, see Chapter 8.

49. **C.** The `coreadm` command is used to configure core file behavior. The `savecore` command is used to save a memory dump following a reboot of the system—this is because the memory dump will normally be stored temporarily in the system swap space and would be overwritten. The command `svcadm restart svc:/system/coreadm:default` would restart the `coreadm` process and `admcore` is a nonexistent command. For more information, see Chapter 9.

50. **B.** `dumpadm` is the command to use to change the default crash dump device. The `crashadm` command does not exist and the file `/var/crash` is the directory normally used for the storing of crash dumps. The `gcore` command is used to create core files from a running process without damaging that process. For more information, see Chapter 9.

51. **C.** The `usermod` command with the `-R` flag is used to add role privileges to a user. `usermod -R adminusr bill` is the correct answer. The commands `modrole` and `moduser` do not exist, and the `rolemod` command is used to modify the specification of a role. For more information, see Chapter 11.

52. **A.** The command `zoneadm -z apps list -v` would display the current status of the zone called `apps`. Answer B would be used to log in to the `apps` zone from the global zone, Answer C would be used to log in to the console of zone `apps` from the global zone, and Answer D is the command that would carry out the installation of zone `apps`. For more information, see Chapter 13, "Solaris Zones."

53. **C.** `/etc/security/user_attr` is the correct answer. The correct path for this RBAC database is `/etc/user_attr`. The other files are valid RBAC database names. For more information, see Chapter 11.

54. **B.** `/etc/nfs/nfslog.conf` is the file that manages NFS logging behavior, although NFS logging is not supported in NFS Version 4. The file `/etc/nfslog` does not exist. `/etc/inetd.conf` is used to configure the `inetd` daemon whilst `/etc/default/nfs` is the file used to configure default parameters for NFS operation. For more information, see Chapter 9.

55. **B.** RAID 1 maintains duplicate sets of all data on separate disk drives. Also known as mirroring. For more information, see Chapter 10, "Managing Storage Volumes."

56. C. RAID 5 is where both parity and data are striped across a set of disks. For more information, see Chapter 10.

57. B. `ldapclient` is used to add a client to the LDAP naming service. The remaining answers are all nonexistent commands. For more information, see Chapter 12.

58. C. The command `svcadm refresh system/system-log` would force the `syslogd` daemon to re-read its configuration file after a change to the file `/etc/syslog.conf` had been made. Answer A would list the details and dependencies of the `system-log` service, answer B would disable the `system-log` service, and answer D is an invalid option to the `syslogd` command.

59. B. The `archive_location` option indicates that a Solaris Flash Archive is being used to install the system and the parameter specifies the network location of the Flash Archive to use for the installation. For more information, see Chapter 14.

60. A, C. Because your system still has 50% of the state database replicas intact, the system will remain running. The system will only panic and must be booted into single user-mode if less than 50% of the replicas are available. The system cannot reboot into multi-user mode unless a majority (half + 1) of the total number of state database replicas are available.

PART III

Appendixes

APPENDIX A

What's on the CD-ROM

The CD features an innovative practice test engine by ExamGear, giving you one of the best tools for assessing your readiness for the exam. The CD also includes a PDF of the entire text of the book accessible from the CD interface.

ExamGear, Exam Prep Edition

ExamGear, Exam Prep Edition is an exam environment developed for Que Certification. In addition to providing a means of evaluating your knowledge of the Exam Prep material, ExamGear, Exam Prep Edition features several innovations that help you improve your mastery of the subject matter.

For example, the practice exams enable you to check your scores by their correspondence to Sun Solaris exam objectives for the Solaris 10 System Administrator exam. In another mode, ExamGear, Exam Prep Edition enables you to obtain immediate feedback on your responses in the form of explanations for the correct and incorrect answers.

ExamGear, Exam Prep Edition is written to the Exam Prep content for this book. It is designed to aid you in assessing how well you understand the Exam Prep material that is related to the Sun exam objectives for Solaris 10 System Administrator exam. ExamGear also presents the common question formats that you will see on the actual exam, including questions that use round option buttons (where you can choose only a single answer from all options displayed) or square checkboxes (where you can choose one or more answers from all options displayed, and the number of options you must choose is often provided). Thus, this tool serves as an excellent method for assessing your knowledge of the Exam Prep content and gives you the experience of taking an electronic exam.

For additional questions online that use the same test engine, please visit `www.unixed.com`.

Glossary

A

Access control list Used in Solaris to provide greater control over file access permissions when traditional Unix file protection is not enough. An ACL provides better file security by enabling you to define file permissions for the file owner, file group, other specific users and groups, and default permissions for each of those categories.

ARP (Address Resolution Protocol) The Internet protocol that dynamically maps Internet addresses to physical (hardware) addresses on local area networks. ARP is limited to networks that support hardware broadcast.

Array Controller A storage array

AutoClient A client system type that caches (locally stores copies of data as it is referenced) all its needed system software from a server. The AutoClient system has a local disk, but the root (`/`) and `/usr` file systems are accessed across the network from a server and are loaded in a local disk cache. Files in the `/` and `/usr` file systems are copied to the cache disk as they are referenced. If a Solstice AutoClient client accesses an application that is not already in its disk cache, that application is downloaded. If the application already resides in the client's disk cache, the application is accessed locally. AutoClient replaced the dataless client in Solaris 2.6.

AutoFS Maps (know each of them) AutoFS files are referred to as maps. These maps are

- **Master map**—Read by the `automount` command during bootup. This map lists the other maps used for establishing the AutoFS.
- **Direct map**—Lists the mount points as absolute pathnames. This map explicitly indicates the mount point of the client.
- **Indirect map**—Lists the mount points as relative pathnames. This map uses a relative path to establish the mount point on the client.
- **Special**—Provides access to entries in `/etc/hosts` or the Federated Naming Services (FNS).

Automated Security Enhancement Tool Examines the startup files to ensure that the path variable is set up correctly and does not contain a dot (`.`) entry for the current directory.

B

Bandwidth A measure of the capacity of a communication channel, which is usually specified in megabytes per second (MB/s).

Block A unit of data that can be transferred by a device, usually 512 bytes long.

Block device A device file that calls for I/O operations based on a defined block size. The block size varies by device, but for a UFS, the default block size is 8KB.

Block size Specifies the size of a section of data that is written to disk or tape at one time. Typical block sizes are 512 bytes or 1024 bytes.

Boot server A server that provides the information that a JumpStart client needs to boot using the network.

Boot The process of loading and executing the operating system—sometimes referred to as *bootstrapping*.

Bootblock The boot program is stored in a predictable area (sectors 1–15) on the system hard drive, CD-ROM, or other bootable device and is referred to as the bootblock (`bootblk`). The bootblock is responsible for loading the secondary boot program (`ufsboot`) into memory, which is located in the UFS on the boot device. Only the root (`/`) file system has an active bootblock, but each file system has space allocated for one.

Bootstrapping The process a computer follows to load and execute the bootable operating system. The name is coined from the phrase "pulling yourself up by your bootstraps." The instructions for the bootstrap procedure are stored in the boot PROM.

Boot server A server system that provides client systems on the same network subnet with the programs and information that they need to start. A boot server is required to install over the network if the install server is on a different subnet than the systems on which Solaris software is to be installed.

Bundled software package A Solaris software package is the standard way to deliver bundled and unbundled software. Packages are administered by using the package administration commands, and they are generally identified by a SUNW*xxx* naming convention when supplied by Sun Microsystems. SUNW is Sun Microsystems' ticker symbol on the stock exchange, hence the SUNW prefix.

Bus A path for transferring data.

Byte A group of adjacent binary digits (bits) operated on by the computer as a unit. The most common-sized byte contains eight binary digits.

C

CDE Process Manager A GUI tool for viewing and managing system processes.

Character device file A device file that calls for I/O operations based on the disk's smallest addressable unit, or sector. Each sector is 512 bytes in size. A character device is also referred to as a raw device.

Check script Used to validate the rules file that is required by the custom JumpStart installation software to match a system to a profile.

Chunk A quantity of information that is handled as a unit by the host and array.

Child process New processes created by a parent process.

Class file A text file that defines how to install the Solaris software on a system.

Client Systems that rely on servers are called clients. In other words, a client is a system that uses remote services from a server.

Client/server Used to describe the relationship between a server and its clients. *See* server and client.

Cluster A cluster of patches (patch cluster), or a cluster of software packages (software cluster).

Concatenation Used to combine two or more files to create one larger file. If partitions are concatenated, the addressing of the component blocks is done on the components sequentially, which means that data is written to the first available stripe until it is full, and then moves to the next available stripe.

Concatenated Stripe A metadevice comprised of both concatenated and striped components.

Configuration group On SPARC systems, software groups are grouped into five configuration groups to make the software installation process easier. During the installation process, you will be asked to install one of the five configuration groups. These five configuration groups are core system support, end-user support, developer system support, entire distribution, and entire distribution plus OEM system support.

Configuration server A server that contains the JumpStart configuration files, used to install networked systems.

Controller A device within the array that manages commands and data transfers from the host, delegates jobs to its processors, and maps the data locations in the array.

Core file A point-in-time copy (snapshot) of the RAM allocated to a process. The copy is written to a more permanent medium, such as a hard disk. A core file is useful in analyzing why a particular program crashed.

A core file is also a disk copy of the address space of a process, at a certain point in time. This information identifies items, such as the task name, task owner, priority, and instruction queue in execution at the time the core file was created.

Crash dump A disk copy of the physical memory of the computer at the time of a fatal system error.

`crontab` file Consists of commands, one per line, that will be executed at regular intervals by the `cron` daemon.

Custom JumpStart Provides a way to install groups of similar systems automatically and identically.

Cylinder A stack of concentric tracks.

Cylinder groups Each file system is divided into cylinder groups with a minimum default size of 16 cylinders per group.

Cylinder group blocks A table in each cylinder group that describes the cylinder group.

D

Data blocks Units of disk space that are used to store data. Regular files, directories, and symbolic links make use of data blocks.

De-encapsulation When a header is removed from each segment received on the way up the layers.

Default printer The printer designated to accept print jobs when a destination printer is not specified.

Default shell The shell that is specified for each user account in the `/etc/passwd` file. When the user logs in, they are automatically placed in their default shell. If no shell is specified for the user, the `/sbin/sh` shell will be their default shell.

Device alias Device pathnames can be long and complex to enter. The concept of device aliases, like Unix aliases, allows a short name to be substituted for a long name. An alias represents an entire device pathname, not a component of it.

Device autoconfiguration This offers many advantages over the manual configuration method used in earlier versions of Unix, in which device drivers were manually added to the kernel, the kernel was recompiled, and the system had to be restarted. *See also* reconfiguration boot.

Device driver A low-level program that allows the kernel to communicate with a specific piece of hardware.

Device hierarchy During a reconfiguration restart, this is created in the `/devices` directory to represent the devices connected to the system.

Device tree Each device has a unique name representing both the type of device and the location of that device in the system addressing structure called the device tree. The OpenBoot firmware builds a device tree for all devices from information gathered at the power-on self-test (POST).

DHCP (Dynamic Host Configuration Protocol) An application-layer protocol that enables individual computers, or clients, on a TCP/IP network to extract an IP address and other network configuration information from a designated and centrally maintained DHCP server or servers. This facility reduces the overhead of maintaining and administering a large IP network.

Disk array A subsystem that contains multiple disk drives, designed to provide performance, high availability, serviceability, or other benefits.

Direct map A type of automount map that lists the mount points as absolute path names. This type of map explicitly indicates the mount point on the client.

Disk block The smallest addressable unit on a disk platter. One sector holds 512 bytes of data. Sectors are also known as disk blocks.

Disk label A special area of every disk that is set aside for storing information about the disk's controller, geometry, and slices.

Disk partition *See* Disk slice.

Disk quota Enables system administrators to control the size of UFSs by limiting the amount of disk space and the number of I-nodes (which roughly corresponds to the number of files) that individual users can acquire.

Disk set A grouping of two hosts and disk drives in which all the drives are accessible by each host in the set.

Disk slice Groupings of cylinders that are commonly used to organize data by function.

Disk-based file system Any file system created on a local disk. Disk-based file systems include UFS, HSFS, PCFS, and UDFs.

Diskless client A client that has no local disk or file systems. The diskless client boots from the server; remotely mounts its root (`/`), `/usr`, and `/export/home` file systems from a server; allocates swap space on the server; and obtains all its data from the server. Any files created are stored on the server.

DNS resolver DNS clients use the dynamic library routines, collectively called the resolver, to locate a remote host. The resolver queries the DNS database on a name server, which eventually returns the host name or IP address of the machine requested by the resolver.

DNS The name service provided by the Internet for Transmission Control Protocol/Internet Protocol (TCP/IP) networks. It was developed so that workstations on the network can be identified by common names instead of Internet addresses.

Domain A part of the Internet naming hierarchy. A domain represents a group of systems on a local network that share administrative files.

Dynamic failover (as it relates to NFS) When high availability for read-only NFS resources is needed, dynamic failover provides an alternate NFS mount point if the primary mount point fails.

E

Encapsulation When a header is added to each segment received on the way down the layers.

Ethernet A standard that defines the physical components a machine uses to access the network and the speed at which the network runs.

F

FDDI A standard for data transmission on fiber-optic lines in a LAN that can extend up to 200km (124 miles).

File access permissions Used in Solaris to provide control over file access.

Filenames The objects most often used to access and manipulate files. A file must have a name that is associated with an I-node. *See* I-node.

File system dump A backup of a file system using the `ufsdump` command.

File system minfree space The portion of a file system that is reserved and held back from users. It is only accessible by root.

File system type Describes the type of file system such as UFS, PROCFS, TMPFS. Many file system administration commands require you to specify the file system type (`fstype`).

File system A structure used to organize and store files on disk.

Finish script Used in a JumpStart installation, this is a user-defined Bourne shell script, specified within the rules file, that performs tasks after the Solaris software is installed on the system, but before the system reboots. You can use finish scripts only with custom JumpStart installations.

Flash archive Provides a method to store a snapshot of the Solaris operating environment complete with all installed patches and applications.

Flash installation A complete snapshot of a Solaris operating environment, including with patches and applications.

Fragment Also referred to as fragmentation. This is the method used by the UFS to allocate disk space efficiently.

Free block Blocks not currently being used as I-nodes, indirect address blocks, or storage blocks are marked as free in the cylinder group map.

Free hog slice A temporary slice that is automatically designated that expands and shrinks to accommodate the slice resizing operations.

Full backup A backup that contains everything on the file system.

Full device name A full device pathname is a series of node names separated by slashes (/). The root of the tree is the machine node, which is not named explicitly but is indicated by a leading slash (/). Each device pathname has this form: `driver-name@unit-address:device-arguments`.

G

Gbyte (Gigabyte) 1,024 Mbytes (or 1,073,741,824 bytes).

Group ID (GID) The primary group number for the group to which the user will belong. This is the group the operating system will assign to files created by the user. GIDs can typically range from 0 to 60,002, but they can go as high as 2,147,483,647.

Group Used to control user access to files and directories. Users who need to share files are placed into the same group. A group can be 1) A collection of users who are referred to by a common name. 2) In NIS+, a collection of users who are collectively given specified access rights to NIS+ objects. NIS+ group information is stored in the NIS+ group table. 3) In Unix, groups determine a user's access to files. There are two types of groups: default user group and standard user group.

H

Hard link A file that has many names that all share the same I-node number.

Hard mount A file system mounted using the `mount -o hard` option. The `hard` option indicates that the retry request is continued until the server responds. The default for the `mount` command is `hard`.

Hardware Port An electrically wired outlet on a piece of equipment into which a plug or cable connects.

Hierarchical namespace Namespace information that is similar in structure to the Unix directory tree. *See* namespace.

Home directory The portion of a file system allocated to a user for storing private files.

Host A node on the network.

Hostname Every system on the network usually has a unique hostname. Hostnames let users refer to any computer on the network by using a short, easily remembered name rather than the host's network IP address. Hostnames should be short, easy to spell, and lowercase, and they should have no more than 64 characters. The `hostname` command determines a system's host.

Hot spare pool A collection of slices (hot spares) reserved for automatic substitution in case of slice failure in either a submirror or RAID5 metadevice. Hot spares are used to increase data availability.

Hot spare A slice reserved to substitute automatically for a failed slice in a submirror or RAID5 metadevice. A hot spare must be a physical slice, not a metadevice.

Hot-pluggable These are devices that can be connected or disconnected while the system is running.

Hot-swappable These devices allow for the connection and disconnection of peripherals or other components without rebooting the operating system.

HSFS High Sierra File System.

Hub The central device through which all hosts in a twisted-pair Ethernet installation are connected. A hub shares bandwidth between all systems that are connected to it. *See* Switch.

I

Incremental backup Backs up only those files that were changed since a previous backup, saving tape space and time.

Indirect map A type of automount map that lists mount points as relative path names. This map uses a relative path to establish the mount point on the client.

Init state When a system begins initialization, it enters one of eight run states—also called init states. Because run state 4 is currently not used, only seven usable run states exist.

Initial installation A Solaris 9 installation method. You perform an initial installation either on a system that does not have an existing Solaris operating system already installed on it or when you want to completely wipe out the existing operating system and reinstall it.

I-node The objects that the Solaris operating environment uses to record information about a file. I-nodes contain information about a file, its owner, permissions, and its size. I-nodes are numbered, and each file system contains its own list of I-nodes.

Install server A server that provides an image of the Solaris operating environment, which the JumpStart client uses as its source of data to install.

Installation media The Solaris 9 operating system software is distributed on CD-ROM and DVD and is referred to as The Installation Media Kit.

Instance name This represents the kernel's abbreviation name for every possible device on the system.

Interactive boot (`boot -a`) Stops and asks for input during the boot process. The system provides a dialog box in which it displays the default boot values and gives you the option of changing them. You might want to boot interactively to make a temporary change to the system file or kernel. Booting interactively enables you to test your changes and recover easily if you have problems.

Interactive installation The Solaris interactive installation program, `suninstall`, guides you step by step through installing the Solaris software.

Interlace The number of blocks on a component of a striped or RAID metadevice that can be simultaneously accessed with the same number of blocks from another component. The interlace value dictates how much data that Solaris Volume Manager places on a component of a striped or RAID metadevice before moving on to the next component.

IP address Each machine on a TCP/IP network has a unique 32-bit Internet address (or IP address) that identifies the machine to its peers on the network. An IP address in IPv4 consists of four numbers that are separated by periods (192.168.0.1, for example). Most often, each part of the IP address is a number between 0 and 225. However, the first number must be less than 224 and the last number cannot be 0.

IPv6 Version 6 of Internet Protocol (IP) that is designed to be an evolutionary step from the current version, IPv4 (version 4).

ISO/OSI model The International Standards Organization (ISO)/Open System Interconnection (OSI) model is an ISO standard for worldwide communications that defines a framework for implementing protocols in seven layers. Control is passed from one layer to the next, starting at the application layer in one station, proceeding to the bottom layer, over the channel to the next station, and back up the hierarchy.

J–K

JavaStation Also known as a zero-administration client, this client has no local file system, and its `/home` is accessed from a server across the network. The JavaStation runs only applications that are 100% pure Java.

Journaling The recording of Unix file system (UFS) updates in a log before the updates are applied to the Unix file system. This allows for increased data recovery in the event of a catastrophic system failure. (Also called *logging*.)

JumpStart client Also referred to as an Install client, the JumpStart client uses the JumpStart automatic installation to install the Solaris operating environment across the network. JumpStart clients require support from a JumpStart server to find an image of the Solaris operating environment to install.

JumpStart server Provides all of the directives for the JumpStart installation, including an image of the Solaris operating environment to install.

Kbyte A Kilobyte, or 1,024 bytes.

Kernel The kernel (covered in detail later in this chapter) is the part of the operating system that remains running at all times until the system is shut down. It is the core and the most important part of the operating system.

Kerberos A security system developed at MIT that authenticates users. It does not provide authorization to services or databases; it establishes identity at logon, which is used throughout the session. Kerberos (also spelled Cerberus) was a fierce, three-headed mastiff who guarded the gates of Hades in Greek mythology.

L

LAN (local area network) Multiple systems at a single geographical site connected together for the purpose of sharing and exchanging data and software.

LAN/WAN Local area network/wide area network. *See* LAN and WAN.

Large file A regular file whose size is greater than or equal to 2GB.

Large file–aware A utility is called large file–aware if it can process large files in the same manner that it does small files. A large file–aware utility can handle large files as input and can generate large files as output. The `newfs`, `mkfs`, `mount`, `umount`, `tunefs`, `labelit`, and `quota` utilities are all large file–aware for UFSs.

Large file–safe A utility is called large file–safe if it causes no data loss or corruption when it encounters a large file. A utility that is large file–safe cannot properly process a large file, so it returns an appropriate error. Some examples of utilities that are not large file–aware but are large file–safe include the `vi` editor and the `mailx` and `lp` commands.

LDAP (Lightweight Directory Access Protocol) This is the latest name-lookup service (directory service) to be added to Solaris.

Live upgrade Provides a method of upgrading while your Solaris system is still running. The original system configuration remains fully functional and unaffected by the upgrade. The upgrade creates a duplicate boot environment that is activated when the system is rebooted. If a failure occurs, you can revert to the original boot environment, thereby eliminating the downtime associated with the normal test and evaluation process.

Local printer A printer that is physically connected to a system and is accessed from that system.

Locale A geographic or political region or community that shares the same language, customs, or cultural conventions (English for the United States is `en_US`, and English for the United Kingdom is `en_UK`).

Logical device name Symbolic links pointing to the physical device name stored in the `/devices` directory. A logical device's name is used to refer to a device when you are entering commands on the command line. All logical device names are stored in the /dev directory.

Logical volume Allows file systems to span multiple disks and provide for improved I/O and reliability compared to the standard Solaris file system.

Logging *See* journaling.

LPD (Line Printer Daemon) A TCP/IP printer protocol that provides print spooling and network printing. Originally developed for Berkeley Unix (BSD Unix), LPD has become the de facto cross-platform printing protocol.

`lpsched` *See* Print Scheduler.

M

MAC address The unique serial number burned into an Ethernet adapter that identifies that network card from all others.

Major device number This indicates the general device class, such as disk, tape, or serial line.

Makefile Used to create the appropriate NIS maps.

Master map A type of automount map that lists the other maps used for establishing the AutoFS. The `autmount` command reads this map at boot time.

Master NIS server The center of the NIS network that is designated as the master server containing the set of maps that get updated.

Mbyte A Megabyte, or 1,024 Kbytes.

Metastate database A database, stored on disk, that records configuration and the state of all metadevices and error conditions. This information is important to the correct operation of Solaris Volume Manager (SVM) and it is replicated. *See also* state database replica.

Metadevice A Solaris Volume Manager (SVM) term used to describe a group of physical slices accessed as a single logical device. Metadevices are used like slices. The metadevice maps logical block addresses to the correct location on one of the physical devices. The type of mapping depends on the configuration of the particular metadevice. Also known as the pseudo, or virtual device in standard Unix terms.

Metadisk A special driver that coordinates I/O to and from physical devices and volumes, enabling applications to treat a volume like a physical device.

Metadriver A pseudo device driver that maps metadevice operations to commands to the metadevice components.

Minor device number This indicates the specific member within a general device class (such as disk, tape, or serial line). All devices managed by a given device driver contain a unique minor number.

Mirror Replicates all writes to a single logical device (the mirror) and then to multiple devices (the submirrors) while distributing read operations. This provides redundancy of data in the event of a disk or hardware failure.

Mounted file system table (`mnttab`) A file system that provides read-only access to the table of mounted file systems for the current host.

Multiuser mode Used to describe a Solaris run state where the system is supporting multiuser operations.

N

Name service switch Used to direct requests to the correct name service in use on the system or network.

Name service A network service that provides a means of identifying and locating resources such as hostnames and IP addresses available to a network. The default name service product available in the Solaris operating environment is Network Information Service Plus (NIS+).

Namespace Stores name service information that users, workstations, and applications must have to communicate across the network. Namespace can also refer to the set of all names in a naming system, such as

NIS+ namespace—A collection of hierarchical network information used by the NIS+ software.

NIS namespace—A collection of nonhierarchical network information used by the NIS software.

DNS—namespace A collection of networked workstations that use the DNS software.

Network address The address, consisting of up to 20 octets, used to locate an Open Systems Interconnection (OSI) transport entity. The address is formatted into an initial domain part that is standardized for each of several addressing domains, and a domain-specific part that is the responsibility of the addressing authority for that domain.

Network class Network addresses are divided into three classes: Class A, Class B, and Class C. This addressing scheme is called classful IPv4 addressing.

Network interface Also referred to as a network adapter or NIC (network interface card). A printed circuit board that plugs into both the clients and servers in a network. It controls the exchange of data between them at the data link level, also known as the *access method* (OSI layers 1 and 2).

Network mask A number used by software to separate the local subnet address from the rest of a given Internet protocol address.

Network port A software network port is an identified doorway (address) for communicating between a program and another communications system or program, often passing through a hardware port. The network port is usually numbered and a standard network implementation such as TCP, UDP, or IP will attach a port number to data it sends. The receiving implementation will guard and listen at the attached port number (doorway) to figure out which program to send data to on its system. A port may send/receive data one direction at a time (simplex) or simultaneously in both directions (duplex). These software network ports may also connect internal programs on a single computer system. In TCP and UDP, the combination of a port and a network address (IP number) is called a socket.

Network printer A printer that is physically attached to the network and has its own hostname and IP address. A network printer provides printing services to print clients without being directly cabled to a print server.

Network protocol The part of the network that you configure but cannot see. It's the software portion of the network that controls data transmission between systems across the network.

Network service A term used to describe services offered by servers to network clients such as FTP, Telnet, and HTTP.

Network-based file system File systems accessed over the network. Typically, they reside on one system (the server) and are accessed by other systems (clients) across the network.

NFS client A system that mounts a remote file system from an NFS server.

NFS daemons Processes that support NFS activities. These daemons can support both NFS client and NFS server activity, NFS server activity alone, or logging of the NFS server activity.

NFS logging Provides a record of all NFS activity on network file systems that have been shared with the logging option enabled.

NFS server Shares resources to be used by NFS clients.

NFS (Network File System) This service lets computers of different architectures, running different operating systems (OSs), share file systems across a network.

NIS client The hosts in the NIS domain, including the master and slave servers.

NIS map Multicolumn tables used to store NIS information.

NIS (Network Information Service) A distributed network information service containing key information about the systems and the users on the network. The NIS database is stored on the master server and all the replica or slave servers.

NIS+ authorization The process of granting NIS+ principals access rights to an NIS+ object.

NIS+ objects Directories, tables, and groups within a namespace.

NIS+ security levels Let NIS+ administrators specify different read, modify, create, and destroy rights to NIS+ objects for each class.

NIS+ This is similar to NIS, but with more features. NIS+ is not an extension of NIS, but a new software program designed to replace NIS.

Node A host or router.

NSCD Speeds up queries of the most common data and the `getent` command to retrieve naming service information from specified databases.

NVRAM (nonvolatile random-access memory) The NVRAM chip has user-definable system parameters and writeable areas for user-controlled diagnostics, macros, and device aliases. The NVRAM is where the system identification information is stored, such as the hostid, Ethernet address, and time-of-day (TOD) clock.

O

OBP (OpenBoot PROM) The hardware-level user interface that you see before the operating system starts. The OpenBoot PROM consists of two 8KB chips on the system board: the startup PROM itself, which contains extensive firmware allowing access to user-written startup drivers and extended diagnostics, and an NVRAM (nonvolatile random-access memory) chip.

OpenBoot The primary task of the OpenBoot firmware is to boot the operating system either from a mass storage device or from the network. *See also* OBP.

P–Q

Packet The basic unit of information to be transferred over the network.

Parallel Simultaneous. Usually applied to a RAID-3 environment where a block of data is transferred by dividing it into smaller blocks, accessing all drives at once and simultaneously transferring the data.

Parent process The main, or primary, program or first process loaded into memory. A parent process forks a child process, which, in turn, can fork other processes.

Parity A method used by RAID5 configurations to provide data redundancy. Typically, a RAID5 configuration stores data blocks and parity blocks. In the case of a missing data block, the missing data can be regenerated using the other data blocks and the parity block.

Partition table This identifies a disk's slices, the slice boundaries (in cylinders), and the total size of the slices.

Password aging A system parameter set by the system administrator in the `/etc/default/password` file that requires users to change their passwords after a certain number of days.

Password encryption The reversible transformation of a user's password from the original (the plaintext) to a difficult-to-interpret format (the ciphertext). It is done as a mechanism for protecting its confidentiality. Encryption uses an encryption algorithm. The encrypted password consists of 13 characters chosen from a 64-character alphabet.

Patchlist file Specifies a file containing a list of patches to install.

PCFS (Personal Computer File System) Allows read and write access to data and programs on DOS-formatted disks that are written for DOS-based personal computers.

Physical device name This represents the full device pathname in the device information hierarchy. Physical device names uniquely identify the physical location of the hardware devices on the system and are maintained in the `/devices` directory. The physical device name contains the hardware information, represented as a series of node names separated by slashes that indicate the path to the device.

Platform group This is a general term used to group Sun systems together based on their hardware architecture. To determine the platform group that your Sun system belongs to, use the `uname -m` command. The system will respond with the platform group and the platform name for your system.

Port *See* network port and hardware port.

POST (power-on self-test) When a system is turned on, the monitor runs a POST that checks such things as the hardware and memory on the system. If no errors are found, the automatic boot process begins.

Power management software Provided in the Solaris environment to automatically save the state of a system and turn it off after it is idle for 30 minutes. On newer systems that comply with the EPA's Energy Star guidelines, the power management software is installed by default. You are then prompted after rebooting to enable or disable the power management software.

Primary group Each user is assigned to a primary group when they log in. This is the group the operating system will assign to files created by the user.

Print client A remote system that sends print requests to a print server.

Print daemon A system process that supports printing activities.

Print Manager A graphical user interface used to manage printers in a name service environment.

Print scheduler The LP print service has a scheduler daemon called `lpsched`. This print scheduler daemon updates the LP system files with information about printer setup and configuration. This dameon schedules all of the local print requests on a print server. It tracks the status of printers and filters on the print server.

Print server A system that has a local printer connected to it, makes the printer available to other systems on the network, and provides spooling for the client's print requests.

Printer class Several locally attached printers that are put into a group. A printer class is helpful if you have several printers sitting next to each other, and it doesn't matter which printer your job goes to.

Process A program in operation.

PROCFS (Process File System) A file system that resides in memory and contains a list of active processes.

Profile A JumpStart configuration file that defines how the Solaris software is installed on the JumpStart client if a system matches the rule. Every rule in the rules file specifies a profile that defines how a system is to be installed when the rule is matched. You usually create a different profile for every rule. However, the same profile can be used in more than one rule. *See also* rules file and rights profile.

PROM (Programmable Read-Only Memory) A permanent memory chip that is programmed, or filled, by the customer rather than by the chip manufacturer. It differs from a ROM, which is programmed at the time of manufacture. PROMs have been mostly superseded by EPROMs, which can be reprogrammed.

R

RAID (Redundant Array of Independent Disks) A disk subsystem that is used to increase performance and/or provide fault tolerance. RAID is a classification of different ways to back up and store data on multiple disk drives. There are seven levels of RAID:

- Level 0: Nonredundant disk array (striping)
- Level 1: Mirrored disk array
- Level 2: Memory-style Error Code Correction (ECC)
- Level 3: Bit-interleaved parity
- Level 4: Block-interleaved parity
- Level 5: Block-interleaved distributed parity
- Level 6: P + Q redundancy

SVM implements RAID levels 0, 1, and 5.

RARP (Reverse ARP) A method by which a client is assigned an IP address based on a lookup of its Ethernet address.

Reconfiguration boot A method of booting a system so that the system recognizes newly added peripheral devices and creates an entry in the `/etc/path_to_inst` file, and the `/dev` and `/devices` directories.

Reconfiguration startup *See* Reconfiguration boot.

Redundancy Duplication for the purpose of achieving fault tolerance. This refers to duplication or addition of components, data, and functions within the array.

Replica One or more additional copies of the state database.

Restricted shell Restricted versions of the Korn shell (rksh) and the Bourne shell (rsh) to limit the operations allowed for a particular user account. Restricted shells are especially useful for ensuring that time-sharing users, or users' guests on a system, have restricted permissions during login sessions.

Rights profile Also referred to as right or profile. A collection of overrides used in RBAC that can be assigned to a role or user. A rights profile can consist of authorizations, commands with set UIDs or GIDs, which are referred to as security attributes, and other rights profiles.

Router A machine that forwards Ethernet packets from one network to another.

RPC (Remote Procedure Call) A protocol that one program can use to request services from another system on the network.

Rules file A text file that contains a rule for each group of systems (or single system) that you want to install automatically using JumpStart. Each rule distinguishes a group of systems, based on one or more system attributes. The rules file links each group to a profile, which is a text file that defines how the Solaris 9 software is to be installed on each system in the group. *See also* profile.

rules.ok file A system generated version of the rules file. The `rules.ok` file is required by the custom JumpStart installation software to match a system to a profile. You must use the check script to create the `rules.ok` file.

Run control script Each `init` state has a corresponding series of run control scripts, referred to as rc scripts and located in the `/sbin` directory, to control each `init` state.

Run state When a system begins initialization, it enters one of eight run states—also called `init` states. Because run state 4 is currently not used, only seven usable run states exist. A run state is also referred to as a run level.

S

SCSI (Small Computer Systems Interface) An interface standard for peripheral devices and computers to communicate with each other.

Secondary group Specifies additional groups, other than the primary group, that a user can belong to. Each user can belong to a maximum of 15 secondary groups.

Secondary swap Additional swap added to a system's primary swap.

Sector *See* disk block.

Secure shell Secure shell, or SSH, is both a computer program and an associated network protocol designed for logging in to and executing commands on a networked computer. Secure shell is designed to replace the earlier rlogin, TELNET, and rsh protocols, which are considered unsecure protocols. SSH provides secure encrypted communications between two untrusted hosts over an unsecure network. Users of SSH can also use it for tunneling, forwarding arbitrary TCP ports and X11 connections over the resultant secure channel, and transferring files using the associated scp or sftp programs. An ssh server, by default, listens on the standard TCP port 22.

Server A system that provides resources, services, or file systems, such as home directories or mailboxes, to other systems on the network.

Shared resource A shared file system on an NFS server.

Shell variable A structure that holds data and is uniquely named by the user within the shell. It holds the data assigned to it until a new value is assigned or the program is finished.

Single-user mode Used to describe a Solaris run state where the system does not support multi-user operations. This run state is used to perform system administration tasks.

Slave NIS server A secondary NIS server that contains all of the maps in case of a failure of the primary server.

SMC (Solaris Management Console) SMC is a graphical user interface designed to ease several routine system administration tasks. When using SMC, the system administrator is presented with a menu-like interface that is much easier to use than the ASCII interface supplied at the command prompt.

Soft mount A file system mounted using the `mount -o soft` option. The `soft` option indicates that the retry request does not continue once the server becomes unresponsive. The default for the `mount` command is `hard`.

Soft partition A new feature of SVM that breaks the traditional eight slices per disk barrier by allowing disks, or logical volumes, to be subdivided into many more partitions.

Software group A logical grouping of the Solaris software (clusters and packages). During a Solaris installation, you can install one of the following software groups: Core, End-user Solaris Software, Developer Solaris Software, Entire Solaris Software, and Entire Solaris Software Group Plus OEM Support.

Software package A Solaris software package is the standard way to deliver bundled and unbundled software. Packages are administered by using the package administration commands, and they are generally identified by a SUNW*xxx* naming convention when supplied by Sun Microsystems. SUNW is Sun Microsystems' ticker symbol on the stock exchange, hence the SUNW prefix.

Software patch A patch is a fix to a reported software problem. Sun will ship several software patches to customers so that problems can be resolved before the next release of software.

Software spool directory For convenience, you can copy frequently installed packages to a spool directory. This way you don't need to use the CD media each time you install the package.

Solaris Volume Manager objects A graphical representation for the state database, metadevice or part of a metadevice, or hot spare pool.

Spool Stands for simultaneous peripheral operations online. For printing, spooling is when an application generates the printer output and sends it to the print spooler. The spooler feeds the print images to the printer, one at a time, at slower printing speeds. The printing is then done in the background while the user interacts with other applications in the foreground.

For software installation, spooling is the process of copying software packages from CD-ROM to a directory on the local disk.

Standalone system Clients that use remote services, such as installation software, from a server don't rely on a server to function. These are referred to as standalone systems.

State database replica A copy of the metadevice state database. Keeping copies of the metadevice state database protects against the loss of state and configuration information critical to metadevice operations.

Sticky bit A permission bit that protects the files within a directory. If the directory has the sticky bit set, a file can be deleted only by the owner of the file, the owner of the directory, or root.

Storage block These occupy space allocated to the file system. *See also* data blocks.

Stripe Accessing several disks at the same time in parallel to gain performance.

Stripe width The amount of data written across a striped or RAID volume. In Solaris Volume Manager, this is the interlace size multiplied by the number of disks in the stripe.

Striping Spreading, or interleaving, logical contiguous blocks of data across multiple independent disk spindles. Striping allows multiple disk controllers to simultaneously access data, improving performance.

Submirror A metadevice that is part of a mirror. *See also* mirror.

SVM (Solaris Volume Manager) Uses virtual disks to manage physical disks and their associated data.

Superblock Stores much of the information about the file system. The superblock resides in the 16 disk sectors (sectors 16–31) that follow the bootblock. The superblock is a table of information that describes the file system.

When a file system is created, each cylinder group replicates the superblock beginning at sector 32. The replication protects the critical data in the superblock against catastrophic loss.

Swap file Physical memory is supplemented by this specially configured file on the physical disk. *See also* swap space.

Swap space Swap space and necessary file system overhead is included in the disk space recommendations for each software group. A minimum of 512MB is required for swap space, but more space might be needed. By default, Solaris Web Start allocates 512MB for swap space. A swap partition or a swap file is used to provide swap space.

Swap Space used as a virtual memory storage area when the system does not have enough physical memory to handle current processes. *See also* swap space.

Switch The central device through which all hosts in a twisted-pair Ethernet installation are connected. Each port on the switch can give full bandwidth to a single server or client station. *See also* hub.

Symbolic link A pointer to files anywhere on the network. The file or directory could exist in another file system, on another disk, or on another system on the network. Symbolic links only contain one type of data: the pathname of the file to which they point. The size of a symbolic link always matches the number of characters in the pathname it contains.

T

TCP/IP (Transmission Control Protocol/Internet Protocol) The protocol suite originally developed for the Internet. It is also called the Internet protocol suite. Solaris networks run on TCP/IP by default.

Terminfo database Describes the capabilities of devices such as printers and terminals.

Throughput A measure of sequential I/O performance, quoted as Mbytes/second.

TMPFS (Temporary File System) A file system that uses local memory for file system reads and writes and is typically much faster than a UFS.

Track A series of sectors positioned end-to-end in a circular path. The number of sectors per track varies with the radius of a track on the platter. The outer tracks are larger and can hold more sectors than the inner tracks.

Trusted host A host from which a user can log in without being required to type in a password.

U

UDF (Universal Disk Format) A file system used for storing information on the optical media technology called DVD (Digital Versatile Disc or Digital Video Disc).

UFS (Unix File System) The default disk-based file system for the Solaris operating environment.

UFS logging The process of storing file system operations to a log before the transactions are applied to the file system.

ufsboot The secondary boot program. It locates and loads the two-part kernel. The kernel consists of a two-piece static core called `genunix` and `unix`.

Unbundled software package A Solaris software package is the standard way to deliver bundled and unbundled software. Packages are administered by using the package administration commands, and they are generally identified by a SUNW*xxx* naming convention when supplied by Sun Microsystems. SUNW is Sun Microsystems' ticker symbol on the stock exchange, hence the SUNW prefix.

Upgrade Performed on a system that is already running Solaris 2.6, Solaris 7, Solaris 8, or a previous release of Solaris 9. An upgrade will save as many modifications as possible from the previous version of Solaris that is currently running on your system. *See also* live upgrade.

User ID (UID) A unique number assigned to each user account. All UIDs must be consistent across the network. The UID is typically a number between 100 and 60,002, but it can go as high as 2,147,483,647.

User initialization file A shell initialization file is a shell script that runs automatically each time the user logs in. The initialization file will set up the work environment and customize the shell environment for the user. The primary job of the shell initialization file is to define the user's shell environment, such as the search path, environment variables, and windowing environment.

User mask Controls the default file permissions assigned to the file or directory.

V–Z

Virtual file system (VFS) Architecture that provides a standard interface for different file system types. The VFS architecture enables the kernel to handle basic operations, such as reading, writing, and listing files, and makes it easier to add new file systems.

Virtual volume Grouping disk partitions across several disks to appear as one single volume to the operating system.

Volume manager Simplifies the use of disks and CDs by automatically mounting them using the `vold` daemon.

Volume name An 8-character name assigned to a disk drive.

Volume A group of physical slices that are accessed as a single logical device by concatenation, striping, mirroring, setting up RAID5 volumes, or logging physical devices. After they are created, volumes are used like slices. The volume maps logical block addresses to the correct location on one of the physical devices. The type of mapping depends on the configuration of the particular volume. Also known as a pseudo device or virtual device in standard Unix terms.

WAN (wide area network) A network that connects multiple local-area networks (LANs) or systems at different geographical sites via phone, fiber-optic, or satellite links.

Warm plug The ability to replace a failed disk drive without powering down the storage array and without rebooting the host computer system. This is an important aspect of high availability. *See* hot pluggable.

Web Start Flash An installation feature that enables you to create a single reference installation (Web Start Flash archive) of the Solaris operating environment on a machine, which is called the master machine. After installing the operating system onto the master machine, you can add or delete software and modify system configuration information as necessary. You then create a Web Start archive from this master machine and can use this archive to replicate that installation on a number of systems, which are called clone machines.

Web Start An installation program located on the Solaris Installation CD-ROM that can be run with a graphical user interface (GUI) or with a command-line interface (CLI). Using Solaris Web Start and Sun's Web browser, you select either a default installation or a customize option to install only the software you want, including the Solaris software group, Solstice utilities, and additional software. You can also use Web Start to upgrade your operating system.

XOR eXclusive OR. A binary mathematical operation performed on data to produce parity information. In RAID level 5, parity is generated from user data and is used to regenerate any user data that is lost due to a drive failure.

SYMBOLS

A

B

C

D

E

F

G

H

I

J

K

L

M

O

P

Q – R

V

X – Y – Z